United States Intelligence

An Encyclopedia

Garland Reference Library
of Social Science

(Vol. 589)

THE GARLAND SERIES ON U.S. MILITARY AFFAIRS presents complete reference coverage of selected military, intelligence, and national security subjects. Beginning with this volume on military intelligence, the multivolume series will discuss these subjects with particular emphasis on contemporary affairs.

Other books in the series:

The United States Army:
A Dictionary

The United States Air Force:
A Dictionary

The United States Navy:
A Dictionary

Command, Control, and
Communications

Series Editor
Bruce W. Watson

UNITED STATES INTELLIGENCE

An Encyclopedia

Edited by
Bruce W. Watson
Susan M. Watson
Gerald W. Hopple

GARLAND PUBLISHING, INC. • NEW YORK & LONDON
1990

The information in this encyclopedia is based on the research of the authors and does not represent the positions or policies of any agency or department of the U.S. government. The information was derived from unclassified publications and sources and is intended to neither confirm nor deny, officially or unofficially, the views of the U.S. government.

United States Intelligence: An Encyclopedia / edited by Bruce W. Watson, Susan M. Watson, Gerald W. Hopple.
  p.   cm. — (Garland reference library of social science : vol. 589)
  Includes bibliographical references.
  ISBN 0-8240-3713-8 (alk. paper)
  1. Intelligence service—United States—Dictionaries. 2. Military intelligence—United States—Dictionaries. I. Watson, Bruce W. II. Watson, Susan M. III. Hopple, Gerald W. IV. Series: Garland reference library of social science : v. 589.
JK468.I6E53   1990
89-28206   327.1'273—dc20

Printed on acid-free, 250-year-life paper
Manufactured in the United States of America

Design by Renata Gomes/Julie Threlkeld

To Robert Beland, Lieutenant Colonel, U.S. Air Force, who rose above the petty service rivalries and tried to show us that we could, too. A superb teacher, officer, and man, he touched all who knew him and will be sorely missed.

Contents

Acknowledgments

This book is dedicated to the late Lieutenant Colonel Robert Beland, U.S. Air Force, who epitomized two aspects of the ideal military intelligence officer. The first was his ability to rise above the parochial views of so many of his contemporaries and to espouse the joint service cause. The second was his endless quest for truth in an earnest attempt to provide the most accurate knowledge to his students. His high standards and devotion made him a truly outstanding professor at the Defense Intelligence College, a teacher respected and admired by both his peers and his students.

This encyclopedia could not have been completed without the efforts of a host of people. We would like to begin by acknowledging Master Sergeant Thomas Baldwin, U.S. Army, and Captain Susan Perrin, U.S. Air Force. Their knowledge of the organizations of the different intelligence entities was invaluable, and the hours they spent in helping us are most appreciated. We would also like to acknowledge Robert Beland, George Pickett, and Mr. Edmund Stewart. The budgetary portions of this book rely heavily on their efforts. In addition, we would like to thank Lieutenant Commander Charles Taylor, U.S. Navy. His detailed research into intelligence collection, command and control, and counterintelligence was most impressive and cleared the clouds over our work on many of the items herein. We would also like to thank Dr. Mark Kauppi, Dr. Ronald Garst, Dr. Max Gross, Lieutenant Colonel Dick Coburn, U.S. Air Force, Lieutenant Colonel Daniel Cummings, U.S. Army, Gunnery Sergeant Stephen Campbell, U.S. Marine Corps, Dr. Karl Pieragostini, First Lieutenant Gregory Lassila, U.S. Air Force, Commander George Witt, U.S. Navy, Wayne Perkins, James McCool, Lieutenant Colonel, U.S. Marine Corps (Retired), James Lucas, and William Liptak, Commander, U.S. Navy (Retired), for their help in this project. In a larger context, we would like to thank and acknowledge the entire faculty, past and present, of the Defense Intelligence College: its commandant, Dr. Howard Roop, Rear Admiral, U.S. Naval Reserve (Retired), its provost, Dr. Robert De Gross, and the many others who have made the college an impressive educational institution and the nation's premier organization in terms of research into the Intelligence Community.

We are also indebted to many for the production of this book. We are most appreciative for the guidance offered by Mr. Gary Kuris and Ms. Kennie Lyman of Garland Publishing. We would like to thank Bruce, Junior, and Jennifer Watson for their hours of proofreading and other help. Finally, we would like to thank Susan M.O. Watson, who spent days helping us prepare and edit this book. We are most thankful for her kind assistance.

Bruce W. Watson

Susan M. Watson

Gerald W. Hopple

Introduction

This encyclopedia is intended for the serious researcher of the U.S. Intelligence Community. As an academic reference, it attempts to discuss all the major terms and entities currently in use. Its scope is the post–World War II period, with an emphasis on the present. However, in order to gain the greatest benefit from the following pages, it is necessary to understand a few salient points about the Community.

In postwar U.S. politics, no issue has been more persistent or troublesome than that of U.S. intelligence. First of all, an Intelligence Community, with its secrecy and covert and clandestine operations, flies in the face of the openness and sense of fair play that is inherent in the American ethic. This, in itself, has created its own history and its own terminology.

Second, there are the interest groups—the President, the Congress, the military services, the civilian federal agencies, and the civilian intelligence entities—that are involved with the Community. The history of each of these groups has had a significant impact on contemporary intelligence affairs, and with that history has come jargon, events, and entities that are noteworthy. All of these appear in the following pages.

Third, there are the troubles of the Intelligence Community—its failed operations and its confrontations with Congress. These, as well, have produced their share of terms that are of interest to the researcher.

Fourth, there is the very nature of intelligence. This covers a panorama that is as large as life itself. Thus, to reduce the research effort of the reader, a few comments on intelligence are in order.

Intelligence is most readily divided into *strategic intelligence* and *tactical intelligence*. Strategic intelligence is of particular interest to national policymakers. It is information on events, threats, and individuals that create major problems for the federal government. Tactical intelligence, on the other hand, is on a lower plane and can be easily divided into two types. The first is *tactical military intelligence*, information that is of interest to the military services—Army, Navy, Air Force, and Marine Corps—and that is of value in reporting on any military threat posed against them. The second type is more difficult to place accurately; it is *covert and clandestine operations*, undercover activity that may be performed to collect information of either tactical or strategic value, or to influence events. In all respects, these operations have produced a huge vocabulary of tactical terms. This book will be used most efficiently if the researcher can first determine whether his or her effort is concerned with strategic or with tactical intelligence.

There are many types of intelligence, including strategic, tactical, operational, scientific and technical, political, economic, sociological, military, and medical intelligence. In fact, it is not inaccurate to say that almost all relevant aspects of human endeavor will fall into some category or type of intelligence. To be aware of the types of intelligence will better prepare the researcher to collect the materials that are needed for a particular research endeavor.

The ways in which intelligence is collected are also of importance. There are, again, many types, such as human, imagery, signals, radar, and acoustical intelligence. Although the researcher often cannot ignore any of these collection methods, an understanding of them and the information they provide may allow the individual to curtail the requisite research time considerably.

In light of the above, we strongly recommend that the reader begin by reading the entry entitled Intelligence. This will provide a focus for further use of this book. In addition, the Tactical Intelligence and Strategic Intelligence entries provide information that may help to focus the research effort. Finally, if the reader is primarily interested in the troubles of the Intelligence Community, then we suggest that he or she begin by reading the following entries: Intelligence Community, Executive Orders on Intelligence, Presidential Oversight, and Congressional Oversight, which should lead to additional entries in this book.

Regardless of whether or not the reader first addresses the entries recommended above, the following should be kept in mind. We have attempted to identify each term in the first sentence of each entry, so that the reader will be able to determine whether the entry is relevant to the research at hand. Such identifications have been provided only for intelligence terms. We have not done this for the entries concerning people or intelligence organizations, because the title of the entry in these cases is self-evident.

This book is divided into the following major sections:

Acronyms. The Intelligence Community has a penchant, indeed a mania, for acronyms. People who come to Washington, D.C., and begin to work in the Community are lost for weeks because they do not understand the acronymic jargon. The current director of Central Intelligence, William Webster, has noted that when he first met Leonard Perroots, who was then the director of the Defense Intelligence Agency, the latter's conversation was so riddled with acronyms that Webster could not understand him.

The list of acronyms that we have prepared deals not only with the Intelligence Community, but also with the *work* of the Intelligence Community. We have done this because we hope that many of our readers will be using this work to research the intelligence that the Community (particularly its military components) has produced. As a result, the list of acronyms is far more extensive and far greater in scope than the list of entries, and it has a strong military bent. Many of the terms have not been included as entries, because they do not bear directly on the Intelligence Community but rather are the technical terms that the Community uses to perform its job. Should one wish to find more information on these terms, we recommend consulting the number of excellent encyclopedic studies on military operations that are available in most reference libraries.

One final note on acronyms. The reader, noticing that many acronyms have more than one meaning, may ask how the intelligence employee remembers them all. The answer is that, first of all, each employee uses only a small number of all the acronyms and is as lost as the layman when it comes to defining all of the terms. Second, for each person the acronym generally has only one meaning or the different meanings are clearly distinguishable. For example, for the naval intelligence analyst, the acronym "SSN" has two meanings. If he is working at the office and reads SSN in an intelligence report, he knows that it means nuclear-powered attack submarine. However, when it comes time to fill out the necessary forms for his security investigation and he comes to the block titled SSN, he will naturally write in his Social Security number. Moreover, the counterintelligence officer who receives this analyst's security papers knows only one meaning for SSN: he expects to see a Social Security number in the box.

We suggest that the researcher use a similar approach. If one encounters an acronym, uses the list in this book, and discovers that there are two or more definitions for the term, then the context in which the acronym is used must be determined. In virtually all cases this context will give a definite idea of the meaning of the acronym. The list can then be used to determine the exact wording.

Major Weapons Systems. A section which lists the major weapons systems has been included, because many research materials use a weapon's name and its numbered designation interchangeably. Since this can cause confusion for a researcher who is not familiar with the systems, the table has been provided for cross-reference purposes.

Chronology. We have provided a chronology of the most significant events in the Intelligence Community since the formation of the Office of the Coordinator of Information in 1941. We hope that this will provide another valuable means of research. Most of the terms, institutions, people, and events mentioned in the chronology appear in the entries and can be easily cross-referenced.

Bibliography. The bibliography contains a complete listing of the sources and references that have been used in this work. It may provide some excellent leads for further research into specific subjects.

Entries. The entries are listed alphabetically, and we have attempted to cross-reference extensively to further assist in the reader's research. The reader will note that some of the entries contain definitions that were created by the Church Committee (the Senate Select Committee to Study Government Operations with Respect to Intelligence Activities). We have provided these in anticipation that some of the readers may use this work in researching the committee or its efforts. We have examined all the definitions that the committee devised, and, when its definition duplicated the established definition, we have merely cited the Church Committee report as one of the references. In these cases, the reader can assume that the committee agreed with the established definition. However, in those cases where the committee devised a different definition, no matter how slight the difference, we have included the committee's definition. We have done this because the committee used its own definitions as one of the bases for its analysis of the Community. In order for the researcher to understand the committee's workings, we feel that it is necessary for him or her to understand its assumptions.

The entries are the result of extensive research into a variety of sources, with the following exceptions. The entry on the National Security Agency relies heavily on *The Puzzle Palace,* by James Bamford, for two reasons. The first is that the book is the result of an outstanding research effort, and it provides a detailed and accurate study of the agency that will endure for years. The second reason is that the agency is so reticent concerning the release of information about its affairs that there is a significant lack of information. Fortunately, Bamford has done much to fill this need.

The second exception concerns the entries on the components of strategic intelligence. Here we have drawn heavily on the research of Jerome K. Clauser and Sandra M. Weir, whose *Intelligence Research Methodology,* completed under contract for the Defense Intelligence School, still stands as the definitive work in its discussion of the components of strategic intelligence.

Appendixes. The appendixes, in almost all cases, are verbatim reproductions of virtually all of the most significant Executive and congressional statements regarding the Intelligence Community after World War II. (The exceptions are (a) that the tables of contents of the pieces have been omitted, and (b) the 1987 report by the Presidential Special Review Board has been abridged because it contained long passages that did not directly pertain to the Intelligence Community.) These documents have been provided because they are not available in any other single reference and because they are of major research value to anyone investigating intelligence legislation, oversight, or scandals, or the origins and history of the Intelligence Community.

In summary, we sincerely hope that this reference will be of major value to research. The subject of U.S. intelligence is both vast and fascinating, and if this work helps to further the public's understanding of the subject, then we will feel that we have accomplished our purpose.

Acronyms

— A —

A-2	Air Force Intelligence
AA	(1) African Office, Current Analysis Section, Bureau of Intelligence and Research, Department of State
	(2) Antiaircraft
	(3) Attack Assessment
AAA	Antiaircraft Artillery
AAAOB	Antiaircraft Artillery Order of Battle
AAB	Air Assault Brigade
AABNCP	Advanced Airborne Command Post
AAC	Alaskan Air Command
AADS	Army Air Defense Staff
AAF	Army Airfield
AAFCE	Allied Air Forces Central Europe (NATO)
AAFIF	Automated Air Facility Intelligence File
AAG	Army Artillery Group
AAGS	Army Air-Ground System
AAH	Advanced Attack Helicopter
AAI	Authorized Active Inventory
AAICV	Armored Amphibious Infantry Combat Vehicle
AALC	Amphibious Assault Landing Craft
AAM	(1) Air-to-Air Missile
	(2) Air Armaments Model
AAMG	Antiair Machinegun
AAO	Army Acquisition Objective
AAP	Allied Publication (NATO)
AARS	Advanced Airborne Radar System
AAS	(1) Area Analysis Study
	(2) Amphibious Area Study
AAW	Antiair Warfare
AAWC	Antiair Warfare Coordinator
AB	Air Base

ABC	(1) Atomic, Biological, and Chemical
	(2) American, British, and Canadian
	(3) Argentina, Brazil, Chile (ABC Countries)
ABCCC	Airborne Battlefield Command and Control Center
ABM	Antiballistic Missile
ABN	Airborne
ABNCP	Airborne Command Post
ABRES	Advanced Ballistic Reentry System
AC	(1) DIA Advisory Committee
	(2) Aircraft
ACB	Armored Cavalry Brigade
ACC	Army Communications Command
ACCHAN	Allied Command Channel (NATO)
ACCS	Automated Command and Control System
ACDA	Arms Control and Disarmament Agency
ACE	(1) Allied Command Europe
	(2) Aviation Combat Element
ACF	Area Coverage File
ACFT	Aircraft
ACI	Airborne Controlled Intercept
ACINT	Acoustical Intelligence
ACL	Allowable Cabin Loads
ACLANT	Allied Command, Atlantic (NATO)
ACM	(1) Anticruise Missile
	(2) Airborne Cruise Missile
	(3) Air Combat Maneuver
ACMI	Air Combat Maneuvering Instrumentation
ACMS	Automated Career Management System
ACOM	Asian Communist; one of four major operational divisions of the National Security Agency's Production

	Organization; now known as B Group
ACOMS	Automated Collection Management System
ACOUSTINT	Acoustical Intelligence
ACP	(1) Area Coordination Paper
	(2) Allied Communication Publication
	(3) Airborne Command Post
	(4) Alternate Command Post
ACR	Armored Cavalry Regiment
ACRV	Armored Command Reconnaissance Vehicle
ACS	Armored Cavalry Squadron
ACSB	Amphibious Contingency Support Brief
ACSC	Air Command and Staff College
ACSI	Assistant Chief of Staff, Intelligence (U.S. Army) (now Deputy Chief of Staff, Intelligence, U.S.Army)
ACV	(1) Armored Command Vehicle
	(2) Air Cushion Vehicle
ACW	(1) Aircraft Control and Warning
	(2) Anticarrier Warfare
AD	(1) Air Defense
	(2) Air Division
	(3) Artillery Division
	(4) Armored Division
	(5) Destroyer Tender
ADA	Air Defense Artillery
ADC	(1) Aide de Campe
	(2) Air Direction Center
	(3) Assistant Division Commander
	(4) Air Data Computer
ADCC	Air Defense Command Center
ADCOM	Aerospace Defense Command
ADD	Air Defense District
ADDISS	Advanced Deployable Digital Imagery Support System
ADF	Automatic Direction Finding
ADG	Deperming Ship
ADISS	Advanced Defense Intelligence Support System
ADIZ	Air Defense Identification Zone
ADLA	Assistant Director (of NSA) for Legal and Legislative Affairs
ADM	Atomic Demolitions Munitions
ADMIN	Administration
ADP	(1) Automatic Data Processing
	(2) Airborne Data Processing
ADPL	Assistant Director (of NSA) for Policy and Liaison
ADPR	Assistant Director (of NSA) for Plans and Resources
ADPS	(1) Automated Data Processing System
	(2) ASARS Deployable Processing Station
ADS	(1) Automated Data System
	(2) Air Defense Sector
ADSS	Aerospace Defense Systems Subcommittee
ADSTAR	Advanced Document Storage and Retrieval System
ADT	(1) Assistant Director (of NSA) for Training
	(2) Active Duty Tour (performed by Reservists)
ADVA	Advanced Soviet; one of the four major operational divisions of NSA's Production Organization; combined with GENS into A Group
ADVAL	Air Defense Evaluation Test
ADZ	Air Defense Zone
AE	(1) Atomic Energy
	(2) Assault Echelon
	(3) Ammunition Ship
	(4) Aerial Exploitation
AEB	Aerial Exploitation Battalion
AEC	Atomic Energy Commission
AECB	Arms Export Control Board
AEDS	Atomic Energy Detection System
AEELS	Airborne ELINT Emitter Location System
AEM	Missile Tender
AEMS	Automated Edge Measurement System
AEROFLOT	Soviet Civil Airline (USSR)
AEV	Armored Engineer Vehicle
AEW	(1) Airborne Early Warning
	(2) Aerial Electronic Warfare
AEW&C	Airborne Early Warning and Control
AF	Air Force
AF ACSI	Air Force Assistant Chief of Staff for Intelligence
AFAITC	Armed Forces Air Intelligence Training Center(Lowry Air Force Base, Colorado)

AFAL	Air Force Armament Laboratory
AFAP	Artillery Fired Atomic Projectile
AFB	(1) Air Force Base
	(2) Airframe Bulletin
	(3) Antifriction Bearing
AFC	Automatic Frequency Control
AFCENT	Allied Forces Central Europe
AFCS	Automatic Flight Control System
AFCSC	Air Force Cryptologic Support Center
AFDB	Auxiliary Floating Drydock (Large)
AFDL	Auxiliary Floating Drydock (Small)
AFDM	Auxiliary Floating Drydock (Medium)
AFDT	AEELS Fixed Downlink Terminal
AFEOC	Air Force Emergency Operations Center
AFESC	Air Force Electronic Security Command
AF ESD	Air Force Electronic Systems Division
AFEUR	Air Force Europe
AFEWC	Air Force Electronic Warfare Center
AFGWC	Air Force Global Weather Center
AFHQ	Air Force Headquarters
AFIA	Air Force Intelligence Agency
AFIC	Air Force Intelligence Center
AFIN	Assistant Chief of Staff, Intelligence Headquarters, U.S. Air Force
AFIO	Association of Former Intelligence Officers
AFIP	Air Force Intelligence Plan
AFIS	Air Force Intelligence Service/Study
AFIT	Air Force Institute of Technology
AFITC	Armed Forces Air Intelligence Training Center
AFLANT	Air Forces, Atlantic
AFLC	Air Force Logistics Command
AFLD	Airfield
AFMIC	Armed Forces Medical Intelligence Center
AFNORTH	Allied Forces Northern Europe (NATO Command)
AFOC	Air Force Operations Center
AFOE	Assault Follow-on Echelon

AFOSI	Air Force Office of Special Investigations
AFOSP	Air Force Office of Security Police
AFOSR	Air Force Office of Scientific Research
AFPC	Air Force Policy Council
AFR	(1) Air Force Reserve
	(2) Air Force Regulation
AFS	Combat Stores Ship
AFSA	Armed Forces Security Agency
AFSAC	(1) Armed Forces Security Agency Council
	(2) Air Force Special Activities Center
AFSAC/IRC	Armed forces Security Council Intelligence Requirements Committee
AFSATCOM	Air Force Satellite Communications System
AFSB	Air Force Staff Board
AFSC	(1) Air Force Systems Command
	(2) Air Force Specialty Code
	(3) Armed Forces Staff College
AFSCO	Air Force Security Clearance Office
AFSOB	Air Force Special Operations Base
AFSOUTH	Allied Forces Southern Europe (NATO Command)
AFSOUTH-COM	Air Force Southern Command
AFTAC	Air Force Technical Applications Center (Patrick Air Force Base, Florida)
AFTFWC	Air Force Tactical Fighter Weapons Center
AFV	Armored Fighting Vehicle
AFWAL	Air Force Wright Aeronautical Laboratory
AFWL	Air Force Weapons Laboratory
AF 5	Fifth Air Force
AF 9 TIS	Air Force Ninth Tactical Intelligence Squadron
AF 460 RTS	Air Force 460th Reconnaissance Technical Squadron
AF 480 RTG	Air Force 480th Reconnaissance Technical Group
AG	(1) Miscellaneous Auxiliary Ship
	(2) Adjutant General
AGB	Icebreaker

AGC	Automatic Gain Control
AGDS	Deep Submarine Support Ship
AGE	Experimental Auxiliary
AGEF	Frigate Research Ship
AGEH	Experimental Auxiliary (Hydrofoil)
AGER	Intelligence Research Ship
AGF	Miscellaneous Command Ship
AGHS	Patrol Combatant Support Ship
AGI	Intelligence Collection Ship
AGL	(1) Buoy Tender
	(2) Above Ground Level
AGM	(1) Missile Range Instrumentation Ship
	(2) Air-to-Ground Missile
AGMR	Major Communications Relay Ship
AGOR	Oceanographic Research Ship
AGOS	(1) Ocean Surveillance Ship
	(2) Air-Ground Operations School (NATO)
	(3) Air-Ground Operations System
AGP	Patrol Craft Tender
AGS	(1) Hydrographic Survey Ship
	(2) Soviet Automatic Grenade Launcher
AGZ	Actual Ground Zero
AH	(1) Hospital Ship
	(2) Alternate Headquarters
AI	(1) Air Intelligence
	(2) Artificial Intelligence
AIA	Army Intelligence Agency
AID	(1) Agency for International Development
	(2) Aerospace Information Digest
	(3) Army Information Digest
	(4) Accident, Incident, Deficiencies
	(5) Active Integral Defense
AIDES	Analyst Intelligence/Information Display and Exploitation System
AIDS	(1) Acoustic Intelligence Data System
	(2) Advanced Identification System
AIF	Automated Installation Intelligence File
AIFV	Armored Infantry Fighting Vehicle

AIG	Address Indicator Group
AII	Area of Influence/Interest
AIIC	USAFE Advanced Imagery Interpretation Course
AIM	ADCOM Intelligence Memorandum
AIMAA	United States Army Armor Infantry, Mechanized Air Assault and Airborne
AIMP	(1) Army Intelligence Management Plan
	(2) Advanced Imagery Management Plan
AIOEC	Association of Iron Ore Exporting Countries
AIPR	Automated Information Processing Request
AIR	American Institute for Research
AIRA	Air Attaché
AIRES	Advanced Imagery Requirements and Exploitation System
AIRLO	Air Liaison Officer
AIRS	Advance Inertial Reference Sphere
AIS	(1) Army Intelligence Survey
	(2) Automatic Indicator System
	(3) Advanced Indications Structure
	(4) Advanced Indications System
AITE	Advanced Indications Technology Experiment
AITPS	Automated Threat Intelligence Production System
AJ	Anti-Jam
AJCC	Alternate Joint Communications Center
AK	(1) Cargo Ship
	(2) Soviet "Kalashnikov" Family of Assault Rifles
AKA	Also Known As
AKL	Light Cargo Ship
AKR	Vehicle Cargo Ship
ALAIRCOM	Alaskan Air Command
ALC	Accounting Legend Code
ALCATS	Automated Lines of Communication and Target System
ALCM	Air-Launched Cruise Missile
ALCOM	Alaskan Command
ALCOP	Alternate Command Post
ALCS	Airborne Launch Control System
ALF	Auxiliary Landing Field

ALFA	Advanced Liaison Forward Area
ALLO	All Others; one of four major operational divisions of NSA's Production Organization; now known as G Group
ALO	(1) Air Liaison Officer
	(2) Authorized Level of Organization
ALOC(s)	Air Line(s) of Communications
ALP	Advanced Language Program
ALSS	Advanced Location Strike System
ALTREV	Altitude Reservation
ALUSNA	American Legation U.S. Naval Attaché
ALUSNLO	American Legation U.S. Naval Liaison Officer
ALWT	Advanced Lightweight Torpedo
ALWTIC	Annual Land Warfare Technical Intelligence Conference
AM	(1) Ante Meridiem
	(2) Amplitude Modulation
AMAB	Air Mobile Assault Brigade
AMASS	Advanced Marine Airborne SIGINT System
AMC	(1) Airspace Management and Control
	(2) Army Material Command (formerly DARCOM)
AMCM	Airborne Mine Countermeasures
AMDT	AEELS Mobile Downlink Terminal
AMF	Allied Command Europe Mobile Force (NATO Command)
AMHS	Automated Message Handling System
AMMO	Ammunition
AMO	Aviation Medical Officer
AMPDS	Automated Message Processing Dissemination System
AMPHI	Aerial Mission Photographic Indoctrination
AMST	Advanced Medium STOL Transport
AN	Net Tender
ANALIT	Analyst-to-Analyst Message Format
ANAUT	Analytical Interest Messages
ANCIB	Army-Navy Communications Intelligence Board
ANCICC	Army-Navy Communications Intelligence Coordinating Committee

ANEX	Analyst-to-Analyst Exchange Message Format
ANFO	Ammonium Nitrate Fuel Oil
ANG	Air National Guard
ANGLICO	Air/Naval Gunfire Liaison Company
ANL	Net Laying Ship
ANMCC	Alternate Military Command Center
ANMIC	Alternate National Military Intelligence Center
ANRPC	Association of Natural Rubber Producing Countries
ANZUS	Australia, New Zealand, United States
AO	(1) Action Officer
	(2) Oiler
	(3) Authenticator Organization
	(4) Area of Operations
	(5) Aerial Observer
AOA	(1) Amphibious Objective Area
	(2) Angle of Attack
	(3) Angle of Arrival
AOB	Air Order of Battle
AOBTS	Air Order of Battle Textual Summary
AOC	(1) Air Officer Commanding (UK)
	(2) Air Operations Center
AOE	Fast Combat Support Ship
AOG	Gasoline Tanker
AOI	Area of Interest
AOP	Area of Probability
AOR	(1) Replenishment Oiler
	(2) Area of Responsibility
AOS	(1) Special Liquids Tanker
	(2) Amphibious Objective Study
AOT	Transport Oiler
AP	(1) Armor Piercing
	(2) Air Police
	(3) Transport Ship
	(4) Associated Press
APB	(1) Self-Propelled Barracks Ship
	(2) All Points Bulletin
	(3) Antipersonnel Bomb
APC	(1) Armored Personnel Carrier
	(2) Area of Positive Control
APDM	Amended Program Decision Memorandum
APDS	Automated Personnel Data Systems

APFSDS	Armor Piercing, Fin Stabilized, Discarding Sabot
AP-I	Armor Piercing Incendiary
APL	Barracks Craft (Non Self-Propelled)
APM	Army Program Memorandum
AP/NSA	Assistant to the President for National Security Affairs
APO	(1) Army Post Office
	(2) Air Post Office
APOD	Aerial Port of Debarkation
APOE	Aerial Port of Embarkation
APPROX	Approximately
APR	Airman Performance Report
APU	Auxiliary Power Unit
APVO	Soviet Air Defense Aviation (USSR)
AR	(1) Advanced Readiness
	(2) Army Regulation
	(3) Action Required
	(4) Repair Ship
	(5) Agent Report
ARA	Assigned Responsible Agency
AR ACSI	Army Assistant Chief of Staff for Intelligence
AR ARDC	Army Armament Research and Development Command
ARB	Battle Damage Repair Ship
ARC	(1) Ad Hoc Requirements Committee
	(2) Cable Ship
	(3) Acquisition Review Committee
	(4) Armored Reconnaissance Carrier
ARCS	(1) Automated Reproduction and Collating System
	(2) Acquisition Radar and Control System
ARD	Auxiliary Repair Drydock
ARDF	Airborne Radio Direction-Finding
ARDM	Auxiliary Repair Drydock
AREUR	Army Europe
AREUR DCSI	Army Europe Deputy Chief of Staff, Intelligence
ARF	Airborne Relay Facility
ARFCOS	Armed Forces Courier Service
ARG	(1) Amphibious Ready Group
	(2) Internal Combustion Repair Ship

ARIS	Advanced Range Instrumentation Ship
ARL	Landing Craft Repair Ship
ARLANT	U.S. Army Forces, Atlantic Command
ARLEA	Army Logistics Evaluation Agency
ARLO	Air Reconnaissance Liaison Officer
ARM	Antiradiation Missile
ARMA	Army Attaché
ARMD	Armored
AR MIA	Army Missile Intelligence Agency
AR MICOM	Army Missile Command
AR MIIA	Army Medical Intelligence and Information Agency
ARMLO	Army Liaison Officer
ARMS	Automated Resource Management System
AR MSIC	Army Missile and Space Intelligence Center
ARO	(1) Area Records Officer
	(2) Auxiliary Readout
ARPA	Advanced Projects
ARPS	Advanced Radar Processing System
ARPV	Advanced Remotely Piloted Vehicle
ARQ	Automatic Repeat Request
ARR	Radiological Repair Ship
ARRCOM	Army Armament Readiness Command
ARRS	(1) Aerospace Rescue and Recovery Service
	(2) Aerial Reconnaissance Reporting System
ARS	Aerial Reconnaissance Satellite
ARSA	Annual Reevaluation of Safe Areas
ARTCC	Air Route Traffic and Control Center
ARTEP	Army Training and Evaluation Program
ARTISS	Advanced Requirements Tasking Information and Support System
ARTOPO	Army Topographic Command
ARTY	Artillery
ARV	(1) Army Recovery Vehicle
	(2) Armored Reconnaissance Vehicle
	(3) Aircraft Repair Ship

AR 2 INF DIV	Army 2nd Infantry Division	**ASDIA**	All-Source Document Index
AR 2 PSY GP	Army 2nd Psychological Operations Group	**ASDIAZ**	All-Source Document Index-Compartmented
AR 4 PSY GP	Army 4th Psychological Operations Group	**ASDIC**	Armed Services Documents Intelligence Center
AR 7 PSY GP	Army 7th Psychological Operations Group	**ASDS**	Automated SIGINT Dissemination System
AR 193 INFBR	Army 193 Infantry Brigade	**ASEAN**	Association of Southeast Asian Nations
AR 361 CAB	Army 361st Civil Affairs Brigade	**ASF**	All-Source Format
AR 488 MID	Army 488th Military Intelligence Detachment	**ASGOBS**	Army Standard Ground Order of Battle System
AR 500 MIG	Army 500th Military Intelligence Group	**ASIC**	All-Source Intelligence Center
AR 501 MIG	Army 501th Military Intelligence Group	**ASIP**	All-Source Imagery Processor
		ASL	Authorized Stock List
AS	(1) Submarine Tender	**ASM**	(1) Air-to-Surface Missile
	(2) Air Surveillance		(2) Antiship Missile
	(3) Aerial Surveillance		(3) Attaché Support Message
ASA	Army Security Agency	**ASMD**	Antiship Missile Defense
ASAC	All-Source Analysis Center	**ASOC**	Attaché Staff Operations Course (Defense Intelligence College)
ASAP	As Soon As Possible		
ASARC	Army Systems Acquisition Review Council	**ASP**	Ammunition Supply Point
ASARS	Advanced Synthetic Aperture Radar System	**ASPAB**	Armed Services Patent Advisory Board
ASART	Analysis Support and Reporting Terminal	**ASPAC**	Asian and Pacific Council
ASAS	All-Source Analysis System	**ASPB**	Assault Patrol Support Boat (Riverine War Craft)
ASAT	(1) Antisatellite	**ASPIC**	Armed Services Personnel Interrogation Center
	(2) Antisatellite Treaty		
ASB	Air Surveillance Broadcast	**ASPJ**	U.S. Airborne Self-Protection Jammer
ASC	Automatic Switching Center	**ASPS**	All-Source Production Section
ASCAS	Automated Security Clearance Approval System	**ASR**	(1) Submarine Rescue Ship
			(2) Airport Surveillance Radar
ASCC	Air Standardization Coordinating Committee	**ASRP**	(1) Airborne SIGINT Reconnaissance Program
ASCM	Antiship Cruise Missile		(2) Airborne SIOP Reconnaissance Plan
ASD(C)	Assistant Secretary of Defense (Comptroller)		
ASD(C3I)	Assistant Secretary of Defense (Command, Control, Communications, and Intelligence)	**ASSIST**	Army System for Standard Intelligence Support Terminals
		ASSM	Antiship Surface Missile
ASD(I)	Assistant Secretary of Defense (Intelligence)	**ASSOTW**	Airfields and Seaplane Stations of the World
ASD(ISA)	Assistant Secretary of Defense (International Security Affairs)	**ASST**	(1) Antiship Surveillance and Tracking
			(2) Assistant
ASD(PA)	Assistant Secretary of Defense (Public Affairs)	**ASSW**	Antisurface Ship Warfare
		ASU	Soviet Airborne Self-Propelled Antitank Gun
ASD(PA&E)	Assistant Secretary of Defense (Public Affairs and Evaluation)	**ASUW**	Antisurface Warfare

ASV	Armored Support Vehicle
ASW	Antisubmarine Warfare
ASWCCS	Antisubmarine Warfare Command and Control System
ASWOC	Antisubmarine Warfare Operations Center
AT	(1) Antitank
	(2) Air Transit
	(3) Simple Antenna (Electronic Component)
	(4) Air Technician
	(5) Awaiting Transportation
ATA	(1) Actual Time of Arrival
	(2) Ocean Tug
	(3) Air Transport Association
ATACS	Analyst-to-Analyst Communications Service
ATAF	Allied Tactical Air Force (NATO Command)
ATB	Air Technical Battalion
ATBM	Antitactical Ballistic Missile
ATC	(1) Air Traffic Control
	(2) Air Target Chart
	(3) Training Command (USAF)
	(4) Mini-Armored Troop Carrier (Riverine Warfare Craft)
ATCH	ASW Torpedo-Carrying Helicopter
ATD	Actual Time of Departure
ATDB	ACE Target Data Base
ATETS	Atomic Heat and Power Plant
ATF	(1) Advanced Tactical Fighter
	(2) Amphibious Task Force
	(3) Fleet Ocean Tug
	(4) Aviation Turbine Fuel
	(5) After the Fact
ATGIN	Atomic Ground Intercept
ATGM	Antitank Guided Missile
ATIC	Aircraft Technical Intelligence Conference
ATIPS	Automated Threat Intelligence Production System (U.S. Army)
ATM	(1) Antitank Missile
	(2) Air Target Materials
	(3) Air Target Mosaic
	(4) Air Crew Training Manuals
ATMG	Arms Transfer Management Group
ATMP	Air Target Materials Program

ATP	(1) Allied Tactical Publication (NATO)
	(2) Ammunition Transfer Points
ATRS	Advanced Tactical Reconnaissance System
ATS	Salvage and Rescue Ship
ATT	Technical Assistance Training Team
AT&T	American Telephone and Telegraph
ATTG	Automated Tactical Target Graphic
AU	Air University
AUM	Air-to-Underwater Missile
AUSCANUKUS	Australia, Canada, United Kingdom, United States
AUTODIN	Automatic Digital Network
AUTOSEVO-COM	Automatic Secure Voice Communications
AUTOVON	Automatic Voice Network
AUTUMN FORGE	NATO Exercise
AUXCP	Auxiliary Command Post
AV	(1) Armored Vehicle
	(2) Audio-Visual
AVF	All Volunteer Force
AVGAS	Aviation Gasoline
AVLB	Armored Bridge-Laying Vehicle
AVMF	Soviet Naval Aviation (USSR)
AVN	Aviation
AVR	Aircraft Rescue Vehicle
AVT	Auxiliary Aircraft Landing Training Ship
AVUM	Aviation Unit Maintenance
AW	(1) Air Warning
	(2) Automatic Weapon(s)
	(3) Water Tanker
	(4) All-Weather
AWACS	Airborne Early Warning and Control System
AWADS	Adverse Weather Aerial Delivery System
AWC	(1) Army War College
	(2) Air War College
AWIR	ADCOM Weekly Intelligence Review Support
AWN	Automated Weather Network
AWOL	Absent Without Leave
AWOP	(1) Absent Without Pay
	(2) Automated Weaponeering Optimization Program

AWS	Air Weather Service
AWT	Water Transport
AWX	All Weather
AXT	Training Ship
AZ	Azimuth

— B —

BA	Budget Authority
BAG	Battalion Artillery Group
BALTAP	Baltic Approaches (NATO Naval Command)
BAO	Basic Attack Option
BAOR	British Army of the Rhine
BAS	Broad Area Search
BASS	Battlefield Surveillance System
BAWB	Bomber Activity Weekly Brief
BB	Battleship
BBBG	Battleship Battle group
BDA	Bomb Damage Assessment
BDE	Brigade
BDP	Battlefield Development Plan
BDS	Base Development Survey
BE	Basic Encyclopedia
BENELUX	Belgium, Netherlands, Luxembourg
BETA	Battlefield Exploitation and Target Acquisition
BFOV	Broad Field of View
BG	Battle Group
BGN	Board on Geographic Names
BGPHES	Battle Group Passive Horizon Extension
BGW	Battlefield Guided Weapon
BI	Background Investigation
BIACC	Basic Integrated Aircraft Command and Control
BICC	Battlefield Information Control Center
BID	Basic Intelligence Division, Central Intelligence Agency
BIF	Basic Imagery File
BIFF	Bistatic Identification Friend or Foe
BIIB	Basic Imagery Interpretation Brief
BIIR	Basic Imagery Interpretation Report

BISS	Basic Intelligence Summary Supplement
BITE	Built-in Test Equipment
BL	Bomb Line
BLEU	Belgium-Luxembourg Economic Union
BLOS	Base Line of Sight
BLSS	Base Level Self-Sufficiency Spares
BLT	Battalion Landing Team
BLUE FLAG	USAF Tactical Training in Air Command and Control
BM	Soviet Truck-Mounted Multiple Rocket Launcher
BMD	(1) Soviet Airborne Combat Vehicle
	(2) Ballistic Missile Defense
BMEWS	Ballistic Missile Early Warning System
BMNT	Beginning Morning Nautical Twilight
BMP	Soviet Armored Infantry Combat Vehicle
BMSS	Ballistic Missiles Systems Subcommittee
BN	Battalion
BND	Bundesrepublik Nachrichtendienst (West German Intelligence Service)
BNDD	Bureau of Narcotics and Dangerous Drugs
BNE	Board of National Estimates
BOA	Broad Ocean Area
BOQ	Bachelor Officers' Quarters
BPA	Blanket Purchase Agreement
BPI	Bits Per Inch
BPS	Basic Psychological Operations Study
BR	Blade Rate
BRAVE SHIELD	U.S. Air Force and U.S. Army Joint Tactical Exercise
BRDM	Soviet Wheeled Amphibious Armored Reconnaissance Vehicle
BRET	Bistatic Reflected Energy Target
BRIGHT STAR	CENTCOM Exercise
BRL	Bomb Release Line
BRP	Bomb Release Point
BRU	Bomb Release Unit
BRUSA	British-United States Agreement
BSD	Battlefield Surveillance Device

BTR	Soviet Armored Personnel Carrier
BUIC	Back-Up Intercept Control
BUNT	British Underground Nuclear Test
BW	(1) Biological Warfare
	(2) Bandwidth
	(3) Beam Width
BWC	Biological Weapons Convention
BWP	Basic Working Paper
BY	Budget Year

— C —

C	Confidential
C3	Command, Control, and Communications
C-C3	Counter Command, Control, and Communications
C&C or C2	Command and Control
C3CM	C3 Countermeasures
C3I	Command, Control, Communications, and Intelligence
C3NET	Command, Control, and Communications Networks
C3S	Command, Control, and Communications Systems
CA	(1) Cryptanalysis
	(2) Covert Action
	(3) Commercial Activities (Program) (DIA)
	(4) Civil Affairs
	(5) Current Analysis
CAA	Concepts Analysis Agency (U.S. Army)
CAB	Compartmented Address Book
CAC	(1) Combined Arms Center
	(2) Collection Advisory Center
CACDA	Combined Arms Combat Development Activity
CACM	Central American Common Market
CAD	Computer-Assisted Design
CADES	COMIREX Automated Management System
CADOB	Consolidated Air Defense Order of Battle
CAG	Carrier Air Group
CAI	Computer-Assisted Instruction
CAM	Computer Assisted Modeling
CAMPS	Computer-Assisted Management Planning System

CAMS	(1) COMIREX Automated Management System
	(2) Communications Area Master Station
CAN	Canadian
CANS	Coastal Air Navigation Supplement
CANT	Chinese Atmospheric Nuclear Test
CANUKUS	Canada, United Kingdom, United States
CAO	(1) Central Actions Office (DIA)
	(2) Coordination of Atomic Operations
CAP	(1) Combat Air Patrol
	(2) Civil Air Patrol
	(3) Communications-Electronics Authorization Program
CAR	Canadian Airborne Regiment
CARC	Corrective Action Review Committee
CARDA	CONUS Airborne Reconnaissance for Damage Assessment
CARG	Crisis Action Review Group
CARIBJIC	Caribbean Joint Intelligence Center
CARICOM	Caribbean Joint Market
CARIFTA	Caribbean Free Trade Association
CARL	Category Assignment Responsibility List
CARP	Computed Air Release Point
CAS	(1) Close Air Support
	(2) Calibrated Air Speed
	(3) Crisis Action System (JCS)
CASS	Collection Analysis Support System
CAST	Catalog of Approved Scientific and Technical Tasks
CAT	(1) Civil Air Transport Line (CIA)
	(2) Crisis Action Team
	(3) Combined Arms Team
CATF	Commander, Amphibious Task force
CATIS	Computer-Aided Tactical Information System
CAV	Cavalry
CBM	Confidence Building Measure(s)
CBNRC	Communications Branch, National Research Council
CBO	Congressional Budget Office

CBR	Chemical, Biological, and Radiological		ics
CBS	Columbia Broadcasting System		(5) Civil Engineer
CBU	Cluster bomb Unit		(6) Corps of Engineers (U.S. Army)
CBW	Chemical and Biological Warfare		(7) Current Exploitation
CC	Command Ship	CEA	Council of Economic Advisors
CCA	Communications Control Authority	CEAO	West African Economic Community
CCC	Command and Control Center	CED	(1) Collection, Exploitation, and Dissemination
CCCC	Centralized COMINT Communications Center		(2) Captured Enemy Document
CCD	(1) Camouflage, Concealment and Deception	CELT	Current Emitter Location Testbed
	(2) Conference of the Committee on Disarmament	CEMA	Council for Mutual Economic Assistance
	(3) Charged Coupled Device	CEN	Center
CCF	Collection Coordination Facility	CENTAG	Central Army Group (NATO)
CCF-SS	Collection Coordination Facility-Support System	CENTCOM	U.S. Central Command
		CENTLANT	Central Sub-Area of Eastern Atlantic Area
CCG	Crisis Coordination Group	C-EO	Communications-Electronics Officer
CCGD	Command, Coast Guard District	CEOI	Communications-Electronics Operation Instructions
CCI	Controlled COMSEC Item		
CCINC	Commander-in-Chief, Pacific	CEP	(1) Circular Error Probable
CCM	(1) Counter-Countermeasures		(2) Construction Electrician (Power)
	(2) Cross-Country Movement		(3) Common Electronic Parts
CCN	Communications Control Number		(4) Civil Emergency Planning
CCP	Consolidated Cryptologic Program		(5) Committee for Energy Policy of OECD
CCPC	Critical Collection Problems Committee	CERP	Combined Economic Reporting Program
CCS	Central Security Service	CESM	Cryptologic Electronic Warfare Support Measures
CCT	Combat Control Team		
CCTC	Command and Control Technical Center	CEST	Contingency Exploitation Support System
CD	(1) Controlled Dissemination	CETA	Chinese-English Translation Assistance
	(2) Certificate of Destruction		
	(3) Civil Defense	CEWI	Combat Electronic Warfare Intelligence
	(4) Committee on Disarmament		
	(5) Collateral Damage	CF	Command Fire
CDE	Conference on Disarmament in Europe	CFA	(1) Combined Field Army (Korea)
CDIP	Consolidated Defense Intelligence Program		(2) Covering Force Area
		CFC	Combined Field Command (Korea)
CDR	Commander		
CDSORG	Civil Direction of Shipping Organization	CFI	Committee on Foreign Intelligence
CE	(1) Counterespionage	CFV	Cavalry Fighting Vehicle
	(2) Circular Error	CG	(1) Consolidated Guidance
	(3) Cost Effectiveness		(2) Commanding General
	(4) Communications-Electron-		(3) Guided Missile Cruiser

CGF	Central Group of Forces (Soviet Forces in Czechoslovakia)
CGN	Guided-Missile Cruiser (Nuclear-Powered)
CH	Aviation Cruiser
CHAN	Channel
CHECKERED FLAG	U.S.-Host Nation Exercise
CHG	Guided-Missile Aviation Cruiser
CHGN	Nuclear-Powered Guided-Missile Aviation Cruiser
CHIP	Communications Handbook for Intelligence Planners
CHN	Nuclear-Powered Aviation Cruiser
CHOP	Change of Operational Control
C-HUMINT	Counter-Human Intelligence
CI	Counterintelligence
CIA	Central Intelligence Agency
CIAP	Central Intelligence Agency Program
CIC	(1) Counterintelligence Corps
	(2) Combat Information Center
	(3) Combined Interrogation Center
CIFAX	Enciphered Facsimile
CIG	Central Intelligence Group
CIIC	Current Intelligence and Indications Center
CIK	Crypto-Ignition Key
CILOP	Conversion in Lieu of Procurement
CIMEX	Civil Military Exercise
C-IMINT	Counter-Imagery Intelligence
CINC	Commander-in-Chief
CINCAD	Commander-in-Chief, Aerospace Defense Command
CINCCFC	Commander-in-Chief, Combined Forces Command, Korea
CINCENT	Commander-in-Chief, Allied Forces Central Europe (NATO)
CINCEUR	Commander-in-Chief, U.S. Forces Europe
CINCHAN	Commander-in-Chief, Channel
CINCLANT	Commander-in-Chief, Atlantic
CINCLANTFLT	Commander-in-Chief, Atlantic Fleet
CINCMAC	Commander-in-Chief, Military Airlift Command
CINCNORAD	Commander-in-Chief, North American Air Defense Command
CINCNORTH	Commander-in-Chief, Allied Forces Northern Europe (NATO)
CINCPAC	Commander-in-Chief, Pacific
CINCPACAF	Commander-in-Chief, Pacific Air Force
CINCPACFLT	Commander-in-Chief, Pacific Fleet
CINCSAC	Commander-in-Chief, Strategic Air Command
CINCSOUTH	Commander-in-Chief, Southern Command
CINCUKAIR	Commander-in-Chief, United Kingdom Air Defense Region (NATO)
CINCUNC	Commander-in-Chief, United Nations Command, Korea
CINCUSAFE	Commander-in-Chief, U.S. Air Forces, Europe
CINCUSAREUR	Commander-in-Chief, U.S. Army, Europe
CINCUSNAVEUR	Commander-in-Chief, U.S. Naval Forces, Europe
CINCWESTLANT	Commander-in-Chief, Western Atlantic
CIOC	Combat Intelligence Operations Center
CIP	(1) Consolidated Intelligence Program
	(2) Critical Intelligence Parameter
	(3) Country Information Package
CIPC	Critical Intelligence Problems Committee
CIPEC	Intergovernmental Council of Copper Exporting Countries
CIPHONY	Enciphered Telephone
CIPR	(1) Consolidated Intelligence Production Requirement
	(2) Counterintelligence Production Registry
CIPS	(1) Counterintelligence Periodic Summary
	(2) Counterintelligence Production Schedule
	(3) Critical Intelligence Parameters
CIR	Continuing Intelligence Requirement
CIRC	Central Information Reference

	and Control
CIRCOL	Central Information Reference and Control On-Line System
CIRIS	Consolidated Intelligence Resources Information System
CIRL	Current Intelligence Requirements List
CIRVIS	Communications Instructions for Reporting Vital Intelligence Sightings
CIS	(1) Country Intelligence Study
	(2) Communications Intercept System
CISR	Communications Intelligence Security Regulation
CIT	Counterintelligence Team
CITS	CENTCOM Imagery Transmission System
CIVISION	Enciphered Television
CJCS	Chairman, Joint Chiefs of Staff
CJTF	Commander, Joint Task Force
CL	(1) Light Cruiser
	(2) Cycle Length
C&LB	Coast and Landing Beaches
CLF	Commander Landing Force
CLSC	COMSEC Logistics Support Company
CLSP	Composite Launch Sequence Plan
CLSU	COMSEC Logistics Support Unit
CM	(1) Countermeasures
	(2) Collection Management
	(3) Memorandum by the Chairman, Joint Chiefs of Staff
	(4) Contract Monitor
CMA	(1) Countermission Analysis
	(2) Collection Management Authority
CMC	(1) Cheyenne Mountain Complex
	(2) Commandant, U.S. Marine Corps
CMCA	Cruise Missile Carrier Aircraft
CMCI	Computed Mission Coverage Index
CMCM	Commandant, U.S. Marine Corps Memorandum
CMCS	COMSEC Material Control System
CMD	Command
CM&D	Collection Management and

	Dissemination
CMEA	Council for Mutual Economic Assistance
CMEC	Captured Material Exploitation Center
CMO	(1) Collection Management Office
	(2) Civil-Military Operations
CMSS	Collection Management Support System
CMT	Crisis Management Teams
CNA	Center for Naval Analyses
CNAD	Conference on NATO Armament Directors
CNI	Commuting NATO Intentions
CNM	Chief of Naval Material
CNO	Chief of Naval Operations
CNOM	Chief of Naval Operations Memorandum
CNOR	Command Not Operationally Ready
CNR	Chief of Naval Research
CNTL	Command Nuclear Target List
CNV	Cryptonet Variable
CNWDI	Critical Nuclear Weapons Design Information
CO	(1) Commanding Officer
	(2) Company
COA	Courses of Action
COB	Close of Business
COBOL	Common Business-Oriented Language
COC	Combat Operations Center
COCKED PISTOL	U.S. Exercise Defense Condition
COCOM	Coordinating Committee
COD	Carrier On-Board Delivery
CODIS	Community of Defense Intelligence Systems
COEA	Cost and Operational Effectiveness Analysis
COG	Continuity of Government
COI	Coordinator of Information (Predecessor of OSS)
COIC	Combat Operations Intelligence Center
COIN	Counterinsurgency
COINS	Community On-Line Intelligence System
COINTELPRO FBI	Domestic Counterintelligence Program

COIR	Commanders' Operational Intelligence Requirements
COLL	Collection
COLLATERAL	All national security information that is protected under the provisions of an Executive Order and for which special intelligence community compartmentation standards have not been formally established
COLOP	Collection Opportunity (Messages)
COM	Computer Output to Microform
COMDT	
COGARD	Commandant, U.S. Coast Guard
COMECON	Council for Mutual Economic Assistance
COMEX	Communications Exercise
COMINFIL	Communist Infiltration; an FBI program of the 1960s
COMINT	Communications Intelligence
COMIREX	Committee on Imagery Requirements and Exploitation
COMIS	Collection Management Information System
COMJAM	Communications Jamming
COMJTF	Commander, Joint Task Force
COMM	Communication
COMMZ	Communications Zone
COMNAVFOR	Commander, Naval Forces
COMNAVINT-COM	Commander, Naval Intelligence Command
COMOR	Committee on Overhead Reconnaissance
COMPASS CALL	U.S. Airborne Communications Jamming System
COMPW	Composite Wing
COMSAT	Communications Satellite
COMSEC	(1) Communications Security
	(2) Office of Communications Security
COMSIXTHFLT	Commander, U.S. Fleet
COMUSFK	Commander, U.S. Forces, Korea
COMUSFOR-CARIB	Commander, U.S. Forces, Caribbean
COMUSJ	Commander, U.S. Forces, Japan
CONCAT	Consolidated Catalog (for SCI Requirements)
CONDECA	Central America Defense Council
CONOPS	Concept of Operations
CONPG	Chairman, Operational Nuclear Planning Group
CONPLAN	(1) Concept Plan
	(2) Contingency Plan
CONSIDO	Consolidated Special Information Dissemination Office
CONTEXT	Conferencing and Text Manipulation System
CONTIC	Continental Army Command Intelligence Center
CONUS	Continental United States
COOP	Contingency of Operations Plan
COP	Command Operation Post
COPG	Chairman, Operational Planners Group
COPRA	Comparative Postwar Recovery Analysis
COPRL	Command Operations Priority Requirements List
COPS	Chief of Operations in the DPP
COR	(1) Central Office of Record
	(2) Command Operationally Ready
CORL	Collection Opportunity Requirements List
COS	Chief of Station
COSCOM	Corps Support Command
COSIN	Control Staff Instructions
COTP	Captain of the Port
COTR	Contracting Officer's Technical Representative
COTS	Container Offloading Transfer System
CP	(1) Contingency Planning
	(2) Command Post
	(3) Character Position
	(4) Communications Processor
	(5) Central Processor
CPBS	Capabilities Programming and Budgeting System
CPC	Coastal Patrol Boat
CPE	Conventional Planning and Execution
CPFL	Contingency Planning Facilities List
CPIC	Coastal Patrol and Interdiction Craft
CPPG	Crisis Pre-Planning Group
CPR	Common Point of Reference
CPS	Collection Problem Set
CPSB	Career Program Selection Board

CPSU	Communist Party of the Soviet Union
CPU	Central Processing Unit
CPX	Command Post Exercise
CR	Crisis Relocation
CRAF	Civil Reserve Air Fleet
CRB	Contingency Reference Book
CRBIF	Crisis Basis Imagery File
CRC	Command and Reporting Center
CRESTED EAGLE	U.S. EUCOM Field Training Exercise
CRIB	Card Reader Insert Board
CRIMP	Crisis Management Plan
CRISCON	Crisis Condition (I&W System)
CRITIC	Critical Intelligence Message
CRITICOMM	Critical Intelligence Communications System
CRMA	Collection Requirements Management Architecture
CRS	(1) COMIREX Requirements Structure
	(2) Central Reports Staff (of CIG)
CRT	(1) Cathode Ray tube (Terminal)
	(2) Combat Readiness Training
CRTA	Chief of Rocket Troops and Artillery
CRYPTA	Cryptanalysis
CS	Countersabotage
CSA	(1) Chief of Staff, Army
	(2) Central Supplies Agency of NATO
	(3) Corps Storage Area
	(4) Cognizant Secure Authority
CSABE	Central and South African Basic Encyclopedia
CSAF	Chief of Staff, Air Force
CSAFM	Chief of Staff, Air Force Memorandum
CSAM	Chief of Staff, Army Memorandum
CSAR	Combat Search and Rescue
CSAW	Cryptologic Support to Amphibious Warfare
CSB	Close Silo Basing
CSC	Community Support Center
CSCE	Conference on Security and Cooperation in Europe
CSCO	Contractor Special Security Officer

CSE	(1) Cryptologic Support Element
	(2) Communications Security Establishment
CSG	(1) Cryptologic Support Group
	(2) Chairman's Staff Group
	(3) Combat Support Group
CSGN	Nuclear Strike Cruiser
C-SIGINT	Counter-Signals Intelligence
CSM	Command Sergeant Major
CSMO	Cryptologic Support to Military Operations
CSO	Composite Signals Organization
CSP	(1) Crisis Staffing Procedures
	(2) Directorate for Command Support and Plans (DIA)
CSPO	Consolidated SAFE Project Office
CSR	(1) Current Situation Room
	(2) Coastal Surveillance Radar
CSS	(1) Communications Security System
	(2) Communications Support System
	(3) Clandestine Services Staff
	(4) Central Security Service
	(5) Combat Service Support (CSS)
CST	Coastal Survey team
CSTIP	Combined Strategic Intelligence Training Program (Defense Intelligence College)
CT	(1) Counterterrorism
	(2) Training Cruiser
CTA	(1) Central Technical Authority
	(2) Common Table of Allowances
CTAK	Cipher Text Auto-Key
CTB	Comprehensive Test Ban
CTBT	Comprehensive Test Ban Treaty
CTCC	Consolidated Telecommunications Center
CTF	Crisis Task Force
CTG	Commander, Task Group
CTH	Aviation Training Cruiser
CTIA	Counter Technical Intelligence Activities
CTOC	Corps Tactical Operations Center
CTOL	Conventional Take-Off and Landing
CTP	Consolidated Telecommunica-

tions Program

CTSCR	Critical Time-Sensitive Collection Requiremnt
CUBIC	Common User Baseline for Intelligence Community
CUDIXS	Common User Digital Information Exchange System
CUSRPG	Canadian-U.S. Regional Planning Group (NATO)
CV	Multipurpose Aircraft Carrier
CVBG	Carrier Battle Group
CVG	Guided-Missile Aircraft Carrier
CVGN	Nuclear-Powered Guided-Missile Aircraft Carrier
CVH	V/STOL Aircraft Carrier
CVHG	Guided-Missile V/STOL Aircraft Carrier
CVHGN	Nuclear-Powered Guided-Missile Aircraft Carrier
CVHN	Nuclear-Powered V/STOL Aircraft Carrier
CVIC	Carrier-Based Intelligence Center
CVL	Light Aircraft Carrier
CVLGN	Nuclear-Powered Guided-Missile Light Aircraft Carrier
CVLN	Nuclear-Powered Light Aircraft Carrier
CVN	Nuclear-Powered Aircraft Carrier
CVRT	Combat Vehicle (Reconnaissance, Tracked)
CVS	Antisubmarine Aircraft Carrier
CVT	Training Aircraft Carrier
CVW	Carrier Air Wing
CW	(1) Chemical Warfare
	(2) Carrier Wave
	(3) Continuous Wave
CWI	Conventional Weapon Index
CWO	Communications Watch Office
CY	Calendar Year
CYCLOPS	Fleet Support Message
CZ	Convergent Zone

— D —

DA	Department of the Army
DAC	Development Assistance Committee of OECD
DACOM	Data Communications
DACT	Dissimilar Air Combat Tactics
DAF	Department of the Air Force
DAG	(1) Defense Special Security Communications Systems Address Group
	(2) Divisional Artillery Group (Soviet)
DAIPR	Department of the Army In-Process Review Programs
DAISY	Daily Summary
DALASP	Defense Advanced Language and Area Studies Program
DAMI-FIM	Foreign Intelligence and Threat Management Division
DAO	(1) Defense Attaché Office
	(2) Division Ammunition Officer
DAP	Designated Acquisition Program
DARCOM	Department of the Army Materiel Development and Readiness Command (now AMC)
DARPA	Defense Advanced Research Projects Agency
DARTS	Digital Antijam Radio Teletype System
DAS	(1) Defense Attaché System
	(2) Defense Audit System
DASC	Direct Air Support Center (Amphibious Operations)
DASD(C³)	Deputy Assistant Secretary of Defense for Command, Control, and Communications
DASPA	Defense Attaché System Property Accounting
DASR	Defense Analysis Special Report
DASVA	Defense Attaché System Vehicle Accounting
DAT	Direct Action Team
DATT	Defense Attaché
DB	Directorate for Research (DIA)
DBC	Data Base Correlation
DBIDI	Data Base Imagery-Derived Information
DBMS	Data Base Management System
DBQ	Data Base Query

DC	Directorate for Collection Management (DIA)
DCA	Defense Communications Agency
DCAPSS	Dual Criteria Aimpoint Selection System
DCI	Director of Central Intelligence
DCIB	Defense Counterintelligence Board
DCID	Director, Central Intelligence Directive
DCII	Defense Central Index of Investigations
DCIS	Defense Criminal Investigative Service
DCL	Defense Communications Link
DCPR	Destination Common Point of Reference
DCS	(1) Defense Communications System
	(2) Deputy Chief of Staff
	(3) Damage Criteria Study
DCSRDA	Deputy Chief of Staff for Research, Development, and Acquisition, DARCOM
DD	(1) Destroyer
	(2) Deputy Director
DDA	(1) CIA Directorate of Administration
	(2) The Deputy Director of Administration
DDC	(1) Defense Documentation Center
	(2) Data Distribution Center
DDCI	Deputy Director of Central Intelligence
D/DCI/A	Deputy Director of Central Intelligence for Administration
D/DCI/CT	Deputy Director of Central Intelligence for Collection Tasking
D/DCI/IC	Deputy Director of Central Intelligence for the Intelligence Community
D/DCI/NI	Deputy Director of Central Intelligence for the National Intelligence
D/DCI/RM	Deputy Director of Central Intelligence for Resource Management
DDF	Deputy Director (of NSA) for Field Management and Evaluation

DDG	Guided-Missile Destroyer
DDGN	Nuclear-Powered Guided-Missile Destroyer
DDH	Aviation Destroyer (ASW)
DDHG	Guided-Missile Aviation Destroyer
DDHGN	Nuclear-Powered Guided-Missile Aviation Destroyer
DDHN	Nuclear-Powered Aviation Destroyer
DDI	(1) Deputy Director for Intelligence (CIA)
	(2) Directorate for Intelligence (CIA)
	(3) Director of Defense Intelligence
D/DIRNSA	Deputy Director of NSA
DDO	(1) Deputy Director for Operations (CIA)
	(2) Directorate for Operations (CIA)
	(3) Deputy Director for Operations (NSA) (Office of Signal Operations)
DDP	(1) Deputy Director for Plans (CIA)
	(2) Directorate for Plans (CIA)
	(3) Defense Dissemination Program
DDPO	Defense Dissemination Program Office
DDPP	Deputy Director for Plans and Policy (NSA)
DDPR	Deputy Director for Plans and Resources (NSA)
DDR	Directorate for Research (CIA)
DDS	(1) Deputy Director for Support (CIA)
	(2) Directorate for Support (CIA)
	(3) Defense Dissemination System
DDS&T	(1) Deputy Director for Science and Technology (CIA and DIA)
	(2) Directorate for Science and Technology (CIA and DIA)
DDT	Training Destroyer
DE	(1) Directorate for Estimates (DIA)
	(2) Damage Expectancy
	(3) Directed Energy
DEA	Drug Enforcement Administration

DEACON	Defense Estimates Analytical Computer On-Line Network
DEB	(1) Defense Estimative Brief
	(2) Digital European Backbone
Decl OADR	Originating Agency's Determination Required for Declassification
DECM	(1) Defense Electronic Countermeasures
	(2) Deceptive Electronic Countermeasures
DECON	Decontamination
DEDAC	Deception and Denial Analysis Committee
DEFCON	(1) Defense Condition
	(2) Defense Readiness Condition
DEFSMAC	Defense Special Missile and Astronautics Center
DEMUX	Demultiplex
DEN	Distant Early Warning
DENAS	Daily European Naval Activity Summary
DEP	(1) Deflection Error Probable
	(2) Defense Estimate for Production
DEPSECDEF	Deputy Secretary of Defense
DES	(1) Digital Exploitation System
	(2) Data Encryption Standard
DESIST	Decision Support and Information System for Terrorism
DET	Detachment
DEW	Distant Early Warning
DF	Direction Finding
DG	Defense Guidance
D/GDIP	General Defense Intelligence Program Staff (DIA)
DGIS	Director General Intelligence and Security
DGU	Downgrade to Unclassified
DGZ	(1) Desired Ground Zero
	(2) Designated Ground Zero
DI	Directorate for Intelligence and External Affairs (DIA)
DIA	Defense Intelligence Agency
DIAC	Defense Intelligence Analysis Center
DIAI	DIA Instruction
DIAIAPPRR	DIA Intelligence Appraisal
DIALOG	Lockheed Corporation Data Base
DIAM	Defense Intelligence Agency Manual

DIANM	DIA Analytical Memorandum
DIAOB	Defense Intelligence Air Order of Battle
DIAOLS	DIA On-Line System
DIAR	DIA Regulation
DIATS	DIA Terrorism Summary
DIB	Defense Intelligence Board
DIC	(1) Defense Intelligence College
	(2) Defense Intelligence Community
	(3) Defense Intelligence Commentary
DICBM	Depressed Intercontinental Ballistic Missile
DIDSRS	Defense Intelligence Dissemination, Storage, and Retrieval System
DIE	Defense Intelligence Estimate
DIEM	Defense Intelligence Estimate Memorandum
DIEOB	Defense Intelligence Electronic Order of Battle
DIEQP	Defense Intelligence Equipment Index
DIESM	Defense Intelligence Estimates Staff Memorandum
DIFAR	(1) Directional Frequency Analysis and Recording System
	(2) Directional Frequency and Ranging
DIFAX	Defense Intelligence Security Facsimile Network
DIFM	Defense Intelligence Functional Manager
DIGOB	Defense Intelligence Ground Order of Battle
DIIP	Defense Intelligence Interoperability Panel
DIIPS	Defense Imagery Interactive Processing System
DIIS	Defense Integrated Intelligence System
DIMOB	Defense Intelligence Missile Order of Battle
DIN	Defense Intelligence Notice
DINDSSCS	Digital Network-Defense Special Security Communications System
DINOB	Defense Intelligence Naval Order of Battle
DINSUM	Daily Intelligence Summary

DIO	Defense Intelligence Officer		Report
DIOBS	Defense Intelligence Order of Battle System		(2) Daily Indications Status Report
DIOP	Defense Intelligence Objectives and Priorities	**DISS**	Digest of Intelligence and Security Services
DIP	Defense Intelligence Plan	**DIST**	Digital Imagery Support Terminal
DIPOLES	Defense Intelligence Photoreconnaissance On-Line Exploitation System	**DISUM**	Daily Intelligence Summary
		DIT	Defense Intelligence Thesaurus
DIPP	Defense Intelligence Projections for Planning	**DITB**	Digital Imagery Test Bed
		DITS	Digital Imagery Transmission System
DIPS	(1) Defense Intelligence Production Schedule	**DIV**	(1) Defense Intelligence Videocassette
	(2) Defense Intelligence Production System		(2) Division
DIR	Defense Intelligence Report	**DIW**	Dead in the Water
DIRDIA	Director, Defense Intelligence Agency	**DJS**	Director, Joint Staff
		DJSM	DJS Memorandum
DIRM	Defense Intelligence Collection Requirements Manual	**DLA**	Defense Logistics Agency
		DLB	Dead Letter Box
DIRNSA/		**DLI**	Defense Language Institute
CHCSS	Director, National Security Agency/Chief, Central Security Service	**DLIFLC**	Defense Language Institute, Foreign Language Center
		DLL	Delegation of Disclosure Letter
DIS	(1) Defense Intelligence School (See Defense Intelligence College)	**DLO**	Defense Liaison Office
		DMA	Defense Mapping Agency
	(2) Defense Intelligence Summary	**DMAAC**	Defense Mapping Agency Aerospace Center
	(3) Defense Investigative Service	**DMAAHTC**	Defense Mapping Agency Hydrographic and Topographic Center
	(4) Daily Intelligence Summary		
	(5) Defence Intelligence Staff (UK)	**DMATC**	Defense Mapping Agency Topographic Center
	(6) Defense Intelligence Service	**DME**	Distance Measuring Equipment
DISC	Daily Intelligence Summary Cable	**DMOB**	Defense Missile Order of Battle
		DMOS	Daily Maritime Intelligence Summary
DISCAS	Defense Intelligence Special Career Automated System		
		DMS	Data Management System
DISCO	Defense Industrial Security Clearance Office	**DMSP**	Defense Meteorological Satellite Program
DISCOM	Division Support Command	**DMZ**	Demilitarized Zone
DISECS	Defense Intelligence Space Exploitation and Correlation System	**DN**	(1) Data Net
			(2) Duplicate Negative
DISES	Defense Intelligence Senior Executive Service	**DNA**	Defense Nuclear Agency
		DND	Department of National Defence (Canada)
DISIDS	Display and Information Distribution System/ Subsystem	**DNI**	Director of Naval Intelligence
		DOA	Date of Arrival
DISOB	Defense Intelligence Space Order of Battle	**DOB**	(1) Depth of Burst
			(2) Date of Birth
DISPLAY	NATO Southern flank Exercise DETERMINATION	**DOC**	Department of Commerce
		DOCKLAMP	Defense Attaché System
DISR	(1) Defense Indications Status		

	Message Channel
DOD	(1) Department of Defense
	(2) Date of Death
	(3) Date of Departure
DODCI	Department of Defense Computer Institute
DODD	Department of Defense Directive
DODIIS	Department of Defense Intelligence Information System
DOE	Department of Energy
DOI	(1) Date of Information
	(2) Duration of Illumination
DONCS	Director of Operations Narcotics Control Reports
DOPS	DIA Outline Plotting System
DOS	(1) Department of State
	(2) Date of Separation
DOT	Department of Transportation
DOUBLE TAKE	U.S. Exercise Defense Condition
DP	(1) Directorate for Plans and Policy (DIA)
	(2) Duplicate Positive
	(3) Development Program
	(4) Displaced Person
	(5) Delegated Production
DPC	Defense Planning Committee (NATO)
DPD	Development Projects Division (CIA)
DPI	Desired Point of Impact
DPIC	Decentralized Pacific Imagery Processing and Interpretation Center
DPOB	Date, Place of Birth
DPP	Delegated Production Program
DPPG	Defense Planning and Policy Guidance (Replaced by the Consolidated Guidance)
DPQ	Defense Planning Questionnaire (NATO)
DPRC	Defense Program Review Committee
DPS	Delegated Production System
DR	Director (DIA)
DRB	Defense Resources Board
DRC	Defense Review Committee (NATO)
DROLS	Defense Research, Development, Test, and Evaluation On-Line System

DRS	Data Relay Satellite
DRSEM	Deployable Receive Segment Engineering Model
DRSP	Defense Reconnaissance Support Center
DRU	Direct Reporting Unit
DS	Direct Support
DSA	(1) Defense Supply Agency
	(2) Direct Service Activities (SIGINT)
	(3) Directed Search Area
	(4) Division Support Area
DSAA	Defense Security Assistance Agency
DSARC	Defense Systems Acquisition Review Council
DSB	(1) Defense Science Board
	(2) Defensive Security Briefing
DSCS	Defense Satellite Communications System
DSD	Defense Signals Directorate
DSE	(1) Directorate for DODIIS Engineering (DIA)
	(2) Direct Support Element
DSG	(1) Defense Steering Group
	(2) Designated
DSI	Directorate for Internal Systems (DIA)
DSIIB	Direct Support Imagery Interpretation Brief
DSIIR	Direct Support Imagery Interpretation Report
DSM	Directorate for DODIIS Management (DIA)
DSP	Defense Support Program
DSPO	Defense Support Project Office
DSR	Defense Source Register
DSRV	Deep Submergence Rescue Vehicle
DSSCC	Defense Special Security Communications Center
DSSCS	Defense Special Security Communications System
DSSS	Defense Special Security System
DSTP	Director Strategic Target Planning
DSU	(1) Directed Support Unit
	(2) Disk Storage Unit
DSV	Deep Submergence Vehicle
DT	(1) Directorate for Scientific and Technical Intelligence (DIA)

	(2) Developmental Test
	(3) Director for Training (DIA)
DTED	Digital Terrain Elevation Data
DTG	Date-Time Group
DTIC	Defense Technical Information Center (formerly Defense Document Center)
DTIR	Defense Technical Intelligence Report
DTNSRDC	David W. Taylor Naval Ship Research and Development Center
DTOC	Division Tactical Operations Center
DTS	(1) Diplomatic Telecommunications System
	(2) Data Transmission System
DU	(1) Decision Unit
	(2) Depleted Uranium
DUSD(P)	Deputy Under-Secretary of Defense (Policy)
DWIP	Defense-Wide Intelligence Plan
DWT	(1) Deadweight Ton
	(2) Division Wing Team
DX	(1) Directorate for Imagery Exploitation (DIA)
	(2) Direct Exchange
DZ/LZ/RZ	Drop/Landing/Recovery Zone
DZS	Drop Zone Study

— E —

EA	Emergency Action(s)
EAC	Echelon Above Corps
EAD	Echelon Above Division
EAM	Emergency Action Message
EAMA	African States Associated with EEC
EAP	(1) East Asia and Pacific Office, Current Analysis Section, Bureau of Intelligence and Research, Department of State
	(2) Emergency Action Plan
	(3) Emergency Action Procedure(s)
EASTLANT	Eastern Atlantic Command
EC	(1) European Community
	(2) Expenditure Center

	(3) Office of Economic Analysis, Assessments and Research Section, Bureau of Intelligence and Research, Department of State
ECAC	Electromagnetic Compatibility Analysis Center
ECC	(1) Eurasian Communist Countries
	(2) European Communist Countries
	(3) European Community Commission
ECCM	Electronic Counter-Countermeasures
ECG	Emergency Coordination Group
ECM	Electronic Countermeasures
ECMO	European Collection Management Office
ECOM	Electronic Computer-Originated Mail
ECOWAS	Economic Community of West African States
ECSC	European Coal and Steel Community
ED	Executive Director (DIA)
EDA	Emergency Dissemination Authority
E-DAY	Start Day of an Exercise
EDPS	ELINT Data Processing System
E&E	Evasion and Escape
EEC	(1) European Economic Community
	(2) East European Countries
EEFI	Essential Elements of Friendly Information
EEI	Essential Elements of Information
EENT	Early Evening Nautical Twilight
EEO	Equal Employment Opportunity
EEOC	Equal Employment Opportunity Commission
EES	Emergency Evacuation Study
EFTA	European Trade Association
EFTO	Encrypted for Transmission Only
EHF	Extremely High Frequency
EI	Effectiveness Index
EIB	External Intelligence Bureau
EIC	Economic Intelligence Committee
EIP	ELINT Improvement Program
ELDO	European Space Vehicle

	Launcher Development Organization
ELECTRO-OPTINT	Electro-Optical Intelligence
ELF	Extremely Low Frequency
ELINT	Electronic Intelligence
ELOS	Extended Line of Sight
ELSEC	Electronic Security
ELV	Expendable Launch Vehicle
EM	(1) Electromagnetic
	(2) Enlisted Man
EMA	European Monetary Agreement
EMATS	Emergency Message Automatic Transmitting System
EMC	Electromagnetic Compatibility
EMCON	Emission Control
EMGTN	Equivalent Megatonnage
EMI	Electromagnetic Interference
EMIDS	Experiment for Management Information Data Systems
EMP	Electromagnetic Pulse
EMR	Electromagnetic Reconnaissance
EMSEC	Emanations Security
EMT	Equivalent Megatonnage
ENDEX	End Date of Exercise
ENIAC	Electronic Numerical Integrator Computer
ENMCC	Expanded National Military Command Center
ENSCE	Enemy Situation Correlation Element
EO	(1) Electro-optics
	(2) Executive Order
EOB	Electronic Order of Battle
EOC	Emergency Operations Center
EOD	Explosive Ordinance Disposal
EOP	Executive Office of the President
EORSAT	ELINT Ocean Reconnaissance Satellite
EOSAT	Earth Observation Satellite
EPA	Environmental Protection Agency
EPF	Exploitation Products File
EPS	ELINT Processing System
EPW	(1) Earth Penetrator Weapon
	(2) Enemy Prisoner of War
ER	(1) Electronic Reconnaissance
	(2) Enhanced Radiation
ERA	(1) Extended Range Ammunition

	(2) Equal Rights Amendment
	(3) Engineering Research Associates
	(4) Economic Research Area
ERADCOM	Electronic Research and Development Command
ERCMS	ELINT Requirements and Capabilities Management System
ERCS	Emergency Rocket Communications System
ERDA	Energy Research and Development Administration
EROS	Earth Resources Observation System
ERP	Effective Power (Radiated)
ERPHO	Earth Resources Photographic Satellite
ERS	Emergency Relocation Site
ERT	Executive Reference Time
ERTS	Earth Resources Technology Satellite
ERW	Enhanced Radiation Weapon
ESA	European Supplies Agency
ESAA	European Special Activities Area (U.S. Air Force)
ESC	Electronic Security Command (U.S. Air Force)
ESF	Environmental Scale Factor
ESG	Electronic Security Group
ESI	Extremely Sensitive Information
ESM	Electronic Warfare Support Measures
ESO	Executive Support Office (DIA)
ESR	ELINT Summary Report
ESRO	European Space Research Organization
ESS	ELINT Support System
ETA	(1) Estimated Time of Arrival
	(2) Equivalent Target Area
ETAWG	ELINT Technical Analysis Working Group
ETC	Estimated Time of Completion
ETD	Estimated Time of Departure
ETDS	Elapsed Time Distribution System
ETF	Enhanced Tactical Fighter
ETI	Estimated Time of Impact
ETII	External to Internal Interface
ETIL	European Target Installation List
ETSC	Electronic and Telecommunications Subcommittee

ETUT	Enhanced Tactical User Terminal
EU	Expenditure Unit
EUCOM	European Command
EUDAC	European Defense Analysis Center
EURATOM	European Atomic Energy Community
EUROCOM	European Communist
EUSA	Eighth United States Army, Korea
EUSC	Effective U.S. Controlled Ships
EVAC	Evacuation
EVS	Electronic Visual Communications
EW	(1) Electronic Warfare
	(2) Early Warning
EWC	Electronic Warfare Center
EW/GCI	Early Warning/Ground Controlled Intercept
EWIR	Electronic Warfare Integrated Reprogramming
EX	Office of the Executive Director, Bureau of Intelligence and Research, Department of State
EXCAP	Exercise Capability (Simulator)
EXCOM	Executive Committee (of the NRO)
EXDIS	Exclusive Distribution
EXOPLAN	Exercise Operations Plan
EXPLAN	Exercise Plan
EXRAND	Exploitation Research and Development (COMIREX)
EXSUBCOM	Exploitation Subcommittee (COMIREX)
EXSUM	Executive Summary

— F —

F	Full Duplex
FA	(1) Field Artillery
	(2) Frontal Aviation (Soviet)
FAA	Federal Aviation Agency
FAAR	Forward Area Alerting Radar
FAAS	Foreign Affairs Administrative Support
FAD	(1) Fleet Air Defense
	(2) Force Activity Designator

FADE OUT	U.S. Exercise Defense Condition
FAE	Fuel Air Explosive
FAI	Fuel Air Incendiary Concussion Bomb
FAMP	Foreign Army Materiel Production
FANT	French Atmospheric Nuclear Test
FANX	Friendship (Airport) Annex of the National Security Agency
FAO	Foreign Area Officer
FAPC	Food and Agriculture Planning Committee (NATO)
FARRP	Forward Area Rearming and Refueling Point
FASC	Forward Area Support Center
FAST	Forward Area Support Team
FAST PACE	U.S. Exercise Defense Condition
FB	Fighter Bomber
FBA	Fighter Bomber Attack
FBI	Federal Bureau of Investigation
FBIS	Foreign Broadcast Information Service
FBM	Fleet Ballistic Missile
FBR	Fast Breeder Reactor
FBS	Forward-Based Systems
FC	Fire Control
FCC	(1) Fleet Command Center
	(2) Federal Communications Commission
FCI	Foreign Counterintelligence
FCZ	Forward Combat Zone
FDBPS	Fleet Data Base Production System
FDC	Fire Detection Center
FDM	Frequency Division Multiplexing
FDOA	Frequency Difference of Arrival
FDX	Full Duplex
FEBA	Forward Edge of Battle Area
FEDS	Front End Distribution System
FEDSIM	Federal Computer Performance Evaluation and Simulation Center
FEMA	Federal Emergency Management Agency
FEWSG	Fleet Electronic Warfare Support Group
FF	Frigate
FFA	Free Fire Area
FFAR	Folding Fin Aerial Rocket

FFG	Guided-Missile Frigate
FFGH	Guided-Missile Aviation Frigate
FFGN	Nuclear-Powered Guided-Missile Frigate
FFH	Aviation Frigate
FFHGN	Nuclear-Powered Guided-Missile Aviation Frigate
FFHN	Nuclear-Powered Aviation Frigate
FFL	Corvette
FFLG	Guided-Missile Corvette
F&FP	Force and Financial Plan
FFR	Radar Picket Frigate
FFT	Training Frigate
FGM	Fiscal Guidance Management (Replaced by the Consolidate Guidance)
FHMA	Family Housing Management Appropriation
FI	Foreign Intelligence
FIC	Fleet Intelligence Center
FICEURLANT	Fleet Intelligence Center, Europe and Atlantic
FICM	Fleet Intelligence Collection Manual
FICPAC	Fleet Intelligence Center, Pacific
FID	Foreign Internal Defense
FIDB	Fundamental Intelligence Data Base
FIO	(1) Foreign Intelligence Officer
	(2) Foreign Intelligence Office (Army)
FIP	Foreign Improvement Plan
FIRF	Future Information Requirements Forecast
FIRMS	Foreign Intelligence Relations Management System
FIS	Foreign Instrumentation Signals
FISA	Foreign Intelligence Surveillance Act
FISINT	Foreign Instrumentation Signals Intelligence
FI&SS	Foreign Intelligence and Security Service(s)
FIST	(1) Fleet Imagery Support Terminal
	(2) Fire Support Team
FLINTLOCK	European Special Forces Operations Exercise
FLIR	Forward Looking Infrared System
FLOT	(1) Forward Line of Troops
	(2) Flotilla

FLR	Forward Looking Radar
FLRA	Federal Labor Relations Authority
FLT	(1) Fleet
	(2) Flight
FLTBCST	Fleet Broadcast
FLTCINC	Fleet Commander-in-Chief
FLTSATCOM	Fleet Satellite Communications System
FM	(1) Foreign Materiel
	(2) Frequency Modulation
	(3) Field Manual
FMA	(1) Foreign Materiel Acquisition
	(2) Foreign Media Analysis
FME	Foreign Materiel Acquisition
FMEC	Foreign Materiel Exploitation Catalog
FMEP	Foreign Materiel Exploitation Program
FMER	Foreign Materiel Exploitation Report
FMF	Fleet Marine Force
FMFLANT	Fleet Marine Force Atlantic
FMP	Foreign Materiel Program
FMPCP	Foreign Military Personnel Contact Program
FMRL	Foreign Materiel Requirements List
FMS	Foreign Military Sales
FMSF	Foreign Military Sales Financing
FNU	First Name Unknown
FO	Forward Observer
FOAMP	Foreign Aerospace Materiel Production
FOAP	Foreign Aircraft Production
FOB	Forward Operational Base
FOBS	Fractional Orbital Bombardment System
FOC	(1) Final Operational Capabilities
	(2) Full Operational Capability
FOCUS	Interagency Review of Defense Attaché Offices
FOD	Foreign Object Damage
FOIA	Freedom of Information Act
FOMA	Foreign Military Assistance
FOMCAT	Foreign Materiel Catalog
FOMP	Foreign Missile Production
FOP	Forward Observation Post
FORDTIS	Foreign Disclosure Technical Information System
FORGE	Force Generation

FORMAT	Foreign Materiel
FORMICA	Foreign Military Intelligence Collection Activity
FORSCOM	U.S. Armed Forces Command
FORSIC	Army Forces Command Intelligence Center
FORSIG	Army Forces Command Intelligence Group
FORSTAT	Force Status and Identity Report
FORT	Force Trends Data Base
FORTRAN	Formula Translator
FOSCAS	Foreign Ship Construction and Shipyards
FOSIC	Fleet Ocean Surveillance Information Center
FOSIC LANT	Fleet Ocean Surveillance Information Center, Atlantic, Norfolk, Virginia
FOSIC PAC	Fleet Ocean Surveillance Information Center, Pacific, Honolulu, Hawaii
FOSIF	Fleet Ocean Surveillance Information Facility
FOSIF Kamisea	Fleet Ocean Surveillance Information Facility, Kamisea, Japan
FOSIF London	Fleet Ocean Surveillance Information Facility, London, UK
FOSIF Rota	Fleet Ocean Surveillance Information Center, Rota, Spain
FOT&E	Follow-On Test and Evaluation
FOTELSYS	Foreign Telecommunications Systems
FOUO	For Official Use Only
FOV	Field of View
FP	Fire Position
FPA	Federal Preparedness Agency
FPE	Force Planning Estimate
FPF	Final Protection Fire
FPL	Fire Protective Line
FPO	Fleet Post Office
FRAGO	Fragmentary Order
FRCOA	Friendly Courses of Action
FRD	(1) Federal Research Division (Library of Congress) (2) Formerly Restricted Data
FRG	Federal Republic of Germany
FRI	Finished Recurring Intelligence
FRIF	Finished Recurring Intelligence File
FRS	(1) Fleet Readiness Squadron

	(2) Federal Research Service
FSCC	Fire Support Coordination Center
FSCL	Fire Support Coordination Line
FSD	Field Support Division
FSE	Fire Support Element
FSHB	Fallout Safe Height Burst
FSK	Frequency Shift Keying
FSL	Foreign Science Library, Columbus, Ohio
FSO	Foreign Service Officer
FSOP	Field Standing Operating Procedure
FST	(1) Future Strategic Targets (2) Future Soviet Tank
FSTC	Foreign Science and Technology Center (U.S. Army)
FSTL	Future Strategic Target List
FSV	Fire Support Vehicle
FTC	Fast Time Constant (ECCM)
FTD	Foreign Technology Division (U.S. Air Force)
FTI	Fixed Target Indicator
FTX	Field Training Exercise
FUNT	French Underground Nuclear Test
FUSS	Fleet Underseas Surveillance System
FUWOB	Forward Unconventional Warfare Operations Base
FV	Fighting Vehicle
FWAIS	Free World Air Intelligence Study
FWAOB	Free World Air Order of Battle
FWVP	Fallout Wind Vector Plot
FY	Fiscal Year
FYDP	Five Year Defense Program
FYI	For Your Information
FYIP	Five-Year Intelligence Plan
FYMOP	Five-Year Master Objectives Plan

— G —

G2	Army Intelligence
G3	Army Operations
GA	Ground Attack
GAD	Guards Artillery Division

GADT	Ground/Air Defense Threat
GAFIA	German Armed Forces Intelligence Agency
GALLANT KNIGHT	CENTCOM Exercise
GAMO	Ground and Amphibious Military Operations
GAO	Government Accounting Office
GAS	Gray Area Systems
GATT	General Agreement on Tariffs and Trade (UN)
GBL	Ground-Based Laser
GBU	Guided Bomb Unit
GC	General Counsel (DIA)
GCA	Ground Controlled Approach
GCC	Government Control Center
GCCS	Government Code and Cipher School
GCE	Ground Combat Element
GCHQ	Government Communications Headquarters (UK)
GCI	Ground Controlled Intercept
GCP	Ground Controlled Processor
GCSB	Government Communications Security Bureau (New Zealand)
GD	Guard
GDIC	General Defense Intelligence Community
GDIP	General Defense Intelligence Program
GDIPP	General Defense Intelligence Proposed Program
GDP	(1) General Defense Plan
	(2) Gross Defense Product
	(3) Ground Defense Position
	(4) Gross Domestic Product
GDR	German Democratic Republic
GDS	General Declassification Schedule
GE	Office of the Geographer, Assessments and Research Section, Bureau of Intelligence and Research, Department of State
GEM	Ground Effects Machine
GENSER	General Service (Communications)
GEOREF	Geographic reference; a worldwide position reference system that may be applied to any map or chart graduated in latitude and longitude regardless of projection
GEP	Ground Entry Point
GFE	Government Furnished Equipment
GFTD	Global Force Trends Data Base
GHZ	Gigahertz
GI	Office of Global Issues, Assessments, and Research Section, Bureau of Intelligence and Research, Department of State
GIPD	General Intelligence Production Division
GIPMIS	General Intelligence Production Management Information System
GITS	General Intelligence Training System
GIUK (Gap)	Greenland-Iceland-United Kingdom (Gap)
GL	Grenade Launcher
GLCM	Ground-Launched Cruise Missile
GLLD	U.S. Ground Laser Locator Designator (for Copperhead)
GLOBAL SHIELD	SAC Exercise
GM	Guided Missile
GMAIC	Guided Missiles/Astronautics Intelligence Committee
GMF	Ground Mobile Forces
GMI	(1) General Medical Intelligence
	(2) General Military Intelligence
GMIC	Guided Missile Intelligence Committee
GMRD	Guards Motorized Rifle Division (Soviet)
GMT	Greenwich Mean Time
GND	Ground
GNP	Gross National Product
GNST	Glossary of Naval Ship Types
GO	Government of (name of country)
GOB	Ground Order of Battle
GOC	General Officer Commanding (U.K.)
GOR	General Operational Requirement
GP	(1) Group
	(2) General Purpose

GPF	General Purpose Forces
GPH	Gallons Per Hour
GPO	Government Printing Office
GPS	Global Positioning System
GPSCS	General Purpose Satellite Communications System
GRA	Geographic Research Area
GROFIS	Ground Forces Intelligence Study
GRT	Gross Registered Tonnage
GRU	Soviet General Staff Intelligence Organization
GS	(1) General Staff
	(2) Geological Survey
	(3) General Support
	(4) General Schedule
	(5) General Service
GSA	General Services Administration
GSE	Ground Support Equipment
GSF	(1) Ground Support Fighter
	(2) Group of Soviet Forces
GSFG	Group of Soviet Forces Germany (East Germany)
GSFM	Group of Soviet Forces, Mongolia
GSP	General Strike Plan
GSR	(1) General Support Reinforcing
	(2) Ground Surveillance Radar
GSRS	U.S. General Support Rocket System
GTD	Guards Tank Division (Soviet)
GW	Guided Weapon
GWC	Global Weather Control
GWIP	Global Weather Intercept System
GZ	Ground Zero

— H —

HAA	Helicopter Alighting Area
HAB	(1) High Altitude Burst
	(2) High Altitude Bombing
	(3) High Air Burst
HAC	House Appropriations Committee
HALE	High Altitude Long Endurance

HALO	High Altitude Low Opening
HAR	Hazardous Activities Restriction
HARV	Harassment Vehicle (Drone)
HASC	House Armed Services Committee
HATS	Heuristic Automated Transportation System
HCF	High Command of Forces
HDL	Harry Diamond Laboratories
HE	High Explosives
HEAT	High-Explosive Antitank
HEI	High Explosive Incendiary
HEL	High Energy Laser
HELIP	HAWK European Limited Improvement Program
HELW	High Energy Laser Weapons
HEMP	High Altitude Electromagnetic Pulse
HERO	Historical Evaluation and Research Organization
HERT	Headquarters Emergency Relocation Team
HET	Heavy Equipment Transporter
HF	High Frequency
HF/DF	High Frequency/Direction Finding
HHC	Headquarters and Headquarters Company
HHD	Headquarters and Headquarters Detachment
HHOC	Headquarters, Headquarters and Operations Company
HH&S	Headquarters and Headquarters Service
HHT	Headquarters and Headquarters Troop
HHW	Higher High Water
HICCD	Hostile Intelligence Collection Capability Display
HIMS	HUMINT Information Management System
HIS	Honeywell Information System
HITS	HUMINT Tasking System
HJ	HONEST JOHN (U.S. Surface-to-Surface Rocket)
HLA/DZ	Helicopter Landing Area/Drop Zone
HLA/DZS	Helicopter Landing Area/Drop Zone Study
HLW	Higher Low Water
HLZ	Helicopter Landing Zone
HMCII	Higher Military Command,

Interior and Islands (Greece)

HMF	Handbook of Military Forces
HMS	Her Majesty's Ship
HNS	Host Nation Support
HOB	Height of Burst
HOC	History of Coverage
HOIS	Hostile Intelligence Service(s)
HOJ	Home on Jam
HOTPHOTO-REP	Hot Photographic Interpretation Report
HOTSIT	Hot Situation Message
HP	(1) Headquarters Pamphlet
	(2) Horsepower
HPSCI	House Permanent Select Committee on Intelligence
HQ	Headquarters
HQJTF	Headquarters, Joint Task Force
HQMC	Headquarters, U.S. Marine Corps
HQMR	HITS Quarterly Management Report
HR	High Resolution
HRC	Human Resources Committee
HRES	House (of Representatives) Resolution
HR/MR	Human Readable/Machine Readable (Data)
HRR	High Resolution Radar
H&S	Headquarters and Service
HTF	How to Fight
HTKP	Hard Target Kill Potential
HTLD	High Technology Light Division
HUAC	House Un-American Activities Committee
HULTEC	Hull-to-Emitter Correlation
HUMINT	Human Intelligence
HVAP	High Velocity Armor Piercing
HVAPFSDS	High Velocity Armor Piercing Fin-Stabilized-Discarding Sabot
HVF	Highly Volatile Fuel
HVT	High Value Targets
HW	High Water
HWY	Highway
HZ	Hertz

— I —

IA	Imagery Analysis
IAA	Latin American Office, Current Analysis Section, Bureau of Intelligence and Research, Department of State
IAB	Intelligence Advisory Board
IAC	(1) Intelligence Advisory Committee
	(2) Intelligence Analysis Center
	(3) Information Analysis Center (Department of Defense)
IADB	Inter-American Defense Board
IAEA	International Atomic Energy Agency
IAG	(1) Intelligence Analysis Group (Formerly ITAD)
	(2) Imagery Analysis Group
IAGC	Instantaneous Automatic Gain Control
IAIPS	Integrated Automated Intelligence Processing System
IAM	Imagery Analysis Memorandum
IAMP	Imagery Acquisition and Management Plan
IAMS	Individual Aerial Mobility System
IAN	Imagery Analysis Notice
IAR	Imagery Analysis Report
IASA	Integrated Assessment of Security Assistance
IASSA	INSCOM Automated Systems Support Activity
IATA	International Air Transport Association
IAW	In Accordance With
IAWG	Interagency Working Group
IBERLANT	Iberian Atlantic Area
IBM	International Business Machines Corporation
IC	(1) Intelligence Community
	(2) Intelligence Collection
	(3) Intelligence Center
	(4) Integrated Circuit
	(5) The Office of Intelligence Coordination, Coordination Section, Bureau of Intelligence and Research, Department of State
ICA	International Communication Agency (now USIA)

ICAF	Industrial College of the Armed Forces		System Communications
ICAO	International Civil Aviation Association	**IDIMS**	Interactive Digital Image Manipulation System
ICBM	Intercontinental Ballistic Missile	**IDN**	Integrated Data Network
ICC	Integrated Communications Center	**IDP**	Intercept Deployment Plan
		IDSCS	Initial Defense Satellite Communications System
ICD	Imitative Communications Deception	**IDSF**	Intelligence Defector Source File
ICDP	Intelligence Career Development Program	**IE**	Intelligence Estimate
ICEP	Intelligence Continuing Education Program	**I&E**	Interrogation and Exploitation
		IEA	International Energy Agreement
ICES	International Cooperation in Ocean Exploration	**IEC**	(1) Intelligence Exchange Conference
ICF	Intelligence Collection Flight		(2) Intelligence Evaluation Committee
ICFTU	International Confederation of Free Trade Unions	**IED**	(1) Improved Explosive Device
ICI	Interagency Committee on Intelligence		(2) Imitative Electronic Deception
ICM	(1) Improved Conventional Munition(s)	**IEEE**	Institute of Electrical and Electronic Engineers
	(2) Intelligence Collection Management	**IEG**	Imagery Exploitation Group
ICM/MM	Intelligence Collection Management/Mission Management	**IEPG**	Independent European Program Group
		IES	Imagery Exploitation System
ICOD	Intelligence Cut-Off Date	**IEW**	Intelligence and Electronic Warfare
ICPR	Initial Common Point of Reference	**IFF**	Identification, Friend or Foe
ICR	Intelligence Collection Requirement	**IFFN**	Identification, Friend or Foe or Neutral
ICRS	(1) Intelligence Collection Requirement System	**INFLIGHTREP**	Inflight Report
	(2) Imagery Collection Requirements Subcommittee (COMIREX)	**IFR**	Instrument Flight Rules
		IFV	Infantry Fighting Vehicle
ICS or IC Staff	Intelligence Community Staff	**IG**	(1) Inspector General
ICTF	Interagency Crisis Task Force		(2) Interdepartmental Group
ICV	Infantry Combat Vehicle		(3) Interagency Group
ID	(1) Identification	**IGCP**	Intelligence Guidance for COMINT Program
	(2) Infantry Division	**IHC**	Intelligence Information Handling Committee
IDA	Institute for Defense Analysis	**IHE**	Insensitive High Explosive
IDB	Integrated Data Base	**IHO**	(1) International Hydrographic Organization
IDC	Interagency Defector Committee		
IDCP	General Defense Career Development Program		(2) In Honor Of
		II	(1) Imagery Interpretation
IDEAS	Intelligence Data Element Authorization Standards		(2) Imagery Interpreter
		IIC	Imagery Interpretation Center
IDEX	Imagery Digital Exploitation System	**IICT**	Interagency Intelligence Committee on Terrorism
IDHS	Intelligence Data Handling System	**IID**	Integrated Information Display
IDHSC	Intelligence Data Handling	**IIDP**	Integrated Intelligence Development Plan (USCINCEUR)

IIE	Installation Identification Element
IIG	Imagery Intelligence Group (Formerly USAIIC)
IIM	Interagency Intelligence Memorandum
IIPD/ITAC	Army Imagery Intelligence Production Division
IIR	(1) Imaging Infrared
	(2) Intelligence Information Report
IIS	(1) IPAC Intelligence Summary
	(2) Intelligence Information Systems (Navy)
IISS	Intelligence Information Subsystem
IITS	Intra-Theater Imagery Transmission System
IIU	Imagery Interpretation Unit
IL	The Office of Intelligence Liaison, Coordination Section, Bureau of Intelligence and Research, Department of State
ILC	International Lines of Communications
ILS	(1) Instrument Landing System
	(2) Integrated Logistic Support
IMA	(1) Institute for Military Assistance
	(2) Individual Mobilization Augmentee
IMET	International Military Education and Training
IMF	International Monetary Fund
IMINT	Imagery Intelligence
IMIS	(1) Intelligence Management Information System
	(2) Integrated Management Information System
IMP	(1) Interface Message Processor
	(2) Input Message Processor
IMS	International Military Staff (NATO)
IN	(1) International Negotiations
	(2) Intelligence
INA	Information Not Available
INCA	Intelligence Communications Architecture
INDICOM	Indications Communications (System)
INF	Intermediate-Range Nuclear Forces

INR	Bureau of Intelligence and Research, Department of State
INR/AR	Assessments and Research Section, Bureau of Intelligence and Research, Department of State
INR/C	Coordination Section, Bureau of Intelligence and Research, Department of State
INR/CA	Current Analysis Section, Bureau of Intelligence and Research, Department of State
INS	(1) Inertial Navigation System
	(2) Immigration and Naturalization Service
INSCOM	Intelligence and Security Command (U.S. Army)
INSIG	Army Intelligence and Security Command Intelligence Group
INSOD	Intelligence Notes for the Secretary of Defense
INST	Instruction
INTCP	Intercept
INTEL	Intelligence
INTELCOM	Worldwide Intelligence Communication
INTELPOST	International Electronic Post
INTELSAT	International Telecommunications Satellite Organization
INTG	Interrogation
INTRA	International Travel by Selected Foreign Officials
INTREP	Intelligence Report
INTSUM	Intelligence Summary
INUT	Indian Nuclear Underground Test
IO	(1) Intelligence Officer
	(2) Indian Ocean
IOA	Indian Ocean Area
IOB	Intelligence Oversight Board
IOC	Initial Operational Capability
IOCTL	Indian Ocean Conventional Target List
IOIC	Integrated Operational Intelligence Center
IONDS	Integrated Operational Nuclear Detection System
IOR	Interorganizational Relationships
IOS	(1) Intelligence Operations Specialist

	(2) International Organization for Standards
IOSS	(1) Integrated Operational Support Study
	(2) Intelligence Organization Stationing Study
IOT&E	Initial Operational Test and Evaluation
IP	(1) Imagery Processing
	(2) Intelligence Problem
	(3) Intelligence Plot
	(4) Issue Papers
	(5) Initial Point
	(6) Intelligence Production
IPA	Intelligence Production Activity
IPAC	Intelligence Center, Pacific
IPB	(1) Intelligence Preparation of the Battlefield
	(2) Intercept Priorities Board
IPC	(1) Industrial Planning Committee
	(2) Intelligence Producers' Council
IPD	Intelligence Planning Document
IPDB	Intelligence Production Data Base
IPF	Integrated Processing Facility
IPIR	(1) Immediate Photo Interpretation Report
	(2) Initial Photographic Interpretation Report
IPL	Information Processing Language
IPP	(1) Intelligence Producer Profile
	(2) Intelligence Production Program
IPR	(1) Intelligence Production Requirement
	(2) In Process Review
IPS	(1) Integrated Program Summary
	(2) Intelligence Production Section
IPSC	Information Processing Standards for Computers
IPSP	Intelligence Priorities for Strategic Planning
IPU	Inter-Parliamentary Union
IPW	Prisoner of War Interrogation
IPWIC	Interagency Prisoner of War Ad Hoc Committee
IR	(1) Intelligence Requirement
	(2) Infrared

	(3) Intelligence Report
	(4) Initial Radiation
	(5) Induced Radiation
	(6) Information Requirements
IRA	Intelligence-Related Activities
IRAC	Intelligence Resources Advisory Committee
IRBM	Intermediate-Range Ballistic Missile
IRC	(1) Intelligence Requirements Committee, Armed Forces Security Agency Council
	(2) International Red Cross
IRCM	Infrared Countermeasures
IRDC	Intelligence Research and Development Council
IRDHS	Imagery-Related Data Handling System (see AIRES)
IRE	The Office of Intelligence Resources, Coordination Section, Bureau of Intelligence and Research, Department of State
IRFLA	Intelligence Information Report File Archive
IRINT	Infrared Intelligence
IRISA	Intelligence Report Index Summary File
IROF	Imagery Reconnaissance Objectives File
IROL	Imagery Reconnaissance Objectives List
IROP	(1) Imagery Reconnaissance Objectives Plan
	(2) Infrared Optical Intelligence
	(3) Imagery Requirements Objectives Program
IRPG	Installation Reference Points Graphics
IRPIA	Intelligence Information Report Photo Index
IRR	Individual Ready Reserve
IRS	(1) Intelligence Research Specialist
	(2) Internal Revenue Service
IS	The Office of Intelligence Support, Bureau of Intelligence and Research, Department of State
ISA	(1) International Security Affairs
	(2) Interservice Support Agreement
	(3) International Studies Association

ISB	Intermediate Staging Base
ISC	Information Science Center
ISD	Information Services Division (FSTC, U.S. Army)
ISE	Intelligence Support Element
ISF	Intelligence Support File
ISIC	Intelligence Support and Indications Center
ISIP	Intelligence Support Interface Program
ISIS	Integrated Signals Intelligence System
ISO	Intelligence Support Office
ISPER	IPAC Special Reports
ISPO	Intelligence Support Program Office
ISS	Intelligence Support System
ITAC	(1) Intelligence and Threat Analysis Center (U.S. Army)
	(2) Intelligence Tracking Analysis and Correlation
ITACIES	Interim Tactical Imagery Exploitation System (U.S. Army)
ITAD/ITAC	Army Intelligence and Threat Analysis Detachment
ITAR	International Traffic in Arms Regulations
ITEP	(1) Interim Tactical ELINT Processor (U.S. Army)
	(2) Integrated Threat Evaluation Program
ITF	Intelligence Task Force
ITG	Interdiction Target Graphic
ITIC-PAC	INSCOM Theater Intelligence Center—Pacific
ITII	Internal-to-Internal Interface
ITP	Intelligence Town Plan
ITSS	Integrated Tactical Surveillance System
ITT	(1) Interrogator Translator Team
	(2) International Telephone and Telegraph Corporation
ITUT	Interim Tactical Users Terminal
IUG	Intelligence Users' Guide
I&W	Indications and Warning
IWD	Intermediate Water Depth
IWTS	Indications and Warning Training System
IWW	Inland Waterway
IX	Unclassified Miscellaneous Ship

— J —

JACC/CP	Joint Airborne Communications Center/Command Post
JACK FROST	Joint Winter Exercise
JAD	Joint Analysis Directorate, JCS (formerly SAGA)
JAEIC	Joint Atomic Energy Intelligence Committee
JAG	Joint Analysis Group
JAI	Joint Administrative Instruction
JAIEG	Joint Atomic Information Exchange Group
JARIC	Joint Air Reconnaissance Interpretation Center (U.K.)
JATF	Joint Amphibious Task Force
JCC	Joint Coordination Center
JCMC	Joint Crisis Management Capability
JCMO	Joint Collection Management Office
JCMPO	Joint Cruise Missile Project Office
JCP	Joint Congressional Committee on Printing
JCRC	Joint Casualty Resolution Center
JCS	Joint Chiefs of Staff
JCSAN	Joint Chiefs of Staff Alert Network
JCSE	Joint Communications Support Element
JCS J-2	Intelligence Functions Filled by DIA
JCS J-3	JCS Operations
JCS J-4	JCS Logistics
JCS J-5	JCS Plans and Policy
JCSM	Joint Chiefs of Staff Memorandum
JDA	(1) Japanese Defense Agency
	(2) Joint Deployment Agency
JEC	Joint Economic Committee
JECC(G)	Joint Exercise Control Center (Group)
JEEP	Joint Emergency Evacuation Plan
JEM	Joint Exercise Manual
JEWC	Joint Electronic Warfare Center
JFC	Joint Fusion Center
JFK CTRMA	John F. Kennedy Center for Military Assistance
JFM	Joint Force Memorandum (Replaced by JPAM)

JFMC	Joint Factory Markings Center		Memorandum
JFMIP	Joint Financial Management Improvement Program	JPO	Joint Project Office
JIB	Joint Intelligence Bureau (Commonwealth Countries)	JPRS	Joint Publications Research Service
JIC	(1) Joint Intelligence Committee	JPSS	Joint Planning Staff for Space
	(2) Joint Intelligence Center	JRC	(1) Joint Reconnaissance Center
JIEP	Joint Intelligence Estimate for Planning		(2) Joint Recovery Center
JIF	Joint Interrogation Facilities	JRDOD	Joint Research and Development Objectives Document (Replaced by Annex F, JSPD)
JIIKS	Joint Imagery Interpretation Key Structure		
JILE	Joint Intelligence Liaison Element	JRS	Joint Reporting Structure
JINTACCS	Joint Interoperability Tactical Command and Control System	JRSC	Jam Resistant Secure Communications
		JS	(1) Joint Staff
JIO	Joint Intelligence Organization		(2) Directorate for JCS Support (DIA)
JIPR	Joint Intelligence Production Requirement	JSAM	Joint Security Assistance Memorandum
JLPPG	Joint Logistics and Personnel Policy and Guidance	JSAMSA	Joint Security Assistance Memorandum Supporting Analysis
JLREID	Joint Long-Range Estimative Intelligence Document	JSCP	Joint Strategic Capabilities Plan
		JSCS	Joint Strategic Connectivity Staff
JLRSA	Joint Long-Range Strategic Appraisal	JSDF	Japanese Self-Defense Force
JLRSS	Joint Long-Range Strategic Study	JSG	Joint Study Group
JMA	Joint Mobilization Augmentation	JSI	Directorate for Current Intelligence (DIA)
JMEM	Joint Munitions Effectiveness Manual	JSL	Directorate for OJCS Intelligence Support (DIA)
JMENS	Joint Mission element Need Statement	JSM	Joint Staff Memorandum
JMO	Joint Management Office	JSO	(1) Directorate for Alert Center Operations (DIA)
JMP	Joint Manpower Program		(2) Directorate for National Military Intelligence Center Operations
JMPAB	Joint Material Priorities Allocation Board		
JMSDF	Japanese Maritime Self-Defense Force	JSOA	Joint Special Operations Agency
JMSNS	Justification for Major System New Start	JSOC	(1) Joint Special Operations Center
			(2) Joint Strategic Operations Center
JNACC	Joint Nuclear Accident Coordinating Center		(3) Joint Strategic Operations Command
JNIDS	Joint National Intelligence Dissemination System	JSOP	Joint Strategic Objective Plan (Replaced by JSPD)
JNMS	Justification for New Mission Start	JSPD	Joint Strategic Planning Document
JNPE	Joint Nuclear Planning Element	JSPDSA	Joint Strategic Planning Document Supporting Analysis
JOC	Joint Operations Center		
JOPES	Joint Operations Planning and Execution System	JSPS	Joint Strategic Planning System
		JSS	Joint Surveillance System
JOPS	Joint Operation Planning System	JSTPS	Joint Strategic Target Planning Staff
JPAM	Joint Program Assessment		

JSW	Directorate for Indications and Warning (DIA)
JTB	Joint Transportation Board
JTCG(ME)	Joint Technical Coordinating Group (for Munitions Effectiveness)
JTD	Joint Table of Distribution (Manning Authorization for a Joint Organization)
JTENS	Joint Service Tactical Exploitation of National Systems
JTF	Joint Task Force
JTFHQ	Joint Task Force Headquarters
JTFP	Joint Tactical Fusion Program
JTIDS	Joint Tactical Information Distribution System
JTLS	Joint Technical Language Service
JUL	July
JUN	June
JUWC	Joint Unconventional Warfare Command
JUWTF	Joint Unconventional Warfare Task Force
JWBCA	Joint Whole Blood Control Agency

— K —

KB	Knowledgeability Brief
KCG	Korean Consultative Group
KDC	Key Distribution Center
KDEI	Key Defense Estimates Issues
KDII	Key Defense Intelligence Issues
KEW	Kinetic Energy Weapon
KG	Kilogram
KGB	Komitet Gosudarstvennoy Bezopastnosti (Soviet Committee for State Security)
KHZ	Kilohertz
KIA	Killed in Action
KIA-BNR	Killed in Action-Body Not Recovered
KILOD	Killed in the Line of Duty
KIP	Key Indigenous Personnel
KIQ	Key Intelligence Questions
KIR	Key Intelligence Requirements
KISS	Korean Intelligence Support

	System
KJ	(1) Kilojoules
	(2) Key Judgments
KM	Kilometer
KM/HR	Kilometers Per Hour
KMR	Kwajalein Missile Range
KN	Knot
KPH	Kilometers Per Hour
KT	(1) Kiloton
	(2) Knot
KTAS	Knots True Air Speed
KW	Kilowatt
KWH	Kilowatt Hours

— L —

LAAIB	Latin American Air Intelligence Brief
LAFTA	Latin American Free Trade Association
LAL	Library Accessions List (DIA)
LAMM	Land Armament and Manpower Model
LAN	Local Area Network
LANDSAT	Land Satellite
LANL	Los Alamos National Laboratory
LANT	Atlantic
LANTCOM	Atlantic Command
LANTCOM EIC	Atlantic Command Electronic Intelligence Center
LANTDAC	Atlantic Command Defense Analysis Center
LANTFLT	U.S. Atlantic Fleet
LAR	(1) Laser Aided Rocket
	(2) Office of Long-Range Assessments and Research, Assessments and Research Section, Bureau of Intelligence and Research, Department of State
LARS	Light Artillery Rocket System
LASER	Light Amplification by Stimulated Emission of Radiation
LASERFAX	CIA-Sponsored Secure System for Transmitting Photos
LASH	Lighter Aboard Ship
LASINT	Laser Intelligence
LASP	Low-Altitude Surveillance Platform

LATIN	LANTCOM Theater Intelligence Network
LAW	Light Antitank Weapon
LC	Library of Congress
LCAC	Landing Craft, Air Cushion
LCC	(1) Amphibious Command Ship
	(2) Logistics Coordination Center
	(3) Life Cycle Cost
	(4) Launch Control Center
LCF	Launch Control Facility
LCM	Medium Landing Craft
LCP	(1) Personnel Landing Craft
	(2) Launching Control Post
LCPR	Ramped Personnel Landing Craft
LCSR	Swimmer Reconnaissance Landing Craft
LCU	Utility Landing Craft
LCW	Special Warfare Support Craft
LD	Line of Departure
LDC	Less Developed Country
LD/LC	Line of Departure/Line of Contact
LDMX	Local Digital Message Exchange
LDR	Leader
LDSD	Lookdown/Shootdown
LDX	Long-Distance Xerox
LEC	LANTCOM ELINT Center
LENSCE	Limited Enemy Situation Correlation Element
LF	(1) Low Frequency
	(2) Launch Facility
LFICS	Landing Force Integrated Communications System
LFM	Landing Force Manual
LFR	Inshore Fire Support Ship
LFS	Amphibious Warfare Fire Support Ship
LGB	Laser-Guided Bomb
LHA	Amphibious Assault Ship (General Purpose)
LHW	Lower High Water
LIC	Low Intensity Conflict
LIMDIS	Limited Distribution
LIMMER	Limited Control of Merchant Shipping
LIPS	Logical Inferences Per Second
LISP	An artificial intelligence programming language
LISS	LANTCOM Intelligence Support

	System
LITES	Laser Intercept and Technical Exploitation System
LITINT	Literature Intelligence
LKA	Amphibious Cargo Ship
LL	Landline
LLLTV	Low Light Level Television
LLNL	Lawrence Livermore National Laboratory
LLW	Lower Low Water
LNG	Liquefied Natural Gas
LNO	Limited Nuclear Option
LNU	Last Name Unknown
LO	(1) Liaison Officer
	(2) Low Observables
LOA	Letter of Agreement
LOB	Line of Bearing
LOC	(1) Line of Communication
	(2) Library of Congress
	(3) Launch Operations Center
	(4) Liaison Officer Coordinator
	(5) Location
	(6) ILS Localizer
LOCD	Lines of Communication Designators
LOCE	Limited Operational Capability in Europe
LOFAR	Low Frequency Analyzing and Recording
LOI	Letter of Instruction
LO/LO	Lift-On/Lift-Off
LORAN	Long Range Navigation
LOROP	Long-Range Oblique Photography
LOS	(1) Law of the Sea
	(2) Line of Sight
LOTS	(1) Lighter Over the Shore
	(2) Logistics Over the Shore
LOW	(1) Laws of War
	(2) Launch on Warning
LP	Listening Post
LPA	Amphibious Personnel Transport
LPAR	Large Phased-Array Radar
LPD	Amphibious Assault Transport Dock
LPG	Liquefied Natural Gas
LPH	Amphibious Assault Ship (Helicopter)
LPI	Low Probability Intercept
LP/OPs	Listening Posts/Observation

	Posts
LPR	Amphibious Transport (Small)
LPS	Logistics Planning Study
LPSS	Amphibious Transport Submarine
LRA	Long Range Aviation (Soviet)
LRAA	Long Range Air Army (Soviet)
LRC	Logistics Readiness Center
LRCM	Long-Range Cruise Missile
LRR	Long-Range Reconnaissance
LRRP	Long-Range Reconnaissance Patrol
LRSP	Long-Range Surveillance Plan
LRSTIA	Long-Range Scientific and Technical Intelligence Assessment
LRTNF	Long-Range Theater Nuclear Force
LRTS	Long-Range Technical Search
LSD	Landing Ship, Dock
LSDV	Swimmer Delivery Vehicle
LSM	Medium Amphibious Assault Landing Ship
LSP	Launch Sequence Plan
LSSC	Light Seal Support
LST	(1) Amphibious Assault Landing Ship
	(2) Local Standard Time
LTBT	Limited Test Ban Treaty
LTC	Lieutenant Colonel (Army)
Lt Col	Lieutenant Colonel (Air Force)
LTDP	NATO Long-Term Defense Plan
LUA	Launch Under Attack
LW	Low Water
LWA	Light Weight Aircraft
LWIR	Long Wavelength Infrared
LWT	Amphibious Warping Tug
LZ	Landing Zone

— M —

M	(1) Meter
	(2) Mach
M5	Office of Security, National Security Agency
M&A	(1) Management and Analysis
	(2) Monitoring and Analysis
MAA	Mission Area Analysis

MAAG	Military Assistance Advisory Group
MAB	Marine Amphibious Brigade
MAC	(1) Military Airlift Command
	(2) Mobile Inshore Undersea Warfare Attack Craft
MACOM	(1) Major Army Command
	(2) Major Command
MAD	(1) Magnetic Anomaly Detector
	(2) Mutual Assured Destruction
MAF	Marine Amphibious Force
MAG	(1) Marine Airlift Group
	(2) Military Assistance Group
	(3) Military Advisory Group
MAGIC	Maritime Air Ground Intelligence Cell
MAGIIC	Mobile Army Ground Imagery Interpretation Center
MAGIS	Marine Air-Ground Intelligence System
MAGTF	Marine Air-Ground Task Force
MAINT	Maintenance
MAJ	Major
MAJCOM	Major Command
MANPADS	Manportable Air Defense System
MAO	Major Attack Option
MAP	Military Assistance Plan
MARAD	Maritime Administration
MARDIS	Modernized Army R&D Information System
MARINTELREP WESTLANT	Maritime Intelligence Report
MARS	(1) Man-hour Accounting and Reporting System
	(2) Military Affiliate Radio System
	(3) Monthly Aerial Reconnaissance Summary
MARSA	Military Assumes Responsibility for Separation of Aircraft
MARSP	Manual of Authorized Recipients of SIGINT Products
MARV	Maneuverable Reentry Vehicle
MASDR	Measurement and Signature Data Requirements
MASH	Mobile Army Surgical Hospital
MASINT	Measurement and Signature Intelligence
MASS	(1) Missile and Space Summary
	(2) Matrix Analysis Subsystem
MAT	Medium Assault Transport

MATSYM	Material Symbol		Chiefs of Staff
MAU	Marine Amphibious Unit	MDLX	Military Demarcation Line Extended
MAW	Marine Air Wing		
MBA	Main Battle Area	MDSP	Master Deployment Security Plan
MBFR	Mutual and Balanced Force Reduction		
		MDW	Military District of Washington
MBO	Management by Objectives	ME	Middle East
MBPS	Megabits Per Second	MEAP	Military Economic Advisory Panel
MBT	Main Battle Tank		
MC	(1) Military Construction (Appropriation)	MEBE	Middle East Basic Encyclopedia
		MECD	Military Equipment Characteristics Document (NATO)
	(2) Military Committee		
	(3) Multichannel	MECH	(1) Mechanized
MCAR	Multichannel Acoustic Array		(2) Mechanical
MCB	Markings Center Brief	MECH MAINT	Mechanical Maintenance
MCC	(1) Mobile Command Center	MED	(1) Message Element Dictionary (JINTACCS)
	(2) Movement Control Center		
MCD	Manipulative Communications Deception		(2) Manipulative Electronic Deception
		MEDEVAC	Medical Evacuation
MCDEC	Marine Corps Development and Education Command	MEDINT	Medical Intelligence
		MEECN	Minimum Essential Emergency Communications Network
MCEB	Military Communications Electronics Board		
		MEFTL	Middle East Force Target List
MCG	Magneto Cumulative Generator	MEIF	Master ELINT Intercept File
MC&G	Mapping, Charting, and Geodesy	MENS	(1) Mission Essential Needs Statement
MCHAN	Multichannel		(2) Mission Element Needs Statement
MCM	(1) Mine Countermeasures		
	(2) Military Committee Memorandum	MER	Maximum Effective Range
		MERADCOM	Mobile Equipment Research and Development Command (U.S. Army)
MCMIP	Marine Corps Master Intelligence Plan		
MCN	Mission Control Number	MERCAST	Merchant Ship Broadcast System
MCP	Mobile Command Post		
MCR	Military Command Region	MERCO	Merchant Ship Reporting and Control System
MCRB	Military Costing Review Board		
MCS	Mine Countermeasures Support Ship	MERINT	Merchant Intelligence
		MERIT	Military Exploitation of Reconnaissance and Intelligence Technology
MCSF	Mobile Cryptologic Support Facility		
MCST	Magnetic Card Selectric Typewriter (IBM)	MERSHIP	Merchant Ship
		METL	Mission Essential Task List
MCTL	Mediterranean Contingency Target List	METSAT	Meteorology Satellite
		METT-T	Mission, Enemy, Terrain, Troops, and Time Available
MCW	Modulated Carrier Wave		
MD	Military District	MF	Medium Frequency
MDCI	Multidisciplinary Counterintelligence	MFP	Major Force Program
		MFR	(1) Memorandum for the Record
MDICs	Military Department Intelligence Chiefs		(2) Mutual Force Reduction
		MG	Machinegun
MDJCS	Memorandum by the Director, Joint Staff for the Joint	MGID	Military Geographic Information

	and Documentation
MGS	Mission Ground Station
MHC	Coastal Mine Hunter
MHD	Magnetohydrodynamics
MHE	Mechanized Handling Equipment
MHV	Miniature Homing Vehicle
MHW(N)(S)	Mean High Water (Nears) (Springs)
MHZ	Megahertz
MI	Military Intelligence
MIA	(1) Missile Intelligence Agency
	(2) Missing in Action
MIB	(1) Military Intelligence Board
	(2) Military Intelligence Battalion
MIBWG	Military Intelligence Board Working Group
MIC	Multinational Intelligence Cell
MICOM	Missile Command (U.S. Army)
MICV	Mechanized Infantry Combat Vehicle
MID	(1) Military Intelligence Division
	(2) Military Intelligence Detachment
MIDEASTFOR	Middle East Force
MIDMS	Machine Independent Data Management System
MIEF	Master Imagery Exchange Format
MIERS	Modernized Imagery Exploitation and Reporting System
MIG	(1) Military Intelligence Group
	(2) Military Intelligence Guide
	(3) Mikoyan (Soviet) Aircraft
MIIA	Medical Intelligence Information Agency (now AFMIC)
MIIDS	Military Intelligence Integrated Data System
MIJI	Meaconing, Intrusion, Jamming, Interference
MILAN	International Antitank Guided-Missile System
MILGP	Military Group
MILSAT(COM)	Military Satellite (Communications)
MILSTAR	U.S. Military Communications Satellite Program
MIP	Management Implementation Plan
MIPIR	Multimission Imagery Photographic Interpretation Report

MIPR	Military Interdepartmental Purchase
MIR	Morning Intelligence Report
MIRV	Multiple Independently Targetable Reentry Vehicle
MIS	(1) Military Intelligence Service
	(2) Military Intelligence Summary
	(3) Management Information System
MISREP	Mission Report
MIT	Mobile Interrogation Team
MITS	(1) Monthly International Terrorism Summary
	(2) MAC Imagery Transmission System
MIUW	Mobile Inshore Undersea Warfare
MJCS	Memorandum for the Joint Chiefs of Staff
MMC	Materiel Management Center
MMI	Main Menu Index
MNU	Middle Name Unknown
MO	Morale Operations
MOA	Memorandum of Agreement
MOB	Missile Order of Battle
MOD	Ministry of Defense
MOP	Memorandum of Policy
MOPP	Mission Oriented Protective Posture
MOS	(1) Military Occupational Specialty
	(2) Maritime Operational Intelligence Summary
MOU	Memorandum of Understanding
MP	Military Police
MPRO	Machine Processing Section of the National Security Agency's Production Organization
MR	Motorized Rifle
MRB	Motorized Rifle Battalion
MRBM	Medium-Range Ballistic Missile
MRC	(1) Movement Report Center
	(2) Military Region Command
	(3) Motorized Rifle Company
MRCA	Multirole Combat Aircraft
MRCS	Medium Resolution Camera System
MRD	Motorized Rifle Division
MRDC	Missile Research and Development Command (U.S. Army)

MRL   Multiple Rocket Launcher
MRLOGAEUR   Minimum Required Logistics
             Augmentation Europe
MRP   Motorized Rifle Platoon
MRR   Motorized Rifle Regiment
MRS   (1) Movement and Reinforce-
             ment Study
             (2) Motorized Rifle Squad
MRT   Mobile Remote Terminal
MRV   Multiple Reentry Vehicle
MS   Morning Summary
MSA   Military Strength Assessment
MSB   Minesweeping Boat
MSC   (1) Military Sealift Command
             (2) Coastal Minesweeper
             (3) Major Subordinate Com-
             mand (NATO)
MSCT   Training Coastal Minesweeper
MSD   Minesweeping Drone
MSDF   Maritime Self-Defense Force
             (Japan)
MSEL   Master Scenario Events List
MSF   Fleet Minesweeper
MSH   Minehunter
MSI   Inshore Minesweeper
MSIC   Missile and Space Intelligence
             Center, Huntsville, Alabama
MSL   (1) Missile
             (2) Mean Sea Level
MSM   Minesweeper (River)
MSN   Mission
MSN CON   Mission Control
MSO   (1) Ocean Minesweeper
             (2) Marine Safety Office
MSPB   Merit System Protection Board
MSR   (1) Patrol Minesweeper
             (2) Main Supply Route
             (3) Missile Site Radar
MSS   (1) Message Support Subsystem
             (2) Specialized Minesweeper
             (3) Moored Sonobuoy System
MSSC   (1) Medium Seal Support Craft
             (2) Specialized Coastal
             Minesweeper
MSSI   Master of Science and Strategic
             Intelligence (Defense
             Intelligence College)
MST   (1) Mutual Security Treaty
             (2) Maintenance Support Team
MT   (1) Metric Ton
             (2) Megaton

             (3) Motor Transport
MTB   Motor Torpedo Boat
MTBF   Mean Time Between Failures
MTCACS   Marine Corps Tactical Com-
             mand and Control System
MTDS   Military Tactical Data System
MTI   Moving Target Indicator
MTIB   Soviet Amphibious Armored
             Tractor
MTL   Mean Tide Level
MT-LB   Soviet Tracked Vehicle
MTMC   Military Traffic Management
             Command
MTOE   Modification Table of Organiza-
             tion and Equipment
MTR   Motorized
MTS   Maritime Tactical Schools
             (NATO)
MTST   Magnetic Tape Selectric
             Typewriter (IBM)
MTT   (1) Military Training Team
             (2) Mobile Training Team
MTTR   Mean Time to Repair
MTZ   Motorized Infantry
MUX   Multiplex
MW   (1) Mine Warfare
             (2) Millimeter Wave
MW/AA   Missile Warning/Attack
             Assessment
MWDS   Missile Warning Display
             Subsystem
MWL   Mean Water Level
MX   Missile, Experimental

— N —

N/A   Not Applicable
NAA   North Atlantic Alliance
NAC   (1) North Atlantic Council
             (NATO)
             (2) No Apparent Change
             (3) National Agency Check
NACAM   National COMSEC Advisory
             Memorandum
NACSIM   National COMSEC Information
             Memorandum
NADGE   NATO Air Defense Ground
             Environment

NAFIS	Naval Forces Intelligence Study
NAI	Named Areas of Interest
NAM	(1) Nonaligned Movement
	(2) Naval Armaments Model
NAMSO	NATO Maintenance and Supply Organization
NAOS	North Atlantic Ocean Station
NARCOG	Narcotics Coordination Group
NAS	Naval Air Station
NASA	National Aeronautics and Space Administration
NASF	NIC Analyst Support Facility
NATO	North Atlantic Treaty Organization
NAVAIR	Naval Air Systems Command
NAVDAC	Naval Data Automation Command
NAVELEX	Naval Electronic Systems Command
NAVEUR	U.S. Naval Forces, Europe
NAVFAC	Naval Shore Facilities
NAVINTCOM	Naval Intelligence Command
NAVMAP	Navy Missile Analysis Program
NAVMAT	Naval Material Command
NAVOCEAN-COMDET	Naval Oceanography Command Detachment
NAVOCEANO	Naval Oceanographic Office
NAVOCFOR-MED	Naval On-Call Force for the Mediterranean (NATO)
NAVOIC	Naval Operational Intelligence Center
NAVOPINCEN	Naval Operations Intelligence Center
NAVSAT	Navigation Satellite
NAVSEA	Naval Sea Systems Command
NAVSEC	Naval Ship Engineering Center
NAVSECGRU	Naval Security Group
NAVSECGRU-COM	Naval Security Group Command
NAVSPACE-COM	Naval Space Command
NAVSPASUR	Naval Space Surveillance Activity
NAVSUPACT	Naval Support Activity
NAVTELCOM	Naval Telecommunications Command
NBC	(1) Nuclear/Biological/Chemical
	(2) National Broadcasting Corporation

NBRG	National Basic Reference Graphic
NBS	National Bureau of Standards
NC	No Change
NCA	National Command Authority
NCAPS	Naval Controls and Protection of Shipping
NCB	Nuclear Contingency Branch
NCC	Navy Command Center
NCCS	Navy Command and Control Systems
NCIC	National Crime Information Center
NCIS	Noncommunications Intercept System
NCO	Noncommissioned Officer
NCOA	(1) Noncommissioned Officers' Academy
	(2) Noncommissioned Officers' Association
NCOIC	Noncommissioned Officer in Charge
NCP	Nuclear Contingency Plan
NCPS	Nuclear Contingency Planning System
NCR	National Capital Region
NCS	(1) National Communications System
	(2) NMIC Control Subsystem
	(3) Naval Control of Shipping
	(4) Network Control Station
	(5) Net Control Station
	(6) National Cryptographic School
NCSC	(1) Navy Command Support Center
	(2) National Computer Security Center
NCSO	Naval Control of Shipping Office
NCTR	Noncooperative Target Recognition
NCWA	NATO Civil Wartime Agency
NCWR	Noncode Word Reporting (Program)
NDA	Nondisclosure Agreements
NDB	Nondirection Beacon
NDCP	Navy Decision Coordinating Paper
NDD	Nuclear Detection Device
NDHQ	National Defense Headquarters
NDP	National Disclosure Policy

NDPC	National Disclosure Policy Committee		Plan
		NIA	National Intelligence Authority
NDRF	National Defense Reserve Fleet	NIAG	NATO Industrial Advisory Group
NDS	(1) Nuclear Detonation Satellite		
	(2) NPIC Data System	NIAM	National Intelligence Analytical Memorandum
NDU	National Defense University		
NEA	Northeast Asia	NIC	(1) National Intelligence Council
NEACP	National Emergency Airborne Command Post		(2) Naval Intelligence Command
NEANMCC	Navy Element Alternate National Military Command Center	NICOLS	NIC On-Line System
		NICS	NATO Integral Communications System
NEC	Northern European Countries	NID	National Intelligence Daily
NEIC	USAFE NATO Equipment Interpretation Course	NIDS	NMCC Information Display System
NEMVAC/		NIE	National Intelligence Estimate
NISH	Noncombatant Emergency and Evacuation	NIEO	New International Economic Order
	Intelligence Support Handbook	NIETB	National Imagery Exploitation Target Base
NEO	Noncombatant Evacuation Operation	NIETS	National Imagery Exploitation Tasking Study
NESA	Near East and South Asia Office,Current Analysis Section, Bureau of	NIHS	NAVEUR Intelligence Highlights Summary
	Intelligence and Research, Department of State	NIIC	NORAD Intelligence Indications Center
NFA	(1) New Fighter Aircraft	NIIDTS	Naval Intelligence Imagery Data Transmission System
	(2) No Forwarding Address		
NFAC	National Foreign Assessment Center	NIIRS	National Imagery Interpretability Rating Scale
NFCS	Nuclear Forces Communications Satellite	NILS	Naval Intelligence Locating Summary
NFI	(1) Not Further Identified	NIM	NORAD Intelligence Memorandum
	(2) No Further Information		
NFIB	National Foreign Intelligence Board	NIO	(1) National Intelligence Officer (CIA)
NFIC	(1) National Foreign Intelligence Council		(2) National Intelligence Office
	(2) National Foreign Intelligence Community	NIP	(1) National Intelligence Priorities
NFIP	National Foreign Intelligence Program		(2) Notice of Intelligence Potential
NFMP	Navy Foreign Material Exploitation Program NFOIO Naval Field Operational Intelligence Office (NAVNFOIO)	NIPE	National Intelligence Programs Evaluation
		NIPIR	Nuclear Intermediate Photo Interpretation Report
		NIPP	National Intelligence Projections for Planning
NGA	NATO Guidelines Area		
NGAZ	NATO Gazetteer	NIPS	Naval Intelligence Processing System
NGF	Northern Group of Forces (Soviet Forces in Poland)	NIPSSA	Naval Intelligence Processing Systems Support Activity
NGFS	Naval Gunfire Support	NIPSTRAFAC	Naval Intelligence Processing Systems Training Facility
NGL	Natural Gas Liquids		
NHCP	National HUMINT Collection		

NIRB	National Intelligence Resources Board	NOB	(1) Naval Order of Battle
			(2) Nuclear Order of Battle
NIS	(1) National Intelligence Survey	NOBTS	Naval Order of Battle Textual Summary
	(2) Naval Investigative Service		
	(3) National Intelligence Summary	NO-CONTRACT	Not Releasable to Contractors/Consultants
	(4) NATO Identification System		
NISAM	Naval Intelligence Systems Architecture Manual	NOD	Night Observation Device
		NOFORN	Not Releasable to Foreign Nationals
NISC	Naval Intelligence Support Center		
		NOIAN	National Operations and Intelligence Analysis Net
NISHQ	Naval Investigative Service Headquarters		
		NOIC	Navy Operational Intelligence Center
NISO	Naval Investigative Service Office		
		NOIWON	National Operations and Intelligence Watch Officers' Network
NISP	NUWEP Intelligence Support Plan		
NISR	National Intelligence Situation Report	NOMS	Nuclear Operations Monitoring System
NIT	National Intelligence Topic	NONCOMM	Noncommunications
NITC	National Intelligence Tasking Center	NORAD	North American Aerospace Defense Command
NKVD	People's Commissariat for Internal Affairs (Narodny Kommissariat Vnutrennykh Del)	NORIP	NORAD Intelligence for Planning Document
		NORSAR	Norwegian Seismic Array
		NORSIB	NORAD Weekly Space Intelligence Bulletin
NLC	National Logistical Command		
NLI	Natural Language Interface	NORTHAG	Northern Army Group
NLT	Not Later Than	NOSC	Naval Ocean Systems Center
NM	Nautical Mile	NOSIC	Naval Ocean Surveillance Information Center
NMC	Naval Material Command		
NMCC	National Military Command Center	NOTAL	Not to All (Message Distribution Restriction)
NMCS	National Military Command System	NPE	Nuclear Planning and Execution
		NPHR	National Foreign Intelligence Plan for Human Resources
NMCSSC	National Military Command Systems Support Center		
		NPIC	National Photographic Interpretation Center
NMI	No Middle Initial		
NMIA	National Military Intelligence Association	NPT	Nonproliferation (of Nuclear Weapons) Treaty
NMIC	National Military Intelligence Center	NR	(1) Research Submarine (Nuclear)
NMICSS	NMIC Support System		(2) Naval Reserve
NMIST	National Military Intelligence Support Team		(3) Nonrecurring
		NRF	Naval Reserve Force
NMN	No Middle Name	NRFI	Nonrecurring Finished Intelligence
NNA	Neutral and Nonaligned		
NNAG	NATO Naval Armaments Group	NRIS	National Radar Interpretability Scale
NNWS	Non-Nuclear Weapons States		
NO	Number	NRL	Naval Research Laboratory
NOA	New Obligational Authority	NRO	National Reconnaissance Office
NOAA	National Oceanographic and Atmospheric Administration	NRT	(1) Near Real Time
			(2) Net Registered Tonnage

NRTSC	Naval Reconnaissance and Technical Support Center	
NSA	(1) National Security Agency	
	(2) Naval Support Activity	
NSA/CSS	National Security Agency/ Central Security Service	
NSAM	National Security Action Memorandum	
NSAPAC	National Security Agency, Pacific	
NSARC	Navy Systems Acquisition Review Council	
NSASAB	National Security Agency Scientific Advisory Board	
NSC	(1) National Security Council	
	(2) Navy Supply Center	
NSCID	National Security Council Intelligence Directive	
NSCIG	National Security Council Interdepartmental Group	
NSCPG	National Security Council Planning Group	
NSDD	National Security Decision Directive	
NSDM	National Security Decision Memorandum	
NSES	National Security Electronic Surveillance	
NSG	(1) National Security Group	
	(2) Naval Security Group	
NSIP	National Senior Intelligence Program (Defense Intelligence College)	
NSO	Non-SIOP Option	
NSOC	National SIGINT Operations Center	
NSPG	National Security Planning Group	
NSRB	National Security Resources Board	
NSRDB	National SIGINT Requirements Data Base	
NSRDC	Naval Ship Research and Development Center	
NSRL	National SIGINT Requirements List	
NSRS	National SIGINT Requirements System	
NSS	NMIC Support System	
NSSD	National Security Study Directive	
NSSE	Navy Special Source ELINT	
NSSM	(1) National Security Study Memorandum	

	(2) Navy Spread Spectrum Modem
NSTDB	National Strategic Target Data Base
NSTG	Nuclear Strike Target Graphic
NSTL	National Strategic Target List
NSW	Naval Special Warfare
NSWC	Navy Surface Weapons Center
NSWG	Naval Special Warfare Group
NSWP	Non-Soviet Warsaw Pact
NSWTC	Naval Special Warfare Task Group
NTB	(1) National Target Base
	(2) Nuclear Test Ban
NTC	(1) National Territorial Command
	(2) National Tasking Center
	(3) Naval Training Center
NTDI	NATO Target Data Inventory
NTDS	Naval Tactical data System
NTI	National Tactical Interface
NTIS	National Technical Information Service
NTISSC	National Telecommunication and Information Systems Security Committee
NTM	National Technical Means
NTMWG	Nuclear Test Monitoring Working Group
NTP	National Tasking Plan
NTPC	National Telemetry Processing Center
NTPR	Nuclear Targeting Policy Review
NTPS	Near Term Maritime Pre-Positioning Ships
NTS	(1) Nuclear Test Site
	(2) Naval Telecommunications System
NUCAP	Nuclear Capabilities Data Base
NUCINT	Nuclear Intelligence
NUDET	(1) Nuclear Detonation
	(2) Nuclear Detection
NUWEAMP	Nuclear Weapons Employment and Acquisition Master Plan
NUWEP	Nuclear Weapons Employment Policy
NW	Nuclear Warfare
NWB	Nuclear Weapons Branch
NWC	(1) National War College
	(2) Naval War College
	(3) Naval Weapons Center

NWFZ	Nuclear Weapons Free Zone
NWIP	Naval Warfare Information Publication
NWIS	Naval Weaponeering Information Sheet
NWP	Naval Warfare Publication
NWRS	Nuclear Weapons Requirement Study
NWS	Nuclear Weapon Site
NWWCSS	Naval Worldwide Command Support System

— O —

O/A	On Or About
OA	Directorate for Operations and Attaches, DIA (now Directorate for Attachés and Operations [DA])
OACSI	Office of the Assistant Chief of Staff, Intelligence
OADR	Originating Agency's Determination Required
OAG	Operations Advisory Group
OAPEC	Organization of Arab Petroleum-Exporting Countries
OAS	Organization of American States
OASD	Office of the Assistant Secretary of Defense
OATS	Operations Analysis for Tactical Support
OAU	Organization of African Unity
OB	Order of Battle
OBC	Optical Bar Camera
OBE	Overtaken by Event
OBJ	Objective
OBS	Ocean Baseline System
OBSN	Observation
OBSUM	Order of Battle Summary
OBU	Ocean Baseline Upgrade
OCA	(1) Ocean Control Authority
	(2) Operational Control Authority
OCAM	Afro-Malagasy and Mauritanian Common Organization
OCB	Operations Coordinating Board
OCD	Office of Collection and Dissemination, CIA

OCEAN SAFARI	NATO Naval Exercise
OCEAN VENTURE	Biennial Joint CINCLANT Exercise
OCI	Office of Current Intelligence
OCJCS	Office of the Chairman, Joint Chiefs of Staff
OCL	Office of Coordination and Liaison
OCMC	Overhead Collection Management Center
OCONUS	Outside CONUS
OCR	Optical Character Reader
OCS	Officer Candidate School
OCU	Operational Conversion Unit
ODC	Office of Defense Cooperation
ODCSOPS	Deputy Chief of Staff for Operations, Plans, Headquarters, Department of the Army
ODECA	Organization of Central American States
ODJS	Office of the Director, Joint Staff
OECD	Organization for Cooperation and Development
OEG	Operational Exposure Guidance
OEIC	Overseas Economic Intelligence Committee
OER	(1) Operational ELINT Requirements
	(2) Office of Economic Research
OET	Office of Emergency Transportation
OFCO	Offensive Counterintelligence Operation
OGC	Office of General Council (DoD)
OHD	Over-the-Horizon Detection Radar
OHD-B	Over-the-Horizon Radar Backscatter
OIC	Officer in Charge
OIR	(1) Operational Intelligence Requirement
	(2) Other Intelligence Requirements
OISS	Operational Intelligence Support System
OJCS	Organization of the Joint Chiefs of Staff
OJT	On-the-Job Training
OKEAN	Soviet Naval exercise

OLC	Oak Leaf Cluster		OPNAV	Office of the Chief of Naval Operations
O&M	Operation and Maintenance (Appropriation)		OPNAVINST	OPNAV Instruction
O&M, A	Operation and Maintenance (Army)		OPORD or OPORDER	Operations Order
O&M, AF	Operation and Maintenance (Air Force)		OPR	Office of Primary Responsibility
OMAT	Ocean Measurements and Array Technology		OPREPS	Operating Reporting System
OMB	Office of Management and Budget		OPS	Operations
			OPSCOMM	Operations Communications
O&M, N	Operation and Maintenance (Navy)		OPS DEPS	Operations Deputies (JCS)
			OPSEC	Operations Security
OMOB	Offensive Missile Order of Battle		OPSEC M&A	Operations Security Management and Analysis
ON	Original Negative		OPTEMPO	Tempo of Operations
ONA	Australia Office of National Assessments		OPTEVFOR	Operational Test and Evaluation Force
ONC	(1) Operational Navigation Chart		OPTINT	Optical Intelligence
			OR	(1) Operational Requirements
	(2) Office of Narcotics Coordinator			(2) Operationally Ready
			ORCON	Originator Controlled
ONE	Office of National Estimates		ORE	(1) Office of Research and Evaluation
ONI	Office of Naval Intelligence			
ONNI	Office of National Narcotics Intelligence			(2) Office of Reports and Estimates
ONOO	Outline NATO Operational Objective		ORI	Operational Readiness Inspection
ONPG	Operational Nuclear Planning Group		ORR	Office of Research and Reports
			OS	(1) Office of Security (DIA)
ONR	Office of Naval Research			(2) Directorate for Security and Counterintelligence (DIA)
OO	Office of Operations, CIA			
OOA	Out of Area		OSAP	Ocean Surveillance Assessment Program
OOB	Opening of Business			
OOK	On/Off Keying		OSC	Office of the Security Council
OP	(1) Observation Post		OSD	Office of the Secretary of Defense
	(2) Operations			
OPC	Office of Policy Coordination, CIA		OSE	Operation Security Evaluation
			OSI	(1) On-Site Inspection
OPCODES	Operational Codes			(2) Office of Special Investigations
OPCOM	Operational Command			
OPCON	Operational Control			(3) Office of Intelligence
OPEC	Organization of Petroleum-Exporting Countries			(4) Office of Scientific Intelligence (CIA, before 1963)
OPFOR	Opposing Force		OSIS	Ocean Surveillance Information System
OPG	Operations Planning Group			
OPI	Office of Primary Interest		OSO	Office of Special Operations, CIA
OPIC-A	Overseas Processing and Interpretation Center—Asia		OSPRA	Ocean Surveillance Pattern Recognition Algorithm
OPINTEL	Operational Intelligence		OSR	Office of Strategic Research
OPLAN	Operations Plan		OSS	Office of Strategic Services
OPM	Office of Personnel Management		OSSC	On-Line System Support Center
			OT	(1) Overseas Territories

(2) Overtime

(3) Operational Test

(4) One Time

(5) Operations Team

(6) Directorate for Training (DIA)

OTEA   Operational Test and Evaluation Agency (U.S. Army)

OTH   Over-the-Horizon

OTH-R   Over-the-Horizon-Radar

OTH-T   Over-the-Horizon-Targeting

OTS   (1) One-Time Source

(2) Officer Training School

OTU   Operational Training Unit

OUO   Official Use Only

OVOP   Overt Operational Proposal

— P —

PA   (1) Privacy Act

(2) Pulse Amplitude

(3) Proper Authority

(4) Proper Authority

P&A   Personnel and Administration

PAC   (1) Pacific

(2) Personnel and Administration Center

PACAF   Pacific Air Forces

PACCS   Post Attack Command and Control System

PACE   Portable Acoustic Collection Equipment

PACFLT   Pacific Fleet

PACOM   Pacific Command

PACOPS   Pacific Air Force Operations

PACTIDES   PACOM Theater Intelligence Data System

PAI   Project Assignment Instruction

PAIS   (1) Personnel Authentication Identification System

(2) Prototype Advanced Indicator System

PAL   Permissive Action Link

PAMIS   Psychological Operations Automated Management Information System

PAO   Product Activity/Operational Code

PAR   (1) Precision Approach Radar

(2) Perimeter Acquisition Radar

(3) Phased-Array Radar

PARCS   Perimeter Acquisition Radar Attack Characterization System

PARMIS   Peacetime Airborne Reconnaissance Management Information System

PARPRO   Peacetime Airborne Reconnaissance Program

PASEP   Passed Separately

PATRON   Patrol Squadron (Navy)

PATWING   Patrol Wing

PB   Particle Beam

PBAC   Program Budget Advisory Committee

PB(A)(H)   Patrol Boat (Air Cushion)(Hydrofoil)

PBCFIA   President's Board of Consultants on Foreign Intelligence Activities

PBD   Program Budget Decision

PBEIST   Planning Board for European Inland Surface Transport

PBN   Public Broadcasting Network

PBOS   Planning Board for Ocean Shipping

PBR   (1) River/Roadstead Patrol Boat (Navy)

(2) Precision Bombing Range

PBV   Post-Boost Vehicle

PBW   Particle Beam Weapon

PC   (1) Patrol Craft

(2) Positive Control

(3) Production Control

PCA   Point of Closest Approach

PCAC   Primary Collection and Analysis Center

PCD   (1) Program Change Decision

(2) Positive Control Document

PCE   Patrol Escort

PCF(A)(H)   Fast Patrol Craft (Air Cushion)(Hydrofoil)

PCFS   Fire Support Patrol Craft

PCG   Planning and Coordinating Group

PCH   Patrol Craft (Hydrofoil)

PCM   Pulse Code Modulation

PCP   (1) Project Concept Proposal

(2) Program Change Proposal

PCR   Program Change Request (Budgeting)

PCS	(1) Publication Control Sheet		(2) Persian Gulf
	(2) Permanent Change of Station		(3) Precision Guidance
	(3) Submarine Chaser	**PGF**	Patrol Ship
PCSF	Fire Support Patrol Craft	**PGG**	Guided-Missile Patrol Combatant
PCT	Training Patrol Craft		
PD	(1) Presidential Directive	**PGH**	Patrol Gunboat (Hydrofoil)
	(2) Probability of Damage	**PGIP**	Post Graduate Intelligence Program
	(3) Pulse Duration		
	(4) Passive Detection	**PGM**	Precision-Guided Munitions
PDB	President's Daily Brief	**PGR**	Reconnaissance Patrol Combatant
PDM	Program Decision Memorandum		
		PHM	Patrol Combatant Missile (Hydrofoil)
PDMS	Point Defense Missile Systems		
PDP	Program Decision Package	**PHOTINT**	Photographic Intelligence
PDS	(1) Protected Distribution System	**PI**	(1) Photographic Interpretation
			(2) Photographic Interpreter
	(2) Production Distribution System	**PIB**	Photo Interpretation Brief
		PIC	Pacific Imagery Processing and Interpretation Center
PDSC	PACOM Data Systems Center		
PE	(1) Probable Error	**PIN**	(1) Preliminary Imagery Nomination File
	(2) Personnel Equipment		
	(3) Program Element		(2) Photographic Intelligence Notes
	(4) Preliminary Exploitation	**PIOB**	President's Intelligence Oversight Board
PEAS	Psychological Operations Effectiveness Analysis Subsystem		
		PIP	Project Implementation Plan
		PIR	(1) Photo Interpretation Report
PEC	Pacific Command Electronic Intelligence Center		(2) Priority Intelligence Requirements
PEG	(1) Photo Exploitation Group	**PK**	(1) Probability of Kill
	(2) Priority Exploitation Group		(2) Soviet Light Machinegun
	(3) Priorities for ELINT Guidance	**PKO**	Peace-Keeping Operation
PEI	Program Enhancement Initiative	**PLA**	Plain-Language Address
PEILS	PACOM Executive Intelligence Summary	**PLL**	Prescribed Load List
		PLO	Palestinian Liberation Organization
PEM	Purchased Equipment Maintenance		
		PLSS	U.S. Precision Location Strike System
PEP	Photographic Exploitation Products		
		PLT	Platoon
PERINTREP	Periodic Intelligence Report	**PM**	(1) Preventive Maintenance
PERM-CERT	Permanent Certification		(2) Preventive Medicine
PERS	Personnel		(3) Program Manager
PESM	Passive Electronic Support Measures		(4) Post Meridiem
			(5) River Monitor
PFADS	Psychological Operations Foreign Area Data Subsystem		(6) Prime Mover
			(7) Project Manager
			(8) Prime Minister
PFIAB	President's Foreign Intelligence Advisory Board	**PMA**	Political-Military Office, Current Analysis Section, Bureau of Intelligence and Research, Department of State
PFLP	Popular Front for the Liberation of Palestine		
PFOD	Presumptive Finding of Death		
PG	(1) Patrol Combatant	**PMF**	Project Management File

PMGM	Program Manager's Guidance Memorandum
PMIS	Personnel Management Information System
PMO	Project Management Office
PMP	Program Management Plan
PMR	Primary Mission Readiness
PMRP	Program Manager's Recommended Program
PMS	(1) Project Management System
	(2) Preventive Maintenance System
PMTC	Pacific Missile Test Center (Navy)
PNE(T)	Peaceful Nuclear Explosion (Treaty)
PNG	Persona Non Grata
PNIOs	Priority National Intelligence Objectives
PNUTS	Possible Nuclear Underground Test Site
PNVS	Pilot Night Vision System
POB	Place of Birth
POC	(1) Point of Contact
	(2) Program of Cooperation
POD	Port of Debarkation
POE	Port of Embarkation
POL	Petroleum, Oils, and Lubricants
POLAD	Political Advisor
POM	(1) Program Objective Memorandum
	(2) Preparation Overseas Movement
POMCUS	Prepositioned Organizational Materiel Configured in Unit Sets
PORTSREP	Ports Reports File (JCS/J-3)
POTBI	Places, Organizations, Things, Biographics, and Intangibles
POTUS	President of the United States
POV	Privately Owned Vehicle
POW	Prisoner of War
PPB	Planning, Programming, and Budgeting
PPBS	Planning, Programming, and Budgeting System
PPG	Planning and Programming Guidance (Replaced by the Consolidated Guidance)
PPGM	Planning and Programming Guidance Memorandum
PPI	Pulse Position Indicator

PPIF	Photo Processing and Interpretation Facility
PPM	(1) Parts Per Million
	(2) Pulse Position Modulation
PQT	Professional Qualification Test
PR	(1) Periodic Review
	(2) Production Review
	(3) Periodic Reinvestigation
PRAM	Allied Mine
PRB	Program Review Board
PRC	(1) Policy Review Committee
	(2) People's Republic of China
	(3) Program Review Committee
PRC(I)	Policy Review Committee (Intelligence) (now SIG(I))
PRD	Production Responsibilities Document
PREMSS	Photo Reconnaissance and Exploitation Management Support System
PRF	Pulse Repetition Frequency
PRI	Pulse Repetition Interval
PRM	President's Review Memorandum
PRO	Protocol Office, DIA
PROD	Office of Production, National Security Agency
PROLOG	Programming Logic
PROPIN	Proprietary Information Involved
PROXIMITY	A type of communications security (COMSEC) test
PRT	Personal Rapid Transit
PRTB	Soviet Mobile Rocket Technical Base
PRTR	Teleprinter
PSAA	Pacific Special Activities Area
PSB	(1) Harbor Patrol Boat
	(2) Psychological Strategy Board
PSC	(1) Primary Subordinate Command (NATO)
	(2) Personnel Service Center
PSI	Pounds Per Square Inch
PSP	Pierced Steel Planking
PSYOP	Psychological Operations
PSYOPGP	Psychological Operations Group
PT	(1) Torpedo Boat
	(2) Part Time
PTG	Missile Attack Boat
PTL	Small Torpedo Boat
PTS	Predicasts Terminal System

PTT	Training torpedo Boat
PV	Physical Vulnerability
PVDS	Physical Vulnerability Data Sheets
PVO	Air Defense (Soviet)
PVTM	Physical Vulnerability Technical Memorandum
PW	(1) Prisoner(s) of War
	(2) Pulse Width
PW/CI/DET	Prisoners of War/Civilian Internees/Detainees
PWI	PACOM Warning Intelligence
PWRS	Prepositioned War Reserve Stock
PY	Program Year

— Q —

Q&A	Question and Answer
QC	Quality Control
QM	Quartermaster
Q-MESSAGE	Classified Message on Navigation Hazard
QPQ	Quid Pro Quo
Q/R	Query/Response
QRC	Quick Reaction Capability
QRG	Quick Response Graphic
QRR	Quick Reaction Requirement
QRT	Quick Reaction Task
QSR	Quick Strike Reconnaissance
QSTAG	Quadripartite Standardization Agreement
QUICKFIX	Airborne HF/VHF intercept direction finding and jamming system
QUICKLOOK	Airborne noncommunications emitter location and identification systems
QUIP	Quarterly Intelligence Production Listing (DIA)

— R —

R	River
RA	Restricted Area
R&A	(1) Research and Analysis (OSS)
	(2) Review and Analysis (in budgeting)
RAAF	Royal Australian Air Force
RABFAC	Radar Beacon Forward Air Controller
RACO	Rear Area Combat Operations
RADAR	Radio Detection and Range
RADAREXREP	Radar Exploitation Report
RADC	Rome Air Development Center
RADCOM	Radio Communications
RADE	Research and Development Division, Office of Research and Development, National Security Agency (now Office of Research and Engineering)
RADIAC	Radioactive Detection, Indication, and Computation
RADINT	Radar Intelligence
RADREL	Radio Relay
RAF	Royal Air Force (U.K.)
RAG	(1) River Assault Group
	(2) Regimental Artillery Group
RAIDS	Rapid Access Imagery Dissemination System
RAM	(1) Rolling Airframe Missile
	(2) Random Access Memory
	(3) Radar Absorbing Materials
RAOC	Rear Area Operations Center
RAP	(1) Rocket Assisted Projectile
	(2) Remedial Action Projects
	(3) Rear Area Protection
RAS	(1) Record Assigned Systems
	(2) Replenishment at Sea
RATT	Radio Teletypewriter/Teleprinter
RAWSII	Raw Statement of Intelligence Interest
RB/ER	Reduced Blast/Enhanced Radiation
RBIF	Red Basic Intelligence File
RC	(1) Radio-Controlled
	(2) Required Capability
	(3) Reserve Component
R&C	Review and Comment
RCA	(1) Riot Control Agent

	(2) Royal Canadian Army
	(3) Radio Corporation of America
RCAF	Royal Canadian Air Force
RCC	(1) Regional Control Center
	(2) Comptroller (DIA)
RCN	Reconnaissance
RCP	Remote Communications Processor
RCRS	Reports, Coordination,and Review Staff,Assessments and Research Section, Bureau of Intelligence and Research, Department of State
RCS	Radar Cross Section
RCSC	Research Crisis Support Center
RCV	Receive Only Station
RCZ	Rear Combat Zone
RD	Restricted Data
R&D	(1) Research and Development
	(2) Office of Research and Development, National Security Agency
RDA	Research, Development, Acquisition
RDC	Rapid Deployment Capability
RDF	(1) Rapid Deployment Force
	(2) Radio Direction Finder(ing)
RDJTF	Rapid Deployment Joint Task Force
RDL	Recurring Document Listing
RDSS	Rapidly Deployed Surveillance System
RDT&E	Research, Development, Test, and Evaluation
R&E	(1) Office of Research and Evaluation, National Security Agency
	(2) Office of Research and Engineering, National Security Agency
READY CAP	Fighter Aircraft in "Standby" Condition
REC	Radioelectronic Combat
RECA(T)	Residual Capability Assessment (Team)
RECCE	Reconnaissance
RECCEXREP	Reconnaissance Exploitation Report
RECI	Radar Emitter Classification Identification (System)
RECON	Reconnaissance

REDCOM	Readiness Command
REDCON	Readiness Condition
RED FLAG	U.S. Technical Flight Training Program Using Stimulated Combat Techniques
REFORGER	(1) U.S. Deployment and Field Training Exercise
	(2) EUCOM Field Training Exercise
REGT	Regiment
REMAB	Remote Marshalling Base
REMP	Research, Engineering, Mathematics, and Physics Division, Office of Research and Development, National Security Agency (now Office of Research and Engineering)
REMS	Remote Sensors
REP	(1) Range Error Probable
	(2) Reserve Exploitation Program
REPRO	Reproduction
REW(S)	Radio Electronic Warfare (Service)
REXMIT	Retransmission
RF	Radio Frequency
RFE/RL	Radio Free Europe/Radio Liberty
RFI	(1) Radio Frequency Interface
	(2) Request for Information
RFP	(1) Remaining Force Potential
	(2) Radio Frequency Pulse
	(3) Request for Proposal
RFPW	Radio Frequency Pulse Weapon
RHR	Directorate for Human Resources (DIA)
RI	Routing Indicator
R&I	Reconnaissance and Intelligence (Panel)
RIF	Reduction in Force
RII	Request for Intelligence Information
RIMPAC	U.S. Naval Exercise
RIMS	Requirements Inventory Management System
RINT	Radar Intelligence
RIP	Register of Intelligence Publications
RISOP	Red Integrated Strategic Operations Plan
RL	(1) Rocket Launcher
	(2) Radio Liberty
RLT	Regimental Landing Team

RM	Resource Management
RMS	Resource Management System
RNAV	Area Navigation
RNO	Regional Nuclear Option
RNP	(1) Radio Navigation Point
	(2) Remote Network Processor
RO	Reporting Officer
ROB	Radar Order of Battle
ROC	(1) Required Operational Capability
	(2) Republic of China
ROCC	Regional Operations Control Center
RODCA	Message Caveat
ROE	Rules of Engagement
ROF	Rate of Fare
ROKUSCFC	Republic of Korea and United States Combined Forces
RON	Remain Overnight
RO/RO	Roll-On/Roll-Off
RORSAT	Radar Ocean Reconnaissance Satellite
ROSS	Refinement of SIGINT Support
ROU	Radius of Uncertainty
ROUND HOUSE	U.S. Exercise Defense Condition
RP	Reference Point
RPC	Regional Reporting Center
RPG	(1) Soviet Shoulder-Fired Antitank Grenade Launcher
	(2) Report Program generator
RPK	Soviet light machinegun, similar in design to the AK rifle
RPM	(1) Revolutions Per Minute
	(2) Rounds Per Minute
RPV	Remotely Piloted Vehicle
RR	(1) Railroad
	(2) Radio Relay
RR/EO	Race Relations/Equal Opportunity
RRF	Ready Reserve Force
RRII	Response to Request for Intelligence Information
RRM	Red Resource Monitoring
RS	Directorate for Resources and Systems (DIA)
RSE	Directorate for DODIIS Engineering (DIA)
RSI, R/S/I	(1) Rationalization, Standardization, and Interoperability
	(2) Directorate for Information Systems (DIA)

RSM	Directorate for DODIIS Planning and Management (DIA)
RSQ	Directorate for Procurement (DIA)
RSTA	Reconnaissance, Surveillance, and Target Acquisition
RT	(1) Real Time
	(2) Radio Telephone
RTASS	Remote Tactical Airborne SIGINT System
RTG	Reconnaissance Technical Group (TAC, USAFE, PACAF)
RTIP	Real Time Interactive Processor
RTOS	Real Time Optical System
RTS	(1) Directorate for Technical Services and Support (DIA)
	(2) Reconnaissance Technical Squadron
	(3) Real-Time Simulator
RTSP	Real-Time Signal Processor
RUM	Resource and Unit Monitoring
RUNT	Russian Underground Nuclear Test
RURPOP	Rural Population File
RV	Reentry Vehicle
RW	(1) Radiological Warfare
	(2) Rotary Wing
RWI	Radio Wire Integration
RWO	Reconnaissance Watch Officer
RZ	Recovery Zone

— S —

SA	(1) Signals Analysis
	(2) Surface-to-Air, used to identify Soviet surface-to-air missiles, e.g., SA-7/GRAIL
	(3) Situation Analysis
	(4) Star Appendices
	(5) Special Activities
	(6) System Analysis
SAB	Subject As Above
SAC	(1) Strategic Air Command
	(2) Scientific Advisory Committee
	(3) Senate Appropriations Committee
SACC	Supporting Arms Coordination

	Center (amphibious warfare)
SACDIN	SAC Digital Network
SACEUR	Supreme Allied Commander, Europe
SACLANT	Supreme Allied Commander, Atlantic
SADT	Structured Analysis Design Technique
SAEDA	Subversion and Espionage Against the U.S. Army and Deliberate Security Violations
SAF	(1) Source Acquisitions File
	(2) Soviet Air Force
SAFE	(1) Support for Analysts' File Environment
	(2) Selected Area for Invasion
SAFF	Safing, Arming, Fuzing, and Firing
SAG	(1) Study Advisory Group
	(2) Surface Action Group
SAGA	Studies, Analysis, and Gaming Agency (JCS)
SAGE	Semiautomatic Ground Environment (Radar)
SAIB	Safe Area Intelligence Brief
SAID	Safe Area Intelligence Description
SAL	(1) Strategic Arms Limitation
	(2) Submarine Alerting and Locating
SALT	Strategic Arms Limitation Treaty
SALUTE	Size, Activity, Location, Unit, Time, and Equipment
SAM	Surface-to-Air Missile
SAMSO	U.S. Air Force Space and Missile Systems Organization
SAO	(1) Special Activities Office(r) (obsolete term)
	(2) Select Attack Option
	(3) Special Access Only
	(4) Security Assistance Organization
SAPAS	Semiautomatic Population Analysis System
SAR	(1) Search and Rescue
	(2) Synthetic Aperture Radar
	(3) Special Access Required
SARK	SAVILLE Advanced Remote Keying (COMSEC term)
SARPF	Strategic Air Relocatable Processing Facility

SART	Strategic Airlift Recovery Team
SAS	(1) Strategic Area Study
	(2) Strategic Aerospace Summary
SATCOM	Satellite Communications
SATCOMA	Satellite Communications Agency (U.S. Army)
SATRAN	Satellite Reconnaissance Advanced Notice
SAVE	Situation Analysis and Vulnerability Estimate
SBDP	Soviet Battlefield Development Plan
SBI	Special Background Investigation
SBI-PR	Special Background Investigation-Periodic Reinvestigation
SBL	Space-Based Laser
SBM	Single-Point Mooring Buoy
SC	(1) Science Committee (NATO)
	(2) Signal Corps
SCA	Service Cryptologic Agency
SCAD	Subsonic Cruise Armed Decoy
SCAMP	(1) Sensor Control and Management Platoon
	(2) Summer Campus, Advanced Mathematics Program, National Security Agency
SCARF	Standard Collection Asset Report Format
SCC	(1) Standing Consultative Commission (SALT)
	(2) Special Coordinating Committee of the National Security Council
	(3) Surveillance Coordination Center
SCC(I)	Special Coordination Committee (Intelligence)
SCE	Service Cryptologic Element
SCG	Special Consultative Group (NATO)
SCI	(1) Special Compartmented Intelligence
	(2) Sensitive Compartmented Information
	(3) Source Code Indicator
SCIBS	Sensitive Compartment Information Billet Structure
SCIF	Sensitive Compartmented Information Facility
SCIM	Subject Codes for Intelligence

	Management
SCIMITAR	System for Countering Interdiction Missiles and Target Radars
SCISO	Sensitive Compartmented Information Security Officer
SCO	Service Cryptologic Organizations
SCP	System Concept Paper
SDA	Ships Destination Authority
SDI	Strategic Defense Initiative
SDIE	Special Defense Intelligence Estimate
SDIN	Special Defense Intelligence Notice
SDIO	Strategic Defense Initiative Organization
SDM	System Development Manager
SDOB	Scaled Depth of Burst
SDR	Source Directed Requirements
SDS	(1) Satellite Data System
	(2) SIGINT Direct Support
SDV	Swimmer Delivery Vehicle
SEA	Southeast Asia
SEAD	Suppression of Enemy Air Defense
SEAL	Sea/Air/Land
SEASTAG	SEATO Standardization Agreement
SEATO	Southeast Asia Treaty Organization
SEAWATCH	NOSIC On-Line Computer System
SEC	Section
SECDEF	Secretary of Defense
SECNAV	Secretary of the Navy
SECOM	Security Committee (CIA)
SEDSCAF	Standard ELINT Data System Codes and Formats
SEEI	Special Essential Elements of Information
SEEK	Soviet Emigré Exploitation Kit
SEI	Specific Emitter Identification
SEIP	Senior Enlisted Intelligence Program
SEIS	Survivable and Enduring Intelligence System
SELA	Latin American Economic System
SELORS	Ship Emitter Locating Reports
SEP	September
SEPA	Soviet Extended Planning Index

SEP BDE	Separate Brigade
SEPS	NATO Selective Employment Plan
SER	Service
SERE	Survival, Evasion, Resistance, and Escape
SES	(1) Surface Effects Ship
	(2) Systems Engineering Study
	(3) Senior Executive Service
	(4) Sensor Employment Squadron
SEWS	SIGINT Electronic Warfare Subsystem
SF	(1) Special Forces
	(2) Standard Form
SFG	Special Forces Group
SFOB	Special Forces Operational Base
SFOD-D	First Special Forces Operational Detachment-Delta
SFR	Statement of Functional Requirement
SFRD	Safe Functional Requirements Document
SGDPS	Second Generation Data Processing System
SGF	Southern Group of Forces (Soviet Forces in Hungary)
SGM	Strategic Guidance Memorandum
SGT	Sergeant
SHAPE	Supreme Headquarters, Allied Powers Europe
SHC	Supreme High Command
SHF	Super High Frequency
SHORAD	Short-Range Air Defense
SI	(1) Special Intelligence
	(2) Secret Intelligence (Unit of OSS)
	(3) Special Instructions
SIB	Special Intelligence Brief
SIC	Scientific Intelligence Committee
SICAM	SIGINT Control and Analysis Module
SICR	Specific Intelligence Collection Requirement
SID(S)	Specific Imagery Dissemination (System)
SIFR	Special Intelligence Functional Requirement
SIG	Senior Interdepartmental Group
SIG-I	Senior Interagency Group for Intelligence

SIGINT	Signals Intelligence
SIGLEX	Special Interest Group on Lexicography, National Security Agency
SIGSEC	Signal Security
SIGTRAN	Special Interest Group on Translation, National Security Agency
SIGVOICE	Special Interest Group on Voice, National Security Agency
SII	Statement of Intelligence Interest
SINGARS	Single Integrated Channel Ground and Airborne Radio Subsystems
SIO	Senior Intelligence Officer
SIOP	Single Integrated Operations Plan
SIPG	Special Intercept Priorities Group, National Security Agency
SIR	Specific Information Requirements
SIRCS	Shipborne Intermediate-Range Combat System
SIRVES	SIGINT Requirements Validation and Evaluation Subcommittee (of SIGINT Committee)
SIS	(1) Signal Intelligence Service
	(2) Significant Indications Summary
	(3) Space Intelligence System
	(4) Secret Intelligence Service (UK)
SI/SAO	Special Intelligence/Special Activities Office
SISS	Survivable Intelligence Support to SIOP
SITMAP	Situation Map
SITREP	Situation Report
SIW	Strategic Intelligence Wing
SJCS	Secretary, Joint Chiefs of Staff
SKCATL	South Korea Conventional Air Target List
SKYLINK	Communications System Provided by the Diplomatic Telecommunications System
SL	Sea Level
SLAR	Side-Looking Airborne Radar
SLBM	Submarine-Launched Ballistic Missile
SLCM	Submarine-Launched Cruise Missile

SLEP	Service Life Extension Program
SLF	Super Low Frequency
SLMM	U.S. Submarine-Launched Mobile Mine
SLOC(s)	Sea Line(s) of Communications
SLR	Side Looking Radar
SLSSM	Submerged-Launched Surface-to-Surface Missile
SM	(1) Memorandum by the Secretary, JCS
	(2) Statute Mile
SMEB	Significant Military Exercise Brief
SMIOC	Senior Military Intelligence Officers' Conference
SMO	Support to Military Operations
SMP	(1) *Soviet Military Power*
	(2) Shipboard Microfilm
SNA	Soviet Naval Aviation
SNAP	Soviet Nuclear Artillery Projectile
SNCCDIPP	Selected Non-Communist Countries DIPP
SNDV	Strategic Nuclear Delivery Vehicles
SNI	Soviet Naval Infantry
SNIE	Special National Intelligence Estimate
SNM	Special Nuclear Materials
SNO	Special Naval Operations
SO	Special Operations
SOA	(1) Speed of Advance
	(2) System Operating Activity
SOADS	Special Operations Automated Data Base
SOB	Space Order of Battle
SOD	(1) Special Operations Detachment
	(2) Special Operations Division
SOF	Special Operations Force
SOFA	Status of Forces Agreement
SOI	(1) Signal Operating Instructions
	(2) Signal of Interest
SOIC	(1) Senior Officials of the Intelligence Community
	(2) Space Operational Intelligence Center
SOISUM	Space Object Identification Summary
SOJ	(1) Sea of Japan
	(2) Stand-Off Jamming
SOLANT	South Atlantic

SOLARS	SAC On-Line Analysis and Retrieval System
SOLID SHIELD	U.S. Joint exercise
SOLIS	SIGINT On-Line Intelligence (or Information) System
SONAR	Sound Navigation and Ranging
SOP	(1) Standing Operating Procedures
	(2) Senior Officer Present
SOPPC	Special Operations Photo Processing Cell
SOS	(1) Save Our Ship
	(2) Squadron Officers' School
SOSS	Satellite Ocean Surveillance System
SOSUS	U.S. Sound Surveillance System
SOTA	SIGINT Operational Tasking Authority
SOTAS	Standoff Target Acquisition System
SOTF	Special Operating Task Force
SOUTHCOM	Southern Command
SOW	Statement of Work
SP	(1) Study Plan (part of the consolidated guidance under PBBS)
	(2) Self-Propelled
	(3) Shore Patrol
SPA	Special PSYOP Analysis
SPACECOM	Space Command
SPADETS	Space Detection and Tracking System
SPADOC	Space Defense Operations Center
SPAWAR	Space and Naval Warfare Systems Command
SPD	Strategic Posture Display
SPEAR	Signal Processing, Evaluation Alert, and Reporting
SPECAT	Special Category (Pneumatic Tube Message Precedence)
SPETSNAZ	Soviet Special Purpose Forces
SPF	Special Purpose Forces
SPG	Special Procedures Group
SPICE	Special Purpose Integrated Communications Equipment
SPINTCOMM	Special Intelligence Communications
SPIREP	Spot Intelligence Report
SPIRES	Special Intelligence Reports
SPOD	Sea Ports of Debarkation
SPOE	Sea Ports of Embarkation

SPRAA	Strategic Plans and Research Analysis Agency (JCS)
SPS	Special PSYOP Study
SPT	Support
SQD	Squad
SQDN	Squadron
SQN	Squadron
SQT	Skill Qualification Test
SRAM	U.S. Short-Range Attack Missile
SRB	Senior Review Board
SRBM	Short-Range Ballistic Missile
SRD	(1) System Requirements Document
	(2) Special Research Detachment (U.S. Army)
SRF	(1) Strategic Rocket Forces (USSR)
	(2) Strategic Reserve Forces
	(3) Secure Reserve Force (U.S.)
SRFTL	Secure Reserve Force Target List
SRP	(1) Sealift Readiness Program
	(2) SIOP Reconnaissance Plan
SRW	Strategic Reconnaissance Wing
SRWG	Standing Requirements Working Group
SS	Diesel-Powered Attack Submarine
SSA	(1) Special Support Activity
	(2) Security Supporting Assistance
	(3) Diesel-Powered Auxiliary Submarine
	(4) Signal Security Agency
SSAC	Auxiliary Submarine (Communications)
SSAG	Auxiliary Submarine
SSAN	(1) Social Security Number
	(2) Nuclear-Powered Auxiliary Submarine
SSB	(1) Ballistic Missile Submarine
	(2) Standard Software Base
	(3) Single Sideband
SSBN	Nuclear-Powered Ballistic Missile-Equipped Submarine
SSC	(1) Coastal Submarine
	(2) Special Security Command
SSCI	Senate Select Committee on Intelligence
SSCN	Nuclear Cruise Missile Submarine
SSF	(1) Special Security File

	(2) Special Service Force
SSG	(1) Special Security Group
	(2) Diesel-Powered Cruise Missile-Equipped Submarine
	(3) Special Study Group
SSGN	Nuclear-Powered Cruise Missile-Equipped Submarine
SSI	Specialty Skill Identifier
SSJ	Self-Screening Jamming
SSLP	Transport Submarine
SSM	(1) Surface-to-Surface Missile
	(2) Midget Submarine
SSMO	SIGINT Support to Military Operations
SSMOB	Surface-to-Surface Missile Order of Battle
SSN	(1) Nuclear-Powered Attack Submarine
	(2) Social Security Number
SSO	Special Security Officer
SSP	SIGINT Support System
SSQ	Auxiliary Submarine, Communications
SSQN	Nuclear-Powered Auxiliary Submarine, Communications
SSR	(1) Radar Picket Submarine
	(2) Secondary Surveillance Radar
	(3) Special Security Representative
SSRS	SIGINT Surveillance and Reporting System
SSS	(1) Staff Summary Sheet
	(2) Systems Science and Software
SST	(1) Training Submarine
	(2) System Specific Threat
	(3) Supersonic Transport
SSU	Strategic Services Unit of the OSS
S&T	Scientific and Technical
STA	Surveillance and Target Acquisition (Platoon) (U.S. Marine Corps)
STAB	Science and Technology Advisory Panel
STANAG	Standardization Agreement (NATO)
STANAV-FORLANT	Standing Naval Forces Atlantic

	(NATO)
STANCIB	State-Army-Navy Communications Intelligence Board
STANS	Soviet Tactical Nuclear Study
STAP	Scientific and Technical Advisory Panel
STAR	System Threat Assessment Report
START	Strategic Arms Reduction Talks
STARTEX	Start Date of an Exercise
STASS	Submarine Towed Array Sonar System
STC	(1) Sensitivity Time Control
	(2) Short Time Constant (ECCM)
STED	Standard Technical Equipment Development Division, Office of Research and Development, National Security Agency (now Office of Research and Engineering)
S&TI	Scientific and Technical Intelligence
STIC	(1) Scientific and Technical Intelligence Committee
	(2) (Naval) Scientific and Technical Intelligence Center
STIISP	Scientific and Technical Intelligence Information Services Program
STINFO	Scientific and Technical Information
STIPS	Scientific and Technical Intelligence Production Schedule
STIR	Scientific and Technical Intelligence Register
STO	Science and Technology Applications
STOL	Short Takeoff and Landing
STOVL	Short Takeoff, Vertical Landing
STP	Soldier's Training Publication
SUAWACS	Soviet AWACS
SUBLANT	Submarine Forces, Atlantic
SUBPAC	Submarine Forces, Pacific
SUM	Surface-to-Underwater Missile
SUPIR	Supplemental Photo Interpretation Report
SUPREMS	Supplemental Preliminary Mission Summary
SURTASS	U.S. Surveillance Towed Array Sonar System
SURVL	Surveillance

SUSLO	Special U.S. Liaison Officer
SVA	Secure Vault Area
SVC	Service
SVD	Soviet Super Rifle
SVOD	Soviet Aircraft Navigation and Landing System
SW	(1) Short Wave
	(2) Surface Warfare
SWA	(1) Southwest Asia
	(2) Southwest Africa
	(3) Secure Working Area
SWAL	Shallow Water Attack Craft, Light
SWAM	Shallow Water Attack Craft, Medium
SWC	(1) Special Warfare Center (U.S. Army)
	(2) Special Warfare Craft
SWCL	Special Warfare Craft, Light
SWCM	Special Warfare Craft, Medium
SWI	Special Weather Intelligence
SWNCC	State, War, Navy Coordinating Committee
SWO	(1) Staff Weather Officer
	(2) Senior Watch Officer
SWS	Strategic Warning Staff
SYS	System

— T —

T	Tank
T^2	Technology Transfer
TA	(1) Traffic Analysis
	(2) Tank Army
	(3) Terrain Avoidance
	(4) Target Analysis
T&A	Transcription and Analysis
TAA	Tactical Air Army (Soviet)
TAACOM	Theater Army Area Command
TAC	(1) Tactical Air Command
	(2) Terrain Analysis Center (U.S. Army)
TACAIR	Tactical Air
TACAMO	U.S. Air Relay Communication System
TACAN	Ultra High Frequency Tactical Air Navigation
TACC	Tactical Air Control Center
TACCP	Tactical Command Post

TACCS	Tactical Airborne Command and Control and Surveillance
TACCTA	Tactical Commander's Terrain Analysis
TACIES	Tactical Imagery Exploitation System
TACINT	Tactical Intelligence (also TACINTEL)
TACOPS	Tactical Air Combat Operations Staff
TACP	Tactical Air Control Party
TACREP	Tactical Report
TACS	Tactical Air Control System
TACSATCOM	Tactical Satellite Communications
TACTAS	U.S. Surface Warship Tactical Towed Array Sonar
TAD	Temporary Additional Duty
TADC	Tactical Air Direction Center (Amphib. Ops)
TADIL	Tactical Data Information Link
TADS	(1) Tactical Air Defense System
	(2) Target Acquisition and Designation System
TAF	Tactical Air Forces
TAFT	Military Assistance and Field Training Team
TAG	Target Actions Group
TALON	U.S. Jet Trainer
TALOS	U.S. Navy Antiair Warfare System (obsolete)
TAOC	Tactical Air Operations Center
TAOR	Tactical Area of Responsibility
TAP	Terrain Analysis Program
TAPS	Technical Analysis Positions System
TARTAR	U.S. Surface-to-Air Missile
TAS	(1) Tactical Airlift Squadron
	(2) Traffic Analysis Survey
	(3) Terminal Access System
	(4) True Air Speed
TASES	Tactical Airborne Signals Exploitation System
TASM	Tactical Air-to-Surface Missile
TASMO	Tactical Air Support of Maritime Operations
TASS	(1) Towed Array Surveillance System
	(2) Tactical Air Support Squadron
	(3) Official News Agency of the USSR

TAT	(1) Terrorist Action Team
	(2) Tactical Analysis Team
	(3) Target Area Tactics
	(4) Transatlantic Telephone Cable
TAVR	Territorial and Army Volunteer Reserve
TB	(1) Tank Battalion
	(2) Tuberculosis
	(3) Technical Bulletin
TBA	To Be Announced
TBD	To Be Determined
T-BIRD	U.S. Jet Trainer (T-33A)
TBM	Tactical Ballistic Missile
TC	(1) Tank Company
	(2) Transportation Corps
	(3) Training Circular
TCAC	Technical Control and Analysis Center
TCAE	Technical Control and Analysis Element
TCAS	Technical Control and Analysis Section
TCC	Telecommunications Center
TCO	Test Control Officer
TCP	(1) Technological Coordinating Paper
	(2) Tactical Cryptographic Program
TCR	Time Critical Requirements
TCT	Tactical Commander's Terminal
TD	(1) Tank Destroyer
	(2) Tank Division
	(3) Transmitter-Distributor
TDA	Table of Distribution and Allowances
TDC	Tactical Digital Computer
TDDP	Tactical Defense Dissemination Program
TDDS	Tactical Defense Dissemination System
TDF	Tactical Data Facsimile
TDI	Target Data Inventory
TDM	Time Division Multiplex
TDOA	Time Difference of Arrival
TDS	Target Data Sheet
TDY	Temporary Duty
TE	(1) Tactical Exploitation
	(2) Task Element
T&E	Test and Evaluation
TEA	Tactical Exploitation Assessment

TEAMPACK	U.S. Ground-Based Signal Intelligence Sensor
TEAMS	Trend and Error Analysis Methodology System
TEAM SPIRIT	U.S. Exercise
TEB	Tactical Exploitation Battalion
TECCE	Tactical Exploitation Collection and Coordination Element
TECOM	Test and Evaluation Command
TECRAS	Technical Reconnaissance and Surveillance
TEDS	Tactical Expendable Drone System
TEL	Transporter-Erector-Launcher
TELAR	Transporter-Erector-Launcher and Radar
TELCON	Telephone Conversation
TELECOM	Telecommunications
TELEFAC	Telecommunications Facility Vulnerability Study
TELINT	Telemetry Intelligence
TEMPEST	A term referring to technical investigations for compromising emanations from electrically operated information processing equipment; such tests are conducted in support of emanations and emission security
TENCAP	Tactical Exploitation of National Capabilities
TEOC	Technical Objective Camera
TEP	Tactical ELINT Processor
TERCOM	Terrain Contour Matching
TEREC	Tactical Electronic Reconnaissance
TERPES	(1) Tactical Electronic Reconnaissance Processing and Evaluation System
	(2) Tactical Electronic Reconnaissance and Exploitation Segment
TET	Transportable Electronic Tower
TEXAS	Tactical Exchange Automation System
TEXTA	Technical Extracts of Traffic
TF	Task Force
TFC	Tactical Fusion Center
TFCC	Tactical Flag Command Center
TFGM	Tentative Fiscal Guidance Memorandum
TFR	Terrain Following Radar

TFS	Tactical Fighter Squadron		**TNF**	Theater Nuclear Forces
TFW	Tactical Fighter Wing		**TO**	Theater of Operations
TFWC	Tactical Fighter Weapons Center		**TOA**	(1) Time of Arrival
TG	Task Group			(2) Total Obligational Authority
T&G	Tracking Guidance			(3) Transportation Operation Agency
TGIF	Transportable Ground Intercept Facility		**TOC**	Tactical Operations Center
TGPF	Transportable Ground Process-ing Facility		**TOE**	(1) Time of Entry
TGS	Transportable Ground System			(2) Table of Organization and Equipment
TI	(1) Technical Intelligence		**TOPCAT**	Tactical Operations Planner for Collection, Analysis, and Tasking
	(2) Target Intelligence			
TIAP	Theater Intelligence Architec-ture Program		**TOR**	Terms of Reference
TIARA	Tactical Intelligence and Related Activities		**TOS**	Tactical Ocean Surveillance
			TOSS	Tactical Operations Support System
TICC	Tactical Information Communi-cations Center		**TOT**	(1) Time on Target
TIDL	Tactical Imagery Data Link			(2) Time of Transmission
TIES	Tactical Information Exchange System		**TPFDD(1)**	Time Phased Force Deployment Data (List)
TIG	Tactical Intelligence Group		**TPP**	Thermal Powerplant
TIHB	Target Intelligence Handbook		**TPPG**	Tentative Planning and Pro-gramming Guidance (Replaced by the Consoli-dated Guidance)
TIIF	Tactical Imagery Interpretation Facility			
TIM	Target Intelligence Material		**TR**	(1) Tank Regiment
TIP	Target Intelligence Package			(2) Transportation Request
TIPE	Tactical Intelligence Product Enhancement		**T-R**	Transmit-Receive
			TRA	Temporary Restricted Area
TIPI	Tactical Information Processing and Interpretation System		**TRADOC**	U.S. Army Training and Doctrine Command
TIPP	Target Intelligence Production Plan		**TRAILBLAZER**	U.S. Ground-Based Signal Intelligence Sensor
TIRSAG	Tactical Intelligence, Reconnais-sance, Surveillance Action Group		**TRAM**	Target Recognition and Attack Multisensor
TIS	(1) Tactical Intelligence Squadron		**TRANS**	Transportation
			TRANS/ANAL	Transcription and Analysis
	(2) Thermal Imaging Site		**TRANSEC**	Transmission Security
TISS	Tactical Intelligence Support Staff		**TREDS**	Tactical Reconnaissance Exploitation Demonstration System
TI/TTR	Target Illumination/Target Tracking Radar		**TRESSCOMM**	Technical Research Ship Special Communications
TJ	Terajoules		**TRIGS**	TR-1 Ground Station
TJS	Tactical Jamming System		**TRI-TAC**	U.S. Joint Tactical Communica-tions Program
TM	(1) Tactical Missile			
	(2) Threat Manager		**TRITAF**	Tactical Air Forces of TAC, USAFE, and PACAF
	(3) Team			
TMDE	Test Measurement and Diagnos-tic Equipment		**TRML**	USAFE Target Reference Material List
TMS	Target Materials Squadron		**TRMS**	Test Resources Management System

TRP	Target Reporting Parameters
TRS	Tactical Reconnaissance Squadron
TRV	Tactical Recovery Vehicle
TRW	Tactical Reconnaissance Wing
TS	Top Secret
TSA	Temporary Secure Area
TSB	Training Support Base
TSC	(1) Tactical Support Center
	(2) Top Secret Control
	(3) Technical Support Center
TSCIXS	Tactical Support Center Information Exchange System
TSCM	Technical Surveillance Counter-measures
TSCO	Top Secret Control Officer
TSCR	Time-Sensitive Collection Requirement
TSCW	Top Secret Code Word
TSD	Technical Services Division
TSDS	Tactical SIGINT Data Support
TSE	Target Support Element
TSEC	Telecommunications Security
TSG	Threat Steering Group
TSM	Technical support Measures
TSP	(1) Transshipment Point
	(2) Threat Support Plan
TSR	(1) Time Sensitive Requirement
	(2) Telecommunications Support Request
TSRS	Tactical Support Reconnaissance System
TSS	(1) Telecommunications Security System
	(2) Time Sharing System
TSSS (TS³)	(1) Tactical Simulator Study Support
	(2) Time-Sensitive Support System
TSWA	Temporary Secure Working Area
TT	(1) Technology Transfer
	(2) Target Track
	(3) Time on Target
TTAC	Technology Transfer Analysis Center
TTAP	Telemetry Technical Analysis Position
TTBT	Threshold Test Ban Treaty
TTI	Tactical Target Illustrations

TTM	Tactical Target Materials
TTMC	Tactical Target Materials Catalog
TTMP	Tactical Target Materials Program
TTPI	Trust Territory of the Pacific Islands
TTY	Teletypewriter
TU	Task Unit
TUHTKP	Time Urgent Hard Target Kill Potential
TUT	Tactical Users Terminal
TV	(1) Target Vulnerability
	(2) Theater of War (Soviet)
	(3) Television
TVD	Theater of Military Operations (Soviet)
TW/AA	Tactical Warning and Attack Assessment
TWG	Threat Working Group
TX	Transmission UAM Underwater-to-Air Missile

— U —

UC	Under Construction
UCIB	USAFE Command Intelligence Brief
UCP	Unified Command Plan
UDEAC	Economic and Customs Union of South Africa
UDIR	USAREUR Daily Intelligence Report
UDT	Underwater Demolition Team
UE	Unit Equipment
UEAC	Union of Central African States
UFO	Unidentified Flying Object
UFR	Unfunded Requirement
UGM	Underwater Guided Missile
UHF	Ultra High Frequency
UI	(1) Unidentified
	(2) Unit of Issue
UIC	Unit Identification Code
UK	United Kingdom
UKLF	United Kingdom Land Forces
UKUSA	United Kingdom-United States Agreement

ULCC	Ultra Large Crude Carrier
ULF	Ultra Low Frequency
UMOP	Unintentional Modulation on Pulse
UN	United Nations
UNIFIL	United Nations Interim Force in Lebanon
UNITAS	Joint U.S.-Latin American Naval Force
URBBO	Urban Area Boundary File
URBPOP	Urban Population File
URD	User Requirements Documents
U&S	Unified and Specified (Command)
US	United States (of America)
USA	(1) United States Army
	(2) United States of America
USACC	U.S. Army Communications Command
USAF	U.S. Air Force
USAFE	U.S. Air Force, Europe
USAFINTEL	U.S. Air Force Intelligence
USAFR	U.S. Air Force Reserve
USAFRED	U.S. Air Force Readiness Command
USAFSO	U.S. Air Force Southern Command
USAFSS	U.S. Air Force Security Service
USAFTAC	(1) U.S. Air Force Technical Applications Center
	(2) U.S. Air Force Tactical Air Command
USAIA	U.S. Army Intelligence Agency
USAIC	U.S. Army Intelligence Command
USAICE	U.S. Army Intelligence Center, Europe
USAICS	U.S. Army Intelligence Center and School
USAINSCOM	U.S. Army Intelligence and Security Command
USAINTA	U.S. Army Intelligence Agency
USAINTC	U.S. Army Intelligence Command
USAISD	United States Army Intelligence School, Fort Devens
USAITAC	U.S. Army Intelligence Threat Analysis Center
USAR	U.S. Army Reserve
USAREUR	U.S. Army, Europe
USARJ	U.S. Army, Japan
USARRED	U.S. Army Forces Readiness Command
USASA	U.S. Army Security Agency
USATAC	U.S. Army Terrain Analysis Center
USATC	United States Air Target Chart
USC	(1) Under Secretaries Committee
	(2) U.S. Code
USCENTCOM	U.S. Central Command
USCIB	U.S. Communications Intelligence Board
USCIB/IC	U.S. Communications Intelligence Board/Intelligence Committee
USCINCENT	Commander-in-Chief, U.S. Central Command
USCINCEUR	Commander-in-Chief, U.S. European Command
USCINCLANT	Commander-in-Chief, Atlantic Command
USCINCPAC	Commander-in-Chief, Pacific Command
USCINCRED-COM	Commander-in-Chief, U.S. Readiness Command
USCINCSO	Commander-in-Chief, U.S. Southern Command
USCINCSPACE	Commander-in-Chief, U.S. Space Command
USCG	U.S. Coast Guard
USCOM-EASTLANT	U.S. Commander, Eastern Atlantic
USDAO	U.S. Defense Attaché Office
USD(P)	Under Secretary of Defense for Policy
USD(R&E)	Under Secretary of Defense for Research and Engineering
USEMB	U.S. Embassy
USEUCOM	U.S. European Command
USFISC	United States Foreign Intelligence Surveillance Court
USFJ	U.S. Forces, Japan
USFK	U.S. Forces, Korea
USG	U.S. Government
USGS	U.S. Geological Survey
USIA	U.S. Information Agency
USIB	U.S. Intelligence Board
USIS	U.S. Information Service
USLAMTCOM	U.S. Atlantic Command
USM	Underwater-to-Surface Missile
USMC	U.S. Marine Corps
USMLM	United States Military Liaison Mission

USN	U.S. Navy
USNAVEUR	U.S. Navy, Europe
USNR	U.S. Naval Reserve
USO	(1) United Service Organization
	(2) Unit Security Officer
USPACOM	U.S. Pacific Command
USREDCOM	U.S. Readiness Command
USS	(1) U.S. Ship
	(2) User Support System
USSID	United States Signals Intelligence Directive
USSIS	United States Signals Intelligence System
USSOUTHCOM	U.S. Southern Command
USSPACECOM	U.S. Space Command
USSS	United States SIGINT System
USW	Undersea Warfare
UT	Users' Terminal
UTIC	USAREUR Tactical Intelligence Center
UTM	Universal Transverse Mercator Grid
UTTAS	Utility Tactical Transport Aircraft System
UV	(1) Ultraviolet
	(2) Unique Variable
UW	(1) Unconventional Warfare
	(2) Underwater
UWOA	Unconventional Warfare Operational Area

— V —

VAB	French Front Armored Vehicle
VDS	Variable Depth Sonar
VDV	Soviet Airborne Forces
VF	Voice Frequency
VFR	Visual Flight Rules
VGK	Supreme High Command (Soviet)
VGW	Variable Geometry Wing
VHF	Very High Frequency
VIN	Vehicle Identification Number
VIP	(1) Very Important Person
	(2) Variable Incentive Payment
	(3) Visual Input Processor
VISINT	Visual Intelligence

VLCC	Very Large Crude Carrier
VLF	Very Low Frequency
VLSI	Very Large Scale Integration (Artificial Intelligence)
VMAQ	Marine Tactical Electronic Warfare Squadron
VMFP	Marine Tactical Reconnaissance Squadron
VMO	(1) Marine Observation Squadron
	(2) Tactical Operations Squadron
VN	Vulnerability Number
VO	(1) Directorate for Management and Operations (DIA)
	(2) Directorate for Operations, Plans, and Training (VO)
VOA	Voice of America
VOCOM	Voice Communications
VOD	Vertical Onboard Delivery
VOR	Very High Frequency Omnidirectional Range
VORTAC	Collocated VOR and TACAN
VP	Directorate for Foreign Intelligence (DIA)
VP-I	International Applications Office (DIA)
VP-S	Staff Operations, Directorate for Foreign Intelligence (VP), DIA
VP-SIA	Systems Interface and Applications Office (DIA)
VP-TPO	Technical Production Office (DIA)
VRBM	Variable-Range Ballistic Missile
V/STOL	Vertical/Short Takeoff and Landing
VTA	Military Transport Aviation (Soviet)
VTOL	Vertical Takeoff and Landing
VTR	Tracked Recovery Vehicle
VULREP	Vulnerability Report
VVS	Soviet Air Forces

— W —

W	(1) A "W" prefix to any ship type designates that it is subordinated to a quasi-military force
	(2) With

WAC	(1) World Aeronautical Chart
	(2) World Area Code
WAG	World Area Grid
WAR	Weekly Activity Report (National Security Agency)
WARM	Wartime Reserve Mode
WASHFAX	Washington Community Facsimile Exchange System
WASP	War Air Service Program
WASSO	WWMCCS ADP Systems Security Officer
WATCHCON	Watch Condition
WATS	Wide Area Telecommunications System
WB	Wide Band
WDCS	Weapons Data Correlation System
WE	Weather
WEA	Western Europe Office, Current Analysis Section, Bureau of Intelligence and Research, Department of State
WEBE	Western European Basic Encyclopedia
WECON	Weather Control
WESTCOM	U.S. Army Western Command
WESTLANT	Western Atlantic Area
WEU	West European Union
WFC	World Food Council
WH	White House
WHCA	White House Communications Agency
WHSR	White House Situation Room
WIA	Wounded in Action
WICS	Worldwide Intelligence Communications System
WIG	Wing-in-Ground Effect
WIN	WWMCCS Intercomputer Network
WINE	Warning and Indications in Europe
WINK	Warning in Korea
WINTEL	Warning Notice—Intelligence Sources and Methods Involved
WINTEX	Winter Exercise
WIP	Weekly Intelligence Production
WIR	Weekly Intelligence Review
WIS	Weekly Intelligence Summary
WISE	Warning Indicators System Europe
WISP	(1) Warning Improvement Study Plan

	(2) Wartime Information Security Program
WISS	WESTCOM Intelligence Support System
WMX	Worldwide Military
WP	Warsaw Pact
WPC	(1) Warsaw Pact Countries
	(2) Word Processing Center
WPM	Words Per Minute
WNRC	Washington National Records Center
WPRS	War Powers Reporting System
WRM	War Reserve Material
WRMS	War Reserve Material Stocks
WRS	(1) Weapons Recommendation Sheet
	(2) War Reserve Stocks
WRSA	War Reserve Stocks for Allies
WRSK	War Readiness Spares Kits
WSAP	Weapons System Acquisition Program
WSEP	Weapon System Evaluation Program
WSI/L	War Supporting Industries and Logistics
WSSIC	Weapons and Space Systems Intelligence Committee
WTM	World Target Mosaic
WWIMS	Worldwide Warning Indicator Monitoring System
WWMCCS	Worldwide Military Command and Control System
WX	Weather

— X —

X-2	Counterintelligence (unit of OSS)
XDM	Exploitation Development Model (in COMSEC)
XLAX	CIRC II System Translation Data Base
XMTR	Transmitter
XO	Executive Officer
XPLT	Exploitation

— Y —

YAG	Miscellaneous Service Craft
YAGE	Experimental Service Craft
YAM	Missile Support Craft
YAMM	Missile Support Barge
YC	Open Barge
YCF	Car Barge
YCK	Lighter Open Cargo
YCV	Lighter Aircraft Transport
YD	Floating Crane
YDG	Deperming/Degaussing Barge
YDT	Diving Tender
YE	Ammunition Lighter
YEN	Ammunition Barge
YF	Covered Lighter
YFB	Ferry
YFDB	Large Floating Drydock
YFDL	Small Floating Drydock
YFDM	Medium Floating Drydock
YFL	Launch
YFN	Covered Barge
YFNB	Large Covered Barge
YFND	Drydock Companion Barge
YFP	Floating Power Barge
YFR	Refrigerated Lighter
YFRN	Refrigerated Barge
YFU	Harbor Utility Transport
YG	Garbage Lighter
YGN	Garbage Barge
YGS	Survey Craft
YGT	Target Service Craft
YGTN	Target Barge
YH	Ambulance Craft
YM	Dredge
YMN	Non-Self-Propelled Dredge
YNC	Net Cargo Craft
YNG	Gate Craft
YO	Fuel Lighter
YON	Fuel Barge
YOS	Oil Storage Barge
YOSR	Nuclear Waste Disposal Barge
YOSS	Submersible Oil Storage Barge
YPD	Floating Pile Driver
YPL	Barracks Barge
YPT	Torpedo Retriever
YR	Floating Workshop Barge
YRC	Cable Tender

YRD	Auxiliary Repair Dock
YRG	Tank Cleaning Craft
YRRN	Radiological Repair Barge
YRS	Salvage Craft
YSR	Sledge Removal Craft
YSS	Surfaced Submersible
YTB	Large Harbor Tug
YTL	Small Harbor Tug
YTM	Medium Harbor Tug
YTR	Fireboat
YTS	Sail Training Craft
YVS	Seaplane Service Craft
YW	Water Lighter
YWN	Water Barge
YXR	Hulk or Relic
YXT	Training Craft

— Z —

Z	Zulu Time
ZBB	Zero Based Budgeting
ZI	Zone of the Interior
ZICON	Zone of the Interior Consumers' Network
ZPU	Soviet Antiaircraft Machinegun
ZSU	Soviet Self-Propelled Antiaircraft Gun
ZU	Soviet Towed Antiaircraft Gun

Major Weapons Systems

—A—

A	NATO names beginning with "A" are used to identify Soviet air-to-air Missiles (ALKALI, ATOLL, etc.)
ACRID	Soviet Air-to-Air Missile (AA-6)
AEGIS	U.S. Navy Antiair Warfare System
ALARM	U.K. Air-Launched Anti-Radiation Missile
ALBATROSS	Czechoslovakian Jet Trainer (L-39)
ALKALI	Soviet Air-to-Air Missile (AA-1)
ALOUETTE	French Helicopter (SA-316B)
ALPHA JET	FRG-French Trainer/Light Attack Aircraft
AMRAAM	U.S. Advanced Medium-Range Air-to-Air Missile
AMX-30	French Main Battle Tank
ANAB	Soviet Air-to-Air Missile (AA-3)
APACHE	U.S. Support Helicopter
APAM	Cluster Bomb Follow-on to ROCKEYE
APEX	Soviet Air-to-Air Missile (AA-7)
APHID	Soviet Air-to-Air Missile (AA-8)
ARGUS	Canadian Maritime Reconnaissance Aircraft (CP-107)
ASH	(1) Advanced Scout Helicopter
	(2) Soviet Air-to-Air Missile (AA-5)
ASRAAM	U.S. Advanced Short-Range Air-to-Air Missile
ASROC	U.S. ASW Missile
ATCA	U.S. Advanced Tanker Cargo Aircraft (KC-10)
ATLANTIC	French Marine Patrol/ASW Aircraft
ATOLL	Soviet Air-to-Air Missile (AA-2)
AUGUSTA	NATO Day/Night Antitank Helicopter
AURORA	Canadian Version of ORION Aircraft

—B—

B	NATO names beginning with "B" are used to identify Soviet bomber aircraft (BLINDER, BACKFIRE, etc.)
BACKFIRE	Soviet Jet Bomber (Tu-22M)
BADGER	Soviet Jet Bomber (Tu-16)
BEAGLE	Soviet Jet Bomber (Il-28)
BEAR	Soviet Turboprop Bomber (Tu-95 and Yu-142)
BISON	Soviet Jet Bomber (M-4)
BLACKBIRD	U.S. Reconnaissance Aircraft (SR-71)
BLACKHAWK	(1) U.S. Utility Helicopter (UH-60A)
	(2) Soviet Jet Bomber
BLINDER	Soviet Jet Bomber (Tu-22)
BLOOD-HOUND	U.K. Surface-to-Air Missile
BLOWPIPE	U.K. Surface-to-Air Missile
BMD	Soviet Airborne Combat Vehicle
BMP	Soviet Armored Combat Vehicle
BRDM	Soviet Armored Reconnaissance Vehicle
BREWER	Soviet Jet Bomber (Yak-28)
BRONCO	U.S. Reconnaissance Aircraft (OV-10)
BTR	Soviet Armored Personnel Carrier
BUCCANEER	U.K. Jet Strike Aircraft
BUCKEYE	U.S. Jet Trainer (T-2)

—C—

C	NATO names beginning with "C" are used to identify Soviet cargo aircraft (COOT, CHARGER, etc.)

CAB	Soviet Propeller Transport (Il-2)
CAMBER	Soviet Jet Transport (Il-86)
CAMEL	Soviet Jet Transport (Tu-104)
CAMP	Soviet Turboprop Transport (An-8)
CANBERRA	U.K. Reconnaissance/Light Bomber
CANDID	Soviet Jet Transport (Il-76)
CAPTOR	U.S. Torpedo Launching ASW Mine
CARELESS	Soviet Jet Transport (Tu-154)
CARIBOU	U.S. Transport (C-7)
CASH	Soviet Turboprop Transport (An-28)
CAT	Soviet Turboprop Transport (An-10)
CENTURION	U.K. Main Battle Tank
CHAPPARRAL	U.S. Air Defense Missile
CHARGER	Soviet Jet Transport (Tu-144)
CHIEFTAIN	U.K. Main Battle Tank
CHINOOK	U.S. Helicopter (CH-47)
CLANK	Soviet Turboprop Transport (An-30)
CLASSIC	Soviet Jet Transport (Il-62)
CLEAT	Soviet Turboprop Transport (Tu-114)
CLINE	Soviet Turboprop Transport (An-32)
CLOBBER	Soviet Jet Transport (Yak-42)
CLOD	Soviet Propeller Transport (An-14)
COACH	Soviet Propeller Transport (Il-12)
COALER	Soviet Jet Transport (An-72/74)
COBRA	(1) U.S. Attack Helicopter (AH-1G)
	(2) FRG Antitank Guided Missile
COCK	Soviet Turboprop Transport (An-22)
CODLING	Soviet Jet Transport (Yak-40)
COKE	Soviet Turboprop Transport (An-24)
COLT	Soviet Propeller Transport (An-2)
COMMANDO	U.S. Wheeler Armored Personnel Carrier
CONDOR	Soviet Heavy-Lift Jet Transport (An-124)
COOKER	Soviet Jet Transport (Tu-110)
COOKPOT	Soviet Jet Transport (Tu-124)
COOT	Soviet Turboprop Transport (Il-18)

CORSAIR II	U.S. Carrier-Based Attack Aircraft (A-7)
CREEK	Soviet Propeller Transport (Yak-12)
CROTALE	French Surface-to-Air Missile
CRUSADER	U.S./French Carrier-Based Fighter Aircraft (F-8)
CRUSTY	Soviet Jet Transport (Tu-134)
CUB	Soviet Turboprop Transport
CUFF	Soviet Turboprop Transport (Be-30)
CURL	Soviet Turboprop Transport (An-26)

— D —

DELTA DART	U.S. Interceptor Aircraft (F-106)
DEXTOR	U.S. Torpedo
DIVAD	U.S. Division Air Defense Gun System (SGT YORK)
DRAGON	U.S. Man-Portable Antitank Guided-Missile System
DRAGONFLY	U.S. Jet Attack Aircraft (A-37)
DRAKEN	Swedish-Built Attack, Intercept, Reconnaissance Aircraft

— E —

EAGLE	U.S. Jet Fighter (F-15)
ETENDARD	French Carrier-Borne Strike Fighter
EXOCET	French Antiship Cruise Missile
EXTENDER	U.S. Tanker/Cargo Aircraft (KC-10A)

— F —

F	NATO names beginning with "F" are used to identify Soviet fighter-type aircraft (FLAGON, FOXBAT, etc.)
FAGOT	Soviet Jet Fighter (MiG-15)
FATMER	Soviet Jet Fighter (MiG-19)

FENCER	Soviet Jet Fighter-Bomber (Su-24)
FIDDLER	Soviet Jet Fighter (Tu-128)
FIGHTING FALCON	U.S. Jet Fighter (F-16)
FINBACK	Chinese Jet Fighter (F-8)
FIREBAR	Soviet Jet Fighter (Yak-28P)
FIRE STREAK	U.K. Air-to-Air Missile
FISHBED	Soviet Jet Fighter (MiG-21)
FISHPOT	Soviet Jet Fighter (Su-9)
FISHPOT C	Soviet Jet Fighter (Su-11)
FITTER A	Soviet Jet Fighter (Su-7)
FITTER B/C/D	Soviet Jet Fighter-Bomber (Su-17)
FITTER C Export	Soviet Jet Fighter (Su-20)
FLAGON	Soviet Jet Fighter (Su-15)
FLANKER	Soviet Jet Fighter (Su-27)
FLOGGER B/E/G	Soviet Jet Fighter (MiG-23)
FLOGGER D/J	Soviet Jet Fighter-Bomber (MiG-27)
FLOGGER F/H	Soviet Jet Fighter (MiG-23)(Export)
FORGER	Soviet Jet V/STOL Fighter (Yak-38)
FOXBAT	Soviet Jet Fighter (MiG-25)
FOXHOUND	Soviet Jet Fighter (MiG-31)
FREEDOM FIGHTER	U.S. Jet Fighter (F-5)
FRESCO	Soviet Jet fighter (MiG-17)
FROG	Soviet Tactical Rocket
FROGFOOT	Soviet Jet Ground-Attack Aircraft (Su-25)
FULCRUM	Soviet Jet Fighter (MiG-29)

— G —

G	NATO names beginning with "G" are used to identify Soviet surface-to-air missiles (GOA, GALOSH, etc.)
GADFLY	Soviet SAM (SA-11)
GAINFUL	Soviet SAM (SA-6)
GALAXY	U.S. Jet Transport (C-5)
GALOSH	Soviet ABM (ABM-1)
GAMMON	Soviet SAM (SA-5)

GANEF	Soviet SAM (SA-4)
GANNET	U.K. Early Warning Aircraft
GASKIN	Soviet SAM (SA-9)
GAZELLE	French/British Helicopter
GECKO	Soviet SAM (SA-8)
GEPARD	FRG Antiaircraft Tank
GOA	Soviet SAM (SA-3/SA-N-1)
GOBLET	Soviet SAM (SA-N-3)
GOPHER	Soviet SAM (SA-13)
GRAIL	Soviet Hand-Held SAM (SA-7)
GREYHOUND	U.S. Transport (C-2)
GRUMBLE	Soviet SAM (SA-10)
GUIDELINE	Soviet SAM (SA-2)
GUILD	Soviet SAM (SA-1)

— H —

H	NATO names beginning with "H" are used to identify Soviet helicopters (HAZE, HOUND, etc.)
HADES	French Battlefield Support Missile
HALO	Soviet Helicopter (Mi-26)
HARE	Soviet Helicopter (Mi-1)
HARKE	Soviet Helicopter (Mi-10)
HARM	U.S. High-Speed Anti-Radiation Missile
HARPOON	U.S. Antiship Cruise Missile
HARRIER	U.S./U.K. V/STOL Attack Fighter (AV-8A)
HAVOC	Soviet Helicopter (Mi-28)
HAWK	(1) Homing-All-the-Way Killer
	(2) U.S. Surface-to-Air Missile
	(3) U.K. Jet Trainer Aircraft
HAWKEYE	U.S. Carrier-Based Turboprop Early Warning Aircraft (E-2)
HAZE	Soviet Helicopter (Mi-14)
HELIX	Soviet Helicopter (Ka-27)
HELLFIRE	U.S. Air-to-Surface Antitank Missile
HEN	Soviet Helicopter (Ka-15)
HERCULES	U.S. Turboprop Transport (C-130)
HIND	Soviet Helicopter (Mi-24)
HIP	Soviet Helicopter (Mi-8)
HOG	Soviet Helicopter (Ka-18)
HOKUM	Soviet Helicopter

HOMER	Soviet Helicopter (Mi-12)
HONEST JOHN	U.S. Surface-to-Surface Rocket
HOODLUM	Soviet Helicopter (Ka-26)
HOOK	Soviet Helicopter (Mi-6)
HOPLITE	Soviet Helicopter (Mi-2)
HORMONE	Soviet Helicopter (Ka-25)
HORNET	U.S. Carrier-Based Jet Fighter (F-18)
HOT	International High Subsonic Optically Guided Tube-Launched (Antitank Missile System)
HOUND	Soviet Helicopter (Mi-4)
HUEY	U.S. Transport Helicopter (UH-1)
HUEY COBRA	U.S. Transport Helicopter (AH-1S)
HURON	U.S. Turboprop Transport

— I —

I-HAWK	Improved HAWK (U.S. Surface-to-Surface Missile)
INDIGO	Italian Surface-to-Air Missile
INTRUDER	U.S. Carrier-Based Jet Attack Aircraft (A-6)
IROQUOIS	U.S. Helicopter (UN-1N)

— J —

JETSTAR	U.S. Jet Transport
JOLLY GREEN	U.S. Transport Helicopter (CH-3) GIANT

— K —

K	NATO names beginning with "K" are used to identify Soviet air-to-surface missiles (KIPPER, KANGAROO, etc.) and Soviet cruisers
KANGAROO	Soviet Air-to-Surface Missile (AS-3)

KAREN	Soviet Air-to-Surface Missile (AS-10)
KEDGE	Soviet Air-to-Surface Missile (AS-14)
KEGLER	Soviet Air-to-Surface Missile (AS-12)
KELT	Soviet Air-to-Surface Missile (AS-5)
KENNEL	Soviet Air-to-Surface Missile (AS-1)
KERRY	Soviet Air-to-Surface Missile (AS-7)
KFIR	Israeli Multipurpose Fighter
KINGFISH	Soviet Air-to-Surface Missile (AS-6)
KIPPER	Soviet Air-to-Surface Missile (AS-2)
KITCHEN	Soviet Air-to-Surface Missile (AS-4)

— L —

LAMPS	U.S. Light Airborne Multipurpose System (ASW Helicopter)
LANCE	U.S. Artillery Support Missile
LEOPARD	FRG Main Battle Tank
LIGHTNING	U.K. Jet Fighter
LYNX	U.K./French General Purpose Helicopter (HAS-2)

— M —

M	NATO names beginning with "M" are used to identify multipurpose aircraft, trainers, and utility craft, etc.(MASCOT, MAYA, etc.)
MADGE	Soviet Maritime Flying Boat (Be-6)
MAESTRO	Soviet Jet Trainer (Yak-28U)
MAGIC	NATO Air-to-Air Missile
MAIL	Soviet Turboprop Maritime Amphibian (Be-12)
MAINSTAY	Soviet AWACS Aircraft
MANDRAKE	Soviet Jet Reconnaissance Aircraft (Yak-27RU)

MANGROVE	Soviet Jet Reconnaissance Aircraft
MARDER	FRG Mechanized Infantry Combat Vehicle
MARTEL	NATO Air-to-Surface Missile
MASCOT	Soviet Jet Trainer (Il-28U)
MASURCA	French Surface-to-Air Missile
MATRA	French Laser-Guided Bomb
MATRA SHAHINE	French Surface-to-Air Missile
MAVERICK	U.S. Air-to-Surface Antiarmor Missile
MAX	Soviet Propeller Trainer (Yak-18T)
MAY	Soviet ASW Maritime Aircraft (Il-38)
MAYA	Czechoslovakian Jet Trainer (L-29)
MENTOR	U.S. Propeller Trainer (T-34)
MESCALERO	U.S. Propeller Trainer
MIDGET	Soviet Jet Trainer (MiG-15U)
MILAN	NATO Antitank Guided Missile
MINUTEMAN	U.S. ICBM
MIRAGE	French Fighter Bomber
MOHAWK	U.S. Turboprop Reconnaissance Aircraft (OV-1)
MONGOL	Soviet Jet Trainer (MiG-21U)
MOOSE	Soviet Propeller Trainer (YaK-11)
MOSS	Soviet AWACS Turboprop Aircraft (Tu-126)
MOUJIK	Soviet Jet Trainer (Su-7U)

— N —

NEACAP	National Emergency Airborne Command Post (E-4)
NIGHTINGALE	U.S. Jet Transport (C-9)
NIKE (HERCULES)	U.S. Surface-to-Air Missile
NIMROD	U.K. ASW Reconnaissance Aircraft

— O —

ORION	U.S. ASW Reconnaissance Aircraft (P-3)
OTOMAT	French Antiship Cruise Missile

— P —

PAH-1	German Antitank Helicopter
PATRIOT	U.S. Surface-to-Air Missile
PAVE KNIFE	U.S. Laser Pod (A-6)
PAVE PAWS	U.S. Phased Array Radar
PAVE SPIKE	U.S. Laser Pod (F-4)
PAVE TACK	U.S. Laser Pod (F-4)
PENGUIN	Norwegian Surface-to-Surface Missile
PERSHING	U.S. Surface-to-Surface Missile
PHALANX	U.S. Navy Close-In Weapons System
PHANTOM	U.S. Jet Attack Fighter (F-4)
PHOENIX	U.S. Navy Long-Range Air-to-Air Missile
PLUTON	French Battlefield Support Missile
POLARIS	U.S. Submarine-Launched Ballistic Missile
POSEIDON	U.S. Submarine-Launched Ballistic Missile
PROWLER	U.S. Carrier-Based ECM Aircraft (A-6B)
PUMA	French General Purpose Helicopter

— Q —

QUICKSTRIKE	U.S. Mine

— R —

RAPIER	U.K. Surface-to-Air Missile System
RAVEN	U.S. Reconnaissance Aircraft (EF-111A)

REDEYE	U.S. Surface-to-Air Missile
RED TOP	U.K. Air-to-Air Missile
ROCKEYE	U.K. Air-to-Ground Missile
ROLAND	U.S. Surface-to-Air Missile

— S —

S	NATO names beginning with "S" are used to identify surface-to-surface missiles (SCARP, SEGO, etc.)
SABER	Soviet IRBM (SS-20)
SABRELINER	U.S. Jet Trainer
SADDLER	Soviet ICBM (SS-7)
SAFEGUARD	U.S. Antiballistic Missile
SAGGER	Soviet Antitank Missile (AT-3)
SALISH	Soviet Tactical Surface-to-Surface Missile (SSC-2a)
SAMARITAN	U.S. Transport
SAMLET	Soviet Coastal Surface-to-Surface Missile (SSC-2b)
SANDAL	Soviet MRBM (SS-4)
SAPWOOD	Soviet ICBM (SS-6)
SARK	Soviet SLBM (SS-N-5)
SARPAC	NATO Antitank Guided Missile
SASIN	Soviet ICBM (SS-8)
SATAN	Soviet ICBM (SS-18)
SAVAGE	Soviet ICBM (SS-13)
SCALEBOARD	Soviet MRBM (SS-12)
SCALPEL	Soviet ICBM (SS-X-24)
SCAMP	Soviet MRBM (SS-X-14)
SCARAB	Soviet SRBM (SS-21)
SCARP	Soviet ICBM (SS-9)
SCIMITAR	U.K. Light Tank
SCORPION	U.K. Light Tank
SCRUBBER	Soviet Antiship Missile (SS-N-1)
SCUD	Soviet Short-Range Surface-to-Surface Missile (SS-1)
SEA CAT	U.K. Surface-to-Air Missile
SEA COBRA	U.S. Helicopter (AH-1)
SEA DART	U.K. Surface-to-Air/Surface-to-Surface Missile
SEA HARRIER	U.K. V/STOL Attack Fighter
SEA KING	U.S. Helicopter (SH-3)
SEA KNIGHT	U.S. Helicopter (CH/UH/-46)
SEA SKUA	U.K. Air-to-Surface Missile
SEA SLUG	U.K. Surface-to-Air Missile
SEA SPARROW	NATO Surface-to-Air Missile (RIM-7H)
SEA SPRITE	U.S. ASW Helicopter
SEA STALLION	U.S. Transport Helicopter (CH-53A)
SEA WOLF	U.K. Surface-to-Air Missile
SEGO	Soviet ICBM (SS-11)
SENTRY	U.S. Reconnaissance Aircraft (E-3A)
SERB	Soviet SLBM (SS-N-6)
SHADDOCK	Soviet Tactical Surface-to-Surface Missile (SSC-1a)
SHAHINE	French Surface-to-Air Missile
SHRIKE	U.S. Anti-Radiation Homing Missile
SHYSTER	Soviet MRBM (SS-3)
SIBLING	Soviet SRBM (SS-2)
SICKLE	Soviet ICBM (SS-X-25)
SIDEWINDER	U.S. Air-to-Air Missile
SINNER	Soviet ICBM (SS-16)
SKEAN	Soviet MRBM (SS-5)
SKIFF	Soviet SLBM (SS-NX-23)
SKY CRANE	U.S. Transport Helicopter
SKYFLASH	NATO Air-to-Air Missile
SKYHAWK	U.S. Carrier-Based Jet Attack Fighter (A-4)
SKYMASTER	U.S. Reconnaissance Aircraft (OV-2A)
SKYTRAIN	U.S. Jet Transport (C-9B)
SKY WARRIOR	U.S. Carrier-Based ECM Aircraft (A-3)
SLAM	U.K. Surface-to-Air Missile
SNAPPER	Soviet Antitank Missile (AT-1)
SNIPE	Soviet SLBM (SS-N-17)
SPANDREL	Soviet Antitank Missile (AT-5)
SPANKER	Soviet ICBM (SS-17)
SPARROW	U.S. Air-to-Air Missile
SPARTAN	U.K. Light Tank (APC)
SPARVIERO	Italian Antitank Guided Missile
SPIDER	Soviet SRBM (SS-23)
SPIGOT	Soviet Antitank Missile (AT-4)
SPIRAL	Soviet Antitank Missile (AT-6)
SRAM	U.S. Short-Range Attack Missile
STANDARD	U.S. Shipborne Surface-to-Surface Missile
STARFIGHTER	U.S. Jet Fighter (F-104)
STARLIFTER	U.S. Jet Transport (C-141)
STILETTO	Soviet ICBM (SS-19)
STINGER	U.S. Surface-to-Air Missile
STINGRAY	Soviet SLBM (SS-N-18)
STRATO-FORTRESS	U.S. Jet Bomber (B-52)

STRATO-TANKER	U.S. Jet Tanker (KC-135)
STURGEON	Soviet SLBM (SS-N-20)
STYX	Soviet Antiship Missile (SS-N-2)
SUBROC	U.S. Submarine-Launched ASW Missile
SWATTER	Soviet Antitank Missile (AT-2)
SWINGFIRE	U.K. Antitank Guided Missile

— T —

TALON	U.S. Jet Trainer
TARTAR	U.S. Surface-to-Air Missile
T-BIRD	U.S. Jet Trainer (T-33A)
TERRIER	U.S. Surface-to-Air Missile
TFX	U.S. Fighter-Bomber (F-111)
THUNDER-BOLT II	U.S. Jet Aircraft (A-10)
TIGER II	U.S. Jet Fighter (F-5E)
TIGERSHARK	U.S. Jet Fighter (F-20)
TITAN	U.S. ICBM
TOMAHAWK	U.S. Antiship/Land Attack Cruise Missile
TOMCAT	U.S. Carrier-Based Jet Fighter (F-14)
TORNADO	U.K./FRG/Italian Fighter-Bomber, Reconnaissance, Intercept Aircraft
TOW	U.S. Tube-Launched, Optically Tracked, Wire-Guided Antitank Weapon
TOW/COBRA	U.S. Helicopter (AH-1S), TOW Missile Launching, Attack
TR-1	U.S. Reconnaissance Aircraft Based on U-2R Airframe
TRACKER	U.S. Propeller Carrier-Based ASW Aircraft

TRIDENT	U.S. SLBM/SSBN System
TURBOLET	Czechoslovakian Turboprop Transport (L-410)
TURBO MENTOR	U.S. Turboprop Trainer (T-34C)

— V —

VIGILANTE	U.S. Jet Reconnaissance Aircraft (A-5)
VIKING	U.S. Carrier-Based Jet ASW Aircraft (S-3A) and COD Aircraft (US-3A)
VOODOO	U.S. Interceptor Aircraft (F-101)
VULCAN	(1) U.S. Mobile Air Defense Gun
	(2) U.K. Medium-Range Bomber

— W —

WALLEYE	U.S. TV-Guided "Smart" Bomb
WARNING STAR	U.S. Reconnaissance Aircraft (EC-121)
WASP	U.K. General Purpose Helicopter (HAS-1)
WEASEL	FRG Light Wheeled Armored Reconnaissance Vehicle
WESSEX	U.K. General Purpose Helicopter (HAS-3)
WILD WEASEL	U.S. Jet Radar Suppression Aircraft (F-4G)

Chronology

1941

February—The Federal Communications Commission establishes the Foreign Broadcast Monitoring Service. This would eventually become the Foreign Broadcast Information Service, a component of the Central Intelligence Agency.

July 11—President Roosevelt establishes the Office of Coordinator of Information and appoints William Donovan as coordinator.

October—The Joint Army-Navy Intelligence Committee of the Joint Army-Navy Board (a predecessor to the Joint Chiefs of Staff) is established.

December 7—Japanese military forces attack Pearl Harbor.

1942

—The Signals Intelligence Service is moved to Arlington Hall Station, Virginia. It will eventually become the Signals Security Agency.

January—The U.S. Army Counterintelligence Corps replaces the Corps of Intelligence Police.

June 13—The Office of Coordinator of Information becomes the Office of Strategic Services (OSS), under a Military Order signed by President Roosevelt.

1944

—State, War, Navy Coordinating Committee, a predecessor of the National Security Council, is established.

November 18—General Donovan issues his plan for a comprehensive, postwar intelligence organization.

1945

October 1—President Truman signs Executive Order 9621, which abolishes the OSS. Its functions are assumed by the Departments of State and War.

December 1—The Interim Research and Intelligence Service, Department of State, was to be abolished under the provisions of Executive Order 9621, issued by President Truman on September 30, 1945. The secretary of state could abolish the functions of the service or transfer them elsewhere in the Department of State, as he saw fit.

1946

—Civil Air Transport, the CIA's air service, is begun in China. It will later be based in Taiwan.

—Signals Intelligence Committee, a Director of Central Intelligence Committee, is established.

—The U.S. Communications Intelligence Board is established.

—The Joint Atomic Energy Intelligence Committee is established.

—The House Military Affairs Committee investigating the attack on Pearl Harbor recommends a separate, central, independent intelligence organization.

—The Office of Special Operations, CIG, is established.

January 22—President Truman signs a Presidential Directive entitled "Coordination of Federal Foreign Intelligence Activities." This directive creates the Central Intelligence Group (CIG), the National Intelligence Authority, and the Intelligence Advisory Board.

January 23—Rear Admiral Sidney W. Souers, U.S. Naval Reserve, becomes the first director of the Central Intelligence Group.

January—President Truman establishes the National Intelligence Authority (NIA), the Central Intelligence Group (CIG), and the Intelligence Advisory Board (IAB).

March 2—Kingman Douglass becomes deputy director of Central Intelligence.

June 10—Lieutenant General Hoyt S. Vandenberg, U.S. Army, relieves Rear Admiral Souers as director of the Central Intelligence Group.

June—The U.S. Communications Intelligence Board is established.

July 11—Kingman Douglass is relieved as deputy director of Central Intelligence.

August—Office of Reports and Estimates is established.

1947

—The Intelligence Advisory Board becomes the Intelligence Advisory Committee (IAC) (it is the predecessor to the National Foreign Intelligence Board [NFIB]).

—The Joint Intelligence Group (JIG), Joint Chiefs of Staff, is established.

January 20—Brigadier General Edwin K. Wright, U.S. Army, becomes deputy director of Central Intelligence.

May 1—Rear Admiral Roscoe H. Hillenkoetter, U.S. Navy, relieves Lieutenant General Vandenberg as director of the Central Intelligence Group.

July 26—The National Security Act is passed. It establishes the National Security Council (NSC), the director of Central Intelligence (DCI), and the Central Intelligence Agency.

September 18—The Central Intelligence Agency (CIA) is established.

October—The CIA is assigned responsibility for the joint military intelligence surveys. These become the National Intelligence Surveys.

1948

—The Director of Central Intelligence Interagency Defector Committee (IDC) is established.

—The 40 Committee of the National Security Council is established.

September 1—The Central Intelligence Agency's Office of Policy Coordination (OPC) is given a covert action charter.

1949

—The Director of Central Intelligence Scientific Estimates Committee is established.

—The Office of Scientific Intelligence, Central Intelligence Agency, is established.

March 9—Brigadier General Wright retires as deputy director of Central Intelligence.

May 20—The Armed Forces Security Agency is established.

June 20—Congress passes the Central Intelligence Agency Act of 1949.

July—Rear Admiral Earl E. Stone, U.S. Navy, becomes director of the National Security Agency.

September—The Soviet Union conducts its first nuclear explosion.

1950

—Harry Gold, a member of the "Atomic Bomb Spy Ring," is convicted and sentenced to 30 years in prison.

—David Greenglass, a member of the "Atomic Bomb Spy Ring," is convicted and sentenced to 15 years in prison.

—The Korean War begins.

—The Joint Intelligence Indications Committee is established by the Joint Chiefs of Staff.

—The Board of National Estimates and Office of National Estimates are established.

—The Office of Research and Reports, CIA, is established.

—The Office of National Estimates is formed to produce National Intelligence Estimates.

April 15—Gustav Adolph Mueller, an Air Force enlisted student, is convicted of espionage and sentenced to five years in prison.

October 7—General Walter Bedell Smith, U.S. Army, relieves Rear Admiral Hillenkoetter as director of Central Intelligence. William H. Jackson becomes the deputy director of Central Intelligence.

October—General Smith reorganizes the CIA.

1951

—The Domestic Contacts Division, CIA, is created.

—The Director of Central Intelligence Economic Intelligence Committee is established.

January—The deputy director for plans position is created in the Central Intelligence Agency. The incumbent heads what will become the clandestine services.

August 3—William H. Jackson is relieved as deputy director of Central Intelligence.

August 23—Allen W. Dulles becomes deputy director of Central Intelligence.

August—Lieutenant General Ralph J. Canine, U.S. Army, relieves Rear Admiral Stone as director of the National Security Agency.

1952

—The Central Intelligence Agency's Office of Policy Coordination and Office of Special Operations are consolidated as the Clandestine Services, which is placed under the deputy director for plans (who later becomes the deputy director for operations [DDO]).

—The Central Intelligence Agency's Directorate for Intelligence is created.

—The Office of Operations (OO) is placed in the CIA's Directorate for Intelligence.

—The Office of Policy Coordination is combined with the Office of Special Operations as the Clandestine Services, under the deputy director for plans.

—The Office of Scientific Intelligence becomes a component of the Directorate for Intelligence, CIA.

—The Office for Research and Reports becomes a component of the Directorate for Intelligence, CIA.

—The Domestic Contacts Division, CIA, becomes part of the Directorate for Intelligence, CIA.

June 13—The Brownell Report, "Survey on Communications Intelligence Activities of the United States Government," is issued.

November 4—A Presidential Directive establishes the National Security Agency (NSA). Lieutenant General Ralph Julian Canine, U.S. Army, becomes the agency's first director, and Rear Admiral Joseph Numa Wegener, U.S. Navy, becomes its first vice director.

November—The CIA's Photographic Intelligence Division is formed.

1953

—The Office of National Estimates is abolished.

—The CIA participates in the Shah of Iran's successful return to power and in the overthrow of Muhammed Mossadeq.

—The CIA conducts successful operations in Costa Rica.

February 9—General Smith ends his tour as director of Central Intelligence in order to become secretary of state.

February 26—Allen W. Dulles becomes director of Central Intelligence.

April 4—An amendment is signed stating that military officers cannot hold the offices of director and deputy director of Central Intelligence concurrently.

April 23—Brigadier General Charles Pearre Cabell, U.S. Air Force, becomes deputy director of Central Intelligence.

April 27—President Eisenhower signs Executive Order 10450, "Security Requirements for Government Employment."

June 19—Julius and Ethel Rosenberg are executed for espionage.

September 2—The Operations Coordinating Board replaces the Psychological Strategy Board, National Security Council.

Autumn—Brigadier General John B. Ackerman, U.S. Air Force, succeeds Rear Admiral Numa Joseph Wegener, U.S. Navy, as vice director of the National Security Agency.

1954

—The position of special assistant to the director of Central Intelligence for community coordination is established.

—The Director of Central Intelligence Watch Committee and the National Indications Center in the Pentagon are established.

—The CIA conducts a successful clandestine operation in Guatemala.

1955

—The first U-2 flight is flown over the USSR.

—The Director of Central Intelligence Ad Hoc Requirements Committee is established.

—National Security Council Directive 5412/1 is issued. It establishes the Planning and Coordination Group, called the 5412 Committee or Special Group.

—The Basic Intelligence Division, Office of Research and Reports, CIA, becomes the Office of Basic Intelligence.

—The Office of Collection and Dissemination, CIA, becomes the Office of Central Reference.

—The Domestic Contacts Division, CIA, becomes the Domestic Contacts Service, CIA.

February—The CIA's Directorate for Administration becomes the Directorate for Support. It assumes the additional responsibilities of training, personnel administration, and communications.

June 29—The Second Hoover Commission Report is issued.

1956

—The DCI Committee on Exchanges is established.

—The DCI Guided Missile Intelligence Committee (GMIC) is established.

—Presidential Executive Order 10656 is signed. It establishes a President's Board of Consultants on Foreign Intelligence Activities.

January 13—President Eisenhower issues Executive Order 10656, which establishes the President's Board of Consultants on Foreign Intelligence Activities.

June—Lieutenant General John A. Samford, U.S. Air Force, succeeds Brigadier General Ackerman as vice director of the National Security Agency.

November—Lieutenant General John A. Samford, U.S. Air Force, relieves Lieutenant General Canine as director of the National Security Agency. Joseph Ream becomes deputy director. The position's title has been changed to deputy director from vice director, and Ream is the first civilian to be assigned to the job.

1957

—The President's Board of Consultants on Foreign Intelligence Activities (PBCFIA) is created by President Eisenhower.

—The Director of Central Intelligence Committee on Overhead Reconnaissance (COMOR) is established.

September 20—George H. French, a U.S. Air Force Captain, is convicted of espionage and is sentenced to life in prison.

October—Dr. Howard T. Engstrom succeeds Joseph H. Ream as deputy director of the National Security Agency.

October—Construction on the CIA complex in Langley, Virginia, is begun.

1958

—The CIA conducts a successful operation in Tibet.

—The Defense Reorganization Act of 1958 is enacted.

—The Intelligence Analysis Committee and the United States Communications Intelligence Board are combined into the new United States Intelligence Board (USIB).

—The Director of Central Intelligence Guided Missile and Astronautics Intelligence Committee (GMAIC) is formed from the old Guided Missile Intelligence Committee (GMIC), which had been in existence since 1956.

August—Dr. Louis W. Tordella succeeds Dr. Engstrom as deputy director of the National Security Agency.

1959

—The Director of Central Intelligence Security Committee is created.

—The Director of Central Intelligence Scientific Intelligence Committee (SIC) replaces the Scientific Estimates Committee, which had existed since 1949.

November 3—The cornerstone of the CIA Headquarters at Langley is laid.

1960

—"The Joint Study Group Report on Foreign Intelligence Activities of the United States Government," known as the "Joint Study Group Report," is issued.

—A U-2 aircraft piloted by Francis Gary Powers is shot down over the Soviet Union, causing a cessation of such reconnaissance flights over the USSR.

—Bernon F. Mitchell, an NSA employee, defects to the Soviet Union.

November—Rear Admiral Laurence H. Frost, U.S. Navy, relieves Lieutenant General Samford as director of the National Security Agency.

1960–1962—The CIA wages Operation Mongoose against Fidel Castro.

1961

—The U.S. photo satellite program becomes operational.

—U.S. reconnaissance satellites become operational.

—The National Photographic Interpretation Center (NPIC) is established.

—The President's Board of Consultants on Foreign Intelligence Activities, which had been established in 1956, becomes the President's Foreign Intelligence Advisory Board (PFIAB).

April 4—The National Security Council formally approves the Bay of Pigs plan.

April 17—The Bay of Pigs operation is launched and fails.

May 4—President Kennedy establishes the President's Foreign Intelligence Advisory Board (PFIAB) in Executive Order 10938.

August 1—The Defense Intelligence Agency is established by Department of Defense Directive 5105.21.

September 20—The first employees move into the new CIA complex at Langley, Virginia.

October—Lieutenant General Joseph F. Carroll, U.S. Air Force, becomes the first director of the Defense Intelligence Agency.

November 29—John A. McCone relieves Allen W. Dulles as director of Central Intelligence.

1962

—Nelson C. Drummond, a Navy yeoman, is arrested for espionage. He is then tried, convicted, and sentenced to life in prison.

January 1—The Department of Defense Central Requirements Registry is established.

January 31—Brigadier General Cabell is relieved as deputy director of Central Intelligence.

April 3—Lieutenant General Marshall S. Carter, U.S. Army, becomes deputy director of Central Intelligence.

April—The CIA Inspector General Lyman Kirkpatrick's working group submits its final recommendations concerning the reorganization of the CIA.

June 30—Lieutenant General Gordon A. Blake, U.S. Air Force, relieves Rear Admiral Frost as director of the National Security Agency.

November 2—The Defense Intelligence School is established.

November 30—The Directorate for Mapping, Charting, and Geodesy, DIA is created.

1963

—The Director of Central Intelligence creates the National Intelligence Programs Evaluation Staff (NIPE).

—Robert D. Haguewood, who worked at the National Security Agency, defects to the Soviet Union.

—The military service chiefs are reduced from members to observers on the U.S. Intelligence Board.

—Secretary of Defense Robert McNamara introduces the PPBS.

—The position of CIA deputy director for science and technology (DDS&T) and the Directorate for Science and Technology are created.

—The Office of Scientific Intelligence, CIA, is transferred from the Directorate for Intelligence to the Directorate for Science and Technology.

January 1—The Defense Intelligence School begins classes.

January 1—The Defense Intelligence Agency Production Center is activated.

February 19—The DIA Automatic Data Processing Center is activated.

July 1—DIA assumes responsibilities as J-2, Joint Chiefs of Staff.

1964

—NSAM 303 is signed. It creates the "303 Committee" to replace the Special Group.

March 31—The DIA Dissemination Center becomes operational.

April 30—The DIA Scientific and Technical Intelligence Directorate is established.

1965

—The Department of Defense-Central Intelligence Agency EXCOM is formed.

—The Office of Operations (OO), CIA, is dissolved.

April 28—Vice Admiral William F. Rayborn, Jr., U.S. Navy, replaces John McCone as director of Central Intelligence.

April 28—Lieutenant General Carter is relieved by Richard Helms as deputy director of Central Intelligence.

June—Lieutenant General Marshall S. Carter, U.S. Army, relieves Lieutenant General Blake as director of the National Security Agency.

1966

June—Brigadier General Ackerman is relieved as vice director of the National Security Agency.

June 30—Richard Helms relieves Vice Admiral Rayborn as director of Central Intelligence.

October 13—Vice Admiral Rufus Taylor, U.S. Navy, becomes deputy director of Central Intelligence.

November 15—The first major agency-wide reorganization of the DIA occurs.

December—The "Foreign Intelligence Collection Requirements: The Inspector General's Survey" (known as the Cunningham Report) is issued.

1967

—The Director of Central Intelligence Committee on Imagery Requirements and Exploitation (COMIREX) is established.

—The Office of Research and Reports, CIA, is dissolved.

—The Office of Strategic Research, Directorate for Intelligence, CIA, is established.

—The Office of Economic Research, Directorate for Intelligence, CIA, is established.

—The Office of Central Reference, CIA, becomes the Central Reference Service, CIA.

—*Katz vs. the United States* is heard by the Supreme Court, which holds that electronic surveillance is a search and seizure.

February—"Report on Strategic Warning" (the Shute Report) is issued.

June—The U.S. Navy intelligence collection ship USS *Liberty* is attacked deliberately by Israeli forces.

June—Herbert W. Boeckenhaupt, an Air Force staff sergeant, is convicted of conspiring to commit espionage and is sentenced to 30 years in prison.

1968

—The Director of Central Intelligence Information Handling Committee is formed.

—HSCIT report on the Defense Intelligence Agency and its Consolidated Intelligence Program (CIP) is issued.

January—The U.S. Navy intelligence collection ship USS *Pueblo* is seized in international waters by North Korean forces and is forced to proceed to a North Korean port.

September—The Defense Intelligence Agency On-Line System (DIAOLS) becomes operational.

1969

January 20—"Report to the Director of Central Intelligence on the Organization of the CIA and the Intelligence Community" is issued.

January 31—Vice Admiral Taylor is relieved as deputy director of Central Intelligence.

May 7—Lieutenant General Robert E. Cushman, Jr., U.S. Marine Corps, becomes deputy director of Central Intelligence.

July 29—"Report on Defense Intelligence" is issued.

August 1—Vice Admiral Noel Gayler, U.S. Navy, succeeds Lieutenant General Carter as director of the National Security Agency.

September—Lieutenant General Donald V. Bennett, U.S. Army, relieves Lieutenant General Carroll as director of the Defense Intelligence Agency.

1970

—President Nixon requests the Bureau of the Budget for a study of the Intelligence Community.

—National Security Decision Memorandum (NSDM) 40 is issued. It creates the "40 Committee," which replaces the 303 Committee of the National Security Council.

—The U.S. Army terminates its domestic intelligence operations.

—The DIA Directorate for Estimates is created.

—The Defense Intelligence Projections for Planning (DIPP) is begun.

July 1—"Report on National Command and Control Capability and Defense Intelligence" by a Blue Ribbon Panel chaired by Gilbert W. Fitzhugh is issued.

July—The second major reorganization of the DIA occurs.

November 1—The DIA creates a separate directorate to produce military estimates.

1971

—The NSA/Central Security Service is created.

—President Nixon directs the director of Central Intelligence to prepare a consolidated intelligence budget, which is to include tactical intelligence.

March 10—"A Review of the Intelligence Community" (the Schlesinger Report) is issued.

July 2—President Nixon signs Executive Order 11605, "Amendment of Executive Order 10450 of April 27, 1953, Relating to Security Requirements for Government Employment."

October 18—Air Force Master Sergeant Walter Perkins is arrested on espionage charges. He is then court-martialed, found guilty, and sentenced to three years in prison.

November 5—President Nixon issues his memorandum "Organization and Management of the U.S. Intelligence Community."

November—Master Sergeant Raymond George DeChamplain, U.S. Air Force, is convicted of espionage and is sentenced to 15 years confinement.

December 15—the President's Foreign Intelligence Advisory Board's (PFIAB's) Economic Intelligence Report is sent to the President.

December 31—Lieutenant General Cushman, Jr., ends his tour of duty as deputy director of Central Intelligence.

1972

—The NIPE staff becomes the Intelligence Community Staff.

—Public Law 92-352 creates the "Study Commission Relating to Foreign Policy" (called the Murphy Commission).

January 21—Director of Central Intelligence Directive (DCID 1/2), "U.S. Intelligence Objectives and Priorities," is issued.

February 17—National Security Council Intelligence Directive (NSCID) 1-8 is revised and reissued. It is still in effect in April 1989.

May 2—Lieutenant General Vernon A. Walters, U.S. Army, becomes deputy director of Central Intelligence.

July 2—The Defense Mapping Agency is created, thereby discontinuing the DIA's responsibilities concerning mapping, charting, and geodesy.

August—Vice Admiral Vincent P. De Poix, U.S. Navy, relieves Lieutenant General Bennett as director of the Defense Intelligence Agency.

August 24—Lieutenant General Samuel C. Phillips, U.S. Air Force, relieves Vice Admiral Gayler as director of the National Security Agency.

1973

—The Technical Services Division, which provides technical support to clandestine activities, is transferred to the Directorate for Science and Technology, CIA.

—The Domestic Contacts Service, CIA, is transferred to the Directorate for Operations, CIA, and is renamed the Domestic Contacts Division, CIA.

—The CRITICOMM/SPINTCOMM network becomes the Digital Network—Defense Special Security Communications System (DINDSCSS).

—The Board of National Estimates, which had been formed in 1950, and the Office of National Estimates are abolished.

—The CIA "Family Jewels" report is prepared.

—The IC Staff is reorganized.

—The Director of Central Intelligence Research and Development Council is established.

—The CIA is involved in the overthrow of the Allende regime in Chile.

February 2—James R. Schlesinger relieves Richard Helms as director of Central Intelligence.

February—The President's Foreign Intelligence Advisory Board (PFIAB) issues its HUMINT report.

March 20—The Senate Foreign Relations Committee begins hearings on ITT, the Central Intelligence Agency, and Chile.

March—Richard Helms becomes U.S. ambassador to Iran.

June—The Net Assessment Group is abolished.

July 2—James R. Schlesinger leaves office as director of Central Intelligence. Lieutenant General Vernon A. Walters, U.S. Army, becomes acting director of Central Intelligence.

August 15—Lieutenant General Lew Allen, Jr., U.S. Air Force, relieves Lieutenant General Phillips as director of the National Security Agency.

September 4—William E. Colby becomes director of Central Intelligence.

December 7—The President's Foreign Intelligence Advisory Board (PFIAB) report on Economic Intelligence (the Cherne Report) is issued.

1974

—The U.S. Army Intelligence Command is discontinued and is replaced by the U.S. Army Intelligence Agency.

—The Key Intelligence Questions (KIQ) program is begun.

—The DCI Watch Committee is disestablished.

—The National Indications Center is disestablished.

—The Director of Central Intelligence Watch Committee is abolished. A special assistant for strategic warning and a Strategic Warning Staff are created.

March—Airman First Class Oliver Everett Grunden, U.S. Air Force, is convicted of espionage. He is dishonorably discharged from the Air Force and receives a five-year prison sentence.

April 21—Benson K. Buffam succeeds Dr. Louis W. Tordella as deputy director of the National Security Agency.

June 4—President Nixon signs Executive Order 11785, "Amending Executive Order 10450, as Amended, Relating to Security Requirements for Government Employment, and for Other Purposes."

September 16—President Ford acknowledges that the CIA conducted operations in Chile.

September—Lieutenant General Daniel O. Graham, U.S. Army, relieves Vice Admiral De Poix as director of the Defense Intelligence Agency.

October 2—The Senate passes the Hughes Amendment to the Foreign Assistance Act. The House passes the Ryan Amendment, which is similar, the following week.

October 30—A comprehensive overhaul of the DIA's production functions, organization, and management is begun.

November 25—The J-2 Support Office, DIA, is created to meet the intelligence needs of the JCS.

December 2—The defense intelligence officers are established.

December 9—The Senate Government Relations Committee holds hearings on the Mansfield-Mathias resolution, which calls for the creation of a "Select Committee to Study Governmental Operations with Respect to Intelligence Activities."

December 17—The differences between the Hughes and Ryan Amendments are resolved.

December 30—The Hughes-Ryan Amendment to the Foreign Assistance Act of 1974 is passed and becomes law.

1975

—The U.S. Army Security Agency (ASA) is disestablished.

—The U.S. Army Intelligence and Security Command is formed.

January 4—President Ford establishes a Presidential Commission to examine CIA operations within the United States. It is chaired by Vice President Nelson Rockefeller and becomes known as the Rockefeller Commission.

January 15—William Colby, director of Central Intelligence, testifies before Congress that provocative CIA domestic operations were discontinued after February 1973.

January 27—The Senate passes Senate Resolution 21 (94th Cong.), which establishes a Senate Select Committee to Study Government Operations with Respect to Intelligence Activities. It is chaired by Senator Frank Church and becomes known as the Church Committee.

February 19—The House of Representatives passes House Resolution 139 (94th Cong.), which establishes the House Select Committee on Intelligence. It is chaired by Representative Lucien Nedzi.

February 19—The Freedom of Information Act is passed.

May 1—Benson K. Buffam is relieved as deputy director of the National Security Agency.

June 10—The Rockefeller Commission Report, which had been submitted to President Ford on June 6, is released. The report states that almost all of the CIA's domestic activities were lawful, but that some were clearly unlawful.

June 17—House Resolution 591 (94th Cong.) is passed. It restaffs the House Select Committee on Intelligence. Representative Otis Pike is named to chair the committee, and it becomes known as the Pike Committee.

June—The Murphy Commission Report is issued.

October 5—The release marking CONTROLLED DISSEMINATION can no longer be used on classified material.

November 2—President Ford dismisses William Colby as director of Central Intelligence.

November 14—Secretary of State Henry Kissinger was cited in contempt of Congress in respect to subpoenaed material on covert activities and in respect to Soviet Union and SALT I.

November 20—The Church Committee releases a report entitled *Alleged Assassination Plots Involving Foreign Leaders.*

December 2—One of two contempt of Congress citations against Kissinger is dropped after an accommodation is reached.

December 4—The Church Committee releases a report entitled *Covert Action in Chile, 1963-1973.*

December 10—The remaining contempt of Congress citation against Kissinger is dropped.

December 19—The Senate adopts the Tunney Amendment, which bars funding of Angolan guerrillas.

December 23—The CIA Station Chief in Greece, Richard S. Welch, is assassinated.

December—Lieutenant General Eugene F. Tighe, U.S. Air Force, relieves Lieutenant General Graham as director of the Defense Intelligence Agency.

1976

—The director of Central Intelligence establishes the National Foreign Intelligence Board.

—The Director of Central intelligence Weapons and Space Systems Intelligence Committee is established.

—The Director of Central Intelligence Scientific and Technical Intelligence Committee is established.

—The Soviet Union increases its naval presence off West Africa after it intercepts communications that indicate opposing forces in the Angolan Civil War intend to attack Soviet arms carrying ships that are delivering weapons to Soviet-backed forces in Angola. From Guinea, this force conducts naval operations in the Gulf of Guinea.

January 29—The Pike Committee report is submitted to the House of Representatives. The House votes to not release the results of the report until President Ford states that its release will not damage U.S. intelligence activities.

January 30—George Bush becomes director of Central Intelligence.

February 16—A portion of the Pike Committee report, which was given to the *Village Voice* by CBS correspondent Daniel Schorr, appears in the *Village Voice.* Additional portions appear on February 23.

February 18—President Ford signs Executive Order 11905, which reorganizes U.S. intelligence. An Intelligence Oversight Board is created and an Operations Advisory Group is established. The President's Foreign Intelligence Advisory Board

(PFIAB) and the U.S. Intelligence Board are abolished.

February 19—The House passes House Resolution 1042 (94th Cong.). It authorizes the House Committee on Standards of Official Conduct to look into the publication of the classified Pike Committee report.

March 1—The Senate Committee on Government Operations reports on Senate Resolution 400 (94th Cong.). The resolution creates a standing Senate Committee on Intelligence.

April 26—The Church Committee releases its *Final Report, Foreign and Military Intelligence.*

April 28—The Church Committee releases its *Final Report, Intelligence Activities and the Rights of Americans.* It maintains that poor oversight of intelligence activities had permitted violations of constitutional rights.

May 19—An amended version of Senate Resolution 400 (94th Cong.) is passed by the Senate. It establishes a Senate Select Committee on Intelligence to monitor intelligence activities.

May—Lieutenant General Samuel V. Wilson, U.S. Army, relieves Lieutenant General Tighe as director of the Defense Intelligence Agency.

July 7—E. Henry Knoche relieves Lieutenant General Walters as deputy director of Central Intelligence.

July—The third major reorganization of the DIA occurs.

December 23—President-Elect Carter announces the nomination of Theodore Sorenson to be the next director of Central Intelligence. The opposition to the Sorenson nomination is immediate and grows as the year ends.

1977

—The U.S. Army Intelligence and Threat Center (ITAC) is created.

January 1—The U.S. Army Intelligence and Security Command is created.

January 17—Theodore Sorenson withdraws his name from nomination as opposition to his appointment increases.

January 20—George Bush leaves the office of director of Central Intelligence. Henry E. Knoche is acting director of Central Intelligence from January 20 until March 9, 1977.

January—Richard Helms concludes his tour as U.S. ambassador to Iran.

February 7—Admiral Stansfield Turner is nominated to the position of director of Central Intelligence.

March 9—Admiral Turner is sworn in as director of Central Intelligence.

March 11—Secretary of Defense Harold Brown reorganizes Defense Intelligence. The Defense Intelligence Agency and the Central Intelligence Agency now are to report to the deputy secretary of defense.

March 25—The final part of the new National Military Intelligence Center is operational.

May 4—President Carter, in Executive Order 11984, abolishes the President's Foreign Intelligence Advisory Board, which had been established in 1955 by President Eisenhower. Carter establishes a three-member Intelligence Oversight Board to act in its place.

May 16—Senate Resolution 1539 (95th Cong.) is introduced. It is the first public intelligence budget, but disclosure is limited to funds concerning the Intelligence Community Staff and the CIA's Retirement and Disability Program.

May 18—The SSCI's first annual report is issued. It says that the intelligence agencies are now accounting properly to Congress and that Executive Oversight appears to be working.

July 5—Vice Admiral Bobby R. Inman, U.S. Navy, succeeds Lieutenant General Allen as Director of the National Security Agency.

July 14—The House passes Resolution 658 (95th Cong.), which creates a House Intelligence Committee. Representative Edward Boland is named as chairman.

July 31—E. Henry Knoch is relieved by John F. Blake as deputy director of Central Intelligence.

August 4—President Carter, in Presidential Directive PD/NSC-17, "Reorganization of the Intelligence Community," provides for additional reorganization of the Intelligence Community. The role of the director of Central Intelligence is strengthened.

August 9—Admiral Stansfield Turner, DCI, announces his intention to reduce the CIA's clandestine Directorate of Operations (DDO) by 800 people.

August—Lieutenant General Wilson ends his tour as director of the Defense Intelligence Agency.

September—Lieutenant General Eugene F. Tighe, Jr., U.S. Air Force, again becomes director of the Defense Intelligence Agency.

October 11—The CIA Directorate of Intelligence is renamed the National Foreign Assessment Center.

October 31—Richard Helms, a former director of Central Intelligence, pleads "no contest" to charges of failing to testify fully and accurately on CIA operations in Chile when he appeared before the Senate Foreign Relations Committee.

October 31—198 employees are fired from the Central Intelligence Agency in a move that is quickly dubbed "the Halloween massacre."

1978

—The Resource Management Staff is created from the Intelligence Community Staff.

—The director of Central Intelligence is given full and exclusive responsibility for the National Foreign Intelligence Program budget.

—National Intelligence Tasking Center is created from the IC Staff.

—Ronald L. Humphrey is convicted of espionage charges and is sentenced to fifteen years in prison.

—William P. Kampiles, an ex-employee of the CIA, is arrested. He is then tried, found guilty in November 1979, and sentenced to 40 years in prison.

January 24—President Carter signs Executive Order 12036. It emphasizes the role of the director of Central Intelligence in establishing priorities for the intelligence budget. The DCI also becomes the special assistant for Central Intelligence. In addition, the order establishes organizations to assist the DCI, defines the missions, functions, and responsibilities for the components of the Intelligence Community, restricts questionable collection techniques and intelligence activities, and provides for further Executive oversight.

February 9—Senate Resolution 2525 (95th Cong.), "The National Intelligence Reorganization and Reform Act of 1978," is introduced. It is a draft of the congressional Intelligence Charter.

February 10—Frank C. Carlucci relieves John F. Blake as deputy director of Central Intelligence.

April 20—The House Intelligence Committee votes against divulging the intelligence funds that it authorized for fiscal year 1979.

May 1—Robert E. Drake succeeds Benson K. Buffam as deputy director of the National Security Agency.

June 28—Presidential Executive Order 12065, "National Security Information," is issued.

September 7—The House passes Resolution 7308 (95th Cong.). This is the House version of the Foreign Intelligence Surveillance Act.

October 5—The Interagency Classification Review Committee issues "Information Security Oversight Office."

October 14—The HPSCI Annual Report is delivered as Rpt. 95-1795.

October 25—The differences between the House and Senate versions having been resolved, the Foreign Intelligence Surveillance Act is passed and becomes law as Public Law 95-511.

1979

—The Murphy Committee (House) holds hearings on the problems of the Intelligence Community.

—Lee Eugene Madsen of the U.S. Navy is arrested on espionage charges. He is then tried, found guilty, and sentenced to eight years in prison.

April—The NTIC issues the first "National HUMINT Tasking Plan."

May 23—Presidential Executive Order 12039, "Foreign Intelligence Electronic Surveillance," is signed by President Carter.

July-August—An internal reorganization is accomplished, creating five directorates in the DIA.

1980

January 1—The National Foreign Intelligence Council (NFAC) is formed.

January—The National Intelligence Council (NIC) is formed.

February 25—The Senate passes Senate Resolution 2284 (H.R. 6588), "The National Intelligence Act of 1980."

April 1—Ann Z. Caracristi becomes deputy director of the National Security Agency, relieving Robert E. Drake.

June 3—The Senate passes Senate Resolution 2284, "The Intelligence Oversight Act of 1980," by a vote of 89 to 1.

October 14—President Reagan signs the "Intelligence Authorization Act for Fiscal Year 1981."

October 15—Public Law 96-456, the "Classified Information Procedures Act," is approved by the 96th Congress and becomes law.

1981

—Congress passes the Intelligence Authorization Act of 1981.

—Joseph G. Helmich, Jr., a U.S. Army warrant officer, is arrested. He is then tried, convicted of espionage offenses, and sentenced to life in prison.

January 20—Admiral Turner leaves office as director of Central Intelligence. John F. Blake is acting director until January 28.

January 28—William J. Casey becomes director of Central Intelligence.

February 5—Frank C. Carlucci ends his tour as deputy director of Central Intelligence.

February 12—Vice Admiral Bobby R. Inman becomes deputy director of Central Intelligence.

March 10—Lieutenant General Lincoln D. Faurer, U.S. Air Force, relieves Vice Admiral Inman as director of the National Security Agency.

April—Ground is broken on the DIA's new Defense Intelligence Analysis Center.

August—Lieutenant General Tighe ends his tour as director of the Defense Intelligence Agency.

September—Lieutenant General James A. Williams, U.S. Army, becomes director of the Defense Intelligence Agency.

October 20—President Reagan signs Executive Order 12331, "The President's Foreign Intelligence Advisory Board," which reestablishes the board by the same name.

December 4—President Reagan signs Executive Order 12333, "United States Intelligence Activities," which makes adjustments in established routines to enable them to conform to his management style.

December 4—President Reagan signs Executive Order 12334, "President's Intelligence Oversight Board," which establishes the board by the same name.

1982

—Congress passes the Intelligence Identities Protection Act of 1982.

April 2—President Reagan signs Executive Order 12356, "National Security Information."

June 10—John McMahon becomes deputy director of Central Intelligence.

June 23—The Intelligence Identities Protection Act of 1982, PL-97-200, is passed by Congress.

July 31—Robert E. Rich relieves Ann Z. Caracristi as deputy director of the National Security Agency.

1983

—The Boland Amendment is attached to the continuing appropriations bill and passes.

—Jeffery L. Pickering, U.S. Navy, is arrested on espionage charges. He is then found guilty and sentenced to five years at hard labor.

—Hans P. Wold, of the U.S. Navy, is arrested. He is then tried, found guilty of espionage, and sentenced to four years at hard labor.

—The Defense Intelligence School is rechartered and renamed the Defense Intelligence College.

—Captain William H. Hughes, Jr., U.S. Air Force, is listed as a deserter. Cleared for access to extremely sensitive intelligence information, Hughes may have defected to the Soviet Union.

—James Durwood Harper, Jr., is arrested for espionage. He is then tried, convicted, and sentenced to life in prison.

—The United States lands Marines in Lebanon. Several hundred Marines die when their headquarters and barracks are blown up.

October 25—U.S. military forces invade Grenada as Operation "Urgent Fury" commences.

1984

—Construction is begun on the second building of the CIA complex in Langley, Virginia.

—Occupancy begins in the DIA's new Defense Intelligence Analysis Center (DIAC).

—Bruce L. Kearn, a naval officer, is arrested, tried, and convicted on espionage charges.

—The Central Intelligence Information Act is passed by Congress.

September 17—A proposed Executive Order, "National Policy on Telecommunications and Automated Information Systems Security," is issued. Although it is never enacted, the order is significant in that it reveals the desires of the National Security Agency. The order would vastly expand the government's control in these areas.

1985

—The U.S. Army Intelligence Agency is reactivated.

—Edward L. Howard, a former employee of the Central Intelligence Agency, defects to the Soviet Union as the FBI is about to arrest him.

January 22—Bruce Edward Tobias, U.S. Navy, is convicted of espionage. Dale Verne Irene, a friend of Tobias, is also convicted.

March 14—Thomas Patrick Cavanagh is convicted of espionage charges and is sentenced to life in prison.

May 17—Jay Clyde Wolff, formerly of the U.S. Navy, is convicted of espionage.

May 31—Alice Michaelson is convicted of espionage.

August 6—Francis Xavier Pizzo, U.S. Navy, is convicted of espionage.

August 9—Arthur James Walker of the Walker spy ring is convicted of espionage.

August 14—Michael Timothy Tobias, Radioman Third Class, U.S. Navy, is convicted of espionage and sentenced to twenty years in prison.

August 26—Edward O. Buchanan is convicted of espionage and is sentenced to prison.

September 27—Sharon Marie Scrange, a CIA employee, is convicted of espionage and is sentenced to five years in prison.

October 17—Samuel Loring Morison, a naval analyst, is convicted of espionage and sentenced to two years in prison.

October 28—President Reagan signs Executive Order 12357, "President's Foreign Intelligence Advisory Board," which made minor changes to Executive Order 12331, revoked that order, and reissued it as Executive Order 12357.

October 28—John Walker, a retired naval warrant officer, is convicted of espionage and sentenced to life imprisonment.

October 28—Michael Walker, son of John Walker, is found guilty of espionage and is sentenced to 25 years in prison.

1986

January 23—Randy Miles Jeffries, a congressional courier, is convicted of espionage and sentenced to ten years in prison.

February 7—Lawrence Wu-Tai Chin, a CIA analyst, is convicted of espionage. He commits suicide while awaiting sentencing.

March 28—John McMahon concludes his tour as deputy director of Central Intelligence.

April 18—Robert M. Gates becomes director of Central Intelligence.

June 4—Jonathan Jay Pollard and his wife, Anne Louise Pollard, are convicted of espionage.

June 5—Ronald William Pelton, formerly of the NSA, is found guilty of espionage and is sentenced to life in prison.

June 19—Richard W. Miller, an FBI agent, is convicted of espionage and is sentenced to life in prison.

July 24—Jerry Alfred Whitworth, of the Walker spy ring, is convicted of espionage and is sentenced to 365 years in prison.

August 6—Bruce Damian Ott, an Air Force sergeant, is found guilty of espionage and is sentenced to 25 years at hard labor.

October 27—Allen Davies, a former Air Force staff sergeant, is arrested on espionage charges. He is then tried, convicted, and sentenced to five years in prison.

December 1—President Reagan signs Executive Order 12575, "President's Special Review Board," which establishes the board to investigate the National Security Council in the wake of the Iran-Contra scandal.

1987

January 29—William Casey's tenure as director of Central Intelligence ends. Robert M. Gates is acting director until May 26.

February 26—The President's Special Review Board that had been established under Executive Order 12575 submits its report. It recommends no major changes in the National Security Council staff structure, but does find fault with the president and several of the major figures in the scandal.

May 6—William Casey dies.

May 26—William H. Webster becomes director of Central Intelligence.

May 28—Allen John Davies, formerly of the Air Force, is convicted of espionage.

July 7-14—Lieutenant Colonel Oliver North, U.S. Marine Corps, testifies before the congressional investigative committee.

1988

—The Boxer Amendment, which is attached to the Fiscal Year 1988 Defense Authorization Bill, becomes law as the bill is approved.

January 27—Senate passes S.1721, which repeals the Hughes-Ryan Amendment and revises procedures for informing Congress about special activities. S.1721 awaits action by the House.

August 17—Pakistani president Zia is killed in the crash of a C-130. Sabotage of the aircraft is a definite possibility.

December 1988—A bomb explodes aboard a Pan American airliner flying over Lockerbie, Scotland, killing all on board. The Guardians of the Islamic Revolution claim responsibility for the bombing and say that it was in response to the downing of an Iranian air bus by the USS *Vincennes* in the Persian Gulf in July 1988.

1989

January—William Webster is retained as director of Central Intelligence by President George Bush.

February—The trial of Lieutenant Colonel Oliver North, U.S. Marine Corps (Retired), begins but legal problems concerning the use of classified material in the defense becomes an immediate and crucial issue.

March 8—Soviet Army Lieutenant Colonel Yuri Pakhtusov, an assistant military attaché in the United States, is arrested for spying. He is declared persona non grata and is expelled from the United States.

March 10—Sharon Rogers, wife of Captain Will Rogers III, U.S. Navy, commanding officer of the USS *Vincennes*, is uninjured when a pipe bomb explodes in her van as she is driving it in San Diego, California. The bombing is believed to be another terrorist response to the downing of an Iranian air bus by the *Vincennes* in the Persian Gulf in July 1988.

Bibliography

Allen, Thomas B., and Polmar, Norman. *Merchants of Treason: America's Secrets for Sale*. New York: Delacorte Press, 1988.

American Bar Association. *Oversight and Accountability of the U.S. Intelligence Agencies: An Evaluation*. Washington, DC: ABA, 1985.

Bamford, James. *The Puzzle Palace: A Report on America's Most Secret Agency*. New York: Penguin Books, 1983.

Becket, Henry S. A. *The Dictionary of Espionage: Spookspeak into English*. New York: Stein and Day, 1986.

Belden, Thomas. "Indications, Warning, and Crisis Options." *International Studies Quarterly* 21, no. 1 (Mar. 1977): 181–98.

Blackburn, N. Glenn. "Computers: A Counterintelligence Concern." Unpublished paper provided to the editors. Washington, DC, 1987.

Boutacoff, David A. "Steering a Course Toward Space." *Defense Electronics* (Mar. 1986): 58–60, 62–63.

Breckinridge, Scott D. *The CIA and the U.S. Intelligence System*. Boulder, CO: Westview Press, 1986.

Brinkley, David A., and Hull, Andrew W. *Estimative Intelligence: A Textbook on the History, Products, Uses, and Writing of Intelligence Estimates*. Columbus, OH: Battelle, 1979.

Central Intelligence Agency. *Central Intelligence Agency Factbook*. Washington, DC: GPO, 1987.

Clancy, Tom. *The Cardinal of the Kremlin*. New York: Putnam, 1988.

Clauser, Jerome K., and Weir, Sandra M. *Intelligence Research Methodology*. State College, PA: HRB-Singer, 1975.

Cline, Ray S. *The CIA Under Reagan, Bush, and Casey*. Washington, DC: Acropolis Books, 1981.

Constantinides, George C. *Intelligence and Espionage: An Analytical Bibliography*. Boulder, CO: Westview Press, 1983.

Corson, William R. *The Armies of Ignorance: The Rise of the American Intelligence Empire*. New York: Dial Press, 1977.

Crawford, David J. *Volunteers: The Betrayal of National Defense Secrets by Air Force Traitors*. Washington, DC: GPO, 1988.

Deacon, Richard. *Spyclopedia: An Encyclopaedia of Spies, Secret Services, Operations, Jargon, and All Subjects Related to the World of Espionage*. London: Macdonald, 1987.

Department of Defense. *Activities of DoD Intelligence Components that Affect U.S. Persons (Department of Defense Directive 5240.1)*. Washington, DC: DoD, 1982.

————. *Keeping the Nation's Secrets: A Report to the Secretary of Defense by the Commission to Review DoD Security Policies and Practices*. Washington, DC: DoD, 1985.

Department of Defense, Defense Intelligence Agency. *Defense Intelligence Agency Manual*. Washington, DC: DIA, 1987.

————. *Defense Intelligence Agency Manual 22-2*. Washington, DC: DIA, 1979.

————. *Defense Intelligence Agency Manual 65-13*. Washington, DC: DIA, 1985.

————. *Organization, Mission, and Key Personnel*. Washington, DC: DIA, 1986.

————. *Training Compendium for General Defense Career Development Program (IDCP) Personnel DOD 1430.10M3-TNG*. Washington, DC: DIA, 1986.

Department of Defense, Defense Intelligence College. *Glossary of Intelligence Terms and Definitions.* Washington, DC: DIC, 1987.

Department of Defense, Information Security Oversight Office. *Directive No. 1: National Security Information.* As reproduced in *Federal Register,* June 25, 1982, pp. 27836– 27841.

Department of Defense, Joint Chiefs of Staff. *Department of Defense Dictionary of Military and Related Terms.* Washington, DC: GPO, 1986.

Department of Defense, National Defense University. *Joint Staff Officer's Guide, 1986.* Washington, DC: GPO, 1986.

Department of Defense, U.S. Army. *AIA: Threat Analysis.* Falls Church, VA: U.S. Army Intelligence Agency, 1987.

————. *Counterintelligence.* Field Manual FM 34-60. Washington, DC: Headquarters, Department of the Army, 1985.

————. *Counter-Signals Intelligence (C-SIGINT) Operations.* Field Manual FM 34-62. Washington, DC: Headquarters, Department of the Army, 1986.

————. *Intelligence and Electronic Warfare Operations.* Field Manual FM 34-1. Washington, DC: Headquarters, Department of the Army, 1984.

————. *Intelligence Imagery.* Field Manual FM 34-55. Washington, DC: Headquarters, Department of the Army, 1985.

————. *Intelligence Interrogation.* Field Manual FM 34-52. Washington, DC: Headquarters, Department of the Army, 1987.

————. *Military Intelligence Battalion Combat Electronic Warfare and Intelligence (Aerial Exploitation) (Corps).* Field Manual FM 34-22. Washington, DC: Headquarters, Department of the Army, 1984.

————. *Military Intelligence Battalion (CEWI) (Operations) (Corps).* Field Manual 34-21. Washington, DC: Headquarters, Department of the Army, 1982.

————. *Military Intelligence Battalion (Combat Electronic Warfare Intelligence) (Division).* Field Manual FM 34-10. Washington, DC: Headquarters, Department of the Army, 1981.

————. *Military Intelligence Battalion (CEWI) (Tactical Exploitation) (Corps): Counterintelligence, Interrogation, Electronic Warfare.* Field Manual FM 34-23. Washington, DC: Headquarters, Department of the Army, 1985.

————. *Military Intelligence Company (Combat Electronic Warfare and Intelligence) (Armored Cavalry Regiment/Separate Brigade).* Field Manual FM 34-30. Washington, DC: Headquarters, Department of the Army, 1983.

————. *Military Intelligence Group (Combat Electronic Warfare and Intelligence) (Corps).* Field Manual FM 34-20. Washington, DC: Headquarters, Department of the Army, 1983.

————. *RDTE Managers Intelligence and Threat Support Guide.* Alexandria, VA: Headquarters, Army Materiel Development and Readiness Command, 1983.

————. *U.S. Army Air Defense Artillery Employment.* Field Manual FM 44-1. Washington, DC: Headquarters, Department of the Army, 1983.

————. *United States Army Intelligence and Threat Analysis Center.* Washington, DC: USAITC, 1987.

Department of State, Bureau of Public Affairs. *Duties of the Secretary of State.* Washington, DC: DoS, 1984.

Dunn, Peter M., and Watson, Bruce W. *American Intervention in Grenada: The Implications of Operation "Urgent Fury."* Boulder, CO: Westview Press, 1985.

Fain, Tyrus G.; Plant, Katharine C.; and Milloy, Ross. *The Intelligence Community: History, Organization, and Issues.* Public Documents Series. New York: R.R. Bowker, 1977.

Gertz, Bill. "Intelligence Operation Red Star of Pelton Trial." *The Washington Times,* June 2, 1986, p. 2A.

Godson, Roy, ed. *Intelligence Problems for the 1980s, Number 1: Elements of Intelligence.* Rev. ed. Washington, DC: National Strategy Information Center, 1983.

————. *Intelligence Problems for the 1980s, Number 2: Analysis and Estimates.* Washington, DC: National Strategy Information Center, 1980.

———. *Intelligence Problems for the 1980s, Number 3: Counterintelligence.* Washington, DC: National Strategy Information Center, 1980.

———. *Intelligence Problems for the 1980s, Number 4: Covert Action.* Washington, DC: National Strategy Information Center, 1981.

———. *Intelligence Problems for the 1980s, Number 5: Clandestine Collection.* Washington, DC: National Strategy Information Center, 1982.

Kent, Sherman. *Strategic Intelligence for American World Policy.* Princeton, NJ: Princeton University Press, 1966.

Kessler, Ronald. *Spy vs. Spy: Stalking Soviet Spies in America.* New York: Charles Scribner's Sons, 1988.

Kornblum, Allan. *Intelligence and the Law: Cases and Materials.* Vol. IV. Washington, DC: DIC, 1987.

Laqueur, Walter. *The Age of Terrorism.* Boston: Little, Brown, 1987.

———. *A World of Secrets.* New York: Basic Books, 1985.

Laubenthal, Sanders A. "Preparing 'the Team': Defense Attache Training." *DIC Newsletter* (Winter 1986): 1-4.

Lefever, Ernest W., and Godson, Roy. *The CIA and the American Ethic: An Unfinished Debate.* Washington, DC: Ethics and Public Policy Center, Georgetown University, 1979.

Lowenthal, Mark M. *U.S. Intelligence: Evolution and Anatomy.* New York: Praeger, 1984.

Maroni, Alice C. *Special Access Programs and the Defense Budget: Understanding the "Black Budget."* Washington, DC: Foreign Affairs and National Defense Division, Congressional Research Service, Library of Congress, 1987.

Martin, Paul H. "Communications-Computer Security." *Journal of Electronic Defense* (June 1987).

Maurer, Alfred C.; Turnstall, Marion D.; and Keagle, James M. *Intelligence Policy and Process.* Boulder, CO: Westview Press, 1985.

Muzerall, Joseph V., and Carty, Thomas P. "COMSEC and Its Need for Key Management." *DP&CS* (Spring 1987).

"National Policy on Telecommunications and Automated Information Systems Security." Proposed Presidential Directive issued Sept. 17, 1984, but never enacted.

Office of the President of the United States. *Executive Order 9621.* Washington, DC, Sept. 25, 1945.

———. *Executive Order 10450, Security Requirements for Government Employment.* Washington, DC, Apr. 27, 1953.

———. *Executive Order 11605, Amendment of Executive Order 10450 of April 27, 1953, Relating to Security Requirements for Government Employment.* Washington, DC, July 2, 1971.

———. *Executive Order 11785, Amending Executive Order No. 10450, as Amended, Relating to Security Requirements for Government Employment, and for Other Purposes.* Washington, DC, June 4, 1974.

———. *Executive Order 11905, United States Foreign Intelligence Activities.* Washington, DC, Feb. 18, 1976.

———. *Executive Order 12036, United States Intelligence Activities.* Washington, DC, Jan. 24, 1978.

———. *Executive Order 12331, President's Foreign Intelligence Advisory Board.* Washington, DC, Oct. 20, 1981.

———. *Executive Order 12356, National Security Information.* Washington, DC, Apr. 2, 1982.

———. *Executive Order 12575, President's Special Review Board.* Washington, DC, Dec. 1, 1986.

———. *Military Order, Office of Strategic Services.* Washington, DC, June 13, 1942.

———. *Order Signed by President Franklin D. Roosevelt, Coordinator of Information.* Washington, DC, July 11, 1941.

———. *Presidential Directive, Coordination of Federal Foreign Intelligence Activities.* Washington, DC, Jan. 22, 1946.

———. *Report of the President's Special Review Board.* Washington, DC: GPO, 1987.

Oseth, John M. "Intelligence and Low Intensity Conflict." *Naval War College Review* (Nov.-Dec. 1984): 19–36.

———. *Regulating U.S. Intelligence Operations: A Study in Definition of the National Interest.* Frankfurt: University of Kentucky Press, 1985.

Pichirallo, Joe. "FBI Details Its Case Against Chin." *The Washington Post*, Nov. 24, 1985, p. A1.

Pickett, George. "Congress, the Budget, and Intelligence." In *Intelligence Policy and Process*, edited by Alfred C. Maurer, Marion D. Turnstall, and James M. Keagle. Boulder, CO: Westview Press, 1985.

Poyer, David. *The Med.* New York: St. Martin's Press, 1988.

Quirk, John; Phillips, David; Cline, Ray; and Pforzheimer, Walter. *The Central Intelligence Agency: A Photographic History.* Guilford, CT: Foreign Intelligence Press, 1986.

Ranelagh, John. *The Agency: The Rise and Decline of the CIA.* New York: Simon and Schuster, 1986.

Reeves, Robert; Anson, Abraham; and Landen, David. *Manual of Remote Sensing.* Falls Church, VA: American Society of Photogrammetry, 1975.

Schmidt, Susan. "Pelton Convicted of Selling Secrets." *The Washington Post*, June 6, 1986, p. A1.

Shenon, Philip. "Former C.I.A. Analyst is Arrested and Accused of Spying for China." *The New York Times*, Nov. 24, 1985.

Treverton, Gregory F. *Covert Action: The Limits of Intervention in the Postwar World.* New York: Basic Books, 1987.

Turner, Stansfield. *Secrecy and Democracy: The CIA in Transition.* Boston: Houghton Mifflin, 1985.

Tyler, Patrick. "Supersecret Work Revealed." *The Washington Post*, May 28, 1986, p. A1.

U.S. Congress. *Intelligence Identities Protection Act of 1982. Public Law 97-200, June 23, 1982.* Washington, DC: GPO, 1982.

U.S. Congress. Senate. *Senate Resolution 400, A Resolution Establishing a Select Committee on Intelligence.* 94th Congress, 1st Sess., 1975.

———. Select Committee to Study Governmental Operations with Respect to Intelligence Activities. *Alleged Assassination Plots Involving Foreign Leaders: An Interim Report of the Select Committee to Study Governmental Operations with Respect to Intelligence Activities.* 94th Congress, 1st sess., Nov. 20, 1975. S. Rept. 94-465.

———. *Final Report of the Senate Select Committee to Study Government Operations with Respect to Intelligence Activities. Report 94-755. Book I, Foreign and Military Intelligence.* Washington, DC: GPO, 1976.

Von Hoene, John P. A. *Intelligence User's Guide.* Washington, DC: DIA, 1983.

Ware, Willis H. "Information Systems, Security, and Privacy." *EDUCOM Bulletin* (Summer 1984).

Warner, John S. "National Security and the First Amendment." Intelligence Profession Series no. 2. McLean, VA: Association of Former Intelligence Officers, 1985.

Watson, Bruce W. *Red Navy at Sea: Soviet Naval Operations on the High Seas, 1956-1980.* Boulder, CO: Westview Press, 1986.

Watson, Bruce W., and Dunn, Peter M. *Military Lessons of the Falkland Islands War: Views from the United States.* Boulder, CO: Westview Press, 1984.

Watson, Bruce W., and Watson, Susan M., eds. *The Soviet Navy: Strengths and Liabilities.* Boulder, CO: Westview Press, 1986.

Wilson, Dick, and Calcaterra, Dennis. "Airborne Command and Control Modernization." *Signal* (Aug. 1987).

The Encyclopedia

—A FORTIORI ANALYSIS is a general intelligence term for an analysis that is deliberately weighted to favor an alternative system when compared to a judgmental "best" system. If the "best" system receives a favorable comparison under the weighted analysis, its position is strengthened. *See also:* Analysis, Intelligence Cycle.

References

Godson, Roy, ed. *Intelligence Problems for the 1980s, Number 1: Elements of Intelligence.* Rev. ed. Washington, DC: National Strategy Information Center, 1983.

—ABORT means to fail to accomplish a mission for any reason other than enemy action. It may occur at any point from the initiation of the operation to the arrival of the mission force at its destination.

References

Department of Defense, Joint Chiefs of Staff. *Department of Defense Dictionary of Military and Related Terms.* Washington, DC: GPO, 1986.

—ACCESS. The official definition of access is the ability or opportunity: (a) to obtain knowledge of classified information; or (b) to be in a place where one would be expected to gain such knowledge; or (c) to sabotage or to interface with the national defense effort. A person does not have access merely by being in a place where classified information is kept, if security measures prevent him or her from gaining knowledge of the information or interfacing with the national defense effort.

Access authorization is a formal act that is required to certify that a person who has been screened and approved for access to classified information is authorized to have access to such information. This act is normally a security briefing or indoctrination, in which the person is cautioned concerning the responsibilities of having such access, is told the meaning of the different classification levels, and is provided other information of a security and counterintelligence nature. The individual is then asked to sign a nondisclosure statement, in which he or she agrees not to divulge the information to anyone who is not cleared for access or does not have a need to know the information.

Access suspension is the temporary removal of one's access to classified information because of a circumstance or incident that has involved the individual and that may have a bearing on the individual's eligibility for access. *See also:* Classification, Classified Information, Code Word, Compromise, Declassification, Disclosure, Downgrade, Freedom of Information Act, Limited Access Area, Need-to-Know, Need-to-Know Principle, No-Lone Zone, Nondisclosure Agreement, Nondiscussion Area, Sanitization, Sanitize, Sanitized Area, Security Certification, Security Classification, Sensitive Compartmented Information, Sensitive Compartmented Information Facility, Two-Person Control.

References

Laqueur, Walter. *A World of Secrets.* New York: Basic Books, Inc., 1985.

Treverton, Gregory F. *Covert Action: The Limits of Intervention in the Postwar World.* New York: Basic Books, Inc., 1987.

Turner, Stansfield. *Secrecy and Democracy: The CIA in Transition.* Boston: Houghton Mifflin, 1985.

—ACCOMMODATION ADDRESS, a term used in clandestine and covert intelligence operations, is a mailing address where an agent can safely and discreetly receive mail. It can also be used for secure communications between agents. In Europe, small shops are often willing to receive such mail for individuals for small fees. According to Henry Becket, the FBI often uses established corporations for such purposes. Interestingly, the Soviet secret service (KGB) no longer uses U.S. Post Office boxes because of the widespread theft in the U.S. postal system. Rather, it now relies on a multitude of private post offices that offer rentals and, in this way, assures the security of its communications. *See also:* Cover Organizations, Illegal Residency, Legal Residency, Live Letter Boxes, Live Letter Drops, Mail Cover, Packed Up, Plumbing, Proprietaries, Proprietary Company, Putting in the Plumbing, Setting Up, Special Activities.

References

Becket, Henry S. A. *The Dictionary of Espionage: Spookspeak into English.* New York: Stein and Day, 1986.

Kessler, Ronald. *Spy vs. Spy: Stalking Soviet Spies in America*. New York: Charles Scribner's Sons, 1988.

Quirk, John; Phillips, David; Cline, Ray; and Pforzheimer, Walter. *The Central Intelligence Agency: A Photographic History*. Guilford, CT: Foreign Intelligence Press, 1986.

Turner, Stansfield. *Secrecy and Democracy: The CIA in Transition*. Boston: Houghton Mifflin, 1985.

—**ACCOUNTABILITY** is the obligation that is imposed upon a security-control officer to keep an accurate record of the documents and materials that he or she possesses and of the people in his or her organization who have been cleared for access to classified material or have been indoctrinated into compartmented intelligence programs. *See also:* Accounting Legend Code, Certificate of Destruction, Inventory, TOP SECRET Control.

References

Department of Defense, Joint Chiefs of Staff. *Department of Defense Dictionary of Military and Related Terms*. Washington, DC: GPO, 1986.

Laqueur, Walter. *A World of Secrets*. New York: Basic Books, 1985.

Treverton, Gregory F. *Covert Action: The Limits of Intervention in the Postwar World*. New York: Basic Books, 1987.

Turner, Stansfield. *Secrecy and Democracy: The CIA in Transition*. Boston: Houghton Mifflin Co., 1985.

—**ACCOUNTING LEGEND CODE (ALC)** is a term used in communications intelligence, communications security, operations security, and signals analysis. It is a numeric code used within the Communications Security (COMSEC) Material Control System to indicate the minimum accounting controls that are required for items of TSEC—nomenclatured COMSEC material. *See also:* Accountability, Certificate of Destruction, TOP SECRET Control.

References

Godson, Roy, ed. *Intelligence Problems for the 1980s, Number 1: Elements of Intelligence*. Rev. ed. Washington, DC: National Strategy Information Center, 1983.

—**ACCREDITATION,** a term used in counterintelligence, counterespionage, and counterinsurgency, means an official authorization that certifies that an area is sufficiently secure to meet or exceed the existing physical security criteria that must be met in order for the area to be designated a Sensitive Compartmented Information Facility (SCIF). *See also:* Sensitive Compartmented Information (SCI), Sensitive Compartmented Information Facility (SCIF).

References

Godson, Roy, ed. *Intelligence Problems for the 1980s, Number 1: Elements of Intelligence*. Rev. ed. Washington, DC: National Strategy Information Center, 1983.

—**ACKERMAN, BRIGADIER JOHN B., U.S. AIR FORCE,** served as the vice director of the National Security Agency from the autumn of 1953 until June 1966. His appointment as a military officer signified the continued dominance of the military in the agency. *See also:* National Security Agency.

References

Bamford, James. *The Puzzle Palace: A Report on America's Most Secret Agency*. New York: Penguin Books, 1983.

—**ACOUSTIC SOURCES,** an electronic surveillance term, refers to the generators of sounds that are made at the location of the original signal transducer. There are two types of acoustic sources: those that emanate unwanted information and noise (for example, an extraneous talker or a background music system), and those that emanate desired information (for example, the primary talker). *See also:* Acoustical Intelligence.

References

Godson, Roy, ed. *Intelligence Problems for the 1980s, Number 1: Elements of Intelligence*. Rev. ed. Washington, DC: National Strategy Information Center, 1983.

Kessler, Michael. *Wiretapping and Electronic Surveillance Commission Studies: Supporting Materials for the Report of the National Commission for the Review of Federal and State Laws Relating to Wiretapping and Electronic Surveillance, Washington, DC, 1976*. Townsend, PA: Loompanics Unlimited, 1976.

Laqueur, Walter. *A World of Secrets*. New York: Basic Books, 1985.

—**ACOUSTIC WARFARE** denotes actions involving the use of underwater acoustic energy to determine, exploit, reduce, or prevent hostile use of the underwater acoustic spectrum; the term also means actions that retain friendly use of the same. There are three divisions within acoustic warfare: (1) Acoustic warfare support measures are actions to search for, intercept, locate, record, and analyze radiated acoustic energy in water for purposes of exploiting such radiations. (2) Acoustic warfare countermeasures are actions that are taken to prevent or reduce an enemy's use of the underwater acoustic spectrum. Such countermeasures involve intentional underwater acoustic emissions for deception and jamming. (3) Acoustic warfare counter-countermeasures are actions that are taken to insure friendly use of the underwater acoustic spectrum despite the enemy's use of underwater acoustic warfare. These involve antiacoustic warfare support measures and antiacoustic warfare countermeasures, though they might not involve underwater acoustic emissions.

References

Department of Defense, Joint Chiefs of Staff. *Department of Defense Dictionary of Military and Related Terms.* Washington, DC: GPO, 1986.

Laqueur, Walter. *A World of Secrets.* New York: Basic Books, 1985.

—**ACOUSTICAL INTELLIGENCE (ACOUSTINT or ACINT)** is intelligence information derived from analyzing acoustic waves that are radiated either intentionally or unintentionally. In naval usage, the term ACINT is used and refers to intelligence derived specifically from the analysis of underwater acoustic waves from ships and submarines. *See also:* Acoustic Sources.

References

Department of Defense, Defense Intelligence College. *Glossary of Intelligence Terms and Definitions.* Washington, DC: DIC, 1987.

Department of Defense, Joint Chiefs of Staff. *Department of Defense Dictionary of Military and Related Terms.* Washington, DC: GPO, 1986.

Laqueur, Walter. *A World of Secrets.* New York: Basic Books, 1985.

—**ACOUSTICAL SURVEILLANCE** is the use of electronic devices, including sound recording, receiving, or transmitting equipment, for collecting information.

References

Department of Defense, Joint Chiefs of Staff. *Department of Defense Dictionary of Military and*

Related Terms. Washington, DC: GPO, 1986.

Laqueur, Walter. *A World of Secrets.* New York: Basic Books, 1985.

Turner, Stansfield. *Secrecy and Democracy: The CIA in Transition.* Boston: Houghton Mifflin, 1985.

U.S. Congress. Senate. *Final Report of the Senate Select Committee to Study Government Operations with Respect to Intelligence Activities. Report 94–755. Book I, Foreign and Military Intelligence.* Washington, DC: GPO, 1976.

—**ACTIONABLE INTELLIGENCE,** a general intelligence term, is information that is of direct use to analysts and customers and can be passed to them without having to go through the entire intelligence production process. Actionable intelligence can address strategic or tactical needs, can support U.S. negotiating teams, or can assist individuals or teams that are concerned with such matters as international terrorism or narcotics. *See also:* Battlefield Intelligence.

References

Department of Defense, Defense Intelligence College. *Glossary of Intelligence Terms and Definitions.* Washington, DC: DIC, 1987.

Laqueur, Walter. *A World of Secrets.* New York: Basic Books, 1985.

Turner, Stansfield. *Secrecy and Democracy: The CIA in Transition.* Boston: Houghton Mifflin, 1985.

—**ACTIVE COUNTERINTELLIGENCE,** a term used in counterintelligence, counterespionage, and counterinsurgency, differs from passive counterintelligence in that its purpose is to counter an ongoing threatening activity by an enemy. There are two types of such active counterintelligence: *investigative activity,* which is conducted with the aim of identifying the hostile action as well as those engaged in it; and *counteractivity,* including counterespionage, countersabotage, and counterterrorism, which are activities directed against enemy actions. *See also:* Counterespionage, Counterinsurgency, Counterintelligence, Countersabotage.

References

Godson, Roy, ed. *Intelligence Problems for the 1980s, Number 1: Elements of Intelligence.* Rev. ed. Washington, DC: National Strategy Information Center, 1983.

———. *Intelligence Problems for the 1980s, Number 3: Counterintelligence.* Washington, DC: National Strategy Information Center, 1980.

Kent, Sherman. *Strategic Intelligence for American World Policy*. Princeton, NJ: Princeton University Press, 1966.

Laqueur, Walter. *A World of Secrets*. New York: Basic Books, 1985.

Treverton, Gregory F. *Covert Action: The Limits of Intervention in the Postwar World*. New York: Basic Books, 1987.

Turner, Stansfield. *Secrecy and Democracy: The CIA in Transition*. Boston: Houghton Mifflin, 1985.

—ACTIVE ELECTRONIC COUNTERMEASURES, a signals intelligence term, is the process of deliberately impairing enemy electronic detection or communications control devices and systems by jamming or deceiving them. *See also:* Jammer.

References

Laqueur, Walter. *A World of Secrets*. New York: Basic Books, 1985.

Treverton, Gregory F. *Covert Action: The Limits of Intervention in the Postwar World*. New York: Basic Books, 1987.

Turner, Stansfield. *Secrecy and Democracy: The CIA in Transition*. Boston: Houghton Mifflin, 1985.

—ACTIVE JAMMING, a term used in communications intelligence, communications security, operations security, and signals analysis, is the intentional radiation or reradiation of electromagnetic waves in order to disrupt or prevent enemies from communicating by preventing them from using a specific portion of the electromagnetic wave spectrum. *See also:* Jammer.

References

Laqueur, Walter. *A World of Secrets*. New York: Basic Books, 1985.

Treverton, Gregory F. *Covert Action: The Limits of Intervention in the Postwar World*. New York: Basic Books, 1987.

Turner, Stansfield. *Secrecy and Democracy: The CIA in Transition*. Boston: Houghton Mifflin, 1985.

—ACTIVE MEASURES (*aktivnoye meropriyatye*) are an aspect of Soviet security operations. These include assassinations, kidnappings, fabrications, deceptions, disinformation ploys, and other measures that are used in the pursuit of Soviet political objectives.

References

Godson, Roy (ed.). *Intelligence Problems for the 1980s, Number 3: Counterintelligence*. Washington, DC: National Strategy Information Center, 1980. *Transition*. Boston: Houghton Mifflin, 1985.

Laqueur, Walter. *A World of Secrets*. New York: Basic Books, 1985.

Turner, Stansfield. *Secrecy and Democracy: The CIA in Transition*. Boston: Houghton Mifflin, 1985.

—ACTIVITIES are units, organizations, or installations that perform functions or missions. For example, a reception center is an activity. The term "activities" is also used for the functions or missions themselves.

References

Department of Defense, Joint Chiefs of Staff. *Department of Defense Dictionary of Military and Related Terms*. Washington, DC: GPO, 1986.

Godson, Roy, ed. *Intelligence Problems for the 1980s, Number 1: Elements of Intelligence*. Rev. ed. Washington, DC: National Strategy Information Center, 1983.

Kent, Sherman. *Strategic Intelligence for American World Policy*. Princeton, NJ: Princeton University Press, 1966.

Laqueur, Walter. *A World of Secrets*. New York: Basic Books, 1985.

Treverton, Gregory F. *Covert Action: The Limits of Intervention in the Postwar World*. New York: Basic Books, 1987.

Turner, Stansfield. *Secrecy and Democracy: The CIA in Transition*. Boston: Houghton Mifflin, 1985.

—AD HOC REQUIREMENTS COMMITTEE (ARC), as defined by the Church Committee, was an interagency group established in 1955 by the special assistant to the director of Central Intelligence to coordinate the collection requirements of the U-2 reconnaissance program. It was succeeded by the Committee on Overhead Reconnaissance (COMOR) in 1960. *See also:* Central Intelligence Agency (CIA).

References

Corson, William R. *The Armies of Ignorance: The Rise of the American Intelligence Empire*. New York: Dial Press, 1977.

Fain, Tyrus G.; Plant, Katharine C.; and Milloy, Ross. *The Intelligence Community: History, Organization, and Issues*. Public Documents Series. New York: R.R. Bowker, 1977.

U.S. Congress. Senate. *Final Report of the Senate Select Committee to Study Government Operations with Respect to Intelligence Activities*. Report 94–755. Book I, *Foreign and Military Intelligence*. Washington, DC: GPO, 1976.

—**ADJUDICATION** is a security term. It is the process of determining a person's eligibility or ineligibility for access to special compartmented intelligence information. *See also:* Background Investigation, National Agency Check, Special Background Investigation.

References

Godson, Roy, ed. *Intelligence Problems for the 1980s, Number 1: Elements of Intelligence.* Rev. ed. Washington, DC: National Strategy Information Center, 1983.

—**ADMINISTRATION AND SUPPORT** is an official term that has been defined by the Defense Intelligence Agency. It means activities relating to the personnel administration, manpower, fiscal, and library functions in support of the agency's intelligence missions. Work in this area is based on the skills particular to the function and requires a minimum knowledge of intelligence functions. *See also:* Defense Intelligence Agency (DIA).

References

Department of Defense, Defense Intelligence Agency. *Defense Intelligence Agency Manual DIAM 22–2.* Washington, DC: DIA, 1979.

Kent, Sherman. *Strategic Intelligence for American World Policy.* Princeton, NJ: Princeton University Press, 1966.

Treverton, Gregory F. *Covert Action: The Limits of Intervention in the Postwar World.* New York: Basic Books, 1987.

Turner, Stansfield. *Secrecy and Democracy: The CIA in Transition.* Boston: Houghton Mifflin, 1985.

—**ADMINISTRATIVE PURPOSES** refers to a decision resulting from Presidential Executive Order 12333, "United States Intelligence Activities," dated December 4, 1981. Information is collected for "administrative purposes" when it is necessary for the administration of a component (a department, office, desk, or any subelement), concerned but it is not collected directly in performance of the intelligence activities assigned to that component. Examples include keeping information relating to the past performance of potential contractors; keeping information to enable components to discharge their public affairs and legislative duties, including maintaining correspondence files; maintaining employee personnel and training records; and maintaining training materials or documents produced at training facilities. *See also:* Executive Orders on Intelligence, Executive Oversight.

References

Department of Defense. *Activities of DoD Intelligence Components that Affect U.S. Persons (Department of Defense Directive 5240.1).* Washington, DC: DoD, 1982.

Laqueur, Walter. *A World of Secrets.* New York: Basic Books, 1985.

Treverton, Gregory F. *Covert Action: The Limits of Intervention in the Postwar World.* New York: Basic Books, 1987.

Turner, Stansfield. *Secrecy and Democracy: The CIA in Transition.* Boston: Houghton Mifflin, 1985.

—**ADMINISTRATIVELY CONTROLLED INFORMATION** is a general intelligence term for privileged but unclassified information that bears such designations as FOR OFFICIAL USE ONLY or LIMITED DISTRIBUTION. The information is assigned such caveats in order to prevent its disclosure to unauthorized persons and its release to the public. *See also:* Classified Information, Collateral, Declassification, Declassification and Downgrading Instructions, Decompartmentation, Downgrade, Ears Only, LIMITED DISTRIBUTION, Need-to-Know, Security Classification, Special Intelligence.

References

Department of Defense, Defense Intelligence College. *Glossary of Intelligence Terms and Definitions.* Washington, DC: DIC, 1987.

—**ADP TECHNICAL TRAINING** is instruction designed to teach people to operate and maintain automatic data processing. The training gives basic technical skills to computer operators, system and application programmers, system analysts, and hardware maintainers. Such training is also defined as a component of one of the ten branches that constitute the National Security Agency. *See also:* Defense Intelligence Agency.

References

Department of Defense, Defense Intelligence Agency. *Defense Intelligence Agency Manual.* Washington, DC: DIA, 1987.

Laqueur, Walter. *A World of Secrets.* New York: Basic Books, 1985.

—**ADP-T SYSTEM TRAINING** is instruction designed to teach technically qualified ADP personnel the procedures and skills that are required to operate and maintain a specific Department of Defense Intelligence Information System (DODIIS) subsystem. The training focuses on the specific hardware and software that comprise a specific DODIIS subsystem. *See also:* Defense Intelligence Agency (DIA).

References

Department of Defense, Defense Intelligence Agency. *Defense Intelligence Agency Manual.* Washington, DC: DIA, 1987.

Laqueur, Walter. *A World of Secrets.* New York: Basic Books, 1985.

—**ADVANCED BASE** is a tactical ground operations term for a base that is located in or near a theater of operations. Its primary mission is to support military operations.

References

Department of Defense, Joint Chiefs of Staff. *Department of Defense Dictionary of Military and Related Terms.* Washington, DC: GPO, 1986.

Poyer, David. *The Med.* New York: St. Martin's Press, 1988.

—**ADVISORY TASKING,** an intelligence term used on the joint intelligence and national level, is a statement of intelligence interest or a request for information that does not have official backing and therefore does not have to be acted upon. It is usually sent by a member organization of the Intelligence Community to a department or agency that has an intelligence or information collection capability but is not a part of the National Foreign Intelligence Program and therefore cannot be tasked officially to respond to the request. *See also:* Requirement, Task, Tasking.

References

Department of Defense, Defense Intelligence College. *Glossary of Intelligence Terms and Definitions.* Washington, DC: DIC, 1987.

—**AERIAL PHOTOGRAPH. Aerial photograph, composite** is an intelligence imagery and photoreconnaissance term for photographs made with one camera having one principal lens and two surrounding and oblique lenses that are symmetrically placed. The photographs from all lenses can be rectified in the printing process to permit assembling them as verticals with the same scale. Composite photography minimizes the distortion that occurs when a single, vertically positioned camera is used. **Aerial photo-**

graph, oblique is an intelligence imagery and photoreconnaissance term. It is a photograph that is taken with the optical axis of the camera directed between the horizontal and the vertical.

High oblique is a photograph in which the apparent horizon is shown, while *low oblique* is one in which the apparent horizon is not shown. Oblique photographs can be used to produce a panorama. **Aerial photograph, vertical** is an intelligence imagery and photoreconnaissance term. It is an aerial photograph that is taken when the optical axis of the camera is approximately perpendicular to the earth's surface and the film is as horizontal as possible. **Aerial photographic mosaic** is an intelligence imagery and photoreconnaissance term for combining two or more overlapping prints to form a single picture. Mosaics can be of significant value in providing an updated picture of a large area to supplement map data. Vertical photographs are usually used and they produce map-like results. However, oblique photographs can be used to produce a panorama. *See also:* Apogee; Basic Cover; Coverage; Fan Camera; Fan Camera Photography; First Light; Image Motion Compensation; Imagery Annotation; Imagery Collateral; Imagery Correlation; Imagery Data Recording; Imagery Exploitation; Imagery Interpretation Key; Imagery Interpreter; KH-11; Last Light; Light Cover; Map; Mosaic; Nadir; Nadir, Ground; Nadir, Map; Nadir, Photograph; National Photographic Interpretation Center (NPIC); Overhead Reconnaissance; Panoramic Air Camera; Photogrammetry; Photographic Coverage; Photographic Intelligence; Photographic Interpretation; Photographic Reading; Photographic Scale; Photographic Strip; Photography; Photomap; Split Cameras; Split Vertical Photography; SR-71 Aircraft; Stereoscopic Cover; Stereoscopic Pair; Stereoscopic vision; Stereoscopy; Strike Photography; Strip plot Titling Strip; U-2 Overhead Reconnaissance Program and U-2 Spy Plane; Zenith.

References

Department of Defense. U.S. Army. *Intelligence Imagery.* Army Field Manual FM 34–55. Washington, DC: Headquarters, Department of the Army, September 9, 1985.

Godson, Roy, ed. *Intelligence Problems for the 1980s, Number 1: Elements of Intelligence.* Rev. ed. Washington, DC: National Strategy Information Center, 1983.

Reeves, Robert; Anson, Abraham; and Landen, David. *Manual of Remote Sensing.* Falls Church, VA: American Society of Photogrammetry, 1975.

—**AERIAL RECONNAISSANCE** is an intelligence imagery and photoreconnaissance term. It is a means of obtaining information, either by aerial photography or by visual observation from the air. *See also:* Aerial Photograph.

References

Department of Defense, U.S. Army. *Intelligence Imagery*. Army Field Manual FM 34–55. Washington, DC: Headquarters, Department of the Army, 1985.

Laqueur, Walter. *A World of Secrets*. New York: Basic Books, 1985.

Reeves, Robert; Anson, Abraham; and Landen, David. *Manual of Remote Sensing*. Falls Church, VA: American Society of Photogrammetry, 1975.

Treverton, Gregory F. *Covert Action: The Limits of Intervention in the Postwar World*. New York: Basic Books, 1987.

Turner, Stansfield. *Secrecy and Democracy: The CIA in Transition*. Boston: Houghton Mifflin, 1985.

—**AERIAL RECONNAISSANCE SATELLITE (ARS).** *See:* KH-11.

—**AERIAL SURVEILLANCE** is an intelligence imagery and photoreconnaissance term for the systematic observation of air, surface, or subsurface areas by visual, electronic, photographic, or other means for intelligence purposes. A surveillance mission is normally performed by a large-area coverage sensor, such as radar, or by visual observation from higher altitudes so that a large ground area can be covered at all times. *See also:* Aerial Photograph.

References

Department of Defense, U.S. Army. *Intelligence Imagery*. Army Field Manual FM 34–55. Washington, DC: Headquarters, Department of the Army, 1985.

Laqueur, Walter. *A World of Secrets*. New York: Basic Books, 1985.

Reeves, Robert; Anson, Abraham; and Landen, David. *Manual of Remote Sensing*. Falls Church, VA: American Society of Photogrammetry, 1975.

Treverton, Gregory F. *Covert Action: The Limits of Intervention in the Postwar World*. New York: Basic Books, 1987.

Turner, Stansfield. *Secrecy and Democracy: The CIA in Transition*. Boston: Houghton Mifflin, 1985.

—**AFGHANISTAN.** The Soviet military involvement in Afghanistan, which began in 1968, was interesting in several respects. It spanned both the Carter and Reagan administrations and curiously reversed the U.S. and Soviet positions that had existed in the Vietnam War. Additionally, the U.S. Intelligence Community was able to act in the Afghan situation without significant interference from the American public, and therefore it was able to conduct a successful operation.

The initial U.S. intelligence performance was not successful, in that the Soviet decision to invade Afghanistan and oust one ruler in favor of another was not foreseen. As a result, the United States was slow in reacting to the invasion.

The Reagan administration successfully handled the Afghan problem in that the performance of both U.S. intelligence and the administration's use of that intelligence were notable. U.S. intelligence identified those Afghan factions and leaders who could most effectively combat the Soviet invasion, and it supported these groups clandestinely. These operations, which are detailed vividly in Tom Clancy's novel, *The Cardinal of the Kremlin*, were extremely successful, causing great demoralization in Soviet forces and the eventual decision to withdraw Soviet troops from Afghanistan.

Equally impressive was the success of the Reagan administration in keeping the magnitude of U.S. involvement under wraps. Thus, there were no detailed public deliberations, and the operation was allowed to progress.

The result was that Soviet expansionism southward from the USSR was effectively thwarted with a low visibility operation in which the U.S. Intelligence Community had performed admirably.

The last Soviet troops were withdrawn from Afghanistan on February 15, 1989. *See also:* Carter, Jimmy; Clandestine Activity; Covert Operation; Reagan, Ronald; Special Activities.

References

Breckinridge, Scott D. *The CIA and the U.S. Intelligence System*. Boulder, CO: Westview Press, 1986.

Brinkley, David A., and Hull, Andrew W. *Estimative Intelligence: A Textbook on the History, Products, Uses and Writing of Intelligence Estimates*. Columbus, OH: Battelle, 1979.

Clancy, Tom. *The Cardinal of the Kremlin*. New York: Putnam, 1988.

Cline, Ray S. *The CIA Under Reagan, Bush, and Casey*. Washington, DC: Acropolis Books, 1981.

Corson, William R. *The Armies of Ignorance: The Rise of the American Intelligence Empire*. New York: Dial Press, 1977.

Godson, Roy, ed. *Intelligence Problems for the 1980s, Number 4: Covert Action*. Washington, DC: National Strategy Information Center, 1981.

Laqueur, Walter. *The Age of Terrorism*. Boston: Little, Brown, 1987.

Lefever, Ernest W., and Godson, Roy. *The CIA and the American Ethic: An Unfinished Debate*. Washington, DC: Ethics and Public Policy Center, Georgetown University, 1979.

Lowenthal, Mark M. *U.S. Intelligence: Evolution and Anatomy*. New York: Praeger, 1984.

Quirk, John; Phillips, David; Cline, Ray; and Pzorzheimer, Walter. *The Central Intelligence Agency: A Photographic History*. Guilford, CT: Foreign Intelligence Press, 1986.

Treverton, Gregory F. *Covert Action: The Limits of Intervention in the Postwar World*. New York: Basic Books, 1987.

Turner, Stansfield. *Secrecy and Democracy: The CIA in Transition*. Boston: Houghton Mifflin, 1985.

Von Hoene, John P.A. *Intelligence User's Guide*. Washington, DC: DIA, 1983.

—**AGEE, PHILIP.** Philip Agee was a CIA agent and field officer in Latin America. After leaving the agency, he wrote *Inside the Company: CIA Diary*, in which he detailed his service in Washington, D.C., Ecuador, Uruguay, and Mexico. As George Constantinides notes, Agee is the only ideological convert to Marxism from the agency who has ever written about its operations. Constantinides also cautions the reader to be wary of many assumptions in and the polemical quality of Agee's book. Nonetheless, there is no doubt that Agee caused a significant amount of damage by publicizing the names of agents and contacts and the names of organizations that the CIA used in its operations. Agee has vowed to expose CIA officers and agents whenever possible and to damage the agency's operations as much as possible.

References

Allen, Thomas B., and Polmar, Norman. *Merchants of Treason: America's Secrets for Sale*. New York: Delacorte Press, 1988.

Constantinides, George C. *Intelligence and Espionage: An Analytical Bibliography*. Boulder, CO: Westview Press, 1983.

Godson, Roy, ed. *Intelligence Problems for the 1980s, Number 1: Elements of Intelligence*. Rev. ed. Washington, DC: National Strategy Information Center, 1983.

Turner, Stansfield. *Secrecy and Democracy: The CIA in Transition*. Boston: Houghton Mifflin, 1985.

—**AGENCY** is a general intelligence term for an organization that collects and processes information. *See also:* Agent, Intelligence Cycle, Source.

References

Department of Defense, Joint Chiefs of Staff. *Department of Defense Dictionary of Military and Related Terms*. Washington, DC: GPO, 1986.

Godson, Roy, ed. *Intelligence Problems for the 1980s, Number 1: Elements of Intelligence*. Rev. ed. Washington, DC: National Strategy Information Center, 1983.

Kent, Sherman. *Strategic Intelligence for American World Policy*. Princeton, NJ: Princeton University Press, 1966.

Laqueur, Walter. *A World of Secrets*. New York: Basic Books, 1985.

Turner, Stansfield. *Secrecy and Democracy: The CIA in Transition*. Boston: Houghton Mifflin, 1985.

—**AGENT** is a term used in clandestine and covert intelligence operations for a person who carries out clandestine intelligence activity under the direction of an intelligence organization but who is not an officer, employee, or co-opted worker of that organization. His usual mission is to obtain or assist in getting valuable intelligence or counterintelligence information. As defined by the Church Committee, an agent is an individual who acts under the direction of an intelligence agency or security service to obtain, or assist in obtaining, information for intelligence or counterintelligence purposes. *See also:* Agent Authentication, Agent in Place, Agent Net, Agent of Influence, Agent Provocateur, Blow, Blown Agent, Burn, Burnt, Cackelbladder, Confusion Agent, Dispatched Agent, Double Agent, Handling Agent, Illegal Agent, Informant, Inside Man, Pocket Litter, Provocation Agent, Pseudonym, Putting in the Plumbing, Recruitment, Recruitment in Place, Special Activities, Walk-in.

References

Clancy, Tom. *The Cardinal of the Kremlin*. New York: Putnam, 1988.

Department of Defense, Defense Intelligence College. *Glossary of Intelligence Terms and Definitions*. Washington, DC: DIC, 1987.

Department of Defense, Joint Chiefs of Staff. *Department of Defense Dictionary of Military and Related Terms*. Washington, DC: GPO, 1986.

Godson, Roy, ed. *Intelligence Problems for the 1980s, Number 1: Elements of Intelligence*. Rev. ed. Washington, DC: National Strategy Information Center, 1983.

Kent, Sherman. *Strategic Intelligence for American World Policy*. Princeton, NJ: Princeton University Press, 1966.

Kessler, Ronald. *Spy vs. Spy: Stalking Soviet Spies in America*. New York: Charles Scribner's Sons, 1988.

Laqueur, Walter. *A World of Secrets*. New York: Basic Books, 1985.

Quirk, John; Phillips, David; Cline, Ray; and Pforzheimer, Walter. *The Central Intelligence Agency: A Photographic History*. Guilford, CT: Foreign Intelligence Press, 1986.

Treverton, Gregory F. *Covert Action: The Limits of Intervention in the Postwar World*. New York: Basic Books, 1987.

Turner, Stansfield. *Secrecy and Democracy: The CIA in Transition*. Boston: Houghton Mifflin, 1985.

U.S. Congress. Senate. *Alleged Assassination Plots Involving Foreign Leaders: An Interim Report of the Select Committee to Study Governmental Operations with Respect to Intelligence Activities*. 94th Congress, 1st sess., Nov. 20, 1975. S. Rept. 94–465.

———. *Final Report of the Senate Select Committee to Study Government Operations with Respect to Intelligence Activities. Report 94–755. Book I, Foreign and Military Intelligence*. Washington, DC: GPO, 1976.

—**AGENT AUTHENTICATION** is a term used in clandestine and covert intelligence operations for the technical-support task of providing an agent with personal documents such as a driver's license and credit cards and with articles such as photographs, attaché cases, and clothing that appear to be authentic and corroborate his assumed identity. *See also:* Agent.

References
Department of Defense, Joint Chiefs of Staff. *Department of Defense Dictionary of Military and Related Terms*. Washington, DC: GPO, 1986.

Turner, Stansfield. *Secrecy and Democracy: The CIA in Transition*. Boston: Houghton Mifflin, 1985.

—**AGENT IN PLACE** is a term used in clandestine and covert intelligence operations for one who agrees to spy for a foreign intelligence agency by continuing to work in his job so that he can pass information. *See also:* Agent.

References
Becket, Henry S. A. *The Dictionary of Espionage: Spookspeak into English*. New York: Stein and Day, 1986.

Clancy, Tom. *The Cardinal of the Kremlin*. New York: Putnam, 1988.

Godson, Roy, ed. *Intelligence Problems for the 1980s, Number 5: Clandestine Collection*. Washington, DC: National Strategy Information Center, 1982.

Turner, Stansfield. *Secrecy and Democracy: The CIA in Transition*. Boston: Houghton Mifflin, 1985.

—**AGENT NET** is a term used in clandestine and covert intelligence operations for a group of agents and other people who operate clandestinely under the direction of one agent. Often only the head agent knows the names of all the people in the net, so that if anyone is caught and interrogated, he or she cannot reveal the names of the other agents. *See also:* Agent.

References
Department of Defense, Joint Chiefs of Staff. *Department of Defense Dictionary of Military and Related Terms*. Washington, DC: GPO, 1986.

Godson, Roy, ed. *Intelligence Problems for the 1980s, Number 5: Clandestine Collection*. Washington, DC: National Strategy Information Center, 1982.

Kessler, Ronald. *Spy vs. Spy: Stalking Soviet Spies in America*. New York: Charles Scribner's Sons, 1988.

Turner, Stansfield. *Secrecy and Democracy: The CIA in Transition*. Boston: Houghton Mifflin, 1985.

—**AGENT OF INFLUENCE** is a term used in covert operations for a person who is manipulated, coerced, or can be used by an intelligence organization to use his position to influence public opinion or decisionmaking in a way that is beneficial to the intelligence organization's country or cause. As defined by the Church Committee, an agent of influence is an individual who can be used to influence covertly foreign officials, opinion molders, organizations, or pressure groups in a way that will generally advance U.S. government objectives, or to undertake specific action in support of U.S. government objectives. *See also:* Agent.

References
Deacon, Richard. *Spyclopedia: An Encyclopaedia of Spies, Secret Services, Operations, Jargon, and All Subjects Related to the World of Espionage*. London: Macdonald, 1987.

Department of Defense, Defense Intelligence College. *Glossary of Intelligence Terms and Definitions*. Washington, DC: DIC, 1987.

Kessler, Ronald. *Spy vs. Spy: Stalking Soviet Spies in America*. New York: Charles Scribner's Sons, 1988.

Turner, Stansfield. *Secrecy and Democracy: The CIA in Transition.* Boston: Houghton Mifflin, 1985.

U.S. Congress. Senate. *Final Report of the Senate Select Committee to Study Government Operations with Respect to Intelligence Activities. Report 94–755. Book I, Foreign and Military Intelligence.* Washington, DC: GPO, 1976.

—**AGENT PROVOCATEUR** is a term used in covert operations for a person who works himself or herself into an organization with the purpose of convincing its members to commit acts that will subject them to punishment. Henry Becket says that the 1950s CIA term for this individual was a "tree-shaker." *See also:* Agent.

References

Allen, Thomas, and Polmar, Norman. *Merchants of Treason: America's Secrets for Sale.* New York: Delacorte Press, 1988.

Becket, Henry S. A. *The Dictionary of Espionage: Spookspeak into English.* New York: Stein and Day, 1986.

Ranelagh, John. *The Agency: The Rise and Decline of the CIA.* New York: Simon and Schuster, 1986.

Turner, Stansfield. *Secrecy and Democracy: The CIA in Transition.* Boston: Houghton Mifflin, 1985.

—**AIR ATTACHÉ** is a member of the Defense Attaché Office, which is part of a U.S. embassy. The air attaché performs attaché duties as they pertain to his service and his military specialty and advises the ambassador on matters pertaining to air power. *See also:* American legation U.S. Naval Attaché (ALUSNA), American legation U.S. Naval Liaison Officer (ALUSNLO), Army Attaché, Attaché Activities, Defense Attaché (DATT), Defense Attaché Office (DAO), Defense Attaché System (DAS), Defense Intelligence Agency (DIA), Persona Non Grata (PNG), United States Country Team.

References

Kent, Sherman. *Strategic Intelligence for American World Policy.* Princeton, NJ: Princeton University Press, 1966.

Laubenthal, Sanders A. "Preparing 'the Team': Defense Attaché Training." *DIC Newsletter* (Winter 1986): 1–4.

—**AIR BATTLE MANAGEMENT** is an Army tactical term that has intelligence significance. Air battle management is a fundamental task of air defense command and control and airspace management that encompasses the principles for the control and coordination of both tactical air and ground-based air defense resources. *See also:* Air Reconnaissance Liaison Officer.

References

Department of Defense, U.S. Army. *U.S. Army Air Defense Artillery Employment.* Field Manual FM 44-1. Washington, DC: Headquarters, Department of the Army, 1983.

Treverton, Gregory F. *Covert Action: The Limits of Intervention in the Postwar World.* New York: Basic Books, 1987.

—**AIR COMMAND AND STAFF COLLEGE,** located at Maxwell Air Force Base, Montgomery, Alabama, is an intermediate-level service school for GS-12 and GS-13 civilians, Army, Marine Corps, and Air Force majors, and Navy lieutenant commanders or selectees for those ranks. The college provides students with the skills, knowledge, and understanding that will enhance their value in responsible command and staff positions. The curriculum covers four areas of study: staff communications and research; national security affairs; command, leadership, and resource management; and military employment. The course runs for 40 weeks. *See also:* Air University.

References

Department of Defense, Defense Intelligence Agency. *Training Compendium for General Defense Career Development Program (IDCP) Personnel DOD 1430.10M3-TNG.* Washington, DC: DIA, 1986.

—**AIR DEFENSE** is an Army tactical term that has intelligence significance. Air defense consists of all the measures that are designed to nullify or reduce the effectiveness of an attack by hostile aircraft or guided missiles after they are airborne.

References

Department of Defense, U.S. Army. *U.S. Army Air Defense Artillery Employment.* Field Manual FM 44-1. Washington, DC: Headquarters, Department of the Army, 1983.

Department of Defense, Joint Chiefs of Staff. *Department of Defense Dictionary of Military and Related Terms.* Washington, DC: GPO, 1986.

Laqueur, Walter. *A World of Secrets.* New York: Basic Books, 1985.

—**AIR DEFENSE IDENTIFICATION ZONE (ADIZ)**, an Air Force intelligence term, is a predetermined airspace within which the identification, location, and control of aircraft is required. Perhaps the most famous ADIZ is that off the U.S. east coast, which in recent years has been the scene of numerous unannounced intrusions by Soviet reconnaissance aircraft as they have proceeded to or from Cuba.

References

Department of Defense, Joint Chiefs of Staff. *Department of Defense Dictionary of Military and Related Terms.* Washington, DC: GPO, 1986.

—**AIR FORCE ELECTRONIC SECURITY COMMAND (AFESC)** is the U.S. Air Force's service cryptologic agency; prior to August 1979 it was called the Air Force Security Service. The AFESC signals intelligence collection activities are done under the operational direction of the National Security Agency, although the command also reports to the U.S. Air Force. While the information that the command collects may be of value to the national intelligence effort, its primary goal is to satisfy U.S. Air Force needs. *See also:* Air Force Intelligence (A-2), National Security Agency (NSA).

References

Bamford, James. *The Puzzle Palace: A Report on America's Most Secret Agency.* New York: Penguin Books, 1983.

Breckinridge, Scott D. *The CIA and the U.S. Intelligence System.* Boulder, CO: Westview Press, 1986.

—**AIR FORCE INTELLIGENCE (A-2)** conducts and manages the collection, processing, analysis, and dissemination of intelligence information to meet the needs of the U.S. Air Force and the national Intelligence Community. Of the military services, the Air Force has the largest intelligence program, and its Foreign Technology Division in Ohio is the leading national source of analysis on foreign aircraft and missiles. The goals of Air Force Intelligence are to provide decisionmakers with information on current and estimated foreign military activities, strategy, tactics, capabilities, and intentions.

Organization. The assistant chief of staff for intelligence, headquarters, U.S. Air Force (ACS/I, HQ USAF) is a major general who also serves as the commander of the Air Force Intelligence Agency (AFIA). Together, the ACS/I, the AFIA commander, and their intelligence directorates provide functional management, oversight, and headquarters review of all Air Force Intelligence activities.

Air Force Intelligence, which employs approximately 15,000 people, is divided into two primary directorates:

The Directorate of Intelligence Plans and Systems is composed of: the Intelligence Resources Management Group; the Plans Division (consisting of Concepts Applications and Current Plans and Force Development); the Systems Division, with its SIGINT, HUMINT, Imagery, and Technical Units; and the Electronic Combat Intelligence Group, which reports directly to the ACS/I.

The Directorate of Estimates is composed of four divisions: Weapons, Space, and Technology; Strategic Threat; Regional Estimates; and General Purpose Threat.

The components of the Air Force Intelligence Agency (AFIA) are the intelligence-producing elements of Air Force Intelligence. These include the following:

Air Force Special Activities Center (AFSAC), located at Fort Belvoir, Virginia, is responsible for the Air Force human intelligence (HUMINT) program *Electronic Security Command (ESC)*, located at Kelly Air Force Base, San Antonio, Texas, is the Air Force's service cryptologic unit. AFESC also has a signals intelligence (SIGINT) function.

Foreign Technology Division (FTD), located at Wright Paterson Air Force Base, Ohio, is the largest of the service scientific and technical intelligence centers. It produces intelligence for both the Air Force and national-level consumers. In addition, the Air Force has a counterintelligence group, the Office of Special Investigations (OSI), which conducts all Air Force investigations and reports directly to the Inspector General. Outside the United States, in the absence of the FBI, the AFOSI has conducted investigations of those civilian groups consisting primarily of Americans living abroad who are considered threats to security.

References

Bamford, James. *The Puzzle Palace: A Report on America's Most Secret Agency.* New York: Penguin Books, 1983.

Breckinridge, Scott D. *The CIA and the U.S. Intelligence System.* Boulder, CO: Westview Press, 1986.

Godson, Roy, ed. *Intelligence Problems for the 1980s, Number 1: Elements of Intelligence*. Rev. ed. Washington, DC: National Strategy Information Center, 1983.

Kent, Sherman. *Strategic Intelligence for American World Policy*. Princeton, NJ: Princeton University Press, 1966.

Laqueur, Walter. *A World of Secrets*. New York: Basic Books, 1985.

Lowenthal, Mark M. *U.S. Intelligence: Evolution and Anatomy*. New York: Praeger, 1984.

Maurer, Alfred C.; Turnstall, Marion D.; and Keagle, James M. *Intelligence Policy and Process*. Boulder, CO: Westview Press, 1985.

Treverton, Gregory F. *Covert Action: The Limits of Intervention in the Postwar World*. New York: Basic Books, 1987.

Turner, Stansfield. *Secrecy and Democracy: The CIA in Transition*. Boston: Houghton Mifflin, 1985.

—AIR FORCE OFFICE OF SPECIAL INVESTIGA-TIONS (AFOSI). *See*: AIR FORCE INTELLIGENCE (A-2).

—AIR FORCES INTELLIGENCE STUDY (AFIS) is produced by the Defense Intelligence Agency's Directorate for Research. It is a comprehensive textual survey of the air forces of the Soviet Union and other countries of great interest to intelligence. The study, which is published annually or biannually, discusses the missions, tasks, organizations, capabilities, policies, and military trends of these air forces.

References
Von Hoene, John P. A. *Intelligence User's Guide*. Washington, DC: DIA, 1983.

—AIR ORDER OF BATTLE, prepared by the Defense Intelligence Agency's Directorate for Research, provides detailed information on the air orders of battle of many countries of the world. Its discussions of military aircraft include their roles, inventories, unit locations, operational readiness, and organizational subordinations. *See also:* Defense Intelligence Agency.

References
Laqueur, Walter. *A World of Secrets*. New York: Basic Books, 1985.

Von Hoene, John P. A. *Intelligence User's Guide*. Washington, DC: DIA, 1983.

—AIR PHOTOGRAPHIC RECONNAISSANCE is the process of obtaining information by means of aerial photography. Air reconnaissance is divided into three types: strategic photographic reconnaissance; tactical photographic reconnaissance; and survey/cartographic photography (air photography that is taken for survey/cartographic purposes and to survey/cartographic standards of accuracy; it may be strategic or tactical in nature). *See also:* Aerial Photograph.

References
Department of Defense, Joint Chiefs of Staff. *Department of Defense Dictionary of Military and Related Terms*. Washington, DC: GPO, 1986.

Department of Defense, U.S. Army. *Intelligence Imagery*. Army Field Manual FM 34–55. Washington, DC: Headquarters, Department of the Army, 1985.

Godson, Roy, ed. *Intelligence Problems for the 1980s, Number 1: Elements of Intelligence*. Rev. ed. Washington, DC: National Strategy Information Center, 1983.

Laqueur, Walter. *The Age of Terrorism*. Boston: Little, Brown, 1987.

————. *A World of Secrets*. New York: Basic Books, 1985.

Treverton, Gregory F. *Covert Action: The Limits of Intervention in the Postwar World*. New York: Basic Books, 1987.

Turner, Stansfield. *Secrecy and Democracy: The CIA in Transition*. Boston: Houghton Mifflin, 1985.

—AIR RECONNAISSANCE LIAISON OFFICER (ARLO) is an Army officer who has received special training in aerial reconnaissance and imagery interpretation and is attached to a tactical air reconnaissance unit. He provides liaison between the ground and air commanders in matters concerning aerial reconnaissance requests. *See also:* Air Battle Management, AirLand Battle.

References
Department of Defense, Joint Chiefs of Staff. *Department of Defense Dictionary of Military and Related Terms*. Washington, DC: GPO, 1986.

Department of Defense. U.S. Army. *Intelligence Imagery*. Army Field Manual FM 34–55. Washington, DC: Headquarters, Department of the Army, 1985.

—AIR UNIVERSITY (AU) is located at Maxwell Air Force Base, Montgomery, Alabama, and offers courses for commissioned officers and civilians.

See also: Air Command and Staff College, Air War College (AWC).

References

Department of Defense, Defense Intelligence Agency. *Training Compendium for General Defense Career Development Program (IDCP) Personnel DOD 1430.10M3-TNG.* Washington, DC: DIA, 1986.

—**AIR WAR COLLEGE (AWC)** is the senior professional school of the U.S. Air Force. Located on Maxwell Air Force Base, Montgomery, Alabama, the college runs a ten-month curriculum that prepares selected officers for eventual assignment to key command and staff assignments where they will be responsible for developing, managing, and deploying air power as a component of national security. The college curriculum includes national security affairs and leadership and management studies. *See also:* Air Command and Staff College, Air University (AU).

References

Department of Defense, Defense Intelligence Agency. *Training Compendium for General Defense Career Development Program (IDCP) Personnel DOD 1430.10M3-TNG.* Washington, DC: DIA, 1986.

—**AIRBORNE EARLY WARNING (AEW)** is the detection of enemy air or surface units by radar and other gear in an aircraft or other airborne vehicle and the transmition of a warning to friendly forces. *See also:* Airborne Early Warning and Control System (AWACS), Indications And Warning (I&W).

References

Department of Defense, Joint Chiefs of Staff. *Department of Defense Dictionary of Military and Related Terms.* Washington, DC: GPO, 1986.

Laqueur, Walter. *A World of Secrets.* New York: Basic Books, 1985.

—**AIRBORNE EARLY WARNING AND CONTROL SYSTEM (AWACS)** consists of a force of airborne early warning aircraft that is equipped with search and height-finding radar and communications equipment for controlling weapons. These planes provide air surveillance and control for friendly forces. *See also:* Airborne Early Warning (AEW), Indications and Warning (I&W).

References

Department of Defense, Joint Chiefs of Staff. *Department of Defense Dictionary of Military and Related Terms.* Washington, DC: GPO, 1986.

Laqueur, Walter. *A World of Secrets.* New York: Basic Books, 1985.

—**AIRFIELDS AND SEAPLANE STATIONS OF THE WORLD (ASSOTW)** is a publication prepared by the Defense Intelligence Agency as part of its Facilities and Installations Studies series. The ASSOTW provides encyclopedic data on major air facilities in Eurasian Communist countries. A parallel study covering Free World countries is prepared by the Defense Mapping Agency. *See also:* Defense Mapping Agency.

References

Von Hoene, John P. A. *Intelligence User's Guide.* Washington, DC: DIA, 1983.

—**AIRLAND BATTLE** is the Army's operational concept that outlines an approach to military operations based on securing or retaining the initiative and exercising it aggressively to defeat the enemy. Two concepts—extending the battlefield, and integrating conventional, nuclear, chemical, and electronic means—are combined to describe a battlefield where the enemy is attacked to the full depth of his formations.

References

Department of Defense, U.S. Army. *U.S. Army Air Defense Artillery Employment.* Field Manual FM 44–1. Washington, DC: Headquarters, Department of the Army, 1983.

—**AIR-TO-AIR MISSILE** is a missile that is launched from an airborne vehicle at a target above the surface of the earth.

References

Department of Defense, Joint Chiefs of Staff. *Department of Defense Dictionary of Military and Related Terms.* Washington, DC: GPO, 1986.

—**AIR-TO-SURFACE MISSILE** is a missile that is launched from an airborne vehicle at a target on the surface of the earth.

References

Department of Defense, Joint Chiefs of Staff. *Department of Defense Dictionary of Military and Related Terms.* Washington, DC: GPO, 1986.

—**ALERT** is a warning or signal of a real or threatened danger, such as an air attack. To alert is to forewarn or to prepare for action.

References

Department of Defense, Joint Chiefs of Staff. *Department of Defense Dictionary of Military and Related Terms*. Washington, DC: GPO, 1986.

—**ALERT CENTER** is an indications and warning (I&W) term. It is a center for reviewing all incoming intelligence information. Such a center has, or has access to, extensive communications for alerting local intelligence personnel and contacting appropriate external reporting sources and other nodes of the Department of Defense I&W system. *See also:* Indications and Warning (I&W), Worldwide Military Command and Control System (WWMCCS).

References

Godson, Roy, ed. *Intelligence Problems for the 1980s, Number 1: Elements of Intelligence*. Rev. ed. Washington, DC: National Strategy Information Center, 1983.

Laqueur, Walter. *A World of Secrets*. New York: Basic Books, 1985.

—**ALERT MEMORANDUM** is an intelligence term used on the joint intelligence and national levels. It is a type of correspondence issued by the director of Central Intelligence to National Security Council-level policymakers to warn them about developments abroad that may be of major concern to the United States. The alert memorandum is coordinated within the Intelligence Community if time permits.

References

Department of Defense, Defense Intelligence College. *Glossary of Intelligence Terms and Definitions*. Washington, DC: DIC, 1987.

Laqueur, Walter. *A World of Secrets*. New York: Basic Books, 1985.

Treverton, Gregory F. *Covert Action: The Limits of Intervention in the Postwar World*. New York: Basic Books, 1987.

Turner, Stansfield. *Secrecy and Democracy: The CIA in Transition*. Boston: Houghton Mifflin, 1985.

—**ALIAS,** a term used in clandestine and covert intelligence operations, means an assumed name, usually consisting of both a first and a last name. *See also:* Accommodation Address, Active Measures, Agent, Agent Authentication, Agent in Place, Agent Net, Agent of Influence, Agent Provocateur, Concealment, Cover, Cover Name, Cover Organizations, Cover Story, Double Agent, Illegal Agent, Informant, Inside Man, Legend, Plumbing, Pocket Litter, Pseudonym, Recruitment, Recruitment in Place, Singleton.

References

Kessler, Ronald. *Spy vs. Spy: Stalking Soviet Spies in America*. New York: Charles Scribner's Sons, 1988.

Turner, Stansfield. *Secrecy and Democracy: The CIA in Transition*. Boston: Houghton Mifflin, 1985.

—**ALLEN, GENERAL LEW, JR., U.S. AIR FORCE,** served as director of the National Security Agency from August 15, 1973, until July 5, 1977. Allen was born on September 30, 1925. A graduate of West Point, he earned his masters and doctoral degrees in physics from the University of Illinois. Most of his early career was spent in the field of nuclear weapons. In December 1961 he was assigned to the Space Technology Office of the director of Defense Research and Engineering, Office of the Secretary of Defense. He then spent several tours in reconnaissance before becoming director of the NSA. Allen spent a good deal of his time as director defending the agency in the ongoing Congressional investigations of the Intelligence Community. Upon being relieved of his position in the NSA, he served briefly as director of the Air Force Systems Command and then became chief of staff of the U.S. Air Force. *See also:* National Security Agency.

References

Bamford, James. *The Puzzle Palace: A Report on America's Most Secret Agency*. New York: Penguin Books, 1983.

Corson, William R. *The Armies of Ignorance: The Rise of the American Intelligence Empire*. New York: Dial Press, 1977.

Turner, Stansfield. *Secrecy and Democracy: The CIA in Transition*. Boston: Houghton Mifflin, 1985.

—**ALLEN, MICHAEL,** a retired naval senior chief radioman, was arrested for selling classified information in 1986. He was tried, convicted, and sentenced to eight years in prison, a fine of $10,000, and forfeiture of his retirement pay.

References

Allen, Thomas B., and Polmar, Norman. *Merchants of Treason: America's Secrets for Sale*. New York: Delacorte Press, 1988.

—**ALLENDE, SALVADOR.** *See*: Chile.

—**ALLOCATION** is an official document that is issued by Headquarters, Department of the Air Force to a major Air Force command or operating agency. It is a funding document and represents cash that can be committed or obligated by the command. *See also:* Appropriation or Fund Account.

References

Godson, Roy, ed. *Intelligence Problems for the 1980s, Number 1: Elements of Intelligence.* Rev. ed. Washington, DC: National Strategy Information Center, 1983.

Kent, Sherman. *Strategic Intelligence for American World Policy.* Princeton, NJ: Princeton University Press, 1966.

Pickett, George. "Congress, the Budget and Intelligence." In *Intelligence Policy and Process,* edited by Alfred C. Maurer, Marion D. Turnstall and James M. Keagle. Boulder, CO: Westview Press, 1985.

—**ALL SOURCE DOCUMENT INDEX (ASDIA)** is a batch and on-line data base that contains over 80,000 records and produces bibliographic listings of materials held in the Defense Intelligence Agency library. Documents contained in the ASDIA include all types of Department of Defense intelligence studies, scientific and technical intelligence studies, handbooks, factbooks, estimates, and orders of battle. Producers of these documents include all Intelligence Community members, other Department of Defense commands, contracted publications, and a host of open-source books and publications. *See also:* All Source Documented Index—Compartmented (ASDIAZ).

References

Von Hoene, John P. A. *Intelligence User's Guide.* Washington, DC: DIA, 1983.

—**ALL SOURCE DOCUMENT INDEX—COM-PARTMENTED (ASDIAZ)** is strictly for compartmented materials and is similar in structure to the All Source Document Index (ASDIA).

References

Von Hoene, John P. A. *Intelligence User's Guide.* Washington, DC: DIA, 1983.

—**ALTERNATE MEET,** a term used in clandestine and covert intelligence operations, is a prearranged meeting that will occur in the event that a regular meeting does not take place. The regular meeting might not take place, for example, if one of the parties is delayed or is unable to shake his or her surveillance. The alternate meet should be approached with some caution, since the failure of the regular meeting to occur as scheduled is out of the ordinary. *See also:* Agent, Agent Authentication, Agent in Place, Agent Net, Agent of Influence, Agent Provocateur, Alias, Blind Dating, Dead Drop, Go-Away, Live Letter Boxes, Live Letter Drops, Mail Cover, Meet Area, Riding Shotgun, Special Activities, Surveillance, Tip-Off, Turned, Walk-Past.

References

Kessler, Ronald. *Spy vs. Spy: Stalking Soviet Spies in America.* New York: Charles Scribner's Sons, 1988.

—**ALTERNATE NATIONAL MILITARY COM-MAND CENTER (ANMCC)** was created so that, in the event that the National Military Command Center is unmanable, there is a means of reestablishing the command and control network. Support and personnel for the ANMCC are provided regularly by the Defense Intelligence Agency's Directorate for Intelligence Support. *See also:* National Military Command Center (NMCC), National Military Intelligence Center (NMIC), Alternate National Military Intelligence Center (ANMIC).

References

Department of Defense, Defense Intelligence Agency. *Organization, Mission and Key Personnel.* Washington, DC: DIA, 1986.

—**ALTERNATE NATIONAL MILITARY INTELLI-GENCE CENTER (ANMIC)** was established to provide a backup in case both the National Military Intelligence Center (NMIC) and the National Military Command Center (NMCC) become inoperable (e.g., because of nuclear attack). The ANMIC has all the necessary communications links with subordinate intelligence facilities, and it is prepared to fulfill the functions of the NMIC if necessary. Support and personnel are provided regularly by the Defense Intelligence Agency's Directorate for Intelligence

Support. *See also:* National Military Intelligence Center (NMIC), National Military Command Center (NMCC), Alternate National Military Command Center (NMCC).

References

Department of Defense, Defense Intelligence Agency. *Organization, Mission and Key Personnel.* Washington, DC: DIA, 1986.

—**ALTERNATIVES,** a general intelligence term, means the ways in which objectives can be obtained. They are options and need not be obvious substitutes for one another or perform the same specific function. For example, to protect civilians against air attack, shelters, defenses, and retaliatory striking power are all alternatives.

References

Godson, Roy, ed. *Intelligence Problems for the 1980s, Number 1: Elements of Intelligence.* Rev. ed. Washington, DC: National Strategy Information Center, 1983.

—**AMERICAN LEGATION U.S. NAVAL ATTACHÉ (ALUSNA)** is a member of the Defense Attaché Office, which is a part of a U.S. embassy. A Navy or Marine Corps officer, he performs attaché duties as they pertain to his service and his military specialty. *See also:* Air Attaché, American Legation U.S. Naval Liaison Officer (ALUSNLO), Army Attaché (ARMA), Attaché Activities, Defense Attaché (DATT), Defense Attaché Office (DAO), Defense Attaché System, Defense Intelligence Agency, Persona Non Grata (PNG), United States Country Team.

References

Laubenthal, Sanders A. "Preparing 'the Team': Defense Attaché Training." *DIC Newsletter* (Winter 1986): 1–4.

—**AMERICAN LEGATION U.S. NAVAL LIAISON OFFICER (ALUSNO)** is a member of the Defense Attaché Office, which is a part of a U.S. embassy. A Navy or Marine Corps officer, he is the assistant naval attaché and performs attaché duties as they pertain to his service and his military specialty. *See also:* Air attaché, American Legation U.S. Naval Attaché (ALUSNA), Army Attaché (ARMA), Attaché Activities, Defense Attaché (DATT), Defense Attaché Office (DAO), Defense Attaché System (DAS), Defense Intelli-

gence Agency (DIA), Persona Non Grata (PNG), United States Country Team.

References

Laubenthal, Sanders A. "Preparing 'the Team': Defense Attaché Training." *DIC Newsletter* (Winter 1986): 1–4.

—**AMPHIBIOUS DEMONSTRATION** is a naval and marine corps intelligence and operational term for a type of amphibious operation that is conducted for the purpose of deceiving the enemy by a show of force.

References

Department of Defense, Joint Chiefs of Staff. *Department of Defense Dictionary of Military and Related Terms.* Washington, DC: GPO, 1986.

Poyer, David. *The Med.* New York: St. Martin's Press, 1988.

—**AMPHIBIOUS OBJECTIVE AREA** is a Navy and Marine Corps intelligence and operations term. It is a defined geographical area within which the areas to be captured by the amphibious task force are located. The amphibious objective area is delineated in the initiating directive in terms of sea, land, and air space.

References

Department of Defense, Joint Chiefs of Staff. *Department of Defense Dictionary of Military and Related Terms.* Washington, DC: GPO, 1986.

Poyer, David. *The Med.* New York: St. Martin's Press, 1988.

—**AMPHIBIOUS OPERATION** is an attack launched from the sea by naval and landing forces that are embarked on ships or craft. The forces land on the shore by accomplishing the following phases:

(1) Planning: the period extending from the time that the initiating directive is issued until embarkation.

(2) Embarkation: the period when the forces, with their equipment and supplies, are embarked on the assigned ships.

(3) Rehearsal: the period when the operation is rehearsed for testing the adequacy of the plans, the timing of detailed operations, the combat readiness of the forces, and the

communications, and for insuring that all echelons are familiar with the plans.

(4) Movement: the period when various components of the amphibious task force move from the embarkation points to the objective area.

(5) Assault: the period between the arrival of major assault forces of the amphibious task force in the objective area and the accomplishment of the amphibious task force mission.

References

Department of Defense, Joint Chiefs of Staff. *Department of Defense Dictionary of Military and Related Terms.* Washington, DC: GPO, 1986.

—**AMPHIBIOUS RECONNAISSANCE,** a term used by Navy and Marine Corps intelligence, is an amphibious landing by a small group (called a unit) in order to secretly collect information and then withdraw and return to headquarters. An amphibious reconnaissance operation was conducted by the Marine Corps before the U.S. landing on Grenada.

References

Department of Defense, Joint Chiefs of Staff. *Department of Defense Dictionary of Military and Related Terms.* Washington, DC: GPO, 1986.

—**AMPHIBIOUS TASK FORCE,** a Navy and Marine Corps intelligence and operations term, is the organization formed to conduct an amphibious operation. The task force always includes Navy forces and a landing force, with their associated aviation, and it may also include Military Sealift Command—provided ships and U.S. Air Force units, when appropriate. David Poyer gives an excellent overview of how an amphibious task force is formed, what the components of such a force are, and how intelligence interacts with operations to enable the force to operate successfully. *See also:* Amphibious Task Force Commander.

References

Department of Defense, Joint Chiefs of Staff. *Department of Defense Dictionary of Military and Related Terms.* Washington, DC: GPO, 1986.

Poyer, David. *The Med.* New York: St. Martin's Press, 1988.

—**AMPHIBIOUS TASK FORCE COMMANDER,** a Navy and Marine Corps intelligence and operations term, is the naval officer who has been designated in the initiating directive as the commander of the amphibious task force. Such a designation is necessary, since there are many different units involved in an amphibious operation, and the assignment gives the commander overall responsibility for the mission. David Poyer provides an excellent description of the responsibilities of the amphibious task force commander. *See also:* Amphibious Task Force.

References

Department of Defense, Joint Chiefs of Staff. *Department of Defense Dictionary of Military and Related Terms.* Washington, DC: GPO, 1986.

Poyer, David. *The Med.* New York: St. Martin's Press, 1988.

—**AMPHIBIOUS TROOPS,** a Navy and Marine Corps intelligence and operations term, refers to the troop components, ground and air, that have been assigned to make a landing in an amphibious operation. The term "amphibious troops" is synonymous with the generic term "landing forces" as it is used in the National Security Act of 1947, as amended. Amphibious troops may be transported to land by airborne means (i.e., helicopter or other aircraft) or by watercraft.

References

Department of Defense, Joint Chiefs of Staff. *Department of Defense Dictionary of Military and Related Terms.* Washington, DC: GPO, 1986.

Poyer, David. *The Med.* New York: St. Martin's Press, 1988.

—**ANALYSIS** is a general intelligence term that has several meanings. (1) Analysis is a process in the production step of the intelligence cycle in which collected information is reviewed to identify significant facts. These are compared and collated with other information, so that logical conclusions can be drawn. (2) In electronic intelligence, analysis is the study of electromagnetic radiations to determine their technical characteristics and their tactical or strategic purpose. (3) Analysis is also an Army tactical intelligence (TACINT) term that means a stage in the intelligence cycle in which information is reviewed to identify significant facts and to derive conclusions therefrom. (4) Analysis, in the Army TACINT context, is also a step in the signals intelligence (SIGINT) process. (5) As defined by the Church Committee, analysis is a stage in the intelligence processing cycle in which information is reviewed to identify significant facts; the information is compared to and collated with other data; and conclusions, which also incorporate the memory and judgment of the intelligence analyst, are drawn from those data. *See also:* Electronic Warfare, Intelligence Cycle, Intelligence Production, SIGINT Process.

References

Department of Defense, Joint Chiefs of Staff. *Department of Defense Dictionary of Military and Related Terms.* Washington, DC: GPO, 1986.

————. *Glossary of Communications-Electronics Terms.* Washington, DC: GPO, 1974.

Department of Defense, U.S. Army. *Counter-Signals Intelligence (C-SIGINT) Operations.* Field Manual FM 34–62. Washington, DC: Headquarters, Department of the Army, 1986.

————. *Military Intelligence Battalion Combat Electronic Warfare and Intelligence (Aerial Exploitation) (Corps).* Field Manual FM 34–22. Washington, DC: Headquarters, Department of the Army, 1984.

————. *Military Intelligence Battalion (Combat Electronic Warfare Intelligence) (Division).* Field Manual FM 34–10. Washington, DC: Headquarters, Department of the Army, 1981.

————. *Military Intelligence Company (Combat Electronic Warfare and Intelligence) (Armored Cavalry Regiment/Separate Brigade).* Field Manual FM 34–30. Washington, DC: Headquarters, Department of the Army, 1983.

Godson, Roy, ed. *Intelligence Problems for the 1980s, Number 1: Elements of Intelligence.* Rev. ed. Washington, DC: National Strategy Information Center, 1983.

————. *Intelligence Problems for the 1980s, Number 3: Counterintelligence.* Washington, DC: National Strategy Information Center, 1980.

Kent, Sherman. *Strategic Intelligence for American World Policy.* Princeton, NJ: Princeton University Press, 1966.

Laqueur, Walter. *A World of Secrets.* New York: Basic Books, 1985.

Quirk, John; Phillips, David; Cline, Ray; and Pforzheimer, Walter. *The Central Intelligence Agency: A Photographic History.* Guilford, CT: Foreign Intelligence Press, 1986.

Treverton, Gregory F. *Covert Action: The Limits of Intervention in the Postwar World.* New York: Basic Books, 1987.

Turner, Stansfield. *Secrecy and Democracy: The CIA in Transition.* Boston: Houghton Mifflin, 1985.

U.S. Congress. Senate. *Final Report of the Senate Select Committee to Study Government Operations with Respect to Intelligence Activities. Report 94–755. Book I, Foreign and Military Intelligence.* Washington, DC: GPO, 1976.

—**ANALYSIS, COMPETITIVE.** *See:* Competitive Analysis.

—**ANALYSIS STAFF.** *See:* Central Analysis Team.

—**ANGOLA.** U.S. intelligence has documented in detail the expansion of Communist insurgency in Angola, which until 1975 was known as Portuguese West Africa. The radical Guinean regime under President Akmed Sekou Toure was created in 1958; the Soviet Navy responded to Toure's request for assistance in 1970, establishing the Soviet West African naval contingent; the Soviet Union also delivered arms to the insurgent Popular Movement for the Liberation of Angola (MPLA) following Angola's independence from Portugal.

In 1976, the Soviets intercepted the communications of the rival Angolan National Liberation Front (FNLA) in which its leader, Holden Roberto, ordered his forces to attempt to interdict the Soviet arms carriers. The Soviet response was both immediate and impressive. The West African naval contingent was bolstered and eventually numbered eight ships, which was adequate for Soviet purposes so long as the United States chose not to react. Cuban troops were conveyed on ships from Cuba to Angola to assist Soviet-backed forces, and a Soviet intelligence collector was deployed to a position midway in the Atlantic so that it could provide navigational assistance to the sealift of Cuban troops. Finally, the Soviets increased their reconnaissance over the North Atlantic, lest the United States attempt to react to the war.

The MPLA soon enjoyed major victories over FNLA forces in battles that may have involved shore bombardment by Soviet naval combatants, and after 1977 the MPLA was faced with merely combatting minor resistance from opposition forces that were operating in southern Angola.

Intelligence reporting had been complete during all of these developments. The U.S. military intelligence entities—Naval Intelligence and the Defense Intelligence Agency—provided a complete picture of Soviet and Cuban military involvement. Likewise, the CIA and other intelligence agencies provided an accurate view of the internal picture in Angola, and the CIA attempted to provide support to forces opposing the MPLA. However, Congressional sentiment, which reflected the mood of the country in the post-Vietnam War period, legislatively barred the Ford administration from actively supporting the anti-MPLA factions. When President Carter took office in 1977, it was doubtful that he could have had much effect on Angola. The Soviet-backed MPLA forces were well on their way to victory, and Congress had made it clear that it would not condone U.S. involvement in the conflict, passing fiscal legislation that forbade the funding of such operations. At any rate, Carter did not attempt to alter this situation, and the MPLA continued to consolidate its gains.

The Angolan operation allowed the Soviets and Cubans to establish an operating pattern that would be used again (e.g., in Ethiopia): the Soviet Union finances and supplies an operation, while Cuba provides the manpower. This approach optimizes the use of available forces, reduces potential public Soviet opposition to the involvement of Soviet troops in Africa, ensures that the most effective troops—mostly Black Cuban troops, rather than xenophobic Soviet troops who often alienate Africans and Asians—will be used, and furthers Castro's image as the leader of the Nonaligned Movement.

In the years since 1977, the United States funded UNITA forces that opposed the Communist Angolan regime. After years of fighting, negotiations were conducted to establish a peace and to disengage the Cuban troops. While the situation remained unstable in the late-1980s, the chances were good that the Cuban troops would leave and that peace would be established. *See also:* Carter, Jimmy; Ethiopia; Ford, Gerald.

References

Breckinridge, Scott D. *The CIA and the U.S. Intelligence System.* Boulder, CO: Westview Press, 1986.

Brinkley, David A., and Hull, Andrew W. *Estimative Intelligence: A Textbook on the History, Products, Uses and Writing of Intelligence Estimates.* Columbus, OH: Battelle, 1979.

Cline, Ray S. *The CIA Under Reagan, Bush, and Casey.* Washington, DC: Acropolis Books, 1981.

Godson, Roy, ed. *Intelligence Problems for the 1980s, Number 3: Counterintelligence.* Washington, DC: National Strategy Information Center, 1980.

———. *Intelligence Problems for the 1980s, Number 4: Covert Action.* Washington, DC: National Strategy Information Center, 1981.

Lefever, Ernest W., and Godson, Roy. *The CIA and the American Ethic: An Unfinished Debate.* Washington, DC: Ethics and Public Policy Center, Georgetown University, 1979.

Lowenthal, Mark M. *U.S. Intelligence: Evolution and Anatomy.* New York: Praeger, 1984.

Treverton, Gregory F. *Covert Action: The Limits of Intervention in the Postwar World.* New York: Basic Books, 1987.

Turner, Stansfield. *Secrecy and Democracy: The CIA in Transition.* Boston: Houghton Mifflin, 1985.

U.S. Congress. Senate. *Alleged Assassination Plots Involving Foreign Leaders: An Interim Report of the Select Committee to Study Governmental Operations with Respect to Intelligence Activities.* 94th Congress, 1st sess., Nov. 20, 1975. S. Rept. 94–465.

Von Hoene, John P. A. *Intelligence User's Guide.* Washington, DC: DIA, 1983.

Watson, Bruce W. *Red Navy at Sea: Soviet Naval Operations on the High Seas, 1956–1980.* Boulder, CO: Westview Press, 1982.

Watson, Bruce W., and Watson, Susan M. *The Soviet Navy: Strengths and Liabilities.* Boulder, CO: Westview Press, 1986.

—**ANNEX** is a document that is appended to an operation order or other document to make it clearer or to provide additional details.

References

Department of Defense, Joint Chiefs of Staff. *Department of Defense Dictionary of Military and Related Terms.* Washington, DC: GPO, 1986.

Godson, Roy, ed. *Intelligence Problems for the 1980s, Number 1: Elements of Intelligence.* Rev. ed. Washington, DC: National Strategy Information Center, 1983.

—**ANNOTATED PRINT** is a photograph on which interpretation details are indicated by words and symbols.

References

Department of Defense, Joint Chiefs of Staff. *Department of Defense Dictionary of Military and Related Terms.* Washington, DC: GPO, 1986.

—**ANNOTATION** is marking (by words or symbols) imagery or drawings for explanatory purposes or to indicate items or areas that are of special importance.

References

Department of Defense, Joint Chiefs of Staff. *Department of Defense Dictionary of Military and Related Terms.* Washington, DC: GPO, 1986.

—ANOMALY. In photoreconnaissance, imagery, SIGINT, and other spheres of intelligence analysis, an anomaly is a deviation of an observed object from its theoretical value. It is due to an abnormality in the observed object or subject.

References
Clancy, Tom. *The Cardinal of the Kremlin*. New York: Putnam, 1988.

Kent, Sherman. *Strategic Intelligence for American World Policy*. Princeton, NJ: Princeton University Press, 1966.

Laqueur, Walter. *A World of Secrets*. New York: Basic Books, 1985.

Reeves, Robert; Anson, Abraham; and Landen, David. *Manual of Remote Sensing*. Falls Church, VA: American Society of Photogrammetry, 1975.

Turner, Stansfield. *Secrecy and Democracy: The CIA in Transition*. Boston: Houghton Mifflin, 1985.

—ANTIAIRCRAFT ARTILLERY ORDER OF BATTLE (AAAOB) is prepared by the Defense Intelligence Agency's Directorate of Research. It provides detailed data on the antiaircraft artillery forces of the Soviet Union and other priority countries. *See also:* Defense Intelligence Agency.

References
Von Hoene, John P. A. *Intelligence User's Guide*. Washington, DC: DIA, 1983.

—ANTISATELLITE (ASAT) is an intelligence imagery and photoreconnaissance term for systems that are designed to neutralize or destroy satellites. These can be destroyed in a variety of ways, such as blowing them up or performing acts that disrupt or destroy the systems they carry on board.

References
Godson, Roy, ed. *Intelligence Problems for the 1980s, Number 1: Elements of Intelligence*. Rev. ed. Washington, DC: National Strategy Information Center, 1983.

—APERIODIC REPORTS are those that are produced as the need arises, rather than at regularly scheduled intervals. They are nonrecurring in nature. An example would be a spot report, which is used to report an unforeseen event that is of interest to the Intelligence Community. *See also:* Precedence, Spot Report.

References
Godson, Roy, ed. *Intelligence Problems for the 1980s, Number 1: Elements of Intelligence*. Rev. ed. Washington, DC: National Strategy Information Center, 1983.

Laqueur, Walter. *A World of Secrets*. New York: Basic Books, 1985.

—APOGEE is an intelligence imagery and photoreconnaissance term. It is the farthest point from the earth in the elliptical orbit of a satellite as it travels around the earth. *See also:* Aerial Photograph.

References
Department of Defense, Joint Chiefs of Staff. *Department of Defense Dictionary of Military and Related Terms*. Washington, DC: GPO, 1986.

Reeves, Robert; Anson, Abraham; and Landen, David. *Manual of Remote Sensing*. Falls Church, VA: American Society of Photogrammetry, 1975.

—APPLIED RESEARCH is a general intelligence term for research that applies practical knowledge, material, or techniques to solving existing or anticipated military problems. *See also:* Research and Development (R&D).

References
Department of Defense, Joint Chiefs of Staff. *Department of Defense Dictionary of Military and Related Terms*. Washington, DC: GPO, 1986.

Kent, Sherman. *Strategic Intelligence for American World Policy*. Princeton, NJ: Princeton University Press, 1966.

—APPRAISAL is a general intelligence term for an impartial analysis of information conducted at each responsible management-control level in order to measure the effectiveness and efficiency of the total process and to determine the correct preventive or corrective action.

References
Godson, Roy, ed. *Intelligence Problems for the 1980s, Number 1: Elements of Intelligence*. Rev. ed. Washington, DC: National Strategy Information Center, 1983.

Kent, Sherman. *Strategic Intelligence for American World Policy*. Princeton, NJ: Princeton University Press, 1966.

Laqueur, Walter. *A World of Secrets*. New York: Basic Books, 1985.

Treverton, Gregory F. *Covert Action: The Limits of Intervention in the Postwar World*. New York: Basic Books, 1987.

Turner, Stansfield. *Secrecy and Democracy: The CIA in Transition*. Boston: Houghton Mifflin, 1985.

—**APPROPRIATION OR FUND ACCOUNT,** in budgeting, is an account that has been established to make money available for paying obligations and for expenditure from the U.S. Treasury. These accounts include not only those to which money is directly appropriated, but also revolving funds and trust funds. A one-year account is available for incurring specified obligations only during a specified fiscal year. A multiple-year account is available for a specified period in excess of one fiscal year. A no-year account is available for an indefinite period of time.

Although the Congressional intelligence committees can oversee projects or programs as decision units, program elements, or justification book categories, they have to translate these into appropriations in order to formulate the authorization bill. Although Congress does authorize programs, it actually appropriates funds to be spent for appropriation accounts such as procurement, research and development, military construction, military pay, and operations and maintenance. Thus, the translation from programs to appropriation accounts is essential to completing the authorization process. *See also:* Defense Guidance (DG); Five-Year Defense Program (FYDP); National Defense Expenditures; National Intelligence Projections for Planning (NIPP); Office of Management and Budget (OMB); Program Budget Decision (PBD).

References

Godson, Roy, ed. *Intelligence Problems for the 1980s, Number 1: Elements of Intelligence*. Rev. ed. Washington, DC: National Strategy Information Center, 1983.

Pickett, George. "Congress, the Budget and Intelligence." In *Intelligence Policy and Process*, edited by Alfred C. Maurer, Marion D. Turnstall and James M. Keagle. Boulder, CO: Westview Press, 1985.

—**APPROPRIATION ACCOUNTING,** in budgeting, is the recording and reporting of governmental financial transactions in terms of appropriation accounts. *See also:* Appropriation or Fund Account.

References

Godson, Roy, ed. *Intelligence Problems for the 1980s, Number 1: Elements of Intelligence*. Rev. ed. Washington, DC: National Strategy Information Center, 1983.

Pickett, George. "Congress, the Budget and Intelligence." In *Intelligence Policy and Process*, edited by Alfred C. Maurer, Marion D. Turnstall and James M. Keagle. Boulder, CO: Westview Press, 1985.

—**APPROVE** is a general intelligence term for the act of authorizing the expenditure of resources to perform a specified task. Also, to approve can also be the act of placing a resource requirement in a proposed major program at a priority level which would result in subsequent congressional funding. *See also:* Appropriation or Fund Account.

References

Department of Defense, Defense Intelligence Agency. *Defense Intelligence Agency Manual*. Washington, DC: DIA, 1987.

Pickett, George. "Congress, the Budget and Intelligence." In *Intelligence Policy and Process*, edited by Alfred C. Maurer, Marion D. Turnstall and James M. Keagle. Boulder, CO: Westview Press, 1985.

—**APPROVED PROGRAMS,** in intelligence budgeting, are individual program elements or other components of the Five-Year Defense Program approved by the secretary of defense and as modified by approved Program Change Decisions and other secretary of defense decisions. They may also be modified by changes approved by the head of a Department of Defense component. *See also:* Appropriation or Fund Account.

References

Godson, Roy, ed. *Intelligence Problems for the 1980s, Number 1: Elements of Intelligence*. Rev. ed. Washington, DC: National Strategy Information Center, 1983.

Pickett, George. "Congress, the Budget and Intelligence." In *Intelligence Policy and Process*, edited by Alfred C. Maurer, Marion D. Turnstall and James M. Keagle. Boulder, CO: Westview Press, 1985.

—**ARBENZ GUZMAN, JACOBO.** *See:* Guatemala.

—**AREA OF INFLUENCE,** an Army tactical intelligence (TACINT) term, means an area where enemy forces that affect current operations are located. *See also:* Area of Interest.

References

Department of Defense, U.S. Army. *Intelligence and Electronic Warfare Operations.* Field Manual FM 34–1. Washington, DC: Headquarters, Department of the Army, 1984.

Laqueur, Walter. *A World of Secrets.* New York: Basic Books, 1985.

—**AREA OF INTELLIGENCE RESPONSIBILITY** is an Army tactical intelligence (TACINT) term for a sector assigned to a commander. It is that commander's responsibility to provide intelligence on the sector if the means are available.

References

Department of Defense, Joint Chiefs of Staff. *Department of Defense Dictionary of Military and Related Terms.* Washington, DC: GPO, 1986.

Laqueur, Walter. *A World of Secrets.* New York: Basic Books, 1985.

—**AREA OF INTEREST,** an Army tactical intelligence (TACINT) term, means an area where enemy forces that have the potential to affect friendly future operations are located. *See also:* Area of Influence.

References

Department of Defense, U.S. Army. *Military Intelligence Battalion (CEWI) (Operations) (Corps).* Field Manual 34–21. Washington, DC: Headquarters, Department of the Army, 1982.

Laqueur, Walter. *A World of Secrets.* New York: Basic Books, 1985.

—**AREA OF OPERATIONS** is an Army intelligence term for a specific part of a war theater in which offensive or defensive military operations are waged in order to fulfill an assigned mission.

References

Department of Defense, Joint Chiefs of Staff. *Department of Defense Dictionary of Military and Related Terms.* Washington, DC: GPO, 1986.

—**ARGUMENT** is a term of logic. The U.S. Intelligence Community has increasingly stressed the importance of logic in intelligence analysis and has begun training in logic. To the Intelligence Community, an argument is simply any group of statements of which one is claimed to follow, or to be correctly inferred, from the others. Any given argument has a structure. This structure is described by using the term "conclusion" to refer to a statement that is affirmed on the basis of the other statements in the argument, which are referred to as premises.

In the area of intelligence analysis and production, the role of argumentation is vital. The National Intelligence Estimate is only one of a family of products that illustrates the absolute necessity of providing policymakers with a carefully constructed argument, or series of arguments, that reveals how premises lead logically to the stated conclusion.

References

Godson, Roy, ed. *Intelligence Problems for the 1980s, Number 1: Elements of Intelligence.* Rev. ed. Washington, DC: National Strategy Information Center, 1983.

Kent, Sherman. *Strategic Intelligence for American World Policy.* Princeton, NJ: Princeton University Press, 1966.

Laqueur, Walter. *A World of Secrets.* New York: Basic Books, 1985.

Turner, Stansfield. *Secrecy and Democracy: The CIA in Transition.* Boston: Houghton Mifflin, 1985.

—**ARLINGTON HALL STATION** was a girls' school that, according to legend, was the first piece of territory taken by the U.S. Army in World War II. Located only a few miles from the Pentagon, the station was ideally situated to serve as an annex for the Department of Defense. A combination of permanent buildings and temporary military structures, it housed several of the Defense Intelligence Agency's analytical offices.

This undesirable situation was remedied when several of the agency's offices were consolidated in the new Defense Intelligence Analysis Center on Bolling Air Force Base, near Anacostia, Maryland. The U.S. Army then had exclusive possession of Arlington Hall Station, where it housed its Intelligence and Security Command, until the station was given to the Department of State in June 1989. *See also:* Defense Intelligence Analysis Center (DIAC), U.S. Army Intelligence and Security Command (INSCOM).

References

Bamford, James. *The Puzzle Palace: A Report on America's Most Secret Agency.* New York: Penguin Books, 1983.

Personal recollection.

—**ARMED FORCES AIR INTELLIGENCE TRAIN-ING CENTER (AFAITC),** at Lowery Air Force Base, Colorado, offers a host of courses in a wide-ranging curriculum. Many of the courses, however, pertain to imagery intelligence analysis and interpretation (for which it has developed its well-deserved reputation), to intelligence analysis, and to targeting. The courses range from a few days to several weeks in length and are geared to all types of intelligence professionals.

References

Department of Defense, Defense Intelligence Agency. *Training Compendium for General Defense Career Development Program (IDCP) Personnel DOD 1430.10M3-TNG.* Washington, DC: DIA, 1986.

—**ARMED FORCES COURIER SERVICE (ARFCOS)** is a joint service of the Army, Navy, and Air Force with the chief of staff of the Army as executive agent. The service provides a means of securely and rapidly transmitting classified and other material that requires protection by a military courier. Although serving as an Armed Forces courier is not considered a job that will promote a military officer to the next rank, it is nonetheless ideal for a person who loves to travel and see the world. *See also:* Courier.

References

Department of Defense, Joint Chiefs of Staff. *Department of Defense Dictionary of Military and Related Terms.* Washington, DC: GPO, 1986.

—**ARMED FORCES INTELLIGENCE** is a general intelligence term for information dealing with foreign armed forces, their personnel, training programs, equipment, bases, capabilities, disposition, manpower levels, and all other pertinent aspects of their strengths and liabilities. In short, it is the integrated study of the organized land, sea, and air forces, both actual and potential, of foreign nations. The Defense Intelligence Agency is primarily responsible for the production of armed forces intelligence. *See also:* Strategic Intelligence.

References

Clauser, Jerome K., and Weir, Sandra M. *Intelligence Research Methodology.* State College, PA: HRB Singer, 1975.

Kent, Sherman. *Strategic Intelligence for American World Policy.* Princeton, NJ: Princeton University Press, 1966.

Laqueur, Walter. *A World of Secrets.* New York: Basic Books, 1985.

Turner, Stansfield. *Secrecy and Democracy: The CIA in Transition.* Boston: Houghton Mifflin, 1985.

—**ARMED FORCES MEDICAL INTELLIGENCE CENTER (AFMIC),** at Fort Detrick, Maryland, was formed from the Army Medical Intelligence and Information Agency. It is a joint organization that provides medical intelligence to all National Foreign Intelligence Community members. Management of the AFMIC is the responsibility of the Army, and it operates under the direction of the Army's surgeon general.

References

Laubenthal, Sanders A. *Survey of Resources for Intelligence Research.* Washington, DC: DIC, 1986.

—**ARMED FORCES SECURITY AGENCY (AFSA)** was the predecessor to the National Security Agency. It was created in 1949 to consolidate the U.S. cryptologic programs.

In 1948, although the nascent signals intelligence (SIGINT) community had great potential, it was still a fragmented composition of contending members. Secretary of Defense James Forrestal attempted unsuccessfully to change the situation. However, on May 20, 1949, his successor, Louis A. Johnson, established the AFSA and placed it under the Joint Chiefs of Staff. Additionally, he created the Armed Forces Security Agency Council (AFSAC) to act as a governing council. James Bamford notes that this created management difficulties that were a major cause of the intelligence failure to forewarn of the invasion of South Korea in 1950. In essence, the U.S. Intelligence Community, though concerned with the Korean situation, failed to notify the SIGINT community, and therefore the latter simply did not report the information that it had. As a result, the AFSAC agreed to create the Intelligence Requirements Committee (IRC), which would convey Intelligence Community needs and priorities to the AFSA. Although this improved the situation to some extent, it still failed to create an acceptable situation. Because of his continued dissatisfaction, President Truman created the Brownell Committee to investigate the SIGINT situation; based on that committee's recommendations, he created the National Security Agency in 1952. *See also:* Brownell Committee, National Security Agency.

References

Bamford, James. *The Puzzle Palace: A Report on America's Most Secret Agency*. New York: Penguin Books, 1983.

U.S. Congress. Senate. *Final Report of the Senate Select Committee to Study Government Operations with Respect to Intelligence Activities. Report 94-755. Book I, Foreign and Military Intelligence*. Washington, DC: GPO, 1976.

—**ARMED RECONNAISSANCE** is an air intelligence term for an air mission that is flown in order to locate and attack targets of opportunity in assigned areas and along ground communications routes. Armed reconnaissance is unique in that its mission is not to attack specific targets.

References

Department of Defense, Joint Chiefs of Staff. *Department of Defense Dictionary of Military and Related Terms*. Washington, DC: GPO, 1986.

—**ARMY.** *See*: U.S. Army.

—**ARMY ATTACHÉ** is a member of the Defense Attaché Office, which is a part of a U.S. embassy. The army attaché performs attaché duties as they pertain to his service and his military specialty. *See also:* Air Attaché, American Legation U.S. Naval Attaché (ALUSNA), American Legation U.S. Naval Liaison Officer (ALUSNLO), Attaché Activities, Defense Attaché (DATT), Defense Attaché Office (DAO), Defense Attaché System (DAS), Defense Intelligence Agency (DIA), Persona Non Grata (PNG), United States Country Team.

References

Kent, Sherman. *Strategic Intelligence for American World Policy*. Princeton, NJ: Princeton University Press, 1966.

Laubenthal, Sanders A. "Preparing 'the Team': Defense Attaché Training." *DIC Newsletter* (Winter 1986): 1–4.

—**ARTIFICIAL INTELLIGENCE (AI)** is a branch of computer science that attempts to simulate human intelligence in a computer-based system. If successful, it will vastly expand the Intelligence Community's analytical capability. LISP is a programming language that is especially popular in the United States and is used by the U.S. Intelligence Community in its artificial intelligence programs.

References

Clancy, Tom. *The Cardinal of the Kremlin*. New York: Putnam, 1988.

Maurer, Alfred C.; Turnstall, Marion D.; and Keagle, James M. *Intelligence Policy and Process*. Boulder, CO: Westview Press, 1985.

Mishkoff, Henry C. *Understanding Artificial Intelligence*. Indianapolis, IN: Howard W. Sams and Co., 1985.

—**ASSASSINATION** is a term used in covert operations. The origin of accepting assassination as a contemporary intelligence operation is obscured and the information is fragmented. Perhaps the most coherent discussion has been provided by Dr. Ray Cline. In regard to Fidel Castro, for example, Cline maintains that it is impossible to discern whether either President Eisenhower or President Kennedy actually intended to authorize his murder. However, Cline says that "the instructions to move against Castro were so explicit and the general atmosphere of urgency was so palpable" that Richard Bissell, the CIA's deputy director for plans, and Sheffield Edwards, the agency's chief of security, thought that they had been authorized to plan Castro's assassination. Cline also notes that the CIA was so unfamiliar with assassinations that none of their "wild schemes" succeeded in assassinating their targets. The agency's endeavors in this field were definitely halted when the Ford administration prohibited such operations, and this proscription was continued by President Carter and President Reagan. *See also:* Church Committee, Executive Orders on Intelligence, Presidential Oversight, Congressional Oversight.

References

American Bar Association. *Oversight and Accountability of the U.S. Intelligence Agencies: An Evaluation*. Washington, DC: ABA, 1985.

Buckley, William F., Jr. *Mongoose, R.I.P.* New York: Random House, 1987, pp. 48–56.

Cline, Ray S. *The CIA Under Reagan, Bush, and Casey*. Washington: Acropolis Books, 1981, pp. 208–15.

Laqueur, Walter. *The Age of Terrorism*. Boston: Little, Brown, 1987.

———. *A World of Secrets*. New York: Basic Books, 1985.

Lefever, Ernest W.; and Godson, Roy. *The CIA and the American Ethic: An Unfinished Debate*. Washington, DC: Ethics and Public Policy Center, Georgetown University, 1979.

Maurer, Alfred C.; Turnstall, Marion D.; and Keagle, James M. *Intelligence Policy and Process.* Boulder, CO: Westview Press, 1985.

Oseth, John M. *Regulating U.S. Intelligence Operations: A Study in the Definition of the National Interest.* Frankfurt: University of Kentucky Press, 1985.

Treverton, Gregory F. *Covert Action: The Limits of Intervention in the Postwar World.* New York: Basic Books, 1987.

Turner, Stansfield. *Secrecy and Democracy: The CIA in Transition.* Boston: Houghton Mifflin, 1985.

—**ASSESSMENT.** In general use, an assessment is an appraisal of the worth of an intelligence activity, source, product, or piece of information. Its value is judged either in terms of how it contributes to a specific goal or in terms of its credibility, reliability, pertinency, and accuracy in terms of intelligence need. When assessment is used in contrast to evaluation, it implies a weighing against resource allocation, expenditure, or risk. In the context of intelligence production, assessment is the part of the process when the analyst determines the reliability and validity of a piece of information. In personnel evaluations, it is the judgment of the motives, qualifications, and characteristics of present or prospective employees or of agents. Assessment is also an Army tactical intelligence (TACINT) term that means an analysis of the security, effectiveness, and potential of an existing or planned intelligence activity. As defined by the Church Committee, an assessment is part of the intelligence process whereby an analyst determines the reliability or validity of a piece of information. An assessment could also be a statement resulting from this process. *See also:* Adjudication, Evaluation, Intelligence Assessment, Intelligence Cycle, Net Assessment.

References

Department of Defense, Defense Intelligence College. *Glossary of Intelligence Terms and Definitions.* Washington, DC: DIC, 1987.

Department of Defense, Joint Chiefs of Staff. *Department of Defense Dictionary of Military and Related Terms.* Washington, DC: GPO, 1986.

Department of Defense, U.S. Army. *Counter-Signals Intelligence (C-SIGINT) Operations.* Field Manual FM 34–62. Washington, DC: Headquarters, Department of the Army, 1986.

————. *Military Intelligence Battalion Combat Electronic Warfare and Intelligence (Aerial Exploitation) (Corps).* Field Manual FM 34-22.

Washington, DC: Headquarters, Department of the Army, 1984.

————. *Military Intelligence Battalion (CEWI) (Tactical Exploitation) (Corps): Counterintelligence, Interrogation, Electronic Warfare.* Field Manual FM 34-23. Washington, DC: Headquarters, Department of the Army, 1985.

————. *Military Intelligence Battalion (Combat Electronic Warfare Intelligence) (Division).* Field Manual FM 34-10. Washington, DC: Headquarters, Department of the Army, 1981.

————. *Military Intelligence Company (Combat Electronic Warfare and Intelligence) (Armored Cavalry Regiment/Separate Brigade).* Field Manual FM 34-30. Washington, DC: Headquarters, Department of the Army, 1983.

Kent, Sherman. *Strategic Intelligence for American World Policy.* Princeton, NJ: Princeton University Press, 1966.

Laqueur, Walter. *A World of Secrets.* New York: Basic Books, 1985.

Quirk, John; Phillips, David; Cline, Ray; and Pforzheimer, Walter. *The Central Intelligence Agency: A Photographic History.* Guilford, CT: Foreign Intelligence Press, 1986.

Treverton, Gregory F. *Covert Action: The Limits of Intervention in the Postwar World.* New York: Basic Books, 1987.

Turner, Stansfield. *Secrecy and Democracy: The CIA in Transition.* Boston: Houghton Mifflin, 1985.

U.S. Congress. Senate. *Final Report of the Senate Select Committee to Study Government Operations with Respect to Intelligence Activities. Report 94–755. Book I, Foreign and Military Intelligence.* Washington, DC: GPO, 1976.

—**ASSET** is any resource, be it a person, a group, a relationship, an instrument, an installation, or a supply, that is used by an intelligence agency in an operational or supporting role. In the CIA, the term is often used to describe a person who contributes to a clandestine mission but who is not a fully controlled agent of the agency. As defined by the Church Committee, an asset is any resource—a person, group, relationship, instrument, installation, or supply—at the disposition of an intelligence agency for use in an operational or supporting role. The term is normally applied to a person who is contributing to a CIA clandestine mission but who is not a fully controlled agent of the agency. *See also:* Asset Management, Intelligence Asset, National Asset.

References

Clancy, Tom. *The Cardinal of the Kremlin.* New York: Putnam, 1988.

Department of Defense, Joint Chiefs of Staff. *Department of Defense Dictionary of Military and Related Terms*. Washington, DC: GPO, 1986.

Godson, Roy, ed. *Intelligence Problems for the 1980s, Number 1: Elements of Intelligence*. Rev. ed. Washington, DC: National Strategy Information Center, 1983.

Kent, Sherman. *Strategic Intelligence for American World Policy*. Princeton, NJ: Princeton University Press, 1966.

Kessler, Ronald. *Spy vs. Spy: Stalking Soviet Spies in America*. New York: Charles Scribner's Sons, 1988.

Laqueur, Walter. *A World of Secrets*. New York: Basic Books, 1985.

Quirk, John; Phillips, David; Cline, Ray; and Pforzheimer, Walter. *The Central Intelligence Agency: A Photographic History*. Guilford, CT: Foreign Intelligence Press, 1986.

Treverton, Gregory F. *Covert Action: The Limits of Intervention in the Postwar World*. New York: Basic Books, 1987.

Turner, Stansfield. *Secrecy and Democracy: The CIA in Transition*. Boston: Houghton Mifflin, 1985.

U.S. Congress. Senate. *Final Report of the Senate Select Committee to Study Government Operations with Respect to Intelligence Activities. Report 94–755. Book I, Foreign and Military Intelligence*. Washington, DC: GPO, 1976.

—**ASSET MANAGEMENT,** an Army tactical intelligence (TACINT) term, means the planning, direction, and control of individual collection, counterintelligence, operations security support, and electronic warfare resources that are necessary for the accomplishment of a mission. Asset management generally is performed by the commander's units with assigned resources that are capable of performing any of the above missions. *See also:* Asset, Asset Tasking.

References

Department of Defense, U.S. Army. *Military Intelligence Company Combat Electronic Warfare and Intelligence) (Armored Cavalry Regiment/ Separate Brigade)*. Field Manual FM 34–30. Washington, DC: Headquarters, Department of Army, 1983.

——. *Military Intelligence Group (Combat Electronic Warfare and Intelligence) (Corps)*. Field Manual FM 34–20. Washington, DC: Headquarters, Department of the Army, 1983.

Kent, Sherman. *Strategic Intelligence for American World Policy*. Princeton, NJ: Princeton University Press, 1966.

Laqueur, Walter. *A World of Secrets*. New York: Basic Books, 1985.

Turner, Stansfield. *Secrecy and Democracy: The CIA in Transition*. Boston: Houghton Mifflin, 1985.

—**ASSET TASKING,** an Army tactical intelligence (TACINT) term, means the assignment of a mission to a specific subordinate element. *See also:* Asset, Asset Management.

References

Department of Defense, U.S. Army. *Intelligence and Electronic Warfare Operations*. Field Manual FM 34-1. Washington, DC: Headquarters, Department of the Army, 1984.

——. *Military Intelligence Battalion (CEWI) (Operations) (Corps)*. Field Manual FM 34–21. Washington, DC: Headquarters, Department of the Army, 1982.

Laqueur, Walter. *A World of Secrets*. New York: Basic Books, 1985.

Turner, Stansfield. *Secrecy and Democracy: The CIA in Transition*. Boston: Houghton Mifflin, 1985.

—**ASSIGNED RESPONSIBLE AGENCY (ARA),** a term used on the joint intelligence and national level in intelligence automation, is the Department of Defense component that is assigned to chair a working group to develop a recommendation to the assistant secretary of defense (comptroller) for standardizing specific data elements and related features. After approval of a specific standard by the secretary of defense (comptroller), the ARA will maintain the standard by evaluating, approving, and coordinating changes in related features.

References

Department of Defense, Defense Intelligence Agency. *Defense Intelligence Agency Manual 65–18*. Washington, DC: DIA, 1984.

Turner, Stansfield. *Secrecy and Democracy: The CIA in Transition*. Boston: Houghton Mifflin, 1985.

—**ASSISTANT CHIEF OF STAFF, INTELLIGENCE (ACSI) (U.S. ARMY),** has been elevated to deputy chief of staff, intelligence. *See:* U.S. Army Intelligence.

—**ASSISTANT CHIEF OF STAFF, INTELLIGENCE (AFIN) (U.S. AIR FORCE).** *See:* Air Force Intelligence (A-2).

—**ASSISTANT SECRETARY OF DEFENSE (COM-MAND, CONTROL, COMMUNICATIONS AND INTELLIGENCE) (ASDC³I).** According to the current Department of Defense directive, the ASDC³I is the principal staff assistant and advisor to the secretary of defense for CC³I policy, requirements, priorities, resources, systems, and programs, including related warning and reconnaissance activities. He is also the principal staff assistant concerning the secretary's responsibilities for the National Communications System (NCS) and defends the C³I program before Congress.

References

Department of Defense. *Keeping the Nation's Secrets: A Report to the Secretary of Defense by the Commission to Review DoD Security Policies and Practices.* Washington, DC: DoD, 1985.

Laqueur, Walter. *A World of Secrets.* New York: Basic Books, 1985.

—**ASSISTANT SECRETARY OF DEFENSE (COMP-TROLLER) (ASD(C))** is the officer within the Office of the Secretary of Defense who is responsible for developing and administering the planning, programming, and budgeting system (PPBS) and other resource management systems. *See also:* Defense Guidance (DG), Office of Management and Budget (OMB).

References

Pickett, George. "Congress, the Budget, and Intelligence." In *Intelligence Policy and Process,* edited by Alfred C. Maurer, Marion D. Turnstall, and James M. Keagle. Boulder, CO: Westview Press, 1985.

—**ASSISTANT TO THE PRESIDENT FOR NA-TIONAL SECURITY AFFAIRS (AP/NSA).** Although often associated with the National Security Council (NSC), the AP/NSA is not one of its members. Indeed, no mention of this position is made in the National Security Act of 1947. Rather, the position was created by President Eisenhower in 1953, and, although its title has been changed over the years, the position has come to be known as the national security advisor.

Under President Eisenhower, the national security advisor served as the principal executive officer of the NSC. In this capacity, he set the agenda, briefed the President on council matters, and supervised the staff.

It was not until President Kennedy, with McGeorge Bundy in the role, that the position took on its current form. Bundy emerged as an important personal advisor to the President on national security affairs, and this introduced an element of direct competition into Bundy's relationship with members of the NSC. Although President Johnson changed the title of the position to simply "special assistant," in the hands of Walt Rostow it continued to play an important role.

President Nixon relied heavily on his national security advisor, maintaining and even enhancing the position's prominence. In that role, Henry Kissinger became a key spokesman for the President's national security policies both to the U.S. press and to foreign governments. Nixon used him to negotiate on behalf of the United States with Vietnam, China, the Soviet Union, and other countries. The roles of spokesman and negotiator had traditionally been the province of the secretary of state, not of the national security advisor. The emerging tension between the two positions was only resolved when Kissinger assumed them both.

Under President Ford, Lieutenant General Brent Scowcroft became national security advisor, with Kissinger remaining as secretary of state. The national security advisor exercised major responsibility for coordinating for the President the advice of his NSC principals and overseeing the process of policy development and implementation within the Executive branch.

President Carter returned in large part to the early Kissinger model, with a resulting increase in tensions with the secretary of state. Carter wanted to take the lead in matters of foreign policy and used his national security advisor as a source of information, ideas, and new initiatives.

Perhaps the most incisive analysis of the position of national security advisor was made by a special review board convened in 1986 by President Reagan to examine the Iran-Contra scandal. The board was composed of Senator John Tower, Senator Edwin Muskie, and Lieutenant General Brent Scowcroft. Their views are fully presented in Appendix W.

References

Laqueur, Walter. *A World of Secrets.* New York: Basic Books, 1985.

Office of the President of the United States. *Report of the President's Special Review Board.* Washington, DC: GPO, 1987.

Treverton, Gregory F. *Covert Action: The Limits of Intervention n the Postwar World.* New York: Basic Books, 1987.

Turner, Stansfield. *Secrecy and Democracy: The CIA in Transition.* Boston: Houghton Mifflin, 1985.

—**ASSOCIATION OF FORMER INTELLIGENCE OFFICERS (AFIO)** is a pro-intelligence lobbying group that was formed during the intelligence investigations in 1975. The AFIO states that it was "formed by former intelligence personnel from the Federal, military, and civilian intelligence and security agencies. Its purpose is to promote public understanding of, and support for, a strong and responsible national intelligence establishment." *See also:* National Military Intelligence Association.

References

Godson, Roy, ed. *Intelligence Problems for the 1980s, Number 5: Clandestine Collection.* Washington, DC: National Strategy Information Center, 1982.

Lowenthal, Mark M. *U.S. Intelligence: Evolution and Anatomy.* New York: Praeger, 1984.

Turner, Stansfield. *Secrecy and Democracy: The CIA in Transition.* Boston: Houghton Mifflin, 1985.

Warner, John S. *National Security and the First Amendment.* McLean, VA: Association of Former Intelligence Officers, 1985.

—**ATTACHMENT,** an Army tactical intelligence (TACINT) term, means an option that can be used to simplify logistic support or to accommodate special command relationships of a temporary nature. Subject to the limitations imposed by the attachment order, the command receiving the attachment order exercises command and control over the attached element as it does over organic elements. In short, attachment places an asset under the temporary control of a command or task force. Orders attaching an element usually specify limitations that are imposed upon the relationship.

References

Department of Defense, U.S. Army. *Military Intelligence Battalion Combat Electronic Warfare and Intelligence (Aerial Exploitation) (Corps).* Field Manual FM 34–22. Washington, DC: Department of the Army, 1984.

————. *Military Intelligence Battalion (CEWI) (Tactical Exploitation) (Corps): Counterintelligence, Interrogation, Electronic Warfare.* Field Manual FM 34–23. Washington, DC: Headquarters, Department of the Army, 1985.

————. *Military Intelligence Battalion (Combat Electronic Warfare Intelligence) (Division).* Field Manual FM 34–10. Washington, DC: Headquarters, Department of the Army, 1981.

————. *Military Intelligence Company (Combat Electronic Warfare and Intelligence) (Armored Cavalry Regiment/Separate Brigade).* Field Manual FM 34–30. Washington, DC: Headquarters, Department of the Army, 1983.

—**ATTACK CARRIER STRIKING FORCES** is a Navy and Marine Corps intelligence and operations term for naval forces, the primary offensive weapon of which is carrier-based aircraft. Ships, other than aircraft carriers, act to support and screen primarily against the submarine and air threats, and secondarily against the surface threat.

References

Department of Defense, Joint Chiefs of Staff. *Department of Defense Dictionary of Military and Related Terms.* Washington, DC: GPO, 1986.

Turner, Stansfield. *Secrecy and Democracy: The CIA in Transition.* Boston: Houghton Mifflin, 1985.

—**AUTHENTICATE,** in electronic surveillance terminology, means a procedure, usually a forensic examination, that seeks to determine whether or not a tape was made in the manner claimed by the parties who are offering it into evidence. Authenticate is also a challenge that is given by voice or electrical means to attest to the authenticity of a message or transmission. *See also:* Authentication, Authentication System.

References

Department of Defense, Joint Chiefs of Staff. *Department of Defense Dictionary of Military and Related Terms.* Washington, DC: GPO, 1986.

Godson, Roy, ed. *Intelligence Problems for the 1980s, Number 1: Elements of Intelligence.* Rev. ed. Washington, DC: National Strategy Information Center, 1983.

Kent, Sherman. *Strategic Intelligence for American World Policy.* Princeton, NJ: Princeton University Press, 1966.

Kessler, Michael. *Wiretapping and Electronic Surveillance Commission Studies: Supporting Materials for the Report of the National Commission for the Review of Federal and State Laws Relating to Wiretapping and Electronic Surveillance, Washington, DC, 1976.* Townsend, PA: Loompanics Unlimited, 1976.

Laqueur, Walter. *A World of Secrets.* New York: Basic Books, 1985.

Treverton, Gregory F. *Covert Action: The Limits of Intervention in the Postwar World.* New York: Basic Books, 1987.

—**AUTHENTICATION** is a communications security measure designed to protect against fraudulent or bogus transmissions and hostile imitative communications deception. Authentication is done by establishing the validity of a transmission, message, station, or designator. It is also a means or method for establishing the eligibility of a station, originator, or individual to receive specific information. Such eligibility can be based upon the receiver's security clearance, his need to know, or other factors. *See also:* Authenticate, Authentication System, Communications Deception.

References

Department of Defense, Defense Intelligence College. *Glossary of Intelligence Terms and Definitions.* Washington, DC: DIC, 1987.

Department of Defense, Joint Chiefs of Staff. *Department of Defense Dictionary of Military and Related Terms.* Washington, DC: GPO, 1986.

Kent, Sherman. *Strategic Intelligence for American World Policy.* Princeton, NJ: Princeton University Press, 1966.

Treverton, Gregory F. *Covert Action: The Limits of Intervention in the Postwar World.* New York: Basic Books, 1987.

—**AUTHENTICATION SYSTEM** is a term used in communications intelligence, communications security, operations security, and signals analysis to describe a cryptosystem or cryptographic process that is used for authentication. *See also:* Authenticate, Communications Deception.

References

Department of Defense, Joint Chiefs of Staff. *Department of Defense Dictionary of Military and Related Terms.* Washington, DC: GPO, 1986.

—**AUTHENTICATOR** is a term used in communications intelligence, communications security, operations security, and signals analysis for a symbol, a group of symbols, or a series of bits that are selected or derived in a prearranged manner and are usually inserted at a predetermined point within a message or transmission for the purpose of attesting to the validity of the message or transmission. *See also:* Authenticate, Authentication System, Communications Deception.

References

Department of Defense, Joint Chiefs of Staff. *Department of Defense Dictionary of Military and Related Terms.* Washington, DC: GPO, 1986.

—**AUTHORIZED** was defined by Congress in the Intelligence Identities Protection Act of 1982: "'Authorized,' when used with respect to access to classified information, means having authority, right, or permission pursuant to the provisions of a statute, Executive order, directive of the head of any department or agency engaged in foreign intelligence or counterintelligence activities, order of any United States court, or provisions of any rule of the House of Representatives or resolution of the Senate which assigns responsibility within the respective House of Congress for the oversight of intelligence activities." *See also:* Access, Background Investigation, Classified Information, Collateral Information, Controlled Area, National Agency Check, Security Clearance, Sensitive Compartmented Information, Special Background Investigation, Special Security Officer.

References

Kent, Sherman. *Strategic Intelligence for American World Policy.* Princeton, NJ: Princeton University Press, 1966.

Turner, Stansfield. *Secrecy and Democracy: The CIA in Transition.* Boston: Houghton Mifflin, 1985.

U.S. Congress. *Intelligence Identities Protection Act of 1982. Public Law 97–200, June 23, 1982.* Washington, DC: GPO, 1982.

—**AUTO-MANUAL CRYPTOSYSTEM** is a term used in communications intelligence, communications security, operations security, and signals analysis to describe a cryptosystem in which a programmable, hand-held device is used to encode and decode messages. *See also:* Code, Cipher, Encipher, Encode, Decipher, Decode.

References

Blackburn, N. Glenn. "Computers: A Counterintelligence Concern." Unpublished paper provided to the editors. Washington, DC, 1987.

Martin, Paul H. "Communications-Computer Security." *Journal of Electronic Defense* (June 1987).

Muzerall, Joseph V., and Carty, Thomas P. "COMSEC and Its Need for Key Management." *DP&CS* (Spring 1987).

Ware, Willis H. "Information Systems, Security, and Privacy." *EDUCOM Bulletin* (Summer 1984).

—AUTOMATED DATA PROCESSING SYSTEM (ADPS) is an Air Force intelligence term. It is the central processing unit (CPU), the associated supporting and supported peripherals (including remote terminals) that are connected electrically to the CPU, and all the computer hardware and software (including system and applications) that are part of any component or components of the system. *See also:* Department of Defense Intelligence Information System (DODIIS).

References

Blackburn, N. Glenn. "Computers: A Counterintelligence Concern." Unpublished paper provided to the editors. Washington, DC, 1987.

Ware, Willis H. "Information Systems, Security, and Privacy." *EDUCOM Bulletin* (Summer 1984).

—AUTOMATED INFORMATION SYSTEMS were defined in "National Policy on Telecommunications and Automated Information Systems Security," a proposed Presidential Directive that was issued on September 17, 1984, as "systems which create, prepare, or manipulate information in electronic form for purposes other than telecommunication, and includes computers, word processing systems, other information handling systems, and associated equipment." *See also:* Automated Data Processing System, Department of Defense Intelligence Information System (DODIIS).

References

"National Policy on Telecommunications and Automated Information Systems Security." Proposed Presidential Directive issued Sept. 17, 1984, but never enacted.

—AUTOMATED INSTALLATIONS INTELLIGENCE FILE (AIF) is a target intelligence program that is managed by the Defense Intelligence Agency's Directorate for Foreign Intelligence (VP). *See also:* Target, Target Acquisition, Target Analysis, Target Correlation, Target Development, Target Intelligence, Target Study, Target System, Targeting.

References

Blackburn, N. Glenn. "Computers: A Counterintelligence Concern." Unpublished paper provided to the editors. Washington, DC, 1987.

Department of Defense, Defense Intelligence Agency. *Organization, Mission and Key Personnel.* Washington, DC: DIA, 1986.

Martin, Paul H. "Communications-Computer Security." *Journal of Electronic Defense* (June 1987).

Muzerall, Joseph V., and Carty, Thomas P. "COMSEC and Its Need for Key Management." *DP&CS* (Spring 1987).

Ware, Willis H. "Information Systems, Security, and Privacy." *EDUCOM Bulletin* (Summer 1984).

—AUTOMATED INSTALLATIONS SYSTEM-BASED INTELLIGENCE PROGRAMS. *See:* Defense Intelligence Agency, *under "Organization."*

—AUTOMATIC DATA PROCESSING SYSTEM SECURITY, a term that is used in counterintelligence, counterespionage, and counterinsurgency, involves all of the technological safeguards and managerial procedures that have been established and are applied to computer hardware, software, and data. These categories include: all hardware and software functions, characteristics, and features; all operational features, accountability procedures, and access controls at the central computer facility; all remote computer and terminal facilities, management constraints, and physical structures and devices; and all the personnel and communication controls needed to provide an acceptable level of protection so that classified information can be kept in the computer system. The purpose of such security is to protect the organization's information and the privacy of those individuals on whom records are kept.

References

Blackburn, N. Glenn. "Computers: A Counterintelligence Concern." Unpublished paper provided to the editors. Washington, DC, 1987.

Department of Defense, Defense Intelligence College. *Glossary of Intelligence Terms and Definitions.* Washington, DC: DIC, 1987.

Martin, Paul H. "Communications-Computer Security." *Journal of Electronic Defense* (June 1987).

Ware, Willis H. "Information Systems, Security, and Privacy." *EDUCOM Bulletin* (Summer 1984).

—AUTOMATIC DIGITAL NETWORK (AUTODIN) is a system that has been built to "meet the requirement and specifications of a Department of Defense store-and-forward message switching system for sensitive compartmented information and other data."

References

Blackburn, N. Glenn. "Computers: A Counterintelligence Concern." Unpublished paper provided to the editors. Washington, DC, 1987.

Martin, Paul H. "Communications-Computer Security." *Journal of Electronic Defense* (June 1987).

Muzerall, Joseph V., and Carty, Thomas P. "COMSEC and Its Need for Key Management." *DP&CS* (Spring 1987).

—**AUTOMATIC DISSEMINATION** is a general intelligence term for the procedures that note previously registered customer requirements to determine the automatic distribution of intelligence materials to user organizations (customers) as they become available. *See also:* Dissemination.

References

Department of Defense, Defense Intelligence Agency. *Defense Intelligence Agency Manual.* Washington, DC: DIA, 1987.

Laqueur, Walter. *A World of Secrets.* New York: Basic Books, 1985.

—**AVAILABLE PUBLICLY** is a general intelligence term that refers to a decision resulting from Presidential Executive Order 12333, "United States Intelligence Activities," dated December 4, 1981. Available publicly is information that has been published or broadcast for general public consumption, is available on request to a member of the general public, could lawfully be seen or heard by an casual observer, or is made available at a meeting open to the general public. In this context, the "general public" also means general availability to persons in a military community even though the military community is not open to the civilian general public. *See also:* Collateral, Security Classification, Unclassified Matter.

References

Department of Defense. *Activities of DoD Intelligence Components that Affect U.S. Persons (Department of Defense Directive 5240.1).* Washington, DC: DoD, 1982.

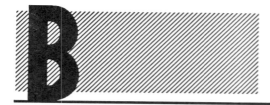

—**B GROUP** is a component of one of the ten branches that constitute the National Security Agency. *See:* National Security Agency.

References

Bamford, James. *The Puzzle Palace: A Report on America's Most Secret Agency.* New York: Penguin Books, 1983.

Laqueur, Walter. *A World of Secrets.* New York: Basic Books, 1985.

—**BABA, ENSIGN STEPHEN A.,** U.S. Navy, was convicted of passing information to South Africa. Apparently motivated by money, he was sentenced to eight years at hard labor in prison. His sentence was subsequently reduced to two years.

References

Allen, Thomas B., and Polmar, Norman. *Merchants of Treason: America's Secrets for Sale.* New York: Delacorte Press, 1988.

Crawford, David J. *Volunteers: The Betrayal of National Defense Secrets by Air Force Traitors.* Washington, DC: GPO, 1988.

—**BACK CHANNEL** is a generic intelligence term that refers to sensitive compartmented information communications systems. *See also:* General Service (GENSER) Communications, Sensitive Compartmented Information, Special Intelligence Communications, Special Security Officer.

References

Department of Defense, Defense Intelligence College. *Glossary of Intelligence Terms and Definitions.* Washington, DC: DIC, 1987.

Turner, Stansfield. *Secrecy and Democracy: The CIA in Transition.* Boston: Houghton Mifflin, 1985.

—**BACKGROUND INVESTIGATION (BI)** is a general intelligence term for an inquiry into the past life of a prospective intelligence agency employee and is required before the person can be given a security clearance. The investigation includes verifying the person's birth date, citizenship, education, employment for the previous five years, and travel information provided by the individual, reviewing all federal agencies for derogatory information, and doing credit and criminal record checks. *See also:* National Agency Check, Special Background Investigation.

References

Allen, Thomas B., and Polmar, Norman. *Merchants of Treason: America's Secrets for Sale.* New York: Delacorte Press, 1988.

Department of Defense, Defense Intelligence College. *Glossary of Intelligence Terms and Definitions.* Washington, DC: DIC, 1987.

Turner, Stansfield. *Secrecy and Democracy: The CIA in Transition.* Boston: Houghton Mifflin, 1985.

—**BACKGROUND USE ONLY** is a general intelligence term for a release marking placed on classified material that had been prepared before October 5, 1975. It was used to protect intelligence and intelligence information, including sources and methods, from extensive dissemination within the U.S. government. The marking meant that the information could not be used in any other document or publication. It was intended solely to control the use of the information and did not affect the dissemination of the document.

References

Department of Defense, Defense Intelligence Agency. *Defense Intelligence Agency Manual.* Washington, DC: DIA, 1987.

—**BACKSTOP** is a term that is used in clandestine and covert intelligence operations to describe an arrangement that is made to support a cover story. Closely representing an alibi, creating a backstop could involve such measures as having people available to verify the details of an agent's cover story. Backstopping, as defined by the Church Committee, is a CIA term for providing appropriate verification and support of cover arrangements for an agent or asset in anticipation of inquiries or other actions which might test the credibility of his cover. *See also:* Agent, Agent Authentication, Agent in Place, Alias, Cover, Cover Name, Cover Story, Pseudonym, Plumbing, Putting in the Plumbing.

References

Allen, Thomas B., and Polmar, Norman. *Merchants of Treason: America's Secrets for Sale.* New York: Delacorte Press, 1988.

Deacon, Richard. *Spyclopedia: An Encyclopedia of Spies, Secret Services, Operations, Jargon, and All Subjects Related to the World of Espionage.* London: Macdonald, 1987.

Kessler, Ronald. *Spy vs. Spy: Stalking Soviet Spies in America.* New York: Charles Scribner's Sons, 1988.

U.S. Congress. Senate. *Final Report of the Senate Select Committee to Study Government Operations with Respect to Intelligence Activities. Report 94-755. Book I, Foreign and Military Intelligence.* Washington, DC: GPO, 1976.

—**BALLISTIC MISSILE** is any missile that does not rely on aerodynamic surfaces to produce lift, and consequently it follows a ballistic trajectory when thrust is terminated.

References

Department of Defense, Joint Chiefs of Staff. *Department of Defense Dictionary of Military and Related Terms.* Washington, DC: GPO, 1986.

—**BALLISTIC MISSILE EARLY WARNING SYSTEM (BMEWS)** is an electronic system for detecting and providing the United States with early warning of an attack by enemy intercontinental ballistic missiles. *See also:* Early Warning, Indications and Warning.

References

Department of Defense, Joint Chiefs of Staff. *Department of Defense Dictionary of Military and Related Terms.* Washington, DC: GPO, 1986.

—**BALLISTIC TRAJECTORY** is the curved path that is traced after the propulsive force is terminated and the body is acted upon by gravity and aerodynamic drag.

References

Department of Defense, Joint Chiefs of Staff. *Department of Defense Dictionary of Military and Related Terms.* Washington, DC: GPO, 1986.

—**BALLOON REFLECTOR,** in electronic warfare, is a balloon-supported confusion reflector that produces fraudulent echoes.

References

Department of Defense, Joint Chiefs of Staff. *Department of Defense Dictionary of Military and Related Terms.* Washington, DC: GPO, 1986.

—**BARNETT, DAVID H.,** worked for the CIA until 1970, with duty in the Far East and the United States. Believing that he had little chance for advancement, he left the agency in 1970 to begin his own business. Failing in this endeavor, he offered to work for Soviet intelligence in 1976. For approximately $90,000, Barnett gave the Soviets the names of several CIA undercover agents and collaborators who were operating in foreign nations; he also gave them information about U.S. intelligence responses to Soviet missile developments. In 1980, Barnett was arrested, found guilty, and sentenced to prison for eighteen years.

References

Allen, Thomas B., and Polmar, Norman. *Merchants of Treason: America's Secrets for Sale.* New York: Delacorte Press, 1988.

Becket, Henry S. A. *The Dictionary of Espionage: Spookspeak into English.* New York: Stein and Day, 1986.

Crawford, David J. *Volunteers: The Betrayal of National Defense Secrets by Air Force Traitors.* Washington, DC: GPO, 1988.

Deacon, Richard. *Spyclopedia: An Encyclopaedia of Spies, Secret Services, Operations, Jargon, and All Subjects Related to the World of Espionage.* London: Macdonald, 1987.

Turner, Stansfield. *Secrecy and Democracy: The CIA in Transition.* Boston: Houghton Mifflin, 1985.

—**BARRAGE JAMMING** is a term used in electronic warfare (EW), to describe the simultaneous jamming of several adjacent channels or frequencies in order to prevent the enemy's reception of radio signals. *See also:* Jammer.

References

Department of Defense, Joint Chiefs of Staff. *Department of Defense Dictionary of Military and Related Terms.* Washington, DC: GPO, 1986.

—**BARRING** is the temporary removal of an individual from a sensitive compartmented information (SCI) environment because he or she has been involved in an incident that may require further investigation and could affect the person's eligibility for access to classified information. *See also:* Access, Authorized, Background Investigation, Personnel Insecurity, Personnel Security, Security, Security Classification.

References

Godson, Roy, ed. *Intelligence Problems for the 1980s, Number 1: Elements of Intelligence.* Rev.

ed. Washington, DC: National Strategy Information Center, 1983.

———. *Intelligence Problems for the 1980s, Number 3: Counterintelligence.* Washington, DC: National Strategy Information Center, 1980.

———. *Intelligence Problems for the 1980s, Number 4: Covert Action.* Washington, DC: National Strategy Information Center, 1981.

—**BASIC COVER (PHOTOGRAMMETRY)** is an intelligence imagery and photoreconnaissance term for photographic and other aerial coverage of any permanent installation or area. Such imagery can be compared to that taken at a later time in order to determine the changes that have taken place. In this way, imagery can be used to monitor and report on the progress of such endeavors as ship building, military or civil construction, or a host of other long-term enterprises that are of intelligence interest. *See also:* Photographic Intelligence.

References

Department of Defense, Defense Intelligence College. *Glossary of Intelligence Terms and Definitions.* Washington, DC: DIC, 1987.

Department of Defense, Joint Chiefs of Staff. *Department of Defense Dictionary of Military and Related Terms.* Washington, DC: GPO, 1986.

Laqueur, Walter. *A World of Secrets.* New York: Basic Books, 1985.

Turner, Stansfield. *Secrecy and Democracy: The CIA in Transition.* Boston: Houghton Mifflin, 1985.

—**BASIC ENCYCLOPEDIA (BE)** is an intelligence term that is used on the joint and national military levels. The Basic Encyclopedia is a compilation of identified installations and physical areas that are of potential significance as object of attack.

References

Department of Defense, Joint Chiefs of Staff. *Department of Defense Dictionary of Military and Related Terms.* Washington, DC: GPO, 1986.

—**BASIC INTELLIGENCE** is a general intelligence term for factual general reference material. It is assembled by collecting encyclopedic information concerning the geography and political, social, economic, and military structures, as well as biographic and cultural material and any information on the resources, capabilities, and

vulnerabilities of a foreign nation or nations. This information is essential because it provides a foundation for planning, policymaking, and military operations. *See also:* Basic Intelligence Production.

References

Corson, William R. *The Armies of Ignorance: The Rise of the American Intelligence Empire.* New York: Dial Press, 1977.

Department of Defense, Defense Intelligence College. *Glossary of Intelligence Terms and Definitions.* Washington, DC: DIC, 1987.

Department of Defense, Joint Chiefs of Staff. *Department of Defense Dictionary of Military and Related Terms.* Washington, DC: GPO, 1986.

Kent, Sherman. *Strategic Intelligence for American World Policy.* Princeton, NJ: Princeton University Press, 1966.

Laqueur, Walter. *A World of Secrets.* New York: Basic Books, 1985.

Treverton, Gregory F. *Covert Action: The Limits of Intervention in the Postwar World.* New York: Basic Books, 1987.

U.S. Congress. Senate. *Final Report of the Senate Select Committee to Study Government Operations with Respect to Intelligence Activities. Report 94-755. Book I, Foreign and Military Intelligence.* Washington, DC: GPO, 1976.

—**BASIC INTELLIGENCE DIVISION (BID),** a component of the Office of Research and Reports (ORR), CIA, was responsible for producing the National Intelligence Surveys. It became the Office of Basic Intelligence in 1955.

References

Fain, Tyrus G.; Plant, Katharine C.; and Milloy, Ross. *The Intelligence Community: History, Organization, and Issues.* Public Documents Series. New York: R.R. Bowker, 1977.

Kent, Sherman. *Strategic Intelligence for American World Policy.* Princeton, NJ: Princeton University Press, 1966.

Laqueur, Walter. *A World of Secrets.* New York: Basic Books, 1985.

—**BASIC INTELLIGENCE PRODUCTION** is an official term that has been defined by the Defense Intelligence Agency. It means applying basic knowledge to a professional discipline, and specifically it means applying the principles and techniques of deductive reasoning and a knowledge of either a geographical area or an occupational specialty to the production of finished intelligence reports and studies. Basic intelligence production includes the research and evaluation of collected information, drawing pertinent inferences from its analysis and, when appropriate, interpreting such inferences within the perspective of planning and policy decisions. *See also:* Basic Intelligence.

References

Corson, William R. *The Armies of Ignorance: The Rise of the American Intelligence Empire.* New York: Dial Press, 1977.

Department of Defense, Defense Intelligence Agency. *Defense Intelligence Agency Manual DIAM 22-2.* Washington, DC: DIA, 1979.

Department of Defense, Joint Chiefs of Staff. *Department of Defense Dictionary of Military and Related Terms.* Washington, DC: GPO, 1986.

Kent, Sherman. *Strategic Intelligence for American World Policy.* Princeton, NJ: Princeton University Press, 1966.

Laqueur, Walter. *A World of Secrets.* New York: Basic Books, 1985.

—**BASIC PSYCHOLOGICAL OPERATIONS STUDY (BPS)** is an Army intelligence term. The BPS is a reference source that briefly describes those characteristics of a country, area, or region that are of greatest value for conducting psychological operations.

References

Department of Defense, Joint Chiefs of Staff. *Department of Defense Dictionary of Military and Related Terms.* Washington, DC: GPO, 1986.

Laqueur, Walter. *A World of Secrets.* New York: Basic Books, 1985.

Lowenthal, Mark M. *U.S. Intelligence: Evolution and Anatomy.* New York: Praeger, 1984.

—**BATTALION LANDING TEAM (BLT)** is a Navy and Marine Corps intelligence and operations term. In an amphibious operation, a BLT is an infantry battalion that is reinforced by the necessary combat support and combat service support elements. The BLT is the basic unit that is used in planning an assault landing.

References

Department of Defense, Joint Chiefs of Staff. *Department of Defense Dictionary of Military and Related Terms.* Washington, DC: GPO, 1986.

Poyer, David. *The Med.* New York: St. Martin's Press, 1988.

—**BATTLEFIELD SURVEILLANCE** is an Army intelligence term. It is the constant, systematic observation of a battle area in order to detect changes or events immediately and then provide timely tactical intelligence information to the operational commander. *See also:* Reconnaissance, Surveillance.

References

Godson, Roy, ed. *Intelligence Problems for the 1980s, Number 1: Clandestine Collection.* Washington, DC: National Strategy Information Center, 1982.

Laqueur, Walter. *A World of Secrets.* New York: Basic Books, Inc., 1985.

—**BAUD,** a term used in communications intelligence, communications security, operations security, and signals analysis, has several meanings. (1) A baud is a unit of signaling speed that is derived from the duration of the shortest code element. Speed in "bauds" is the number of code elements per second. (2) Baud is also the unit of modulation rate. (3) Baud can be the shortest element used in forming code characters. (4) Finally, a baud can be a bit, single element, or impulse. *See also:* Baud-Based System.

References

Blackburn, N. Glenn. "Computers: A Counterintelligence Concern." Unpublished paper provided to the editors. Washington, DC, 1987.

Martin, Paul H. "Communications-Computer Security." *Journal of Electronic Defense* (June 1987).

Muzerall, Joseph V., and Carty, Thomas P. "COMSEC and Its Need for Key Management." *DP&CS* (Spring 1987).

Ware, Willis H. "Information Systems, Security, and Privacy." *EDUCOM Bulletin* (Summer 1984).

—**BAUD-BASED SYSTEM,** a term used in communications intelligence, communications security, operations security, and signals analysis, is a means of transmitting intelligence. It uses a predetermined number of unit elements ("bauds") for transmitting each character or function.

References

Blackburn, N. Glenn. "Computers: A Counterintelligence Concern." Unpublished paper provided to the editors. Washington, DC, 1987.

Martin, Paul H. "Communications-Computer Security." *Journal of Electronic Defense* (June 1987).

Muzerall, Joseph V., and Carty, Thomas P. "COMSEC and Its Need for Key Management." *DP&CS* (Spring 1987).

Ware, Willis H. "Information Systems, Security, and Privacy." *EDUCOM Bulletin* (Summer 1984).

—**BAY OF PIGS** refers to the attempted invasion of Cuba in 1961; it was a CIA paramilitary operation that failed miserably and had catastrophic results. Its origins date back to the Eisenhower administration in 1960, when the CIA was ordered to establish a guerrilla warfare training program for hundreds of anti-Castro Cuban refugees. Eisenhower approved the training program as a contingency plan and left its execution to President Kennedy. In November 1960, the concept of guerrilla operations was abandoned and the Cubans were assembled into a 1,400-man armed brigade that was prepared for an invasion in the Bay of Pigs, along Cuba's southwest coast. According to Ray Cline, the operation, which had the approval of the Joint Chiefs of Staff and of Allen Dulles, then director of Central Intelligence, was the responsibility of the deputy director for plans (DDP). Cline assessed this to be an unsound procedure, because it did not include other, more knowledgeable elements of the CIA. He states that the plan was formally approved at an April 4, 1961, meeting of the National Security Council, which was attended by all the appropriate officials, including President Kennedy, Secretary of State Dean Rusk, Secretary of Defense Robert McNamara, General Lyman Lemnitzer, Chairman of the Joint Chiefs of Staff, William Fulbright of the Senate Foreign Relations Committee, White House Assistant Arthur Schlesinger, Jr., and Allen Dulles. The operation was launched on April 17. In a change to the plan that amounted to an unsuccessful attempt to hide U.S. involvement, U.S. air cover and backup forces were not provided. To make matters worse, the Cuban Air Force was not completely destroyed by the invading forces. As a result, in spite of a heroic effort by those forces, they never managed to get beyond the beaches, and the expected support from anti-Castro Cubans on the island never materialized. The Bay of Pigs should have taught the CIA many lessons about launching full-scale military operations. In addition, it demonstrated that Castro was, indeed, able to defend his regime from U.S. or U.S.-sponsored incursions, thereby encouraging the Soviet Union to play a greater role in Cuba, and possibly sparking the events that eventually led to the Cuban missile crisis of 1962. Finally, the operation diffused U.S. sentiment concerning "doing something about Castro," thereby furthering the security of the Castro regime. *See also:* Kennedy, John F.; Mongoose.

References

American Bar Association. *Oversight and Accountability of the U.S. Intelligence Agencies: An Evaluation.* Washington, DC: ABA, 1985.

Cline, Ray. *The CIA Under Reagan, Bush, and Casey.* Washington, DC: Acropolis Books, 1981.

Corson, William R. *The Armies of Ignorance: The Rise of the American Intelligence Empire.* New York: Dial Press, 1977.

Godson, Roy, ed. *Intelligence Problems for the 1980s, Number 4: Covert Action.* Washington, DC: National Strategy Information Center, 1981.

Laqueur, Walter. *A World of Secrets.* New York: Basic Books, 1985.

Maurer, Alfred C.; Turnstall, Marion D.; and Keagle, James M. *Intelligence Policy and Process.* Boulder, CO: Westview Press, 1985.

Treverton, Gregory F. *Covert Action: The Limits of Intervention in the Postwar World.* New York: Basic Books, 1987.

Turner, Stansfield. *Secrecy and Democracy: The CIA in Transition.* Boston: Houghton Mifflin, 1985.

—**BEACHHEAD,** a Navy and Marine Corps intelligence and operations term, is a designated area on a hostile shore that, when seized and held, insures the continuous landing of troops and material and provides the maneuvering space required for subsequent offensive operations ashore. David Poyer gives a vivid and comprehensive description of a beachhead as it is viewed by the amphibious task force commander, by his staff officer, and, most emotionally, by one of the Marines who actually hits the beach. Poyer's excellent book gives much information about how the Marines train for such operations and about the types of intelligence they need to conduct the operation.

References

Department of Defense, Joint Chiefs of Staff. *Department of Defense Dictionary of Military and Related Terms.* Washington, DC: GPO, 1986.

Poyer, David. *The Med.* New York: St. Martin's Press, 1988.

—**BEAM RIDER** is a missile that is guided by a radio or radar beam.

References

Department of Defense, Joint Chiefs of Staff. *Department of Defense Dictionary of Military and Related Terms.* Washington, DC: GPO, 1986.

—**BEIRUT, LEBANON.** *See:* Lebanon.

—**BELL, WILLIAM HOLDEN,** an employee of Hughes Aircraft, was convicted of passing information to Polish intelligence. Apparently motivated by money, Bell was sentenced to eight years in prison.

References

Allen, Thomas B., and Polmar, Norman. *Merchants of Treason: America's Secrets for Sale.* New York: Delacorte Press, 1988.

Crawford, David J. *Volunteers: The Betrayal of National Defense Secrets by Air Force Traitors.* Washington, DC: GPO, 1988.

Deacon, Richard. *Spyclopedia: An Encyclopaedia of Spies, Secret Services, Operations, Jargon, and All Subjects Related to the World of Espionage.* London: Macdonald, 1987.

—**BERLIN DEMOCRATIC CLUB, ET AL. VS. BROWN** is perhaps the most famous of the 1970s litigations against U.S. intelligence activities. It was based on the revelations of a former Army counterintelligence agent, in which he alleged that the Army had conducted various operations, including wiretapping, mail- opening, penetrating civilian groups covertly, and surveilling Americans and Europeans who were believed to be promoting desertions and a lack of discipline in U.S. Army units. The lawsuit was stalled for six years by delaying tactics on the part of the defense and was finally settled out of court in 1980. However, one of the pronouncements of the court, had it been held in effect, would have had widespread implications for U.S. intelligence operations overseas. In it, a federal district court judge held that U.S. electronic surveillance of American civilians overseas must be subject to the Fourth Amendment.

References

Oseth, John M. *Regulating U.S. Intelligence Operations: A Study in the Definition of the National Interest.* Frankfurt: University of Kentucky Press, 1985.

—**BETWEEN THE LINES ENTRY,** a term used in counterintelligence, counterespionage, and counterinsurgency in the context of automatic data system security, refers to a situation in which a penetrator of an ADP system who has tapped into the communications lines waits until a legitimate user is finished but has not signed off the computer. The penetrator then seizes control of the lines and acts like a legitimate user.

References

Blackburn, N. Glenn. "Computers: A Counterintelligence Concern." Unpublished paper provided to the editors. Washington, DC, 1987.

—**BIAS,** a baud-based system term used in communications intelligence, communications security, operations security, and signals analysis, is a distortion characteristic that results in the lengthening of the mark elements and a corresponding shortening of the space elements, or vice versa. *See also:* Mark Bias.

References

Laqueur, Walter. *A World of Secrets.* New York: Basic Books, 1985.

—**BIGOT LIST,** a term used in clandestine and covert intelligence operations, is a highly restricted list of persons who have access to a particular and highly sensitive type of information. "Bigot" is intended to mean narrow, and the list is intended to maintain tight control of the circulation of documents and to insure that everyone reading them has a genuine "need to know." *See also:* Access, Authorized, Classification, Classified Information, Code Word, Compromise, Declassification, Disclosure, Downgrade, Freedom of Information Act, Limited Access Area, Need-to-Know, Need-to-Know Principle, No-Lone Zone, Nondisclosure Agreement, Nondiscussion Area, Sanitization, Sanitize, Sanitized Area, Security Certification, Security Classification, Sensitive Compartmented Information, Sensitive Compartmented Information Facility, Two-Person Control.

References

Becket, Henry S. A. *The Dictionary of Espionage: Spookspeak into English.* New York: Stein and Day, 1986.

Quirk, John; Phillips, David; Cline, Ray; and Pforzheimer, Walter. *The Central Intelligence Agency: A Photographic History.* Guilford, CT: Foreign Intelligence Press, 1986.

Turner, Stansfield. *Secrecy and Democracy: The CIA in Transition.* Boston: Houghton Mifflin, 1985.

U.S. Congress. Senate. *Final Report of the Senate Select Committee to Study Government Operations*

with Respect to Intelligence Activities. Report 94-755. Book I, Foreign and Military Intelligence. Washington, DC: GPO, 1976.

—**BILLET** is a job. It is the way the federal government defines its workload and determines the numbers of people that it needs. The justification of a billet is made in terms of work hours and the responsibilities assigned. When a billet is approved, a person can be hired to do the job. In intelligence security, the federal billet structure, is used as a basis for determining whether an individual needs access to sensitive compartmented information. By examining the duties of the billet, a determination can be made concerning the need for access to certain types of information. Once formal approval has been granted that recognizes the necessity of the holder of the billet (the incumbent, in governmental parlance) to have access to a type of information, then the agency can request permission to indoctrinate the incumbent. At that point, assuming that a background investigation has been made on the employee, the employee's file is reviewed and a determination is made concerning granting him or her access to the information. If the determination is positive, the individual is indoctrinated and granted access to the information. Finally, if the individual is moved out of the billet for any reason (transfer, promotion, etc.), he or she is no longer eligible for access, because the need for such access was determined by the duties of the billet. In this case, the individual is either moved administratively to another approved billet or is debriefed and is no longer allowed access to the information. The system is an excellent one because, by emphasizing the billet, the number of people granted access is restricted, and those who do not have a need to know are excluded. Additionally, on a psychological plane, the individual does not feel hurt, because the judgment concerning denial of access is not made against him or her; instead, it is made against the billet he or she is occupying. Thus the individual has less cause to think that he or she is the object of discrimination.

A **billet realignment** is a means of keeping an existing sensitive compartmented information (SCI) billet structure current. Realignment is the administrative transfer of a billet from one element of an organization to another in order to reflect a personnel transfer that has taken place. In this case, there have been no changes in the duties or responsibilities of the individual who holds the position and the billet therefore still requires access to SCI.

A **billet redesignation** is the cancellation of an established sensitive compartmented information (SCI) billet and the creation of a new billet that has different duties and therefore has a different "need to know" requirement. For example, the cancellation of an intelligence analyst billet and the creation of an intelligence supervisor billet would be a billet redesignation.

References

Department of Defense, Defense Intelligence College. *Glossary of Intelligence Terms and Definitions.* Washington, DC: DIC, 1987.

Department of Defense, Joint Chiefs of Staff. *Department of Defense Dictionary of Military and Related Terms.* Washington, DC: GPO, 1986.

Laqueur, Walter. *A World of Secrets.* New York: Basic Books, 1985.

Treverton, Gregory F. *Covert Action: The Limits of Intervention in the Postwar World.* New York: Basic Books, 1987.

Turner, Stansfield. *Secrecy and Democracy: The CIA in Transition.* Boston: Houghton Mifflin, 1985.

—**BI-MODAL** is a statistical or quantitative methodological term that is often used in intelligence analysis. A bi-modal frequency distribution is one that has two or more score values or two score classes that have higher frequencies than any other score values or score classes. A bi-modal frequency polygon would thus have two peaks.

References

Blackburn, N. Glenn. "Computers: A Counterintelligence Concern." Unpublished paper provided to the editors. Washington, DC, 1987.

Martin, Paul H. "Communications-Computer Security." *Journal of Electronic Defense* (June 1987).

Muzerall, Joseph V., and Carty, Thomas P. "COMSEC and Its Need for Key Management." *DP&CS* (Spring 1987).

Ware, Willis H. "Information Systems, Security, and Privacy." *EDUCOM Bulletin* (Summer 1984).

—**BIOGRAPHIC LEVERAGE** is a CIA euphemism for blackmail. *See also:* Blackmail.

References

Becket, Henry S. A. *The Dictionary of Espionage: Spookspeak into English.* New York: Stein and Day, 1986.

Deacon, Richard. *Spyclopedia: An Encyclopedia of Spies, Secret Services, Operations, Jargon, and All Subjects Related to the World of Espionage.* London: Macdonald, 1987.

Treverton, Gregory F. *Covert Action: The Limits of Intervention in the Postwar World.* New York: Basic Books, 1987.

—**BIOGRAPHICAL INTELLIGENCE** is a component of strategic intelligence. It involves intelligence that is collected on the views, traits, habits, skills, importance, relationships, health, and curriculum vitae of foreign individuals who are of actual or potential interest to the U.S. government. People are studied collectively under the sociological and political components of strategic intelligence, and to a lesser degree under economic, armed forces, and scientific intelligence. The Defense Intelligence Agency has primary responsibility for producing biographical intelligence on foreign military people, and the CIA maintains biographic files on all other people.

In answering many intelligence problems, the knowledge of people as individuals is a principal means of solution. The background and personal history of the successful leaders of a revolution, for example, may provide the only means of determining, for example, whether a new government will be more or less friendly to the United States than the old. Or if, at a delicate phase of negotiations between two governments, one of the envoys is replaced, the record of the new delegate may provide a valuable key to the probable courses of action of the government concerned. In making such deductions, the knowledge of the background and associations of the individuals involved is the essential contribution of biographic intelligence.

Biographic intelligence is not limited to monitoring individuals who are prominent. Many problems can often be solved with a knowledge of persons who are in themselves obscure. For example, a subversive organization often cannot be identified as such solely by its announced program or by the identification of individuals who are serving as "fronts" in its directorate. The real key to the nature of the organization may lie in the recognition of certain personnel on the working level who have served in similar capacities in other organizations that are known to be subversive. Another facet of the same problem is found in recognizing the fact that there are many people currently in obscure positions in the political, military, economic, and scientific fields who are destined to advance to positions of leadership. The significance of the elevation to power of one of these individuals could not possibly be assessed unless intelligence of his or her character, training, and experience had already been collected while he or she was an underling.

Extensive dossiers cannot be maintained on more than a small fraction of the approximately three billion people in the world. Selection of those on whom records will be kept must be based on a continuing process of critical search, selection, and elimination. In the case of prominent people, information is often readily available in considerable detail. However, this does not lead intelligence personnel to feel that their mission has been completed because they have copied what has already been reported. A continual effort is made to unearth obscure but important information regarding them, since this may be the key to understanding their personalities and the means by which their reactions to certain situations may be predicted. In the case of obscure individuals, the task of collecting even minimal information will be difficult—not only because they are obscure, but also because their governments may wish to keep them obscure.

The primary collection of biographic information is simplified by the fact that human interest in personalities is universal and intense. A great deal of such collection is done by the press, and much more appears as the by-product of other intelligence activities. However, it has only been through the development of imaginative and painstaking techniques of selection, evaluation, presentation, and exploitation that this information has been made to yield its highest value to strategic intelligence. *See also:* Strategic Intelligence.

References

Clauser, Jerome K., and Weir, Sandra M. *Intelligence Research Methodology.* State College, PA: HRB Singer, 1975.

Department of Defense, Defense Intelligence College. *Glossary of Intelligence Terms and Definitions.* Washington, DC: DIC, 1987.

Department of Defense, Joint Chiefs of Staff. *Department of Defense Dictionary of Military and Related Terms.* Washington, DC: GPO, 1986.

Godson, Roy, ed. *Intelligence Problems for the 1980s, Number 4: Covert Action.* Washington, DC: National Strategy Information Center, 1981.

Kent, Sherman. *Strategic Intelligence for American World Policy*. Princeton, NJ: Princeton University Press, 1966.

Laqueur, Walter. *A World of Secrets*. New York: Basic Books, 1985.

Treverton, Gregory F. *Covert Action: The Limits of Intervention in the Postwar World*. New York: Basic Books, 1987.

Turner, Stansfield. *Secrecy and Democracy: The CIA in Transition*. Boston: Houghton Mifflin, 1985.

—**BIOLOGICAL AGENT,** as defined by the Church Committee, is a microorganism that causes disease in humans, plants, or animals or that causes a deterioration of materiel. **Biological operations**, as defined by the Church Committee, are the employment of biological agents to produce casualties in humans or animals, and damage to plants or materiel; these operations may also mean a defense against such an attack. **Biological warfare**, as defined by the Church Committee, is the use of organisms, toxic biological products, or plant growth regulators to cause death or injury to humans, animals, or plants; it may also be a defense against such action. **Biological weapon**, as defined by the Church Committee, is one that projects, disperses, or disseminates a biological agent.

References

American Bar Association. *Oversight and Accountability of the U.S. Intelligence Agencies: An Evaluation*. Washington, DC: ABA, 1985.

Department of Defense, Joint Chiefs of Staff. *Department of Defense Dictionary of Military and Related Terms*. Washington, DC: GPO, 1986.

Laqueur, Walter. *The Age of Terrorism*. Boston: Little, Brown, 1987.

Maurer, Alfred C.; Turnstall, Marion D.; and Keagle, James M. *Intelligence Policy and Process*. Boulder, CO: Westview Press, 1985.

U.S. Congress. Senate. *Final Report of the Senate Select Committee to Study Government Operations with Respect to Intelligence Activities. Report 94-755. Book I, Foreign and Military Intelligence*. Washington, DC: GPO, 1976.

—**BIT,** a baud-based system term used in communications intelligence, communications security, operations security, and signals analysis, is an abbreviation for binary digit. A bit is a unit of information that is equal to one binary decision, or the designation of one of two possible and equally likely values or states (such as 1 or 0), or anything used to store or convey information.

References

Blackburn, N. Glenn. "Computers: A Counterintelligence Concern." Unpublished paper provided to the editors. Washington, DC, 1987.

Martin, Paul H. "Communications-Computer Security." *Journal of Electronic Defense* (June 1987).

Muzerall, Joseph V., and Carty, Thomas P. "COMSEC and Its Need for Key Management." *DP&CS* (Spring 1987).

Ware, Willis H. "Information Systems, Security, and Privacy." *EDUCOM Bulletin* (Summer 1984).

—**BLACK** is a term used in clandestine and covert intelligence operations to describe the concealment of—rather than cover for—an activity.

References

Department of Defense, Joint Chiefs of Staff. *Department of Defense Dictionary of Military and Related Terms*. Washington, DC: GPO, 1986.

Quirk, John; Phillips, David; Cline, Ray; and Pforzheimer, Walter. *The Central Intelligence Agency: A Photographic History*. Guilford, CT: Foreign Intelligence Press, 1986.

U.S. Congress. Senate. *Final Report of the Senate Select Committee to Study Government Operations with Respect to Intelligence Activities. Report 94-755. Book I, Foreign and Military Intelligence*. Washington, DC: GPO, 1976.

—**BLACK BAG JOB** is a term used in clandestine and covert intelligence operations to describe a surreptitious entry without a warrant. It is usually done in order to search for photographs and other incriminating or valuable documents, rather than to install microphones. *See also:* Agent, Bug, Bugging, Concealment Devices, Lock Studies, Sound Man, Sound School, Special Activities, Surreptitious Entry.

References

Allen, Thomas B., and Polmar, Norman. *Merchants of Treason: America's Secrets for Sale*. New York: Delacorte Press, 1988.

Becket, Henry S. A. *The Dictionary of Espionage: Spookspeak into English*. New York: Stein and Day, 1986.

Deacon, Richard. *Spyclopedia: An Encyclopaedia of Spies, Secret Services, Operations, Jargon, and All Subjects Related to the World of Espionage*. London: Macdonald, 1987.

Laqueur, Walter. *A World of Secrets*. New York: Basic Books, 1985.

Quirk, John; Phillips, David; Cline, Ray; and Pforzheimer, Walter. *The Central Intelligence Agency: A Photographic History*. Guilford, CT: Foreign Intelligence Press, 1986.

Treverton, Gregory F. *Covert Action: The Limits of Intervention in the Postwar World*. New York: Basic Books, 1987.

U.S. Congress. Senate. *Final Report of the Senate Select Committee to Study Government Operations with Respect to Intelligence Activities. Report 94-755. Book I, Foreign and Military Intelligence*. Washington, DC: GPO, 1976.

—**BLACK BAG OPERATION (BLACK OPERATION)** is a CIA term for an illicit operation, such as passing funds to a foreign political party. *See also:* Agent of Influence, Agent Provocateur, Cacklebladder, Confusion Agent, Co-opted Worker, Co-optees, Illegal Operations, Infiltration, Singleton, Snitch Jacket.

References

Becket, Henry S. A. *The Dictionary of Espionage: Spookspeak into English*. New York: Stein and Day, 1986.

Deacon, Richard. *Spyclopedia: An Encyclopedia of Spies, Secret Services, Operations, Jargon, and All Subjects Related to the World of Espionage*. London: Macdonald, 1987.

Turner, Stansfield. *Secrecy and Democracy: The CIA in Transition*. Boston: Houghton Mifflin Co., 1985.

—**BLACK BULK FACILITY,** in communications security (COMSEC), is a telecommunications facility that uses cryptoequipment to protect the multichannel trunks that are passing encrypted or unclassified information.

References

Blackburn, N. Glenn. "Computers: A Counterintelligence Concern." Unpublished paper provided to the editors. Washington, DC, 1987.

Martin, Paul H. "Communications-Computer Security." *Journal of Electronic Defense* (June 1987).

Muzerall, Joseph V., and Carty, Thomas P. "COMSEC and Its Need for Key Management." *DP&CS* (Spring 1987).

Ware, Willis H. "Information Systems, Security, and Privacy." *EDUCOM Bulletin* (Summer 1984).

—**BLACK DESIGNATION,** in communications security (COMSEC), is a designation applied to all telecommunications circuits, components, equipment, and systems that handle only encrypted or unclassified signals. It is also applied to telecommunications areas in which no classified signals occur.

References

Turner, Stansfield. *Secrecy and Democracy: The CIA in Transition*. Boston: Houghton Mifflin, 1985.

—**BLACK FORCES** is an intelligence term used to denote those units representing Warsaw Pact forces participating in military exercises.

References

Department of Defense, Joint Chiefs of Staff. *Department of Defense Dictionary of Military and Related Terms*. Washington, DC: GPO, 1986.

—**BLACK LIST,** as defined by the Church Committee, is an official counterintelligence listing of actual or potential hostile collaborators, sympathizers, intelligence suspects, and other persons who are viewed as threatening to the security of friendly military forces.

References

Department of Defense, Joint Chiefs of Staff. *Department of Defense Dictionary of Military and Related Terms*. Washington, DC: GPO, 1986.

Treverton, Gregory F. *Covert Action: The Limits of Intervention in the Postwar World*. New York: Basic Books, 1987.

U.S. Congress. Senate. *Final Report of the Senate Select Committee to Study Government Operations with Respect to Intelligence Activities. Report 94-755. Book I, Foreign and Military Intelligence*. Washington, DC: GPO, 1976.

—**BLACK PROGRAM** is a generic intelligence term for a special access program, the very existence and purpose of which may be classified. "Black program" is a term that has no official status in any Department of Defense policy or regulation. It is an expression that is used colloquially by some defense analysts to mean all programs for which funding figures are classified at some level. *See also:* Special Activities.

References

Clancy, Tom. *The Cardinal of the Kremlin*. New York: Putnam, 1988.

Laqueur, Walter. *A World of Secrets.* New York: Basic Books, 1985.

Maroni, Alice C. *Special Access Programs: Understanding the "Black Budget."* Washington, DC: Foreign Affairs and National Defense Division, Congressional Research Service, Library of Congress, 1987.

—**BLACK PROPAGANDA,** is a term used in clandestine and covert intelligence operations. Black propaganda results when the source of the propaganda is shielded or misrepresented so that it cannot be attributed to him. If no source is given, then it is called gray propaganda. As defined by the Church Committee, black propaganda is that which purports to emanate from a source other than the true one. *See also:* Gray Propaganda, White Propaganda.

References

Becket, Henry S. A. *The Dictionary of Espionage: Spookspeak into English.* New York: Stein and Day, 1986.

Department of Defense, Joint Chiefs of Staff. *Department of Defense Dictionary of Military and Related Terms.* Washington, DC: GPO, 1986.

Godson, Roy, ed. *Intelligence Problems for the 1980s, Number 4: Covert Action.* Washington, DC: National Strategy Information Center, 1981.

Quirk, John; Phillips, David; Cline, Ray; and Pforzheimer, Walter. *The Central Intelligence Agency: A Photographic History.* Guilford, CT: Foreign Intelligence Press, 1986.

Treverton, Gregory F. *Covert Action: The Limits of Intervention in the Postwar World.* New York: Basic Books, 1987.

U.S. Congress. Senate. *Final Report of the Senate Select Committee to Study Government Operations with Respect to Intelligence Activities. Report 94-755. Book I, Foreign and Military Intelligence.* Washington, DC: GPO, 1976.

—**BLACK SIGNAL** is an Air Force intelligence term meaning an encrypted or secure emission. *See also:* Communications Security, Decryption, Encryption.

References

Blackburn, N. Glenn. "Computers: A Counterintelligence Concern." Unpublished paper provided to the editors. Washington, DC, 1987.

Department of Defense, Defense Intelligence College. *Glossary of Intelligence Terms and Definitions.* Washington, DC: DIC, 1987.

Martin, Paul H. "Communications-Computer Security." *Journal of Electronic Defense* (June 1987).

—**BLACK TRAINEE** is the CIA nickname given to a foreigner who is recruited for CIA undercover training and is trained at the CIA "farm" (Camp Peary) in Virginia. At one time, according to Richard Deacon, these trainees were not supposed to know that they were even in the United States.

References

Deacon, Richard. *Spyclopedia: An Encyclopedia of Spies, Secret Services, Operations, Jargon, and All Subjects Related to the World of Espionage.* London: Macdonald, 1987.

—**BLACKMAIL** is a term used in clandestine and covert intelligence operations to describe the use of derogatory information to force a person to work for an intelligence service. *See also:* Biographic Leverage.

References

American Bar Association. *Oversight and Accountability of the U.S. Intelligence Agencies: An Evaluation.* Washington, DC: ABA, 1985.

Maurer, Alfred C.; Turnstall, Marion D.; and Keagle, James M. *Intelligence Policy and Process.* Boulder, CO: Westview Press, 1985.

Treverton, Gregory F. *Covert Action: The Limits of Intervention in the Postwar World.* New York: Basic Books, 1987.

U.S. Congress. Senate. *Final Report of the Senate Select Committee to Study Government Operations with Respect to Intelligence Activities. Report 94-755. Book I, Foreign and Military Intelligence.* Washington, DC: GPO, 1976.

—**BLAKE, LIEUTENANT GENERAL GORDON A., U.S. AIR FORCE,** served as the director of the National Security Agency from June 30, 1962, until June 1, 1965. Before this assignment, he had served as commander of the Army Airways Communications System in World War II and as director of Air Force Communications from 1953 to 1957. In 1957 he had been appointed commander of the U.S. Air Force Security Service, NSA's air arm.

References

Bamford, James. *The Puzzle Palace: A Report on America's Most Secret Agency.* New York: Penguin Books, 1983.

—**BLAKE, JOHN F.,** served as deputy director of Central Intelligence from July 31, 1977, until February 10, 1978.

References

Turner, Stansfield. *Secrecy and Democracy: The CIA in Transition*. Boston: Houghton Mifflin, 1985.

—**BLANK PASS** is a baud-based system term used in communications intelligence, communications security, operations security, and signals analysis. It is the automatic insertion of a blank by the transmitting equipment that compensates for the difference in speed between the equipment and the intelligence being presented to it.

References

Blackburn, N. Glenn. "Computers: A Counterintelligence Concern." Unpublished paper provided to the editors. Washington, DC, 1987.

Martin, Paul H. "Communications-Computer Security." *Journal of Electronic Defense* (June 1987).

Muzerall, Joseph V., and Carty, Thomas P. "COMSEC and Its Need for Key Management." *DP&CS* (Spring 1987).

Ware, Willis H. "Information Systems, Security, and Privacy." *EDUCOM Bulletin* (Summer 1984).

—**BLANKET PURCHASE AGREEMENTS (BPA).** See: Defense Intelligence Agency.

—**BLEEP BOX** is a term used in clandestine and covert intelligence operations to describe a mechanism used by agents for telephone tapping and for placing telephone calls anywhere in the world without paying.

References

Deacon, Richard. *Spyclopedia: An Encyclopedia of Spies, Secret Services, Operations, Jargon, and All Subjects Related to the World of Espionage*. London: Macdonald, 1987.

—**BLIND DATING** is a term used in clandestine and covert intelligence operations to describe a situation in which an intelligence officer agrees to meet someone at a place chosen by that person. The greatest risk is that the intelligence officer will be kidnapped, and therefore the recommended procedure is that the first meeting be held in a public place so that neither party is jeopardized.

References

Becket, Henry S. A. *The Dictionary of Espionage: Spookspeak into English*. New York: Stein and Day, 1986.

—**BLIND MEMORANDUM** is a memorandum written on stationery that does not have a letterhead, a signature, or any indication of where the information came from. Intelligence agencies often use blind memoranda to keep informal records, since individual responsibility cannot be assigned. Additionally, these can be easily destroyed in case of an investigation because they have not been given a control number and are not accountable.

References

Becket, Henry S. A. *The Dictionary of Espionage: Spookspeak into English*. New York: Stein and Day, 1986.

—**BLOW** is a term used in clandestine and covert intelligence operations. It means to expose, usually unintentionally, the personnel, installations, or other aspects of a clandestine organization or activity. *See also:* Agent, Agent Authentication, Agent in Place, Agent Net, Agent of Influence, Agent Provocateur, Blown Agent, Burn, Burnt, Confusion Agent, Dispatched Agent, Double Agent, Handling Agent, Illegal Agent, Informant, Inside Man, Pocket Litter, Provocation Agent, Pseudonym, Putting in the Plumbing, Recruitment, Recruitment in Place, Special Activities, Walk-In.

References

Department of Defense, Joint Chiefs of Staff. *Department of Defense Dictionary of Military and Related Terms*. Washington, DC: GPO, 1986.

Quirk, John; Phillips, David; Cline, Ray; and Pforzheimer, Walter. *The Central Intelligence Agency: A Photographic History*. Guilford, CT: Foreign Intelligence Press, 1986.

U.S. Congress. Senate. *Final Report of the Senate Select Committee to Study Government Operations with Respect to Intelligence Activities. Report 94-755. Book I, Foreign and Military Intelligence*. Washington, DC: GPO, 1976.

—**BLOWN** is a term that is used in clandestine and covert intelligence operations. It means an agent whose cover has been broken or a network of spies that has been infiltrated. *See also:* Blow.

References

Becket, Henry S. A. *The Dictionary of Espionage: Spookspeak into English.* New York: Stein and Day, 1986.

Crawford, David J. *Volunteers: The Betrayal of National Defense Secrets by Air Force Traitors.* Washington, DC: GPO, 1988.

Deacon, Richard. *Spyclopedia: An Encyclopedia of Spies, Secret Services, Operations, Jargon, and All Subjects Related to the World of Espionage.* London: Macdonald, 1987.

—**BLOWN AGENT** is a term that is used in clandestine and covert intelligence operations to describe an agent whose identity has been revealed to the enemy. *See also:* Blow.

References

Allen, Thomas B., and Polmar, Norman. *Merchants of Treason: America's Secrets for Sale.* New York: Delacorte Press, 1988.

Becket, Henry S. A. *The Dictionary of Espionage: Spookspeak into English.* New York: Stein and Day, 1986.

Crawford, David J. *Volunteers: The Betrayal of National Defense Secrets by Air Force Traitors.* Washington, DC: GPO, 1988.

Kessler, Ronald. *Spy vs. Spy: Stalking Soviet Spies in America.* New York: Charles Scribner's Sons, 1988.

—**BOARD OF ANALYSTS** was a group composed of seven senior analysts in the Office of the Coordinator of Information (COI). Created by the American attorney William Donovan during World War II, the COI was a forerunner of the senior intelligence estimative groups. *See also:* Central Intelligence Agency; Coordinator of Information; Donovan, William; Executive Orders on Intelligence.

References

Corson, William R. *The Armies of Ignorance: The Rise of the American Intelligence Empire.* New York: Dial Press, 1977.

Laqueur, Walter. *A World of Secrets.* New York: Basic Books, 1985.

Lowenthal, Mark M. *U.S. Intelligence: Evolution and Anatomy.* New York: Praeger, 1984.

—**BOARD OF NATIONAL ESTIMATES (BNE)** was established in 1950 by Director of Central Intelligence Walter Bedell Smith, and its members were responsible for reviewing National Intelligence Estimates for the director of Central Intelligence. The BNE was dissolved in 1973. *See also:* National Intelligence Estimates.

References

American Bar Association. *Oversight and Accountability of the U.S. Intelligence Agencies: An Evaluation.* Washington, DC: ABA, 1985.

Laqueur, Walter. *A World of Secrets.* New York: Basic Books, 1985.

Lowenthal, Mark M. *U.S. Intelligence: Evolution and Anatomy.* New York: Praeger, 1984.

Maurer, Alfred C.; Turnstall, Marion D.; and Keagle, James M. *Intelligence Policy and Process.* Boulder, CO: Westview Press, 1985.

Treverton, Gregory F. *Covert Action: The Limits of Intervention in the Postwar World.* New York: Basic Books, 1987.

U.S. Congress. Senate. *Final Report of the Senate Select Committee to Study Government Operations with Respect to Intelligence Activities. Report 94-755. Book I, Foreign and Military Intelligence.* Washington, DC: GPO, 1976.

—**BOECKENHAUPT, HERBERT,** was a communications specialist and crypto-repairman assigned to the 33rd Communications Squadron, March Air Force Base, California. He was observed meeting with a Soviet secret service (GRU) agent on two occasions, and he was apprehended on October 24, 1966, in Riverside, California. The subsequent investigation revealed that he had passed a significant amount of classified information, including reports and photographs of reports and documents, from October 1962 until July 1963, while he was stationed at Sidi Slimane, Morocco. In return, the Soviets paid him less than $12,000. Although the evidence is inconclusive, it appears that Boeckenhaupt continued to provide information to the Soviets until his apprehension. At his trial, he claimed that immaturity and his frustration with not having been promoted were the reasons for his betrayal. He admitted to having given signal books, maps, instruments, sketches, and photographs to the Soviets. He received a 30-year sentence for his crimes.

References

Allen, Thomas B., and Polmar, Norman. *Merchants of Treason: America's Secrets for Sale.* New York: Delacorte Press, 1988.

Crawford, David J. *Volunteers: The Betrayal of National Defense Secrets by Air Force Traitors.* Washington, DC: GPO, 1988.

—**BOGIE** is a term used in clandestine and covert intelligence operations to describe a visitor whose identity is unknown.

References

Kessler, Ronald. *Spy vs. Spy: Stalking Soviet Spies in America.* New York: Charles Scribner's Sons, 1988.

—**BOGUS MESSAGE,** in Communications Security (COMSEC), is a message sent for some purpose other than for its content; it may consist of dummy groups of material or meaningless text.

References

Blackburn, N. Glenn. "Computers: A Counterintelligence Concern." Unpublished paper provided to the editors. Washington, DC, 1987.

Martin, Paul H. "Communications-Computer Security." *Journal of Electronic Defense* (June 1987).

Muzerall, Joseph V., and Carty, Thomas P. "COMSEC and Its Need for Key Management." *DP&CS* (Spring 1987).

Ware, Willis H. "Information Systems, Security, and Privacy." *EDUCOM Bulletin* (Summer 1984).

—**BOLAND AMENDMENT.** The Boland Amendment was attached to the appropriations bill for 1983, and it restricted severely the Executive freedom of action in Central America. It stated: "None of the funds provided in this Act may be used by the Central Intelligence Agency or the Department of Defense to furnish military equipment, military training or advice, or other support for military activities, to any group or individual, not part of a country's armed forces, for the purpose of overthrowing the Government of Nicaragua or provoking a military exchange between Nicaragua and Honduras."

The significance of the amendment was that it was another assertion by Congress that it would play a significant role in U.S. foreign policy. The restrictions of the Boland Amendment were a catalyst for the Iran-Contra operation, for example, in that this was an attempt to circumvent Boland and actively influence events in Latin America. *See also:* Congressional Oversight.

References

American Bar Association. *Oversight and Accountability of the U.S. Intelligence Agencies: An Evaluation.* Washington, DC: ABA, 1985.

Maurer, Alfred C.; Turnstall, Marion D.; and Keagle, James M. *Intelligence Policy and Process.* Boulder, CO: Westview Press, 1985.

Treverton, Gregory F. *Covert Action: The Limits of Intervention in the Postwar World.* New York: Basic Books, 1987.

Turner, Stansfield. *Secrecy and Democracy: The CIA in Transition.* Boston: Houghton Mifflin, 1985.

—**BOMBER INTELLIGENCE** is a term used in counterintelligence, counterespionage, and counterinsurgency to describe information that is used to defeat hostile foreign intelligence activities and to protect information from espionage, people from subversion, and installations or materiel from sabotage.

References

Kent, Sherman. *Strategic Intelligence for American World Policy.* Princeton, NJ: Princeton University Press, 1966.

—**BONAFIDES** are documents, information, or actions that are offered by someone to demonstrate his good faith, identity, dependability, honesty, or motivation. *See also:* Agent, Agent Authentication, Agent in Place, Agent Net, Agent of Influence, Agent Provocateur, Alias, Establishing Bonafides, Penetration, Penetration Aids, Pocket Litter, Special Activities.

References

Allen, Thomas B., and Polmar, Norman. *Merchants of Treason: America's Secrets for Sale.* New York: Delacorte Press, 1988.

Becket, Henry S. A. *The Dictionary of Espionage: Spookspeak into English.* New York: Stein and Day, 1986.

Deacon, Richard. *Spyclopedia: An Encyclopedia of Spies, Secret Services, Operations, Jargon, and All Subjects Related to the World of Espionage.* London: Macdonald, 1987.

Kessler, Ronald. *Spy vs. Spy: Stalking Soviet Spies in America.* New York: Charles Scribner's Sons, 1988.

Turner, Stansfield. *Secrecy and Democracy: The CIA in Transition.* Boston: Houghton Mifflin, 1985.

—**BORDER CROSSERS,** a term used in clandestine and covert intelligence operations, has two meanings. (1) Boarder crossers are people who live close to a frontier and have to cross it frequently for legitimate reasons. (2) In clandestine terminology, a border crosser is also an agent who attempts to cross the border into an enemy nation covertly with the intention of collecting and transmitting or sending information back to friendly forces.

References

Becket, Henry S. A. *The Dictionary of Espionage: Spookspeak into English.* New York: Stein and Day, 1986.

Department of Defense, Joint Chiefs of Staff. *Department of Defense Dictionary of Military and Related Terms.* Washington, DC: GPO, 1986.

U.S. Congress. Senate. *Final Report of the Senate Select Committee to Study Government Operations with Respect to Intelligence Activities. Report 94-755. Book I, Foreign and Military Intelligence.* Washington, DC: GPO, 1976.

—**BORGER, HAROLD NOAH,** was sentenced by a German court to serve 30 months in prison for attempting to obtain classified U.S. defense information for the East German intelligence service.

References

Crawford, David J. *Volunteers: The Betrayal of National Defense Secrets by Air Force Traitors.* Washington, DC: GPO, 1988.

—**BOXER AMENDMENT** to the Fiscal Year 1988 Defense Authorization Bill (adopted by the House of Representatives as Sec. 807) was incorporated into the final version of the Fiscal Year 1988-89 National Defense Authorization Act. That act required the secretary of defense to provide the chairmen and ranking minority members of the four key defense committees with a report on all existing special access programs, to be followed in subsequent years with annual notice and justification for new special access programs.

References

Maroni, Alice C. *Special Access Programs: Understanding the "Black Budget."* Washington, DC: Foreign Affairs and National Defense Division, Congressional Research Service, Library of Congress, 1987.

—**BOYCE, CHRISTOPHER,** sold secrets to the Soviet Union while employed by a company that was under contract with the CIA. Boyce and his partner, Andrew D. Lee, were arrested in 1977. Boyce was tried, convicted, and sentenced to 40 years in prison.

References

Allen, Thomas B., and Polmar, Norman. *Merchants of Treason: America's Secrets for Sale.* New York: Delacorte Press, 1988.

Deacon, Richard. *Spyclopedia: An Encyclopedia of Spies, Secret Services, Operations, Jargon, and All Subjects Related to the World of Espionage.* London: Macdonald, 1987.

Godson, Roy, ed. *Intelligence Problems for the 1980s, Number 3: Counterintelligence.* Washington, DC: National Strategy Information Center, 1980.

————. *Intelligence Problems for the 1980s, Number 5: Clandestine Collection.* Washington, DC: National Strategy Information Center, 1982.

Lefever, Ernest W., and Godson, Roy. *The CIA and the American Ethic: An Unfinished Debate.* Washington, DC: Ethics and Public Policy Center, Georgetown University, 1979.

Turner, Stansfield. *Secrecy and Democracy: The CIA in Transition.* Boston: Houghton Mifflin, 1985.

—**BRACEY, ARNOLD,** while a Marine Corps guard at the U.S. Embassy in Moscow, was implicated with Sergeant Clayton J. Lonetree on suspicion of espionage. Charges against Bracey were dismissed on June 12, 1987.

References

Allen, Thomas B., and Polmar, Norman. *Merchants of Treason: America's Secrets for Sale.* New York: Delacorte Press, 1988.

Becket, Henry S. A. *The Dictionary of Espionage: Spookspeak into English.* New York: Stein and Day, 1986.

Deacon, Richard. *Spyclopedia: An Encyclopedia of Spies, Secret Services, Operations, Jargon, and All Subjects Related to the World of Espionage.* London: Macdonald, 1987.

—**BREVITY CODE/BREVITY LIST,** in communications security (COMSEC), is a code that is used solely for the purpose of shortening the length of a message, rather than to conceal the message's content.

References

Cline, Ray S. *The CIA Under Reagan, Bush, and Casey.* Washington, DC: Acropolis Books, 1981.

—**BRIEFING,** in FBI parlance, is the preparation of an individual for a specific operation by describing the entire scenario, including the situation that will be encountered, the methods to be employed, and the mission, purpose, and objective of the operation. A briefing is usually given orally, with the necessary graphics. A briefing can also be a specific lecture in which an individual or individuals are informed about the particulars of an event, or it can be a lecture that is planned beforehand and delivered at scheduled intervals in order to inform an individual or individuals of the relevant events that have occurred since the last briefing.

References

Kessler, Ronald. *Spy vs. Spy: Stalking Soviet Spies in America.* New York: Charles Scribner's Sons, 1988.

Laqueur, Walter. *A World of Secrets.* New York: Basic Books, 1985.

Turner, Stansfield. *Secrecy and Democracy: The CIA in Transition.* Boston: Houghton Mifflin, 1985.

—**BROWNELL COMMITTEE.** In the early postwar years, although the nascent signals intelligence (SIGINT) community had great potential, it was a fragmented composition of contending members in which interservice military rivalry was the order of the day. As a result of his dissatisfaction concerning SIGINT's performance at the outbreak of the Korean War, President Truman appointed George A. Brownell to head a committee to investigate the SIGINT situation and make recommendations. Brownell's report firmly and correctly criticized the military services and the Joint Chiefs of Staff. After considering several proposals, the Brownell Committee recommended that the secretary of defense be made the executive agent for communications intelligence, that the Armed Forces Security Agency Council (AFSAC) be abolished, and that the director of Armed Forces Security Agency (AFSA) be given far greater authority. The military services would be allowed to retain their service SIGINT organizations within the greater organizational framework. Truman accepted the committee's recommendations with only one major exception, that the name of the organization be changed to the National Security Agency.

References

Bamford, James. *The Puzzle Palace: A Report on America's Most Secret Agency.* New York: Penguin Books, 1983.

—**BROWSING** is a counterintelligence term used in the context of automatic data processing system (ADPS) security and refers to an incident where a legitimate system user attempts to gain access to classified files for which the individual has no authorization. For example, an individual who has a CONFIDENTIAL security clearance browses through the system until he or she gains entry to a SECRET file.

References

Blackburn, N. Glenn. "Computers: A Counterintelligence Concern." Unpublished paper provided to the editors. Washington, DC, 1987.

—**BRUSH CONTACT,** in FBI terminology, is a brief, discreet meeting between intelligence officers in order to pass information or documents. It is also called a brief encounter or brush pass. *See also:* Agent, Alternate Meet, Go-Away, Live Letter Boxes, Live Letter Drops, Pavement Artists, Shadow, Shaking off the Dogs, Surveillance, Walk-Past.

References

Clancy, Tom. *The Cardinal of the Kremlin.* New York: Putnam, 1988.

Kessler, Ronald. *Spy vs. Spy: Stalking Soviet Spies in America.* New York: Charles Scribner's Sons, 1988.

—**BRUTE FORCE JAMMING** is a term used in electronic warfare (EW) operations to describe jamming or blocking radio signals with high power, either with a single high-powered transmitter or by cascading large numbers of jammers so that the enemy cannot receive radio signals. *See also:* Jammer.

References

Blackburn, N. Glenn. "Computers: A Counterintelligence Concern." Unpublished paper provided to the editors. Washington, DC, 1987.

Martin, Paul H. "Communications-Computer Security." *Journal of Electronic Defense* (June 1987).

Muzerall, Joseph V., and Carty, Thomas P. "COMSEC and Its Need for Key Management." *DP&CS* (Spring 1987).

Ware, Willis H. "Information Systems, Security, and Privacy." *EDUCOM Bulletin* (Summer 1984).

—**BUCHANAN, EDWARD OWEN,** was court-martialed and found guilty on August 26, 1985, of attempting to commit espionage; he was sentenced to prison for 30 months and a dishonorable discharge from the Air Force. Buchanan had attempted repeatedly to contact the East German and Soviet embassies with offers to provide them with classified information. He was finally intercepted and arrested by Air Force counterintelligence agents posing as Soviet agents.

References

Crawford, David J. *Volunteers: The Betrayal of National Defense Secrets by Air Force Traitors.* Washington, DC: GPO, 1988.

—**BUDGET** is a general intelligence term for a proposed plan by an organization for a specified period of time that reflects the anticipated resources and estimates how they will be spent in the pursuit of the organization's objectives. *See also:* Defense Guidance, Five-Year Defense Program; National Defense Expenditures; National Intelligence Projections for Planning (NIPP); Office of Management and Budget (OMB).

References

American Bar Association. *Oversight and Accountability of the U.S. Intelligence Agencies: An Evaluation.* Washington, DC: ABA, 1985.

Laqueur, Walter. *A World of Secrets.* New York: Basic Books, 1985.

Lefever, Ernest W., and Godson, Roy. *The CIA and the American Ethic: An Unfinished Debate.* Washington, DC: Ethics and Public Policy Center, Georgetown University, 1979.

Maurer, Alfred C.; Turnstall, Marion D.; and Keagle, James M. *Intelligence Policy and Process.* Boulder, CO: Westview Press, 1985.

Pickett, George. "Congress, the Budget and Intelligence." In *Intelligence Policy and Process,* edited by Alfred C. Maurer, Marion D. Turnstall, and James M. Keagle. Boulder, CO: Westview Press, 1985.

Treverton, Gregory F. *Covert Action: The Limits of Intervention in the Postwar World.* New York: Basic Books, 1987.

Turner, Stansfield. *Secrecy and Democracy: The CIA in Transition.* Boston: Houghton Mifflin, 1985.

—**BUDGET ACTIVITY,** an intelligence budgeting term, is a function or activity that is funded under an appropriation category in the budget. *See also:* Budget.

—**BUDGET AUTHORITY** is a general intelligence term for the authority provided by Congress, mainly in the form of appropriations, that allows the federal agencies to incur obligations. Budget authority is composed of New Obligational Authority (NOA), plus loan authority (which is authority to incur obligations for loans). *See also:* Budget.

—**BUDGET CYCLE,** a general intelligence term, is the time necessary to formulate, review, present, and secure approval of the fiscal program. *See also:* Budget.

—**BUDGET ESTIMATE SUBMISSION** is a general intelligence term for a revision of the costs of the Program Objective Memorandum (POM) as modified by the Program Decision Memorandum (PDM). Such adjustments, including Congressional actions that have an impact on the POM and PDM positions, are made in accordance with the direction of the Office of the Secretary of Defense. *See also:* Budget, Program Decision Memorandum (PDM), Program Objective Memorandum (POM).

—**BUDGET YEAR** is the fiscal year that is covered by the budget estimate. A budget year begins on October 1 and ends September 30 of the following year. It is used by the federal government for accounting purposes. *See also:* Budget.

—**BUDGETING,** for purposes of the Planning, Programming, and Budgeting System (PPBS), is the process of determining a short-range, detailed allocation of resources in order to execute or complete an organization's assigned missions. *See also:* Budget.

—**BUFFHAM, BENSON K.,** served as deputy director of the National Security Agency from April 21, 1974, to May 1, 1975.

References

Bamford, James. *The Puzzle Palace: A Report on America's Most Secret Agency.* New York: Penguin Books, 1983.

—**BUG** is a term used in clandestine and covert intelligence operations and has several meanings. (1) A bug is a microphone, concealed listening device, or audio surveillance device that can be used to eavesdrop. (2) To bug means to install such a device in order to overhear a subject's conversations. *See also:* Bugging, Electronic Surveillance.

References

Clancy, Tom. *The Cardinal of the Kremlin.* New York: Putnam, 1988.

Department of Defense, Joint Chiefs of Staff. *Department of Defense Dictionary of Military and Related Terms.* Washington, DC: GPO, 1986.

Quirk, John; Phillips, David; Cline, Ray; and Pforzheimer, Walter. *The Central Intelligence Agency: A Photographic History.* Guilford, CT: Foreign Intelligence Press.

Turner, Stansfield. *Secrecy and Democracy: The CIA in Transition.* Boston: Houghton Mifflin, 1985.

U.S. Congress. Senate. *Final Report of the Senate Select Committee to Study Government Operations with Respect to Intelligence Activities. Report 94-755. Book I, Foreign and Military Intelligence.* Washington, DC: GPO, 1976.

—**BUGGING** is a term used in clandestine and covert intelligence operations to describe the entire spectrum of eavesdropping, from telephone taps to electronic surveillance devices.

References

Clancy, Tom. *The Cardinal of the Kremlin.* New York: Putnam, 1988.

Deacon, Richard. *Spyclopedia: An Encyclopedia of Spies, Secret Services, Operations, Jargon, and All Subjects Related to the World of Espionage.* London: Macdonald, 1987.

Department of Defense, Joint Chiefs of Staff. *Department of Defense Dictionary of Military and Related Terms.* Washington, DC: GPO, 1986.

Quirk, John; Phillips, David; Cline, Ray; and Pzorzheimer, Walter. *The Central Intelligence Agency: A Photographic History.* Guilford, CT: Foreign Intelligence Press.

Treverton, Gregory F. *Covert Action: The Limits of Intervention in the Postwar World.* New York: Basic Books, 1987.

Turner, Stansfield. *Secrecy and Democracy: The CIA in Transition.* Boston: Houghton Mifflin, 1985.

U.S. Congress. Senate. *Final Report of the Senate Select Committee to Study Government Operations with Respect to Intelligence Activities. Report 94-755. Book I, Foreign and Military Intelligence.* Washington, DC: GPO, 1976.

—**BUREAU OF INTELLIGENCE AND RESEARCH (INR), DEPARTMENT OF STATE.**

Mission

The INR has two primary responsibilities: (1) to provide raw and finished intelligence to the Department of State (DoS) from the Intelligence Community, to produce finished intelligence of its own for the DoS, and to participate in writing community-wide assessments and estimates; and (2) to coordinate U.S. intelligence activities for the DoS to insure that they support U.S. policy interests.

In the intelligence field, the focus is on timely, policy-oriented research. Through close working relationships with other officials in the DoS—beginning with the secretary, deputy secretary, and under secretaries and reaching out to all subordinate levels—the INR is continuously aware of the key problems facing policy officials and adjusts its work priorities accordingly.

In the coordination field, the INR is in liaison with the Central Intelligence Agency (CIA), the Defense Intelligence Agency (DIA), the Federal Bureau of Investigation (FBI), and other members of the Intelligence Community. It represents the DoS on the National Foreign Intelligence Board (NFIB), the National Foreign Intelligence Council (NFIC), and the committees of the director of Central Intelligence that work on programs, priorities, and substantive problems in intelligence collection and analysis. The INR also prepares the DoS's senior officers for meetings of the National Security Council's committees.

Thus, the INR is the organization specifically designed within the DoS to supply intelligence information to policy needs, to provide a professional intelligence analytical perspective of developments abroad, and to insure that the DoS both benefits from and contributes to the Intelligence Community. It differs from many other parts of the Community in that it has no field representatives to collect intelligence. Rather, for its daily briefing papers, special analyses, and other studies, the INR uses information gathered by the Foreign Service, CIA, Department of Defense intelligence components, FBI, and Foreign Broadcast Information Service, as well as information available in scholarly publications and in the press. Although INR papers are sent to other agencies represented on the National Security Council (NSC) and to the NSC staff, its output is geared to the specific needs and responsibilities of the secretary of state and the secretary's principal assistants.

Contributions

The INR makes three contributions to the foreign policy process. First, it receives information from all parts of the world and systematically selects and analyzes relevant material. Because of its size and organization, the INR is capable of expeditiously processing geographical and functional information that is relevant to current foreign policy questions.

The INR provides input into the DoS's position concerning foreign policy issues and trends. This means that there is an overlap between the INR and other bureaus, which also, within their fields of responsibility, process and analyze information. This overlap is deliberate and forms the basis for the second major INR contribution.

In the tradition of checks and balances, the DoS needed an alternative producer of information and interpretation that paralleled the historic sources in the geographic and functional bureaus—a source whose view, conditioned by the particular qualities of analytical work, would complement and on occasion differ from the positions and opinions of bureaus whose central focus was the formulation of policy. Secretary of State George Marshall, who developed the framework for the INR's organization, deliberately allowed for the development of an independent INR position, and subsequent secretaries have endorsed Marshall's position.

The demand in the DoS for INR products shows that most officers find it useful to check their positions against a viewpoint arrived at in an organization separate enough to render an independent judgement but close enough to appreciate their problems. The outer limits of the INR's activity in this field are marked by the tradition that, although the INR may assess the prospective consequences of alternative U.S. policies, it does not itself formulate or recommend foreign policy in the way that the other bureaus do, nor does it design courses of action.

Finally, the INR concentrates in a single unit the staff work necessary to assist the DoS in its relations with the Intelligence Community and all of the latter's complex technological and operational processes. It is a two-way street. The INR, through ramified connections with the agencies that make up the Community, insures that the DoS receives all of the relevant information that these agencies collect and produce. Equally important, the INR acts to fulfill the DoS's obligations toward the Community agencies.

Bureau Organization

The INR is headed by a Director, who has the rank and authority of an assistant secretary of state, and four deputy assistant secretaries. The director participates in the regular staff meetings conducted by the secretary and the deputy sec-

retary. As the secretary's senior advisor on intelligence matters, the Director is responsible for representing the DoS on the NFIB and on other interagency intelligence groups. The director handles intelligence matters with appropriate elements of the NSC staff and, with the senior INR deputy, leads a staff of about 320 people. (About 200 of these are foreign affairs or intelligence analysis personnel; the rest are clerical, administrative, and other support staff.) The INR staff is grouped in three major sections, each under one of the other deputy assistant secretaries.

The INR's structure reflects its principal responsibilities. One deputy is responsible for correct analysis output. A second supervises analysis involving longer term assessments and research, both in the INR and from the academic world. The third deputy guides coordination activities relating to the other intelligence agencies' operations abroad.

Current Analysis. The largest part of the INR's staff is directed by the deputy assistant secretary for current analysis (INR/CA). Six of the seven offices in this grouping correspond to the principal geographic areas of the world: Africa (AA); Latin America (IAA); East Asia and the Pacific (EAP); the Soviet Union and Eastern Europe (SEE); Western Europe (WEA); and the Near East and South Asia (NESA). The seventh is the Office of Political-Military Analysis (PMA).

The primary function of these offices is to produce analyses of developments and issues that are, or will be, of concern to the policymaker. CA offices perform "traditional" research in that they acquire information and evaluate, store, retrieve, and use it for the benefit of their readers. They produce finished intelligence in that their work is based on classified information as well as on more conventional open sources, is directed to issues of immediate or potential concern to policymakers, and is intended to analyze developments and not merely chronicle them. These offices are responsible for preparing the regional and other special summaries mentioned above, for briefing senior officers, and for preparing the INR contributions to Community-wide estimates and assessments.

CA analysts have a particular responsibility for commenting on current developments and on issues of current concern to policymakers. Their special contribution is to lend perspective and depth to events by putting them in a broader, policy-relevant context, judging whether they reflect the continuation or interruption of a trend, and estimating their likely future course.

In practice, the boundaries between "current" analysis and other analytical work are difficult to define and analysis of a fast-breaking situation, for example, may involve placing events in long-term perspective, and a long-range assessment may be the prerequisite to a decision on a current and even urgent issue. The common denominator is the application of specialized knowledge and technical expertise to the analysis of foreign policy situations.

As substantive experts, therefore, CA analysts also undertake longer-range studies and assessments. When performing in that capacity, they operate under the guidance and direction of the deputy assistant secretary for assessments and research.

Assessments and Research. The deputy assistant secretary for assessments and research (INR/AR) has the primary responsibility for INR's long-range analytical studies, as noted above. In addition, this deputy directs the following offices and staffs.

The Office of Long-Range Assessments and Research (LAR). The LAR prepares its own long-range assessments on selected topics, occasionally contributes to assessments prepared elsewhere in the INR, and commissions from contractors and consultants those that cannot be done in the INR. The office also manages a program for contract research studies and conferences on issues identified by other DoS bureaus and units. Finally, the LAR is the staff through which the DoS discharges the secretary of state's responsibilities concerning the coordination of all U.S. government-supported research on foreign affairs.

The Office of Economic Analysis (EC). The EC produces reports for policymakers on current and longer-range issues involving such international economic concerns as foreign economic policies, business cycles, trade, financial affairs, food, population, energy, and economic relations between the industrialized countries and the developing nations. The EC uses econometric modeling to assess the effects of alternate economic policies.

The Office of the Geographer (GE). The GE prepares studies of policy issues associated with physical, cultural, economic, and political geography; the law of the sea; U.S. maritime issues; and international boundaries and jurisdictional problems. It produces maps and reviews maps and charts produced by other agencies to insure consistency in nomenclature and in matters of sovereignty. It represents the DoS and the U.S. government at international geographic and cartographic forums and, as appropriate, provides geographic expertise to foreign governments.

The Office of Global Issues (GI). The GI produces finished intelligence on selected transnational, regional, and global topics. Its reports and briefings deal with political issues of importance to the United States that are raised in international forums and with such functional issues as the political psychology of conflict, international terrorism, science and technology, narcotics, human rights and refugees, oceans, and the environment.

The Reports, Coordination and Review Staff (RCRS). The RCRS is responsible for the management and final production of the INR's formal reports, either regular series (*Current Analyses, Assessments and Research, Policy Assessments*) or special publications. Its principal concerns include editorial review, typography, printing, and distributing these reports.

Coordination. The staff directed by the deputy assistant secretary for coordination (INR/C) functions as the focal point for other elements of the Community, other areas of the DoS, and missions overseas on the conduct and direction of all U.S. intelligence collection activities having significance for foreign affairs. It coordinates the DoS's role, including the secretary's participation, in the National Security Planning Group, which coordinates special intelligence activities and sensitive intelligence collection operations, and in the Senior Interagency Group for Intelligence, which establishes priorities and reviews intelligence and counterintelligence programs. To accomplish these missions, INR/C is organized into the following components:

The Office of Intelligence Liaison (IL). The IL coordinates proposals for special intelligence activities. Its basic responsibility in connection with these programs is to insure consideration of their support of and implications for U.S. foreign policy. The IL participates in briefings on intelligence matters for intelligence officers going to and returning from overseas posts. It also handles liaison with designated foreign intelligence representatives.

The Office of Intelligence Coordination (IC). The IC works with the DIA and the FBI on intelligence problems of mutual concern. It represents the DoS in Community coordination of priorities for national intelligence collection and production, and it works with other agencies on human source collection efforts. It manages the DoS's effort to counter anti-U.S. propaganda; serves as the focal point for foreign service reporting plans and evaluations; coordinates the U.S. government's map and publications procurement abroad; represents the DoS in handling defector cases; and processes requests for biographic data and other Community intelligence production.

The Office of Intelligence Resources (IRE). The IRE provides staff support, representation, and coordination for the DoS's interests in technical intelligence programs and the National Intelligence Budget. It works closely with other Community agencies, concerned areas of the DoS, and overseas missions in planning, deploying, and evaluating technical collection activities. Finally, it advises DoS officers on the use of intelligence produced by major technical systems.

Special Functions

Apart from the responsibilities managed by the deputy assistant secretaries for current analysis, assessments and research, and coordination, two offices in the INR serve bureau-wide needs. They report directly to the senior deputy assistant director.

The Office of the Executive Director (EX) handles all INR administrative and management activities, including organization, budget and fiscal, personnel, training, security, and general administrative support services. The executive director represents the INR in these areas within the DoS and the Intelligence Community. This officer also manages a student intern work-study program in which a limited number of outstanding university students spend from three to four months working as junior-level analysts in the INR's regional and functional offices.

The Office of Intelligence Support (IS) is the DoS's center for receiving intelligence information, in both documentary and electrical form, and for processing and disseminating this intelligence under the requisite security safeguards. Supported by other INR offices, most of which have space and personnel within the center, the IS insures that DoS officers have speedy access to urgent intelligence items as well as appropriate INR comments and studies. The IS staffs the INR's Watch Office, which is collocated with the 24-hour Operations Center in the DoS's Executive Secretariat.

Reports

The INR produces reports that are designed to furnish intelligence information and analysis to policy officers. Some of these reports have exclusive distribution; others are distributed widely within the government and, when classified, outside the government. Besides its regular publications, the INR prepares studies in the form of memoranda for senior officers, some in response to ad hoc requests for the INR's judgments, others initiated by the INR.

Although the INR undertakes many types of work, it stresses carefully drafted, succinct analytic reports that will directly assist DoS policy officers in their work. It seeks to provide an independent viewpoint based on the use of all information available.

Among the INR's regular publications are:

- *The Morning Summary*, prepared in collaboration with the DoS's Executive Secretariat. This daily publication is intended to inform the secretary of state and his principal deputies of current events and current intelligence and to supply them with tightly drafted analyses assessing the importance of developments and trends. The first part of the *Summary* consists of short gist-and-comment reports based on newly available information. The second part usually consists of three one-page essays drafted by INR analysts. This highly classified publication is also circulated to a few top officials in other foreign policy agencies.

- Regional and functional summaries, prepared by the analytical offices of the INR on a daily, weekly, or biweekly basis. In the past, these have included *African Trends, Arab-Israeli Highlights, Central American Highlights, East Asia and Pacific Highlights, Global Issues Review, Inter-American Highlights, Politico-Military Analyses, Science and Technology,* and *Soviet Weekly.* These serial publications consist of short essays or brief analytical items and gists of significant intelligence reports. They are designed to keep the senior officers who follow these issues up-to-date in ways that minimize demands on their time.

- Single-subject reports published under three distinctive mastheads. *Current Analyses* includes papers that analyze recent or ongoing events and assess their prospects and implications in the next six months. Analysts rely primarily on current intelligence in preparing these reports. *Assessments and Research* includes papers that assess past trends or project the course of events beyond six months. These reports include those for which the analyst has done substantial background or in-depth research on broader, long-range issues. *Policy Assessments* includes papers that analyze the context or results of past policies (retrospective analyses) or that assess comparative policies or policy options.

Studies in these series vary in length; may contain specially prepared maps, charts, and other visual aids; are generally circulated throughout the government, including U.S. missions abroad; and sometimes consist of the text or the digest of a study done under contract by a nongovernment expert.

- Geographic studies. The INR's Office of the Geographer issues special studies on land and maritime boundaries that are important basic research tools for American and foreign cartographers.

Briefings and Intelligence Community Activities

The INR closely interacts with geographic and functional bureaus of the DoS and with the other intelligence agencies. The INR's position as part of both the DoS and the Intelligence Community facilitates its efforts to draft studies of direct pertinence to policy officers.

Part of the INR's work consists of briefings given to the policy officers. This may include the INR director's participation in the secretary of state's regular staff meetings, INR office directors' daily meetings with assistant and deputy assistant secretaries, and meetings of individual analysts with country directors or desk officers. INR officers comment on developments and issues that have been revealed or illuminated by intelligence. They call to the attention of and discuss with policy officers any important raw intelligence reports and analysis received from other agencies. Through these contacts, INR officers can identify issues that should be further studied by analysts within the INR or elsewhere in the Intelligence Community. Many INR papers are written in response to questions raised in briefings or meetings. Papers are also prompted by informal conversations, phone calls, cables, and memoranda.

INR analysts work closely with other segments of the Intelligence Community in many ways, but perhaps most importantly by contributing to the preparation of such interagency assessments as National Intelligence Estimates (NIEs).

NIEs, coordinated among the intelligence agencies and reviewed by the NFIB, present the most senior official judgment of the community on major problem areas related to foreign affairs and national security. They may deal with political, economic, and strategic issues or may focus on a single event or problem, a country, a region, or a worldwide issue. At every stage the INR is involved, from helping a DoS officer who wishes to frame a request for an NIE to the final step when the INR director participates on the NFIB with fellow intelligence agency heads in discussing and defining the contents of the final text. INR analysts participate in interagency working groups to determine terms of reference for the NIEs; they often submit written or oral contributions; and they spend much time in interagency meetings at which draft estimates are revised and differing assessments aired prior to NFIB consideration.

References

Department of State. *INR: Intelligence and Research in the Department of State*. Washington, DC: GPO, 1984.

Kent, Sherman. *Strategic Intelligence for American World Policy*. Princeton, NJ: Princeton University Press, 1966.

Laqueur, Walter. *A World of Secrets*. New York: Basic Books, 1985.

Lefever, Ernest W., and Godson, Roy. *The CIA and the American Ethic: An Unfinished Debate*. Washington, DC: Ethics and Public Policy Center, Georgetown University, 1979.

Lowenthal, Mark M. *U.S. Intelligence: Evolution and Anatomy*. New York: Praeger, 1984.

Quirk, John; Phillips, David; Cline, Ray; and Pforzheimer, Walter. *The Central Intelligence Agency: A Photographic History*. Guilford, CT: Foreign Intelligence Press, 1986.

Treverton, Gregory F. *Covert Action: The Limits of Intervention in the Postwar World*. New York: Basic Books, 1987.

Turner, Stansfield. *Secrecy and Democracy: The CIA in Transition*. Boston: Houghton Mifflin, 1985.

—**BURN** is a term used in clandestine and covert intelligence operations. To burn is to deliberately sacrifice an agent in order to protect a more important, valuable, or productive spy. *See also:* Agent, Agent Authentication, Agent in Place,

Agent Net, Agent of Influence, Agent Provocateur, Blow, Blown Agent, Burnt, Confusion Agent, Dispatched Agent, Double Agent, Handling Agent, Illegal Agent, Informant, Inside Man, Provocation Agent, Special Activities.

References

Becket, Henry S. A. *The Dictionary of Espionage: Spookspeak into English.* New York: Stein and Day, 1986.

Clancy, Tom. *The Cardinal of the Kremlin.* New York: Putnam, 1988.

Deacon, Richard. *Spyclopedia: An Encyclopedia of Spies, Secret Services, Operations, Jargon, and All Subjects Related to the World of Espionage.* London: Macdonald, 1987.

Department of Defense, Joint Chiefs of Staff. *Department of Defense Dictionary of Military and Related Terms.* Washington, DC: GPO, 1986.

Turner, Stansfield. *Secrecy and Democracy: The CIA in Transition.* Boston: Houghton Mifflin, 1985.

U.S. Congress. Senate. *Final Report of the Senate Select Committee to Study Government Operations with Respect to Intelligence Activities. Report 94-755. Book I, Foreign and Military Intelligence.* Washington, DC: GPO, 1976.

—**BURN NOTICE** is an official statement by one intelligence agency to other agencies, domestic or foreign, that an individual or a group is unreliable for any of a variety of reasons.

References

Department of Defense, Joint Chiefs of Staff. *Department of Defense Dictionary of Military and Related Terms.* Washington, DC: GPO, 1986.

—**BURNT** is a term used in clandestine and covert intelligence operations to describe an agent who has either been discovered or so severely compromised that he is no longer effective. In Tom Clancy's novel, *The Cardinal of the Kremlin,* the Cardinal burns Colonel Penkovsky, the famous Soviet spy, because Penkovsky has already been detected and will be arrested anyway. By burning him, the Cardinal is able to further establish his own credibility. *See also:* Agent, Agent Authentication, Agent in Place, Agent Net, Agent of Influence, Agent Provocateur, Blow, Blown Agent, Burn, Confusion Agent, Dispatched Agent, Double Agent, Handling Agent, Illegal Agent, Informant, Inside Man, Provocation Agent, Pseudonym, Special Activities.

References

Clancy, Tom. *The Cardinal of the Kremlin.* New York: Putnam, 1988.

Deacon, Richard. *Spyclopedia: An Encyclopedia of Spies, Secret Services, Operations, Jargon, and All Subjects Related to the World of Espionage.* London: Macdonald, 1987.

Department of Defense, Joint Chiefs of Staff. *Department of Defense Dictionary of Military and Related Terms.* Washington, DC: GPO, 1986.

U.S. Congress. Senate. *Final Report of the Senate Select Committee to Study Government Operations with Respect to Intelligence Activities. Report 94-755. Book I, Foreign and Military Intelligence.* Washington, DC: GPO, 1976.

—**BURST TRANSMISSION** is a preset message that is transmitted so rapidly that it prevents enemy direction-finding surveillance from locating the sender.

References

Quirk, John; Phillips, David; Cline, Ray; and Pforzheimer, Walter. *The Central Intelligence Agency: A Photographic History.* Guilford, CT: Foreign Intelligence Press, 1986.

—**BUSH, GEORGE HERBERT WALKER,** was born on June 12, 1924 in Milton, Massachusetts. He served as a naval aviator in the Pacific in World War II and subsequently graduated from Yale University in 1948. Bush spent his early years in private business and then spent four years in Congress (1966–1970) as the representative from Texas's 7th District. In 1971 he was appointed as ambassador to the United Nations, serving there until 1972. In 1973 he became the chairman of the Republican National Committee, but he left this position in 1974 to become chief of the U.S. Liaison Office in the People's Republic of China. On November 3, 1975, he was appointed by President Ford to be the director of Central Intelligence (DCI) after Ford dismissed William Colby. Bush's appointment was confirmed by the Senate on January 27, 1976, and he was sworn in on January 30. It was a political appointment, however, made as a reaction during an ongoing intelligence scandal, and Bush's tenure was so short that he had little effect on the agency. He left office as part of the personnel turnover that occurred when President Carter took office, and he was replaced by Admiral Stansfield Turner, U.S. Navy.

On January 20, 1981, Bush was sworn in as vice president of the United States, serving in this office during both terms of the Reagan administration. In November 1988 he was elected president of the United States, and, in terms of job experience, was the most qualified person ever to assume that position.

References

American Bar Association. *Oversight and Accountability of the U.S. Intelligence Agencies: An Evaluation.* Washington, DC: ABA, 1985.

Breckinridge, Scott D. *The CIA and the U.S. Intelligence System.* Boulder, CO: Westview Press, 1986.

Brinkley, David A., and Hull, Andrew W. *Estimative Intelligence: A Textbook on the History, Products, Uses, and Writing of Intelligence Estimates.* Columbus, OH: Battelle, 1979.

Cline, Ray S. *The CIA Under Reagan, Bush, and Casey.* Washington, DC: Acropolis Books, 1981.

Crawford, David J. *Volunteers: The Betrayal of National Defense Secrets by Air Force Traitors.* Washington, DC: GPO, 1988.

Laqueur, Walter. *A World of Secrets.* New York: Basic Books, 1985.

Lefever, Ernest W., and Godson, Roy. *The CIA and the American Ethic: An Unfinished Debate.* Washington, DC: Ethics and Public Policy Center, Georgetown University, 1979.

Lowenthal, Mark M. *U.S. Intelligence: Evolution and Anatomy.* New York: Praeger, 1984.

Maurer, Alfred C.; Turnstall, Marion D.; and Keagle, James M. *Intelligence Policy and Process.* Boulder, CO: Westview Press, 1985.

Quirk, John; Phillips, David; Cline, Ray; and Pforzheimer, Walter. *The Central Intelligence Agency: A Photographic History.* Guilford, CT: Foreign Intelligence Press, 1986.

Turner, Stansfield. *Secrecy and Democracy: The CIA in Transition.* Boston: Houghton Mifflin, 1985.

U.S. Congress. Senate. *Alleged Assassination Plots Involving Foreign Leaders: An Interim Report of the Select Committee to Study Governmental Operations with Respect to Intelligence Activities.* 94th Congress. 1st sess., Nov. 20, 1975. S. Rept. 94-465.

Von Hoene, John P. A. *Intelligence User's Guide.* Washington, DC: DIA, 1983.

—**BUTENKO, JOHN,** a contractor working for the U.S. government, was convicted in 1964 of passing classified information concerning the Strategic Air Command to the Soviet secret service (KGB). He was apparently motivated by ideological reasons. He was sentenced to 30 years in prison for his crimes.

References

Allen, Thomas B. and Polmar, Norman. *Merchants of Treason: America's Secrets for Sale.* New York: Delacorte Press, 1988.

Crawford, David J. *Volunteers: The Betrayal of National Defense Secrets by Air Force Traitors.* Washington, DC: GPO, 1988.

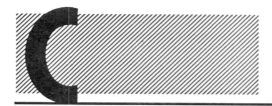

—CABELL, GENERAL CHARLES PEARRE, U.S. AIR FORCE, served as deputy director of Central Intelligence from April 23, 1953, until January 31, 1962. *See also:* Central Intelligence Agency.

References

American Bar Association. *Oversight and Accountability of the U.S. Intelligence Agencies: An Evaluation.* Washington, DC: ABA, 1985.

Corson, William R. *The Armies of Ignorance: The Rise of the American Intelligence Empire.* New York: Dial Press, 1977.

Godson, Roy, ed. *Intelligence Problems for the 1980s, Number 1: Elements of Intelligence.* Rev. ed. Washington, DC: National Strategy Information Center, 1983.

Lefever, Ernest W., and Godson, Roy. *The CIA and the American Ethic: An Unfinished Debate.* Washington, DC: Ethics and Public Policy Center, Georgetown University, 1979.

Maurer, Alfred C.; Turnstall, Marion D.; and Keagle, James M. *Intelligence Policy and Process.* Boulder, CO: Westview Press, 1985.

Turner, Stansfield. *Secrecy and Democracy: The CIA in Transition.* Boston: Houghton Mifflin, 1985.

—CACKLEBLADDER is a term used in clandestine and covert intelligence operations. According to Richard Deacon, cacklebladder is jargon for disguising a live body to look like a corpse after the enemy has been induced to shoot a dummy corpse. Chicken blood is often used to smear over the live body. It is a ploy often used to blackmail or force a confession from an agent. *See also:* Biographic Leverage, Blackmail, Dirty Tricks, Pigeon, Plumbing, Putting in the Plumbing, Recruitment, Recruitment in Place, Snitch Jacket.

References

Deacon, Richard. *Spyclopedia: An Encyclopedia of Spies, Secret Services, Operations, Jargon, and All Subjects Related to the World of Espionage.* London: Macdonald, Ltd., 1987.

—CALL SIGN, in communications and communications security (COMSEC), is the symbol used to identify a member of a communications net. It is any combination of characters or pronounceable words that identifies a communications facility, a command, an authority, an activity, or a unit; it is used primarily for establishing and maintaining communications. *See also:* Communications Security.

References

Department of Defense, Joint Chiefs of Staff. *Department of Defense Dictionary of Military and Related Terms.* Washington, DC: GPO, 1986.

—CALL-SIGN CIPHER, in communications and communications security (COMSEC), is a cryptosystem used to encipher or decipher call signs, address groups, or address-indicating groups. *See also:* Call Sign.

References

Blackburn, N. Glenn. "Computers: A Counterintelligence Concern." Unpublished paper provided to the editors. Washington, DC, 1987.

Martin, Paul H. "Communications-Computer Security." *Journal of Electronic Defense* (June 1987).

Muzerall, Joseph V., and Carty, Thomas P. "COMSEC and Its Need for Key Management." *DP&CS* (Spring 1987).

Ware, Willis H. "Information Systems, Security, and Privacy." *EDUCOM Bulletin* (Summer 1984).

—CAMOUFLAGE is a general intelligence term for the use of concealment and disguise to hide troops, material, equipment, and installations in order to minimize the possibility of their detection or identification. It includes taking advantage of the natural environment as well as applying natural and artificial materials.

References

American Bar Association. *Oversight and Accountability of the U.S. Intelligence Agencies: An Evaluation.* Washington, DC: ABA, 1985.

Department of Defense, Joint Chiefs of Staff. *Department of Defense Dictionary of Military and Related Terms.* Washington, DC: GPO, 1986.

Maurer, Alfred C.; Turnstall, Marion D.; and Keagle, James M. *Intelligence Policy and Process.* Boulder, CO: Westview Press, 1985.

—**CAMOUFLAGE DETECTION PHOTOGRAPHY** is the use of a special type of film (usually infrared film) that is designed to detect camouflage.

References

Department of Defense, Joint Chiefs of Staff. *Department of Defense Dictionary of Military and Related Terms.* Washington, DC: GPO, 1986.

—**CAMP PEARY** is a CIA training facility on a narrow neck of land between the James and York rivers near Williamsburg, Virginia. A Seabee training camp during World War II, it became a CIA facility in the early 1950s. The CIA tore down the ramshackle shacks then present and built red brick buildings that give the camp the look of a small college. Agency employees call Camp Peary "the farm." *See also:* Central Intelligence Agency.

References

Becket, Henry S. A. *The Dictionary of Espionage: Spookspeak into English.* New York: Stein and Day, 1986.

Clancy, Tom. *The Cardinal of the Kremlin.* New York: Putnam, 1988.

Ranelagh, John. *The Agency: The Rise and Decline of the CIA.* New York: Simon and Schuster, 1986.

Turner, Stansfield. *Secrecy and Democracy: The CIA in Transition.* Boston: Houghton Mifflin, 1985.

—**CANAL,** a baud-based system term used in communications intelligence, communications security, operations security, and signals analysis, is one of the communications arteries that are transmitted simultaneously by using double frequency shift (DFS) keying. *See also:* Communications Security.

References

Blackburn, N. Glenn. "Computers: A Counterintelligence Concern." Unpublished paper provided to the editors. Washington, DC, 1987.

Martin, Paul H. "Communications-Computer Security." *Journal of Electronic Defense* (June 1987).

Muzerall, Joseph V., and Carty, Thomas P. "COMSEC and Its Need for Key Management." *DP&CS* (Spring 1987).

Ware, Willis H. "Information Systems, Security, and Privacy." *EDUCOM Bulletin* (Summer 1984).

—**CANINE, LIEUTENANT GENERAL RALPH J., U.S. ARMY,** a graduate of Northwestern University, served as director of the National Security Agency from November 1952 until November 1956. Canine spent most of his career as a ground soldier, and he had commanded artillery units in France in World War I and at the Battle of the Bulge in World War II. While he lacked a scientific background, he had intelligence experience, having served as deputy chief of staff for Army intelligence. *See also:* National Security Agency.

References

Bamford, James. *The Puzzle Palace: A Report on America's Most Secret Agency.* New York: Penguin Books, 1983.

—**CANISTER,** in communications security (COMSEC), is a type of protective package used for cryptovariables in tape form that are designated "CRYPTO." *See also:* Communications Security.

References

Blackburn, N. Glenn. "Computers: A Counterintelligence Concern." Unpublished paper provided to the editors. Washington, DC, 1987.

Martin, Paul H. "Communications-Computer Security." *Journal of Electronic Defense* (June 1987).

Muzerall, Joseph V., and Carty, Thomas P. "COMSEC and Its Need for Key Management." *DP&CS* (Spring 1987).

Ware, Willis H. "Information Systems, Security, and Privacy." *EDUCOM Bulletin* (Summer 1984).

—**CANNON** is a term used in clandestine and covert intelligence operations. A cannon is a professional thief who steals the money or reward that was given to an enemy agent or informant in exchange for information. Cannons are often used by intelligence services that are short of funds. *See also:* Clandestine Operation.

References

Allen, Thomas, and Polmar, Norman. *Merchants of Treason: America's Secrets for Sale.* New York: Delacorte Press, 1988.

Becket, Henry S. A. *The Dictionary of Espionage: Spookspeak into English.* New York: Stein and Day, 1986.

Deacon, Richard. *Spyclopedia: An Encyclopedia of Spies, Secret Services, Operations, Jargon, and All Subjects Related to the World of Espionage.* London: Macdonald, 1987.

—CAPABILITIES PROGRAMMING AND BUD-GETING SYSTEM (CPBS) is the system used to create the General Defense Intelligence Program (GDIP) and the National Foreign Intelligence Program (NFIP) budgets. An extensive program, the CPBS has stipulated document submissions that are required from the programs' components, staffs that process these submissions and prepare proposed programs for review by the director of Central Intelligence, and a capability to monitor the accomplishments of the programs' components in fulfilling the requirements stated in their budget submissions. *See also:* Defense Guidance (DG); Five-Year Defense Program (FYDP); National Defense Expenditures; National Intelligence Projections for Planning (NIPP); Office of Management and Budget (OMB); Program Budget Decision (PBD).

References

Maurer, Alfred C.; Turnstall, Marion D.; and Keagle, James M. *Intelligence Policy and Process.* Boulder, CO: Westview Press, 1985.

Pickett, George. "Congress, the Budget and Intelligence." In *Intelligence Policy and Process,* edited by Alfred C. Maurer, Marion D. Turnstall, and James M. Keagle. Boulder, CO: Westview Press, 1985.

Wilson, Dick, and Calcaterra, Dennis. "Airborne Command and Control Modernization." *Signal* (Aug. 1987).

—CAPABILITY is the ability to accomplish a specified course of action. It may or may not be accompanied by an intention.

References

Department of Defense, Joint Chiefs of Staff. *Department of Defense Dictionary of Military and Related Terms.* Washington, DC: GPO, 1986.

Kent, Sherman. *Strategic Intelligence for American World Policy.* Princeton, NJ: Princeton University Press, 1966.

—CARACRISTI, ANN Z. served as deputy director of the National Security Agency from April 1980 to July 1982. A graduate of Russell Sage College, Caracristi had been a signals intelligence (SIGINT) professional since 1942 and had served as chief of the Office of SIGINT Research and later as deputy chief of A Group, the major SIGINT analysis group, before assuming the position as deputy director. She was succeeded by Robert E. Rich. *See also:* National Security Agency (NSA).

References

Bamford, James. *The Puzzle Palace: A Report on America's Most Secret Agency.* New York: Penguin Books, 1983.

—CARBONS are paper that produce secret writing when they are treated chemically. *See also:* Agent, Agent Authentication, Agent in Place, Agent Net, Ciphers, Codes, Dead Drop, Edible Paper, Flaps and Seals, Flaps and Seals Man, Illegal Communication, Letter Drop, Live Letter Boxes, Live Letter Drops, Mail Cover, Secret Writing.

References

Becket, Henry S. A. *The Dictionary of Espionage: Spookspeak into English.* New York: Stein and Day, 1986.

Deacon, Richard. *Spyclopedia: An Encyclopedia of Spies, Secret Services, Operations, Jargon, and All Subjects Related to the World of Espionage.* London: Macdonald, 1987.

—CARD READER INSERT BOARD (CRIB), in communications security (COMSEC), is a removable component on some machine cryptosystems that is installed in place of the card reader circuit plate in order to alter the cryptovariable provided by the key card. *See also:* Communications Security.

References

Blackburn, N. Glenn. "Computers: A Counterintelligence Concern." Unpublished paper provided to the editors. Washington, DC, 1987.

Martin, Paul H. "Communications-Computer Security." *Journal of Electronic Defense* (June 1987).

Muzerall, Joseph V., and Carty, Thomas P. "COMSEC and Its Need for Key Management." *DP&CS* (Spring 1987).

Ware, Willis H. "Information Systems, Security, and Privacy." *EDUCOM Bulletin* (Summer 1984).

—CARTER, JIMMY. Like his predecessors, President Carter worked actively to solve the problem of presidential oversight. Carter came to office in the wake of the intelligence scandal associated with Watergate and the presidential and congressional investigations, and attempted to define a new role for the Intelligence Community, as that entity emerged from the devastating scandals. When his initial choice for director of

Central Intelligence (DCI), Theodore Sorenson, withdrew his name from consideration in the face of stiff potential congressional opposition, Carter nominated Admiral Stansfield Turner, who was approved by Congress.

Carter's first reform occurred in May 1977, when he abolished the President's Foreign Intelligence Advisory Board (PFIAB), claiming that, with the creation of the standing congressional committees, the PFIAB had become redundant. This was followed by a reorganization in August 1977, in which Carter attempted to augment the DCI's power, and then the highly significant Executive Order 12036, which the President signed on January 24, 1978. The order, which appears as Appendix K, gave the DCI exclusive control over the National Foreign Intelligence Program budget. This, the second such order that attempted to administer the Intelligence Community, clearly defined what the Community could and could not do. *See also:* Executive Oversight.

References

American Bar Association. *Oversight and Accountability of the U.S. Intelligence Agencies: An Evaluation.* Washington, DC: ABA, 1985.

Breckinridge, Scott D. *The CIA and the U.S. Intelligence System.* Boulder, CO: Westview Press, 1986.

Brinkley, David A., and Hull, Andrew W. *Estimative Intelligence: A Textbook on the History, Products, Uses and Writing of Intelligence Estimates.* Columbus, OH: Battelle, 1979.

Cline, Ray S. *The CIA Under Reagan, Bush, and Casey.* Washington, DC: Acropolis Books, 1981.

Corson, William R. *The Armies of Ignorance: The Rise of the American Intelligence Empire.* New York: Dial Press, 1977.

Crawford, David J. *Volunteers: The Betrayal of National Defense Secrets by Air Force Traitors.* Washington, DC: GPO, 1988.

Godson, Roy, ed. *Intelligence Problems for the 1980s, Number 2: Analysis and Estimates.* Washington, DC: National Strategy Information Center, 1980.

———. *Intelligence Problems for the 1980s, Number 4: Covert Action.* Washington, DC: National Strategy Information Center, 1981.

Laqueur, Walter. *A World of Secrets.* New York: Basic Books, 1985.

Lowenthal, Mark M. *U.S. Intelligence: Evolution and Anatomy.* New York: Praeger, 1984.

Maurer, Alfred C.; Turnstall, Marion D.; and Keagle, James M. *Intelligence Policy and Process.* Boulder, CO: Westview Press, 1985.

Treverton, Gregory F. *Covert Action: The Limits of Intervention in the Postwar World.* New York: Basic Books, 1987.

Turner, Stansfield. *Secrecy and Democracy: The CIA in Transition.* Boston: Houghton Mifflin, 1985.

U.S. Congress. Senate. *Alleged Assassination Plots Involving Foreign Leaders: An Interim Report of the Select Committee to Study Governmental Operations with Respect to Intelligence Activities.* 94th Congress, 1st sess., Nov. 20, 1975. S. Rept. 94-465.

Von Hoene, John P. A. *Intelligence User's Guide.* Washington, DC: DIA, 1983.

—**CARTER, LIEUTENANT GENERAL MARSHALL S., U.S. ARMY,** graduated from West Point and received a masters degree in engineering from MIT. He served as deputy director of Central Intelligence from April 3, 1962 until April 28, 1965, under John McCone. When President Johnson replaced McCone with Vice Admiral William Rayborn, Carter was without a job, because military officers cannot serve concurrently as both director and deputy director of Central Intelligence. Thus he accepted the offer to be director of the National Security Agency in June 1965. In August 1969 he retired from the NSA and was succeeded by Vice Admiral Noel Gayler, U.S. Navy. *See also:* Central Intelligence Agency.

References

Bamford, James. *The Puzzle Palace: A Report on America's Most Secret Agency.* New York: Penguin Books, 1983.

—**CARTOGRAPHIC INTELLIGENCE** is a general term for intelligence that is derived from maps and charts of areas outside the United States and its territorial waters. *See also:* Mapping, Charting, Geodesy.

References

Department of Defense, Defense Intelligence College. *Glossary of Intelligence Terms and Definitions.* Washington, DC: DIC, 1987.

Kent, Sherman. *Strategic Intelligence for American World Policy.* Princeton, NJ: Princeton University Press, 1966.

Treverton, Gregory F. *Covert Action: The Limits of Intervention in the Postwar World.* New York: Basic Books, 1987.

Turner, Stansfield. *Secrecy and Democracy: The CIA in Transition.* Boston: Houghton Mifflin, 1985.

—**"CARVE-OUT" CONTRACT** is a general intelligence term for a type of classified contract that is issued in connection with an approved special access program in which the Defense Investigative Service (DIS) has been relieved of inspection responsibility in whole or in part under the Defense Industrial Security Program. *See also:* Security.

References

Maroni, Alice C. *Special Access Programs: Understanding the "Black Budget."* Washington, DC: Foreign Affairs and National Defense Division, Congressional Research Service, Library of Congress, 1987.

—**CASCIO, GIUSEPPE,** an Air Force staff sergeant, was convicted on June 8, 1953, of conspiracy to pass secrets to Communist agents. He was sentenced to twenty years at hard labor and was given a dishonorable discharge. Cascio had tried to sell classified flight-test data concerning the F-86E Sabre jet to North Korean intelligence service officers, but he was apprehended before he could pass the information.

References

Crawford, David J. *Volunteers: The Betrayal of National Defense Secrets by Air Force Traitors.* Washington, DC: GPO, 1988.

—**CASE** is a general intelligence term that has two meanings. (1) A case is an intelligence operation in its entirety, and (2) it is also a record of the development, methods, and objectives of an operation. *See also:* Black Bag Operation, Case Officer, Cover Story, Double Agent, Handling Agent, Naked, Packed Up, Processing the Take, Putting in the Plumbing.

References

Department of Defense, Joint Chiefs of Staff. *Department of Defense Dictionary of Military and Related Terms.* Washington, DC: GPO, 1986.

Kent, Sherman. *Strategic Intelligence for American World Policy.* Princeton, NJ: Princeton University Press, 1966.

Quirk, John; Phillips, David; Cline, Ray; and Pforzheimer, Walter. *The Central Intelligence Agency: A Photographic History.* Guilford, CT: Foreign Intelligence Press, 1986.

Turner, Stansfield. *Secrecy and Democracy: The CIA in Transition.* Boston: Houghton Mifflin, 1985.

U.S. Congress. Senate. *Final Report of the Senate Select Committee to Study Government Operations with Respect to Intelligence Activities. Report 94-*

755. Book I, Foreign and Military Intelligence. Washington, DC: GPO, 1976.

—**CASE OFFICER** is a term used in clandestine and covert intelligence operations. It has three slightly different meanings. (1) A case officer can be a professional employee of an intelligence organization who is responsible for directing an agent operation. (2) In CIA terminology, the case officer is the person in charge of agents collecting intelligence or performing other clandestine activities. As such, he acts as the link between Washington, D.C., and the information it wants or the actions it desires. The case officer has no contact with the enemy. Rather, his purposes are to direct the operation and to provide agents with the resources they need to accomplish their mission. Ideally, the case officer is the agents' only contact with the parent intelligence agency, because involving other people can create organizational and management problems. The case officer reports to the chief of station. (3) In FBI terminology, a case officer can either be a headquarters case officer or a field case officer. *See also:* Case.

References

Allen, Thomas B., and Polmar, Norman. *Merchants of Treason: America's Secrets for Sale.* New York: Delacorte Press, 1988.

Becket, Henry S. A. *The Dictionary of Espionage: Spookspeak into English.* New York: Stein and Day, 1986.

Clancy, Tom. *The Cardinal of the Kremlin.* New York: Putnam, 1988.

Department of Defense, Defense Intelligence College. *Glossary of Intelligence Terms and Definitions.* Washington, DC: DIC, 1987.

Department of Defense, Joint Chiefs of Staff. *Department of Defense Dictionary of Military and Related Terms.* Washington, DC: GPO, 1986.

Kessler, Ronald. *Spy vs. Spy: Stalking Soviet Spies in America.* New York: Charles Scribner's Sons, 1988.

Laqueur, Walter. *A World of Secrets.* New York: Basic Books, 1985.

Quirk, John; Phillips, David; Cline, Ray; and Pforzheimer, Walter. *The Central Intelligence Agency: A Photographic History.* Guilford, CT: Foreign Intelligence Press, 1986.

Treverton, Gregory F. *Covert Action: The Limits of Intervention in the Postwar World.* New York: Basic Books, 1987.

Turner, Stansfield. *Secrecy and Democracy: The CIA in Transition.* Boston: Houghton Mifflin, 1985.

U.S. Congress. Senate. *Final Report of the Senate Select Committee to Study Government Operations with Respect to Intelligence Activities. Report 94-755. Book I, Foreign and Military Intelligence.* Washington, DC: Government Printing Office, 1976.

—CASEY, WILLIAM JOSEPH, was born on March 13, 1913 in New York City. He earned a Bachelor of Science degree from Fordham University in 1934 and a Bachelor of Law degree from St. John's University in 1937. His early career involved law and business, and he was commissioned in the Naval Reserve in 1943. During World War II, he served with the Office of Strategic Services (OSS), becoming chief of its Special Intelligence Branch in the European theater of operations in 1944. In 1948, he was appointed as associate general counsel at the European headquarters of the Marshall Plan. He subsequently left government service, but returned in 1971 to become chairman of the Securities and Exchange Commission, a position he held until 1973, when he was made under secretary of state for economic affairs. He left in 1974 to become president and chairman of the Export-Import Bank of the United States. In 1976 and 1977, Casey served as a member of the President's Foreign Intelligence Advisory Board, and he became Ronald Reagan's campaign manager in 1980. On January 13, 1981, he was appointed by the President to be director of Central Intelligence. His appointment was confirmed by the Senate on January 27, 1981, and he was sworn in on January 28.

Casey was one of the more colorful directors. His tenure was hallmarked by attempting to maintain the secrecy of CIA programs and the agency's freedom from Congress. In the early years of his tenure, this led to repeated run-ins with Congress that were highlighted by disagreements with Senator Barry Goldwater (R-Ariz.). Goldwater, a conservative, was placed in the unfortunate position of trying to maintain secrecy while controlling Casey. In 1986 Casey's involvement in the Iran-Contra scandal was made public. In 1987 it was announced that Casey had terminal cancer, and he was hospitalized during much of the hearings concerning the scandal. The hearings did reveal that Casey was a major participant in the operation and that he, Lieutenant Colonel Oliver North, U.S. Marine Corps (who was then attached to the National Security Council), and others had begun an operation that circumvented congressional control and was outside the control of the CIA. Casey's condition continued to deteriorate, and he died before he could testify before the congressional investigative committee. Since he did not make a statement concerning his involvement, his actions in this matter remain shrouded in secrecy. *See also:* Central Intelligence Agency.

References

American Bar Association. *Oversight and Accountability of the U.S. Intelligence Agencies: An Evaluation.* Washington, DC: ABA, 1985.

Laqueur, Walter. *A World of Secrets.* New York: Basic Books, 1985.

Quirk, John; Phillips, David; Cline, Ray; and Pforzheimer, Walter. *The Central Intelligence Agency: A Photographic History.* Guilford, CT: Foreign Intelligence Press, 1986.

Treverton, Gregory F. *Covert Action: The Limits of Intervention in the Postwar World.* New York: Basic Books, 1987.

Turner, Stansfield. *Secrecy and Democracy: The CIA in Transition.* Boston: Houghton Mifflin, 1985.

—CASH BUDGET, FEDERAL, is an intelligence budgeting term. It is a consolidated statement showing the cash income and the cash outgo of the federal government. It excludes certain budgetary receipts and expenditures that are noncash in nature, such as intragovernmental transfers and accrued interest on savings bonds. The cash receipts and cash expenditures of trust funds are included. *See also:* Budget.

References

Pickett, George. "Congress, the Budget, and Intelligence." In *Intelligence Policy and Process,* edited by Alfred C. Maurer, Marion D. Turnstall, and James M. Keagle. Boulder, CO: Westview Press, 1985.

—CASTRO, FIDEL. *See:* Mongoose.

—CATALOG OF APPROVED SCIENTIFIC AND TECHNICAL TASKS (CAST) is a four-volume publication containing Department of Defense scientific and technical intelligence production tasking. Its inclusion in the CAST means that a requirement has been identified and that financing has been approved for the requirement. However, it does not necessarily mean that work is being done on the project, because this would depend on the priority assigned to the project (i.e., how important it is considered), whether there is enough information available, and whether it is feasible to do the project. Thus, it is merely a listing of Defense Intelligence Agency-assigned production tasks that have been forwarded to scientific and technical production elements of the military services for possible action. *See also:* Defense Intelligence Agency.

References

Pickett, George. "Congress, the Budget, and Intelligence." In *Intelligence Policy and Process*, edited by Alfred C. Maurer, Marion D. Turnstall, and James M. Keagle. Boulder, CO: Westview Press, 1985.

Von Hoene, John P. A. *Intelligence User's Guide*. Washington, DC: DIA, 1983.

—**CAUTERIZE** is a term used in clandestine and covert intelligence operations. It means to remove compromised agents and to take them to safety. *See also:* Agent, Agent Authentication, Agent in Place, Agent Net, Agent of Influence, Agent Provocateur, Alias, Blow, Blown Agent, Burn, Burnt, Discard, Doubled, Exfiltration, Go To Ground, Graduated, Naked, Rolling Up the Net, Turned.

References

Becket, Henry S. A. *The Dictionary of Espionage: Spookspeak into English*. New York: Stein and Day, 1986.

Deacon, Richard. *Spyclopedia: An Encyclopedia of Spies, Secret Services, Operations, Jargon, and All Subjects Related to the World of Espionage*. London: Macdonald, 1987.

Ranelagh, John. *The Agency: The Rise and Decline of the CIA*. New York: Simon and Schuster, 1986.

—**CAVANAGH, THOMAS PATRICK,** an employee with the Northrop Corporation, was arrested in Los Angeles, California, on December 18, 1984, while trying to pass classified information on the stealth bomber. He was convicted on espionage charges on March 14, 1985, and sentenced to life in prison.

References

Allen, Thomas B., and Polmar, Norman. *Merchants of Treason: America's Secrets for Sale*. New York: Delacorte Press, 1988.

Crawford, David J. *Volunteers: The Betrayal of National Defense Secrets by Air Force Traitors*. Washington, DC: GPO, 1988.

—**CELL** is a small group of people who work together for clandestine or subversive purposes.

References

Department of Defense, Joint Chiefs of Staff. *Department of Defense Dictionary of Military and Related Terms*. Washington, DC: GPO, 1986.

—**CENTER** is a general intelligence term with two meanings. (1) The Center is the Soviet secret service (KGB) term for its headquarters at 2 Dzerzhinsky Square in Moscow; it is also called "Moscow Center." (2) In FBI terminology, a center is an intelligence service headquarters.

References

Becket, Henry S. A. *The Dictionary of Espionage: Spookspeak into English*. New York: Stein and Day, 1986.

Clancy, Tom. *The Cardinal of the Kremlin*. New York: Putnam, 1988.

Kessler, Ronald. *Spy vs. Spy: Stalking Soviet Spies in America*. New York: Charles Scribner's Sons, 1988.

—**CENTER FOR NAVAL ANALYSIS (CNA)** has its origins in World War II, when German submarines were inflicting heavy losses on Allied convoys. Impressed by the British methods of studying military operations, the United States created the Antisubmarine Warfare Operations Research Group in 1942. By 1945 it had become the Operations Evaluation Group, was studying the whole range of naval operations, and was taken over by the Massachusetts Institute of Technology. The present CNA was formed in 1962, and its management and direction were transferred to the Franklin Institute of the State of Pennsylvania and later to the University of Rochester. A reorientation occurred when the management of the CNA passed to the Hudson Institute in Indianapolis, Indiana, in 1984. As a division of the institute, it continues its program of operations research, systems analysis, and program analysis for the Navy and other government agencies. The CNA is currently staffed with both active-duty naval personnel and civilian analysts. It is located in Alexandria, Virginia.

References

Laubenthal, Saunders A. *Survey of Resources for Intelligence Research*. Washington, DC: DIC, 1986.

—**CENTRAL ACTIONS OFFICE (CAO)**. *See:* Defense Intelligence Agency, *under "Organization."*

—**CENTRAL INFORMATION REFERENCE AND CONTROL (CIRC) SYSTEM** supports the intelligence and research and development communities, other government agencies, and government contractors by maintaining a central source of references to scientific and technical intelligence information. The Defense Intelligence Agency manages the Scientific and Technical Intelligence Information Services Program, of which the CIRC is a part. The Air Force System Command's Foreign Technology Division (FTD) is the executive agent for the CIRC.

The more sophisticated CIRC II system is an automated index of publications, reports, and documents. Its data base consists of over six million references to scientific and technical documents that date from 1957 to the present. About 300,000 open source and classified references are added each year. The following are among the types of materials that are maintained in the CIRC system:

- Open-source materials. The CIRC system has open literature from the USSR, Eastern Europe, and the People's Republic of China concerning the natural sciences and engineering, with particular interest in military application. Open sources on military equipment are covered on a worldwide basis. Abstracts of open-source material may be read and printed at any remote terminal location.
- Most of the open-source documents that are referenced by the CIRC are stored at the Foreign Science Library (FSL) in Columbus, Ohio; however, the FTD often enters material from abstract journals into the CIRC without having a full text copy of the original document. The rationale is that it is better to know that a document exists and not be able to readily provide it than not to know of its existence. The CIRC entry on an open-source document provides the source of the data.
- Classified materials. Although about 85 percent of the CIRC II system consists of unclassified information, it does include other infirmation of all classification levels up to special compartmented information (SCI) material. This classified information consists of intelligence information reports, sensor analysis reports, finished intelligence products, and other materials of scientific and technical value. The classified materials are often entered into the CIRC II as complete documents, but documents that are over two pages long are reduced to substantive abstracts or abstracts for on-line review.
- Translations. The CIRC II system includes a translation data base called XLAX. This data base permits on-line reference to unclassified documents that have been translated. The file also provides the capability to locate existing translations so that costly and time-consuming new translations do not have to be initiated.
- Current awareness. The CIRC II profile-dissemination system offers continuing dissemination of current information that has been generated by a standing request, or profile, which is a statement of information requirements.

See also: Defense Intelligence Agency.

References

Department of Defense, U.S. Army. *RDTE Managers Intelligence and Threat Support Guide.* Alexandria, VA: Headquarters, Army Matériel Development and Readiness Command, 1983.

—**CENTRAL INTELLIGENCE AGENCY (CIA)**

History

Even before the attack on Pearl Harbor, President Franklin D. Roosevelt was concerned about U.S. intelligence deficiencies. The debacle at Pearl Harbor merely furthered these doubts. As a result, he asked a New York lawyer, William J. Donovan, to draft a plan for an intelligence service. From this request the concept for the Office of Strategic Services (OSS) was developed. The OSS was established in June 1942 and was given the mission of collecting and analyzing strategic information and of conducting special operations that were not assigned to other agencies. During World War II it provided policymakers with the essential facts and national estimates that were necessary to conduct the war, and it also often provided direct assistance to American forces in military campaigns. However, the OSS was never given complete jurisdiction over all U.S. foreign intelligence activities. For example, since the 1930s, the FBI had been responsible for intelligence work in Latin America, and the military services also jealously guarded their areas of responsibility. As a result of this provincialism and other factors, the OSS was inhibited greatly in its operations during the war.

The OSS was disbanded in 1945 and its functions were given to the State and War Departments. However, Donovan realized the need for a centralized intelligence system and submitted a proposal to Roosevelt that called for the separation of the OSS from the Joint Chiefs of Staff. The new organization, which would be responsible directly to the President, would collect intelligence overtly and covertly and would "provide intelligence guidance, determine national intelligence objectives, and correlate the intelligence information that was collected by all government agencies." According to Donovan, the agency would coordinate all the intelligence services, would conduct subversive operations abroad, but would have "no police or law enforcement functions, either at home or abroad."

Donovan's plan was very unpopular. The military services opposed a complete merger, the State Department claimed that it should direct all peacetime operations that affected foreign relations, and the FBI supported a system in which the military services would control military intelligence worldwide and it would handle all civilian activities.

In response to this debate, President Harry Truman established the Central Intelligence Group (CIG) in January 1946 and directed it to coordinate existing departmental intelligence and to supplement their operations. The CIG was to operate under the direction of the National Intelligence Authority, which was composed of a presidential representative, and the secretaries of state, war, and the Navy. Rear Admiral Sidney W. Souers, U.S. Naval Reserve, who was then the deputy chief of naval intelligence, was appointed as the first director of Central Intelligence. The major weakness of the CIG was that its funds and staff were provided by other departments, which also had their own intelligence organizations. Twenty months later, both the NIA and the CIG were disestablished, and, under the provisions of the National Security Act of 1947, the National Security Council (NSC) and the Central Intelligence Agency (CIA) were established.

Most of the act's provisions followed the original Donovan plan of 1944 and the Presidential Directive creating the CIG. In addition, it stated that the director and deputy director of Central Intelligence were to be appointed by the President and confirmed by the Senate. An amend-

ment that was signed on April 4, 1953 stipulated that these individuals could be either civilians or military, but that military officers could not hold both offices concurrently.

The initial organizational structure included a number of administrative functions and four major operating components:

The Office of Reports and Estimates (ORE) was initially responsible for all finished intelligence production. The direct forerunner of all the intelligence producing offices now in existence, it was subdivided repeatedly as the production function grew in size and was diversified in responsibility. The office was initially formed in the CIG by personnel who were transferred from the State Department and from the military services.

The Office of Special Operations (OSO) was derived from what remained of the wartime Office of Strategic Services (OSS), which had been attached to the War Department as the Strategic Services Unit in the immediate postwar years. This office was responsible for espionage and counterespionage. Following the practice that had been established in the OSS, worldwide communications and security support also were assigned to this operating office.

The Office of Operations (OO) was responsible for overt and domestic collection of foreign intelligence. It, too, was formed partly out of the remnants of the OSS structure that had been attached to the Pentagon and had included a coordinator of domestic collection activity that became the Contact Division. It also included the broadcast monitoring capability of the Foreign Broadcast Information Service that was transferred from the War Department and the foreign document centers that were taken over from the Army and Navy and merged into the Foreign Documents Division.

The Office of Collection and Dissemination (OCD) was responsible for establishing intelligence collection priorities, coordinating the collection efforts of the various agencies, and organizing the dissemination or distribution of both raw intelligence and finished reports. This office soon assumed control of the reference and records centers as well.

As additional activities and assets were transferred to the CIA, they were added to the existing structure. For example, when joint Military Intelligence Surveys became a CIA responsibility in October 1947, the National Intelligence Survey program was organized in a Basic Intelligence

Division of the Office of Reports and Estimates.

The NSC, which had been established concurrently with the CIA, began issuing a series of directives in December 1947 that had a great deal to do with the subsequent shaping of the CIA's structure and missions. One of the most significant of these directives ordered an immediate expansion in covert operations and paramilitary activities. In response, on September 1, 1948, the Office of Policy Coordination (OPC) was established. It had a unique relationship with the rest of the CIA, since the NSC ordered that it remain as independent of the remainder of the organization as possible and placed it under the policy direction of the Departments of State and Defense. As a result, during its first two years, the OPC's policy guidance came directly from State and Defense, although its chain of command ran through the director of Central Intelligence. It was during this period that, under the OPC, such CIA activities as Radio Free Europe, the Committee for Free Asia, Radio Liberty, the Asia Foundation, and the youth, student, and labor programs of the Agency were begun.

Shortly after the establishment of the OPC, a Hoover Commission Task Force began making recommendations on national security organization, and these were partially endorsed by the commission itself in 1949. A separate National Intelligence Survey Group headed by Allen Dulles filed its own report with the NSC in January 1949. The NSC subsequently directed a merger of the Office of Special Operations, the Office of Policy Coordination, and the Contact Branch. However, this could not be accomplished under the original CIA charter, and no major change was made until General Walter Bedell Smith took over as director of Central Intelligence in October 1950.

In 1949 the Central Intelligence Agency Act, which supplemented the 1947 act, was passed. Additional provisions were also passed that exempted the CIA from many of the usual limitations on expending federal funds and permitted the CIA to use confidential fiscal and administrative procedures. In addition, the legislation also provided that CIA funds could be included in the budgets of other departments and then transferred to the agency without the restrictions placed on the initial appropriation. This legislation was the statutory authority for the secrecy of the CIA's budget. The 1949 act also exempted the agency from having to disclose its "organization, functions, names, officials, titles, salaries and numbers of personnel employed," thereby further protecting intelligence sources and methods from disclosure.

The creation of the CIA occurred at a time when the leadership of the Soviet Union was directing its attention to Europe. Between 1945 and 1948 it consolidated its military and political control of most of Eastern Europe and threatened to move against Greece, Turkey, Iran, Yugoslavia, and Berlin. Italy was seen as crucial to U.S. policy in the region, and President Truman approved providing covert assistance to those groups opposing the Communists in national elections. The CIA provided financial and technical assistance to the Christian Democrats and other moderate groups, which were victorious in the April 1949 parliamentary elections.

Following the success in Italy, George F. Kennan, then director of the Policy Planning Staff, Department of State, supported the creation of a permanent covert political action department that would conduct paramilitary operations and political and economic warfare. It was established in the CIA and was named the Office of Policy Coordination.

In addition to the above activities, the CIA's European operations also included support for Radio Free Europe and Radio Liberty, which provided news and political analysis to listeners in Eastern Europe and the Soviet Union.

Concurrently, in China the CIA sponsored paramilitary operations by providing aircraft, boats, and an agent network with the goal of impeding Chinese operations in Korea.

The First Three Directors of Central Intelligence

Concerning the leadership of the organization, the initial years reflected great fluidity at the top.

The first director of Central Intelligence (DCI), Rear Admiral Sidney W. Souers, held the office for only four months (January 23–June 10, 1946) before retiring from the Navy.

Lieutenant General Hoyt S. Vandenberg succeeded Souers as the DCI in June 1946. More aggressive than Souers, Vandenberg appeared to view the position as a stepping stone to his goal of becoming chief of staff of the newly formed Air Force. Vandenberg did manage to gain greater budget independence for the CIG and expanded the group's clandestine collection, research, and analysis roles. Thus, the CIG's function changed from merely coordinating national estimates to producing intelligence. Additionally, the Office of Research and Evaluation was formed, and the CIG continued to expand in size and scope. Finally, under Vandenberg, the CIG produced its first national estimate, which dealt with Soviet intentions and capabilities.

Vandenberg also played a pivotal role in delineating the proposed CIA's role in intelligence. Through his influence, the National Security Act of 1947 stated that the agency would have the following duties: advise the National Security Council on intelligence activities; make recommendations to the National Security Council on coordinating intelligence activities; correlate, evaluate, and disseminate intelligence; perform intelligence functions that the National Security Council felt could best be handled by a central intelligence organization; and perform such other duties as the National Security Council directed.

Although the act had identified the CIA as a coordinator of intelligence, it became apparent during Rear Admiral Roscoe H. Hillenkoetter's tenure (May 1, 1947–October 7, 1950) that the DCI lacked the bureaucratic power to effect such coordination. As a result, the CIA was prompted to move into the area of current intelligence production. This, in turn, resulted in ignoring intelligence estimates, and a study group initiated by President Truman recommended in 1949 that the agency be reorganized.

The Tenure of Walter Bedell Smith

General. The failure to foresee the invasion of South Korea in June 1950 prompted further criticism of the CIA. In October 1950, General Walter Bedell Smith became the DCI. Smith, who had been Eisenhower's chief of staff when Eisenhower was supreme commander in Europe and then had served as U.S. ambassador to the Soviet Union, was aggressive and an extremely competent administrator. With his deputy DCI, William Jackson, Smith instituted a number of reforms. He created the Office of National Estimates, whose only task was to produce coordinated national estimates. An Office of Research and Reports was created to report on economic changes in the Soviet bloc, and in 1952 the Directorate for Intelligence (DDI) was formed to produce finished intelligence.

During Smith's tenure the CIA assumed a more permanent form. There were now two primary groups: operations and analysis. It was up to his successor, Allen Dulles, to further expand these initiatives.

Highlights. The consensus of opinion is that the appointment of Smith as director was an excellent one. He served until February 9, 1953, and during his tenure, the CIA reacted successfully to a crisis in Iran and was transformed into an effective service much along the lines initially envisioned by General Donovan.

Concerning the Iranian crisis, when the Shah was driven from Iran by the forces of leftist premier Mohammed Mossadegh (supported by the Iranian Communist Party and the Soviet Union), the CIA mounted a counterattack by hiring demonstrators to intimidate Mossadegh's supporters and instructing the Shah's forces in ways to take over the local radio station in order to prepare the nation for the Shah's triumphant return.

Agency Organizational Innovations. In respect to organization, when Smith assumed office, the existence of both the OSO and the OPC meant that two clandestine organizations were responding to separate chains of command while working within many of the same foreign countries. This situation had caused continual difficulties—especially when the two offices were competing for the same potential agents. Smith immediately ordered that all orders to the OPC be passed through him, and he designated a number of senior representatives abroad to coordinate the separate activities. The integration of the OPC and the OSO had begun by mid-1951, and a complete integration was ordered in July 1952. Nonetheless, some overseas stations continued to report directly to the DCI through overseas representatives until 1954. This new joint organization was named the Clandestine Services, and within it an International Organizations Division was activated in June 1954 to handle student, youth, and labor programs.

Smith also created two new deputy directors, one for administration and one for operations. The latter was redesignated the deputy director for plans (DDP) in January 1951 and headed what became the Clandestine Services.

Meanwhile, reorganization of the intelligence production offices was also being accomplished. The Office of Research and Estimates was divided into the Office of National Estimates, which was responsible for national-level policy-related papers that projected analysis into the future, and the Office of Research and Reports (ORR), which handled economic and geographic intelligence and the National Intelligence Survey Program. A new Office of Current Intelligence was added in January 1951. A year later, a deputy director for intelligence (DDI) was named, with supervision over the above offices as well as the Office of Scientific Intelligence, the Office of Collection and Dissemination, and the Office of Intelligence Coordination, which had been directly under the DCI. In March 1952 the Office of Operations, which controlled such overt functions as domestic contacts, the Foreign Broadcast Information Service, and the Foreign Documents Division, was placed under the DDI. Moreover, in November 1952 the Photographic Intelligence Division was established within the ORR's Geographic Research Area, to be followed by an Office of Basic Intelligence that was formed in 1955.

Smith also created the Office of National Estimates and initiated a daily report for the President that summarized the most important developments affecting U.S. interests.

The Tenure of Allen Dulles

General. Smith left the directorship in February 1953 in order to become secretary of state. His successor, Allen Dulles, had served in the OSS and had been brought to the CIA from his private law practice by Smith. Dulles's tenure from February 26, 1953, to November 29, 1961, continued many of Smith's innovations and provided greater long-term direction for the CIA.

Highlights. Dulles differed from his predecessors in that he had previous operational intelligence experience. He had served in the OSS in Switzerland, where he directed intelligence operations against Germany. Because of his experience, his interests were primarily operational, and during his tenure the agency conducted many operations that were intended to replace a government that was hostile to the United States with one that was more friendly. These included a successful operation in Iran in 1953 that brought the Shah back to power, successful operations in Costa Rica in 1953 and Guatemala in 1954, and unsuccessful operations in Indonesia in 1958, Tibet in 1958, and operation Mongoose against Castro's Cuba in 1960 and 1961.

Dulles's final years as DCI were troubled by two issues: the missile gap, and the Bay of Pigs invasion. The missile gap issue centered on the strategic balance between the Soviet Union and the United States. Through the efforts of Senator Stuart Symington and Senator John Kennedy, this became a campaign issue in the 1960 presidential election. President Eisenhower, who had

sufficient overhead reconnaissance to know that there was no gap, could not present this evidence because of its classification and therefore was unable to squelch the issue. After Kennedy became president, his administration revealed that a gap, indeed, did not exist.

The Bay of Pigs invasion can be viewed in many lights, and, as President Kennedy said in its aftermath, there was sufficient blame to go around for all concerned. From the intelligence and CIA perspectives, the invasion was the culmination of similar paramilitary operations that had been conducted in Iran, Guatemala, and elsewhere in the 1950s. What set it apart was that it was larger and less well conceived. The abysmal failure of the operation led to a reevaluation of the CIA's role in such operations and a movement away from large-scale paramilitary operations.

Agency organizational innovations. Between 1950 and 1952 the CIA had grown markedly, and the administrative support functions had increased along with the other activities. In February 1955 the responsibilities for training, personnel administration, and communications were centralized in the Directorate for Administration, which was renamed the Directorate for Support. By 1955, therefore, the basic structure of the current agency had been established. The director had three functional deputies, each in charge of a directorate. Overt collection, analysis, and production of finished intelligence were centralized in the Intelligence Directorate. Other intelligence collection—both espionage and the rapidly growing technical forms—were located in the Plans Directorate. Finally, the Support Directorate provided administrative services of common concern as well as specialized support to various units.

Much of this structure still exists. Over time, however, functions have been shifted from one directorate to another, realigned within directorates, or eliminated. These have usually occurred for one of two reasons: (1) decisions or recommendations have been received from other parts of the governmental structure, most often from the President, the National Security Council, the Congress, or from a succession of special commissions and internal study groups; or (2) changes in organizational philosophy have resulted from personnel changes. Various changes have been made concerning the CIA's organization, but all have reflected a combination of three approaches: the approach of grouping similar functions; the approach of grouping organizations by common interest (e.g., by geographical region); and the approach of grouping organizations so that there were close organizational links between the supplier of a service and the principal customer.

Likewise, changes in the priorities that have been assigned to particular missions or intelligence targets have also resulted in changes in the size or the authority of the organizational components. Significant growth in a particular area has led to occasional divisions of one unit into smaller ones, in order to provide for more effective control.

In the six years following the establishment of this framework, most organizational changes were minor. The positions of senior representative of the DCI abroad were eliminated in 1957. A Photographic Interpretation Center, which combined the functions from several CIA components, including the Photo Intelligence Division, was established within the DDI in 1958. This, in turn, was replaced by the National Photographic Interpretation Center (NPIC) in 1961, reflecting the increase in production workload that was caused by the U-2 and other overhead reconnaissance programs. Finally, the personnel and responsibilities involved in the development of technical collection services— primarily aircraft—were transferred from the office of the DCI to the Plans Directorate.

The Tenure of John A. McCone

General. John A. McCone succeeded Allen Dulles on November 29, 1961, and served until April 28, 1965.

Highlights. The appointment of McCone augured a significant change in the agency's orientation. McCone, who had pursued a successful career in business and government, was more interested in intelligence production than in operations, and this had a decidedly positive effect on the quality of the agency's intelligence output. In 1963 he established the National Intelligence Programs Evaluation (NIPE) to evaluate and review Intelligence Community programs, their cost-effectiveness, and the effectiveness of the U.S. Intelligence Board. Additionally, McCone took an active interest in the production of the National Intelligence Estimates, leading to a much more accurate intelligence picture of Cuba during the missile crisis in 1962 than had existed in 1961 during the Bay of Pigs invasion.

McCone's influence declined significantly after President Kennedy's assassination. President Johnson had less interest in intelligence than did Kennedy, and he preferred to work through the Departments of State and Defense. When McCone and Johnson disagreed over U.S. participation in Vietnam, with McCone arguing for a direct approach to the problem and Johnson preferring an incremental approach concerning U.S. involvement, McCone resigned.

Organizational innovations and changes. Late in 1961, McCone established a new working group chaired by CIA inspector general Lyman Kirkpatrick to study the agency's and Intelligence Community's organization and activities. The group's final recommendations, which were submitted in April 1962, led to the last major reorganization of the CIA.

Even before the study was completed, one major decision had been made. Technological advances had been so numerous and so rapid in the 1950s that they presented new opportunities for intelligence collection by machines. Reconnaissance aircraft had been developed within the agency, and collection of electronic intelligence was another rapidly growing area. Technology had also made new kinds of information available for analysis and had created a need for more analysis by scientifically trained people. McCone designated a deputy director for research, with initial responsibility over elements drawn from the DDP and additional responsibilities to be determined after the completion of the study, in February 1962. The Office of Research and Development, the Office of Electronic Intelligence, and the Office of Special Activities (responsible for overhead reconnaissance activities) were established immediately, and the Office of Scientific Intelligence (from DDI) and automatic data processing activities (from Support and the Comptroller) were added in 1963. With the establishment of the Foreign Missile and Space Analysis Center later that year, the renamed Directorate of Science and Technology assumed the basic form that it still maintains.

The Kirkpatrick study also prompted a major strengthening of the Office of the Director. The General Counsel's Office, Audit Staff, Comptroller, Office of the Budget, Program Analysis and Manpower, and the U.S. Intelligence Board Secretariat were added to it. By late 1962, the position of an executive director-comptroller had been established and his role as third in command of the CIA had been delineated. The Kirkpatrick study also prompted a centralization of paramilitary activities, an organization to provide a command mechanism for future contingencies, and the establishment of a Domestic Operations Division, to develop contacts with foreign nationals in the United States.

By the end of 1963 the agency's organization had settled into a pattern that it would keep for a decade. Four directorates existed. These were distinguished primarily by function, but units performing services were collocated frequently with their customers. The agency's central direction was strong, with an executive director-comptroller playing a major role in all agency activities, and the Board of National Estimates reporting directly to the director, although the supporting Office of National Estimates remained in the Intelligence Directorate for about another year.

The Tenure of William F. Rayborn, Jr.

General. Vice Admiral William F. Rayborn, Jr., U.S. Navy (Retired), became the DCI on April 28, 1965, and served until June 30, 1966.

Highlights. Rayborn had been extremely successful in his management of the Polaris missile program, but he had little knowledge of international affairs and no intelligence background. As Mark Lowenthal astutely observed in *U.S. Intelligence: Evolution and Anatomy*, Rayborn "simply was not taken very seriously by his subordinates or, eventually, by the President himself." He left in little over a year.

The Tenure of Richard Helms

General. Richard Helms became DCI on June 30, 1966, and served for almost seven years, retiring on February 2, 1973.

Highlights. Helms had been in intelligence since joining the Office of Strategic Services in 1942; he was the first career officer to become the DCI. However, his operational background was carried over into his tenure in the CIA, and the focus of the agency was shifted again toward operations. In the late 1960's and early 1970s, Vietnam dominated the intelligence world. When Nixon became president, he shifted the emphasis to the White House and the National Security Council, but he did increase Helms's power by creating two organizations. The first was the Intelligence Resources Advisory Committee (IRAC), to assist the "DCI on the preparation of a consolidated intelligence program budget." The second innovation, which was introduced by Helms, was the creation of the Intelligence Community Staff in 1972. With the decline of U.S. involvement in Vietnam in 1972 and Nixon's use of the CIA in the Watergate crimes, the intelligence focus became blurred. In 1973 Helms was designated ambassador to Iran, and he was replaced as the DCI by James R. Schlesinger.

Organizational innovations and changes. The CIA's organizational arrangements remained largely static from 1964 until 1973, although the growing emphasis on analysis led to further subdivisions in the analytical offices. The DDI's Office of Operations was reorganized and renamed the Domestic Contact Office in mid-1965. The Office of Basic Intelligence was enlarged and took over the agency's geographic responsibilities from the Office of Research and Reports. The latter was divided in 1967 into the Office of Economic Research and the Office of Strategic Research. In the Directorate for Science and Technology, the Office of Special Projects was established in 1965 to conduct overhead reconnaissance, a duty that had been handled previously by a staff. Staffs to address special needs were added to the Plans Directorate. Responsibility for proprietary organizations was transferred from the Domestic Operations Division to other DDP components in December 1971, and that division was renamed the Foreign Resources Division the following month. Some mechanism for coordinating and evaluating national foreign intelligence activities had existed since the establishment of the CIA. In 1972 this took the form of the Intelligence Community Staff in the Office of the Director.

Activities related to Southeast Asia grew and substantially contracted during this period. Operationally, such changes were reflected in the creation of a special assistant to the DCI for Vietnam affairs with a supporting staff and in the formation of a number of new low-level components throughout the agency.

The Tenure of James R. Schlesinger

General. James R. Schlesinger became the DCI on February 2, 1973, and served until July 2, 1973. He was succeeded by Lieutenant General Vernon A. Walters, U.S. Army, the deputy director, who served as acting DCI until William E. Colby took office on September 4, 1973.

Highlights. Although Schlesinger served as the DCI for only five months, his tenure had a decided effect on the Intelligence Community. He reduced drastically the size of the Directorate for Operations and the analytic staff, and he took an active role in the production of the National Intelligence Estimates. Schlesinger would probably have had an even more dramatic affect on the agency had he been permitted to remain as the DCI, but President Nixon appointed him as secretary of defense in the spring of 1973.

Organizational innovations and changes. The CIA's most recent changes were begun by Schlesinger. He instituted a number of organizational studies and directed a number of transfers. Some of these were accomplished during his tenure, while others were carried out by William Colby.

The following organizational moves and personnel reductions were initiated by Schlesinger:

- The Domestic Contact Service was transferred from the Directorate for Intelligence (DDI) to the Directorate for Plans (DDP). The staff was reduced and DDI was redesignated the Directorate for Operations.
- Three technical activities—technical services, communications research and development, and the National Photographic Interpretation Center (NPIC)—were transferred to the Science and Technology Directorate. This directorate also merged certain functions of the Office of Scientific Intelligence with the Foreign Missile and Space Analysis Center and established the Office of Weapons Intelligence. The Office of Special Projects was changed into the Office of Development and Engineering, which provides agency-wide engineering and system development support.
- A new Office of Political Research was established in the Directorate of Intelligence.
- Computer services, which had been fragmented, were transferred—with the largest elements in the Directorate for Science and Technology—to the Support Directorate. And the Support Directorate itself went through two name changes, first to Management and Services, and subsequently to the Directorate for Administration.
- The Board and Office of National Estimates were abolished and replaced by a group of senior functional and geographic specialists called National Intelligence Officers (NIOs), who were drawn partially from outside of the CIA. Both the senior NIO and the head of the Intelligence Community Staff were named deputies to the DCI.
- The position of executive director-comptroller was abolished. Many of its functions were redistributed within the Office of the DCI and the Directorate of Administration. A Management Committee composed of the DCI, his principal deputy, the four deputies in charge of directorates, the comptroller, the general counsel, and the inspector general was established to advise the DCI on management policy questions.
- For budgetary reasons, a decision was made to terminate the National Intelligence Survey program in the Office of Basic and Geographic Intelligence. As a result, the geographic intelligence unit was redesignated the Office of Geographic and Cartographic Research.

Thus, in February 1975 the agency's structure was generally the same as it had been in 1965. However, there was a stricter adherence to combining similar functions than there had been in earlier years. Management direction and control were decentralized. The staff structure was now considerably reduced and simplified, and the number of full-time personnel had been reduced substantially.

The Tenure of William E. Colby

General. William E. Colby served as the DCI from September 4, 1973, until January 30, 1976.

Highlights. Colby, like Richard Helms, was a professional intelligence officer. Although he had spent his life in operations, he had served as Schlesinger's deputy and thus continued many of Schlesinger's initiatives. The most dramatic accomplishments during his tenure were abolishing the Board and the Office of National Estimates, replacing them with the National Intelligence Officer (NIO) system. Under the new system, there were thirteen NIOs who had a functional or regional area and were responsible to the DCI for intelligence collection and production in their area.

Colby's greatest task was to respond to the presidential and congressional committees that had been formed to investigate intelligence activities. The initial request came from President Ford, who asked for an accounting shortly after he took office in 1974. Colby responded by submitting a detailed list of all CIA transgressions that had been prepared for his predecessor, James Schlesinger. This report was so comprehensive that it became known as the "Family Jewels," and many in the CIA were opposed to providing such detailed information. The subsequent congressional investigations created considerable friction between the White House and Congress. The White House position was epitomized by Secretary of State Henry Kissinger, who favored limiting the information given to Congress to only that which was requested. Colby's position, on the other hand, was to be as open with Congress as possible. This divergence of opinion was to be Colby's downfall, and he was dismissed on November 2, 1975, but stayed on until George Bush became the DCI in January 1976.

The Tenure of George Bush

General. George Bush became the DCI on January 30, 1976. He served for less than a year, leaving office on January 20, 1977. He was succeeded by E. Henry Knoche, the deputy director, who served as acting DCI until Admiral Stansfield Turner, U.S. Navy, took office on March 9, 1977.

Highlights. George Bush, who replaced William Colby as the DCI in November 1975, was a political appointment that was made as a reaction to the ongoing intelligence scandal. Bush's tenure was so short that he had little effect on the agency. He left office as part of the turnover that occurred when President Carter took office.

The Tenure of Stansfield Turner

General. Admiral Stansfield Turner served as the DCI from March 9, 1977, until January 20, 1981.

Highlights. Turner, an old classmate of Jimmy Carter from the days when the President had attended Annapolis, became DCI after Carter unsuccessfully attempted to gain congressional approval of Theodore Sorenson for the position. Arriving from the Naval War College, Turner brought with him a strong determination to make the corrections in the system that he perceived as necessary. In August 1977 he announced that he would reduce the CIA staff by 800 positions, which would come from the Directorate for Operations. On October 31 he fired 198 employees in a move that was quickly dubbed the Halloween Massacre.

One of the Republican positions in the election of 1980 was that the restrictions that had been placed on the Intelligence Community were both unwarranted and detrimental. This stance contrasted so starkly with Turner's performance as the DCI that it was a certainty he would be replaced if the Republicans won the election. When they did, President-elect Reagan promptly nominated William Casey to be the DCI.

The Tenure of William J. Casey

General. William J. Casey served as the DCI from January 28, 1981, until January 29, 1987.

Highlights. Casey was one of the more colorful directors. His tenure was hallmarked by attempting to maintain the secrecy of CIA programs and the agency's freedom from Congress. In the early years of his tenure, this led to repeated run-ins with Congress that were highlighted by disagreements with Senator Barry Goldwater (R-Ariz.). Goldwater, a conservative, was placed in the unfortunate position of trying to maintain secrecy while controlling Casey. In 1986 Casey's involvement in the Iran-Contra scandal was made public. In 1987 it was announced that Casey had terminal cancer, and he was hospitalized during much of the hearings concerning the scandal. The hearings did reveal that Casey was a major participant in the operation and that he, Lieutenant Colonel Oliver North, U.S. Marine Corps (who was then attached to the National Security Council), and others had begun an operation that circumvented congressional control and was outside the control of the CIA. Casey's condition continued to deteriorate, and he died before he could testify before the congressional investigative committee. Since he did not make a statement concerning his involvement, his actions in this matter remain shrouded in secrecy.

The Tenure of William Webster

General. William Webster became the DCI on May 26, 1987.

He had not wanted to be the DCI, and he was not President Reagan's first choice for the job. However, with the death of William Casey and the Iran-Contra hearings, the CIA was in disarray, and Webster was known for his excellent job of revitalizing the FBI in the aftermath of J. Edgar Hoover. Webster, whose wife had died in 1984, had decided to retire from the FBI and return to the practice of law. Those close to him say that, when he was offered the directorship, he was not eager to accept it. However, after discussing it with his children, Webster accepted the post.

Webster's appointment was not greeted warmly by many of the professionals at the agency, who felt that his approach would probably inhibit agency operations. However, his first eighteen months as director demonstrated that, while he intended to obey the law, he did not intend to unreasonably restrict the agency's covert and clandestine activities. His stated position was that such activities must be accomplished in accordance with existing law and must be of such nature that they could be explained to and accepted by the American people, in the event that the operation was blown.

In summary, much of the criticism of Webster's appointment had subsided by the spring of 1989. The changes that he had made at the agency had apparently been accepted by the rank and file and had not been drastic. Webster appeared to be an excellent administrator, and, most important, he had kept the CIA out of the spotlight, providing a respite that it sorely needed.

Organization

The organization of the CIA includes an executive or headquarters element, and four directorates.

Executive Element. The executive element is composed of the director of Central Intelligence, the deputy director of Central Intelligence, and the executive director, who exercise authority over the four directorates (for Operations, Science and Technology, Intelligence, and Administration). In addition, there are several staff elements that do not exercise authority over the directorates, but fulfill essential duties for the agency.

Director of Central Intelligence (DCI). The DCI is the President's principal foreign intelligence advisor. He is appointed by the President with the consent of Congress to be the head of the Intelligence Community and director of the CIA and to discharge his responsibilities as they are prescribed by law and by presidential and National Security Council directives. (For information on the people who have served as the DCI and the dates of their service, see above in this entry.)

Deputy director of Central Intelligence (DDCI). The DDCI is appointed by the President, with the advice and consent of the Senate, to act as the DCI in the absence or disability of that person. The DCI and DDCI usually divide the DCI's duties as the DCI chooses. The DDCI also represents the CIA on the National Foreign Intelligence Board. The following individuals have served as DDCI:

Kingman Douglass (acting), March 2, 1946–July 11, 1946.

Brigadier General Edwin K. Wright, U.S. Army, January 20, 1947–March 9, 1949.

The Honorable William H. Jackson, October 7, 1950–August 3, 1951.

The Honorable Allen W. Dulles, August 23, 1951–February 26, 1953.

General Charles Pearre Cabell, U.S. Air Force, April 23, 1953–January 31, 1962.

Lieutenant General Marshall S. Carter, U.S. Army, April 3, 1962–April 28, 1965.

The Honorable Richard Helms, April 28, 1965–June 30, 1966.

Vice Admiral Rufus L. Taylor, U.S. Navy, October 13, 1966–January 31, 1969.

Lieutenant General Robert E. Cushman, Jr., U.S. Marine Corps, May 7, 1969–December 31, 1971.

Lieutenant General Vernon A. Walters, U.S. Army, May 2, 1972–July 7, 1976 (served as acting DCI July 1–September 4, 1973).

The Honorable E. Henry Knoche, July 7, 1976–July 31, 1977 (served as acting DCI January 20–March 9, 1977).

John F. Blake (acting), July 31, 1977–February 10, 1978.

The Honorable Frank C. Carlucci, February 10, 1978–February 5, 1981.

Admiral Bobby Inman, U.S. Navy, February 12, 1981–June 10, 1982.

The Honorable John N. McMahon, June 10, 1982–March 28, 1986.

The Honorable Robert M. Gates, April 18, 1986–.

Executive director. The executive director is appointed by the DCI to oversee the daily operations of the CIA. He coordinates the activities of the directorates and monitors the development and execution of the agency's annual program.

Staff elements.

- The director, Intelligence Community Staff is appointed by the DCI to head an interagency staff that assists and advises him on matters pertaining to his duties as the senior intelligence officer who is responsible for a coordinated, national intelligence effort by the Intelligence Community.
- The National Intelligence Council (NIC) was created in January 1980. It combines the features of the Board of National Estimates and the National Intelligence Officer system with the aim of producing more accurate National Intelligence Estimates (NIEs). The number of national intelligence officers (NIOs) has been reduced from thirteen to eight, and each of them is responsible for producing NIEs for his geographical area. The council reviews the NIEs for quality and has four generalist NIOs-at-large to perform this task.
- The general counsel is the CIA's legal officer. He provides legal advice to the DCI and legal guidance and counsel to all employees on issues concerning the propriety and legality of the agency's operations, so that these are consistent with the Constitution, the laws of the United States, applicable executive

orders, and agency rules and regulations. He also reviews proposed legislation and directives that will affect the agency. His office monitors the agency's adherence to the Privacy and Freedom of Information acts and advises the agency's Publications Review Board, which is charged with approving the writings of agency employees for release to the public.

- The inspector general (IG) is the DCI's investigative officer. He assists in improving the agency's performance and acts to insure that its activities are in compliance with the law and existing regulations. The IG inspects the agency's offices and components to determine how well each is fulfilling its duties, and he assesses whether organizational changes are needed. He also conducts special investigations and studies when directed by the DCI.
- The Public Affairs Office is the point of contact for the public and the news media. It provides unclassified agency studies and schedules media, academic, and business appointments with the appropriate agency personnel.
- The Congressional Affairs Office staffs and monitors the completion of congressional queries and requests.
- The comptroller is responsible for the agency's planning, programming, and budget. He also develops and maintains the agency's financial control systems.

The Directorates.

Directorate for Operations (DDO). The DDO is responsible for clandestinely collecting foreign intelligence (usually by human agents), conducting counterintelligence abroad, and engaging in special activities or clandestine activities conducted abroad to influence individuals or events in support of U.S. foreign policy objectives. The directorate is often called the Clandestine Service. The deputy director for operations is the head of the directorate and is also referred to as the DDO.

Directorate for Science and Technology (DDS&T). The DDS&T is responsible for research, development, and operation of technical collection systems and for producing finished scientific and technical intelligence. The deputy director for science and technology is the head of the directorate and is also referred to as the DDS&T. This directorate has the following offices:

- The Office of Research and Development is in charge of conducting basic and applied scientific and technical research in chemistry, computer science, aeronautics, photogrammetry, communications, and a host of other fields.
- The Office of Research and Engineering designs and operates the agency's technical collection systems.
- The Foreign Broadcast Information Service (FBIS) operates a worldwide network of broadcast monitoring units that are responsible for reviewing foreign media. The information is selected based on a set of intelligence requirements and is translated and disseminated to consumers. The bulk of FBIS reports are unclassified and are available to the public as "Daily Reports" for the world's geographic areas for a fee from the National Technical Information Service of the U.S. Department of Commerce.

FBIS products are of two major categories. The first, FBIS reports, provide summaries of the most important news of a particular nation. The collection includes daily reports of the following translation series: China, Eastern Europe, the Soviet Union, Asia and the Pacific, the Middle East and Africa, Latin America, Western Europe, and South Asia. The second category involves publications issued by the Joint Publications Research Service (JPRS). While JPRS also issues periodic reports, it produces reports that are longer than FBIS items and are much more factual and in greater depth than FBIS materials. The JPRS collection includes: Worldwide Daily Reports, China Reports, USSR Reports (General), USSR Reports (Scientific and Technical), East European Reports, West European Reports, Latin America Reports, Asia Reports, Near East and North Africa Reports, and Miscellaneous Reports.

Together the FBIS and JPRS reports provide an excellent research source of primary and secondary materials for the academic researcher or professional analyst.

- The Office of SIGINT Operations supports the National Security Agency in collecting information on all communications intelligence (COMINT), electronics intelligence (ELINT), telemetry intelligence (TELINT), and foreign instrumentation signals intelligence (FISINT).
- The Office of Technical Service accomplishes the technical research, development, and engineering of instruments and devices used in

clandestine operations.

- The National Photographic Interpretation Center is staffed by CIA and military personnel and provides service to the entire Intelligence Community. It analyzes photography taken by overhead reconnaissance vehicles.

Directorate for Intelligence (DDI). The DDI is responsible for analyzing and producing finished national intelligence, including foreign and international political, economic, scientific, weapons, and related military intelligence, as well as other types of intelligence of interest to the President and policymakers. The head of the directorate is the deputy director for intelligence and is also referred to as the DDI. Since the DDI and his directorate are not under the control of another department, in theory they can produce truly objective intelligence. The DDI is also responsible for the CIA's input into National Intelligence Estimates, which are produced by the National Intelligence Council. In addition, he represents the director of Central Intelligence in matters of substantive intelligence in the National Security Council, in the Executive branch of the cabinet, with Congress, with civilian organizations and with the public. The directorate has the following offices:

- The Office of Soviet Analysis, Office of European Analysis, Office of Near Eastern and South Asian Analysis, Office of East Asian Analysis, and Office of African and Latin American Analysis accomplish political, economic, biographic, sociological, military, and other analyses of selected countries in their respective geographic areas.
- The Office of Scientific and Weapons Research analyzes the design, production, performance characteristics, deployment capabilities, and endurance and maintenance of foreign weapons and space systems. It also analyzes and reports on nuclear weapons, energy and proliferation, technology transfer, tactical and general purpose weapons, strategic forces, strategic offensive and defensive weapon systems, antisubmarine warfare weapons, scientific policy, and physical and life sciences.
- The Office of Global Issues conducts analysis and prepares studies on international economic, geographic, and technological issues, including international trade and development and the commodity markets. It also analyzes and reports on special topics,

such as low-intensity conflict, terrorism, narcotics production, movement and distribution, weapons transfers and sales, and political instability.

- The Office of Imagery Analysis interprets and analyzes photography and imagery and prepares the appropriate reports. The subjects covered in these reports cover the entire spectrum of intelligence areas, from weapons systems, deployments and movements of military forces to agricultural, industrial, commercial, transportation and telecommunications studies and reports on other topics of intelligence interest.
- The Office of Current Production and Analytic Support manages and staffs the CIA's operations center on a 24-hours-a-day basis. The center is prepared to react to crises at all times and has near-constant communications with agency offices around the world and with Department of Defense (DoD) and non-DoD indications and warning centers. The office also provides support to agency analysts in such areas as mathematical statistics, operations research, decision analysis, econometrics, and political methodology.
- The Office of Information Resources provides research backup for the other offices.
- The Office of Leadership Analysis offers biographic and other data on selected national leaders.

Directorate for Administration (DDA). The DDA is responsible for finance, medical services, communications, training, and security for CIA personnel and facilities. It is headed by the deputy director for administration, who is also called the DDA. He provides the same services for elements of the Intelligence Community outside of the CIA but under the jurisdiction of the director of Central Intelligence. The directorate is composed of the following offices:

- The Office of Medical Services administers the agency's medical and health program, including physical examinations of new employees, periodic examinations of all employees, emergency health care, administration of flu shots and other preventive medicine, and psychiatric diagnosis and consultation. It also provides medical support in operations and intelligence production. Finally, the Office of Medical Services administers and maintains the agency's overseas medical program, which provides medical and health care for employees stationed overseas.

- The Office of Security is responsible for personnel and physical security. It conducts investigations of those seeking employment at the agency, conducts routine, periodic polygraph testing of employees, issues security clearances and badges, conducts inspections of agency offices to insure that existing regulations concerning the care and storage of classified material are obeyed, examines and orders new security safes and containers and other physical security equipment, maintains the agency's alarm and antipenetration systems, administers the agency's computer and ADP emanations security programs, and fulfills all other personnel and physical security duties as required.

- The Office of Training and Education manages and administers the agency's training program. This includes training in intelligence collection, analysis, research and production, foreign language courses, courses in writing and speaking, and other training or education courses as required.

- The Office of Finance is responsible for all of the agency's financial matters, including its budget, accounting, auditing, employee payroll, and overseas expenditures.

- The Office of Logistics fulfills many of the functions normally found in an organization's supply department, and much more. It provides for offices, buildings, and complexes, procures almost all supply items required by the agency, handles all agency travel requirements, handles overseas contracting, and runs the agency's publication and print shop.

- The Office of Information Technology develops, operates, and maintains the agency's information processing systems and its manual and automated information storage and retrieval systems both in the United States and overseas.

- The Office of Personnel/OEEO maintains and supervises the agency's nationwide recruitment program. In addition, it manages the personnel evaluation, promotion, and assignment policies and programs, develops staffing and management procedures, and operates the employee benefits and services programs. It also provides against discrimination and insures the agency's compliance with equal employment opportunity programs and regulations.

- The Office of Communications provides and maintains the agency's worldwide communications system, including all communications facilities, cable facilities, agent radios and communications devices, and microwave and satellite equipment.

The CIA Seal

Section 2 of the Central Intelligence Agency Act of 1949 provided for a seal of office for the agency. The design of the seal was approved and set forth in President Truman's Executive Order of February 11, 1950. The order described the seal in heraldic terms as follows:

Shield: Argent, a compass rose of sixteen points gules.

Crest: On a wreath argent and gules and American bald eagle's head erased proper.

Below the shield on a gold color scroll the inscription "United States of America" in red letters, and encircling the shield and crest at the top the inscription "Central Intelligence Agency" in white letters.

All on a circular blue background with a narrow gold edge.

The interpretation of the CIA seal is as follows: The American Eagle is the national bird and is a symbol of strength and alertness. The radiating spokes of the compass rose depict the coverage of intelligence data from all areas of the world to a central point.

CIA Medals

The CIA awards ten medals:

The Distinguished Intelligence Cross is awarded for a voluntary act or acts of exceptional heroism involving the acceptance of existing dangers with conspicuous fortitude and exemplary courage.

The Distinguished Intelligence Medal is awarded for performance of outstanding services or achievement of a distinctly exceptional nature in a duty or responsibility.

The Intelligence Star is awarded for a voluntary act or acts of courage performed under hazardous conditions or for outstanding achievements or services rendered with distinction under conditions of grave risk.

The Intelligence Medal of Merit is awarded for the performance of especially meritorious service or for an act or an achievement conspicuously above normal duties.

The Career Intelligence Medal is awarded for a cumulative record of service that reflects exceptional achievement.

The Intelligence Commendation Medal is awarded for performance of exceptionally commendable service or for an act or an achievement significantly above normal duties that results in an important contribution to the mission of the agency.

The Exceptional Service Medallion is awarded for injury or death resulting from service in an area of hazard.

The Gold Retirement Medallion is awarded for a career of 35 years or more with the agency.

The Silver Retirement Medallion is awarded for a career of 25 years or more with the agency.

The Bronze Retirement Medallion is awarded for a career of at least 15 but less than 25 years with the agency.

The CIA Credo:

We are the Central Intelligence Agency.

We produce timely and high quality intelligence for the President and Government of the United States.

We provide objective and unbiased evaluations and are always open to new perceptions and ready to challenge conventional wisdom.

We perform special intelligence tasks at the request of the President.

We conduct our activities and ourselves according to the highest standards of integrity, morality and honor and according to the spirit and letter of our law and Constitution.

We measure our success by our contribution to the protection and enhancement of American values, security and national interest.

We believe our people are the Agency's most important resource. We seek the best and work to make them better. We subordinate our desire for public recognition to the need for confidentiality. We strive for continuing professional improvement. We give unfailing loyalty to each other and to our common purpose.

We seek through our leaders to stimulate initiative, a commitment to excellence and a propensity for action; to protect and reward Agency personnel for their special responsibilities, contributions, and sacrifices; to promote a sense of mutual trust and shared responsibility.

We get our inspiration and commitment to excellence from the inscription in our foyer: "And Ye shall know the truth and the truth shall make you free." *See also:* Bay of Pigs; Bush, George; Carter, Jimmy; Casey, William J.; Central Intelligence Group; Colby, William E.; Congressional Oversight; Director of Central Intelligence; Donovan, William; Dulles, Allen; Eisenhower, Dwight D.; Executive Orders on Intelligence; Executive Oversight; "Family Jewels"; Ford, Gerald; Helms, Richard; Iran-Contra Scandal; Johnson, Lyndon B; Kennedy, John F.; McCone, John A.; Missile Gap; Mongoose; National Intelligence Authority; National Security Act; National Security Council; Nixon, Richard; Office of Strategic Services; Pearl Harbor; Radio Free Europe and Radio Liberty; Rayborn, William F., Jr.; Reagan, Ronald; Roosevelt, Franklin D.; Schlesinger, James R.; Smith, Walter Bedell; Souers, Sidney W.; Truman, Harry; Turner, Stansfield; Vandenberg, Hoyt S.; Walters, Vernon A.; Webster, William.

References

Allen, Thomas B., and Polmar, Norman. *Merchants of Treason: America's Secrets for Sale.* New York: Delacorte Press, 1988.

American Bar Association. *Oversight and Accountability of the U.S. Intelligence Agencies: An Evaluation.* Washington, DC: ABA, 1985.

Central Intelligence Agency. *Fact Book on Intelligence.* Washington, DC: CIA, 1987.

"Cleaning Up the Mess." *Newsweek,* October 12, 1987, pp. 24-28.

Corson, William R. *The Armies of Ignorance: The Rise of the American Intelligence Empire.* New York: Dial Press, 1977.

Deacon, Richard. *Spyclopedia: An Encyclopedia of Spies, Secret Services, Operations, Jargon, and All Subjects Related to the World of Espionage.* London: Macdonald, 1987.

Department of Defense, Defense Intelligence College. *Glossary of Intelligence Terms and Definitions.* Washington, DC: DIC, 1987.

"The Director: 'We're Not Out of Business.'" *Newsweek,* October 12, 1987, pp. 29–30, 35.

Godson, Roy, ed. *Intelligence Problems for the 1980s, Number 2 Analysis and Estimates.* Washington, DC: National Strategy Information Center, 1980.

———. *Intelligence Problems for the 1980s, Number 5: Clandestine Collection.* Washington, DC: National Strategy Information Center, 1982.

Kent, Sherman. *Strategic Intelligence for American World Policy.* Princeton, NJ: Princeton University Press, 1966.

Laqueur, Walter. *A World of Secrets.* New York: Basic Books, 1985.

Lefever, Ernest W., and Godson, Roy. *The CIA and the American Ethic: An Unfinished Debate.*

Washington, DC: Ethics and Public Policy Center, Georgetown University, 1979.

Lowenthal, Mark M. *U.S. Intelligence: Evolution and Anatomy.* New York: Praeger, 1984.

Maurer, Alfred C.; Turnstall, Marion D.; and Keagle, James M. *Intelligence Policy and Process.* Boulder, CO: Westview Press, 1985.

Quirk, John; Phillips, David; Cline, Ray; and Pforzheimer, Walter. *The Central Intelligence Agency: A Photographic History.* Guilford, CT: Foreign Intelligence Press, 1986.

Treverton, Gregory F. *Covert Action: The Limits of Intervention in the Postwar World.* New York: Basic Books, 1987.

Turner, Stansfield. *Secrecy and Democracy: The CIA in Transition.* Boston: Houghton Mifflin, 1985.

—**CENTRAL INTELLIGENCE AGENCY ACT OF 1949, 50 U.S.C.A. 403A,** vastly expanded the capability and authority of the CIA. Included in the act were important provisions concerning funding and a provision that exempted the agency from having to divulge information concerning its organization and the number of individuals it employed.

References

American Bar Association. *Oversight and Accountability of the U.S. Intelligence Agencies: An Evaluation.* Washington, DC: ABA, 1985.

Corson, William R. *The Armies of Ignorance: The Rise of the American Intelligence Empire.* New York: Dial Press, 1977.

Kent, Sherman. *Strategic Intelligence for American World Policy.* Princeton, NJ: Princeton University Press, 1966.

Laqueur, Walter. *A World of Secrets.* New York: Basic Books, 1985.

Lefever, Ernest W., and Godson, Roy. *The CIA and the American Ethic: An Unfinished Debate.* Washington, DC: Ethics and Public Policy Center, Georgetown University, 1979.

Maurer, Alfred C.; Turnstall, Marion D.; and Keagle, James M. *Intelligence Policy and Process.* Boulder, CO: Westview Press, 1985.

Treverton, Gregory F. *Covert Action: The Limits of Intervention in the Postwar World.* New York: Basic Books, 1987.

Turner, Stansfield. *Secrecy and Democracy: The CIA in Transition.* Boston: Houghton Mifflin, 1985.

Warner, John S. "National Security and the First Amendment." The Intelligence Profession Series. no. 2. McLean, VA: Association of Former Intelligence Officers, 1986.

—**CENTRAL INTELLIGENCE AGENCY PROGRAM (CIAP).** *See:* National Foreign Intelligence Program.

—**CENTRAL INTELLIGENCE GROUP (CIG),** created by President Truman in an Executive Order on January 22, 1946, was the immediate predecessor to the Central Intelligence Agency. It operated under the National Intelligence Authority (NIA), which was established at the same time.

General William Donovan, who had headed the Office of Strategic Services during World War II, had submitted a plan for a centralized intelligence agency. However, Donovan's plan was very unpopular. The military services opposed a complete merger, the State Department claimed that it should direct all peacetime operations that affected foreign relations, and the FBI supported a system in which the military services would control military intelligence worldwide and it would handle all civilian activities.

In response to this debate, President Harry Truman established the CIG in 1946 and directed it to coordinate existing departmental intelligence and to supplement their operations. The CIG was to operate under the direction of the NIA, which was composed of a presidential representative and the secretaries of State, War, and the Navy. Rear Admiral Sidney W. Souers, U.S. Naval Reserve, who was then the deputy chief of Naval Intelligence, was appointed as the first director of Central Intelligence. The major weakness of the CIG was that its funds and staff were provided by other departments, which also had their own intelligence organizations. Twenty months later, both the NIA and the CIG were disestablished, and, under the provisions of the National Security Act of 1947, the National Security Council (NSC) and the Central Intelligence Agency (CIA) were established. *See also:* Central Intelligence Agency.

References

Kent, Sherman. *Strategic Intelligence for American World Policy.* Princeton, NJ: Princeton University Press, 1966.

Laqueur, Walter. *A World of Secrets.* New York: Basic Books, 1985.

Lowenthal, Mark M. *U.S. Intelligence: Evolution and Anatomy.* New York: Praeger, 1984.

Quirk, John; Phillips, David; Cline, Ray; and Pforzheimer, Walter. *The Central Intelligence Agency: A Photographic History.* Guilford, CT: Foreign Intelligence Press, 1986.

Treverton, Gregory F. *Covert Action: The Limits of Intervention in the Postwar World.* New York: Basic Books, 1987.

U.S. Congress. Senate. *Final Report of the Senate Select Committee to Study Government Operations with Respect to Intelligence Activities. Report 94-755. Book I, Foreign and Military Intelligence.* Washington, DC: GPO, 1976.

—**CENTRAL INTELLIGENCE INFORMATION ACT OF 1984.** When Congress passed the Freedom of Information Act (FOIA) in 1966, it permitted the public great access to Intelligence Community files. By the early 1980s it was perceived that the FOIA had gone too far and that, unless it was amended, the public would continue to have access to very sensitive intelligence files. The modification to the FOIA was the Central Intelligence Information Act of 1984. In it, the operational files of the CIA were exempted from the FOIA.

The 1984 act defined "operational files" as: "(1) files of the Directorate of Operations which document the conduct of foreign intelligence or counterintelligence operations or intelligence or security liaison arrangements or information exchanges with foreign governments or their intelligence or security services; (2) files of the Directorate for Science and Technology which document the means by which foreign intelligence or counterintelligence is collected through scientific and technical systems; and (3) files of the Office of Security which document investigations conducted to determine the suitability of potential foreign intelligence or counterintelligence sources; except that files which are the sole repository of disseminated intelligence are not operational files."

However, the act stipulated that operational files would still be subject to search and review if a request were made by a U.S. citizen or lawfully admitted alien who requested information about himself or herself, or if the subject of the investigation involved congressional oversight into matters of illegality or impropriety concerning the Intelligence Community. There were additional provisions that provided requesters recourse in the courts if they felt they were being denied information improperly and that required the director of Central Intelligence to review or have reviewed the operational files every ten years to determine if any files should be removed from this category. *See also:* Freedom of Information Act.

References

U.S. Congress. *Central Intelligence Information Act. Public Law 98-477, October 15, 1984.* Washington, DC: GPO, 1984.

—**CENTRAL OFFICE OF RECORD (COR),** in communications security (COMSEC), is the activity within a department or agency that is charged with the responsibility of maintaining records of accountability for all COMSEC material that has been received in or has been generated in the department or agency. *See also:* Communications Security.

References

Turner, Stansfield. *Secrecy and Democracy: The CIA in Transition.* Boston: Houghton Mifflin, 1985.

—**CENTRAL REPORTS STAFF (CRS)** was a component of the Central Intelligence Group that was responsible for correlating and evaluating information that was received from other intelligence agencies and services. *See also:* Central Intelligence Agency, Central Intelligence Group.

References

Fain, Tyrus G.; Plant, Katharine C.; and Milloy, Ross. *The Intelligence Community: History, Organization, and Issues.* Public Documents Series. New York: R.R. Bowker, 1977.

Turner, Stansfield. *Secrecy and Democracy: The CIA in Transition.* Boston: Houghton Mifflin, 1985.

—**CERTIFICATE OF DESTRUCTION** is a general intelligence term. All classified material must be held in custody from the time it is created until it is destroyed. Material is passed from one authorized person to another by means of an accountability system, in which the receiver signs for and provides a receipt to the provider of the material. When the material is no longer needed and can be destroyed, it is inventoried, destroyed, and a notation is made on a certificate of destruction. The following information is required on the certificate: title and control number of the document, classification, date of destruction, and persons witnessing and destroying the material. The certificate of destruction is the official record of the disposition of the material. *See also:* Classification; Classification Authority; Classification Review; Classified Information.

References

Blackburn, N. Glenn. "Computers: A Counterintelligence Concern." An unpublished manuscript provided to the editors, Washington, DC, 1987.

Godson, Roy, ed. *Intelligence Problems for the 1980s, Number 1: Elements of Intelligence*. Rev. ed. Washington, DC: National Strategy Information Center, 1983.

—**CHAD (CHADDED TAPE),** is a baud-based system term used in communications intelligence, communications security, operations security, and signals analysis. It is tape that is used in printing telegraph/teletypewriter operations. The perforations are completely severed from the tape, making holes that represent characters. *See also:* Chadless Tape, Communications Security (COMSEC).

References

Blackburn, N. Glenn. "Computers: A Counterintelligence Concern." Unpublished paper provided to the editors. Washington, DC, 1987.

Martin, Paul H. "Communications-Computer Security." *Journal of Electronic Defense* (June 1987).

Muzerall, Joseph V., and Carty, Thomas P. "COMSEC and Its Need for Key Management." *DP&CS* (Spring 1987).

Ware, Willis H. "Information Systems, Security, and Privacy." *EDUCOM Bulletin* (Summer 1984).

—**CHADLESS TAPE** is a baud-based system term used in communications intelligence, communications security, operations security, and signals analysis. It is tape that is used in printing telegraph/teleprinter operations. The perforations are not completely severed from the tape, thereby permitting the printing of characters on the tape. *See also:* Chad (Chadded Tape).

References

Blackburn, N. Glenn. "Computers: A Counterintelligence Concern." Unpublished paper provided to the editors. Washington, DC, 1987.

Martin, Paul H. "Communications-Computer Security." *Journal of Electronic Defense* (June 1987).

Muzerall, Joseph V., and Carty, Thomas P. "COMSEC and Its Need for Key Management." *DP&CS* (Spring 1987).

Ware, Willis H. "Information Systems, Security, and Privacy." *EDUCOM Bulletin* (Summer 1984).

—**CHAFF** is a term used in signals intelligence (SIGINT). It is composed of radar confusion reflectors: thin, narrow metallic strips of various lengths and frequency responses that are used to reflect echoes and create confusion. On naval combatants, chaff launchers fire chaff to confuse and deflect incoming missiles. *See also:* Jammer.

References

Department of Defense, Joint Chiefs of Staff. *Department of Defense Dictionary of Military and Related Terms*. Washington, DC: GPO, 1986.

—**CHAFF ELEMENT (DIPOLE)** is one resonant piece of chaff material. *See also:* Chaff.

References

Department of Defense, Joint Chiefs of Staff. *Department of Defense Dictionary of Military and Related Terms*. Washington, DC: GPO, 1986.

—**CHAIRMAN, JOINT CHIEFS OF STAFF (C/JCS)** is appointed by the President from the officers of the regular components of the Armed Forces. He serves at the pleasure of the President and may be appointed for one additional term. He is the ranking officer in the Armed Forces, but he has no command authority over the Joint Chiefs of Staff or any of the Armed Forces. Although he lacks command authority and his responsibilities are not precisely defined, his influence has grown over the years, especially as JCS spokesman and advisor to the secretary of defense, National Security Council, and the President. He prepares the agenda and presides over JCS meetings. His intelligence or J-2 requirements have been fulfilled by the Defense Intelligence Agency since 1963, when the director of that agency was given this responsibility and the JCS J-2 was disestablished. *See also:* Defense Intelligence Agency, Joint Force, Joint Force Memorandum, Joint Intelligence Estimate for Planning, Joint Intelligence Liaison Element, Joint Long-Range Estimative Intelligence Document, Joint Long-Range Strategic Appraisal, Joint Operational Planning System, Joint Program Assessment Memorandum, Joint Strategic Capabilities Plan, Joint Strategic Objectives Plan, Joint Strategic Planning Document, Joint Strategic Planning Document Supporting Analysis, Joint Strategic Planning System, National Military Command Center, National Military Intelligence Center, Specified Command, Unified Command.

References

Godson, Roy, ed. *Intelligence Problems for the 1980s, Number 1: Elements of Intelligence.* Rev. ed. Washington, DC: National Strategy Information Center, 1983.

Laqueur, Walter. *A World of Secrets.* New York: Basic Books, 1985.

Treverton, Gregory F. *Covert Action: The Limits of Intervention in the Postwar World.* New York: Basic Books, 1987.

Turner, Stansfield. *Secrecy and Democracy: The CIA in Transition.* Boston: Houghton Mifflin, 1985.

—**CHALLENGE** is a process carried out by one unit or person with the purpose of determining the identity of another and whether the intentions of that person or entity are friendly or hostile.

References

Department of Defense, Joint Chiefs of Staff. *Department of Defense Dictionary of Military and Related Terms.* Washington, DC: GPO, 1986.

—**CHALLENGE AND REPLY AUTHENTICATION,** in communications security (COMSEC), is a prearranged procedure whereby one communicator requests authentication from another communicator, and the second establishes his validity by replying correctly. *See also:* Communications Security.

References

Blackburn, N. Glenn. "Computers: A Counterintelligence Concern." An unpublished manuscript provided to the editors, Washington, DC, 1987.

—**CHANGE OF OPERATIONAL CONTROL (CHOP),** a general Navy and Marine Corps operations term, is the time and date (GMT) at which the responsibility for operational control of a force or units passes from one operational control authority to another. CHOP is a common acronym used both officially and in informal conversation. Variations include IN-CHOP and OUT-CHOP, particularly when referring to duty in the Mediterranean Sea or western Pacific. To IN-CHOP the Med means to become officially subordinated to the commander of the U.S. Sixth Fleet and this in turn means that, if ordered, the ship or unit will respond to Mediterranean crises and other operations. To OUT-CHOP the Med means to officially drop one's subordination to the Sixth Fleet commander, and most often means that the ship is transiting homeward. In *The Med,* David Poyer conveys the emotional context of the word CHOP, indicating that to IN-CHOP is to become one of the peacekeepers of the Mediterranean, with all the danger that it can involve, while OUT-CHOPPING means to be relieved of the burdens and the dangers of that responsibility.

References

Department of Defense, Joint Chiefs of Staff. *Department of Defense Dictionary of Military and Related Terms.* Washington, DC: GPO, 1986.

Poyer, David. *The Med.* New York: St. Martin's Press, 1988.

—**CHANNEL (CHAN)** is a baud-based system term used in communications intelligence, communications security, operations security, and signals analysis, and it has three meanings. (1) A channel is a single path for transmitting electrical signals. Channel may signify either a one-way or a two-way path, providing communications in one direction only or in two directions. (2) A channel is also a path along which information, particularly a series of digits or characters, may flow. (3) In TDM teleprinter systems, a channel is that portion of time allotted to a signal to carry one stream of intelligence. *See also:* Communications Security.

References

Department of Defense, Joint Chiefs of Staff. *Department of Defense Dictionary of Military and Related Terms.* Washington, DC: GPO, 1986.

—**CHANNEL SPEED** is a baud-based system term used in communications intelligence, communications security, operations security, and signals analysis. It is a signal parameter that is given in words per minute (the number of words that can be sent in a channel in a minute). A word is six characters for purposes of measurement. *See also:* Communications Security.

References

Blackburn, N. Glenn. "Computers: A Counterintelligence Concern." Unpublished paper provided to the editors. Washington, DC, 1987.

Martin, Paul H. "Communications-Computer Security." *Journal of Electronic Defense* (June 1987).

Muzerall, Joseph V., and Carty, Thomas P. "COMSEC and Its Need for Key Management." *DP&CS* (Spring 1987).

Ware, Willis H. "Information Systems, Security, and Privacy." *EDUCOM Bulletin* (Summer 1984).

—**CHARACTER** is a baud-based system term used in communications intelligence, communications security, operations security, and signals analysis. It is any letter, figure, or symbol that is represented by a series of signal impulses. *See also:* Communications Security.

References

Blackburn, N. Glenn. "Computers: A Counterintelligence Concern." Unpublished paper provided to the editors. Washington, DC, 1987.

Ware, Willis H. "Information Systems, Security, and Privacy." *EDUCOM Bulletin* (Summer 1984).

—**CHARTERING AUTHORITY** is the General Defense Intelligence Community (GDIC) component official (senior intelligence officer) who has supervisory jurisdiction over the functional sponsor of a development program. The Chartering Authority approves and issues the Program Manager (Coordinator) Charter and the System Development (Coordinator) Charter. The Chartering Authority is responsible for spending the resources approved through the GDIP programming and budgeting processes for GDIC program and system development efforts. *See also:* General Defense Intelligence Community (GDIC), General Defense Intelligence Program (GDIP).

References

Department of Defense, Defense Intelligence Agency. *Defense Intelligence Agency Manual.* Washington, DC: DIA, 1987.

Kent, Sherman. *Strategic Intelligence for American World Policy.* Princeton, NJ: Princeton University Press, 1966.

—**CHATTER** is a baud-based system term used in communications intelligence, communications security, operations security, and signals analysis. Chatter is any informal message between communications operators. *See also:* Communications Security.

References

Blackburn, N. Glenn. "Computers: A Counterintelligence Concern." An unpublished manuscript provided to the editors, Washington, DC, 1987.

Martin, Paul H. "Communications-Computer Security." *Journal of Electronic Defense* (June 1987).

—**CHATTER ROLL** is paper used for informal communications on secure teletype circuits. Such a roll and system are quite important, although they deal with informal communications. They allow the communicators to line up systems and to discuss, when necessary, the countless other details and problems that are associated with lining up communications systems. *See also:* Communications Security.

References

Blackburn, N. Glenn. "Computers: A Counterintelligence Concern." An unpublished manuscript provided to the editors, Washington, DC, 1987.

Martin, Paul H. "Communications-Computer Security." *Journal of Electronic Defense* (June 1987).

—**CHECK DECRYPTION,** in communications security (COMSEC), is used in off-line cryptographic operations. It is the process of insuring that a message has been properly encrypted by decrypting and checking it before it is transmitted. *See also:* Communications Security.

References

Blackburn, N. Glenn. "Computers: A Counterintelligence Concern." Unpublished paper provided to the editors. Washington, DC, 1987.

Martin, Paul H. "Communications-Computer Security." *Journal of Electronic Defense* (June 1987).

Muzerall, Joseph V., and Carty, Thomas P. "COMSEC and Its Need for Key Management." *DP&CS* (Spring 1987).

Ware, Willis H. "Information Systems, Security, and Privacy." *EDUCOM Bulletin* (Summer 1984).

—**CHECK WORD,** in communications security (COMSEC), is a group of characters or bits that are used to verify that the cryptovariable has been properly filled into a cryptographic system. *See also:* Communications Security.

References

Blackburn, N. Glenn. "Computers: A Counterintelligence Concern." Unpublished paper provided to the editors. Washington, DC, 1987.

Martin, Paul H. "Communications-Computer Security." *Journal of Electronic Defense* (June 1987).

Muzerall, Joseph V., and Carty, Thomas P. "COMSEC and Its Need for Key Management." *DP&CS* (Spring 1987).

Ware, Willis H. "Information Systems, Security, and Privacy." *EDUCOM Bulletin* (Summer 1984).

—**CHEMICAL AGENT,** as defined by the Church Committee, is a chemical compound that; when disseminated, causes incapacitating, lethal, or damaging effects on humans, animals, plants, or materials. *See also:* Chemical Operations.

References

Department of Defense, Joint Chiefs of Staff. *Department of Defense Dictionary of Military and Related Terms.* Washington, DC: GPO, 1986.

Godson, Roy, ed. *Intelligence Problems for the 1980s, Number 1: Elements of Intelligence.* Rev. ed. Washington, DC: National Strategy Information Center, 1983.

Laqueur, Walter. *The Age of Terrorism.* Boston: Little, Brown, 1987.

U.S. Congress. Senate. *Final Report of the Senate Select Committee to Study Government Operations with Respect to Intelligence Activities. Report 94-755. Book I, Foreign and Military Intelligence.* Washington, DC: GPO, 1976.

—**CHEMICAL OPERATIONS,** as defined by the Church Committee, is the use of chemical agents—excluding riot control agents—to kill or incapacitate humans or animals, or to deny the use of facilities, materials, or areas. *See also:* Chemical Agent.

References

Department of Defense, Joint Chiefs of Staff. *Department of Defense Dictionary of Military and Related Terms.* Washington, DC: GPO, 1986.

Godson, Roy, ed. *Intelligence Problems for the 1980s, Number 1: Elements of Intelligence.* Rev. ed. Washington, DC: National Strategy Information Center, 1983.

Laqueur, Walter. *The Age of Terrorism.* Boston: Little, Brown, 1987.

U.S. Congress. Senate. *Final Report of the Senate Select Committee to Study Government Operations with Respect to Intelligence Activities. Report 94-755. Book I, Foreign and Military Intelligence.* Washington, DC: GPO, 1976.

—**CHIEF OF BASE** is a CIA agent who is in charge of a field office that is subordinate to the CIA station in a country. *See also:* Agent, Agent Net, Black Bag Job, Black Bag Operation, Case Officer, Chief of Outpost, Chief of Station, Company, Cover Organizations, Handling Agent, Illegal Agent, Illegal Net, Illegal Support Officer, Recruitment, Recruitment in Place, Special Activities, Third Country Operation.

References

Becket, Henry S. A. *The Dictionary of Espionage: Spookspeak into English.* New York: Stein and Day, 1986.

Breckinridge, Scott D. *The CIA and the U.S. Intelligence System.* Boulder, CO: Westview Press, 1986.

Clancy, Tom. *The Cardinal of the Kremlin.* New York: Putnam, 1988.

Corson, William R. *The Armies of Ignorance: The Rise of the American Intelligence Empire.* New York: Dial Press, 1977.

Deacon, Richard. *Spyclopedia: An Encyclopedia of Spies, Secret Services, Operations, Jargon, and All Subjects Related to the World of Espionage.* London: Macdonald, 1987.

Godson, Roy, ed. *Intelligence Problems for the 1980s, Number 1: Elements of Intelligence.* Rev. ed. Washington, DC: National Strategy Information Center, 1983.

———. *Intelligence Problems for the 1980s, Number 5: Clandestine Collection.* Washington, DC: National Strategy Information Center, 1982.

Laqueur, Walter. *The Age of Terrorism.* Boston: Little, Brown, 1987.

Ranelagh, John. *The Agency: The Rise and Decline of the CIA.* New York: Simon and Schuster, 1986.

Treverton, Gregory F. *Covert Action: The Limits of Intervention in the Postwar World.* New York: Basic Books, 1987.

Turner, Stansfield. *Secrecy and Democracy: The CIA in Transition.* Boston: Houghton Mifflin, 1985.

—**CHIEF OF OUTPOST** is the CIA agent who is in charge of a field office that is subordinate to the CIA station in a country. An outpost is smaller than a base. *See also:* Chief of Base.

References

Becket, Henry S. A. *The Dictionary of Espionage: Spookspeak into English.* New York: Stein and Day, 1986.

Clancy, Tom. *The Cardinal of the Kremlin.* New York: Putnam, 1988.

Deacon, Richard. *Spyclopedia: An Encyclopedia of Spies, Secret Services, Operations, Jargon, and All Subjects Related to the World of Espionage.* London: Macdonald, 1987.

Godson, Roy, ed. *Intelligence Problems for the 1980s, Number 1: Elements of Intelligence.* Rev. ed. Washington, DC: National Strategy Information Center, 1983.

———. *Intelligence Problems for the 1980s, Number 5: Clandestine Collection.* Washington, DC: National Strategy Information Center, 1982.

Ranelagh, John. *The Agency: The Rise and Decline of the CIA*. New York: Simon Schuster, 1986.

Treverton, Gregory F. *Covert Action: The Limits of Intervention in the Postwar World*. New York: Basic Books, 1987.

Turner, Stansfield. *Secrecy and Democracy: The CIA in Transition*. Boston: Houghton Mifflin, 1985.

—**CHIEF OF STATION** is a CIA position title for an individual, usually a career intelligence officer, who is operating under cover in a U.S. embassy. He is usually the senior member of the agency's presence in a country, and his subordinates often include case officers, who in turn deal with agents. In addition, there may be outposts, field offices in the country that are subordinate to the station, that are also under his supervision. *See also:* Chief of Base.

References

Becket, Henry S. A. *The Dictionary of Espionage: Spookspeak into English*. New York: Stein and Day, 1986.

Clancy, Tom. *The Cardinal of the Kremlin*. New York: Putnam, 1988.

Deacon, Richard. *Spyclopedia: An Encyclopedia of Spies, Secret Services, Operations, Jargon, and All Subjects Related to the World of Espionage*. London: Macdonald, 1987.

Godson, Roy, ed. *Intelligence Problems for the 1980s, Number 1: Elements of Intelligence*. Rev. ed. Washington, DC: National Strategy Information Center, 1983.

———. *Intelligence Problems for the 1980s, Number 3: Counterintelligence*. Washington, DC: National Strategy Information Center, 1980.

———. *Intelligence Problems for the 1980s, Number 5: Clandestine Collection*. Washington, DC: National Strategy Information Center, 1982.

Laqueur, Walter. *A World of Secrets*. Boston: Little, Brown, 1985.

Quirk, John; Phillips, David; Cline, Ray; and Pforzheimer, Walter. *The Central Intelligence Agency: A Photographic History*. Guilford, CT: Foreign Intelligence Press, 1986.

Treverton, Gregory F. *Covert Action: The Limits of Intervention in the Postwar World*. New York: Basic Books, 1987.

Turner, Stansfield. *Secrecy and Democracy: The CIA in Transition*. Boston: Houghton Mifflin, 1985.

—**CHILE.** U.S. involvement in the deposition of Salvador Allende Gossens in 1973 has been detailed by the Church Committee. President Nixon expressed deep concern over Allende's Marxism and his bid for the presidency, yet CIA efforts failed to prevent Allende's election in 1970, and his subsequent radical reforms supported Nixon's fears. The CIA was involved in the military coup d'état that deposed Allende in 1973. However, the evidence that the editors have uncovered indicates that the CIA was not directly involved in Allende's death; as Scott Breckinridge notes, Allende's wife subsequently stated that her husband had, indeed, committed suicide. *See also:* Special Activities.

References

Breckinridge, Scott D. *The CIA and the U.S. Intelligence System*. Boulder, CO: Westview Press, 1986.

Corson, William R. *The Armies of Ignorance: The Rise of the American Intelligence Empire*. New York: Dial Press, 1977.

Godson, Roy, ed. *Intelligence Problems for the 1980s, Number 1: Elements of Intelligence*. Rev. ed. Washington, DC: National Strategy Information Center, 1983.

———. *Intelligence Problems for the 1980s, Number 4: Covert Action*. Washington, DC: National Strategy Information Center, 1981.

Laqueur, Walter. *A World of Secrets*. Boston: Little, Brown, 1985.

Treverton, Gregory F. *Covert Action: The Limits of Intervention in the Postwar World*. New York: Basic Books, 1987.

Turner, Stansfield. *Secrecy and Democracy: The CIA in Transition*. Boston: Houghton Mifflin, 1985.

U.S. Congress. Senate. *Final Report of the Senate Select Committee to Study Government Operations with Respect to Intelligence Activities. Report 94-755. Book I, Foreign and Military Intelligence*. Washington, DC: GPO, 1976.

—**CHIN, LARRY WU-TAI,** an analyst with the CIA, was arrested in Alexandria, Virginia, on November 22, 1985. He was accused of spying for the People's Republic of China for nearly 30 years and was convicted on espionage charges on February 7, 1986. Chin had been paid more than $140,000 for the information that he had provided. While awaiting his sentence on February 21, 1986, he committed suicide in his cell.

References

Allen, Thomas B., and Polmar, Norman. *Merchants of Treason: America's Secrets for Sale*. New York: Delacorte Press, 1988.

Crawford, David J. *Volunteers: The Betrayal of National Defense Secrets by Air Force Traitors*. Washington, DC: GPO, 1988.

Pichirallo, Joe. "FBI Details Its Case Against Chin." *The Washington Post*, Nov. 24, 1985, p. A1.

Shenon, Philip. "Former C.I.A. Analyst is Arrested and Accused of Spying for China." *The New York Times*, Nov. 24, 1985.

—**CHURCH COMMITTEE.** During the Johnson and Nixon administrations, the United States was stricken with social turmoil and demonstrations against the Vietnam war. In reaction, some elements of the Intelligence Community conducted operations within the United States, and some of these activities were questionable in their legality.

Such domestic involvement went even further in the Watergate scandal. Here was a case in which the Nixon administration used the CIA's assets in a domestic operation that was clearly illegal. The result was Nixon's eventual resignation, but the affair's effect on the Intelligence Community was devastating.

As Watergate unraveled, it became obvious that the Intelligence Community had so exceeded its authority that its operations were patently illegal. Both the Senate and the House of Representatives formed investigative committees, and these bodies not only investigated Watergate but also examined all domestic intelligence activities that had been waged by the Intelligence Community in the 1960s and 1970s. The result was a definite shift in the focus of presidential and congressional oversight from concern about the quality of the intelligence produced (a traditional concern) to concern over the types of activities the Intelligence Community performed.

The Senate created the Select Committee to Study Government Operations with Respect to Intelligence Activities, chaired by Senator Frank Church. It concentrated on intelligence abuses and illegalities. Its sister investigatory group in the House, chaired by Otis Pike, focused on intelligence management, organization, and the quality of intelligence products.

The Pike Committee issued its report on January 29, 1976, recommending that the Defense Intelligence Agency be abolished, that the director of Central Intelligence (DCI) be separated from CIA so that he could concentrate on his management responsibilities, and that congressional and presidential oversight be enhanced. Soon thereafter the Church Committee completed its investigation. Its report, issued in April 1976, was voluminous, and among its recommendations were that legislative charters be written for each of the intelligence agencies, that the DCI be separated from the CIA, that the DCI's authority over the entire Intelligence Community be strengthened, that the analysis and operations functions in the CIA be separated, that congressional consent be required for all covert operations, and that additional oversight be established.

Mark Lowenthal's assessment of the two committees is the most insightful and profound that has yet to appear. He believes that the Church Committee was the better of the two, in that it produced a detailed 2,685-page report that considered the CIA in its entirety. However, he does criticize the Church Committee for emphasizing the sensational—assassinations, toxic agents, and so forth—in its hearings. Conversely, Lowenthal feels that the Pike Committee, while it failed to prevent the leaking of its report to the *Village Voice* and thereby lost a considerable degree of credibility, did concentrate on the crucial issue of the quality of intelligence. *See also:* Congressional Oversight.

References

American Bar Association. *Oversight and Accountability of the U.S. Intelligence Agencies: An Evaluation.* Washington, DC: ABA, 1985.

Breckinridge, Scott D. *The CIA and the U.S. Intelligence System.* Boulder, CO: Westview Press, 1986.

Brinkley, David A., and Hull, Andrew W. *Estimative Intelligence: A Textbook on the History, Products, Uses and Writing of Intelligence Estimates.* Columbus, OH: Battelle, 1979.

Cline, Ray S. *The CIA Under Reagan, Bush, and Casey.* Washington, DC: Acropolis Books, 1981.

Crawford, David J. *Volunteers: The Betrayal of National Defense Secrets by Air Force Traitors.* Washington, DC: GPO, 1988.

Godson, Roy, ed. *Intelligence Problems for the 1980s, Number 1: Elements of Intelligence.* Rev. ed. Washington, DC: National Strategy Information Center, 1983.

——— *Intelligence Problems for the 1980s, Number 2: Analysis and Estimates.* Washington, DC: National Strategy Information Center, 1980.

Lowenthal, Mark M. *U.S. Intelligence: Evolution and Anatomy.* New York: Praeger, 1984.

Maurer, Alfred C.; Turnstall, Marion D.; and Keagle, James M. *Intelligence Policy and Process.* Boulder, CO: Westview Press, 1985.

U.S. Congress. Senate. *Final Report of the Senate Select Committee to Study Government Operations with Respect to Intelligence Activities. Report 94-755. Book I, Foreign and Military Intelligence.* Washington, DC: GPO, 1976.

Von Hoene, John P. A. *Intelligence User's Guide*. Washington, DC: DIA, 1983.

—**CIPHER** is a term used in signals intelligence, communications security, communications intelligence, operations security, and signals analysis. It is any cryptographic system in which arbitrary symbols or groups of symbols represent units of plain text. The plain text is encoded in order to obscure or conceal its meaning. A cipher can be applied to plain textual material such as letters and numbers. The ciphered material either has no intrinsic meaning or its meaning is disregarded if the material produces one or more real words. *See also:* Code, Communications Security (COMSEC), Decipher, Decode, Encipher, Encode.

References

Clancy, Tom. *The Cardinal of the Kremlin*. New York: Putnam, 1988.

Corson, William R. *The Armies of Ignorance: The Rise of the American Intelligence Empire*. New York: Dial Press, 1977.

Department of Defense, Defense Intelligence College. *Glossary of Intelligence Terms and Definitions*. Washington, DC: DIC, 1987.

Department of Defense, Joint Chiefs of Staff. *Department of Defense Dictionary of Military and Related Terms*. Washington, DC: GPO, 1986.

Godson, Roy, ed. *Intelligence Problems for the 1980s, Number 1: Elements of Intelligence*. Rev. ed. Washington, DC: National Strategy Information Center, 1983.

Kent, Sherman. *Strategic Intelligence for American World Policy*. Princeton, NJ: Princeton University Press, 1966.

Kessler, Ronald. *Spy vs. Spy: Stalking Soviet Spies in America*. New York: Charles Scribner's Sons, 1988.

Laqueur, Walter. *The Age of Terrorism*. Boston: Little, Brown, 1987.

———. *A World of Secrets*. New York: Basic Books, 1985.

Lefever, Ernest W., and Godson, Roy. *The CIA and the American Ethic: An Unfinished Debate*. Washington, DC: Ethics and Public Policy Center, Georgetown University, 1979.

Treverton, Gregory F. *Covert Action: The Limits of Intervention in the Postwar World*. New York: Basic Books, 1987.

Turner, Stansfield. *Secrecy and Democracy: The CIA in Transition*. Boston: Houghton Mifflin, 1985.

U.S. Congress. Senate. *Final Report of the Senate Select Committee to Study Government Operations with Respect to Intelligence Activities. Report 94-755. Book I, Foreign and Military Intelligence*. Washington, DC: GPO, 1976.

—**CIPHER GROUP** is a term used in signals intelligence, communications security, communications intelligence, operations security, and signals analysis. It is a group of letters or numbers (usually five in number) that is used in encrypted versions of messages. The group is protected by off-line manual and machine cryptosystems to facilitate transmission or encryption/decryption. *See also:* Cipher.

References

Department of Defense, Joint Chiefs of Staff. *Department of Defense Dictionary of Military and Related Terms*. Washington, DC: GPO, 1986.

Godson, Roy, ed. *Intelligence Problems for the 1980s, Number 1: Elements of Intelligence*. Rev. ed. Washington, DC: National Strategy Information Center, 1983.

U.S. Congress. Senate. *Final Report of the Senate Select Committee to Study Government Operations with Respect to Intelligence Activities. Report 94-755. Book I, Foreign and Military Intelligence*. Washington, DC: GPO, 1976.

—**CIPHER SYSTEM** is a term used in signals intelligence, communications security, communications intelligence, operations security, and signals analysis. It is a cryptosystem in which the cryptographic treatment is applied to plain text elements. *See also:* Cipher, Communications Security (COMSEC).

References

Department of Defense, Joint Chiefs of Staff. *Department of Defense Dictionary of Military and Related Terms*. Washington, DC: GPO, 1986.

Godson, Roy, ed. *Intelligence Problems for the 1980s, Number 1: Elements of Intelligence*. Rev. ed. Washington, DC: National Strategy Information Center, 1983.

U.S. Congress. Senate. *Final Report of the Senate Select Committee to Study Government Operations with Respect to Intelligence Activities. Report 94-755. Book I, Foreign and Military Intelligence*. Washington, DC: GPO, 1976.

—**CIPHER TEXT** is a term used in signals intelligence, communications security, communications intelligence, operations security, and signals analysis. It is enciphered information. *See also:* Cipher, Communications Security (COMSEC).

References

Blackburn, N. Glenn. "Computers: A Counterintelligence Concern." Unpublished paper provided to the editors. Washington, DC, 1987.

Martin, Paul H. "Communications-Computer Security." *Journal of Electronic Defense* (June 1987).

Muzerall, Joseph V., and Carty, Thomas P. "COMSEC and Its Need for Key Management." *DP&CS* (Spring 1987).

Ware, Willis H. "Information Systems, Security, and Privacy." *EDUCOM Bulletin* (Summer 1984).

—**CIPHER TEXT AUTO-KEY (CTAK)** is a term used in signals intelligence, communications security, communications intelligence, operations security, and signals analysis. It is a cryptographic logic that uses previous cipher text to produce a key. *See also:* Cipher, Communications Security (COMSEC).

References

Blackburn, N. Glenn. "Computers: A Counterintelligence Concern." Unpublished paper provided to the editors. Washington, DC, 1987.

Martin, Paul H. "Communications-Computer Security." *Journal of Electronic Defense* (June 1987).

Muzerall, Joseph V., and Carty, Thomas P. "COMSEC and Its Need for Key Management." *DP&CS* (Spring 1987).

Ware, Willis H. "Information Systems, Security, and Privacy." *EDUCOM Bulletin* (Summer 1984).

—**CIPHONY** is a term used in signals intelligence, communications security, communications intelligence, operations security, and signals analysis. It is the process of enciphering digitized audio signals. *See also:* Cipher, Communications Security (COMSEC).

References

Blackburn, N. Glenn. "Computers: A Counterintelligence Concern." Unpublished paper provided to the editors. Washington, DC, 1987.

Martin, Paul H. "Communications-Computer Security." *Journal of Electronic Defense* (June 1987).

Muzerall, Joseph V., and Carty, Thomas P. "COMSEC and Its Need for Key Management." *DP&CS* (Spring 1987).

Ware, Willis H. "Information Systems, Security, and Privacy." *EDUCOM Bulletin* (Summer 1984).

—**CIRCUMVENTION** is a counterintelligence term used in the context of automatic data processing (ADP) system security and refers to a situation in which a penetrator of an ADP system attempts to circumvent security controls by probing for "trap doors" in the system that will allow him to enter without going through the prescribed security controls.

References

Blackburn, N. Glenn. "Computers: A Counterintelligence Concern." Unpublished manuscript provided to the editors, Washington, DC, 1987.

—**CIVIL AIR TRANSPORT (CAT),** according to Richard Deacon, is the CIA's air service. It was founded in China in 1946 and was later based in Taiwan, where it supported clandestine operations in Korea, Vietnam, and other Asian nations. *See also:* Central Intelligence Agency.

References

Becket, Henry S. A. *The Dictionary of Espionage: Spookspeak into English.* New York: Stein and Day, 1986.

Deacon, Richard. *Spyclopedia: An Encyclopedia of Spies, Secret Services, Operations, Jargon, and All Subjects Related to the World of Espionage.* London: Macdonald, 1987.

Ranelagh, John. *The Agency: The Rise and Decline of the CIA.* New York: Simon and Schuster, 1986.

—**CLANDESTINE ACTIVITY** means secret or hidden operations. In intelligence parlance, the phrase *clandestine operation* is preferred, since operations are pre-planned activities. *See also:* Clandestine Operation.

—**CLANDESTINE COLLECTION** is the secret or covert procurement of intelligence information so that the target or enemy is unaware that the collated information has been compromised. *See also:* Clandestine Operation.

—**CLANDESTINE COMMUNICATION** is any type of signal, message, or other communication that is sent or given in support of a clandestine operation. *See also:* Clandestine Operation.

—**CLANDESTINE INTELLIGENCE** is intelligence information collected secretly. *See also:* Clandestine Operation.

—**CLANDESTINE OPERATION** is a preplanned secret intelligence, counterintelligence, or other information-collection activity or a covert political, economic, propaganda, or paramilitary operation conducted in a way that insures that the operation remains a secret. A clandestine operation encompasses both clandestine collection and covert action. *See also:* Clandestine Activity, Clandestine Collection, Clandestine Communication, Clandestine Intelligence, Special Activities.

References

Department of Defense, Joint Chiefs of Staff. *Department of Defense Dictionary of Military and Related Terms.* Washington, DC: GPO, 1986.

Godson, Roy, ed. *Intelligence Problems for the 1980s, Number 1: Elements of Intelligence.* Rev. ed. Washington, DC: National Strategy Information Center, 1983.

———. *Intelligence Problems for the 1980s, Number 3: Counterintelligence.* Washington, DC: National Strategy Information Center, 1980.

———. *Intelligence Problems for the 1980s, Number 5: Clandestine Collection.* Washington, DC: National Strategy Information Center, 1982.

Kent, Sherman. *Strategic Intelligence for American World Policy.* Princeton, NJ: Princeton University Press, 1966.

Laqueur, Walter. *The Age of Terrorism.* Boston: Little, Brown, 1987.

———. *A World of Secrets.* New York: Basic Books, 1985.

Lefever, Ernest W., and Godson, Roy. *The CIA and the American Ethic: An Unfinished Debate.* Washington, DC: Ethics and Public Policy Center, Georgetown University, 1979.

Quirk, John; Phillips, David; Cline, Ray; and Pforzheimer, Walter. *The Central Intelligence Agency: A Photographic History.* Guilford, CT: Foreign Intelligence Press, 1986.

Treverton, Gregory F. *Covert Action: The Limits of Intervention in the Postwar World.* New York: Basic Books, 1987.

Turner, Stansfield. *Secrecy and Democracy: The CIA in Transition.* Boston: Houghton Mifflin, 1985.

U.S. Congress. Senate. *Final Report of the Senate Select Committee to Study Government Operations with Respect to Intelligence Activities. Report 94-755. Book I, Foreign and Military Intelligence.* Washington, DC: GPO, 1976.

—**CLANDESTINE SERVICES** is sometimes referred to as the CIA Operations Directorate. It is that part of the CIA that engages in clandestine operations. *See also:* Central Intelligence Agency.

References

Corson, William R. *The Armies of Ignorance: The Rise of the American Intelligence Empire.* New York: Dial Press, 1977.

Godson, Roy, ed. *Intelligence Problems for the 1980s, Number 1: Elements of Intelligence.* Rev. ed. Washington, DC: National Strategy Information Center, 1983.

———. *Intelligence Problems for the 1980s, Number 3: Counterintelligence.* Washington, DC: National Strategy Information Center, 1980.

———. *Intelligence Problems for the 1980s, Number 5: Clandestine Collection.* Washington, DC: National Strategy Information Center, 1982.

Kent, Sherman. *Strategic Intelligence for American World Policy.* Princeton, NJ: Princeton University Press, 1966.

Laqueur, Walter. *The Age of Terrorism.* Boston: Little, Brown, 1987.

———. *A World of Secrets.* New York: Basic Books, 1985.

Lefever, Ernest W., and Godson, Roy. *The CIA and the American Ethic: An Unfinished Debate.* Washington, DC: Ethics and Public Policy Center, Georgetown University, 1979.

Treverton, Gregory F. *Covert Action: The Limits of Intervention in the Postwar World.* New York, Basic Books, 1987.

Turner, Stansfield. *Secrecy and Democracy: The CIA in Transition.* Boston: Houghton Mifflin, 1985.

—**CLARK AMENDMENT,** Section 118 of the International Security and Development Cooperation Act of 1980, entitled "Military and Paramilitary Operations in Angola," placed heavy restrictions on any U.S. assistance to Angola. The amendment stated that no assistance could be provided unless: (1) the President determined that such assistance would benefit the national security interests of the United States; (2) the President submitted a report to the House Committee on Foreign Affairs and the Senate Committee of Foreign Relations containing: (a) a description of the amount and type of assistance that would be furnished and (b) a certification that providing such assistance would be important to U.S. national security, with reasons supporting this position. (3) Congress would then, through joint resolution, approve or disapprove providing the assistance.

The significance of the Clark Amendment was twofold. First, it effectively barred the President from providing assistance to Angola, thereby simplifying the military problem that Communist forces had in the nation's civil war, because they did not have to fear U.S. involvement or U.S. support for the opposing forces. Second and more important, it represented a significant congressional encroachment on the right of the President to make foreign policy. This was significant because it meant that foreign policy formulation now would be influenced by the individuals who composed the two houses of Congress, rather than the few in the White House, and would therefore be much less consistent in its thrust. Equally important, it signaled congressional intentions to continue this role in the future. This had obvious and serious effects on U.S. support to the Nicaraguan Contras, and it precipitated the Iran-Contra incident, in which the National Security Council staff attempted to circumvent congressional restrictions in order to support the Nicaraguan rebels. *See also:* Congressional Oversight.

References

Corson, William R. *The Armies of Ignorance: The Rise of the American Intelligence Empire.* New York: Dial Press, 1977.

Treverton, Gregory F. *Covert Action: The Limits of Intervention in the Postwar World.* New York: Basic Books, 1987.

Turner, Stansfield. *Secrecy and Democracy: The CIA in Transition.* Boston: Houghton Mifflin, 1985.

U.S. Congress. *International Security and Development Cooperation Act of 1980.* Section 662. U.S.C. 2422, 1980.

—**CLASS LIMITS** is a statistical or quantitative methodological term that is often used in intelligence analysis. It means the smallest and largest values that go into any given class.

References

Blackburn, N. Glenn. "Computers: A Counterintelligence Concern." Unpublished manuscript provided to the editors, Washington, DC, 1987.

—**CLASS MARK** is a statistical or quantitative methodological term that is often used in intelligence analysis. It means the midpoint of a class in a frequency distribution, the average of the lower and the upper limits.

References

Blackburn, N. Glenn. "Computers: A Counterintelligence Concern." Unpublished manuscript provided to the editors, Washington, DC, 1987.

—**CLASSIFICATION** is a general intelligence term. The official definition of classification is that it "reflects the fact that a determination has been made that the official information contained in the document requires, in the interests of national security, a degree of protection against unauthorized disclosure." The three security designations are CONFIDENTIAL, SECRET, and TOP SECRET, which are normally referred to as security classifications. The originator of the document usually assigns the security classification, along with downgrading instructions that indicate when the material might be reduced to a lower classification and when it will be declassified. The classification is clearly stamped on each page of the material. In some cases, individual paragraphs of a document will be assigned classifications, so that it will be easier to downgrade the document to a lower security classification by removing the more highly classified material or even to sanitize the document to unclassified by removing all classified material. *See also:* Access, Authorized, Classification Authority, Classification Review, Classified Information, Code Word, Compromise, Declassification, Disclosure, Downgrade, Freedom of Information Act, Limited Access Area, Need-to-Know, Need-to-Know Principle, No-Lone Zone, Nondisclosure Agreement, Nondiscussion Area, Sanitization, Sanitize, Sanitized Area, Security Certification, Security Classification, Sensitive Compartmented Information, Sensitive Compartmented Information Facility, Two-Person Control.

References

Department of Defense, Defense Intelligence College. *Glossary of Intelligence Terms and Definitions.* Washington, DC: DIC, 1987.

Department of Defense, Joint Chiefs of Staff. *Department of Defense Dictionary of Military and Related Terms.* Washington, DC: GPO, 1986.

Godson, Roy, ed. *Intelligence Problems for the 1980s, Number 1: Elements of Intelligence.* Rev. ed. Washington, DC: National Strategy Information Center, 1983.

Kent, Sherman. *Strategic Intelligence for American World Policy.* Princeton, NJ: Princeton University Press, 1966.

—**CLASSIFICATION AUTHORITY,** a general intelligence term, is an official within the Executive branch of the government who has been authorized by an Executive Order to classify information or material. Obviously, he delegates this authority to his subordinates, since the total volume of classified material is enormous and is well beyond the capability of one person to process. *See also:* Classification.

References

Department of Defense, Defense Intelligence College. *Glossary of Intelligence Terms and Definitions.* Washington, DC: DIC, 1987.

Department of Defense, Joint Chiefs of Staff. *Department of Defense Dictionary of Military and Related Terms.* Washington, DC: GPO, 1986.

Turner, Stansfield. *Secrecy and Democracy: The CIA in Transition.* Boston: Houghton Mifflin, 1985.

—**CLASSIFICATION REVIEW** is a general intelligence term. It is the review of a document to determine if it can be downgraded (reduced in classification level) or declared to be unclassified. Classification review is a time-consuming process and often prompts delays in the release of information. *See also:* Classification.

References

Department of Defense, Joint Chiefs of Staff. *Department of Defense Dictionary of Military and Related Terms.* Washington, DC: GPO, 1986.

Turner, Stansfield. *Secrecy and Democracy: The CIA in Transition.* Boston: Houghton Mifflin, 1985.

—**CLASSIFIED INFORMATION** was defined by Congress in the Intelligence Identities Protection Act of 1982 as "information or material designated and clearly marked or clearly represented, pursuant to the provisions of a statute or Executive order (or a regulation or order issued pursuant to a statute or Executive order), as requiring a specific degree of protection against unauthorized disclosure for reasons of national security." An alternative official definition is "official information which has been determined to require protection against unauthorized disclosure in the interests of national security. Classified information is clearly designated as such by assigning a security classification to the information." *See also:* Classification.

References

Department of Defense, Defense Intelligence College. *Glossary of Intelligence Terms and Definitions.* Washington, DC: DIC, 1987.

Department of Defense, Joint Chiefs of Staff. *Department of Defense Dictionary of Military and Related Terms.* Washington, DC: GPO, 1986.

Godson, Roy, ed. *Intelligence Problems for the 1980s, Number 1: Elements of Intelligence.* Rev.

ed. Washington, DC: National Strategy Information Center, 1983.

Treverton, Gregory F. *Covert Action: The Limits of Intervention in the Postwar World.* New York: Basic Books, 1987.

U.S. Congress. *Intelligence Identities Protection Act of 1982. Public Law 97-200, June 23, 1982.* Washington, DC: GPO, 1982.

—**CLASSIFIED INFORMATION PROCEDURES ACT.** *See:* Public Law 96-456.

—**CLASSIFIED MATTER.** *See:* Classified Information.

—**CLEAN** is a term used in clandestine and covert intelligence operations to describe an agent, a safe house, a letter drop, or some other object that has never been used operationally and therefore is unknown to the enemy. *See also:* Concealment, Go To Ground, Handling Agent, Illegal Residency, Legal, Legal Residency, Suitable Cover, Surfacing.

References

Becket, Henry S. A. *The Dictionary of Espionage: Spookspeak into English.* New York: Stein and Day, 1986.

Deacon, Richard. *Spyclopedia: An Encyclopedia of Spies, Secret Services, Operations, Jargon, and All Subjects Related to the World of Espionage.* London: Macdonald, 1987.

—**CLEAR,** a general intelligence term, is a verb that means to give a person a security clearance. *See also:* Access, Authorized, Background Investigation, Billet, Clearance, Compartmentation, Debriefing, Defense Industrial Security Clearance Office, Defense Security Briefing, Defense Investigative Service, Need-to-Know, Need-to-Know Principle, No-Lone Zone, Nondisclosure Agreement, Personnel Insecurity, Personnel Security, Security, Security Classification, Special Sensitive Compartmented Information (SCI), Sensitive Compartmented Information Facility (SCIF), Security Officer, Special Security Office System, TOP SECRET Code Word, TOP SECRET Control Officer.

References

Department of Defense, Joint Chiefs of Staff. *Department of Defense Dictionary of Military and Related Terms.* Washington, DC: GPO, 1986.

Godson, Roy, ed. *Intelligence Problems for the 1980s, Number 1: Elements of Intelligence.* Rev.

ed. Washington, DC: National Strategy Information Center, 1983.

U.S. Congress. Senate. *Final Report of the Senate Select Committee to Study Government Operations with Respect to Intelligence Activities. Report 94-755. Book I, Foreign and Military Intelligence.* Washington, DC: GPO, 1976.

—**CLEAR TEXT.** *See:* Plain Text.

—**CLEARANCE** is a general intelligence term for a determination that a person is eligible, under the standards of current Director of Central Intelligence directives and Department of Defense regulations, for access to classified information. However, clearance does not imply a need-to-know. *See also:* Clear.

References

Department of Defense, Joint Chiefs of Staff. *Department of Defense Dictionary of Military and Related Terms.* Washington, DC: GPO, 1986.

Godson, Roy, ed. *Intelligence Problems for the 1980s, Number 1: Elements of Intelligence.* Rev. ed. Washington, DC: National Strategy Information Center, 1983.

—**CLOSE AIR SUPPORT** is air action against enemy targets that are located close to friendly forces. Close air support is requested and approved by the support unit commander, and it is controlled by the forward air controller.

References

Department of Defense, Joint Chiefs of Staff. *Department of Defense Dictionary of Military and Related Terms.* Washington, DC: GPO, 1986.

Poyer, David. *The Med.* New York: St. Martin's Press, 1988.

—**CLOSED STORAGE** is a general intelligence term for the storage of classified material in locked security containers (safes) within an accredited facility when the facility is not occupied by authorized personnel. Storage includes all classified waste (burn bags), reusable carbon paper, typewriter ribbons, and, of course, all classified documents. *See also:* Classification, Secure Area.

References

Blackburn, N. Glenn. "Computers: A Counterintelligence Concern." Unpublished manuscript provided to the editors, Washington, DC, 1987.

—**COBBLER** is a term used in clandestine and covert intelligence operations to describe a forger of passports. *See also:* Agent Authentication, Cover, Cover Name, Cover Organizations, Cover Story, Establishing Bonafides, Pocket Litter.

References

Becket, Henry S. A. *The Dictionary of Espionage: Spookspeak into English.* New York: Stein and Day, 1986.

Deacon, Richard. *Spyclopedia: An Encyclopedia of Spies, Secret Services, Operations, Jargon, and All Subjects Related to the World of Espionage.* London: Macdonald, 1987.

Ranelagh, John. *The Agency: The Rise and Decline of the CIA.* New York: Simon and Schuster, 1986.

—**COBERLY, ALAN D.,** a Marine Corps deserter, walked into the Soviet Embassy in Manila in 1983. He was tried for desertion and other acts and received an eighteen-month sentence.

References

Allen, Thomas B., and Polmar, Norman. *Merchants of Treason: America's Secrets for Sale.* New York: Delacorte Press, 1988.

Crawford, David J. *Volunteers: The Betrayal of National Defense Secrets by Air Force Traitors.* Washington, DC: GPO, 1988.

—**CODE** is a general intelligence term that has two meanings. (1) A code is a cryptographic system in which arbitrary groups of signals or cryptographic equivalents, which are usually called code groups, are substituted for textual material such as words, phrases, or sentences. The code groups typically consist of meaningless combinations of letters or numbers or a combination of both. A code can be used for brevity, as in the case of semaphore codes, which reduce considerably the amount of flag waving, or it can be used for security.

Codes have three distinctly different applications: (a) In the broadest sense, coding is a means of converting information into a form suitable for communications or encryption. Examples of such codes would be coded speech, morse code, or typewriter codes. In this case, no security is provided. (b) Another application involves brevity lists. These are codes used to reduce the length of time that is required to transmit information. An example would be long, stereotypical sentences that can be reduced to a few characters. In this case as well, no security is provided. (c) The final application is the cryptosystem. Here cryptographic equivalents are substituted for plain text information. In this case, security is provided.

(2) A code is also a baud-based system term used in communications intelligence, communications security, operations security, and signals analysis. It means, in electrical or electronic communications, a system of unique arrangements of signal impulses, each arrangement of which represents a predetermined character or function. *See also:* Cipher, Communications Security, Decipher, Decode, Encipher, Encode.

References

American Bar Association. *Oversight and Accountability of the U.S. Intelligence Agencies: An Evaluation.* Washington, DC: ABA, 1985.

Clancy, Tom. *The Cardinal of the Kremlin.* New York: Putnam, 1988.

Department of Defense, Defense Intelligence College. *Glossary of Intelligence Terms and Definitions.* Washington, DC: DIC 1987.

Department of Defense, Joint Chiefs of Staff. *Department of Defense Dictionary of Military and Related Terms.* Washington, DC: GPO, 1986.

Godson, Roy, ed. *Intelligence Problems for the 1980s, Number 1: Elements of Intelligence.* Rev. ed. Washington, DC: National Strategy Information Center, 1983.

Maurer, Alfred C.; Turnstall, Marion D.; and Keagle, James M. *Intelligence Policy and Process.* Boulder, CO: Westview Press, 1985.

U.S. Congress. Senate. *Final Report of the Senate Select Committee to Study Government Operations with Respect to Intelligence Activities. Report 94-755. Book I, Foreign and Military Intelligence.* Washington, DC: GPO, 1976.

—**CODE BOOK,** in communications security is a book or other document that contains plain and code equivalents that are systematically arranged. It can also mean a technique of machine encryption that employs word substitution. *See also:* Code.

References

American Bar Association. *Oversight and Accountability of the U.S. Intelligence Agencies: An Evaluation.* Washington, DC: ABA, 1985.

Maurer, Alfred C.; Turnstall, Marion D.; and Keagle, James M. *Intelligence Policy and Process.* Boulder, CO: Westview Press, 1985.

—**CODE GROUP,** in communications security, is a group of letters or numbers, or both, that is assigned in a code system to represent a plain text element, which may be a word, phrase, or sentence. *See also:* Code.

References

American Bar Association. *Oversight and Accountability of the U.S. Intelligence Agencies: An Evaluation.* Washington, DC: ABA, 1985.

Maurer, Alfred C.; Turnstall, Marion D.; and Keagle, James M. *Intelligence Policy and Process.* Boulder, CO: Westview Press, 1985.

—**CODE TEXT,** a signals analysis term, is the result of transforming plain text into secret or hidden form. *See also:* Code.

References

American Bar Association. *Oversight and Accountability of the U.S. Intelligence Agencies: An Evaluation.* Washington, DC: ABA, 1985.

Maurer, Alfred C.; Turnstall, Marion D.; and Keagle, James M. *Intelligence Policy and Process.* Boulder, CO: Westview Press, 1985.

—**CODE VOCABULARY,** in communications security, is the set of plain text items to which code equivalents are to be assigned in a code system. *See also:* Code.

References

American Bar Association. *Oversight and Accountability of the U.S. Intelligence Agencies: An Evaluation.* Washington, DC: ABA, 1985.

Maurer, Alfred C.; Turnstall, Marion D.; and Keagle, James M. *Intelligence Policy and Process.* Boulder, CO: Westview Press, 1985.

—**CODE WORD** has several distinct meanings. (1) "Codeword" is any of a series of designated words or terms that are used along with a security classification to indicate that the material being conveyed in the documents, briefings, or by other means has been collected by a sensitive method or has been received from a sensitive source. The codeword thus indicates that the material is of a certain type of sensitive compartmented information (SCI) and therefore its distribution must be extremely limited. (2) A code word is a word or term that has a prearranged meaning other than its actual definition(s). It has been chosen to conceal the identity of a function or action and is therefore different than a cover name, which is used to conceal the identity of a person, organization, or installation. (3) A code word is a term that has a classified meaning in order to safeguard the intentions and information concerning a planned operation. After the operation is conducted and made public, the code word is usually declassified. Examples of code words are "Urgent Fury" for the U.S. operation in Grenada and "El Dorado Canyon" for the U.S. air attacks on Libya. (4) A code word may also be a word that conveys a meaning other than its conventional one. In this case, the word is agreed upon by the participants beforehand, and the use of the word is intended to increase security. *See also:* Access, Authorized, Classification, Classified Information, Compromise, Cover, Declassification, Disclosure, Downgrade, Freedom of Information Act, Limited Access Area, Need-to-Know, Need-to-Know Principle, No-Lone Zone, Nondisclosure Agreement, Nondiscussion Area, Sanitization, Sanitize, Sanitized Area, Security Certification, Security Classification, Sensitive Compartmented Information, Sensitive Compartmented Information Facility, Two-Person Control.

References

Allen, Thomas B., and Polmar, Norman. *Merchants of Treason: America's Secrets for Sale.* New York: Delacorte Press, 1988.

American Bar Association. *Oversight and Accountability of the U.S. Intelligence Agencies: An Evaluation.* Washington, DC: ABA, 1985.

Department of Defense, Defense Intelligence College. *Glossary of Intelligence Terms and Definitions.* Washington, DC: DIC, 1987.

Department of Defense, Department of the Air Force. *Communications-Electronics Terminology.* Washington, DC: DAF, 1973.

Department of Defense, Joint Chiefs of Staff. *Department of Defense Dictionary of Military and Related Terms.* Washington, DC: GPO, 1986.

Godson, Roy, ed. *Intelligence Problems for the 1980s, Number 1: Elements of Intelligence.* Rev. ed. Washington, DC: National Strategy Information Center, 1983.

Kessler, Ronald. *Spy vs. Spy: Stalking Soviet Spies in America.* New York: Charles Scribner's Sons, 1988.

Maurer, Alfred C.; Turnstall, Marion D.; and Keagle, James M. *Intelligence Policy and Process.* Boulder, CO: Westview Press, 1985.

U.S. Congress. Senate. *Final Report of the Senate Select Committee to Study Government Operations with Respect to Intelligence Activities. Report 94-755. Book I, Foreign and Military Intelligence.* Washington, DC: GPO, 1976.

—**COINTELPRO** was an FBI term for the bureau's "counterintelligence program" in the 1960s and 1970s. It was directed against antiwar and radical groups, ranging from pacifists to black militants to white supremests. The program, which lasted from 1956 until 1971, used techniques that the FBI had developed for use against hostile foreign agents; it included infiltrating organizations and disrupting them through covert means. The defunct program was singled out for special criticism by the Church Committee in 1976. *See also:* COMINFIL, Rabble Rouser Index.

References

American Bar Association. *Oversight and Accountability of the U.S. Intelligence Agencies: An Evaluation.* Washington, DC: ABA, 1985.

Becket, Henry S. A. *The Dictionary of Espionage: Spookspeak into English.* New York: Stein and Day, 1986.

Corson, William R. *The Armies of Ignorance: The Rise of the American Intelligence Empire.* New York: Dial Press, 1977.

Deacon, Richard. *Spyclopedia: An Encyclopedia of Spies, Secret Services, Operations, Jargon, and All Subjects Related to the World of Espionage.* London: Macdonald, 1987.

Maurer, Alfred C.; Turnstall, Marion D.; and Keagle, James M. *Intelligence Policy and Process.* Boulder, CO: Westview Press, 1985.

Ranelagh, John. *The Agency: The Rise and Decline of the CIA.* New York: Simon and Schuster, 1986.

—**COLBY, WILLIAM,** was born on January 20, 1920, in St. Paul, Minnesota. He graduated from Princeton University in 1940 with a Bachelor of Arts degree and from Columbia University with a Bachelor of Law degree in 1947. He was commissioned in the U.S. Army in 1941 and served with the Office of Strategic Services (OSS) from 1943 to 1945. He worked in private practice from 1947 until 1949, when he joined the National Labor Relations Board, serving there until 1950. In 1950, he joined the Central Intelligence Agency (CIA) and served as chief of the Far East Division from 1962 until 1967. He then left the CIA and was assigned to the Agency for International Development as director of Civil Operations and Rural Development Support in Saigon in 1968. He served in this capacity, with the rank of ambassador, until 1971. He served as executive director-comptroller in 1972 and 1973, before being appointed deputy director for Operations, CIA, in 1973. On May 10, 1973, he was appointed as director of Central Intelligence

(DCI) by President Nixon. His appointment was confirmed by the U.S. Senate on August 1, and he was sworn in on September 4, 1973. He served until January 30, 1976, when he returned to private law practice.

Colby's most dramatic accomplishments as DCI were abolishing the Board and the Office of National Estimates, and replacing them with the National Intelligence Officer (NIO) system. Under the new system, there were thirteen NIOs. Each had a functional or regional area and was responsible to the DCI for intelligence collection and production in his area.

Colby's greatest task was to respond to the presidential and congressional committees that had been formed to investigate intelligence activities. The initial request came from President Ford, who asked for an accounting shortly after he took office in 1974. Colby responded by submitting a detailed list of all CIA transgressions that had been prepared for his predecessor, James Schlesinger. This report was so comprehensive that it became known as the "Family Jewels," and many in the CIA were opposed to providing such detailed information. The subsequent congressional investigations created considerable friction between the White House and Congress. The White House position was epitomized by Secretary of State Henry Kissinger, who favored limiting the information given to Congress to only that which was requested. Colby's position, on the other hand, was to be as open with Congress as possible. This divergence of opinion was to be Colby's downfall, and he was dismissed on November 2, 1975. *See also:* Central Intelligence Agency.

References

American Bar Association. *Oversight and Accountability of the U.S. Intelligence Agencies: An Evaluation.* Washington, DC: ABA, 1985.

Breckinridge, Scott D. *The CIA and the U.S. Intelligence System.* Boulder, CO: Westview Press, 1986.

Brinkley, David A., and Hull, Andrew W. *Estimative Intelligence: A Textbook on the History, Products, Uses and Writing of Intelligence Estimates.* Columbus, OH: Battelle, 1979.

Cline, Ray S. *The CIA Under Reagan, Bush, and Casey.* Washington, DC: Acropolis Books, 1981.

Corson, William R. *The Armies of Ignorance: The Rise of the American Intelligence Empire.* New York: Dial Press, 1977.

Crawford, David J. *Volunteers: The Betrayal of National Defense Secrets by Air Force Traitors.* Washington, DC: GPO, 1988.

Godson, Roy, ed. *Intelligence Problems for the 1980s, Number 1: Elements of Intelligence.* Rev. ed. Washington, DC: National Strategy Information Center, 1983.

———. *Intelligence Problems for the 1980s, Number 2: Analysis and Estimates.* Washington, DC: National Strategy Information Center, 1980.

———. *Intelligence Problems for the 1980s, Number 4: Covert Action.* Washington, DC: National Strategy Information Center, 1981.

Laqueur, Walter. *A World of Secrets.* New York: Basic Books, 1985.

Lowenthal, Mark M. *U.S. Intelligence: Evolution and Anatomy.* New York: Praeger, 1984.

Maurer, Alfred C., Turnstall, Marion D.; and Keagle, James M. *Intelligence Policy and Process.* Boulder, CO: Westview Press, 1985.

Quirk, John; Phillips, David; Cline, Ray; and Pforzheimer, Walter. *The Central Intelligence Agency: A Photographic History.* Guilford, CT: Foreign Intelligence Press, 1986.

Treverton, Gregory F. *Covert Action: The Limits of Intervention in the Postwar World.* New York: Basic Books, 1987.

Turner, Stansfield. *Secrecy and Democracy: The CIA in Transition.* Boston: Houghton Mifflin, 1985.

U.S. Congress. Senate. *Final Report of the Senate Select Committee to Study Government Operations with Respect to Intelligence Activities. Report 94-755. Book I, Foreign and Military Intelligence.* Washington, DC: GPO, 1976.

Von Hoene, John P. A. *Intelligence User's Guide.* Washington, DC: DIA, 1983.

—**COLD APPROACH** is a term used in clandestine and covert intelligence operations. It is an attempt to recruit a foreign national without any prior indication that he will accept the offer. The cold approach is a very risky operation, with a low probability of success. *See also:* Agent, Case Officer, Co-opted Worker, Co-optees, Cultivation, Double Agent, Handling Agent, Infiltration, Informant, Inside Man, Recruitment, Recruitment in Place, Special Activities.

References

Becket, Henry S. A. *The Dictionary of Espionage: Spookspeak into English.* New York: Stein and Day, 1986.

Turner, Stansfield. *Secrecy and Democracy: The CIA in Transition.* Boston: Houghton Mifflin, 1985.

—**COLLATERAL INFORMATION** is all national security information that has been classified under the provisions of an Executive Order for which

Intelligence Community special systems of compartmentation (sensitive compartmented information [SCI]) are not formally established. Collateral information is less sensitive than SCI and therefore requires less stringent security and storage procedures. An alternative definition is that it is information that is classified CONFIDENTIAL, SECRET, or TOP SECRET in accordance with Department of Defense Regulation 5200.1. *See also:* Access, Authorized, Classification, Classified Information, Code Word, Compromise, Declassification, Disclosure, Downgrade, Freedom of Information Act, Limited Access Area, Need-to-Know, Need-to-Know Principle, No-Lone Zone, Nondisclosure Agreement, Nondiscussion Area, Sanitization, Sanitize, Sanitized Area, Security Certification, Security Classification, Sensitive Compartmented Information, Sensitive Compartmented Information Facility, Two-Person Control.

References

Department of Defense, Defense Intelligence Agency. *Defense Intelligence Agency Manual.* Washington, DC: DIA, 1987.

Department of Defense, Defense Intelligence College. *Glossary of Intelligence Terms and Definitions.* Washington, DC: DIC, Defense Intelligence College, 1987.

Godson, Roy, ed. *Intelligence Problems for the 1980s, Number 1: Elements of Intelligence.* Rev. ed. Washington, DC: National Strategy Information Center, 1983.

Laqueur, Walter. *A World of Secrets.* New York: Basic Books, 1985.

Treverton, Gregory F. *Covert Action: The Limits of Intervention in the Postwar World.* New York: Basic Books, 1987.

—**COLLATION** is a general intelligence term. It is the grouping together, often chronologically, of related items of information in order to provide a record of events and to facilitate further intelligence processing. As defined by the Church Committee, collation is the assembly of facts to determine the relationships among them in order to derive intelligence and facilitate further processing of intelligence information. *See also:* Intelligence Cycle, Intelligence Production.

References

Department of Defense, Joint Chiefs of Staff. *Department of Defense Dictionary of Military and Related Terms.* Washington, DC: GPO, 1986.

Godson, Roy, ed. *Intelligence Problems for the 1980s, Number 1: Elements of Intelligence.* Rev. ed. Washington, DC: National Strategy Information Center, 1983.

Kent, Sherman. *Strategic Intelligence for American World Policy.* Princeton, NJ: Princeton University Press, 1966.

Treverton, Gregory F. *Covert Action: The Limits of Intervention in the Postwar World.* New York: Basic Books, 1987.

U.S. Congress. Senate. *Final Report of the Senate Select Committee to Study Government Operations with Respect to Intelligence Activities. Report 94-755. Book I, Foreign and Military Intelligence.* Washington, DC: GPO, 1976.

—**COLLECTION** is a general intelligence term that has several meanings. (1) Collection is gathering information and delivering it to the proper intelligence unit so that it can be made into intelligence. (2) Collection may also be gathering, analyzing, and disseminating non-publicly available information without the permission of the subject and delivering that information to the proper intelligence unit for processing. (3) In weapons systems, collection is using equipment or instruments to gather data concerning the testing and operation of foreign weapon systems. (4) In electronic intelligence, collection is gathering information from radars, navigation aids, countermeasures equipment and other electronic devices of an enemy or a potential enemy, except for communications equipment. (5) In respect to collecting information about U.S. persons under the provisions of Presidential Executive Order 12333 of December 4, 1981, information is considered to have been collected when it has been received for use by an employee of a Department of Defense component in the course of his official duties. Thus, information volunteered to a Department of Defense intelligence component by a cooperating source would be considered collected under this procedure when an employee of such a component officially accepts, in some manner, such information for use within his component. Data by electronic means is "collected" only when it has been processed into intelligible form. (6) Collection is also an Army tactical intelligence (TACINT) term that means acquiring information and providing it to intelligence processing and/or production elements. (7) Finally, as defined by the Church Committee, collection is the acquisition of information by any means and its delivery to the proper intelligence processing unit for use in the production of intelligence. *See also:* Collection Agency, Collection Plan, Collection Requirement, Intelligence Cycle.

References

Department of Defense. *Activities of DoD Intelligence Components that Affect U.S. Persons (Department of Defense Directive 5240.1).* Washington, DC: DoD, 1982.

Department of Defense, Defense Intelligence Agency. *Defense Intelligence Agency Manual.* Washington, DC: DIA, 1987.

Department of Defense, Defense Intelligence College. *Glossary of Intelligence Terms and Definitions.* Washington, DC: DIC, 1987.

Department of Defense, Joint Chiefs of Staff. *Department of Defense Dictionary of Military and Related Terms.* Washington, DC: GPO, 1986.

Department of Defense, U.S. Army. *Counter-Signals Intelligence (C-SIGINT) Operations.* Field Manual FM 34-62. Washington, DC: Headquarters, Department of the Army, 1986.

————. *Military Intelligence Battalion Combat Electronic Warfare and Intelligence (Aerial Exploitation) (Corps).* Field Manual FM 34-22. Washington, DC: Headquarters, Department of the Army, 1984.

————. *Military Intelligence Battalion (CEWI) (Tactical Exploitation) (Corps): Counterintelligence, Interrogation, Electronic Warfare.* Field Manual FM 34-23. Washington, DC: Headquarters, Department of the Army, 1985.

————. *Military Intelligence Battalion (Combat Electronic Warfare Intelligence) (Division).* Field Manual FM 34-10. Washington, DC: Headquarters, Department of the Army, 1981.

————. *Military Intelligence Company (Combat Electronic Warfare and Intelligence) (Armored Cavalry Regiment/Separate Brigade).* Field Manual FM 34-30. Washington, DC: Headquarters, Department of the Army, 1983.

Godson, Roy, ed. *Intelligence Problems for the 1980s, Number 1: Elements of Intelligence.* Rev. ed. Washington, DC: National Strategy Information Center, 1983.

Lefever, Ernest W., and Godson, Roy. *The CIA and the American Ethic: An Unfinished Debate.* Washington, DC: Ethics and Public Policy Center, Georgetown University, 1979.

National Security Agency. *Limitations and Procedures in Signals Intelligence Operations of the USSS.* Washington, DC: GPO, 1976.

Quirk, John; Phillips, David; Cline, Ray; and Pforzheimer, Walter. *The Central Intelligence Agency: A Photographic History.* Guilford, CT: Foreign Intelligence Press, 1986.

U.S. Congress. Senate. *Final Report of the Senate Select Committee to Study Government Operations with Respect to Intelligence Activities. Report 94-755. Book I, Foreign and Military Intelligence.* Washington, DC: GPO, 1976.

—**COLLECTION AGENCY** is a general intelligence term for any individual or organization that has access to information and collects it for an intelligence agency. *See also:* Central Intelligence Agency, Collection, Defense Intelligence Agency, Intelligence Collection, Intelligence Cycle.

References

Department of Defense, Joint Chiefs of Staff. *Department of Defense Dictionary of Military and Related Terms.* Washington, DC: GPO, 1986.

Godson, Roy, ed. *Intelligence Problems for the 1980s, Number 1: Elements of Intelligence.* Rev. ed. Washington, DC: National Strategy Information Center, 1983.

Lefever, Ernest W., and Godson, Roy. *The CIA and the American Ethic: An Unfinished Debate.* Washington, DC: Ethics and Public Policy Center, Georgetown University, 1979.

Turner, Stansfield. *Secrecy and Democracy: The CIA in Transition.* Boston: Houghton Mifflin, 1985.

—**COLLECTION COORDINATION FACILITY (CCF).** *See:* Defense Intelligence Agency.

—**COLLECTION GUIDANCE.** *See:* Guidance.

—**COLLECTION MANAGEMENT AND DISSEMINATION SECTION (CM&D SECTION),** on the Army Corps level, works under the staff supervision of the G2, performs mission management for intelligence operations, and disseminates combat information and intelligence. Mission management provides for the direction and control of corps intelligence collection operations. It is based on the requirements that have been identified in the Essential Elements of Information (EEI).

The CM&D Section plans missions based on identified requirements and available collection resources. Requirements for information are translated into specific collection missions by the section. When mission planning is completed, the CM&D Section prepares and transmits the mission tasking, and then monitors the status of the collection effort. The CM&D section also provides rapid dissemination of information. It coordinates directly with the fire support element to provide an immediate exchange of target information. *See also:* Collection Agency.

References

Department of Defense, U.S. Army. *Military Intelligence Group (Combat Electronic Warfare and Intelligence) (Corps).* Field Manual FM 34-20. Washington, DC: Headquarters, Department of the Army, 1983.

—**COLLECTION PLAN** is a term used in intelligence collection and acquisition to describe a scheme for collecting information from all available sources in order to fulfill an intelligence requirement. Once the sources are identified, the requirement is written as a request to those sources asking them to submit the necessary information. *See also:* Collection Agency.

References

Department of Defense, Joint Chiefs of Staff. *Department of Defense Dictionary of Military and Related Terms.* Washington, DC: GPO, 1986.

Godson, Roy, ed. *Intelligence Problems for the 1980s, Number 1: Elements of Intelligence.* Rev. ed. Washington, DC: National Strategy Information Center, 1983.

Treverton, Gregory F. *Covert Action: The Limits of Intervention in the Postwar World.* New York: Basic Books, 1987.

Turner, Stansfield. *Secrecy and Democracy: The CIA in Transition.* Boston: Houghton Mifflin, 1985.

—**COLLECTION REQUIREMENT** is a term used in intelligence collection and acquisition. It is the way a need for intelligence information is officially expressed. It is a written description of the problem and an implicit authorization to use intelligence resources to get the required information. Collection requirements are often originated by intelligence analysts, but must be approved at least at the supervisory level. The procedure is designed to process the requirements rapidly, while permitting accountability of the resources spent on specific requirements. *See also:* Collection Agency, Intelligence Requirement.

References

Department of Defense, Defense Intelligence College. *Glossary of Intelligence Terms and Definitions.* Washington, DC: DIC, 1987.

Kent, Sherman. *Strategic Intelligence for American World Policy.* Princeton, NJ: Princeton University Press, 1966.

Turner, Stansfield. *Secrecy and Democracy: The CIA in Transition.* Boston: Houghton Mifflin, 1985.

—**COLLECTIONS** is an official term that has been defined by the Defense Intelligence Agency for one of its functional areas. It means "activities relating to the review, development, coordination, supervision, registration, or validation of collection requirements or procedures; programs requiring collection via technical means or collection activities involving human resources; [and] the publication or review of collection manuals and guides." *See also:* Collection Agency.

References

Department of Defense, Defense Intelligence Agency. *Defense Intelligence Agency Manual 22-2.* Washington, DC: DIA, 1979.

—**COMBAT ELECTRONIC WARFARE INTELLIGENCE (CEWI).** In 1975, the U.S. Army Security Agency (USASA) was broken up in a significant reorganization of Army Intelligence. On the tactical level, USASA assets were merged with other army intelligence resources to form multidiscipline CEWI units. The goal was to provide better intelligence to field commanders by combining all the available intelligence and security resources into formations that would support the divisions and corps. *See also:* Army Security Agency.

References

Finnegan, John P. *Military Intelligence: A Picture History.* Arlington, VA: U.S. Army Intelligence and Security Command, 1984.

—**COMBAT INFORMATION** is an Army tactical intelligence term. Combat information is raw data that can be passed directly to combat and combat support units for artillery fire and maneuver, without interpretation, analysis, or integration with other data. *See also:* Combat Intelligence, Operational Intelligence.

References

Department of Defense, Department of the Army. *Intelligence and Electronic Warfare Operations.* Field Manual FM 34-1. Washington, DC: Headquarters, Department of the Army, 1984.

———. *Military Intelligence Battalion (CEWI) (Operations) (Corps).* Field Manual FM 34-21. Washington, DC: Headquarters, Department of the Army, 1982.

Department of Defense, Joint Chiefs of Staff. *Department of Defense Dictionary of Military and Related Terms.* Washington, DC: GPO, 1986.

Godson, Roy, ed. *Intelligence Problems for the 1980s, Number 1: Elements of Intelligence.* Rev.

ed. Washington, DC: National Strategy Information Center, 1983.

—**COMBAT INTELLIGENCE** is a general intelligence term that has two meanings. (1) It is an Army tactical intelligence (TACINT) term that refers to unevaluated data and therefore is not intelligence. Because it is so highly perishable or because the tactical situation is so critical, the information must be provided immediately to a tactical commander, because it cannot be processed into tactical intelligence in time to satisfy the commander's tactical intelligence requirements. Combat information can be used for immediate artillery fire and maneuver without processing. (2) Combat intelligence is knowledge of the enemy, weather, and the area's geographical features that is needed by a commander so that he can plan and conduct combat operations. *See also:* Combat Information, Tactical Intelligence.

References

Department of Defense, Defense Intelligence College. *Glossary of Intelligence Terms and Definitions.* Washington, DC: DIC, 1987.

Department of Defense, Joint Chiefs of Staff. *Department of Defense Dictionary of Military and Related Terms.* Washington, DC: GPO, 1986.

Department of Defense, U.S. Army. *Military Intelligence Battalion Combat Electronic Warfare and Intelligence (Aerial Exploitation) (Corps).* Field Manual FM 34-22. Washington, DC: Headquarters, Department of the Army, 1984.

———. *Military Intelligence Battalion (CEWI) (Operations) (Corps).* Field Manual FM 34-21. Washington, DC: Headquarters, Department of the Army, 1982.

———. *Military Intelligence Battalion (CEWI) (Tactical Exploitation) (Corps): Counterintelligence, Interrogation, Electronic Warfare.* Field Manual FM 34-23. Washington, DC: Headquarters, Department of the Army, 1985.

———. *Military Intelligence Battalion (Combat Electronic Warfare Intelligence) (Division).* Field Manual FM 34-10. Washington, DC: Headquarters, Department of the Army, 1981.

———. *Military Intelligence Company (Combat Electronic Warfare and Intelligence) (Armored Cavalry Regiment/Separate Brigade).* Field Manual FM 34-30. Washington, DC: Headquarters, Department of the Army, 1983.

———. *Military Intelligence Group (Combat Electronic Warfare and Intelligence) (Corps).* Field Manual FM 34-20. Washington, DC: Headquarters, Department of the Army, 1983.

Godson, Roy, ed. *Intelligence Problems for the 1980s, Number 1: Elements of Intelligence.* Rev. ed. Washington, DC: National Strategy Information Center, 1983.

Kent, Sherman. *Strategic Intelligence for American World Policy.* Princeton, NJ: Princeton University Press, 1966.

—**COMBAT SERVICE SUPPORT TROOPS** are units that render support to combat units in supply, maintenance, transportation, hospitalization, and related service matters.

References

Department of Defense, Joint Chiefs of Staff. *Department of Defense Dictionary of Military and Related Terms.* Washington, DC: GPO, 1986.

Poyer, David. *The Med.* New York: St. Martin's Press, 1988.

—**COMBAT SURVEILLANCE** is a continuous, all-weather, day-and-night, systematic watch over the battle area to provide timely information for tactical combat operations.

References

Department of Defense, Joint Chiefs of Staff. *Department of Defense Dictionary of Military and Related Terms.* Washington, DC: GPO, 1986.

—**COMBINED FORCE** is a military force that is composed of elements of two or more allied nations. When all allies or services are not involved, then the participating services are identified (e.g., combined navies).

References

Department of Defense, Joint Chiefs of Staff. *Department of Defense Dictionary of Military and Related Terms.* Washington, DC: GPO, 1986.

—**COMBINED OBSTACLES OVERLAY** is an Army tactical intelligence (TACINT) term. It is an overlay for a map that depicts the most probable areas of passability and impassability to enemy forces as a result of terrain and weather conditions. The combined obstacles overlay file contains coordinate data describing boundaries of all impassable areas and descriptions of the types of obstacles that are present.

References

Department of Defense, U.S. Army. *Counter-Signals Intelligence (C-SIGINT) Operations.* Field Manual

FM 34-62. Washington, DC: Headquarters, Department of the Army, 1986.

————. *Military Intelligence Battalion Combat Electronic Warfare and Intelligence (Aerial Exploitation) (Corps).* Field Manual FM 34-22. Washington, DC: Headquarters, Department of the Army, 1984.

————. *Military Intelligence Company (Combat Electronic Warfare and Intelligence) (Armored Cavalry Regiment/Separate Brigade).* Field Manual FM 34-30. Washington, DC: Headquarters, Department of the Army, 1983.

—**COMINFIL** was an FBI acronym for a program conducted in the 1960s to counter Communist infiltration of mass organizations such as the National Association for the Advancement of Colored People (NAACP), the United Farm Workers, and the Boy Scouts of America. According to Becket, the initial approach was to inform a leader in the group of the attempted infiltration and to name the Communist agent. Later, the FBI exposed both the Communist agent and the infiltrated organization for purposes of embarrassment. *See also:* COINTELPRO.

References
Becket, Henry S. A. *The Dictionary of Espionage: Spookspeak into English.* New York: Stein and Day, 1986.

Treverton, Gregory F. *Covert Action: The Limits of Intervention in the Postwar World.* New York: Basic Books, 1987.

—**COMINT.** *See:* Communications Intelligence.

—**COMMAND** is a general intelligence term that has two meanings. (1) A command is a unit or units, an organization, or an area under the direction of one individual. (2) Command is the authority that a military commander lawfully exercises over his subordinates by virtue of his rank or assignment. Command includes the responsibility and authority for planning, organizing, directing, coordinating, and controlling military forces in order to accomplish the missions that have been assigned to the commander.

References
Department of Defense, Joint Chiefs of Staff. *Department of Defense Dictionary of Military and Related Terms.* Washington, DC: GPO, 1986.

Godson, Roy, ed. *Intelligence Problems for the 1980s, Number 1: Elements of Intelligence.* Rev. ed. Washington, DC: National Strategy Information Center, 1983.

Turner, Stansfield. *Secrecy and Democracy: The CIA in Transition.* Boston: Houghton Mifflin, 1985.

U.S. Congress. Senate. *Final Report of the Senate Select Committee to Study Government Operations with Respect to Intelligence Activities. Report 94-755. Book I, Foreign and Military Intelligence.* Washington, DC: GPO, 1976.

—**COMMAND AND CONTROL (C&C OR C²)** is the exercising of authority and direction by a properly designated commander over the forces assigned to him as he accomplishes his mission. Command and control functions are fulfilled by organizing personnel, equipment, communications, and facilities and writing procedures so that a commander can plan, direct, and coordinate the forces assigned to him. Command and control is an also an Army tactical intelligence (TACINT) term that means functions performed through the arrangement of personnel, equipment, communications, facilities, and procedures that provide for the direction of combat operations. *See also:* Command, Control, and Communications Countermeasures (C³CM); Command, Control, Communications and Intelligence (C³I); Communications Security (COMSEC).

References
Department of Defense, Joint Chiefs of Staff. *Department of Defense Dictionary of Military and Related Terms.* Washington, DC: GPO, 1986.

Department of Defense, U.S. Army. *Military Intelligence Battalion Combat Electronic Warfare and Intelligence (Aerial Exploitation) (Corps).* Field Manual FM 34-22. Washington, DC: Headquarters, Department of the Army, 1984.

————. *Military Intelligence Battalion (CEWI) (Tactical Exploitation) (Corps): Counterintelligence, Interrogation, Electronic Warfare.* Field Manual FM 34-23. Washington, DC: Headquarters, Department of the Army, 1985.

————. *Military Intelligence Battalion (Combat Electronic Warfare Intelligence) (Division).* Field Manual FM 34-10. Washington, DC: Headquarters, Department of the Army, 1981.

————. *Military Intelligence Company (Combat Electronic Warfare and Intelligence) (Armored Cavalry Regiment/Separate Brigade).* Field Manual FM 34-30. Washington, DC: Headquarters, Department of the Army, 1983.

————. *Military Intelligence Group (Combat Electronic Warfare and Intelligence) (Corps).* Field Manual FM 34-20. Washington, DC: Headquarters, Department of the Army, 1983.

Godson, Roy, ed. *Intelligence Problems for the 1980s, Number 1: Elements of Intelligence.* Rev. ed. Washington, DC: National Strategy Information Center, 1983.

Turner, Stansfield. *Secrecy and Democracy: The CIA in Transition.* Boston: Houghton Mifflin, 1985.

U.S. Congress. Senate. *Final Report of the Senate Select Committee to Study Government Operations with Respect to Intelligence Activities. Report 94-755. Book I, Foreign and Military Intelligence.* Washington, DC: GPO, 1976.

—**COMMAND CHANNELS** are the operational chains of command as defined by the Joint Chiefs of Staff.

References

Department of Defense, Defense Intelligence Agency. *Defense Intelligence Agency Manual.* Washington, DC: DIA, 1987.

—**COMMAND, CONTROL, AND COMMUNICATIONS COUNTERMEASURES (C³CM)** are the combined use of operations security, military deception, jamming, and physical destruction supported by intelligence to deny information and to influence, damage, or destroy enemy command, control, and communications (C³) capabilities while protecting one's own C³ capabilities from similar action by the enemy. There are two divisions within C³CM: (1) counter C³, which is that division of C³CM that comprises measures taken to deny adversary commanders and other decisionmakers the ability to command and control their forces effectively; (2) C³ protection, which is that division of C³CM that comprises measures taken to maintain the effectiveness of friendly C³ despite both adversary and friendly counter-C³ actions. *See also:* Command and Control.

References

Department of Defense, Joint Chiefs of Staff. Department of *Defense Dictionary of Military and Related Terms.* Washington, DC: GPO, 1986.

Department of Defense, U.S. Army. *Counter-Signals Intelligence (C-SIGINT) Operations.* Field Manual FM 34-62. Washington, DC: Headquarters, Department of the Army, 1986.

—**COMMAND, CONTROL, AND COMMUNICATIONS NETWORK (C³NET)** means the different command and control entities and the systems that permit these entities to communicate with each other. Currently there is considerable con-

cern about the reliability of U.S. secure communications (in terms of whether they are truly secure and whether they will continue to perform in intense combat), and about the fact that the United States does not have great redundancy or duplication in its systems. This means that if one of the systems is disrupted, there may be no alternative means of communication.

In the modern era of computer and electronic systems, CC³Nets are, on the one hand, more secure than in the past, given the advances in electronics; on the other hand, these same systems are vulnerable, particularly in nuclear attacks, and may not function adequately under certain wartime conditions. *See also:* Command and Control.

References

Blackburn, N. Glenn. "Computers: A Counterintelligence Concern." Unpublished paper provided to the editors. Washington, DC, 1987.

Godson, Roy, ed. *Intelligence Problems for the 1980s, Number 1: Elements of Intelligence.* Rev. ed. Washington, DC: National Strategy Information Center, 1983.

—**COMMAND, CONTROL, AND COMMUNICATIONS SYSTEMS (C³S)** are the individual communications and control systems that a commander and his staff need in order to direct operations. Such systems are grouped to form command, control, and communications networks (C³ Nets). *See also:* Command and Control.

References

Blackburn, N. Glenn. "Computers: A Counterintelligence Concern." Unpublished paper provided to the editors. Washington, DC, 1987.

—**COMMAND, CONTROL, COMMUNICATIONS, AND INTELLIGENCE (C³I)** has relevance on both the tactical and the strategic levels. It involves the entire system, all the people, properly organized, and all the equipment, intelligence, communications, facilities, and writing procedures that a commander needs in order to plan, direct, and coordinate the forces that are assigned to him. *See also:* Command and Control.

References

Department of Defense, Joint Chiefs of Staff. Department of *Defense Dictionary of Military and Related Terms.* Washington, DC: GPO, 1986.

U.S. Congress. Senate. *Final Report of the Senate Select Committee to Study Government Operations*

with Respect to Intelligence Activities. Report 94-755. Book I, Foreign and Military Intelligence. Washington, DC: GPO, 1976.

—**COMMANDER, NAVAL INTELLIGENCE COMMAND (COMNAVINTCOM).** *See:* Naval Intelligence.

—**COMMERCIAL ACTIVITIES (CA) PROGRAM.** *See:* Defense Intelligence Agency.

—**COMMITTEE ON FOREIGN INTELLIGENCE (CFI)** was created by President Ford in his Executive Order 11905, dated February 18, 1976. Chaired by the director of Central Intelligence (DCI) and consisting of the deputy secretary of defense for Intelligence and the deputy assistant to the President for national security affairs, the CFI was to control the preparation and resource allocation of the budget for the National Foreign Intelligence Program (NFIP), was to establish priorities for national intelligence collection and production, and was to provide guidance concerning the relationship between tactical and national intelligence. The committee was responsible for the DCI's Intelligence Community management and resource allocation functions from 1976 to 1978. *See also:* Central Intelligence Agency; Executive Order 11905; Executive Oversight; Ford, Gerald.

References

Corson, William R. *The Armies of Ignorance: The Rise of the American Intelligence Empire.* New York: Dial Press, 1977.

Lowenthal, Mark M. *U.S. Intelligence: Evolution and Anatomy.* New York: Praeger, 1984.

Turner, Stansfield. *Secrecy and Democracy: The CIA in Transition.* Boston: Houghton Mifflin, 1985.

White House, *Executive Order 11905, United States Foreign Intelligence Activities.* Washington, DC, February 18, 1976.

—**COMMITTEE ON IMAGERY REQUIREMENTS AND EXPLOITATION (COMIREX),** as defined by the Church Committee, is one of three intelligence collection committees that were formerly under the United States Intelligence Board (USIB), dealing with photographic intelligence. It was established in 1967 to succeed the Committee on Overhead Reconnaissance (COMOR) as the part of the USIB that was responsible for the management of collection planning.

COMIREX establishes policy on national imagery collection resources and products for the director of Central Intelligence. COMIREX is currently one of four IC Staff collection committees. The other three are the SIGINT, HUMINT, and COMINT committees. *See also:* Central Intelligence Agency.

References

Corson, William R. *The Armies of Ignorance: The Rise of the American Intelligence Empire.* New York: Dial Press, 1977.

Fain, Tyrus G.; Plant, Katharine C.; and Milloy, Ross. *The Intelligence Community: History, Organization, and Issues.* Public Documents Series. New York: R.R. Bowker, 1977.

U.S. Congress. Senate. *Final Report of the Senate Select Committee to Study Government Operations with Respect to Intelligence Activities. Report 94-755. Book I, Foreign and Military Intelligence.* Washington, DC: GPO, 1976.

—**COMMITTEE ON OVERHEAD RECONNAISSANCE (COMOR)** was part of the United States Intelligence Board (USIB) that was established in 1960 to coordinate intelligence collection requirements among the departments for the development and operation of all overhead systems. It was replaced by the Committee on Imagery Requirements and Exploitation (COMIREX) in 1967. *See also:* Central Intelligence Agency.

References

Corson, William R. *The Armies of Ignorance: The Rise of the American Intelligence Empire.* New York: Dial Press, 1977.

Fain, Tyrus G.; Plant, Katharine C.; and Milloy, Ross. *The Intelligence Community: History, Organization, and Issues.* Public Documents Series. New York: R.R. Bowker, 1977.

—**COMMO** is the CIA's Office of Communications. According to Henry Becket, COMMO provides communications between CIA headquarters in Langley, Virginia, and its offices overseas and "between headquarters and sensitive agents abroad with whom regular contact is impracticable or a threat to their security." Today much of COMMO's traffic is by satellite. *See also:* Central Intelligence Agency, Communications Security (COMSEC).

References

Becket, Henry S. A. *The Dictionary of Espionage: Spookspeak into English.* New York: Stein and Day, 1986.

—**COMMON FILL DEVICES,** in communications security, are a family of devices that have been developed to read in, transfer, and store keying variables. *See also:* Communications Security.

References

Blackburn, N. Glenn. "Computers: A Counterintelligence Concern." Unpublished paper provided to the editors. Washington, DC, 1987.

Martin, Paul H. "Communications-Computer Security." *Journal of Electronic Defense* (June 1987).

Muzerall, Joseph V., and Carty, Thomas P. "COMSEC and Its Need for Key Management." *DP&CS* (Spring 1987).

Ware, Willis H. "Information Systems, Security, and Privacy." *EDUCOM Bulletin* (Summer 1984).

—**COMMUNICATIONS,** as defined by the Church Committee, are "the methods or means of conveying information from one person or place to another. This term does not include direct, unassisted conversation or correspondence through nonmilitary postal agencies." *See also:* Communications Security.

References

Godson, Roy, ed. *Intelligence Problems for the 1980s, Number 1: Elements of Intelligence.* Rev. ed. Washington, DC: National Strategy Information Center, 1983.

U.S. Congress. Senate. *Final Report of the Senate Select Committee to Study Government Operations with Respect to Intelligence Activities. Report 94-755. Book I, Foreign and Military Intelligence.* Washington, DC: GPO, 1976.

—**COMMUNICATIONS CENTER,** as defined by the Church Committee, is "a facility that is responsible for receiving, transmitting, and delivering messages; it normally contains a message section, a cryptographic section, and a sending and receiving section, using electronic communications devices." *See also:* Communications Security.

References

Godson, Roy, ed. *Intelligence Problems for the 1980s, Number 1: Elements of Intelligence.* Rev. ed. Washington, DC: National Strategy Information Center, 1983.

U.S. Congress. Senate. *Final Report of the Senate Select Committee to Study Government Operations with Respect to Intelligence Activities. Report 94-755. Book I, Foreign and Military Intelligence.* Washington, DC: GPO, 1976.

—**COMMUNICATIONS COVER,** in communications security, is a technique of concealing or altering communications so that unauthorized parties cannot collect information that would be of value. *See also:* Communications Security.

References

Godson, Roy, ed. *Intelligence Problems for the 1980s, Number 1: Elements of Intelligence.* Rev. ed. Washington, DC: National Strategy Information Center, 1983.

Laqueur, Walter. *A World of Secrets.* New York: Basic Books, 1985.

—**COMMUNICATIONS DECEPTION** is a term used in signals intelligence, communications security, communications intelligence, operations security, and signals analysis. It is transmitting, retransmitting, altering, absorbing, or manipulating telecommunications. It is intentionally done in order to cause a misinterpretation of the telecommunications. There are two types of communications deception: (1) Imitative communications deception is intruding into foreign communications channels with signals or traffic that imitate the foreign communications in order to deceive the enemy; (2) manipulative communications deception is altering or simulating friendly communications in order to deceive the enemy. *See also:* Communications Security.

References

Department of Defense, Defense Intelligence College. *Glossary of Intelligence Terms and Definitions.* Washington, DC: DIC, 1987.

Godson, Roy, ed. *Intelligence Problems for the 1980s, Number 1: Elements of Intelligence.* Rev. ed. Washington, DC: National Strategy Information Center, 1983.

Laqueur, Walter. *A World of Secrets.* New York: Basic Books, 1985.

—**COMMUNICATIONS-ELECTRONICS (C-E)** are all the equipment and gear needed for formal and informal secure electronic communications. *See also:* Communications Security.

References

Blackburn, N. Glenn. "Computers: A Counterintelligence Concern." Unpublished paper provided to the editors. Washington, DC, 1987.

Martin, Paul H. "Communications-Computer Security." *Journal of Electronic Defense* (June 1987).

Muzerall, Joseph V., and Carty, Thomas P. "COMSEC and Its Need for Key Management." *DP&CS* (Spring 1987).

Ware, Willis H. "Information Systems, Security, and Privacy." *EDUCOM Bulletin* (Summer 1984).

—**COMMUNICATIONS INTELLIGENCE (COM-INT).** The official definition of COMINT is intelligence and technical information that is derived from foreign communications by other than the intended recipients. It does not include monitoring foreign public media or communications intercepts that are obtained in the course of counterintelligence investigations within the United States. A more precise definition was supplied by the Senate Select Committee on Intelligence in 1976, when it said:

Communications intelligence is technical and intelligence information derived from foreign communications by other than the intended recipients:

A. Foreign Communications are all communications except: (1) Those of the governments of the United States and the British Commonwealth, (2) Those exchanged among private organizations and nationals, acting in a private capacity of the United States and the British Commonwealth, and (3) Those of nationals of the United States and the British Commonwealth appointed or detailed by their governments to serve in the international organizations.

B. COMINT activities are those which produce COMINT by collecting and processing foreign communications passed by radio, wire, or other electromagnetic means, and by the processing of foreign encrypted communications. However transmitted, collection comprises search, intercept and direction finding. Processing comprises range estimation, transmitter/operator identification, signal analysis, traffic analysis, cryptanalysis, decryption, study of the plain text, the fusion of these processes, and the reporting of the results.

C. Exceptions to COMINT and COMINT activities. COMINT and COMINT activities defined here do not include (1) Intercept and processing of unencrypted written communications, except written plain text versions of communications which have been encrypted or are intended for subsequent encryption. (2) Intercept and processing of press, propaganda, and other public broadcasts, except for encrypted or "hidden meaning" passages in such broadcasts. (3) Operations conducted by the United States, United Kingdom or Commonwealth security authorities. (4) Censorship. (5) The intercept and study of non-communications transmissions (ELINT) *See also:* Communications Security.

References

Allen, Thomas B., and Polmar, Norman. *Merchants of Treason: America's Secrets for Sale.* New York: Delacorte Press, 1988.

American Bar Association. *Oversight and Accountability of the U.S. Intelligence Agencies: An Evaluation.* Washington, DC: ABA, 1985.

Bamford, James. *The Puzzle Palace: A Report on America's Most Secret Agency.* New York: Penguin Books, 1983.

Corson, William R. *The Armies of Ignorance: The Rise of the American Intelligence Empire.* New York: Dial Press, 1977.

Department of Defense, Defense Intelligence College. *Glossary of Intelligence Terms and Definitions.* Washington, DC: DIC, 1987.

Department of Defense, U.S. Army. *Counter-Signals Intelligence (C-SIGINT) Operations.* Field Manual FM 34-62. Washington, DC: Headquarters, Department of the Army, 1986.

————. *Military Intelligence Battalion Combat Electronic Warfare and Intelligence (Aerial Exploitation) (Corps).* Field Manual FM 34-22. Washington, DC: Headquarters, Department of the Army, 1984.

————. *Military Intelligence Battalion (CEWI) (Tactical Exploitation) (Corps): Counterintelligence, Interrogation, Electronic Warfare.* Field Manual FM 34-23. Washington, DC: Headquarters, Department of the Army, 1985.

————. *Military Intelligence Battalion (Combat Electronic Warfare Intelligence) (Division).* Field Manual FM 34-10. Washington, DC: Headquarters, Department of the Army, 1981.

————. *Military Intelligence Company (Combat Electronic Warfare and Intelligence) (Armored Cavalry Regiment/Separate Brigade).* Field Manual FM 34-30. Washington, DC: Headquarters, Department of the Army, 1983.

Godson, Roy, ed. *Intelligence Problems for the 1980s, Number 1: Elements of Intelligence.* Rev. ed. Washington, DC: National Strategy Information Center, 1983.

————. *Intelligence Problems for the 1980s, Number 3: Counterintelligence.* Washington, DC: National Strategy Information Center, 1980.

————. *Intelligence Problems for the 1980s, Number 5: Clandestine Collection.* Washington, DC: National Strategy Information Center, 1982.

Kessler, Ronald. *Spy vs. Spy: Stalking Soviet Spies in America.* New York: Charles Scribner's Sons, 1988.

Laqueur, Walter. *A World of Secrets.* New York: Basic Books, Inc., 1985.

Maurer, Alfred C.; Turnstall, Marion D.; and Keagle, James M. *Intelligence Policy and Process.* Boulder, CO: Westview Press, 1985.

U.S. Congress. Senate. *Final Report of the Senate Select Committee to Study Government Operations with Respect to Intelligence Activities. Report 94-755. Book I, Foreign and Military Intelligence.* Washington, DC: GPO, 1976.

—COMMUNICATIONS INTELLIGENCE DATA BASE is that part of the technical and intelligence information that has been intercepted from foreign communications, analyzed, and judged to be of value to intercept, analysis, and reporting activities. This does not include information taken from press, propaganda, or public broadcasts. *See also:* Communications Security.

References

Department of Defense, Joint Chiefs of Staff. Department of *Defense Dictionary of Military and Related Terms.* Washington, DC: GPO, 1986.

Laqueur, Walter. *A World of Secrets.* New York: Basic Books, 1985.

—COMMUNICATIONS INTERCEPTION, as defined by the Church Committee, is the raw data of communications intelligence (COMINT). It is information that has been taken from a communications system by someone other than the intended recipients. Communications intercepts, when received, are placed into the intelligence processing cycle in order to produce COMINT. *See also:* Communications Security.

References

Godson, Roy, ed. *Intelligence Problems for the 1980s, Number 1: Elements of Intelligence.* Rev. ed. Washington, DC: National Strategy Information Center, 1983.

———. *Intelligence Problems for the 1980s, Number 3: Counterintelligence.* Washington, DC: National Strategy Information Center, 1980.

Laqueur, Walter. *A World of Secrets.* New York: Basic Books, 1985.

U.S. Congress. Senate. *Final Report of the Senate Select Committee to Study Government Operations with Respect to Intelligence Activities. Report 94-755. Book I, Foreign and Military Intelligence.* Washington, DC: GPO, 1976.

—COMMUNICATIONS JAMMING (COMJAM) is that part of electronic jamming that is directed against enemy communications so that they cannot receive information. *See also:* Jammer.

References

Blackburn, N. Glenn. "Computers: A Counterintelligence Concern." Unpublished paper provided to the editors. Washington, DC, 1987.

Muzerall, Joseph V., and Carty, Thomas P. "COMSEC and Its Need for Key Management." *DP&CS* (Spring 1987).

—COMMUNICATIONS PRIVACY, in communications security, is the protection afforded to information that is transmitted in a secure telecommunications system or network in order to conceal it from persons within the system or network. *See also:* Communications Security.

References

Blackburn, N. Glenn. "Computers: A Counterintelligence Concern." Unpublished paper provided to the editors. Washington, DC, 1987.

Muzerall, Joseph V., and Carty, Thomas P. "COMSEC and Its Need for Key Management." *DP&CS* (Spring 1987).

—COMMUNICATIONS PROFILE, in communications security (COMSEC), is an analytic model of the communications associated with an organization or activity as they might appear to a hostile signals intelligence (SIGINT) organization. The model is the result of a systematic examination of applied COMSEC measures, communications content and patterns, and the functions that they reflect.

References

Department of Defense, U.S. Army. *Counter-Signals Intelligence (C-SIGINT) Operations.* Field Manual FM 34-62. Washington, DC: Headquarters, Department of the Army, 1986.

———. *Military Intelligence Battalion Combat Electronic Warfare and Intelligence (Aerial Exploitation) (Corps).* Field Manual FM 34-22. Washington, DC: Headquarters, Department of the Army, 1984.

———. *Military Intelligence Company (Combat Electronic Warfare and Intelligence) (Armored Cavalry Regiment/Separate Brigade).* Field Manual FM 34-30. Washington, DC: Headquarters, Department of the Army, 1983.

—COMMUNICATIONS PROTECTION, in communications security (COMSEC), is applying COMSEC measures to telecommunications in order to deny unauthorized persons access to unclassified information that may be of value, to prevent disruption, or to ensure the authenticity of such telecommunications. *See also:* Communications Security.

References

Laqueur, Walter. *A World of Secrets.* New York: Basic Books, 1985.

—**COMMUNICATIONS SATELLITE (COMSAT)** is an orbiting vehicle that relays signals between communications stations. There are two types: active communications satellites, which receive, regenerate, and retransmit signals between stations; and passive communications satellites, which reflect communications between stations.

References

Department of Defense, Joint Chiefs of Staff. Department of *Defense Dictionary of Military and Related Terms.* Washington, DC: GPO, 1986.

Godson, Roy, ed. *Intelligence Problems for the 1980s, Number 1: Elements of Intelligence.* Rev. ed. Washington, DC: National Strategy Information Center, 1983.

Laqueur, Walter. *A World of Secrets.* New York: Basic Books, 1985.

Turner, Stansfield. *Secrecy and Democracy: The CIA in Transition.* Boston: Houghton Mifflin, 1985.

—**COMMUNICATIONS SECURITY (COMSEC)** is the protection that results from all efforts designed to prevent unauthorized individuals from gaining access to and analyzing the volume and content of specific information of intelligence value. COMSEC also involves attempts to mislead unauthorized persons when they analyze this information if they manage to gain access to it, and it involves the authenticating of the subject information. The protection of U.S. telecommunications and other communications from exploitation by foreign intelligence services and from unauthorized disclosure is one of the responsibilities of the National Security Agency. It includes cryptosecurity, emission security, and the physical security of classified communications security materials, equipment and documents. COMSEC is also an Army tactical intelligence (TACINT) term that means the protective measures that are taken to deny unauthorized persons information derived from U.S. government telecommunications that are related to the national security, and to ensure the authenticity of such communications. Such protection results from the application of security measures (including cryptosecurity, transmissions security, and emissions security) to electrical systems generating, handling, processing, or using national security-related information. It also includes applying physical security measures to communications security information or materials. As defined by the Church Committee, COMSEC "is the protection of United States telecommunications and other communications from exploitation by foreign intelligence services and from unauthorized disclosure. COMSEC is one of the missions of the National Security Agency. It includes cryptosecurity, transmission security, emission security, and physical security of classified equipment, material, and documents." **COMSEC account** is an administrative entity, identified by an account number, that is used to account for custody and control of COMSEC material. **COMSEC aids** are all COMSEC material, other than the equipment and devices, that perform or assist the user in performing cryptographic functions or that relate to associated functions or devices. COMSEC aids are often required for producing, operating, or maintaining cryptosystems or cryptosystem components. Some examples are COMSEC keying material, call-sign/frequency systems, and supporting documentation, such as operating and maintenance manuals. **COMSEC assessment** is a determination of the relative significance of telecommunications vulnerabilities and the threats thereto. **COMSEC control program** means a set of instructions or routines for a computer that controls or affects externally performed functions of key generation, cryptovariable generation and distribution, message encryption/decryption, or authentication. **COMSEC custodian** means the individual who is designated by proper authority to be responsible for the receipt, transfer, accountability, safeguarding, and destruction of the COMSEC material that is issued to a COMSEC account. **COMSEC end item** means a part or combination of component parts and/or material that is ready for its intended use in a COMSEC application. **COMSEC equipment** means equipment designed to provide security to telecommunications by converting information to a form that is unintelligible to an unauthorized interceptor and by reconverting such information to its original form for authorized recipients, as well as the equipment designed specifically to aid in, or is an essential element of, the conversion process. COMSEC equipment is crypto-equipment, crypto-ancillary equipment, cryptoproduction equipment, and authentication equipment. **COMSEC evaluation** is an assessment of the effectiveness of the COMSEC measures that have been applied to a particular telecommunications system, and of the need, if any, for applying additional COMSEC measures. **COMSEC facility** is a facility that contains classified COMSEC material. **COMSEC firmware** is the program information that is contained in a Programmable Read-Only Memory (PROM), Read-Only Memory (ROM), or a similar device that incorporates a COMSEC function. **COMSEC information** is all the information concerning COMSEC and all COMSEC material. **COMSEC insecurity** is an occurrence that jeopardizes the security of COMSEC material or the secure electrical transmission of national security or national security-related information. **COMSEC material** includes COMSEC aids, equipments and components thereof, and devices that are identifiable by the Telecommunications Security (TSEC) nomenclature system or a similar system of a U.S. department or agency, foreign government or international organization. **COMSEC Material Control System (CMCS)** is the logistic system through which accountable COMSEC material is distributed, controlled and safeguarded. It consists of all COMSEC Central Offices of Record, cryptologistic depots and COMSEC accounts and subaccounts. **COMSEC measures** are all cryptographic, transmission security, emission security, and physical security techniques that are employed to protect telecommunications. **COMSEC monitoring** is the act of listening to, copying or recording transmissions of one's own official telecommunications to provide material for analysis in order to determine the degree of security being provided to those transmissions. It is one of the techniques of COMSEC surveillance. **COMSEC profile** is the identification of all COMSEC measures and materials that are available for a given operation, system, or organization, and a determination of the amount and type of use of those measures and materials. **COMSEC signals acquisition and analysis** is the acquiring of radio frequency propagation and its subsequent analysis to determine empirically the vulnerability of the transmission media to interception by foreign intelligence services. This process includes cataloging the transmission spectrum and taking signal parametric measurements as required. It does not include acquiring information carried on the system. It is one of the techniques of COMSEC surveillance. **COMSEC software** consists of the computer or microprocessor instructions and/or routines which con-

trol or perform COMSEC and COMSEC-related functions and associated documentation. **COMSEC surveillance** is the systematic examination of telecommunications to determine the adequacy of COMSEC measures, to identify COMSEC deficiencies, to provide data from which to predict the effectiveness of proposed COMSEC measures, and to confirm the adequacy of such measures after they are implemented. **COMSEC survey** has two meanings. (1) In one sense, it is the application of COMSEC analysis and assessment techniques to a specific operation, function, or program. (2) It also means an examination and inspection of a physical location in order to determine whether alterations and modifications are necessary to make it acceptable for the installation and operation of COMSEC equipment. **COMSEC system** is the combination of all measures that are intended to provide communications security for a specific telecommunications system, including the associated cryptographic, transmission, emission, computer and physical security measures, as well as the COMSEC support system (documentation, doctrine, keying material protection and distribution, and equipment engineering, production, distribution, modification, and maintenance).

References

Allen, Thomas B., and Polmar, Norman. *Merchants of Treason: America's Secrets for Sale.* New York: Delacorte Press, 1988.

Blackburn, N. Glenn. "Computers: A Counterintelligence Concern." Unpublished paper provided to the editors. Washington, DC, 1987.

Department of Defense. *Activities of DoD Intelligence Components that Affect U.S. Persons (Department of Defense Directive 5240.1).* Washington, DC: DoD, 1982.

Department of Defense, Joint Chiefs of Staff. *Department of Defense Dictionary of Military and Related Terms.* Washington, DC: GPO, 1986.

Department of Defense, U.S. Army. *Counterintelligence.* Field Manual FM 34-60. Washington, DC: Headquarters, Department of the Army, 1985.

———. *Counter-Signals Intelligence (C-SIGINT) Operations.* Field Manual FM 34-62. Washington, DC: Headquarters, Department of the Army, 1986.

———. *Military Intelligence Battalion Combat Electronic Warfare and Intelligence (Aerial Exploitation) (Corps).* Field Manual FM 34-22. Washington, DC: Headquarters, Department of the Army, 1984.

———. *Military Intelligence Battalion (CEWI) (Tactical Exploitation) (Corps): Counterintelligence, Interrogation, Electronic Warfare.* Field Manual FM

34-23. Washington, DC: Headquarters, Department of the Army, 1985.

————. *Military Intelligence Company (Combat Electronic Warfare and Intelligence) (Armored) Cavalry Regiment/Separate Brigade)*. Field Manual FM 34-30. Washington, DC: Headquarters, Department of the Army, 1983.

Godson, Roy, ed., *Intelligence Problems for the 1980s, Number 1: Elements of Intelligence*. Rev. ed. Washington, DC: National Strategy Information Center, 1983.

Kessler, Ronald. *Spy vs. Spy: Stalking Soviet Spies in America*. New York: Charles Scribner's Sons, 1988.

Laqueur, Walter. *A World of Secrets*. New York: Basic Books, 1985.

Martin, Paul H. "Communications-Computer Security." *Journal of Electronic Defense* (June 1987).

Muzerall, Joseph V., and Carty, Thomas P. "COMSEC and Its Need for Key Management." *DP&CS* (Spring 1987).

Office of the President of the United States. *Executive Order 12036, U.S. Intelligence Activities*. Washington, DC, January 24, 1978.

U.S. Congress. Senate. *Final Report of the Senate Select Committee to Study Government Operations with Respect to Intelligence Activities. Report 94-755. Book I, Foreign and Military Intelligence*. Washington, DC: GPO, 1976.

Ware, Willis H. "Information Systems, Security, and Privacy." *EDUCOM Bulletin* (Summer 1984).

—**COMMUNICATIONS SECURITY EQUIPMENT** provides security for telecommunications by converting the information transmitted to an unintelligible form at the transmitting station, and reconverting it back into its original form at the receiving station. Communications security equipment includes cryptoequipment, cryptoancilliary equipment, cryptoproduction equipment, and authentication equipment. *See also:* Communications Security.

References

Department of Defense, Joint Chiefs of Staff. *Department of Defense Dictionary of Military and Related Terms*. Washington, DC: GPO, 1986.

—**COMMUNICATIONS SECURITY MATERIAL** includes all the documents devices, equipment, and cryptomaterial used in setting up and maintaining a secure communications system. *See also:* Communications Security.

References

Department of Defense, Joint Chiefs of Staff. *Department of Defense Dictionary of Military and Related Terms*. Washington, DC: GPO, 1986.

Laqueur, Walter. *A World of Secrets*. New York: Basic Books, 1985.

—**COMMUNICATIONS SECURITY MONITORING** is listening to or recording one's own transmissions in order to determine if the communication security measures are adequate. *See also:* Communications Security.

References

Department of Defense, Joint Chiefs of Staff. *Department of Defense Dictionary of Military and Related Terms*. Washington, DC: GPO, 1986.

Laqueur, Walter. *A World of Secrets*. New York: Basic Books, 1985.

—**COMMUNICATIONS SECURITY SIGNAL ACQUISITION AND ANALYSIS** is collecting and analyzing communications signals to determine whether they can be intercepted by the enemy. It involves monitoring the transmission spectrum and recording signals, but does not include collecting the information on these frequencies. It is one of the techniques of communications security surveillance. *See also:* Communications Security, Communications Security Surveillance.

References

Department of Defense, Defense Intelligence College. *Glossary of Intelligence Terms and Definitions*. Washington, DC: DIC, 1987.

—**COMMUNICATIONS SECURITY SURVEILLANCE** involves systematically examining one's own telecommunications and automatic data processing systems in order to determine whether the communications security measures are adequate, to identify any communications deficiencies, to provide information from which one can predict whether proposed security measures will be effective, and to confirm the adequacy of these security measures after they are implemented. *See also:* Communications Security.

References

Department of Defense, Defense Intelligence College. *Glossary of Intelligence Terms and Definitions*. Washington, DC: DIC, 1987.

—**COMMUNITY DEVELOPMENT** is a program-system development effort that involves simultaneous changes in the intelligence operations or ADP-T architectures of two or more GDIC components. *See also:* General Defense Intelligence Community (GDIC), General Defense Intelligence Program (GDIP).

References

Department of Defense, Defense Intelligence Agency. *Defense Intelligence Agency Manual.* Washington, DC: DIA, 1987.

—**COMMUNITY ON-LINE INTELLIGENCE SYSTEM (COINS)** is a network of Intelligence Community computer-based information storage and retrieval systems that have been interconnected for interagency sharing of machine-formatted files that are available to NSA, CIA, Department of State, and Department of Defense analysts. COINS was a management tool that was initially met with resistance from some Intelligence Community members. Recognizing that the intelligence organizations had all invested in a variety of automated systems, COINS was an attempt to integrate these systems into one where communication was possible. Officially objecting to the system because of the perceived impact it would have on their computer systems, many organizations actually were opposed to COINS because it would grant other intelligence organizations access to their files; it was perceived as a significant threat to an organization's control and influence. Nonetheless, despite the opposition, COINS was established. DIAOLS (the DIA On-Line System) and COINS eventually became major data acquisition systems. *See also:* Defense Intelligence Agency.

References

Department of Defense, Defense Intelligence College. *Glossary of Intelligence Terms and Definitions.* Washington, DC: DIC, 1987.

—**COMPANY** is an insiders' name for the Central Intelligence Agency. The term is now somewhat passé. Other nicknames for the CIA are "The Agency" or "Langley," which is the Virginia town in which the CIA headquarters are located.

References

Becket, Henry S. A. *The Dictionary of Espionage: Spookspeak into English.* New York: Stein and Day, 1986.

Deacon, Richard. *Spyclopedia: An Encyclopedia of Spies, Secret Services, Operations, Jargon, and All Subjects Related to the World of Espionage.* London: Macdonald, 1987.

Godson, Roy, ed., *Intelligence Problems for the 1980s, Number 1: Elements of Intelligence.* Rev. ed. Washington, DC: National Strategy Information Center, 1983.

Laqueur, Walter. *A World of Secrets.* New York: Basic Books, 1985.

Quirk, John; Phillips, David; Cline, Ray; and Pforzheimer, Walter. *The Central Intelligence Agency: A Photographic History.* Guilford, CT: Foreign Intelligence Press, 1986.

Treverton, Gregory F. *Covert Action: The Limits of Intervention in the Postwar World.* New York: Basic Books, 1987.

—**COMPARTMENTATION** is a general intelligence term that is used in several contexts. (1) Compartmentation is a means of further restricting intelligence information to a strict need-to-know basis. It is the practice of establishing special channels for handling sensitive intelligence information. These channels are limited to individuals with a specific need for such information and who are therefore given special security clearances that give them access to it. Compartmented systems are established by or are under the cognizance of the director of Central Intelligence and are intended to protect sensitive information or sensitive intelligence sources, methods, or analytical procedures of foreign intelligence programs. Implied in compartmentation is that divulging the information, sources, methods, or procedures would destroy an entire, very valuable type of intelligence and must therefore be protected under stringent safeguards. Compartmentation security measures not only include the above-described measures for clearing personnel for access to a certain type of information, but they also involve particularly stringent measures for storing and safeguarding the information. (2) In signals intelligence (SIGINT), compartmentation has a more specific meaning. Here it is the special protection given to the production and distribution of especially sensitive SIGINT material because of its source, method of processing, or content. (3) In general security, it has still another meaning. Here compartmentation is establishing and managing an intelligence organization so that information about the employees, organization, or activities of one component is made available to the organization's other components only to the extent that is required for these other components to do their jobs. (4) As defined by the Church Committee, compartmentation is the practice of establishing special channels for handling sensitive intelligence information. The channels are limited to individuals with a specific need for such information and who are therefore given special security clearances in order to have access to it. *See also:* Authorized, Classification, Classification Authority, Classification Review, Classified Information, Closed Storage, Communications Security, Compromise, Controlled Area, Controlled Dissemination, Debriefing, Declassification, Decompartmentation, Information Security, Limited Access Area, Nondisclosure Agreement, Physical Security, Secure Area, Secure Vault Area, Secure Working Area, Security, Security Certification, Security Classification, Security Clearance, Sensitive Compartmented Information, Sensitive Compartmented Information Facility, Special Security Officer, Special Security Officer System, TOP SECRET Code Word, TOP SECRET Control, TOP SECRET Control Officer, Vault Door.

References

Allen, Thomas B., and Polmar, Norman. *Merchants of Treason: America's Secrets for Sale.* New York: Delacorte Press, 1988.

American Bar Association. *Oversight and Accountability of the U.S. Intelligence Agencies: An Evaluation.* Washington, DC: ABA, 1985.

Department of Defense, Defense Intelligence College. *Glossary of Intelligence Terms and Definitions.* Washington, DC: DIC, 1987.

Department of Defense, Joint Chiefs of Staff. *Department of Defense Dictionary of Military and Related Terms.* Washington, DC: GPO, 1986.

Godson, Roy, ed., *Intelligence Problems for the 1980s, Number 1: Elements of Intelligence.* Rev. ed. Washington, DC: National Strategy Information Center, 1983.

Kessler, Ronald. *Spy vs. Spy: Stalking Soviet Spies in America.* New York: Charles Scribner's Sons, 1988.

Laqueur, Walter. *A World of Secrets.* New York: Basic Books, 1985.

Treverton, Gregory F. *Covert Action: The Limits of Intervention in the Postwar World.* New York: Basic Books, 1987.

Turner, Stansfield. *Secrecy and Democracy: The CIA in Transition.* Boston: Houghton Mifflin, 1985.

U.S. Congress. Senate. *Final Report of the Senate Select Committee to Study Government Operations with Respect to Intelligence Activities. Report 94-755. Book I, Foreign and Military Intelligence.* Washington, DC: GPO, 1976.

—**COMPELLING NEED** is a requirement that an individual be granted access to sensitive compartmented information (SCI) when that person does not meet personnel security standards. The requirement must show that the benefits to be gained outweigh the risks involved. A compelling need exists when denying access would have an adverse impact on the organization. *See also:* Compartmentation.

References

Maurer, Alfred C.; Turnstall, Marion D.; and Keagle, James M. *Intelligence Policy and Process.* Boulder, CO: Westview Press, 1985.

—**COMPETITIVE ANALYSIS** is a term used in intelligence analysis. Supporters of competitive analysis maintain that U.S. estimates have not been accurate because alternative views have not been considered. The individuals believe that by creating competitive, centralized analytic agencies and having them produce independent analyses that would be competitive, the Intelligence Community would produce more accurate estimates.

References

American Bar Association. *Oversight and Accountability of the U.S. Intelligence Agencies: An Evaluation.* Washington, DC: ABA, 1985.

Lefever, Ernest W., and Godson, Roy. *The CIA and the American Ethic: An Unfinished Debate.* Washington, DC: Ethics and Public Policy Center, Georgetown University, 1979.

Maurer, Alfred C.; Turnstall, Marion D.; and Keagle, James M. *Intelligence Policy and Process.* Boulder, CO: Westview Press, 1985.

Treverton, Gregory F. *Covert Action: The Limits of Intervention in the Postwar World.* New York: Basic Books, 1987.

Turner, Stansfield. *Secrecy and Democracy: The CIA in Transition.* Boston: Houghton Mifflin, 1985.

—**COMPILATION** occurs when several pieces of information that are unclassified by themselves are combined, resulting in a classified piece of information.

References

Department of Defense, Joint Chiefs of Staff. *Department of Defense Dictionary of Military and Related Terms.* Washington, DC: GPO, 1986.

Turner, Stansfield. *Secrecy and Democracy: The CIA in Transition.* Boston: Houghton Mifflin, 1985.

Von Hoene, John P. A. *Intelligence User's Guide.* Washington, DC: DIA, 1983.

—**COMPLEX BARRAGE JAMMING** is an electronic warfare term. It is jamming that is caused by several jamming carriers with different modulations. *See also:* Jamming.

References

Blackburn, N. Glenn. "Computers: A Counterintelligence Concern." Unpublished paper provided to the editors. Washington, DC, 1987.

—**COMPOUND,** a baud-based system term used in communications intelligence, communications security, operations security, and signals analysis, is a transmission containing two or more sequenced groups, each consisting of two or more interlaced channels, or one or more interlaced channels followed by a sequential channel. *See also:* Communications Security.

References

Blackburn, N. Glenn. "Computers: A Counterintelligence Concern." Unpublished paper provided to the editors. Washington, DC, 1987.

Ware, Willis H. "Information Systems, Security, and Privacy." *EDUCOM Bulletin* (Summer 1984).

—**COMPROMISE** is a general intelligence term that has several meanings. (1) Compromise can be the same as unauthorized disclosure if it involves exposing classified information or activities to people who are not cleared for access to it. (2) In clandestine and covert intelligence activities, it is the enemy's detection of a safe house, an agent, or an intelligence technique. (3) In communications security, it is the known or suspected exposure of clandestine personnel, installations or other assets, or of classified material to an unauthorized person. (4) As defined by the Church Committee, compromise is a known or suspected exposure of clandestine personnel, installations or other assets, or of classified information or material, to an unauthorized person. *See also:* Access, Authorized, Classification, Classified Information, Code Word, Declassification, Disclosure, Downgrade, Freedom of Information Act, Limited Access Area, Need-to-Know, Need-to-Know Principle, No-Lone Zone, Nondisclosure Agreement, Nondiscussion Area, Sanitization, Sanitize, Sanitized Area, Security Certification, Security Classification, Sensitive Compartmented Information, Sensitive Compartmented Information Facility, Two-Person Control.

References

Allen, Thomas B., and Polmar, Norman. Merchants of Treaso*n: America's Secrets for Sale.* New York: Delacorte Press, 1988.

Becket, Henry S. A. *The Dictionary of Espionage: Spookspeak into English.* New York: Stein and Day, 1986.

Clancy, Tom. *The Cardinal of the Kremlin.* New York: Putnam, 1988.

Department of Defense, Defense Intelligence College. *Glossary of Intelligence Terms and Definitions.* Washington, DC: DIC, 1987.

Department of Defense, Joint Chiefs of Staff. *Department of Defense Dictionary of Military and Related Terms.* Washington, DC: GPO, 1986.

Godson, Roy, ed., *Intelligence Problems for the 1980s, Number 1: Elements of Intelligence.* Rev. ed. Washington, DC: National Strategy Information Center, 1983.

Turner, Stansfield. *Secrecy and Democracy: The CIA in Transition.* Boston: Houghton Mifflin, 1985.

U.S. Congress. Senate. *Final Report of the Senate Select Committee to Study Government Operations with Respect to Intelligence Activities. Report 94-755. Book I, Foreign and Military Intelligence.* Washington, DC: GPO, 1976.

—**COMPROMISING EMANATIONS** is a term used in signals intelligence, communications security, and operations security. Such emanations are unintentional emissions from information-processing equipment that could disclose the information being transmitted, received, or handled. For example, in the 1960s and early 1970s, the older IBM typewriters that carried the letters on a ball would draw different amounts of current each time a different letter was struck. Thus, by monitoring the flow of electric current leading to the typewriter, one could determine the keys that were being struck and could then determine the entire text. A simple procedure altered the machines so that they would not divulge this information by insuring that every key struck would draw the same amount of current. *See also:* Communications Security.

References

Department of Defense, Defense Intelligence College. *Glossary of Intelligence Terms and Definitions.* Washington, DC: DIC, 1987.

Department of Defense, U.S. Army. *Counter-Signals Intelligence (C-SIGINT) Operations.* Field Manual FM 34-62. Washington, DC: Headquarters, Department of the Army, 1986.

————. *Military Intelligence Battalion Combat Electronic Warfare and Intelligence (Aerial Exploitation) (Corps)*. Field Manual FM 34-22. Washington, DC: Headquarters, Department of the Army, 1984.

————. *Military Intelligence Company (Combat Electronic Warfare and Intelligence) (Armored) Cavalry Regiment/Separate Brigade)*. Field Manual FM 34-30. Washington, DC: Headquarters, Department of the Army, 1983.

—**COMPTROLLER.** *See:* Central Intelligence Agency and Defense Intelligence Agency.

—**COMPUTER CRYPTOGRAPHY,** in communications security, is the use of a cryptoalgorithm in a computer, microprocessor, or microcomputer to perform encryption or decryption, to protect information or to authenticate users or sources of information. *See also:* Communications Security.

References

Maurer, Alfred C.; Turnstall, Marion D.; and Keagle, James M. *Intelligence Policy and Process*. Boulder, CO: Westview Press, 1985.

—**COMPUTER SECURITY (COMPUSEC),** in communications security, is the protection resulting from all measures designed to prevent deliberate or inadvertent unauthorized disclosure, acquisition, manipulation, modification, or loss of information contained in a computer system, as well as measures designed to prevent denial of authorized use of the system. The National Security Agency is the responsible agency for all COMPUSEC policy for the Department of Defense and for any systems using national security information. *See also:* Communications Security.

References

American Bar Association. *Oversight and Accountability of the U.S. Intelligence Agencies: An Evaluation*. Washington, DC: ABA, 1985.

Department of Defense, Defense Intelligence College. *Glossary of Intelligence Terms and Definitions*. Washington, DC: DIC, 1987.

Godson, Roy, ed. *Intelligence Problems for the 1980s, Number 1: Elements of Intelligence*. Rev. ed. Washington, DC: National Strategy Information Center, 1983.

Laqueur, Walter. *A World of Secrets*. New York: Basic Books, 1985.

Maurer, Alfred C.; Turnstall, Marion D.; and Keagle, James M. *Intelligence Policy and Process*. Boulder, CO: Westview Press, 1985.

—**COMSEC.** *See:* Communications Security.

—**CONCEALMENT,** as defined by the Church Committee, is the provision of protection from observation only. This is similar to the official Department of Defense definition, which is the protection from observation or surveillance. *See also:* Concealment Devices, Cover, Cover Name, Cover Organizations, Cover Story, Go to Ground, Suitable Cover.

References

Department of Defense, Joint Chiefs of Staff. *Department of Defense Dictionary of Military and Related Terms*. Washington, DC: GPO, 1986.

Treverton, Gregory F. *Covert Action: The Limits of Intervention in the Postwar World*. New York: Basic Books, 1987.

U.S. Congress. Senate. *Final Report of the Senate Select Committee to Study Government Operations with Respect to Intelligence Activities. Report 94-755. Book I, Foreign and Military Intelligence*. Washington, DC: GPO, 1976.

—**CONCEALMENT DEVICES** are innocuous objects that are used to hide material or equipment. They are also called containers.

References

Becket, Henry S. A. *The Dictionary of Espionage: Spookspeak into English*. New York: Stein and Day, 1986.

Deacon, Richard. *Spyclopedia: An Encyclopedia of Spies, Secret Services, Operations, Jargon, and All Subjects Related to the World of Espionage*. London: Macdonald, 1987.

Kessler, Ronald. *Spy vs. Spy: Stalking Soviet Spies in America*. New York: Charles Scribner's Sons, 1988.

—**CONDUCT OF INTELLIGENCE ACTIVITIES.** *See:* Executive Order 12036.

—**CONFIDENTIAL.** *See:* Security Classification.

—**CONFIDENTIAL SOURCES** is a term used in clandestine intelligence operations to describe people who supply an intelligence agency information that they collect at their jobs. These individuals might be bankers, telephone company employees, landlords, customs and immigrations personnel, hotel employees, newspaper writers and editors or any others who might have information to offer. *See also:* Agent in Place, Agent Net, Agent of Influence, Agent Provocateur, Co-opted Worker, Co-optees, Defector, Double Agent, Illegal Agent, Informant, Inside Man, Keeping Books, Ladies, Legal, Not Witting, Pigeon, Recruitment, Recruitment in Place, Special Activities, Turned, Walk-in.

References

Becket, Henry S. A. *The Dictionary of Espionage: Spookspeak into English.* New York: Stein and Day, 1986.

Godson, Roy, ed. *Intelligence Problems for the 1980s, Number 1: Elements of Intelligence.* Rev. ed. Washington, DC: National Strategy Information Center, 1983.

Turner, Stansfield. *Secrecy and Democracy: The CIA in Transition.* Boston: Houghton Mifflin, 1985.

—**CONFIGURATION** is a general intelligence term that has two meanings. (1) It is the physical and functional characteristics of systems or equipment as achieved in the hardware or software as described in the appropriate documentation. (2) Configuration is also defined as the complete technical description required to fabricate, test, accept, operate, maintain, and logistically support systems or equipment.

References

Pickett, George. "Congress, the Budget and Intelligence." In *Intelligence Policy and Process,* edited by Alfred C. Maurer, Marion D. Turnstall, and James M. Keagle. Boulder, CO: Westview Press, 1985.

—**CONFIRMATION OF INFORMATION** is a general intelligence term that describes an occurrence in which a piece of information is verified because the same information is reported by another source that is independent from the first reporter. The reliability of the second reporter is of course taken into consideration when confirming the first piece of information. Collating items from independent sources is an excellent means of establishing the validity of each piece of information and of weeding out erroneous data.

References

Department of Defense, Defense Intelligence College. *Glossary of Intelligence Terms and Definitions.* Washington, DC: DIC, 1987.

Department of Defense, Joint Chiefs of Staff. *Department of Defense Dictionary of Military and Related Terms.* Washington, DC: GPO, 1986.

Godson, Roy, ed., *Intelligence Problems for the 1980s, Number 1: Elements of Intelligence.* Rev. ed. Washington, DC: National Strategy Information Center, 1983.

—**CONFUSION AGENT,** as defined by the Church Committee, "is an individual who is dispatched by his sponsor to confound the intelligence or counterintelligence apparatus of another country rather than to collect and transmit information." *See also:* Agent, Agent Authentication, Agent in Place, Agent Net, Agent of Influence, Agent Provocateur, Blow, Blown Agent, Burn, Burnt, Dispatched Agent, Double Agent, Handling Agent, Illegal Agent, Informant, Inside Man, Pocket Litter, Provocation Agent, Pseudonym, Putting in the Plumbing, Recruitment, Recruitment in Place, Special Activities.

References

Department of Defense, Joint Chiefs of Staff. *Department of Defense Dictionary of Military and Related Terms.* Washington, DC: GPO, 1986.

Treverton, Gregory F. *Covert Action: The Limits of Intervention in the Postwar World.* New York: Basic Books, 1987.

Turner, Stansfield. *Secrecy and Democracy: The CIA in Transition.* Boston: Houghton Mifflin, 1985.

U.S. Congress. Senate. *Final Report of the Senate Select Committee to Study Government Operations with Respect to Intelligence Activities. Report 94-755. Book I, Foreign and Military Intelligence.* Washington, DC: GPO, 1976.

—**CONGRESSIONAL COMMITTEES ON INTELLIGENCE.** *See:* House Permanent Select Committee on Intelligence, Senate Select Committee on Intelligence.

—**CONGRESSIONAL NOTIFICATION** pertains to the requirement of the Intelligence Community to notify Congress when it conducts certain types of activities. *See also:* Congressional Oversight.

References

Godson, Roy, ed., *Intelligence Problems for the 1980s, Number 1: Elements of Intelligence.* Rev. ed. Washington, DC: National Strategy Information Center, 1983.

Laqueur, Walter. *A World of Secrets.* New York: Basic Books, 1985.

Lefever, Ernest W., and Godson, Roy. *The CIA and the American Ethic: An Unfinished Debate.*

Washington, DC: Ethics and Public Policy Center, Georgetown University, 1979.

Turner, Stansfield. *Secrecy and Democracy: The CIA in Transition.* Boston: Houghton Mifflin, 1985.

—**CONGRESSIONAL OVERSIGHT.** Since World War II, the issue of oversight of the Intelligence Community has been a chronic and complex problem. It involves not only the relations of the Intelligence Community with the organs of government, but also the competition between the organs of government, specifically the White House and Congress, as to who would oversee the Intelligence Community. Superimposed on this debate has been the issue of the type of oversight that should be established. Should it monitor the quality of intelligence output, or should it monitor the types of operations the Community conducts?

In the early postwar years, the presidency worked actively for the minimization of the congressional role in oversight. President Truman's orders disbanding the Office of Strategic Services and creating the Central Intelligence Group, his appointment of the directors of Central Intelligence, and his other policies all indicated that he was determined to see that oversight of intelligence remained a duty of the Executive branch of government. Presidents Eisenhower and Kennedy continued this approach, and they created presidential boards to oversee the Intelligence Community.

For its part, Congress appeared content to allow the White House to take the lead in intelligence oversight. To the extent that it did get involved, Congress, like the White House, concerned itself with the quality of the intelligence that the community produced.

This situation changed drastically in the 1960s and 1970s, when the White House and Congress competed for oversight of the Community. The focus of oversight shifted from the quality of the intelligence that was produced to the types of operations that the Community accomplished. There were several reasons for this shift; among the most significant was the Vietnam War and the tremendous unrest that it caused in the United States. The Central Intelligence Agency (CIA) had previously involved itself domestically in that it had supported organizations such as the National Student Association and had subsidized U.S. publishers. But now the entire Intelligence Community became involved in domestic affairs in a much more significant way. Army intelligence conducted domestic programs that were targeted against the antiwar movement, the Federal Bureau of Investigation (FBI) conducted its COINTELPRO operation against the same groups, and other intelligence entities were involved in domestic politics as well. Indeed, this involvement had several results: it blurred the distinction between foreign and domestic operations; it detracted from foreign intelligence operations; and it politicized the Intelligence Community to the extent that it was now vulnerable to domestic political pressure.

That these results had occurred was evident in the next phase of intelligence involvement, the Watergate operation. There the White House asked for and was given assistance in an intelligence operation that was not only illegal but was also totally within the realm of domestic American politics, an arena in which the Intelligence Community simply did not belong. When the operation was made public, Congress reacted. However, that reaction was not limited to Watergate: it involved a comprehensive congressional review of intelligence operations that looked back to all activities that had been conducted in the 1950s, 1960s, and 1970s.

Another issue that shifted the focus of oversight to the types of operations in which the Community engaged was the CIA involvement in the fall of the Allende regime in Chile in 1973. As a result, in 1974 Congress passed the Hughes-Ryan Amendment, which stated that, before funds could be expended on any type of CIA operation in a foreign nation other than an operation solely for intelligence collection, the President had to be certain that the operation was important to the national security and had to notify the House Foreign Affairs Committee and the Senate Foreign Relations Committee of this finding in a timely fashion. In essence, the amendment expanded considerably congressional oversight of the CIA's covert action operations.

However, subsequent events expanded this oversight even further. Following the departure of President Nixon from office, President Ford demanded a full accounting from the CIA concerning any activities that might be improper or illegal. James Schlesinger, when he had been the director of Central Intelligence (DCI) during the Nixon administration, had demanded a similar accounting and had used that report to begin reforming the CIA, but he had never released it to the public. Now, when President Ford demanded an accounting, Director of Central Intelligence

William Colby gave Ford the Schlesinger report, which became known as the "Family Jewels."

The revelations in this report prompted considerably greater congressional involvement. Both houses created investigative committees. The House of Representatives created the Select Committee on Intelligence, which was briefly chaired by Lucien Nedzi, but was then chaired by Otis Pike. Concurrently, the Senate created the Select Committee to Study Government Operations with Respect to Intelligence Activities, chaired by Frank Church. The Church Committee concentrated on intelligence abuses and illegalities, while the Pike Committee focused on intelligence management, organization, and the quality of intelligence products.

The Pike Committee issued its report on January 29, 1976, recommending that the Defense Intelligence Agency be abolished, that the DCI be separated from the CIA so that he could concentrate on his management responsibilities, and that congressional and presidential oversight be enhanced.

Soon thereafter the Church Committee completed its investigation. Its report, issued in April 1976, was voluminous, and among its recommendations were that legislative charters be required for all of the intelligence agencies, that the DCI be separated from the CIA, that a strengthening of the DCI's authority over the entire Intelligence Community occur, that analysis and operations be separated within the CIA, and that congressional consent for all covert operations be required, and that additional oversight be established.

Mark Lowenthal's assessment of the two committees is the most insightful and profound that has yet to appear. He believes that the Church Committee was the better of the two, in that it produced a detailed 2,685-page report that considered the CIA in its entirety. However, he does criticize the Church Committee for emphasizing the sensational—assassinations, toxic agents, and so forth—in its hearings. Conversely, Lowenthal feels that the Pike Committee, while it failed to prevent the leaking of its report to the *Village Voice* and thereby lost a considerable degree of credibility, did concentrate on the crucial issue of the quality of intelligence.

Congressional oversight was continued into the Carter administration. The Senate's Select Committee reported in May 1977 that the intelligence agencies were now properly accountable to Congress and that presidential oversight was working—relatively high marks when one considers the recent past. Meanwhile, the House, at the encouragement of the White House, created its Permanent Select Committee on Intelligence, and both committees worked on charter legislation for the intelligence agencies. The result was S.2525, the National Intelligence Reform and Reorganization Act of 1978. Among the bill's provisions, those that called for renaming the DCI the director of National Intelligence and separating him from the CIA and strict controls over covert and clandestine operations were sufficiently controversial that they stalled the bill in Congress. Although S.2525 was never enacted, it was the climax of the congressional foray into the Intelligence Community; it was a bill that was extremely significant in its reflection of congressional attitudes.

Congressional oversight continued into the late 1970s, with the major incidents being Senator Church's concern about the Intelligence Community's failure to report the presence of a Soviet brigade in Cuba and the Community's failure to foresee the fall of the Shah in Iran. As the Reagan administration settled in, it appeared that congressional oversight was not only relaxing but was shifting its focus back to concern over the quality of intelligence produced, rather than the types of operations that the community conducted. However, all this changed once more, as news of the Iran-Contra operation was made public.

When news of the operation broke, Congress again convened a committee to investigate. Initially, much of the public expected a replay of the Watergate hearings. Certainly the evidence suggested that, even if the operation was not illegal, it was certainly very questionable. And the primary players—Lieutenant Colonel Oliver North, U.S. Marine Corps, retired General Seecord, Admiral Poindexter and others—freely admitted their involvement in the deception. However, ultimately both the Watergate and the Iran-Contra hearings were played on the political rather than the legal plane, and here, unlike Watergate, the Iran-Contra investigation failed to discredit the players or, by extension, the operation itself.

Even more important, however, was the failure of the committee to address the crucial issue: how could a small group, regardless of the validity of its motives, have managed to short-circuit an entire system of congressional and presidential oversight in order to accomplish the operation? This issue was extremely important in that it indicated that similar exploits were possible in the future. Yet, Congress never set in motion the deliberative body or committee that might have examined this and established procedures that would preclude similar operations in the future.

This failure, in turn, brings into question the greater issue of whether the nation can rely on Congress to provide adequate oversight of the Intelligence Community. The following two factors argue against Congress's ability to play such a role. First, those instances of intense congressional attention have been characterized by political grandstanding, a lack of knowledge of the Intelligence Community, and a lack of appreciation for the problems that the Community faces. As a result, the actions of Congress have largely been detrimental to the Community but have not resolved the fundamental problem of the control of the Community by the U.S. government.

Second, the involvement of Congress has furthered the politicalization of the Intelligence Community. The deliberations of Congress have been along party lines, in which one political party attacked and another defended the Community. This has inevitably led to the dependence of the Community on domestic American political factions, which can and may have had a definite effect on subsequent intelligence production. It may be very difficult to produce intelligence that conflicts with or undermines a political position when the proponents of that position have been your staunchest defenders in past congressional attacks. Indeed, the Intelligence Community must be allowed to remain aloof from U.S. policy and must not be forced into a corner where it must skew its intelligence findings in order to support a given policy. And yet it is difficult if not impossible for the Community to maintain its independence if it is continually forced to seek allies in Congress during the periodic excursions of the latter into intelligence affairs.

In the aftermath of the Iran-Contra affair, two significant events occurred. One was prompted by President Reagan, who appointed a special three-man board in 1987 to investigate the National Security Council, the National Security Council staff, and the assistant to the president for National Security Affairs. Composed of Senator John Tower, Senator Edmund Muskie, and Lieutenant General Brent Scowcroft, the board submitted a profound report, considering the severe financial and time restrictions under which it operated. (Excerpts are provided in Appendix W.) In its report, the board addressed the problem of leaks, stating the following:

The obsession with secrecy and preoccupation with leaks threaten to paralyze the government in its handling of covert operations. Unfortunately, the concern is not misplaced. The selective leak has become a principal means of waging bureaucratic warfare. Opponents of an operation kill it with a leak; supporters seek to build support through the same means.

We have witnessed over the past years a significant deterioration in the integrity of process. Rather than a means to obtain results more satisfactory than the position of any of the individual departments, it has frequently become something to be manipulated to reach a specific outcome. The leak becomes a primary instrument of that process.

This practice is destructive of orderly governance. It can only be reversed if the most senior officials take the lead. If senior decision-makers set a clear example and demand compliance, subordinates are more likely to conform.

Most recent administrations have had carefully drawn procedures for the consideration of covert activities. The Reagan Administration established such procedures in January, 1985, then promptly ignored them in their consideration of the Iran initiative.

The Board then addressed the problem of leaks when special activities were reported to Congress, stating:

There is a natural tension between the desire for secrecy and the need to consult Congress on covert operations. Presidents seem to become increasingly concerned about leaks of classified information as their administrations progress. They blame Congress disproportionately. Various cabinet officials from prior administrations indicated to the Board that they believe Congress bears no more blame than the Executive Branch.

However, the number of Members and staff involved in reviewing covert activities is large; it provides cause for concern and a convenient excuse for Presidents to avoid Congressional consultation.

Nonetheless, the Board still seemed to realize that a problem existed. Its final recommendation concerning Congress was that "Congress consider replacing the existing Intelligence Committees of the respective Houses with a new joint committee with a restricted staff to oversee the intelligence community, patterned after the Joint Committee on Atomic Energy that existed until the mid-1970s."

The second result of the Iran-Contra affair was congressional action. On January 27, 1988, the Senate passed S.1721, which would repeal the Hughes-Ryan Amendment and establish new procedures concerning the President's reporting to Congress concerning special activities. While it was firm in its requirements on presidential action, the bill was mild in tone, and it did not require congressional confirmation of the assistant to the president for National Security Affairs, as many had wished.

Thus, while the Iran-Contra affair had its effect on White House–Congressional relations vis-à-vis special activities, it had not prompted any major change in the existing structure.

References

Breckinridge, Scott D. *The CIA and the U.S. Intelligence System.* Boulder, CO: Westview Press, 1986.

Brinkley, David A., and Hull, Andrew W. *Estimative Intelligence: A Textbook on the History, Products, Uses and Writing of Intelligence Estimates.* Columbus, OH: Battelle, 1979.

Cline, Ray S. *The CIA Under Reagan, Bush, and Casey.* Washington, DC: Acropolis Books, 1981.

Crawford, David J. *Volunteers: The Betrayal of National Defense Secrets by Air Force Traitors.* Washington, DC: GPO, 1988.

Department of Defense, Joint Chiefs of Staff. *Department of Defense Dictionary of Military and Related Terms.* Washington, DC: GPO, 1986.

Godson, Roy, ed., *Intelligence Problems for the 1980s, Number 1: Elements of Intelligence.* Rev. ed. Washington, DC: National Strategy Information Center, 1983.

Laqueur, Walter. *A World of Secrets.* New York: Basic Books, 1985.

Lefever, Ernest W., and Godson, Roy. *The CIA and the American Ethic: An Unfinished Debate.* Washington, DC: Ethics and Public Policy Center, Georgetown University, 1979.

Lowenthal, Mark M. *U.S. Intelligence: Evolution and Anatomy.* New York: Praeger, 1984.

Office of the President of the United States. *Report of the President's Special Review Board.* Washington, DC: GPO, Feb. 26, 1987.

Turner, Stansfield. *Secrecy and Democracy: The CIA in Transition.* Boston: Houghton Mifflin, 1985.

U.S. Congress. Senate. *Final Report of the Senate Select Committee to Study Government Operations with Respect to Intelligence Activities. Report 94-755. Book I, Foreign and Military Intelligence.* Washington, DC: GPO, 1976.

Von Hoene, John P. A. *Intelligence User's Guide.* Washington, DC: DIA, 1983.

—CONSENSUAL ELECTRONIC SURVEILLANCE is a term used in clandestine intelligence operations to describe a wiretapping or bugging where one party in the conversation consents to the monitoring.

References

Becket, Henry S. A. *The Dictionary of Espionage: Spookspeak into English.* New York: Stein and Day, 1986.

Deacon, Richard. *Spyclopedia: An Encyclopedia of Spies, Secret Services, Operations, Jargon, and All Subjects Related to the World of Espionage.* London: Macdonald, 1987.

Ranelagh, John. *The Agency: The Rise and Decline of the CIA.* New York: Simon and Schuster, 1986.

—CONSENT refers to a decision resulting from Presidential Executive Order 12333, "United States Intelligence Activities," dated December 4, 1981. It is the agreement by a person or organization to permit Department of Defense intelligence components to take particular actions that affect the person.

References

Department of Defense. *Activities of DoD Intelligence Components that Affect U.S. Persons (Department of Defense Directive 5240.1).* Washington, DC: DoD, 1982.

Laqueur, Walter. *A World of Secrets.* New York: Basic Books, 1985.

Turner, Stansfield. *Secrecy and Democracy: The CIA in Transition.* Boston: Houghton Mifflin, 1985.

—CONSOLIDATED CRYPTOLOGIC PROGRAM (CCP) is prepared by the National Security Agency's Office of Programs and Resources (DDPR). *See also:* Communications Security, National Foreign Intelligence Program.

References

American Bar Association. *Oversight and Accountability of the U.S. Intelligence Agencies: An Evaluation.* Washington, DC: ABA, 1985.

Bamford, James. *The Puzzle Palace: A Report on America's Most Secret Agency.* New York: Penguin Books, 1983.

Maurer, Alfred C.; Turnstall, Marion D.; and Keagle, James M. *Intelligence Policy and Process.* Boulder, CO: Westview Press, 1985.

—CONSOLIDATED INTELLIGENCE RESOURCES INFORMATION SYSTEM (CIRIS) is an automated management data system that is used to identify and display the expected distribution of all intelligence resources (funds, personnel, equipment programs, etc.) within the National Foreign Intelligence Program. *See also:* Defense Intelligence Agency.

References

Von Hoene, John P. A. *Intelligence User's Guide.* Washington, DC: DIA, 1983.

—CONSOLIDATED TELECOMMUNICATIONS CENTER (CTCC) is a telecommunications center that handles both collateral and sensitive compartmented information (SCI). *See also:* Communications Security.

References

Blackburn, N. Glenn. "Computers: A Counterintelligence Concern." Unpublished manuscript provided to the editors. Washington, DC, 1987.

—CONSTANT DOLLARS is a term used in intelligence budgeting. A statistical series is said to be expressed in constant dollars when the effect of changes in the purchasing power of the dollar has been removed. Usually the data are expressed in terms of a selected year or set of years. *See also:* Capabilities Programming and Budgeting System (CPBS).

References

Lowenthal, Mark M. *U.S. Intelligence: Evolution and Anatomy.* New York: Praeger, 1984.

Pickett, George. "Congress, the Budget, and Intelligence." In *Intelligence Policy and Process,* edited by Alfred C. Maurer, Marion D. Turnstall, and James M. Keagle. Boulder, CO: Westview Press, 1985.

—CONSTRAINT, in intelligence budgeting, is a resource limitation, which may be specific (e.g., the supply of skilled manpower or of a particular metal) or general (e.g., total available funds). *See also:* Capabilities Programming and Budgeting System (CPBS).

References

Pickett, George. "Congress, the Budget, and Intelligence." In *Intelligence Policy and Process,* edited by Alfred C. Maurer, Marion D. Turnstall, and James M. Keagle. Boulder, CO: Westview Press, 1985.

—CONSULTANT is an individual who is not a U.S. government employee but who provides a service to a governmental agency or department. The individual is normally under personal contract to a particular agency or military department, but he can also be on loan from an industrial organization. The consultant's services are normally provided for a particular project or service that is related to his expertise, rather than in connection with a negotiated contract.

References

Godson, Roy, ed. *Intelligence Problems for the 1980s, Number 1: Elements of Intelligence.* Rev. ed. Washington, DC: National Strategy Information Center, 1983.

Laqueur, Walter. *A World of Secrets.* New York: Basic Books, 1985.

Turner, Stansfield. *Secrecy and Democracy: The CIA in Transition.* Boston: Houghton Mifflin, 1985.

—CONSUMER is an obsolete term for customer. As defined by the Church Committee, a consumer is "a person or agency that uses information or intelligence that is produced by either its own staff or other agencies." *See also:* Customer.

References

American Bar Association. *Oversight and Accountability of the U.S. Intelligence Agencies: An Evaluation.* Washington, DC: ABA, 1985.

Department of Defense, Joint Chiefs of Staff. *Department of Defense Dictionary of Military and Related Terms.* Washington, DC: GPO, 1986.

Godson, Roy, ed. *Intelligence Problems for the 1980s, Number 2: Analysis and Estimates.* Washington, DC: National Strategy Information Center, 1980.

Kent, Sherman. *Strategic Intelligence for American World Policy.* Princeton, NJ: Princeton University Press, 1966.

Maurer, Alfred C.; Turnstall, Marion D.; and Keagle, James M. *Intelligence Policy and Process.* Boulder, CO: Westview Press, 1985.

U.S. Congress. Senate. *Final Report of the Senate Select Committee to Study Government Operations with Respect to Intelligence Activities. Report 94-755. Book I, Foreign and Military Intelligence.* Washington, DC: GPO, 1976.

—CONTAINERS. *See:* Concealment Devices.

—CONTINENTAL UNITED STATES (CONUS), as defined by the Church Committee, is a military term that refers to U.S. territory, including adjacent territorial waters, located within the North American continent between Canada and Mexico.

References

Department of Defense, Joint Chiefs of Staff. *Department of Defense Dictionary of Military and Related Terms.* Washington, DC: GPO, 1986.

U.S. Congress. Senate. *Final Report of the Senate Select Committee to Study Government Operations with Respect to Intelligence Activities. Report 94-755. Book I, Foreign and Military Intelligence.* Washington, DC: GPO, 1976.

—**CONTINGENCY KEY,** in communications security (COMSEC), means the keying material that is held for use on a cryptonet that is planned for establishment under specific operational conditions or in support of specific contingency plans. *See also*: Communications Security.

References
Blackburn, N. Glenn. "Computers: A Counterintelligence Concern." Unpublished manuscript provided to the editors. Washington, DC, 1987.

—**CONTINUING INTELLIGENCE REQUIREMENT (CIR)** is one that has been validated (approved) as an intelligence requirement and one that cannot be permanently satisfied in a single intelligence collection and production effort. Rather, it generally pertains to an evolving or continuing action on the part of the enemy, one that will require continual monitoring over an extended period.

References
Laqueur, Walter. *A World of Secrets.* New York: Basic Books, 1985.

—**CONTRACT MONITOR (CM)** is a military person or U.S. government civilian employee who monitors a government contract with a contractor. The person serves as the government's point of contact for the contractor and makes sure that the services or materials the contractor delivers meet the contract's specifications. *See also:* Contractor.

References
Turner, Stansfield. *Secrecy and Democracy: The CIA in Transition.* Boston: Houghton Mifflin, 1985.

—**CONTRACT REQUIREMENTS REVIEW BOARD.** *See also:* Defense Intelligence Agency.

—**CONTRACTOR** is a general intelligence term for an industrial, educational, commercial, or other entity that has executed a contract with a user agency or a Department of Defense Security Agreement with a Department of Defense agency or activity. *See also:* Contract Monitor.

References
Department of Defense, Defense Intelligence Agency. *Defense Intelligence Agency Manual.* Washington, DC: DIA, 1987.

Turner, Stansfield. *Secrecy and Democracy: The CIA in Transition.* Boston: Houghton Mifflin, 1985.

—**CONTROL** is a term used in clandestine and covert intelligence operations to describe the physical or psychological pressure that is exerted on an agent or group to insure that he obeys the directions of an intelligence agency or service.

References
Allen, Thomas B., and Polmar, Norman. *Merchants of Treason: America's Secrets for Sale.* New York: Delacorte Press, 1988.

Becket, Henry S. A. *The Dictionary of Espionage: Spookspeak into English.* New York: Stein and Day, 1986.

Department of Defense, Joint Chiefs of Staff. *Department of Defense Dictionary of Military and Related Terms.* Washington, DC: GPO, 1986.

Godson, Roy, ed. *Intelligence Problems for the 1980s, Number 1: Elements of Intelligence.* Rev. ed. Washington, DC: National Strategy Information Center, 1983.

Quirk, John; Phillips, David; Cline, Ray; and Pforzheimer, Walter. *The Central Intelligence Agency: A Photographic History.* Guilford, CT: Foreign Intelligence Press, 1986.

Turner, Stansfield. *Secrecy and Democracy: The CIA in Transition.* Boston: Houghton Mifflin, 1985.

U.S. Congress. Senate. *Final Report of the Senate Select Committee to Study Government Operations with Respect to Intelligence Activities. Report 94-755. Book I, Foreign and Military Intelligence.* Washington, DC: GPO, 1976.

—**CONTROLLED AREA,** in communications security (COMSEC), means an area or space to which access is physically restricted or controlled. Restricting the access of people to an area in this manner is one of several means that are employed to insure document security. *See also:* Access, Authorized, Classification, Classified Information, Code Word, Compromise, Declassification, Disclosure, Downgrade, Freedom of Information Act, Limited Access Area, Need-to-Know, Need-to-Know Principle, No-Lone Zone, Nondisclosure Agreement, Nondiscussion Area, Sanitization, Sanitize, Sanitized Area, Security Certification, Security Classification, Sensitive

Compartmented Information, Sensitive Compartmented Information Facility, Two-Person Control.

References

Blackburn, N. Glenn. "Computers: A Counterintelligence Concern." An unpublished manuscript provided to the editors. Washington, DC, 1987.

—**CONTROLLED COMSEC ITEM (CCI),** in communications security (COMSEC) means a marking that is applied to those unclassified end items and assemblies that perform critical COMSEC functions and require access controls and physical security protection to insure their continued safety and integrity. *See also:* Communications Security.

References

Blackburn, N. Glenn. "Computers: A Counterintelligence Concern." Unpublished manuscript provided to the editors. Washington, DC, 1987.

Muzerall, Joseph V., and Carty, Thomas P. "COMSEC and Its Need for Key Management." *DP&CS* (Spring 1987).

Ware, Willis H. "Information Systems, Security, and Privacy." *EDUCOM Bulletin* (Summer 1984).

—**CONTROLLED DISSEMINATION (CD)** was a general intelligence term for a release marking used on materials prepared before October 5, 1975. It was used to protect intelligence and intelligence information that was disseminated within the U.S. government where source protection, including the proprietary interest of commercial sources, would warrant limiting the dissemination of the document. The marking was also applied for dissemination control purposes to assist in identifying that intelligence material which by category or classification was, by USIB-approved policy and other directives, prohibited from dissemination to contractors. The source of the policy was Director of Central Intelligence Directive (DCID) 1/7. *See also:* Access, Authorized, Classification, Classified Information, Code Word, Compromise, Declassification, Disclosure, Downgrade, Freedom of Information Act, Limited Access Area, Need-to-Know, Need-to-Know Principle, No-Lone Zone, Nondisclosure Agreement, Nondiscussion Area, Sanitization, Sanitize, Sanitized Area, Security Certification, Security Classification, Sensitive Compartmented Information, Sensitive Compartmented Information Facility, Two-Person Control.

References

Department of Defense, Defense Intelligence Agency. *Defense Intelligence Agency Manual.* Washington, DC: DIA, 1987.

Godson, Roy, ed. *Intelligence Problems for the 1980s, Number 1: Elements of Intelligence.* Rev. ed. Washington, DC: National Strategy Information Center, 1983.

Von Hoene, John P. A. *Intelligence User's Guide.* Washington, DC: DIA, 1983.

—**CONTROLLING AUTHORITY,** in communications security (COMSEC), means the organization that is responsible for establishing and operating a cryptonet. *See also:* Communications Security.

References

Blackburn, N. Glenn. "Computers: A Counterintelligence Concern." Unpublished manuscript provided to the editors. Washington, DC, 1987.

—**COOKE, SECOND LIEUTENANT CHRISTOPHER M., U.S. AIR FORCE,** gathered classified security information in 1980 and 1981, which he hoped to pass to Soviet agents. Repeated attempts to get the Soviets to meet him failed, and he was finally apprehended. In his interrogation, he requested and was given immunity and therefore was not court-martialed. (Thomas Allen and Norman Polmar state that Cooke's interrogation was mismanaged and that the evidence was therefore inadmissible. Cooke, they state, was released from the Air Force.)

References

Allen, Thomas B., and Polmar, Norman. *Merchants of Treason: America's Secrets for Sale.* New York: Delacorte Press, 1988.

Crawford, David J. *Volunteers: The Betrayal of National Defense Secrets by Air Force Traitors.* Washington, DC: GPO, 1988.

—**COOPERATING SOURCES** is a term used in clandestine and covert intelligence and counterintelligence operations to describe persons or organizations that knowingly and voluntarily provide information to Department of Defense components, or access to information, at the request of such components on their own initiative. These include government agencies, law enforcement authorities, credit agencies, academic institutions, employers, and foreign governments. This definition was established as a result of Presidential Executive Order 12333, "United States Intelligence Activities," December 4, 1981. *See also:* Co-opted Worker, Co-optees, Cultivation, Disaffected Person, Double Agent, False Flag, Granny, Informant, Inside Man, Pigeon, Recruitment, Recruitment in Place, Sleeper, Special Activities.

References

Department of Defense. *Activities of DoD Intelligence Components that Affect U.S. Persons (Department of Defense Directive 5240.1).* Washington, DC: DoD, 1982.

Turner, Stansfield. *Secrecy and Democracy: The CIA in Transition.* Boston: Houghton Mifflin, 1985.

—**CO-OPTED WORKER** is a term used in clandestine and covert intelligence operations to describe a citizen of a country who, while he is not an officer or employee of his country's intelligence service, assists that service on a temporary or regular basis. In most cases, he is an official of that country, but he could be in another profession. In FBI terminology, he may also be called a co-opted agent or a co-optee. *See also:* Cooperating Sources.

References

Department of Defense, Defense Intelligence College. *Glossary of Intelligence Terms and Definitions.* Washington, DC: DIC, 1987.

Kessler, Ronald. *Spy vs. Spy: Stalking Soviet Spies in America.* New York: Charles Scribner's Sons, 1988.

Treverton, Gregory F. *Covert Action: The Limits of Intervention in the Postwar World.* New York: Basic Books, 1987.

—**CO-OPTEES** is a term used in clandestine and covert intelligence operations to describe Soviet diplomatic personnel serving in a foreign embassy who are not KGB employees but who will follow KGB orders when asked. *See also:* Cooperating Sources.

References

Becket, Henry S. A. *The Dictionary of Espionage: Spookspeak into English.* New York: Stein and Day, 1986.

Turner, Stansfield. *Secrecy and Democracy: The CIA in Transition.* Boston: Houghton Mifflin, 1985.

—**COORDINATION** is a general intelligence term that has two meanings. (1) In general, coordination is the act of obtaining concurrence from one or more groups, organizations, or agencies concerning a proposal or an activity over which they have some responsibility. In coordination, these bodies may concur, contribute, or not concur. In government parlance, it is often referred to as "staffing a paper." (2) In intelligence production, coordination is the act or process by which the person or body that wrote a draft of an estimate, assessment, or report gets the opinions of other producers on the quality of the product. Coordination is intended to make the product factually more accurate, to clarify the judgments made, to resolve disagreements on issues, or to sharpen the statements of disagreement on major unresolved issues. *See also:* Intelligence Cycle.

References

Department of Defense, Defense Intelligence College, *Glossary of Intelligence Terms and Definitions.* Washington, DC: DIC, 1987.

Kent, Sherman. *Strategic Intelligence for American World Policy.* Princeton, NJ: Princeton University Press, 1966.

—**COORDINATOR OF INFORMATION (COI)** was the position held by William J. Donovan in 1941 and 1942 prior to the creation of the Office of Strategic Services. *See also:* Donovan, William; Office of Strategic Services.

References

Corson, William R. *The Armies of Ignorance: The Rise of the American Intelligence Empire.* New York: Dial Press, 1977.

Lowenthal, Mark M. *U.S. Intelligence: Evolution and Anatomy.* New York: Praeger, 1984.

—**CORDREY, ROBERT E., U.S. MARINE CORPS,** was stationed at a training school at Camp Lejeune, North Carolina, and attempted to contact the Soviet, East German, Polish, and Czechoslovakian intelligence services, offering to provide classified information. He was sentenced to twelve years in prison at hard labor, but the charges were reduced to two years in accordance with a pretrial agreement.

References

Allen, Thomas B., and Polmar, Norman. *Merchants of Treason: America's Secrets for Sale.* New York: Delacorte Press, 1988.

Crawford, David J. *Volunteers: The Betrayal of National Defense Secrets by Air Force Traitors.* Washington, DC: GPO, 1988.

—**CORNER REFLECTOR (PASSIVE)** is a term used in electronic warfare and communications security. (1) A corner reflector can be a device made in the form of three perpendicular planes, like the three sides of a cube that meet at a corner. Because of this shape, it returns a very strong radar echo and is used for such purposes. (2) A corner reflector may also be a device consisting of two flat surfaces meeting at a right angle. Such a reflector, when used with dipole antennas, adds directivity to a radiation pattern. This will allow a transmitter to direct the signal in a specific direction, thereby reducing the chances of its interception by the enemy. *See also:* Communications Security.

References
Department of Defense, Joint Chiefs of Staff. *Department of Defense Dictionary of Military and Related Terms.* Washington, DC: GPO, 1986.

—**CORPS** may be the highest Army operational headquarters in combat operations and as such has tactical, logistic, and administrative responsibilities. It is generally the first level of command where information from national and tactical intelligence systems are brought together. The corps uses this information to plan and allocate resources for operations up to 72 hours in the future. Defending corps commanders direct, coordinate, and support operations conducted by divisions against assaulting enemy divisions.

References
Department of Defense, U.S. Army. *Military Intelligence Group (Combat Electronic Warfare and Intelligence) (Corps).* Field Manual FM 34-20. Washington, DC: Headquarters, Department of the Army, 1983.

—**COST,** in intelligence budgeting, means goods or services used or consumed. *See also:* Capabilities Programming and Budgeting System (CPBS).

References
Treverton, Gregory F. *Covert Action: The Limits of Intervention in the Postwar World.* New York: Basic Books, 1987.
Turner, Stansfield. *Secrecy and Democracy: The CIA in Transition.* Boston: Houghton Mifflin, 1985.

—**COST ACCOUNTING,** in intelligence budgeting, is the recording and reporting of financial transactions in terms of the cost of goods and services used or otherwise applied in carrying out programs and activities during a specified period. *See also:* Capabilities Programming and Budgeting System (CPBS).

References
Treverton, Gregory F. *Covert Action: The Limits of Intervention in the Postwar World.* New York: Basic Books, 1987.
Turner, Stansfield. *Secrecy and Democracy: The CIA in Transition.* Boston: Houghton Mifflin, 1985.

—**COST ANALYSIS,** in intelligence budgeting, is the systematic examination of cost (total resource implications) of interrelated activities and equipments to determine the relative costs of alternative systems, organizations, and force structures. Cost analysis is not designed to provide the precise measurements required for budgetary purposes. *See also:* Capabilities Programming and Budgeting System (CPBS).

References
Treverton, Gregory F. *Covert Action: The Limits of Intervention in the Postwar World.* New York: Basic Books, 1987.
Turner, Stansfield. *Secrecy and Democracy: The CIA in Transition.* Boston: Houghton Mifflin, 1985.

—**COST EFFECTIVENESS/ANALYSIS,** in intelligence budgeting, is the quantitative examination of alternative prospective systems for the purpose of identifying the preferred system and its associated equipment, organizations, etc. The examination aims at finding more precise answers to a question and not at justifying a conclusion. The analytical process includes tradeoffs among alternatives, design of additional alternatives, and the measurement of the effectiveness and cost of the alternatives. *See also:* Capabilities Programming and Budgeting System (CPBS).

References
Treverton, Gregory F. *Covert Action: The Limits of Intervention in the Postwar World.* New York: Basic Books, 1987.
Turner, Stansfield. *Secrecy and Democracy: The CIA in Transition.* Boston: Houghton Mifflin, 1985.

—**COUNTER COMMAND, CONTROL, AND COMMUNICATIONS (C-C³).** *See:* Command, Control, and Communications Countermeasures.

—**COUNTERDECEPTION** is an attempt to negate or diminish the effects of a foreign deception operation. It does not include identifying the foreign deception operation.

References

American Bar Association. *Oversight and Accountability of the U.S. Intelligence Agencies: An Evaluation.* Washington, DC: ABA, 1985.

Department of Defense, Joint Chiefs of Staff. *Department of Defense Dictionary of Military and Related Terms.* Washington, DC: GPO, 1986.

Laqueur, Walter. *A World of Secrets.* New York: Basic Books, 1985.

Maurer, Alfred C.; Turnstall, Marion D.; and Keagle, James M. *Intelligence Policy and Process.* Boulder, CO: Westview Press, 1985.

Treverton, Gregory F. *Covert Action: The Limits of Intervention in the Postwar World.* New York: Basic Books, 1987.

—**COUNTERESPIONAGE (CE)** is that aspect of counterintelligence concerned with aggressive operations against another intelligence service in order to reduce its effectiveness or to detect and neutralize foreign espionage. This is accomplished by identifying, penetrating, manipulating, deceiving, or repressing people, groups, or organizations conducting espionage in order to destroy, neutralize, exploit, or prevent further activity.

References

Allen, Thomas B., and Polmar, Norman. *Merchants of Treason: America's Secrets for Sale.* New York: Delacorte Press, 1988.

American Bar Association. *Oversight and Accountability of the U.S. Intelligence Agencies: An Evaluation.* Washington, DC: ABA, 1985.

Corson, William R. *The Armies of Ignorance: The Rise of the American Intelligence Empire.* New York: Dial Press, 1977.

Department of Defense, Joint Chiefs of Staff. *Department of Defense Dictionary of Military and Related Terms.* Washington, DC: GPO, 1986.

Godson, Roy, ed. *Intelligence Problems for the 1980s, Number 1: Elements of Intelligence.* Rev. ed. Washington, DC: National Strategy Information Center, 1983.

———. *Intelligence Problems for the 1980s, Number 3: Counterintelligence.* Washington, DC: National Strategy Information Center, 1980.

———. *Intelligence Problems for the 1980s, Number 4: Covert Action.* Washington, DC: National Strategy Information Center, 1981.

Kent, Sherman. *Strategic Intelligence for American World Policy.* Princeton, NJ: Princeton University Press, 1966.

Laqueur, Walter. *The Age of Terrorism.* Boston: Little, Brown, 1987.

Maurer, Alfred C.; Turnstall, Marion D.; and Keagle, James M. *Intelligence Policy and Process.* Boulder, CO: Westview Press, 1985.

Treverton, Gregory F. *Covert Action: The Limits of Intervention in the Postwar World.* New York: Basic Books, 1987.

U.S. Congress. Senate. *Final Report of the Senate Select Committee to Study Government Operations with Respect to Intelligence Activities. Report 94-755. Book I, Foreign and Military Intelligence.* Washington, DC: GPO, 1976.

—**COUNTERGUERRILLA WARFARE** entails operations waged by a government's armed forces, paramilitary forces, or nonmilitary forces against guerrillas.

References

American Bar Association. *Oversight and Accountability of the U.S. Intelligence Agencies: An Evaluation.* Washington, DC: ABA, 1985.

Becket, Henry S. A. *The Dictionary of Espionage: Spookspeak into English.* New York: Stein and Day, 1986.

Department of Defense, Joint Chiefs of Staff. *Department of Defense Dictionary of Military and Related Terms.* Washington, DC: GPO, 1986.

Godson, Roy, ed. *Intelligence Problems for the 1980s, Number 1: Elements of Intelligence.* Rev. ed. Washington, DC: National Strategy Information Center, 1983.

———. *Intelligence Problems for the 1980s, Number 4: Covert Action.* Washington, DC: National Strategy Information Center, 1981.

Laqueur, Walter. *The Age of Terrorism.* Boston: Little, Brown, 1987.

Maurer, Alfred C.; Turnstall, Marion D.; and Keagle, James M. *Intelligence Policy and Process.* Boulder, CO: Westview Press, 1985.

Treverton, Gregory F. *Covert Action: The Limits of Intervention in the Postwar World.* New York: Basic Books, 1987.

U.S. Congress. Senate. *Final Report of the Senate Select Committee to Study Government Operations with Respect to Intelligence Activities. Report 94-755. Book I, Foreign and Military Intelligence.* Washington, DC: GPO, 1976.

—**COUNTER-HUMAN INTELLIGENCE (C-HUMINT)** is an Army tactical intelligence (TAC-INT) term that means the actions taken to determine enemy HUMINT collection capabilities and activities, the assessment of friendly vulnerabilities, and the subsequent development and recommendations or the implementation of countermeasures. It includes counterintelligence special operations, liaison, counterinterrogation, countervisual, counterolfactory and counter-acoustical means, security, and counter-intelligence screening.

References

American Bar Association. *Oversight and Accountability of the U.S. Intelligence Agencies: An Evaluation.* Washington, DC: ABA, 1985.

Department of Defense, U.S. Army. *Counterintelligence.* Field Manual FM 34-60. Washington, DC: Headquarters, Department of the Army, 1985.

———. *Counter-Signals Intelligence (C-SIGINT) Operations.* Field Manual FM 34-62. Washington, DC: Headquarters, Department of the Army, 1986.

Godson, Roy, ed. *Intelligence Problems for the 1980s, Number 3: Counterintelligence.* Washington, DC: National Strategy Information Center, 1980.

Maurer, Alfred C.; Turnstall, Marion D.; and Keagle, James M. *Intelligence Policy and Process.* Boulder, CO: Westview Press, 1985.

—**COUNTER-IMAGERY INTELLIGENCE (COUNTER-IMINT)** is an Army tactical intelligence (TACINT) term that means the actions taken to determine enemy imagery intelligence capabilities and activities, including surveillance radar, photo, and infrared systems. It is also the assessment of friendly operations to identify patterns and signatures. The resulting vulnerabilities are used for subsequent development and recommendations for countermeasures. Counter-IMINT operations include determining enemy surveillance radar, photo, thermal, and infrared systems capabilities; assessing friendly operations to identify patterns and signatures and the vulnerabilities identified by them; and the subsequent development and recommendation of countermeasures. Successful counter-IMINT operations rely heavily on pattern and movement analysis and evaluation and on signature suppression actions.

References

American Bar Association. *Oversight and Accountability of the U.S. Intelligence Agencies: An Evaluation.* Washington, DC: ABA, 1985.

Department of Defense, U.S. Army. *Counterintelligence.* Field Manual FM 34-60. Washington, DC: Headquarters, Department of the Army, 1985.

———. *Counter-Signals Intelligence (C-SIGINT) Operations.* Field Manual FM 34-62. Washington, DC: Headquarters, Department of the Army, 1986.

Maurer, Alfred C.; Turnstall, Marion D.; and Keagle, James M. *Intelligence Policy and Process.* Boulder, CO: Westview Press, 1985.

—**COUNTERINSURGENCY (COIN)** is a term used to describe the military, paramilitary, political, economic, psychological, and civic actions that a government takes to defeat rebellion and subversion within the nation.

References

American Bar Association. *Oversight and Accountability of the U.S. Intelligence Agencies: An Evaluation.* Washington, DC: ABA, 1985.

Corson, William R. *The Armies of Ignorance: The Rise of the American Intelligence Empire.* New York: Dial Press, 1977.

Department of Defense, Joint Chiefs of Staff. *Department of Defense Dictionary of Military and Related Terms.* Washington, DC: GPO, 1986.

Godson, Roy, ed. *Intelligence Problems for the 1980s, Number 1: Elements of Intelligence.* Rev. ed. Washington, DC: National Strategy Information Center, 1983.

———. *Intelligence Problems for the 1980s, Number 4: Covert Action.* Washington, DC: National Strategy Information Center, 1981.

Laqueur, Walter. *A World of Secrets.* New York: Basic Books, 1985.

Maurer, Alfred C.; Turnstall, Marion D.; and Keagle, James M. *Intelligence Policy and Process.* Boulder, CO: Westview Press, 1985.

Treverton, Gregory F. *Covert Action: The Limits of Intervention in the Postwar World.* New York: Basic Books, 1985.

U.S. Congress. Senate. *Final Report of the Senate Select Committee to Study Government Operations with Respect to Intelligence Activities.* Report 94-755. Book I, *Foreign and Military Intelligence.* Washington, DC: GPO, 1976.

—**COUNTERINTELLIGENCE (CI).** (1) Counterintelligence is gathering information and conducting activities to protect against espionage, other clandestine activities, sabotage, international terrorist activities, and assassinations conducted by or for foreign powers. It does not include personnel, physical, document, or communications security programs. (2) Counterintelligence is also an Army tactical intelligence (TACINT) term that has two meanings: (a) Counterintelligence is those activities intended to detect, evaluate, counteract, or prevent hostile intelligence collection, subversion, sabotage, international terrorism, or assassination that is conducted by or on behalf of any foreign power, organization or person operating to the detriment of the U.S. Army. It includes the identification of the hostile multidiscipline intelligence collection threat, the determination of friendly vulnerabilities to that threat, and the recommendation and evaluation of security measures. (b) Counterintelligence is those activities concerned with identifying and countering the threat to security posed by hostile intelligence services or organizations or by individuals engaged in espionage, sabotage, or subversion. (3) As defined by the Church Committee, counterintelligence involves activities that are conducted to destroy the effectiveness of foreign intelligence operations and to protect information against espionage, individuals against subversion, and installations against sabotage. The term also refers to information developed by or used in counterintelligence operations. *See also:* Counterespionage, Countersabotage, Countersubversion, Foreign Counterintelligence.

References

Allen, Thomas B., and Polmar, Norman. *Merchants of Treason: America's Secrets for Sale.* New York: Delacorte Press, 1988.

American Bar Association. *Oversight and Accountability of the U.S. Intelligence Agencies: An Evaluation.* Washington, DC: ABA, 1985.

Clancy, Tom. *The Cardinal of the Kremlin.* New York: Putnam, 1988.

Corson, William R. *The Armies of Ignorance: The Rise of the American Intelligence Empire.* New York: Dial Press, 1977.

Department of Defense. *Activities of DoD Intelligence Components that Affect U.S. Persons (Department of Defense Directive 5240.1).* Washington, DC: DoD, 1982.

Department of Defense, Defense Intelligence College. *Glossary of Intelligence Terms and Definitions.* Washington, DC: DIC, 1987.

Department of Defense, Joint Chiefs of Staff. *Department of Defense Dictionary of Military and Related Terms.* Washington, DC: GPO, 1986.

Department of Defense, U.S. Army. *Counter-Signals Intelligence (C-SIGINT) Operations.* Field Manual FM 34-62. Washington, DC: Headquarters, Department of the Army, 1986.

————. *Intelligence and Electronic Warfare Operations.* Field Manual FM 34-1. Washington, DC: Headquarters, Department of the Army, 1984.

————. *Military Intelligence Battalion (Combat Electronic Warfare Intelligence) (Division).* Field Manual FM 34-10. Washington, DC: Headquarters, Department of the Army, 1981.

————. *Military Intelligence Battalion Combat Electronic Warfare and Intelligence (Aerial Exploitation) (Corps).* Field Manual FM 34-22. Washington, DC: Headquarters, Department of the Army, 1984.

————. *Military Intelligence Company (Combat Electronic Warfare and Intelligence) (Armored Cavalry Regiment/Separate Brigade).* Field Manual FM 34-30. Washington, DC: Headquarters, Department of the Army, 1983.

————. *Military Intelligence Battalion (CEWI) (Tactical Exploitation) (Corps): Counterintelligence, Interrogation, Electronic Warfare.* Field Manual FM 34-23. Washington, DC: Headquarters, Department of the Army, 1985.

Godson, Roy, ed. *Intelligence Problems for the 1980s, Number 1: Elements of Intelligence.* Rev. ed. Washington, DC: National Strategy Information Center, 1983.

————. *Intelligence Problems for the 1980s, Number 3: Counterintelligence.* Washington, DC: National Strategy Information Center, 1980.

Kent, Sherman. *Strategic Intelligence for American World Policy.* Princeton, NJ: Princeton University Press, 1966.

Kessler, Ronald. *Spy vs. Spy: Stalking Soviet Spies in America.* New York: Charles Scribner's Sons, 1988.

Laqueur, Walter. *A World of Secrets.* New York: Basic Books, 1985.

Lefever, Ernest W., and Godson, Roy. *The CIA and the American Ethic: An Unfinished Debate.* Washington, DC: Ethics and Public Policy Center, Georgetown University, 1979.

Maurer, Alfred C.; Turnstall, Marion D.; and Keagle, James M. *Intelligence Policy and Process.* Boulder, CO: Westview Press, 1985.

Treverton, Gregory F. *Covert Action: The Limits of Intervention in the Postwar World.* New York: Basic Books, 1985.

Turner, Stansfield. *Secrecy and Democracy: The CIA in Transition.* Boston: Houghton Mifflin, 1985.

U.S. Congress. Senate. *Final Report of the Senate Select Committee to Study Government Operations with Respect to Intelligence Activities. Report 94-755. Book I, Foreign and Military Intelligence.* Washington, DC: GPO, 1976.

—**COUNTERINTELLIGENCE AND SECURITY** is an official term that has been defined by the Defense Intelligence Agency for one of its functional areas. It means "activities devoted to defending against, destroying, neutralizing, or controlling through the exploitation of human sources, inimical foreign intelligence operations, and safeguarding information, personnel, material, and installations against the espionage, sabotage, or subversive activities of foreign powers and disaffected or dissident groups or individuals which constitute a threat to the national security." *See also:* Communications Security, Counterintelligence.

References

American Bar Association. *Oversight and Accountability of the U.S. Intelligence Agencies: An Evaluation.* Washington, DC: ABA, 1985.

Corson, William R. *The Armies of Ignorance: The Rise of the American Intelligence Empire.* New York: Dial Press, 1977.

Department of Defense, Defense Intelligence Agency. *Defense Intelligence Agency Manual 22-2.* Washington, DC: DIA, 1979.

Godson, Roy, ed. *Intelligence Problems for the 1980s, Number 1: Elements of Intelligence.* Rev. ed. Washington, DC: National Strategy Information Center, 1983.

————. *Intelligence Problems for the 1980s, Number 3: Counterintelligence.* Washington, DC: National Strategy Information Center, 1980.

————. *Intelligence Problems for the 1980s, Number 4: Covert Action.* Washington, DC: National Strategy Information Center, 1981.

Laqueur, Walter. *A World of Secrets.* New York: Basic Books, 1985.

Lefever, Ernest W., and Godson, Roy. *The CIA and the American Ethic: An Unfinished Debate.* Washington, DC: Ethics and Public Policy Center, Georgetown University, 1979.

Maurer, Alfred C.; Turnstall, Marion D.; and Keagle, James M. *Intelligence Policy and Process.* Boulder, CO: Westview Press, 1985.

Treverton, Gregory F. *Covert Action: The Limits of Intervention in the Postwar World.* New York: Basic Books, 1985.

Turner, Stansfield. *Secrecy and Democracy: The CIA in Transition.* Boston: Houghton Mifflin, 1985.

Treverton, Gregory F. *Covert Action: The Limits of Intervention in the Postwar World.* New York: Basic Books, 1985.

Turner, Stansfield. *Secrecy and Democracy: The CIA in Transition.* Boston: Houghton Mifflin, 1985.

Von Hoene, John P. A. *Intelligence User's Guide.* Washington, DC: DIA, 1983.

—COUNTERINTELLIGENCE INFORMATION is information, regardless of its source (HUMINT, COMINT, ELINT, etc.), that is of value to counterintelligence forces. *See also:* Counterintelligence.

—COUNTERINTELLIGENCE INVESTIGATION refers to a decision resulting from Presidential Executive Order 12333, "United States Intelligence Activities," dated December 4, 1981. It includes information gathered and activities conducted to protect against espionage, other intelligence activities, sabotage, or assassinations conducted for or on behalf of foreign powers, organizations, or persons, or international terrorist activities, but not including personnel, physical, document, or communications security programs. *See also:* Counterintelligence.

—COUNTERINTELLIGENCE MEMORANDUMS are studies and assessments of foreign intelligence organizations, operational capabilities and techniques, specific espionage cases, collection targets or other operational objectives, U.S. vulnerabilities and compromises/losses, and countermeasures considerations. Most of these memorandums are widely distributed. *See also:* Counterintelligence.

—COUNTERINTELLIGENCE BRIEF is a short, summary report of significant counterintelligence matters and usually addresses a single development, situation, or event.

References

American Bar Association. *Oversight and Accountability of the U.S. Intelligence Agencies: An Evaluation.* Washington, DC: ABA, 1985.

Godson, Roy, ed. *Intelligence Problems for the 1980s, Number 3: Counterintelligence.* Washington, DC: National Strategy Information Center, 1980.

Lefever, Ernest W., and Godson, Roy. *The CIA and the American Ethic: An Unfinished Debate.* Washington, DC: Ethics and Public Policy Center, Georgetown University, 1979.

Maurer, Alfred C.; Turnstall, Marion D.; and Keagle, James M. *Intelligence Policy and Process.* Boulder, CO: Westview Press, 1985.

—COUNTERINTELLIGENCE PRODUCTION SCHEDULE (CIPS) is a Defense Intelligence Agency (DIA) product. Published annually, it lists all proposed counterintelligence publications that are scheduled for production by the DIA and the military services for the next fiscal year as well as for future fiscal years. The CIPS is distributed to production managers, resource planning offices, and selected customers.

References

American Bar Association. *Oversight and Accountability of the U.S. Intelligence Agencies: An Evaluation.* Washington, DC: ABA, 1985.

Lefever, Ernest W., and Godson, Roy. *The CIA and the American Ethic: An Unfinished Debate.* Washington, DC: Ethics and Public Policy Center, Georgetown University, 1979.

Turner, Stansfield. *Secrecy and Democracy: The CIA in Transition.* Boston: Houghton Mifflin, 1985.

Von Hoene, John P. A. *Intelligence User's Guide.* Washington, DC: DIA, 1983.

—**COUNTERINTELLIGENCE PUBLICATIONS REGISTRY (CIPR)** is a Defense Intelligence Agency (DIA) management document. It lists all counterintelligence publications produced by the DIA and the Departments of the Army, Navy, and Air Force. It is published annually.

References

Brinkley, David A., and Hull, Andrew W. *Estimative Intelligence: A Textbook on the History, Products, Uses and Writing of Intelligence Estimates.* Columbus, OH: Battelle, 1979.

Turner, Stansfield. *Secrecy and Democracy: The CIA in Transition.* Boston: Houghton Mifflin, 1985.

Von Hoene, John P. A. *Intelligence User's Guide.* Washington, DC: DIA, 1983.

—**COUNTERINTELLIGENCE STAFF (CI STAFF)** is a component of the Directorate of Plans of the CIA that, until recently, maintained virtual control over counterintelligence operations.

References

Fain, Tyrus G.; Plant, Katharine C.; and Milloy, Ross. *The Intelligence Community: History, Organization, and Issues.* Public Documents Series. New York: R.R. Bowker, 1977.

Godson, Roy, ed. *Intelligence Problems for the 1980s, Number 3: Counterintelligence.* Washington, DC: National Strategy Information Center, 1980.

Maurer, Alfred C.; Turnstall, Marion D.; and Keagle, James M. *Intelligence Policy and Process.* Boulder, CO: Westview Press, 1985.

Treverton, Gregory F. *Covert Action: The Limits of Intervention in the Postwar World.* New York: Basic Books, 1987.

Turner, Stansfield. *Secrecy and Democracy: The CIA in Transition.* Boston: Houghton Mifflin, 1985.

Von Hoene, John P. A. *Intelligence User's Guide.* Washington, DC: DIA, 1983.

—**COUNTERINTERVENTION** is a generic term used to describe covert or clandestine operations intended to deny success to another nation that has intervened in the affairs of a third nation. Because many types of counterintervention operations are opposed by a portion of the U.S. public and Congress, they are often a point of contention when U.S. intelligence operations are made public. They are, nonetheless, an integral part of U.S. intelligence activities. *See also:* Case, Case Officer, Center, Chief of Base, Chief of Outpost, Chief of Station, Covert, False Flag, Fifth Column, Flap Potential, Illegal Agent, Illegal Operations, Infiltration, Ringing the Gong, Rolling Up the Net, Shaking the Tree, Special Activities, Third Country Operation.

References

American Bar Association. *Oversight and Accountability of the U.S. Intelligence Agencies: An Evaluation.* Washington, DC: ABA, 1985.

Breckinridge, Scott D. *The CIA and the U.S. Intelligence System.* Boulder, CO: Westview Press, 1986.

Godson, Roy, ed. *Intelligence Problems for the 1980s, Number 1: Elements of Intelligence.* Rev. ed. Washington, DC: National Strategy Information Center, 1983.

Laqueur, Walter. *A World of Secrets.* New York: Basic Books, 1985.

Maurer, Alfred C.; Turnstall, Marion D.; and Keagle, James M. *Intelligence Policy and Process.* Boulder, CO: Westview Press, 1985.

—**COUNTERMEASURES (CM)** are a type of military activity in which devices or techniques are used to impair the enemy's operational effectiveness. *See also:* Counterintelligence.

—**COUNTERRECONNAISSANCE** is the sum of all the efforts taken to prevent the enemy's observing a force, area, or place.

References

Department of Defense, Joint Chiefs of Staff. *Department of Defense Dictionary of Military and Related Terms.* Washington, DC: GPO, 1986.

Laqueur, Walter. *A World of Secrets.* New York: Basic Books, 1985.

U.S. Congress. Senate. *Final Report of the Senate Select Committee to Study Government Operations with Respect to Intelligence Activities. Report 94-755. Book I, Foreign and Military Intelligence.* Washington, DC: GPO, 1976.

—**COUNTERSABOTAGE (CS)** is the part of counterintelligence that detects, destroys, neutralizes, or prevents sabotage by identifying, penetrating, manipulating, deceiving, and repressing groups or organizations suspected of conducting it. *See also:* Counterintelligence.

—**COUNTERSIGN** is a secret challenge and its reply.

References

Department of Defense, Joint Chiefs of Staff. *Department of Defense Dictionary of Military and Related Terms.* Washington, DC: GPO, 1986.

—**COUNTER-SIGNALS INTELLIGENCE (C-SIGINT)** is an Army tactical intelligence (TAC-INT) term that means those actions employed to determine enemy signals intelligence and related electronic warfare (EW) capabilities and activities, to assess friendly operations, to identify patterns and signatures and the resulting vulnerabilities for subsequent development and recommendation of countermeasures, and to evaluate the effectiveness of the applied countermeasure. Recommendations to counter the hostile SIGINT threat are provided to the G3 (operations) by the G2 (intelligence). They can include both offensive (active) measures—such as electronic countermeasures (ECM) to include jamming or deception, or targeting for fire or maneuver—and defensive (passive) measures—such as improved electronic counter-countermeasures (ECCM) or protective command, control, and communications countermeasures. *See also:* Communications Security.

References

American Bar Association. *Oversight and Accountability of the U.S. Intelligence Agencies: An Evaluation.* Washington, DC: ABA, 1985.

Department of Defense, U.S. Army. *Counterintelligence.* Field Manual FM 34-60. Washington, DC: Headquarters, Department of the Army, 1985.

———. *Counter-Signals Intelligence (C-SIGINT) Operations.* Field Manual FM 34-62. Washington, DC: Headquarters, Department of the Army, 1986.

Maurer, Alfred C.; Turnstall, Marion D.; and Keagle, James M. *Intelligence Policy and Process.* Boulder, CO: Westview Press, 1985.

—**COUNTER-SPY,** according to Richard Deacon, is a spy who is put in place so that he can betray or mislead opposing spies. *See also:* Double Agent.

References

American Bar Association. *Oversight and Accountability of the U.S. Intelligence Agencies: An Evaluation.* Washington, DC: ABA, 1985.

Becket, Henry S. A. *The Dictionary of Espionage: Spookspeak into English.* New York: Stein and Day, 1986.

Deacon, Richard. *Spyclopedia: An Encyclopedia of Spies, Secret Services, Operations, Jargon, and All Subjects Related to the World of Espionage.* London: Macdonald, 1987.

Maurer, Alfred C.; Turnstall, Marion D.; and Keagle, James M. *Intelligence Policy and Process.* Boulder, CO: Westview Press, 1985.

—**COUNTERSUBVERSION,** as defined by the Church Committee, is "that part of counterintelligence that is designed to destroy the effectiveness of subversive activities through the detection, identification, exploitation, penetration, manipulation, deception, and repression of individuals, groups, or organizations conducting or capable of conducting such activities."

References

Department of Defense, Joint Chiefs of Staff. *Department of Defense Dictionary of Military and Related Terms.* Washington, DC: GPO, 1986.

U.S. Congress. Senate. *Final Report of the Senate Select Committee to Study Government Operations with Respect to Intelligence Activities. Report 94-755. Book I, Foreign and Military Intelligence.* Washington, DC: GPO, 1976.

—**COUNTERSURVEILLANCE** is a term used in clandestine and covert intelligence operations to describe the process of insuring that an agent is not being followed when he goes to meet a contact. *See also:* Alternate Meet, Go-Away, Make, Meet Area, Movements Analysis, Pavement Artists, Riding Shotgun, Shadow, Shaking Off the Dogs, Surround, Surveillance.

References

American Bar Association. *Oversight and Accountability of the U.S. Intelligence Agencies: An Evaluation.* Washington, DC: ABA, 1985.

Becket, Henry S. A. *The Dictionary of Espionage: Spookspeak into English.* New York: Stein and Day, 1986.

Clancy, Tom. *The Cardinal of the Kremlin.* New York: Putnam, 1988.

Department of Defense, Joint Chiefs of Staff. *Department of Defense Dictionary of Military and Related Terms.* Washington, DC: GPO, 1986.

Godson, Roy, ed. *Intelligence Problems for the 1980s, Number 1: Elements of Intelligence.* Rev. ed. Washington, DC: National Strategy Information Center, 1983.

———. *Intelligence Problems for the 1980s, Number 3: Counterintelligence.* Washington, DC: National Strategy Information Center, 1980.

Maurer, Alfred C.; Turnstall, Marion D.; and Keagle, James M. *Intelligence Policy and Process.* Boulder, CO: Westview Press, 1985.

Treverton, Gregory F. *Covert Action: The Limits of Intervention in the Postwar World.* New York: Basic Books, 1987.

—COUNTERSURVEILLANCE MEASURES is an Army tactical intelligence (TACINT) term that refers to the security techniques designed and routinely employed to prevent or deceive the hostile observation of friendly operations or activities in order to protect the true status of those operations. Countersurveillance measures are normally listed in the unit's standard operating procedures (SOP) and include camouflage, smoke, disrupters, listening posts/observation posts (LP/OPs), frequent patrolling, and signal security (SIGSEC) procedures. *See also:* Countersurveillance.

References

American Bar Association. *Oversight and Accountability of the U.S. Intelligence Agencies: An Evaluation.* Washington, DC: ABA, 1985.

Department of Defense, U.S. Army. *Counter-Signals Intelligence (C-SIGINT) Operations.* Field Manual FM 34-62. Washington, DC: Headquarters, Department of the Army, 1986.

Maurer, Alfred C.; Turnstall, Marion D.; and Keagle, James M. *Intelligence Policy and Process.* Boulder, CO: Westview Press, 1985.

—COUNTRY INTELLIGENCE STUDY (CIS) is produced by the Defense Intelligence Agency. Each study deals with a single nation and is composed of five sections: history; environment; economic system; government; and politics. The CIS replaced the old Area Handbooks. *See also:* Defense Intelligence Agency.

References

American Bar Association. *Oversight and Accountability of the U.S. Intelligence Agencies: An Evaluation.* Washington, DC: ABA, 1985.

Kent, Sherman. *Strategic Intelligence for American World Policy.* Princeton, NJ: Princeton University Press, 1966.

Turner, Stansfield. *Secrecy and Democracy: The CIA in Transition.* Boston: Houghton Mifflin, 1985.

—COUPS. In six cases, the United States has supported coups d'état in foreign nations: Jacobo Arbenz Guzman of Guatemala in 1953; Muhammed Mossadeq of Iran in 1954; Fidel Castro of Cuba in 1961–62; Rafael Trujillo of the Dominican Republic in 1961; Ngo Dinh Diem of South Vietnam in 1962; and Salvador Allende Gossens of Chile in 1973.

References

Breckinridge, Scott D. *The CIA and the U.S. Intelligence System.* Boulder, CO: Westview Press, 1986.

Turner, Stansfield. *Secrecy and Democracy: The CIA in Transition.* Boston: Houghton Mifflin, 1985.

—COURIER is a general intelligence term for a messenger who is responsible for the secure physical transmission and delivery of documents or material. The courier hand-carries the information to its destination. *See also:* Armed Forces Courier Service.

References

Becket, Henry S. A. *The Dictionary of Espionage: Spookspeak into English.* New York: Stein and Day, 1986.

Department of Defense, Joint Chiefs of Staff. *Department of Defense Dictionary of Military and Related Terms.* Washington, DC: GPO, 1986.

Quirk, John; Phillips, David; Cline, Ray; and Pforzheimer, Walter. *The Central Intelligence Agency: A Photographic History.* Guilford, CT: Foreign Intelligence Press, 1986.

U.S. Congress. Senate. *Final Report of the Senate Select Committee to Study Government Operations with Respect to Intelligence Activities. Report 94-755. Book I, Foreign and Military Intelligence.* Washington, DC: GPO, 1976.

—COURSE OF ACTION has four meanings. (1) A course of action is any sequence of activities that an individual or a unit may follow. (2) It may also be a possible plan that is open to an individual or a command that would accomplish or would be related to the accomplishment of the assigned mission. (3) It can be the scheme that has been adopted to accomplish a job or mission. (4) It can be a line of conduct in an engagement.

References

Department of Defense, Joint Chiefs of Staff. *Department of Defense Dictionary of Military and Related Terms.* Washington, DC: GPO, 1986.

U.S. Congress. Senate. *Final Report of the Senate Select Committee to Study Government Operations with Respect to Intelligence Activities. Report 94-755. Book I, Foreign and Military Intelligence.* Washington, DC: GPO, 1976.

—**COUSINS** is the British Secret Intelligence Service (SIS) nickname for the Central Intelligence Agency.

References

Deacon, Richard. *Spyclopedia: An Encyclopedia of Spies, Secret Services, Operations, Jargon, and All Subjects Related to the World of Espionage.* London: Macdonald, 1987.

Turner, Stansfield. *Secrecy and Democracy: The CIA in Transition.* Boston: Houghton Mifflin, 1985.

—**COVER.** In clandestine and covert intelligence, cover is a disguise or role assumed by a person, organization, or installation to cover the fact that he (or it) is engaged in clandestine operations. Henry Becket maintains, for example, that as many as 70 percent of the diplomatic billets in the Soviet embassies in Washington, London, Paris, Tokyo, and Mexico City are actually filled by Soviet intelligence agents who are using their diplomatic titles as cover. In Army tactical intelligence (TACINT), cover means those measures necessary to protect a person, plan, operation, formation, or installation from the enemy intelligence effort and from the leakage of information. *See also:* Agent, Agent in Place, Agent Net, Agent of Influence, Agent Provocateur, Alias, Case, Case Officer, Center, Chief of Base, Chief of Outpost, Chief of Station, Clean, Company, Concealment, Concealment Devices, Confusion Agent, Co-opted Worker, Co-optees, Cover Name, Cover Organizations, Cover Story, Defector, Disaffected Person, Discard, Dispatched Agent, Double Agent, Doubled, Establishing Bonafides, Illegal Agent, Illegal Communication, Illegal Net, Illegal Operations, Illegal Residency, Illegal Support Officer, Infiltration, Informant, Inside Man, Keeping Books, Ladies, Legal, Legal Residency, Mole, Penetration, Plumbing, Pocket Litter, Putting in the Plumbing, Silent School, Singleton, Special Activities, Submerge, Suitable Cover, Surfacing.

References

Becket, Henry S. A. *The Dictionary of Espionage: Spookspeak into English.* New York: Stein and Day, 1986.

Clancy, Tom. *The Cardinal of the Kremlin.* New York: Putnam, 1988.

Department of Defense, Defense Intelligence College. *Glossary of Intelligence Terms and Definitions.* Washington, DC: DIC, 1987.

Department of Defense, Joint Chiefs of Staff. *Department of Defense Dictionary of Military and Related Terms.* Washington, DC: GPO, 1986.

Department of Defense, U.S. Army. *Counter-Signals Intelligence (C-SIGINT) Operations.* Field Manual FM 34-62. Washington, DC: Headquarters, Department of the Army, 1986.

Godson, Roy, ed. *Intelligence Problems for the 1980s, Number 4: Covert Action.* Washington, DC: National Strategy Information Center, 1981.

Kessler, Ronald. *Spy vs. Spy: Stalking Soviet Spies in America.* New York: Charles Scribner's Sons, 1988.

Laqueur, Walter. *A World of Secrets.* New York: Basic Books, Inc., 1985.

Turner, Stansfield. *Secrecy and Democracy: The CIA in Transition.* Boston: Houghton Mifflin, 1985.

U.S. Congress. Senate. *Final Report of the Senate Select Committee to Study Government Operations with Respect to Intelligence Activities. Report 94-755. Book I, Foreign and Military Intelligence.* Washington, DC: GPO, 1976.

—**COVER NAME** is a term used in clandestine and covert intelligence operations. It is a pseudonym used by an agent for security purposes. According to Henry Becket, this name is used in the general files, and the agent's true identity is recorded only in a tightly controlled central security registry.

References

Becket, Henry S. A. *The Dictionary of Espionage: Spookspeak into English.* New York: Stein and Day, 1986.

Deacon, Richard. *Spyclopedia: An Encyclopedia of Spies, Secret Services, Operations, Jargon, and All Subjects Related to the World of Espionage.* London: Macdonald, 1987.

Ranelagh, John. *The Agency: The Rise and Decline of the CIA.* New York: Simon and Schuster, 1986.

—**COVER ORGANIZATIONS** is a term used in clandestine and covert intelligence operations. Such organizations are groups created solely to provide cover for a covert agent. They may be small, one-man corporations or law firms, or huge businesses. They must be of a nature that provides the agent or agents working for it with reasonable excuses for traveling often and for keeping unorthodox hours. At a minimum, there must be an office and a phone, so that superficial inquiries will not expose the agent or agents.

References

Becket, Henry S. A. *The Dictionary of Espionage: Spookspeak into English.* New York: Stein and Day, 1986.

Deacon, Richard. *Spyclopedia: An Encyclopedia of Spies, Secret Services, Operations, Jargon, and All

Subjects Related to the World of Espionage.
London: Macdonald, 1987.

Ranelagh, John. *The Agency: The Rise and Decline of the CIA.* New York: Simon and Schuster, 1986.

—**COVER STORY** is a term used in clandestine and covert intelligence operations. It is a plausible explanation that is used when an operation fails. For example, Henry Becket says that the U.S. statement that Gary Powers's U-2 mission over the USSR in 1960 was really a weather reconnaissance aircraft that had drifted off course was a cover story. This one backfired when the Soviets produced both Powers and pieces of the aircraft. *See also:* Legend.

References

Becket, Henry S. A. *The Dictionary of Espionage: Spookspeak into English.* New York: Stein and Day, 1986.

Deacon, Richard. *Spyclopedia: An Encyclopedia of Spies, Secret Services, Operations, Jargon, and All Subjects Related to the World of Espionage.* London: Macdonald, 1987.

Kessler, Ronald. *Spy vs. Spy: Stalking Soviet Spies in America.* New York: Charles Scribner's Sons, 1988.

Ranelagh, John. *The Agency: The Rise and Decline of the CIA.* New York: Simon and Schuster, 1986.

—**COVERAGE** is the ground area that is represented on imagery, photomaps, mosaics, maps, or other geographical presentation systems. Coverage is also the extent to which intelligence information is available in respect to any specified area of interest. *See also:* Aerial Photograph.

References

Department of Defense, Joint Chiefs of Staff. *Department of Defense Dictionary of Military and Related Terms.* Washington, DC: GPO, 1986.

Godson, Roy, ed. *Intelligence Problems for the 1980s, Number 1: Elements of Intelligence.* Rev. ed. Washington, DC: National Strategy Information Center, 1983.

U.S. Congress. Senate. *Final Report of the Senate Select Committee to Study Government Operations with Respect to Intelligence Activities. Report 94-755. Book I, Foreign and Military Intelligence.* Washington, DC: GPO, 1976.

—**COVERING FORCE AREA** is an Army tactical intelligence (TACINT) term that means the operational area that is forward of the forward edge of the main battle area.

References

Department of Defense, U.S. Army. *Military Intelligence Battalion Combat Electronic Warfare and Intelligence (Aerial Exploitation) (Corps).* Field Manual FM 34-22. Washington, DC: Headquarters, Department of the Army, 1984.

———. *Military Intelligence Battalion (CEWI) (Tactical Exploitation) (Corps): Counterintelligence, Interrogation, Electronic Warfare.* Field Manual FM 34-23. Washington, DC: Headquarters, Department of the Army, 1985.

———. *Military Intelligence Battalion (Combat Electronic Warfare Intelligence) (Division).* Field Manual FM 34-10. Washington, DC: Headquarters, Department of the Army, 1981.

———. *Military Intelligence Company (Combat Electronic Warfare and Intelligence) (Armored Cavalry Regiment/Separate Brigade).* Field Manual FM 34-30. Washington, DC: Headquarters, Department of the Army, 1983.

———. *Military Intelligence Group (Combat Electronic Warfare and Intelligence) (Corps).* Field Manual FM 34-20. Washington, DC: Headquarters, Department of the Army, 1983.

—**COVERT.** *See:* Clandestine Operation.

—**COVERT ACTION** is a clandestine operation designed to influence foreign governments, events, organizations, or persons to support U.S. foreign policy. It may involve political, economic, propaganda, or paramilitary activities. Covert action is called *special activities* in Executive Order No. 12333. *See also:* Clandestine Operation, Covert Operation, Executive Order No. 12033.

References

Deacon, Richard. *Spyclopedia: An Encyclopedia of Spies, Secret Services, Operations, Jargon, and All Subjects Related to the World of Espionage.* London: Macdonald, 1987.

Department of Defense, Defense Intelligence College. *Glossary of Intelligence Terms and Definitions.* Washington, DC: DIC, 1987.

Godson, Roy, ed. *Intelligence Problems for the 1980s, Number 1: Elements of Intelligence.* Rev. ed. Washington, DC: National Strategy Information Center, 1983.

———. *Intelligence Problems for the 1980s, Number 3: 3: Counterintelligence.* Washington, DC: National Strategy Information Center, 1980.

———. *Intelligence Problems for the 1980s, Number 4: Covert Action.* Washington, DC: National Strategy Information Center, 1981.

Laqueur, Walter. *The Age of Terrorism.* Boston: Little, Brown, 1987.

———. *A World of Secrets*. New York: Basic Books, 1985.

Lefever, Ernest W., and Godson, Roy. *The CIA and the American Ethic: An Unfinished Debate*. Washington, DC: Ethics and Public Policy Center, Georgetown University, 1979.

Treverton, Gregory F. *Covert Action: The Limits of Intervention in the Postwar World*. New York: Basic Books, 1987.

Turner, Stansfield. *Secrecy and Democracy: The CIA in Transition*. Boston: Houghton Mifflin, 1985.

U.S. Congress. Senate. *Final Report of the Senate Select Committee to Study Government Operations with Respect to Intelligence Activities. Report 94-755. Book I, Foreign and Military Intelligence*. Washington, DC: GPO, 1976.

—**COVERT ACTION STAFF (CA STAFF)** is a component of the Directorate for Plans of the CIA. It is responsible for reviewing covert action projects for the directorate as well as managing and controlling some field operations. *See also:* Central Intelligence Agency.

References

Fain, Tyrus G.; Plant, Katharine C.; and Milloy, Ross. *The Intelligence Community: History, Organization, and Issues*. Public Documents Series. New York: R.R. Bowker, 1977.

Godson, Roy, ed. *Intelligence Problems for the 1980s, Number 3: Counterintelligence*. Washington, DC: National Strategy Information Center, 1980.

Lefever, Ernest W., and Godson, Roy. *The CIA and the American Ethic: An Unfinished Debate*. Washington, DC: Ethics and Public Policy Center, Georgetown University, 1979.

Treverton, Gregory F. *Covert Action: The Limits of Intervention in the Postwar World*. New York: Basic Books, 1987.

Turner, Stansfield. *Secrecy and Democracy: The CIA in Transition*. Boston: Houghton Mifflin, 1985.

—**COVERT AGENT** was defined by Congress in the Intelligence Identities Protection Act of 1982 as: "(A) an officer or employee of an intelligence agency or a member of the Armed Forces assigned to duty with an intelligence agency (i) whose identity as such an officer, employee, or member is classified information, and (ii) who is serving outside the United States or has within the last five years served outside the United States; or (B) a United States citizen whose intelligence relationship to the United States is classified information, and (i) who resides and acts outside the United States as an agent of, or informant or source of operational assistance to, an intelligence agency, or (ii) who is at the time of the disclosure acting as an agent of, or informant to, the foreign counterintelligence or foreign counterterrorism components of the Federal Bureau of Investigation; or (C) an individual, other than a United States citizen, whose past or present intelligence relationship to the United States is classified information and who is a present or former agent of, or a present or former informant or source of operational assistance to, an intelligence agency." *See also:* Covert Operation.

References

U.S. Congress. *Intelligence Identities Protection Act of 1982. Public Law 97-200, June 23, 1982*. Washington, DC: GPO, 1982.

—**COVERT OPERATION** is a covert action. It provides a cover story to hide the real purpose of an agent's mission. In contrast to a clandestine operation, no effort is made to conceal a covert operation from view. Rather, the agent relies on his wits to avoid detection. Henry Becket provides the best definition when he quotes Christopher Felix, a former CIA employee, who said, "The working distinction between the two forms . . . is that a clandestine operation is hidden, but not disguised, and a covert operation is disguised, but not hidden." As defined by the Church Committee, covert operations are "operations planned and executed against foreign governments, installations, and individuals so as to conceal the identity of the sponsor or else to permit the sponsor's plausible denial of the operation. The terms covert action, covert operation, clandestine operation and clandestine activity are sometimes used interchangeably." *See also:* Cover, Cover Name, Cover Organizations, Cover Story, Double Agent, Executive Action, Fifth Column, Illegal Agent, Illegal Communication, Illegal Net, Illegal Operations, Illegal Residency, Illegal Support Officer, Infiltration, Informant, Inside Man, Legal, Legal Residency, Legend, Legitimate, Mole, Moonlight Extradition, Mozhno Girls, Penetration, Plumbing, Putting in the Plumbing, Raven, Recruitment, Recruitment in Place, Silent School, Singleton, Sisters, Sleeper, Sound Man, Sound School, Special Activities, Stable, Sterile Funds, Sterile Telephone, Sterility Coding, Sterilize, Suitable Cover, Surreptitious Entry, Surround, Surveillance, Swallow, Swallow's Nest, Taxi, Terminate with Extreme Prejudice, Third Country Operation.

References

Becket, Henry S. A. *The Dictionary of Espionage: Spookspeak into English*. New York: Stein and Day, 1986.

Department of Defense, Defense Intelligence College. *Glossary of Intelligence Terms and Definitions*. Washington, DC: DIC, 1987.

Department of Defense, Joint Chiefs of Staff. *Department of Defense Dictionary of Military and Related Terms*. Washington, DC: GPO, 1986.

Godson, Roy, ed. *Intelligence Problems for the 1980s, Number 1: Elements of Intelligence*. Rev. ed. Washington, DC: National Strategy Information Center, 1983.

———. *Intelligence Problems for the 1980s, Number 3: 3: Counterintelligence*. Washington, DC: National Strategy Information Center, 1980.

Kent, Sherman. *Strategic Intelligence for American World Policy*. Princeton, NJ: Princeton University Press, 1966.

Laqueur, Walter. *The Age of Terrorism*. Boston: Little, Brown, 1987.

———. *A World of Secrets*. New York: Basic Books, 1985.

Lefever, Ernest W., and Godson, Roy. *The CIA and the American Ethic: An Unfinished Debate*. Washington, DC: Ethics and Public Policy Center, Georgetown University, 1979.

Treverton, Gregory F. *Covert Action: The Limits of Intervention in the Postwar World*. New York: Basic Books, 1987.

Turner, Stansfield. *Secrecy and Democracy: The CIA in Transition*. Boston: Houghton Mifflin, 1985.

U.S. Congress. Senate. *Final Report of the Senate Select Committee to Study Government Operations with Respect to Intelligence Activities. Report 94-755. Book I, Foreign and Military Intelligence*. Washington, DC: GPO, 1976.

—**CRIME RECORDS DIVISION** is the FBI's division that is responsible for contacts with the high-level media. It is located in FBI headquarters in Washington, DC.

References

Becket, Henry S. A. *The Dictionary of Espionage: Spookspeak into English*. New York: Stein and Day, 1986.

—**CRISIS,** as defined by the Department of Defense, is "an incident or situation involving a threat to the United States, its territories, and possessions that rapidly develops and creates a condition of such diplomatic, economic, political or military importance to the U.S. government that commitment of U.S. military forces and resources is contemplated to achieve U.S. national objectives."

References

U.S. Department of Defense, National Defense University. *Joint Staff Officer's Guide, 1986*. Washington, DC: GPO, 1986.

—**CRITICAL COMSEC FUNCTION,** in communications security (COMSEC), means a machine cryptosystem function that must be performed properly in order to prevent the loss of COMSEC protection. *See also:* Communications Security.

References

Blackburn, N. Glenn. "Computers: A Counterintelligence Concern." Unpublished paper provided to the editors. Washington, DC, 1987.

Martin, Paul H. "Communications-Computer Security." *Journal of Electronic Defense* (June 1987).

Muzerall, Joseph V., and Carty, Thomas P. "COMSEC and Its Need for Key Management." *DP&CS* (Spring 1987).

Ware, Willis H. "Information Systems, Security, and Privacy." *EDUCOM Bulletin* (Summer 1984).

—**CRITICAL INFORMATION,** in communications security (COMSEC), means information or data that must be protected in order to keep an adversary from gaining a significant military, political, or technical advantage. *See also:* Communications Security.

References

Blackburn, N. Glenn. "Computers: A Counterintelligence Concern." Unpublished paper provided to the editors. Washington, DC, 1987.

Godson, Roy, ed. *Intelligence Problems for the 1980s, Number 1: Elements of Intelligence*. Rev. ed. Washington, DC: National Strategy Information Center, 1983.

Martin, Paul H. "Communications-Computer Security." *Journal of Electronic Defense* (June 1987).

Muzerall, Joseph V., and Carty, Thomas P. "COMSEC and Its Need for Key Management." *DP&CS* (Spring 1987).

Ware, Willis H. "Information Systems, Security, and Privacy." *EDUCOM Bulletin* (Summer 1984).

—**CRITICAL INTELLIGENCE,** on the strategic level, is intelligence of such urgent importance to the security of the United States that it is transmitted at the highest priority to the President and other national decisionmaking officials before it is passed through normal evaluative channels. On the tactical level, critical intelligence is intelligence that requires the immediate attention of the commander so that he can react in time to actions by a potential or actual enemy. It includes but is not limited to the following: strong indications that hostilities are about to break out; indications that aggression is about to occur against a nation friendly to the United States; indications of the impending use of nuclear or biological weapons; and the occurrence of significant events in potentially hostile nations that may lead to modifying U.S. nuclear strike plans.

References

Department of Defense, Defense Intelligence College. *Glossary of Intelligence Terms and Definitions*. Washington, DC: DIC, 1987.

Department of Defense, Joint Chiefs of Staff. *Department of Defense Dictionary of Military and Related Terms*. Washington, DC: GPO, 1986.

Kent, Sherman. *Strategic Intelligence for American World Policy*. Princeton, NJ: Princeton University Press, 1966.

Godson, Roy, ed. *Intelligence Problems for the 1980s, Number 1: Elements of Intelligence*. Rev. ed. Washington, DC: National Strategy Information Center, 1983.

Treverton, Gregory F. *Covert Action: The Limits of Intervention in the Postwar World*. New York: Basic Books, 1987.

U.S. Congress. Senate. *Final Report of the Senate Select Committee to Study Government Operations with Respect to Intelligence Activities. Report 94-755. Book I, Foreign and Military Intelligence*. Washington, DC: GPO, 1976.

—**CRITICAL INTELLIGENCE COMMUNICA-TIONS SYSTEM (CRITICOMM)** is specifically designed to handle critical intelligence and is the responsibility of the director of the National Security Agency. The NSA's Office of Telecommunications and Computer Services administers the network. CRITICOMM is a worldwide circuit that is designed to flash to the President and a selected number of other high-level consumers news of an event within ten minutes of its occurrence. In 1973, the CRITICOMM/SPINTCOMM network became the Digital Network–Defense Special Security Communications System (DINDSSCS). *See also:* Communications Security.

References

Bamford, James. *The Puzzle Palace: A Report on America's Most Secret Agency*. New York: Penguin Books, 1983.

Department of Defense, Defense Intelligence College. *Glossary of Intelligence Terms and Definitions*. Washington, DC: DIC, 1987.

———. *Joint Intelligence: A Book of Supportive Readings*. Washington, DC: DIC, 1986.

—**CRITICAL INTELLIGENCE MESSAGE (CRITIC)** contains information about a situation that so critically affects the security interests of the United States or its allies that it may require the immediate attention of the President. It is sent within the Critical Intelligence Communications System. *See also:* Communications Security.

References

Department of Defense, Defense Intelligence College. *Glossary of Intelligence Terms and Definitions*. Washington, DC: DIC, 1987.

—**CRITICAL INTELLIGENCE PARAMETERS (CIPS)**, an Army intelligence term, means those threat parameters that are identified by service program management elements—such as numbers, types, mix, or characteristics of actual or projected enemy systems—that most strongly influence the effectiveness, survivability, security, or cost of a U.S. system.

References

Department of Defense, U.S. Army. *RDTE Managers Intelligence and Threat Support Guide*. Alexandria, VA: Headquarters, Army Matériel Development and Readiness Command, 1983.

Laqueur, Walter. *A World of Secrets*. New York: Basic Books, 1985.

—**CRITICAL-PRIMARY ELEMENTS**, in target intelligence, are those parts of the target that, if they are left undamaged, will allow the target to continue to function and to fulfill its mission. If a radar site, for example, were a target, then the radar facility and its support facilities would be the critical primary elements, while the mess hall would be a secondary element.

References

Maurer, Alfred C.; Turnstall, Marion D.; and Keagle, James M. *Intelligence Policy and Process*. Boulder, CO: Westview Press, 1985.

—**CRYPT INTELLIGENCE** is intelligence that has been derived from cryptanalysis or decryption. *See also:* Communications Security.

References

Laqueur, Walter. *A World of Secrets*. New York: Basic Books, 1985.

—**CRYPTANALYSIS (CA)** is converting encrypted messages into plain text when the encryption system or encryption key is unknown. In FBI terminology, this is called cryptoanalysis. In communications security (COMSEC), its purpose is to evaluate the adequacy of the security protection that it is intended to provide or to discover weaknesses or vulnerabilities that could be exploited to defeat or lessen that protection. *See also:* Communications Security.

References

Department of Defense, Defense Intelligence College. *Glossary of Intelligence Terms and Definitions.* Washington, DC: DIC, 1987.

Department of Defense, Joint Chiefs of Staff. *Department of Defense Dictionary of Military and Related Terms.* Washington, DC: GPO, 1986.

Godson, Roy, ed. *Intelligence Problems for the 1980s, Number 1: Elements of Intelligence.* Rev. ed. Washington, DC: National Strategy Information Center, 1983.

Kessler, Ronald. *Spy vs. Spy: Stalking Soviet Spies in America.* New York: Charles Scribner's Sons, 1988.

Laqueur, Walter. *A World of Secrets.* New York: Basic Books, 1985.

U.S. Congress. Senate. *Final Report of the Senate Select Committee to Study Government Operations with Respect to Intelligence Activities. Report 94-755. Book I, Foreign and Military Intelligence.* Washington, DC: GPO, 1976.

—**CRYPTO** is a designation applied to classified, cryptographic information that is so sensitive that it requires special rules for access and handling. *See also:* Communications Security.

References

Department of Defense, Defense Intelligence College. *Glossary of Intelligence Terms and Definitions.* Washington, DC: DIC, 1987.

—**CRYPTO-ALARM,** in communications security (COMSEC), means a circuit or device in crypto-equipment that detects failures or aberrations in the logic or operation of the crypto-equipment. It may inhibit transmission or may provide a visible or audible signal. *See also:* Communications Security (COMSEC).

References

Blackburn, N. Glenn. "Computers: A Counterintelligence Concern." Unpublished paper provided to the editors. Washington, DC, 1987.

Muzerall, Joseph V., and Carty, Thomas P. "COMSEC and Its Need for Key Management." *DP&CS* (Spring 1987).

—**CRYPTO-ALGORITHM,** in communications security (COMSEC), means a well-defined procedure or sequence of rules or steps that are used to produce cipher text from plain text and vice versa. *See also:* Communications Security.

References

Blackburn, N. Glenn. "Computers: A Counterintelligence Concern." Unpublished paper provided to the editors. Washington, DC, 1987.

—**CRYPTO-ANCILLARY EQUIPMENT,** in communications security (COMSEC), is equipment designed specifically to facilitate the efficient or reliable operation of crypto-equipment, but which does not perform cryptographic functions. Crypto-ancillary equipment can also be equipment that is designed specifically to convert information to a form that is suitable for processing by crypto-equipment. *See also:* Communications Security.

References

Blackburn, N. Glenn. "Computers: A Counterintelligence Concern." Unpublished paper provided to the editors. Washington, DC, 1987.

—**CRYPTOCHANNEL** is a complete system of crypto-communications between two or more entities. It is the basic unit in naval cryptographic communications and is analogous to a radio circuit. *See also:* Communications Security.

References

Corson, William R. *The Armies of Ignorance: The Rise of the American Intelligence Empire.* New York: Dial Press, 1977.

Department of Defense, Joint Chiefs of Staff. *Department of Defense Dictionary of Military and Related Terms.* Washington, DC: GPO, 1986.

Laqueur, Walter. *A World of Secrets.* New York: Basic Books, 1985.

—**CRYPTODATE,** in communications security (COMSEC), means the date that determines the specific key to be employed in a cryptosystem. *See also:* Communications Security.

References

Corson, William R. *The Armies of Ignorance: The Rise of the American Intelligence Empire.* New York: Dial Press, 1977.

Laqueur, Walter. *A World of Secrets.* New York: Basic Books, 1985.

—**CRYPTO-EQUIPMENT,** in communications security (COMSEC), means any piece of equipment that uses a cryptographic logic. *See also:* Communications Security.

References

Corson, William R. *The Armies of Ignorance: The Rise of the American Intelligence Empire.* New York: Dial Press, 1977.

—**CRYPTOGRAM,** a signals analysis term, is a single enciphered message with emphasis on transmission. It is the final product that will be transmitted. *See also:* Communications Security.

References

Corson, William R. *The Armies of Ignorance: The Rise of the American Intelligence Empire.* New York: Dial Press, 1977.

Laqueur, Walter. *A World of Secrets.* New York: Basic Books, 1985.

—**CRYPTOGRAPHIC INFORMATION** is detailed information of cryptographic techniques, processes, systems, equipment, functions, and capabilities, and all cryptomaterial. (Detailed means that disclosure of the information to unauthorized persons could reveal specific cryptographic features of classified crypto-equipment, or reveal weaknesses in equipment that could allow unauthorized decryption of encrypted traffic, or aid significantly in enemy cryptanalysis of a cryptosystem or of a specific message.) *See also:* Communications Security.

References

Corson, William R. *The Armies of Ignorance: The Rise of the American Intelligence Empire.* New York: Dial Press, 1977.

Department of Defense, Defense Intelligence College. *Glossary of Intelligence Terms and Definitions.* Washington, DC: DIC, 1987.

Department of Defense, Joint Chiefs of Staff. *Department of Defense Dictionary of Military and Related Terms.* Washington, DC: GPO, 1986.

Laqueur, Walter. *A World of Secrets.* New York: Basic Books, 1985.

—**CRYPTOGRAPHIC LOGIC,** in communications security (COMSEC), means a deterministic logic by which information may be converted to unintelligible form and reconverted to intelligible form. (This is sometimes referred to as "cryptoprinciple.") *See also:* Communications Security.

References

Corson, William R. *The Armies of Ignorance: The Rise of the American Intelligence Empire.* New York: Dial Press, 1977.

Department of Defense, Joint Chiefs of Staff. *Department of Defense Dictionary of Military and Related Terms.* Washington, DC: GPO, 1986.

Laqueur, Walter. *A World of Secrets.* New York: Basic Books, 1985.

—**CRYPTOGRAPHY.** (1) Cryptography is a branch of cryptology that encompasses the vast variety of means and methods used to make plain text unintelligible to unauthorized parties and the means and methods used to reconvert the same text back into intelligent text. (2) It is also the application of such means and methods in ways other than cryptanalysis. (3) It also refers to the design and use of cryptosystems. (4) As defined by the Church Committee, cryptography is the enciphering of plain text so that it will be unintelligible to an unauthorized recipient. *See also:* Communications Security.

References

Blackburn, N. Glenn. "Computers: A Counterintelligence Concern." Unpublished paper provided to the editors. Washington, DC, 1987.

Corson, William R. *The Armies of Ignorance: The Rise of the American Intelligence Empire.* New York: Dial Press, 1977.

Department of Defense, Defense Intelligence College. *Glossary of Intelligence Terms and Definitions.* Washington, DC: DIC, 1987.

Department of Defense, Joint Chiefs of Staff. *Department of Defense Dictionary of Military and Related Terms.* Washington, DC: GPO, 1986.

Godson, Roy, ed. *Intelligence Problems for the 1980s, Number 1: Elements of Intelligence.* Rev. ed. Washington, DC: National Strategy Information Center, 1983.

Laqueur, Walter. *A World of Secrets.* New York: Basic Books, Inc., 1985.

Martin, Paul H. "Communications-Computer Security." *Journal of Electronic Defense* (June 1987).

Muzerall, Joseph V., and Carty, Thomas P. "COMSEC and Its Need for Key Management." *DP&CS* (Spring 1987).

U.S. Congress. Senate. *Final Report of the Senate Select Committee to Study Government Operations with Respect to Intelligence Activities. Report 94-755. Book I, Foreign and Military Intelligence.* Washington, DC: GPO, 1976.

Ware, Willis H. "Information Systems, Security, and Privacy." *EDUCOM Bulletin* (Summer 1984).

—**CRYPTOGUARD,** in communications security (COMSEC), is an activity that is responsible for decrypting, encrypting in another cryptosystem, and relaying telecommunications for other activities that do not hold compatible cryptosystems. A cryptoguard can also be an activity that is responsible for providing secure communications services for other activities. *See also:* Communications Security.

References

Blackburn, N. Glenn. "Computers: A Counterintelligence Concern." Unpublished paper provided to the editors. Washington, DC, 1987.

Corson, William R. *The Armies of Ignorance: The Rise of the American Intelligence Empire.* New York: Dial Press, 1977.

Laqueur, Walter. *A World of Secrets.* New York: Basic Books, 1985.

Martin, Paul H. "Communications-Computer Security." *Journal of Electronic Defense* (June 1987).

Muzerall, Joseph V., and Carty, Thomas P. "COMSEC and Its Need for Key Management." *DP&CS* (Spring 1987).

Ware, Willis H. "Information Systems, Security, and Privacy." *EDUCOM Bulletin* (Summer 1984).

—**CRYPTO-IGNITION KEY (CIK),** in communications security (COMSEC), means a device or variable that splits or alters the cryptovariable so that keyed crypto-equipment may be left unattended when the CIK is removed. *See also:* Communications Security.

References

Blackburn, N. Glenn. "Computers: A Counterintelligence Concern." Unpublished paper provided to the editors. Washington, DC, 1987.

Corson, William R. *The Armies of Ignorance: The Rise of the American Intelligence Empire.* New York: Dial Press, 1977.

Martin, Paul H. "Communications-Computer Security." *Journal of Electronic Defense* (June 1987).

Muzerall, Joseph V., and Carty, Thomas P. "COMSEC and Its Need for Key Management." *DP&CS* (Spring 1987).

Ware, Willis H. "Information Systems, Security, and Privacy." *EDUCOM Bulletin* (Summer 1984).

—**CRYPTO-INSECURITY,** in communications security (COMSEC), means an equipment malfunction or operator error that adversely affects the security of a cryptosystem. *See also:* Communications Security.

References

Blackburn, N. Glenn. "Computers: A Counterintelligence Concern." Unpublished paper provided to the editors. Washington, DC, 1987.

Corson, William R. *The Armies of Ignorance: The Rise of the American Intelligence Empire.* New York: Dial Press, 1977.

Laqueur, Walter. *A World of Secrets.* New York: Basic Books, 1985.

Martin, Paul H. "Communications-Computer Security." *Journal of Electronic Defense* (June 1987).

Muzerall, Joseph V., and Carty, Thomas P. "COMSEC and Its Need for Key Management." *DP&CS* (Spring 1987).

Ware, Willis H. "Information Systems, Security, and Privacy." *EDUCOM Bulletin* (Summer 1984).

—**CRYPTOLOGIC ACTIVITIES** are the operations needed to produce signals intelligence and to maintain signals security. *See also:* Communications Security.

References

Blackburn, N. Glenn. "Computers: A Counterintelligence Concern." Unpublished paper provided to the editors. Washington, DC, 1987.

Corson, William R. *The Armies of Ignorance: The Rise of the American Intelligence Empire.* New York: Dial Press, 1977.

Department of Defense, Defense Intelligence College. *Glossary of Intelligence Terms and Definitions.* Washington, DC: DIC, 1987.

Martin, Paul H. "Communications-Computer Security." *Journal of Electronic Defense* (June 1987).

Muzerall, Joseph V., and Carty, Thomas P. "COMSEC and Its Need for Key Management." *DP&CS* (Spring 1987).

Ware, Willis H. "Information Systems, Security, and Privacy." *EDUCOM Bulletin* (Summer 1984).

—**CRYPTOLOGY.** (1) As defined by the Department of Defense, cryptology is the science of secret communications. (2) In communications security (COMSEC), it means the science that deals with hidden, disguised, or encrypted communications. It embraces communications security and communications intelligence. (3) As defined by the Church Committee, cryptology is "the science that includes cryptoanalysis and cryptography, and embraces communications intelligence and communications security." *See also:* Communications Security.

References

Corson, William R. *The Armies of Ignorance: The Rise of the American Intelligence Empire.* New York: Dial Press, 1977.

Department of Defense, Joint Chiefs of Staff. *Department of Defense Dictionary of Military and Related Terms.* Washington, DC: GPO, 1986.

Godson, Roy, ed. *Intelligence Problems for the 1980s, Number 1: Elements of Intelligence.* Rev. ed. Washington, DC: National Strategy Information Center, 1983.

Kessler, Ronald. *Spy vs. Spy: Stalking Soviet Spies in America.* New York: Charles Scribner's Sons, 1988.

Laqueur, Walter. *A World of Secrets.* New York: Basic Books, 1985.

U.S. Congress. Senate. *Final Report of the Senate Select Committee to Study Government Operations with Respect to Intelligence Activities. Report 94-755. Book I, Foreign and Military Intelligence.* Washington, DC: GPO, 1976.

—**CRYPTOMATERIAL** is all communications security (COMSEC) material (including documents, devices, and equipment) that contains the cryptographic information needed to encrypt, decrypt, or authenticate communications. The material is marked CRYPTO or any other way that indicates that it has cryptographic information. *See also:* Communications Security.

References

Blackburn, N. Glenn. "Computers: A Counterintelligence Concern." Unpublished paper provided to the editors. Washington, DC, 1987.

Department of Defense, Defense Intelligence College. *Glossary of Intelligence Terms and Definitions.* Washington, DC: DIC, 1987.

Department of Defense, Department of the Air Force. *Communications-Electronics Terminology.* Washington, DC: GPO, 1973.

Department of Defense, Joint Chiefs of Staff. *Department of Defense Dictionary of Military and Related Terms.* Washington, DC: GPO, 1986.

Laqueur, Walter. *A World of Secrets.* New York: Basic Books, 1985.

Martin, Paul H. "Communications-Computer Security." *Journal of Electronic Defense* (June 1987).

Muzerall, Joseph V., and Carty, Thomas P. "COMSEC and Its Need for Key Management." *DP&CS* (Spring 1987).

U.S. Congress. Senate. *Final Report of the Senate Select Committee to Study Government Operations with Respect to Intelligence Activities. Report 94-755. Book I, Foreign and Military Intelligence.* Washington, DC: GPO, 1976.

Ware, Willis H. "Information Systems, Security, and Privacy." *EDUCOM Bulletin* (Summer 1984).

—**CRYPTONET,** in communications security (COMSEC), means two or more activities that hold the same keying material and therefore can communicate. *See also:* Communications Security.

References

Blackburn, N. Glenn. "Computers: A Counterintelligence Concern." Unpublished paper provided to the editors. Washington, DC, 1987.

Martin, Paul H. "Communications-Computer Security." *Journal of Electronic Defense* (June 1987).

Muzerall, Joseph V., and Carty, Thomas P. "COMSEC and Its Need for Key Management." *DP&CS* (Spring 1987).

Ware, Willis H. "Information Systems, Security, and Privacy." *EDUCOM Bulletin* (Summer 1984).

—**CRYPTONET COMPARTMENTATION,** in communications security (COMSEC), means the limiting of the size of a cryptonet (i.e., the number of holders of a certain cryptovariable) as a means of controlling the volume of traffic protected by that cryptovariable or limiting the distribution of cryptovariables to specific user communities. *See also:* Communications Security.

References

Blackburn, N. Glenn. "Computers: A Counterintelligence Concern." Unpublished paper provided to the editors. Washington, DC, 1987.

Martin, Paul H. "Communications-Computer Security." *Journal of Electronic Defense* (June 1987).

Muzerall, Joseph V., and Carty, Thomas P. "COMSEC and Its Need for Key Management." *DP&CS* (Spring 1987).

Ware, Willis H. "Information Systems, Security, and Privacy." *EDUCOM Bulletin* (Summer 1984).

—**CRYPTONET CONTROLLER,** in communications security (COMSEC), means the operator of a communications terminal who is responsible for generating and distributing cryptovariables in electrical form. *See also:* Communications Security.

References

Blackburn, N. Glenn. "Computers: A Counterintelligence Concern." Unpublished paper provided to the editors. Washington, DC, 1987.

Martin, Paul H. "Communications-Computer

Security." *Journal of Electronic Defense* (June 1987).

Muzerall, Joseph V., and Carty, Thomas P. "COMSEC and Its Need for Key Management." *DP&CS* (Spring 1987).

Ware, Willis H. "Information Systems, Security, and Privacy." *EDUCOM Bulletin* (Summer 1984).

—**CRYPTONET VARIABLE (CNV),** in communications security (COMSEC), means a cryptovariable that is held in common by all members of a secure communications net. This variable is usually used to secure all intra-net communications. *See also:* Communications Security.

References

Blackburn, N. Glenn. "Computers: A Counterintelligence Concern." Unpublished paper provided to the editors. Washington, DC, 1987.

Martin, Paul H. "Communications-Computer Security." *Journal of Electronic Defense* (June 1987).

Muzerall, Joseph V., and Carty, Thomas P. "COMSEC and Its Need for Key Management." *DP&CS* (Spring 1987).

Ware, Willis H. "Information Systems, Security, and Privacy." *EDUCOM Bulletin* (Summer 1984).

—**CRYPTONYM,** in FBI terminology, is a code word or symbol that is used to conceal operations, projects, organizations, or individuals. *See also:* Pseudonym.

References

Kessler, Ronald. *Spy vs. Spy: Stalking Soviet Spies in America.* New York: Charles Scribner's Sons, 1988.

—**CRYPTOPERIOD,** in communications security (COMSEC), means the time span during which a specific cryptovariable is authorized for use or in which the cryptovariables for a given system may remain in effect. *See also:* Communications Security.

References

Blackburn, N. Glenn. "Computers: A Counterintelligence Concern." Unpublished paper provided to the editors. Washington, DC, 1987.

Martin, Paul H. "Communications-Computer Security." *Journal of Electronic Defense* (June 1987).

Muzerall, Joseph V., and Carty, Thomas P. "COMSEC and Its Need for Key Management." *DP&CS* (Spring 1987).

Ware, Willis H. "Information Systems, Security, and Privacy." *EDUCOM Bulletin* (Summer 1984).

—**CRYPTOPRODUCTION EQUIPMENT,** in communications security (COMSEC), means equipment and components thereof that are specifically designed for, and used in, manufacturing and the associated testing of keying material in hard copy form. *See also:* Communications Security.

References

Laqueur, Walter. *A World of Secrets.* New York: Basic Books, 1985.

—**CRYPTOSECURITY** is a component of communications security (COMSEC) and is the result of providing technically sound cryptosystems and using them under proper security procedures. *See also:* Communications Security.

References

Department of Defense, Joint Chiefs of Staff. *Department of Defense Dictionary of Military and Related Terms.* Washington, DC: GPO, 1986.

Laqueur, Walter. *A World of Secrets.* New York: Basic Books, 1985.

U.S. Congress. Senate. *Final Report of the Senate Select Committee to Study Government Operations with Respect to Intelligence Activities. Report 94-755. Book I, Foreign and Military Intelligence.* Washington, DC: GPO, 1976.

—**CRYPTOSERVICE MESSAGE,** in communications security (COMSEC), means a message that is (usually encrypted and) transmitted between cryptocenters requesting or supplying information concerning the irregularities in message encryption or decryption. *See also:* Communications Security.

References

Blackburn, N. Glenn. "Computers: A Counterintelligence Concern." Unpublished paper provided to the editors. Washington, DC, 1987.

Martin, Paul H. "Communications-Computer Security." *Journal of Electronic Defense* (June 1987).

Muzerall, Joseph V., and Carty, Thomas P. "COMSEC and Its Need for Key Management." *DP&CS* (Spring 1987).

Ware, Willis H. "Information Systems, Security, and Privacy." *EDUCOM Bulletin* (Summer 1984).

—**CRYPTOSYSTEM,** in communications security (COMSEC), is an entire system or unit that provides a single means of encrypting and decrypting material. It includes the equipment, their removable parts, the operating instructions, maintenance manuals, and any mechanical or electrical method or device that is used to disguise the system or its functions. *See also:* Communications Security.

References

Department of Defense, Joint Chiefs of Staff. *Department of Defense Dictionary of Military and Related Terms.* Washington, DC: GPO, 1986.

Laqueur, Walter. *A World of Secrets.* New York: Basic Books, Inc., 1985.

U.S. Congress. Senate. *Final Report of the Senate Select Committee to Study Government Operations with Respect to Intelligence Activities. Report 94-755. Book I, Foreign and Military Intelligence.* Washington, DC: GPO, 1976.

—**CRYPTOVARIABLE,** in communications security (COMSEC), means a sequence of random binary bits that are used to initially set up and periodically change permutations in crypto-equipment for purposes of encrypting or decrypting electronic signals. *See also:* Communications Security.

References

Blackburn, N. Glenn. "Computers: A Counterintelligence Concern." Unpublished paper provided to the editors. Washington, DC, 1987.

Laqueur, Walter. *A World of Secrets.* New York: Basic Books, 1985.

Martin, Paul H. "Communications-Computer Security." *Journal of Electronic Defense* (June 1987).

Muzerall, Joseph V., and Carty, Thomas P. "COMSEC and Its Need for Key Management." *DP&CS* (Spring 1987).

Ware, Willis H. "Information Systems, Security, and Privacy." *EDUCOM Bulletin* (Summer 1984).

—**CRYPTOVARIABLE UPDATING,** in communications security (COMSEC), means a periodic cryptovariable modification that is performed automatically or manually to protect past traffic. *See also:* Communications Security.

References

Blackburn, N. Glenn. "Computers: A Counterintelligence Concern." Unpublished paper provided to the editors. Washington, DC, 1987.

Martin, Paul H. "Communications-Computer Security." *Journal of Electronic Defense* (June 1987).

Muzerall, Joseph V., and Carty, Thomas P. "COMSEC and Its Need for Key Management." *DP&CS* (Spring 1987).

Ware, Willis H. "Information Systems, Security, and Privacy." *EDUCOM Bulletin* (Summer 1984).

—**CUBA.** *See:* Mongoose.

—**CULTIVATION** is a term that is used in clandestine and covert intelligence operations to describe the process of establishing a relationship with a potential defector or a possible source of information. It begins with a demonstration of friendship and a tangible offer, such as dinner or a trip.

References

Becket, Henry S. A. *The Dictionary of Espionage: Spookspeak into English.* New York: Stein and Day, 1986.

Department of Defense, Joint Chiefs of Staff. *Department of Defense Dictionary of Military and Related Terms.* Washington, DC: GPO, 1986.

Kessler, Ronald. *Spy vs. Spy: Stalking Soviet Spies in America.* New York: Charles Scribner's Sons, 1988.

—**CURRENT INTELLIGENCE** is intelligence of all types and forms concerning events of immediate interest. Since it is often highly time-perishable, it is usually disseminated without evaluation and interpretation, since these processes could consume so much time that they would render the intelligence worthless. Although there is no time cutoff concerning current intelligence, such information covers events that are rarely more than 48 hours old. As defined by the Church Committee, current intelligence is "summaries and analyses of recent events."

References

American Bar Association. *Oversight and Accountability of the U.S. Intelligence Agencies: An Evaluation.* Washington, DC: ABA, 1985.

Corson, William R. *The Armies of Ignorance: The Rise of the American Intelligence Empire.* New York: Dial Press, 1977.

Department of Defense, Joint Chiefs of Staff. *Department of Defense Dictionary of Military and Related Terms.* Washington, DC: GPO, 1986.

Godson, Roy, ed. *Intelligence Problems for the 1980s, Number 1: Elements of Intelligence.* Rev. ed. Washington, DC: National Strategy Information Center, 1983.

Kent, Sherman. *Strategic Intelligence for American World Policy.* Princeton, NJ: Princeton University Press, 1966.

Laqueur, Walter. *A World of Secrets.* New York: Basic Books, 1985.

Maurer, Alfred C.; Turnstall, Marion D.; and Keagle, James M. *Intelligence Policy and Process.* Boulder, CO: Westview Press, 1985.

Treverton, Gregory F. *Covert Action: The Limits of Intervention in the Postwar World*. New York: Basic Books, 1987.

Turner, Stansfield. *Secrecy and Democracy: The CIA in Transition*. Boston: Houghton Mifflin, 1985.

U.S. Congress. Senate. *Final Report of the Senate Select Committee to Study Government Operations with Respect to Intelligence Activities. Report 94-755. Book I, Foreign and Military Intelligence*. Washington, DC: GPO, 1976.

—**CURRENT INTELLIGENCE AND INDICATIONS** is an official term that has been defined by the Defense Intelligence Agency for one of its functional areas. It means "activities relating to information, in varying degrees of evaluation, which bear on the intention of a potentially hostile force to adopt or reject a course of action; or on an impending crisis."

References

Kent, Sherman. *Strategic Intelligence for American World Policy*. Princeton, NJ: Princeton University Press, 1966.

Laqueur, Walter. *A World of Secrets*. New York: Basic Books, 1985.

Treverton, Gregory F. *Covert Action: The Limits of Intervention in the Postwar World*. New York: Basic Books, 1987.

Turner, Stansfield. *Secrecy and Democracy: The CIA in Transition*. Boston: Houghton Mifflin, 1985.

Department of Defense, Defense Intelligence Agency. *Defense Intelligence Agency Manual 22-2*. Washington, DC: DIA, 1979.

—**CURRENT INTELLIGENCE REQUIREMENTS LIST (CIRL)** was a statement of immediate intelligence interests, which served as an itemization of the consumer's special information interests. It was taken over by the U.S. Intelligence Board and then by the National Foreign Intelligence Board.

References

Breckinridge, Scott D. *The CIA and the U.S. Intelligence System*. Boulder, CO: Westview Press, 1986.

Laqueur, Walter. *A World of Secrets*. New York: Basic Books, 1985.

Treverton, Gregory F. *Covert Action: The Limits of Intervention in the Postwar World*. New York: Basic Books, 1987.

—**CURRENT/OPERATIONAL INTELLIGENCE** is an indications and warning (I&W) term. It is intelligence that is required for the final planning and execution of all types of operations. *See also:* Indications and Warning.

References

Godson, Roy, ed. *Intelligence Problems for the 1980s, Number 1: Elements of Intelligence*. Rev. ed. Washington, DC: National Strategy Information Center, 1983.

Kent, Sherman. *Strategic Intelligence for American World Policy*. Princeton, NJ: Princeton University Press, 1966.

Laqueur, Walter. *A World of Secrets*. New York: Basic Books, 1985.

—**CUSTODIAL DETENTION LIST** was an FBI list of individuals whom the bureau felt it might have to arrest in wartime. The list was composed of both aliens and American citizens. Its name was changed in 1946 to "Security Index," later to the "Reserve Index," and finally to the "Communist Index." By 1951 more than 15,000 people, mostly Communist Party (USA) members and Puerto Rican nationalists, were on the list. *See also:* COINTELPRO, Rabble Rouser Index.

References

Becket, Henry S. A. *The Dictionary of Espionage: Spookspeak into English*. New York: Stein and Day, 1986.

Deacon, Richard. *Spyclopedia: An Encyclopedia of Spies, Secret Services, Operations, Jargon, and All Subjects Related to the World of Espionage*. London: Macdonald, 1987.

Ranelagh, John. *The Agency: The Rise and Decline of the CIA*. New York: Simon and Schuster, 1986.

—**CUSTOMER** is a general intelligence term for an authorized person who uses intelligence or intelligence information either to produce other intelligence or to make decisions. Customer is the same as user, consumer, or requester, and has replaced these terms as the official term used in the Department of Defense.

References

Department of Defense, Defense Intelligence Agency. *Defense Intelligence Agency Manual*. Washington, DC: DIA, 1987.

Department of Defense, Defense Intelligence College. *Glossary of Intelligence Terms and Definitions*. Washington, DC: DIC, 1987.

Department of Defense, U.S. Army. *RDTE Managers Intelligence and Threat Support Guide*. Alexandria,

VA: Headquarters, Army Matériel Development and Readiness Command, 1983.

Godson, Roy, ed. *Intelligence Problems for the 1980s, Number 1: Elements of Intelligence*. Rev. ed. Washington, DC: National Strategy Information Center, 1983.

Kent, Sherman. *Strategic Intelligence for American World Policy*. Princeton, NJ: Princeton University Press, 1966.

Laqueur, Walter. *A World of Secrets*. New York: Basic Books, 1985.

—**CUTOUT** is a term that is used in clandestine and covert intelligence operations to describe a person who is used to conceal contact between the members of a clandestine activity or organization. A cutout is a go-between whose existence makes it unnecessary for an agent to know the identity of his superiors. There are two types of cutout systems. In a block cutout, the contact knows the names of all agents working in an individual operation or cell; in a chain cutout, the contact knows only one agent and the others are recruited sequentially, so an agent knows only the persons directly above and below him. *See also:* Agent, Agent Net, Cover, Special Activities.

References

Becket, Henry S. A. *The Dictionary of Espionage: Spookspeak into English*. New York: Stein and Day, 1986.

Deacon, Richard. *Spyclopedia: An Encyclopedia of Spies, Secret Services, Operations, Jargon, and All Subjects Related to the World of Espionage*. London: Macdonald, 1987.

Kessler, Ronald. *Spy vs. Spy: Stalking Soviet Spies in America*. New York: Charles Scribner's Sons, 1988.

Treverton, Gregory F. *Covert Action: The Limits of Intervention in the Postwar World*. New York: Basic Books, 1987.

Turner, Stansfield. *Secrecy and Democracy: The CIA in Transition*. Boston: Houghton Mifflin, 1985.

U.S. Congress. Senate. *Final Report of the Senate Select Committee to Study Government Operations with Respect to Intelligence Activities. Report 94-755. Book I, Foreign and Military Intelligence*. Washington, DC: GPO, 1976.

—**CW JAMMING** is an electronic warfare (EW) term that means continuous wave jamming. It involves the transmission of constant amplitude, constant frequency, unmodulated jamming signals in order to change the signal-to-noise ratio of a receiver. Successful CW jamming will create so much noise that communications cannot be received. *See also:* Communications Security.

References

Blackburn, N. Glenn. "Computers: A Counterintelligence Concern." Unpublished paper provided to the editors. Washington, DC, 1987.

—**CYCLE,** a baud-based system term used in communications intelligence, communications security, operations security, and signals analysis, has two meanings. (1) A cycle, in communications systems, is the part of a transmission that is formed by one complete revolution of the commutator or its electric counterpart. (2) A cycle is also a round of internal operations of a machine that ends with the machine in its original state, as when a character is typed on a keyboard, causing the commutator to proceed through one complete revolution. *See also:* Communications Security.

References

Kent, Sherman. *Strategic Intelligence for American World Policy*. Princeton, NJ: Princeton University Press, 1966.

Laqueur, Walter. *A World of Secrets*. New York: Basic Books, 1985.

—**CYCLE LENGTH (CL),** a baud-based system term used in communications intelligence, communications security, operations security, and signals analysis, is the time required to complete one cycle. It is normally stated in milliseconds (MS). *See also:* Communications Security.

References

Blackburn, N. Glenn. "Computers: A Counterintelligence Concern." Unpublished paper provided to the editors. Washington, DC, 1987.

Martin, Paul H. "Communications-Computer Security." *Journal of Electronic Defense* (June 1987).

Muzerall, Joseph V., and Carty, Thomas P. "COMSEC and Its Need for Key Management." *DP&CS* (Spring 1987).

Ware, Willis H. "Information Systems, Security, and Privacy." *EDUCOM Bulletin* (Summer 1984).

—DAILY INDICATIONS STATUS REPORT (DISR) is a message sent by the Defense Intelligence Agency to the Joint Chiefs of Staff, White House, Department of Defense (DoD), and other commands that gives the status of current warning problems to DoD indications and warning system members. It is a two-part message, with the first providing an overview and the second containing detailed assessments of specific warning problems. *See also:* Defense Intelligence Agency, Indications and Warning.

References

Von Hoene, John P. A. *Intelligence User's Guide.* Washington, DC: Defense Intelligence Agency, 1983.

—DAILY INTELLIGENCE SUMMARY (DINSUM) provides a daily analysis of crisis situations and a summary of relevant intelligence information that was produced during the previous 24 hours. It is sent to the Joint Chiefs of Staff, the military services, and selected other government agencies. *See also:* Defense Intelligence Agency.

References

Department of Defense, National Defense University. *Joint Staff Officer's Guide, 1986.* Washington, DC: GPO, 1986.

Treverton, Gregory F. *Covert Action: The Limits of Intervention in the Postwar World.* New York: Basic Books, 1987.

Turner, Stansfield. *Secrecy and Democracy: The CIA in Transition.* Boston: Houghton Mifflin, 1985.

—DAILY MARITIME INTELLIGENCE SUMMARY (DMOS) is a daily report produced by the Navy Operations Intelligence Center (NOIC) in Suitland, Maryland. An all-source report, it presents a complete summary of all the significant Soviet and East European naval activity that has occurred over the previous 24-hour period. The NOIC is a 24-hour, seven-day-a-week watch center, and the DMOS is therefore produced by all watches. The Highlights, containing the most

significant activity and the Mediterranean summary, are produced during normal working hours, eastern standard time; the Atlantic summary is produced on the evening watch; and the Pacific and Indian Ocean summaries are produced on the midwatch (midnight to 8 a.m., local time). The DMOS is considered to be one of Naval Intelligence's most authoritative documents and is sent to the Intelligence Community, to concerned national leaders, and to the field commands.

—DAILY SUMMARY OF SIGNIFICANT UNCONVENTIONAL WARFARE AND CIVIL DISTURBANCE ACTIVITIES synopsizes significant incidents involving terrorist groups and tactics, or terrorist activities by violence-oriented groups worldwide and provides limited commentary on these incidents. It is not widely distributed in the Intelligence Community.

References

Turner, Stansfield. *Secrecy and Democracy: The CIA in Transition.* Boston: Houghton Mifflin, 1985.

Von Hoene, John P. A. *Intelligence User's Guide.* Washington, DC: Defense Intelligence Agency, 1983.

—DAMAGE ASSESSMENT is a term used in clandestine and covert intelligence operations, in counterintelligence, counterespionage, and counterinsurgency operations, and in general military operations. (1) In the counterintelligence, counterespionage, and counterinsurgency context, a damage assessment is an evaluation of the impact of a compromise in terms of the loss of intelligence information, sources, or methods. It may describe measures to minimize the damage and make recommendations concerning preventing future compromises. (2) In the clandestine and covert intelligence context, a damage assessment is an act performed in order to determine the amount of damage that has been done to an operation because a portion of it has been blown or revealed to the enemy. (3) In the military context, it is an appraisal of the effects of an attack on one or more elements of a nation's strength (military, economic, and political) to determine the residual capability for further operations. *See also:* Blow, Blown Agent, Burn, Burnt, Damage Control, Doubled, Packed Up, Rolling Up the Net, Surround, Surveillance, Turned.

References

Clancy, Tom. *The Cardinal of the Kremlin.* New York: Putnam, 1988.

Department of Defense, Defense Intelligence College. *Glossary of Intelligence Terms and Definitions.* Washington, DC: DIC, 1987.

Turner, Stansfield. *Secrecy and Democracy: The CIA in Transition.* Boston: Houghton Mifflin, 1985.

—**DAMAGE CONTROL** is a term that is used in clandestine and covert intelligence operations. It is the means by which an intelligence organization attempts to minimize the harmful results of an aborted or failed operation. Such means are generally put into effect after a damage assessment has been performed. *See also:* Damage Assessment.

References

Becket, Henry S. A. *The Dictionary of Espionage: Spookspeak into English.* New York: Stein and Day, 1986.

Clancy, Tom. *The Cardinal of the Kremlin.* New York: Putnam, 1988.

Turner, Stansfield. *Secrecy and Democracy: The CIA in Transition.* Boston: Houghton Mifflin, 1985.

—**DANGLE** is a term used in clandestine and covert intelligence operations for a person who approaches an intelligence agency in a way implying that he wants to be recruited. The danger is that he may well be working for a hostile intelligence organization and has been sent to learn about the organization he is contacting. *See also:* Agent, Agent Authentication, Agent in Place, Agent of Influence, Agent Provocateur, Alias, Co-opted Worker, Co-optees, Defector, Disaffected Person, Double Agent, Illegal Agent, Infiltration, Informant, Inside Man, Litmus Test, Penetration, Recruitment, Shopworn Goods.

References

Becket, Henry S. A. *The Dictionary of Espionage: Spookspeak into English.* New York: Stein and Day, 1986.

Deacon, Richard. *Spyclopedia: An Encyclopedia of Spies, Secret Services, Operations, Jargon, and All Subjects Related to the World of Espionage.* London: Macdonald, 1987.

Ranelagh, John. *The Agency: The Rise and Decline of the CIA.* New York: Simon and Schuster, 1986.

—**DATA** is a statistical or quantitative methodological term that is often used in intelligence analysis. It describes the raw material of statistics. Data are numbers that provide numerical values for any characteristic of a sample or a population. *See also:* Intelligence Information.

References

Blackburn, N. Glenn. "Computers: A Counterintelligence Concern." Unpublished paper provided to the editors. Washington, DC, 1987.

Department of Defense, Joint Chiefs of Staff. *Department of Defense Dictionary of Military and Related Terms.* Washington, DC: GPO, 1986.

Godson, Roy, ed. *Intelligence Problems for the 1980s, Number 1: Elements of Intelligence.* Rev. ed. Washington, DC: National Strategy Information Center, 1983.

—**DATA ARRAY** is a statistical or quantitative methodological term that is often used in intelligence analysis. It means the arrangement of data by observations in either ascending or descending order. *See also:* Data.

References

Blackburn, N. Glenn. "Computers: A Counterintelligence Concern." Unpublished paper provided to the editors. Washington, DC, 1987.

Laqueur, Walter. *A World of Secrets.* New York: Basic Books, 1985.

—**DATA BASE** is a term used in artificial intelligence and computer-based systems and means the information that is stored in a computer for subsequent retrieval. *See also:* Data.

References

Godson, Roy, ed. *Intelligence Problems for the 1980s, Number 1: Elements of Intelligence.* Rev. ed. Washington, DC: National Strategy Information Center, 1983.

Kent, Sherman. *Strategic Intelligence for American World Policy.* Princeton, NJ: Princeton University Press, 1966.

Laqueur, Walter. *A World of Secrets.* New York: Basic Books, 1985.

Mishkoff, Henry C. *Understanding Artificial Intelligence.* Indianapolis, IN: Howard W. Sams, 1985.

—**DATA CHAIN,** in intelligence automation, is a name or title given to the use of a combination of two or more logically related standard data elements, data use identifiers, or other data chains. For example, the data chain "Date" is made from the combination of the data elements "Year," "Month," and "Day," in that order. *See also:* Data.

References

Department of Defense, Defense Intelligence Agency. *Defense Intelligence Agency Manual 65-18*. Washington, DC: DIA, 1984.

Laqueur, Walter. *A World of Secrets*. New York: Basic Books, 1985.

—**DATA ENCRYPTION STANDARD (DES)** in communications security (COMSEC), means an unclassified crypto-algorithm that is published by the National Bureau of Standards for the protection of certain U.S. government information. *See also:* Communications Security.

References

Blackburn, N. Glenn. "Computers: A Counterintelligence Concern." Unpublished paper provided to the editors. Washington, DC, 1987.

Martin, Paul H. "Communications-Computer Security." *Journal of Electronic Defense* (June 1987).

Muzerall, Joseph V., and Carty, Thomas P. "COMSEC and Its Need for Key Management." *DP&CS* (Spring 1987).

Ware, Willis H. "Information Systems, Security, and Privacy." *EDUCOM Bulletin* (Summer 1984).

—**DATA HANDLING SYSTEM ARCHITECTURE** is a framework of data handling technology that is designed to receive, route, present, manipulate, store, retrieve, and disseminate data in a functional architecture. *See also:* Automatic Data Processing, Department of Defense Intelligence Information System.

References

Department of Defense, Defense Intelligence Agency. *Defense Intelligence Agency Manual*. Washington, DC: DIA, 1987.

—**DATA ITEM,** in intelligence automation, is a subunit of descriptive information or value that is classified under a data element. For example, the data element "Army Service Grade" contains data elements such as "sergeant," "captain," "major," and "colonel." *See also:* Data.

References

Department of Defense, Defense Intelligence Agency. *Defense Intelligence Agency Manual 65-18*. Washington, DC: DIA, 1984.

Department of Defense, Joint Chiefs of Staff. *Department of Defense Dictionary of Military and Related Terms*. Washington, DC: GPO, 1986.

Laqueur, Walter. *A World of Secrets*. New York: Basic Books, 1985.

—**DATA POINT** is a statistical or quantitative methodological term often used in intelligence analysis. It is a single observation from a data set. *See also:* Data.

References

Blackburn, N. Glenn. "Computers: A Counterintelligence Concern." Unpublished paper provided to the editors. Washington, DC, 1987.

Godson, Roy, ed. *Intelligence Problems for the 1980s, Number 1: Elements of Intelligence*. Rev. ed. Washington, DC: National Strategy Information Center, 1983.

—**DATA SET** is a statistical or quantitative methodological term often used in intelligence analysis. It is a correlation of data. *See also:* Data.

References

Blackburn, N. Glenn. "Computers: A Counterintelligence Concern." Unpublished paper provided to the editors. Washington, DC, 1987.

Godson, Roy, ed. *Intelligence Problems for the 1980s, Number 1: Elements of Intelligence*. Rev. ed. Washington, DC: National Strategy Information Center, 1983.

—**DATA SYSTEM,** in intelligence automation, is the combination of personnel efforts, forms, formats, instructions and procedures, data elements and related codes, communications, and data processing equipment that provides an organized and interconnected means, whether automated, manual, or a mixture of these, for recording, collecting, processing, and communicating data. *See also:* Automatic Data Processing, Department of Defense Intelligence Information System.

References

Department of Defense, Defense Intelligence Agency. *Defense Intelligence Agency Manual 65-18*. Washington, DC: DIA, 1984.

Godson, Roy, ed. *Intelligence Problems for the 1980s, Number 1: Elements of Intelligence*. Rev. ed. Washington, DC: National Strategy Information Center, 1983.

Kent, Sherman. *Strategic Intelligence for American World Policy*. Princeton, NJ: Princeton University Press, 1966.

Laqueur, Walter. *A World of Secrets*. New York: Basic Books, 1985.

—**DATA USE IDENTIFIER,** in intelligence automation, is the name given to the use of a data element in a data system. For example, the data element "Country of the World," when used in a system, may be assigned the data use identifier "Country of Location" or "Country of Allegiance." *See also:* Data System.

References

Department of Defense, Defense Intelligence Agency. *Defense Intelligence Agency Manual 65-18.* Washington, DC: DIA, 1984.

—**DAVIES, ALLEN,** a former Air Force staff sergeant, was arrested on October 27, 1986, while attempting to deliver classified U.S. military information to an undercover agent who was posing as a Soviet official. He was tried, convicted, and sentenced to five years in prison.

References

Allen, Thomas B., and Polmar, Norman. *Merchants of Treason: America's Secrets for Sale.* New York: Delacorte Press, 1988.

Crawford, David J. *Volunteers: The Betrayal of National Defense Secrets by Air Force Traitors.* Washington, DC: GPO, 1988.

—**D-DAY** is the unnamed day on which a particular operation commences or is to commence. An operation may be the commencement of hostilities, the date of a major military effort, the execution date of an operation, or the date the operations phase is implemented by land assault, air strike, naval bombardment, parachute assault, or amphibious assault. The highest command or headquarters responsible for coordinating the planning will specify the exact meaning of D-day within the aforementioned definition. If more than one event is mentioned in a single plan, the secondary events will be keyed to the primary event by adding or subtracting days as necessary. The letter "D" will be the only one used to denote the above. The command or headquarters directly responsible for the execution of the operation, if other than the one coordinating the planning, will do so in light of the meanings specified by the highest planning headquarters. Time in plans will be indicated by a letter that shows the unit of time employed and figures, with a minus or a plus sign, to indicate the time before or after the referenced event. For example, if "D" is for a particular day and "H" for an hour, D+7 means seven days after D-day, and H-2 means two hours before "H" hour.

References

Department of Defense, Joint Chiefs of Staff. *Department of Defense Dictionary of Military and Related Terms.* Washington, DC: GPO, 1986.

—**DEAD DROP** is a term used in clandestine and covert intelligence operations. It is a covert procedure in which an agent leaves a message or material in a safe location for retrieval by another agent or controller at a later time. In FBI terminology, a dead drop is also called a dead letter box (DLB) or simply a drop. *See also:* Accommodation Address, Letter Drop, Live Letter Boxes, Live Letter Drops, Mail Cover.

References

Becket, Henry S. A. *The Dictionary of Espionage: Spookspeak into English.* New York: Stein and Day, 1986.

Godson, Roy, ed. *Intelligence Problems for the 1980s, Number 1: Elements of Intelligence.* Rev. ed. Washington, DC: National Strategy Information Center, 1983.

Kessler, Ronald. *Spy vs. Spy: Stalking Soviet Spies in America.* New York: Charles Scribner's Sons, 1988.

Turner, Stansfield. *Secrecy and Democracy: The CIA in Transition.* Boston: Houghton Mifflin, 1985.

—**DEBRIEFING,** a general intelligence term, is an interview of someone who has completed an intelligence assignment or one who has intelligence information. In respect to intelligence employees, it is a process of informing an individual that: (1) he or she no longer has a need to know classified material; or (2) he or she continues to be bound by all the security directives and public law that pertains to the security of the classified information that the person has seen unless the person has been released from that obligation by competent authority.

References

Clancy, Tom. *The Cardinal of the Kremlin.* New York: Putnam, 1988.

Godson, Roy, ed. *Intelligence Problems for the 1980s, Number 1: Elements of Intelligence.* Rev. ed. Washington, DC: National Strategy Information Center, 1983.

Kessler, Ronald. *Spy vs. Spy: Stalking Soviet Spies in America.* New York: Charles Scribner's Sons, 1988.

—**DECEPTION** is a general intelligence term that has applicability but different meanings in Army tactical intelligence, in counterintelligence, counterespionage, and counterinsurgency, and in signals intelligence, communications security, communications intelligence, operations security, and signals analysis. (1) Deception encompasses those measures that mislead the enemy by manipulating, distorting, or falsifying information or evidence with the hope of prompting him to react in a manner that is prejudicial to his interests. (2) Deception is also an Army tactical intelligence (TACINT) term that means the deliberate planning of interdependent activities in order to deny the enemy the ability to collect factual information and to provide him with misleading or false information in order to achieve tactical surprise. The term "deception" denotes active manipulation, distortion, or falsification of evidence to the enemy concerning U.S. intentions and capabilities, while denying him true information. (3) Deception is also a counterintelligence term used in the context of automatic data processing (ADP) system security. It refers to a situation in which a penetrator of an ADP system, using his own computer equipment, masquerades as a legitimate user. He must have access to system procedural guides in order to succeed if proper hardware and software security controls are built into the system. *See also:* Communications Deception, Electronic Countermeasures, Manipulative Deception.

References

American Bar Association. *Oversight and Accountability of the U.S. Intelligence Agencies: An Evaluation.* Washington, DC: ABA, 1985.

Department of Defense, U.S. Army. *Counter-Signals Intelligence (C-SIGINT) Operations.* Field Manual FM 34-62, Washington, DC: Headquarters, Department of the Army, 1986.

———. *Intelligence and Electronic Warfare Operations.* Field Manual FM 34-1. Washington, DC: Headquarters, Department of the Army, 1984.

———. *Military Intelligence Battalion Combat Electronic Warfare and Intelligence (Aerial Exploitation) (Corps).* Field Manual FM 34-22. Washington, DC: Headquarters, Department of the Army, 1984.

———. *Military Intelligence Battalion (Combat Electronic Warfare Intelligence) (Division).* Field Manual FM 34-10. Washington, DC: Headquarters, Department of the Army, 1981.

———. *Military Intelligence Battalion (CEWI) (Operations) (Corps).* Field Manual FM 34-21. Washington, DC: Headquarters, Department of the Army, 1982.

———. *Military Intelligence Battalion (CEWI) (Tactical Exploitation) (Corps): Counterintelligence, Interrogation, Electronic Warfare.* Field Manual FM 34-23. Washington, DC: Headquarters, Department of the Army, 1985.

———. *Military Intelligence Company (Combat Electronic Warfare and Intelligence) (Armored Cavalry Regiment/Separate Brigade).* Field Manual FM 34-30. Washington, DC: Headquarters, Department of the Army, 1983.

———. *Military Intelligence Group (Combat Electronic Warfare and Intelligence) (Corps).* Field Manual FM 34-20. Washington, DC: Headquarters, Department of the Army, 1983.

Godson, Roy, ed. *Intelligence Problems for the 1980s, Number 1: Elements of Intelligence.* Rev. ed. Washington, DC: National Strategy Information Center, 1983.

———. *Intelligence Problems for the 1980s, Number 2: Analysis and Estimates.* Washington, DC: National Strategy Information Center, 1980.

Laqueur, Walter. *A World of Secrets.* New York: Basic Books, 1985.

Lefever, Ernest W., and Godson, Roy. *The CIA and the American Ethic: An Unfinished Debate.* Washington, DC: Ethics and Public Policy Center, Georgetown University, 1979.

U.S. Congress. Senate. *Final Report of the Senate Select Committee to Study Government Operations with Respect to Intelligence Activities.* Report 94-755. Book I, Foreign and Military Intelligence. Washington, DC: GPO, 1976.

—**DECEPTION JAMMER** is a term used in signals intelligence (SIGINT). It is a specialized type of radar jammer used primarily against weapons control radars and missile homing systems. It attempts to create a "more profitable target" for the weapon to home in on, rather than attempting to obliterate the target information. *See also:* Jammer.

References

Laqueur, Walter. *A World of Secrets.* New York: Basic Books, 1985.

—**DECEPTION MATERIAL** is a term used in clandestine and covert intelligence operations. Deception material is information passed to an intelligence service or to a government that is deliberately meant to mislead that party.

References

Kessler, Ronald. *Spy vs. Spy: Stalking Soviet Spies in America.* New York: Charles Scribner's Sons, 1988.

—**DECHAMPLAIN, RAYMOND GEORGE,** was apprehended in Bangkok, Thailand while on his way to deliver classified material to a Soviet agent. An administrative specialist, DeChamplain had passed large quantities of classified material while stationed at the Joint U.S. Military Advisory Group (JUSMAG) in Bangkok. He had received $3,800 from the Soviets, with promises of additional payments. He was tried, convicted, and sentenced to fifteen years in confinement. Upon review, the sentence was reduced to seven years at hard labor.

References

Crawford, David J. *Volunteers: The Betrayal of National Defense Secrets by Air Force Traitors.* Washington, DC: GPO, 1988.

—**DECIPHER,** in communications security (COMSEC), means to convert enciphered text into plain text by means of a cipher system. *See also:* Cipher, Code, Communications Security (COMSEC), Decode, Encipher, Encode.

References

Blackburn, N. Glenn. "Computers: A Counterintelligence Concern." Unpublished paper provided to the editors. Washington, DC, 1987.

Department of Defense, Defense Intelligence College. *Glossary of Intelligence Terms and Definitions.* Washington, DC: DIC, 1987.

Godson, Roy, ed. *Intelligence Problems for the 1980s, Number 1: Elements of Intelligence.* Rev. ed. Washington, DC: National Strategy Information Center, 1983.

Laqueur, Walter. *A World of Secrets.* New York: Basic Books, 1985.

Martin, Paul H. "Communications-Computer Security." *Journal of Electronic Defense* (June 1987).

Muzerall, Joseph V., and Carty, Thomas P. "COMSEC and Its Need for Key Management." *DP&CS* (Spring 1987).

Ware, Willis H. "Information Systems, Security, and Privacy." *EDUCOM Bulletin* (Summer 1984).

—**DECISION UNITS** is an intelligence budgeting term. The Carter administration's use of Zero Based Budgeting required the intelligence activities to be divided into specific units. For example, all manpower, administrative, and other supporting costs of a 200-man analysis group could be in one unit; a major computer for the group could be in another unit. These units were then ranked in priority order. When the President decided on the total budget, the units were funded in priority order until the budget was committed. The remaining units (and, therefore, their activities) were dropped. Although the director of Central Intelligence grouped National Foreign Intelligence Program (NFIP) activities into small units that were focused on intelligence, the Department of Defense included its Intelligence Related Activities (IRA) projects into very large units that also contained nonintelligence activities. Thus, decision units were needed to provide some type of correlating mechanism between the different systems. *See also:* Appropriation or Fund Account.

References

Pickett, George. "Congress, the Budget, and Intelligence." In *Intelligence Policy and Process,* edited by Alfred C. Maurer, Marion D. Turnstall, and James M. Keagle. Boulder, CO: Westview Press, 1985.

—**DECLASSIFICATION** is a general intelligence term. It is the result of a decision to declare official information unclassified on the basis that its disclosure is no longer detrimental to national security. It is thereby removed from the protective status that has been afforded by its security classification. *See also:* Access, Authorized, Classification, Classified Information, Code Word, Collateral, Compromise, Disclosure, Downgrade, Freedom of Information Act, Limited Access Area, Need-to-Know, Need-to-Know Principle, No-Lone Zone, Nondisclosure Agreement, Nondiscussion Area, Sanitization, Sanitize, Sanitized Area, Security Certification, Security Classification, Sensitive Compartmented Information, Sensitive Compartmented Information Facility, Two-Person Control.

References

American Bar Association. *Oversight and Accountability of the U.S. Intelligence Agencies: An Evaluation.* Washington, DC: ABA, 1985.

Department of Defense, Defense Intelligence College. *Glossary of Intelligence Terms and Definitions.* Washington, DC: DIC, 1987.

Department of Defense, Information Security Oversight Office. *Directive No. 1: National Security Information.* As reproduced in *Federal Register,* June 25, 1982, pp. 27836–27841.

Department of Defense, Joint Chiefs of Staff. *Department of Defense Dictionary of Military and Related Terms.* Washington, DC: GPO, 1986.

Godson, Roy, ed. *Intelligence Problems for the 1980s, Number 1: Elements of Intelligence*. Rev. ed. Washington, DC: National Strategy Information Center, 1983.

Turner, Stansfield. *Secrecy and Democracy: The CIA in Transition*. Boston: Houghton Mifflin, 1985.

—**DECLASSIFICATION AND DOWNGRADING INSTRUCTIONS** are notations that appear on a classified document that will tell when the material may be downgraded to a lower classification and when it may be declassified. In the case of sensitive information that cannot be automatically declassified, there will be a notation indicating that the document is excluded or exempt from the general downgrading system and must be reviewed before it is downgraded or declared to be unclassified. *See also:* Declassification.

References

Department of Defense, Information Security Oversight Office. *Directive No. 1: National Security Information*. As reproduced in *Federal Register*, June 25, 1982, pp. 27836–27841.

—**DECODE** is a term used in clandestine and covert intelligence operations and in signals intelligence, communications security, communications intelligence, operations security, and signals analysis. It means to convert an encoded message back into plain text by using a code system. *See also:* Cipher, Code, Communications Security (COMSEC), Decipher, Encipher, Encode.

References

Clancy, Tom. *The Cardinal of the Kremlin*. New York: Putnam, 1988.

Department of Defense, Defense Intelligence College. *Glossary of Intelligence Terms and Definitions*. Washington, DC: DIC, 1987.

Godson, Roy, ed. *Intelligence Problems for the 1980s, Number 1: Elements of Intelligence*. Rev. ed. Washington, DC: National Strategy Information Center, 1983.

Laqueur, Walter. *A World of Secrets*. New York: Basic Books, 1985.

—**DECOMPARTMENTATION** is a general intelligence term. It is the removal of information from a compartmentation system without altering the information. *See also:* Compartmentation.

References

Department of Defense, Defense Intelligence College. *Glossary of Intelligence Terms and Definitions*. Washington, DC: DIC, 1987.

Laqueur, Walter. *A World of Secrets*. New York: Basic Books, 1985.

Treverton, Gregory F. *Covert Action: The Limits of Intervention in the Postwar World*. New York: Basic Books, 1987.

Turner, Stansfield. *Secrecy and Democracy: The CIA in Transition*. Boston: Houghton Mifflin, 1985.

—**DECRYPT** is a term used in signals intelligence, communications security, communications intelligence, operations security, and signals analysis. It means to transform an encrypted communication into plain text by means of a cryptosystem. The term decrypt encompasses the terms decipher and decode. *See also:* Cipher, Code, Communications Security, Decipher, Decode, Encipher, Encode, Encrypt.

References

Department of Defense, Defense Intelligence College. *Glossary of Intelligence Terms and Definitions*. Washington, DC: DIC, 1987.

Godson, Roy, ed. *Intelligence Problems for the 1980s, Number 1: Elements of Intelligence*. Rev. ed. Washington, DC: National Strategy Information Center, 1983.

Martin, Paul H. "Communications-Computer Security." *Journal of Electronic Defense* (June 1987).

Muzerall, Joseph V., and Carty, Thomas P. "COMSEC and Its Need for Key Management." *DP&CS* (Spring 1987).

U.S. Congress. Senate. *Final Report of the Senate Select Committee to Study Government Operations with Respect to Intelligence Activities. Report 94-755. Book I, Foreign and Military Intelligence*. Washington, DC: GPO, 1976.

—**DEDICATED MODE.** An automatic data processing (ADP) system operates in a dedicated mode when the central computer facility and all of its dedicated peripheral devices and remote terminals are exclusively used and controlled by a specific user, or group of users, for the processing of one particular type of sensitive compartmented information (SCI). All other users with access to the system will have to meet the appropriate security and need-to-know requirements in order to use the system. *See also:* Sensitive Compartmented Information, Sensitive Compartmented Information Facility.

References

Martin, Paul H. "Communications-Computer Security." *Journal of Electronic Defense* (June 1987).

Muzerall, Joseph V., and Carty, Thomas P. "COMSEC and Its Need for Key Management." *DP&CS* (Spring 1987).

—**DEFECTION,** in FBI terminology, is an abandonment of loyalty, allegiance, or duty to one's country. *See also:* Co-opted Worker, Co-optees, Defector, Informant, Inside Man, Recruitment, Recruitment in Place, Walk-in.

References

Godson, Roy, ed. *Intelligence Problems for the 1980s, Number 1: Elements of Intelligence.* Rev. ed. Washington, DC: National Strategy Information Center, 1983.

Kessler, Ronald. *Spy vs. Spy: Stalking Soviet Spies in America.* New York: Charles Scribner's Sons, 1988.

—**DEFECTOR** is a term used in clandestine and covert intelligence operations to describe a person who has deserted his cause or his country for political or other reasons. He may have information of interest to U.S. intelligence. The official U.S. definition says that the defector is outside his nation's jurisdiction and control and is unwilling to return; however, this is not always the case. For example, while a "walk-in defector" arrives unannounced and brings information with him, a "defector in place" may play the role of a defector, but may actually be an agent who continues to work for his cause or country.

Handling defectors is one of the more difficult tasks of an intelligence agency. The first problem is to establish that the defector is genuine and not an agent. This is not an easy endeavor, and in some cases it is never determined with certainty. For example, in the case of Nicholas Shadrin, a Soviet naval officer who defected to the United States, it appears that the U.S. government was convinced of his authenticity. However, years later, Shadrin was picked up by the KGB in Vienna in an incident that is still controversial.

Once a defector's bonafides are established, the intelligence agency will often try to convince him to remain in place in his job and country so that he can pass along intelligence information. Henry Becket notes that this approach is sometimes successful and can produce dramatic results. For example, the CIA convinced Soviet colonel Oleg Penkovsky to continue working in his assigned position for almost two years after he indicated that he wanted to defect. During that time, he passed along some of the USSR's most guarded secrets. However, it is far more likely that the defector will refuse and will demand asylum. In this case, the intelligence agency must make several determinations. Defectors will involve great expenses in order to transport them safely to the West, debrief them, and then reestablish them. Here, a defector's rank or position will often determine his intelligence value and, with it, his conveyance to freedom.

Once a defector is accepted by an intelligence service and is brought to safety, he is then "debriefed." This generally involves many months of interviews, in which the defector's information is checked and rechecked in order to determine its validity. After his knowledge is exhausted, he is relocated and given a new identity and a living subsidy for several years so that he can reestablish himself.

Becket notes that Western intelligence publicizes only a fraction of all those who defect each year, and the Soviet Union is therefore seldom absolutely certain of the whereabouts of a Soviet officer or civilian who disappears. The usual Soviet approach in such situations is to state publicly that the defector has died in an accident. If news of the defection is released by the Western press, then the approach will shift to vilifying the individual. These attacks can range from accusations of theft and sexual deviation to such minor flaws as abusing his family or psychological problems.

Thus, while the potential intelligence value of a defector can be very high, he does not come without risks. A good agent in place, if accepted as a defector, can pass along information that can grossly mislead an intelligence organization. This, in turn, can not only affect dramatically the validity and accuracy of the intelligence produced, but can also, if the agent is discovered or revealed, jaundice the intelligence organization against future genuine defectors who have valuable information to reveal. *See also:* Defection; Disaffected Person; Emigré; Refugee; Penkovsky, Oleg; Shadrin, Nicholas.

References

Becket, Henry S. A. *The Dictionary of Espionage: Spookspeak into English.* New York: Stein and Day, 1986.

Deacon, Richard. *Spyclopedia: An Encyclopedia of Spies, Secret Services, Operations, Jargon, and All Subjects Related to the World of Espionage.* London: Macdonald, 1987.

Department of Defense, Defense Intelligence College. *Glossary of Intelligence Terms and Definitions.* Washington, DC: DIC, 1987.

Department of Defense, Joint Chiefs of Staff. *Department of Defense Dictionary of Military and Related Terms.* Washington, DC: GPO, 1986.

Kessler, Ronald. *Spy vs. Spy: Stalking Soviet Spies in America.* New York: Charles Scribner's Sons, 1988.

Turner, Stansfield. *Secrecy and Democracy: The CIA in Transition.* Boston: Houghton Mifflin, 1985.

U.S. Congress. Senate. *Final Report of the Senate Select Committee to Study Government Operations with Respect to Intelligence Activities. Report 94-755. Book I, Foreign and Military Intelligence.* Washington, DC: GPO, 1976.

—**DEFENSE ATTACHÉ (DATT)** is a member of the Defense Attaché Office, which is a part of a U.S. embassy. The defense attaché may be an Army, Navy, Air Force, or Marine Corps officer. He is the senior military officer in his attaché office and is responsible for the supervision of his office and for the attachés and other people assigned to it. *See also:* Defense Attaché Office, Defense Attaché System.

References

Godson, Roy, ed. *Intelligence Problems for the 1980s, Number 1: Elements of Intelligence.* Rev. ed. Washington, DC: National Strategy Information Center, 1983.

Kent, Sherman. *Strategic Intelligence for American World Policy.* Princeton, NJ: Princeton University Press, 1966.

Laubenthal, Sanders A. "Preparing 'the Team': Defense Attaché Training." *DIC Newsletter* (Winter 1986): 1–4.

—**DEFENSE ATTACHÉ OFFICE (DAO)** is a part of a U.S. embassy. It is composed of a defense attaché (DATT) and possibly one or more service attachés (Army attaché, air attaché, and/or naval attaché). *See also:* Defense Attaché System.

References

Godson, Roy, ed. *Intelligence Problems for the 1980s, Number 1: Elements of Intelligence.* Rev. ed. Washington, DC: National Strategy Information Center, 1983.

Kent, Sherman. *Strategic Intelligence for American World Policy.* Princeton, NJ: Princeton University Press, 1966.

Laubenthal, Sanders A. "Preparing 'the Team': Defense Attaché Training." *DIC Newsletter* (Winter 1986): 1–4.

—**DEFENSE ATTACHÉ SYSTEM (DAS)** trains, supports, and supervises the personnel and the Defense Attaché Offices that are found in U.S. embassies around the world.

The term "attaché" dates from the era when French was still the international language of diplomacy, and it designated an individual "attached" to his governmental representative overseas. The United States has had military attachés since 1872, when a U.S. naval officer was accredited in London. However, until the mid-1960s, each service maintained its own office in the embassy. At that time the Defense Intelligence Agency assumed operational control of all attachés and grouped them in one joint service Defense Attaché Office for each country. Each office is headed by a defense attaché (DATT), who is in charge of the office as a whole and is also the attaché for his own service. The service attachés, assistant attachés, and their staffs of warrant officers, noncommissioned officers, petty officers, and civilians serve in 96 Defense Attaché Offices in U.S. embassies worldwide. They function as a team, part of the larger "country team" under the ambassador.

The attaché role is fourfold. Attachés observe and report military and politico-military information that is readily available. In this sense, they are the information gatherers or collectors for the Joint Chiefs of Staff. Additionally, the attachés represent the Department of Defense and the military services; advise the ambassador on military and politico-military matters; and, in some countries, administer the military assistance and sales programs.

The size of the "team" can vary greatly. In some countries, the office may be as small as one officer; in others, such as those in the United Kingdom or France, there may be as many as fifteen or twenty people.

The preparation for an attaché assignment is extensive, but it varies in accordance with the requirements for a given country, the service, and the officer's existing knowledge. After a thorough screening by his or her service board, the prospective attaché is screened for assignment by the DAS. The attaché is then often sent to graduate school to become an area specialist in the country to which he will be assigned. He or she is then sent to the military's language school at Monterey, California, or to the State Department's Foreign Service Institute in Roslyn, Virginia, for language training. This is intensive training. The Russian language course, for example, is 47 weeks and purports to teach at a rate of one college semester of language every two weeks. The attaché then attends the Attaché Course at the Defense Intelligence College. Here the curriculum has been designed to give each graduate a sound base of knowledge concerning attaché duties, activities, and responsibilities— the knowledge that is essential for all attaché students regardless of his or her future position or duty location. This ranges from budget and fiscal operations of the Defense Attaché Office to procedures for handling U.S. Navy ship visits to foreign countries, from the organization of a diplomatic mission to family adjustment to the embassy lifestyle. Observation and reporting, representation and relations, and many other aspects of the Defense Attaché Office environment are included. In recent years, there has been an increased emphasis on security awareness and counter-terrorist action, including hands-on training in defensive driving. Additionally, there are guest speakers, field trips, practical exercises, and many hours allotted to individual country research.

In addition to training the attaché, there is extensive training available to the attaché's spouse. This focuses on the personal and professional aspects of the attaché mission and on the host country. The course is taken on a voluntary basis as time permits, and language training is also available.

If a prospective attaché is completely untrained when he or she enters the system, the training, including two years of graduate school, a year of language, and the attaché course and additional training can take up to four years. After the officer serves a tour as an attaché, he or she will likely return to the Defense Intelligence Agency for his or her next tour, so that the government can take further advantage of the training that it has invested in the officer.

In addition to the attachés, the Defense Attaché Office support staff also receives extensive training. The Defense Intelligence College offers a seven-week Attaché Staff Operations Course (ASOC) for noncommissioned officers, warrant officers, and civilian research technicians, that is virtually all professional training in attaché support, including budgeting, finance, housing, vehicles, support for the embassy, experience with a standardized worldwide file plan, and reporting formats. *See also:* Air Attaché, Army Attaché, Country Team, Defense Attaché.

References
Kent, Sherman. *Strategic Intelligence for American World Policy.* Princeton, NJ: Princeton University Press, 1966.

Laubenthal, Sanders A. "Preparing 'the Team': Defense Attaché Training." *DIC Newsletter* (Winter 1986): 1–4.

Von Hoene, John P. A. *Intelligence User's Guide.* Washington, DC: Defense Intelligence Agency, 1983.

—**DEFENSE CONDITION (DEFCON).** *See:* Defense Readiness Condition.

—**DEFENSE COUNTERINTELLIGENCE BOARD** coordinates the Department of Defense foreign counterintelligence activities. It is chaired by a representative of the deputy undersecretary of defense for policy.

References
Godson, Roy, ed. *Intelligence Problems for the 1980s, Number 1: Elements of Intelligence.* Rev. ed. Washington, DC: National Strategy Information Center, 1983.

—**DEFENSE DOCUMENT CENTER (DDC)** is an on-line system consisting of four data banks that are associated with the Department of Defense research, development, test, and evaluation (RDT&E) program. The information in the system includes technical summaries of research and development projects currently in production, formal reports on completed RDT&E projects sponsored by the Department of Defense, and descriptions of projects that are being produced by Department of Defense contractors. *See also:* Department of Defense Intelligence Information System.

References
Von Hoene, John P. A. *Intelligence User's Guide.* Washington, DC: DIA, 1983.

—**DEFENSE ESTIMATIVE BRIEF (DEB)** is prepared by the Defense Intelligence Agency's Directorate for Estimates. It is usually about two pages long and is a "mini-estimate" that tackles a contentious issue on a quick-reaction basis. *See also:* Estimates.

References

Brinkley, David A., and Hull, Andrew W. *Estimative Intelligence: A Textbook on the History, Products, Uses and Writing of Intelligence Estimates.* Columbus, OH: Battelle, 1979.

Godson, Roy, ed. *Intelligence Problems for the 1980s, Number 1: Elements of Intelligence.* Rev. ed. Washington, DC: National Strategy Information Center, 1983.

—**DEFENSE GUIDANCE (DG)** is the guidance that the secretary of defense provides the Department of Defense components in January of each year. It is a part of the budgeting process and contains his views after he has read the Joint Chiefs of Staff Joint Strategic Planning Document, which contains their views on military strategy and recommendations to be considered in the secretary's drafting of the DG. After it is coordinated, a final draft of the DG is issued in March. It contains an authoritative statement of the fundamental strategy, issues, and rationale underlying the defense program as seen by the leadership of the Department of Defense. It culminates the planning phase of the budget process and provides definitive guidance, including fiscal restraints, for developing the Program Objective Memorandum by the military departments of the defense agencies, and it continues as the primary guidance until it is revised or modified by subsequent secretary of defense decisions.

The secretary's guidance to the Department of Defense covers several areas, including policy guidance, views on strategy, force planning, resource planning, fiscal guidance, and his views on major issues.

All Department of Defense elements help to develop the DG. Drafting teams review and develop sections of the guidance, and a DG steering group and the Defense Resources Board resolve issues. The guidance is designed to link all the planning pieces together in a coherent package, and its purpose is to guide resource allocation decisions, to provide guidance to the services when they are developing their programs, and to provide guidance to the secretary of defense and the Joint Chiefs of Staff when they are conducting their program review. Thus, it is designed to guide resource allocation decisions that occur during the programming and budgeting phases.

Thus, the DG is fiscal guidance that is provided at the Total Obligational Authority (TOA) level for each of the next five years. (TOA is the total money required to execute each program.) This dollar total reflects presidential and Office of Management and Budget decisions concerning the total amount of real growth and the inflation rates to be used when developing the service program. This fiscal guidance provides the overall constraint, or dollar ceiling, within which the service program must be constructed. *See also:* Appropriation or Fund Account.

References

Godson, Roy, ed. *Intelligence Problems for the 1980s, Number 1: Elements of Intelligence.* Rev. ed. Washington, DC: National Strategy Information Center, 1983.

Pickett, George. "Congress, the Budget, and Intelligence." In *Intelligence Policy and Process,* edited by Alfred C. Maurer, Marion D. Turnstall, and James M. Keagle. Boulder, CO: Westview Press, 1985.

—**DEFENSE INDUSTRIAL SECURITY CLEARANCE OFFICE (DISCO)** is the Department of Defense office that is responsible for industrial security clearances for contractor personnel and for facility security and clearances. *See also:* Access, Authorized, Background Investigation, Billet, Clearance, Compartmentation, Compromise, Debriefing, Defense Security Briefing, Defense Investigative Service, Lawful Investigation, "Least Intrusive Means."

References

Allen, Thomas B., and Polmar, Norman. *Merchants of Treason: America's Secrets for Sale.* New York: Delacorte Press, 1988.

Godson, Roy, ed. *Intelligence Problems for the 1980s, Number 1: Elements of Intelligence.* Rev. ed. Washington, DC: National Strategy Information Center, 1983.

—**DEFENSE INTELLIGENCE AGENCY (DIA).** The mission of the DIA is defined as follows:
  • to satisfy the foreign military and military-related intelligence requirements of the secretary of defense, the Joint Chiefs of Staff, the Unified and Specified Commands, other Department of Defense components, and, as appropriate, nondefense agencies. This is done through internal production or through tasking other defense components and coordination with other intelligence agencies.
  • to provide military intelligence for national foreign intelligence and counterintelligence products.

- to coordinate all Department of Defense intelligence collection requirements for departmental needs.
- to manage and operate the Defense Attaché System.
- to provide foreign intelligence and counterintelligence staff support to the Joint Chiefs of Staff.

There are three aspects of the mission that have caused chronic problems for the agency. The first pertains to the number of organizations that it must support. The DIA is responsible to so many disparate entities that it has had difficulties focusing on its responsibilities, directing its resources, and satisfying all of its requirements. It must fulfill its responsibilities as the J-2 (or intelligence) arm of the Joint Chiefs of Staff and therefore must direct its attention to satisfying the national-level needs of the Washington community. However, at times the agency's preoccupation with this requirement has caused it to neglect its responsibilities to the field, specifically to the Unified and Specified Commands, and this had led to the infamous "intelligence shortfalls" or intelligence failures, where the agency failed either to foresee or to adequately report to the field commands indications of impending crises. The sheer number of entities that rely on the DIA remains a problem, which continued internal reorganizations in the agency have affected with mixed success.

The second problem concerns the many types of intelligence that the agency is responsible for. In general, it is responsible for the production of all military intelligence, biographical intelligence on military figures, transportation and telecommunications intelligence, military geographic intelligence, and scientific and technical intelligence, which it is to produce in concord with the scientific and technical organizations of the different services. In each category, it produces current, in-depth, estimative, and basic intelligence. The result is that there are a multitude of requirements demanding to be satisfied, which in turn creates significant managerial and budgetary problems, as the DIA attempts to continually prioritize thousands of competing requirements in hundreds of different categories. In sum, the situation is fraught with peril and, although the agency's managerial record has been impressive, shortfalls are bound to occur occasionally, and when they do, the adverse reaction is both counterproductive and demoralizing to the agency's leaders and staff.

The third problem pertains to the DIA's relationships with the services. Created in order to manage the service intelligence organizations and to provide or compel better communications between them, the agency has often been resented. The situation is even worse, because while it must rely on the services for all its military officers, which accounts for a significant portion of its staff, the services' detailing policies are often characterized by actions that are not beneficial to the agency and are detrimental to its success. In spite of this, the agency is expected to function and is continually compared to the Central Intelligence Agency, which has complete control over its personnel selection. In sum, given the above liabilities over which it has no control, it is noteworthy that the DIA has functioned as well as it has.

History.

The DIA was created by the secretary of defense in 1961. However, the planning for such an organization preceded this event by several years. The centralization of U.S. intelligence activities following World War II led to the creation of the Central Intelligence Agency and National Security Council in 1947 and of the National Security Agency in 1952. However, a lack of management efficiency and poor quality of intelligence products often characterized military intelligence after the war. In examining the national security structure, the 1948 Hoover Commission reported "disturbing inadequacies" in intelligence coordination and control. An amendment to the National Security Act of 1945, among other things, sought to improve coordination and better define the intelligence responsibilities of the Joint Chiefs of Staff (JCS). Numerous studies followed in the 1950s that reexamined the coordination and control issue as well as the organizational structure under which military intelligence activities operated.

In 1953, the secretary of defense, in an attempt to improve the coordination of the Department of Defense Intelligence Community, appointed an assistant to the secretary of defense for special operations (OSO). This individual was tasked with providing intelligence staff support to the secretary in respect to his duties as a member of the National Security Council. The OSO did not produce intelligence himself but was a point of coordination for Department of Defense intelligence activities and for liaison with the civilian Intelligence Community.

During this period, the Joint Chiefs of Staff had a very small intelligence staff, called the Joint Intelligence Group (JIG), which had been created at the end of World War II. However, due to its small size it was incapable of effectively coordinating the military service intelligence efforts.

Thus the three military departments operated separate intelligence organizations that were relatively autonomous. They separately collected, produced, and disseminated intelligence for their individual use. Additionally, each service provided its products to the secretary of defense, the Unified and Specified Commands, and other governmental agencies. There was little coordination between them, and there was little quality control over the intelligence that each produced. Additionally, the system was considered triplicative, costly, and did not provide for unified military intelligence estimates at any level of government. Rather, the service positions were often divergent and often reflected their parochial service views. Moreover, the services were opposed to an integration of the intelligence effort, as this would likely affect their relative strengths in the continuous interservice rivalry. This situation was continued until 1958, as each service separately collected, produced, and disseminated intelligence in support of its forces. The Defense Reorganization Act of 1958 was the result of several actions that showed concern for the vague authority of the secretary of defense. The act removed all doubts concerning the secretary's authority, while the Joint Chiefs of Staff assumed responsibility for intelligence support to the Unified and Specified Commands. The JIG became the J-2 of the Joint Staff. However, its small size forced it to delegate much of its support responsibility to the military services. In 1958, the national Intelligence Community also was significantly modified with the creation of the United States Intelligence Board. However, the prescribed procedures frequently required the secretary of defense to review the dissenting opinions of the service intelligence chiefs. The launch of Sputnik, and mushrooming technological advances—particularly in communications and information availability, missile gap theories, and increasing world tensions—underscored the need for a system that would provide reliable intelligence. Consequently, in 1959, Secretary of Defense Thomas S. Gates became concerned that the increased intelligence requirements of the Unified and Specified Commands, the Joint Chiefs of Staff, and the

Office of the Secretary of Defense were not receiving the proper emphasis. He asked the Joint Chiefs of Staff to review all the military requirements of all elements of the Department of Defense. Furthermore, in May 1960, President Eisenhower appointed a special task force to the Joint Study Group (JSG), to examine the organizational and managerial aspects of the Intelligence Community, including military intelligence coordination and cost effectiveness.

The JSG found that intelligence channels still followed the old chain of command from service headquarters to service components in the field, although the Defense Reorganization Act of 1958 had established a new operational chain of command from the secretary of defense through the Joint Chiefs of Staff to the commanders in chief. Additionally, after extensive investigation, the JSG found that improved coordination and resource control was needed. The JSG advanced the concept of a new intelligence organization as a primary point of contact for the military intelligence community that would have broad managerial powers over the intelligence programs and activities of Department of Defense components.

One of the recommendations of the task force was to bring the military intelligence organizations under the Department of Defense as the Defense Reorganization Act of 1958 had required.

The group's report also strongly urged that the above-described intelligence organization be created.

On February 8, 1961, Secretary of Defense Robert S. McNamara advised the Joint Chiefs of Staff of his decision to establish a Defense Intelligence Agency and tasked them with developing a concept plan that would extensively integrate the military intelligence efforts of all department elements. The JCS completed this assignment by July, and Department of Defense Directive 5105.21, "Defense Intelligence Agency," was published on August 1, and was to be effective on October 1, 1961.

According to the plan, the new Defense Intelligence Agency would report to the secretary of defense through the Joint Chiefs of Staff. It would be a union—not a confederation—of defense intelligence and counterintelligence activities, and it would not add administrative layering within the Defense Intelligence Community. The transfer of functions and resources from the services would be completed on a time-phased basis to avoid degrading the effectiveness of defense intelligence during the transition.

Thus the DIA was established to unify the intelligence efforts of the Department of Defense; strengthen Department of Defense capabilities for collection, production, and dissemination of intelligence; provide the most efficient allocation of Department of Defense resources; improve the management of those resources; and eliminate any unnecessary duplication of effort. Its mission was the continuous task of collecting, processing, evaluating, analyzing, integrating, producing, and disseminating military intelligence for the Department of Defense. The OSO was disestablished on October 31, 1961, and the DIA assumed its defense intelligence coordination duties.

The agency evolved on a carefully planned and phased schedule that required about three years before becoming fully operational in all assigned functional areas. Organizational milestones included:

Jan. 1, 1962: the Department of Defense Central Requirements Registry was established.

Jan. 3, 1962: an Excepted Service Appointment System was approved.

Nov. 2, 1962: the Defense Intelligence School was established. The school was activated on January 1, 1963.

November 30, 1962: a Mapping, Charting, and Geodesy Directorate was added to the agency.

Jan. 1, 1963: the agency's Production Center was activated.

Feb. 19, 1963: the Automatic Data Processing Center was established.

Feb. 1, 1964: the Intelligence Career Development Program was started.

Mar. 31, 1964: the agency's Dissemination Center became operational.

Apr. 30, 1964: the agency's Scientific and Technical Intelligence Directorate was established.

Dec. 12, 1964: the Defense Attaché System (DAS) was established by a Department of Defense Directive. The agency assumed responsibility for the DAS on July 1, 1965.

The DIA assumed the staff support functions of the J-2 Joint Staff on July 1, 1963, following the disestablishment of the J-2. The first major agency-wide reorganization occurred on November 15, 1966, in an effort to streamline the agency and improve the reaction time of those elements producing military intelligence.

The DIA was the most significant development in military intelligence since World War II, but it had shaky beginnings. The concept of a central intelligence authority within the Department of Defense was sound, but U.S. intelligence and the nation were embarking on a new and hazardous era. Two of the great issues of our times immediately faced the new agency—for example, the prospect of nuclear war over the placement of Soviet missiles in Cuba, and U.S. involvement in Vietnam. Moreover, the services' displeasure over the loss of functions and resources to the DIA, and concerns that tactical intelligence needs would not be met, placed additional pressure on the fledgling agency. As a result, during the 1960s, the DIA focused on organizational consolidation and on satisfying consumer requirements with quality products.

Throughout the 1960s, the Department of Defense studied many ways to improve defense intelligence, which led to the DIA's second major reorganization in July 1970. The early 1970s were transitional years in that the agency's focus shifted from the consolidation of internal and external management roles to that of establishing the agency as a credible producer of national intelligence. This proved difficult at first, since sweeping manpower reductions reduced the agency's manpower by 31 percent from 1968 to 1975, causing mission reductions and organizational restructuring. Defense intelligence underwent other changes.

The President's Blue Ribbon Defense Panel reported in July 1970 the need for a single entity within the Office of the Secretary of Defense with staff responsibility for all Department of Defense intelligence responsibilities, particularly in resource management. On November 3, 1971, an assistant secretary of defense (intelligence) was established, "to supervise defense intelligence programs . . . and to provide the principal point for management and policy coordination with the Director of Central Intelligence, CIA and other intelligence officials outside the Department of Defense."

In November 1971, President Nixon reorganized the Intelligence Community to improve its efficiency and effectiveness. The Presidential Directive extended the responsibilities of the director of Central Intelligence to "planning, reviewing, coordinating and evaluating all intelligence programs and activities" of the Intelligence Community, including the production of national intelligence and the preparation of a consolidated intelligence program budget to include tactical intelligence. Additional turbulence was created in the National Intelligence Community by an intense congressional review in 1975–76.

While the DIA remained unscathed by the congressional investigation, the impact on the overall Intelligence Community amounted to greater oversight and succession of legislative actions that would extend into the 1980s. The issuing of Executive Order 11905 in February 1976 prompted the third major reorganization of the agency in July 1976. In the first charter change since 1964, Department of Defense Directive 5105.21 was revised in December 1976 to recognize the DIA as the primary intelligence authority in military inputs to national intelligence products.

Agency milestones in the 1970s included:

Nov. 1, 1970: an independent directorate for producing military estimates was established.

July 2, 1972: the Defense Mapping Agency was created, thereby discontinuing the DIA's responsibility in mapping, charting and geodesy.

Oct. 30, 1974: a comprehensive overhaul of the DIA's production functions, organization, and management was begun.

Nov. 25, 1974: the J-2 support office was established to support the intelligence needs of the Joint Chiefs of Staff.

Dec. 2, 1974: Defense Intelligence Officers were established to act as the director's personal senior staff representatives on substantive intelligence matters.

Mar. 25, 1977: the final portion of the modernized National Military Intelligence Center became operational.

Jan. 24, 1978: Executive Order 12036 established the Intelligence Community as it currently exists, and clarified the DIA's national and departmental intelligence responsibilities.

July-Aug. 1979: an internal reorganization of the agency established the five current directorates. The charter revision of May 19, 1977 detailed the DIA's relationship with the Joint Chiefs of Staff and the Office of the Secretary of Defense. Specifically, staff supervision of the DIA was exercised for the secretary of defense by the under secretary of defense (research and engineering) with respect to resources and by the under secretary of defense for policy with respect to policy matters.

The congressional appropriation of funding for a new building in fiscal years 1981 and 1982 symbolized a new era of institutional maturity and achievement for the DIA. Groundbreaking occurred on April 21, 1981, and the Defense Intelligence Analysis Center became operational in 1984. As the DIA entered the 1980s, resources became less available than in 1961, but capabili-

ties were greater. Emphasis on automated data systems to keep stride with the worldwide explosion of information and technology elevated the DIA's stake in the formulation of national security policy. A greater role in tactical as well as national intelligence, emerging concern for looking beyond the near-term, the advent of a Defense Intelligence Senior Executive Service, and the growing credibility of the agency's products signaled a coming of age for the organization.

As of 1990, the mission of the DIA is to satisfy the foreign military and military-related intelligence requirements of the secretary of defense, the Joint Chiefs of Staff, the Unified and Specified Commands, other defense components, and, as appropriate, nondefense agencies. This is done through internal production or through other defense components in coordination with other intelligence agencies. Moreover, the DIA provides military intelligence for national foreign intelligence and counterintelligence products; provides staff support to the Joint Chiefs of Staff; coordinates all Department of Defense intelligence collection requirements for departmental needs; and operates the Defense Attaché System. All of the DIA's functional responsibilities are encompassed within the broad areas of collection, production, and support. Although production is not the initial step in the intelligence process, it comprises the major portion of DIA resources. The DIA employs both military and civilian personnel, of which the latter comprise about 59 percent of the total. Among the military, one-third are enlisted. The Army accounts for 39 percent, the Navy for 23 percent, the Air Force for 36 percent, and the Marine Corps for 2 percent of the military manpower. Most officers and civilians hold bachelor's degrees and one-half and one-third, respectively, have earned master's degrees. This training includes the disciplines of business, the biological and physical sciences, mathematics, history, photography, medicine, logistics, the legal field, and data automation.

The Directors of the Defense Intelligence Agency.

From its inception to 1990, there have been ten directors of the DIA:

Joseph F. Carroll, Lieutenant General, U.S. Air Force, Oct. 1961–Sept. 1969.

Donald V. Bennett, Lieutenant General, U.S. Army, Sept. 1969–Aug. 1972.

Vincent P. De Poix, Vice Admiral, U.S. Navy, Aug. 1972–Sept. 1974.

Daniel O. Graham, Lieutenant General, U.S. Army, Sept. 1974–Dec. 1975.

Eugene F. Tighe, Jr., Lieutenant General, U.S. Air Force, Dec. 1975–May 1976.

Samuel V. Wilson, Lieutenant General, U.S. Army, May 1976–Aug. 1977.

Eugene F. Tighe, Jr., Lieutenant General, U.S. Air Force, Sept. 1977–Aug. 1981.

James A. Williams, Lieutenant General, U.S. Army, Sept. 1982–Oct. 1985.

Leonard Perroots, Lieutenant General, U.S. Air Force, Oct. 1985–Dec. 1988.

Howard E. Soyster, Lieutenant General, U.S. Army, Dec. 1988–present.

Organization.

In order to accomplish its duties, the Agency is organized into major elements as follows:

Command Element. Within the Command Element, there are three major positions: the deputy director, the executive director, and the secretariat.

The deputy director (DD) is to serve as the principal assistant to the director in all aspects of agency programs. His functions include: acting as the director's principal assistant; exercising supervision over all agency programs; coordinating the efforts of the major directorates; disseminating the guidance and decisions of the director; and representing the director during his absence.

The executive director (ED) is to serve as the principal coordinating staff assistant to the director and deputy director. The ED:

- is the principal staff assistant to the director and deputy director and has overall responsibility for the daily management of the agency's internal operations and activities.
- identifies, assigns, reviews, and implements the agency's short- and long-range plans involving the entire agency.
- coordinates the efforts of the major staff elements and insures that there is the most effective and efficient organizational management possible so that the agency can meet its operational responsibilities.
- oversees the acquisition, management, and direction of all the agency's resources.
- reviews all staff correspondence and actions that require Command Element approval.
- is the agency's senior official in respect to information security.

- supervises the Directorate for Security and Counterintelligence.
- coordinates and resolves internal management and operational issues that involve more than one directorate and similar issues involving coordination with another agency or department.
- supervises the Secretariat.
  The secretariat's mission is to assist the Command Element and to provide administrative and support services. In fulfilling this mission, the secretariat has the following duties:
- its Central Actions Office (CAO) receives and reviews all formal and informal requests for information. After determining which office in the agency should appropriately respond, it tasks that office to respond to the request, assigns a suspense date and ensures that the response is completed.
- its Protocol Office (PRO) advises on all matters concerning the proper ceremonial forms, courtesies, and etiquette that should be shown to senior visitors to the agency.
- its Executive Support Office (ESO) provides administrative support to the Command Element in the areas of correspondence management, security, personnel, budget, records management, and logistics.

The General Defense Intelligence Program Staff (D/GDIP). The mission of this staff is to act independently of the agency in all matters relating to developing and managing the program and to provide staff support to the director so that he can fulfill his responsibilities as the program's manager. Concerning this mission, the staff has the following duties. It:

- writes, publishes, and distributes the program manager's Guidance Memorandum and all other general defense policy and instructions concerning GDIP planning, programming, and budgeting.
- reviews and evaluates the general intelligence programs of the military services, the Unified and Specified Commands, and the agency to insure that they conform to current policy and program guidance, that they accomplish their goals and objectives, and that they stay within budget appropriations. It also develops program alternatives, if these are needed.
- prioritizes the programs for the director and recommends additional programs for the GDIP.

- prepares and presents the GDIP budget.
- prepares the GDIP congressional budget-justification books.
- prepares GDIP congressional testimony.
- tasks GDIP organizations to meet the program responsibilities and to respond when Congress requests information.
- identifies and studies resource issues within the GDIP and forms working groups, task forces, and ad hoc committees to deal with program issues and problems.
- tasks the agency, the military services, and other Department of Defense organizations for support for GDIP planning, programming, and budgeting actions.
- serves as the GDIP management office and coordinates among the relevant offices of the Office of the Secretary of Defense, the Office of Management and Budget, the Intelligence Community Staff, the military services, defense agencies, congressional oversight and appropriations committees, and other offices as necessary.
- coordinates and approves policy, plans, procedures, instructions, and tasking that has been imposed on GDIP activities and coordinates the program's planning and programming matters.
- tasks the agency's managers to support, evaluate, and advise on the effect of GDIP collection and other programs on intelligence production, on the compliance of these programs and their budgets with intelligence guidance, and on the relationships between the GDIP and other intelligence activities. The staff can also direct the managers to evaluate the existing intelligence capabilities.

The Inspector General (IG). The mission of the IG is to investigate and report on matters that affect the agency's performance of its mission as well as the state of the agency's efficiency, economy, and discipline, and to perform other duties that the director assigns. In fulfilling this mission, the IG:

- writes the policies and procedures for inspections, investigations, inquiries, requests for assistance, and complaints, and it monitors the agency's self-inspection system.
- insures that the agency complies with Executive Order 12333, United States Intelligence Activities; Executive Order 12065, National Security Information; the Privacy Act of 1974; and the Freedom of Information Act.

- inspects all DIA offices to promote economy, efficiency, and effectiveness and to detect and prevent fraud, waste, and abuse.
- conducts criminal investigations of known or suspected fraud within the agency that is not investigated by the Defense Criminal Investigative Service (DCIS).
- holds inspections to assess the performance of the Defense Attaché Offices and Liaison Detachments, as well as special inspections, investigations, and inquiries to determine the operational and administrative effectiveness of all elements of the agency.
- prepares and submits the required periodic and special reports to the Intelligence Oversight Board under the provisions of Executive Order 12334, President's Intelligence Oversight Board, and to Congress under the provisions of Public Law 95-452, the Inspector General Act of 1978.
- manages the agency's complaint program and receives and processes requests for assistance. This program does not include Civil Service grievances or discrimination in equal employment opportunity.
- is the focal point for Department of Defense hotline referrals that concern the agency.
- represents the agency in its dealings with other inspectors general, and equivalent inspection and investigation offices in the Department of Defense, the Joint Chiefs of Staff, the military services, the Department of State, the Central Intelligence Agency, and other governmental organizations.

The Defense Intelligence Officers (DIOs). The mission of the DIOs is to serve as the primary substantive intelligence advisors to the director and deputy director concerning their geographical and functional areas of responsibility. They represent the director and deputy director with intelligence consumers within the Department of Defense, with other members of the Intelligence Community, with other Executive departments and agencies, and with international organizations and foreign consumers. In fulfilling this mission, the DIOs:

- act as senior advisors to the director and deputy director and prepare specialized intelligence reports on issues that involve the assigned responsibilities of more than one element of the agency.

- support the key intelligence users in the Office of the Secretary of Defense and the Joint Chiefs of Staff in order to insure that the agency and the Intelligence Community respond to their intelligence requirements.
- interact with the National Intelligence Officers (NIOs) on substantive matters to insure that there is effective defense representation in national intelligence matters.
- serve as the director's and deputy director's personal representatives with the National Security Council, the Unified and Specified Commands, and the military services.
- represent the director and deputy director in intelligence negotiations and exchanges with allied and international organizations.
- review the defense intelligence products to insure quality, timeliness, and relevance to consumer needs.

The General Counsel (GC). The GC provides legal advice to the director concerning matters that affect the agency's ability to fulfill its mission. In accomplishing this mission, the GC:

- is the agency's legal advisor and reports directly to the director.
- provides legal advice on substantive and procedural questions concerning the DIA and concerning its relationships with other government agencies and private institutions.
- prepares the agency's position on legislation that affects it, including budget and fiscal legislation.
- represents the agency in legal and public policy matters and serves as the legal liaison officer with other departments and agencies.
- serves as the designated agency ethics official.
- interprets laws, Executive Orders, and Defense Department Directives.
- advises the director concerning the requirements to be met in areas allowing for administrative discretion.
- monitors the agency's responsiveness under the Freedom of Information and Privacy acts.
- coordinates the agency's defense with the Justice Department in all law suits.
- accomplishes the oversight functions assigned in the Executive Orders and in implementing agency regulations.
- coordinates and approves proposed acquisitions and is a member of the Contract Review Board.

Directorate for Security and Counterintelligence (OS). The missions of the OS are to produce counterintelligence and counterterrorism analysis, to provide counterterrorism staff support, and to provide coordination between the Office of the Secretary of Defense, the Joint Chiefs of Staff, agencies under the Joint Chiefs of Staff's cognizance, and the Defense Attaché System. It is also responsible for the agency's physical, TEMPEST, information, document, and personnel security programs; it manages the sensitive compartmented information (SCI) programs; it oversees the security of the agency's special access programs; and it serves as the principal Department of Defense advisor on TEMPEST matters. In fulfilling this mission, the OS:

- provides counterintelligence staff support to the Office of the Secretary of Defense, the Office of the Joint Chiefs of Staff, and the Unified and Specified Commands. It represents the chairman of the Joint Chiefs of Staff on national level counterintelligence working groups and manages the Department of Defense counterintelligence production program.
- acts as the counterintelligence staff for the Office of Joint Chiefs of Staff.
- manages antiterrorism and personnel and defensive security measures.
- manages the Department of Defense's Strategic MDCI Analysis Center.
- establishes policy, procedures, and quality control for the light armored vehicle program.
- reviews, coordinates, develops, and provides counterintelligence policy and guidance to the Unified and Specified Commands and the agency, including the Defense Attaché System.
- produces joint and defense-level counterintelligence analyses of foreign intelligence threats, maintains the Department of Defense counterintelligence data base, and publishes a counterintelligence production registry.
- provides defensive security, counterintelligence, and attaché training support for the Defense Attaché System and makes periodic security assistance visits to the Defense Attaché Offices and attaché residences worldwide.
- conducts pre-employment personnel security interviews, security inspections, and surveys of agency offices, runs the agency's security violation program, and conducts investigations when there have been unauthorized disclosures of classified information. It also conducts

investigations of allegations concerning agency personnel and runs the agency's security education, identification badge, and polygraph programs.

- manages the DIA TEMPEST program. In respect to sensitive compartmented information (SCI), it has several responsibilities, including developing Intelligence Community and Department of Defense personnel, physical, information, and TEMPEST security policies, accrediting all Department of Defense SCI facilities worldwide, conducting inspections and monitoring TEMPEST and the physical security of all DIA facilities, and providing guards at the agency's facilities.
- manages the SCI billets, indoctrinates and debriefs all personnel in the Office of the Secretary of Defense, the Office of the Joint Chiefs of Staff, and the defense agencies (except the National Security Agency) that have access to SCI material, and approves the use of SCI in tactical training exercises.
- establishes SCI security policy (except for the National Security Agency, which has its own security program) and oversees SCI security and training for the entire Department of Defense.
- manages the agency's polygraph program.

Defense Intelligence College (DIC). For details, see the Defense Intelligence College entry.

Comptroller (OC). The missions of the OC are to act as a focal point concerning all facets of the Planning, Programming, and Budgeting System (PPBS); to provide financial management services for the agency; to exercise overall staff responsibility for managing approved resources, management analysis, and cost analysis functions of the agency; to provide basic management services for the agency; and to act as agency competition advocate. In fulfilling its mission, the OC:

- reviews and analyzes DIA programs to insure that the optimal means of achieving the approved goals and objectives are included.
- prepares the Program Objective Memorandum (POM) for the DIA National Foreign Intelligence Program (NFIP) and non-NFIP requirements. It prepares agency rebuttals to director of Central Intelligence and secretary of defense decisions, and it incorporates the final decisions in the Five-Year Defense Program (FYDP) update and budget development.

- prepares and submits the DIA program and budget.
- prepares the agency's budget estimates, prepares and promulgates guidance and budget memoranda, and presents and defends the budget to the director of Central Intelligence, the Office of the Secretary of Defense, the Office of Management and Budget, and congressional committees, and prepares rebuttals as necessary.
- manages and monitors the execution of the agency's financial plan.
- conducts management assistance studies within the agency and insures that sound management principles are implemented.
- serves as the focal point for matters relating to defense audits of the use of agency resources.
- provides management services, including the Project Management System, the Contract Requirements Review Board, and the Commercial Activities Program.
- provides support to the Directorate for Resources and Systems concerning the areas of Information Resources Management and the agency's Internal Management Control Program pursuant to the Federal Manager's Financial Integrity Act.
- establishes the agency's financial policy and provides accounting for agency resources.
- acts as agency competition advocate pursuant to the Competition in Contracting Act.
- serves as the agency's focal point for debt collection and the credit card program.

Directorate for Operations, Plans, and Training (VO). The missions of the VO are to manage the collection requirements sent to the agency; to develop and operate an all-source collection management system; to develop and coordinate intelligence planning and support during crises and war; to direct the agency's functional managers for SIGINT, IMINT, HUMINT, MASINT, and training; to implement the Department of Defense HUMINT plan; to develop policy, plans, and programs for defense intelligence activities, including Tactical Intelligence and Related Activities (TIARA); to be responsible for the Department of Defense intelligence training program; to supervise the intelligence program concerned with intelligence on American POWs and MIAs; and to direct and supervise the directorates assigned to it. The VO is directly responsible to the agency's Command Element, and it oversees four additional directorates:

The Directorate for Collection Management (DC) manages the agency's collection resources in order to fulfill current and projected Department of Defense (DoD) intelligence requirements. In accomplishing this mission, the DC:

- processes all DoD intelligence collection requirements.
- coordinates with the military services, Unified and Specified Commands, and other DoD components to insure that the collection program is meeting their needs.
- operates the Collection Coordination Facility (CCF), which tasks the collection systems and operations.
- serves as the agency's point of contact on all matters pertaining to future collection requirements.
- develops or assists in developing national and DoD collection programs.
- insures coordination between DoD and other collection programs.
- provides guidance for certain sensitive security systems that protect collection sources, methods, and products.
- provides a DIA component to the Defense Special Missile and Astronautics Center (DEFSMAC).
- is responsible for imagery collection, processing, and dissemination for DIA and leads the DoD Intelligence Community in all imagery matters.

The Directorate for Training (OT) implements and directs all of the agency's internal training programs.

The Directorate for Command Support and Plans (CSP) provides on-scene representation for the DIA director to insure that the Unified and Specified Commands receive the intelligence support that they need, and it manages the agency's participation in TENCAP, NMIST, and other programs.

The Command Representatives (VO-CR) provide a focal point for coordination and monitoring the agency's activities with the Unified and Specified Commands and with NATO/SHAPE headquarters.

The Intelligence Communications Architecture Project Office (VO-I). The mission of the VO-I is to develop a worldwide communications architecture (INCA) to improve the dissemination of national and tactical intelligence to operational commanders in peace, crisis, and war. The VO-I accomplishes this mission in that it:

- develops an intelligence communications architecture and monitors related DoD communications architectural efforts.
- evaluates intelligence communications program proposals and initiatives to insure compliance with approved intelligence and communications architectures.
- examines intelligence communications deficiencies and shortfalls to provide a sound basis for a comprehensive upgrade of intelligence communications support programs, systems, and procedures.
- examines the advantages and disadvantages of providing intelligence support communications organic to the intelligence infrastructure.
- represents the director of the DIA in policy discussions related to intelligence communications requirements and architecture.
- develops technical proposals for contractual assistance and manages contractual activities.
- develops input to Defense Guidance that provides guidance to DoD activities on intelligence communications.
- develops the INCA program and conducts liaison with program managers, review authorities, congressional oversight committees, the Intelligence Community, and defense participants.
- recommends improvements in intelligence communications interoperability within the Intelligence Community and in support of operational commanders.
- reviews intelligence plans, programs, and budgets relating to DoD intelligence communications requirements.
- conducts exercises and field tests to evaluate new systems, concepts, and doctrinal alternatives.

The Directorate for Foreign Intelligence (VP). The mission of VP is to support Department of Defense (DoD) and national-level planners, decisionmakers, and operational elements by producing on a worldwide basis all-source, finished basic military intelligence, scientific and technical intelligence, and all DoD estimates and DoD contributions to the National Estimates. The VP also establishes policy for and manages DoD worldwide general, and scientific and technical intelligence production. Moreover, it directs the production of the DIA's contributions to national military intelligence in coordination with other DIA and external or-ganizations, as appropriate. Finally, the VP directs the development and insures the maintenance of the military intelligence data bases.

In fulfilling these missions, it oversees the production and affairs of its directorates and thus is responsible for the production of those items and services that are listed on their entries. In addition, the VP does the following:

- its staff operations (VP-S) support the deputy director for foreign intelligence (VP) and the subordinate directorates in determining their roles, organizational structures, and personnel resources. It also provides fiscal management support. Moreover, it recommends planning concepts, policies, and alternatives in the foregoing areas to sustain and improve current and future VP production. Finally, it measures VP mission accomplishment and expenditure efforts and coordinates to insure unity of effort concerning VP collection requirements.
- its International Applications Office (VP-1) is a focal point for analyzing and assessing Soviet strategic cover, concealment and deception, and related indirect conflict activities that are aimed at attaining Soviet strategic political-military objectives. It provides all-source finished intelligence and substantive, estimative intelligence on this subject area. It also participates in interagency studies.
- its Systems Interface and Applications Office (VP-SIA) provides overall staff responsibility for VP ADP systems policy, planning, programming, development, design, modification, refinement, application requirements, hardware prioritization and allocation, and user training. It is also the VP's focal point for ADP systems support activities. Finally, it manages the worldwide Automated Installations Intelligence File (AIF) and associated target intelligence programs. It is the Project Management Office for the Military Intelligence Integrated Data System (MIIDS).
- its Technical Production Office (VP-TPO) operates as the senior staff and management advisor and representative of the deputy director for foreign intelligence and director for all matters involving intelligence production support to electronic warfare and command, control, and communica-

tions countermeasures (CC³CM). It implements, manages, and coordinates intelligence production within the agency and with the National Security Agency (NSA) in support of the Joint Chiefs of Staff (JCS) "Plan for Integrated Intelligence Support to EW and C³CM," JSCM 46-85, and other JCS taskings as appropriate. It responds to policy guidance and designs and directs in-house agency VP assignments in a manner consistent with the JCS, commanders-in-chiefs', and military services' electronic warfare and C³CM programs and plans.

- its Threat Assessment Office (VP-TAO) provides a focal point for validated threat support for planning and systems acquisition activities.

The Directorate for Estimates (DE). The missions of the DE are to develop and produce all DoD intelligence estimates and DoD contributions to national intelligence and international estimates; to produce long-range threat forecasts and provide intelligence support for the DoD system acquisition process; to initiate estimates of future trends in foreign force structures, weapons systems, overall military capabilities, strategy, and defense policy to alert national and DoD planners and decisionmakers to developments that might affect the national security of the United States; and to produce special publications designed for senior-level Executive branch and DoD officials.

In fulfilling these missions, the DE:

- develops and produces DIA contributions to National Intelligence Estimates (NIEs), Special National Intelligence Estimates (SNIEs), and other national intelligence estimative papers within the purview of the National Foreign Intelligence Board (NFIB).
- develops and produces Defence Intelligence Estimates (DIEs) and Special Defense Intelligence Estimates (SDIEs) with the Service Intelligence Organizations and Defense Intelligence Estimative Memoranda (DIEMs) and Defense Estimative Briefs (DEBs).
- provides intelligence support to the OSD, JCS, and the Defense System Acquisition Review Council (DSARC) for the DoD system acquisition process. Serves as the intelligence advisor on the DSARC. Validates threat assessments produced by the military services for systems acquisition programs.
- develops and produces estimates to satisfy the requirements of the Joint

Strategic Planning System (JSPS) of the Joint Staff and the intelligence portions of National Security Council (NSC) requirements on the OSD and the JCS.

- develops and integrates DoD military intelligence estimates and estimative contributions for, and represents the NFIB and JCS at negotiations with international military organizations of which the United States is a member.
- develops and produces all-source, military-related intelligence publications specifically designed for senior-level Executive branch and DoD officials.
- provides the DIA interface with the National Intelligence Officers (NIOs), Central Intelligence Agency (CIA), Intelligence and Research (INR) Division of the Department of State, National Security Agency (NSA), and cognizant DoD elements on intelligence estimative issues.
- manages the development of automated data bases for force trend analyses and projections.

The Directorate for Research (DB). The DB's mission is to provide all-source military intelligence and wide-ranging geographical and functional expertise relevant to the intelligence needs of the national command authorities to the Office of the Secretary of Defense, to the Joint Chiefs of Staff, to Congress, to the commanders-in-chief of the Unified and Specified Commands, to the military services; and to other U.S. government agencies. In fulfilling this mission, the DB:

- produces all-source, finished military intelligence and maintains data bases on order of battle, military doctrine, strategy and tactics, C^3, equipment and logistics, biographs, economics, material production and assistance programs, terrorism, and narcotics trafficking.
- provides tailored, substantive intelligence for national-level studies, current/indications and warning intelligence, estimative intelligence products, special studies, and departmental or other consumer needs.
- formulates nuclear, conventional, and special warfare target intelligence policy and plans. Performs physical vulnerability research and bomb damage assessment studies.
- insures the development and maintenance of automated intelligence files. Serves as the point of contact and action office for mapping and charting matters.
- manages certain major Department of

Defense-wide intelligence systems, to include serving as executive agent for the worldwide Automated Installations System-Based Target Intelligence Programs, and the Delegated Production Program with its automated Defense Intelligence Order-of-Battle System.

- develops a single DoD general intelligence production program that focuses on priority defense needs, reduces unnecessary redundancy among producers, and improves the intelligence end product.
- provides major staffing, analytical, and administrative contributions to DoD public diplomacy programs.
- performs a wide variety of hosting, representational, and administrative functions in support of substantive conferences, intelligence exchanges, NATO dissemination programs, and other related projects.
- provides consultative and management expertise to staff and evaluate current and proposed NFIP and GDIP programs covering a wide spectrum of topical disciplines.
- provides direct analytical and staffing support to Department of Defense operational components, other agencies, and DIA directorates during contingency and crisis operations.
- provides staffing, scenario development assistance, and facilities support for U.S. and multinational military exercises.
- provides key participation in the directing and evaluation of collection. Assists in defense attaché training and provides direct on-station support to selected U.S. Defense Attaché Offices.

The Directorate for Imagery Exploitation (DX). The DX's mission is to be responsible for the exploitation of multisensor imagery and production of imagery-derived intelligence products in support of DIA analysts, the director of the DIA, the chairman of the Joint Chiefs of Staff, the secretary of defense and, as required, the Unified and Specified Commands, military departments, non-DoD agencies, and the Committee on Imagery Requirements and Exploitation (COMIREX). It also provides administrative management over DIA personnel assigned to the imagery exploitation elements of the National Photographic Interpretation Center (NPIC). In fulfilling this mission, the DX:

- provides time-sensitive, imagery-derived intelligence and detailed imagery analysis on foreign military capabilities, including order of battle, transportation and logistics, and force dispositions.

- produces tailored imagery-derived intelligence to support special operations, unconventional warfare planning, counterterrorism, and certain activities related to narcotics.
- produces third-phase basic imagery reports in accordance with National Tasking Plan responsibilities, as levied by COMIREX.
- participates in national-level imagery-related committees and chairs the DoD Imagery Interpretation Keys Committee.
- provides support services in the form of photogrammetric products and procedures, imagery equipment analysis maintenance and logistics, and editorial review for internal use and external customers, as required.
- develops and evaluates imagery exploitation equipment, support systems, applications, and techniques.
- conducts or participates in imagery quality and utility evaluations pertaining to new collection systems, formats, and films.
- exercises administrative management over DIA personnel assigned to the imagery exploitation elements of the National Photographic Exploitation Center.

The Directorate for Scientific and Technical Intelligence (DT). The DT's mission is to develop and maintain policies and procedures for DoD production of scientific and technical (S&T) intelligence covering foreign developments in basic and applied sciences and technologies with warfare potential; characteristics, capabilities, and limitations of all weapon systems, subsystems, and associated material; research and development related thereto; production methods employed in the manufacturing process; and overall weapon systems and equipment effectiveness. It also provides all-source finished scientific and technical intelligence to the office of the Secretary of Defense, Office of the Joint Chiefs of Staff, military departments, Unified and Specified Commands, and other DoD and non-DoD activities through direct production or through management and technical direction of the production efforts assigned to the military departments. In fulfilling this mission, the DT:

- reviews and validates the requirements for S&T intelligence; produces or tasks the S&T intelligence centers of the military departments in accordance with established production responsibilities;

and develops annual production schedules in coordination with the military departments to implement assigned production tasking.

- reviews and approves service-produced S&T intelligence and integrates it to provide selected assessments of combined military threat systems capabilities.
- coordinates the DoD Scientific and Technical Intelligence Information Services Program (STIISP), the Foreign Material Exploitation Program (FMEP), and the distribution of technical sensor data to DoD S&T production centers.
- reviews DoD S&T intelligence resources for validity and accuracy in terms of production requirements satisfaction and submits recommendations to appropriate resource management authorities.
- serves as a single point of contact within the DIA for all matters concerning the S&T intelligence production elements of the military departments.
- serves as the director's special assistant on matters concerning the DIA Scientific Advisory Committee (SAC) and provides administrative and technical support to the SAC.
- maintains liaison with other DoD agencies, the CIA, and other government elements to facilitate coordination and cooperation on S&T intelligence production matters and provides membership on National Foreign Intelligence Board (NFIB) technical committees, subcommittees, and working groups.

Directorate for JCS Support (JS). The missions of the JS are to serve as the DIA focal point for the Joint Staff; to maintain close relationships with all offices of the Organization of the Joint Chiefs of Staff (OJCS); and to insure prompt and responsive DIA participation in intelligence matters. In fulfilling these missions, the JS:

- provides all-source DoD and national-level current indications and warning (I&W) intelligence. It also provides analytical support to the National Military Intelligence Center (NMIC) on a 24-hour basis and interfaces with DoD and non-DoD agencies on substantive I&W matters.
- supervises the DoD I&W system and monitors its upgrade, including the development of new concepts, methodologies, and techniques to improve I&W performance.

- manages and operates the NMIC, a 24-hour-a-day I&W center that is responsible for providing time-sensitive intelligence to the National Military Command Center, secretary of defense, Joint Chiefs of Staff, Unified and Specified Commands, and military services. Additionally, it is tasked to provide support to the National Military Command Center (NMCC).

Directorate for OJCS Intelligence Support (JSJ). The JSJ serves as the DIA focal point for the Joint Staff. It maintains close relations with eleven offices of the Organization of the Joint Chiefs of Staff (OJCS) and insures prompt and responsive DIA participation and support in intelligence matters. In fulfilling this mission, the JSJ:

- insures that intelligence support, including intelligence policy planning, organization, and programming to the OJCS, is facilitated and expedited.
- retains primary responsibility for all actions assigned to the DIA by the JCS or OJCS, except for those that exceed the expertise of personnel assigned or require a level of work effort beyond the capabilities of the office to respond within the suspense date established.
- assigns collaborative action responsibilities to appropriate directorates when required to satisfy a Joint Staff requirement.
- conducts continuous coordination and liaison with the National Security Agency/Central Security Service representatives to insure their participation and cooperation in pertinent Joint Staff actions.
- provides direct, crisis-related intelligence support to the OJCS, related Unified Commands, and selected military forces.
- provides support and personnel to the National Military Command Center (NMCC), the Alternate Military Command Center (ANMCC), and the National Emergency Airborne Command Post (NEACP).
- is the DIA point of contact for intelligence support to Joint Special Operations Agency (JSOA) and Special Operations Forces (SOF). It also maintains the DIA focal point system and protects associated SPECAT information and material for the SOF.

Directorate for Current Intelligence (JSI). The JSI provides all-source DoD and national-level current indications and warning (I&W) intelligence. It provides analytical support to the Na-

tional Military Intelligence Center (NMIC) on a 24-hour basis. It interfaces with both DoD and non-DoD agencies on substantive I&W matters. In fulfilling this mission, the JSI:

- provides the Morning Summary, daily Defense Intelligence Notices, and Warning Reports and intelligence appraisals, as required. It also contributes to the National Intelligence Daily and provides I&W intelligence to the secretary of defense, the Joint Chiefs of Staff (JCS), and other DoD consumers.
- provides daily briefings on current intelligence subjects to the secretary of defense, Joint Chiefs of Staff, and other DoD officials.
- provides analytical support to the National Military Intelligence Center (NMIC) and the National Military Command Center (NMCC) on a 24-hour basis, including task forces.
- assesses, coordinates, produces, and integrates all-source current and I&W intelligence on a worldwide basis.
- provides current and I&W intelligence support to NATO and selected friendly foreign governments.
- prepares and presents intelligence briefings for selected foreign defense attachés in Washington, DC.

Directorate for Indications and Warning (JSW). The mission of the JSW is to provide authoritative advice and planning regarding the accomplishment of the agency's indications and warning (I&W) mission. In fulfilling this mission, the JSW:

- supervises the Department of Defense (DoD) I&W system and monitors its upgrade to include the development of new concepts, methodologies and techniques to improve I&W performance. It also maintains the effectiveness of the U.S. I&W effort.
- serves as the administrator of the Worldwide Warning Indicator Monitoring System (WWIMS).
- manages the advanced technological applications systems and establishes developmental concepts, long-term goals and priorities, and operational uses for systems already under development.
- participates in inter- or intra-agency study groups and task forces dealing with management issues relating to the NMIC and the DoD I&W system.
- develops analytical methodologies and automated systems to enhance the use of electronic intelligence (ELINT) and the all-source production of I&W and current intelligence.

- provides ELINT analytical support throughout the DIA and the DoD I&W system.

Directorate for NMIC Operations (JSO). The mission of the JSO is to manage and operate the National Military Intelligence Center (NMIC), a 24-hour-a-day I&W center, which is responsible for providing time-sensitive intelligence to the National Military Command Center (NMCC), secretary of defense, Joint Chiefs of Staff, Unified and Specified Commands and military services. To accomplish these services, the JSO:

- insures the continuity of operation of the NMIC. Provides policy and operational guidance to the five Alert Teams on duty.
- provides direct intelligence support to the NMCC.
- serves as the central point of contact for the DIA during nonduty hours.
- insures that the NMIC fully cooperates with other Washington area operations centers, including the White House Situation Room, Central Intelligence Agency, Department of State, and National Security Agency.
- participates in continuity of government planning concerned with crisis intelligence support.
- provides administrative and training support to all personnel assigned to the NMIC.
- coordinates the establishment of and provides administrative support for all intelligence task force organizations formed in response to DIA plans.
- manages the NMIC support system (NSS) and establishes policy and guidance for the use of other on-line ADP systems in the NMIC.
- supervises the operational application of the Worldwide Warning Indicator Monitoring System (WWIMS) in the NMIC.
- provides command briefings on NMIC operations to visiting officials.
- serves as the DIA representative to the DoD I&W system.

Directorate for External Relations (DI). The mission of the DI involves managing DIA key relationships; insuring effective and responsive intelligence support to key users of defense intelligence; being the liaison with policy-level consumers in the OSD, DoD, legislative branch, Unified and Specified Commands, foreign intelligence agencies and attachés, and offices and delegations involved in international arms control negotiations; and participating in key intelligence community committees. To accomplish this mission, the DI:

- serves as a single DIA focal point to provide tailored, anticipatory defense intelligence support to the secretary of defense as well as to other principals in the OSD and on the NSC staff.
- supports and interacts with Unified and Specified Commands and insures that all needs for national intelligence support are met. Serves as the DIA counterpart to Military Service TENCAP offices. Insures that all intelligence needs of the JCS exercise program are met, and represents the DIA on the Joint Exercise Control Group during JCS-directed exercises.
- insures that the defense intelligence requirements of the House and Senate are fully supported by the DIA; informs the intelligence branch of key defense intelligence issues; insures effective interaction between the DIA leadership and the legislative branch; serves as the DIA point of contact for public affairs and as a focal point for intelligence support to the assistant secretary of defense for public affairs.
- conducts foreign intelligence liaison, serving as the primary point of contact for foreign representatives conducting business with DoD activities; manages foreign disclosures and manages military exchange agreements with foreign intelligence agencies.
- provides defense intelligence support to U.S. policy offices and U.S. delegations involved in international negotiations of security issues.
- participates in and supports the National Foreign Intelligence Board (NFIB), National Foreign Intelligence Council (NFIC), Military Intelligence Board (MIB), and Critical Intelligence Problems Committee (CIPC).

Directorate for Resources and Systems (RS). The mission of the RS is to provide for the acquisition, management, and control of the DIA's support and resource management programs and to insure the effective and economical execution of the several Department of Defense management responsibilities assigned to the agency. The latter includes structuring a worldwide intelligence information systems architecture, managing the Department of Defense Intelligence Information System (DODIIS), and developing and maintaining intelligence systems mid- and long-range plans; managing a worldwide secure intelligence communications network, and managing and operating a worldwide intelligence dissemination program. In addition, the RS:

- provides agency-wide support services including comptroller activities for the agency; developing, implementing and operating agency computer systems and facilities; operating and maintaining agency communications files; operating, and maintaining a precision photographic laboratory and DoD central film depository; and providing and managing personnel and providing support services to include logistics, contract information, graphics, printing, information control, dissemination, central reference, and space administration. It also provides construction management of DIA facilities and serves in the capacity of head contracting activity for the agency.
- develops a worldwide intelligence communications architecture (INCA) to improve the dissemination of national and tactical intelligence to operational commanders in peace, crisis, and war.

Directorate for Technical Services and Support (RTS). The RTS provides the DIA and selected Department of Defense (DoD) intelligence activities with graphic arts products and services, including published intelligence books and pamphlets and audiovisual products. It provides DoD intelligence elements with a specialized intelligence reference library, intelligence document distribution, dissemination, and translation services. Additionally, it operates and manages the DoD central depository for all intelligence imagery, the National Area Coverage Data File, DoD imagery standards laboratory, and the DIA photographic laboratories. It provides imagery coverage analysis, specialized photographic reproduction, and imagery-technology support as services of common concern for the DoD and the Intelligence Community. Finally, it provides the DIA with centralized logistics, travel, engineering, and specialized management support services. In fulfilling this mission, the RTS:

- designs, formats, and prepares publications, graphics, and audiovisual presentations along with those composition and printing and video services that are required to support intelligence production programs.
- provides dissemination, bibliographic, translation, and intelligence reference services for the DoD and Intelligence Community on a worldwide basis. Indexes and catalogs intelligence publications and open-source documents.

- provides all DIA logistic services, including supply, maintenance, and property accountability.
- formulates and monitors intelligence imagery processing, handling, and identification standards for the DoD.
- provides centralized photographic processing and reproduction of new and archival imagery for the DIA, DoD, Intelligence Community, and other government activities.
- indexes all aerial imagery, maintains automated index files of all DoD and nationally acquired imagery, and provides coverage research on imagery held in the DIA's Central DoD Depository. Conducts worldwide DoD compartmented transshipment of specialized imagery materials and facilitates Intelligence Community silver recovery from film.
- provides general service message service, mail distribution, classified material destruction, correspondence control, and Washington area courier service.
- manages the DIA top secret and NATO registers.
- provides DoD imagery evaluations and other imagery related technical assistance to field units to optimize DoD imagery collection and processing.
- provides engineering and space management, acquisition, maintenance, design, funding, and management of government, military and privately leased facilities. Provides travel, transportation, records, forms, and management services for the DIA.
- manages the DIA's release of information under the Privacy and Freedom of Information acts.
- provides video processing equipment and expertise to ease the production of approved intelligence products in video format. Provides for integration of video capability and audio, visual, and teleconferencing requirements having a compartmented intelligence base.
- manages the DoD intelligence dissemination program.
- manages the DIA contractor release of intelligence information program.

Directorate for Human Resources (RHR). The RHR exercises overall staff responsibility for all aspects of manpower resource management and organizational and functional analyses for the agency. It develops and implements DIA policies, procedures, and programs for personnel management of both military and civilian employees. It provides military (active and reserve) and civilian personnel to work at the agency, and it plans and develops the agency's career development program. In fulfilling this mission, the RHR:

- develops and recommends organizational plans, structures and functional alignments to perform the DIA mission and develops human resources-related legislative initiatives where appropriate.
- conducts manpower studies within the agency and insures the development and implementation of the DIA manpower program.
- develops and maintains the DIA Joint Manpower Program (JMP) and the Joint Table of Distribution (JTD).
- manages and monitors DIA requirements for military positions that require an advanced academic degree. Provides DIA functional management of the Air Force's Advanced Academic Degree Management System. Oversees agency submissions to the Army Educational Requirements Board, the Navy Subspecialty Review Board, and the Marine Corps Special Education Program.
- participates in program and budget development and financial reviews for all DIA program elements and activities to insure that minimum manpower needed to perform required missions is identified and requested.
- develops, recommends, and promulgates policy and procedures for developing the Defense Intelligence Senior Executive Service (DISES), including executive position determination and prioritization.
- plans, directs, implements, and evaluates the development and operation of the agency's military and civilian personnel programs and services.
- provides technical advice and counsel to agency operating officials and employees at all levels on all matters pertaining to position establishment, position classification, and position and pay management.
- plans and conducts recruitment activities in response to current and projected DIA civilian staffing requirements.
- develops and evaluates a comprehensive career development enhancement program for civilian and military personnel. Develops the necessary support systems to allow managers to more effectively exercise their personnel resource management responsibilities.
- formulates, coordinates, and implements policies and procedures for the management of the DIA Military and Civilian Reserve Program. Requisitions, assigns, and administers all Individual Mobilization Augmentees.
- manages the agency personnel management information system to meet overall personnel information requirements.
- conducts awards programs for agency personnel.

Directorate for Procurement (RSQ). The RSQ manages the agency's procurement program for both appropriated and nonappropriated funds, establishes and implements procurement policy and procedures, and insures effective and responsive contracting support. In fulfilling this mission, the RSQ:

- formulates and publishes procurement policy and procedures within the framework of the Federal Acquisition Regulation (FAR) and the DoD FAR Supplement.
- executes, administers, or terminates contracts and makes related determinations and findings.
- provides contracting support to the Department of Defense Intelligence Information System (DODIIS) community and other selected intelligence activities.
- establishes and administers Blanket Purchase Agreements (BPAs) for use by delegated personnel.
- provides advice and assistance relating to procurement planning and preparation of required documents for contract execution.
- implements the Small Business and Disadvantaged Business Programs within the agency.

The Directorate for Information Systems (DS). The DS provides engineering support for developing and enhancing the Department of Defense Intelligence Information System (DODIIS).

The Directorate for DODIIS Management (DSM). The mission of DSM is to be responsible for the management of the DODIIS. In addition, it conducts mid- and long-term planning for the orderly development of the DODIIS; develops policies, concepts, planning guidance, and management procedures; and performs management analyses and reviews of management, technical, and resource issues related to the modernization and maintenance of the worldwide integrated DODIIS and its component parts. The DSM provides ADP-T and resource recommendations to the General Defense Intelligence Program (GDIP) manager. Additionally, with respect to DODIIS/GDIP ADP-T, it provides representation in designated intelligence community, interdepartmental, and other government-sponsored activities related to intelligence information systems. In fulfilling this mission, the DSM:

- develops and maintains the DODIIS master plan.
- provides command representation and liaison services and acts as the DIA focal point to the Unified and Specified Commands for intelligence information system matters.
- provides ADP planning support to Intelligence Community functional managers and manages the integration of new ADP support capabilities into the DODIIS architecture.
- reviews and provides recommendations, as ADP-T functional manager, on the ADP-T portions of the GDIP.
- provides support in the preparation of congressional justification documents.
- develops the pertinent directives, regulations, and procedures that govern the management and administration of the DODIIS.
- maintains reference information on DODIIS subsystems.
- develops concepts, architecture, and plans for DODIIS systems interface with command and control systems.
- conducts DODIIS managers' conferences and provides DODIIS information exchange, documentation, and services.
- establishes DODIIS training policy.
- provides technical and administrative support to the Joint National Intelligence Development Staff (JNIDS).

The Directorate for DODIIS Engineering (DSE). The DSE provides engineering management and support for developing and enhancing the DODIIS to insure overall system operability, the elimination of duplicate efforts, the development of interfaces with tactical intelligence systems, and improved intelligence information processing and exchange capabilities. In fulfilling this mission, the DSE:

- develops and publishes overall DODIIS systems specifications.
- develops and publishes DODIIS software development, hardware, and data element standards.
- develops and publishes tactical interface criteria.

- provides liaison between the DIA and the Joint Chiefs of Staff Program to achieve Joint Interoperability of Tactical Command and Control Systems (JINTACCS).
- provides for the development of the DODIIS network and its daily operational management.
- develops and publishes configuration management procedures.
- manages the DOD AN/GYQ-21(V) program.
- manages the DODIIS technology sharing program.
- establishes DODIIS security policy and accomplishes security accreditation actions.
- provides for the maintenance of inventories and libraries of DODIIS standard common and site-unique software.
- participates in user groups and configuration control boards of all DODIIS executive agents.
- provides special technical support to the DODIIS community.
- serves as DODIIS executive agent for the model 204 data base management system.
- defines communications interfaces of national, tactical, and command and control systems of the DODIIS.
- develops communications procedures for intelligence systems including those for SPINTCOMM.

Directorate for Internal Systems (DSI). The mission of the DSI is to provide for the effective and efficient development, maintenance, and operation of DIA information system services, including establishing policy, plans, procedures, and programs governing communication services and capabilities, automated intelligence information handling systems, and office technologies. Additionally, it manages the worldwide special intelligence communications (SPINTCOMM) portion of the Defense Special Security Communications System (DSSCS). It also administers and operates the DIA communications security program and operates all DIA computer equipment and facilities. In fulfilling this mission, the DSI:

- formulates objectives and policy governing the acquisition, operation, and use of agency information systems. It also prepares and coordinates plans for managing, acquiring, developing, and operating future information system services and capabilities.
- reviews and evaluates existing information systems for cost effective-

ness and ability to meet user needs; develops, in conjunction with user organizations, programs and plans to meet future information requirements.

- plans and supports acquiring, implementing, and using office technology within the DIA, including personal computers, word processing, office communications equipment and systems, video, and facsimile capabilities. Provides centralized services to the users of office technology, including training, acquisition, maintenance, and initial set-up and operation.
- designs, tests, implements, and operates intelligence communications systems for the DIA and other supported DoD intelligence agencies.
- designs, develops, tests, and implements automated intelligence information systems based on approved requirements supporting the DIA and other defense and national intelligence activities.
- manages, operates, and maintains DIA information system computers and associated equipment, communications and telecommunications equipment, and systems and office automation/ technology equipment.
- operates and maintains the DIA SPINTCOMM facilities in support of DoD, JCS, DIA, and other defense activities. Installs and maintains communications services, telephones, terminals, and other telecommunications equipment.
- monitors, evaluates, and participates in research and development activities in communications and office technologies, data processing hardware and software, and information system sciences and practices to determine the applicability of advanced techniques to agency information system needs.

Directorate for Attachés and Operations (DA). The DA provides human intelligence information. In doing so, the DA:

- acts as the DoD HUMINT manager, develops the DoD HUMINT program, and issues DoD HUMINT guidance.
- handles General Defense Intelligence Program (GDIP) matters pertaining to the HUMINT program.
- issues DIA instructions and regulations regarding the HUMINT program.
- manages and conducts HUMINT collection activities and tasking of the DoD HUMINT collection system.

- operates the Defense Attaché System and is the system's point of contact for other departments, services, and agencies.

The DIA Shield.

The shield is circular, with a narrow red border and a background of dark blue. On the background is affixed a green and light blue representation of the world, with two red atomic ellipses. Through the poles of the earth penetrate a gold torch. Beneath the world is placed an olive wreath, and above the world are thirteen white stars. Just inside the rim on the dark blue background is written "Defense Intelligence Agency" and "United States of America" in gold letters. The symbolism is as follows: The initial letters of Defense Intelligence Agency also comprise the Greek word "dia," which means divided into two parts. In this instance, the flaming gold torch represents knowledge (i.e., intelligence) lighting the way of the "known" light blue-green world against the darkness or "unknown" symbolized by the dark blue background—the "area of truth" that is the worldwide mission of the agency. The red atomic ellipses symbolize the scientific and technical aspects of intelligence today and of the future. The thirteen stars and the wreath are adopted from the Department of Defense seal and are used to identify the agency as a Department of Defense organization.

References

American Bar Association. *Oversight and Accountability of the U.S. Intelligence Agencies: An Evaluation.* Washington, DC: ABA, 1985.

Corson, William R. *The Armies of Ignorance: The Rise of the American Intelligence Empire.* New York: Dial Press, 1977.

Department of Defense, Defense Intelligence Agency. *History of the Defense Intelligence Agency.* Washington, DC: DIA, 1985.

Department of Defense, Defense Intelligence Agency. *Organization, Mission and Key Personnel.* Washington, DC: DIA, 1987.

Department of Defense, Defense Intelligence College. *Defense Intelligence College 1987-1988 Catalog.* Washington, DC: DIC, 1987.

Fain, Tyrus G.; Plant, Katharine C.; and Milloy, Ross. *The Intelligence Community: History, Organization, and Issues.* Public Documents Series. New York: R.R. Bowker, 1977.

Godson, Roy, ed. *Intelligence Problems for the 1980s, Number 2: Analysis and Estimates.* Washington, DC: National Strategy Information Center, 1980.

————. *Intelligence Problems for the 1980s, Number 5: Clandestine Collection.* Washington, DC: National Strategy Information Center, 1982.

Laqueur, Walter. *A World of Secrets.* New York: Basic Books, 1985.

Lefever, Ernest W., and Godson, Roy. *The CIA and the American Ethic: An Unfinished Debate.* Washington, DC: Ethics and Public Policy Center, Georgetown University, 1979.

Lowenthal, Mark M. *U.S. Intelligence: Evolution and Anatomy.* New York: Praeger Publishers, 1984.

Maurer, Alfred C.; Turnstall, Marion D.; and Keagle, James M. *Intelligence Policy and Process.* Boulder, CO: Westview Press, 1985.

Quirk, John; Phillips, David; Cline, Ray; and Pforzheimer, Walter. *The Central Intelligence Agency: A Photographic History.* Guilford, CT: Foreign Intelligence Press, 1986.

Treverton, Gregory F. *Covert Action: The Limits of Intervention in the Postwar World.* New York: Basic Books, 1987.

Turner, Stansfield. *Secrecy and Democracy: The CIA in Transition.* Boston: Houghton Mifflin, 1985.

U.S. Congress. Senate. *Final Report of the Senate Select Committee to Study Government Operations with Respect to Intelligence Activities. Report 94-755. Book I, Foreign and Military Intelligence.* Washington, DC: GPO, 1976.

—**DEFENSE INTELLIGENCE AGENCY AS J-2, JOINT CHIEFS OF STAFF.** In 1963, in an attempt to consolidate intelligence resources and streamline intelligence management, the J-2 intelligence organization of the Joint Chiefs of Staff was disbanded, and its duties were passed to the director of the Defense Intelligence Agency (DIA). This made the DIA a major actor in current intelligence collection, analysis, and production. It also created some mission problems over the years, as the DIA attempted to balance its requirements to the Joint Chiefs of Staff and national leaders with its duties concerning the Unified and Specified Commands and other entities in the field. The DIA maintains the National Military Intelligence Center (NMIC) on a 24-hour basis in order to insure adequate support to both the Joint Chiefs of Staff and the field commands. *See also:* Chairman, Joint Chiefs of Staff.

References

Department of Defense, National Defense University. *Joint Staff Officer's Guide, 1986.* Washington, DC: GPO, 1986.

Laqueur, Walter. *A World of Secrets.* New York: Basic Books, 1985.

—**DEFENSE INTELLIGENCE AGENCY INTELLIGENCE APPRAISAL (DIAIAPPR)** provides a timely assessment of a situation or development to national-level decisionmakers in the Washington area and to the major military commands around the world. It normally discusses a single subject and provides a more comprehensive and detailed assessment than other current intelligence publications. It may be written in response to a specific request or may be self-initiated in response to anticipated user requirements. It may be written at any classification level, and it is sent by message to those outside the Washington area. *See also:* Defense Intelligence Agency.

References

Von Hoene, John P. A. *Intelligence User's Guide.* Washington, DC: DIA, 1983.

—**DEFENSE INTELLIGENCE AGENCY MILITARY AND CIVILIAN RESERVE PROGRAM.** *See:* Defense Intelligence Agency.

—**DEFENSE INTELLIGENCE AGENCY ON-LINE SYSTEM (DIAOLS)** became operational in September 1968. It is a general purpose automated system that provides service to DIA analysts as well as to other organizations in the Intelligence Community and interfaces with the Community On-Line Intelligence System (COINS). It offers over 2,700 users access to a broad range of intelligence data bases that can be used in intelligence production. Examples of the information available in DIAOLS include ground, naval, and air order-of-battle data, information on foreign installations, library reference, and biographic data files. Accessing over 160 files and providing rapid response and remote batch operations to over 800 keyboard terminals and 12 remote batch terminal locations in Washington, Europe, the Pacific, and military installations throughout the United States, DIAOLS offers a full range of retrieval and output capabilities. *See also:* Defense Intelligence Agency.

References

Von Hoene, John P. A. *Intelligence User's Guide.* Washington, DC: DIA, 1983.

—**DEFENSE INTELLIGENCE AGENCY PERIODIC INTELLIGENCE SUMMARY (DIA INTSUM)** is a report on foreign crisis situations that could have an immediate effect on U.S. planning and operations. The INTSUM is provided to the Joint Chiefs of Staff, the Unified and Specified Commands, the military services, U.S. commanders worldwide, and selected U.S. government agencies. *See also:* Defense Intelligence Agency.

References

Department of Defense, National Defense University. *Joint Staff Officer's Guide, 1986.* Washington, DC: GPO, 1986.

Laqueur, Walter. *A World of Secrets.* New York: Basic Books, 1985.

Turner, Stansfield. *Secrecy and Democracy: The CIA in Transition.* Boston: Houghton Mifflin, 1985.

—**DEFENSE INTELLIGENCE AGENCY SECURITY EDUCATION AND SELF-INSPECTION PROGRAM.** *See:* Defense Intelligence Agency.

—**DEFENSE INTELLIGENCE AIR ORDER OF BATTLE (DIAOB)** is a part of the Defense Intelligence Order of Battle System (DIOBS) of the Defense Intelligence Agency On-Line System (DIAOLS), which provides analysts access to detailed equipment inventories of foreign air forces. *See also:* Defense Intelligence Agency.

References

Laqueur, Walter. *A World of Secrets.* New York: Basic Books, 1985.

Von Hoene, John P. A. *Intelligence User's Guide.* Washington, DC: DIA, 1983.

—**DEFENSE INTELLIGENCE ANALYSIS CENTER (DIAC),** located on Bolling Air Force Base in Washington, DC, is the result of seventeen years of planning. It is unique in that it houses both standard office space and a highly complex industrial plant. Work on the building's design began in 1975, ground was broken in April 1981, and occupancy began in 1984. The design concept includes a combined system of modular and specialized types of space. The modular areas contain the administrative and analytical offices of the DIA, and the specialized spaces are used by service-oriented offices, such as the photo lab, printing plant, and computer center.

The building was designed to minimize the walking distances and to group together offices with similar functions. The DIA's employees and visitors enter the building on the second floor and proceed through security control points to their designations. There are several levels of security in the building, ranging from nonsecure to compartmented intelligence areas. While the first floor is clad in granite for structural support, the remaining levels are clad in a light silver-colored panel system that contains large, fixed glass windows. This, and the building's modular design, give the building a unique appearance.

Completion of the DIAC marked the first time in the DIA's history that its major elements were housed in a single facility. This has caused a drastic improvement in the quality of the agency's output. Nevertheless, the building has proven too small for the agency's expanding functions and growing staff, and an addition is planned for completion in the early 1990s. The foresight inherent in the building's original modular plans facilitates the integration of the addition into the building's total design. *See also:* Defense Intelligence Agency.

References

Department of Defense, Defense Intelligence Agency. *Defense Intelligence Analysis Center.* (A public relations statement concerning the DIAC.) Washington, DC: DIA, 1983.

—**DEFENSE INTELLIGENCE ANALYTICAL MEMORANDUM (DIAM)** is a detailed analysis of a complex subject. It is often speculative or tentative in nature but is not considered to be an estimate. The DIAM is characterized by great detail and is therefore intended for desk officers and technical specialists. *See also:* Defense Intelligence Agency.

References

Brinkley, David A. and Hull, Andrew W. *Estimative Intelligence: A Textbook on the History, Products, Uses, and Writing of Intelligence Estimates.* Columbus, OH: Battelle, 1979.

Turner, Stansfield. *Secrecy and Democracy: The CIA in Transition.* Boston: Houghton Mifflin, 1985.

—**DEFENSE INTELLIGENCE COLLEGE (DIC).** The DIC's mission is to train Department of Defense military and civilian personnel for assignment to Department of Defense and other national and international intelligence agency command, staff, and policymaking positions.

In a decision that combined the U.S. Army Strategic Intelligence School and the U.S. Naval Intelligence School, the Defense Intelligence

School was established in 1963. The size of the school grew and the quality of its faculty and curriculum continued to improve, so that by the early 1980s it was offering twenty programs and had a student body of 2,000 people made up of entry, mid-level, and senior military and civilian intelligence specialists. The school made great strides under its commandant, Colonel Lee Badgett, U.S. Air Force, and its provost, Dr. Robert L. De Gross, and was rechartered and renamed as the Defense Intelligence College in 1983. Under Badgett's and De Gross's guidance, the DIC was accredited by the Middle States Association of Colleges and Schools, developed an impressive research and publications program, and vastly increased its Master of Science of Strategic Intelligence program. In 1984, the DIC moved to its current quarters in the Defense Intelligence Analysis Center on Bolling Air Force Base in Washington, DC. It now offers intelligence programs on both the graduate and undergraduate levels on both a full- and part-time basis to U.S. military personnel, Department of Defense and other federal agency civilians, and officers from many other countries. In 1987, it was decided to civilianize the position of commandant in order to provide greater continuity. Howard Roop, Ed.D., Rear Admiral, U.S. Naval Reserve (Retired), the first incumbent, took office in 1988. Since 1963, over 40,000 people have attended the institution, and more than 2,000 have completed the graduate program.

As of 1990, the DIC offers students an opportunity to pursue professional graduate study on a full- or part-time basis by attending the Postgraduate Intelligence Program (PGIP) or the Master of Science of Strategic Intelligence (MSSI) program. Students enrolling in the DIC's graduate program may earn a concentration certificate by completing a series of specified courses, a diploma by completing the PGIP course work requirements, or the MSSI by completing all degree requirements. The college offers a plethora of educational and training courses and programs that span from one day to 40 weeks in length. The following are among the major programs:

Master of Science of Strategic Intelligence (MSSI) degree program. This program provides military personnel and civilians with a graduate-level program of study in the principles of strategic intelligence, methodologies of intelligence assessment, and the role and functions of intelligence in joint operations. The program requirements include attending sixteen graduate courses

and completing a research thesis or a nonthesis option.

Postgraduate Intelligence Program (PGIP). The PGIP is a 40-week course of study for professional civilians and military intelligence specialists. The goal of the program is to prepare students for mid-career assignments in the planning, direction, collection, production, and dissemination of defense intelligence at the national and international level. The PGIP includes courses on the U.S. national security structure; the national foreign intelligence community; collection, production, and dissemination phases of the intelligence cycle; the fundamentals of intelligence indications and warning; aspects of international terrorism; assessment of key world areas; management of intelligence resources; basic elements of statistical analysis and probability theory; and introduction to intelligence ADP systems. Ten subject-area concentrations and a certificate in indications and warning are offered to students enrolled in the PGIP.

Combined Strategic Intelligence Training Program (CSTIP). This program is intended specifically for foreign military students of the grades of O–5 (lieutenant colonel) and below.

Senior Enlisted Intelligence Program (SEIP). The SEIP is a 41-week program that prepares senior noncommissioned officers for key national and joint-level assignments through a program of advanced study.

References

American Bar Association. *Oversight and Accountability of the U.S. Intelligence Agencies: An Evaluation.* Washington, DC: ABA, 1985.

Corson, William R. *The Armies of Ignorance: The Rise of the American Intelligence Empire.* New York: Dial Press, 1977.

Department of Defense, Defense Intelligence Agency. *Defense Intelligence Agency Manual.* Washington, DC: DIA, 1987.

————. *Training Compendium for General Defense Career Development Program (IDCP) Personnel DOD 1430.10M3-TNG.* Washington, DC: DIA, 1986.

Maurer, Alfred C.; Turnstall, Marion D.; and Keagle, James M. *Intelligence Policy and Process.* Boulder, CO: Westview Press, 1985.

Von Hoene, John P. A. *Intelligence User's Guide.* Washington, DC: DIA, 1983.

—DEFENSE INTELLIGENCE COMMUNITY (DIC) is composed of the Defense Intelligence Agency (DIA), National Security Agency (NSA), Army, Navy, Air Force, and Marine Corps intelligence offices, and Department of Defense (DoD) collectors of specialized intelligence through reconnaissance programs. *See also:* Air Force Intelligence, Central Intelligence Agency, Defense Intelligence Agency, National Security Agency, Naval Intelligence, U.S. Army Intelligence.

References

Department of Defense, Defense Intelligence College. *Glossary of Intelligence Terms and Definitions.* Washington, DC: DIC, 1987.

Godson, Roy, ed. *Intelligence Problems for the 1980s, Number 1: Elements of Intelligence.* Rev. ed. Washington, DC: National Strategy Information Center, 1983.

Kent, Sherman. *Strategic Intelligence for American World Policy.* Princeton, NJ: Princeton University Press, 1966.

Laqueur, Walter. *A World of Secrets.* New York: Basic Books, 1985.

Turner, Stansfield. *Secrecy and Democracy: The CIA in Transition.* Boston: Houghton Mifflin, 1985.

—**DEFENSE INTELLIGENCE ELECTRONIC ORDER OF BATTLE (DIEOB)** is part of the Defense Intelligence Order of Battle System (DIOBS) of the Defense Intelligence Agency On-Line System (DIAOLS), which provides analysts access to detailed information on the capabilities of foreign forces. *See also:* Defense Intelligence Agency.

References

Laqueur, Walter. *A World of Secrets.* New York: Basic Books, 1985.

Von Hoene, John P. A. *Intelligence User's Guide.* Washington, DC: DIA, 1983.

—**DEFENSE INTELLIGENCE ESTIMATE (DIE)** is the Defense Intelligence Agency's counterpart to the National Intelligence Estimate (NIE). DIEs were begun in late 1969 or early 1970 as a means for the DIA to express independent positions on estimates and as a way for the DIA to establish its positions on issues prior to U.S. Intelligence Board (USIB) meetings.

The subjects of DIEs are defense-related topics that are narrower in scope than NIEs and often address in detail topics that NIEs discuss only briefly. DIEs differ from NIEs in that they are self-initiated in the DIA, rather than being requested by consumers, as NIEs are. DIEs are usually only 25–30 pages long, considerably shorter than NIEs, which can run to several hundred pages. DIEs are drafted by the Directorate for Estimates,

are circulated throughout the DIA, and are sent to the military services for comment. Should a service strongly disagree with a position in a DIE, it can comment on that disagreement, either by footnoting the objection or preparing a detailed account of the objection for inclusion in the DIE. The DIE is meant for a rather select audience. It is written with the secretary of defense in mind, but in reality it is used by many different levels of the Department of Defense and military services. DIEs are also meant to support the director of the DIA when he attends National Foreign Intelligence Board (NFIB) meetings or when he coordinates with the directors of other intelligence organizations. *See also:* Defense Intelligence Agency.

References

Brinkley, David A., and Hull, Andrew W. *Estimative Intelligence: A Textbook on the History, Products, Uses, and Writing of Intelligence Estimates.* Columbus, OH: Battelle, 1979.

—**DEFENSE INTELLIGENCE ESTIMATE MEMORANDUM (DIEM)** is prepared by the Defense Intelligence Agency's Directorate for Estimates. It usually covers an important topic or issue that requires an immediate response and is therefore not coordinated within the DIA or with the military services. Often it is written in response to a single event, such as a coup or an assassination. *See also:* Defense Intelligence Agency.

References

Brinkley, David A., and Hull, Andrew W. *Estimative Intelligence: A Textbook on the History, Products, Uses, and Writing of Intelligence Estimates.* Columbus, OH: Battelle, 1979.

Department of Defense, Defense Intelligence Agency. *Defense Intelligence Agency Manual.* Washington, DC: DIA, 1987.

Kent, Sherman. *Strategic Intelligence for American World Policy.* Princeton, NJ: Princeton University Press, 1966.

—**DEFENSE INTELLIGENCE ESTIMATES STAFF MEMORANDUM (DIESM)** is the least formal of the reports prepared by the Defense Intelligence Agency's Directorate for Estimates. The DIESM is intended to stimulate thought within the directorate concerning issues or matters that are not yet completely clear or have not developed sufficiently to warrant a more complete estimate. Because they are unofficial "thought pieces," they are not circulated outside of the DIA. *See also:* Defense Intelligence Agency.

References

Brinkley, David A., and Hull, Andrew W. *Estimative Intelligence: A Textbook on the History, Products, Uses, and Writing of Intelligence Estimates.* Columbus, OH: Battelle, 1979.

Laqueur, Walter. *A World of Secrets.* New York: Basic Books, 1985.

—**DEFENSE INTELLIGENCE FUNCTIONAL MANAGER (DIFM)** is a Defense Intelligence Agency official who has been appointed by the director of the DIA to oversee a specific operational (functional) area within the General Defense Intelligence Community (GDIC). *See also:* Defense Intelligence Agency, General Defense Intelligence Community.

References

Department of Defense, Defense Intelligence Agency. *Defense Intelligence Agency Manual.* Washington, DC: DIA, 1987.

Laqueur, Walter. *A World of Secrets.* New York: Basic Books, 1985.

—**DEFENSE INTELLIGENCE GROUND ORDER OF BATTLE (DIGOB)** is part of the Defense Intelligence Order of Battle System (DIOBS) of the Defense Intelligence Agency On-Line System (DIAOLS), which provides analysts access to detailed equipment inventories of ground forces. *See also:* Defense Intelligence Agency.

References

Laqueur, Walter. *A World of Secrets.* New York: Basic Books, 1985.

Von Hoene, John P. A. *Intelligence User's Guide.* Washington, DC: DIA, 1983.

—**DEFENSE INTELLIGENCE HANDBOOKS** are produced by the Defense Intelligence Agency. They discuss various foreign military systems, the organization of forces, manpower, military security forces, weapons, and equipment, training and tactics, and uniforms, insignia, and decorations. *See also:* Defense Intelligence Agency.

References

Von Hoene, John P. A. *Intelligence User's Guide.* Washington, DC: DIA, 1983.

—**DEFENSE INTELLIGENCE MISSILE ORDER OF BATTLE (DIMOB)** is part of the Defense Intelligence Order of Battle System (DIOBS) of the Defense Intelligence Agency On-Line System (DIAOLS), which provides analysts access to detailed equipment inventories of missile forces. *See also:* Defense Intelligence Agency.

References

Laqueur, Walter. *A World of Secrets.* New York: Basic Books, 1985.

Von Hoene, John P. A. *Intelligence User's Guide.* Washington, DC: DIA, 1983.

—**DEFENSE INTELLIGENCE NAVAL ORDER OF BATTLE (DINOB)** is part of the Defense Intelligence Order of Battle System (DIOBS) of the Defense Intelligence agency On-Line System (DIAOLS), which provides analysts access to detailed equipment inventories of naval forces. *See also:* Defense Intelligence Agency.

References

Von Hoene, John P. A. *Intelligence User's Guide.* Washington, DC: DIA, 1983.

—**DEFENSE INTELLIGENCE NOTICE (DIN)** provides current, finished intelligence on developments that could have a significant impact on current and future planning and operations. Prepared by the Defense Intelligence Agency and generally covering only one event or situation, the purpose of the DIN is to report on significant developments, explain why they occurred, and assess their impact on the United States or U.S. interests. It is sent to the Joint Chiefs of Staff, the Unified and Specified Commands, the military services, and selected other U.S. government agencies. Among the organizations that prepare such notices are the DIA's Directorate for Current Intelligence. *See also:* Defense Intelligence Agency.

References

Department of Defense, Defense Intelligence Agency. *Organization, Mission, and Key Personnel.* Washington, DC: DIA, 1986.

Department of Defense, National Defense University. *Joint Staff Officer's Guide, 1986.* Washington, DC: GPO, 1986.

Laqueur, Walter. *A World of Secrets.* New York: Basic Books, 1985.

Von Hoene, John P. A. *Intelligence User's Guide.* Washington, DC: DIA, 1983.

—**DEFENSE INTELLIGENCE OBJECTIVES AND PRIORITIES (DIOP)**, as defined by the Church Committee, is a single statement of intelligence requirements that is compiled by the Defense Intelligence Agency for use by all Department of Defense intelligence components. *See also:* Defense Intelligence Agency.

References

U.S. Congress. Senate. *Final Report of the Senate Select Committee to Study Government Operations with Respect to Intelligence Activities. Report 94-755. Book I, Foreign and Military Intelligence.* Washington, DC: GPO, 1976.

—**DEFENSE INTELLIGENCE OFFICER (DIO)**. *See:* Defense Intelligence Agency.

—**DEFENSE INTELLIGENCE ORDER OF BATTLE SYSTEM (DIOBS)** is part of the Delegated Production Program and is managed by the Directorate for Research of the Defense Intelligence Agency. *See also:* Defense Intelligence Agency.

References

Department of Defense, Defense Intelligence Agency. *Organization, Mission, and Key Personnel.* Washington, DC: DIA, 1986.

Laqueur, Walter. *A World of Secrets.* New York: Basic Books, 1985.

—**DEFENSE INTELLIGENCE PRODUCTION SYSTEM (DIPS)** is a Defense Intelligence Agency management document. It is a two-volume publication that lists the Department of Defense general intelligence production that is scheduled for production. *See also:* Defense Intelligence Agency.

References

Laqueur, Walter. *A World of Secrets.* New York: Basic Books, 1985.

Von Hoene, John P. A. *Intelligence User's Guide.* Washington, DC: DIA, 1983.

—**DEFENSE INTELLIGENCE PROJECTIONS FOR PLANNING (DIPP)** is produced by the Defense Intelligence Agency's Directorate for Estimates. Published in several volumes, it focuses on the force structure and composition of NATO, Soviet, Warsaw Pact, and Chinese communist armed forces. The DIPP appeared in 1970 along with the creation of the DIA's Directorate for Estimates, but a forerunner of the DIPP extends back several years to the CIA's National Intelligence Projections for Planning. The DIPP was needed when reporting responsibility shifted from the CIA to the DIA in 1970.

The DIPP is very different from other types of estimates produced by the DIA. For example, it consists primarily of numbers, with very little narrative, and has a very rigid format that presents projections for a ten-year period. It contains forecasts of military forces, weapon-systems, and weapon systems characteristics for short- and mid-range planning. *See also:* Defense Intelligence Agency.

References

Brinkley, David A., and Hull, Andrew W. *Estimative Intelligence: A Textbook on the History, Products, Uses, and Writing of Intelligence Estimates.* Columbus, OH: Battelle, 1979.

Laqueur, Walter. *A World of Secrets.* New York: Basic Books, 1985.

Von Hoene, John P. A. *Intelligence User's Guide.* Washington, DC: DIA, 1983.

—**DEFENSE INTELLIGENCE REPORT (DIR)** is a timely analytical study of a specific subject or development that has military implications or significance. It is a concise, interpretive study that is issued on a one-time basis. *See also:* Defense Intelligence Agency.

References

Laqueur, Walter. *A World of Secrets.* New York: Basic Books, 1985.

Von Hoene, John P. A. *Intelligence User's Guide.* Washington, DC: DIA, 1983.

—**DEFENSE INTELLIGENCE SCHOOL (DIS)**. *See:* Defense Intelligence College (DIC).

—**DEFENSE INTELLIGENCE SPACE ORDER OF BATTLE (DISOB)** is part of the Defense Intelligence Order of Battle System (DIOBS) of the Defense Intelligence Agency On-Line System (DIAOLS), which provides analysts access to detailed information about the few nations currently involved in space activity. *See also:* Defense Intelligence Agency.

References

Laqueur, Walter. *A World of Secrets.* New York: Basic Books, 1985.

Von Hoene, John P. A. *Intelligence User's Guide.* Washington, DC: DIA, 1983.

—**DEFENSE INTELLIGENCE THESAURUS (DIT)** is a standard subject listing of approximately 4,000 terms that is heavily weighted toward military subjects and used for dissemination, storage, and retrieval of intelligence material. *See also:* Defense Intelligence Agency.

References

Department of Defense, Defense Intelligence Agency. *Defense Intelligence Agency Manual.* Washington, DC: DIA, 1987.

—**DEFENSE INTELLIGENCE THESAURUS (DIT) WORKSHEET,** formerly referred to as a Statement of Intelligence Interest, is a method by which authorized recipients can identify the intelligence and intelligence information that they need according to subject and geographic areas. *See also:* Defense Intelligence Agency.

References

Department of Defense, Defense Intelligence Agency. *Defense Intelligence Agency Manual.* Washington, DC: DIA, 1987.

—**DEFENSE INVESTIGATIVE SERVICE (DIS)** is in charge of conducting background investigations inside the United States for clearance of military and civilian personnel in the Department of Defense. The DIS relies on the military services for investigations outside the United States. *See also:* Access, Authorized, Background Investigation, Billet, Clearance, Compartmentation, Compromise, Debriefing, Defense Industrial Security Clearance Office, Defense Security Briefing, Lawful Investigation, "Least Intrusive Means," Nondisclosure Agreement, Personnel Security, Security, Sensitive Compartmented Information.

References

Allen, Thomas B., and Polmar, Norman. *Merchants of Treason: America's Secrets for Sale.* New York: Delacorte Press, 1988.

Breckinridge, Scott D. *The CIA and the U.S. Intelligence System.* Boulder, CO: Westview Press, 1986.

Corson, William R. *The Armies of Ignorance: The Rise of the American Intelligence Empire.* New York: Dial Press, 1977.

Laqueur, Walter. *A World of Secrets.* New York: Basic Books, 1985.

Maroni, Alice C. *Special Access Programs: Understanding the "Black Budget."* Washington, DC: Foreign Affairs and National Defense Division, Congressional Research Service, Library of Congress, 1987.

—**DEFENSE LANGUAGE INSTITUTE, FOREIGN LANGUAGE CENTER (DLIFLC),** located in Monterey, California, offers language training in over 30 languages. Course lengths vary from 25 to 47 weeks, depending on the difficulty of the language and the level of proficiency that is desired. Students at the institute are trained to fulfill a variety of military intelligence billets and positions in the attaché system.

References

Defense Intelligence Agency. *Training Compendium for General Defense Career Development Program (IDCP) Personnel DOD 1430.10M3-TNG.* Washington, DC: DIA, 1986.

—**DEFENSE MAPPING AGENCY (DMA)** is not a major intelligence producer. However, the maps it produces are of considerable value to military commanders and intelligence analysts.

References

Breckinridge, Scott D. *The CIA and the U.S. Intelligence System.* Boulder, CO: Westview Press, 1986.

Corson, William R. *The Armies of Ignorance: The Rise of the American Intelligence Empire.* New York: Dial Press, 1977.

—**DEFENSE READINESS CONDITION (DEFCON)** is a standard system of progressive alert postures for use by the Joint Chiefs of Staff, commanders of the Unified and Specified Commands, and the military services. The conditions match situations of varying degrees of severity and are identified by the short titles DEFCON 5, 4, 3, 2, or 1, with 5 being the lowest posture and 1 being at war. As each higher DEFCON is put into effect, military forces react accordingly. DEFCON 5 is a very low condition, and in the Navy it would be set for a ship only when it was in the yards or unable to get underway and accomplish its mission. DEFCON 4 is a normal state of peacetime preparedness. Troops in the field, aircraft aloft, and ships at sea would normally have watches and readiness conditions set that would conform to DEFCON 4. DEFCON 3 is a posture of heightened alert and was set, for example, in 1973, when the United States was unsure of Soviet intentions during the Yom Kippur War in October of that year. DEFCON 2 is a posture that is assumed when hostilities are imminent, and DEFCON 1 is combat.

References

Department of Defense, National Defense University. *Joint Staff Officer's Guide, 1986.* Washington, DC: GPO, 1986.

Godson, Roy, ed. *Intelligence Problems for the 1980s, Number 1: Elements of Intelligence.* Rev. ed. Washington, DC: National Strategy Information Center, 1983.

—**DEFENSE RESOURCES BOARD (DRB)** has a role in intelligence program budgeting. As the secretary of defense's corporate review body, it acts as a board of directors and helps the secretary of defense manage the Planning, Programing, and Budgeting System (PPBS) by reviewing planning issues and conducting program and budget reviews. In addition, the DRB helps the secretary manage the systems acquisition process and assists him in insuring that the acquisition of major systems is more closely aligned with the PPBS.

The DRB consists of the following members: assistant secretary of defense (Chairman); secretary of the Army; secretary of the Navy; secretary of the Air Force; chairman, Joint Chiefs of Staff; under secretary of defense (policy); under secretary of defense (research and engineering); assistant secretary of defense (acquisition and logistics); assistant secretary of defense (command, control, communications and intelligence); assistant secretary of defense (comptroller); assistant secretary of defense (health affairs); assistant secretary of defense (international security affairs); assistant secretary of defense (international security policy); assistant secretary of defense (manpower); assistant secretary of defense (research and technology); assistant secretary of defense (reserve affairs); general counsel; director, Program Analysis and Evaluation; director, Strategic Defense Initiative; director, Operational Test and Evaluation; and associate director (OMB), National Security and International Affairs.

The participation of the Office of Management and Budget (OMB) is very useful. Since the OMB has the responsibility for developing the President's budget, its participation on the DRB, in the PPBS, and in budget reviews eliminates the need for an additional OMB review following the completion of the Department of Defense action. This unique procedure allows the secretary of defense to submit the defense budget later than any other executive department.

Under the Reagan administration, the DRB had greater power than in the past because the deputy secretary of defense was given decision-making authority, whereas formerly the decisions had to be made by the secretary of defense. *See also:* Appropriation or Fund Account.

References

Godson, Roy, ed. *Intelligence Problems for the 1980s, Number 1: Elements of Intelligence.* Rev. ed. Washington, DC: National Strategy Information Center, 1983.

Pickett, George. "Congress, the Budget, and Intelligence." In *Intelligence Policy and Process,* edited by Alfred C. Maurer, Marion D. Turnstall and James M. Keagle. Boulder, CO: Westview Press, 1985.

—**DEFENSE SECURITY BRIEFINGS** are formal briefings that alert intelligence personnel of the potential for harassment, provocation, or entrapment in the areas that they are about to visit. Also known as Foreign Travel Briefings, they are based on the actual experience of previous travelers, when available, and include information on the courses of action that will be helpful in reducing the chances of adverse security or personnel consequences.

References

Godson, Roy, ed. *Intelligence Problems for the 1980s, Number 1: Elements of Intelligence.* Rev. ed. Washington, DC: National Strategy Information Center, 1983.

Laqueur, Walter. *A World of Secrets.* New York: Basic Books, 1985.

—**DEFENSE SPECIAL SECURITY COMMUNICATIONS SYSTEM (DSSCS)** is a worldwide, special purpose communications system for processing SIGINT and CRITIC messages and other sensitive or private information. It uses the terminals and relay facilities of CRITICOMM, managed by the director of the National Security Agency (DIRNSA); of SPINTCOMM, managed by the director of the Defense Intelligence Agency, and the capability that has been engineered into the DCS Automatic Digital Network (AUTODIN), which is managed by the director of the Defense Communications Agency (DCA). *See also:* Automatic Digital Network; Critical Intelligence Communications System (CRITICOMM); Critical Intelligence Message (CRITIC); Director, National Security Agency; Director, Defense Intelligence Agency; Special Intelligence Communications (SPINTCOMM).

References

Blackburn, N. Glenn. "Computers: A Counterintelligence Concern." Unpublished manuscript provided to the editors. Washington, DC, 1987.

Muzerall, Joseph V., and Carty, Thomas P. "COMSEC and Its Need for Key Management." *DP&CS* (Spring 1987).

Ware, Willis H. "Information Systems, Security, and Privacy." *EDUCOM Bulletin* (Summer 1984).

—**DEFENSE SPECIAL SECURITY SYSTEM (DSSS)** controls sensitive compartmented information and disseminates the same within the Department of Defense. *See also:* Communications Security, Sensitive Compartmented Information.

References

Blackburn, N. Glenn. "Computers: A Counterintelligence Concern." Unpublished manuscript provided to the editors. Washington, DC, 1987.

—**DEFENSE TECHNICAL INFORMATION CENTER (DTIC)** is a component of the Department of Defense scientific and technical intelligence program. Its data system provides summaries and information of ongoing and completed research projects.

The DTIC provides access to and transfer of scientific and technical information for Department of Defense personnel, contractors, and other U.S. government agency personnel. DTIC services include current awareness through the selected dissemination of information, retrospective search of the DTIC reference data bases, and retrieval and distribution of hard copy documents.

All research and development (R&D) organizations as well as many other military and civilian agencies regularly submit their completed reports to the DTIC. Many of the reports that are submitted are actually written by foreign sources or contain information from foreign sources. The bulk of the foreign information that is available pertains to non-communist countries that have connections with the United States. However, some material that is relevant to the USSR and communist bloc is included. For example, the Army's Foreign Science and Technology Center (FSTC), the Navy's Naval Technical Information Support Center (NTIC), and the Air Force's Foreign Technology Division (FTD) submit most of their translations to the DTIC for inclusion in their technical reports data base. *See also:* Scientific and Technical Intelligence.

References

Department of Defense, U.S. Army. *RDTE Managers Intelligence and Threat Support Guide*. Alexandria, VA: Headquarters, Army Matériel Development and Readiness Command, 1983.

Von Hoene, John P. A. *Intelligence User's Guide*. Washington, DC: DIA, 1983.

—**DEFENSE TECHNICAL INTELLIGENCE REPORT (DTIR)** is a report of a completed research project. It contains complete information about the nature of the project, the methodology employed and the results of the research effort.

References

Department of Defense, Defense Intelligence Agency. *Defense Intelligence Agency Manual*. Washington, DC: DIA, 1987.

Von Hoene, John P. A. *Intelligence User's Guide*. Washington, DC: DIA, 1983.

—**DEFINITION** is an intelligence imagery interpretation term. It is the degree of sharpness or clarity of an image. *See also:* Aerial Photograph, Composite.

References

Godson, Roy, ed. *Intelligence Problems for the 1980s, Number 1: Elements of Intelligence*. Rev. ed. Washington, DC: National Strategy Information Center, 1983.

Laqueur, Walter. *A World of Secrets*. New York: Basic Books, 1985.

—**DEGAUSS** is to demagnetize. The term is used in reference to demagnetizing tapes, thereby erasing them.

References

Department of Defense, Joint Chiefs of Staff. *Department of Defense Dictionary of Military and Related Terms*. Washington, DC: GPO, 1986.

—**DELETION** is an electronic surveillance term. It means the physical removal of a segment of a tape or the destruction of a portion of a recording. *See also:* Electronic Surveillance.

References

Kessler, Michael. *Wiretapping and Electronic Surveillance Commission Studies: Supporting Materials for the Report of the National Commission for the Review of Federal and State Laws Relating to Wiretapping and Electronic Surveillance, Washington, DC, 1976*. Townsend, PA: Loompanics Unlimited, 1976.

—**DEMILITARIZED ZONE (DMZ)** is a defined area where stationing or concentrating military forces or establishing military facilities of any kind is prohibited. Perhaps the most famous of the demilitarized zones is the one separating North and South Korea; it has been the scene of numerous confrontations between North Korean and U.N. forces.

References

Godson, Roy, ed. *Intelligence Problems for the 1980s, Number 1: Elements of Intelligence.* Rev. ed. Washington, DC: National Strategy Information Center, 1983.

—**DEMOTE MAXIMALLY** is to purge by killing. *See also:* Active Measures, Assassination, Executive Action, Terminate with Extreme Prejudice.

References

Becket, Henry S. A. *The Dictionary of Espionage: Spookspeak into English.* New York: Stein and Day, 1986.

Deacon, Richard. *Spyclopedia: An Encyclopedia of Spies, Secret Services, Operations, Jargon, and All Subjects Related to the World of Espionage.* London: Macdonald, 1987.

Ranelagh, John. *The Agency: The Rise and Decline of the CIA.* New York: Simon and Schuster, 1986.

Turner, Stansfield. *Secrecy and Democracy: The CIA in Transition.* Boston: Houghton Mifflin, 1985.

—**DEMULTIPLEX (DEMUX),** a baud-based system term used in communications intelligence, communications security, operations security, and signals analysis, is the process of separating and extracting individual channels of a multiplex signal. *See also:* Communications Security.

References

Blackburn, N. Glenn. "Computers: A Counterintelligence Concern." Unpublished manuscript provided to the editors. Washington, DC, 1987.

Martin, Paul H. "Communications-Computer Security." *Journal of Electronic Defense* (June 1987).

Ware, Willis H. "Information Systems, Security, and Privacy." *EDUCOM Bulletin* (Summer 1984).

—**DENIABILITY** is the deliberate use of euphemisms that give the President of the United States or other high officials grounds for denying knowledge of covert activities that were discussed at a meeting that they attended. The existence of deniability is necessary, since presidents and other high officials will have to become involved

in sensitive intelligence operations, and if these go awry, it is beneficial to remove the President from blame so that his administration is not fatally crippled. However, employing deniability is not without its cost, since the official then leaves himself open to accusations of incompetence and mismanagement because a failed and possibly flawed operation was allowed to occur without his knowledge—not a sign of a tight watch.

References

Becket, Henry S. A. *The Dictionary of Espionage: Spookspeak into English.* New York: Stein and Day, 1986.

Turner, Stansfield. *Secrecy and Democracy: The CIA in Transition.* Boston: Houghton Mifflin, 1985.

—**DENIED AREA** is a term used in clandestine and covert intelligence operations to describe a country where internal security is so strict that foreign intelligence agents dare not contact each other in person, relying instead on dead drops and other methods to maintain contact and pass information. The Soviet Union, People's Republic of China, Cuba, and Vietnam are probably denied areas. *See also:* Dead Drop, Letter Drop, Live Letter Drops.

References

Becket, Henry S. A. *The Dictionary of Espionage: Spookspeak into English.* New York: Stein and Day, 1986.

Deacon, Richard. *Spyclopedia: An Encyclopedia of Spies, Secret Services, Operations, Jargon, and All Subjects Related to the World of Espionage.* London: Macdonald, 1987.

Godson, Roy, ed. *Intelligence Problems for the 1980s, Number 1: Elements of Intelligence.* Rev. ed. Washington, DC: National Strategy Information Center, 1983.

Ranelagh, John. *The Agency: The Rise and Decline of the CIA.* New York: Simon and Schuster, 1986.

—**DEPARTMENT OF DEFENSE COMPONENTS** is a definition resulting from Presidential Executive Order 12333, "United States Intelligence Activities," dated December 4, 1981. It includes the Office of the Secretary of Defense, each of the military departments, the Organization of the Joint Chiefs of Staff, the Unified and Specified Commands, and the defense agencies.

References

American Bar Association. *Oversight and Accountability of the U.S. Intelligence Agencies: An Evaluation.* Washington, DC: ABA, 1985.

Department of Defense. *Activities of DoD Intelligence Components that Affect U.S. Persons (Department of Defense Directive 5240.1).* Washington, DC: DoD, 1982.

Godson, Roy, ed. *Intelligence Problems for the 1980s, Number 1: Elements of Intelligence.* Rev. ed. Washington, DC: National Strategy Information Center, 1983.

Laqueur, Walter. *A World of Secrets.* New York: Basic Books, 1985.

Maurer, Alfred C.; Turnstall, Marion D.; and Keagle, James M. *Intelligence Policy and Process.* Boulder, CO: Westview Press, 1985.

Treverton, Gregory F. *Covert Action: The Limits of Intervention in the Postwar World.* New York: Basic Books, 1987.

Turner, Stansfield. *Secrecy and Democracy: The CIA in Transition.* Boston: Houghton Mifflin, 1985.

—DEPARTMENT OF DEFENSE COMPUTER INSTITUTE (DODCI), located on the U.S. Navy Yard in Washington, DC, offers a group of courses that run in length from three days to four weeks. The institute's curriculum deals entirely with instruction concerning Department of Defense computer systems and programs. The students are military officers and career civilian professionals.

References

Defense Intelligence Agency. *Training Compendium for General Defense Career Development Program (IDCP) Personnel DOD 1430.10M3-TNG.* Washington, DC: DIA, 1986.

—DEPARTMENT OF DEFENSE DIRECTIVE 5240.1 was issued on December 3, 1982, and was titled "Activities of Department of Defense Components that Affect U.S. Persons." Its purpose was to provide policy and the authority under which Department of Defense intelligence components could collect, retain, and disseminate information about U.S. persons. It was the instruction that implemented the guidance provided in Executive Order 12333. It placed strict limits on the types of activities that could occur and on the types of people who could be targeted.

References

Department of Defense. *Activities of DoD Intelligence Components that Affect U.S. Persons (Department of Defense Directive 5240.1).* Washington, DC: DoD, 1982.

—DEPARTMENT OF DEFENSE INTELLIGENCE is the intelligence and intelligence information that is produced by the military intelligence and counterintelligence operations and activities of the Department of Defense.

References

Department of Defense, Defense Intelligence Agency. *Defense Intelligence Agency Manual.* Washington, DC: DIA, 1987.

Godson, Roy, ed. *Intelligence Problems for the 1980s, Number 1: Elements of Intelligence.* Rev. ed. Washington, DC: National Strategy Information Center, 1983.

———. *Intelligence Problems for the 1980s, Number 2: Analysis and Estimates.* Washington, DC: National Strategy Information Center, 1980.

Laqueur, Walter. *A World of Secrets.* New York: Basic Books, 1985.

Turner, Stansfield. *Secrecy and Democracy: The CIA in Transition.* Boston: Houghton Mifflin, 1985.

—DEPARTMENT OF DEFENSE INTELLIGENCE COMPONENTS were identified in Presidential Executive Order 12333, "United States Intelligence Activities," dated December 4, 1981. They include the following: the National Security Agency/Central Security Service; the Defense Intelligence Agency; the offices within the Department of Defense for the collection of specialized national foreign intelligence through reconnaissance programs; the deputy chief of staff for intelligence, Army General Staff; the Office of Naval intelligence; the assistant chief of staff, intelligence, U.S. Air Force; the Army Intelligence and Security Command; the Naval Intelligence Command; the Naval Security Group Command; the director of intelligence, U.S. Marine Corps; the Air Force Intelligence Service; the Electronic Security Command; the counterintelligence elements of the Naval Security and Investigative Command (NSIC); the counterintelligence elements of the Air Force Office of Special Investigations; the 650th Military Intelligence Group, SHAPE; and other organizations, staffs, and offices when used for foreign intelligence or counterintelligence purposes.

References

Department of Defense. *Activities of DoD Intelligence Components that Affect U.S. Persons (Department of Defense Directive 5240.1).* Washington, DC: DoD, 1982.

Maroni, Alice C. *Special Access Programs: Understanding the "Black Budget."* Washington, DC: Foreign Affairs and National Defense Division, Congressional Research Service, Library of Congress, 1987.

—**DEPARTMENT OF DEFENSE INTELLIGENCE INFORMATION SYSTEM (DODIIS)** is composed of all Department of Defense employees, equipment, procedures, computer programs, and communications that prepare and forward intelligence to military commanders and national-level decisionmakers. The DODIIS is managed by the Defense Intelligence Agency's Directorate for Resources and Systems (RS), while the DODIIS Master Plan is developed and maintained by the Directorate for DODIIS Planning and Management, DIA. Additionally, engineering management and support for DODIIS is provided by the Directorate for DODIIS Engineering, DIA. Finally, contracting assistance is provided by the DIA's Directorate for Procurement (RSQ).

The DODIIS encompasses those ADP systems and related telecommunications systems that are used to support general intelligence collection, exploitation, production, and management and are not under the purview of the National Security Agency or the service cryptologic activities. In a sense, the DODIIS is a federation of members of operational intelligence systems that involve people, procedures, hardware, software, and telecommunications. The DODIIS is funded largely through the General Defense Intelligence Program (GDIP).

Some of the typical DODIIS community functions include:

Command support, including intelligence and warning information, targeting data, current intelligence information, and estimative data.

Exploitation of intelligence, including providing imagery, signals intelligence (SIGINT), acoustical, and telemetry data.

Intelligence data base support, including delegated production of intelligence and files on national level systems.

Scientific and technical intelligence support, including data on materials, technology assessment, medical intelligence, and weapons system capabilities.

The DODIIS' current scope includes 55 sites, such as those at the DIA, the military service intelligence headquarters, and the Unified and Specified Commands. It has 60 mainframe host computers, 200 minicomputers, and comprises 55 major ADP systems and projects.

The DODIIS is an evolving system, and there are several dynamic factors that affect its future development. Among these are increasing data volumes, new consumers (particularly in the realm of tactical intelligence), the continual changes in the components of the Intelligence Community and their expanding needs, and new information systems technologies.

The DODIIS network's goal is to allow any analyst at any location to access the required data at any time by using a standard query language. In order to meet this goal, the DODIIS is continually enhancing its integrated information handling capability in order to further its responsiveness to decisionmakers from the tactical to the national levels. However, it still faces many challenges, particularly in the areas of information system security, integrating planning and management, and redundancy and survivability. *See also:* Defense Intelligence Agency.

References

Department of Defense, Defense Intelligence Agency. *Organization, Mission, and Key Personnel.* Washington, DC: DIA, 1986.

Department of Defense, Joint Chiefs of Staff. *Department of Defense Dictionary of Military and Related Terms.* Washington, DC: GPO, 1986.

—**DEPARTMENT OF DEFENSE INTELLIGENCE INFORMATION SYSTEM (DODIIS) EXECUTIVE AGENT** is a general Defense Intelligence Community (GDIC) organization that has accepted the DODIIS Manager tasking to perform management functions for standard or common DODIIS software as a service of common concern to the DODIIS community. *See also:* Defense Intelligence Agency.

References

Department of Defense, Defense Intelligence Agency. *Defense Intelligence Agency Manual.* Washington, DC: DIA, 1987.

—**DEPARTMENT OF DEFENSE INTELLIGENCE INFORMATION SYSTEM (DODIIS) MANAGER** is the Defense Intelligence Agency Deputy Director for Resources and Systems (DIA/RS). The manager's staff is composed of the Defense Intelligence Agency (DIA) Assistant Deputy Director for DODIIS Planning and Management (RSM) and the DIA Assistant Deputy Director for DODIIS Engineering (RSE). *See also:* Defense Intelligence Agency.

References

Department of Defense, Defense Intelligence
Agency. *Defense Intelligence Agency Manual.*
Washington, DC: DIA, 1987.

—**DEPARTMENT OF DEFENSE INTELLIGENCE INFORMATION SYSTEM (DODIIS) SUBSYSTEM** is an intelligence support system that functions as an integral part of the DODIIS and is operated and maintained in whole or in part by resources acquired through the General Defense Intelligence Program (GDIP). It can receive, route, display, manipulate, store and retrieve, and disseminate intelligence data, as required. DODIIS subsystems are characterized by the application of general purpose (large, mini, and micro) computers, peripheral equipment, and automated storage and retrieval equipment.

While automation is a distinguishing characteristic of DODIIS subsystems, individual system components may be either automated or manually operated. Microcomputers used for production and administrative control operations, or those that are integrated into intelligence processing operations or equipment, are excluded. *See also:* Defense Intelligence Agency.

References

Department of Defense, Defense Intelligence
Agency. *Defense Intelligence Agency Manual.*
Washington, DC: DIA, 1987.

Department of Defense, Joint Chiefs of Staff.
*Department of Defense Dictionary of Military and
Related Terms.* Washington, DC: GPO, 1986.

—**DEPARTMENT OF DEFENSE SECURITY REVIEW COMMISSION** was established by Secretary of Defense Caspar Weinberger just after the arrest of the Walker spy ring. The commission was directed to "conduct a review and evaluation of Department of Defense security policies and procedures" and "identify any systematic vulnerabilities or weaknesses in the Department of Defense security programs, including an analysis of lessons learned from incidents which have occurred recently, and make recommendations for change, as appropriate." The commission, chaired by General Richard G. Stilwell, U.S. Army (Retired), was composed of fourteen commissioners and an appropriate support staff. The commission held seventeen formal sessions between June 26 and November 6, 1985. It also conducted several separate interviews in order to establish its position. Its major findings were that:

- "Requests for security clearance must be reduced and controlled." In this respect, it recommended that a Top Secret billet control structure be established so that clearances would be with positions, rather than with individuals; contractors be required to provide specific justifications when requesting security clearances; and limited, one-time, short-duration access be authorized to specific information at the next higher security category in order to meet operational contingencies.
- The quality and frequency of background investigations of intelligence employees should be improved. In this respect, it suggested that the scope of the investigation for a Secret clearance be expanded to include a credit check and inquiries of past and present employers; the research into behavioral science be intensified to improve investigative techniques; and the backlog of reinvestigations for access to Top Secret and SCI access be reduced and a plan for reinvestigating people holding Secret clearances be developed.
- The Department of Defense's most sensitive information must be accorded a higher priority in "attention and resources." Concerning this finding, the commission recommended that Congress grant the secretary of defense greater authority concerning the use of polygraph testing; the appropriate Department of Defense components develop a reliability program; and Special Access Programs be reviewed and revalidated, with standardized procedures and standards developed to insure uniform oversight.
- The adjudication process concerning security clearance determinations should be improved. Here the commission recommended that more precise and effective adjudicative standards be developed; and adjudicators be trained properly.
- Controls for classified material should be improved. Here the commission recommended that there be a uniform Department of Defense accounting system for Secret material; the retention of classified materials for more than five years be prohibited unless they are permanently valuable records of the government; employees not be

permitted to work alone in areas containing Top Secret or SCI materials; and procedures for checking briefcases and other personal effects be established to see if classified material is being removed from intelligence facilities.

- Additional measures should be instituted to counter the effectiveness of hostile intelligence activities that are directed at the Department of Defense. Here the commission recommended that efforts be made to limit the size and freedom of movement of the diplomatic presence of potentially hostile nations; the funding for counterintelligence analysis be increased; all cleared personnel be required to report on their foreign travel and their contacts with foreign nationals; and the size and effectiveness of the security awareness program be increased.

- The professionalism of security personnel should be enhanced. Here the commission recommended that training programs be established.

- Basic research must be increased to guide security policy and practice. Here, the specific recommendations were that the Defense Security Institute and its research and development program concerning personnel investigations be expanded; and increased funding be provided for the National Computer Security Center's research and development program.

- More effective action should be taken against those who violate the security rules. Here the specific recommendations were to continue to urge Congress to enact legislation to enhance criminal enforcement of those who disclose security information without permission; to withhold payments to contractors until they comply with Department of Defense security requirements; and to revoke, if necessary, clearances of contractors who continue to display indifference.

- Security is critically dependent on the actions of commanders and supervisors at all levels. Here the commission recommended that all agencies and departments conduct a one-time security inspection to see how classified material is being handled; and commanders and supervisors be instructed to use the appropriate enforcement remedies for those who violate security requirements.

References

Corson, William R. *The Armies of Ignorance: The Rise of the American Intelligence Empire.* New York: Dial Press, 1977.

Dixon, James H. *National Security Policy Formulation: Institutions, Processes, and Issues.* Washington, DC: National Defense University, 1984.

Godson, Roy, ed. *Intelligence Problems for the 1980s, Number 1: Elements of Intelligence.* Rev. ed. Washington, DC: National Strategy Information Center, 1983.

—**DEPARTMENT OF ENERGY (DOE)** openly collects political, economic, and technical information concerning foreign energy matters. While the DOE does produce some foreign intelligence and provides technical and analytical research capabilities to other intelligence operations, it is primarily an intelligence customer.

References

American Bar Association. *Oversight and Accountability of the U.S. Intelligence Agencies: An Evaluation.* Washington, DC: ABA, 1985.

Corson, William R. *The Armies of Ignorance: The Rise of the American Intelligence Empire.* New York: Dial Press, 1977.

Dixon, James H. *National Security Policy Formulation: Institutions, Processes, and Issues.* Washington, DC: National Defense University, 1984.

Laqueur, Walter. *A World of Secrets.* New York: Basic Books, 1985.

Lowenthal, Mark M. *U.S. Intelligence: Evolution and Anatomy.* New York: Praeger Publishers, 1984.

Maurer, Alfred C.; Turnstall, Marion D.; and Keagle, James M. *Intelligence Policy and Process.* Boulder, CO: Westview Press, 1985.

Oseth, John M. *Regulating U.S. Intelligence Operations: A Study in the Definition of the National Interest.* Frankfurt: University of Kentucky Press, 1985.

Quirk, John; Phillips, David; Cline, Ray; and Pforzheimer, Walter. *The Central Intelligence Agency: A Photographic History.* Guilford, CT: Foreign Intelligence Press, 1986.

Treverton, Gregory F. *Covert Action: The Limits of Intervention in the Postwar World.* New York: Basic Books, 1987.

Turner, Stansfield. *Secrecy and Democracy: The CIA in Transition.* Boston: Houghton Mifflin, 1985.

—**DEPARTMENT OF STATE,** specifically its Bureau of Intelligence and Research, produces political and some economic intelligence to meet departmental needs. It also coordinates the department's relations with other foreign intelligence operations, disseminates reports received from U.S. diplomatic and consular posts abroad, and participates in preparing National Intelligence Estimates.

In addition, the secretary of state has several duties and responsibilities, many of which require intelligence support. His duties are to serve as the President's principal advisor on foreign policy; to conduct negotiations relating to U.S. foreign affairs; to grant and issue passports to American citizens; to advise the President on the appointment of U.S. ambassadors, ministers, counsuls, and other diplomatic representatives; to advise the President regarding the acceptance, recall, and dismissal, of the representatives of foreign governments; to personally participate in or direct American representatives to international conferences, organizations, and agencies; to negotiate, interpret, and terminate treaties and agreements; to insure protection by the U.S. government of American citizens, property, and interests in foreign states; to supervise the administration of U.S. immigration laws abroad; to provide information to American citizens regarding the political, economic, social, cultural, and humanitarian conditions in foreign countries; to inform Congress and the American public on the conduct of U.S. foreign relations; to promote beneficial economic intercourse between the United States and other countries; to administer the Department of State; and to supervise the Foreign Service of the United States. *See also:* Bureau of Intelligence and Research.

References

American Bar Association. *Oversight and Accountability of the U.S. Intelligence Agencies: An Evaluation.* Washington, DC: ABA, 1985.

Corson, William R. *The Armies of Ignorance: The Rise of the American Intelligence Empire.* New York: Dial Press, 1977.

Department of State, Bureau of Public Affairs. *Duties of the Secretary of State.* Washington, DC: Department of State, 1984.

Dixon, James. *National Security Policy Formulation: Institutions, Processes, and Issues.* Washington, DC: National Defense University, 1984.

Godson, Roy, ed. *Intelligence Problems for the 1980s, Number 2: Analysis and Estimates.* Washington, DC: National Strategy Information Center, 1980.

Kent, Sherman. *Strategic Intelligence for American World Policy.* Princeton, NJ: Princeton University Press, 1966.

Laqueur, Walter. *A World of Secrets.* New York: Basic Books, 1985.

Lowenthal, Mark M. *U.S. Intelligence: Evolution and Anatomy.* New York: Praeger, 1984.

Maurer, Alfred C.; Turnstall, Marion D.; and Keagle, James M. *Intelligence Policy and Process.* Boulder, CO: Westview Press, 1985.

Oseth, John M. *Regulating U.S. Intelligence Operations: A Study in the Definition of the National Interest.* Frankfurt: University of Kentucky Press, 1985.

Quirk, John; Phillips, David; Cline, Ray; and Pforzheimer, Walter. *The Central Intelligence Agency: A Photographic History.* Guilford, CT: Foreign Intelligence Press, 1986.

Treverton, Gregory F. *Covert Action: The Limits of Intervention in the Postwar World.* New York: Basic Books, 1987.

Turner, Stansfield. *Secrecy and Democracy: The CIA in Transition.* Boston: Houghton Mifflin, 1985.

—DEPARTMENT OF THE TREASURY openly collects foreign financial and monetary information and helps the State Department to collect economic data. It assists in producing national intelligence for the President and senior policymakers and insures, through the Secret Service, that the President, Office of the President, and other officials are not being surveilled by hostile intelligence or other organizations. In addition, the Secret Service and other departments conduct very low-level intelligence activities. The Secret Service, in addition to its responsibilities concerning the President, collects information and handles investigations concerning the counterfeiting of U.S. currency, including credit card fraud. There are approximately 1,500 Secret Service agents stationed in field offices around the United States.

The Department of the Treasury's Office of Protective Intelligence collects, evaluates, and stores protective security data that helps the Secret Service keep track of suspected individuals and groups.

The U.S. Customs Service conducts investigations concerning fraud, smuggling, and cargo thefts. Its intelligence experts monitor the production of narcotics overseas, technology transfer, and money laundering. Agents in the Bureau of Alcohol, Tobacco, and Firearms are involved in investigations concerning bombings and the illegal possession of firearms and explosives. *See also:* Economic Intelligence.

References

American Bar Association. *Oversight and Account-ability of the U.S. Intelligence Agencies: An Evaluation.* Washington, DC: ABA, 1985.

Corson, William R. *The Armies of Ignorance: The Rise of the American Intelligence Empire.* New York: Dial Press, 1977.

Department of Defense, Defense Intelligence College. *Joint Intelligence: A Book of Supportive Readings.* Washington, DC: DIC, 1986.

Kent, Sherman. *Strategic Intelligence for American World Policy.* Princeton, NJ: Princeton University Press, 1966.

Laqueur, Walter. *A World of Secrets.* New York: Basic Books, 1985.

Lowenthal, Mark M. *U.S. Intelligence: Evolution and Anatomy.* New York: Praeger, 1984.

Maurer, Alfred C.; Turnstall, Marion D.; and Keagle, James M. *Intelligence Policy and Process.* Boulder, CO: Westview Press, 1985.

Quirk, John; Phillips, David; Cline, Ray; and Pforzheimer, Walter. *The Central Intelligence Agency: A Photographic History.* Guilford, CT: Foreign Intelligence Press, 1986.

Treverton, Gregory F. *Covert Action: The Limits of Intervention in the Postwar World.* New York: Basic Books, 1987.

Turner, Stansfield. *Secrecy and Democracy: The CIA in Transition.* Boston: Houghton Mifflin, 1985.

—**DEPARTMENTAL INTELLIGENCE** is a general intelligence term for intelligence that governmental departments and agencies produce in order to accomplish their missions and accomplish the duties that they have been assigned.

References

Becket, Henry S. A. *The Dictionary of Espionage: Spookspeak into English.* New York: Stein and Day, 1986.

Department of Defense, Joint Chiefs of Staff. *Department of Defense Dictionary of Military and Related Terms.* Washington, DC: GPO, 1986.

Kent, Sherman. *Strategic Intelligence for American World Policy.* Princeton, NJ: Princeton University Press, 1966.

Turner, Stansfield. *Secrecy and Democracy: The CIA in Transition.* Boston: Houghton Mifflin, 1985.

U.S. Congress. Senate. *Final Report of the Senate Select Committee to Study Government Operations with Respect to Intelligence Activities. Report 94-755. Book I, Foreign and Military Intelligence.* Washington, DC: GPO, 1976.

—**DEPUTY DIRECTOR FOR ADMINISTRATION (DDA).** *See:* Central Intelligence Agency.

—**DEPUTY DIRECTOR FOR INTELLIGENCE (DDI).** *See:* Central Intelligence Agency.

—**DEPUTY DIRECTOR FOR OPERATIONS (DDO).** *See:* Central Intelligence Agency.

—**DEPUTY DIRECTOR FOR PLANS (DDP)** was the predecessor of the deputy director of operations (DDO). It was renamed in 1973.

References

Lowenthal, Mark M. *U.S. Intelligence: Evolution and Anatomy.* New York: Praeger, 1984.

—**DEPUTY DIRECTOR FOR SCIENCE AND TECHNOLOGY (DDS&T).** *See:* Central Intelligence Agency.

—**DEPUTY DIRECTOR FOR CENTRAL INTELLIGENCE (DDCI).** *See:* Central Intelligence Agency.

—**DEPUTY UNDER SECRETARY OF DEFENSE FOR POLICY (DUSD(P))** shares responsibility for the development of security policy for the Department of Defense with the assistant secretary of defense for command, control, communications, and intelligence (ASD(C³I)). He is also responsible for staff supervision for all Department of Defense counterintelligence policy and is responsible for the Defense Investigative Service. *See also:* Assistant Secretary of Defense (command, control, communications, and intelligence) (ASD(C³I)).

References

Corson, William R. *The Armies of Ignorance: The Rise of the American Intelligence Empire.* New York: Dial Press, 1977.

Godson, Roy, ed. *Intelligence Problems for the 1980s, Number 1: Elements of Intelligence.* Rev. ed. Washington, DC: National Strategy Information Center, 1983.

—**DEROGATORY INFORMATION** is an intelligence security term. It is information concerning an individual that indicates that granting the individual access to classified information may not be consistent with the interests of national security. *See also:* Access, Authorized, Background Investigation, Clearance, Debriefing, Lawful Investigation, "Least Intrusive Means," Personnel Security, Security.

References

Corson, William R. *The Armies of Ignorance: The Rise of the American Intelligence Empire.* New York: Dial Press, 1977.

Godson, Roy, ed. *Intelligence Problems for the 1980s, Number 1: Elements of Intelligence.* Rev. ed. Washington, DC: National Strategy Information Center, 1983.

Turner, Stansfield. *Secrecy and Democracy: The CIA in Transition.* Boston: Houghton Mifflin, 1985.

—**DES DEVICE,** in communications security (COMSEC), means the hardware part or subassembly that implements the DES algorithm. *See also:* Communications Security.

References

Martin, Paul H. "Communications-Computer Security." *Journal of Electronic Defense* (June 1987).

Muzerall, Joseph V., and Carty, Thomas P. "COMSEC and Its Need for Key Management." *DP&CS* (Spring 1987).

Ware, Willis H. "Information Systems, Security, and Privacy." *EDUCOM Bulletin* (Summer 1984).

—**DES EQUIPMENT,** in communications security (COMSEC), means equipment embodying one or more DES devices and associated controls and power supplies that are used to implement the DES algorithm in a cryptosystem. *See also:* Communications Security.

References

Martin, Paul H. "Communications-Computer Security." *Journal of Electronic Defense* (June 1987).

Muzerall, Joseph V., and Carty, Thomas P. "COMSEC and Its Need for Key Management." *DP&CS* (Spring 1987).

Ware, Willis H. "Information Systems, Security, and Privacy." *EDUCOM Bulletin* (Summer 1984).

—**DESCRIPTIVE STATISTICS** is a statistical or quantitative methodological term that is often used in intelligence analysis. It is the branch of statistics that involves summarizing, tabulating, organizing, and graphing data for the purpose of describing a sample of objects or individuals that have been measured or observed. In descriptive statistics, no attempt is made to infer the characteristics of objects or individuals that have not been measured or observed.

References

Pickett, George. "Congress, the Budget, and Intelligence." In *Intelligence Policy and Process,* edited by Alfred C. Maurer, Marion D. Turnstall, and James M. Keagle. Boulder, CO: Westview Press, 1985.

—**DESIGNATED AGENCY ETHICS OFFICIAL.** *See:* Central Intelligence Agency.

—**DESTABILIZATION** is a term used in clandestine and covert intelligence operations to describe the use of overt political and economic actions to undermine a foreign government. *See also:* Agent, Agent in Place, Agent Net, Agent of Influence, Agent Provocateur, Case, Case Officer, Cover, Cover Name, Cover Organizations, Cover Story, Dirty Tricks, Illegal Operations, Illegal Residency, Illegal Support Officer, Infiltration, Provocation Agent, Special Activities, Third Country Operation.

References

Becket, Henry S. A. *The Dictionary of Espionage: Spookspeak into English.* New York: Stein and Day, 1986.

Deacon, Richard. *Spyclopedia: An Encyclopedia of Spies, Secret Services, Operations, Jargon, and All Subjects Related to the World of Espionage.* London: Macdonald, 1987.

Department of Defense, Defense Intelligence Agency. *Defense Intelligence Agency Manual.* Washington, DC: DIA, 1987.

Ranelagh, John. *The Agency: The Rise and Decline of the CIA.* New York: Simon and Schuster, 1986.

Turner, Stansfield. *Secrecy and Democracy: The CIA in Transition.* Boston: Houghton Mifflin, 1985.

—**DETAILED REPORT** is an intelligence imagery and photoreconnaissance term. In photographic interpretation, it is a comprehensive analytical intelligence report that describes in detail the interpretation of photography that usually covers a single subject, target, or target complex. *See also:* Basic Cover, Coverage, Imagery Annotation, Imagery Correlation, Imagery Data Recording, Imagery Exploitation, Imagery Intelligence,

Imagery Interpretation Key, Imagery Interpreter, Photogrammetry, Photographic Coverage, Photographic Intelligence, Photographic Interpretation, Photographic Reading, Photographic Scale, Photographic Strip, Photography, Strip Plot, Titling Strip.

References

Department of Defense, Joint Chiefs of Staff. *Department of Defense Dictionary of Military and Related Terms.* Washington, DC: GPO, 1986.

—**DETECTION,** in imagery interpretation, means the discovery of an object but does not mean that the object has been identified. *See also:* Detailed Report.

References

Department of Defense, Joint Chiefs of Staff. *Department of Defense Dictionary of Military and Related Terms.* Washington, DC: GPO, 1986.

Godson, Roy, ed. *Intelligence Problems for the 1980s, Number 3: Counterintelligence.* Washington, DC: National Strategy Information Center, 1980.

Laqueur, Walter. *A World of Secrets.* New York: Basic Books, 1985.

—**DEVELOP** is a covert and clandestine intelligence term. It means to cultivate a sympathizer into becoming an agent. *See also:* Agent, Agent in Place, Agent of Influence, Agent Provocateur, Co-opted Worker, Co-optees, Cultivation, False Flag, Informant, Inside Man, Provocation Agent, Special Activities, Walk-in.

References

Becket, Henry S. A. *The Dictionary of Espionage: Spookspeak into English.* New York: Stein and Day, 1986.

Deacon, Richard. *Spyclopedia: An Encyclopedia of Spies, Secret Services, Operations, Jargon, and All Subjects Related to the World of Espionage.* London: Macdonald, 1987.

Ranelagh, John. *The Agency: The Rise and Decline of the CIA.* New York: Simon and Schuster, 1986.

Treverton, Gregory F. *Covert Action: The Limits of Intervention in the Postwar World.* New York: Basic Books, 1987.

—**DEVELOPMENT PROJECTS DIVISION (DPD),** Central Intelligence Agency, was a component of the Directorate for Plans and was responsible for overhead reconnaissance. It was transferred to the Directorate for Science and Technology in 1963. *See also:* Central Intelligence Agency.

References

Fain, Tyrus G.; Plant, Katharine C.; and Milloy, Ross. *The Intelligence Community: History, Organization, and Issues.* Public Documents Series. New York: R.R. Bowker, 1977.

—**DIA FACT BOOK-COMMUNIST WORLD FORCES,** produced by the Defense Intelligence Agency, is a desk-top reference containing a summary of essential information concerning the size and capabilities of Communist military forces worldwide. Emphasis is placed on the current order of battle and on the characteristics and performance of major Communist weapons systems and other military equipment. *See also:* Defense Intelligence Agency.

References

Von Hoene, John P. A. *Intelligence User's Guide.* Washington, DC: DIA, 1983.

—**DIA LEXICON** is designed as a basic reference tool for military intelligence professionals. It contains the definitions of acronyms, words, phrases, abbreviations, and nomenclature that are used commonly in the military environment. It is updated and published as necessary. All the acronyms from this lexicon and a host more are included in the acronym section of this encyclopedia. *See also:* Defense Intelligence Agency.

References

Von Hoene, John P. A. *Intelligence User's Guide.* Washington, DC: DIA, 1983.

—**DIA POINT OF CONTACT PAMPHLET** is a listing of all Defense Intelligence Agency points of contact with their telephone numbers. *See also:* Defense Intelligence Agency.

References

Von Hoene, John P. A. *Intelligence User's Guide.* Washington, DC: DIA, 1983.

—**DIPLEX,** a baud-based system term used in communications intelligence, communications security, operations security, and signals analysis, is a two-channel time division multiplex signal, in which the intelligence elements of a basic single-channel system have been split, allowing for two-channel operation using an interlaced element arrangement. *See also:* Communications Security.

References

Muzerall, Joseph V., and Carty, Thomas P. "COMSEC and Its Need for Key Management." *DP&CS* (Spring 1987).

—**DIRECT AIR SUPPORT CENTER,** a Navy and Marine Corps tactical operations entity, is a subordinate operational component of the tactical air control system that is designed for controlling and directing close air support and other direct air support operations. The center is under the operational control of a tactical air control or tactical air direction center and is normally located near the command post of the supported ground unit.

References

Department of Defense, Joint Chiefs of Staff. *Department of Defense Dictionary of Military and Related Terms.* Washington, DC: GPO, 1986.

—**DIRECT SUPPORT** is an Army tactical intelligence (TACINT) term that means providing a priority response to requests from a supported unit. A military intelligence element in direct support remains under the operational control of its parent organization.

References

Department of Defense, Joint Chiefs of Staff. *Department of Defense Dictionary of Military and Related Terms.* Washington, DC: GPO, 1986.

Department of Defense, U.S. Army. *Intelligence and Electronic Warfare Operations.* Field Manual FM 34-1. Washington, DC: Headquarters, Department of the Army, 1984.

———. *Military Intelligence Battalion Combat Electronic Warfare and Intelligence (Aerial Exploitation) (Corps).* Field Manual FM 34-22. Washington, DC: Headquarters, Department of the Army, 1984.

———. *Military Intelligence Battalion (CEWI) (Operations) (Corps).* Field Manual 34-21. Washington, DC: Headquarters, Department of the Army, 1982.

———. *Military Intelligence Battalion (Combat Electronic Warfare Intelligence) (Division).* Field Manual FM 34-10. Washington, DC: Headquarters, Department of the Army, 1981.

———. *Military Intelligence Battalion (CEWI) (Tactical Exploitation) (Corps): Counterintelligence, Interrogation, Electronic Warfare.* Field Manual FM 34-23. Washington, DC: Headquarters, Department of the Army, 1985.

———. *Military Intelligence Company (Combat Electronic Warfare and Intelligence) (Armored Cavalry Regiment/Separate Brigade).* Field Manual FM 34-30. Washington, DC: Headquarters, Department of the Army, 1983.

———. *Military Intelligence Group (Combat Electronic Warfare and Intelligence) (Corps).* Field Manual FM 34-20. Washington, DC: Headquarters, Department of the Army, 1983.

—**DIRECTION (INTELLIGENCE CYCLE)** is a general intelligence term. It involves determining which intelligence requirements are most important and therefore should be satisfied, preparing a collection plan to guide all concerned in fulfilling these requirements, issuing orders and requests for information from intelligence collection agencies, and continuously monitoring the progress of the collecting agencies in collecting the information. *See also:* Intelligence, Intelligence Cycle.

References

Laqueur, Walter. *A World of Secrets.* New York: Basic Books, 1985.

Turner, Stansfield. *Secrecy and Democracy: The CIA in Transition.* Boston: Houghton Mifflin, 1985.

—**DIRECTION FINDING (DF)** is a procedure for obtaining bearings on radio transmitters with the use of a directional antenna and a display unit on an intercept receiver or ancillary equipment. In the Army tactical intelligence (TACINT) context, DF is a step in the signals intelligence (SIGINT) process. *See:* SIGINT Process.

References

Department of Defense, Defense Intelligence College. *Glossary of Intelligence Terms and Definitions.* Washington, DC: DIC, 1987.

Department of Defense, Joint Chiefs of Staff. *Department of Defense Dictionary of Military and Related Terms.* Washington, DC: GPO, 1986.

Department of Defense, U.S. Army. *Counter-Signals Intelligence (C-SIGINT) Operations.* Field Manual FM 34-62. Washington, DC: Headquarters, Department of the Army, 1986.

———. *Military Intelligence Battalion (Combat Electronic Warfare Intelligence) (Division).* Field Manual FM 34-10. Washington, DC: Headquarters, Department of the Army, 1981.

———. *Military Intelligence Company (Combat Electronic Warfare and Intelligence) (Armored Cavalry Regiment/Separate Brigade).* Field Manual FM 34-30. Washington, DC: Headquarters, Department of the Army, 1983.

—DIRECTIVE, as defined by the Church Committee, is "any executive branch communication which initiates or governs departmental or agency action, conduct, or procedure."

References

Department of Defense, Joint Chiefs of Staff. *Department of Defense Dictionary of Military and Related Terms.* Washington, DC: GPO, 1986.

Laqueur, Walter. *A World of Secrets.* New York: Basic Books, 1985.

Turner, Stansfield. *Secrecy and Democracy: The CIA in Transition.* Boston: Houghton Mifflin, 1985.

U.S. Congress. Senate. *Final Report of the Senate Select Committee to Study Government Operations with Respect to Intelligence Activities. Report 94-755. Book I, Foreign and Military Intelligence.* Washington, DC: GPO, 1976.

—DIRECTOR (DR) (DIA). *See:* Defense Intelligence Agency.

—DIRECTOR, NATIONAL SECURITY AGENCY/ CHIEF, CENTRAL SECURITY SERVICE. *See:* National Security Agency.

—DIRECTOR OF CENTRAL INTELLIGENCE (DCI). *See:* Central Intelligence Agency.

—DIRECTOR OF CENTRAL INTELLIGENCE COMMITTEE is any one of several committees that have been created by the director of Central Intelligence (DCI) to advise him and to perform whatever functions he determines. DCI committees usually deal with Intelligence Community concerns, and their terms of reference are usually specified in DCI directives. Members of the DCI committees may be drawn from all components of the Intelligence Community. *See also:* Director of Central Intelligence Directive.

References

Department of Defense, Defense Intelligence College. *Glossary of Intelligence Terms and Definitions.* Washington, DC: DIC, 1987.

Kent, Sherman. *Strategic Intelligence for American World Policy.* Princeton, NJ: Princeton University Press, 1966.

Laqueur, Walter. *A World of Secrets.* New York: Basic Books, 1985.

Turner, Stansfield. *Secrecy and Democracy: The CIA in Transition.* Boston: Houghton Mifflin, 1985.

—DIRECTOR OF CENTRAL INTELLIGENCE DIRECTIVE (DCID) is an instruction issued by the director of Central Intelligence. It outlines the general policies and procedures that are to be followed by the agencies and organizations that have been placed under his direction and overview. It is usually more specific than a National Security Council Intelligence Directive (NSCID).

References

Becket, Henry S. A. *The Dictionary of Espionage: Spookspeak into English.* New York: Stein and Day, 1986.

Department of Defense, Defense Intelligence College. *Glossary of Intelligence Terms and Definitions.* Washington, DC: DIC, 1987.

Fain, Tyrus G.; Plant, Katharine C.; and Milloy, Ross. *The Intelligence Community: History, Organization, and Issues.* Public Documents Series. New York: R.R. Bowker, 1977.

Laqueur, Walter. *A World of Secrets.* New York: Basic Books, 1985.

Turner, Stansfield. *Secrecy and Democracy: The CIA in Transition.* Boston: Houghton Mifflin, 1985.

U.S. Congress. Senate. *Final Report of the Senate Select Committee to Study Government Operations with Respect to Intelligence Activities. Report 94-755. Book I, Foreign and Military Intelligence.* Washington, DC: GPO, 1976.

—DIRECTOR, OFFICE OF MANAGEMENT AND BUDGET was to be given several responsibilities under a proposed Presidential Directive entitled "National Policy on Telecommunications and Automated Information Systems Security," which appeared on September 17, 1984, but was never put into effect. The directive expressed concern for the lack of automated information systems and telecommunications security, and it established two committees and two positions to work toward strengthening the existing security in these areas. In it, the director of the OMB was directed to "(1) Specify data to be provided during the annual budget review by the departments and agencies on programs and budgets relating to telecommunications systems security and automated information systems security of the departments and agencies of the government; (2) Consolidate and provide such data to the National Manager via the Executive Agent; and (3) Review for consistency with this Directive and amend as appropriate, OMB Circular A-71 (Transmittal Memorandum No. 1), OMB Circular A-76, as amended, and other OMB policies and regulations which may pertain to the subject matter herein."

References

"National Policy on Telecommunications and Automated Information Systems Security." Proposed Presidential Directive, September 17, 1984.

—**DIRECTOR OF NAVAL INTELLIGENCE (DNI).** *See:* Naval Intelligence, Office of Naval Intelligence.

—**DIRECTORATE FOR ADMINISTRATION,** Central Intelligence Agency, was established in 1950 and was assigned responsibility for personnel, budgetary, security, medical services, and logistical support aspects of the agency's overseas operations. *See also:* Central Intelligence Agency.

References

Fain, Tyrus G.; Plant, Katharine C.; and Milloy, Ross. *The Intelligence Community: History, Organization, and Issues.* Public Documents Series. New York: R.R. Bowker, 1977.

—**DIRECTORATE FOR ALERT CENTER OPERATIONS (JSO).** *See:* Defense Intelligence Agency.

—**DIRECTORATE FOR COLLECTION MANAGEMENT (DC).** *See:* Defense Intelligence Agency.

—**DIRECTORATE FOR CURRENT INTELLIGENCE (JSI).** *See:* Defense Intelligence Agency.

—**DIRECTORATE FOR DODIIS ENGINEERING.** *See:* Defense Intelligence Agency.

—**DIRECTORATE FOR DODIIS PLANNING AND MANAGEMENT.** *See:* Defense Intelligence Agency.

—**DIRECTORATE FOR ESTIMATES (DE).** *See:* Defense Intelligence Agency.

—**DIRECTORATE FOR EXTERNAL RELATIONS (DI).** *See:* Defense Intelligence Agency.

—**DIRECTORATE FOR FOREIGN INTELLIGENCE (VP).** *See:* Defense Intelligence Agency.

—**DIRECTORATE FOR HUMAN RESOURCES (RHR).** *See:* Defense Intelligence Agency.

—**DIRECTORATE FOR IMAGERY EXPLOITATION (DX).** *See:* Defense Intelligence Agency.

—**DIRECTORATE FOR INDICATIONS AND WARNING (JSW).** *See:* Defense Intelligence Agency.

—**DIRECTORATE FOR INFORMATION SYSTEMS (RSI).** *See:* Defense Intelligence Agency.

—**DIRECTORATE FOR INTELLIGENCE (DDI).** *See:* Central Intelligence Agency.

—**DIRECTORATE FOR INTELLIGENCE AND EXTERNAL AFFAIRS (DI).** *See:* Defense Intelligence Agency.

—**DIRECTORATE FOR JCS SUPPORT (JS).** *See:* Defense Intelligence Agency.

—**DIRECTORATE FOR MANAGEMENT AND OPERATIONS (VO).** *See:* Defense Intelligence Agency.

—**DIRECTORATE FOR NMIC OPERATIONS (ISO).** *See:* Defense Intelligence Agency.

—**DIRECTORATE FOR OJCS INTELLIGENCE SUPPORT (JSJ).** *See:* Defense Intelligence Agency.

—**DIRECTORATE FOR OPERATIONS (DDO).** *See:* Defense Intelligence Agency.

—**DIRECTORATE FOR OPERATIONS, PLANS, AND TRAINING (VO).** *See:* Defense Intelligence Agency.

—**DIRECTORATE FOR PLANS (DDP),** Central Intelligence Agency, was created in 1952 from the integration of the Office of Special Operations (OSO) and the Office of Policy Coordination (OPC). It was also known as the "Clandestine Service." It was renamed the Directorate of Operations (DDO) in 1973. *See also:* Central Intelligence Agency.

References

Corson, William R. *The Armies of Ignorance: The Rise of the American Intelligence Empire.* New York: Dial Press, 1977.

Fain, Tyrus G.; Plant, Katharine C.; and Milloy, Ross. *The Intelligence Community: History, Organization, and Issues.* Public Documents Series. New York: R.R. Bowker, 1977.

Godson, Roy, ed. *Intelligence Problems for the 1980s, Number 1: Elements of Intelligence.* Rev. ed. Washington, DC: National Strategy Information Center, 1983.

Lowenthal, Mark M. *U.S. Intelligence: Evolution and Anatomy.* New York: Praeger, 1984.

—**DIRECTORATE FOR PLANS AND POLICY (DP).** *See:* Defense Intelligence Agency.

—**DIRECTORATE FOR PROCUREMENT (RSQ).** *See:* Defense Intelligence Agency.

—**DIRECTORATE FOR RESEARCH (DDR),** Central Intelligence Agency, was created in 1962 and was the immediate predecessor to the Directorate for Science and Technology. *See also:* Central Intelligence Agency.

References

Corson, William R. *The Armies of Ignorance: The Rise of the American Intelligence Empire.* New York: Dial Press, 1977.

Fain, Tyrus G.; Plant, Katharine C.; and Milloy, Ross. *The Intelligence Community: History, Organization, and Issues.* Public Documents Series. New York: R.R. Bowker, 1977.

Godson, Roy, ed. *Intelligence Problems for the 1980s, Number 1: Elements of Intelligence.* Rev. ed. Washington, DC: National Strategy Information Center, 1983.

Lowenthal, Mark M. *U.S. Intelligence: Evolution and Anatomy.* New York: Praeger, 1984.

—**DIRECTORATE FOR RESOURCES AND SYSTEMS (RS).** *See:* Defense Intelligence Agency.

—**DIRECTORATE FOR SCIENCE AND TECHNOLOGY (DDS&T).** *See:* Central Intelligence Agency, Defense Intelligence Agency.

—**DIRECTORATE FOR SCIENTIFIC AND TECHNICAL INTELLIGENCE (DT).** *See:* Defense Intelligence Agency.

—**DIRECTORATE FOR SECURITY AND COUNTERINTELLIGENCE (OS).** *See:* Defense Intelligence Agency.

—**DIRECTORATE FOR TECHNICAL SERVICES AND SUPPORT (RTS).** *See:* Defense Intelligence Agency.

—**DIRECTORATE FOR TRAINING.** *See:* Defense Intelligence Agency.

—**DIRECTORATE OF ADMINISTRATION (DDA).** *See:* Central Intelligence Agency.

—**DIRECTORATE OF ATTACHÉS.** *See:* Defense Intelligence Agency.

—**DIRECTORATE OF RESEARCH (DB).** *See:* Defense Intelligence Agency.

—**DIRECTORATE OF SUPPORT (DDS).** *See:* Central Intelligence Agency.

—**DIRTY TRICKS** is a term used in clandestine and covert intelligence operations. Dirty tricks concern "black operations" and is a generic term to describe the gamut of counterespionage skullduggery. It can include breaking into an apartment or home to illegally install bugging devices. *See also:* Black Bag Job, Black Bag Operation, Black List, Blackmail, Cacklebladder, Case, Case Officer, Executive Action, Flap Potential, Fur-lined Seat Cover, Granny, Heavy Mob, Heavy Squad, Honey Trap, Ladies, Lion Tamer, Mozhno Girls, Paroles, Pavement Artists, Pigeon, Raven, Scalp Hunters, Shaking the Tree, Sheep Dipping, Sisters, Sleeper, Snitch Jacket, Swallow, Swallow's Nest, Taxi, Tell-tale, Terminate with Extreme Prejudice, Third Country Operation.

References

Becket, Henry S. A. *The Dictionary of Espionage: Spookspeak into English.* New York: Stein and Day, 1986.

Corson, William R. *The Armies of Ignorance: The Rise of the American Intelligence Empire.* New York: Dial Press, 1977. 1977.

Deacon, Richard. *Spyclopedia: An Encyclopedia of Spies, Secret Services, Operations, Jargon, and All Subjects Related to the World of Espionage.* London: Macdonald, 1987.

Ranelagh, John. *The Agency: The Rise and Decline of the CIA.* New York: Simon and Schuster, 1986.

Treverton, Gregory F. *Covert Action: The Limits of Intervention in the Postwar World.* New York: Basic Books, 1987.

—**DISAFFECTED PERSON** is a term used in clandestine and covert intelligence operations to describe an individual who is disenchanted or dissatisfied with his current position or situation and therefore may be exploitable for intelligence purposes, in that he might be willing to become an agent or defector. The term assumes that the person works with or has access to classified or sensitive information. *See also:* Walk-in.

References

Department of Defense, Defense Intelligence College. *Glossary of Intelligence Terms and Definitions.* Washington, DC: DIC, 1987.

—**DISCARD** is a term used in clandestine and covert intelligence operations to describe an agent who is betrayed by his own service in order to protect another, more valuable agent or source of information. *See also:* Agent, Blow, Blown Agent, Bug, Bugging, Burn, Burnt, Snitch Jacket.

References

Becket, Henry S. A. *The Dictionary of Espionage: Spookspeak into English.* New York: Stein and Day, 1986.

Deacon, Richard. *Spyclopedia: An Encyclopedia of Spies, Secret Services, Operations, Jargon, and All Subjects Related to the World of Espionage.* London: Macdonald, 1987.

Ranelagh, John. *The Agency: The Rise and Decline of the CIA.* New York: Simon and Schuster, 1986.

—**DISCLOSURE** is a general intelligence term for the authorized release of classified information through approved channels. Disclosure was also defined by Congress in the Intelligence Identities Protection Act of 1982 as "to communicate, provide, impart, transmit, transfer, convey, publish, or otherwise make available." *See also:* Access, Authorized, Classification, Classified Information, Code Word, Compromise, Declassification, Downgrade, Freedom of Information Act, Limited Access Area, Need-to-Know, Need-to-Know Principle, No-Lone Zone, Nondisclosure Agreement, Nondiscussion Area, Sanitization, Sanitize, Sanitized Area, Security Certification, Security Classification, Sensitive Compartmented Information, Sensitive Compartmented Information Facility, Two-Person Control.

References

Corson, William R. *The Armies of Ignorance: The Rise of the American Intelligence Empire.* New York: Dial Press, 1977.

Department of Defense, Defense Intelligence College. *Glossary of Intelligence Terms and Definitions.* Washington, DC: DIC, 1987.

Godson, Roy, ed. *Intelligence Problems for the 1980s, Number 1: Elements of Intelligence.* Rev. ed. Washington, DC: National Strategy Information Center, 1983.

U.S. Congress. *Intelligence Identities Protection Act of 1982. Public Law 97-200, June 23, 1982.* Washington, DC: GPO, 1982.

—**DISINFORMATION** is a term used in clandestine and covert intelligence operations to describe manufactured, false evidence that is used to discredit your opponent. In FBI terminology, it is misinformation that has been prepared by an intelligence agency with the goal of misleading, deluding, disrupting, or undermining confidence in individuals, organizations, or governments. *See also:* Agent, Flap Potential, Sanctification, Snitch Jacket, Third Country Operation.

References

Becket, Henry S. A. *The Dictionary of Espionage: Spookspeak into English.* New York: Stein and Day, 1986.

Corson, William R. *The Armies of Ignorance: The Rise of the American Intelligence Empire.* New York: Dial Press, 1977.

Deacon, Richard. *Spyclopedia: An Encyclopedia of Spies, Secret Services, Operations, Jargon, and All Subjects Related to the World of Espionage.* London: Macdonald, 1987.

Godson, Roy, ed. *Intelligence Problems for the 1980s, Number 1: Elements of Intelligence.* Rev. ed. Washington, DC: National Strategy Information Center, 1983.

Kessler, Ronald. *Spy vs. Spy: Stalking Soviet Spies in America.* New York: Charles Scribner's Sons, 1988.

Laqueur, Walter. *A World of Secrets.* New York: Basic Books, 1985.

Maurer, Alfred C.; Turnstall, Marion D.; and Keagle, James M. *Intelligence Policy and Process.* Boulder, CO: Westview Press, 1985.

Treverton, Gregory F. *Covert Action: The Limits of Intervention in the Postwar World.* New York: Basic Books, 1987.

Turner, Stansfield. *Secrecy and Democracy: The CIA in Transition.* Boston: Houghton Mifflin, 1985.

—**DISPATCHED AGENT** is a term used in clandestine and covert intelligence operations. A dispatched agent is one who contacts a rival organization, claiming that he wants to defect, when he actually is attempting to penetrate the rival organization. *See also:* Agent, Agent Authentication, Agent in Place, Agent Net, Agent of Influence, Agent Provocateur, Blow, Blown Agent, Burn, Burnt, Confusion Agent, Double Agent, Handling Agent, Illegal Agent, Informant, Inside Man, Pocket Litter, Provocation Agent, Pseudonym, Putting in the Plumbing, Recruitment, Recruitment in Place, Special Activities, Walk-in.

References

Becket, Henry S. A. *The Dictionary of Espionage: Spookspeak into English.* New York: Stein and Day, 1986.

Deacon, Richard. *Spyclopedia: An Encyclopedia of Spies, Secret Services, Operations, Jargon, and All Subjects Related to the World of Espionage.* London: Macdonald, 1987.

Kessler, Ronald. *Spy vs. Spy: Stalking Soviet Spies in America.* New York: Charles Scribner's Sons, 1988.

Ranelagh, John. *The Agency: The Rise and Decline of the CIA.* New York: Simon and Schuster, 1986.

Turner, Stansfield. *Secrecy and Democracy: The CIA in Transition.* Boston: Houghton Mifflin, 1985.

—**DISPERSION** is a statistical or quantitative methodological term often used in intelligence analysis. It is the scatter or variability in a set of data.

References

Department of Defense, Joint Chiefs of Staff. *Department of Defense Dictionary of Military and Related Terms.* Washington, DC: GPO, 1986.

—**DISPOSAL** is a CIA term for dismissing a non-career agent, who is usually not an American but who has worked for American intelligence. *See also:* Central Intelligence Agency.

References

Becket, Henry S. A. *The Dictionary of Espionage: Spookspeak into English.* New York: Stein and Day, 1986.

Deacon, Richard. *Spyclopedia: An Encyclopedia of Spies, Secret Services, Operations, Jargon, and All Subjects Related to the World of Espionage.* London: Macdonald, 1987.

Ranelagh, John. *The Agency: The Rise and Decline of the CIA.* New York: Simon and Schuster, 1986.

—**DISPOSITION** is a tactical intelligence term. It is the location of the elements of a command and is usually depicted in terms of the exact location of each unit headquarters and the deployment of the forces subordinate to it.

References

Department of Defense, Joint Chiefs of Staff. *Department of Defense Dictionary of Military and Related Terms.* Washington, DC: GPO, 1986.

—**DISSEMINATION** is the timely delivery of intelligence in the appropriate oral, written, or graphic form and by suitable means to those who need it. Dissemination is also a step in the Army tactical intelligence (TACINT) signals intelligence (SIGINT) process. As defined by the Defense Intelligence Agency, dissemination is an official term for one of its functional areas. It means "activities relating to the development of criteria for, and the conveyance of intelligence information and intelligence in suitable form, graphic or written, to authorized recipients. This includes the original receipt, analysis for customer determination based on validated requirements, reproduction, and distribution." *See also:* Intelligence Cycle, SIGINT Process.

References

Department of Defense, Defense Intelligence Agency. *Defense Intelligence Agency Manual 22-2.* Washington, DC: DIA, 1979.

Department of Defense, U.S. Army. *Counter-Signals Intelligence (C-SIGINT) Operations.* Field Manual FM 34-62, 3 February 1986. Washington, DC: Headquarters, Department of the Army, 1986.

———. *Military Intelligence Battalion Combat Electronic Warfare and Intelligence (Aerial Exploitation) (Corps).* Field Manual FM 34-22. Washington, DC: Headquarters, Department of the Army, 1984.

———. *Military Intelligence Battalion (Combat Electronic Warfare Intelligence) (Division).* Field

Manual FM 34-10. Washington, DC: Headquarters, Department of the Army, 1981.

———. *Military Intelligence Battalion (CEWI) (Tactical Exploitation) (Corps): Counterintelligence, Interrogation, Electronic Warfare.* Field Manual FM 34-23. Washington, DC: Headquarters, Department of the Army, 1985.

———. *Military Intelligence Company (Combat Electronic Warfare and Intelligence) (Armored Cavalry Regiment/Separate Brigade).* Field Manual FM 34-30. Washington, DC: Headquarters, Department of the Army, 1983.

Kent, Sherman. *Strategic Intelligence for American World Policy.* Princeton, NJ: Princeton University Press, 1966.

Laqueur, Walter. *A World of Secrets.* New York: Basic Books, 1985.

U.S. Congress. Senate. *Final Report of the Senate Select Committee to Study Government Operations with Respect to Intelligence Activities. Report 94-755. Book I, Foreign and Military Intelligence.* Washington, DC: GPO, 1976.

—**DISSEMINATION PROGRAM MANAGER** is a general intelligence term for a military service- or Unified or Specified Command-level manager who validates intelligence requirements for subordinate units and assists them in getting the intelligence that they need in a timely fashion. *See also:* Defense Intelligence Agency.

References

Department of Defense, Defense Intelligence Agency. *Defense Intelligence Agency Manual.* Washington, DC: DIA, 1987.

Laqueur, Walter. *A World of Secrets.* New York: Basic Books, 1985.

—**DIVERSION** is a deliberate, premeditated distraction that is intended to draw the enemy's attention away from another occurrence or operation. *See also:* Agent, Case, Case Officer, Concealment, Concealment Devices, Cover, Cover Name, Cover Organizations, Cover Story, Damage Control, False Confirmation, Mole, Paper Mill, Plumbing, Pocket Litter, Putting in the Plumbing, Snitch Jacket.

References

Clancy, Tom. *The Cardinal of the Kremlin.* New York: Putnam, 1988.

Department of Defense, Joint Chiefs of Staff. *Department of Defense Dictionary of Military and Related Terms.* Washington, DC: GPO, 1986.

—**DOCTOR** is a term used in clandestine and covert intelligence operations. It is an euphemism for the police. *See also:* Hospital, Zoo.

References

Becket, Henry S. A. *The Dictionary of Espionage: Spookspeak into English.* New York: Stein and Day, 1986.

Deacon, Richard. *Spyclopedia: An Encyclopedia of Spies, Secret Services, Operations, Jargon, and All Subjects Related to the World of Espionage.* London: Macdonald, 1987.

—**DOCTRINE,** in Army tactical intelligence (TAC-INT) terminology, means the fundamental principles by which military forces or elements of military forces guide their actions in support of national objectives. Doctrine is authoritative but requires judgment in its application.

References

Department of Defense, Joint Chiefs of Staff. *Department of Defense Dictionary of Military and Related Terms.* Washington, DC: GPO, 1986.

Department of Defense, U.S. Army. *Army Air Defense Artillery Employment.* Field Manual FM 44-1. Washington, DC: Headquarters, Department of the Army, 1983.

———. *Counter-Signals Intelligence (C-SIGINT) Operations.* Field Manual FM 34-62. Washington, DC: Headquarters, Department of the Army, 1986.

—**DOCUMENTATION** is a term used in clandestine and covert intelligence operations to describe documents, personal effects, and other materials that are given to an individual to support his cover story. *See also:* Cover, Cover Name, Cover Organizations, Cover Story, Establishing Bonafides, Legend, Paper Mill, Pseudonym, Plumbing, Pocket Litter, Putting in the Plumbing.

References

Becket, Henry S. A. *The Dictionary of Espionage: Spookspeak into English.* New York: Stein and Day, 1986.

Deacon, Richard. *Spyclopedia: An Encyclopedia of Spies, Secret Services, Operations, Jargon, and All Subjects Related to the World of Espionage.* London: Macdonald, 1987.

Kessler, Ronald. *Spy vs. Spy: Stalking Soviet Spies in America.* New York: Charles Scribner's Sons, 1988.

Ranelagh, John. *The Agency: The Rise and Decline of the CIA.* New York: Simon and Schuster, 1986.

—**DOMESTIC ACTIVITIES** is a general intelligence term for activities that take place within the United States that do not involve a significant connection with a foreign power, organization, or person.

References

American Bar Association. *Oversight and Accountability of the U.S. Intelligence Agencies: An Evaluation.* Washington, DC: ABA, 1985.

Corson, William R. *The Armies of Ignorance: The Rise of the American Intelligence Empire.* New York: Dial Press, 1977.

Department of Defense. *Activities of DoD Intelligence Components that Affect U.S. Persons (Department of Defense Directive 5240.1).* Washington, DC: DoD, 1982.

Laqueur, Walter. *The Age of Terrorism.* Boston: Little, Brown, 1987.

————. *A World of Secrets.* New York: Basic Books, 1985.

Lefever, Ernest W., and Godson, Roy. *The CIA and the American Ethic: An Unfinished Debate.* Washington, DC: Ethics and Public Policy Center, Georgetown University, 1979.

Maurer, Alfred C.; Turnstall, Marion D.; and Keagle, James M. *Intelligence Policy and Process.* Boulder, CO: Westview Press, 1985.

Treverton, Gregory F. *Covert Action: The Limits of Intervention in the Postwar World.* New York: Basic Books, 1987.

Turner, Stansfield. *Secrecy and Democracy: The CIA in Transition.* Boston: Houghton Mifflin, 1985.

—**DOMESTIC COLLECTION** is a general intelligence term for acquiring foreign intelligence information within the United States from government or private organizations or individuals who understand that the intelligence is being collected by the United States government and who are willing to share such information.

References

American Bar Association. *Oversight and Accountability of the U.S. Intelligence Agencies: An Evaluation.* Washington, DC: ABA, 1985.

Corson, William R. *The Armies of Ignorance: The Rise of the American Intelligence Empire.* New York: Dial Press, 1977.

Department of Defense, Defense Intelligence College. *Glossary of Intelligence Terms and Definitions.* Washington, DC: DIC, 1987.

Lefever, Ernest W., and Godson, Roy. *The CIA and the American Ethic: An Unfinished Debate.* Washington, DC: Ethics and Public Policy Center, Georgetown University, 1979.

Maurer, Alfred C.; Turnstall, Marion D.; and Keagle, James M. *Intelligence Policy and Process.* Boulder, CO: Westview Press, 1985.

Treverton, Gregory F. *Covert Action: The Limits of Intervention in the Postwar World.* New York: Basic Books, 1987.

Turner, Stansfield. *Secrecy and Democracy: The CIA in Transition.* Boston: Houghton Mifflin, 1985.

—**DOMESTIC CONTACTS DIVISION** is a component of the Central Intelligence Agency that overtly collects information in the United States from U.S. travelers and those with contacts overseas who are willing to share their knowledge. *See also:* Central Intelligence Agency.

References

Breckinridge, Scott D. *The CIA and the U.S. Intelligence System.* Boulder, CO: Westview Press, 1986.

—**DOMESTIC CONTACTS SERVICE** was a component of the Central Intelligence Group (CIG). It was responsible for soliciting domestic sources for foreign intelligence information. It was renamed the Domestic Contacts Division in 1951 and became a component of the Directorate for Intelligence in 1952. It was renamed the Domestic Contact Service in 1965 and was transferred to the Directorate of Operations (DDO) in 1973, when it was renamed the Domestic Contacts Division. *See also:* Central Intelligence Agency.

References

Fain, Tyrus G.; Plant, Katharine C.; and Milloy, Ross. *The Intelligence Community: History, Organization, and Issues.* Public Documents Series. New York: R.R. Bowker, 1977.

—**DOMESTIC EMERGENCIES,** as defined by the Church Committee, are "emergencies occurring within the United States, its territories, or possessions, which affect the public welfare. Such emergencies may arise from enemy attack, insurrection, civil disturbances, natural disasters (earthquakes, floods), fire, or other comparable emergencies which endanger life and property or disrupt the normal processes of government."

References

Department of Defense, Joint Chiefs of Staff. *Department of Defense Dictionary of Military and Related Terms.* Washington, DC: GPO, 1986.

Turner, Stansfield. *Secrecy and Democracy: The CIA in Transition.* Boston: Houghton Mifflin, 1985.

U.S. Congress. Senate. *Final Report of the Senate Select Committee to Study Government Operations with Respect to Intelligence Activities. Report 94-755. Book I, Foreign and Military Intelligence.* Washington, DC: GPO, 1976.

—**DOMESTIC INTELLIGENCE** is a general intelligence term for intelligence relating to activities or conditions within the United States that threaten the internal security and might require the use of troops. It also means intelligence related to the activities of agencies or individuals that are potentially or actually harmful to the security of the Department of Defense.

References

American Bar Association. *Oversight and Accountability of the U.S. Intelligence Agencies: An Evaluation.* Washington, DC: ABA, 1985.

Department of Defense, Joint Chiefs of Staff. *Department of Defense Dictionary of Military and Related Terms.* Washington, DC: GPO, 1986.

Laqueur, Walter. *The Age of Terrorism.* Boston: Little, Brown, 1987.

———. *A World of Secrets.* New York: Basic Books, 1985.

Lefever, Ernest W., and Godson, Roy. *The CIA and the American Ethic: An Unfinished Debate.* Washington, DC: Ethics and Public Policy Center, Georgetown University, 1979.

Maurer, Alfred C.; Turnstall, Marion D.; and Keagle, James M. *Intelligence Policy and Process.* Boulder, CO: Westview Press, 1985.

Treverton, Gregory F. *Covert Action: The Limits of Intervention in the Postwar World.* New York: Basic Books, 1987.

Turner, Stansfield. *Secrecy and Democracy: The CIA in Transition.* Boston: Houghton Mifflin, 1985.

U.S. Congress. Senate. *Final Report of the Senate Select Committee to Study Government Operations with Respect to Intelligence Activities. Report 94-755. Book I, Foreign and Military Intelligence.* Washington, DC: GPO, 1976.

—**DOMINICAN REPUBLIC.** Scott Breckinridge notes that President Eisenhower was concerned that Rafael Trujillo was a weakness in the U.S. attempt to halt the spread of communism in the Caribbean basin. The continued association of the United States with Trujillo's harsh, dictatorial regime worked against U.S. policy and prestige in the region. Both the State Department and the Central Intelligence Agency had dialogues with Trujillo's opponents and encouraged them to oust him. President Kennedy's administration took over the plan when it was well underway and, according to Breckinridge, knew that the plotters intended to kill Trujillo, but did not attempt to prevent this. The coup occurred in 1961 and Trujillo was killed in an ambush. *See also:* Assassination.

References

Breckinridge, Scott D. *The CIA and the U.S. Intelligence System.* Boulder, CO: Westview Press, 1986.

Treverton, Gregory F. *Covert Action: The Limits of Intervention in the Postwar World.* New York: Basic Books, 1987.

Turner, Stansfield. *Secrecy and Democracy: The CIA in Transition.* Boston: Houghton Mifflin, 1985.

U.S. Congress. Senate. *Alleged Assassination Plots Involving Foreign Leaders: An Interim Report of the Select Committee to Study Governmental Operations with Respect to Intelligence Activities.* 94th Congress, 1st sess., Nov. 20, 1975. S. Rept. 94-465.

—**DONOVAN, WILLIAM J.,** who had been awarded the Congressional Medal of Honor for his actions in World War I, played a pivotal role in the U.S. intelligence effort in World War II.

Donovan was born on January 1, 1883, in Buffalo, New York. He graduated from Columbia College and law school and began practicing law in Buffalo. However, with the outbreak of World War I, Donovan's life was altered considerably. Even before the United States became involved in the war, Donovan was traveling throughout Europe, reporting on U.S. relief efforts. In 1916, his national guard unit was mobilized, first to fight on the Mexican front and then to fight in Europe. Donovan saw heavy fighting, was wounded, and won the Distinguished Service Cross, the Purple Heart, and the Congressional Medal of Honor. After the war, he returned to law and entered politics, running unsuccessfully for the New York governorship in 1932.

However, with the coming of World War II, Donovan's attention again turned to intelligence, and he developed his proposal for a centralized intelligence organization, which he passed to his friend Frank Knox. Knox, in turn, passed the proposal to President Roosevelt. The President had also been thinking along the same lines and had even considered Vincent Astor, Fiorello La Guardia, and Nelson Rockefeller to head the organization. Donovan's plan was warmly received by Roosevelt, who created the Office of Coordinator of Information (COI) and appointed

Donovan to head the office. As coordinator, Donovan established two traditions. First, he drew heavily on the academic community; second, he created a seven-member Board of Analysts, which was the forerunner of many later estimative bodies.

The Japanese attack on Pearl Harbor demonstrated vividly the need for a centralized intelligence unit. As a result, on June 13, 1942, Roosevelt, by military order, created the Office of Strategic Services (OSS) and placed it under the Joint Chiefs of Staff.

In spite of Donovan's ambition and efforts, the contribution of the OSS to the war was modest. The OSS operated under several handicaps. First of all, it was one of several intelligence organizations and had to vie with the others, particularly the Federal Bureau of Investigation and the Army G-2, for attention and resources. Second, by operating under the Joint Chiefs of Staff, it competed with the Joint Intelligence Committee, which has been created specifically to meet JCS intelligence needs. Third, it was an organization that espoused the use of propaganda, covert operations, and subversion—methods that a sleepy, provincial America had not yet accepted to be either necessary or "American."

Although the OSS was not an overwhelming success, it did make several contributions. It trained an entire generation of postwar analytical intelligence analysts under wartime conditions. Moreover, it demonstrated the utility of combining intelligence collection and operations in one organization. Finally, by merely surviving and contributing, it continued the viability of a centralized intelligence organization as a way of organizing the national intelligence community.

In spite of these contributions, however, the OSS could not survive the end of the war. On September 20, 1945, President Truman ordered the termination of OSS operations on October 1 of that year, and many of its functions were quickly claimed by the State and War departments.

Donovan became an assistant prosecutor at the Nuremberg Trials after the war, but he left before the trials began. He then returned to his law practice but accepted an ambassadorship to Thailand in 1953, serving there until September 1954. He died on February 8, 1959, and is buried in Arlington National Cemetery. *See also:* Central Intelligence Agency, Office of Strategic Services.

References

Corson, William R. *The Armies of Ignorance: The Rise of the American Intelligence Empire.* New York: Dial Press, 1977.

Laqueur, Walter. *A World of Secrets.* New York: Basic Books, 1985.

Lowenthal, Mark M. *U.S. Intelligence: Evolution and Anatomy.* New York: Praeger, 1984.

Treverton, Gregory F. *Covert Action: The Limits of Intervention in the Postwar World.* New York: Basic Books, 1987.

—**DOORKNOCKER** is a nickname given to an agent assigned to do personnel security reviews in order to determine that a person who needs a security clearance has no criminal or nefarious incidents in his past. The process begins when the individual completes a background investigation form, is fingerprinted and submits supportive documents. Each of the items on the form must be verified by an investigative officer from the military services (if the person is in the military), the Civil Service Commission (if the person is to be a civil servant), or the FBI (if he is to work for the bureau). To be an investigative officer is one of the least glamorous jobs in intelligence. *See also:* Access, Background Investigation, Clearance, Lawful Investigation, Nondisclosure Agreement, Personnel Security, Security.

References

Becket, Henry S. A. *The Dictionary of Espionage: Spookspeak into English.* New York: Stein and Day, 1986.

Deacon, Richard. *Spyclopedia: An Encyclopedia of Spies, Secret Services, Operations, Jargon, and All Subjects Related to the World of Espionage.* London: Macdonald, 1987.

Kessler, Ronald. *Spy vs. Spy: Stalking Soviet Spies in America.* New York: Charles Scribner's Sons, 1988.

Ranelagh, John. *The Agency: The Rise and Decline of the CIA.* New York: Simon and Schuster, 1986.

Turner, Stansfield. *Secrecy and Democracy: The CIA in Transition.* Boston: Houghton Mifflin, 1985.

—**DOUBLE AGENT** is a term used in clandestine and covert intelligence operations. In the past, a double agent usually was an individual who freelanced by working for two sides without either knowing about the other. More recently, the term has come to mean an individual who appears to be working for both sides, but is actually working for only one agency. In this capacity, his purpose is to pass false or misleading information, as well as to collect intelligence about the other side. Being a double agent is one of the most dangerous jobs in the intelligence business. Working under cover, he is constantly forced to prove his worth to the enemy organization. He hopes that he can do this without compromising his own side or endangering its interests. Yet, he is continually called upon to produce, and he must provide a minimum of information to avoid suspicion. The psychological pressures and physical dangers to which the double agent is exposed are therefore considerable. *See also:* Agent, Agent Authentication, Agent in Place, Agent Net, Agent of Influence, Agent Provocateur, Blow, Blown Agent, Burn, Burnt, Confusion Agent, Dispatched Agent, Handling Agent, Illegal Agent, Informant, Inside Man, Pocket Litter, Provocation Agent, Pseudonym, Putting in the Plumbing, Recruitment, Recruitment in Place, Special Activities, Walk-in.

References

American Bar Association. *Oversight and Accountability of the U.S. Intelligence Agencies: An Evaluation.* Washington, DC: ABA, 1985.

Becket, Henry S. A. *The Dictionary of Espionage: Spookspeak into English.* New York: Stein and Day, 1986.

Clancy, Tom. *The Cardinal of the Kremlin.* New York: Putnam, 1988.

Deacon, Richard. *Spyclopedia: An Encyclopedia of Spies, Secret Services, Operations, Jargon, and All Subjects Related to the World of Espionage.* London: Macdonald, 1987.

Department of Defense, Joint Chiefs of Staff. *Department of Defense Dictionary of Military and Related Terms.* Washington, DC: GPO, 1986.

Godson, Roy, ed. *Intelligence Problems for the 1980s, Number 1: Elements of Intelligence.* Rev. ed. Washington, DC: National Strategy Information Center, 1983.

————. *Intelligence Problems for the 1980s, Number 3: Counterintelligence.* Washington, DC: National Strategy Information Center, 1980.

————. *Intelligence Problems for the 1980s, Number 4: Covert Action.* Washington, DC: National Strategy Information Center, 1981.

Kessler, Ronald. *Spy vs. Spy: Stalking Soviet Spies in America.* New York: Charles Scribner's Sons, 1988.

Maurer, Alfred C.; Turnstall, Marion D.; and Keagle, James M. *Intelligence Policy and Process.* Boulder, CO: Westview Press, 1985.

Treverton, Gregory F. *Covert Action: The Limits of Intervention in the Postwar World.* New York: Basic Books, 1987.

Turner, Stansfield. *Secrecy and Democracy: The CIA in Transition.* Boston: Houghton Mifflin, 1985.

U.S. Congress. Senate. *Final Report of the Senate Select Committee to Study Government Operations with Respect to Intelligence Activities. Report 94-755. Book I, Foreign and Military Intelligence.* Washington, DC: GPO, 1976.

—**DOUBLED** is a term used in clandestine and covert intelligence operations. Doubled is when an agent passes bogus messages to his home controller. These messages are usually supplied by his captors. *See also:* Agent, Biographic Leverage, Blackmail, Blow, Blown Agent, Bug, Bugging, Burn, Burnt, Co-opted Worker, Co-optees, Damage Assessment, Damage Control, Discard, Dispatched Agent, Double Agent, Doubled, Special Activities, Toss, Turned.

References

Becket, Henry S. A. *The Dictionary of Espionage: Spookspeak into English.* New York: Stein and Day, 1986.

Clancy, Tom. *The Cardinal of the Kremlin.* New York: Putnam, 1988.

Turner, Stansfield. *Secrecy and Democracy: The CIA in Transition.* Boston: Houghton Mifflin, 1985.

—**DOUGLASS, KINGMAN** served as deputy director of Central Intelligence from March 2 until July 11, 1946. *See also:* Central Intelligence Agency.

—**DOWNGRADE** is the process of changing a security classification from a higher to a lower classification. Some classified material is automatically downgraded after a period of time; other material is excluded from such an automatic procedure and must be reviewed and personally downgraded. *See also:* Access, Authorized, Classification, Classified Information, Code Word, Compromise, Declassification, Disclosure, Freedom of Information Act, Limited Access Area, Need-to-Know, Need-to-Know Principle, No-Lone Zone, Nondisclosure Agreement, Nondiscussion Area, Sanitization, Sanitize, Sanitized Area, Security Certification, Security Classification, Sensitive Compartmented Information, Sensitive Compartmented Information Facility, Two-Person Control.

References

Department of Defense, Defense Intelligence College. *Glossary of Intelligence Terms and Definitions.* Washington, DC: DIC, 1987.

Department of Defense, Joint Chiefs of Staff. *Department of Defense Dictionary of Military and Related Terms.* Washington, DC: GPO, 1986.

Godson, Roy, ed. *Intelligence Problems for the 1980s, Number 1: Elements of Intelligence.* Rev. ed. Washington, DC: National Strategy Information Center, 1983.

—**DRAFTER,** in message preparation, is the individual whose thoughts will be conveyed by message to the receiver. He prepares his thoughts in the form of a message and then passes it to the releasing official, who determines that the thoughts, indeed, should be passed by message, and then releases the message so that it may be transmitted to the receiver.

References

Department of Defense, Defense Intelligence Agency. *Defense Intelligence Agency Manual.* Washington, DC: DIA, 1984.

Department of Defense, Joint Chiefs of Staff. *Department of Defense Dictionary of Military and Related Terms.* Washington, DC: GPO, 1986.

—**DRAKE, ROBERT E.,** served as deputy director of the National Security Agency from May 1, 1978, until April 1, 1980. *See also:* National Security Agency.

References

Bamford, James. *The Puzzle Palace: A Report on America's Most Secret Agency.* New York: Penguin Books, 1983.

—**DRONE** is an intelligence imagery and photoreconnaissance term for a land, sea, or air vehicle that is usually unmanned and is remotely or automatically controlled. *See also:* Aerial Photograph.

References

Department of Defense, Joint Chiefs of Staff. *Department of Defense Dictionary of Military and Related Terms.* Washington, DC: GPO, 1986.

—**DROP** is a term used in clandestine and covert intelligence operations that has two meanings. (1) To drop is to clandestinely transfer intelligence information. Leaving material in a secret place for someone to pick up is a dead drop, while passing material to another person is a live drop. (2) In the CIA, drop means success in a black operation. *See also:* Agent, Black Bag Job, Black Bag Operation, Case, Case Officer, Chief of Outpost, Chief of Station, Dead Drop, Debriefing, Illegal Operations, Illegal Residency, Illegal Support Officer, Legal, Legal Residency, Legend, Letter Drop, Live Letter Boxes, Live Letter Drops, Mail Cover, Packed Up, Processing the Take, Run Down a Case.

References

Becket, Henry S. A. *The Dictionary of Espionage: Spookspeak into English.* New York: Stein and Day, 1986.

Clancy, Tom. *The Cardinal of the Kremlin.* New York: Putnam, 1988.

Deacon, Richard. *Spyclopedia: An Encyclopedia of Spies, Secret Services, Operations, Jargon, and All Subjects Related to the World of Espionage.* London: Macdonald, 1987.

Turner, Stansfield. *Secrecy and Democracy: The CIA in Transition.* Boston: Houghton Mifflin, 1985.

—**DROP ACCOUNTABILITY,** in communications security (COMSEC), means an accounting procedure by which a COMSEC account or subaccount receiving accountable COMSEC material assumes all responsibility after initial receipt and provides no further accounting to the central office of record. *See also:* Communications Security.

References

Martin, Paul H. "Communications-Computer Security." *Journal of Electronic Defense* (June 1987).

Muzerall, Joseph V., and Carty, Thomas P. "COMSEC and Its Need for Key Management." *DP&CS* (Spring 1987).

—**DRUMMOND, NELSON C.,** a naval yeoman, was convicted of passing classified information to the Soviets in 1957. He was motivated by monetary desires. Arrested in 1962, he was tried, convicted, and sentenced to life in prison.

References

Allen, Thomas B., and Polmar, Norman. *Merchants of Treason: America's Secrets for Sale.* New York: Delacorte Press, 1988.

Crawford, David J. *Volunteers: The Betrayal of National Defense Secrets by Air Force Traitors.* Washington, DC: GPO, 1988.

—**DRY CLEANING** is a term used in clandestine and covert intelligence operations. It encompasses the various techniques an agent uses to shake off his pursuers or to determine whether he is being followed. *See also:* Agent, Alternate Meet, Blind Dating, Clean, Meet Area, Movements Analysis, Riding Shotgun, Shadow, Shaking Off the Dogs, Special Activities, Surround, Surveillance, Walk-Past.

References

Becket, Henry S. A. *The Dictionary of Espionage: Spookspeak into English.* New York: Stein and Day, 1986.

Kessler, Ronald. *Spy vs. Spy: Stalking Soviet Spies in America.* New York: Charles Scribner's Sons, 1988.

Turner, Stansfield. *Secrecy and Democracy: The CIA in Transition.* Boston: Houghton Mifflin, 1985.

—**DRY RUN,** in covert and counterintelligence operations, is a rehearsal for an operation or an operation that produces no results. In intelligence dissemination, a dry run is a rehearsal for a briefing.

References

Kessler, Ronald. *Spy vs. Spy: Stalking Soviet Spies in America.* New York: Charles Scribner's Sons, 1988.

—**DUBBERSTEIN, WALDO H.,** a former employee of the Defense Intelligence Agency and the Central Intelligence Agency, was convicted of passing classified information to Libya. He may have been motivated by financial desires.

References

Allen, Thomas B., and Polmar, Norman. *Merchants of Treason: America's Secrets for Sale.* New York: Delacorte Press, 1988.

Crawford, David J. *Volunteers: The Betrayal of National Defense Secrets by Air Force Traitors.* Washington, DC: GPO, 1988.

—**DUD** is a term used in clandestine and covert intelligence operations to describe a person who contacts an intelligence agency and agrees to pass information, but who never appears again. *See also:* Agent, Agent Authentication, Co-opted Worker, Co-optees, Disaffected Person, Double Agent, Handling Agent, Mole, Nash, Recruitment, Recruitment in Place, Singleton, Sleeper, Walk-in.

References

Becket, Henry S. A. *The Dictionary of Espionage: Spookspeak into English.* New York: Stein and Day, 1986.

Deacon, Richard. *Spyclopedia: An Encyclopedia of Spies, Secret Services, Operations, Jargon, and All Subjects Related to the World of Espionage.* London: Macdonald, 1987.

Kessler, Ronald. *Spy vs. Spy: Stalking Soviet Spies in America.* New York: Charles Scribner's Sons, 1988.

Ranelagh, John. *The Agency: The Rise and Decline of the CIA.* New York: Simon and Schuster, 1986.

—**DUE PROCESS** is a security term. It means advising an individual that he or she has been determined to be ineligible for access to special compartmented information (SCI), informing the individual of the reasons for the denial, and affording the individual the opportunity to appeal that decision. *See also:* Sensitive Compartmented Information.

—**DULLES, ALLEN W.,** was born on April 7, 1893, in Watertown, New York. He received a Bachelor of Arts degree in 1914, a Master of Arts degree from Princeton University in 1916, and a Bachelor of Law degree from George Washington University in 1926. From 1916 until 1926, he served in the Diplomatic Service, Department of State; he practiced law in New York from 1926 until 1942, when he was appointed to head the Office of Strategic Services (OSS) office in Berne, Switzerland. In 1946, he returned to his law practice. In December 1950, he was appointed as deputy director for plans, Central Intelligence Agency, and was promoted to deputy director of Central Intelligence on August 23, 1951. On February 10, 1953, President Eisenhower appointed him director of Central Intelligence (DCI). The appointment was confirmed by the Senate on February 23, and he was sworn in on February 26, 1953. He retired on November 29, 1961 and returned to private life and writing. He subsequently served on the President's Commission on the Assassination of President Kennedy in 1963 and 1964. He died on January 28, 1969.

Dulles differed from his predecessors as DCI in that he had previous operational intelligence experience. He had served in the OSS in Switzerland, where he directed intelligence operations against Germany. Because of his experience, his interests were primarily operational, and during his tenure the agency conducted many operations that were intended to replace a government that was hostile to the United States with one that was more friendly. These included a successful operation in Iran in 1953 that brought the Shah back to power, successful operations in Costa Rica in 1953 and Guatemala in 1954, and unsuccessful operations in Indonesia in 1958, Tibet in

1958, and operation *Mongoose* against Castro's Cuba in 1960 and 1961.

Dulles's final years as DCI were troubled by two issues: the missile gap, and the Bay of Pigs invasion. The missile gap issue centered on the strategic balance between the Soviet Union and the United States. Senator Stuart Symington and Senator John Kennedy made this a campaign issue in the 1960 presidential election, accusing the Eisenhower administration of not adequately protecting the country and allowing the Soviets to gain a strategic military advantage. President Eisenhower, who had sufficient evidence (having received overhead reconnaissance) to know that there was no gap, could not present this case because of the high classification of the photography and therefore was unable to squelch the issue. After Kennedy became President, his administration revealed that a gap, indeed, did not exist.

The Bay of Pigs invasion was the last of a series of CIA-sponsored paramilitary operations that had been conducted in Iran, Guatemala, and elsewhere in the 1950s. What set it apart was that it was larger and less well conceived. The abysmal failure of the operation led to a reevaluation of the CIA's role in such operations and a movement away from large-scale paramilitary operations. *See also:* Central Intelligence Agency, Mongoose.

References

American Bar Association. *Oversight and Accountability of the U.S. Intelligence Agencies: An Evaluation.* Washington, DC: ABA, 1985.

Breckinridge, Scott D. *The CIA and the U.S. Intelligence System.* Boulder, CO: Westview Press, 1986.

Brinkley, David A., and Hull, Andrew W. *Estimative Intelligence: A Textbook on the History, Products, Uses and Writing of Intelligence Estimates.* Columbus, OH: Battelle, 1979.

Cline, Ray S. *The CIA Under Reagan, Bush, and Casey.* Washington, DC: Acropolis Books, 1981.

Corson, William R. *The Armies of Ignorance: The Rise of the American Intelligence Empire.* New York: Dial Press, 1977.

Laqueur, Walter. *A World of Secrets.* New York: Basic Books, 1985.

Lowenthal, Mark M. *U.S. Intelligence: Evolution and Anatomy.* New York: Praeger, 1984.

Maurer, Alfred C.; Turnstall, Marion D.; and Keagle, James M. *Intelligence Policy and Process.* Boulder, CO: Westview Press, 1985.

Quirk, John; Phillips, David; Cline, Ray; and Pforzheimer, Walter. *The Central Intelligence Agency: A Photographic History.* Guilford, CN: Foreign Intelligence Press, 1986.

Treverton, Gregory F. *Covert Action: The Limits of Intervention in the Postwar World.* New York: Basic Books, 1987.

U.S. Congress. Senate. *Alleged Assassination Plots Involving Foreign Leaders: An Interim Report of the Select Committee to Study Governmental Operations with Respect to Intelligence Activities.* 94th Congress, 1st sess., Nov. 20, 1975. S. Rept. 94-465.

U.S. Congress. Senate. *Final Report of the Senate Select Committee to Study Government Operations with Respect to Intelligence Activities. Report 94-755. Book I, Foreign and Military Intelligence.* Washington, DC: GPO, 1976.

Von Hoene, John P. A. *Intelligence User's Guide.* Washington, DC: DIA, 1983.

—**DUMMY GROUP,** in communications security (COMSEC), means a group having the appearance of a valid code or cipher group but having no plain-text significance. *See also:* Communications Security.

References

Muzerall, Joseph V., and Carty, Thomas P. "COMSEC and Its Need for Key Management." *DP&CS* (Spring 1987).

Ware, Willis H. "Information Systems, Security, and Privacy." *EDUCOM Bulletin* (Summer 1984).

—**DUPLEX,** a baud-based system term used in communications intelligence, communications security, operations security, and signals analysis, is a circuit on which simultaneous transmission and reception in both directions is possible. *See also:* communications security.

References

Muzerall, Joseph V., and Carty, Thomas P. "COMSEC and Its Need for Key Management." *DP&CS* (Spring 1987).

—**DYNAMO SPORTS CLUB** is the KGB team that participates in track and field and other sporting events in the Soviet Union. *See also:* KGB.

References

Becket, Henry S. A. *The Dictionary of Espionage: Spookspeak into English.* New York: Stein and Day, 1986.

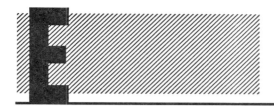

Deacon, Richard. *Spyclopedia: An Encyclopedia of Spies, Secret Services, Operations, Jargon, and All Subjects Related to the World of Espionage.* London: Macdonald, 1987.

Ranelagh, John. *The Agency: The Rise and Decline of the CIA.* New York: Simon and Schuster, 1986.

—**EARLY WARNING (EW)** is the early or timely notification of the launch or approach of unknown weapons or weapons carriers. *See also:* Early Warning Radar, Indications and Warning.

References

Department of Defense, Joint Chiefs of Staff. *Department of Defense Dictionary of Military and Related Terms.* Washington, DC: GPO, 1986.

Godson, Roy, ed. *Intelligence Problems for the 1980s, Number 1: Elements of Intelligence.* Rev. ed. Washington, DC: National Strategy Information Center, 1983.

—**EARLY WARNING RADAR** is a system that covers the skies in all directions and elevations in order to detect approaching aircraft or missiles early enough for fighter planes to be in the air and ready to intercept them, or, in the case of missiles, early enough so that defensive measures can be taken. *See also:* Early Warning, Indications and Warning.

References

Department of Defense, Joint Chiefs of Staff. *Department of Defense Dictionary of Military and Related Terms.* Washington, DC: GPO, 1986.

—**EARS ONLY** is information so sensitive that it is not written down or published. EARS ONLY is not an official classification. *See also:* Access, Authorized, Classification, Classified Information, Code Word, Compromise, Declassification, Disclosure, Downgrade, Freedom of Information Act, Limited Access Area, Need-to-Know, Need-to-Know Principle, No-Lone Zone, Nondisclosure Agreement, Nondiscussion Area, Sanitization, Sanitize, Sanitized Area, Security Certification, Security Classification, Sensitive Compartmented Information, Sensitive Compartmented Information Facility, Two-Person Control.

References

Becket, Henry S. A. *The Dictionary of Espionage: Spookspeak into English.* New York: Stein and Day, 1986.

—**EARTH OBSERVATION SATELLITE (EOSAT)** is a joint venture of Hughes Aircraft Company and the RCA Corporation for the purpose of establishing a U.S. privately owned operational land observation and data service program. The program involves a series of unmanned satellites (LANDSATs) that provide a full range of photographic and digital products.

LANDSAT products are handled by the Defense Mapping Agency, which distributes these products to other government agencies.

Department of Defense activities to which satellite-sensed data are applied cover virtually the full range of military functions. LANDSAT images cover approximately 13,000 square miles, but various levels of detail can be examined, depending on the goal of the interpreter. The four application areas that are most significant are navigation, geographic change detection and classification, terrain analysis, and coastal bathymetry.

References

Earth Observation Satellite Company. *EOSAT Information Sheet.* Lantham, MD: EOSC, 1985.

Turner, Stansfield. *Secrecy and Democracy: The CIA in Transition.* Boston: Houghton Mifflin, 1985.

—**EAVESDROPPING.** *See:* Electronic Surveillance.

—**ECONOMIC ACTION** is the planned use of economic measures that are designed to influence the policies or actions of another state. Such actions might include those that are intended to impair the war-making potential of a hostile power or those intended to generate economic stability within a friendly power.

References

Department of Defense, Joint Chiefs of Staff. *Department of Defense Dictionary of Military and Related Terms.* Washington, DC: GPO, 1986.

—**ECONOMIC INTELLIGENCE,** a component of strategic intelligence, is foreign intelligence concerning the production, distribution, and consumption of goods and services, labor, finance, taxation, and other aspects of a nation's economy or of the international economic system. The State Department is the primary producer of economic intelligence on the free world, while the Central Intelligence Agency has reporting responsibility for communist countries.

Economics is the science of production, distribution, and use of wealth—the material means of satisfying human desires. It analyzes factors of production and determines how they can be used to produce the things that satisfy these material wants. Thus economics deals with the basic aspects of human living, of relations between people and nations, and it deals with their competition for a share of the world's resources. That competition has been, and continues to be, a major cause of war. From this, then, we can say that **economic intelligence** is intelligence that deals with the extent and use of the natural and human resources and the potential of nations. The position of the United States as a major economic power makes it inevitable that almost any economic development impinges in some way upon our position in international affairs. For this reason, the study of the national economy of foreign nations is one of the most important tasks in strategic intelligence. Economic weapons can be among the most effective means of international conflict short of direct military action, and economic potential is perhaps the best single measure of a nation's strategic capabilities.

Economic intelligence serves three related purposes in the design of policies to preserve our national security:

(1) To estimate the magnitude of possible present or future military or other threats to ourselves and our allies. A potential enemy can undertake and successfully carry out only those operations— military or otherwise—that its economy is capable of mounting and sustaining. In the very short run, national strength may be measured in terms of manpower that can be mobilized and stocks of weapons and military supplies that are available. In modern times, however, it has come to be recognized that military potential for anything but the briefest campaigns depends on the total resources of a nation—resources that are necessary to sustain the civilian economy as well as those that are necessary to produce and operate the weapons of war. An objective appraisal of the nature and magnitude of any actual or potential threats to our interests is necessary if our policy planners are to appreciate realistically the magnitude of the necessary defense effort which must be sustained in order to preserve our freedom and defend our national interests.

(2) To assist in estimating the intentions of a potential enemy. This is a difficult problem, despite the deceptive simplicity of the concept. The economic resources of a potential enemy and their disposition offer him a selection of a range of possible or probable courses of action. For example, efforts to achieve a state of military preparedness do not necessarily foretell the advent of military aggression. Military preparedness makes aggression possible, but not inevitable. Thus, while it is possible to establish the outside limits of the range of possibilities and even to develop estimates of probabilities based on the existence of key indications, it would be foolhardy indeed to assume that analysis of economic indications of the intentions of a government has reached a level at all close to an exact science.

(3) To assist in estimating the probable development of the relative strengths of the Soviet bloc and all other foreign economies for the next few years. These comparative estimates are needed by U.S. policymakers for guidance in developing those political policies that will offer the best chance of achieving the objectives without hostilities. Questions of relative economic strength are obviously basic to the development of such a policy. There are equally grave dangers in a serious overestimation of future economic strength, because either may produce policies that are more likely to bring on war than would a more accurate estimate.

Economic Warfare

Economic warfare may take several forms. It may consist of diplomatic and financial pressures that are designed to induce neutral countries to cease trading with the enemy. It may take the form of the preclusive buying policy that the United States applied during World War II to keep critical materials away from the enemy. Or it may go to the extreme of military action that is directed toward the seizure or destruction of the enemy's economic resources. For these purposes, it is necessary to know the strong and weak points of national economies and of international economic relations.

The intelligence officer gives the military operational planners accurate information on the location and character of steel plants, freight yards, oil refineries, power stations, chemical plants, and other industrial installations. Moreover, his or her study of a particular country reveals industrial bottlenecks and the degree to which the military effort would be hampered by the loss of certain materials or specific facilities. The answers to certain questions will help in assessing the capabilities, vulnerabilities, and probable courses of action of a nation. Intelligence wants to know what raw materials are available, in what quantities and from what sources. The Intelligence Community usually makes a distinction between basic foodstuffs and basic industrial materials. The list of industrial raw materials is divided into three groups: the metallic minerals, such as copper; the nonmetallic minerals, such as coal; and the organic substances, such as wood, rubber, and hides.

The most dependable supply of a raw material usually lies within a country's own boundaries. In peacetime a nation can usually get materials from abroad, but during a war transportation may be obstructed by a blockade, a lack of shipping, or congestion of railroads and ports. Since it is usually uncertain as to which side will control the sea lanes, estimates of a nation's raw material potential must take into account the possible disruption of lines of communications to foreign sources of supply.

It is also important to know what industrial capacity is available and its limitations from the perspective of war goods production. A nation's industrial capacity is a product of the skillful use of manpower, natural resources, and capital. But high industrial potential does not result automatically from the possession of these elements. Some countries—China, for example—have abundant manpower and extensive deposits of minerals but are deficient in mines and factories. On the other hand, countries like the Netherlands have important industries despite a lack of key raw materials.

The adaptability of a nation's productive capacity to meet the demands of war depends to a considerable degree on its peacetime economic policies. Sometimes competitive private enterprise has been relied on with relatively little governmental interference in order to achieve the maximum degree of industrial development. In the United States, this policy has resulted in a high degree of efficiency and an industrial establishment that is well adjusted to competition. A possible shortcoming of such an economic policy is the underdevelopment of production in some lines that are of paramount importance in wartime.

In contrast to a policy of relying on private initiative, there are many degrees of government control. Through various degrees of control, including government ownership, a nation may achieve a close approximation to a war economy in time of peace. This situation prevailed in Germany prior to 1939. The USSR has been on such an economic basis for a generation.

Once a war has begun, even a country committed to the principle of free enterprise finds it necessary to impose controls. There are ways, however, in which such a country may prepare in advance for the adjustment of peacetime industry to wartime needs. Examples are stockpiling strategic materials and the peacetime placement of "educational" orders for minor quantities of military equipment to familiarize manufacturers with the problems that will be encountered in wartime. Advance planning for an industrial mobilization can help a nation avoid shortages in essential items in wartime.

The ability to produce goods depends on many considerations in addition to the availability of raw materials and a nation's industrial capacity. Among the most important of these are: the availability of labor, especially skilled workers; an adequate transportation system; stability of the country's financial structure; and efficiency in executing the country's economic policies.

Economic Mobilization

The ability to recognize when a nation is mobilizing economically for war is vital as one significant indication of its probable course of action. The term *economic mobilization* means the changing of a nation's war potential into actual war energies. The aim of a war economy is to insure the maximum use of the nation's total resources, human as well as material, in the effort to defeat the enemy.

Economic mobilization for war requires at least four steps. First, available manpower must be used to provide adequate personnel for the armed forces and simultaneously to allot sufficient workers to produce war materials and essential civilian goods. Labor must be directed into the necessary channels through a system of freezes, priorities, and drafts. Second, to curtail civilian production and expand war production, the flow of raw materials must be controlled so that essential production is supplied adequately. Third, as an aid to financing the war and to smooth the operation of the economic system, it is necessary to establish a system of price controls. Fourth, the rationing of scarce civilian goods is imperative to insure the maximum efficiency and highest morale of the population.

For economic mobilization for war, the totalitarian countries with their controlled economic systems are in a much better technical position than the free enterprise economies. Even in peacetime, they have numerous controls already in operation that govern investments, production, foreign trade, prices, wages, and employment.

Sources of Economic Intelligence

Economic intelligence can be useful only to the extent that the information is both timely and reliable. This fundamental fact highlights the importance of collecting intelligence, making collection no less important to intelligence production than the analytical process.

The number one priority area for United States intelligence today is the Soviet Union and its communist allies. These countries share a highly developed sense of security consciousness, with the result that information of all kinds, including economic data, is sharply curtailed.

This is not to say that the open Soviet publications that are available to the Intelligence Community are not useful; on the contrary, they provide a substantial portion of the information that is currently received. The point is that through the control of such public media as newspapers and trade journals the Soviet authorities have created wide gaps in our knowledge. Information about certain fields of activity such as armaments is very tightly controlled, including even information about industries that are only indirectly related to armaments. One of these, for example, is the extraction and manufacture of nonferrous metals.

The selective nature of published information that has been received about the Soviet bloc has placed a high premium on the capability of attachés and reporting officers who are stationed in the bloc countries, since their observations and insights offer the greatest chance of filling intelligence gaps. Other sources, of course, come

into play, such as foreign broadcasts, occasional defectors, commercial contacts, and clandestine sources. These are used in different ways and with varying degrees of effectiveness, depending both on the type of opportunity and on the nature of the economic problem to be solved. The most reliable source of economic intelligence on the bloc, however, has undoubtedly been and probably will continue to be published information that is interpreted and supplemented by informed attachés and economic reporting officer reports. *See also:* Strategic Intelligence.

References

Clauser, Jerome K. and Weir, Sandra M. *Intelligence Research Methodology.* State College, PA: HRB Singer, 1975.

Department of Defense, Defense Intelligence College. *Glossary of Intelligence Terms and Definitions.* Washington, DC: DIC, 1987.

Department of Defense, Joint Chiefs of Staff. *Department of Defense Dictionary of Military and Related Terms.* Washington, DC: GPO, 1986.

Godson, Roy, ed. *Intelligence Problems for the 1980s, Number 1: Elements of Intelligence.* Rev. ed. Washington, DC: National Strategy Information Center, 1983.

———. *Intelligence Problems for the 1980s, Number 4: Covert Action.* Washington, DC: National Strategy Information Center, 1981.

Kent, Sherman. *Strategic Intelligence for American World Policy.* Princeton, NJ: Princeton University Press, 1966.

Laqueur, Walter. *A World of Secrets.* New York: Basic Books, 1985.

Treverton, Gregory F. *Covert Action: The Limits of Intervention in the Postwar World.* New York: Basic Books, 1987.

Turner, Stansfield. *Secrecy and Democracy: The CIA in Transition.* Boston: Houghton Mifflin, 1985.

U.S. Congress. Senate. *Final Report of the Senate Select Committee to Study Government Operations with Respect to Intelligence Activities. Report 94-755. Book I, Foreign and Military Intelligence.* Washington, DC: GPO, 1976.

—ECONOMIC INTELLIGENCE COMMITTEE (EIC) is a subcommittee of the Intelligence Advisory Committee (IAC) that was created in 1951. Its duties were to accomplish interdepartmental coordination of economic intelligence efforts, and to produce economic intelligence. The EIC was continued under the United States Intelligence Board (USIB). *See also:* Central Intelligence Agency, Director of Central Intelligence Committee.

References

Fain, Tyrus G.; Plant, Katharine C.; and Milloy, Ross. *The Intelligence Community: History, Organization, and Issues.* Public Documents Series. New York: R.R. Bowker, 1977.

Turner, Stansfield. *Secrecy and Democracy: The CIA in Transition.* Boston: Houghton Mifflin, 1985.

—**ECONOMIC MOBILIZATION** is the process of preparing for and carrying out such changes in the organization and functioning of the national economy as are necessary to provide for the most effective use of resources in a national emergency.

References

Department of Defense, Joint Chiefs of Staff. *Department of Defense Dictionary of Military and Related Terms.* Washington, DC: GPO, 1986.

Godson, Roy, ed. *Intelligence Problems for the 1980s, Number 1: Elements of Intelligence.* Rev. ed. Washington, DC: National Strategy Information Center, 1983.

—**ECONOMIC POTENTIAL** is the total capacity of a nation to produce goods and services.

References

Department of Defense, Joint Chiefs of Staff. *Department of Defense Dictionary of Military and Related Terms.* Washington, DC: GPO, 1986.

—**ECONOMIC RESEARCH AREA (ERA),** Central Intelligence Agency, was established in 1950 as a component of the Office of Research and Reports (ORR) and was responsible for the production of economic intelligence. The ERA was eventually developed into the Office of Economic Research (OER). *See also:* Central Intelligence Agency.

References

Fain, Tyrus G.; Plant, Katharine C.; and Milloy, Ross. *The Intelligence Community: History, Organization, and Issues.* Public Documents Series. New York: R.R. Bowker, 1977.

—**ECONOMIC WARFARE.** *See:* Economic Intelligence.

—**EDIBLE PAPER** is a term used in clandestine and covert intelligence operations to describe a water-soluble paper that can be swallowed by an intelligence agent in an emergency. According to Henry Becket, the paper does not dissolve easily, to the discomfort of the diner.

References

Becket, Henry S. A. *The Dictionary of Espionage: Spookspeak into English.* New York: Stein and Day, 1986.

Deacon, Richard. *Spyclopedia: An Encyclopedia of Spies, Secret Services, Operations, Jargon, and All Subjects Related to the World of Espionage.* London: Macdonald, 1987.

Ranelagh, John. *The Agency: The Rise and Decline of the CIA.* New York: Simon and Schuster, 1986.

—**EISENHOWER, DWIGHT DAVID.** President Eisenhower's administration was hallmarked by managerial boards, and this penchant was evident in his approach to the Intelligence Community. In 1957, he created the President's Board of Consultants on Foreign Intelligence Activities (PBCFIA), composed of a group of experienced private citizens who were tasked to review periodically the nation's intelligence activities. He also created the United States Intelligence Board in 1958, in an unsuccessful attempt to increase the power of the director of Central Intelligence. President Eisenhower deserves high marks for his handling of the Intelligence Community. Throughout his tenure, the Community did not become involved in domestic politics. His choice of Alan Dulles to replace General Walter Bedell Smith in 1953 was, on the whole, an astute one, although Dulles's background as an intelligence operative in World War II prompted him to concentrate on intelligence operations, at the expense of the CIA's efforts in the realm of intelligence estimates. However, Dulles did continue many of the initiatives begun by General Smith, to the benefit of the CIA.

During Eisenhower's administration, the CIA undertook several operations that were staged to replace governments that were antagonistic to the United States with ones that were friendly. These were the successful operation in Iran in 1953 that brought the Shah back to power, successful operations in Costa Rica in 1953 and Guatemala in 1954, and unsuccessful efforts in Indonesia and Tibet in 1958.

Perhaps the most significant intelligence development of the Eisenhower administration proved to be the most embarrassing to the President. This was the highly successful U-2 overhead reconnaissance program. Initially, Eisenhower had questioned the viability of the program and had expressed his wish to have several U-2s penetrate Soviet airspace concurrently in a one-time reconnaissance effort. However, he demurred and U-2 missions were flown in a highly successful collection program that ended when Francis Gary Powers was shot down over the Soviet Union. At first the administration claimed that the mission had been a weather flight, but when the Soviet Union produced both the plane and Powers, the United States had to admit that it had been spying. The results were cataclysmal, in that a Soviet-American summit conference was scuttled, the Soviet-American dialogue was suspended until Eisenhower left office, and, most important, U.S. reconnaissance efforts over the USSR were suspended until the advent of reconnaissance satellites in the early 1960s.

In spite of this incident, Eisenhower must be assessed as being one of the most skillful postwar presidents in his handling of the U.S. Intelligence Community. *See also:* Executive Oversight.

References

American Bar Association. *Oversight and Accountability of the U.S. Intelligence Agencies: An Evaluation.* Washington, DC: ABA, 1985.

Breckinridge, Scott D. *The CIA and the U.S. Intelligence System.* Boulder, CO: Westview Press, 1986.

Brinkley, David A., and Hull, Andrew W. *Estimative Intelligence: A Textbook on the History, Products, Uses, and Writing of Intelligence Estimates.* Columbus, OH: Battelle, 1979.

Cline, Ray S. *The CIA Under Reagan, Bush, and Casey.* Washington, DC: Acropolis Books, 1981.

Corson, William R. *The Armies of Ignorance: The Rise of the American Intelligence Empire.* New York: Dial Press, 1977.

Laqueur, Walter. *A World of Secrets.* New York: Basic Books, 1985.

Lowenthal, Mark M. *U.S. Intelligence: Evolution and Anatomy.* New York: Praeger, 1984.

Maurer, Alfred C.; Turnstall, Marion D.; and Keagle, James M. *Intelligence Policy and Process.* Boulder, CO: Westview Press, 1985.

Treverton, Gregory F. *Covert Action: The Limits of Intervention in the Postwar World.* New York: Basic Books, 1987.

U.S. Congress. Senate. *Alleged Assassination Plots Involving Foreign Leaders: An Interim Report of the Select Committee to Study Governmental Operations with Respect to Intelligence Activities.* 94th Congress, 1st sess., Nov. 20, 1975. S. Rept. 94-465.

Von Hoene, John P. *A Intelligence User's Guide.* Washington, DC: DIA, 1983.

—ELECTRICAL AND ELECTROMECHANICAL EQUIPMENT refers to all electrical and electromechanical devices that are used to handle unencrypted information, including but not limited to end terminal equipment, patches, interface units, automated switches, multiplexers, minicomputers, and computer systems. *See also:* Communications Security.

References

Laqueur, Walter. *A World of Secrets.* New York: Basic Books, 1985.

—ELECTRICAL SIGNAL is an electronic surveillance term that means the electrical equivalent of the source signal. *See also:* Communications Security.

References

Kessler, Michael. *Wiretapping and Electronic Surveillance Commission Studies: Supporting Materials for the Report of the National Commission for the Review of Federal and State Laws Relating to Wiretapping and Electronic Surveillance, Washington, DC, 1976.* Townsend, PA: Loompanics Unlimited, 1976.

Laqueur, Walter. *A World of Secrets.* New York: Basic Books, 1985.

—ELECTROMAGNETIC refers to electronic systems whose electricity is produced by magnetism. *See also:* Communications Security.

References

Laqueur, Walter. *A World of Secrets.* New York: Basic Books, 1985.

—ELECTROMAGNETIC COMPATIBILITY (EMC) is the compatibility of different systems with each other electromagnetically. It is desirable for different systems on a single platform to be compatible so that they do not damage each other. *See also:* Communications Security.

References

Department of Defense, Joint Chiefs of Staff. *Department of Defense Dictionary of Military and Related Terms.* Washington, DC: GPO, 1986.

Godson, Roy, ed. *Intelligence Problems for the 1980s, Number 1: Elements of Intelligence.* Rev. ed. Washington, DC: National Strategy Information Center, 1983.

—ELECTROMAGNETIC EMISSIONS, as defined by Army tactical intelligence (TACINT), are fields of electric and magnetic energy that travel through space. Depending on their frequency and rate of oscillation they are known as radio waves, gamma rays, X rays, ultraviolet rays, infrared light, or radar waves. *See also:* Communications Security.

References

Godson, Roy, ed. *Intelligence Problems for the 1980s, Number 1: Elements of Intelligence.* Rev. ed. Washington, DC: National Strategy Information Center, 1983.

Department of Defense, U.S. Army. *Counter-Signals Intelligence (C-SIGINT) Operations.* Field Manual FM 34-62. Washington, DC: Headquarters, Department of the Army, 1986.

———. *Military Intelligence Battalion Combat Electronic Warfare and Intelligence (Aerial Exploitation) (Corps).* Field Manual FM 34-22. Washington, DC: Headquarters, Department of the Army, 1984.

———. *Military Intelligence Company (Combat Electronic Warfare and Intelligence) (Armored Cavalry Regiment/Separate Brigade).* Field Manual FM 34-30. Washington, DC: Headquarters, Department of the Army, 1983.

—**ELECTROMAGNETIC PULSE (EMP)** is an electronic wave generated by a nuclear detonation that induces a current in any electrical conductor. An EMP can temporarily disrupt or overload and damage components of electronic equipment if they are not properly protected. *See also:* Communications Security.

References

Department of Defense, Joint Chiefs of Staff. *Department of Defense Dictionary of Military and Related Terms.* Washington, DC: GPO, 1986.

Department of Defense, U.S. Army. *U.S. Army Air Defense Artillery Employment.* Field Manual FM 44-1. Washington, DC: Headquarters, Department of the Army, 1983.

—**ELECTROMAGNETIC RADIATION** is a term used in signals intelligence, communications security, operations security, and signals analysis. It is radiation composed of oscillating electric and magnetic fields. Such waves, which include radar and radio waves, are propagated at the speed of light. *See also:* Communications Security.

References

Department of Defense, Joint Chiefs of Staff. *Department of Defense Dictionary of Military and Related Terms.* Washington, DC: GPO, 1986.

Godson, Roy, ed. *Intelligence Problems for the 1980s, Number 1: Elements of Intelligence.* Rev. ed. Washington, DC: National Strategy Information Center, 1983.

—**ELECTROMAGNETIC SPECTRUM** is a term that is used in electronic warfare, signals intelligence, communications security, operations security, and signals analysis. It is the frequencies (or wavelengths) present in a given electromagnetic radiation. A particular spectrum might include only a single frequency or could include a range of frequencies. As defined by the Church Committee, electromagnetic spectrum, has a slightly different meaning: "It is the frequencies (or wavelengths) present in a given electromagnetic radiation (radiation made up of oscillating electric and magnetic fields and propagated with the speed of light—such as radar or radio waves). A particular spectrum could include a single frequency, or a broad range of frequencies." *See also:* Communications Security.

References

Department of Defense, Joint Chiefs of Staff. *Department of Defense Dictionary of Military and Related Terms.* Washington, DC: GPO, 1986.

U.S. Congress. Senate. *Final Report of the Senate Select Committee to Study Government Operations with Respect to Intelligence Activities. Report 94-755. Book I, Foreign and Military Intelligence.* Washington, DC: GPO, 1976.

—**ELECTRONIC CAMOUFLAGE** is an electronic warfare term. It is the use of radar absorbent or reflecting materials in order to change the radar echoing properties of a surface. The purpose is to prevent the detection of the surface if it is hit by a radar signal. *See also:* Electronic Warfare.

References

Department of Defense, Defense Intelligence College. *Analyst Working Guide.* Washington, DC: DIC, 1987.

Godson, Roy, ed. *Intelligence Problems for the 1980s, Number 1: Elements of Intelligence.* Rev. ed. Washington, DC: National Strategy Information Center, 1983.

—**ELECTRONIC COUNTER-COUNTERMEASURES (ECCM)** is that division of electronic warfare involving actions taken to insure the effective use of the electromagnetic spectrum despite an adversary's use of electronic countermeasures. *See also:* Electronic Countermeasures.

—**ELECTRONIC COUNTERMEASURES (ECM)** are a division of electronic warfare that involve actions taken to prevent or reduce an enemy's use of the electromagnetic spectrum. Electronic countermeasures include *electronic jamming,* which is the deliberate radiation, reradiation, or reflection of electromagnetic energy in order to impair the enemy's use of his electronic equipment, and *electronic deception,* which is similar but is meant to mislead the enemy so that he misinterprets the information he receives from his electronic systems. Among the types of electronic deception, three are noteworthy. Manipulative deception involves altering or simulating friendly electromagnetic radiations in order to deceive an adversary. Simulative electronic deception involves actions that simulate real or fictional friendly capabilities in order to mislead the enemy. Imitative deception involves introducing radiations into enemy channels that imitate his own emissions. *See also:* Communications Security, Electronic Warfare.

References

Deacon, Richard. *Spyclopedia: An Encyclopedia of Spies, Secret Services, Operations, Jargon, and All Subjects Related to the World of Espionage.* London: Macdonald, 1987.

Department of Defense, Defense Intelligence College. *Glossary of Intelligence Terms and Definitions.* Washington, DC: DIC, 1987.

Department of Defense, Joint Chiefs of Staff. *Department of Defense Dictionary of Military and Related Terms.* Washington, DC: GPO, 1986.

Department of Defense, U.S. Army. *Counter-Signals Intelligence (C-SIGINT) Operations.* Field Manual FM 34-62. Washington, DC: Headquarters, Department of the Army, 1986.

————. *Military Intelligence Battalion Combat Electronic Warfare and Intelligence (Aerial Exploitation) (Corps).* Field Manual FM 34-22. Washington, DC: Headquarters, Department of the Army, 1984.

————. *Military Intelligence Battalion (Combat Electronic Warfare Intelligence) (Division).* Field Manual FM 34-10. Washington, DC: Headquarters, Department of the Army, 1981.

————. *Military Intelligence Battalion (CEWI) (Operations) (Corps).* Field Manual FM 34-21. Washington, DC: Headquarters, Department of the Army, 1982.

————. *Military Intelligence Battalion (CEWI) (Tactical Exploitation) (Corps): Counterintelligence, Interrogation, Electronic Warfare.* Field Manual FM 34-23. Washington, DC: Headquarters, Department of the Army, 1985.

————. *Military Intelligence Company (Combat Electronic Warfare and Intelligence) (Armored Cavalry Regiment/Separate Brigade).* Field Manual FM 34-30. Washington, DC: Headquarters, Department of the Army, 1983.

————. *Military Intelligence Group (Combat Electronic Warfare and Intelligence) (Corps).* Field Manual FM 34-20. Washington, DC: Headquarters, Department of the Army, 1983.

————. *Intelligence and Electronic Warfare Operations.* Field Manual FM 34-1. Washington, DC: Headquarters, Department of the Army, 1984.

Godson, Roy, ed. *Intelligence Problems for the 1980s, Number 1: Elements of Intelligence.* Rev. ed. Washington, DC: National Strategy Information Center, 1983.

—**ELECTRONIC DECEPTION** is an Army tactical intelligence (TACINT) term that means the deliberate radiation, reradiation, alteration, suppression, absorption, denial, enhancement, or reflection of electromagnetic energy in a manner that is intended to convey misleading information or to deny the receipt of valid information by an enemy or by enemy electronics-dependent weapons. Among the types of electronic deception are manipulative electronic deception, simulated electronic deception, and imitative deception. *See also:* Electronic Countermeasures.

—**ELECTRONIC EMISSION SECURITY** involves measures taken to protect all transmissions from interception and electronic analysis. *See also:* Communications Security.

References

Department of Defense, Defense Intelligence College. *Glossary of Intelligence Terms and Definitions.* Washington, DC: DIC, 1987.

Department of Defense, Joint Chiefs of Staff. *Department of Defense Dictionary of Military and Related Terms.* Washington, DC: GPO, 1986.

—**ELECTRONIC INTELLIGENCE (ELINT),** in the general sense, is technical and intelligence information derived from foreign electromagnetic radiations other than those involving communications and those from atomic detonations and radioactive sources. ELINT is part of the National Security Agency/Central Security Service Signals Intelligence Mission. In the Army tactical intelligence (TACINT) sense, the term is defined somewhat more specifically as the intercepting and processing of noncommunications signals in order to determine the intentions, capabilities, and locations as well as the equipment characteristics and functions of the transmitters. *See also:* Communications Security.

References

Department of Defense, Defense Intelligence College. *Glossary of Intelligence Terms and Definitions*. Washington, DC: DIC, 1987.

Department of Defense, Joint Chiefs of Staff. *Department of Defense Dictionary of Military and Related Terms*. Washington, DC: GPO, 1986.

Department of Defense, U.S. Army. *Counter-Signals Intelligence (C-SIGINT) Operations*. Field Manual FM 34-62. Washington, DC: Headquarters, Department of the Army, 1986.

———. *Military Intelligence Battalion Combat Electronic Warfare and Intelligence (Aerial Exploitation) (Corps)*. Field Manual FM 34-22. Washington, DC: Headquarters, Department of the Army, 1984.

———. *Military Intelligence Battalion (Combat Electronic Warfare Intelligence) (Division)*. Field Manual FM 34-10. Washington, DC: Headquarters, Department of the Army, 1981.

———. *Military Intelligence Battalion (CEWI) (Operations) (Corps)*. Field Manual FM 34-21. Washington, DC: Headquarters, Department of the Army, 1982.

———. *Military Intelligence Company (Combat Electronic Warfare and Intelligence) (Armored Cavalry Regiment/Separate Brigade)*. Field Manual FM 34-30. Washington, DC: Headquarters, Department of the Army, 1983.

———. *Military Intelligence Group (Combat Electronic Warfare and Intelligence) (Corps)*. Field Manual FM 34-20. Washington, DC: Headquarters, Department of the Army, 1983.

———. *Intelligence and Electronic Warfare Operations*. Field Manual FM 34-1. Washington, DC: Headquarters, Department of the Army, 1984.

Godson, Roy, ed. *Intelligence Problems for the 1980s, Number 1: Elements of Intelligence*. Rev. ed. Washington, DC: National Strategy Information Center, 1983.

—**ELECTRONIC JAMMING** is an electronic warfare term. It is the deliberate radiation, re-radiation, or reflection of electromagnetic signals with the aim of impairing the enemy's use of his electronic devices. *See also:* Electronic Countermeasures, Jamming.

References

Department of Defense, Joint Chiefs of Staff. *Department of Defense Dictionary of Military and Related Terms*. Washington, DC: GPO, 1986.

U.S. Congress. Senate. *Final Report of the Senate Select Committee to Study Government Operations with Respect to Intelligence Activities. Report 94-755. Book I, Foreign and Military Intelligence*. Washington, DC: GPO, 1976.

—**ELECTRONIC LINE OF SIGHT,** as defined by the Church Committee, is the path that is traveled by electromagnetic waves that is not subject to reflection or refraction by the atmosphere.

References

Department of Defense, Joint Chiefs of Staff. *Department of Defense Dictionary of Military and Related Terms*. Washington, DC: GPO, 1986.

U.S. Congress. Senate. *Final Report of the Senate Select Committee to Study Government Operations with Respect to Intelligence Activities. Report 94-755. Book I, Foreign and Military Intelligence*. Washington, DC: GPO, 1976.

—**ELECTRONIC ORDER OF BATTLE (EOB)** is a listing of a foreign nation's noncommunications electronic devices. The listing includes name or nomenclature of the emitter, its location, site designation, the function of the site, and any other pertinent information that has military significance. *See also:* Defense Intelligence Agency.

References

Department of Defense, Defense Intelligence College. *Glossary of Intelligence Terms and Definitions*. Washington, DC: DIC, 1987.

Godson, Roy, ed. *Intelligence Problems for the 1980s, Number 1: Elements of Intelligence*. Rev. ed. Washington, DC: National Strategy Information Center, 1983.

—**ELECTRONIC RECONNAISSANCE (ER)** is an electronic warfare term. It means detecting, collecting, identifying, evaluating and locating electromagnetic signals other than communications signals and radiation from nuclear detonations and radioactive sources. *See also:* Electronic Warfare.

References

Department of Defense, Joint Chiefs of Staff. *Department of Defense Dictionary of Military and Related Terms*. Washington, DC: GPO, 1986.

Laqueur, Walter. *A World of Secrets*. New York: Basic Books, 1985.

—**ELECTRONIC SECURITY (ELSEC)** is a term used in counterintelligence, counterespionage, and counterinsurgency to describe the protection that results from all the measures taken to deny unauthorized persons access to information of military value that might be derived from their intercepting and analyzing one's noncommunications electromagnetic radiations. *See also:* Communications Security.

References

Department of Defense, Defense Intelligence College. *Glossary of Intelligence Terms and Definitions.* Washington, DC: DIC, 1987.

Department of Defense, Joint Chiefs of Staff. *Department of Defense Dictionary of Military and Related Terms.* Washington, DC: GPO, 1986.

Department of Defense, U.S. Army. *Counterintelligence.* Field Manual FM 34-60. Washington, DC: Headquarters, Department of the Army, 1985.

Godson, Roy, ed. *Intelligence Problems for the 1980s, Number 1: Elements of Intelligence.* Rev. ed. Washington, DC: National Strategy Information Center, 1983.

U.S. Congress. Senate. *Final Report of the Senate Select Committee to Study Government Operations with Respect to Intelligence Activities. Report 94-755. Book I, Foreign and Military Intelligence.* Washington, DC: GPO, 1976.

—**ELECTRONIC SURVEILLANCE** is a term used in clandestine intelligence operations and has two meanings. (1) Electronic surveillance, or eavesdropping, means monitoring private communications by electronic means in situations where the subject neither consents nor knows that his or her conversations are being overheard. Electronic surveillance does not include the use of radio direction finding equipment solely to determine the location of a transmitter. (2) A second definition for electronic surveillance evolved from Presidential Executive Order 12333, "United States Intelligence Activities," dated December 4, 1981, which concerned the surveillance of U.S. citizens by U.S. intelligence agencies. It states that "electronic surveillance is acquiring nonpublic communications by electronic means without the consent of a person who is a party to an electronic communication or, in the case of nonelectronic communication, without the consent of a person who is visibly present at the place of communication, but not including the use of radio direction finding equipment solely to determine the location of a transmitter. (Electronic surveillance within the United States is subject to the definitions in the Foreign Intelligence Surveillance Act of 1978.)"

References

Department of Defense. *Activities of DoD Intelligence Components that Affect U.S. Persons (Department of Defense Directive 5240.1).* Washington, DC: DoD, 1982.

Department of Defense, Defense Intelligence College. *Glossary of Intelligence Terms and Definitions.* Washington, DC: DIC, 1987.

Department of Defense, Joint Chiefs of Staff. *Department of Defense Dictionary of Military and Related Terms.* Washington, DC: GPO, 1986.

Godson, Roy, ed. *Intelligence Problems for the 1980s, Number 1: Elements of Intelligence.* Rev. ed. Washington, DC: National Strategy Information Center, 1983.

Maurer, Alfred C.; Turnstall, Marion D.; and Keagle, James M. *Intelligence Policy and Process.* Boulder, CO: Westview Press, 1985.

U.S. Congress. Senate. *Final Report of the Senate Select Committee to Study Government Operations with Respect to Intelligence Activities. Report 94-755. Book I, Foreign and Military Intelligence.* Washington, DC: GPO, 1976.

—**ELECTRONIC WARFARE (EW)** is a form of military action involving the use electromagnetic energy to determine, exploit, reduce, or prevent the enemy's use of the electromagnetic spectrum while insuring that friendly forces still can use the same spectrum. There are three divisions in electronic warfare: electronic warfare support measures (ESM); electronic countermeasures (ECM); and electronic counter-countermeasures (ECCM). *See also:* Communications Security, Electronic Counter-Countermeasures, Electronic Countermeasures, Electronic Warfare Support Measures.

References

Department of Defense, Defense Intelligence College. *Glossary of Intelligence Terms and Definitions.* Washington, DC: DIC, 1987.

Department of Defense, Joint Chiefs of Staff. *Department of Defense Dictionary of Military and Related Terms.* Washington, DC: GPO, 1986.

Department of Defense, U.S. Army. *Counter-Signals Intelligence (C-SIGINT) Operations.* Field Manual FM 34-62. Washington, DC: Headquarters, Department of the Army, 1986.

———. *Military Intelligence Battalion Combat Electronic Warfare and Intelligence (Aerial Exploitation) (Corps).* Field Manual FM 34-22. Washington, DC: Headquarters, Department of the Army, 1984.

———. *Military Intelligence Battalion (Combat Electronic Warfare Intelligence) (Division).* Field Manual FM 34-10. Washington, DC: Headquarters, Department of the Army, 1981.

————. *Military Intelligence Battalion (CEWI) (Operations) (Corps).* Field Manual FM 34-21. Washington, DC: Headquarters, Department of the Army, 1982.

————. *Military Intelligence Company (Combat Electronic Warfare and Intelligence) (Armored Cavalry Regiment/Separate Brigade).* Field Manual FM 34-30. Washington, DC: Headquarters, Department of the Army, 1983.

————. *Military Intelligence Group (Combat Electronic Warfare and Intelligence) (Corps).* Field Manual FM 34-20. Washington, DC: Headquarters, U.S. Army, 1983.

————. *Intelligence and Electronic Warfare Operations.* Field Manual FM 34-1. Washington, DC: Headquarters, Department of the Army, 1984.

Godson, Roy, ed. *Intelligence Problems for the 1980s, Number 1: Elements of Intelligence.* Rev. ed. Washington, DC: National Strategy Information Center, 1983.

Laqueur, Walter. *A World of Secrets.* New York: Basic Books, 1985.

U.S. Congress. Senate. *Final Report of the Senate Select Committee to Study Government Operations with Respect to Intelligence Activities. Report 94-755. Book I, Foreign and Military Intelligence.* Washington, DC: GPO, 1976.

—**ELECTRONIC WARFARE SUPPORT MEASURES (ESM)** are a part of electronic warfare involving actions taken to search for, intercept, locate, and immediately identify radiated electromagnetic energy for the purposes of immediate threat recognition. These measures provide information required for immediate action involving electronic countermeasures (ECM), electronic counter-countermeasures (ECCM), avoidance, targeting, and other tactical endeavors. In Army tactical intelligence (TACINT), direction finding of radios and radars is an ESM technique. *See also:* Communications Security, Electronic Warfare.

—**ELECTRO-OPTICAL INTELLIGENCE (ELECTRO-OPTINT)** is intelligence information derived from information collected by optically monitoring the electromagnetic spectrum from ultraviolet (0.01 micrometers) through far (long wavelength) infrared (1,000 micrometers). *See also:* Optical Intelligence.

References
Department of Defense, Defense Intelligence College. *Glossary of Intelligence Terms and Definitions.* Washington, DC: DIC, 1987.

—**ELEMENT** is a general intelligence term that has several meanings. (1) Within the Defense Intelligence Agency, an element is a directorate, division, branch or section, as appropriate. (2) Element is also a communications security (COMSEC) term that means a subdivision of COMSEC equipment, assembly, or subassembly that normally consists of a single or a group of replaceable parts. It is a removable item that is necessary for the operation of the equipment but does not necessarily perform a complete function by itself. (3) Element is also a baud-based system term that is used in communications intelligence, communications security, operations security, and signals analysis. It is a unit of measurement and is the signal impulse of the shortest intentional duration occurring in a teleprinter or similar telegraphic system. (4) Finally, an element is a target intelligence term that pertains to the target that is to be destroyed. In this context, it is the smallest subdivision of a military unit that can be tactically maneuvered independently. Elements are the physical and functional components of an installation or site that are related to other elements by proximity or function. *See also:* Protection Elements, Primary Elements, Secondary Elements, Critical Primary Elements, Vulnerable Elements, Vulnerable-Critical Elements.

References
Department of Defense, Joint Chiefs of Staff. *Department of Defense Dictionary of Military and Related Terms.* Washington, DC: GPO, 1986.

Godson, Roy, ed. *Intelligence Problems for the 1980s, Number 1: Elements of Intelligence.* Rev. ed. Washington, DC: National Strategy Information Center, 1983.

U.S. Congress. Senate. *Final Report of the Senate Select Committee to Study Government Operations with Respect to Intelligence Activities. Report 94-755. Book I, Foreign and Military Intelligence.* Washington, DC: GPO, 1976.

—**ELEMENTS OF NATIONAL POWER** are all the means that are available for employment in the pursuit of national objectives.

References
Department of Defense, Joint Chiefs of Staff. *Department of Defense Dictionary of Military and Related Terms.* Washington, DC: GPO, 1986.

—**ELICITATION** is a term used in clandestine and covert intelligence operations. It means getting intelligence from a person or group without disclosing the true purpose of the conversation. It is a human intelligence (HUMINT) collection technique that is overt, unless the collector uses a false identity.

References

Department of Defense, Joint Chiefs of Staff. *Department of Defense Dictionary of Military and Related Terms.* Washington, DC: GPO, 1986.

Quirk, John; Phillips, David; Cline, Ray; and Pforzheimer, Walter. *The Central Intelligence Agency: A Photographic History.* Guilford, CT: Foreign Intelligence Press, 1986.

U.S. Congress. Senate. *Final Report of the Senate Select Committee to Study Government Operations with Respect to Intelligence Activities. Report 94-755. Book I, Foreign and Military Intelligence.* Washington, DC: GPO, 1976.

—**ELIGIBILITY** pertains to intelligence security matters. It is a term that is synonymous with "eligible for access to sensitive compartmented information." *See also:* Adjudication, Background Investigation, National Agency Check, Special Background Investigation.

References

Department of Defense, Defense Intelligence College. *Glossary of Intelligence Terms and Definitions.* Washington, DC: DIC, 1987.

—**ELINT.** *See:* Electronic Intelligence.

—**ELLIS, ROBERT W.,** while stationed at Moffett Field Naval Air Station, offered to sell classified information to the Soviets in 1983. He was dishonorably discharged and sentenced to five years in prison. The sentence was subsequently reduced to three years.

References

Allen, Thomas B., and Polmar, Norman. *Merchants of Treason: America's Secrets for Sale.* New York: Delacorte Press, 1988.

—**ELLSBERG CASE** concerned a government suit to prevent publication of the *Pentagon Papers* by Daniel Ellsberg, a collection of military documents pertaining to the Vietnam War. The papers were published widely throughout the United States.

References

Breckinridge, Scott D. *The CIA and the U.S. Intelligence System.* Boulder, CO: Westview Press, 1986.

Godson, Roy, ed. *Intelligence Problems for the 1980s, Number 2: Analysis and Estimates.* Washington, DC: National Strategy Information Center, 1980.

—**EMANATIONS SECURITY (EMSEC)** is a term used in counterintelligence and counterespionage to describe the protection that results from all the measures that are designed to deny unauthorized individuals access to information. The use of EMSEC implies that the conversations, if intercepted and analyzed, would be of intelligence value. EMSEC does not include measures regarding cryptographic equipment or telecommunications systems, which are protected under other programs. *See also:* Communications Security, Emission Security.

References

Department of Defense, Defense Intelligence College. *Glossary of Intelligence Terms and Definitions.* Washington, DC: DIC, 1987.

—**EMERGENCY ACCESS** is an intelligence security term. It is the requirement for an individual to have access to sensitive compartmented information before the completion of his special background investigation (SBI). The completion of the SBI is normally required before access is granted, so that the adjudicator can be certain that there is no derogatory information in respect to the person's past that would preclude the granting of access. However, in some situations, for example when one military officer relieves another on short notice or when a civilian is hired to work on an unforeseen and highly important project, it is mandatory for the command to seek emergency access. In such a request, the command must explain the adverse consequences that will occur if the person is not granted access. (In the case of the reporting officer, denial of access would prevent him from relieving the officer who is departing the command, thereby creating a gap in that capability. In the case of the newly hired employee, denial of access would mean that work cannot begin on the project.)

Once the request is received by the investigative command, an examination is made concerning how far the investigation has advanced (which will indicate whether there is enough information to make a reasonable judgment) and whether any derogatory information has been discovered. This, coupled with the strength of the command's justification for its request, will be used to determine whether an emergency access can be approved. *See also:* Access.

References

Department of Defense, Defense Intelligence College. *Glossary of Intelligence Terms and Definitions.* Washington, DC: DIC, 1987.

—**EMERGENCY ACTION PLAN (EAP)** is to be used during natural disasters, hostilities, and other emergencies. The plan stresses the importance of personnel safety, provides for safeguarding sensitive compartmented information (SCI), and discusses the evacuation or destruction of this material if this is necessary. The plan will also identify the items that are to be destroyed and the priority order in which they are to be destroyed. Finally it will discuss procedures for conducting exercises, orientations, and inspections. *See also:* Sensitive Compartmented Information.

References

Department of Defense, Defense Intelligence College. *Glossary of Intelligence Terms and Definitions.* Washington, DC: DIC, 1987.

—**EMERGENCY PRIORITY** is a category of immediate mission request that takes precedence over all other priorities. An enemy breakthrough would be an emergency priority.

References

Department of Defense, Joint Chiefs of Staff. *Department of Defense Dictionary of Military and Related Terms.* Washington, DC: GPO, 1986.

—**EMERGENCY RELOCATION SITE (ERS)** is an area that has been designated as a location where sensitive compartmented information (SCI) may be used during emergencies that require relocating the facility to another place. *See also:* Emergency Action Plan.

References

Department of Defense, Joint Chiefs of Staff. *Department of Defense Dictionary of Military and Related Terms.* Washington, DC: GPO, 1986.

—**EMIGRÉ** is a person who leaves his country legally and intends to permanently resettle elsewhere.

References

Department of Defense, Defense Intelligence College. *Glossary of Intelligence Terms and Definitions.* Washington, DC: DIC, 1987.

Turner, Stansfield. *Secrecy and Democracy: The CIA in Transition.* Boston: Houghton Mifflin, 1985.

—**EMISSION CONTROL** is an Army tactical intelligence (TACINT) term that means the selective and controlled use of electromagnetic, acoustic, or other emitters to optimize command and control capabilities while minimizing, for operations security, detection by enemy sensors; to minimize mutual interference among friendly systems; and/or to execute a military deception plan. *See also:* Communications Security.

References

Department of Defense, Joint Chiefs of Staff. *Department of Defense Dictionary of Military and Related Terms.* Washington, DC: GPO, 1986.

Department of Defense, U.S. Army. *Counter-Signals Intelligence (C-SIGINT) Operations.* Field Manual FM 34-62. Washington, DC: Headquarters, Department of the Army, 1986.

———. *Military Intelligence Battalion Combat Electronic Warfare and Intelligence (Aerial Exploitation) (Corps).* Field Manual FM 34-22. Washington, DC: Headquarters, Department of the Army, 1984.

———. *Military Intelligence Company (Combat Electronic Warfare and Intelligence) (Armored Cavalry Regiment/Separate Brigade).* Field Manual FM 34-30. Washington, DC: Headquarters, Department of the Army, 1983.

Godson, Roy, ed. *Intelligence Problems for the 1980s, Number 1: Elements of Intelligence.* Rev. ed. Washington, DC: National Strategy Information Center, 1983.

Laqueur, Walter. *A World of Secrets.* New York: Basic Books, 1985.

—**EMISSION SECURITY (EMSEC)**, in communications security (COMSEC), means that part of COMSEC involving measures taken to deny unauthorized parties access to information passed on cryptographic equipment and telecommunications systems. *See also:* Communications Security.

References

Department of Defense, Defense Intelligence College. *Glossary of Intelligence Terms and Definitions.* Washington, DC: DIC, 1987.

Department of Defense, Joint Chiefs of Staff. *Department of Defense Dictionary of Military and Related Terms.* Washington, DC: GPO, 1986.

Department of Defense, U.S. Army. *Counter-Signals Intelligence (C-SIGINT) Operations.* Field Manual FM 34-62. Washington, DC: Headquarters, Department of the Army, 1986.

Godson, Roy, ed. *Intelligence Problems for the 1980s, Number 1: Elements of Intelligence.* Rev. ed. Washington, DC: National Strategy Information Center, 1983.

Laqueur, Walter. *A World of Secrets.* New York: Basic Books, 1985.

U.S. Congress. Senate. *Final Report of the Senate Select Committee to Study Government Operations with Respect to Intelligence Activities. Report 94-755. Book I, Foreign and Military Intelligence.* Washington, DC: GPO, 1976.

—EMPLOYEE is a definition that evolved from Presidential Executive Order 12333, "United States Intelligence Activities," dated December 4, 1981, which governs the types of surveillance activities that U.S. intelligence agencies can use on U.S. citizens. In this context, an employee is a person employed by, assigned to, or acting for an agency within the intelligence community, including contractors and other persons otherwise acting at the direction of such an agency. *See also:* Agent, Blown Agent, Case Officer, Chief of Base, Chief of Outpost, Chief of Station, Company, Confusion Agent, Co-Opted Worker, Co-Optees, Defector, Disaffected Person, Dispatched Agent, Double Agent, Illegal Agent, Illegal Support Officer, Informant, Inside Man, Ladies, Nash, Raven, Recruitment, Recruitment in Place, Swallow, Taxi, Special Activities.

References

Godson, Roy, ed. *Intelligence Problems for the 1980s, Number 1: Elements of Intelligence.* Rev. ed. Washington, DC: National Strategy Information Center, 1983.

Kessler, Ronald. *Spy vs. Spy: Stalking Soviet Spies in America.* New York: Charles Scribner's Sons, 1988.

Turner, Stansfield. *Secrecy and Democracy: The CIA in Transition.* Boston: Houghton Mifflin, 1985.

U.S. Government, Department of Defense. *Activities of DoD Intelligence Components that Affect U.S. Persons (Department of Defense Directive 5240.1).* Washington, DC: DoD, 1982.

—ENCIPHER, in communications security (COMSEC), means to encrypt or convert plain text into unintelligible form by using a cipher system. *See also:* Cipher, Communications Security.

References

Department of Defense, Defense Intelligence College. *Glossary of Intelligence Terms and Definitions.* Washington, DC: DIC, 1987.

Department of Defense, Joint Chiefs of Staff. *Department of Defense Dictionary of Military and Related Terms.* Washington, DC: GPO, 1986.

Godson, Roy, ed. *Intelligence Problems for the 1980s, Number 1: Elements of Intelligence.* Rev. ed. Washington, DC: National Strategy Information Center, 1983.

U.S. Congress. Senate. *Final Report of the Senate Select Committee to Study Government Operations with Respect to Intelligence Activities. Report 94-755. Book I, Foreign and Military Intelligence.* Washington, DC: GPO, 1976.

—ENCODE, in communications security (COMSEC), means the process of converting plain text into a different form (encoded text) by means of a code. *See also:* Communications Security.

References

Department of Defense, Defense Intelligence College. *Glossary of Intelligence Terms and Definitions.* Washington, DC: DIC, 1987.

Godson, Roy, ed. *Intelligence Problems for the 1980s, Number 1: Elements of Intelligence.* Rev. ed. Washington, DC: National Strategy Information Center, 1983.

—ENCRYPT, in communications security (COMSEC), means to convert plain text into a different, unintelligible form (encrypted form) in order to conceal its meaning. Note that the term "encrypt" encompasses the terms "encipher" and "encode." *See also:* Communications Security.

References

Department of Defense, Defense Intelligence College. *Glossary of Intelligence Terms and Definitions.* Washington, DC: DIC, 1987.

Department of Defense, Joint Chiefs of Staff. *Department of Defense Dictionary of Military and Related Terms.* Washington, DC: GPO, 1986.

Godson, Roy, ed. *Intelligence Problems for the 1980s, Number 1: Elements of Intelligence.* Rev. ed. Washington, DC: National Strategy Information Center, 1983.

Maurer, Alfred C.; Turnstall, Marion D.; and Keagle, James M. *Intelligence Policy and Process.* Boulder, CO: Westview Press, 1985.

U.S. Congress. Senate. *Final Report of the Senate Select Committee to Study Government Operations with Respect to Intelligence Activities. Report 94-755. Book I, Foreign and Military Intelligence.* Washington, DC: GPO, 1976.

—**ENCRYPTED FOR TRANSMISSION ONLY (EFTO)** is used only on unclassified messages. The procedure is authorized within the Department of Defense, including the National Security Agency and the Federal Aviation Administration, and is acceptable for the delivery of U.S. military originated messages by the General Services Administration. It is applied to unclassified information that is considered, for any reason, to be sufficiently sensitive that it should be encrypted while being transmitted. *See also:* Communications Security.

References

Department of Defense, Defense Intelligence Agency. *Defense Intelligence Agency Manual.* Washington, DC: DIA, 1987.

—**END PRODUCT.** *See:* Finished Intelligence.

—**END-TO-END ENCRYPTION,** in communications security (COMSEC), means the protection of information that is passed in a secure telecommunications system by cryptographic means from the point of origin to the point of destination. *See also:* Communications Security.

References

Martin, Paul H. "Communications-Computer Security." *Journal of Electronic Defense* (June 1987).

Muzerall, Joseph V., and Carty, Thomas P. "COMSEC and Its Need for Key Management." *DP&CS* (Spring 1987). Ware, Willis H. "Information Systems, Security, and Privacy." *EDUCOM Bulletin* (Summer 1984).

—**END-TO-END SECURITY,** in communications security (COMSEC), means the protection of information that is passed in a secure telecommunications system by a cryptographic or a protected distribution system from the point of origin to the point of destination. *See also:* Communications Security.

References

Martin, Paul H. "Communications-Computer Security." *Journal of Electronic Defense* (June 1987).

Muzerall, Joseph V., and Carty, Thomas P. "COMSEC and Its Need for Key Management." *DP&CS* (Spring 1987).

—**ENEMY CAPABILITIES** is a general intelligence term that has two meanings. (1) Enemy capabilities are those courses of action open to the enemy that, if adopted, will adversely affect the accomplishment of a friendly mission. The term "capabilities" includes not only the general courses of action open to the enemy, such as attack, defense, or withdrawal, but also all the options available to him under each course of action. Enemy capabilities are considered with due respect to all known factors that can affect military operations, including time, space, weather, terrain, and the strength and disposition of enemy forces. (2) On the strategic level, the capabilities of a nation are the courses of action that are within that nation's power to accomplish its national objectives in both peace and war.

References

Department of Defense, Joint Chiefs of Staff. *Department of Defense Dictionary of Military and Related Terms.* Washington, DC: GPO, 1986.

Godson, Roy, ed. *Intelligence Problems for the 1980s, Number 1: Elements of Intelligence.* Rev. ed. Washington, DC: National Strategy Information Center, 1983.

U.S. Congress. Senate. *Final Report of the Senate Select Committee to Study Government Operations with Respect to Intelligence Activities. Report 94-755. Book I, Foreign and Military Intelligence.* Washington, DC: GPO, 1976.

—**ENERGY INTELLIGENCE** is intelligence related to the technical, economic, and political capabilities and programs of foreign countries concerning the development, use, and sale of basic and advanced energy resources and technologies. Energy intelligence is specifically concerned with the location and size of foreign energy resources; how these resources are used and allocated; foreign governments' energy policies, plans, and programs; any new or improved foreign energy technologies; and the economic and security aspects of foreign energy supply, demand, production, distribution, and use.

References

Department of Defense, Defense Intelligence College. *Glossary of Intelligence Terms and Definitions.* Washington, DC: DIC, 1987.

Godson, Roy, ed. *Intelligence Problems for the 1980s, Number 1: Elements of Intelligence.* Rev. ed. Washington, DC: National Strategy Information Center, 1983.

Laqueur, Walter. *A World of Secrets.* New York: Basic Books, 1985.

Treverton, Gregory F. *Covert Action: The Limits of Intervention in the Postwar World*. New York: Basic Books, 1987.

U.S. Congress. Senate. *Final Report of the Senate Select Committee to Study Government Operations with Respect to Intelligence Activities. Report 94-755. Book I, Foreign and Military Intelligence*. Washington, DC: GPO, 1976.

—**ENGSTROM, DR. HOWARD T.,** served as deputy director of the National Security Agency from October 1957 until August 1958. His selection as a civilian indicated that the civilian faction of the agency was continuing to exert its influence over the military.

References

Bamford, James. *The Puzzle Palace: A Report on America's Most Secret Agency*. New York: Penguin Books, 1983.

—**ENTITY,** as defined by the Church Committee, is a company, firm, corporation, institution, bank, or foundation.

References

U.S. Congress. Senate. *Final Report of the Senate Select Committee to Study Government Operations with Respect to Intelligence Activities. Report 94-755. Book I, Foreign and Military Intelligence*. Washington, DC: GPO, 1976.

—**ESCAPE AND EVASION.** *See:* Evasion and Escape.

—**ESCORT** is a general intelligence term for an employee of an intelligence agency who escorts or accompanies an uncleared visitor (one who either does not have a security clearance or one whose security clearance cannot be confirmed) through the security area of the agency. An escort is assigned when it is necessary to grant the visitor access to the area. The escort must insure that the visitor sees no classified material and is not given the opportunity to steal documents or materials. Such visitors are usually maintenance, repair, or cleaning personnel.

References

Department of Defense, Joint Chiefs of Staff. *Department of Defense Dictionary of Military and Related Terms*. Washington, DC: GPO, 1986.

Godson, Roy, ed. *Intelligence Problems for the 1980s, Number 1: Elements of Intelligence*. Rev. ed. Washington, DC: National Strategy Information Center, 1983.

—**ESCORT JAMMING** is an electronic warfare term. It means jamming that is performed by an aircraft carrying sophisticated electronic gear in order to protect other accompanying aircraft that it is protecting. *See also:* Jamming.

References

Department of Defense, U.S. Army. *Counter-Signals Intelligence (C-SIGINT) Operations*. Field Manual FM 34-62. Washington, DC: Headquarters, Department of the Army, 1986.

————. *Military Intelligence Battalion Combat Electronic Warfare and Intelligence (Aerial Exploitation) (Corps)*. Field Manual FM 34-22. Washington, DC: Headquarters, Department of the Army, 1984.

————. *Military Intelligence Company (Combat Electronic Warfare and Intelligence) (Armored Cavalry Regiment/Separate Brigade)*. Field Manual FM 34-30. Washington, DC: Headquarters, Department of the Army, 1983.

Godson, Roy, ed. *Intelligence Problems for the 1980s, Number 1: Elements of Intelligence*. Rev. ed. Washington, DC: National Strategy Information Center, 1983.

—**ESPIONAGE** is "activity that is conducted with the goal of clandestinely acquiring information of intelligence value. Espionage activity is considered unlawful by the country against which it is committed." As defined by the Church Committee, espionage is "clandestine intelligence collection activity. This term is often interchanged with 'clandestine collection.'" The Defense Investigative Review Council, in its Study Report No. 9 dated May 5, 1971, established another definition for espionage. It said that espionage is "overt, covert, or clandestine activity that is designed to obtain information relating to the national defense with the intent or reason to believe that it will be used to the injury of the United States or to the advantage of a foreign nation." *See also:* Active Measures, Agent, Agent in Place, Agent Net, Agent of Influence, Agent Provocateur, Biographic Leverage, Black Bag Job, Black Bag Operation, Blackmail, Bug, Bugging, Cacklebladder, Case, Case Officer, Center, Company, Confusion Agent, Co-Opted Worker, Co-Optees, Cover Organizations, Cover Story, Dirty Tricks, Double Agent, Farm, Firm, Handling Agent, Honey Trap, Illegal Agent, Illegal Net, Illegal Operations, Infiltration, Informant, Inside Man, Ladies, Mole, Moonlight Extradition, Mozhno Girls, Mugbooks, Penetration, Plumbing, Putting in the Plumbing, Setting Up,

Shaking the Tree, Sheep Dipping, Sisters, Sleeper, Snitch Jacket, Soap, Sound Man, Sound School, Special Activities, Stable, Stringer, Stroller, Surreptitious Entry, Surround, Surveillance, Swallow, Swallow's Nest, Taxi, Terminate with Extreme Prejudice, Third Country Operation.

References

Department of Defense, Defense Intelligence College. *Glossary of Intelligence Terms and Definitions.* Washington, DC: DIC, 1987.

Department of Defense, Joint Chiefs of Staff. *Department of Defense Dictionary of Military and Related Terms.* Washington, DC: GPO, 1986.

Godson, Roy, ed. *Intelligence Problems for the 1980s, Number 1: Elements of Intelligence.* Rev. ed. Washington, DC: National Strategy Information Center, 1983.

Kessler, Ronald. *Spy vs. Spy: Stalking Soviet Spies in America.* New York: Charles Scribner's Sons, 1988.

Kent, Sherman. *Strategic Intelligence for American World Policy.* Princeton, NJ: Princeton University Press, 1966.

Laqueur, Walter. *A World of Secrets.* New York: Basic Books, 1985.

Treverton, Gregory F. *Covert Action: The Limits of Intervention in the Postwar World.* New York: Basic Books, 1987.

Turner, Stansfield. *Secrecy and Democracy: The CIA in Transition.* Boston: Houghton Mifflin, 1985.

U.S. Congress. Senate. *Final Report of the Senate Select Committee to Study Government Operations with Respect to Intelligence Activities. Report 94-755. Book I, Foreign and Military Intelligence.* Washington, DC: GPO, 1976.

—**ESPIONAGE AGAINST THE UNITED STATES** is "overt, covert or clandestine activity that is designed to obtain information relating to the national defense with intent or reason to believe that it will be used to the injury of the United States or to the advantage of a foreign nation." Espionage crimes are discussed in Chapter 37 of Title 18, U.S. Code. *See also:* Espionage.

References

Department of Defense, Joint Chiefs of Staff. *Department of Defense Dictionary of Military and Related Terms.* Washington, DC: GPO, 1986.

Godson, Roy, ed. *Intelligence Problems for the 1980s, Number 1: Elements of Intelligence.* Rev. ed. Washington, DC: National Strategy Information Center, 1983.

Kent, Sherman. *Strategic Intelligence for American World Policy.* Princeton, NJ: Princeton University Press, 1966.

Laqueur, Walter. *A World of Secrets.* New York: Basic Books, 1985.

Treverton, Gregory F. *Covert Action: The Limits of Intervention in the Postwar World.* New York: Basic Books, 1987.

Turner, Stansfield. *Secrecy and Democracy: The CIA in Transition.* Boston: Houghton Mifflin, 1985.

—**ESPIONAGE BRANCH OF THE CIA.** *See:* Central Intelligence Agency.

—**ESSENTIAL ELEMENTS OF FRIENDLY INFORMATION (EEFI)** is a term used in counterintelligence, counterespionage, counterinsurgency, and tactical intelligence. They are the key questions concerning friendly intentions and military capabilities that are likely to be asked by enemy planners and decisionmakers. *See also:* Essential Elements of Information.

—**ESSENTIAL ELEMENTS OF INFORMATION (EEI)** is a general intelligence term for those items of intelligence information that concern a foreign power, forces, targets, or the foreign physical environment that are absolutely vital for timely and accurate decisionmaking. *See also:* Information Requirements.

References

Department of Defense, Joint Chiefs of Staff. *Department of Defense Dictionary of Military and Related Terms.* Washington, DC: GPO, 1986.

Kessler, Ronald. *Spy vs. Spy: Stalking Soviet Spies in America.* New York: Charles Scribner's Sons, 1988.

Department of Defense, U.S. Army. *Military Intelligence Battalion (Combat Electronic Warfare Intelligence) (Division).* Field Manual FM 34-10. Washington, DC: Headquarters, Department of the Army, 1981.

————. *Military Intelligence Battalion Combat Electronic Warfare and Intelligence (Aerial Exploitation) (Corps).* Field Manual FM 34-22. Washington, DC: Headquarters, Department of the Army, 1984.

————. *Military Intelligence Company (Combat Electronic Warfare and Intelligence) (Armored Cavalry Regiment/Separate Brigade).* Field Manual FM 34-30. Washington, DC: Headquarters, Department of the Army, 1983.

————. *Military Intelligence Battalion (CEWI) (Tactical Exploitation) (Corps): Counterintelligence, Interrogation, Electronic Warfare.* Field Manual FM 34-23. Washington, DC: Headquarters, Department of the Army, 1985.

Godson, Roy, ed. *Intelligence Problems for the 1980s, Number 1: Elements of Intelligence.* Rev. ed. Washington, DC: National Strategy Information Center, 1983.

—**ESTABLISHED SOURCE** is a person whom the FBI has previously used as an informant and therefore is considered reliable. *See also:* Agent, Agent Authentication, Agent in Place, Agent Net, Agent of Influence, Agent Provocateur, Confusion Agent, Co-Opted Worker, Co-Optees, Defector, Disaffected Person, Dispatched Agent, Double Agent, Establishing Bonafides, Illegal Agent, Illegal Support Officer, Informant, Inside Man, Ladies, Litmus Test, Mole, Mozhno Girls, Nash, Pigeon, Plumbing, Processing the Take, Provocation Agent, Putting in the Plumbing, Raven, Shaking the Tree, Shopworn Goods, Singleton, Sisters, Soap.

References

Becket, Henry S. A. *The Dictionary of Espionage: Spookspeak into English.* New York: Stein and Day, 1986.

Deacon, Richard. *Spyclopedia: An Encyclopedia of Spies, Secret Services, Operations, Jargon, and All Subjects Related to the World of Espionage.* London: Macdonald, 1987.

—**ESTABLISHING BONA FIDES** is a term used in clandestine and covert intelligence operations to describe when agents who do not know each other use recognition signals, such as specific newspapers or magazines, when they meet in order to establish contact.

References

Becket, Henry S. A. *The Dictionary of Espionage: Spookspeak into English.* New York: Stein and Day, 1986.

Deacon, Richard. *Spyclopedia: An Encyclopedia of Spies, Secret Services, Operations, Jargon, and All Subjects Related to the World of Espionage.* London: Macdonald, 1987.

Ranelagh, John. *The Agency: The Rise and Decline of the CIA.* New York: Simon and Schuster, 1986.

—**ESTIMATE** is a general intelligence term that has four definitions. (1) An estimate is an analysis of a foreign situation, development or trend that identifies its major elements, interprets its significance, and appraises the future possibilities and the possible results of the various actions that might be taken. (2) An estimate is also an appraisal of the capabilities, vulnerabilities and potential courses of action of a foreign nation or group of nations that result from a specific national plan, policy, decision or contemplated course of action. (3) An estimate is also an analysis of an actual or contemplated clandestine operation in relation to the situation in which it is or would be conducted in order to identify and appraise such factors as available and needed assets and potential obstacles, accomplishments and consequences. (4) As defined by the Church Committee, estimating is an effort to appraise and analyze the future possibilities or courses of action in a situation under study and the various results or consequences of foreign or U.S. actions relating to that situation. This analysis of such a foreign situation would consider its development and trends to identify major elements, interpret the significance of the situation, and evaluate the future possibilities and prospective results of various actions which might be taken, including clandestine operations. *See also:* Intelligence Cycle, Intelligence Estimate.

References

Department of Defense, Joint Chiefs of Staff. *Department of Defense Dictionary of Military and Related Terms.* Washington, DC: GPO, 1986.

Godson, Roy, ed. *Intelligence Problems for the 1980s, Number 1: Elements of Intelligence.* Rev. ed. Washington, DC: National Strategy Information Center, 1983.

Kent, Sherman. *Strategic Intelligence for American World Policy.* Princeton, NJ: Princeton University Press, 1966.

Laqueur, Walter. *A World of Secrets.* New York: Basic Books, 1985.

Treverton, Gregory F. *Covert Action: The Limits of Intervention in the Postwar World.* New York: Basic Books, 1987.

Turner, Stansfield. *Secrecy and Democracy: The CIA in Transition.* Boston: Houghton Mifflin, 1985.

—**ESTIMATIVE INTELLIGENCE** is a general intelligence term. It is the type of intelligence that projects or forecasts probable future foreign courses of action and developments and discusses their implications for the United States or U.S. interests. Estimative intelligence may or may not be coordinated within the Intelligence Community and may be either national or departmental intelligence. *See also:* Defense Intelligence Agency, Intelligence.

References

Department of Defense, Defense Intelligence College. *Glossary of Intelligence Terms and Definitions.* Washington, DC: DIC, 1987.

Godson, Roy, ed. *Intelligence Problems for the 1980s, Number 1: Elements of Intelligence.* Rev. ed. Washington, DC: National Strategy Information Center, 1983.

Kent, Sherman. *Strategic Intelligence for American World Policy.* Princeton, NJ: Princeton University Press, 1966.

Laqueur, Walter. *A World of Secrets.* New York: Basic Books, 1985.

Treverton, Gregory F. *Covert Action: The Limits of Intervention in the Postwar World.* New York: Basic Books, 1987.

Turner, Stansfield. *Secrecy and Democracy: The CIA in Transition.* Boston: Houghton Mifflin, 1985.

—**ETHIOPIA.** The Ethiopian episode has its origins in an Ethiopian-Somali conflict over a border region, the Ogaden desert. In 1969, when the Soviet Union was asked to provide assistance to the Marxist Somali government, it correctly assessed that the Somali-Ethiopian animosity, if handled properly, could be a means of furthering Soviet influence in Somalia. Such a policy seemed well founded, since the radical Somali regime was facing the conservative Ethiopian regime of Emperor Haile Selassie in a traditional radical-conservative Third World confrontation.

The Soviet policy was quite successful. From 1969 until 1977, the Soviets enjoyed the use of the port facilities at Berbera, staged aircraft from an airfield just outside of Berbera for reconnaissance operations over the Indian Ocean region, began constructing a missile storage and support facility, and established a communications complex in the vicinity of Berbera that was ideal for the command and control of Soviet naval forces in the region.

However, things began to sour in 1974, when a radical regime headed by Mengistu Haile Mariam deposed the emperor and established itself in power. The Soviet Union now found itself in an unenviable position, in that it was allied with two nations that were at war with each other. The Soviet policy of attempting to assuage both nations failed, and the Soviet Navy was expelled from Somalia in November 1977 as the Ogaden War became more violent.

Throughout this period, the U.S. Intelligence Community accurately and consistently reported on the ongoing events. After the expulsion of the Soviet Navy, Somalia turned to the United States for assistance, which was denied. The Soviets conducted massive air and sea lifts of supplies to Ethiopia, shipped Cuban troops from Angola and Cuba to Ethiopia, sent Soviet Air Force pilots to relieve Cuban pilots, who were flying air defense missions over Havana, so that the Cuban pilots could fly tactical combat missions in Ethiopia, and established a Soviet high command under Soviet General Vasiliy Petrov, in what was an extremely complex crisis response. And the Soviets were rewarded for their efforts. As of 1990, the Soviet Navy operates from its facilities on Dahalak Island, an Ethiopian island due east of Massawa that sits astride the sea lanes that run northward and southward through the Red Sea. Having successfully bridged the transition from Somalia to Ethiopia, the Soviet Indian Ocean Squadron continues as a factor in the Indian Ocean regional balance of power.

References

Breckinridge, Scott D. *The CIA and the U.S. Intelligence System.* Boulder, CO: Westview Press, 1986.

Brinkley, David A., and Hull, Andrew W. *Estimative Intelligence: A Textbook on the History, Products, Uses, and Writing of Intelligence Estimates.* Columbus, OH: Battelle, 1979.

Clancy, Thomas. *The Cardinal of the Kremlin.* New York: Putnam, 1988.

Cline, Ray S. *The CIA Under Reagan, Bush, and Casey.* Washington, DC: Acropolis Books, 1981.

Crawford, David J. *Volunteers: The Betrayal of National Defense Secrets by Air Force Traitors.* Washington, DC: GPO, 1988.

Godson, Roy, ed. *Intelligence Problems for the 1980s, Number 3: Counterintelligence.* Washington, DC: National Strategy Information Center, 1980.

———. *Intelligence Problems for the 1980s, Number 4: Covert Action.* Washington, DC: National Strategy Information Center, 1981.

Laqueur, Walter. *A World of Secrets.* New York: Basic Books, 1985.

Lowenthal, Mark M. *U.S. Intelligence: Evolution and Anatomy.* New York: Praeger, 1984.

Quirk, John; Phillips, David; Cline, Ray; and Pforzheimer, Walter. *The Central Intelligence Agency: A Photographic History.* Guilford, CT: Foreign Intelligence Press, 1986.

Ranelagh, John. *The Agency: The Rise and Decline of the CIA.* New York: Simon and Schuster, 1986.

Treverton, Gregory F. *Covert Action: The Limits of Intervention in the Postwar World.* New York: Basic Books, 1987.

Turner, Stansfield. *Secrecy and Democracy: The CIA in Transition*. Boston: Houghton Mifflin, 1985.

U.S. Congress. Senate. *Alleged Assassination Plots Involving Foreign Leaders: An Interim Report of the Select Committee to Study Governmental Operations with Respect to Intelligence Activities.* 94th Congress. 1st sess., Nov. 20, 1975. S. Rept. 94-465.

———. *Final Report of the Senate Select Committee to Study Government Operations with Respect to Intelligence Activities. Report 94-755. Book I, Foreign and Military Intelligence*. Washington, DC: GPO, 1976.

Von Hoene, John P. A. *Intelligence User's Guide.* Washington, DC: DIA, 1983.

Watson, Bruce W. *Red Navy at Sea: Soviet Naval Operations on the High Seas, 1956-1980*. Boulder, CO: Westview Press, 1982.

Watson, Bruce W., and Watson, Susan M., eds. *The Soviet Navy: Strengths and Liabilities*. Boulder, CO: Westview Press, 1986.

—**EVADER** is a term used in clandestine and covert intelligence operations to describe any person isolated in hostile or unfriendly territory who eludes capture. *See also:* Agent, Blow, Blown Agent, Concealment, Concealment Devices, Cover, Cover Name, Cover Organizations, Cover Story, Damage Assessment, Damage Control, Doubled, Evasion and Escape, Evasion and Escape Intelligence, Go Private, Go to Ground, Mole, Moonlight Extradition, Movements Analysis, Pavement Artists, Shadow, Shaking off the Dogs, Sign of Life Signal, Special Activities, Submerge, Suitable Cover, Surfacing, Surround, Surveillance, Turned, What's Your Twenty?

References
Department of Defense, Joint Chiefs of Staff. *Department of Defense Dictionary of Military and Related Terms*. Washington, DC: GPO, 1986.

—**EVALUATION (INTELLIGENCE)** involves appraising a piece of information in terms of its credibility, reliability, pertinency, and accuracy. This involves appraisals or evaluations at several stages in the intelligence process. Initial evaluations are made by agents, case officers, and reporting officers and are based on the reliability of the source of the information and the accuracy of the information, and on other facts and information that are available at or close to the operational level. Subsequent evaluations by intelligence analysts are intended to verify the accuracy of the information, and these apprais-

als may actually change the information into intelligence. Appraisals or evaluations of information or intelligence are made by a standard letter-number system. The source's reliability is graded from A to F, while the information's accuracy is graded from 1 to 6. The grades are as follows:

Reliability of the source: A, completely reliable; B, usually reliable; C, fairly reliable; D, not usually reliable; E, reliability cannot be judged. *Accuracy of the information*: 1, confirmed by other sources; 2, probably true; 3, possibly true; 4, doubtful; 5, truth cannot be judged.

Thus, the information that is "probably true" and has been received from a "completely reliable source" would be rated as A2 or A-2. *See also:* Intelligence Cycle.

References
Department of Defense, Joint Chiefs of Staff. *Department of Defense Dictionary of Military and Related Terms*. Washington, DC: GPO, 1986.

Godson, Roy, ed. *Intelligence Problems for the 1980s, Number 1: Elements of Intelligence*. Rev. ed. Washington, DC: National Strategy Information Center, 1983.

Kent, Sherman. *Strategic Intelligence for American World Policy*. Princeton, NJ: Princeton University Press, 1966.

Treverton, Gregory F. *Covert Action: The Limits of Intervention in the Postwar World*. New York: Basic Books, 1987.

—**EVALUATION OF DATA BASE ADEQUACY** is produced by the Defense Intelligence Agency and is updated annually. It contains the current assessments of the adequacy of the basic military and scientific and technical (S&T) intelligence data bases. *See also:* Defense Intelligence Agency.

References
Turner, Stansfield. *Secrecy and Democracy: The CIA in Transition*. Boston: Houghton Mifflin, 1985.

Von Hoene, John P. A. *Intelligence User's Guide*. Washington, DC: DIA, 1983.

—**EVASION AND ESCAPE (E&E)** are the means by which military personnel and selected individuals can pass from enemy-held or hostile areas to friendly areas. *See also:* Evader, Evasion and Escape Intelligence.

References
Deacon, Richard. *Spyclopedia: An Encyclopedia of Spies, Secret Services, Operations, Jargon, and All Subjects Related to the World of Espionage*. London: Macdonald, 1987.

Department of Defense, Defense Intelligence College. *Glossary of Intelligence Terms and Definitions.* Washington, DC: DIC, 1987.

Department of Defense, Joint Chiefs of Staff. *Department of Defense Dictionary of Military and Related Terms.* Washington, DC: GPO, 1986.

—**EVASION AND ESCAPE INTELLIGENCE** is processed intelligence information that has been prepared to help people avoid capture if they are lost in enemy-held territory or to escape from the enemy if they are captured. *See also:* Evader, Evasion and Escape.

References

Department of Defense, Defense Intelligence College. *Glossary of Intelligence Terms and Definitions.* Washington, DC: DIC, 1987.

Department of Defense, Joint Chiefs of Staff. *Department of Defense Dictionary of Military and Related Terms.* Washington, DC: GPO, 1986.

—**EVASION AND ESCAPE NET** is an organization within enemy-held territory or hostile areas that operates to receive, move, and exfiltrate military personnel and other individuals to friendly territory and control.

References

Department of Defense, Joint Chiefs of Staff. *Department of Defense Dictionary of Military and Related Terms.* Washington, DC: GPO, 1986.

—**EVASION AND ESCAPE ROUTE** is a course of travel, which may or may not be preplanned, that an escapee or evader uses in an attempt to escape from enemy-held territory and to return to friendly lines.

References

Department of Defense, Joint Chiefs of Staff. *Department of Defense Dictionary of Military and Related Terms.* Washington, DC: GPO, 1986.

—**EXECUTIVE ACTION** is a term used in clandestine and covert intelligence operations. It is an euphemism for assassination. As defined by the Church Committee, executive action is "generally a euphemism for assassination, and was used by the Central Intelligence Agency to describe a program aimed at overthrowing certain foreign leaders, by assassinating them if necessary." *See also:* Active Measures, Assassi-

nation, Demote Maximally, Special Activities, Terminate with Extreme Prejudice.

References

Godson, Roy, ed. *Intelligence Problems for the 1980s, Number 1: Elements of Intelligence.* Rev. ed. Washington, DC: National Strategy Information Center, 1983.

Treverton, Gregory F. *Covert Action: The Limits of Intervention in the Postwar World.* New York: Basic Books, 1987.

Quirk, John; Phillips, David; Cline, Ray; and Pforzheimer, Walter. *The Central Intelligence Agency: A Photographic History.* Guilford, CT: Foreign Intelligence Press, 1986.

U.S. Congress. Senate. *Final Report of the Senate Select Committee to Study Government Operations with Respect to Intelligence Activities. Report 94-755. Book I, Foreign and Military Intelligence.* Washington, DC: GPO, 1976.

—**EXECUTIVE COMMITTEE (EXCOM)** was a group of three individuals—the Director of Central Intelligence, an Assistant Secretary of Defense and the President's Scientific Advisor—that was established in 1969 to make decisions concerning U.S. reconnaissance programs. *See also:* Central Intelligence Agency.

References

Breckinridge, Scott D. *The CIA and the U.S. Intelligence System.* Boulder, CO: Westview Press, 1986.

Fain, Tyrus G.; Plant, Katharine C.; and Milloy, Ross. *The Intelligence Community: History, Organization, and Issues.* Public Documents Series. New York: R.R. Bowker, 1977.

—**EXECUTIVE DIRECTOR.** *See:* Central Intelligence Agency, Defense Intelligence Agency.

—**EXECUTIVE ORDERS ON INTELLIGENCE.** One of the means most often used by the President to change the Intelligence Community has been the Executive Order. Initially this was a seldom used method, however, since the Ford administration, every President has issued an Executive Order which has modified the Intelligence Community to his liking. Following are some of the most significant Executive Orders affecting the Intelligence Community; they are also reproduced as appendixes to this encyclopedia. *See also:* Military Order signed June 13, 1942; Presidential Order signed July 11, 1941; Presidential Order signed January 22, 1946.

—**EXECUTIVE ORDER 9621,** September 30, 1945, was issued by President Truman in the wake of World War II. The order disbanded the Office of Strategic Services (OSS) and reassigned its functions to other agencies and departments. An Interim Research and Intelligence Service was established at the Department of State, and it was given the functions of the Research and Analysis Branch and the Presentation Branch of the OSS, except for such functions performed in Austria and Germany. The Interim Research and Intelligence Service was to be abolished on December 31, 1945, and the secretary of state could either abolish the functions of the service or transfer them elsewhere within the Department of State, as he saw fit. The remaining functions and staff of the OSS were transferred to the Department of War, the secretary of which was given the power to either abolish them or retain them within his own organization.

This Executive Order not only signified an inauspicious end to the OSS, but also atomized rather than centralized U.S. intelligence. In one sense, President Truman's order reflected American distrust of clandestine intelligence and indicated that the United States was still groping with the problem of assuming a position of world leadership in the post-World War II period. This distrust and the associated issue of creating a responsible central intelligence entity was a chronic problem that would trouble presidents for four decades. In respect to the wartime trend of centralizing U.S. intelligence, this order effectively reversed that trend, resulting in a fragmented community. *See also:* Executive Oversight and Office of Strategic Services.

References

Office of the President of the United States. *Executive Order 9621.* Washington, DC, Sept. 25, 1945.

—**EXECUTIVE ORDER 10450,** April 27, 1953, "Security Requirements for Government Employment," was issued by President Eisenhower. The order consisted of the following major points:

1. The head of each government department and agency should establish a personnel screening program to insure that the employment of each of his employees was in the best interests of national security.
2. Civilian employees should be subject to extensive security investigations of their backgrounds.
3. Those employees who failed to receive acceptable investigations could be suspended from employment.
4. An adverse finding could be based on, but was not limited to: (a) evidence of dishonesty or unreliability; (b) deliberate misrepresentations, omissions, or falsifications of material fact on the security forms; (c) evidence of criminal, infamous, immoral, dishonest, or notoriously disgraceful conduct, or drug addiction, habitual use of intoxicants to excess, sexual perversion, or financial irresponsibility; (d) evidence of a judgment of insanity without evidence of a cure; (e) evidence that the individual could be unduly coerced; (f) evidence of association with a saboteur, spy, traitor, seditionist, anarchist, revolutionist, or a secret agent of a foreign government; (g) evidence that the individual had committed an act of treason, sabotage, espionage, or sedition, or had helped another person to commit such an act; (h) evidence that the individual advocated the use of force to overthrow the U.S. government; (i) membership in a subversive organization; (j) evidence that the individual disclosed classified information without authorization; and (k) evidence that the individual is serving the interests of another nation over those of the United States.

The order represented a determined attempt to screen federal employees to insure their reliability. Although challenged in the courts, the order went a long way toward prompting the development of adequate personnel screening procedures for employees in sensitive security and intelligence positions. The order was amended by President Nixon in his Executive Orders 11605 and 11785. *See also:* Executive Oversight, Personnel Security.

References

Office of the President of the United States. *Executive Order 10450, Security Requirements for Government Employment.* Washington, DC, Apr. 27, 1953.

—**EXECUTIVE ORDER 11605,** July 2, 1971, "Amendment of Executive Order 10450 of April 27, 1953, Relating to Security Requirements for Government Employment," was issued by President Nixon. The order consisted of the following major points:

1. It specified the types of subversive organizations that had been mentioned in the earlier order, stating that these organizations were totalitarian, fascist, communist, subversive, or had adopted a policy of unlawfully advocating the commission of acts of force or violence to deny others their rights, or sought to overthrow the government.
2. The head of each agency would be provided with a list of the names of such organizations.
3. The Subversive Activities Control Board would conduct hearings at the request of the attorney general in order to decide whether an organization belonged on the list.
4. In making a determination, the board could decide that an organization sought to deny people their rights or sought to overthrow the government if it (a) committed violent or illegal acts in order to deny others their rights; (b) damaged or destroyed property or injured people; (c) was working for the overthrow of the U.S. government or a state government; or (d) committed acts of treason, rebellion, insurrection, seditious conspiracy, riot or disorder, sabotage, trading with the enemy, obstructing the enlistment of others into the service of the United States, or impeding officers of the United States.
5. The board could determine that an organization was totalitarian if it found that the organization engaged in activities that sought to establish an autocratic system of government in which control was centered in a single group or party and allowed no effective representation by the opposition.
6. The board could determine that an organization was fascist if it sought by unlawful means to establish a government that was characterized by rigid one-party dictatorship, suppression of the opposition, state ownership of property, and the fostering of racism.
7. The board could determine that an organization was communist if it espoused the principles of Marxism-Leninism, sought to establish a dictatorship of the proletariat, and sought to establish a single authoritarian party.
8. The board could determine that an organization was subversive if it found that the organization was working for the overthrow of the U.S. government by unlawful means.

The order clarified greatly the intention of the earlier Executive Order by noting exactly which types of organizational political conduct were considered objectionable and by stating how a determination was to be made. At a time when the nation had barely emerged from the tumult of the 1960s and many revolutionary sects were still committing unlawful acts, this order clarified the government's stand on the types of organizations and activities that it would seek to counter. *See also:* Executive Oversight, Personnel Security.

References

Office of the President of the United States. *Executive Order 11605, Amendment of Executive Order 10450 of April 27, 1953, Relating to Security Requirements for Government Employment.* Washington, DC, July 2, 1971.

—**EXECUTIVE ORDER 11785,** June 4, 1974, "Amending Executive Order 10450, as Amended, Relating to Security Requirements for Government Employment, and for Other Purposes," was issued by President Nixon. The order revoked Executive Order 11605. The most significant additional aspects were:

1. Neither the attorney general nor the Subversive Activities Control Board nor any other agency could designate organizations or circulate a list of designated organizations.
2. The list of organizations was abolished.
3. The provision concerning actions against organizations that sought to deny others their ability to exercise their rights or sought to overthrow the government was softened.

The order was required because so much of Executive Order 11605 had been overruled in the courts that, in essence, there was no standing instruction on the issue. This order attempted to establish a new policy that would not be declared unlawful.

References

Office of the President of the United States. *Executive Order 11785, Amending Executive Order No. 10450, as Amended, Relating to Security Requirements for Government Employment, and for Other Purposes.* Washington, DC, June 4, 1974.

Turner, Stansfield. *Secrecy and Democracy: The CIA in Transition.* Boston: Houghton Mifflin, 1985.

—**EXECUTIVE ORDER 11905,** February 18, 1976, "United States Foreign Intelligence Activities," was issued by President Ford. The order consisted of the following major points:

1. The National Security Council was to conduct a semiannual review of intelligence policies and particularly of "special activities in support of national foreign policy objectives." In doing so, the council was to consider the needs of the intelligence users and the "continued appropriateness" of each activity.

2. The Committee on Foreign Intelligence (CFI) was established. Chaired by the director of Central Intelligence and consisting of the deputy secretary of defense for intelligence and the deputy assistant to the President for national security affairs, the CFI was to control the preparation and resource allocation of the budget for the National Foreign Intelligence Program (NFIP), establish priorities for national intelligence collection and production, and provide guidance concerning the relationship between tactical and national intelligence.

3. The Operations Advisory Group was established. Composed of the assistant to the President for national security affairs, the secretary of state, the secretary of defense, the chairman of the Joint Chiefs of Staff, and the director of Central Intelligence, its chairman was to be designated by the President. This group was to develop a policy recommendation for the President prior to his decision on special activities, approve specific sensitive intelligence collection operations, and review ongoing special activities and sensitive collection operations periodically to ensure that they should be continued.

4. The Intelligence Oversight Board was established. Composed of three members from outside the government, it was to receive reports from the inspectors general and general counsels of the Intelligence Community regarding intelligence activities that raised questions of legality or propriety. They were to report any evidence of such illegal or improper activities to the attorney general immediately and were to routinely report to the attorney general and the President at least quarterly on their findings.

5. The director of Central Intelligence was to remain as the President's chief advisor on foreign intelligence. He was to ensure the proper implementation of special activities.

6. To assist the director of Central Intelligence in fulfilling his duties, the position of deputy director of Central Intelligence was created. His purpose was to assume responsibility for the day-to-day operation of the Central Intelligence Agency so that the director could devote his talents to accomplishing his other responsibilities.

7. The responsibilities of the Central Intelligence Agency, the Department of State, the Department of the Treasury, the Department of Defense, the Energy Research and Development Administration, and the Federal Bureau of Investigation were discussed in detail.

8. Several restrictions were placed on the Intelligence Community. (a) Foreign intelligence agencies were prohibited from conducting physical surveillance of U.S. citizens unless such surveillance met stringent guidelines; conducting electronic surveillance of U.S. citizens, unless it, too, met stringent guidelines; conducting unconsented physical searches in the United States and of U.S. citizens overseas, unless they were lawful searches that were approved by the attorney general; opening mail or examining envelopes of mail that is in the U.S. postal channels, except in accordance with applicable laws and regulations; examining federal tax returns, except in accordance with applicable statutes and regulations; and assassinating anyone. (b) Heavy restrictions were placed on the following activities by foreign intelligence agencies, namely, infiltrating or participating in organizations in the United States for the purpose of reporting on or influencing its members; or collecting information on U.S. citizens.

Executive Order 11905 was issued by President Ford in the wake of the Watergate investigation and of the Church and Pike committees' investigations. The order was an attempt, on the one hand, to make the changes necessary to bring the Intelligence Community under presidential control and, on the other hand, to ward off additional congressional interference in the affairs of the Intelligence Community. In this latter aim, the President was fairly successful, because although the Church Committee conducted extensive sessions that divulged a great deal of information concerning intelligence operations, information that many considered to be damaging to the Intelligence Community's operations, the committee's recommendation for restrictive charter legislation was never passed by Congress. Thus, the trend of greater congressional involvement in and control of the Intelligence Community was effectively attenuated. *See also:* Executive Oversight.

References

Godson, Roy, ed. *Intelligence Problems for the 1980s, Number 1: Elements of Intelligence*. Rev. ed. Washington, DC: National Strategy Information Center, 1983.

————. *Intelligence Problems for the 1980s, Number 2: Analysis and Estimates*. Washington, DC: National Strategy Information Center, 1980.

Laqueur, Walter. *A World of Secrets*. New York: Basic Books, 1985.

Lefever, Ernest W., and Godson, Roy. *The CIA and the American Ethic: An Unfinished Debate*. Washington, DC: Ethics and Public Policy Center, Georgetown University, 1979.

Office of the President of the United States. *Executive Order 11905, United States Foreign Intelligence Activities*. Washington, DC, Feb. 18, 1976.

Turner, Stansfield. *Secrecy and Democracy: The CIA in Transition*. Boston: Houghton Mifflin, 1985.

—**EXECUTIVE ORDER 12036,** January 24, 1978, "United States Intelligence Activities," was signed by President Carter. The order was perhaps the most stringent and restrictive of any Executive Order ever issued concerning the Intelligence Community.

The order established two committees. The first, the NSC Policy Review Committee (PRC) was to be chaired by the director of Central Intelligence and was composed of the vice president, the secretary of defense, the secretary of the treasury, the assistant to the President for national security affairs, the chairman of the Joint Chiefs of Staff, and other members, as appropriate. Its duties were to establish requirements and priorities for national foreign intelligence; review the budget proposals for the National Foreign Intelligence Program; conduct periodic reviews of intelligence products in order to assess their quality and responsiveness to intelligence requirements; and report annually on the activities of the National Security Council.

The second committee was the Special Coordination Committee (SCC). It was chaired by the assistant to the President for national security affairs and was composed of the statutory members of the National Security Council and other senior officials, as appropriate. The duties of the SCC were to review every special activity that the Intelligence Community or National Security Council proposed and to make recommendations to the President (when meeting for this purpose, the SCC was to be composed of the secretary of state, secretary of defense, attorney general, director of Management and Budget, assistant to the President for national security affairs, chairman of the Joint Chiefs of Staff, and director of Central Intelligence); review sensitive foreign intelligence collection operations (when meeting for this purpose, only the secretary of state, the secretary of defense, the attorney general, the assistant to the President for national security affairs, the director of Central Intelligence, and such other members as designated by the chairman were to meet); develop policy for conducting counterintelligence (when meeting in this capacity, the members were to include the secretary of state, secretary of defense, attorney general, director of the Office of Management and Budget, assistant to the President for national security affairs, chairman of the Joint Chiefs of Staff, director of Central Intelligence, and the director of the Federal Bureau of Investigation). Its responsibilities in this respect were to develop standards and doctrine for counterintelligence activity; resolve interagency differences; develop an annual threat assessment that would include an assessment of U.S. counterintelligence efforts; and approve specific counterintelligence activities. The SCC was also to conduct annual reviews of special activities and sensitive intelligence collection operations and report on these to the NSC, and it was to conduct such other actions as the President requested.

Additionally, the order established a National Foreign Intelligence Board and a National Intelligence Tasking Center. The board was to be chaired by the director of Central Intelligence and was to be staffed by members of the Intelligence Community. Its purpose was to review the intelligence budget and various intelligence matters.

The National Intelligence Tasking Center was to be directed by the director of Central Intelligence. It was to be staffed by civilian and military personnel from the intelligence agencies, and its purpose was to assist the director of Central Intelligence in translating intelligence requirements and priorities into collection objectives;

assigning targets and objectives to collection organizations; ensuring the timely dissemination of intelligence; providing advisory tasking to other agencies having intelligence information; and resolving conflicts among members of the Intelligence Community.

The order also detailed the responsibilities of the director of Central Intelligence and gave him exclusive control over the intelligence budget. It then specified the duties of the Department of State, the Central Intelligence Agency, the Department of the Treasury, the Department of Defense, the Department of Energy, the Federal Bureau of Investigation, and the Drug Enforcement Administration.

However, it was the second section of the order that provided the most restrictive guidance. Entitled "Restrictions on Intelligence Activities," it discussed adherence to the law and then placed restrictions on electronic surveillance, physical searches, and mail and physical surveillance, which were to be conducted by the "least intrusive means." It also placed restrictions on the acquisition of tax information and on conducting medical experimentation, and it prohibited political assassinations.

The focus of the order was then shifted to oversight, and the Intelligence Oversight Board (IOB) was reaffirmed. Composed of three members from outside the government, the board's duties were to review the practices and procedures of the inspectors general and general counsels and to oversee the practices of the intelligence agencies to ensure that they were legal and proper. To reiterate, no other Executive Order has discussed in such detail the responsibilities of all major intelligence entities. Nor has any other order developed as many restrictions as did Executive Order 12036. Thus, its greatest significance was the restrictions that it placed on intelligence activities. The tone of the order and its detail reflected the President's distrust of the Intelligence Community and reflected the general dissatisfaction with the Community in the wake of the congressional investigations of intelligence activities.

The order was also significant for the additional responsibilities that it assigned to the director of Central Intelligence. The most significant matter was his gaining control of the budget, which gave him considerable power over the affairs of the other intelligence agencies. In this respect, the bill furthered the trend of centralizing the U.S. Intelligence Community. *See also:* Executive Oversight.

References

American Bar Association. *Oversight and Accountability of the U.S. Intelligence Agencies: An Evaluation.* Washington, DC: ABA, 1985.

Godson, Roy, ed. *Intelligence Problems for the 1980s, Number 1: Elements of Intelligence.* Rev. ed. Washington, DC: National Strategy Information Center, 1983.

———. *Intelligence Problems for the 1980s, Number 3: Counterintelligence.* Washington, DC: National Strategy Information Center, 1980.

Laqueur, Walter. *A World of Secrets.* New York: Basic Books, 1985.

Maurer, Alfred C.; Turnstall, Marion D.; and Keagle, James M. *Intelligence Policy and Process.* Boulder, CO: Westview Press, 1985.

Office of the President of the United States. *Executive Order 12036, United States Intelligence Activities.* Washington, DC, January 24, 1978.

Treverton, Gregory F. *Covert Action: The Limits of Intervention in the Postwar World.* New York: Basic Books, 1987.

Turner, Stansfield. *Secrecy and Democracy: The CIA in Transition.* Boston: Houghton Mifflin, 1985.

—**EXECUTIVE ORDER 12331,** October 20, 1981, "The President's Foreign Intelligence Advisory Board," was signed by President Reagan. The order reestablished the President's Foreign Intelligence Advisory Board. According to the Executive Order, the members of the board were to serve at the pleasure of the President and the President would choose a chairman and a vice chairman from among the members. The purpose of the board was to assess the quality, quantity, and adequacy of intelligence collection, analysis, and estimates, of counterintelligence and of other intelligence activities. The board was given the authority to continually review the performance of all intelligence agencies involved in the collection, evaluation, and production of intelligence or the execution of intelligence policy. It would report directly to the President periodically, but at least semiannually. This Executive Order is important for two reasons. First, it reflected the President's attitude toward the Intelligence Community, his concern that adequate oversight be established and that this oversight rest firmly in the Executive branch. The second significant aspect of the order was that it reflected the President's desire to adapt the Community to his working style. *See also:* Executive Oversight, President's Foreign Intelligence Advisory Board.

References

Office of the President of the United States. *Executive Order 12331, President's Foreign Intelligence Advisory Board.* Washington, DC, Oct. 20, 1981.

Turner, Stansfield. *Secrecy and Democracy: The CIA in Transition.* Boston: Houghton Mifflin, 1985.

—**EXECUTIVE ORDER 12333,** December 4, 1981, "United States Intelligence Activities," was signed by President Reagan. The order defined the duties of the National Security Council and stated that the council would form the committees that it considered appropriate to consider and provide recommendations to the President concerning special activities. The order continued by defining the responsibilities of the Intelligence Community, the director of Central Intelligence, the Central Intelligence Agency, the Department of State, the Department of Defense, the Department of the Treasury, the National Security Agency, the Defense Intelligence Agency, the Department of Energy, and the Federal Bureau of Investigation.

The order was significant for two reasons. First, it detailed the responsibilities of each component of the Intelligence Community, reflecting the President's concern for adequate oversight. Second, the order enabled the President to redirect the Intelligence Community so that it conformed more closely to his managerial and creative styles. Similar bills had been issued by Presidents Ford and Carter. Executive Order 12333 reflected the President's preference for committees that would process intelligence and present him with options from which he could choose. *See also:* Executive Oversight.

References

American Bar Association. *Oversight and Accountability of the U.S. Intelligence Agencies: An Evaluation.* Washington, DC: ABA, 1985.

Maurer, Alfred C.; Turnstall, Marion D.; and Keagle, James M. *Intelligence Policy and Process.* Boulder, CO: Westview Press, 1985.

Office of the President of the United States. *Executive Order 12333, United States Intelligence Activities.* Washington, DC, Dec. 4, 1981.

Treverton, Gregory F. *Covert Action: The Limits of Intervention in the Postwar World.* New York: Basic Books, 1987.

—**EXECUTIVE ORDER 12334,** December 4, 1981, "President's Intelligence Oversight Board," was signed by President Reagan. The order established the President's Intelligence Oversight Board (IOB). Composed of three members, including one member of the President's Foreign Intelligence Advisory Board (PFIAB), it was to serve as an additional mechanism of presidential oversight of the Intelligence Community. The members were to serve at the pleasure of the President and were to have a full-time staff. The duties of the IOB were to inform the President of any activities that were in violation of existing laws and forward reports of such activity to the attorney general; review guidelines and procedures within the Intelligence Community concerning the legality of intelligence activities; and conduct investigations as necessary into unlawful activity. The order reflected President Reagan's determination to provide for adequate oversight of the Intelligence Community and his intention to see that oversight resided in the White House and not Congress. *See also:* Executive Oversight.

References

Office of the President of the United States. *Executive Order 12334, President's Intelligence Oversight Board.* Washington, DC, Dec. 4, 1981.

—**EXECUTIVE ORDER 12356,** April 2, 1982, "National Security Information," was signed by President Reagan. The order prescribed a uniform system for classifying, declassifying, and safeguarding national security information. The order redefined the classification levels of CONFIDENTIAL, SECRET, and TOP SECRET, established classification authorities, and detailed procedures for downgrading and declassifying information. The significance of this order was not what it prescribed but what it implied. The emphasis of the order, as it discussed procedures for downgrading and declassifying information, was definitely on providing adequate security for national security information. This was in contrast to the trend of the Carter administration, which favored the Freedom of Information Act. The implication was that if Congress wished to consider modifying the act, the President would certainly welcome such changes. Taken together with the Reagan administration's stand on lie detector tests and its position on the disclosure of information on sensitive intelligence methods and operations, the order signified a significant turn toward restricting public access to information concerning the Intelligence Community and its operations. *See also:* Security.

References
Office of the President of the United States.
*Executive Order 12356, National Security
Information.* Washington, DC, Apr. 2, 1982.

—EXECUTIVE ORDER 12537, October 28,1985, "President's Foreign Intelligence Advisory Board," was signed by President Reagan. The order revoked Executive Order 12331 of October 20, 1981, which had reestablished the President's Foreign Intelligence Advisory Board (PFIAB), and then again reestablished the PFIAB. This Executive Order was virtually identical to Executive Order 12331; the only differences were that 12537 discussed more fully the terms of membership of the PFIAB members. It limited the total membership to fourteen members, but this was subsequently increased to sixteen by amendment. The order was, in many respects, a bureaucratic exercise, in that it replaced a 1981 order that President Reagan had issued on the same subject. Nonetheless, it reflected the President's continued commitment to oversight of the Intelligence Community as well as his intention to minimize the congressional role in such oversight by seeing that the White House provided sufficient monitoring of the same. *See also:* Executive Oversight, President's Foreign Intelligence Advisory Board.

References
Office of the President of the United States.
*Executive Order 12537, President's Foreign
Intelligence Oversight Board.* Washington, DC,
Oct. 28, 1985.

—EXECUTIVE ORDER 12575, December 1, 1986, "President's Special Review Board," was signed by President Reagan. Issued in the wake of the Iran-Contra scandal in which several National Security Council (NSC) staff members and the National Security Advisor had been implicated, the order created a three-man special board to investigate the NSC. The most relevant aspects of the order were that:

1. It established a three-man board, and the President was to choose a chairman from them.
2. The functions of the board were to examine the future role of the National Security Council staff; conduct an extensive study of the NSC staff in the "development, coordination, oversight, and conduct of foreign and national security policy; review and examine the role of the NSC staff in operational

activities, particularly those that were "extremely sensitive diplomatic, military, and intelligence missions"; and provide recommendations to the President.
3. It required the board to report to the President in 30 days.

The President was under a great deal of pressure to react to the Iran-Contra scandal. By creating the special board, he probably hoped that he would demonstrate that he had, indeed, reacted. Additionally, by appointing three extremely respected individuals—Senator John Tower (who was made Chairman), Senator Edmund Muskie, and Lieutenant General Brent Scowcroft—the President averted accusations that the board would whitewash the issue. Conversely, the fact that the President gave the board only 30 days to complete its investigation and to report indicated that he wished to hurry its proceedings and to report as quickly as possible and thereby hopefully defuse the issue. *See also:* Executive Oversight, Iran-Contra Scandal, National Security Council.

References
Office of the President of the United States.
*Executive Order 12575, President's Special Review
Board.* Washington, DC, Dec. 1, 1986.

—EXECUTIVE OVERSIGHT has been a problem that has plagued all of the postwar presidents. President Truman, possibly fearing the dangers of a centralized intelligence organization, disbanded the Office of Strategic Services in 1945 and placed its branches within the Departments of State and War. It was Truman's hope that the Department of State would take the lead in centralized intelligence collection and production. When this did not occur, Truman favored the creation of the Central Intelligence Group, which later became the Central Intelligence Agency.

Until the 1970s, presidential oversight was concerned with the quality of U.S. intelligence, not whether U.S. intelligence activities were lawful. The first manifestation of this concern was the creation of the President's Board of Consultants on Foreign Intelligence Activities (PBCFIA) by President Eisenhower. It was to be staffed by a group of experienced private citizens who would periodically review U.S. intelligence activities. President Eisenhower also created the United States Intelligence Board in 1958, in an unsuccessful attempt to increase the power of the director of Central Intelligence.

President Kennedy permitted the members of Eisenhower's PBCFIA to resign when he took office in 1961, and he did not restaff the board. However, after the Bay of Pigs fiasco, he created the President's Foreign Intelligence Advisory Board (PFIAB), which resumed the duties of the old PBCFIA in evaluating U.S. intelligence activities and agencies. Like his predecessors, Kennedy's purpose in oversight was to improve the quality of the material that the Intelligence Community produced. President Johnson did not share Kennedy's interest in intelligence and preferred to work with his secretaries of defense and state, rather than with the intelligence chiefs. However, Johnson, who was occupied by the progress of the Vietnam War, demonstrated considerable concern over the Community's inability to reach a consensus concerning North Vietnamese military capabilities.

It was during the Johnson administration and into the Nixon administration that the United States was stricken with domestic turmoil and demonstrations against the war. In reaction, some elements of the Intelligence Community became involved in domestic operations, and some of these were questionable in their legality. (Some years later, the Church Committee was particularly critical of the Federal Bureau of Investigation's COINTELPRO operation and of the waging of domestic operations by Army Intelligence and the Central Intelligence Agency.) Such domestic involvement went even further in the Watergate scandal. Here was a case in which the Nixon administration used CIA assets in a domestic operation that was highly questionable. The result was President Nixon's eventual resignation, but its affect on the Intelligence Community was devastating.

As Watergate unraveled, it became obvious that the Intelligence Community had exceeded its authority. Both the Senate and the House formed investigative committees, and these bodies not only investigated Watergate but also scrutinized all domestic intelligence activities that had been waged by the Intelligence Community in the 1960s and 1970s. The result was a definite shift in the focus of presidential and congressional oversight from concern about the quality of the intelligence produced to concern over the types of activities the Intelligence Community performed.

In 1974, President Ford, who had only been in office for about four months but who had inherited the intelligence crisis from his predecessor, requested a report from William Colby, who was then serving as the director of Central Intelligence (DCI). Colby submitted a report that had been prepared by the agency for his predecessor, James Schlesinger; this document has often been referred to as the "Family Jewels." After reviewing the report, Ford established a presidential panel, chaired by Vice President Nelson Rockefeller, to investigate the CIA's domestic activities and operations.

In June 1975, the Rockefeller report was submitted. It confirmed the accusations of illegal CIA activities, including domestic surveillance and spying. Among the commission's recommendations was one that called for a Joint Oversight Committee in Congress to oversee intelligence activities.

As the intelligence scandal worsened, President Ford took several steps. He dismissed Colby as DCI on November 2, 1975, replacing him with George Bush. Additionally, he issued Executive Order 11905 on February 8, 1976. This, the first public Executive directive on intelligence responsibilities and functions, reaffirmed the DCI's primary role in intelligence, abolished the United States Intelligence Board, the National Security Council Intelligence Committee, the Intelligence Resources Advisory Committee, and the "40" Committee, and created a new United States Intelligence Board. The DCI's management was handled through a new Committee on Foreign Intelligence (CFI), which reported to the National Security Council. An Intelligence Oversight Board was also created to monitor intelligence activity.

President Carter also worked actively to solve the problem of presidential oversight. He attempted to define a new role for the Intelligence Community as that entity emerged from the devastating scandals. When his initial choice for DCI, Theodore Sorenson, withdrew his nomination in the face of stiff potential congressional opposition, Carter nominated Admiral Stansfield Turner, who was approved by Congress.

Carter's first reform occurred in May 1977, when he abolished the President's Foreign Intelligence Advisory Board (PFIAB). This was followed by a reorganization in August 1977, in which he attempted to augment the DCI's power, and then the highly significant Executive Order 12036, which the President signed on January 24, 1978. That Executive Order (see Appendix K) gave the DCI exclusive control over the National Foreign Intelligence Program budget.

President Reagan inherited a difficult situation from Carter. The Intelligence Community had been decimated by the congressional and presidential investigations and by the intelligence failures in Iran and the Soviet brigade in Cuba. Reagan shifted the focus of presidential oversight away from the types of intelligence operations that were being conducted to the quality of intelligence collection, analysis, and reporting. His appointment of William Casey, although controversial, initially had a positive affect on the CIA. The President then issued Executive Order 12333 on December 4, 1981. In addition, he continued the Intelligence Oversight Board in Executive Order 12334. Finally, Reagan restored the President's Foreign Intelligence Advisory Board (PFIAB) and directed its focus toward contributing constructively to improving the quality of U.S. intelligence.

As Reagan left office in 1989, the issue of presidential oversight still had not been resolved. Indeed, the dual problems of overseeing the Intelligence Community's production of good intelligence and the problem of insuring that the community was not politicized to the extent that it produced politically influenced intelligence (intelligence that would support political policies, rather than accurate intelligence) still remained a problem. It was one that confronted George Bush as he began his tenure as President in 1989.

References

Breckinridge, Scott D. *The CIA and the U.S. Intelligence System.* Boulder, CO: Westview Press, 1986.

Central Intelligence Agency. *Central Intelligence Agency Factbook.* Washington, DC: GPO, 1987.

Cline, Ray S. *The CIA Under Reagan, Bush, and Casey.* Washington, DC: Acropolis Books, 1981.

Godson, Roy, ed. *Intelligence Problems for the 1980s, Number 5: Clandestine Collection.* Washington, DC: National Strategy Information Center, 1982.

Lowenthal, Mark M. *U.S. Intelligence: Evolution and Anatomy.* New York: Praeger, 1984.

Oseth, John M. *Regulating U.S. Intelligence Operations: A Study in the Definition of the National Interest.* Frankfort: University of Kentucky Press, 1985.

Treverton, Gregory F. *Covert Action: The Limits of Intervention in the Postwar World.* New York: Basic Books, 1987.

Turner, Stansfield. *Secrecy and Democracy: The CIA in Transition.* Boston: Houghton Mifflin, 1985.

Von Hoene, John P. A. *Intelligence User's Guide.* Washington, DC: DIA, 1983.

—**EXECUTIVE SUPPORT OFFICE (ESO).** *See:* Defense Intelligence Agency.

—**EXFILTRATION** is a term used in clandestine and covert intelligence operations to describe smuggling an agent out of an unfriendly country. *See also:* Evasion and Escape, Evasion and Escape Intelligence, Moonlight Extradition.

References

Becket, Henry S. A. *The Dictionary of Espionage: Spookspeak into English.* New York: Stein and Day, 1986.

Deacon, Richard. *Spyclopedia: An Encyclopedia of Spies, Secret Services, Operations, Jargon, and All Subjects Related to the World of Espionage.* London: Macdonald, 1987.

Department of Defense, Joint Chiefs of Staff. *Department of Defense Dictionary of Military and Related Terms.* Washington, DC: GPO, 1986.

—**EXPENSES** is a term used in clandestine and covert intelligence operations. Expenses is a tactic for entrapping an intelligence target so that he or she will work for an intelligence agency. Usually the recruiter asks for something unclassified, such as a directory, and pays the target for his trouble. After several such requests and payments, the target is asked to sign a receipt for the payment, being told that the recruiter will then be able to obtain reimbursement. Once the target signs, he is trapped and can be forced to accomplish clandestine activities. *See also:* Agent, Biographic Leverage, Blackmail, Blow, Blown Agent, Burn, Burnt, Co-Opted Worker, Co-Optees, Cultivation, Doubled, Recruitment, Recruitment in Place, Special Activities.

References

Becket, Henry S. A. *The Dictionary of Espionage: Spookspeak into English.* New York: Stein and Day, 1986.

—**EXPLOITATION,** in general, is the process of obtaining intelligence information from any source and taking advantage of it for tactical or strategic purposes. However, in signals intelligence (SIGINT), exploitation means producing information from encrypted messages where the encryption system is unknown. It includes decryption, translation, and the solution of specific controls such as indicators and specific keys. *See also:* Intelligence Cycle, Signals Intelligence.

References

Becket, Henry S. A. *The Dictionary of Espionage: Spookspeak into English.* New York: Stein and Day, 1986.

Department of Defense, Defense Intelligence College. *Glossary of Intelligence Terms and Definitions.* Washington, DC: DIC, 1987.

Department of Defense, Joint Chiefs of Staff. *Department of Defense Dictionary of Military and Related Terms.* Washington, DC: GPO, 1986.

Godson, Roy, ed. *Intelligence Problems for the 1980s, Number 1: Elements of Intelligence.* Rev. ed. Washington, DC: National Strategy Information Center, 1983.

Laqueur, Walter. *A World of Secrets.* New York: Basic Books, 1985.

U.S. Congress. Senate. *Final Report of the Senate Select Committee to Study Government Operations with Respect to Intelligence Activities. Report 94-755. Book I, Foreign and Military Intelligence.* Washington, DC: GPO, 1976.

—**EXPOSED AREA** is a geographic area that is in danger of being overrun by hostile forces, or where the local political or military situation poses a real threat to the security of sensitive compartmented information (SCI) located there or to SCI activities conducted there.

References

Department of Defense, U.S. Army. *Counter-Signals Intelligence (C-SIGINT) Operations.* Field Manual FM 34-62. Washington, DC: Headquarters, Department of the Army, 1986.

———. *Military Intelligence Battalion Combat Electronic Warfare and Intelligence (Aerial Exploitation) (Corps).* Field Manual FM 34-22. Washington, DC: Headquarters, Department of the Army, 1984.

———. *Military Intelligence Company (Combat Electronic Warfare and Intelligence) (Armored Cavalry Regiment/Separate Brigade).* Field Manual FM 34-30. Washington, DC: Headquarters, Department of the Army, 1983.

—**EXTERMINATORS** is a term used in clandestine and covert intelligence operations for individuals who debug offices, objects, and other materials that are believed to be bugged. *See also:* Bug, Bugging, Concealment Devices, Electronic Surveillance, Sound Man, Sound School, Special Activities.

References

Godson, Roy, ed. *Intelligence Problems for the 1980s, Number 1: Elements of Intelligence.* Rev. ed. Washington, DC: National Strategy Information Center, 1983.

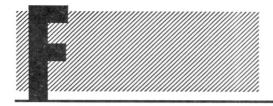

—**FABRICATOR** is a term used in clandestine intelligence operations to describe an agent who provides false information. *See also:* Agent, Cover, Cover Name, Cover Organizations, Cover Story, Establishing Bonafides, Legend, Litmus Test, Mole, Rumor, Shopworn Goods.

References

Department of Defense, Joint Chiefs of Staff. *Department of Defense Dictionary of Military and Related Terms.* Washington, DC: GPO, 1986.

Quirk, John; Phillips, David; Cline, Ray; and Pforzheimer, Walter. *The Central Intelligence Agency: A Photographic History.* Guilford, CT: Foreign Intelligence Press, 1986.

—**FAILURE.** *See:* Intelligence Failure.

—**FALSE CONFIRMATION** is a term used in clandestine and covert intelligence operations. It is a phase in a disinformation or deception operation that is intended to give credence to an item of information that an agency is trying to pass to the other side. Ideally, the false confirmation would come from a source that appeared both reputable and not identifiable with the agency. *See also:* Agent, Agent Authentication, Agent in Place, Cover, Cover Name, Cover Organizations, Cover Story, Establishing Bonafides, Infiltration, Legend, Playback, Plumbing, Pocket Litter, Putting in the Plumbing, Setting Up, Special Activities, Suitable Cover.

References

Becket, Henry S. A. *The Dictionary of Espionage: Spookspeak into English.* New York: Stein and Day, 1986.

Deacon, Richard. *Spyclopedia: An Encyclopedia of Spies, Secret Services, Operations, Jargon, and All Subjects Related to the World of Espionage.* London: Macdonald, 1987.

Ranelagh, John. *The Agency: The Rise and Decline of the CIA.* New York: Simon and Schuster, 1986.

—**FALSE FLAG** is a term used in clandestine and covert intelligence operations. A false flag occurs when an agent or informer is recruited by telling him that he is actually working for another country or interest. False flagging is done when the individual will not work for the agency that needs his services. An excellent example of false flagging was created by Frederick Forsyth in his novel, *The Fourth Protocol.* In it, British intelligence discovers that a high-ranking British government employee has been passing classified intelligence information to a member of the South African Embassy. One of the book's climactic scenes occurs when the British employee is told that the embassy contact is actually an agent for the Soviet KGB and that the information he had passed had not been sent to South Africa, but to Moscow. *See also:* Agent, Double Agent, Handling Agent, Informant, Inside Man, Putting in the Plumbing, Recruitment, Recruitment in Place, Special Activities.

References

Becket, Henry S. A. *The Dictionary of Espionage: Spookspeak into English.* New York: Stein and Day, 1986.

Clancy, Tom. *The Cardinal of the Kremlin.* New York: Putnam, 1988.

Forsyth, Frederick. *The Fourth Protocol.* New York: Viking, 1984.

Kessler, Ronald. *Spy vs. Spy: Stalking Soviet Spies in America.* New York: Charles Scribner's Sons, 1988.

Quirk, John; Phillips, David; Cline, Ray; and Pforzheimer, Walter. *The Central Intelligence Agency: A Photographic History.* Guilford, CT: Foreign Intelligence Press, 1986.

Treverton, Gregory F. *Covert Action: The Limits of Intervention in the Postwar World.* New York: Basic Books, 1987.

—**FALSE TARGET,** in electronic warfare, is any jamming phenomenon that appears in some or all respects to be a true target on the receiving system element. False targets are not necessarily due to deceptive jamming. *See also:* Electronic Warfare.

References

Muzerall, Joseph V., and Carty, Thomas P. "COMSEC and Its Need for Key Management." *DP&CS* (Spring 1987).

—**"FAMILY JEWELS"** was a list of transgressions that the Central Intelligence Agency prepared in 1973, after it was revealed that Gordon Liddy and Howard Hunt had used the agency's facilities in some of their illegal Watergate activities. James Schlesinger, then the director of Central Intelligence, ordered that all illegal operations that had occurred be reported to him. These were passed to the CIA's inspector general, who composed a document of almost 700 pages, involving about 300 different instances of illegal activity. A few months later, Schlesinger's successor, William Colby, released the document to the Rockefeller Commission, which was investigating the CIA's activities. According to Henry Becket, Colby's action created widespread demoralization within the agency. *See also:* Central Intelligence Agency, Congressional Oversight, Executive Oversight.

References

American Bar Association. *Oversight and Accountability of the U.S. Intelligence Agencies: An Evaluation.* Washington, DC: ABA, 1985.

Becket, Henry S. A. *The Dictionary of Espionage: Spookspeak into English.* New York: Stein and Day, 1986.

Godson, Roy, ed. *Intelligence Problems for the 1980s, Number 1: Elements of Intelligence.* Rev. ed. Washington, DC: National Strategy Information Center, 1983.

Laqueur, Walter. *A World of Secrets.* New York: Basic Books, 1985.

Maurer, Alfred C.; Turnstall, Marion D.; and Keagle, James M. *Intelligence Policy and Process.* Boulder, CO: Westview Press, 1985.

Turner, Stansfield. *Secrecy and Democracy: The CIA in Transition.* Boston: Houghton Mifflin, 1985.

—**FAN CAMERA** is an intelligence imagery and photoreconnaissance term for an assembly of three or more cameras that are systematically disposed at fixed angles relative to each other so as to provide wide lateral coverage with overlapping images. *See also:* Aerial Photograph.

References

Department of Defense, Joint Chiefs of Staff. *Department of Defense Dictionary of Military and Related Terms.* Washington, DC: GPO, 1986.

Von Hoene, John P. A. *Intelligence User's Guide.* Washington, DC: DIA, 1983.

—**THE FARM** is Camp Peary, the Central Intelligence Agency training school in Virginia. *See also:* Camp Peary.

References

Becket, Henry S. A. *The Dictionary of Espionage: Spookspeak into English.* New York: Stein and Day, 1986.

Quirk, John; Phillips, David; Cline, Ray; and Pforzheimer, Walter. *The Central Intelligence Agency: A Photographic History.* Guilford, CT: Foreign Intelligence Press, 1986.

Turner, Stansfield. *Secrecy and Democracy: The CIA in Transition.* Boston: Houghton Mifflin, 1985.

—**FAURER, LIEUTENANT GENERAL LINCOLN D., U.S. AIR FORCE,** became the director of the National Security Agency on March 10, 1981. Born in Medford, Massachusetts, Faurer had attended West Point and subsequently earned a master's degree in engineering management from Rensselaer Polytechnic Institute and a second master's in international affairs from George Washington University. Faurer spent most of his career in intelligence and strategic reconnaissance assignments before being assigned to the Defense Intelligence Agency in 1964. In 1974, he returned to the agency to become its deputy director for intelligence, and then he became its vice director for production. In 1977, he was transferred to Europe, where he was chief of intelligence for the U.S. European Command and then deputy chairman of NATO's Military Committee in Brussels. In 1981, he was selected as director, NSA. *See also:* National Security Agency.

References

Bamford, James. *The Puzzle Palace: A Report on America's Most Secret Agency.* New York: Penguin Books, 1983.

—**FEDERAL BUREAU OF INVESTIGATION (FBI)** was established in 1908 as the Bureau of Intelligence within the Department of Justice. It was reorganized as the FBI in 1924 under J. Edgar Hoover and was given national counterintelligence responsibilities in 1939. It has the primary responsibility for counterintelligence within the United States and is the agency charged with the responsibility for collecting, producing, and disseminating intelligence about foreign intelligence activities within the United States. This includes detecting, penetrating, preventing and neutralizing, by lawful means, espionage, sabotage, and other clandestine intelligence activities directed against the United States by hostile foreign intelligence services. The FBI works closely with the Central Intelligence Agency, which has primary responsibility for counterintelligence outside of the United States. While the

FBI occasionally conducts counterintelligence activities outside the United States, it does so in coordination with the CIA and the military services.

References

Allen, Thomas B., and Polmar, Norman. *Merchants of Treason: America's Secrets for Sale.* New York: Delacorte Press, 1988.

American Bar Association. *Oversight and Accountability of the U.S. Intelligence Agencies: An Evaluation.* Washington, DC: ABA, 1985.

Deacon, Richard. *Spyclopedia: An Encyclopedia of Spies, Secret Services, Operations, Jargon, and All Subjects Related to the World of Espionage.* London: Macdonald, 1987.

Godson, Roy, ed. *Intelligence Problems for the 1980s, Number 1: Elements of Intelligence.* Rev. ed. Washington, DC: National Strategy Information Center, 1983.

————. *Intelligence Problems for the 1980s, Number 3: Counterintelligence.* Washington, DC: National Strategy Information Center, 1980.

Kent, Sherman. *Strategic Intelligence for American World Policy.* Princeton, NJ: Princeton University Press, 1966.

Laqueur, Walter. *A World of Secrets.* New York: Basic Books, 1985.

Lefever, Ernest W., and Godson, Roy. *The CIA and the American Ethic: An Unfinished Debate.* Washington, DC: Ethics and Public Policy Center, Georgetown University, 1979.

Lowenthal, Mark M. *U.S. Intelligence: Evolution and Anatomy.* New York: Praeger, 1984.

Maurer, Alfred C.; Turnstall, Marion D.; and Keagle, James M. *Intelligence Policy and Process.* Boulder, CO: Westview Press, 1985.

Treverton, Gregory F. *Covert Action: The Limits of Intervention in the Postwar World.* New York: Basic Books, 1987.

Turner, Stansfield. *Secrecy and Democracy: The CIA in Transition.* Boston: Houghton Mifflin, 1985.

—**FEDERAL INTELLIGENCE AGENCY** is the NATO name for the West German Bundesnachrichtendienst (BND).

References

Deacon, Richard. *Spyclopedia: An Encyclopedia of Spies, Secret Services, Operations, Jargon, and All Subjects Related to the World of Espionage.* London: Macdonald, 1987.

—**FEED MATERIAL** is data that is generally true but unimportant. It is given to someone to pass to an intelligence agency so that he or she can establish credibility with that service. This is some-times called build-up material. *See also:* Agent, Agent Authentication, Agent in Place, Establishing Bonafides, False Confirmation, Legend, Plumbing, Pocket Litter, Putting in the Plumbing, Setting Up, Special Activities.

References

Becket, Henry S. A. *The Dictionary of Espionage: Spookspeak into English.* New York: Stein and Day, 1986.

Deacon, Richard. *Spyclopedia: An Encyclopedia of Spies, Secret Services, Operations, Jargon, and All Subjects Related to the World of Espionage.* London: Macdonald, 1987.

Kessler, Ronald. *Spy vs. Spy: Stalking Soviet Spies in America.* New York: Charles Scribner's Sons, 1988.

Ranelagh, John. *The Agency: The Rise and Decline of the CIA.* New York: Simon and Schuster, 1986.

—**FEEDBACK AGENT** is a term used in clandestine and covert intelligence operations. It is an enemy agent who is planted in a rival intelligence organization and reports back to his own agency concerning the effectiveness of its counterintelligence program. *See also:* Agent Authentication, Agent in Place, Agent Provocateur, Cover, Cover Name, Cover Organizations, Cover Story, Damage Assessment, Damage Control, Double Agent, Infiltration, Informant, Inside Man, Recruitment, Recruitment in Place, Singleton, Sleeper, Special Activities.

References

Becket, Henry S. A. *The Dictionary of Espionage: Spookspeak into English.* New York: Stein and Day, 1986.

Deacon, Richard. *Spyclopedia: An Encyclopedia of Spies, Secret Services, Operations, Jargon, and All Subjects Related to the World of Espionage.* London: Macdonald, 1987.

Kessler, Ronald. *Spy vs. Spy: Stalking Soviet Spies in America.* New York: Charles Scribner's Sons, 1988.

Ranelagh, John. *The Agency: The Rise and Decline of the CIA.* New York: Simon and Schuster, 1986.

—**FIELD** is a term used in clandestine and covert intelligence operations. It is the foreign territory where an agent is on assignment. *See also:* Case, Case Officer, Chief of Base, Chief of Outpost, Chief of Station, Company, Special Activities.

References

Becket, Henry S. A. *The Dictionary of Espionage: Spookspeak into English.* New York: Stein and Day, 1986.

Clancy, Tom. *The Cardinal of the Kremlin*. New York: Putnam, 1988.

Deacon, Richard. *Spyclopedia: An Encyclopedia of Spies, Secret Services, Operations, Jargon, and All Subjects Related to the World of Espionage*. London: Macdonald, 1987.

Godson, Roy, ed. *Intelligence Problems for the 1980s, Number 1: Elements of Intelligence*. Rev. ed. Washington, DC: National Strategy Information Center, 1983.

Treverton, Gregory F. *Covert Action: The Limits of Intervention in the Postwar World*. New York: Basic Books, 1987.

Turner, Stansfield. *Secrecy and Democracy: The CIA in Transition*. Boston: Houghton Mifflin, 1985.

—**FIELD INFORMATION REPORT** is the basic field report of a Central Intelligence Agency operative. It is sent directly to the local agency station, reviewed by the Chief of Station, and then pouched, or sent by courier, to the agency's headquarters at Langley. *See also:* Field.

References

Becket, Henry S. A. *The Dictionary of Espionage: Spookspeak into English*. New York: Stein and Day, 1986.

Ranelagh, John. *The Agency: The Rise and Decline of the CIA*. New York: Simon and Schuster, 1986.

Treverton, Gregory F. *Covert Action: The Limits of Intervention in the Postwar World*. New York: Basic Books, 1987.

—**FIELD OFFICER** is a generic term that means an operational agent or spy, in contrast to a nonoperational intelligence person, such as an estimator, analyst, or imagery interpreter. *See also:* Field.

References

Clancy, Tom. *The Cardinal of the Kremlin*. New York: Putnam, 1988.

Godson, Roy, ed. *Intelligence Problems for the 1980s, Number 1: Elements of Intelligence*. Rev. ed. Washington, DC: National Strategy Information Center, 1983.

Treverton, Gregory F. *Covert Action: The Limits of Intervention in the Postwar World*. New York: Basic Books, 1987.

Turner, Stansfield. *Secrecy and Democracy: The CIA in Transition*. Boston: Houghton Mifflin, 1985.

—**FIFTH COLUMN** means subversives who are willing to work for the enemy within their own country. According to Henry Becket, the term is now passe and has been replaced by the term "agent of influence." *See also:* Agent of Influence, Defector, Double Agent, Inside Man, Mole, Recruitment, Recruitment in Place, Special Activities, Turned.

References

Becket, Henry S. A. *The Dictionary of Espionage: Spookspeak into English*. New York: Stein and Day, 1986.

Turner, Stansfield. *Secrecy and Democracy: The CIA in Transition*. Boston: Houghton Mifflin, 1985.

—**FINISHED INTELLIGENCE** is a general intelligence term. Generally, it is the intelligence product and is the result of the production step in the intelligence cycle. However, to the Army, it is intelligence information that has been "evaluated, analyzed, integrated, interpreted and formatted for issue." *See also:* Intelligence Cycle.

References

Department of Defense, Defense Intelligence College. *Glossary of Intelligence Terms and Definitions*. Washington, DC: DIC, 1987.

Godson, Roy, ed. *Intelligence Problems for the 1980s, Number 1: Elements of Intelligence*. Rev. ed. Washington, DC: National Strategy Information Center, 1983.

Kent, Sherman. *Strategic Intelligence for American World Policy*. Princeton, NJ: Princeton University Press, 1966.

Treverton, Gregory F. *Covert Action: The Limits of Intervention in the Postwar World*. New York: Basic Books, 1987.

—**FINISHED INTELLIGENCE PUBLICATIONS** refers to completed and published intelligence studies, including but not limited to intelligence studies, orders of battle, estimates, factbooks, and other products and publications. *See also:* Finished Intelligence.

References

Brinkley, David A., and Hull, Andrew W. *Estimative Intelligence: A Textbook on the History, Products, Uses and Writing of Intelligence Estimates*. Columbus, OH: Battelle, 1979.

Godson, Roy, ed. *Intelligence Problems for the 1980s, Number 1: Elements of Intelligence*. Rev. ed. Washington, DC: National Strategy Information Center, 1983.

Kent, Sherman. *Strategic Intelligence for American World Policy.* Princeton, NJ: Princeton University Press, 1966.

Treverton, Gregory F. *Covert Action: The Limits of Intervention in the Postwar World.* New York: Basic Books, 1987.

Turner, Stansfield. *Secrecy and Democracy: The CIA in Transition.* Boston: Houghton Mifflin, 1985.

—**FINISHED RECURRING INTELLIGENCE (FRI)** is evaluated intelligence that is either produced on a recurring basis and generally covers the same subject areas, or is frequently revised. *See also:* Finished Intelligence.

References

Department of Defense, U.S. Army. *RDTE Managers Intelligence and Threat Support Guide.* Alexandria, VA: Headquarters, Army Materiel Development and Readiness Command, 1983.

Godson, Roy, ed. *Intelligence Problems for the 1980s, Number 1: Elements of Intelligence.* Rev. ed. Washington, DC: National Strategy Information Center, 1983.

—**FIREFLY** is a term used in clandestine and covert intelligence operations to describe a chemical that ignites after it has been mixed with gasoline. According to Henry Becket, it was quite effective in OSS operations during World War II and is still available in the CIA.

References

Becket, Henry S. A. *The Dictionary of Espionage: Spookspeak into English.* New York: Stein and Day, 1986.

—**FIRM** is a euphemism for the British Secret Service that is used by its agents.

References

Deacon, Richard. *Spyclopedia: An Encyclopedia of Spies, Secret Services, Operations, Jargon, and All Subjects Related to the World of Espionage.* London: Macdonald, 1987.

Turner, Stansfield. *Secrecy and Democracy: The CIA in Transition.* Boston: Houghton Mifflin, 1985.

—**FIRST LIGHT** is a term used in imagery and photoreconnaissance. It is the beginning of nautical twilight, that is, when the center of the morning sun is 12 degrees below the horizon. *See also:* Aerial Photograph.

References

Department of Defense, Joint Chiefs of Staff. *Department of Defense Dictionary of Military and Related Terms.* Washington, DC: GPO, 1986.

—**FISCAL GUIDANCE** is an intelligence budgeting term. It is the biannual guidance that is issued by the secretary of defense that provides fiscal constraints on the Joint Chiefs of Staff, the military departments, and the defense agencies in their formulating of force structures and the Five-Year Defense Program (FYDP). *See also:* Appropriation or Fund Account.

References

Pickett, George. "Congress, the Budget, and Intelligence." In *Intelligence Policy and Process,* edited by Alfred C. Maurer, Marion D. Turnstall, and James M. Keagle. Boulder, CO: Westview Press, 1985.

—**FISCAL YEAR** is a term used in intelligence budgeting. It is the twelve-month period that begins on October 1 of one calendar year and ends on September 30 of the next calendar year. *See also:* Fiscal Guidance.

References

Pickett, George. "Congress, the Budget, and Intelligence." In *Intelligence Policy and Process,* edited by Alfred C. Maurer, Marion D. Turnstall, and James M. Keagle. Boulder, CO: Westview Press, 1985.

Turner, Stansfield. *Secrecy and Democracy: The CIA in Transition.* Boston: Houghton Mifflin, 1985.

—**FIVE-YEAR DEFENSE PROGRAM (FYDP)** covers procurement and construction projected for a five-year period beyond the budget year. The FYDP consists of summary tables supported by detailed submissions of the military departments and other Department of Defense components. The FYDP is formally approved by the secretary of defense and is binding, for programming purposes, on all components of the Department of Defense. The base program was approved in July 1962 and is changed as necessary through the Program Change Control Process. Each of the three segments of the Planning, Programming, and Budgeting System (PPBS) contributes toward attaining the ultimate objective of providing the operational commanders with the best mix of forces and support possible within existing fiscal constraints.

Planning identifies the threat that will face the United States for the next five to twenty years, assesses U.S. capability to counter that threat, and recommends the forces that will be necessary to defeat it. Planning highlights the critical needs and examines the risks if the recommended goals are not attained. This data helps to guide resource decisions.

Programming matches the available dollars against the most critical needs and develops a five-year resource proposal. After this proposal is approved, it becomes the basis of subsequent budgeting actions.

Budgeting refines the detailed costs and develops the service estimate that is required to accomplish the approved program. Following review and approval, it serves as the input to the President's budget. In this budgeting segment, the service staffs play a major role in defending the budget submission before Congress and in executing the congressional appropriation legislation.

The FYDP is the basic Department of Defense programming document. It is an integrated and coordinated program that involves forces, costs, manpower, procurement, and construction. Its structure is to present the financial horizon out to five years (out to eight years for force tables), and it portrays the data in two ways. First, it presents it in the form of a major force program (MFP) for Department of Defense review. There are ten MFPs, each consisting of several program elements (PEs). The PEs are the basic building blocks of the system, and there are over 1,600 of them in the Department of Defense. The MFPs and PEs are presented in a way that facilitates internal Department of Defense program review. The ten MFPs are strategic forces; general purpose forces; intelligence and communications; airlift/sealift forces; guard and reserve forces; research and development; central supply and maintenance; training, medical, and other general personnel activities; administration and associated activities; and support of other nations.

Second, the FYDP presents the data in the form of appropriations for congressional review. The FYDP is updated three times a year. In January, it is updated to reflect the President's budget. This becomes the departure point for developing the service program for the next budget year. In May, it is again updated to reflect the Program Objective Memorandum (POM), and in September, it is updated a final time to reflect the service budget estimates. The assistant secretary of defense (comptroller) maintains the

FYDP, while the services provide the updated data. *See also:* Fiscal Guidance.

References

Department of Defense, Defense Intelligence Agency. *Organization, Mission, and Key Personnel.* Washington, DC: DIA, 1986.

Laqueur, Walter. *A World of Secrets.* New York: Basic Books, 1985.

Pickett, George. "Congress, the Budget, and Intelligence." In *Intelligence Policy and Process,* edited by Alfred C. Maurer, Marion D. Turnstall, and James M. Keagle. Boulder, CO: Westview Press, 1985.

—**FIX** is a clandestine and covert intelligence operations term that describes a person who has been compromised and will therefore work for an intelligence agency. Used as a verb, it means to compromise, blackmail, or con someone. *See also:* Agent in Place, Agent of Influence, Biographic Leverage, Blackmail, Blow, Blown Agent, Co-Opted Worker, Co-Optees, Double Agent, Doubled, Recruitment, Recruitment in Place, Special Activities, Turned.

References

Becket, Henry S. A. *The Dictionary of Espionage: Spookspeak into English.* New York: Stein and Day, 1986.

Deacon, Richard. *Spyclopedia: An Encyclopedia of Spies, Secret Services, Operations, Jargon, and All Subjects Related to the World of Espionage.* London: Macdonald, 1987.

—**FLAP** is a term used in clandestine and covert intelligence operations to describe the commotion, controversy, or publicity that results from a bungled or mismanaged intelligence operation. In current intelligence, a flap is jargon for a crisis. *See also:* Flap Potential.

References

Godson, Roy, ed. *Intelligence Problems for the 1980s, Number 1: Elements of Intelligence.* Rev. ed. Washington, DC: National Strategy Information Center, 1983.

Quirk, John; Phillips, David; Cline, Ray; and Pforzheimer, Walter. *The Central Intelligence Agency: A Photographic History.* Guilford, CT: Foreign Intelligence Press, 1986.

Turner, Stansfield. *Secrecy and Democracy: The CIA in Transition.* Boston: Houghton Mifflin, 1985.

—**FLAP POTENTIAL** is a term used in clandestine and covert intelligence operations to describe the degree of embarrassment that an intelligence agency may suffer when a questionable activity is made public or when an agent defects. *See also:* Flap.

References

Becket, Henry S. A. *The Dictionary of Espionage: Spookspeak into English.* New York: Stein and Day, 1986.

Deacon, Richard. *Spyclopedia: An Encyclopedia of Spies, Secret Services, Operations, Jargon, and All Subjects Related to the World of Espionage.* London: Macdonald, 1987.

Kessler, Ronald. *Spy vs. Spy: Stalking Soviet Spies in America.* New York: Charles Scribner's Sons, 1988.

Ranelagh, John. *The Agency: The Rise and Decline of the CIA.* New York: Simon and Schuster, 1986.

—**FLAPS AND SEALS** is a mail opening course that is taught by the Central Intelligence Agency. In it, an agent is taught to open and remove the contents of envelopes rapidly, but in such a way that the contents can be replaced and the envelope resealed without the addressee's realizing that his or her mail has been opened. Pierre Salinger and Leonard Gross provide a detailed discussion of flaps and seals in their novel, *Mortal Games.* They explain that, once the glue on an envelope is loosened, a stick is inserted in the envelope and the contents are rolled onto the stick and then extracted. After the contents are read, the reverse process is followed and the envelope is resealed. *See also:* Flaps and Seals Man.

References

Becket, Henry S. A. *The Dictionary of Espionage: Spookspeak into English.* New York: Stein and Day, 1986.

Deacon, Richard. *Spyclopedia: An Encyclopedia of Spies, Secret Services, Operations, Jargon, and All Subjects Related to the World of Espionage.* London: Macdonald, 1987.

Kessler, Ronald. *Spy vs. Spy: Stalking Soviet Spies in America.* New York: Charles Scribner's Sons, 1988.

Salinger, Pierre, and Gross, Leonard. *Mortal Games.* New York: Doubleday, 1988.

—**FLAPS AND SEALS MAN** is a term used in clandestine and covert intelligence operations for a person who is expert at the undetected opening and closing of mail. *See also:* Flaps and Seals.

References

Becket, Henry S. A. *The Dictionary of Espionage: Spookspeak into English.* New York: Stein and Day, 1986.

Deacon, Richard. *Spyclopedia: An Encyclopedia of Spies, Secret Services, Operations, Jargon, and All Subjects Related to the World of Espionage.* London: Macdonald, 1987.

Kessler, Ronald. *Spy vs. Spy: Stalking Soviet Spies in America.* New York: Charles Scribner's Sons, 1988.

Ranelagh, John. *The Agency: The Rise and Decline of the CIA.* New York: Simon and Schuster, 1986.

—**FLEET OCEAN SURVEILLANCE INFORMA-TION CENTER (FOSIC)** is part of the Navy's Ocean Surveillance Information System (OSIS), a complex network of undersea, surface, and airborne sensor systems that monitor the world's oceans and tracks naval and merchant activity. At the top of this system is the Navy Operational Intelligence Center (NOIC), which is located in Suitland, Maryland. The NOIC maintains information on naval and merchant activity worldwide and supports both the fleet intelligence facilities and the national Intelligence Community.

On the next level, there are the FOSICs. There are two of these, in Norfolk, Virginia, and Honolulu, Hawaii. They offer direct support to fleet commanders of the Atlantic and Pacific fleets (LANTFLT and PACFLT), respectively. FOSIC LANT monitors all activity in the Atlantic, FOSIC PAC monitors all activity in the Pacific, and both monitor portions of the Indian Ocean. The FOSICs maintain round-the-clock watches on all maritime activity, issue periodic reports on the same, and issue special reports on unusual events or high-interest activities when they occur.

In addition to the FOSICs, there are Fleet Ocean Surveillance Information Facilities (FOSIFs) in areas where there is high-interest maritime activity. *See also:* Fleet Ocean Surveillance Information Facility (FOSIF), Navy Operational Intelligence Center (NOIC), Ocean Surveillance Information System (OSIS).

—**FLEET OCEAN SURVEILLANCE INFORMA-TION FACILITY (FOSIF)** is part of the U.S. Navy's Ocean Surveillance Information System (OSIS). At the head of the system is the Navy Operational Intelligence Center (NOIC). There are also Fleet Ocean Surveillance Information Centers (FOSICs) in Norfolk, Virginia, and Honolulu, Hawaii, which monitor activity in the

Atlantic and Pacific oceans, respectively. Finally, there are FOSIFs, which monitor naval and merchant activity in high-interest areas. There are three such facilities: FOSIF Rota (Spain), which monitors activity in the Mediterranean Sea; FOSIF London, which monitors activity in the Baltic, North, and Norwegian seas; and FOSIF Kamisea (Japan), which monitors activity in the Sea of Japan. *See also:* Fleet Ocean Surveillance Information Center (FOSIC), Navy Operational Intelligence Center (NOIC), Ocean Surveillance Information Center (FOSIC).

—**FLOATER** is a clandestine and covert intelligence term for a person who is used for an occasional intelligence job. A floater often performs a low-level job and is often unaware that he is being used. *See also:* Disaffected Person, Fur-Lined Seat Cover, Granny, Heavy Mob, Honey Trap, Ladies, Lion Tamer, Mozhno Girls, Musician, Naked, Nash, Notionals, Not Witting, Paroles, Pavement Artists, Recruitment, Recruitment in Place, Riding Shotgun, Sisters, Sleeper, Stringer, Stroller, Taxi.

References

Becket, Henry S. A. *The Dictionary of Espionage: Spookspeak into English.* New York: Stein and Day, 1986.

Deacon, Richard. *Spyclopedia: An Encyclopedia of Spies, Secret Services, Operations, Jargon, and All Subjects Related to the World of Espionage.* London: Macdonald, 1987.

Kessler, Ronald. *Spy vs. Spy: Stalking Soviet Spies in America.* New York: Charles Scribner's Sons, 1988.

Ranelagh, John. *The Agency: The Rise and Decline of the CIA.* New York: Simon and Schuster, 1986.

—**FLOATING CONTACT** is a term used in counterintelligence, counterespionage, and counterinsurgency, as well as in clandestine and covert intelligence operations, to describe a person who is being followed who suddenly gets into a passing bus, car, or taxi. *See also:* Agent, Agent Provocateur, Blow, Blown Agent, Burn, Burnt, Make, Pavement Artists, Shaking off the Dogs, Surveillance.

References

Becket, Henry S. A. *The Dictionary of Espionage: Spookspeak into English.* New York: Stein and Day, 1986.

Deacon, Richard. *Spyclopedia: An Encyclopedia of Spies, Secret Services, Operations, Jargon, and All Subjects Related to the World of Espionage.* London: Macdonald, 1987.

Kessler, Ronald. *Spy vs. Spy: Stalking Soviet Spies in America.* New York: Charles Scribner's Sons, 1988.

Ranelagh, John. *The Agency: The Rise and Decline of the CIA.* New York: Simon and Schuster, 1986.

—**FLUTTER** is a term that has two intelligence meanings. (1) Flutter is to conduct a lie detector or polygraph test. Henry Becket says that it is administered to employees who have access to sensitive material when they are hired and then yearly after that. However, polygraph testing became very popular in the mid-1980s, as the government feared that more and more of its employees were taking drugs. While most intelligence employees saw the need for such testing, many resented the types of personal questions that were asked. Specifically, one routine, labeled the "lifestyle test," questioned intimately the types of sexual activity that an employee engaged in with his or her spouse. Many justifiably asked whether their employers had gone too far. While the accuracy of the lie detector is undetermined, it is an effective tool for use within the intelligence agencies. (2) In electronic surveillance, flutter is the frequency modulation of tones that are present in the record signal. The modulation is caused by eccentricities of rotating parts in the tape recorder. *See also:* Fluttered, Litmus Test.

References

Becket, Henry S. A. *The Dictionary of Espionage: Spookspeak into English.* New York: Stein and Day, 1986.

Godson, Roy, ed. *Intelligence Problems for the 1980s, Number 1: Elements of Intelligence.* Rev. ed. Washington, DC: National Strategy Information Center, 1983.

Kessler, Michael. *Wiretapping and Electronic Surveillance Commission Studies: Supporting Materials for the Report of the National Commission for the Review of Federal and State Laws Relating to Wiretapping and Electronic Surveillance, Washington, DC, 1976.* Townsend, PA: Loompanics Unlimited, 1976.

Quirk, John; Phillips, David; Cline, Ray; and Pforzheimer, Walter. *The Central Intelligence Agency: A Photographic History.* Guilford, CT: Foreign Intelligence Press, 1986.

Treverton, Gregory F. *Covert Action: The Limits of Intervention in the Postwar World.* New York: Basic Books, 1987.

Turner, Stansfield. *Secrecy and Democracy: The CIA in Transition.* Boston: Houghton Mifflin, 1985.

—**FLUTTERED** is a term used in clandestine and covert intelligence operations. Fluttered means to be examined by a lie detector. *See also:* Flutter.

References
Becket, Henry S. A. *The Dictionary of Espionage: Spookspeak into English.* New York: Stein and Day, 1986.

Deacon, Richard. *Spyclopedia: An Encyclopedia of Spies, Secret Services, Operations, Jargon, and All Subjects Related to the World of Espionage.* London: Macdonald, 1987.

Kessler, Ronald. *Spy vs. Spy: Stalking Soviet Spies in America.* New York: Charles Scribner's Sons, 1988.

Ranelagh, John. *The Agency: The Rise and Decline of the CIA.* New York: Simon and Schuster, 1986.

Treverton, Gregory F. *Covert Action: The Limits of Intervention in the Postwar World.* New York: Basic Books, 1987.

Turner, Stansfield. *Secrecy and Democracy: The CIA in Transition.* Boston: Houghton Mifflin, 1985.

—**FOR OFFICIAL USE ONLY (FOUO).** *See:* Security Classification.

—**FORCE,** for purposes of intelligence budgeting and the Planning, Programming, and Budgeting System (PPBS), means those units (kinds of units) that are identified in the force tabs of the secretary of defense's Five-Year Defense Program (FYDP). These units are the major combat-oriented forces and airlift and sealift forces. *See also:* Fiscal Guidance.

References
Pickett, George. "Congress, the Budget, and Intelligence." In *Intelligence Policy and Process,* edited by Alfred C. Maurer, Marion D. Turnstall, and James M. Keagle. Boulder, CO: Westview Press, 1985.

—**FORCE AND FINANCIAL PLAN (F&FP)** is the data base that describes the Five-Year Defense Plan (FYDP). *See also:* Fiscal Guidance.

References
Pickett, George. "Congress, the Budget, and Intelligence." In *Intelligence Policy and Process,* edited by Alfred C. Maurer, Marion D. Turnstall, and James M. Keagle. Boulder, CO: Westview Press, 1985.

—**FORCE DEVELOPMENT STUDIES** are published quarterly on Soviet forces and semiannually on the forces of the People's Republic of China by the Defense Intelligence Agency. They present concise overviews of the most significant military developments in both the strategic and the general purpose forces of these nations. These developments are placed in perspective against overall projections, trends, and comparative data. *See also:* Defense Intelligence Agency.

References
Von Hoene, John P. A. *Intelligence User's Guide.* Washington, DC: DIA, 1983.

—**FORD, GERALD.** Like his predecessors, President Ford grappled with the problem of presidential oversight of the Intelligence Community. However, for him this was an imperative, in that he inherited the White House from a man who had been driven from it by the Watergate scandal, an incident in which the Intelligence Community had been significantly involved. In 1974, when he had only been in office for about four months, Ford requested a report from William Colby, who was then serving as the director of Central Intelligence (DCI). Colby submitted a report that had been prepared by the agency for his predecessor, James Schlesinger, a document often referred to as the "Family Jewels." After reviewing the report, Ford established a presidential panel chaired by Vice President Nelson Rockefeller to investigate the CIA's domestic activities and operations.

In June 1975, the Rockefeller Report was submitted. It confirmed the accusations of illegal CIA activities, including domestic surveillance and spying. Among the commission's recommendations was one that called for a Joint Oversight Committee in Congress to oversee intelligence activities.

As the intelligence scandal worsened, President Ford took several steps. He dismissed Colby as DCI on November 2, 1975, replacing him with George Bush. Additionally, he issued Executive Order 11905 on February 18, 1976. This, the first public Executive directive on intelligence responsibilities and functions, reaffirmed the DCI's primary role in intelligence, abolished the United States Intelligence Board, the National Security Council Intelligence Committee, the IRAC, and the "40" Committee, and created a new United States Intelligence Board. The DCI's management was handled through a new Committee on Foreign Intelligence (CFI), which reported to the National Security Council. An Intelligence Oversight Board was also created to monitor intelligence activity.

In summary, Ford should be given high marks for his handling of the Intelligence Community problem. His dismissal of Colby was based on his belief that Colby was revealing too much to Congress and that Colby's dismissal was therefore a damage control operation that attempted to limit the damage caused by the congressional hearings. Ford's management of the problem was a reflection of his background, which had spanned both the White House and the Congress and had provided him with an exceptionally broad view of the government. His bureaucratic oversight efforts, as reflected in his Executive Order, were much more realistic than those of his predecessor, and his appointment of Bush to head the CIA and Rockefeller to head the presidential investigative commission were strokes of political genius that did much to defuse the crisis. Thus, in the final analysis, Ford stands among the best of the postwar presidents in his management of the Intelligence Community. *See also:* Presidential Oversight.

References

American Bar Association. *Oversight and Accountability of the U.S. Intelligence Agencies: An Evaluation.* Washington, DC: ABA, 1985.

Breckinridge, Scott D. *The CIA and the U.S. Intelligence System.* Boulder, CO: Westview Press, 1986.

Brinkley, David A., and Hull, Andrew W. *Estimative Intelligence: A Textbook on the History, Products, Uses and Writing of Intelligence Estimates.* Columbus, OH: Battelle, 1979.

Cline, Ray S. *The CIA Under Reagan, Bush, and Casey.* Washington, DC: Acropolis Books, 1981.

Corson, William R. *The Armies of Ignorance: The Rise of the American Intelligence Empire.* New York: Dial Press, 1977.

Crawford, David J. *Volunteers: The Betrayal of National Defense Secrets by Air Force Traitors.* Washington, DC: GPO, 1988.

Godson, Roy, ed. *Intelligence Problems for the 1980s, Number 1: Elements of Intelligence.* Rev. ed. Washington, DC: National Strategy Information Center, 1983.

Laqueur, Walter. *A World of Secrets.* New York: Basic Books, 1985.

Lowenthal, Mark M. *U.S. Intelligence: Evolution and Anatomy.* New York: Praeger, 1984.

Maurer, Alfred C.; Turnstall, Marion D.; and Keagle, James M. *Intelligence Policy and Process.* Boulder, CO: Westview Press, 1985.

Treverton, Gregory F. *Covert Action: The Limits of Intervention in the Postwar World.* New York: Basic Books, 1987.

Turner, Stansfield. *Secrecy and Democracy: The CIA in Transition.* Boston: Houghton Mifflin, 1985.

U.S. Congress. Senate. *Alleged Assassination Plots Involving Foreign Leaders: An Interim Report of the Select Committee to Study Governmental Operations with Respect to Intelligence Activities.* 94th Congress, 1st sess., Nov. 20, 1975. S. Rept. 94-465.

Von Hoene, John P. A. *Intelligence User's Guide.* Washington, DC: DIA, 1983.

—**FORECASTS.** *See:* Estimative Intelligence, Intelligence Estimates.

—**FOREIGN AFFAIRS COMMUNITY** is composed of the U.S. government departments, agencies, and other entities that are represented in U.S. diplomatic missions abroad, and of those that may not be represented abroad but are significantly involved in international activities with the governments of other nations.

References

Department of Defense, Defense Intelligence College. *Glossary of Intelligence Terms and Definitions.* Washington, DC: DIC, 1987.

Godson, Roy, ed. *Intelligence Problems for the 1980s, Number 1: Elements of Intelligence.* Rev. ed. Washington, DC: National Strategy Information Center, 1983.

Laqueur, Walter. *A World of Secrets.* New York: Basic Books, 1985.

Treverton, Gregory F. *Covert Action: The Limits of Intervention in the Postwar World.* New York: Basic Books, 1987.

Turner, Stansfield. *Secrecy and Democracy: The CIA in Transition.* Boston: Houghton Mifflin, 1985.

—**FOREIGN AIRCRAFT PRODUCTION (FOAP)** is published by the Defense Intelligence Agency as part of its military economic and production series. The FOAP reports on aircraft production and research and development activities by country. *See also:* Defense Intelligence Agency.

References

Von Hoene, John P. A. *Intelligence User's Guide.* Washington, DC: DIA, 1983.

—**FOREIGN ARMY MATERIEL PRODUCTION (FAMP)** is produced by the Defense Intelligence Agency. It is a worldwide study that presents all types of data on ground forces' material production, and it also discusses the capabilities of each nation's ground forces. *See also:* Defense Intelligence Agency.

References

Von Hoene, John P. A. *Intelligence User's Guide.* Washington, DC: DIA, 1983.

—**FOREIGN BROADCAST INFORMATION DIVISION** was an element of the Central Intelligence Group (CIG) that monitored overseas broadcasts. It became a part of the Directorate for Intelligence (DDI) in 1952 and was renamed the Foreign Broadcast Information Service (FBIS) in 1965. *See also:* Central Intelligence Agency.

References

Corson, William R. *The Armies of Ignorance: The Rise of the American Intelligence Empire.* New York: Dial Press, 1977.

Fain, Tyrus G.; Plant, Katharine C.; and Milloy, Ross. *The Intelligence Community: History, Organization, and Issues.* Public Documents Series. New York: R.R. Bowker, 1977.

Godson, Roy, ed. *Intelligence Problems for the 1980s, Number 1: Elements of Intelligence.* Rev. ed. Washington, DC: National Strategy Information Center, 1983.

Kent, Sherman. *Strategic Intelligence for American World Policy.* Princeton, NJ: Princeton University Press, 1966.

Treverton, Gregory F. *Covert Action: The Limits of Intervention in the Postwar World.* New York: Basic Books, 1987.

Turner, Stansfield. *Secrecy and Democracy: The CIA in Transition.* Boston: Houghton Mifflin, 1985.

—**FOREIGN BROADCAST INFORMATION SERVICE.** *See:* Central Intelligence Agency *under* Directorate for Science and Technology.

—**FOREIGN COUNTERINTELLIGENCE (FCI)** is a general intelligence term that includes both the intelligence activity and the finished intelligence that is produced as a result of these operations. Foreign counterintelligence is intended to detect, counteract, and prevent espionage and other clandestine intelligence activities, sabotage, international terrorist activities, or assassinations conducted on behalf of foreign powers, organizations, or persons. Foreign counterintel-

ligence does not include personnel, physical, document, or communications security programs. *See also:* Communications Security, Counterintelligence.

References

Department of Defense, Defense Intelligence College. *Glossary of Intelligence Terms and Definitions.* Washington, DC: DIC, 1987.

Godson, Roy, ed. *Intelligence Problems for the 1980s, Number 1: Elements of Intelligence.* Rev. ed. Washington, DC: National Strategy Information Center, 1983.

———. *Intelligence Problems for the 1980s, Number 3: Counterintelligence.* Washington, DC: National Strategy Information Center, 1980.

———. *Intelligence Problems for the 1980s, Number 4: Covert Action.* Washington, DC: National Strategy Information Center, 1981.

———. *Intelligence Problems for the 1980s, Number 5: Clandestine Collection.* Washington, DC: National Strategy Information Center, 1982.

Laqueur, Walter. *A World of Secrets.* New York: Basic Books, 1985.

Turner, Stansfield. *Secrecy and Democracy: The CIA in Transition.* Boston: Houghton Mifflin, 1985.

—**FOREIGN INSTRUMENTATION SIGNALS (FIS)** is a technical intelligence term for electromagnetic signals that are associated with testing and operationally deploying non-U.S. aerospace, surface, and subsurface systems that may have either military or civilian application. It includes but is not limited to telemetry, beaconry, electronic interrogation, tracking/fusing/arming command system, and video data link signals. *See also:* Telemetry Intelligence.

References

Department of Defense, Defense Intelligence College. *Glossary of Intelligence Terms and Definitions.* Washington, DC: DIC, 1987.

Godson, Roy, ed. *Intelligence Problems for the 1980s, Number 1: Elements of Intelligence.* Rev. ed. Washington, DC: National Strategy Information Center, 1983.

—**FOREIGN INSTRUMENTATION SIGNALS INTELLIGENCE (FISINT)** is the technical and intelligence information that is derived from processing intercepted foreign instrumentation signals.

References

Department of Defense, Defense Intelligence College. *Glossary of Intelligence Terms and Definitions.* Washington, DC: DIC, 1987.

—FOREIGN INSTRUMENTATION SIGNALS (FIS) INTELLIGENCE INFORMATION REPORTING is all FIS raw data and products, including original and duplicate analog and digital recordings; data displays and listings; field reports; intercept listings; results of signals analysis, data manipulation, and data analysis; and product reports.

References

Muzerall, Joseph V., and Carty, Thomas P. "COMSEC and Its Need for Key Management." *DP&CS* (Spring 1987). Ware, Willis H. "Information Systems, Security, and Privacy." *EDUCOM Bulletin* (Summer 1984).

—FOREIGN INSTRUMENTATION SIGNALS (FIS) INTERNALS are preselected measurements from onboard engineering sensors or guidance computer calculations that are superimposed (or "modulated") on a radio carrier and are transmitted to specially configured instrumentation sites on the ground. The measurement data are separated (or "demodulated") from the radio signal and are displayed for study by test and evaluation engineers.

References

U.S. Congress. *Central Intelligence Information Act. Public Law 98-477, October 15, 1984.* Washington, DC: GPO, 1984.

—FOREIGN INTELLIGENCE (FI) is a general intelligence term with several meanings. (1) It is the product that results from collecting, evaluating, analyzing, integrating, and interpreting intelligence information about a foreign power that is of value to U.S. national security, foreign relations, or economic interests and that is provided by a government intelligence agency. (2) The U.S. Army defines foreign intelligence in a slightly different way. Foreign intelligence includes all evaluated information concerning one or more aspects of foreign nations, foreign materiel, or areas of operations of immediate or potential significance to the accomplishment of the Army mission, and is obtained and disseminated through intelligence channels. (3) Foreign intelligence is a term that has caused considerable disagreement in congressional investigations of the Intelligence Community. The Church Committee defined it merely as "intelligence concerning areas outside the United States." (4) A more complete definition that also infers greater latitude for intelligence operations is given by the U.S. Signals Intelligence Directive. It defines foreign intelligence as:

a. Information concerning the capabilities, intentions and activities of any foreign power, or of any non-U.S. person, whether within or outside the United States or concerning areas outside the United States.
b. Information relating to the ability of the United States to protect itself against actual or potential attack or other hostile acts of a foreign power or its agents.
c. Information with respect to foreign powers or non-U.S. persons which because of its importance is deemed essential to the security of the United States or the conduct of its foreign affairs.
d. Information relating to the ability of the United States to defend itself against the activities of foreign intelligence services.

(5) An alternative definition resulted from Presidential Executive Order 12333, "United States Intelligence Activities," dated December 4, 1981. It defined foreign intelligence as "information relating to the capabilities, intentions and activities of foreign powers, organizations or persons, but not including counterintelligence except for information on international terrorist activities." *See also:* Intelligence Cycle.

References

Department of Defense. *Activities of DoD Intelligence Components that Affect U.S. Persons (Department of Defense Directive 5240.1).* Washington, DC: DoD, 1982.

Department of Defense, Defense Intelligence College. *Glossary of Intelligence Terms and Definitions.* Washington, DC: DIC, 1987.

Department of Defense, Joint Chiefs of Staff. *Department of Defense Dictionary of Military and Related Terms.* Washington, DC: GPO, 1986.

Department of Defense, U.S. Army. *RDTE Managers Intelligence and Threat Support Guide.* Alexandria, VA: Headquarters, Army Materiel Development and Readiness Command, 1983.

Godson, Roy, ed. *Intelligence Problems for the 1980s, Number 1: Elements of Intelligence.* Rev. ed. Washington, DC: National Strategy Information Center, 1983.

———. *Intelligence Problems for the 1980s, Number 2: Analysis and Estimates.* Washington, DC: National Strategy Information Center, 1980.

———. *Intelligence Problems for the 1980s, Number 3: Counterintelligence.* Washington, DC: National Strategy Information Center, 1980.

———. *Intelligence Problems for the 1980s, Number 4: Covert Action.* Washington, DC: National Strategy Information Center, 1981.

———. *Intelligence Problems for the 1980s, Number 5: Clandestine Collection.* Washington, DC: National Strategy Information Center, 1982.

Kent, Sherman. *Strategic Intelligence for American World Policy.* Princeton, NJ: Princeton University Press, 1966.

Laqueur, Walter. *A World of Secrets.* New York: Basic Books, 1985.

Turner, Stansfield. *Secrecy and Democracy: The CIA in Transition.* Boston: Houghton Mifflin, 1985.

U.S. Congress. Senate. *Final Report of the Senate Select Committee to Study Government Operations with Respect to Intelligence Activities. Report 94-755. Book I, Foreign and Military Intelligence.* Washington, DC: GPO, 1976.

—**FOREIGN INTELLIGENCE SERVICE** is the general intelligence term for an organization of a foreign government that conducts intelligence activity. *See also:* Federal Intelligence Agency, Government Communications Headquarters, KGB.

References

Department of Defense, Defense Intelligence College. *Glossary of Intelligence Terms and Definitions.* Washington, DC: DIC, 1987.

—**FOREIGN INTELLIGENCE SURVEILLANCE ACT (FISA)** of 1978 instituted judicial review of proposals for electronic surveillance by the Intelligence Community within the United States. Under it, the attorney general was to approve government applications for electronic surveillance, accompanied by the appropriate justifications and certifications. The application then went to a "FISA court," where it was reviewed. If approved by the court, then the court would issue warrants permitting electronic surveillance activities that met the requisite standards.

In 1984, the Senate Select Committee on Intelligence reviewed the effectiveness of the FISA during its first five years of existence and concluded that it had achieved its initial purposes of protecting the rights of the individual on the one hand and that it had resolved the legal uncertainties that had inhibited electronic surveillance on the other. *See also:* Congressional Oversight.

References

American Bar Association. *Oversight and Accountability of the U.S. Intelligence Agencies: An Evaluation.* Washington, DC: ABA, 1985.

Godson, Roy, ed. *Intelligence Problems for the 1980s, Number 1: Elements of Intelligence.* Rev.

ed. Washington, DC: National Strategy Information Center, 1983.

Kornblum, Allan. *Intelligence and the Law: Cases and Materials.* Vol. IV. Washington, DC: DIC, 1987.

Lefever, Ernest W., and Godson, Roy. *The CIA and the American Ethic: An Unfinished Debate.* Washington, DC: Ethics and Public Policy Center, Georgetown University, 1979.

Maurer, Alfred C.; Turnstall, Marion D.; and Keagle, James M. *Intelligence Policy and Process.* Boulder, CO: Westview Press, 1985.

Oseth, John M. *Regulating U.S. Intelligence Operations: A Study in the Definition of the National Interest.* Frankfurt: University of Kentucky Press, 1985.

U.S. Congress. Senate. *The Foreign Intelligence Surveillance Act of 1978: The First Five Years: Report of the Select Committee on Intelligence, U.S. Senate.* Washington, DC: GPO, 1984.

—**FOREIGN INTERNAL DEFENSE** is a general intelligence term. It occurs when the military and civilian agencies of a government participate in any of the action programs taken by another country to free and protect its society from subversion, lawlessness, and insurgency.

References

American Bar Association. *Oversight and Accountability of the U.S. Intelligence Agencies: An Evaluation.* Washington, DC: ABA, 1985.

Department of Defense, Joint Chiefs of Staff. *Department of Defense Dictionary of Military and Related Terms.* Washington, DC: GPO, 1986.

Godson, Roy, ed. *Intelligence Problems for the 1980s, Number 1: Elements of Intelligence.* Rev. ed. Washington, DC: National Strategy Information Center, 1983.

Maurer, Alfred C.; Turnstall, Marion D.; and Keagle, James M. *Intelligence Policy and Process.* Boulder, CO: Westview Press, 1985.

Treverton, Gregory F. *Covert Action: The Limits of Intervention in the Postwar World.* New York: Basic Books, 1987.

Turner, Stansfield. *Secrecy and Democracy: The CIA in Transition.* Boston: Houghton Mifflin, 1985.

—**FOREIGN MATERIEL (FM OR FORMAT),** in the broader sense, means not only the materiel (equipment), but also the maintenance, operations, and support of the equipment. Since most of the sophisticated military equipment in use today is produced by relatively few nations, it is also important to evaluate the equipment mix in order to assess the degree of compatibility of several systems from different sources. *See also:* Intelligence Cycle, Scientific and Technical Intelligence.

References

Pickett, George. "Congress, the Budget, and Intelligence." In *Intelligence Policy and Process,* edited by Alfred C. Maurer, Marion D. Turnstall, and James M. Keagle. Boulder, CO: Westview Press, 1985.

—**FOREIGN MATERIEL ACQUISITION (FMA)** means acquiring foreign weapon systems for research, testing, and evaluation purposes. Each of the services has a facility for testing such equipment once it has been acquired. Such acquisition and testing, if it can be accomplished, provides the optimal means of understanding and defeating a system produced by a potential adversary. *See also:* Foreign Materiel.

References

Pickett, George. "Congress, the Budget, and Intelligence." In *Intelligence Policy and Process,* edited by Alfred C. Maurer, Marion D. Turnstall, and James M. Keagle. Boulder, CO: Westview Press, 1985.

—**FOREIGN MATERIEL EXPLOITATION CATALOG (FMEC)** is a document that provides a multiservice compilation of foreign materiel exploitation reports that have been published by the components of the Department of Defense and the Central Intelligence Agency. *See also:* Foreign Materiel.

References

Von Hoene, John P. A. *Intelligence User's Guide.* Washington, DC: DIA, 1983.

—**FOREIGN MATERIEL EXPLOITATION PROGRAM (FMEP)** is coordinated by the Directorate for Scientific and Technical Intelligence (DT), Defense Intelligence Agency. *See also:* Foreign Materiel.

References

Department of Defense, Defense Intelligence Agency. *Organization, Mission, and Key Personnel.* Washington, DC: DIA, 1986.

Department of Defense, U.S. Army. *AIA: Threat Analysis.* Falls Church, VA: U.S. Army Intelligence Agency, 1987.

—**FOREIGN MATERIEL EXPLOITATION REPORT (FMER)** is the report produced by a facility after it has examined, tested, and analyzed a given piece of foreign materiel. Such a report discusses the capabilities and limitations of the system and is invaluable in producing systems to defeat the system. *See also:* Foreign Materiel.

References

Department of Defense, U.S. Army. *AIA: Threat Analysis.* Falls Church, VA: U.S. Army Intelligence Agency, 1987.

—**FOREIGN MATERIEL INTELLIGENCE** is the intelligence that results from exploiting foreign materiel. *See also:* Exploitation, Foreign Materiel.

References

Department of Defense, Defense Intelligence College. *Glossary of Intelligence Terms and Definitions.* Washington, DC: DIC, 1987.

—**FOREIGN MILITARY ASSISTANCE (FOMA)** is published by the Defense Intelligence Agency as part of its Military Economic and Production Studies series. The FOMA provides detailed information on worldwide foreign military assistance, excluding U.S. data. *See also:* Defense Intelligence Agency.

References

Treverton, Gregory F. *Covert Action: The Limits of Intervention in the Postwar World.* New York: Basic Books, 1987.

Von Hoene, John P. A. *Intelligence User's Guide.* Washington, DC: DIA, 1983.

—**FOREIGN MISSILE PRODUCTION (FOMP)** is published by the Defense Intelligence Agency as part of its Military Economic and Production Studies series. The FOMP contains information about missile manufacturing and research and development activities by country. *See also:* Defense Intelligence Agency.

References

Von Hoene, John P. A. *Intelligence User's Guide.* Washington, DC: DIA, 1983.

—**FOREIGN OFFICIAL** is a person acting officially on behalf of a foreign power and is attached to a foreign diplomatic establishment or one that is under the control of a foreign power, or who is employed by a public international organization.

See also: Chief of Base, Chief of Outpost, Chief of Station, Cover, Cover Name, Cover Organizations, Illegal Agent, Illegal Communication, Illegal Net, Illegal Operations, Illegal Residency, Illegal Support Officer, Legal, Legal Residency, Moonlight Extradition, Pudding, Pudding Club, Third Country Operation.

References

Department of Defense, Defense Intelligence College. *Glossary of Intelligence Terms and Definitions.* Washington, DC: DIC, 1987.

—**FOREIGN POWER** is a definition that resulted from Presidential Executive Order 12333, "United States Intelligence Activities," dated December 4, 1981. It is any foreign government, regardless of whether it is recognized by the United States, foreign-based political party or faction of such a party, foreign military force, foreign-based terrorist group, or any organization composed in major part of any such entity or entities.

References

Department of Defense. *Activities of DoD Intelligence Components that Affect U.S. Persons (Department of Defense Directive 5240.1).* Washington, DC: DoD, 1982.

Godson, Roy, ed. *Intelligence Problems for the 1980s, Number 1: Elements of Intelligence.* Rev. ed. Washington, DC: National Strategy Information Center, 1983.

Turner, Stansfield. *Secrecy and Democracy: The CIA in Transition.* Boston: Houghton Mifflin, 1985.

—**FOREIGN SCIENCE AND TECHNOLOGY CENTER (FSTC), U.S. ARMY,** is the Army's scientific and technical intelligence center. It explores foreign developments in the sciences, engineering, and the applied technologies. FSTC analyzes the current, projected, and assigned foreign ground force systems and related sciences and technologies. It also implements the Army's foreign materiel exploitation program.

Its Information Services Division (ISD) provides vital and comprehensive information support to the research, development, test, and evaluation (RDTE) efforts through the Army's Foreign Intelligence Office (FIO) system. The ISD manages the Army's acquisition of intelligence materials through the Statement of Intelligence Interest (SII), maintains an extensive library of foreign intelligence and open-source scientific and technical materials, supports both Army research and development and intelligence needs

for translations, and has access to an extensive system for search and retrieval of documents throughout the Intelligence Community, the rest of the federal government, and private library systems. The ISD is the principal source for scientific and technical documents that are not available in local intelligence files or in the local technical library. *See also:* Scientific and Technical Intelligence.

References

Department of Defense, U.S. Army. *AIA: Threat Analysis.* Falls Church, VA: U.S. Army Intelligence Agency, 1987. *RDTE Managers Intelligence and Threat Support Guide.* Alexandria, VA: Headquarters, Army Materiel Development and Readiness Command, 1983.

—**FOREIGN SERVICE OFFICER (FSO)** is a diplomatic professional in the State Department.

References

Laqueur, Walter. *A World of Secrets.* New York: Basic Books, 1985.

Lowenthal, Mark M. *U.S. Intelligence: Evolution and Anatomy.* New York: Praeger, 1984.

Turner, Stansfield. *Secrecy and Democracy: The CIA in Transition.* Boston: Houghton Mifflin, 1985.

—**FOREIGN TECHNOLOGY DIVISION (FTD).** *See:* Air Force Intelligence.

—**FOREIGN TELECOMMUNICATION SYSTEMS (FOTELSYS)** is a publication prepared by the Defense Intelligence Agency as part of its Facilities and Installations Studies series. FOTELSYS presents an analysis of the civil and military telecommunications structure and facilities of a geographic region. *See also:* Defense Intelligence Agency, Transportation and Telecommunications Systems.

References

Von Hoene, John P. A. *Intelligence User's Guide.* Washington, DC: DIA, 1983.

—**FORMERLY RESTRICTED DATA (FRD)** is information that has been removed from the RESTRICTED DATA category after a joint decision has been made by the Department of Energy and the Department of Defense that such information relates primarily to the military use of atomic weapons and that such information can be adequately protected as classified defense information. *See also:* Restricted Data.

References

Department of Defense, Defense Intelligence Agency. *Defense Intelligence Agency Manual.* Washington, DC: DIA, 1986.

Department of Defense, Joint Chiefs of Staff. *Department of Defense Dictionary of Military and Related Terms.* Washington, DC: GPO, 1986.

—**FORT HOLABIRD,** known as "The Bird," was originally an Army locomotive repair depot on the outskirts of Baltimore, Maryland. At various times it housed the Army Intelligence Command, the Army Intelligence School, and various other activities. Fort Holabird, as such, no longer exists. The Army's intelligence school and some of its other elements are now located in impressive facilities at Fort Huachuca, Arizona.

References

Becket, Henry S. A. *The Dictionary of Espionage: Spookspeak into English.* New York: Stein and Day, 1986.

Von Hoene, John P. A. *Intelligence User's Guide.* Washington, DC: DIA, 1983.

—**"40" COMMITTEE,** of the National Security Council, was created in 1948 to review proposed covert operations. As such, it was a vital part of presidential oversight of the Intelligence Community. It was abolished in 1970. *See also:* National Security Council.

References

Laqueur, Walter. *A World of Secrets.* New York: Basic Books, 1985.

Lowenthal, Mark M. *U.S. Intelligence: Evolution and Anatomy.* New York: Praeger, 1984.

Treverton, Gregory F. *Covert Action: The Limits of Intervention in the Postwar World.* New York: Basic Books, 1987.

—**FORWARD LINE OF OWN TROOPS (FLOT)** is an Army term for a line that indicates the most forward positions of friendly forces in any kind of military operation at a specific time. These positions may be occupied by elements of the covering force or the advanced guard.

References

Department of Defense, U.S. Army. *Intelligence and Electronic Warfare Operations.* Field Manual FM 34-1. Washington, DC: Headquarters, Department of the Army, 1984.

————. *Military Intelligence Battalion Combat Electronic Warfare and Intelligence (Aerial Exploitation) (Corps).* Field Manual FM 34-22. Washington, DC: Headquarters, Department of the Army, 1984.

————. *Military Intelligence Battalion (Combat Electronic Warfare Intelligence) (Division).* Field Manual FM 34-10. Washington, DC: Headquarters, Department of the Army, 1981.

————. *Military Intelligence Battalion (CEWI) (Operations) (Corps).* Field Manual FM 34-21. Washington, DC: Headquarters, Department of the Army, 1982.

————. *Military Intelligence Battalion (CEWI) (Tactical Exploitation) (Corps): Counterintelligence, Interrogation, Electronic Warfare.* Field Manual FM 34-23. Washington, DC: Headquarters, Department of the Army, 1985.

————. *Military Intelligence Group (Combat Electronic Warfare and Intelligence) (Corps).* Field Manual FM 34-20. Washington, DC: Headquarters, Department of the Army, 1983.

—**FORWARD LOOKING INFRARED SYSTEM (FLIR)** is an intelligence imagery and photoreconnaissance system, an infrared imagery system that scans the scene by internal means. It can be spaceborne, airborne, seaborne, mounted on a ground vehicle, or placed at a fixed site. Its field of view is determined by the optics used, the scanning mechanism, and the dimensions of the detector array. *See also:* Side-Looking Airborne Radar.

References

Department of Defense, Defense Intelligence College. *Glossary of Intelligence Terms and Definitions.* Washington, DC: DIC, 1987.

—**FRAME,** in photography, is a single exposure that is contained within a continuous sequence of photographs.

References

Department of Defense, Joint Chiefs of Staff. *Department of Defense Dictionary of Military and Related Terms.* Washington, DC: GPO, 1986.

—**FREEDOM OF INFORMATION ACT (FOIA),** passed in 1966 and amended substantially in 1974, established procedures for releasing government information to people who requested it and were outside the government. The FOIA established specific provisions concerning how an agency would inform the public, in the *Fed-*

eral Register, of its procedures for obtaining information. Additionally, it provided for punishment by law of those individuals who illegally withheld information from the public. Finally, it required each agency to report to Congress annually concerning the number of FOIA cases in which the requests for information were refused. *See also:* Access, Authorized, Classification, Classified Information, Code Word, Compromise, Declassification, Disclosure, Downgrade, Limited Access Area, Need-To-Know, Need-to-Know Principle, No-Lone Zone, Nondisclosure Agreement, Nondiscussion Area, Sanitization, Sanitize, Sanitized Area, Security Certification, Security Classification, Sensitive Compartmented Information, Sensitive Compartmented Information Facility, Two-Person Control.

References

American Bar Association. *Oversight and Accountability of the U.S. Intelligence Agencies: An Evaluation.* Washington, DC: ABA, 1985.

Godson, Roy, ed. *Intelligence Problems for the 1980s, Number 1: Elements of Intelligence.* Rev. ed. Washington, DC: National Strategy Information Center, 1983.

Lowenthal, Mark M. *U.S. Intelligence: Evolution and Anatomy.* New York: Praeger, 1984.

Maurer, Alfred C.; Turnstall, Marion D.; and Keagle, James M. *Intelligence Policy and Process.* Boulder, CO: Westview Press, 1985.

Oseth, John M. *Regulating U.S. Intelligence Operations: A Study in the Definition of the National Interest.* Frankfurt: University of Kentucky Press, 1985.

Turner, Stansfield. *Secrecy and Democracy: The CIA in Transition.* Boston: Houghton Mifflin, 1985.

—**FRENCH, GEORGE H.,** an Air Force captain, was apprehended in April 1957 by Air Force and federal agents posing as Soviet agents. French had offered to pass classified defense information, and subsequent searches revealed that he had 60 classified documents. He appears to have been motivated by financial difficulties and gambling debts. He was convicted of espionage on September 20, 1957, and received a life sentence. The court martial sentence was later reduced to ten years.

References

Allen, Thomas B., and Polmar, Norman. *Merchants of Treason: America's Secrets for Sale.* New York: Delacorte Press, 1988.

Crawford, David J. *Volunteers: The Betrayal of National Defense Secrets by Air Force Traitors.* Washington, DC: GPO, 1988.

—**FRIEND** is a term used in clandestine and covert intelligence operations to describe a person who is willing to work for an intelligence agency by influencing a foreign government. His motivation is, in almost all cases, ideological. *See also:* Agent, Agent of Influence, Case, Case Officer, Co-Opted Worker, Co-Optees, Double Agent, Informant, Inside Man, Mole, Nash, Recruitment, Recruitment in Place, Sleeper, Special Activities.

References

Becket, Henry S. A. *The Dictionary of Espionage: Spookspeak into English.* New York: Stein and Day, 1986.

Deacon, Richard. *Spyclopedia: An Encyclopedia of Spies, Secret Services, Operations, Jargon, and All Subjects Related to the World of Espionage.* London: Macdonald, 1987.

Ranelagh, John. *The Agency: The Rise and Decline of the CIA.* New York: Simon and Schuster, 1986.

—**FROST, VICE ADMIRAL LAURENCE H., U.S. NAVY,** served as the director of the National Security Agency (NSA) from November 1960 to June 30, 1962. A graduate of Annapolis, Frost had an extensive communications background. Awarded a Bronze and two Silver Stars for his duty as commanding officer of the destroyer USS *Weller* in the Pacific in World War II, Frost subsequently served in several intelligence billets, then served as chief of staff at the NSA from 1953 to 1955. He then returned to the Navy, serving as director of Naval Intelligence. In 1960, he accepted assignment as director of the NSA. Following a dispute with the Pentagon in 1962, Frost was reassigned to the Potomac River Naval Command, from which he retired. *See also:* National Security Agency.

References

Bamford, James. *The Puzzle Palace: A Report on America's Most Secret Agency.* New York: Penguin Books, 1983.

—**FULL OPERATIONAL CAPABILITY (FOC)** is the point at which a Department of Defense Intelligence Information System (DODIIS) subsystem satisfies all functional design requirements and is accepted for operational use by the functional sponsor. *See also:* Defense Intelligence Agency.

References

Department of Defense, Defense Intelligence Agency. *Defense Intelligence Agency Manual.* Washington, DC: DIA, 1987.

—**FUMIGATE** is a term used in counterintelligence operations to describe the use of electronic devices to locate and remove or neutralize listening devices from a room or area. *See also:* Bug, Bugging, Burn, Burnt, Clean, Concealment Devices, Damage Assessment, Damage Control, Exterminators, Harmonica Bug, Sound Man, Sound School, Special Activities, Sterile Telephone, Sterility Coding, Sterilize.

References

Becket, Henry S. A. *The Dictionary of Espionage: Spookspeak into English.* New York: Stein and Day, 1986.

Deacon, Richard. *Spyclopedia: An Encyclopedia of Spies, Secret Services, Operations, Jargon, and All Subjects Related to the World of Espionage.* London: Macdonald, 1987.

—**FUNCTIONAL ARCHITECTURE** is a general intelligence term for an operational and organizational framework of activity and events that are designed to accomplish a predefined purpose. *See also:* Defense Intelligence Agency.

References

Department of Defense, Defense Intelligence Agency. *Defense Intelligence Agency Manual.* Washington, DC: DIA, 1987.

—**FUNCTIONAL SPONSOR** is the General Defense Intelligence Community (GDIC) functional manager who initiates a Statement of Functional Requirement (SFR) that is subsequently validated and approved. He is the sponsor of a GDIC Program and System Development effort. *See also:* Defense Intelligence Agency.

References

Department of Defense, Defense Intelligence Agency. *Defense Intelligence Agency Manual.* Washington, DC: DIA, 1987.

—**FUNDAMENTAL INTELLIGENCE DATA BASE** is maintained by the Defense Intelligence Agency. It is a structured framework of basic data elements, the lowest level of intelligence that must be maintained on an area. It provides a founda-tion on which to build when a low priority suddenly demands increased attention. *See also:* Defense Intelligence Agency.

References

Von Hoene, John P. A. *Intelligence User's Guide.* Washington, DC: DIA, 1983.

—**FUR-LINED SEAT COVER** is a term that is used in clandestine and covert intelligence operations. It is a euphemistic reference to an agent who has a female passenger. *See also:* Honey Trap, Ladies, Raven, Sisters, Swallow, Swallow's Nest, Taxi.

References

Deacon, Richard. *Spyclopedia: An Encyclopedia of Spies, Secret Services, Operations, Jargon, and All Subjects Related to the World of Espionage.* London: Macdonald, 1987.

—**FUSION,** a term often used in the Department of Defense, means integrating intelligence information from several sources in order to produce a single intelligence product. *See also:* Intelligence Cycle.

References

Department of Defense, Defense Intelligence College. *Glossary of Intelligence Terms and Definitions.* Washington, DC: DIC, 1987.

Godson, Roy, ed. *Intelligence Problems for the 1980s, Number 1: Elements of Intelligence.* Rev. ed. Washington, DC: National Strategy Information Center, 1983.

—**FUSION CENTER** is a Department of Defense term for an organization that is responsible for integrating compartmented intelligence information with all other intelligence information in the support of military operations. *See also:* Intelligence Cycle.

References

Department of Defense, Defense Intelligence College. *Glossary of Intelligence Terms and Definitions.* Washington, DC: DIC, 1987.

Godson, Roy, ed. *Intelligence Problems for the 1980s, Number 1: Elements of Intelligence.* Rev. ed. Washington, DC: National Strategy Information Center, 1983.

G

Clancy, Tom. *The Cardinal of the Kremlin.* New York: Putnam, 1988.

Deacon, Richard. *Spyclopedia: An Encyclopedia of Spies, Secret Services, Operations, Jargon, and All Subjects Related to the World of Espionage.* London: Macdonald, 1987.

—**G GROUP** is a component of one of the ten branches that constitute the National Security Agency. *See:* National Security Agency.

References

Bamford, James. *The Puzzle Palace: A Report on America's Most Secret Agency.* New York: Penguin Books, 1983.

—**G2, ASSISTANT CHIEF OF STAFF, INTELLIGENCE,** is the principal staff officer for the commander on all military intelligence (MI) matters. The G2 acquires intelligence information and data; analyzes and evaluates it; and presents the assessment evaluation and recommendation to the commander.

References

Department of Defense, U.S. Army. *Staff Organizations and Operations.* Field Manual FM 101-5. Washington, DC: Headquarters, Department of the Army, 1984.

—**G3, ASSISTANT CHIEF OF STAFF, OPERATIONS,** is the principal staff officer for the commander in matters concerning operations, plans, organization, and training. The nature of the operations officer's responsibilities requires a high degree of coordination with other staff members.

References

Department of Defense, U.S. Army. *Staff Organizations and Operations.* Field Manual FM 101-5. Washington, DC: Headquarters, Department of the Army, 1984.

—**GAME** is a term used in clandestine and covert intelligence operations. The game is the intelligence game or intelligence world. A person is said to be in the game if he works in intelligence. *See also:* Special Activities.

References

Becket, Henry S. A. *The Dictionary of Espionage: Spookspeak into English.* New York: Stein and Day, 1986.

—**GAP** is an electronic surveillance term that means a segment of a recording in which the character of the recorded material changes for no apparent reason.

References

Kessler, Michael. *Wiretapping and Electronic Surveillance Commission Studies: Supporting Materials for the Report of the National Commission for the Review of Federal and State Laws Relating to Wiretapping and Electronic Surveillance, Washington, DC, 1976.* Townsend, PA: Loompanics Unlimited, 1976.

—**GARBLE,** a term used in communications intelligence, communications security, operations security, and signals analysis, is the mutilation of any part of a message or transmitted intelligence. *See also:* Communications Security.

References

Department of Defense, Joint Chiefs of Staff. *Department of Defense Dictionary of Military and Related Terms.* Washington, DC: GPO, 1986.

—**GAYLER, VICE ADMIRAL NOEL, U.S. NAVY,** served as the director of the National Security Agency (NSA) from August 1, 1969, until August 24, 1972. Born on December 25, 1914, Gayler had graduated from the Naval Academy, had spent most of his career as a fighter pilot, and had been awarded three Silver Stars for his service in World War II. His postwar tours included serving as aide to Secretary of the Navy Thomas S. Gates, Jr., as naval attaché to London, and as deputy director of the Joint Strategic Planning Staff. Gayler was unlike his predecessors at the NSA. They had been assigned to the agency as their twilight tour, the last major job before retirement. Gayler was young enough to anticipate an additional major tour before his retirement. Three years into his tour as director, Gayler was selected for the prestigious assignment as commander in chief, Pacific. Thus, beginning with Gayler, the directorship was no longer a dead-end job. Rather, it became a springboard to four-star rank. *See also:* National Security Agency.

References

Bamford, James. *The Puzzle Palace: A Report on America's Most Secret Agency.* New York: Penguin Books, 1983.

—**GENERAL COUNSEL.** *See:* Central Intelligence Agency, Defense Intelligence Agency.

—**GENERAL DECLASSIFICATION SCHEDULE (GDS).** When collateral material (material that is not within sensitive compartmented information channels) is classified, it comes under a general declassification schedule. This means that its classification will be lowered at specific time intervals and that it will be declassified after a certain date. Should the originator believe that the information is sufficiently sensitive that it should not be downgraded and declassified automatically, he or she can request that it be exempted from the GDS. In this case, the classification cannot be changed without a specific review and assessment of the document. *See also:* Classification, Classification Authority, Classification Review, Classified Information, Declassification, Declassification and Downgrading Instructions, Physical Security, Security Classification.

References

Department of Defense, Defense Intelligence Agency. *Defense Intelligence Agency Manual.* Washington, DC: DIA, 1987.

Godson, Roy, ed. *Intelligence Problems for the 1980s, Number 1: Elements of Intelligence.* Rev. ed. Washington, DC: National Strategy Information Center, 1983.

Maurer, Alfred C.; Turnstall, Marion D.; and Keagle, James M. *Intelligence Policy and Process.* Boulder, CO: Westview Press, 1985.

—**GENERAL DEFENSE INTELLIGENCE COMMUNITY (GDIC)** is the Defense Intelligence Agency and those commands, activities, and elements of the military services, Unified and Specified Commands, and their subordinated Unified and Component Commands that are funded through the General Defense Intelligence Program (GDIP). GDIC members are tasked with collecting, exploiting, producing, and disseminating intelligence and intelligence information to military operational commanders and national-level decisionmakers.

References

American Bar Association. *Oversight and Accountability of the U.S. Intelligence Agencies: An Evaluation.* Washington, DC: ABA, 1985.

Department of Defense, Defense Intelligence Agency. *Defense Intelligence Agency Manual.* Washington, DC: DIA, 1987.

Godson, Roy, ed. *Intelligence Problems for the 1980s, Number 1: Elements of Intelligence.* Rev. ed. Washington, DC: National Strategy Information Center, 1983.

Laqueur, Walter. *A World of Secrets.* New York: Basic Books, 1985.

Maurer, Alfred C.; Turnstall, Marion D.; and Keagle, James M. *Intelligence Policy and Process.* Boulder, CO: Westview Press, 1985.

—**GENERAL DEFENSE INTELLIGENCE COMMUNITY FUNCTIONAL MANAGER** is a GDIC component official who is responsible for both the structure and operation of GDIC component functional architecture.

References

American Bar Association. *Oversight and Accountability of the U.S. Intelligence Agencies: An Evaluation.* Washington, DC: ABA, 1985.

Department of Defense, Defense Intelligence Agency. *Defense Intelligence Agency Manual.* Washington, DC: DIA, 1987.

Laqueur, Walter. *A World of Secrets.* New York: Basic Books, 1985.

Maurer, Alfred C.; Turnstall, Marion D.; and Keagle, James M. *Intelligence Policy and Process.* Boulder, CO: Westview Press, 1985.

—**GENERAL DEFENSE INTELLIGENCE PROGRAM (GDIP)** is one of a number of specialized programs that have been developed in order to manage Department of Defense general intelligence resources. The detailed resource management responsibilities for the GDIP have been given to the director of the Defense Intelligence Agency (DIA). The DIA ensures proper intelligence support to the Joint Chiefs of Staff (JCS) by submitting intelligence requirements in its GDIP submission to the Planning, Programming, and Budgeting System (PPBS). In its role as a financial management tool, the GDIP is the budget for defense intelligence activities. It is the general intelligence portion of the DoD Major Force Program 3, Communications and Intelligence, and a part of the larger National Foreign Intelligence Program (NFIP). The director of the DIA is program manager for the GDIP and is assisted by the General Defense Intelligence Program Staff (D/GDIP). *See also:* National Foreign Intelligence Program.

References

American Bar Association. *Oversight and Accountability of the U.S. Intelligence Agencies: An Evaluation.* Washington, DC: ABA, 1985.

Department of Defense, Defense Intelligence Agency. *Defense Intelligence Agency Manual.* Washington, DC: DIA, 1987.

Godson, Roy, ed. *Intelligence Problems for the 1980s, Number 1: Elements of Intelligence.* Rev. ed. Washington, DC: National Strategy Information Center, 1983.

Laqueur, Walter. *A World of Secrets.* New York: Basic Books, 1985.

Lowenthal, Mark M. *U.S. Intelligence: Evolution and Anatomy.* New York: Praeger, 1984.

Maurer, Alfred C.; Turnstall, Marion D.; and Keagle, James M. *Intelligence Policy and Process.* Boulder, CO: Westview Press, 1985.

—**GENERAL DEFENSE INTELLIGENCE PROGRAM STAFF (D/GDIP)** is a body that assists in preparing the General Defense Intelligence Program (GDIP). It receives the budget submissions from the GDIP components, processes them, combines them into the General Defense Intelligence Proposed Program (GDIPP), and prepares the GDIPP for submission to the director of Central Intelligence. It then oversees the administration of the GDIP once it is approved. *See also:* Defense Intelligence Agency.

References

American Bar Association. *Oversight and Accountability of the U.S. Intelligence Agencies: An Evaluation.* Washington, DC: ABA, 1985.

Laqueur, Walter. *A World of Secrets.* New York: Basic Books, 1985.

Maurer, Alfred C.; Turnstall, Marion D.; and Keagle, James M. *Intelligence Policy and Process.* Boulder, CO: Westview Press, 1985.

—**GENERAL DEFENSE INTELLIGENCE PROPOSED PROGRAM (GDIPP)** is the first opportunity that the General Defense Intelligence Program (GDIP) components have to submit their budget requirements annually. It is submitted to the GDIP Staff in April or May of each year and forms the basis of the GDIP manager's budget forecast, which is submitted to the director of Central Intelligence in May or June.

References

American Bar Association. *Oversight and Accountability of the U.S. Intelligence Agencies: An Evaluation.* Washington, DC: ABA, 1985.

Laqueur, Walter. *A World of Secrets.* New York: Basic Books, 1985.

Maurer, Alfred C.; Turnstall, Marion D.; and Keagle, James M. *Intelligence Policy and Process.* Boulder, CO: Westview Press, 1985.

—**GENERAL INTELLIGENCE** is military intelligence covering (1) military capabilities, including orders of battle, organization, training, tactics, and all other factors bearing on military strength and effectiveness; (2) area and terrain intelligence, including urban areas, coasts, and landing beaches, and medical/environmental, meteorological, and geological intelligence; (3) transportation in all modes; (4) materiel production and support industries, telecommunications, and military economics; (5) location and identification of military-related installations; (6) government control; (7) evasion and escape; (8) threats and forecasts; and (9) indications.

References

American Bar Association. *Oversight and Accountability of the U.S. Intelligence Agencies: An Evaluation.* Washington, DC: ABA, 1985.

Department of Defense, U.S. Army. *RDTE Managers Intelligence and Threat Support Guide.* Alexandria, VA: Headquarters, Army Materiel Development and Readiness Command, 1983.

Godson, Roy, ed. *Intelligence Problems for the 1980s, Number 1: Elements of Intelligence.* Rev. ed. Washington, DC: National Strategy Information Center, 1983.

Maurer, Alfred C.; Turnstall, Marion D.; and Keagle, James M. *Intelligence Policy and Process.* Boulder, CO: Westview Press, 1985.

Turner, Stansfield. *Secrecy and Democracy: The CIA in Transition.* Boston: Houghton Mifflin, 1985.

—**GENERAL INTELLIGENCE CAREER DEVELOPMENT PROGRAM.** *See:* Defense Intelligence Agency *under* Directorate for Training (OT).

—**GENERAL INTELLIGENCE TRAINING SYSTEM (GITS).** *See:* Defense Intelligence Agency *under* Directorate for Training (OT).

—**GENERAL MEDICAL INTELLIGENCE (GMI).** *See:* Medical Intelligence.

—**GENERAL SERVICE (GENSER)** is a worldwide communications system for processing unclassified and collateral message traffic.

References

Department of Defense, Defense Intelligence Agency. *Defense Intelligence Agency Manual.* Washington, DC: DIA, 1987.

Godson, Roy, ed. *Intelligence Problems for the 1980s, Number 1: Elements of Intelligence.* Rev. ed. Washington, DC: National Strategy Information Center, 1983.

—**GENERAL SUPPORT** is an Army tactical intelligence (TACINT) term that means providing support to the combat force as a whole as directed by the combat force commander and task-organized by the military intelligence (MI) team leader. General support provides MI support that is responsive to the force commander. It is the most standardized of the standard tactical missions.

References

Department of Defense, Joint Chiefs of Staff. *Department of Defense Dictionary of Military and Related Terms.* Washington, DC: GPO, 1986.

Department of Defense, U.S. Army. *Intelligence and Electronic Warfare Operations.* Field Manual FM 34-1. Washington, DC: Headquarters, Department of the Army, 1984.

———. *Military Intelligence Battalion Combat Electronic Warfare and Intelligence (Aerial Exploitation) (Corps).* Field Manual FM 34-22. Washington, DC: Headquarters, Department of the Army, 1984.

———. *Military Intelligence Battalion (Combat Electronic Warfare Intelligence) (Division).* Field Manual FM 34-10. Washington, DC: Headquarters, Department of the Army, 1981.

———. *Military Intelligence Battalion (CEWI) (Operations) (Corps).* Field Manual FM 34-21. Washington, DC: Headquarters, Department of the Army, 1982.

———. *Military Intelligence Battalion (CEWI) (Tactical Exploitation) (Corps): Counterintelligence, Interrogation, Electronic Warfare.* Field Manual FM 34-23. Washington, DC: Headquarters, Department of the Army, 1985.

———. *Military Intelligence Company (Combat Electronic Warfare and Intelligence) (Armored Cavalry Regiment/Separate Brigade).* Field Manual FM 34-30. Washington, DC: Headquarters, Department of the Army, 1983.

———. *Military Intelligence Group (Combat Electronic Warfare and Intelligence) (Corps).* Field Manual FM 34-20. Washington, DC: Headquarters, Department of the Army, 1983.

—**GENERAL SUPPORT REINFORCING** is an Army tactical intelligence (TACINT) term that means providing support to the combat force as a whole, with secondary emphasis on supporting another military intelligence (MI) unit or element. An MI unit with an assigned general support reinforcing mission responds to the needs of the combat force commander and is task organized by the MI commander. It responds to requests from the reinforced MI unit or element as a secondary priority. The general support reinforcing MI unit remains under the operational control of the MI commander. *See also:* General Support.

—**GEOGRAPHIC RESEARCH AREA (GRA),** Central Intelligence Agency, was created in 1950 as a part of the Office of Research and Reports (ORR). In 1965, it was transferred to the Office of Basic Intelligence (OBI), which was renamed the Office of Basic and Geographic Intelligence (IBGI). The IBGI became the Office of Geographic and Cartographic Research in 1974. *See also:* Central Intelligence Agency.

References

Fain, Tyrus G.; Plant, Katharine C.; and Milloy, Ross. *The Intelligence Community: History, Organization, and Issues.* Public Documents Series. New York: R.R. Bowker, 1977.

—**GEOGRAPHIC(AL) INTELLIGENCE,** a component of strategic intelligence, is foreign intelligence dealing with the location, description, and analysis and cultural factors of the world, including terrain, climate, natural resources, transportation, boundaries, and population distribution, and their changes through time. The agency primarily responsible for the production of military geographical intelligence is the Defense Intelligence Agency.

In order to understand geographical intelligence, it is necessary to understand how the Intelligence Community defines geography. To it, geography is the science of describing the land, sea, and air and the distribution of plant and animal life, including humans and their industries. To the Intelligence Community, geography is a synthetic science that relies on the results of specialized sciences such as astronomy, physics, geology, oceanography, meteorology, biology, and bacteriology for its data.

In this context, military geographic intelligence is the military evaluation of all geographic factors that in any way may influence military operations. Military geography, in the sense that it is used in strategic intelligence, embraces all aspects of the physical environment, both natural and artificial. It is concerned not only with the factors of position, size, shape, boundaries, weather, climate, land forms, drainage, vegetation and surface materials, but also with the cultural factors that have altered the landscape or terrain. Military geographic intelligence in its broadest terms is so inclusive in its fields of interest as to be practically synonymous with strategic intelligence. Both have the same objective: to determine the strategic capabilities, vulnerabilities, and probable courses of action of nations and their peoples. In arriving at an estimate, both consider all elements of the human environment, including the relatively abstract factors as well as the more obvious elements of the natural and cultural landscape.

Concerning the production of geographical intelligence, the principal function of the military geographer is to evaluate the effect of the physical landscape on military operations. Strategic intelligence on economic, political, and sociological factors is produced largely by specialists in those fields. A geographic interpretation of the work of these specialists, however, contributes to the selection of strategic areas as military objectives and enters into the determination of the routes to them. The vulnerability or defensibility of military objectives is interpreted by the military geographer after a thorough analysis and evaluation of any one or all of the following factors:

Location, Size, and Shape of Boundaries

The location of an area relative to the historical centers of gravity has shaped the destiny of individual nations and of whole regions. The place of a nation on a world trade route, for example, influences its political policies, economic development, and human technology. Militarily, location may limit the accessibility of an area by land, yet the area may be readily accessible by air or water.

The importance of size of an area is affected by the destiny of the transportation net and the dispersion of vital centers. These latter factors may determine whether space can be exchanged for time by the defenders in ground operations. (Perhaps the greatest example of this factor is the way the Russians and later the Soviets used their land so effectively in war. By withdrawing and burning the land, they forced the French under

Napoleon and the Germans under Hitler to continually extend their supply lines, which became ever more vulnerable to interdiction.) However, a vast expanse of land alone does not provide great strength, because modern power is based to a large extent on productive facilities that are not necessarily a corollary of size. Perhaps the greatest example of this factor is Saudi Arabia, which consists of a huge area that is rich in oil but has many national strategic problems. Air power has changed the effect of this factor, and the use of other new weapons will probably do likewise.

The shape of an area, either alone or in combination with other geographic factors, has significant influence on basic military plans. The advantages of a compact shape as opposed to a long, narrow one are readily apparent from both an offensive and defensive point of view. For example, the Norwegians and Chileans must consider the huge length and narrow width of their nations as major factors in the strategic calculations concerning their nations' defenses. Almost equally important is the shape of a vital part of a given country, since it may provide the key to the control of the entire nation.

Whether a boundary follows a river, the crest of a mountain range, or a straight line across a plane, its most obvious military significance is mainly with respect to ground operations. However, the immediate military importance of boundaries and particularly the ease of identifying them is not to be minimized in relation to air operations, where enemy territory adjoins nonenemy areas and national interests can be gravely damaged through bombing error.

Coasts and Landing Beaches

Intelligence on the physical characteristics of coasts and landing beaches forms an integral part of military geographic intelligence. It is of key importance to strategic planners in selecting the type of operations to be undertaken and in evaluating the risk involved.

Accurate data on coasts and landing beaches are vital for planning amphibious operations because of the role they play in permitting access to enemy-held areas. Also, they substitute for or complement ports in the initial phase of a campaign. In defensive planning, coasts and landing beaches affect the disposition and capabilities of the defender.

The component data required for a beach are its location, near-shore approaches, tidal data, length and width, gradient and underwater slope, materials and trafficability, and the nature of obstructions. The terrain flanking and backing the beach determines its exits.

While beach intelligence is primarily concerned with physical characteristics, coastal description is concerned also with the cultural features such as road nets, railroads, airfields, towns, harbors, and anchorages. It is necessary to include a coastal description of the entire area in order to relate the beaches to the surrounding terrain.

Weather and Climate

The importance of weather and climate in relation to strategic planning make them extremely significant factors of military geographic intelligence. Weather refers to the meteorological conditions (wind, temperature, rain, snow, etc.) affecting an area at a given time or for a short period of time. Climate refers to the frequency of occurrence and range of meteorological conditions affecting an area over a long period of time.

Data on temperature, precipitation, clouds, fog, humidity, and winds and their effect on air, airborne, and amphibious operations, transportation facilities, physical condition of troops, equipment performance, storage and supply of equipment, clothing and shelter for personnel, disease, morale, reconnaissance, and other operations are the chief components of climate and weather intelligence. The significance of special weather phenomena such as typhoons, monsoons, hurricanes, tornadoes, and sandstorms is also important.

Climate and weather influence strategic planning indirectly also through their effect on the economic, sociological, and political character of an area. Although these factors are given consideration in economic, sociological, and political intelligence, military geographical intelligence considers the significance of their interrelationships. Complete strategic planning is, therefore, dependent upon knowledge of both the indirect and direct military implications of weather and climate.

Topography

Within this category of geographic intelligence, emphasis is placed on determining the military significance of such factors as relief, drainage, vegetation, and soil traficability.

Relief, landforms, and drainage patterns. Among the environmental factors of major significance to military operations are the size, configuration, and operational implications of land reforms and the arrangement of drainage features. Not only do relief features confine or facilitate military operations, but they may also affect such other militarily significant geographic factors as climate. A major element in military geographic analysis is the evaluation of information regarding the shape, height, degree of slope, and trends of relief and drainage features in relation to such problems as determining locations for airheads and beachheads, bivouac areas, specific obstacles to ground movement, and the logical directions for the advance or withdrawal of enemy forces.

Drainage characteristics. The significance of lakes, streams, canals, and swamps as barriers or as navigable waterways reflect such conditions as seasonal depths, currents, widths, bottom characteristics, ice conditions, banks, shorelines, and vegetation in relation to military operations.

Water resources. Data on water resources involve quantitative and qualitative values of such factors as potability, contamination, turbidity, mineral content, and seasonability of supply.

Soil and rocks. Scientific soil and geological surveys from which military interpretation can be derived exist in few countries. Hence, descriptions and samples of soils and rocks together with evaluations in terms of their militarily significant properties are best derived from field observations and collection. Important data of intelligence interest are as follows: rapidity of soil drainage and thickness and character of surface materials as they affect or would affect the construction of roads, airstrips, emplacements, trenches, foxholes and minefields; availability of sand or gravel for road building, emplacement repair, and construction; and the precise nature of the soil as to its effects on the rates of wear of tires, shoes, moving parts, and other types of equipment.

Vegetation. Accurate information on the vegetation of an area is essential for anticipating such military problems as the degree of ease or difficulty of moving men and equipment, the ability to effect strategic and tactical surprise, the availability of concealment from ground and air observation, the extent to which mechanized and motorized equipment may be employed, the suitability for air landings and air drops, and a host of other problems. Characteristics such as heights, density of sand, stem diameters, coloration, rooting strength, and cultivation practices evaluated in terms of military significance are essential data. For example, much of this data would be crucial for estimates of the construction difficulties to be anticipated, the ease or difficulty that should be anticipated in moving one's trucks and vehicles, the problems that will occur concerning concealment of men and equipment, and the potential fire hazard existing in the area.

Cultural features. Such features as mines, quarries, tombs, burial mounds, ditches, hedge rows, terraces, and roads, which occur in sufficient concentration to be of importance in the planning of military operations, are seldom described in terms that bring out their military significance—if data on them are available at all.

Special physical phenomena. Information concerning such factors as seismic disturbances, volcanic phenomena, permafrost, and other factors peculiar to an area assumes military significance in many instances in relation to the extent and frequency of such phenomena.

Urban Areas

The heterogeneity of this subject necessitates close attention. The military significance of such factors as the distribution and pattern of cities and towns, the general characteristics of urban and rural settlement, and the main types of towns is obvious.

Main types of towns. Towns are classified according to the factors of function, physical characteristics, vulnerabilities, and defensibility. The purpose of this classification is to determine the key strategic towns or cities and their relative importance. Some examples of the detail to be considered in the evaluation of urban areas under the foregoing major factors are use (industrial, commercial, administrative, political, or combination); pattern (radial, rectangular, etc.); construction (frame, masonry, etc.); utilities (water, power, sanitation, etc.); and population (districted, scattered, etc.).

Strategic towns. The principal militarily significant towns can be defined on the basis of the above information. The defining of key towns is, in effect, a culmination of geographic intelligence and is indispensable to the military planner for determining the defensibility of the town, its political and industrial relationship to the nation, and the effect of its expansion or destruction upon the economy or war effort of the nation concerned.

Military Geographic Regions

The military geographic region is conceived to be an area in which the combination of environmental conditions is sufficiently uniform to per-

mit or require throughout its extent the use of the same general mode of military operations or kinds of warfare and of the same general types of equipment and personnel. The delineation of such regions requires not only a full understanding of the environmental factors involved, but also an understanding of the military factors concerned. Although the size of a country is not necessarily a factor in determining the number of military geographic regions that it may include, the large countries rather than the small countries are more likely to include more than one such region. Research analysts can distinguish between areas having different environmental complexes, but the delimitation of such regions and the validity of the military characterization can be appreciably refined through the field observation of intelligence personnel who assess the areas in terms of their military aspects. In preparing an analysis of each military region, all aspects of military intelligence must be considered. The description of a region in terms of well-known regions—parts of the United States—greatly enhances the value of the intelligence produced.

Strategic Areas, Approaches, and Internal Routes

The efforts of geographic intelligence to assess a country's capabilities and vulnerabilities focus on those areas to which strategic significance attaches for any particular reason. An adjunct to such an assessment includes an evaluation of the external approaches and internal routes directed against it, and particularly against its strategic areas. This aspect of geographic intelligence is subject to change and must be continuously under review to ensure that the assessments of areas and the approaches thereto correctly reflect current conditions. *See also:* Strategic Intelligence.

References

Clauser, Jerome K., and Weir, Sandra M. *Intelligence Research Methodology.* State College, PA: HRB-Singer, 1975.

Department of Defense, Defense Intelligence College. *Glossary of Intelligence Terms and Definitions.* Washington, DC: DIC, 1987.

Godson, Roy, ed. *Intelligence Problems for the 1980s, Number 1: Elements of Intelligence.* Rev. ed. Washington, DC: National Strategy Information Center, 1983.

Kent, Sherman. *Strategic Intelligence for American World Policy.* Princeton, NJ: Princeton University Press, 1966.

—**GESSNER, GEORGE J.,** attached to the Army, was convicted of passing classified information to a foreign intelligence service. His motivation was disgruntlement with his status. Arrested in 1962, he was given a 21-year prison sentence.

References

Crawford, David J. *Volunteers: The Betrayal of National Defense Secrets by Air Force Traitors.* Washington, DC: GPO, 1988.

—**GLOBAL VARIABLE,** in communications security (COMSEC), means a cryptovariable that is intended for emergency use by an entire communications net when the supporting key generation facility is unavailable or inoperable. *See also:* Communications Security.

References

Martin, Paul H. "Communications-Computer Security." *Journal of Electronic Defense* (June 1987).

Muzerall, Joseph V., and Carty, Thomas P. "COMSEC and Its Need for Key Management." *DP&CS* (Spring 1987).

—**GO PRIVATE** is a term used in clandestine and covert intelligence operations. It means to leave an intelligence agency and to attempt to establish a new identity in a new place. A continuing theme on the popular television show "The Equalizer" of the mid-1980s was that the hero had "gone private" and that he knew so much that his intelligence organization was not sure that he should be allowed to live. In reality, the CIA has an extensive job-placement service for agents who wish to retire, and it actively works to assist them should they need it. *See also:* Agent, Case Officer, Debriefing, Graduated, Special Activities.

References

Becket, Henry S. A. *The Dictionary of Espionage: Spookspeak into English.* New York: Stein and Day, 1986.

Deacon, Richard. *Spyclopedia: An Encyclopedia of Spies, Secret Services, Operations, Jargon, and All Subjects Related to the World of Espionage.* London: Macdonald, 1987.

Ranelagh, John. *The Agency: The Rise and Decline of the CIA.* New York: Simon and Schuster, 1986.

—**GO TO GROUND** is a term used in clandestine and covert intelligence operations. It means to disappear or to go into hiding. When the individ-

ual reappears, he is said to have "surfaced." *See also:* Case, Case Officer, Clean, Cover, Cover Name, Cover Organizations, Cover Story, Damage Assessment, Damage Control, Shaking off the Dogs, Sterile Funds, Sterile Telephone, Sterility Coding, Sterilize, Submerge, Suitable Cover, Surfacing.

References

Becket, Henry S. A. *The Dictionary of Espionage: Spookspeak into English.* New York: Stein and Day, 1986.

Deacon, Richard. *Spyclopedia: An Encyclopedia of Spies, Secret Services, Operations, Jargon, and All Subjects Related to the World of Espionage.* London: Macdonald, 1987.

Ranelagh, John. *The Agency: The Rise and Decline of the CIA.* New York: Simon and Schuster, 1986.

—**GO-AWAY** is a term used in clandestine and covert intelligence operations. It is a signal that an agent gives to his contact to indicate that it is unwise to meet as they had planned. The meeting is often cancelled because the agent feels that he is being followed, and the signal is given by some gesture of the hand. *See also:* Agent, Alternate Meet, Clean, Doubled, Meet Area, Movements Analysis, Sterile, Sterilize, Submerge, Walk-past.

References

Becket, Henry S. A. *The Dictionary of Espionage: Spookspeak into English.* New York: Stein and Day, 1986.

Clancy, Tom. *The Cardinal of the Kremlin.* New York: Putnam, 1988.

—**GOLD, HARRY,** was a member of the "Atomic Spy Ring," headed by Julius and Ethel Rosenberg. A chemist who worked for Soviet intelligence from 1934 to 1945, Gold received information about the U.S. atomic bomb program from Klaus Fuchs. He was arrested in 1950, was sentenced to 30 years in prison, and was released in 1965.

References

Allen, Thomas B., and Polmar, Norman. *Merchants of Treason: America's Secrets for Sale.* New York: Delacorte Press, 1988.

Deacon, Richard. *Spyclopedia: An Encyclopedia of Spies, Secret Services, Operations, Jargon, and All Subjects Related to the World of Espionage.* London: Macdonald, 1987.

—**GOVERNMENT COMMUNICATIONS HEAD-QUARTERS (GCHQ)** is the British communications intelligence organization and is headquartered at Cheltenham. It has a worldwide network of spies, bases, ships, planes, and satellites and is part of a network (of which the United States, Canada, and Australia are also members) that has divided the world into areas of responsibility. The GCHQ has large listening staffs of more than 1,000 members on Cyprus and in Hong Kong and Berlin. There are smaller stations on Ascension Island and in Oman.

References

American Bar Association. *Oversight and Accountability of the U.S. Intelligence Agencies: An Evaluation.* Washington, DC: ABA, 1985.

Deacon, Richard. *Spyclopedia: An Encyclopedia of Spies, Secret Services, Operations, Jargon, and All Subjects Related to the World of Espionage.* London: Macdonald, 1987.

Laqueur, Walter. *A World of Secrets.* New York: Basic Books, 1985.

Maurer, Alfred C.; Turnstall, Marion D.; and Keagle, James M. *Intelligence Policy and Process.* Boulder, CO: Westview Press, 1985.

Turner, Stansfield. *Secrecy and Democracy: The CIA in Transition.* Boston: Houghton Mifflin, 1985.

—**GRADUATED** is a term used in clandestine and covert intelligence operations. It means that a Soviet mole has been able to move from one position to a more sensitive position and therefore will be of greater value.

References

Becket, Henry S. A. *The Dictionary of Espionage: Spookspeak into English.* New York: Stein and Day, 1986.

—**GRANNY** is a non–Central Intelligence Agency employee.

References

Becket, Henry S. A. *The Dictionary of Espionage: Spookspeak into English.* New York: Stein and Day, 1986.

—**GRAY PROPAGANDA** is a term used in clandestine and covert intelligence operations. It is propaganda in which the source is either not given or is deliberately confusing. *See also:* Black Propaganda, White Propaganda.

References

Becket, Henry S. A. *The Dictionary of Espionage: Spookspeak into English.* New York: Stein and Day, 1986.

Ranelagh, John. *The Agency: The Rise and Decline of the CIA.* New York: Simon and Schuster, 1986.

—**GRAYMAIL** occurs when a person who is being accused of an intelligence-related offense threatens to reveal classified information in open court in an attempt to force the government to drop its case. The ploy worked successfully for many defendants in the 1970s but has been considerably less successful since Congress passed the Classified Information Procedures Act. *See also:* Public Law 96-456.

References

Becket, Henry S. A. *The Dictionary of Espionage: Spookspeak into English.* New York: Stein and Day, 1986.

Treverton, Gregory F. *Covert Action: The Limits of Intervention in the Postwar World.* New York: Basic Books, 1987.

—**GREENGLASS, DAVID,** was implicated by Harry Gold as a source of atomic bomb secrets. Greenglass was Julius Rosenberg's brother-in-law and a member of the "Atomic Spy Ring"; he was convicted and received a fifteen-year sentence in 1950. He was released from prison in 1960.

References

Allen, Thomas B., and Polmar, Norman. *Merchants of Treason: America's Secrets for Sale.* New York: Delacorte Press, 1988.

—**GRENADA.** The record of the Intelligence Community in the Grenada invasion, Operation "Urgent Fury," was not without its shortcomings, but ultimately it was successful.

In the period prior to the operation, military intelligence reported fully and consistently on Cuban construction of an airfield on the island. This facility, which would have been long enough to support Soviet Tu-95 Bear D long-range aircraft that were deployed frequently to Cuba and that provided the Soviet Union with a significant regional reconnaissance capability, was considered a threat to U.S. regional security. Concurrently, intelligence was also reporting on the radical Marxist regime of Maurice Bishop and its attempted communization of Grenada. Then, in September 1983, the factional rivalry within Bishop's government intensified, and the political situation began to unravel. On October 23, 1983, the United States received a formal request from five members of the Organization of Eastern Caribbean States to intervene on Grenada. The United States responded rapidly and deployed Navy, Marine Corps, Army and Air Force power in a joint operation that had as its goal the occupation of the island. In the ensuing military operation, a total of 7,335 U.S. personnel were landed on the island, of which 18 were killed in the action.

In contrast to the excellent record that the Intelligence Community had sustained in the period before the invasion, the Community now had several problems. The exercise was conceived so rapidly that intelligence had difficulty responding. With its resources focused on the Soviet Union, its focus on supporting the national leadership rather than the operational commands in the field, and with a naval intelligence community that relied heavily on technical means for collecting intelligence while underrating and possibly even distrusting human intelligence, intelligence was less than satisfactory. All of the millions of dollars that had been invested in "national technical means," a euphemism for intelligence reconnaissance programs, could not adequately support the U.S. fighting forces.

The following were among the most significant military intelligence problems: (1) No information was provided on the Bishop regime. U.S. operating forces were operating in a vacuum and were not aware of the split in the ranks of Bishop's forces. (2) There was too much reliance on technical systems and not enough emphasis on human intelligence. Tourists who had recently visited Grenada and students who were home from the medical school located on the island were never contacted by the government for information that they might have concerning recent events and conditions on the island. (3) The physical support (briefings, maps, and other data) that the Intelligence Community provided was clearly inadequate. The Marines, for example, were provided extremely out-of-date maps that turned to pulpy masses when the Marines tried to use them in the rain. This resulted in two lapses that were potentially very serious. First, U.S. combat forces were not informed that there were two medical school campuses with American students. Thus U.S. forces liberated one campus soon after the invasion but did not liberate the other campus until the next day because they were unaware that it existed. In the interim, the campus was held by Grenadians, who had plenty of time to kill the students, if they had wished to. Second, after receiving fire from a building, U.S. forces bombed an insane asylum. They later reported that they were not aware that the building was used for such purposes. Had they known, they probably would have used other means to clear the enemy from the building. The resulting deaths of patients was a blot on an otherwise very successful operation.

In assessing this intelligence support, it is important to note that "Urgent Fury" again demonstrated the Intelligence Community's recurring problem of adequately supporting both the national leadership and the fighting forces. Additionally, the detrimental effects of the Community's overreliance (particularly on the part of Naval Intelligence), on technical systems, and a tendency to underuse and even distrust human intelligence was again demonstrated. Here the Intelligence Community was primarily to blame, but the National Security Council should have been aware of the Community's weaknesses and should have been more alert, as this might have resulted in more satisfactory intelligence support to U.S. fighting forces.

In the political realm, in contrast to the military picture, intelligence support to Operation "Urgent Fury" was a complete success. Captured enemy documents and weapons confirmed the intelligence estimates that there was, indeed, a very real threat of the use of the island for the expansion of communist subversion.

As a result, Grenada was a significant political success for several reasons. First, it showed that the United States was willing to act in the Western Hemisphere, and it went far toward repairing the damage that the Carter administration had done to the Monroe Doctrine when it invoked and then failed to uphold it in its reaction to the presence of the Soviet brigade in Cuba in 1979. Second, it effectively stopped the spread of communist subversion in the eastern region of the Caribbean basin. Third, it had the support of several of the nations of the region. Finally, it had the support of the Grenadians. This was vividly demonstrated when President Reagan subsequently visited the island and over 90 percent of the Grenadians turned out to thank him for their liberation.

In summary, intelligence support to the Grenadian invasion was a mixed success. Full, accurate, and consistent military intelligence reporting in the period before the invasion yielded to unsatisfactory intelligence support during the actual operation. On the other hand, the political and strategic estimates of the potential danger of the Bishop regime and its unpopularity with the other nations of the region were very accurate and, when heeded, contributed to a military operation that in the final analysis was a first-rate use of military power for political effect.

References

Breckinridge, Scott D. *The CIA and the U.S. Intelligence System.* Boulder, CO: Westview Press, 1986.

Brinkley, David A., and Hull, Andrew W. *Estimative Intelligence: A Textbook on the History, Products, Uses and Writing of Intelligence Estimates.* Columbus, OH: Battelle, 1979.

Clancy, Thomas. *The Cardinal of the Kremlin.* New York: Putnam, 1988.

Cline, Ray S. *The CIA Under Reagan, Bush, and Casey.* Washington, DC: Acropolis Books, 1981.

Crawford, David J. *Volunteers: The Betrayal of National Defense Secrets by Air Force Traitors.* Washington, DC: GPO, 1988.

Dunn, Peter M., and Watson, Bruce W. *American Intervention in Grenada: The Implications of Operation "Urgent Fury."* Boulder, CO: Westview Press, 1985.

Lowenthal, Mark M. *U.S. Intelligence: Evolution and Anatomy.* New York: Praeger, 1984.

Quirk, John; Phillips, David; Cline, Ray; and Pforzheimer, Walter. *The Central Intelligence Agency: A Photographic History.* Guilford, CT: Foreign Intelligence Press, 1986.

Treverton, Gregory F. *Covert Action: The Limits of Intervention in the Postwar World.* New York: Basic Books, 1987.

Turner, Stansfield. *Secrecy and Democracy: The CIA in Transition.* Boston: Houghton Mifflin, 1985.

U.S. Congress. Senate. *Alleged Assassination Plots Involving Foreign Leaders: An Interim Report of the Select Committee to Study Governmental Operations with Respect to Intelligence Activities.* 94th Congress, 1st sess., Nov. 20, 1975. S. Rept. 94-465.

Von Hoene, John P. A. *Intelligence User's Guide.* Washington, DC: DIA, 1983.

Watson, Bruce W. *Red Navy at Sea: Soviet Naval Operations on the High Seas, 1956–1980.* Boulder, CO: Westview Press, 1982.

Watson, Bruce W., and Dunn, Peter M. *Military Lessons of the Falkland Islands War: Views from the United States.* Boulder, CO: Westview Press, 1984.

—**GRINDER** is a term used in clandestine and covert intelligence operations to describe a debriefing room that is used to interrogate defectors. Henry Becket asserts that the Central Intelligence Agency maintains several such rooms in safe houses in the suburbs of Washington, DC. While in the grinder, the defector, fed and housed in adjacent rooms, is asked to repeat his story continually, while his information is checked against verifiable information. An excellent representation of a Soviet KGB grinder is shown in the final scenes of the movie "No Way Out," in which the agent is housed in a grinder in the vicinity of Alexandria, Virginia, and is forced to reiterate his story to KGB agents. *See also:* Debriefing.

References

Becket, Henry S. A. *The Dictionary of Espionage: Spookspeak into English.* New York: Stein and Day, 1986.

Ranelagh, John. *The Agency: The Rise and Decline of the CIA.* New York: Simon and Schuster, 1986.

—**GROUND CONTROLLED INTERCEPTION (GCI)** is a technique that permits the control of friendly aircraft or missiles for the purposes of insuring interception.

References

Department of Defense, Joint Chiefs of Staff. *Department of Defense Dictionary of Military and Related Terms.* Washington, DC: GPO, 1986.

—**GROUND FORCES INTELLIGENCE STUDY (GROFIS)** provides a good summary of ground forces' compositions, identifications, and strengths. These studies are categorized both by regions and by countries of the world. Published annually or biennially, they cover the missions, tasks, organization, capabilities, policies, and military trends of the subject nation or region. *See also:* Defense Intelligence Agency.

References

Von Hoene, John P. A. *Intelligence User's Guide.* Washington, DC: DIA, 1983.

—**GROUND ORDER OF BATTLE (GOB)** is a Defense Intelligence Agency publication. It is published by country or region and provides detailed information on a nation's army forces, the army's command structure, its territorial and tactical organization, and the distribution of its units. *See also:* Defense Intelligence Agency.

References

Von Hoene, John P. A. *Intelligence User's Guide.* Washington, DC: DIA, 1983.

—**GROUND RESOLUTION** is an intelligence imagery and photoreconnaissance term. It is a measurement of the smallest detail that can be distinguished on the ground by a sensor system under specific conditions. *See also:* Aerial Photograph.

References

Von Hoene, John P. A. *Intelligence User's Guide.* Washington, DC: DIA, 1983.

—**GROUND RETURN** is a term used in radar intelligence (RADINT). Ground return are radar echoes that are reflected from the ground or terrain. They are also called ground clutter.*See also:* Electronic Intelligence.

References

Department of Defense, Joint Chiefs of Staff. *Department of Defense Dictionary of Military and Related Terms.* Washington, DC: GPO, 1986.

Reeves, Robert; Anson, Abraham; and Landen, David. *Manual of Remote Sensing.* Falls Church, VA: American Society of Photogrammetry, 1975.

—**GROUND TRUTH** is an intelligence imagery and photoreconnaissance term. It is an imprecise term that refers to information obtained on surface or subsurface features that aid in interpreting imagery. It is misleading because of the use of the word "truth," which gives it undeserved validity. More acceptable terms are "ground data" or "ground information."*See also:* Ground Resolution.

References

Reeves, Robert; Anson, Abraham; and Landen, David. *Manual of Remote Sensing.* Falls Church, VA: American Society of Photogrammetry, 1975.

—**GRU (GLAVNOE RAZVEDYVATELNOE UPRAVLENIE),** the Soviet military intelligence group, is the chief intelligence directorate of the Soviet General Staff. Headquartered in Moscow, it has greater resources for collecting foreign intelligence than the KGB. Much of the GRU's work is accomplished by Soviet military attachés who are stationed in embassies around the world.

References

Brinkley, David A., and Hull, Andrew W. *Estimative Intelligence: A Textbook on the History, Products, Uses and Writing of Intelligence Estimates.* Columbus, OH: Battelle, 1979.

Deacon, Richard. *Spyclopedia: An Encyclopedia of Spies, Secret Services, Operations, Jargon, and All Subjects Related to the World of Espionage.* London: Macdonald, 1987.

—**GRUNDEN, OLIVER EVERETT,** an Airman First Class, was apprehended in September 1973 by Air Force agents posing as Soviet intelligence officers as he attempted to sell them classified information concerning the U-2 aircraft. He appears to have been motivated by financial gain. In March 1974 a court-martial convicted Grunden and awarded him a dishonorable discharge and a five-year prison sentence.

References

Allen, Thomas B., and Polmar, Norman. *Merchants of Treason: America's Secrets for Sale.* New York: Delacorte Press, 1988.

Crawford, David J. *Volunteers: The Betrayal of National Defense Secrets by Air Force Traitors.* Washington, DC: GPO, 1988.

—**GUARDRAIL** aircraft is an Army tactical intelligence (TACINT) aircraft that provides collection and emitter location information on enemy communications systems. It intercepts enemy high frequency (HF), VHF, and UHF communications emitters and locates HF and VHF communications emitters. It processes the information and reports it to users over secure, direct communications in near real time. The system consists of a remotely controlled collection and data transmitting system aboard an RU-21 or RC-12 aircraft; ground support and maintenance equipment; an integrated processing facility (IPF); and a tactical commander's terminal (TCT).

References

Department of Defense, U.S. Army. *Military Intelligence Battalion Combat Electronic Warfare and Intelligence (Aerial Exploitation) (Corps).* Field Manual FM 34-22. Washington, DC: Headquarters, Department of the Army, 1984.

—**GUATEMALA.** The overthrow of Jacobo Arbenz Guzman in 1954 was one of six coups d'état that were waged with U.S. assistance. The Eisenhower administration, concerned about Arbenz's radical leftist orientation and Guatemalan instability, assisted a small insurgent force, bolstered with considerable propaganda, to overthrow Arbenz. Feeling that he could not defeat the force, Arbenz fled the capital. *See also:* Central Intelligence Agency.

References

American Bar Association. *Oversight and Accountability of the U.S. Intelligence Agencies: An Evaluation.* Washington, DC: ABA, 1985.

Breckinridge, Scott D. *The CIA and the U.S. Intelligence System.* Boulder, CO: Westview Press, 1986.

Laqueur, Walter. *The Age of Terrorism.* Boston: Little, Brown, 1987.

————. *A World of Secrets.* New York: Basic Books, 1985.

Maurer, Alfred C.; Turnstall, Marion D.; and Keagle, James M. *Intelligence Policy and Process.* Boulder, CO: Westview Press, 1985.

Treverton, Gregory F. *Covert Action: The Limits of Intervention in the Postwar World.* New York: Basic Books, 1987.

Turner, Stansfield. *Secrecy and Democracy: The CIA in Transition.* Boston: Houghton Mifflin, 1985.

—**GUERRILLA OPERATIONS** are activities conducted by guerrillas, lightly armed indigenous forces who are operating in an area that is controlled by a hostile central government or an occupying foreign power. *See also:* Guerrilla Warfare, Guerrillas.

References

Godson, Roy, ed. *Intelligence Problems for the 1980s, Number 1: Elements of Intelligence.* Rev. ed. Washington, DC: National Strategy Information Center, 1983.

————. *Intelligence Problems for the 1980s, Number 4: Covert Action.* Washington, DC: National Strategy Information Center, 1981.

Laqueur, Walter. *The Age of Terrorism.* Boston: Little, Brown, 1987.

Oseth, John M. *Regulating U.S. Intelligence Operations: A Study in the Definition of the National Interest.* Frankfurt: University of Kentucky Press, 1985.

Treverton, Gregory F. *Covert Action: The Limits of Intervention in the Postwar World.* New York: Basic Books, 1987.

Turner, Stansfield. *Secrecy and Democracy: The CIA in Transition.* Boston: Houghton Mifflin, 1985.

—**GUERRILLA WARFARE** is the sum of the hostilities conducted by lightly armed indigenous forces operating in an area controlled by a hostile central government or an occupying foreign power. The guerrilla is fundamentally an offensive weapon of war who has a superior knowledge of the terrain and the element of surprise. This allows him the ability to mount hit-and-run operations with great effectiveness. *See also:* Guerrilla Operations, Guerrillas.

References

American Bar Association. *Oversight and Accountability of the U.S. Intelligence Agencies: An Evaluation.* Washington, DC: ABA, 1985.

Department of Defense, Joint Chiefs of Staff. *Department of Defense Dictionary of Military and Related Terms.* Washington, DC: GPO, 1986.

Godson, Roy, ed. *Intelligence Problems for the 1980s, Number 1: Elements of Intelligence.* Rev. ed. Washington, DC: National Strategy Information Center, 1983.

————. *Intelligence Problems for the 1980s, Number 4: Covert Action.* Washington, DC: National Strategy Information Center, 1981.

Laqueur, Walter. *The Age of Terrorism.* Boston: Little, Brown, 1987.

Maurer, Alfred C.; Turnstall, Marion D.; and Keagle, James M. *Intelligence Policy and Process.* Boulder, CO: Westview Press, 1985.

Treverton, Gregory F. *Covert Action: The Limits of Intervention in the Postwar World.* New York: Basic Books, 1987.

Turner, Stansfield. *Secrecy and Democracy: The CIA in Transition.* Boston: Houghton Mifflin, 1985.

U.S. Congress. Senate. *Final Report of the Senate Select Committee to Study Government Operations with Respect to Intelligence Activities. Report 94-755. Book I, Foreign and Military Intelligence.* Washington, DC: GPO, 1976.

—**GUERRILLAS** are an organized force in enemy territory that conduct commando and paramilitary operations. Guerrilla forces are usually not strong enough to conduct more assertive operations, and thus wage these types of low-level conflict. As defined by the Church Committee, a guerrilla is "a combat participant in guerrilla warfare."

References

Becket, Henry S. A. *The Dictionary of Espionage: Spookspeak into English.* New York: Stein and Day, 1986.

Godson, Roy, ed. *Intelligence Problems for the 1980s, Number 1: Elements of Intelligence.* Rev. ed. Washington, DC: National Strategy Information Center, 1983.

————. *Intelligence Problems for the 1980s, Number 4: Covert Action.* Washington, DC: National Strategy Information Center, 1981.

Laqueur, Walter. *The Age of Terrorism*. Boston: Little, Brown, 1987.

———. *A World of Secrets*. New York: Basic Books, 1985.

Treverton, Gregory F. *Covert Action: The Limits of Intervention in the Postwar World*. New York: Basic Books, 1987.

Turner, Stansfield. *Secrecy and Democracy: The CIA in Transition*. Boston: Houghton Mifflin, 1985.

U.S. Congress. Senate. *Final Report of the Senate Select Committee to Study Government Operations with Respect to Intelligence Activities. Report 94-755. Book I, Foreign and Military Intelligence.* Washington, DC: GPO, 1976.

—**GUIDANCE** is advice that identifies, interprets, clarifies, or expands on an information need. In collection, it can also mean the general direction of the intelligence effort. As defined by the Church Committee, guidance is the "general direction of an intelligence effort, particularly in the area of collection." *See also:* Information Need, Intelligence Cycle.

References

Department of Defense, Defense Intelligence College. *Glossary of Intelligence Terms and Definitions*. Washington, DC: DIC, 1987.

Department of Defense, Joint Chiefs of Staff. *Department of Defense Dictionary of Military and Related Terms*. Washington, DC: GPO, 1986.

Kent, Sherman. *Strategic Intelligence for American World Policy*. Princeton, NJ: Princeton University Press, 1966.

Treverton, Gregory F. *Covert Action: The Limits of Intervention in the Postwar World*. New York: Basic Books, 1987.

Turner, Stansfield. *Secrecy and Democracy: The CIA in Transition*. Boston: Houghton Mifflin, 1985.

U.S. Congress. Senate. *Final Report of the Senate Select Committee to Study Government Operations with Respect to Intelligence Activities. Report 94-755. Book I, Foreign and Military Intelligence.* Washington, DC: GPO, 1976.

—**GUIDED MISSILES AND ASTRONAUTICS INTELLIGENCE COMMITTEE (GMAIC)** was a United States Intelligence Board subcommittee established in 1958, succeeding the Guided Missiles Intelligence Committee (GMIC). It was responsible for the interdepartmental coordination of intelligence that was related to guided missiles. *See also:* Central Intelligence Agency.

References

Fain, Tyrus G.; Plant, Katharine C.; and Milloy, Ross. *The Intelligence Community: History, Organization, and Issues*. Public Documents Series. New York: R.R. Bowker, 1977.

—**GUIDED MISSILES INTELLIGENCE COMMITTEE (GMIC)** was an Intelligence Advisory Committee (IAC) subcommittee that was established in 1956. It was responsible for the interdepartmental coordination of intelligence relating to guided missiles. It was replaced by the Guided Missiles and Astronautics Intelligence Committee (GMAIC) in 1958. *See also:* Central Intelligence Agency.

References

Fain, Tyrus G.; Plant, Katharine C.; and Milloy, Ross. *The Intelligence Community: History, Organization, and Issues*. Public Documents Series. New York: R.R. Bowker, 1977.

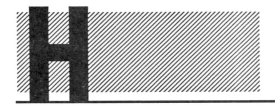

—**HAGUEWOOD, ROBERT D.,** a naval petty officer, was sentenced for attempting to sell government secrets in 1986. In a plea bargain, he received a two-year sentence and a dishonorable discharge.

References
Allen, Thomas B., and Polmar, Norman. *Merchants of Treason: America's Secrets for Sale*. New York: Delacorte Press, 1988.

Crawford, David J. *Volunteers: The Betrayal of National Defense Secrets by Air Force Traitors*. Washington, DC: GPO, 1988.

—**HAMILTON, VICTOR N.,** who worked at the National Security Agency, defected to the Soviet Union in 1963. *See also:* National Security Agency.

References
Allen, Thomas B., and Polmar, Norman. *Merchants of Treason: America's Secrets for Sale*. New York: Delacorte Press, 1988.

Crawford, David J. *Volunteers: The Betrayal of National Defense Secrets by Air Force Traitors*. Washington, DC: GPO, 1988.

—**HAND RECEIPT** is a communications security (COMSEC) term for a document used to record a local or a temporary transfer of COMSEC material from a COMSEC custodian to a user. *See also:* Certificate of Destruction, Classification, Courier.

References
Martin, Paul H. "Communications-Computer Security." *Journal of Electronic Defense* (June 1987).

Von Hoene, John P. A. *Intelligence User's Guide*. Washington, DC: DIA, 1983.

—**HANDLING AGENT (OR HANDLER)** is an FBI agent who is responsible for handling the undercover activities of an informant. He not only receives information from the informant, but also directs the informant's activities. *See also:* Agent, Agent in Place, Agent Net, Agent of Influence, Agent Provocateur, Confusion Agent, Dispatched Agent, Double Agent, Illegal Agent, Informant, Inside Man, Provocation Agent, Pseudonym, Recruitment, Recruitment in Place, Special Activities, Walk-in.

References
Becket, Henry S. A. *The Dictionary of Espionage: Spookspeak into English*. New York: Stein and Day, 1986.

Clancy, Tom. *The Cardinal of the Kremlin*. New York: Putnam, 1988.

Kessler, Ronald. *Spy vs. Spy: Stalking Soviet Spies in America*. New York: Charles Scribner's Sons, 1988.

—**HARD COPY DOCUMENT** is any document that is initially published and distributed in paper form and that is not stored or transmitted by electrical means.

References
Von Hoene, John P. A. *Intelligence User's Guide*. Washington, DC: DIA, 1983.

—**HARD TARGETS** are secret and closed societies, such as Iran, Libya, and the communist nations. They are contrasted against "soft targets," which are the open societies of neutral and allied nations. *See also:* Intelligence Collection.

References
Becket, Henry S. A. *The Dictionary of Espionage: Spookspeak into English*. New York: Stein and Day, 1986.

Deacon, Richard. *Spyclopedia: An Encyclopedia of Spies, Secret Services, Operations, Jargon, and All Subjects Related to the World of Espionage*. London: Macdonald, 1987.

Ranelagh, John. *The Agency: The Rise and Decline of the CIA*. New York: Simon and Schuster, 1986.

—**HARMONICA BUG** is an electronic surveillance term. It is a very small transmitter, or bug, that can be placed inside a telephone mouthpiece. *See also:* Bug, Bugging.

References
Becket, Henry S. A. *The Dictionary of Espionage: Spookspeak into English*. New York: Stein and Day, 1986.

Deacon, Richard. *Spyclopedia: An Encyclopedia of Spies, Secret Services, Operations, Jargon, and All Subjects Related to the World of Espionage*. London: Macdonald, 1987.

Godson, Roy, ed. *Intelligence Problems for the 1980s, Number 1: Elements of Intelligence.* Rev. ed. Washington, DC: National Strategy Information Center, 1983.

—**HARPER, JAMES DURWOOD, JR.,** was convicted of passing classified information to Polish intelligence agents for monetary reward. He was arrested in 1983, convicted, and given a life sentence in prison.

References

Allen, Thomas B., and Polmar, Norman. *Merchants of Treason: America's Secrets for Sale.* New York: Delacorte Press, 1988.

Crawford, David J. *Volunteers: The Betrayal of National Defense Secrets by Air Force Traitors.* Washington, DC: GPO, 1988.

—**HARRIS, ULYSSES L.,** attached to the Army, was convicted of espionage offenses in 1967 and was given a seven-year prison sentence. His apparent motivation was expected monetary gain.

References

Crawford, David J. *Volunteers: The Betrayal of National Defense Secrets by Air Force Traitors.* Washington, DC: GPO, 1988.

—**HAZARDOUS ACTIVITIES** include assignments or visits to, and travel through, certain specified nations that are either hostile to the United States or are experiencing significant unrest. The list of such nations is continually updated, and it is the responsibility of the individual to determine whether his or her destination is on the list. Hazardous activities also include assignment or travel in combat zones or other areas where hostilities are taking place, duties behind hostile lines, and duties or travel in isolated or exposed areas where persons cannot reasonably be protected against hostile action.

While some consider such a designation to be an inconvenience or an encroachment upon their freedom, it is actually a very rational concept. The list of areas has traditionally been short, and has been limited only to those areas that presented the greatest danger to an individual. *See also:* Hazardous Activities Restriction.

References

Von Hoene, John P. A. *Intelligence User's Guide.* Washington, DC: DIA, 1983.

—**HAZARDOUS ACTIVITIES RESTRICTION (HAR)** is one of several security measures that have been rescinded over the years. A HAR was a restriction that was placed on an individual during the time that he or she was permitted access to sensitive compartmented information and for a period of time after that access terminated. The period assigned after access termination was contingent on the sensitivity of the information that the person had seen, and normally was computed in terms of years. The HAR was very unpopular because it often interfered with military careers in that military personnel were not allowed to go to combat and other "career-enhancing" assignments because of their HARs. As a result, there were many who deliberately avoided an intelligence assignment for fear that it would destroy their careers. *See also:* Hazardous Activities.

References

Von Hoene, John P. A. *Intelligence User's Guide.* Washington, DC: DIA, 1983.

—**HEAVY MOB (OR HEAVY SQUAD)** is a term used in clandestine and covert intelligence operations. It is the CIA "muscle" and is used when the agency expects trouble or feels that it may have to use force. During the Iran-Contra investigations, the Navy's counterpart to the "heavy mob" was seen often on television as it guarded Lieutenant Colonel Oliver North, U.S. Marine Corps. These individuals were so conspicuous that one concludes that they were meant to be seen, in the hopes that their detection would avert any attempts on North's life. *See also:* Knuckle Dragger.

References

Becket, Henry S. A. *The Dictionary of Espionage: Spookspeak into English.* New York: Stein and Day, 1986.

Deacon, Richard. *Spyclopedia: An Encyclopedia of Spies, Secret Services, Operations, Jargon, and All Subjects Related to the World of Espionage.* London: Macdonald, 1987.

Ranelagh, John. *The Agency: The Rise and Decline of the CIA.* New York: Simon and Schuster, 1986.

—**HEEL LIFT** is a term used in clandestine and covert intelligence operations. It is a thick slab of leather that is worn in a shoe, a CIA device that forces the wearer to walk with a limp. It is one of the means that one can use to alter his or her appearance. *See also:* Tongue-Tangler.

References

Becket, Henry S. A. *The Dictionary of Espionage: Spookspeak into English.* New York: Stein and Day, 1986.

—**HELICOPTER DIRECTION CENTER,** an amphibious operations entity, is an air operations installation that is under the overall control of the Tactical Air Control Center (TACC), the Tactical Air Direction Center (TADC), or the Direct Air Support Center (DASC), as appropriate, from which the control and direction of helicopter operations are exercised.

References

Department of Defense, Joint Chiefs of Staff. *Department of Defense Dictionary of Military and Related Terms.* Washington, DC: GPO, 1986.

—**HELICOPTER SUPPORT TEAM** is a Marine Corps task organization that is formed and equipped for use in a landing and movement of helicopter-borne troops, equipment, and supplies and to evacuate selected casualties and prisoners of war. It may be built around a nucleus of shore party and helicopter landing zone control personnel. The Army counterpart is the air mobile support party.

References

Department of Defense, Joint Chiefs of Staff. *Department of Defense Dictionary of Military and Related Terms.* Washington, DC: GPO, 1986.

—**HELMICH, JOSEPH G., JR.,** a U.S. Army warrant officer, was convicted of espionage offenses concerning passing classified information to the Soviet KGB in the 1960s. He was motivated by expectations of monetary gain. Arrested in 1981, he was sentenced to life in prison.

References

Allen, Thomas B., and Polmar, Norman. *Merchants of Treason: America's Secrets for Sale.* New York: Delacorte Press, 1988.

Crawford, David J. *Volunteers: The Betrayal of National Defense Secrets by Air Force Traitors.* Washington, DC: GPO, 1988.

Godson, Roy, ed. *Intelligence Problems for the 1980s, Number 1: Elements of Intelligence.* Rev. ed. Washington, DC: National Strategy Information Center, 1983.

———. *Intelligence Problems for the 1980s, Number 5: Clandestine Collection.* Washington, DC: National Strategy Information Center, 1982.

—**HELMS, RICHARD,** was born on March 30, 1913, in St. Davids, Pennsylvania. He attended Williams College, earning a bachelor of arts in 1935. His early career was as a journalist, and he was commissioned in the U.S. Naval Reserve in 1942. He served with the Office of Strategic Services and its successors from 1943 until 1946. He then pursued a career in the Central Intelligence Agency and served as deputy director for plans from 1962 to 1965 and as deputy director of Central Intelligence from April 28, 1965, until June 30, 1966. He was appointed director of Central Intelligence (DCI) by President Johnson on June 18, 1966. The appointment was approved by the Senate on June 28, and he was sworn in on June 30, 1966. He served as the DCI until his retirement on February 2, 1973. He served as ambassador to Iran from March 1973 until January 1977. He then became a private consultant and, in 1983, became a member of the President's Commission on Strategic Forces.

President Johnson's choice of Helms as a replacement for Admiral William F. Rayborn, Jr., U.S. Navy, was an excellent one. Helms, who had been in intelligence since joining the Office of Strategic Services in 1942, was the first career officer to become the DCI. However, his operational background was carried over into his tenure as the DCI, and the focus of the agency was shifted back toward operations. During Helms's tenure as the DCI, Vietnam dominated the intelligence world. When Nixon became President, he shifted the emphasis to the White House and the National Security Council, but he did increase Helms's power by creating two organizations: the Intelligence Resources Advisory Committee (IRAC) to assist the DCI on the preparation of a consolidated intelligence program budget, and the Intelligence Community Staff. With the decline of U.S. involvement in Vietnam in 1972, and with the use of the CIA in the Watergate crimes, the intelligence focus became blurred. *See also:* Central Intelligence Agency.

References

American Bar Association. *Oversight and Accountability of the U.S. Intelligence Agencies: An Evaluation.* Washington, DC: ABA, 1985.

Breckinridge, Scott D. *The CIA and the U.S. Intelligence System.* Boulder, CO: Westview Press, 1986.

Brinkley, David A., and Hull, Andrew W. *Estimative Intelligence: A Textbook on the History, Products, Uses and Writing of Intelligence Estimates.* Columbus, OH: Battelle, 1979.

Cline, Ray S. *The CIA Under Reagan, Bush, and Casey.* Washington, DC: Acropolis Books, 1981.

Crawford, David J. *Volunteers: The Betrayal of National Defense Secrets by Air Force Traitors.* Washington, DC: GPO, 1988.

Godson, Roy, ed. *Intelligence Problems for the 1980s, Number 1: Elements of Intelligence.* Rev. ed. Washington, DC: National Strategy Information Center, 1983.

Lefever, Ernest W., and Godson, Roy. *The CIA and the American Ethic: An Unfinished Debate.* Washington, DC: Ethics and Public Policy Center, Georgetown University, 1979.

Lowenthal, Mark M. *U.S. Intelligence: Evolution and Anatomy.* New York: Praeger, 1984.

Maurer, Alfred C.; Turnstall, Marion D.; and Keagle, James M. *Intelligence Policy and Process.* Boulder, CO: Westview Press, 1985.

Treverton, Gregory F. *Covert Action: The Limits of Intervention in the Postwar World.* New York: Basic Books, 1987.

Turner, Stansfield. *Secrecy and Democracy: The CIA in Transition.* Boston: Houghton Mifflin, 1985.

U.S. Congress. Senate. *Alleged Assassination Plots Involving Foreign Leaders: An Interim Report of the Select Committee to Study Governmental Operations with Respect to Intelligence Activities.* 94th Congress, 1st sess., Nov. 20, 1975. S. Rept. 94-465.

Von Hoene, John P. A. *Intelligence User's Guide.* Washington, DC: DIA, 1983.

—HIDING PLACE. *See:* Drop.

—HIGH FREQUENCY/DIRECTION FINDING (HF/DF) is exploring the high- frequency spectrum for emitter signals in order to determine their directions and locations. HF/DF is used extensively in maritime reconnaissance to determine the approximate direction or bearing of a transmitting antenna. When a DF station obtains a line of bearing (LOB), it provides an approximate direction to the emitter, but not the distance. However, when two or more stations are located at significantly different directions from the emitter, then the LOBs from each can provide an accurate location. HF/DF location reports are a major and very significant input into the maritime surveillance and locations files. Normally when HF/DF is reported, the reporter will provide his rating of the locating data, using a rating system from A (excellent) to C (poor). In the vernacular, "super charlie DF" is considered so poor a fix that it is almost worthless. *See also:* Intelligence Collection.

References

Department of Defense, U.S. Army. *Counter-Signals Intelligence (C-SIGINT) Operations.* Field Manual FM 34-62. Washington, DC: Headquarters, Department of the Army, 1986.

—HIGH RISK ENVIRONMENT, in communications security (COMSEC), means a geographical area or a specific location in which there are too few friendly security forces to ensure the safeguarding of installed machine cryptosystems. *See also:* Communications Security.

References

Martin, Paul H. "Communications-Computer Security." *Journal of Electronic Defense* (June 1987).

Ware, Willis H. "Information Systems, Security, and Privacy." *EDUCOM Bulletin* (Summer 1984).

—HILLENKOETTER, RADM ROSCOE H., U.S. NAVY, was born on May 8, 1897, in St. Louis, Missouri. He graduated from the U.S. Naval Academy in 1919. His navy career included several tours as assistant naval attaché and naval attaché to France in the 1930s and 1940s, and a tour as officer in charge of intelligence on the staff of Admiral Chester Nimitz, Commander-in-Chief, Pacific Ocean Area, from September 1942 to March 1943. He was promoted to rear admiral on November 29, 1946, and was appointed director of Central Intelligence (DCI) by President Truman on April 30, 1947. Hillenkoetter lacked the assertiveness in Washington politics that his successor, Lieutenant General Hoyt Vandenberg, U.S. Air Force, demonstrated, and he only served as the DCI until October 7, 1950. As a result, his tenure was too short for Hillenkoetter to have a great impact on the CIG. He resigned to become the Commander Navy Task Force in the Korean War. He served in this capacity from November 1950 until September 1951. He was promoted to vice admiral on April 9, 1956, became inspector general of the Navy on August 1 of that year, and then retired from the Navy on May 1, 1957. He then pursued a career in private business, and he died on June 18, 1982. *See also:* Central Intelligence Agency.

References

American Bar Association. *Oversight and Accountability of the U.S. Intelligence Agencies: An Evaluation.* Washington, DC: ABA, 1985.

Breckinridge, Scott D. *The CIA and the U.S. Intelligence System.* Boulder, CO: Westview Press, 1986.

Brinkley, David A., and Hull, Andrew W. *Estimative Intelligence: A Textbook on the History, Products, Uses and Writing of Intelligence Estimates.* Columbus, OH: Battelle, 1979.

Cline, Ray S. *The CIA Under Reagan, Bush, and Casey.* Washington, DC: Acropolis Books, 1981.

Crawford, David J. *Volunteers: The Betrayal of National Defense Secrets by Air Force Traitors.* Washington, DC: GPO, 1988.

Lowenthal, Mark M. *U.S. Intelligence: Evolution and Anatomy.* New York: Praeger, 1984.

Maurer, Alfred C.; Turnstall, Marion D.; and Keagle, James M. *Intelligence Policy and Process.* Boulder, CO: Westview Press, 1985.

Quirk, John; Phillips, David; Cline, Ray; and Pforzheimer, Walter. *The Central Intelligence Agency: A Photographic History.* Guilford, CT: Foreign Intelligence Press, 1986.

U.S. Congress. Senate. *Alleged Assassination Plots Involving Foreign Leaders: An Interim Report of the Select Committee to Study Governmental Operations with Respect to Intelligence Activities.* 94th Congress, 1st sess., Nov. 20, 1975. S. Rept. 94-465.

Von Hoene, John P. A. *Intelligence User's Guide.* Washington, DC: DIA, 1983.

—**HILSMAN, ROGER,** took charge of the Department of State's Bureau of Intelligence and Research (INR) in 1961. An advocate of a closer relationship between intelligence and policymaking, Hilsman drastically redirected the thrust of the bureau. He discontinued the National Intelligence Survey program and reduced the size of the bureau. His changes significantly reshaped the INR and set the pattern that still exists in the organization. *See also:* Bureau of Intelligence and Research, National Intelligence Estimate.

References

American Bar Association. *Oversight and Accountability of the U.S. Intelligence Agencies: An Evaluation.* Washington, DC: ABA, 1985.

Lowenthal, Mark M. *U.S. Intelligence: Evolution and Anatomy.* New York: Praeger, 1984.

Maurer, Alfred C.; Turnstall, Marion D.; and Keagle, James M. *Intelligence Policy and Process.* Boulder, CO: Westview Press, 1985.

Treverton, Gregory F. *Covert Action: The Limits of Intervention in the Postwar World.* New York: Basic Books, 1987.

—**HOLOCRYPTIC,** a signals analysis term, is an unbreakable code. In a holocryptic system, it is absolutely necessary to have the key, or the code cannot be broken.

References

Department of Defense, U.S. Army. *AIA: Threat Analysis.* Falls Church, VA: U.S. Army Intelligence Agency, 1987.

Martin, Paul H. "Communications-Computer Security." *Journal of Electronic Defense* (June 1987).

Muzerall, Joseph V., and Carty, Thomas P. "COMSEC and Its Need for Key Management." *DP&CS* (Spring 1987). Von Hoene, John P. A. *Intelligence User's Guide.* Washington, DC: DIA, 1983.

Ware, Willis H. "Information Systems, Security, and Privacy." *EDUCOM Bulletin* (Summer 1984).

—**HOMOPHONE,** a signals analysis term, is a plain-text term that may have more than one symbol. The alternative symbols are called nomophones.

References

Department of Defense, U.S. Army. *AIA: Threat Analysis.* Falls Church, VA: U.S. Army Intelligence Agency, 1987.

Martin, Paul H. "Communications-Computer Security." *Journal of Electronic Defense* (June 1987).

Muzerall, Joseph V., and Carty, Thomas P. "COMSEC and Its Need for Key Management." *DP&CS* (Spring 1987).

Ware, Willis H. "Information Systems, Security, and Privacy." *EDUCOM Bulletin* (Summer 1984).

—**HONEY TRAP** is a term used in clandestine and covert intelligence operations for an operation that is intended to compromise an opponent sexually. It is usually done to compromise someone so that he or she can be blackmailed. One of the criteria used in selecting U.S. attachés for duty in Moscow or Eastern Europe is to insure that they are married and that their wives accompany them so that the chances of honey trap operations are reduced. *See also:* Biographic Leverage, Ladies, Mozhno Girls, Raven, Sisters, Swallow, Swallow's Nest, Taxi.

References

Becket, Henry S. A. *The Dictionary of Espionage: Spookspeak into English.* New York: Stein and Day, 1986.

Deacon, Richard. *Spyclopedia: An Encyclopedia of Spies, Secret Services, Operations, Jargon, and All Subjects Related to the World of Espionage.* London: Macdonald, 1987.

Quirk, John; Phillips, David; Cline, Ray; and Pforzheimer, Walter. *The Central Intelligence Agency: A Photographic History.* Guilford, CT: Foreign Intelligence Press, 1986.

Ranelagh, John. *The Agency: The Rise and Decline of the CIA.* New York: Simon and Schuster, 1986.

—**HORIZON** is an intelligence imagery and photoreconnaissance term. It is the apparent or visible junction between the earth and the sky. It approximates the true horizon only when the point of vision is very close to sea level. *See also:* Aerial Photograph.

References

Department of Defense, Joint Chiefs of Staff. *Department of Defense Dictionary of Military and Related Terms.* Washington, DC: GPO, 1986.

Reeves, Robert; Anson, Abraham; and Landen, David. *Manual of Remote Sensing.* Falls Church, VA: American Society of Photogrammetry, 1975.

—**HORTON, BRIAN P.,** a naval intelligence specialist, was convicted of espionage offenses concerning the sale of classified material to the U.S.S.R. intelligence service. He was sentenced to six years in prison.

References

Allen, Thomas B., and Polmar, Norman. *Merchants of Treason: America's Secrets for Sale.* New York: Delacorte Press, 1988.

Crawford, David J. *Volunteers: The Betrayal of National Defense Secrets by Air Force Traitors.* Washington, DC: GPO, 1988.

—**HOSPITAL,** a term used in clandestine and covert intelligence operations, is a euphemism for prison.

References

Becket, Henry S. A. *The Dictionary of Espionage: Spookspeak into English.* New York: Stein and Day, 1986.

Deacon, Richard. *Spyclopedia: An Encyclopedia of Spies, Secret Services, Operations, Jargon, and All Subjects Related to the World of Espionage.* London: Macdonald, 1987.

Ranelagh, John. *The Agency: The Rise and Decline of the CIA.* New York: Simon and Schuster, 1986.

—**HOSTAGE** is a person held as a pledge that certain terms or agreements will be kept.

References

Department of Defense, Joint Chiefs of Staff. *Department of Defense Dictionary of Military and Related Terms.* Washington, DC: GPO, 1986.

Godson, Roy, ed. *Intelligence Problems for the 1980s, Number 1: Elements of Intelligence.* Rev. ed. Washington, DC: National Strategy Information Center, 1983.

Laqueur, Walter. *The Age of Terrorism.* Boston: Little, Brown, 1987.

———. *A World of Secrets.* New York: Basic Books, 1985.

Treverton, Gregory F. *Covert Action: The Limits of Intervention in the Postwar World.* New York: Basic Books, 1987.

—**HOSTILE COGNIZANT AGENT,** in communications security (COMSEC), means a person who is authorized access to national security or national security–related information and who intentionally makes it available to an unauthorized party.

References

Martin, Paul H. "Communications-Computer Security." *Journal of Electronic Defense* (June 1987).

Von Hoene, John P. A. *Intelligence User's Guide.* Washington, DC: DIA, 1983.

Ware, Willis H. "Information Systems, Security, and Privacy." *EDUCOM Bulletin* (Summer 1984).

—**HOT PHOTOGRAPHIC INTERPRETATION REPORT (HOTPHOTOREP)** is a preliminary unformatted report of significant information from tactical reconnaissance imagery dispatched prior to the compilation of the Initial Photo Interpretation Report. It should pertain to a single objective, event, or activity of significant interest to justify immediate reporting. *See also:* Imagery Intelligence, Imagery Interpreter, Photographic Intelligence.

References

Department of Defense, Joint Chiefs of Staff. *Department of Defense Dictionary of Military and Related Terms.* Washington, DC: GPO, 1986.

—**HOUSE PERMANENT SELECT COMMITTEE ON INTELLIGENCE.** From the inception of the Central Intelligence Group in the years immediately after the end of World War II, congressional oversight of intelligence was sporadic and was focused on attempting to improve the quality of the intelligence that was produced. However, when news of the Watergate operation was revealed in the early 1970s, congressional oversight became much greater, resulting in two committees: the Church Committee in the Senate, and the Pike Committee in the House. The Church Committee, in its investigation, focused on intelligence abuses, while the Pike Committee concerned itself with intelligence organization and the quality of the intelligence produced by the Intelligence Community. Although both of these committees completed their investigations and submitted their final reports, congressional oversight was continued into the Carter administration. The Senate maintained a Select Committee on Intelligence in 1976; the House created its own Permanent Select Committee on Intelligence in 1977. During the Carter years, both committees worked on charter legislation for the intelligence agencies. The result was S.2525, the National Intelligence Reform and Reorganization Act of 1978. Among the bill's provisions, those that called for renaming the director of Central Intelligence as the director of National Intelligence and separating him from the CIA, as well as strict controls over covert and clandestine operations, were sufficiently controversial that they stalled the bill in Congress. Although S.2525 was never enacted, it was the climax of congressional action against the Intelligence Community.

The House committee has been continued and is one of the two primary vehicles of congressional oversight of the Intelligence Community. *See also:* Congressional Oversight.

References

American Bar Association. *Oversight and Accountability of the U.S. Intelligence Agencies: An Evaluation.* Washington, DC: ABA, 1985.

Breckinridge, Scott D. *The CIA and the U.S. Intelligence System.* Boulder, CO: Westview Press, 1986.

Brinkley, David A., and Hull, Andrew W. *Estimative Intelligence: A Textbook on the History, Products, Uses, and Writing of Intelligence Estimates.* Columbus, OH: Battelle, 1979.

Cline, Ray S. *The CIA Under Reagan, Bush, and Casey.* Washington, DC: Acropolis Books, 1981.

Crawford, David J. *Volunteers: The Betrayal of National Defense Secrets by Air Force Traitors.* Washington, DC: GPO, 1988.

Godson, Roy, ed. *Intelligence Problems for the 1980s, Number 1: Elements of Intelligence.* Rev.

ed. Washington, DC: National Strategy Information Center, 1983.

Lefever, Ernest W., and Godson, Roy. *The CIA and the American Ethic: An Unfinished Debate.* Washington, DC: Ethics and Public Policy Center, Georgetown University, 1979.

Lowenthal, Mark M. *U.S. Intelligence: Evolution and Anatomy.* New York: Praeger, 1984.

Maurer, Alfred C.; Turnstall, Marion D.; and Keagle, James M. *Intelligence Policy and Process.* Boulder, CO: Westview Press, 1985.

Quirk, John; Phillips, David; Cline, Ray; and Pforzheimer, Walter. *The Central Intelligence Agency: A Photographic History.* Guilford, CT: Foreign Intelligence Press, 1986.

U.S. Congress. Senate. *Alleged Assassination Plots Involving Foreign Leaders: An Interim Report of the Select Committee to Study Governmental Operations with Respect to Intelligence Activities.* 94th Congress, 1st sess., Nov. 20, 1975. S. Rept. 94-465.

Von Hoene, John P. A. *Intelligence User's Guide.* Washington, DC: DIA, 1983.

—**HOUSE RESOLUTION (HRES) 658,** passed on July 14, 1977, established the House Permanent Select Committee on Intelligence (HPSCI). Passed a year and a half after Senate Resolution 400, which established the Senate Select Committee on Intelligence, HRES 658 emulated much of the language in the Senate resolution. However, it did differ in two significant respects. First, it inserted the word "permanent" in the title of the House committee, which gave it more prestige among the standing committees in the House. Second, it gave the committee authority over the budget, prominently mentioned "intelligence-related activities," and did not exclude congressional involvement in tactical intelligence. This amounted to a significant expansion of the House's role over the military services.

The House committee was to consist of thirteen members, in contrast to sixteen in the Senate. Of these, one member each was to also be a member of the Armed Services, International Relations, Judiciary, and Appropriations committees. Unlike the Senate, there was no mention of a party balance. Rather, the composition of the committee was to reflect the overall party balance existent in the House. *See also:* Congressional Oversight.

References

Maurer, Alfred C.; Turnstall, Marion D.; and Keagle, James M. *Intelligence Policy and Process.* Boulder, CO: Westview Press, 1985.

—HOUSE SELECT COMMITTEE ON INTELLIGENCE. *See:* Pike Committee.

—HOWARD, EDWARD L., a former employee of the Central Intelligence Agency, offered to work for the Soviet Union. He defected to the Soviet Union in 1985, as the FBI was about to arrest him. Howard provided the Soviets with the names of many of the CIA's agents in place in the Soviet Union and detailed information concerning the agency's operations in that country. The result was severe damage to the agency's operations in the Soviet Union and the executions of several Soviet citizens.

References

Allen, Thomas B., and Polmar, Norman. *Merchants of Treason: America's Secrets for Sale.* New York: Delacorte Press, 1988.

Becket, Henry S. A. *The Dictionary of Espionage: Spookspeak into English.* New York: Stein and Day, 1986.

Crawford, David J. *Volunteers: The Betrayal of National Defense Secrets by Air Force Traitors.* Washington, DC: GPO, 1988.

Deacon, Richard. *Spyclopedia: An Encyclopedia of Spies, Secret Services, Operations, Jargon, and All Subjects Related to the World of Espionage.* London: Macdonald, 1987.

—HUGHES, CAPTAIN WILLIAM H., JR., U.S. AIR FORCE, cleared for access to extremely sensitive communications information, disappeared after being sent to the Netherlands. He was listed as a deserter in 1983.

References

Allen, Thomas B., and Polmar, Norman. *Merchants of Treason: America's Secrets for Sale.* New York: Delacorte Press, 1988.

—HUGHES-RYAN AMENDMENT. Congressional oversight of the Intelligence Community has been a continuing theme of congressional proceedings since the earliest post–World War II days. However, the focus of this oversight had been on attempts to improve the quality of the intelligence that the Community produced. This focus shifted in 1974 from concern over the quality of intelligence to the types of operations in which the Community was engaged. The issues that prompted this shift were the involvement of the CIA in the fall of the Allende regime in Chile in 1973, and the agency's involvement in the Watergate affair. The result of congressional involvement came in 1974, when it passed the Hughes-Ryan Amendment to the Foreign Assistance Act of 1961, which stated that before funds could be expended on any type of CIA operations in foreign nations other than one that was solely for intelligence collection, the President had to be certain that the operation was important to national security and had to notify the House Foreign Affairs Committee and the Senate Foreign Relations Committee of his finding in a timely fashion. The significance of the amendment was that it considerably expanded congressional oversight of the CIA's covert action operations and was therefore a challenge to presidential influence and oversight over the Community. Additionally, it was a milestone that indicated that, if necessary, Congress would play a much greater role in Intelligence Community affairs. *See also:* Congressional Oversight.

References

Breckinridge, Scott D. *The CIA and the U.S. Intelligence System.* Boulder, CO: Westview Press, 1986.

Brinkley, David A., and Hull, Andrew W. *Estimative Intelligence: A Textbook on the History, Products, Uses and Writing of Intelligence Estimates.* Columbus, OH: Battelle, 1979.

Cline, Ray S. *The CIA Under Reagan, Bush, and Casey.* Washington, DC: Acropolis Books, 1981.

Crawford, David J. *Volunteers: The Betrayal of National Defense Secrets by Air Force Traitors.* Washington, DC: GPO, 1988.

Godson, Roy, ed. *Intelligence Problems for the 1980s, Number 1: Elements of Intelligence.* Rev. ed. Washington, DC: National Strategy Information Center, 1983.

Lefever, Ernest W., and Godson, Roy. *The CIA and the American Ethic: An Unfinished Debate.* Washington, DC: Ethics and Public Policy Center, Georgetown University, 1979.

Lowenthal, Mark M. *U.S. Intelligence: Evolution and Anatomy.* New York: Praeger, 1984.

Treverton, Gregory F. *Covert Action: The Limits of Intervention in the Postwar World.* New York: Basic Books, 1987.

Turner, Stansfield. *Secrecy and Democracy: The CIA in Transition.* Boston: Houghton Mifflin, 1985.

U.S. Congress. Senate. *Alleged Assassination Plots Involving Foreign Leaders: An Interim Report of the Select Committee to Study Governmental Operations with Respect to Intelligence Activities.* 94th Congress, 1st sess., Nov. 20, 1975. S. Rept. 94-465.

Von Hoene, John P. A. *Intelligence User's Guide.* Washington, DC: DIA, 1983.

—**HUMAN COLLECTION.** *See:* Human Intelligence.

—**HUMAN INTELLIGENCE (HUMINT)** is a category of intelligence information that is provided by human beings, rather than by technical or other means. A justifiable criticism that has been made of the U.S. Intelligence Community is that it relies too heavily on technical systems for its intelligence information and does not sufficiently exploit human sources of information. An excellent example of this is seen when the British performance in the Falkland Islands War and the U.S. performance in the Grenada operation are contrasted. In the Falklands conflict, the British took pains to exploit all sources of information. This included interviewing two retired school teachers who had just returned from the islands as well as scientists who had recently conducted research in the region. These sources were able to provide valuable information about existing road conditions, the terrain, and other environmental aspects that are so valuable in conducting military operations.

In regard to Grenada, on the other hand, the United States did not even attempt to identify human sources of information in many cases. The result was that U.S. forces hit the island with outdated maps, U.S. aircraft bombed an insane asylum, and one of two school campuses with U.S. medical students was not liberated until a day after the invasion *because U.S. forces were unaware of the existence of the second campus.* There were many students who had recently returned from Grenada who could have filled these shortfalls or gaps in intelligence information, but they were not contacted. Additionally, some who came forth to volunteer information were ignored.

The predilection of the U.S. Intelligence Community to favor empirical data that can be collected by systems and to distrust the "softer" intelligence that HUMINT has to offer is a very real problem. Recently, greater attention has been paid to this valuable resource, but there is a great deal of additional valuable information that is ignored. *See also:* Human Resources Collection, Human Source Reporting.

References
American Bar Association. *Oversight and Accountability of the U.S. Intelligence Agencies: An Evaluation.* Washington, DC: ABA, 1985.

Corson, William R. *The Armies of Ignorance: The Rise of the American Intelligence Empire.* New York: Dial Press, 1977.

Department of Defense, Defense Intelligence College. *Glossary of Intelligence Terms and Definitions.* Washington, DC: DIC, 1987.

Godson, Roy, ed. *Intelligence Problems for the 1980s, Number 1: Elements of Intelligence.* Rev. ed. Washington, DC: National Strategy Information Center, 1983.

———. *Intelligence Problems for the 1980s, Number 2: Analysis and Estimates.* Washington, DC: National Strategy Information Center, 1980.

———. *Intelligence Problems for the 1980s, Number 3: Counterintelligence.* Washington, DC: National Strategy Information Center, 1980.

———. *Intelligence Problems for the 1980s, Number 5: Clandestine Collection.* Washington, DC: National Strategy Information Center, 1982.

Kent, Sherman. *Strategic Intelligence for American World Policy.* Princeton, NJ: Princeton University Press, 1966.

Laqueur, Walter. *A World of Secrets.* New York: Basic Books, 1985.

Lowenthal, Mark M. *U.S. Intelligence: Evolution and Anatomy.* New York: Praeger, 1984.

Maurer, Alfred C.; Turnstall, Marion D.; and Keagle, James M. *Intelligence Policy and Process.* Boulder, CO: Westview Press, 1985.

Treverton, Gregory F. *Covert Action: The Limits of Intervention in the Postwar World.* New York: Basic Books, 1987.

Turner, Stansfield. *Secrecy and Democracy: The CIA in Transition.* Boston: Houghton Mifflin, 1985.

—**HUMAN INTELLIGENCE COMMITTEE,** a committee of the U.S. Intelligence Board, was created with some reluctance on the part of the director of Central Intelligence because of the sensitive nature of human clandestine operations. It later became the Human Resources Committee.

References
Breckinridge, Scott D. *The CIA and the U.S. Intelligence System.* Boulder, CO: Westview Press, 1986.

Godson, Roy, ed. *Intelligence Problems for the 1980s, Number 1: Elements of Intelligence.* Rev. ed. Washington, DC: National Strategy Information Center, 1983.

———. *Intelligence Problems for the 1980s, Number 5: Clandestine Collection.* Washington, DC: National Strategy Information Center, 1982.

Kent, Sherman. *Strategic Intelligence for American World Policy.* Princeton, NJ: Princeton University Press, 1966.

Laqueur, Walter. *A World of Secrets.* New York: Basic Books, 1985.

Turner, Stansfield. *Secrecy and Democracy: The CIA in Transition.* Boston: Houghton Mifflin, 1985.

—**HUMAN RESOURCES COLLECTION** is a general intelligence term for all the activity associated with collecting information from human sources. *See also:* Human Intelligence (HUMINT).

—**HUMAN SOURCE** is a general intelligence term for a person who knowingly or unknowingly provides information of potential intelligence value to an intelligence agency or activity. *See also:* Agent, Co-Opted Worker, Co-Optees, Disaffected Person, Mole, Pigeon, Recruitment, Recruitment in Place.

References

Department of Defense, Defense Intelligence College. *Glossary of Intelligence Terms and Definitions.* Washington, DC: DIC, 1987.

Godson, Roy, ed. *Intelligence Problems for the 1980s, Number 1: Elements of Intelligence.* Rev. ed. Washington, DC: National Strategy Information Center, 1983.

————. *Intelligence Problems for the 1980s, Number 2: Analysis and Estimates.* Washington, DC: National Strategy Information Center, 1980.

————. *Intelligence Problems for the 1980s, Number 3: Counterintelligence.* Washington, DC: National Strategy Information Center, 1980.

————. *Intelligence Problems for the 1980s, Number 5: Clandestine Collection.* Washington, DC: National Strategy Information Center, 1982.

Kent, Sherman. *Strategic Intelligence for American World Policy.* Princeton, NJ: Princeton University Press, 1966.

Laqueur, Walter. *A World of Secrets.* New York: Basic Books, 1985.

Turner, Stansfield. *Secrecy and Democracy: The CIA in Transition.* Boston: Houghton Mifflin, 1985.

—**HUMAN SOURCE REPORTING** is a general intelligence term. It is the flow of intelligence information from those who gather it to the customer. It may come from collectors who are in or are outside the Intelligence Community. *See also:* Human Source.

—**HUMINT.** *See:* Human Intelligence.

—**HUMPHREY, RONALD L.,** an employee of the U.S. Information Service, was convicted in 1978 of espionage offenses concerning passing classified information to Vietnamese intelligence. He was apparently motivated by family ties. He was sentenced to fifteen years in prison.

References

Allen, Thomas B., and Polmar, Norman. *Merchants of Treason: America's Secrets for Sale.* New York: Delacorte Press, 1988.

Crawford, David J. *Volunteers: The Betrayal of National Defense Secrets by Air Force Traitors.* Washington, DC: GPO, 1988.

Turner, Stansfield. *Secrecy and Democracy: The CIA in Transition.* Boston: Houghton Mifflin, 1985.

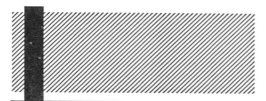

Muzerall, Joseph V., and Carty, Thomas P. "COMSEC and Its Need for Key Management." *DP&CS* (Spring 1987).

Ware, Willis H. "Information Systems, Security, and Privacy." *EDUCOM Bulletin* (Summer 1984).

—**ILLEGAL** is a term used in clandestine and covert intelligence operations to describe an officer or employee of an intelligence organization who is sent abroad and has no overt connection with either his intelligence organization or the government that sponsors the intelligence organization. *See also:* Agent, Agent Authentication, Agent in Place, Agent of Influence, Agent Provocateur, Between the Lines Entry, Cover, Cover Name, Cover Organizations, Cover Story, Go to Ground, Illegal Agent, Illegal Communication, Illegal Net, Illegal Operations, Illegal Residency, Illegal Support Officer, Infiltration, Penetration, Provocation Agent, Sign of Life Signal, Singleton, Special Activities, Submerge, Suitable Cover, Third Country Operation.

References

Allen, Thomas B., and Polmar, Norman. *Merchants of Treason: America's Secrets for Sale.* New York: Delacorte Press, 1988.

Department of Defense, Defense Intelligence College. *Glossary of Intelligence Terms and Definitions.* Washington, DC: DIC, 1987.

Kessler, Ronald. *Spy vs. Spy: Stalking Soviet Spies in America.* New York: Charles Scribner's Sons, 1988.

—**ILLEGAL AGENT** is an agent who is controlled by an illegal residency or by the headquarters of an intelligence organization. *See also:* Agent, Agent Authentication, Agent in Place, Agent Net, Agent of Influence, Agent Provocateur, Confusion Agent, Dispatched Agent, Double Agent, Handling Agent, Informant, Inside Man, Provocation Agent, Pseudonym, Recruitment, Recruitment in Place, Special Activities, Walk-in.

References

Department of Defense, Defense Intelligence College. *Glossary of Intelligence Terms and Definitions.* Washington, DC: DIC, 1987.

Kessler, Ronald. *Spy vs. Spy: Stalking Soviet Spies in America.* New York: Charles Scribner's Sons, 1988.

—**ILLEGAL COMMUNICATION** is a term used in clandestine and covert intelligence operations to describe an electronic communication or signal made without the legal permission of the nation from which it is sent. *See also:* Illegal, Illegal Agent.

—**IDENTIFICATION.** (1) In imagery interpretation, identification is the discrimination between objects within a particular type or class. (2) Identification is also an Army tactical intelligence (TACINT) term that means the analysis of the content of the communications or the signal characteristics of an emitter in order to identify the signal for further exploitation. Analysis can be as simple as identifying a language or as complicated as determining a special code that is used by a unit. (3) In the context of definition (2), it is a step in the Army TACINT signals intelligence (SIGINT) process. *See also*: SIGINT Process.

References

Department of Defense, Joint Chiefs of Staff. *Department of Defense Dictionary of Military and Related Terms.* Washington, DC: GPO, 1986.

Department of Defense, U.S. Army. *Counter-Signals Intelligence (C-SIGINT) Operations.* Field Manual FM 34-62. Washington, DC: Headquarters, Department of the Army, 1986.

———. *Military Intelligence Battalion (Combat Electronic Warfare Intelligence) (Division).* Field Manual FM 34-10. Washington, DC: Headquarters, Department of the Army, 1981.

———. *Military Intelligence Company (Combat Electronic Warfare and Intelligence) (Armored Cavalry Regiment/Separate Brigade).* Field Manual FM 34-30. Washington, DC: Headquarters, Department of the Army, 1983.

Reeves, Robert; Anson, Abraham; and Landen, David. *Manual of Remote Sensing.* Falls Church, VA: American Society of Photogrammetry, 1975.

—**IDLE,** a baud-based system term used in communications intelligence, communications security, operations security, and signals analysis, is a signal condition in which a communications system is activated but no intelligence is being sent. *See also:* Communications Security.

References

Department of Defense, U.S. Army. *AIA: Threat Analysis.* Falls Church, VA: U.S. Army Intelligence Agency, 1987.

References

Department of Defense, Defense Intelligence College. *Glossary of Intelligence Terms and Definitions.* Washington, DC: DIC, 1987.

—**ILLEGAL NET** is an intelligence collecting unit that is operating under the control of an illegal residency. *See also:* Illegal, Illegal Agent, Illegal Communication, Illegal Residency.

References

Becket, Henry S. A. *The Dictionary of Espionage: Spookspeak into English.* New York: Stein and Day, 1986.

Deacon, Richard. *Spyclopedia: An Encyclopedia of Spies, Secret Services, Operations, Jargon, and All Subjects Related to the World of Espionage.* London: Macdonald, 1987.

Kessler, Ronald. *Spy vs. Spy: Stalking Soviet Spies in America.* New York: Charles Scribner's Sons, 1988.

—**ILLEGAL OPERATIONS** are activities conducted by intelligence officers, employees, or agents who are under the control of an illegal residency or of an intelligence agency. *See also:* Illegal.

References

Becket, Henry S. A. *The Dictionary of Espionage: Spookspeak into English.* New York: Stein and Day, 1986.

Kessler, Ronald. *Spy vs. Spy: Stalking Soviet Spies in America.* New York: Charles Scribner's Sons, 1988.

Ranelagh, John. *The Agency: The Rise and Decline of the CIA.* New York: Simon and Schuster, 1986.

—**ILLEGAL RESIDENCY** is a term used in clandestine and covert intelligence operations. It is an intelligence apparatus that is established in a foreign nation and composed of one or more intelligence officers. It has no overt connection with the sponsoring intelligence agency or with the intelligence agency's government. *See also:* Illegal, Legal Residency.

References

Department of Defense, Defense Intelligence College. *Glossary of Intelligence Terms and Definitions.* Washington, DC: DIC, 1987.

—**ILLEGAL SUPPORT OFFICER** is an intelligence officer who is assigned to a legal residency. His mission is to support illegals by supplying them with their everyday essentials and to gather information that will help the illegals avoid detection. *See also:* Illegal.

References

Becket, Henry S. A. *The Dictionary of Espionage: Spookspeak into English.* New York: Stein and Day, 1986.

Deacon, Richard. *Spyclopedia: An Encyclopedia of Spies, Secret Services, Operations, Jargon, and All Subjects Related to the World of Espionage.* London: Macdonald, 1987.

Kessler, Ronald. *Spy vs. Spy: Stalking Soviet Spies in America.* New York: Charles Scribner's Sons, 1988.

Ranelagh, John. *The Agency: The Rise and Decline of the CIA.* New York: Simon and Schuster, 1986.

—**ILLICIT COMMUNICATION** is a type of clandestine communication. It is an electronic communication or signal that is sent in support of a clandestine operation. *See also:* Music Box, Musician, Piano Concerto, Piano Study, Quick Trip Around the Horn, Sign of Life Signal, Sterile Telephone, Thirty Threes, What's Your Twenty?

References

Becket, Henry S. A. *The Dictionary of Espionage: Spookspeak into English.* New York: Stein and Day, 1986.

Deacon, Richard. *Spyclopedia: An Encyclopedia of Spies, Secret Services, Operations, Jargon, and All Subjects Related to the World of Espionage.* London: Macdonald, 1987.

Department of Defense, Defense Intelligence College. *Glossary of Intelligence Terms and Definitions.* Washington, DC: DIC, 1987.

Kessler, Ronald. *Spy vs. Spy: Stalking Soviet Spies in America.* New York: Charles Scribner's Sons, 1988.

Ranelagh, John. *The Agency: The Rise and Decline of the CIA.* New York: Simon and Schuster, 1986.

—**IMAGE** is a representation of an object by electronic or optical means on film, electronic display devices, or other media. *See also:* Aerial Photograph.

References

Department of Defense, Defense Intelligence College. *Glossary of Intelligence Terms and Definitions.* Washington, DC: DIC, 1987.

Department of Defense, Joint Chiefs of Staff. *Department of Defense Dictionary of Military and Related Terms.* Washington, DC: GPO, 1986.

Department of Defense, U.S. Army. *Intelligence Imagery.* Field Manual FM 34-55. Washington, DC: Headquarters, Department of the Army, 1985.

Reeves, Robert; Anson, Abraham; and Landen, David. *Manual of Remote Sensing.* Falls Church, VA: American Society of Photogrammetry, 1975.

U.S. Congress. Senate. *Final Report of the Senate Select Committee to Study Government Operations with Respect to Intelligence Activities. Report 94-755. Book I, Foreign and Military Intelligence.* Washington, DC: GPO, 1976.

—**IMAGE MOTION COMPENSATION** is movement that is intentionally imparted to a film at a rate that will compensate for the forward motion of an aircraft or space vehicle when photographing ground objects. *See also:* Image.

References

Department of Defense, Joint Chiefs of Staff. *Department of Defense Dictionary of Military and Related Terms.* Washington, DC: GPO, 1986.

Department of Defense, U.S. Army. *Intelligence Imagery.* Field Manual FM 34-55. Washington, DC: Headquarters, Department of the Army, 1985.

Reeves, Robert; Anson, Abraham; and Landen, David. *Manual of Remote Sensing.* Falls Church, VA: American Society of Photogrammetry, 1975.

—**IMAGERY** are representations of objects that are reproduced electronically or optically on film, electronic display devices, or other media. *See also:* Image.

References

Department of Defense, Defense Intelligence College. *Glossary of Intelligence Terms and Definitions.* Washington, DC: DIC, 1987.

Department of Defense, Joint Chiefs of Staff. *Department of Defense Dictionary of Military and Related Terms.* Washington, DC: GPO, 1986.

Department of Defense, U.S. Army. *Intelligence Imagery.* Field Manual FM 34-55. Washington, DC: Headquarters, Department of the Army, 1985.

Reeves, Robert; Anson, Abraham; and Landen, David. *Manual of Remote Sensing.* Falls Church, VA: American Society of Photogrammetry, 1975.

U.S. Congress. Senate. *Final Report of the Senate Select Committee to Study Government Operations with Respect to Intelligence Activities. Report 94-755. Book I, Foreign and Military Intelligence.* Washington, DC: GPO, 1976.

—**IMAGERY ANNOTATION** is an intelligence imagery and photoreconnaissance term for the material or information that is written on the imagery. It is often necessary to amplify the written report. The following annotations are required on imagery produced by the U.S. Army: a titling strip that includes a grid reference or the geographic coordinates of the target or object; a reference point to illustrate the geographical reference that is quoted in the titling strip; the target category and description; an orientation aid in the form of an arrowhead; and interpretation annotations that indicate the individual target category item. *See also:* Image.

References

Department of Defense, U.S. Army. *Intelligence Imagery.* Field Manual FM 34-55. Washington, DC: Headquarters, Department of the Army, 1985.

Reeves, Robert; Anson, Abraham; and Landen, David. *Manual of Remote Sensing.* Falls Church, VA: American Society of Photogrammetry, 1975.

—**IMAGERY COLLATERAL** are the referenced materials that support imagery interpretation. *See also:* Image.

References

Department of Defense, Joint Chiefs of Staff. *Department of Defense Dictionary of Military and Related Terms.* Washington, DC: GPO, 1986.

Department of Defense, U.S. Army. *Intelligence Imagery.* Field Manual FM 34-55. Washington, DC: Headquarters, Department of the Army, 1985.

—**IMAGERY CORRELATION** is the mutual relationship between the different signatures on imagery from different types of sensors in terms of position and the physical characteristics signified. *See also:* Image.

References

Department of Defense, Joint Chiefs of Staff. *Department of Defense Dictionary of Military and Related Terms.* Washington, DC: GPO, 1986.

Department of Defense, U.S. Army. *Intelligence Imagery.* Field Manual FM 34-55. Washington, DC: Headquarters, Department of the Army, 1985.

Reeves, Robert; Anson, Abraham; and Landen, David. *Manual of Remote Sensing.* Falls Church, VA: American Society of Photogrammetry, 1975.

—**IMAGERY DATA RECORDING** is transposing information relating to the airborne vehicle and sensor, such as speed, height, tilt, position, and time, to the matrix block on the sensor record at the moment that the imagery is acquired. *See also:* Image.

References

Department of Defense, Joint Chiefs of Staff. *Department of Defense Dictionary of Military and Related Terms.* Washington, DC: GPO, 1986.

Department of Defense, U.S. Army. *Intelligence Imagery*. Field Manual FM 34-55. Washington, DC: Headquarters, Department of the Army, 1985.

Reeves, Robert; Anson, Abraham; and Landen, David. *Manual of Remote Sensing*. Falls Church, VA: American Society of Photogrammetry, 1975.

—**IMAGERY EXPLOITATION** is the process of processing and printing imagery, assembling it into imagery packs, identifying, interpreting, measuring, extracting information, preparing reports, and disseminating the information to the customer. *See also:* Image.

References

Department of Defense, Joint Chiefs of Staff. *Department of Defense Dictionary of Military and Related Terms*. Washington, DC: GPO, 1986.

Department of Defense, U.S. Army. *Intelligence Imagery*. Field Manual FM 34-55. Washington, DC: Headquarters, Department of the Army, 1985.

Reeves, Robert; Anson, Abraham; and Landen, David. *Manual of Remote Sensing*. Falls Church, VA: American Society of Photogrammetry, 1975.

—**IMAGERY INTELLIGENCE (IMINT)** are the collected products of imagery interpretation that have been processed for intelligence use by an imagery interpreter or imagery analyst. *See also:* Image.

References

Department of Defense, U.S. Army. *Intelligence Imagery*. Field Manual FM 34-55. Washington, DC: Headquarters, Department of the Army, 1985.

————. *Military Intelligence Battalion (CEWI) (Operations) (Corps)*. Field Manual FM 34-21. Washington, DC: Headquarters, Department of the Army, 1982.

Reeves, Robert; Anson, Abraham; and Landen, David. *Manual of Remote Sensing*. Falls Church, VA: American Society of Photogrammetry, 1975.

—**IMAGERY INTERPRETATION (II)** is the process of locating, recognizing, identifying, and describing objects, activities, and terrain that appears on imagery. *See also:* Image.

References

Department of Defense, Joint Chiefs of Staff. *Department of Defense Dictionary of Military and Related Terms*. Washington, DC: GPO, 1986.

Department of Defense, U.S. Army. *Intelligence Imagery*. Field Manual FM 34-55. Washington, DC: Headquarters, Department of the Army, 1985.

Reeves, Robert; Anson, Abraham; and Landen, David. *Manual of Remote Sensing*. Falls Church, VA: American Society of Photogrammetry, 1975.

—**IMAGERY INTERPRETATION KEY** is any diagram, chart, table, list, or set of examples that are used to help imagery interpreters to identify quickly objects that are visible on imagery. *See also:* Image.

References

Department of Defense, Joint Chiefs of Staff. *Department of Defense Dictionary of Military and Related Terms*. Washington, DC: GPO, 1986.

Department of Defense, U.S. Army. *Intelligence Imagery*. Field Manual FM 34-55. Washington, DC: Headquarters, Department of the Army, 1985.

—**IMAGERY INTERPRETER (II)** is an individual trained to examine photography and other imagery in order to locate, recognize, identify, and describe objects, activities, and terrain of intelligence interest. *See also:* Image.

References

Department of Defense, Joint Chiefs of Staff. *Department of Defense Dictionary of Military and Related Terms*. Washington, DC: GPO, 1986.

Department of Defense, U.S. Army. *Intelligence Imagery*. Field Manual FM 34-55. Washington, DC: Headquarters, Department of the Army, 1985.

Reeves, Robert; Anson, Abraham; and Landen, David. *Manual of Remote Sensing*. Falls Church, VA: American Society of Photogrammetry, 1975.

—**IMAGERY PACK** is an intelligence imagery and photoreconnaissance term. It is an assembly of records from different imagery sensors that cover the same target area. *See also:* Image.

References

Department of Defense, Joint Chiefs of Staff. *Department of Defense Dictionary of Military and Related Terms*. Washington, DC: GPO, 1986.

Department of Defense, U.S. Army. *Intelligence Imagery*. Field Manual FM 34-55. Washington, DC: Headquarters, Department of the Army, 1985.

—**IMITATIVE COMMUNICATIONS DECEPTION (ICD),** in electronic warfare (EW), means intruding on communications channels for deceptive purposes by introducing signals or traffic that imitate other communications. *See also:* Communications Deception, Electronic Warfare.

References

Department of Defense, U.S. Army. *Counter-Signals Intelligence (C-SIGINT) Operations.* Field Manual FM 34-62. Washington, DC: Headquarters, Department of the Army, 1986.

———. *Military Intelligence Battalion Combat Electronic Warfare and Intelligence (Aerial Exploitation) (Corps).* Field Manual FM 34-22. Washington, DC: Headquarters, Department of the Army, 1984.

———. *Military Intelligence Battalion (Combat Electronic Warfare Intelligence) (Division).* Field Manual FM 34-10. Washington, DC: Headquarters, Department of the Army, 1981.

———. *Military Intelligence Battalion (CEWI) (Tactical Exploitation) (Corps): Counterintelligence, Interrogation, Electronic Warfare.* Field Manual FM 34-23. Washington, DC: Headquarters, Department of the Army, 1985.

———. *Military Intelligence Company (Combat Electronic Warfare and Intelligence) (Armored Cavalry Regiment/Separate Brigade).* Field Manual FM 34-30. Washington, DC: Headquarters, Department of the Army, 1983.

———. *Military Intelligence Group (Combat Electronic Warfare and Intelligence) (Corps).* Field Manual FM 34-20. Washington, DC: Headquarters, Department of the Army, 1983.

—**IMITATIVE DECEPTION,** in electronic warfare (EW), is introducing electromagnetic radiations that imitate enemy emissions into enemy channels. *See also:* Electronic Warfare.

References

Department of Defense, Defense Intelligence College. *Glossary of Intelligence Terms and Definitions.* Washington, DC: DIC, 1987.

Department of Defense, U.S. Army. *Counter-Signals Intelligence (C-SIGINT) Operations.* Field Manual FM 34-62, 3 February 1986. Washington, DC: Headquarters, Department of the Army, 1986.

———. *Military Intelligence Battalion (Combat Electronic Warfare Intelligence) (Division).* Field Manual FM 34-10, 3 July 1981. Washington, DC: Headquarters, Department of the Army, 1981.

———. *Military Intelligence Battalion Combat Electronic Warfare and Intelligence (Aerial Exploitation) (Corps).* Field Manual FM 34-22, 19 March 1984. Washington, DC: Headquarters, Department of the Army, 1984.

———. *Military Intelligence Battalion (CEWI) (Tactical Exploitation) (Corps): Counterintelligence, Interrogation, Electronic Warfare.* Field Manual FM 34-23, 21 January 1985. Washington, DC: Headquarters, Department of the Army, 1985.

———. *Military Intelligence Company (Combat Electronic Warfare and Intelligence) (Armored Cavalry Regiment/Separate Brigade).* Field Manual FM 34-30. Washington, DC: Headquarters, Department of the Army, 1983.

———. *Military Intelligence Group (Combat Electronic Warfare and Intelligence) (Corps).* Field Manual FM 34-20. Washington, DC: Headquarters, Department of the Army, 1983.

—**IMMEDIATE MESSAGE** is a precedence category reserved for messages relating to situations that gravely affect the security of national or allied forces or people and that require immediate delivery to the addressees. *See also:* Precedence.

References

Department of Defense, Joint Chiefs of Staff. *Department of Defense Dictionary of Military and Related Terms.* Washington, DC: GPO, 1986.

—**INCREMENTAL COST,** in intelligence budgeting, is the added cost of a change in the level or nature of activity. Incremental costs can refer to any type of change: adding a new product, changing distribution channels, or adding new machinery are some examples. Although they are sometimes interpreted to be the same as marginal cost, the latter has a much more limited meaning, in that it refers to the cost of an added unit of output. *See also:* Budget.

References

Pickett, George. "Congress, the Budget, and Intelligence." In *Intelligence Policy and Process,* edited by Alfred C. Maurer, Marion D. Turnstall, and James M. Keagle. Boulder, CO: Westview Press, 1985.

—**INCUMBENT,** in the context of sensitive compartmented information (SCI), is an individual who is occupying an SCI billet. *See also:* Billet.

References

Department of Defense, Defense Intelligence College. *Glossary of Intelligence Terms and Definitions.* Washington, DC: DIC, 1987.

—**INDEX NUMBER,** in intelligence budgeting, is a magnitude expressed as a percentage of the corresponding magnitude in some "base" period. The base is usually designated as equal to 100. *See also:* Incremental Cost.

References

Pickett, George. "Congress, the Budget, and Intelligence." In *Intelligence Policy and Process*, edited by Alfred C. Maurer, Marion D. Turnstall, and James M. Keagle. Boulder, CO: Westview Press, 1985.

—**INDICATION** is an indications and warning (I&W) term. It is a specific action that has been observed or that can be inferred from intelligence sources which is related to the preparation for or the rejection of hostile activity. There is a relationship between *indication* and *indicator*. An indicator in I&W is something that we might expect the enemy to do and therefore watch for. An indication is an indicator that has actually occurred. *See also:* Indicator.

References

Laqueur, Walter. *A World of Secrets*. New York: Basic Books, 1985.

Treverton, Gregory F. *Covert Action: The Limits of Intervention in the Postwar World*. New York: Basic Books, 1987.

—**INDICATIONS (INTELLIGENCE),** according to the Church Committee, means "information in various degrees of evaluation which bears on the intention of a potential enemy to adopt or reject a course of action." Intelligence indications is also an intelligence and warning (I&W) term. Here it means "that specialized form of current and estimative intelligence which seeks to discern, in advance, the intent of any foreign country to initiate hostilities, or to produce a crisis which might give rise to hostilities or to action by U.S. forces." *See also:* Indications and Warning.

References

Department of Defense, Joint Chiefs of Staff. *Department of Defense Dictionary of Military and Related Terms*. Washington, DC: GPO, 1986.

Laqueur, Walter. *A World of Secrets*. New York: Basic Books, 1985.

Treverton, Gregory F. *Covert Action: The Limits of Intervention in the Postwar World*. New York: Basic Books, 1987.

—**INDICATIONS AND WARNING (I&W)** are intelligence activities that are tasked with detecting and reporting time-sensitive intelligence on foreign events that could threaten U.S. or allied military, economic, or political interests, or U.S. citizens abroad. It includes the timely warning of hostile enemy actions or intentions; imminent hostilities; serious insurgency; nuclear or nonnuclear attack on the United States, its overseas forces, or allies; hostile reactions to U.S. reconnaissance activities; terrorist attacks; and other similar activities. *See also:* Indications.

References

American Bar Association. *Oversight and Accountability of the U.S. Intelligence Agencies: An Evaluation*. Washington, DC: ABA, 1985.

Department of Defense, Defense Intelligence College. *Glossary of Intelligence Terms and Definitions*. Washington, DC: DIC, 1987.

Department of Defense, Joint Chiefs of Staff. *Department of Defense Dictionary of Military and Related Terms*. Washington, DC: GPO, 1986.

Kent, Sherman. *Strategic Intelligence for American World Policy*. Princeton, NJ: Princeton University Press, 1966.

Laqueur, Walter. *The Age of Terrorism*. Boston: Little, Brown, 1987.

———. *A World of Secrets*. New York: Basic Books, 1985.

Treverton, Gregory F. *Covert Action: The Limits of Intervention in the Postwar World*. New York: Basic Books, 1987.

Turner, Stansfield. *Secrecy and Democracy: The CIA in Transition*. Boston: Houghton Mifflin, 1985.

—**INDICATIONS AND WARNING INTELLIGENCE** is information that alerts or warns of an impending course of action by a foreign power that is detrimental to the interests of the United States. This information is the product of a recognition and correlation of threat indications and the synthesis of a threat posture. *See also:* Indications, Indications and Warning.

—**INDICATIONS AND WARNING SYSTEM** is an associated grouping into a network of intelligence production facilities with analytical resources that are capable of contributing to or developing indications and warning intelligence and of disseminating this product within their own command and to all other facilities, organizations, or commands within the Department of Defense network. *See also:* Indications, Indications and Warning.

References

Department of Defense, Defense Intelligence College. *Glossary of Intelligence Terms and Definitions.* Washington, DC: DIC, 1987.

Laqueur, Walter. *A World of Secrets.* New York: Basic Books, 1985.

—**INDICATIONS CENTER** is an indications and warning (I&W) term. It is an intelligence situation room or plot, distinguished by around-the-clock operations, highly qualified personnel, comprehensive communications, concentration on all aspects of possible enemy attack or other situations that might require action by U.S. forces, and adherence to procedures established for operation of the Department of Defense indications system. The indications center is the focal point for performing the operational intelligence functions of a command. *See also:* Alert Center, Watch Center.

References

Department of Defense, Defense Intelligence College. *Glossary of Intelligence Terms and Definitions.* Washington, DC: DIC, 1987.

Laqueur, Walter. *A World of Secrets.* New York: Basic Books, 1985.

—**INDICATIONS WATCH OFFICER** is an indications and warning (I&W) term. Such an officer serves in an indications center. The senior indications officer is the command's intelligence duty officer and is the duty representative of the commander in intelligence matters. An indications officer is trained to identify indications of hostilities and to cope with other intelligence that requires immediate attention. *See also:* Alert Center, Watch Center.

References

Department of Defense, Defense Intelligence College. *Glossary of Intelligence Terms and Definitions.* Washington, DC: DIC, 1987.

Laqueur, Walter. *A World of Secrets.* New York: Basic Books, 1985.

—**INDICATOR,** in general intelligence usage, is an item of information that reflects on the intention or capability of a potential enemy to adopt or reject a course of action. In Army tactical intelligence (TACINT), the term has the above meaning and can also mean activities that can contribute to the determination of a friendly course of action. In indications and warning (I&W), an indicator is an action—specific, generalized, or theoretical—that an enemy might be expected to take in preparation for an aggressive act. It is a hypothetical event or action that may be necessary to establish a threat. For any potential threat, various indicators may be necessary. For one case, certain indicators may be observed, yet in another situation, different indicators may be expected. These potential actions are referred to as indicators, and lists of indicators have been developed to aid the warning analyst in performing his or her job. When an indicator is observed as actually occurring, then it is referred to as an indication. For example, an indicator may be the deployment of artillery to forward areas. When this action is actually observed, it is then called an indication.

References

Department of Defense, Joint Chiefs of Staff. *Department of Defense Dictionary of Military and Related Terms.* Washington, DC: GPO, 1986.

Department of Defense, U.S. Army. *Counter-Signals Intelligence (C-SIGINT) Operations.* Field Manual FM 34-62. Washington, DC: Headquarters, Department of the Army, 1986.

———. *Military Intelligence Battalion (CEWI) (Tactical Exploitation) (Corps): Counterintelligence, Interrogation, Electronic Warfare.* Field Manual FM 34-23. Washington, DC: Headquarters, Department of the Army, 1985.

———. *Military Intelligence Company (Combat Electronic Warfare and Intelligence) (Armored Cavalry Regiment/Separate Brigade).* Field Manual FM 34-30. Washington, DC: Headquarters, Department of the Army, 1983.

Laqueur, Walter. *A World of Secrets.* New York: Basic Books, 1985.

—**INDICATOR ELEMENT,** a term used in communications intelligence, communications security, operations security, and signals analysis, is an element that is used to indicate different traffic conditions. *See also:* Communications Security.

References

Department of Defense, Defense Intelligence College. *Glossary of Intelligence Terms and Definitions.* Washington, DC: DIC, 1987.

Department of Defense, U.S. Army. *Counter-Signals Intelligence (C-SIGINT) Operations.* Field Manual

FM 34-62. Washington, DC: Headquarters, Department of the Army, 1986.

————. *Military Intelligence Battalion Combat Electronic Warfare and Intelligence (Aerial Exploitation) (Corps)*. Field Manual FM 34-22. Washington, DC: Headquarters, Department of the Army, 1984.

————. *Military Intelligence Battalion (Combat Electronic Warfare Intelligence) (Division)*. Field Manual FM 34-10. Washington, DC: Headquarters, Department of the Army, 1981.

————. *Military Intelligence Battalion (CEWI) (Tactical Exploitation) (Corps): Counterintelligence, Interrogation, Electronic Warfare*. Field Manual FM 34-23. Washington, DC: Headquarters, Department of the Army, 1985.

————. *Military Intelligence Company (Combat Electronic Warfare and Intelligence) (Armored Cavalry Regiment/Separate Brigade)*. Field Manual FM 34-30. Washington, DC: Headquarters, Department of the Army, 1983.

————. *Military Intelligence Group (Combat Electronic Warfare and Intelligence) (Corps)*. Field Manual FM 34-20. Washington, DC: Headquarters, Department of the Army, 1983.

Laqueur, Walter. *A World of Secrets*. New York: Basic Books, 1985.

—**INDICATOR LIST** is an indications and warning (I&W) term. It is a list of factors or acts (military, political, economic, diplomatic, and internal actions) that a foreign power might be expected to take if it intended to initiate hostilities. These factors are logical or plausible moves or acts, based on U.S. reasoning, or observed during past conflicts or crises, or based on the results of intelligence assessments of enemy strategic offensive military doctrine and strategic standard operating procedures. *See also:* Indications, Indications and Warning.

References

Department of Defense, Defense Intelligence College. *Glossary of Intelligence Terms and Definitions*. Washington, DC: DIC, 1987.

Department of Defense, U.S. Army. *Counter-Signals Intelligence (C-SIGINT) Operations*. Field Manual FM 34-62. Washington, DC: Headquarters, Department of the Army, 1986.

————. *Military Intelligence Battalion Combat Electronic Warfare and Intelligence (Aerial Exploitation) (Corps)*. Field Manual FM 34-22. Washington, DC: Headquarters, Department of the Army, 1984.

————. *Military Intelligence Battalion (Combat Electronic Warfare Intelligence) (Division)*. Field Manual FM 34-10. Washington, DC: Headquarters, Department of the Army, 1981.

————. *Military Intelligence Battalion (CEWI) (Tactical Exploitation) (Corps): Counterintelligence, Interrogation, Electronic Warfare*. Field Manual FM 34-23. Washington, DC: Headquarters, Department of the Army, 1985.

————. *Military Intelligence Company (Combat Electronic Warfare and Intelligence) (Armored Cavalry Regiment/Separate Brigade)*. Field Manual FM 34-30. Washington, DC: Headquarters, Department of the Army, 1983.

————. *Military Intelligence Group (Combat Electronic Warfare and Intelligence) (Corps)*. Field Manual FM 34-20. Washington, DC: Headquarters, Department of the Army, 1983.

—**INDICATOR ORGANIZATION** is a term used in counterintelligence, counterespionage, and counterinsurgency to describe a group that is identified as typical of other organizations that are working toward a common political or philosophical goal. If intelligence assets are limited, then an intelligence agency will single out one such organization for extensive coverage on the theory that the other groups will be conducting similar activities. *See also:* Piggybacking.

References

Becket, Henry S. A. *The Dictionary of Espionage: Spookspeak into English*. New York: Stein and Day, 1986.

—**INDOCTRINATION** is the initial instruction that a person experiences before being granted access to sensitive compartmented information (SCI). The indoctrination concerns the unique nature of SCI, its unusual sensitivity, and the special security regulations and practices that are required for handling this information. *See also:* Access, Authorized, Background Investigation, Billet, Clearance, Briefing, Debriefing, Defense Security Briefings, Need-to-Know, Need-to-Know Principle, Nondisclosure Agreement, Personnel Insecurity, Personnel Security, Security, Security Classification, Sensitive Compartmented Information (SCI), Special Security Office System, TOP SECRET Code Word, TOP SECRET Control.

References

Department of Defense, Defense Intelligence College. *Glossary of Intelligence Terms and Definitions.* Washington, DC: DIC, 1987.

—**INDUSTRIAL COLLEGE OF THE ARMED FORCES (ICAF)** is a part of the National Defense University, Fort Lesley J. McNair, Washington, DC. The college runs a ten-month course for officers in the ranks of lieutenant colonel/commander and colonel/captain. It is the only senior service college course that is dedicated to the study of mobilization planning and management and the management of resources for national security. The primary goal of the college is to enhance the preparation of selected military officers and career civilians for positions of high trust in the federal government. Economics, public administration, quantitative methods, manpower, and personnel management subjects are taught. The course focuses on material and manpower with emphasis on mobilization and emergency preparedness planning. Attention is also given to Department of Defense resource management philosophy, practices, and systems to be used in developing skilled public sector executives. *See also:* National Defense University.

References

Defense Intelligence Agency. *Training Compendium for General Defense Career Development Program (IDCP) Personnel DOD 1430.10M3-TNG.* Washington, DC: DIA, 1986.

—**INFILTRATION,** a term used in clandestine and covert intelligence operations, has several meanings. (1) In intelligence, infiltration is placing an agent or another person in a target area in hostile territory. It usually involves crossing a frontier or other guarded line. There are three types of infiltration. Black infiltration means infiltrating clandestinely. Grey infiltration means infiltrating through a legal crossing point but using false identification. White infiltration means infiltrating legally. (2) Infiltration is also the movement through or into an area or territory by either friendly or enemy troops or organizations. The movement is made, either by small groups or individuals, at extended or irregular intervals. When used with respect to the enemy, it infers that contact is avoided. (3) As defined by the Church Committee, infiltration is stated in a slightly different way. To the committee, infiltration is "the placing of an agent or other person in a target area within hostile territory or within

targeted groups or organizations." *See also:* Accommodation Address, Agent, Agent Authentication, Agent in Place, Agent Net, Agent of Influence, Agent Provocateur, Alias, Between the Lines Entry, Biographic Leverage, Concealment, Cover, Cover Name, Cover Organizations, Cover Story, Double Agent, Exfiltration, Illegal Agent, Illegal Communication, Illegal Net, Illegal Operations, Illegal Residency, Illegal Support Officer, Penetration, Shaking Off the Dogs, Sign of Life Signal, Silent School, Singleton, Special Activities, Submerge, Third Country Operation.

References

Department of Defense, Joint Chiefs of Staff. *Department of Defense Dictionary of Military and Related Terms.* Washington, DC: GPO, 1986.

U.S. Congress. Senate. *Final Report of the Senate Select Committee to Study Government Operations with Respect to Intelligence Activities. Report 94-755. Book I, Foreign and Military Intelligence.* Washington, DC: GPO, 1976.

—**INFORMANT,** a term used in clandestine and covert intelligence operations, has three meanings. (1) An informant is a person who wittingly or unwittingly provides information to an agent, a clandestine service, or the police. (2) In intelligence reporting, an informant is a person who has provided specific information and is cited as a source. (3) In the Intelligence Identities Protection Act of 1982, Congress defined informant as "any individual who furnishes information to an intelligence agency in the course of a confidential relationship protecting the identity of such individual from public disclosure." *See also:* Agent, Agent Authentication, Agent in Place, Agent Net, Agent of Influence, Dispatched Agent, Double Agent, Handling Agent, Illegal Agent, Inside Man, Provocation Agent, Pseudonym, Recruitment, Recruitment in Place, Special Activities, Walk-in.

References

Department of Defense, Joint Chiefs of Staff. *Department of Defense Dictionary of Military and Related Terms.* Washington, DC: GPO, 1986.

Turner, Stansfield. Secrecy and Democracy: *The CIA in Transition.* Boston: Houghton Mifflin, 1985.

U.S. Congress. *Intelligence Identities Protection Act of 1982. Public Law 97-200, June 23, 1982.* Washington, DC: GPO, 1982.

U.S. Congress. Senate. *Final Report of the Senate Select Committee to Study Government Operations with Respect to Intelligence Activities. Report 94-755. Book I, Foreign and Military Intelligence.* Washington, DC: GPO, 1976.

—**INFORMATION** is a general intelligence term for all types of unevaluated material at all levels of reliability from any source of potential intelligence information. As defined by the Church Committee, information is stated somewhat differently. To the committee, information is "raw, unevaluated data at all levels of reliability and from all kinds of sources, such as observation, rumors, reports, and photographs, which, when processed, may produce intelligence." *See also:* Intelligence Cycle, Intelligence Information.

References

Department of Defense, Defense Intelligence Agency. *Defense Intelligence Agency Manual.* Washington, DC: DIA, 1987.

Department of Defense, Defense Intelligence College. *Glossary of Intelligence Terms and Definitions.* Washington, DC: DIC, 1987.

Department of Defense, Joint Chiefs of Staff. *Department of Defense Dictionary of Military and Related Terms.* Washington, DC: GPO, 1986.

Kent, Sherman. *Strategic Intelligence for American World Policy.* Princeton, NJ: Princeton University Press, 1966.

Laqueur, Walter. *A World of Secrets.* New York: Basic Books, 1985.

Treverton, Gregory F. *Covert Action: The Limits of Intervention in the Postwar World.* New York: Basic Books, 1987.

U.S. Congress. Senate. *Final Report of the Senate Select Committee to Study Government Operations with Respect to Intelligence Activities. Report 94-755. Book I, Foreign and Military Intelligence.* Washington, DC: GPO, 1976.

—**INFORMATION HANDLING.** *See:* Department of Defense Intelligence Information System (DODIIS).

—**INFORMATION INCONSISTENCY,** in electronic surveillance, is a condition that exists when the content of a recording differs from the statements, sounds, or events recalled by one of the subject talkers. *See also:* Electronic Surveillance.

References

Kessler, Michael. *Wiretapping and Electronic Surveillance Commission Studies: Supporting Materials for the Report of the National Commission for the Review of Federal and State Laws Relating to Wiretapping and Electronic Surveillance, Washington, DC, 1976.* Townsend, PA: Loompanics Unlimited, 1976.

—**INFORMATION NEED** is a gap in the knowledge of the intelligence analyst. *See also:* Information Requirements.

References

Kent, Sherman. *Strategic Intelligence for American World Policy.* Princeton, NJ: Princeton University Press, 1966.

Laqueur, Walter. *A World of Secrets.* New York: Basic Books, 1985.

Treverton, Gregory F. *Covert Action: The Limits of Intervention in the Postwar World.* New York: Basic Books, 1987.

Turner, Stansfield. *Secrecy and Democracy: The CIA in Transition.* Boston: Houghton Mifflin, 1985.

—**INFORMATION PROCESSING.** *See:* Intelligence Cycle.

—**INFORMATION REPORT** is a report used to forward raw information that has been collected to fulfill intelligence requirements. *See also:* Intelligence, Intelligence Cycle.

References

Department of Defense, Joint Chiefs of Staff. *Department of Defense Dictionary of Military and Related Terms.* Washington, DC: GPO, 1986.

Laqueur, Walter. *A World of Secrets.* New York: Basic Books, 1985.

Treverton, Gregory F. *Covert Action: The Limits of Intervention in the Postwar World.* New York: Basic Books, 1987.

—**INFORMATION REQUIREMENTS** is a tactical intelligence term. They are items of information regarding the enemy and his environment that need to be collected and processed in order to meet the intelligence requirements of the commander. *See also:* Priority Intelligence Requirements.

References

Department of Defense, Joint Chiefs of Staff. *Department of Defense Dictionary of Military and Related Terms.* Washington, DC: GPO, 1986.

Laqueur, Walter. *A World of Secrets.* New York: Basic Books, 1985.

Treverton, Gregory F. *Covert Action: The Limits of Intervention in the Postwar World.* New York: Basic Books, 1987.

—**INFORMATION SECURITY,** on the joint intelligence level, is "the process of safeguarding knowledge against unauthorized disclosure; or the result of any system of administrative policies and procedures for identifying, controlling and protecting from unauthorized disclosure or release to the public, information that is authorized protection by executive order or statute." Information security is also an Army tactical intelligence (TACINT) term that means the prevention of disclosures of operational information through written, verbal, or graphic communications. Restrictions are placed on personnel and the release of operational information to safeguard against unintentional disclosure of data to the enemy. *See also:* Closed Storage, Communications Security, Compartmentation, Nondisclosure Agreement, Secure Vault Area.

References

Department of Defense, Defense Intelligence College. *Glossary of Intelligence Terms and Definitions.* Washington, DC: DIC, 1987.

Department of Defense, Joint Chiefs of Staff. *Department of Defense Dictionary of Military and Related Terms.* Washington, DC: GPO, 1986.

Department of Defense, U.S. Army. *Military Intelligence Battalion Combat Electronic Warfare and Intelligence (Aerial Exploitation) (Corps).* Field Manual FM 34-22. Washington, DC: Headquarters, Department of the Army, 1984.

————. *Military Intelligence Battalion (Combat Electronic Warfare Intelligence) (Division).* Field Manual FM 34-10. Washington, DC: Headquarters, Department of the Army, 1981.

————. *Military Intelligence Battalion (CEWI) (Tactical Exploitation) (Corps): Counterintelligence, Interrogation, Electronic Warfare.* Field Manual FM 34-23. Washington, DC: Headquarters, Department of the Army, 1985.

————. *Military Intelligence Company (Combat Electronic Warfare and Intelligence) (Armored Cavalry Regiment/Separate Brigade).* Field Manual FM 34-30. Washington, DC: Headquarters, Department of the Army, 1983.

————. *Military Intelligence Group (Combat Electronic Warfare and Intelligence) (Corps).* Field Manual FM 34-20. Washington, DC: Headquarters, Department of the Army, 1983.

U.S. Congress. Senate. *Final Report of the Senate Select Committee to Study Government Operations with Respect to Intelligence Activities. Report 94-755. Book I, Foreign and Military Intelligence.* Washington, DC: GPO, 1976.

—**INFORMATION SECURITY OVERSIGHT OFFICE** promulgates instructions concerning the classification of intelligence information in order to insure that there is uniform and consistent classification of the material. *See also:* Information Security.

References

U.S. Government. Information Security Oversight Office. *Directive Number 1: National Security Information.* Washington, DC: Federal Register, June 25, 1982, pp. 27836–27841.

—**INFORMATION SYSTEM** is a general intelligence term. Such a system comprises all personnel, equipment, and resources involved in the provision of information and in the collection, processing, production, and dissemination of intelligence in support of the consumer. *See also:* Intelligence Cycle.

References

Department of Defense, Defense Intelligence College. *Glossary of Intelligence Terms and Definitions.* Washington, DC: DIC, 1987.

Treverton, Gregory F. *Covert Action: The Limits of Intervention in the Postwar World.* New York: Basic Books, 1987.

—**INFORMER** is a clandestine and covert intelligence operations term for a person who intentionally discloses to the police or to a security service information about persons or activities that are considered suspect. An informer often is motivated by the expectation of a financial reward. *See also:* Agent, Agent Authentication, Agent in Place, Agent of Influence, Agent Provocateur, Co-Opted Worker, Co-Optees, Defector, Disaffected Person, Double Agent, Illegal Agent, Inside Man, Lion Tamer, Mole, Nash, Penetration, Turned, Walk-in.

References

Department of Defense, Joint Chiefs of Staff. *Department of Defense Dictionary of Military and Related Terms.* Washington, DC: GPO, 1986.

Treverton, Gregory F. *Covert Action: The Limits of Intervention in the Postwar World.* New York: Basic Books, 1987.

Turner, Stansfield. *Secrecy and Democracy: The CIA in Transition.* Boston: Houghton Mifflin, 1985.

U.S. Congress. Senate. *Final Report of the Senate Select Committee to Study Government Operations with Respect to Intelligence Activities. Report 94-755. Book I, Foreign and Military Intelligence.* Washington, DC: GPO, 1976.

—INFRARED (IR) pertains to or designates those rays of light that are just beyond the red end of the visible spectrum and that are emitted by a hot body. They are invisible and are detected by their thermal and photographic effects. Their wavelengths are longer than those of visible light and shorter than those of radio waves. *See also:* Infrared Intelligence.

References

Department of Defense, U.S. Army. *Intelligence Imagery*. Field Manual FM 34-55. Washington, DC: Headquarters, Department of the Army, 1985.

Reeves, Robert; Anson, Abraham; and Landen, David. *Manual of Remote Sensing*. Falls Church, VA: American Society of Photogrammetry, 1975.

—INFRARED COUNTERMEASURES (IRCM) are countermeasures used specifically against threats operating in the infrared spectrum.

References

Department of Defense, U.S. Army. *Intelligence Imagery*. Field Manual FM 34-55. Washington, DC: Headquarters, Department of the Army, 1985.

—INFRARED DETECTOR is a thermal device used for observing and measuring infrared radiation.

References

Department of Defense, U.S. Army. *Intelligence Imagery*. Field Manual FM 34-55. Washington, DC: Headquarters, Department of the Army, 1985.

—INFRARED FILM is used in intelligence imagery and photoreconnaissance. It is a film that has an emulsion that is especially sensitive to "near-infrared." It is used to photograph through haze, because of the penetrating power of infrared light, and in camouflage detection to distinguish between living vegetation and dead vegetation or artificial green pigment. *See also:* Infrared Intelligence.

References

Department of Defense, Joint Chiefs of Staff. *Department of Defense Dictionary of Military and Related Terms*. Washington, DC: GPO, 1986.

Department of Defense, U.S. Army. *Intelligence Imagery*. Field Manual FM 34-55. Washington, DC: Headquarters, Department of the Army, 1985.

—INFRARED IMAGERY is an intelligence imagery and photoreconnaissance term for the imagery that is produced as a result of sensing electro-magnetic radiations that are emitted or reflected from a target surface in the infrared position of the electromagnetic spectrum (approximately 0.72 to 1,000 microns). *See also:* Infrared Intelligence.

References

Department of Defense, Joint Chiefs of Staff. *Department of Defense Dictionary of Military and Related Terms*. Washington, DC: GPO, 1986.

Department of Defense, U.S. Army. *Intelligence Imagery*. Field Manual FM 34-55. Washington, DC: Headquarters, Department of the Army, 1985.

—INFRARED IMAGING is an intelligence imagery and photoreconnaissance term for the remote sensing of radiant temperatures. An electronic sensor is used to produce detailed or general intelligence coverage of an area or target by sensing apparent temperature differences between terrain features and military or cultural features of the terrain.

Infrared imagery sensors are passive. They do not generate their own illumination like radar. This reduces their vulnerability to detection by the enemy, but lower natural energy levels in the thermal region generally require that missions be flown at low altitude over enemy targets. Some types of infrared sensors have a limited standoff capability. Infrared systems can be operated by day or night and have the capability to see through light atmospheric conditions. *See also:* Infrared Intelligence.

References

Department of Defense, U.S. Army. *Intelligence Imagery*. Field Manual FM 34-55. Washington, DC: Headquarters, Department of the Army, 1985.

—INFRARED INTELLIGENCE (IRINT) is an intelligence imagery and photoreconnaissance term for the intelligence information that is gleaned from the detection of infrared energy that is radiated, reradiated, or reflected from the surface of the earth. By comparing the minute differences between the amounts of energy radiated by an object and its background, an image of the object can be projected for recording on film or for a television-like display. Since virtually every object and terrain feature radiates a different level of energy, high resolution images can be produced. The quality of the imagery nearly equals that of photography, but infrared imagery systems have far greater capabilities than photographic systems, since they are immune to many conditions, such as smoke, darkness, clouds, fog, and vegetation, that can block photography.

References

Department of Defense, Joint Chiefs of Staff. *Department of Defense Dictionary of Military and Related Terms.* Washington, DC: GPO, 1986.

Department of Defense, U.S. Army. *Intelligence Imagery.* Field Manual FM 34-55. Washington, DC: Headquarters, Department of the Army, 1985.

—**INFRARED LINESCAN SYSTEM** is an intelligence imagery and photoreconnaissance term for a passive airborne infrared recording system that scans across the ground beneath the flight path, adding successive lines to the record as the vehicle advances along the flight path. *See also:* Infrared Intelligence.

References

Department of Defense, Joint Chiefs of Staff. *Department of Defense Dictionary of Military and Related Terms.* Washington, DC: GPO, 1986.

Department of Defense, U.S. Army. *Intelligence Imagery.* Field Manual FM 34-55. Washington, DC: Headquarters, Department of the Army, 1985.

—**INFRARED PHOTOGRAPHY** is photography that uses an optical system and direct image recording on film sensitive to near-infrared wavelength (infrared film). Infrared photography should not be confused with infrared imagery. *See also:* Infrared Intelligence.

References

Department of Defense, Joint Chiefs of Staff. *Department of Defense Dictionary of Military and Related Terms.* Washington, DC: GPO, 1986.

Department of Defense, U.S. Army. *Intelligence Imagery.* Field Manual FM 34-55. Washington, DC: Headquarters, Department of the Army, 1985.

—**INFRARED RADIATION** is radiation that is emitted or reflected in the infrared portion of the electromagnetic spectrum.

References

Department of Defense, Joint Chiefs of Staff. *Department of Defense Dictionary of Military and Related Terms.* Washington, DC: GPO, 1986.

Department of Defense, U.S. Army. *Intelligence Imagery.* Field Manual FM 34-55. Washington, DC: Headquarters, Department of the Army, 1985.

—**INITIAL OPERATING CAPABILITY (IOC)** is the point at which a Department of Defense Intelligence Information System (DODIIS) subsystem is initially turned over to the functional users for mission support operations. The IOC system contains basic data handling capabilities in satisfaction of stated functional design requirements but requires additional development before it reaches full operational capability (FOC). *See also:* Defense Intelligence Agency, Department of Defense Intelligence Information System (DODIIS).

References

Department of Defense, Joint Chiefs of Staff. *Department of Defense Dictionary of Military and Related Terms.* Washington, DC: GPO, 1986.

Department of Defense, Defense Intelligence Agency. *Defense Intelligence Agency Manual.* Washington, DC: DIA, 1987.

—**INITIAL PHOTO INTERPRETATION REPORT** is an intelligence imagery and photoreconnaissance term. It is a first-phase interpretation report, and appears after the Joint Tactical Reconnaissance/Surveillance Mission Report. It presents the results of the initial reading of new imagery to answer the specific requirements for which the mission was requested. *See also:* Initial Programmed Interpretation Report (IPIR).

References

Department of Defense, Joint Chiefs of Staff. *Department of Defense Dictionary of Military and Related Terms.* Washington, DC: GPO, 1986.

Department of Defense, U.S. Army. *Intelligence Imagery.* Field Manual FM 34-55. Washington, DC: Headquarters, Department of the Army, 1985.

—**INITIAL PROGRAMMED INTERPRETATION REPORT (IPIR)** is an intelligence imagery and photoreconnaissance term for a report that provides information on mission objectives that are not mentioned in other reports. An IPIR is requested when extensive or detailed data from a systematic review of sensor imagery is needed, and the rapid response required by the Reconnaissance Exploitation Report would be hindered by the format, size, or quantity of the imagery involved. *See also:* Image, Radar Exploitation Report (RADAREXREP), Reconnaissance Exploitation Report (RECCEXREP), Supplemental Programmed Interpretation Report (SUPIR).

References

Department of Defense, Joint Chiefs of Staff. *Department of Defense Dictionary of Military and Related Terms.* Washington, DC: GPO, 1986.

Department of Defense, U.S. Army. *Intelligence Imagery.* Field Manual FM 34-55. Washington, DC: Headquarters, Department of the Army, 1985.

—**INITIALIZATION VECTOR,** in communications security (COMSEC), means a group of signals that are used to define the starting point of an encryption process within data encryption standard (DES) equipment. *See also:* Communications Security.

References

Department of Defense, U.S. Army. *Military Intelligence Battalion (CEWI) (Tactical Exploitation) (Corps): Counterintelligence, Interrogation, Electronic Warfare.* Field Manual FM 34-23. Washington, DC: Headquarters, Department of the Army, 1985.

————. *Military Intelligence Battalion (Combat Electronic Warfare Intelligence) (Division).* Field Manual FM 34-10. Washington, DC: Headquarters, Department of the Army, 1981.

————. *Military Intelligence Company (Combat Electronic Warfare and Intelligence) (Armored Cavalry Regiment/Separate Brigade).* Field Manual FM 34-30. Washington, DC: Headquarters, Department of the Army, 1983.

—**INITIATING DIRECTIVE,** in tactical amphibious operations, is the directive that begins the process of an amphibious operation. It is issued by the commander of a command that has been established by the Joint Chiefs of Staff or by other commanders so authorized by the Joint Chiefs of Staff or by other higher authority.

References

Department of Defense, Defense Intelligence College. *Glossary of Intelligence Terms and Definitions.* Washington, DC: DIC, 1987.

—**INNOCUOUS MECHANISM** is an electronic surveillance term. It is an undesired, naturally occurring event or condition that may affect a tape or its perceptual interpretation. *See also:* Electronic Surveillance.

References

Kessler, Michael. *Wiretapping and Electronic Surveillance Commission Studies: Supporting Materials for the Report of the National Commis-* *sion for the Review of Federal and State Laws Relating to Wiretapping and Electronic Surveillance, Washington, DC, 1976.* Townsend, PA: Loompanics Unlimited, 1976.

—**INSIDE MAN** is a CIA case officer who works out of a U.S. embassy abroad and who has State Department cover. *See also:* Agent, Agent Net, Case Officer, Chief of Base, Chief of Outpost, Chief of Station, Company, Cover, Cover Name, Cover Organizations, Cover Story, Illegal Agent, Illegal Communication, Illegal Net, Illegal Operations, Illegal Residency, Illegal Support Officer, Infiltration, Informant, Legitimate, Mole, Proprietaries, Proprietary Company, Special Activities, Third Country Operation.

References

Becket, Henry S. A. *The Dictionary of Espionage: Spookspeak into English.* New York: Stein and Day, 1986.

—**INSPECTION,** in arms control, is a physical process of determining compliance with arms control measures.

References

Department of Defense, Joint Chiefs of Staff. *Department of Defense Dictionary of Military and Related Terms.* Washington, DC: GPO, 1986.

—**INSPECTOR GENERAL (IG).** *See:* Central Intelligence Agency, Defense Intelligence Agency.

—**INSPIRE** is a term used in clandestine and covert intelligence operations. To inspire is to fool a detected enemy agent into accepting false information and passing it along to his superiors as valid information. *See also:* Alias, Cover, Cover Name, Cover Organizations, Cover Story, False Confirmation, Legend, Processing the Take, Sanctification, Shopping List, Shopworn Goods, Special Activities.

References

Becket, Henry S. A. *The Dictionary of Espionage: Spookspeak into English.* New York: Stein and Day, 1986.

Deacon, Richard. *Spyclopedia: An Encyclopedia of Spies, Secret Services, Operations, Jargon, and All Subjects Related to the World of Espionage.* London: Macdonald, 1987.

Kessler, Ronald. *Spy vs. Spy: Stalking Soviet Spies in America.* New York: Charles Scribner's Sons, 1988.

Ranelagh, John. *The Agency: The Rise and Decline of the CIA.* New York: Simon and Schuster, 1986.

—**INSTALLATION** is a target intelligence term that pertains to the target that is to be destroyed. An installation is a grouping of facilities, located in the same vicinity, that support particular functions. Installations may be elements of a base. In another sense, installations are fixed and consist of a single function or group of functions that are collocated at the same coordinates or are located in geographic proximity. *See also:* Target Intelligence.

References

Department of Defense, Joint Chiefs of Staff. *Department of Defense Dictionary of Military and Related Terms.* Washington, DC: GPO, 1986.

—**INSURGENCY** is a term used in counterintelligence, counterespionage, and counterinsurgency and has two meanings. (1) Insurgency is an organized movement that is aimed at the overthrow of a constituted government through the use of subversion or armed conflict. (2) Insurgency is also a condition resulting from a revolt or insurrection against a constituted government that falls short of a civil war. *See also:* Counterinsurgency.

References

American Bar Association. *Oversight and Accountability of the U.S. Intelligence Agencies: An Evaluation.* Washington, DC: ABA, 1985.

Department of Defense, Joint Chiefs of Staff. *Department of Defense Dictionary of Military and Related Terms.* Washington, DC: GPO, 1986.

Godson, Roy, ed. *Intelligence Problems for the 1980s, Number 3: Counterintelligence.* Washington, DC: National Strategy Information Center, 1980.

Maurer, Alfred C.; Turnstall, Marion D.; and Keagle, James M. *Intelligence Policy and Process.* Boulder, CO: Westview Press, 1985.

Turner, Stansfield. *Secrecy and Democracy: The CIA in Transition.* Boston: Houghton Mifflin, 1985.

U.S. Congress. Senate. *Final Report of the Senate Select Committee to Study Government Operations with Respect to Intelligence Activities. Report 94-755. Book I, Foreign and Military Intelligence.* Washington, DC: GPO, 1976.

—**INTEGRATED COMSEC EQUIPMENT,** in communications security (COMSEC), means cryptographic equipment or circuitry that has been incorporated into other equipment and whose primary purpose or function is not cryptographic. *See also:* Communications Security.

References

Department of Defense, U.S. Army. *AIA: Threat Analysis.* Falls Church, VA: U.S. Army Intelligence Agency, 1987.

Muzerall, Joseph V., and Carty, Thomas P. "COMSEC and Its Need for Key Management." *DP&CS* (Spring 1987).

Ware, Willis H. "Information Systems, Security, and Privacy." *EDUCOM Bulletin* (Summer 1984).

—**INTEGRATED FUNCTIONAL TRAINING** is instruction given to employees who use the Department of Defense Intelligence Information System (DODIIS). This instruction integrates training in the functional intelligence discipline with training on how to best use the current or projected ADP-T capabilities to perform those intelligence functions. *See also:* Defense Intelligence Agency, Department of Defense Intelligence Information System (DODIIS).

References

Department of Defense, Defense Intelligence Agency. *Defense Intelligence Agency Manual.* Washington, DC: DIA, 1987.

—**INTEGRATED OPERATIONAL SUPPORT STUDY (IOSS)** is produced by the Defense Intelligence Agency and is an excellent source of geographic intelligence. It presents integrated military analyses of transportation networks, LOCs, and associated cultural and military geographic features of a region or country. *See also:* Defense Intelligence Agency.

References

Von Hoene, John P. A. *Intelligence User's Guide.* Washington, DC: DIA, 1983.

—**INTEGRATED STAFF** is one in which people are assigned to staff posts regardless of their nationality or service.

References

Department of Defense, Joint Chiefs of Staff. *Department of Defense Dictionary of Military and Related Terms.* Washington, DC: GPO, 1986.

—**INTEGRATED WARFARE** occurs when opposing forces employ both conventional and unconventional weapons in combat.

References

Department of Defense, Joint Chiefs of Staff. *Department of Defense Dictionary of Military and Related Terms.* Washington, DC: GPO, 1986.

—**INTEGRATION** is a general intelligence term that has two meanings. (1) Integration is a stage in the intelligence cycle in which a pattern is formed through selecting and combining evaluated information. (2) In photography, integration is the combining of several photographic images into a single image. *See also:* Image, Intelligence Cycle.

References

Department of Defense, Joint Chiefs of Staff. *Department of Defense Dictionary of Military and Related Terms.* Washington, DC: GPO, 1986.

Kent, Sherman. *Strategic Intelligence for American World Policy.* Princeton, NJ: Princeton University Press, 1966.

—**INTELLIGENCE.** To begin, intelligence should be differentiated from information and intelligence information. Information is unevaluated material of every type. Intelligence information is information that has not been processed into intelligence, but may be of intelligence value. Finally, intelligence is the product that results or the knowledge that is derived from the cyclical processing of information. Sherman Kent maintains that intelligence has three definitional subsets: knowledge (the knowledge that our nation must have for proper decisionmaking); institution (the physical organization of people who are pursuing a certain type of knowledge); and activity (the actions of collection, evaluation, research, analysis, study, presentation, and more).

On the strategic level, intelligence is the product resulting from collecting, processing, integrating, analyzing, evaluating, and interpreting available information concerning foreign countries or areas, hostile or potentially hostile forces or elements, and areas of actual or potential operations. The term is also applied to the activity that results from the product and the organizations that are engaged in such activity. On the Army tactical intelligence (TACINT) level, the term is similarly defined, but also includes information on weather and terrain. In the TACINT context, intelligence is considered immediately or potentially significant to military planning and operations.

According to the Church Committee, intelligence was defined as "the product resulting from the collection, collation, evaluation, analysis, integration, and interpretation of all collected information."

The many types of intelligence include the following, many of which are discussed fully under their own headings: acoustical intelligence (ACOUSTINT or ACINT), actionable intelligence, basic intelligence, biographical intelligence, cartographic intelligence, combat intelligence, communications intelligence (COMINT), counterintelligence (CI), critical intelligence, current intelligence, departmental intelligence, domestic intelligence, economic intelligence, electronic intelligence (ELINT), electro-optical intelligence (ELECTRO-OPTINT), energy intelligence, estimative intelligence, evasion and escape intelligence, finished intelligence, foreign counterintelligence (FCI), foreign instrumentation and signals intelligence (FISINT), foreign intelligence (FI), foreign material (FORMAT) intelligence, geographical intelligence, human intelligence (HUMINT), imagery intelligence (IMINT), joint intelligence, laser intelligence (LASINT), literature intelligence, measurement and signature intelligence (MASINT), medical intelligence (MEDINT), military intelligence (MI), national intelligence, nuclear intelligence (NUCINT), nuclear proliferation intelligence, operational intelligence (OPINTEL), optical intelligence (OPTINT), photographic intelligence (PHOTINT), political intelligence, positive intelligence, radar intelligence (RADINT), radiation intelligence (RINT), raw intelligence, scientific and technical (S&T) intelligence, signals intelligence (SIGINT), sociological intelligence, special intelligence (SI), strategic intelligence, tactical intelligence (TACINTEL), target intelligence, technical intelligence (TI), telemetry intelligence (TELINT). *See also:* Intelligence Cycle.

References

American Bar Association. *Oversight and Accountability of the U.S. Intelligence Agencies: An Evaluation.* Washington, DC: ABA, 1985.

Corson, William R. *The Armies of Ignorance: The Rise of the American Intelligence Empire.* New York: Dial Press, 1977.

Department of Defense, Defense Intelligence Agency. *Defense Intelligence Agency Manual.* Washington, DC: DIA, 1987.

Department of Defense, Defense Intelligence College. *Glossary of Intelligence Terms and Definitions.* Washington, DC: DIC, 1987.

Department of Defense, Joint Chiefs of Staff. *Department of Defense Dictionary of Military and Related Terms.* Washington, DC: GPO, 1986.

Kent, Sherman. *Strategic Intelligence for American World Policy.* Princeton, NJ: Princeton University Press, 1966.

Laqueur, Walter. *A World of Secrets.* New York: Basic Books, 1985.

Treverton, Gregory F. *Covert Action: The Limits of Intervention in the Postwar World.* New York: Basic Books, 1987.

Turner, Stansfield. *Secrecy and Democracy: The CIA in Transition.* Boston: Houghton Mifflin, 1985.

U.S. Congress. Senate. *Final Report of the Senate Select Committee to Study Government Operations with Respect to Intelligence Activities. Report 94-755. Book I, Foreign and Military Intelligence.* Washington, DC: GPO, 1976.

—**INTELLIGENCE ACTIVITIES.** (1) Intelligence Activities are any or all of the activities accomplished by intelligence organizations. In June 1977, U.S. Senate Resolution 400 defined intelligence activities as: "(A) the collection, analysis, production, dissemination or use of information which relates to any foreign country, or any government, political group, party, military force, movement, or other association in such foreign country, and which relates to the defense, foreign policy, national security, or related policies of the United States, and other activity which is in support of these activities; (B) activities taken to counter similar activities directed against the United States; (C) covert or clandestine activities affecting the relations of the United States with any foreign government, political group, parity, military force, movement or other association; (D) the collection, analysis, production, dissemination or use of information about the activities of persons within the United States, its territories and possessions, or nationals of the United States abroad whose political and related activities pose, or may be considered by any department, agency, bureau, office, division, instrumentality or employee of the United States to pose, a threat to the internal security of the United States, and covert or clandestine activities directed against such persons. Such term does not include tactical foreign military intelligence serving no national policymaking function." (2) Intelligence activities are the activities of Department of Defense intelligence components that are authorized under Presidential Executive Order 12333, of December 4, 1981.

References

American Bar Association. *Oversight and Accountability of the U.S. Intelligence Agencies: An Evaluation.* Washington, DC: ABA, 1985.

Department of Defense. *Activities of DoD Intelligence Components that Affect U.S. Persons (Department of Defense Directive 5240.1).* Washington, DC: DoD, 1982.

Department of Defense, Defense Intelligence College. *Glossary of Intelligence Terms and Definitions.* Washington, DC: DIC, 1987.

Kent, Sherman. *Strategic Intelligence for American World Policy.* Princeton, NJ: Princeton University Press, 1966.

Laqueur, Walter. *A World of Secrets.* New York: Basic Books, 1985.

Treverton, Gregory F. *Covert Action: The Limits of Intervention in the Postwar World.* New York: Basic Books, 1987.

Turner, Stansfield. *Secrecy and Democracy: The CIA in Transition.* Boston: Houghton Mifflin, 1985.

—**INTELLIGENCE ADVISORY BOARD (IAB)** existed during the period of the Central Intelligence Group as an advisory group for the director of Central Intelligence. It was composed of the heads of the military and civilian intelligence agencies. *See also:* Central Intelligence Agency.

References

American Bar Association. *Oversight and Accountability of the U.S. Intelligence Agencies: An Evaluation.* Washington, DC: ABA, 1985.

Corson, William R. *The Armies of Ignorance: The Rise of the American Intelligence Empire.* New York: Dial Press, 1977.

Fain, Tyrus G.; Plant, Katharine C.; and Milloy, Ross. *The Intelligence Community: History, Organization, and Issues.* Public Documents Series. New York: R.R. Bowker, 1977.

Laqueur, Walter. *A World of Secrets.* New York: Basic Books, 1985.

Lowenthal, Mark M. *U.S. Intelligence: Evolution and Anatomy.* New York: Praeger, 1984.

Maurer, Alfred C.; Turnstall, Marion D.; and Keagle, James M. *Intelligence Policy and Process.* Boulder, CO: Westview Press, 1985.

Treverton, Gregory F. *Covert Action: The Limits of Intervention in the Postwar World.* New York: Basic Books, 1987.

Turner, Stansfield. *Secrecy and Democracy: The CIA in Transition.* Boston: Houghton Mifflin, 1985.

—INTELLIGENCE ADVISORY COMMITTEE (IAC) was the successor to the Intelligence Advisory Board. It was founded in 1947, with the purpose of assisting the director of Central Intelligence to coordinate intelligence and set intelligence requirements. It was replaced by the United States Intelligence Board in 1958. *See also:* Central Intelligence Agency.

References

American Bar Association. *Oversight and Accountability of the U.S. Intelligence Agencies: An Evaluation.* Washington, DC: ABA, 1985.

Corson, William R. *The Armies of Ignorance: The Rise of the American Intelligence Empire.* New York: Dial Press, 1977.

Fain, Tyrus G.; Plant, Katharine C.; and Milloy, Ross. *The Intelligence Community: History, Organization, and Issues.* Public Documents Series. New York: R.R. Bowker, 1977.

Laqueur, Walter. *A World of Secrets.* New York: Basic Books, 1985.

Lowenthal, Mark M. *U.S. Intelligence: Evolution and Anatomy.* New York: Praeger, 1984.

Maurer, Alfred C.; Turnstall, Marion D.; and Keagle, James M. *Intelligence Policy and Process.* Boulder, CO: Westview Press, 1985.

Turner, Stansfield. *Secrecy and Democracy: The CIA in Transition.* Boston: Houghton Mifflin, 1985.

—INTELLIGENCE AGENCY is a component organization of the Intelligence Community. *See also:* Intelligence Community.

References

American Bar Association. *Oversight and Accountability of the U.S. Intelligence Agencies: An Evaluation.* Washington, DC: ABA, 1985.

Department of Defense, Defense Intelligence College. *Glossary of Intelligence Terms and Definitions.* Washington, DC: DIC, 1987.

Laqueur, Walter. *A World of Secrets.* New York: Basic Books, 1985.

Maurer, Alfred C.; Turnstall, Marion D.; and Keagle, James M. *Intelligence Policy and Process.* Boulder, CO: Westview Press, 1985.

Treverton, Gregory F. *Covert Action: The Limits of Intervention in the Postwar World.* New York: Basic Books, 1987.

Turner, Stansfield. *Secrecy and Democracy: The CIA in Transition.* Boston: Houghton Mifflin, 1985.

—INTELLIGENCE AND SECURITY COMMAND (INSCOM). *See:* U.S. Army Intelligence and Security Command.

—INTELLIGENCE ANNEX is a supporting document of an operation plan or order that provides detailed information on the enemy situation, assignment of intelligence tasks, and intelligence administrative procedures.

References

American Bar Association. *Oversight and Accountability of the U.S. Intelligence Agencies: An Evaluation.* Washington, DC: ABA, 1985.

Department of Defense, Joint Chiefs of Staff. *Department of Defense Dictionary of Military and Related Terms.* Washington, DC: GPO, 1986.

Maurer, Alfred C.; Turnstall, Marion D.; and Keagle, James M. *Intelligence Policy and Process.* Boulder, CO: Westview Press, 1985.

U.S. Congress. Senate. *Final Report of the Senate Select Committee to Study Government Operations with Respect to Intelligence Activities. Report 94-755. Book I, Foreign and Military Intelligence.* Washington, DC: GPO, 1976.

—INTELLIGENCE ASSESSMENT is a category of intelligence production that is found in most analytical studies dealing with subjects that have policy significance. It is based on a thorough analysis of the subject matter, but, unlike intelligence assessments, does not attempt to project future developments and their implications. It is usually coordinated within the producing intelligence organization but may not be coordinated with other intelligence agencies. *See also:* Estimative Intelligence.

—INTELLIGENCE ASSET is any resource, be it a person, group, instrument, installation, or technical system, that can be used by an intelligence organization.

References

American Bar Association. *Oversight and Accountability of the U.S. Intelligence Agencies: An Evaluation.* Washington, DC: ABA, 1985.

Department of Defense, Defense Intelligence College. *Glossary of Intelligence Terms and Definitions.* Washington, DC: DIC, 1987.

Kent, Sherman. *Strategic Intelligence for American World Policy.* Princeton, NJ: Princeton University Press, 1966.

Laqueur, Walter. *A World of Secrets.* New York: Basic Books, 1985.

Maurer, Alfred C.; Turnstall, Marion D.; and Keagle, James M. *Intelligence Policy and Process.* Boulder, CO: Westview Press, 1985.

Treverton, Gregory F. *Covert Action: The Limits of Intervention in the Postwar World.* New York: Basic Books, 1987.

Turner, Stansfield. *Secrecy and Democracy: The CIA in Transition.* Boston: Houghton Mifflin, 1985.

—INTELLIGENCE AUTHORIZATION ACT OF 1981, Public Law 96-450, reduced the reporting on presidential approval of covert action operations from eight congressional committees to two, the House and Senate intelligence committees. A presidential finding concerning the operation and prior notification to Congress were still required under this act. Additionally, the two committees were to be kept fully and currently informed of all significant intelligence activities, including "intelligence failures."

References

American Bar Association. *Oversight and Accountability of the U.S. Intelligence Agencies: An Evaluation.* Washington, DC: ABA, 1985.

Maurer, Alfred C.; Turnstall, Marion D.; and Keagle, James M. *Intelligence Policy and Process.* Boulder, CO: Westview Press, 1985.

Turner, Stansfield. *Secrecy and Democracy: The CIA in Transition.* Boston: Houghton Mifflin, 1985.

—INTELLIGENCE CAREER DEVELOPMENT PROGRAM (ICDP) is a Department of Defense program that is intended to train and retain intelligence employees. It is under the direction of the Defense Intelligence Agency's Directorate for Training (OT). *See also:* Defense Intelligence Agency.

References

American Bar Association. *Oversight and Accountability of the U.S. Intelligence Agencies: An Evaluation.* Washington, DC: ABA, 1985.

Department of Defense, Defense Intelligence Agency. *Defense Intelligence Agency Manual.* Washington, DC: DIA, 1987.

Maurer, Alfred C.; Turnstall, Marion D.; and Keagle, James M. *Intelligence Policy and Process.* Boulder, CO: Westview Press, 1985.

—INTELLIGENCE COLLECTION (IC) is the gathering of information by all means (SIGINT, HUMINT, PHOTINT, etc.) and from all sources (from unclassified or open sources to the most highly classified sources available) that pertain to a given intelligence problem and the delivery

of the same to the appropriate office or facility for processing and production. *See also:* Intelligence, Intelligence Cycle.

References

American Bar Association. *Oversight and Accountability of the U.S. Intelligence Agencies: An Evaluation.* Washington, DC: ABA, 1985.

Kent, Sherman. *Strategic Intelligence for American World Policy.* Princeton, NJ: Princeton University Press, 1966.

Laqueur, Walter. *A World of Secrets.* New York: Basic Books, 1985.

Lowenthal, Mark M. *U.S. Intelligence: Evolution and Anatomy.* New York: Praeger, 1984.

Maurer, Alfred C.; Turnstall, Marion D.; and Keagle, James M. *Intelligence Policy and Process.* Boulder, CO: Westview Press, 1985.

Oseth, John M. *Regulating U.S. Intelligence Operations: A Study in the Definition of the National Interest.* Frankfurt: University of Kentucky Press, 1985.

Treverton, Gregory F. *Covert Action: The Limits of Intervention in the Postwar World.* New York: Basic Books, 1987.

Turner, Stansfield. *Secrecy and Democracy: The CIA in Transition.* Boston: Houghton Mifflin, 1985.

—INTELLIGENCE COLLECTION PLAN is a plan for gathering information from all available sources in order to satisfy an intelligence requirement. Specifically, it is a logical plan for transforming the essential elements of information into orders or requests to sources for information within a required time limit. *See also:* Intelligence, Intelligence Cycle.

References

U.S. Congress. Senate. *Final Report of the Senate Select Committee to Study Government Operations with Respect to Intelligence Activities. Report 94-755. Book I, Foreign and Military Intelligence.* Washington, DC: GPO, 1976.

American Bar Association. *Oversight and Accountability of the U.S. Intelligence Agencies: An Evaluation.* Washington, DC: ABA, 1985.

Department of Defense, Joint Chiefs of Staff. *Department of Defense Dictionary of Military and Related Terms.* Washington, DC: GPO, 1986.

Kent, Sherman. *Strategic Intelligence for American World Policy.* Princeton, NJ: Princeton University Press, 1966.

Maurer, Alfred C.; Turnstall, Marion D.; and Keagle, James M. *Intelligence Policy and Process.* Boulder, CO: Westview Press, 1985.

—**INTELLIGENCE COLLECTION REQUIREMENT (ICR)** is the means by which an intelligence analyst expresses an intelligence need to the intelligence collector. The ICR discusses the specific information shortfall, addresses the precise information needed in detail, and provides a time frame of when the information is needed. The analyst will also provide any other information that might assist the collector in fulfilling the requirement. The ICR has replaced the Specific Intelligence Collection Requirement (SICR). *See also:* Intelligence, Intelligence Cycle.

References

American Bar Association. *Oversight and Accountability of the U.S. Intelligence Agencies: An Evaluation.* Washington, DC: ABA, 1985.

Department of Defense, Joint Chiefs of Staff. *Department of Defense Dictionary of Military and Related Terms.* Washington, DC: GPO, 1986.

Kent, Sherman. *Strategic Intelligence for American World Policy.* Princeton, NJ: Princeton University Press, 1966.

Maurer, Alfred C.; Turnstall, Marion D.; and Keagle, James M. *Intelligence Policy and Process.* Boulder, CO: Westview Press, 1985.

U.S. Congress. Senate. *Final Report of the Senate Select Committee to Study Government Operations with Respect to Intelligence Activities. Report 94-755. Book I, Foreign and Military Intelligence.* Washington, DC: GPO, 1976.

—**INTELLIGENCE COLLECTION REQUIREMENT SYSTEM (ICRS)** is the system employed by the Defense Intelligence Agency to manage Intelligence Collection Requirements (ICRs). It provides for processing and validating ICRs that are submitted by intelligence analysts, directing collectors to satisfy the requirements, monitoring the collectors' progress, and determining whether the collectors' responses truly satisfy the analysts' requirements. *See also:* Defense Intelligence Agency.

References

American Bar Association. *Oversight and Accountability of the U.S. Intelligence Agencies: An Evaluation.* Washington, DC: ABA, 1985.

Kent, Sherman. *Strategic Intelligence for American World Policy.* Princeton, NJ: Princeton University Press, 1966.

Maurer, Alfred C.; Turnstall, Marion D.; and Keagle, James M. *Intelligence Policy and Process.* Boulder, CO: Westview Press, 1985.

Turner, Stansfield. *Secrecy and Democracy: The CIA in Transition.* Boston: Houghton Mifflin, 1985.

—**INTELLIGENCE COLLECTION SHIP (OR INTELLIGENCE COLLECTOR)** Many collection systems are used to gather intelligence on maritime affairs. One of the most versatile is the intelligence collection ship, a vessel that is specially configured and equipped with electronic and other sensing equipment and deployed to patrol areas where it can collect intelligence. Both the United States and the Soviet Union make great use of such ships for intelligence collection.

The United States has used intelligence collectors for decades. These have been used primarily to collect intelligence concerning the Soviet Union, Warsaw Pact nations, and other communist nations, but they have also been used to gather intelligence concerning other nations as well. For years, these ships were either unarmed or very lightly armed. However, two incidents, involving the USS *Pueblo* and the USS *Liberty*, forced a change in this procedure. The USS *Liberty* was attacked by Israeli forces off the Egyptian coast in 1967, and the USS *Pueblo* was seized in international waters off North Korea by the North Koreans in 1968. More recent U.S. intelligence collection patrols have been conducted by more heavily armed ships.

Likewise, the Soviet Union has used intelligence collectors extensively. The early classes were converted fishing trawlers that had been equipped with electronic sensing equipment. The more modern classes are much larger, have an on-board intelligence processing capability, and are more heavily armed. Today, the Soviet Union has the world's largest fleet of intelligence collection ships.

The Soviets deploy their collection ships extensively. The earliest patrols were intended to collect intelligence about U.S. and NATO operations. A patrol was established along the U.S. east coast in the late 1950s to collect information about the U.S. space program while steaming off Cape Canaveral, and about U.S. naval and army activity while steaming up and down the coast. The collectors would steam as far north as Newport, Rhode Island, to fulfill this mission. Another patrol was established off the English coast to monitor the deployments of U.S. ballistic submarines from Holy Loch. In the 1960s, a patrol was established off Rota, Spain, to monitor U.S. ballistic submarine movements out of Rota and maritime traffic through the Strait of Gibraltar. A similar patrol was established off Guam, in the Pacific, to monitor U.S. ballistic missile submarine movements. During the U.S. involvement in Vietnam, the Soviet Navy patrolled off the shores of Vietnam and the Philippines to collect against U.S. Army, Navy, and Air Force and South Vietnamese forces. Finally, the Soviets have also had patrols off the Middle East to collect information against Israel, Lebanon, and Egypt, and off the U.S. west coast to monitor activities in the U.S. Army, Navy, and Air Force bases situated there.

In summary, intelligence collectors have been of inestimable value to both the Soviet Union and the United States for purposes of maritime intelligence collection.

References

Department of the Navy, Office of the Chief of Naval Operations. *Understanding Soviet Naval Developments*. Washington, DC: GPO, 1985.

Watson, Bruce W. *Red Navy at Sea: Soviet Naval Operations on the High Seas, 1956–1980*. Boulder, CO: Westview Press, 1982.

Watson, Bruce W., and Watson, Susan M. *The Soviet Navy: Strengths and Liabilities*. Boulder, CO: Westview Press, 1986.

—**INTELLIGENCE COLLECTOR** is a person, organization, or group that gathers intelligence information. An intelligence collector is part of the collection part of the intelligence cycle. *See also:* Intelligence Cycle, Intelligence Collection Ships.

References

Department of Defense, Defense Intelligence College. *Glossary of Intelligence Terms and Definitions*. Washington, DC: DIC, 1987.

—**INTELLIGENCE COMMITTEE** was an outgrowth of President Nixon's management style. Unlike President Johnson, who preferred a minimal organization, Nixon preferred a large and formal National Security Council (NSC) structure. This network eventually included an Intelligence Committee, which was directed by Assistant for National Security Affairs Henry A. Kissinger, and provided guidance for national intelligence needs and continuing evaluations of intelligence products. *See also:* National Security Council; Nixon, Richard M.

References

American Bar Association. *Oversight and Accountability of the U.S. Intelligence Agencies: An Evaluation*. Washington, DC: ABA, 1985.

Laqueur, Walter. *A World of Secrets*. New York: Basic Books, 1985.

Lowenthal, Mark M. *U.S. Intelligence: Evolution and Anatomy*. New York: Praeger, 1984.

Maurer, Alfred C.; Turnstall, Marion D.; and Keagle, James M. *Intelligence Policy and Process*. Boulder, CO: Westview Press, 1985.

—**INTELLIGENCE COMMUNICATIONS ARCHITECTURE (INCA)** is developed by the Defense Intelligence Agency's Intelligence Communications Architecture Project Office (RS-P). It is a program that aims at rapidly disseminating, national and tactical intelligence to the operational commanders in peace, crisis, and war. *See also:* Communications Security, Defense Intelligence Agency.

References

Department of Defense, Defense Intelligence Agency. *Organization, Mission, and Key Personnel*. Washington, DC: DIA, 1986.

—**INTELLIGENCE COMMUNICATIONS ARCHITECTURE PROJECT OFFICE.** *See:* Defense Intelligence Agency.

—**INTELLIGENCE COMMUNITY (IC)** is a term that refers to the following Executive branch organizations and activities: the Central Intelligence Agency (CIA); the National Security Agency (NSA); the Defense Intelligence Agency (DIA); offices within the Department of Defense for the collection of specialized national foreign intelligence through reconnaissance programs; the Bureau of Intelligence and Research (INR) of the Department of State; intelligence elements of the military services; intelligence elements of the Federal Bureau of Investigation (FBI); intelligence elements of the Department of the Treasury; intelligence elements of the Department of Energy; and staff elements of the Office of the Director of Central Intelligence.

The concept of an Intelligence Community is unique in the government in that it is composed for the most part of elements that have their primary institutional homes in various departments and agencies of the Executive branch. Many of them differ from others in significant ways, but together they conduct the variety of activities that add up to the entire U.S. intelligence effort.

It is the duty of the director of Central Intelligence to make certain that the Community achieves its goal of providing national leaders with the most reliable and accurate intelligence possible. *See also:* Central Intelligence Agency, Defense Intelligence Agency, Director of Central Intelligence.

References

American Bar Association. *Oversight and Accountability of the U.S. Intelligence Agencies: An Evaluation.* Washington, DC: ABA, 1985.

Department of Defense, Defense Intelligence Agency. *Defense Intelligence Agency Manual.* Washington, DC: DIA, 1987.

Department of Defense, Defense Intelligence College. *Glossary of Intelligence Terms and Definitions.* Washington, DC: DIC, 1987.

Maurer, Alfred C.; Turnstall, Marion D.; and Keagle, James M. *Intelligence Policy and Process.* Boulder, CO: Westview Press, 1985.

Turner, Stansfield. *Secrecy and Democracy: The CIA in Transition.* Boston: Houghton Mifflin, 1985.

—INTELLIGENCE COMMUNITY STAFF (ICS OR IC STAFF) is the organization under the direction and control of the director of Central Intelligence (DCI). It was formed in 1972 as a replacement for the National Intelligence Programs Evaluation (NIPE) Staff. Its purpose is to assist the DCI in accomplishing his responsibilities concerning the Intelligence Community. The ICS is composed of eight major offices: Assessment and Evaluation, Community Coordination, Collection, HUMINT (human intelligence), Imagery Collection and Exploitation, Planning, Program Budget Coordination, and SIGINT (signals intelligence) Collection. *See also:* Director of Central Intelligence.

References

American Bar Association. *Oversight and Accountability of the U.S. Intelligence Agencies: An Evaluation.* Washington, DC: ABA, 1985.

Department of Defense, Defense Intelligence Agency. *Defense Intelligence Agency Manual.* Washington, DC: DIA, 1987.

Department of Defense, Defense Intelligence College. *Glossary of Intelligence Terms and Definitions.* Washington, DC: DIC, 1987.

Maurer, Alfred C.; Turnstall, Marion D.; and Keagle, James M. *Intelligence Policy and Process.* Boulder, CO: Westview Press, 1985.

Turner, Stansfield. *Secrecy and Democracy: The CIA in Transition.* Boston: Houghton Mifflin, 1985.

—INTELLIGENCE CONSUMER. *See:* Customer.

—INTELLIGENCE CONTINGENCY FUNDS are appropriated funds to be used for intelligence activities that are unforeseen at the time of the budget and when the use of other funds is not applicable or would either jeopardize or impede the mission of the intelligence unit. Such funds are almost invariably used for clandestine activity. *See also:* Incremental Cost.

References

American Bar Association. *Oversight and Accountability of the U.S. Intelligence Agencies: An Evaluation.* Washington, DC: ABA, 1985.

Department of Defense, Joint Chiefs of Staff. *Department of Defense Dictionary of Military and Related Terms.* Washington, DC: GPO, 1986.

Maurer, Alfred C.; Turnstall, Marion D.; and Keagle, James M. *Intelligence Policy and Process.* Boulder, CO: Westview Press, 1985.

U.S. Congress. Senate. *Final Report of the Senate Select Committee to Study Government Operations with Respect to Intelligence Activities. Report 94-755. Book I, Foreign and Military Intelligence.* Washington, DC: GPO, 1976.

—INTELLIGENCE CUT-OFF DATE (ICOD) is the date and the time of the intelligence used in a report or product. It usually is the date and time of the last piece of intelligence received, but if intelligence reporting has been sporadic and the reporter feels that he has not received all of the available information, he will state this in his report. The ICOD is particularly important in current intelligence reporting, where events tend to move along at a brisk pace and information becomes dated very rapidly. However, it is of great use to any analyst, because it provides a ready reference to when the information was produced, and he can then judge whether this has any effect on the value of the intelligence that he is using.

References

American Bar Association. *Oversight and Accountability of the U.S. Intelligence Agencies: An Evaluation.* Washington, DC: ABA, 1985.

Department of Defense, Joint Chiefs of Staff. *Department of Defense Dictionary of Military and Related Terms.* Washington, DC: GPO, 1986.

Maurer, Alfred C.; Turnstall, Marion D.; and Keagle, James M. *Intelligence Policy and Process.* Boulder, CO: Westview Press, 1985.

—INTELLIGENCE CYCLE is the process by which information is gathered, converted into intelligence, and delivered to the customer. There are usually five steps in the cycle:

Planning and direction. An intelligence agency first determines that a need for intelligence information exists. Its people prepare a collection plan, which defines the needs, makes suggestions concerning information collection, and provides other advice and guidelines. Funding is approved, orders are issued, requests are sent to the collection entities asking them to gather information, and continuous monitoring of the collection entities' progress is maintained.

Collection. Information or intelligence information is gathered and delivered to the production or processing activity.

Processing. The collected information is converted into a form more suitable for intelligence production.

Production. The information is converted into finished intelligence through integrating, analyzing, evaluating, and interpreting all available information. Intelligence products are prepared in response to known or anticipated customer requirements.

Dissemination. The finished intelligence products (in oral, written, or graphic form) are distributed to departmental and agency intelligence consumers. *See also:* Information, Intelligence, Intelligence Information.

References

Department of Defense, Defense Intelligence College. *Glossary of Intelligence Terms and Definitions.* Washington, DC: DIC, 1987.

Department of Defense, Joint Chiefs of Staff. *Department of Defense Dictionary of Military and Related Terms.* Washington, DC: GPO, 1986.

Maurer, Alfred C.; Turnstall, Marion D.; and Keagle, James M. *Intelligence Policy and Process.* Boulder, CO: Westview Press, 1985.

U.S. Congress. Senate. *Final Report of the Senate Select Committee to Study Government Operations with Respect to Intelligence Activities. Report 94-755. Book I, Foreign and Military Intelligence.* Washington, DC: GPO, 1976.

—**INTELLIGENCE DATA BASE** is all of the intelligence data and finished intelligence products at a given organization.

References

Department of Defense, Joint Chiefs of Staff. *Department of Defense Dictionary of Military and Related Terms.* Washington, DC: GPO, 1986.

Maurer, Alfred C.; Turnstall, Marion D.; and Keagle, James M. *Intelligence Policy and Process.* Boulder, CO: Westview Press, 1985.

U.S. Congress. Senate. *Final Report of the Senate Select Committee to Study Government Operations with Respect to Intelligence Activities. Report 94-755. Book I, Foreign and Military Intelligence.* Washington, DC: GPO, 1976.

—**INTELLIGENCE DATA HANDLING SYSTEM (IDHS)** is an information system that processes and manipulates raw information and intelligence data. It is usually composed of general purpose computers, peripheral equipment, and automated storage and retrieval equipment for documents and photographs. While automation is the distinguishing characteristic of an intelligence data handling system, the system's individual components may or may not be automated. The term is synonymous with the Department of Defense Intelligence Information System (DODIIS) or a DODIIS subsystem. *See also:* Department of Defense Intelligence Information System.

References

Department of Defense, Defense Intelligence Agency. *Defense Intelligence Agency Manual.* Washington, DC: DIA, 1985.

Department of Defense, Joint Chiefs of Staff. *Department of Defense Dictionary of Military and Related Terms.* Washington, DC: GPO, 1986.

Maurer, Alfred C.; Turnstall, Marion D.; and Keagle, James M. *Intelligence Policy and Process.* Boulder, CO: Westview Press, 1985.

U.S. Congress. Senate. *Final Report of the Senate Select Committee to Study Government Operations with Respect to Intelligence Activities. Report 94-755. Book I, Foreign and Military Intelligence.* Washington, DC: GPO, 1976.

—**INTELLIGENCE DATA HANDLING SYSTEMS** is an official term that has been defined by the Defense Intelligence Agency for one of its functional areas. It means "activities relating to the processing of intelligence data among and between humans and machines. This includes the functions of receipt from collection sources, transformation, coding, storage, search, retrieval, manipulation, presentation, and the function of dissemination where an interface between humans and machines is involved." *See also:* Defense Intelligence Agency.

References

Department of Defense, Defense Intelligence Agency. *Defense Intelligence Agency Manual 22-2.* Washington, DC: DIA, 1979.

Department of Defense, Joint Chiefs of Staff. *Department of Defense Dictionary of Military and Related Terms.* Washington, DC: GPO, 1986.

Maurer, Alfred C.; Turnstall, Marion D.; and Keagle, James M. *Intelligence Policy and Process.* Boulder, CO: Westview Press, 1985.

—**INTELLIGENCE DISSEMINATION** is the conveyance of intelligence in suitable, usable form to the agencies needing it. Intelligence dissemination includes identifying consumers having an intelligence requirement for the intelligence at hand. *See also:* Intelligence Cycle.

References

Department of Defense, Defense Intelligence Agency. *Defense Intelligence Agency Manual.* Washington, DC: DIA, 1987.

Kent, Sherman. *Strategic Intelligence for American World Policy.* Princeton, NJ: Princeton University Press, 1966.

Laqueur, Walter. *A World of Secrets.* New York: Basic Books, 1985.

Treverton, Gregory F. *Covert Action: The Limits of Intervention in the Postwar World.* New York: Basic Books, 1987.

Turner, Stansfield. *Secrecy and Democracy: The CIA in Transition.* Boston: Houghton Mifflin, 1985.

—**INTELLIGENCE DOCUMENTS** are paper or microform copies of substantive intelligence reports, studies, publications, and information reports produced by or for the Defense Intelligence Agency, intelligence elements of the military services, Unified and Specified Commands, Central Intelligence Agency, Bureau of Intelligence and Research, Department of State, and intelligence agencies of foreign nations.

References

American Bar Association. *Oversight and Accountability of the U.S. Intelligence Agencies: An Evaluation.* Washington, DC: ABA, 1985.

Department of Defense, Defense Intelligence Agency. *Defense Intelligence Agency Manual.* Washington, DC: DIA, 1987.

Kent, Sherman. *Strategic Intelligence for American World Policy.* Princeton, NJ: Princeton University Press, 1966.

Maurer, Alfred C.; Turnstall, Marion D.; and Keagle, James M. *Intelligence Policy and Process.* Boulder, CO: Westview Press, 1985.

—**INTELLIGENCE EDUCATION** is an official term that has been defined by the Defense Intelligence Agency for one of its functional areas. It means "activities relating to intelligence education at the Defense Intelligence College, its predecessors, the Military Departments or other Government Agencies."

References

Department of Defense, Defense Intelligence Agency. *Defense Intelligence Agency Manual 22-2.* Washington, DC: DIA, 1979.

—**INTELLIGENCE ESTIMATE (IE)** is the product of estimative intelligence. It is prepared by appraising the elements of intelligence relating to a specific situation or condition in order to determine the courses of action that are open to an enemy or probable enemy, as well as their probable order of adoption. In other words, it is intelligence that predicts the degree of likelihood of possible future events, developments, or courses of action and their implications and consequences. *See also:* Estimate, Estimative Intelligence.

References

Department of Defense, Defense Intelligence College. *Glossary of Intelligence Terms and Definitions.* Washington, DC: DIC, 1987.

Department of Defense, Joint Chiefs of Staff. *Department of Defense Dictionary of Military and Related Terms.* Washington, DC: GPO, 1986.

Kent, Sherman. *Strategic Intelligence for American World Policy.* Princeton, NJ: Princeton University Press, 1966.

Laqueur, Walter. *A World of Secrets.* New York: Basic Books, 1985.

Maurer, Alfred C.; Turnstall, Marion D.; and Keagle, James M. *Intelligence Policy and Process.* Boulder, CO: Westview Press, 1985.

Turner, Stansfield. *Secrecy and Democracy: The CIA in Transition.* Boston: Houghton Mifflin, 1985.

U.S. Congress. Senate. *Final Report of the Senate Select Committee to Study Government Operations with Respect to Intelligence Activities. Report 94-755. Book I, Foreign and Military Intelligence.* Washington, DC: GPO, 1976.

—**INTELLIGENCE IDENTITIES PROTECTION ACT OF 1982,** PL-97-200, of June 23, 1982, made it a crime for people, including journalists, to seek out and publicize the names of U.S. intelligence agents. It does not punish anyone for inadvertent disclosures, but only those who make this a part of an activity that is aimed at harming U.S. intelligence.

The bill, which was passed as an amendment to the National Security Act of 1947, delineates various punishments for different acts of disclosure, with the maximum sentence being a fine of $50,000 and imprisonment for not more than ten years, or both.

References

American Bar Association. *Oversight and Accountability of the U.S. Intelligence Agencies: An Evaluation.* Washington, DC: ABA, 1985.

Kornblum, Allan. *Intelligence and the Law: Cases and Materials.* Vol. IV. Washington, DC: DIC, 1987.

Laqueur, Walter. *A World of Secrets.* New York: Basic Books, 1985.

Maurer, Alfred C.; Turnstall, Marion D.; and Keagle, James M. *Intelligence Policy and Process.* Boulder, CO: Westview Press, 1985.

Oseth, John M. *Regulating U.S. Intelligence Operations: A Study in the Definition of the National Interest.* Frankfurt: University of Kentucky Press, 1985.

U.S. Congress. *Intelligence Identities Protection Act of 1982. Public Law 97-200, June 23, 1982.* Washington, DC: GPO, 1982.

—**INTELLIGENCE INFORMATION** is information of potential intelligence value concerning the capabilities, intentions, and activities of any foreign power or organization, or of their personnel. *See also:* Information, Intelligence.

References

American Bar Association. *Oversight and Accountability of the U.S. Intelligence Agencies: An Evaluation.* Washington, DC: ABA, 1985.

Corson, William R. *The Armies of Ignorance: The Rise of the American Intelligence Empire.* New York: Dial Press, 1977.

Department of Defense, Defense Intelligence College. *Glossary of Intelligence Terms and Definitions.* Washington, DC: DIC, 1987.

Kent, Sherman. *Strategic Intelligence for American World Policy.* Princeton, NJ: Princeton University Press, 1966.

Maurer, Alfred C.; Turnstall, Marion D.; and Keagle, James M. *Intelligence Policy and Process.* Boulder, CO: Westview Press, 1985.

Treverton, Gregory F. *Covert Action: The Limits of Intervention in the Postwar World.* New York: Basic Books, 1987.

Turner, Stansfield. *Secrecy and Democracy: The CIA in Transition.* Boston: Houghton Mifflin, 1985.

—**INTELLIGENCE INFORMATION HANDLING COMMITTEE (IHC).** *See:* Director of Central Intelligence Committee.

—**INTELLIGENCE INFORMATION REPORT (IIR)** is the final product resulting from the collection step of the intelligence cycle. It is a report used to forward the raw information collected to fulfill intelligence requirements. *See also:* Intelligence Report.

References

Department of Defense, Defense Intelligence Agency. *Defense Intelligence Agency Manual.* Washington, DC: DIA, 1987.

Department of Defense, Defense Intelligence College. *Glossary of Intelligence Terms and Definitions.* Washington, DC: DIC, 1987.

Department of Defense, U.S. Army. *RDTE Managers Intelligence and Threat Support Guide.* Alexandria, VA: Headquarters, Army Materiel Development and Readiness Command, 1983.

Maurer, Alfred C.; Turnstall, Marion D.; and Keagle, James M. *Intelligence Policy and Process.* Boulder, CO: Westview Press, 1985.

—**INTELLIGENCE INFORMATION REPORT FILE ARCHIVE (IRFLA)** are files containing identification and content-identification data for Department of Defense and Central Intelligence Agency intelligence reports received between July 1, 1965, and September 1, 1971. Over 778,000 records of Department of Defense and Central Intelligence Agency intelligence information reports are contained in the file, which is accessed by batch mode.

References

Department of Defense, Defense Intelligence Agency. *Defense Intelligence Agency Manual.* Washington, DC: DIA, 1987.

Von Hoene, John P. A. *Intelligence User's Guide.* Washington, DC: DIA, 1983.

—**INTELLIGENCE JOURNAL** is a chronological log of intelligence activities that covers a specific period (usually 24 hours). It is an index of reports and messages that have been received and transmitted, important events that have occurred, and actions that have been taken. The journal is a permanent and official record. *See also:* Journal.

References

Department of Defense, Joint Chiefs of Staff. *Department of Defense Dictionary of Military and Related Terms.* Washington, DC: GPO, 1986.

Department of Defense, U.S. Army. *Intelligence and Electronic Warfare Operations.* Field Manual FM 34-1. Washington, DC: Headquarters, Department of the Army, 1984.

—**INTELLIGENCE OFFICER (IO)** is a professional (vice clerical) employee of an intelligence organization who is engaged in intelligence activities. *See also:* Analyst.

References

Department of Defense, Defense Intelligence College. *Glossary of Intelligence Terms and Definitions.* Washington, DC: DIC, 1987.

Maurer, Alfred C.; Turnstall, Marion D.; and Keagle, James M. *Intelligence Policy and Process.* Boulder, CO: Westview Press, 1985.

—**INTELLIGENCE ORGANIZATION** is any organization, agency, group, or other entity that is involved in intelligence activity. *See also:* Foreign Intelligence Service, Intelligence Agency.

References

Department of Defense, Defense Intelligence College. *Glossary of Intelligence Terms and Definitions.* Washington, DC: DIC, 1987.

Maurer, Alfred C.; Turnstall, Marion D.; and Keagle, James M. *Intelligence Policy and Process.* Boulder, CO: Westview Press, 1985.

—**INTELLIGENCE OVERSIGHT ACT OF 1980,** which was passed as Title V of the National Security Act of 1947 (950 U.S.C. 413), "Accountability for Intelligence Activities," stated that the director of Central intelligence and the heads of all intelligence departments and agencies would (1) keep the Select Committee on Intelligence of the U.S. Senate and the Permanent Select Committee on Intelligence of the U.S. House of Representatives fully informed of all intelligence activities that were currently being performed. (There was one exemption to this clause. If the President determined that he wished to limit the dissemination of information concerning an operation, then he could opt to inform only the chairmen, the ranking minority members of the intelligence committees, and the House and Senate majority and minority leaders.); (2) furnish any information that was requested by Congress so that Congress could be assured that it had effective oversight controls; (3) report to Congress promptly of any intelligence failure, along with the actions that would be taken to preclude a repeat of the failure in the future; and (4) Congress would create the procedures necessary to ensure the security of the information that was provided by the Intelligence Committees.

In one sense, the significance of the act was that it reflected Congress's continued unease concerning its ability to monitor adequately the operations of the U.S. Intelligence Community. In another, the act was the result of S.2525, in which almost 300 pages of material was reduced to the act. In this respect, in the wake of the Soviet invasion of Afghanistan, the Soviet Brigade in Cuba, and the Iran hostage crisis, the act reflected congressional recognition that the Executive needed flexibility in order to respond adequately to such episodes.

References

American Bar Association. *Oversight and Accountability of the U.S. Intelligence Agencies: An Evaluation.* Washington, DC: ABA, 1985.

Laqueur, Walter. *A World of Secrets.* New York: Basic Books, 1985.

Maurer, Alfred C.; Turnstall, Marion D.; and Keagle, James M. *Intelligence Policy and Process.* Boulder, CO: Westview Press, 1985.

Treverton, Gregory F. *Covert Action: The Limits of Intervention in the Postwar World.* New York: Basic Books, 1987.

Turner, Stansfield. *Secrecy and Democracy: The CIA in Transition.* Boston: Houghton Mifflin, 1985.

—**INTELLIGENCE OVERSIGHT BOARD (IOB)** is a body that was created by President Ford under Executive Order 11905, dated February 18, 1976, and entitled "United States Foreign Intelligence Activities." The purpose of the IOB was to inform and advise the President on the legality and propriety of an intelligence activity. It consists of three members from outside the government who are appointed by the President. One of these, who serves as chairman, is also a member of the President's Foreign Intelligence Advisory Board. The IOB was responsible for discovering and reporting to the President any intelligence activities or operations that were legally questionable in terms of the Constitution, the laws of the United States, or Presidential Executive

Orders, or that raised questions of propriety. According to the Executive Order, the IOB was to report any evidence of such illegal or improper activities to the attorney general immediately and was to routinely report to the attorney general and the President at least quarterly on its findings. The board was also charged with reviewing the internal guidelines and direction of the Intelligence Community. It is a permanent, nonpartisan body.

The duties of the IOB were redefined in Executive Order 12036, "United States Intelligence Activities," signed by President Jimmy Carter on January 24, 1978. Still composed of three members from outside the government, the board's duties are to review the practices and procedures of the inspectors general and general counsels and to oversee the practices of the intelligence agencies to ensure that they are legal and proper. The IOB was continued by President Reagan and is currently governed by Executive Order 12334.

References

American Bar Association. *Oversight and Accountability of the U.S. Intelligence Agencies: An Evaluation.* Washington, DC: ABA, 1985.

Laqueur, Walter. *A World of Secrets.* New York: Basic Books, 1985.

Lowenthal, Mark M. *U.S. Intelligence: Evolution and Anatomy.* New York: Praeger, 1984.

Maurer, Alfred C.; Turnstall, Marion D.; and Keagle, James M. *Intelligence Policy and Process.* Boulder, CO: Westview Press, 1985.

Office of the President of the United States. *Executive Order 11905, United States Foreign Intelligence Activities.* Washington, DC, Feb. 18, 1976.

———. *Executive Order 12036, United States Intelligence Activities.* Washington, DC, Jan. 24, 1978.

Treverton, Gregory F. *Covert Action: The Limits of Intervention in the Postwar World.* New York: Basic Books, 1987.

Turner, Stansfield. *Secrecy and Democracy: The CIA in Transition.* Boston: Houghton Mifflin, 1985.

—**INTELLIGENCE POLICY** is a generic term that means the selection of intelligence objectives or goals and of the means calculated to achieve them.

References

Maurer, Alfred C.; Turnstall, Marion D.; and Keagle, James M. *Intelligence Policy and Process.* Boulder, CO: Westview Press, 1985.

Turner, Stansfield. *Secrecy and Democracy: The CIA in Transition.* Boston: Houghton Mifflin, 1985.

—**INTELLIGENCE PREPARATION OF THE BATTLEFIELD (IPB)** is an Army tactical intelligence (TACINT) term that means the detailed analysis of enemy, weather, and terrain in specific geographic areas. It provides an analytical tool for relating changes in enemy doctrine and capabilities to specific terrain and weather scenarios.

References

Department of Defense, U.S. Army. *Intelligence and Electronic Warfare Operations.* Field Manual FM 34-1. Washington, DC: Headquarters, Department of the Army, 1984.

———. *Military Intelligence Battalion (Combat Electronic Warfare Intelligence) (Division).* Field Manual FM 34-10. Washington, DC: Headquarters, Department of the Army, 1981.

———. *Military Intelligence Battalion (CEWI) (Operations) (Corps).* Field Manual FM 34-21. Washington, DC: Headquarters, Department of the Army, 1982.

———. *Military Intelligence Battalion (CEWI) (Tactical Exploitation) (Corps): Counterintelligence, Interrogation, Electronic Warfare.* Field Manual FM 34-23. Washington, DC: Headquarters, Department of the Army, 1985.

———. *Military Intelligence Company (Combat Electronic Warfare and Intelligence) (Armored Cavalry Regiment/Separate Brigade).* Field Manual FM 34-30. Washington, DC: Headquarters, Department of the Army, 1983.

———. *Military Intelligence Group (Combat Electronic Warfare and Intelligence) (Corps).* Field Manual FM 34-20. Washington, DC: Headquarters, Department of the Army, 1983.

—**INTELLIGENCE PRIORITIES FOR STRATEGIC PLANNING (IPSP)** is one of seven documents, listed under the Joint Strategic Planning System (JSPS), that make up the system. The IPSP is a comprehensive document that discusses the military intelligence priorities in order to support the tasking of Department of Defense intelligence production, collection, and support activities in the short- and mid-term. Additionally, it provides advice to the secretary of defense on the military intelligence priorities that are required to carry out the strategy in the Joint Strategic Planning Document (JSPD), and it advises the military services and the commanders-in-chief on what their intelligence requirements and priorities ought to be. Finally, the IPSP provides prioritized collection and production guidance for intelligence activities that are necessary to support the Joint Intelligence Estimate for Planning (JIEP). The IPSP is prepared by the Defense Intelligence Agency and is approved by the Joint Chiefs of Staff. *See also:* Joint Strategic Planning System.

References

Department of Defense, National Defense University. *Joint Staff Officer's Guide, 1986.* Washington, DC: GPO, 1986.

Kent, Sherman. *Strategic Intelligence for American World Policy.* Princeton, NJ: Princeton University Press, 1966.

Laqueur, Walter. *A World of Secrets.* New York: Basic Books, 1985.

Treverton, Gregory F. *Covert Action: The Limits of Intervention in the Postwar World.* New York: Basic Books, 1987.

—**INTELLIGENCE PROCESS,** as defined by the Church Committee, is composed of those steps by which information is collected, converted into intelligence, and then disseminated. *See also:* Intelligence Cycle.

References

Kent, Sherman. *Strategic Intelligence for American World Policy.* Princeton, NJ: Princeton University Press, 1966.

Maurer, Alfred C.; Turnstall, Marion D.; and Keagle, James M. *Intelligence Policy and Process.* Boulder, CO: Westview Press, 1985.

U.S. Congress. Senate. *Final Report of the Senate Select Committee to Study Government Operations with Respect to Intelligence Activities. Report 94-755. Book I, Foreign and Military Intelligence.* Washington, DC: GPO, 1976.

—**INTELLIGENCE PRODUCER** is an organization or agency that participates in the production step of the intelligence cycle. *See also:* Intelligence Cycle.

References

Department of Defense, Defense Intelligence College. *Glossary of Intelligence Terms and Definitions.* Washington, DC: DIC, 1987.

—**INTELLIGENCE PRODUCER'S COUNCIL** advises the director of Central Intelligence on the quality of intelligence. It reports to the director through the deputy director for intelligence. *See also:* Central Intelligence Agency.

References

Lowenthal, Mark M. *U.S. Intelligence: Evolution and Anatomy.* New York: Praeger, 1984.

Maurer, Alfred C.; Turnstall, Marion D.; and Keagle, James M. *Intelligence Policy and Process.* Boulder, CO: Westview Press, 1985.

—**INTELLIGENCE PRODUCT** is the result of intelligence analysis. It is finished intelligence that is ready for presentation to the customer. *See also:* Intelligence Cycle, Intelligence Production.

References

Maurer, Alfred C.; Turnstall, Marion D.; and Keagle, James M. *Intelligence Policy and Process.* Boulder, CO: Westview Press, 1985.

—**INTELLIGENCE PRODUCTION REQUIREMENT (IPR)** is a form printed by the Department of Defense and completed by the intelligence customer. It is the means by which a customer describes his or her requirement to the Defense Intelligence Agency (DIA). This requirement is a stated need for the production of intelligence on a general or specific subject, program, system, or weapon. The requirement is then approved and processed by the DIA.

The IPR is the preferred way to establish a long-term requirement (long-term requirements are those of sufficient importance to warrant the scheduling of products in the appropriate general or scientific and technical intelligence production program, and which necessitate the application of considerable analytical resources to satisfy).

References

Department of Defense, U.S. Army. *RDTE Managers Intelligence and Threat Support Guide.* Alexandria, VA: Headquarters, Army Materiel Development and Readiness Command, 1983.

Maurer, Alfred C.; Turnstall, Marion D.; and Keagle, James M. *Intelligence Policy and Process.* Boulder, CO: Westview Press, 1985.

—**INTELLIGENCE-RELATED ACTIVITIES (IRA)** are endeavors that are specifically excluded from the National Foreign Intelligence Program (NFIP) that respond to departmental or agency tasking for time-sensitive information on foreign activities and that respond to national Intelligence

Community advisory tasking of collection capabilities. IRA have a primary mission of supporting departmental or agency missions or operational forces, of training personnel for intelligence duties, and of being devoted to research and development for intelligence and related capabilities. Specifically excluded from these activities are programs that are so closely integrated with a weapon system that their primary function is to provide targeting data for immediate use.

In 1974–76, the House Appropriations Committee (HAC), in an attempt to get the Department of Defense to report on intelligence systems (such as the SR-71 Blackbird) that were not reported in the intelligence budget, created a budget category called IRA. Also included in IRA were the Navy's surveillance systems that tracked Soviet submarines and the warning systems that were used by the Department of Defense to monitor bombers, missiles, and satellites. Between 1976 and 1980, more systems were added to IRA, and by 1980 the Department of Defense had embraced IRA as a management tool to coordinate and control a wide range of service intelligence activities.

References

American Bar Association. *Oversight and Accountability of the U.S. Intelligence Agencies: An Evaluation.* Washington, DC: ABA, 1985.

Department of Defense, Joint Chiefs of Staff. *Department of Defense Dictionary of Military and Related Terms.* Washington, DC: GPO, 1986.

Laqueur, Walter. *A World of Secrets.* New York: Basic Books, 1985.

Maurer, Alfred C.; Turnstall, Marion D.; and Keagle, James M. *Intelligence Policy and Process.* Boulder, CO: Westview Press, 1985.

Treverton, Gregory F. *Covert Action: The Limits of Intervention in the Postwar World.* New York: Basic Books, 1987.

—**INTELLIGENCE REPORT (IR)** is a product of the production step of the intelligence cycle. On the tactical level, an intelligence report, called an INTREP, is a specific report of information, usually on a single item, that is made at any level of command in tactical operations and is disseminated as rapidly as possible in keeping with the timeliness of the information. *See also:* Intelligence Information Report.

References

Department of Defense, Defense Intelligence College. *Glossary of Intelligence Terms and Definitions.* Washington, DC: DIC, 1987.

Department of Defense, Joint Chiefs of Staff. *Department of Defense Dictionary of Military and Related Terms.* Washington, DC: GPO, 1986.

Maurer, Alfred C.; Turnstall, Marion D.; and Keagle, James M. *Intelligence Policy and Process.* Boulder, CO: Westview Press, 1985.

—**INTELLIGENCE REPORT EVALUATION FORM** is the means by which intelligence customers and analysts can evaluate the reporting from the field collectors.

References

Department of Defense, Joint Chiefs of Staff. *Department of Defense Dictionary of Military and Related Terms.* Washington, DC: GPO, 1986.

Department of Defense, Defense Intelligence College. *Glossary of Intelligence Terms and Definitions.* Washington, DC: DIC, 1987.

—**INTELLIGENCE REPORT INDEX SUMMARY (IRISA)** is a computerized on-line and batch index to Department of Defense and Central Intelligence Agency intelligence information reports from September 1, 1971, to the present. The total file has about 1,900,000 reports, of which 300,000 of the most current are on-line.

References

Department of Defense, Defense Intelligence Agency. *Defense Intelligence Agency Manual.* Washington, DC: DIA, 1987.

—**INTELLIGENCE REPORTING** is preparing and sending information by any means. More commonly, the term is limited to reports that are prepared by an intelligence collector and transmitted by him or her to headquarters, and by this component of the intelligence structure to one or more intelligence-producing centers or facilities. Thus, even in this limited sense, reporting embraces both collection and dissemination. The term is applied to normal and specialist intelligence reports. *See also:* Normal Intelligence Reports, Specialist Intelligence Reports.

References

American Bar Association. *Oversight and Accountability of the U.S. Intelligence Agencies: An Evaluation.* Washington, DC: ABA, 1985.

Department of Defense, Joint Chiefs of Staff. *Department of Defense Dictionary of Military and Related Terms.* Washington, DC: GPO, 1986.

Kent, Sherman. *Strategic Intelligence for American World Policy.* Princeton, NJ: Princeton University Press, 1966.

Maurer, Alfred C.; Turnstall, Marion D.; and Keagle, James M. *Intelligence Policy and Process*. Boulder, CO: Westview Press, 1985.

Treverton, Gregory F. *Covert Action: The Limits of Intervention in the Postwar World*. New York: Basic Books, 1987.

—**INTELLIGENCE REQUIREMENT (IR)** is any subject for which there is a need to collect intelligence information and produce intelligence. It may appear as a consumer statement of intelligence need for which information is not readily available. *See also:* Essential Elements of Information.

References

Department of Defense, Defense Intelligence College. *Glossary of Intelligence Terms and Definitions*. Washington, DC: DIC, 1987.

Department of Defense, Joint Chiefs of Staff. *Department of Defense Dictionary of Military and Related Terms*. Washington, DC: GPO, 1986.

Kent, Sherman. *Strategic Intelligence for American World Policy*. Princeton, NJ: Princeton University Press, 1966.

Laqueur, Walter. *A World of Secrets*. New York: Basic Books, 1985.

Treverton, Gregory F. *Covert Action: The Limits of Intervention in the Postwar World*. New York: Basic Books, 1987.

U.S. Congress. Senate. *Final Report of the Senate Select Committee to Study Government Operations with Respect to Intelligence Activities. Report 94-755. Book I, Foreign and Military Intelligence*. Washington, DC: GPO, 1976.

—**INTELLIGENCE RESEARCH AND DEVELOPMENT COUNCIL (IRDC).** *See:* Director of Central Intelligence Committee.

—**INTELLIGENCE RESOURCES ADVISORY COMMITTEE (IRAC)** was an interdepartmental group established in 1971 to advise the director of Central Intelligence in preparing a consolidated intelligence program budget for the President. Its members included representatives from the Departments of State and Defense, the Office of Management and Budget, and the Central Intelligence Agency. It was abolished by President Ford's Executive Order No. 11905 of February 2, 1976. *See also:* Central Intelligence Agency.

References

American Bar Association. *Oversight and Accountability of the U.S. Intelligence Agencies: An Evaluation*. Washington, DC: ABA, 1985.

Corson, William R. *The Armies of Ignorance: The Rise of the American Intelligence Empire*. New York: Dial Press, 1977.

Fain, Tyrus G.; Plant, Katharine C.; and Milloy, Ross. *The Intelligence Community: History, Organization, and Issues*. Public Documents Series. New York: R.R. Bowker, 1977.

Lowenthal, Mark M. *U.S. Intelligence: Evolution and Anatomy*. New York: Praeger, 1984.

Maurer, Alfred C.; Turnstall, Marion D.; and Keagle, James M. *Intelligence Policy and Process*. Boulder, CO: Westview Press, 1985.

U.S. Congress. Senate. *Final Report of the Senate Select Committee to Study Government Operations with Respect to Intelligence Activities. Report 94-755. Book I, Foreign and Military Intelligence*. Washington, DC: GPO, 1976.

—**INTELLIGENCE SUBJECT CODE** is a system of subject and area references that are used to index the information contained in intelligence reports as required by a general intelligence document reference service. *See also:* Intelligence Reports.

References

American Bar Association. *Oversight and Accountability of the U.S. Intelligence Agencies: An Evaluation*. Washington, DC: ABA, 1985.

Department of Defense, Defense Intelligence Agency. *Defense Intelligence Agency Manual*. Washington, DC: DIA, 1987.

Department of Defense, Joint Chiefs of Staff. *Department of Defense Dictionary of Military and Related Terms*. Washington, DC: GPO, 1986.

Maurer, Alfred C.; Turnstall, Marion D.; and Keagle, James M. *Intelligence Policy and Process*. Boulder, CO: Westview Press, 1985.

—**INTELLIGENCE SUMMARY (INTSUM)** is a specific report that provides a summary of intelligence items at frequent intervals. *See also:* Intelligence.

References

American Bar Association. *Oversight and Accountability of the U.S. Intelligence Agencies: An Evaluation*. Washington, DC: ABA, 1985.

Department of Defense, Defense Intelligence Agency. *Defense Intelligence Agency Manual*. Washington, DC: DIA, 1987.

Department of Defense, Joint Chiefs of Staff. *Department of Defense Dictionary of Military and Related Terms.* Washington, DC: GPO, 1986.

Maurer, Alfred C.; Turnstall, Marion D.; and Keagle, James M. *Intelligence Policy and Process.* Boulder, CO: Westview Press, 1985.

—**INTELLIGENCE TARGETING** pertains to the target that is to be destroyed. It is the part of an overall process that is accomplished by target intelligence officers and specialists. Though aspects of targeting are performed by the U.S. Army, Navy, Marine Corps, and Allied personnel, only the U.S. Air Force has an officer and a noncommissioned officer career field specialty that is devoted specifically to targeting. The functions that constitute intelligence targeting include target analysis, weaponeering, management of materials, and other related functions. *See also:* Targeting.

References

American Bar Association. *Oversight and Accountability of the U.S. Intelligence Agencies: An Evaluation.* Washington, DC: ABA, 1985.

Department of Defense, Defense Intelligence Agency. *Defense Intelligence Agency Manual.* Washington, DC: DIA, 1987.

Maurer, Alfred C.; Turnstall, Marion D.; and Keagle, James M. *Intelligence Policy and Process.* Boulder, CO: Westview Press, 1985.

—**INTELLIGENCE USER.** *See:* Customer.

—**INTELLIGENCE USER'S GUIDE (IUG),** published by the Defense Intelligence Agency (DIA), acquaints the reader with the various defense intelligence products and provides information on how authorized organizations may obtain finished intelligence products and support. Its aim is to help the intelligence user or operator who does not have an intelligence staff. The missions, responsibilities, and organization of the DIA, as well as its relationships with other agencies, have been included to aid the user in understanding the DIA role within the Intelligence Community. *See also:* Defense Intelligence Agency.

References

Department of Defense, Defense Intelligence Agency. *Defense Intelligence Agency Manual.* Washington, DC: DIA, 1987.

—**INTENTION,** as a general intelligence term, is an aim or design to execute a specific course of action. In the indications and warning (I&W) context, intention means an adversary's purpose, plan, commitment, or design for action. I&W is concerned with the intentions of the leader or decisionmaker, with the intentions of nations, and with the foreign policies of nations. *See also:* Indications and Warning.

References

Department of Defense, Joint Chiefs of Staff. *Department of Defense Dictionary of Military and Related Terms.* Washington, DC: GPO, 1986.

Kent, Sherman. *Strategic Intelligence for American World Policy.* Princeton, NJ: Princeton University Press, 1966.

Laqueur, Walter. *A World of Secrets.* New York: Basic Books, 1985.

Treverton, Gregory F. *Covert Action: The Limits of Intervention in the Postwar World.* New York: Basic Books, 1987.

—**INTERACTIVE ANALYSIS** is a study performed by, or under the auspices of, service program management elements to examine the interaction between a proposed U.S. system and the threat it is intended to encounter during its operational lifetime.

References

Department of Defense, U.S. Army. *RDTE Managers Intelligence and Threat Support Guide.* Alexandria, VA: Headquarters, Army Materiel Development and Readiness Command, 1983.

—**INTERAGENCY DEFECTOR COMMITTEE (IDC).** *See:* Director of Central Intelligence Committee.

—**INTERAGENCY GROUPS (IGS)** were established to assist the Senior Interagency Group for Intelligence (SIG-I) by considering individual policy issues. Each group consists of SIG members and, upon invitation of the group's chairman, others who have specific responsibilities for the issues being considered. A representative of the director of Central Intelligence chairs the meetings that deal with national foreign intelligence. A representative of the Federal Bureau of Investigation chairs those that deal with counterintelligence, except for international terrorism, which is divided between a State Department representative for terrorism abroad and an attorney general representative for terrorism in the United States. Any number of IGs may be established, and they, in turn, may establish working groups as needed to provide support to the National Security Council.

References

Corson, William R. *The Armies of Ignorance: The Rise of the American Intelligence Empire*. New York: Dial Press, 1977.

Laqueur, Walter. *A World of Secrets*. New York: Basic Books, 1985.

Maurer, Alfred C.; Turnstall, Marion D.; and Keagle, James M. *Intelligence Policy and Process*. Boulder, CO: Westview Press, 1985.

Treverton, Gregory F. *Covert Action: The Limits of Intervention in the Postwar World*. New York: Basic Books, 1987.

—**INTERAGENCY INTELLIGENCE MEMORANDUM (IIM)** is a national intelligence assessment or estimate that is produced by a national intelligence officer.

References

Corson, William R. *The Armies of Ignorance: The Rise of the American Intelligence Empire*. New York: Dial Press, 1977.

Department of Defense, Defense Intelligence College. *Glossary of Intelligence Terms and Definitions*. Washington, DC: DIC, 1987.

Laqueur, Walter. *A World of Secrets*. New York: Basic Books, 1985.

Treverton, Gregory F. *Covert Action: The Limits of Intervention in the Postwar World*. New York: Basic Books, 1987.

Turner, Stansfield. *Secrecy and Democracy: The CIA in Transition*. Boston: Houghton Mifflin, 1985.

—**INTERCEPT STATION,** in signals intelligence (SIGINT), is one that intercepts or collects communications or noncommunications transmissions for intelligence purposes.

References

Department of Defense, Defense Intelligence College. *Glossary of Intelligence Terms and Definitions*. Washington, DC: DIC, 1987.

Turner, Stansfield. *Secrecy and Democracy: The CIA in Transition*. Boston: Houghton Mifflin, 1985.

—**INTERCEPTION.** In a general sense, interception means acquiring electromagnetic signals such as radio signals with electronic collection equipment for intelligence purposes and without the consent of the signaler. Interception is also an Army tactical intelligence (TACINT) term that means the act of listening, copying, or recording emissions by someone other than the intended party. The goals of interception are to collect emissions for information content; determine the locations and characteristics of the emitters; determine the parameter, structure, and functions of the emissions; and determine the organizational or individual identities of communications or noncommunications emitters. In the context of TACINT, interception is a step in the Army signals intelligence (SIGINT) process. *See also:* SIGINT Process.

References

Department of Defense, Defense Intelligence College. *Glossary of Intelligence Terms and Definitions*. Washington, DC: DIC, 1987.

Department of Defense, Joint Chiefs of Staff. *Department of Defense Dictionary of Military and Related Terms*. Washington, DC: GPO, 1986.

Department of Defense, U.S. Army. *Counter-Signals Intelligence (C-SIGINT) Operations*. Field Manual FM 34-62. Washington, DC: Headquarters, Department of the Army, 1986.

———. *Military Intelligence Battalion (Combat Electronic Warfare Intelligence) (Division)*. Field Manual FM 34-10. Washington, DC: Headquarters, Department of the Army, 1981.

———. *Military Intelligence Battalion (CEWI) (Tactical Exploitation) (Corps): Counterintelligence, Interrogation, Electronic Warfare*. Field Manual FM 34-23. Washington, DC: Headquarters, Department of the Army, 1985.

———. *Military Intelligence Company (Combat Electronic Warfare and Intelligence) (Armored Cavalry Regiment/Separate Brigade)*. Field Manual FM 34-30. Washington, DC: Headquarters, Department of the Army, 1983.

Lowenthal, Mark M. *U.S. Intelligence: Evolution and Anatomy*. New York: Praeger, 1984.

Quirk, John; Phillips, David; Cline, Ray; and Pforzheimer, Walter. *The Central Intelligence Agency: A Photographic History*. Guilford, CT: Foreign Intelligence Press, 1986.

U.S. Congress. Senate. *Final Report of the Senate Select Committee to Study Government Operations with Respect to Intelligence Activities. Report 94-755. Book I, Foreign and Military Intelligence*. Washington, DC: GPO, 1976.

—**INTERCONTINENTAL BALLISTIC MISSILE (ICBM)** is a ballistic missile with a range of about 3,000 to 8,000 nautical miles.

References

Department of Defense, Joint Chiefs of Staff. *Department of Defense Dictionary of Military and Related Terms.* Washington, DC: GPO, 1986.

—**INTERDEPARTMENTAL COORDINATING AND PLANNING STAFF,** a component of the Central Intelligence Group, handled the administrative aspects of the group's contacts with other intelligence entities. *See also:* Central Intelligence Agency.

References

Corson, William R. *The Armies of Ignorance: The Rise of the American Intelligence Empire.* New York: Dial Press, 1977.

Fain, Tyrus G.; Plant, Katharine C.; and Milloy, Ross. *The Intelligence Community: History, Organization, and Issues.* Public Documents Series. New York: R.R. Bowker, 1977.

—**INTERDEPARTMENTAL INTELLIGENCE** is a general intelligence term for integrated departmental intelligence that is needed by departments or agencies of the U.S. government so that they can fulfill their duties, but exceeds the capability of a single department to produce. As defined by the Church Committee, interdepartmental intelligence has a slightly different meaning. Here it "is the synthesis of departmental intelligence which is required by departments and agencies of the United States Government for performance of their missions. Such intelligence is viewed as transcending the exclusive production competence of a single department or agency." *See also:* Departmental Intelligence.

References

Corson, William R. *The Armies of Ignorance: The Rise of the American Intelligence Empire.* New York: Dial Press, 1977.

Department of Defense, Joint Chiefs of Staff. *Department of Defense Dictionary of Military and Related Terms.* Washington, DC: GPO, 1986.

Kent, Sherman. *Strategic Intelligence for American World Policy.* Princeton, NJ: Princeton University Press, 1966.

U.S. Congress. Senate. *Final Report of the Senate Select Committee to Study Government Operations with Respect to Intelligence Activities. Report 94-755. Book I, Foreign and Military Intelligence.* Washington, DC: GPO, 1976.

—**INTERFACE** is a boundary or point common to two or more similar or dissimilar command and control systems, subsystems, or other entities against which or at which necessary information flow takes place. Perhaps one of the most overused words in Washington, interface has come to mean cooperate with, and it is synonymous with interact, cooperate, or coordinate.

References

Department of Defense, Joint Chiefs of Staff. *Department of Defense Dictionary of Military and Related Terms.* Washington, DC: GPO, 1986.

Laqueur, Walter. *A World of Secrets.* New York: Basic Books, 1985.

—**INTERFERENCE** is any disturbance that causes undesirable responses in electronic equipment. It is also called babble, clutter, cosmic noise, crosstalk, jitter, or static.

References

Department of Defense, Joint Chiefs of Staff. *Department of Defense Dictionary of Military and Related Terms.* Washington, DC: GPO, 1986.

—**INTERIM RESEARCH AND INTELLIGENCE SERVICE** was formed in 1945 in the State Department out of the Research and Analysis Section of the Office of Strategic Services and other wartime intelligence analytical groups. It was an early intelligence branch of the Department of State and was established in the State Department because President Truman hoped that the department would take the lead in intelligence in the postwar era. *See also:* Central Intelligence Service; Truman, Harry.

References

Corson, William R. *The Armies of Ignorance: The Rise of the American Intelligence Empire.* New York: Dial Press, 1977.

Lowenthal, Mark M. *U.S. Intelligence: Evolution and Anatomy.* New York: Praeger, 1984.

—**INTERNATIONAL ESTIMATES.** The U.S. Intelligence Community participates in developing a few international estimates in cooperation with friendly governments or with existing alliances. On the alliance level, the United States participates in the preparation of the annual NATO threat document (MC 161), which is used in NATO planning. On the bilateral level, the United States and Canada prepare estimates on the air threat to North America, which are used by the North American Defense Command. Additional estimates are prepared with other countries, most notably the United Kingdom, Australia, and the Federal Republic of Germany. The drafting of these estimates differs from the preparation of U.S. estimates in two respects. First, they are prepared by multinational committees; second, U.S. estimators do not seek to come up with new material when developing these estimates. Rather, the U.S. position is established before the U.S. delegation goes to the conference. *See also:* Estimate, Estimative Intelligence.

References

Brinkley, David A., and Hull, Andrew W. *Estimative Intelligence: A Textbook on the History, Products, Uses and Writing of Intelligence Estimates.* Columbus, OH: Battelle, 1979.

Treverton, Gregory F. *Covert Action: The Limits of Intervention in the Postwar World.* New York: Basic Books, 1987.

—**INTERNATIONAL LINES OF COMMUNICATION (ILC)** are those communications services that are under the supervision of the International Telecommunications Union and that carry paid public communications traffic between different countries. They are also known as International Civil Communications, International Commercial Communications, Internationally Leased Communications, International Service of Public Correspondence, and commercial communications. *See also:* Transportation and Telecommunications Intelligence.

References

Department of Defense, Defense Intelligence College. *Glossary of Intelligence Terms and Definitions.* Washington, DC: DIC, 1987.

U.S. Congress. Senate. *Final Report of the Senate Select Committee to Study Government Operations with Respect to Intelligence Activities. Report 94-755. Book I, Foreign and Military Intelligence.* Washington, DC: GPO, 1976.

—**INTERNATIONAL NARCOTICS ACTIVITIES** is a term that resulted from Presidential Executive Order 12333, "United States Intelligence Activities," dated December 4, 1981, which delineated the types of activities U.S. intelligence agencies could conduct concerning U.S. citizens. The term refers to activities outside the United States to produce, transfer, or sell narcotics or other substances controlled in accordance with Title 21, U.S. Code, Sections 811 and 812.

References

Department of Defense. *Activities of DoD Intelligence Components that Affect U.S. Persons (Department of Defense Directive 5240.1).* Washington, DC: DoD, 1982.

—**INTERNATIONAL TERRORISM** involves the use of violence or force against the institutions of a government in order to alter or overthrow the system. Terrorism is inexpensive to wage and may be the conventional war of the future. The objectives of terrorism are to spread fear, to create alarm, and to publicize and advance a cause. The most often exercised capabilities of terrorist organizations are bombing facilities and installations, kidnapping and assassinating individuals, stealing weapons, and robbing banks. The criteria in choosing a target are most often the attractiveness of the target and the risk involved in accomplishing the operation. *See also:* Terrorism.

References

Laqueur, Walter. *The Age of Terrorism.* Boston: Little, Brown, 1987.

———. *A World of Secrets.* New York: Basic Books, 1985.

Treverton, Gregory F. *Covert Action: The Limits of Intervention in the Postwar World.* New York: Basic Books, 1987.

—**INTERNATIONAL TERRORIST ACTIVITY** is the calculated use of violence or the threat of violence to achieve political goals through fear, intimidation, or coercion. It usually involves a criminal act that is often symbolic in nature and is meant to influence an audience beyond the immediate victims. International terrorism transcends national boundaries in the carrying out of the act, the purpose of the act, the nationalities of the victims, or the resolution of an incident. The act is usually designed to attract wide publicity in order to focus attention on the existence, cause, or demands of the perpetrators.

Executive Order 12036, signed by President Carter on January 26, 1978, gave a more elaborate definition of terrorist activities. It said that they were "any activity or activities which: (a) involves killing, causing bodily harm, kidnapping or violent destruction of property or an attempt or credible threat to commit such acts; and (b) appears intended to endanger a protectee of the Secret Service or Department of State or to further political, social or economic goals by intimidating or coercing a civilian population or any segment thereof, influencing the policy of a government or international organization by intimidation or coercion, or obtaining widespread publicity for a group or cause; and (c) transcends national boundaries in terms of the means by which it is accomplished, the civilian population, government, or international organization it appears intended to coerce or intimidate, or the locale in which its perpetrators operate or seek asylum."

Another definition was provided by the Department of Defense when it responded to Executive Order 12333, dated December 4, 1981. It stated that international terrorist activities were "activities undertaken by or in support of terrorists or terrorist organizations that occur totally outside the United States, or that transcend national boundaries in terms of the means by which they are accomplished, the persons they appear intended to coerce or intimidate, or the locale in which the perpetrators operate or seek asylum." *See also:* Terrorism.

References

Department of Defense. *Activities of DoD Intelligence Components that Affect U.S. Persons (Department of Defense Directive 5240.1).* Washington, DC: DoD, 1982.

Department of Defense, Defense Intelligence College. *Glossary of Intelligence Terms and Definitions.* Washington, DC: DIC, 1987.

Laqueur, Walter. *The Age of Terrorism.* Boston: Little, Brown, 1987.

———. Laqueur, Walter. *A World of Secrets.* New York: Basic Books, 1985.

Treverton, Gregory F. *Covert Action: The Limits of Intervention in the Postwar World.* New York: Basic Books, 1987.

—**INTERPRETABILITY,** in intelligence imagery and photoreconnaissance, is the suitability of imagery for interpretation with respect to answering adequately the requirements of the customer. Interpretability is assessed in terms of quality and scale, according to the following scale:

Poor: denotes imagery that is unsuitable for interpretation to answer adequately the customer's requirements concerning a given type of target.

Fair: denotes imagery that is suitable for interpretation to answer customer requirements concerning a target but with only average detail.

Good: denotes imagery that is suitable for interpretation to answer customer requirements concerning a target in considerable detail.

Excellent: denotes imagery that is suitable for interpretation to answer customer requirements concerning a target in complete detail. *See also:* Image.

References

Department of Defense, Joint Chiefs of Staff. *Department of Defense Dictionary of Military and Related Terms.* Washington, DC: GPO, 1986.

Kent, Sherman. *Strategic Intelligence for American World Policy.* Princeton, NJ: Princeton University Press, 1966.

—**INTERPRETATION** is a general intelligence term for a process in the production step of the intelligence cycle in which the significance of information or intelligence information is weighted relative to the available body of knowledge. *See also:* Intelligence Cycle.

References

Department of Defense, Joint Chiefs of Staff. *Department of Defense Dictionary of Military and Related Terms.* Washington, DC: GPO, 1986.

Kent, Sherman. *Strategic Intelligence for American World Policy.* Princeton, NJ: Princeton University Press, 1966.

Treverton, Gregory F. *Covert Action: The Limits of Intervention in the Postwar World.* New York: Basic Books, 1987.

—**INTERROGATION** is the art of questioning and examining a source to obtain the maximum amount of usable information. The goal of any interrogation is to obtain usable and reliable information in a lawful manner and in the least amount of time. Interrogations are of many types, including the interview, the debriefing, and elicitation.

References

Department of Defense, Joint Chiefs of Staff. *Department of Defense Dictionary of Military and Related Terms.* Washington, DC: GPO, 1986.

Department of Defense, U.S. Army. *Intelligence Interrogation.* Field Manual FM 34-52. Washington, DC: Headquarters, Department of the Army, 1987.

Quirk, John; Phillips, David; Cline, Ray; and Pforzheimer, Walter. *The Central Intelligence Agency: A Photographic History.* Guilford, CT: Foreign Intelligence Press, 1986.

U.S. Congress. Senate. *Final Report of the Senate Select Committee to Study Government Operations with Respect to Intelligence Activities. Report 94-755. Book I, Foreign and Military Intelligence.* Washington, DC: GPO, 1976.

—**INTERROGATION SIGNAL** is a sign that is passed by one agent to another in order to identify himself. It is normally followed by either a response signal from the other agent or a wave off signal, indicating that it is not safe to meet.

References

Clancy, Tom. *The Cardinal of the Kremlin.* New York: Putnam, 1988.

—**INTERVIEW,** as defined by the Church Committee, is "the gathering of information from an individual who knows that he or she is giving information, although not often with awareness of the true connection or purposes of the interviewer. This is generally an overt collection technique, unless the interviewer is not what he or she purports to be."

References

Department of Defense, Joint Chiefs of Staff. *Department of Defense Dictionary of Military and Related Terms.* Washington, DC: GPO, 1986.

U.S. Congress. Senate. *Final Report of the Senate Select Committee to Study Government Operations with Respect to Intelligence Activities. Report 94-755. Book I, Foreign and Military Intelligence.* Washington, DC: GPO, 1976.

—**INTRUSION DETECTION SYSTEM,** in communications security (COMSEC), means a system that is designed to detect and signal the entry of unauthorized persons into a protected area. In layman terms, an intrusion detection system is most often called a security alarm, although some are referred to as sensor alarms or video systems. *See also:* Communications Security.

References

Department of Defense, U.S. Army. *AIA: Threat Analysis.* Falls Church, VA: U.S. Army Intelligence Agency, 1987.

Martin, Paul H. "Communications-Computer Security." *Journal of Electronic Defense* (June 1987).

Muzerall, Joseph V., and Carty, Thomas P. "COMSEC and Its Need for Key Management." *DP&CS* (Spring 1987).

Ware, Willis H. "Information Systems, Security, and Privacy." *EDUCOM Bulletin* (Summer 1984).

—**INVENTORY** is a communications security (COMSEC) term that has two meanings. (1) An inventory can be a listing of each item of COMSEC material that is accountable or charged to a COMSEC account. (2) An inventory can also be an act or process in which the physical verification of the presence of each line item of accountable COMSEC material that is charged to an account is identified and checked against a copy of the COMSEC account listing. *See also:* Communications Security (COMSEC).

References

Department of Defense, U.S. Army. *AIA: Threat Analysis.* Falls Church, VA: U.S. Army Intelligence Agency, 1987.

Martin, Paul H. "Communications-Computer Security." *Journal of Electronic Defense* (June 1987).

Muzerall, Joseph V., and Carty, Thomas P. "COMSEC and Its Need for Key Management." *DP&CS* (Spring 1987).

Ware, Willis H. "Information Systems, Security, and Privacy." *EDUCOM Bulletin* (Summer 1984).

—**INVESTIGATION** is a duly authorized, systematized, detailed examination or inquiry to uncover facts and determine the truth of a matter. This may include collecting, processing, storing, recording, analyzing, evaluating, producing, and disseminating the authorized information.

References

Department of Defense, Joint Chiefs of Staff. *Department of Defense Dictionary of Military and Related Terms.* Washington, DC: GPO, 1986.

—**IRAN.** Iran was a rather continuous intelligence theme during most of the postwar presidential administrations. Additionally, the inability of U.S. intelligence to accurately assess the political situation in Iran often amounted to a debilitating factor in U.S. foreign policy formulation.

During the Truman administration, the first instance occurred as the Soviet Union exerted pressure on the region, with particular attention to Iran, Turkey, and Greece. President Truman responded by deploying naval power to the region. These measures effectively thwarted Soviet designs on the area.

During the Eisenhower administration, the Iranian focus shifted to the domestic scene. In one of its more successful operations, the Central Intelligence Agency assisted in deposing a radical Iranian regime and reinstalling the Shah on the throne.

The policies of the Shah were ambitious and, in many ways, can be compared to those of the nineteenth-century Russian tsars. The Shah's intentions were to modernize his country as quickly as possible, and his policy was, in essence, a revolution that was forcefully imposed on the nation. Education and literacy were stressed, and college students were sent to the West for additional education. The goal was to create as quickly as possible an educated base that was capable of modernizing the nation. However, just as in the Russian experience, the Shah's policies, dictatorially imposed, created internal instability. Two outcomes seemed likely: either the Shah would succeed, thereby creating a modern conservative Islamic nation; or his policies would fail, leading to his fall and the ascendancy of either a radical left or a conservative Islamic regime.

The policies of the Shah appeared successful, and much progress was made in the 1950s and 1960s. Iran was modernized and, with significant U.S. military assistance, became a regional power. By the time that President Nixon came to office, Iran had emerged as an impressive power, and a tenet of the Nixon-Kissinger policy in the Indian Ocean–Persian Gulf region was to rely on Iran as an ally that would insure regional stability. However, intelligence began to report that the Shah's position might not be as secure as had been believed, and one of the first public indications of a U.S. response was Richard Helms's decision to resign as director of Central Intelligence in order to become the U.S. ambassador to Iran.

The situation became critical during the Ford and Carter administrations, as increasing sociological change and dislocations created greater turmoil. It appears that, while U.S. intelligence perceived and reported on the situation's deterioration, it underestimated the true severity of the situation, because the rise of the Ayatollah Khomeini, the storming and occupation of the U.S. Embassy, and the capture of embassy personnel was not foreseen. The staff itself had not perceived the danger of the situation and was unable to fully destroy sensitive intelligence files that, when repaired and read by the extremists, only worsened the crisis.

The resulting chain of events was complex. An attempt to free the hostages ended in disaster as the rescue mission had an aircraft accident in the Iranian desert. Although the full details of the mission have not yet been released, those that have been provided indicate that the exercise, a joint operation, was undertaken without clearly defined lines of authority and that, as the endeavor began to sour, the confused chain of command further impeded the subsequent actions of the rescuers. The result was that the mission was aborted, and most of the rescuers proceeded to safety. The hostage affair was resolved when the hostages were released on U.S. Presidential Inauguration Day in 1981.

This resolution gave President Reagan greater latitude in the ensuing period. The Reagan administration informally pursued a low-visibility, conciliatory policy in the hopes of repairing the relationship. However, in President Reagan's second term in office, several factors came together to bring Iran back into the headlines. The first had to do with Iran. Embroiled in a bloody war with Iraq, Iran found its military equipment continually deteriorating because it was composed primarily of U.S.-made equipment, and with the cessation of U.S.-Irani relations, spare parts and repairs were very difficult to acquire. Second, the Reagan administration wanted the return of the U.S. hostages who were being held in the Middle East. Third, the administration had become very concerned about the spread of communism in Central America, and sought a means of combatting the Nicaraguan government of Daniel Ortega. However, due to the intelligence abuses of the 1960s and 1970s, Congress had passed restrictive legislation that governed what both the Intelligence Community and the White House could do without congressional approval.

In a covert operation intended to address all three concerns, a plan that is now known as the Iran-Contra operation was waged. An extremely complex endeavor, the operation involved the following: selling the needed arms to Iran in return for U.S. hostages; filtering the money gained from the arms sales through Israel (with the assistance of the Israeli government) into Swiss bank accounts; establishing a huge infrastructure that would use the money to buy arms and then deliver them to the Contras, who were fighting against the communist Nicaraguan government; keeping the entire operation from Congress; keeping the operation secret from the Intelligence Community; supervising the entire operation from the National Security Council; either deceiving the President by keeping the knowledge of the operation from him, or providing him with "plausible deniability." The operation soured after only one of the hostages was released, and soon thereafter the administration went public.

The final stage of U.S.-Iranian activity occurred late in President Reagan's second term. This involved the mining of the Persian Gulf and the strafing of innocent merchant ships by Irani extremists. The United States responded almost immediately by sending a naval force to the region. However, subsequent operations by this force demonstrated several problems in U.S. tactical intelligence. First, U.S. naval ships had less than complete success in protecting shipping from the mines, and then the USS *Stark* was hit by an Iraqi air-launched missile. Subsequent operations included U.S. naval bombardment of oil rigs known to have Irani terrorists aboard, and then, in the summer of 1988, the downing of an Irani airliner by a U.S. surface-to-air missile, because it was believed to be an inbound hostile Irani aircraft.

As a result, in 1989, the Irani-U.S. relationship remained at a low point, with the United States, still willing to attempt a reconciliation, and an unconfident Iran, emerging from the Iran-Iraq War, still at loggerheads. The death of the Ayatollah in June 1989 ushered in a period of uncertainty. It was up to President Bush to see if anything could be salvaged from the situation, and up to the Intelligence Community to attempt to further improve the completeness and accuracy of its reporting on Iran.

References

Breckinridge, Scott D. *The CIA and the U.S. Intelligence System*. Boulder, CO: Westview Press, 1986.

Brinkley, David A., and Hull, Andrew W. *Estimative Intelligence: A Textbook on the History, Products, Uses and Writing of Intelligence Estimates*. Columbus, OH: Battelle, 1979.

Corson, William R. *The Armies of Ignorance: The Rise of the American Intelligence Empire*. New York: Dial Press, 1977.

Crawford, David J. *Volunteers: The Betrayal of National Defense Secrets by Air Force Traitors*. Washington, DC: GPO, 1988.

Godson, Roy, ed. *Intelligence Problems for the 1980s, Number 2: Analysis and Estimates*. Washington, DC: National Strategy Information Center, 1980.

———. *Intelligence Problems for the 1980s, Number 4: Covert Action*. Washington, DC: National Strategy Information Center, 1981.

Laqueur, Walter. *The Age of Terrorism*. Boston: Little, Brown, 1987.

———. *A World of Secrets*. New York: Basic Books, 1985.

Lefever, Ernest W., and Godson, Roy. *The CIA and the American Ethic: An Unfinished Debate*. Washington, DC: Ethics and Public Policy Center, Georgetown University, 1979.

Lowenthal, Mark M. *U.S. Intelligence: Evolution and Anatomy*. New York: Praeger, 1984.

Quirk, John; Phillips, David; Cline, Ray; and Pforzheimer, Walter. *The Central Intelligence Agency: A Photographic History*. Guilford, CT: Foreign Intelligence Press, 1986.

Treverton, Gregory F. *Covert Action: The Limits of Intervention in the Postwar World*. New York: Basic Books, 1987.

Turner, Stansfield. *Secrecy and Democracy: The CIA in Transition*. Boston: Houghton Mifflin, 1985.

Von Hoene, John P. A. *Intelligence User's Guide*. Washington, DC: DIA, 1983.

U.S. Congress. Senate. *Alleged Assassination Plots Involving Foreign Leaders: An Interim Report of the Select Committee to Study Governmental Operations with Respect to Intelligence Activities*. 94th Congress, 1st sess., Nov. 20, 1975. S. Rept. 94-465.

—IRAN-CONTRA SCANDAL. *See:* Iran.

—IRREGULARLY SUPERCEDED KEYING MATERIAL, in communications security (COMSEC), means keying material that is used on an "as needed" basis, rather than during a specified period of time. *See also:* Communications Security.

References

Department of Defense, U.S. Army. *AIA: Threat Analysis*. Falls Church, VA: U.S. Army Intelligence Agency, 1987.

Martin, Paul H. "Communications-Computer Security." *Journal of Electronic Defense* (June 1987).

Muzerall, Joseph V., and Carty, Thomas P. "COMSEC and Its Need for Key Management." *DP&CS* (Spring 1987).

Ware, Willis H. "Information Systems, Security, and Privacy." *EDUCOM Bulletin* (Summer 1984).

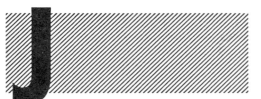

—**JACKSON, WILLIAM H.** served as deputy director of Central Intelligence from October 7, 1950, until August 3, 1951. *See also:* Central Intelligence Agency.

References

Corson, William R. *The Armies of Ignorance: The Rise of the American Intelligence Empire*. New York: Dial Press, 1977.

Treverton, Gregory F. *Covert Action: The Limits of Intervention in the Postwar World*. New York: Basic Books, 1987.

—**JAMMER,** in electronic warfare, is an electronic device that intentionally introduces unwanted signals into a radio or receiver for the purpose of denying information. *See also:* Active Electronic Countermeasures, Active Jamming, Brute Force Jamming, Communications Jamming, Complex Barrage Jamming, Deception Jammer, Electronic Jamming, Escort Jamming, Jammer Band (Width), Jamming, Jamming Effectiveness, Jamming Platform, Jamming Signal, Jamming Target, Multitarget Jamming, Noise Jamming, Noise Modulated Jamming, Passive Jamming, Repeater Jammer, Self-Protection Jamming, Spot Jamming, Sweep Jamming.

References

Department of Defense, Joint Chiefs of Staff. *Department of Defense Dictionary of Military and Related Terms*. Washington, DC: GPO, 1986.

Department of Defense, U.S. Army. *Intelligence and Electronic Warfare Operations*. Field Manual FM 34-1. Washington, DC: Headquarters, Department of the Army, 1984.

———. *Military Intelligence Battalion Combat Electronic Warfare and Intelligence (Aerial Exploitation) (Corps)*. Field Manual FM 34-22. Washington, DC: Headquarters, Department of the Army, 1984.

———. *Military Intelligence Battalion (Combat Electronic Warfare Intelligence) (Division)*. Field Manual FM 34-10. Washington, DC: Headquarters, Department of the Army, 1981.

———. *Military Intelligence Battalion (CEWI) (Operations) (Corps)*. Field Manual FM 34-21.

Washington, DC: Headquarters, Department of the Army, 1982.

———. *Military Intelligence Company (Combat Electronic Warfare and Intelligence) (Armored Cavalry Regiment/Separate Brigade)*. Field Manual FM 34-30. Washington, DC: Headquarters, Department of the Army, 1983.

———. *Military Intelligence Group (Combat Electronic Warfare and Intelligence) (Corps)*. Field Manual FM 34-20. Washington, DC: Headquarters, Department of the Army, 1983.

—**JAMMER BAND (WIDTH),** in electronic warfare, is a band of frequency in which the output of the jammer is concentrated. *See also:* Jammer.

—**JAMMING,** in Army tactical intelligence (TACINT), means "the deliberate radiation, reradiation, or reflection of electromagnetic energy with the object of impairing the use of electronic devices by the enemy." Jamming is an electronic countermeasure (ECM). *See also:* Jammer.

—**JAMMING EFFECTIVENESS,** in electronic warfare (EW), is the percentage of information in a text message that is incorrectly received. *See also:* Jammer.

—**JAMMING PLATFORM,** in electronic warfare, is that vehicle or other source from which jamming emanates. *See also:* Jammer.

—**JAMMING SIGNAL,** in electronic warfare (EW), is the electromagnetic wave propagated by a jammer to transmit energy to a communications or noncommunications receiver for interference purposes. *See also:* Jammer.

—**JAMMING TARGET,** in electronic warfare, is any receiving system or set of receiving systems that is intended for interference or jamming. *See also:* Jammer.

—**JEFFRIES, RANDY MILES,** a congressional courier, was arrested in Washington, DC, on December 20, 1985, for espionage. He was convicted on January 23, 1986, and was sentenced to ten years in prison.

References

Allen, Thomas B., and Polmar, Norman. *Merchants of Treason: America's Secrets for Sale*. New York: Delacorte Press, 1988.

Crawford, David J. *Volunteers: The Betrayal of National Defense Secrets by Air Force Traitors.* Washington, DC: GPO, 1988.

—**JOCK STRAP MEDAL** is a decoration that has been awarded to a clandestine agent or operative of the Central Intelligence Agency. These medals are held by the agency until the agent retires and possibly longer, if the national security warrants. According to Henry Becket, they are called "jock strap medals" because they can only be worn there so as not to be revealed. *See also:* Central Intelligence Agency.

References

Becket, Henry S. A. *The Dictionary of Espionage: Spookspeak into English.* New York: Stein and Day, 1986.

—**JOHNSON, LYNDON.** In contrast to President Kennedy, President Johnson showed relatively little interest in intelligence matters. His organizational style was to work through his secretaries of state and defense and his national security advisor, rather than intimately with his director of Central Intelligence (DCI). This deemphasis of intelligence led to friction between the President and John McCone, who was then serving as DCI. Matters came to a breaking point when McCone and Johnson disagreed over U.S. policy toward Vietnam (with Johnson wanting incremental escalations in U.S. involvement and McCone wanting a more definitive program), and McCone resigned. Johnson appointed Vice Admiral William Rayborn, who left office in a little over a year. Johnson then appointed Richard Helms, a career intelligence officer, to the position. Although he had an operational background, Helms did maintain a balance between the operational and analytical duties of the CIA.

In terms of organizational style, President Johnson preferred to work with a minimal staff. In the final analysis, he is assessed as having a rather neutral effect on the Intelligence Community, save for the fact that he appointed Helms as DCI. *See also:* Executive Oversight.

References

American Bar Association. *Oversight and Accountability of the U.S. Intelligence Agencies: An Evaluation.* Washington, DC: ABA, 1985.

Breckinridge, Scott D. *The CIA and the U.S. Intelligence System.* Boulder, CO: Westview Press, 1986.

Brinkley, David A., and Hull, Andrew W. *Estimative Intelligence: A Textbook on the History, Products, Uses and Writing of Intelligence Estimates.*

Columbus, OH: Battelle, 1979.

Cline, Ray S. *The CIA Under Reagan, Bush, and Casey.* Washington, DC: Acropolis Books, 1981.

Corson, William R. *The Armies of Ignorance: The Rise of the American Intelligence Empire.* New York: Dial Press, 1977.

Crawford, David J. *Volunteers: The Betrayal of National Defense Secrets by Air Force Traitors.* Washington, DC: GPO, 1988.

Godson, Roy, ed. *Intelligence Problems for the 1980s, Number 2: Analysis and Estimates.* Washington, DC: National Strategy Information Center, 1980.

Laqueur, Walter. *A World of Secrets.* New York: Basic Books, 1985.

Lowenthal, Mark M. *U.S. Intelligence: Evolution and Anatomy.* New York: Praeger, 1984.

Maurer, Alfred C.; Turnstall, Marion D.; and Keagle, James M. *Intelligence Policy and Process.* Boulder, CO: Westview Press, 1985.

Treverton, Gregory F. *Covert Action: The Limits of Intervention in the Postwar World.* New York: Basic Books, 1987.

Turner, Stansfield. *Secrecy and Democracy: The CIA in Transition.* Boston: Houghton Mifflin, 1985.

U.S. Congress. Senate. *Alleged Assassination Plots Involving Foreign Leaders: An Interim Report of the Select Committee to Study Governmental Operations with Respect to Intelligence Activities.* 94th Congress, 1st sess., Nov. 20, 1975. S. Rept. 94-465.

————. Senate. *Final Report of the Senate Select Committee to Study Government Operations with Respect to Intelligence Activities. Report 94-755. Book I, Foreign and Military Intelligence.* Washington, DC: GPO, 1976.

Von Hoene, John P. A. *Intelligence User's Guide.* Washington, DC: DIA, 1983.

—**JOHNSON, ROBERT,** attached to the U.S. Army, was convicted of espionage charges concerning passing classified information to the Soviet KGB. Johnson was disgruntled and was also motivated by expected monetary gain. He was sentenced to 25 years in prison, but in 1972 he was stabbed to death in his prison cell by his son.

References

Allen, Thomas B., and Polmar, Norman. *Merchants of Treason: America's Secrets for Sale.* New York: Delacorte Press, 1988.

Corson, William R. *The Armies of Ignorance: The Rise of the American Intelligence Empire.* New York: Dial Press, 1977.

Crawford, David J. *Volunteers: The Betrayal of National Defense Secrets by Air Force Traitors.* Washington, DC: GPO, 1988.

—**JOINT AMPHIBIOUS TASK FORCE (JATF)** is an amphibious warfare term for a temporary grouping of units of two or more military services under a single commander that is organized for the purpose of accomplishing an amphibious landing assault on enemy shores.

References

Department of Defense, Joint Chiefs of Staff. *Department of Defense Dictionary of Military and Related Terms.* Washington, DC: GPO, 1986.

—**JOINT ANALYSIS GROUP (JAG)** was an interdepartmental study group established in 1962 for the purpose of providing regular assessments on future Soviet and Chinese military strengths.

References

Fain, Tyrus G.; Plant, Katharine C.; and Milloy, Ross. *The Intelligence Community: History, Organization, and Issues.* Public Documents Series. New York: R.R. Bowker, 1977.

—**JOINT ATOMIC ENERGY INTELLIGENCE COMMITTEE (JAEIC),** a subcommittee of the United States Intelligence Board (USIB), was responsible for the interdepartmental coordination of intelligence relating to atomic energy.

References

Fain, Tyrus G.; Plant, Katharine C.; and Milloy, Ross. *The Intelligence Community: History, Organization, and Issues.* Public Documents Series. New York: R.R. Bowker, 1977.

—**JOINT CHIEFS OF STAFF, J-2.** *See:* Defense Intelligence Agency.

—**JOINT FORCE** is a generic term applied to a force that is composed of significant elements of the Army, Navy, Marine Corps, and Air Force, or any two of these services. The joint force operates under a single commander who is authorized to exercise united command or operational control over such a joint task force. *See also:* Joint Force Memorandum (JFM); Joint Intelligence; Joint Intelligence Estimate for Planning (JIEP); Joint Intelligence Liaison Element (JILE); Joint Long-Range Estimative Intelligence Document (JLREID); Joint Long-Range Strategic Appraisal (JLRSA); Joint Operational Intelligence Agency; Joint Operations Center; Joint Operational Planning System (JOPS); Joint Program Assessment Memorandum (JPAM); Joint Research and Development Objective Document (JRDOD); Joint Security Assistance Memorandum (JSAM); Joint Stra-

tegic Capabilities Plan (JSCP); Joint Strategic Objectives Plan (JSOP); Joint Strategic Planning Document (JSPD); Joint Strategic Planning Document Supporting Analysis (JSPDSA); Joint Strategic Planning System (JSPS); Joint Strategic Target Planning Staff (JSTPS); Joint Tactical Information Distribution System (JTIDS); Joint Task Force.

References

Department of Defense, Joint Chiefs of Staff. *Department of Defense Dictionary of Military and Related Terms.* Washington, DC: GPO, 1986.

Department of Defense, National Defense University. *Joint Staff Officer's Guide, 1986.* Washington, DC: GPO, 1986.

—**JOINT FORCE MEMORANDUM (JFM)** is a document prepared annually by the Joint Chiefs of Staff (JCS) and submitted to the secretary of defense. It provides recommendations concerning the Joint Force Program within the fiscal guidance that has been provided by the secretary of defense. *See also:* Joint Force.

References

Department of Defense, National Defense University. *Joint Staff Officer's Guide, 1986.* Washington, DC: GPO, 1986.

Pickett, George. "Congress, the Budget and Intelligence." In *Intelligence Policy and Process,* edited by Alfred C. Maurer, Marion D. Turnstall, and James M. Keagle. Boulder, CO: Westview Press, 1985.

—**JOINT INTELLIGENCE** is a general intelligence term that has two meanings. (1) In the military context, joint intelligence is intelligence produced by more than one military service of the same nation. (2) In the context of the Intelligence Community, joint intelligence is intelligence produced by intelligence organizations of more than one country. *See also:* Joint Force.

References

Corson, William R. *The Armies of Ignorance: The Rise of the American Intelligence Empire.* New York: Dial Press, 1977.

Department of Defense, Defense Intelligence College. *Glossary of Intelligence Terms and Definitions.* Washington, DC: DIC, 1987.

Department of Defense, Joint Chiefs of Staff. *Department of Defense Dictionary of Military and Related Terms.* Washington, DC: GPO, 1986.

U.S. Congress. Senate. *Final Report of the Senate Select Committee to Study Government Operations with Respect to Intelligence Activities. Report 94-755. Book I, Foreign and Military Intelligence.* Washington, DC: GPO, 1976.

—**JOINT INTELLIGENCE ESTIMATE FOR PLAN-NING (JIEP)** is one of seven documents, listed under Joint Strategic Planning System (JSPS), that make up the system. The JIEP contains detailed estimative intelligence that concentrates on possible worldwide situations and developments that could affect U.S. security interests in the near- and mid-term periods.

Providing detailed estimative intelligence for the short- and mid-range periods, the JIEP is the principal intelligence basis for the development of the Joint Strategic Planning Document (JSPD), the Joint Program Assessment Memorandum (JPAM) and the Joint Strategic Capabilities Plan (JSCP) and is used at the beginning of each planning cycle. Prepared annually by the Joint Staff Services of the Defense Intelligence Agency, it is submitted to the Joint Chiefs of Staff (JCS) for approval.

Content. The JIEP is composed of world power relationships, regional estimates of capabilities and likely courses of action, and regional treaty organizations. The JIEP concentrates on world-wide situations and developments that could affect U.S. security interests. It includes a global appraisal with an estimate of the world situation and the nature of the military threat. Additionally, there are regional appraisals, including estimates of the external and internal threats to countries of significance to the United States. Third, there are estimates of the Warsaw Pact and Asian communist military forces and potential threats in the Middle East, Persian Gulf, Korea, and various Third World regions, including the Soviet capability to project forces into these regions.

Organization. The JIEP is a single document with seven parts: global appraisal; regional appraisals; USSR, Warsaw Pact; People's Republic of China; North Korea; Southeast Asia; and Cuba. The JIEP presents the principal threat on which the JCS builds, in subsequent documents, recommendations on strategy to overcome the threat and to fulfill U.S. military objectives and planning forces to carry out the strategy. The JIEP is published in December, at the start of the Planning, Programming, and Budgeting sequence.

The JIEP Supplement provides additional estimative intelligence that consists of discussions of significant changes in intelligence that have occurred between the annual publications of the JIEP, the military capabilities and vulnerabilities of selected countries, and force tables for se-lected countries. The JIEP Supplement is not a JCS-approved document. *See also:* Joint Force.

References

Department of Defense, National Defense University. *Joint Staff Officer's Guide, 1986.* Washington, DC: GPO, 1986.

U.S. Congress. Senate. *Final Report of the Senate Select Committee to Study Government Operations with Respect to Intelligence Activities. Report 94-755. Book I, Foreign and Military Intelligence.* Washington, DC: GPO, 1976.

—**JOINT INTELLIGENCE LIAISON ELEMENT (JILE)** is a coordinating contingent that is provided by the Central Intelligence Agency to support a unified command or joint task force. *See also:* Joint Force.

References

Department of Defense, Joint Chiefs of Staff. *Department of Defense Dictionary of Military and Related Terms.* Washington, DC: GPO, 1986.

Department of Defense, National Defense University. *Joint Staff Officer's Guide, 1986.* Washington, DC: GPO, 1986.

—**JOINT LONG-RANGE ESTIMATIVE INTELLI-GENCE DOCUMENT (JLREID)** existed until 1975. It was a Joint Chiefs of Staff document that attempted to project out to twenty years. It is now incorporated into the Joint Long-Range Strategic Appraisal. *See also:* Joint Force.

References

Department of Defense, National Defense University. *Joint Staff Officer's Guide, 1986.* Washington, DC: GPO, 1986.

—**JOINT LONG-RANGE STRATEGIC APPRAIS-AL (JLRSA)** is one of seven documents, listed under Joint Strategic Planning System (JSPS), that make up the system. It is a Joint Chiefs of Staff document that projects out to between ten and twenty years. Its format involves an executive summary, a global and regional appraisal, an alternative environments section that presents different scenarios for the structure of the international system, and an alternative strategic considerations section, which examines key considerations that are likely to have an impact on the United States in the next ten to twenty years. Reviewed biannually, it is revised every four years.

Providing a basis for the transition from mid-range to long-range strategic planning, the JLRSA is intended to stimulate more sharply focused strategic studies and analyses and to influence the development of and provide supporting analysis for the mid-range Joint Strategic Planning Document (JSPD) and the Joint Strategic Planning Document Supporting Analysis (JSPDSA). The document provides a framework for identifying and outlining broad force structuring implications and development of a baseline for assessing military policies, plans, and programs having both mid-range and long-range implications. *See also:* Joint Force.

References

Department of Defense, National Defense University. *Joint Staff Officer's Guide, 1986.* Washington, DC: GPO, 1986.

Pickett, George. "Congress, the Budget, and Intelligence." In *Intelligence Policy and Process,* edited by Alfred C. Maurer, Marion D. Turnstall, and James M. Keagle. Boulder, CO: Westview Press, 1985.

—**JOINT OPERATIONAL INTELLIGENCE AGENCY** is an intelligence agency in which two or more services are integrated to furnish the operational intelligence that is essential to a commander of a joint force and to supplement the intelligence available from the subordinate forces of the command. *See also:* Joint Force.

References

Department of Defense, Joint Chiefs of Staff. *Department of Defense Dictionary of Military and Related Terms.* Washington, DC: GPO, 1986.

—**JOINT OPERATIONS CENTER (JOC)** is a facility staffed by personnel from more than one armed service and is a component of a joint force commander's headquarters. It is established for planning, monitoring, and guiding the execution of the commander's decisions. *See also:* Joint Force.

References

Department of Defense, Joint Chiefs of Staff. *Department of Defense Dictionary of Military and Related Terms.* Washington, DC: GPO, 1986.

Department of Defense, National Defense University. *Joint Staff Officer's Guide, 1986.* Washington, DC: GPO, 1986.

Fain, Tyrus G.; Plant, Katharine C.; and Milloy, Ross. *The Intelligence Community: History, Organization, and Issues.* Public Documents Series. New York: R.R. Bowker, 1977.

—**JOINT OPERATIONAL PLANNING SYSTEM (JOPS).** Operation plans for possible deployment and use of U.S. military forces overseas are normally prepared in peacetime using a deliberate planning process. When situations become sufficiently grave for the United States to consider using military force, existing plans are adjusted or new courses of action are considered to meet time-sensitive requirements. The military planning system used to support joint military operation planning and crisis management is the JOPS. The objective is the timely development of adequate, suitable, and feasible operation plans (OPLANs) and orders by the Joint Chiefs of Staff (JCS), the commanders of the Unified and Specified Commands, and the Joint Task Force (JTF) commanders.

To meet this objective, the JOPS accomplishes seven things. First, it establishes the joint planning process. Second, it prescribes standard formats and minimum content. Third, it provides standard data files and common functional programs. Fourth, it provides for the effective refinement and review of operation plans and for review of noncombatant evacuation operation plans, continuity of operations plans, and disaster relief plans that are submitted to fulfill the assigned planning tasks that have been assigned or approved by the JCS. Fifth, it provides for testing the transportation feasibility of operation plans. Sixth, it provides for reporting and processing shortfalls and limiting factors. Finally, it provides procedures for the timely conversion of operation plans (OPLANs) into operation orders (OPORDs), when applicable, in a time of national crisis.

Planning is a continuous process. It begins when a task is assigned and ends only when the requirements for the plan are canceled or when the plan is implemented. Planning is accomplished by following a deliberate series of steps that lead a commander and his planning staff step-by-step through the planning process. The staff will produce either an operational plan in concept format (CONPLAN) or an operation plan in complete format (OPLAN), depending on the level of planning detail that is required by the JCS.

When an OPLAN is conceived, it is based on an existing or an expected situation and, as the plan is being developed, it is built with forces that are designated for the operation. A plan will remain current only as long as the conditions at the time of planning remain the same. Consequently, a plan cannot be "put on the shelf" to gather dust after it has been produced. It must be reexamined periodically to ensure that the information in the plan is still current and that it still satisfies the original need. Maintaining the currency of the plan is the responsibility of the commander who prepared it, but new or revised intelligence is submitted by various members of the planning community. Maintenance of the movement plan is coordinated by the Joint Deployment Agency (JDA). The JCS requires an annual review of all JCS-directed plans, and they can direct the revision of any plan on an ad hoc basis. Maintenance and review of existing plans is normally the most time-consuming task of the staff officer. Even though an existing CONPLAN or OPLAN is current, it must be modified at the time of implementation.

Deliberate planning begins when a commander receives JSCP tasking, and it ends when the plan and its supporting plans have been completed and approved. The JSCP initiates the planning process, which normally consists of five phases:

Initiating phase. Planning tasks are assigned and major combat forces and strategic transportation forces are identified for planning purposes.

Concept development phase. The planning guidance is issued, courses of military action are proposed and tested, information and intelligence on factors that could affect the mission are collected and analyzed, and a concept of operations is developed, reviewed, approved, and distributed.

Plan development phase. All forces are selected and time-phased, support requirements are determined, and strategic transportation capabilities are tested. All data produced and collected are entered into the plan's Time Phased Force and Deployment Data (TPFDD) computer file. The TPFDD and the written portions of the plan, which are documented during this phase, make up the OPLAN in complete format.

Plan review phase. Plans are submitted to the tasking authority, are formally reviewed, and are approved for implementation.

Supporting plans phase. All required supporting plans are completed, documented in the appropriate format, and submitted to and approved by the reviewing authority. *See also:* Joint Force.

References

Department of Defense, National Defense University. *Joint Staff Officer's Guide, 1986.* Washington, DC: GPO, 1986.

Pickett, George. "Congress, the Budget, and Intelligence." In *Intelligence Policy and Process,* edited by Alfred C. Maurer, Marion D. Turnstall, and James M. Keagle. Boulder, CO: Westview Press, 1985.

—**JOINT PROBABILITY** is a term that is sometimes used in intelligence budgeting. It is the probability that two or more specified events will occur simultaneously. *See also:* Budget.

References

Brinkley, David A., and Hull, Andrew W. *Estimative Intelligence: A Textbook on the History, Products, Uses, and Writing of Intelligence Estimates.* Columbus, OH: Battelle, 1979.

Department of Defense, National Defense University. *Joint Staff Officer's Guide, 1986.* Washington, DC: GPO, 1986.

—**JOINT PROGRAM ASSESSMENT MEMORANDUM (JPAM).** The JPAM is one of seven documents, listed under Joint Strategic Planning System (JSPS), that make up the system. It provides the views of the Joint Chiefs of Staff (JCS) on the balance of the composite Program Objectives Memorandum (POM) force recommendations of the military services. Primarily the JCS will comment on the ability of the total POM forces to execute the national military strategy, assess the risk represented by these forces, examine the forces' composite capability, and make specified recommendations as to which capabilities require further emphasis. The JPAM provides the views of the JCS on the adequacy of the total forces contained in the service POMs. It is not intended to be a critique of the military department POMs. Rather, it is an assessment of the capabilities generated by the composite POMs to execute the national military strategy and an estimate of the risks inherent in those force capabilities. Unified and Specified Commanders are invited to comment on the composite POMs as they relate to the current strategy.

The JPAM follows the publication of the POMs by 30 days and, as indicated, provides substantive recommendations on the composite POM force after detailed analysis of the military POMs, including mobility force analysis, has been accomplished. In the same time-frame as the JPAM, but under separate cover, the JCS advice on the nuclear weapons stockpile is provided to the Office of the Secretary of Defense. *See also:* Joint Force.

References

Department of Defense, National Defense University. *Joint Staff Officer's Guide, 1986.* Washington, DC: GPO, 1986.

Pickett, George. "Congress, the Budget, and Intelligence." In *Intelligence Policy and Process,* edited by Alfred C. Maurer, Marion D. Turnstall, and James M. Keagle. Boulder, CO: Westview Press, 1985.

—**JOINT PUBLICATIONS RESEARCH SERVICE (JPRS).** *See:* Central Intelligence Agency.

—**JOINT RESEARCH AND DEVELOPMENT OBJECTIVE DOCUMENT (JRDOD)** is prepared annually by the Joint Chiefs of Staff (JCS) and submitted to the secretary of defense. It concerns the research and development objectives that are necessary to carry out the strategy and force recommendations in the Joint Strategic Objectives Plan (JSOP). *See also:* Joint Force.

References

Department of Defense, National Defense University. *Joint Staff Officer's Guide, 1986.* Washington, DC: GPO, 1986.

—**JOINT SECURITY ASSISTANCE MEMORANDUM (JSAM)** is one of seven documents, listed under Joint Strategic Planning System (JSPS), that make up the system. It is a Joint Chiefs of Staff (JCS) funding document that has significance for the Intelligence Community. The JSAM provides JCS views on funding levels for U.S.-financed security assistance programs, security assistance manning levels, and key arms transfer policy matters that have been established in the Joint Strategic Planning Document Supporting Analysis (JSPDSA), the Integrated Assessment of Security Assistance (IASA) submitted annually by in-country teams, and unified commanders' comments and recommendations. This military assessment is based on an analysis of U.S. military interests, security assistance objectives, and desired force levels for friendly and allied nations. It addresses security assistance objectives, programs and priorities on a worldwide, regional, and individual country basis, and includes an assessment of alternate levels of funding.

The JSAM, together with the JSPDSA, provides the initial integration of security assistance planning with U.S. national security interests and military planning. The JSAM is structured to facilitate its use during interagency budget development and deliberations by the Arms Export Control Board (AECB) during the summer and fall. The AECB is an interagency advisory body that makes recommendations to the secretary of state on all security assistance plans, programs, budget, and legislative proposals.

The JSAM is drawn from an internal JCS document, the Joint Security Assistance Memorandum Supporting Analysis (JSAMSA), which provides the supporting analysis of individual country security assistance funding levels that are recommended in the JSAM. *See also:* Joint Force.

References

Department of Defense, National Defense University. *Joint Staff Officer's Guide, 1986.* Washington, DC: GPO, 1986.

—**JOINT STRATEGIC CAPABILITIES PLAN (JSCP)** provides Joint Chiefs of Staff (JCS) guidance to the commanders of the Unified and Specified Commands and the chiefs of the military services. It is a short-range plan that is prepared by the JCS J-5 and is based on the Joint Intelligence Estimate for Planning (JIEP), projected forces available, and subsequent secretary of defense guidance. It is divided into two volumes: Volume I is entitled "Concepts, Tasks, and Planning Guidance," and Volume II is "Forces." It also has fourteen supporting annexes: (A) Intelligence; (B) Logistics; (C) Nuclear; (D) Psychological Operations; (E) Unconventional Warfare; (F) Chemical Warfare; Nuclear, Biological and Chemical Defense; Riot Control Agents; and Herbicides; (G) Mapping, Charting, and Geodesy; (H) Nuclear Weapons Damage Considerations, Civil Defense, Recovery and Reconstitution CONUS; (I) Communications and Electronics; (J) Mobility; (K) Military Deception; (L) Civil Affairs; (M) Electronic Warfare; and (N) Mobilization.

The JSCP is reviewed and published annually in March and is a document that is critical to the commanders of the Unified and Specified Commands and to the services because it describes what major forces will be available for planning purposes. Additionally, it assigns tasks, provides planning guidance for the development of operation plans to accomplish those tasks, and gives planning guidance to the services for support of the Unified and Specified Commands in the execution of their assigned tasks. The JSCP also includes a section that presents the military objectives, the strategic concepts, and the national strategy for employing current forces.

The JSCP tasking is based on the capabilities of available forces, intelligence reports, and guidance by the secretary of defense. It directs the development of operational plans to support national security objectives by assigning tasks to the Unified and Specified Commanders. This document initiates the Joint Operational Planning System (JOPS). *See also:* Joint Force.

References

Department of Defense, National Defense University. *Joint Staff Officer's Guide, 1986.* Washington, DC: GPO, 1986.

—JOINT STRATEGIC OBJECTIVES PLAN (JSOP),

prepared annually, provides the advice of the Joint Chiefs of Staff to the President and the secretary of defense on the military strategy and force objectives that are necessary for attaining the national security objectives of the United States. In addition to recommendations on major forces, it includes the rationale supporting the forces and assessment of risks associated therewith, costs and manpower estimates, and other supporting data. The JSOP is published in two volumes: Volume I is entitled Strategy, and Volume II is Analysis and Force Tabulations. *See also:* Joint Force.

References

Department of Defense, National Defense University. *Joint Staff Officer's Guide, 1986.* Washington, DC: GPO, 1986.

—JOINT STRATEGIC PLANNING DOCUMENT

(JSPD) is one of seven documents, listed under Joint Strategic Planning System (JSPS), that make up the system. The JSPD conveys to the President, the National Security Council, and the secretary of defense the Joint Chiefs of Staff (JCS) position on the military strategy and force structure required to support the national security objectives. It is the basis of major policy discussion with the secretary of defense and is timed to precede the publication of the Defense Guidance (DG). It is published in two volumes. The first, JSPDSA I, Strategy and Force Planning Guidance, provides JCS views on national defense objectives, policies, strategy, and planning for the mid-range period. It addresses previous versions of the DG, provides JCS advice on national defense matters, and contains a recommended national military strategy. Volume I consists of military objectives, JCS threat ap-

praisal, military strategy, and force planning guidance to the commanders-in-chief (CinCs) and the services.

The second volume is JSPDSA II, Analysis and Force Requirements. It is force-oriented and contains JCS views on the military requirements that must be met to support national objectives and to execute the stated national strategy with a reasonable degree of success. It is derived from CinC and service inputs, assesses the capabilities and associated risks of the programmed force against the planning force, and makes appropriate planning recommendations to the secretary of defense. The volume also contains risk reduction measures, since the required resources needed to achieve the planning force are usually not available, and the programmed force will therefore have a lesser capability to execute the national military strategy. The volume also supports the Planning, Programming, and Budgeting System (PPBS) with JCS advice. In addition to the basic volume, there are separate annexes that provide military assessments and advice in the following functional areas: (A) Intelligence; (B) Nuclear; (C) Command, Control, and Communications; (D) Research and Development; (E) Mapping, Charting, and Geodesy; and (F) Manpower and Personnel.

The JSPD is noteworthy for several reasons. First, it provides the secretary of defense, the National Security Council, and the President with JCS advice on U.S. policy, national military strategy, and force recommendations. Second, it establishes a JCS position as a reference for presidential and National Security Council–directed actions. Third, it provides JCS recommendations to the Office of the Secretary of Defense that influences the development of the Defense Guidance. Fourth, it includes recommendations for risk reduction measures in respect to which mission or program areas should receive emphasis if additional funds become available. Finally, it requires CinC and service involvement in its development. *See also:* Joint Force.

References

Department of Defense, National Defense University. *Joint Staff Officer's Guide, 1986.* Washington, DC: GPO, 1986.

—JOINT STRATEGIC PLANNING DOCUMENT

SUPPORTING ANALYSIS (JSPDSA) is an internal document of the Joint Chiefs of Staff (JCS) and contains the principal supporting analysis for the

Joint Strategic Planning Document (JSPD). Prepared under the direction of the J-5, it provides the basis for drafting the JSPD and establishes the JCS position on national security matters. The JSPDSA is published biannually, is reviewed annually as required by changes to defense policy, strategy, or force planning requirements, and contains three parts: Part I, Strategy and Force Planning Guidance; Part II, Analysis and Force Requirements–Minimum Risk Force; and Part III, Analysis and Force Requirements–Planning Force.

Part I provides military planners with the perception of the JCS on national military objectives, strategy, and planning guidance as stated in the previous Defense Guidance (DG). Additionally, it provides specific perceived strategy and force planning guidance to the commanders of the Unified and Specified Commands to guide their preparation of Parts II and III.

In Parts II and III, the JCS develop planning force levels, together with their underlying analysis and rationale, which they consider necessary to support the national military strategy with a reasonable assurance of success. In developing the Planning Force in Part III, forces that are required to execute the strategy at minimum risk are used as an essential reference. The coalition aspects of the strategy are considered and the contribution of Allied and friendly forces are included. The entire process reflects the input provided by the services and the Unified and Specified Commanders as directed in JSPDSA I. The manpower requirements and costs that are associated with the planning force are compared with the most recent Five-Year Defense Plan (FYDP) force to include an assessment of the program force capabilities and associated risks. These risks provide the basis for JCS recommended changes to the DG. *See also:* Joint Force.

References

Department of Defense, National Defense
  University. *Joint Staff Officer's Guide, 1986.*
  Washington, DC: GPO, 1986.

—JOINT STRATEGIC PLANNING SYSTEM (JSPS) is the means by which the Joint Chiefs of Staff (JCS) give military advice to the President and the secretary of defense, establish the strategic basis for the secretary of defense's Defense Guidance (DG), develop the guidance and allot forces for contingency planning and operations in the near term, and develop the continuity necessary for the preparation of the next JCS cycle. Many of the

system's estimates are produced by the Directorate for Estimates (DE) of the Defense Intelligence Agency.

The JCS are charged by the National Security Act of 1947 with preparing strategic plans and for providing for the strategic direction of U.S. Armed Forces. The JCS use a series of documents that make up the JSPS in order to accomplish their strategic planning responsibilities. The combination of all these documents and their interrelationships constitute the framework for the JSPS.

The JSPS consists of seven documents: the Joint Long-Range Strategic Appraisal (JLRSA); the Joint Intelligence Estimate for Planning (JIEP); the Intelligence Priorities for Strategic Planning (IPSP); the Joint Strategic Planning Document (JSPD); the Joint Strategic Planning Document Supporting Analysis (JSPDSA); the Joint Program Assessment Memorandum (JPAM); and the Joint Security Assistance Memorandum (JSAM). The publication dates are contingent on the Program/Budget Review Schedule, which is published annually by the Office of the Secretary of Defense. *See also:* Joint Force.

References

Department of Defense, Defense Intelligence
  Agency. *Organization, Mission, and Key Personnel.*
  Washington, DC: DIA, 1986.

Department of Defense, National Defense
  University. *Joint Staff Officer's Guide, 1986.*
  Washington, DC: GPO, 1986.

—JOINT STRATEGIC TARGET PLANNING STAFF (JSTPS) is located at Offutt Air Force Base, Nebraska, and is concerned with identifying strategic targets and placing them in the U.S. strategic target system. *See also:* Joint Force.

References

Department of Defense, National Defense
  University. *Joint Staff Officer's Guide, 1986.*
  Washington, DC: GPO, 1986.

—JOINT TACTICAL INFORMATION DISTRIBUTION SYSTEM (JTIDS) is an intelligence term used on the joint intelligence and national level to describe a tri-service (Army, Navy, and Air Force) system that provides jam resistance and communication, navigation, and identification capabilities in the tactical intelligence environment. In order to enhance military operations, the JTIDS capabilities include pseudo-noise, nodeless information distribution, high data rate, frequency hopping, and crypto-secure communications. *See also:* Joint Force.

References
Department of Defense, National Defense
University. *Joint Staff Officer's Guide, 1986.*
Washington, DC: GPO, 1986.

—**JOINT TASK FORCE** is an intelligence term used on the joint intelligence and national level to describe a force composed of personnel from the Army, Navy, Air Force, or Marine Corps (at least two services) that has been designated as such by the secretary of defense or a commander of a Unified Command, a Specified Command, or an existing task force. *See also:* Joint Force.

References
Department of Defense, Joint Chiefs of Staff.
*Department of Defense Dictionary of Military and
Related Terms.* Washington, DC: GPO, 1986.

Department of Defense, National Defense
University. *Joint Staff Officer's Guide, 1986.*
Washington, DC: GPO, 1986.

Fain, Tyrus G.; Plant, Katharine C.; and Milloy, Ross.
*The Intelligence Community: History, Organiza-
tion, and Issues.* Public Documents Series. New
York: R.R. Bowker, 1977.

—**JONES, JOHN P.,** an Air Force staff sergeant, was arrested along with Staff Sergeant Giuseppe E. Cascio in Taegu, Korea, for attempting to pass classified information to the North Koreans. Jones was found to be insane and not competent to stand trial, and thus he was never tried.

References
Crawford, David J. *Volunteers: The Betrayal of
National Defense Secrets by Air Force Traitors.*
Washington, DC: GPO, 1988.

—**JOURNAL,** in the Army tactical intelligence (TACINT) context, is a permanent, chronological record of each message and document that enters a counter-signals intelligence (C-SIGINT) section. It provides a cross-reference—a complete compilation of all incoming reports for the purpose of future recovery. It covers a specified time, which is usually a 24-hour period. *See also:* Intelligence Journal.

References
Department of Defense, Joint Chiefs of Staff.
*Department of Defense Dictionary of Military and
Related Terms.* Washington, DC: GPO, 1986.

Department of Defense, U.S. Army. *Intelligence and
Electronic Warfare Operations.* Field Manual FM
34-1. Washington, DC: Headquarters, Department
of the Army, 1984.

————. *Military Intelligence Battalion Combat
Electronic Warfare and Intelligence (Aerial
Exploitation) (Corps).* Field Manual FM 34-22.
Washington, DC: Headquarters, Department of the
Army, 1984.

————. *Military Intelligence Battalion (Combat
Electronic Warfare Intelligence) (Division).* Field
Manual FM 34-10. Washington, DC: Headquarters,
Department of the Army, 1981.

————. *Military Intelligence Battalion (CEWI)
(Operations) (Corps).* Field Manual FM 34-21.
Washington, DC: Headquarters, Department of the
Army, 1982.

————. *Military Intelligence Company (Combat
Electronic Warfare and Intelligence) (Armored
Cavalry Regiment/Separate Brigade).* Field Manual
FM 34-30. Washington, DC: Headquarters,
Department of the Army, 1983.

————. *Military Intelligence Group (Combat
Electronic Warfare and Intelligence) (Corps).* Field
Manual FM 34-20. Washington, DC: Headquarters,
Department of the Army, 1983.

—**JUSTIFICATION BOOK CATEGORIES.** During the Carter administration, the director of Central Intelligence and the secretary of defense submitted annually several thousand-page descriptions of intelligence programs in the National Foreign Intelligence Program (NFIP) and in Intelligence Related Activities (IRA). Because the justification book categories in the NFIP and IRA volumes could be different, the process of monitoring all of this became a very complex problem. *See also:* Appropriation or Fund Account, Decision Units, Program Elements (PEs), Zero Based Budgeting.

References
Godson, Roy, ed. *Intelligence Problems for the
1980s, Number 3: Counterintelligence.* Washington, DC: National Strategy Information Center,
1980.

Maurer, Alfred C.; Turnstall, Marion D.; and Keagle,
James M. *Intelligence Policy and Process.* Boulder,
CO: Westview Press, 1985.

Pickett, George. "Congress, the Budget, and
Intelligence." In *Intelligence Policy and Process,*
edited by Alfred C. Maurer, Marion D. Turnstall,
and James M. Keagle. Boulder, CO: Westview
Press, 1985.

Turner, Stansfield. *Secrecy and Democracy: The CIA
in Transition.* Boston: Houghton Mifflin, 1985.

—KAMPILES, WILLIAM P., was a low-level employee of the Central Intelligence Agency who sold a technical manual about U.S. surveillance satellites to the Soviet Union. He was arrested in 1978, was tried, and in November 1979 was sentenced to 40 years in prison.

References

Allen, Thomas B., and Polmar, Norman. *Merchants of Treason: America's Secrets for Sale.* New York: Delacorte Press, 1988.

Becket, Henry S. A. *The Dictionary of Espionage: Spookspeak into English.* New York: Stein and Day, 1986.

Deacon, Richard. *Spyclopedia: An Encyclopedia of Spies, Secret Services, Operations, Jargon, and All Subjects Related to the World of Espionage.* London: Macdonald, 1987.

Kessler, Ronald. *Spy vs. Spy: Stalking Soviet Spies in America.* New York: Charles Scribner's Sons, 1988.

Lefever, Ernest W., and Godson, Roy. *The CIA and the American Ethic: An Unfinished Debate.* Washington, DC: Ethics and Public Policy Center, Georgetown University, 1979.

Ranelagh, John. *The Agency: The Rise and Decline of the CIA.* New York: Simon and Schuster, 1986.

—*KATZ VS. UNITED STATES* was a 1967 Supreme Court decision that held that electronic surveillance was a search and seizure within the meaning of the Fourth Amendment and that the results of domestic electronic surveillance activities were therefore inadmissable in court if the probable cause and warrant requirements of the Fourth Amendment had not been satisfied. Since the decision affected criminal investigations, not intelligence activities, the question of whether the Court would limit such intelligence activities was still undecided. Nonetheless, *Katz vs. United States* indicated that the Court, if pressed, might well limit such activity. *See also:* Executive Orders on Intelligence, Surveillance.

References

Kornblum, Allan. *Intelligence and the Law: Cases and Materials.* Vol. IV. Washington, DC: DIC, 1987.

Oseth, John M. *Regulating U.S. Intelligence Operations: A Study in Definition of the National Interest.* Frankfurt: University of Kentucky Press, 1985.

—KAUFMANN, JOSEPH PATRICK, an Air Force captain, was trained by East German and Soviet intelligence officers to collect classified U.S. defense information. However, before he could operate, one of the East German officers defected and divulged that Kaufmann was committing espionage. Kaufmann was tried by court-martial in 1962 and received a twenty-year sentence. On appeal, the sentence was reduced to two years.

References

Allen, Thomas B., and Polmar, Norman. *Merchants of Treason: America's Secrets for Sale.* New York: Delacorte Press, 1988.

Crawford, David J. *Volunteers: The Betrayal of National Defense Secrets by Air Force Traitors.* Washington, DC: GPO, 1988.

—KEARN, BRUCE L., a U.S. naval officer, left his ship in 1984 with secret documents and cryptographic material. He was arrested in 1984 and was tried, convicted, and given a dishonorable discharge and a four-year prison sentence.

References

Allen, Thomas B., and Polmar, Norman. *Merchants of Treason: America's Secrets for Sale.* New York: Delacorte Press, 1988.

Crawford, David J. *Volunteers: The Betrayal of National Defense Secrets by Air Force Traitors.* Washington, DC: GPO, 1988.

—KEEPING BOOKS is a term used in clandestine and covert intelligence operations to describe the process of keeping tabs on hostile intelligence agents who are operating in one's territory. *See also:* Agent, Center, Demote Maximally, Heavy Mob, Movements Analysis, Piggyback Entry, Piggybacking, Surround, Surveillance, Terminate with Extreme Prejudice.

References

Becket, Henry S. A. The Dictionary *of Espionage: Spookspeak into English.* New York: Stein and Day, 1986.

Deacon, Richard. *Spyclopedia: An Encyclopedia of Spies, Secret Services, Operations, Jargon, and All Subjects Related to the World of Espionage.* London: Macdonald, 1987.

Quirk, John; Phillips, David; Cline, Ray; and Pforzheimer, Walter. *The Central Intelligence Agency: A Photographic History.* Guilford, CT: Foreign Intelligence Press, 1986.

—**KENNEDY, JOHN F.** President Kennedy's initial relationship with the Intelligence Community was unsuccessful. Inheriting an evolving plan concerning the Bay of Pigs invasion from the Eisenhower administration, Kennedy approved this, the most ambitious paramilitary operation that the CIA had yet attempted. After the failure of the operation, Kennedy paid greater attention to presidential oversight of the Intelligence Community. Upon taking office, he had not restaffed Eisenhower's oversight body, the President's Board of Consultants on Foreign Intelligence Activities (PBCFIA). However, after the Bay of Pigs affair, Kennedy allowed Allen Dulles to resign as director of Central Intelligence and appointed John McCone to the position. McCone redirected the focus of the CIA toward the production of intelligence estimates, and he so improved the agency's efforts that a year later, in 1962, its reporting during the Cuban missile crisis was quite accurate, in vivid contrast to its analysis of Cuba before the Bay of Pigs. Kennedy also established the President's Foreign Intelligence Advisory Board (PFIAB) in May 1961, which had much the same responsibilities as Eisenhower's PBCFIA in respect to monitoring intelligence quality. In addition, the National Intelligence Programs Evaluation (NIPE) office was established in 1963 to review and evaluate Intelligence Community programs, their cost-effectiveness, and the effectiveness of the United States Intelligence Board in implementing the priority national intelligence objectives.

Elsewhere, Kennedy's appointment of Robert McNamara as secretary of defense had a significant long-range effect on military intelligence. In 1961, the Defense Intelligence Agency was established to manage the production of military intelligence. It has since assumed an even greater role in the management and production of military intelligence.

In summary, in respect to the men he appointed to intelligence positions, Kennedy should be given high marks. In addition, his efforts with Robert McNamara in creating the Defense Intelligence Agency were commendable. His micromanagement of intelligence (personally viewing U-2 photography and the like) was counterproductive and distracting to the Intelligence Community, but was a minor flaw in an otherwise impressive record that benefited American intelligence. *See also:* Bay of Pigs; Helms, Richard; McCone, John; Mongoose; President's Board of Consultants in Foreign Intelligence Activities (PBCFIA).

References

American Bar Association. *Oversight and Accountability of the U.S. Intelligence Agencies: An Evaluation.* Washington, DC: ABA, 1985.

Breckinridge, Scott D. *The CIA and the U.S. Intelligence System.* Boulder, CO: Westview Press, 1986.

Brinkley, David A., and Hull, Andrew W. *Estimative Intelligence: A Textbook on the History, Products, Uses and Writing of Intelligence Estimates.* Columbus, OH: Battelle, 1979.

Cline, Ray S. *The CIA Under Reagan, Bush, and Casey.* Washington, DC: Acropolis Books, 1981.

Corson, William R. *The Armies of Ignorance: The Rise of the American Intelligence Empire.* New York: Dial Press, 1977.

Crawford, David J. *Volunteers: The Betrayal of National Defense Secrets by Air Force Traitors.* Washington, DC: GPO, 1988.

Godson, Roy, ed. *Intelligence Problems for the 1980s, Number 2: Analysis and Estimates.* Washington, DC: National Strategy Information Center, 1980.

Laqueur, Walter. *A World of Secrets.* New York: Basic Books, 1985.

Lowenthal, Mark M. *U.S. Intelligence: Evolution and Anatomy.* New York: Praeger, 1984.

Maurer, Alfred C.; Turnstall, Marion D.; and Keagle, James M. *Intelligence Policy and Process.* Boulder, CO: Westview Press, 1985.

Treverton, Gregory F. *Covert Action: The Limits of Intervention in the Postwar World.* New York: Basic Books, 1987.

Turner, Stansfield. *Secrecy and Democracy: The CIA in Transition.* Boston: Houghton Mifflin, 1985.

U.S. Congress. Senate. *Alleged Assassination Plots Involving Foreign Leaders: An Interim Report of the Select Committee to Study Governmental Operations with Respect to Intelligence Activities.* 94th Congress, 1st sess., Nov. 20, 1975. S. Rept. 94-465.

U.S. Congress. Senate. *Final Report of the Senate Select Committee to Study Government Operations with Respect to Intelligence Activities. Report 94-755. Book I, Foreign and Military Intelligence.* Washington, DC: GPO, 1976.

Von Hoene, John P. A. *Intelligence User's Guide.* Washington, DC: DIA, 1983.

—**KEY,** in communications security (COMSEC), means a sequence of symbols or their electrical or mechanical equivalents that, in a machine or auto-manual cryptosystem, is combined with plain text in order to produce cipher text. Key is often used informally as a synonym for keying material or a cryptovariable. *See also:* Key-Auto-Key.

References

Martin, Paul H. "Communications-Computer Security." *Journal of Electronic Defense* (June 1987).

Muzerall, Joseph V., and Carty, Thomas P. "COMSEC and Its Need for Key Management." *DP&CS* (Spring 1987).

—**KEY AREA** is an area that is of paramount importance in a military operation.

References

Department of Defense, Joint Chiefs of Staff. *Department of Defense Dictionary of Military and Related Terms.* Washington, DC: GPO, 1986.

—**KEY-AUTO-KEY,** in communications security (COMSEC), means a cryptographic logic that uses a previous key to produce a key. *See also:* Key, Key Card.

References

Martin, Paul H. "Communications-Computer Security." *Journal of Electronic Defense* (June 1987).

Muzerall, Joseph V., and Carty, Thomas P. "COMSEC and Its Need for Key Management." *DP&CS* (Spring 1987).

—**KEY CARD,** in communications security (COMSEC), means a card that contains a pattern of punched holes, which establishes the cryptovariable for a specific cryptonet at a specific time. *See also:* Key.

References

Martin, Paul H. "Communications-Computer Security." *Journal of Electronic Defense* (June 1987).

Muzerall, Joseph V., and Carty, Thomas P. "COMSEC and Its Need for Key Management." *DP&CS* (Spring 1987).

—**KEY CYCLE,** in communications security (COMSEC), means a periodic sequence of key derived from a key generator in its successive states. One period is the key cycle and is usually marked by a return of the key generator to a former state. *See also:* Key.

References

Martin, Paul H. "Communications-Computer Security." *Journal of Electronic Defense* (June 1987).

Muzerall, Joseph V., and Carty, Thomas P. "COMSEC and Its Need for Key Management." *DP&CS* (Spring 1987).

—**KEY DISTRIBUTION CENTER (KDC),** in communications security (COMSEC), means a COMSEC facility that generates and distributes cryptovariables in electrical form. *See also:* Key.

References

Martin, Paul H. "Communications-Computer Security." *Journal of Electronic Defense* (June 1987).

Muzerall, Joseph V., and Carty, Thomas P. "COMSEC and Its Need for Key Management." *DP&CS* (Spring 1987).

—**KEY GENERATOR,** in communications security (COMSEC), means a device or algorithm that uses a series of mathematical rules to deterministically produce a pseudo-random sequence of variables. *See also:* Key.

References

Martin, Paul H. "Communications-Computer Security." *Journal of Electronic Defense* (June 1987).

Muzerall, Joseph V., and Carty, Thomas P. "COMSEC and Its Need for Key Management." *DP&CS* (Spring 1987).

—**KEY INTELLIGENCE QUESTIONS (KIQ)** is an intelligence term for questions of major interest to national policymakers and are defined by the director of Central Intelligence. The KIQ program was begun in 1974 to produce intelligence on these questions. They were similar to the military's essential elements of information and were replaced by the National Intelligence Topics of Current Interest. *See also:* Essential Elements of Information.

References

Corson, William R. *The Armies of Ignorance: The Rise of the American Intelligence Empire.* New York: Dial Press, 1977.

Fain, Tyrus G.; Plant, Katharine C.; and Milloy, Ross. *The Intelligence Community: History, Organiza-*

tion, and Issues. Public Documents Series. New York: R.R. Bowker, 1977.

U.S. Congress. Senate. *Final Report of the Senate Select Committee to Study Government Operations with Respect to Intelligence Activities. Report 94-755. Book I, Foreign and Military Intelligence.* Washington, DC: GPO, 1976.

—**KEY LIST,** in communications security (COMSEC), means a printed series of key settings for a specific cryptonet at a specified time that is produced in a list, padded or tape form. *See also:* Key.

References

Martin, Paul H. "Communications-Computer Security." *Journal of Electronic Defense* (June 1987).

Muzerall, Joseph V., and Carty, Thomas P. "COMSEC and Its Need for Key Management." *DP&CS* (Spring 1987).

—**KEY POINT** is a concentrated site or installation, the destruction or capture of which would seriously affect the war effort or the success of an operation.

References

Department of Defense, Joint Chiefs of Staff. *Department of Defense Dictionary of Military and Related Terms.* Washington, DC: GPO, 1986.

—**KEY TAPE,** in communications security (COMSEC), means a paper, mylar, or magnetic tape that contains the key for a specific cryptonet at a specific time. *See also:* Key.

References

Martin, Paul H. "Communications-Computer Security." *Journal of Electronic Defense* (June 1987).

Muzerall, Joseph V., and Carty, Thomas P. "COMSEC and Its Need for Key Management." *DP&CS* (Spring 1987).

—**KEY TERRAIN** is any locality or area, the seizure or retention of which affords a marked advantage to either combatant.

References

Department of Defense, Joint Chiefs of Staff. *Department of Defense Dictionary of Military and Related Terms.* Washington, DC: GPO, 1986.

—**KEYING MATERIAL,** in communications security (COMSEC), means a type of COMSEC aid that supplies either an encoding means for manual and auto-manual cryptosystems or cryptovariables for machine cryptosystems. *See also:* Key.

References

Martin, Paul H. "Communications-Computer Security." *Journal of Electronic Defense* (June 1987).

Muzerall, Joseph V., and Carty, Thomas P. "COMSEC and Its Need for Key Management." *DP&CS* (Spring 1987).

—**KEYING SPEED,** a baud-based system term used in communications intelligence, communications security, operations security, and signals analysis, is used to define the modulation rate (in bauds) for certain communications systems. It is the maximum number of mark and space unit elements per second, and is computed by dividing the element length (in milliseconds) into 1,000.

References

Martin, Paul H. "Communications-Computer Security." *Journal of Electronic Defense* (June 1987).

Muzerall, Joseph V., and Carty, Thomas P. "COMSEC and Its Need for Key Management." *DP&CS* (Spring 1987).

—**KEYING VARIABLES.** *See:* Cryptovariable.

—**KEYSTREAM,** in communications security (COMSEC), means the sequence of key that is produced by a key generator. *See also:* Key.

References

Martin, Paul H. "Communications-Computer Security." *Journal of Electronic Defense* (June 1987).

Muzerall, Joseph V., and Carty, Thomas P. "COMSEC and Its Need for Key Management." *DP&CS* (Spring 1987).

—**KGB (KOMITET GOSUDARSTVENNOY BEZOPASTNOSTI)** is the Soviet Committee for State Security. It is a vast organization that covers espionage and counterespionage duties and details border guards. *See also:* Center.

References

Deacon, Richard. *Spyclopedia: An Encyclopedia of Spies, Secret Services, Operations, Jargon, and All Subjects Related to the World of Espionage.* London: Macdonald, 1987.

Godson, Roy, *Intelligence Problems for the 1980s, Number 3: Counterintelligence.* Washington, DC: National Strategy Information Center, 1980.

————.*Intelligence Problems for the 1980s, Number 4: Covert Action.* Washington, DC: National Strategy Information Center, 1981.

————.*Intelligence Problems for the 1980s, Number 5: Clandestine Collection.* Washington, DC: National Strategy Information Center, 1982.

Laqueur, Walter. *A World of Secrets.* New York: Basic Books, 1985.

Turner, Stansfield. *Secrecy and Democracy: The CIA in Transition.* Boston: Houghton Mifflin, 1985.

—**KH-11** is a satellite system that plays the major role in the current U.S. satellite reconnaissance program. In 1978, William Kampiles, a CIA employee, sold a manual describing the KH-11 system to the Soviet Union. The compromise of the manual to the Soviet Union was potentially an extremely great security breach, because it may have provided the Soviets with additional details of the system that could allow them to develop more effective methods of defeating the capability. *See also:* Kampiles, William.

References

Crawford, David J. *Volunteers: The Betrayal of National Defense Secrets by Air Force Traitors.* Washington, DC: GPO, 1988.

Laqueur, Walter. *A World of Secrets.* New York: Basic Books, 1985.

Lowenthal, Mark M. *U.S. Intelligence: Evolution and Anatomy.* New York: Praeger, 1984.

Turner, Stansfield. *Secrecy and Democracy: The CIA in Transition.* Boston: Houghton Mifflin, 1985.

—**KNOCHE, E. HENRY,** served as deputy director of Central Intelligence from July 7, 1976, until July 31, 1977. *See also:* Central Intelligence Agency.

References

Turner, Stansfield. *Secrecy and Democracy: The CIA in Transition.* Boston: Houghton Mifflin, 1985.

—**KNUCKLE DRAGGER,** according to Henry Becket, is a paramilitary soldier working for the Central Intelligence Agency. The term is derogatory and means that these people are "such apes that their knuckles drag on the ground when they walk."

References

Becket, Henry S. A. *The Dictionary of Espionage: Spookspeak into English.* New York: Stein and Day, 1986.

Deacon, Richard. *Spyclopedia: An Encyclopedia of Spies, Secret Services, Operations, Jargon, and All Subjects Related to the World of Espionage.* London: Macdonald, 1987.

Ranelagh, John. *The Agency: The Rise and Decline of the CIA.* New York: Simon and Schuster, 1986.

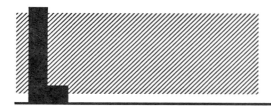

—LADIES is a term used in clandestine and covert intelligence operations. Ladies is a euphemism for women intelligence operatives who attempt to compromise intelligence targets. Such an effort may or may not involve seducing the target. *See also:* Agent, Biographic Leverage, Fur-Lined Seat Cover, Honey Trap, Mozhno Girls, Raven, Sisters, Swallow, Swallow's Nest, Taxi.

References

Deacon, Richard. *Spyclopedia: An Encyclopedia of Spies, Secret Services, Operations, Jargon, and All Subjects Related to the World of Espionage.* London: Macdonald, 1987.

—LANDING FORCE COMMANDER is the officer who is designated in the initiating directive to command the landing force.

References

Department of Defense, Joint Chiefs of Staff. *Department of Defense Dictionary of Military and Related Terms.* Washington, DC: GPO, 1986.

—LANDSAT SATELLITE. *See:* Earth Observation Satellite.

—LANGLEY HEADQUARTERS of the Central Intelligence Agency was designed in the mid-1950s by the New York firm of Harrison and Abramovitz, the designers of the United Nations building. Located about eight miles from downtown Washington, the building and grounds were envisioned by Director of Central Intelligence Allen W. Dulles as projecting the atmosphere of a college campus.

Construction of Langley was begun in October 1957 and completed in November 1963. The cornerstone was laid on November 3, 1959, and concrete and Georgia marble were used in the main lobby and corridor. Although the building was completed during the presidency of Dwight D. Eisenhower, whose name appears on the cornerstone, the building was commissioned by his predecessor, President Harry S. Truman. Personal messages of gratitude and approbation to the agency from these two presidents and their successors are hung along the first floor corridor.

A biblical verse characterizing the intelligence mission in a free society is etched in the wall of the central lobby. It reads: "And ye shall know the truth/and the truth shall make you free./John VIII-XXXII." Also on the wall of the central lobby is a bas-relief bust of Allen Dulles, since the building was erected during his period in office.

Engraved in the same wall are memorial stars, each honoring a CIA employee whose life was lost in the service of his country. The names of several of these Americans can never be revealed.

The research library at Langley consists of 60,000 cataloged titles, 110,000 volumes, and 1,700 newspapers and journal subscriptions. The emphasis is on basic and current information about foreign countries, including a selection of foreign newspapers, telephone directories, and encyclopedias.

The art work in the building is selected and hung by the CIA Fine Arts Committee. The majority of the collection is abstract, with an emphasis on color studies.

The original Langley building consists of a million square feet, while the building and grounds comprise 219 acres. A second building, begun in the spring of 1984, has added an additional 1.1 million square feet. It consists of two seven-story office towers that are connected by a four-story podium that contains technical support facilities and an employee services concourse. The project was designed by the Detroit architectural and engineering firm of Smith, Hinchman, and Grills.

References

Central Intelligence Agency. *Central Intelligence Agency Factbook.* Washington, DC: GPO, 1987.

Godson, Roy, ed. *Intelligence Problems for the 1980s, Number 1: Elements of Intelligence.* Rev. ed. Washington, DC: National Strategy Information Center, 1983.

————. *Intelligence Problems for the 1980s, Number 3: Counterintelligence.* Washington, DC: National Strategy Information Center, 1980.

—LASER INTELLIGENCE (LASINT) is a term used in measurement and signature intelligence (MASINT). It is a subcategory of electro-opint intelligence and is the technical and intelligence information that is derived from laser systems. *See also:* Signals Intelligence.

References

Department of Defense, Defense Intelligence College. *Glossary of Intelligence Terms and Definitions.* Washington, DC: DIC, 1987.

Godson, Roy, ed. *Intelligence Problems for the 1980s, Number 1: Elements of Intelligence.* Rev. ed. Washington, DC: National Strategy Information Center, 1983.

—**LAST LIGHT** is a term used in intelligence imagery and photoreconnaissance. It is the end of evening nautical twilight, that is, when the center of the evening sun is 12 degrees below the horizon. *See also:* Aerial Photograph.

References

Reeves, Robert; Anson, Abraham; and Landen, David. *Manual of Remote Sensing.* Falls Church, VA: American Society of Photogrammetry, 1975.

—**LATCH/RELEASE (START-STOP),** a baud-based system term used in communications intelligence, communications security, operations security, and signals analysis, pertains to a system that requires at least two additional impulses (one at the beginning and one or more at the end of a cycle) to maintain speed adjustment between transmitting and receiving teleprinters. *See also:* Communications Security.

References

Department of Defense, U.S. Army. *AIA: Threat Analysis.* Falls Church, VA: U.S. Army Intelligence Agency, 1987.

——— *Counter-Signals Intelligence (C-SIGINT) Operations.* Field Manual FM 34-62. Washington, DC: Headquarters, Department of the Army, 1986.

—**LATCHED CONDITION** is a baud-based system term used in communications intelligence, communications security, operations security, and signals analysis. It is a signal condition where all elements of a channel are in an energized state. This condition is associated with those system using additional elements to start or stop a receiving printer. *See also:* Communications Security.

References

Department of Defense, U.S. Army. *AIA: Threat Analysis.* Falls Church, VA: U.S. Army Intelligence Agency, 1987.

——— *Counter-Signals Intelligence (C-SIGINT) Operations.* Field Manual FM 34-62. Washington, DC: Headquarters, Department of the Army, 1986.

—**LAWFUL INVESTIGATION** is a definition resulting from Presidential Executive Order 12333, "United States Intelligence Activities," dated December 4, 1981, which defined the types of activities U.S. intelligence organizations could conduct concerning U.S. citizens. An inquiry qualifies as a lawful investigation if the subject of the investigation is within Department of Defense investigative jurisdiction; if it is conducted by a Department of Defense component that is authorized to conduct the particular type of investigation concerned (for example, counterintelligence, personnel security, physical security, or communications security); and if the investigation is conducted in accordance with applicable law and policy, including Executive Order 12333 and Department of Defense Regulation 5240.1.

References

Department of Defense. *Activities of DoD Intelligence Components that Affect U.S. Persons (Department of Defense Directive 5240.1).* Washington, DC: DoD, 1982.

Godson, Roy, ed. *Intelligence Problems for the 1980s, Number 1: Elements of Intelligence.* Rev. ed. Washington, DC: National Strategy Information Center, 1983.

Treverton, Gregory F. *Covert Action: The Limits of Intervention in the Postwar World.* New York: Basic Books, 1987.

Turner, Stansfield. *Secrecy and Democracy: The CIA in Transition.* Boston: Houghton Mifflin, 1985.

—**LEAKS,** a term used in counterintelligence, counterespionage, and counterinsurgency, has two definitions. (1) Leaks are deliberate or accidental disclosures of classified information. (2) Leaks are also used in another context. Like the first definition, the second deals with divulging classified information, but refers to the release of information to the public by a government source. At times, the President will "leak" or divulge classified information if this will support or justify an action that he is about to take. In another context, an interested party will divulge information in order to weaken the support for an opponent's stand. This type of bureaucratic warfare can be very damaging and has been a major factor in the Executive's not informing

Congress of special operations, a euphemism for covert operations. For example, in 1976 the Pike Committee's inability to keep its report confidential until it could be cleared by security lent credence to these misgivings.

One of the most definitive statements that have been made on leaks appeared in February 1987, in the final report of the President's Special Board, composed of Senator John Tower, Senator Edmund Muskie, and Lieutenant General Brent Scowcroft, that was created to investigate the National Security Advisor, the National Security Council, and the National Security Council staff in the wake of the Iran-Contra affair. The Board stated:

> The obsession with secrecy and preoccupation with leaks threaten to paralyze the government in its handling of covert operations. Unfortunately, the concern is not misplaced. The selective leak has become a principal means of waging bureaucratic warfare. Opponents of an operation kill it with a leak; supporters seek to build support through the same means.

> We have witnessed over the past years a significant deterioration in the integrity of process. Rather than a means to obtain results more satisfactory than the position of any of the individual departments, it has frequently become something to be manipulated to reach a specific outcome. The leak becomes a primary instrument of that process.

> This practice is destructive of orderly governance. It can only be reversed if the most senior officials take the lead. If senior decision-makers set a clear example and demand compliance, subordinates are more likely to conform.

> Most recent administrations have had carefully drawn procedures for the consideration of covert activities. The Reagan Administration established such procedures in January, 1985, then promptly ignored them in their consideration of the Iran initiative.

See also: Congressional Oversight, Executive Orders on Intelligence, Executive Oversight.

References

American Bar Association. *Oversight and Accountability of the U.S. Intelligence Agencies: An Evaluation.* Washington, DC: ABA, 1985.

Becket, Henry S. A. *The Dictionary of Espionage: Spookspeak into English.* New York: Stein and Day, 1986.

Clancy, Tom. *The Cardinal of the Kremlin.* New York: Putnam, 1988.

Godson, Roy, ed. *Intelligence Problems for the 1980s, Number 1: Elements of Intelligence.* Rev. ed. Washington, DC: National Strategy Information Center, 1983.

Office of the President of the United States. *Report of the President's Special Review Board.* Washington, DC: GPO, Feb. 26, 1987.

Treverton, Gregory F. *Covert Action: The Limits of Intervention in the Postwar World.* New York: Basic Books, 1987.

Turner, Stansfield. *Secrecy and Democracy: The CIA in Transition.* Boston: Houghton Mifflin, 1985.

—**LEARNING CURVE,** in intelligence budgeting, is the unit cost-cumulative quantity relationship for estimating costs. It is generally used to predict or describe the decrease in the cost of a unit as the number of units produced increases.

References

Pickett, George. "Congress, the Budget, and Intelligence." In *Intelligence Policy and Process,* edited by Alfred C. Maurer, Marion D. Turnstall, and James M. Keagle. Boulder, CO: Westview Press, 1985.

—**"LEAST INTRUSIVE MEANS"** rule was imposed by the Carter administration on intelligence activities. It stated that, in intelligence collection, the operators were required to choose techniques in an order of precedence shaped by concern for possible impact on citizens' rights. In general, this means the following:

> To the extent feasible, such information shall be collected from publicly available information or with the consent of the person concerned; if information from these sources is not reasonable or sufficient, such information may be collected from cooperating sources; if such information from cooperating sources is not feasible or sufficient, such information may be collected, as appropriate, using other lawful investigative techniques that do not require a judicial warrant or the approval of the Attorney General; then if collection through use of these techniques is not feasible or sufficient, approval for use of investigative techniques that do require a judicial warrant or the approval of the Attorney General may be sought.

See also: Congressional Oversight.

References

Department of Defense. *Activities of DoD Intelligence Components that Affect U.S. Persons (Department of Defense Directive 5240.1).* Washington, DC: DoD, 1982.

Godson, Roy, ed. *Intelligence Problems for the 1980s, Number 1: Elements of Intelligence.* Rev. ed. Washington, DC: National Strategy Information Center, 1983.

Oseth, John M. *Regulating U.S. Intelligence Operations: A Study in Definition of the National Interest.* Frankfurt: University of Kentucky Press, 1985.

Turner, Stansfield. *Secrecy and Democracy: The CIA in Transition.* Boston: Houghton Mifflin, 1985.

—**LEBANON.** In 1983, the United States landed Marines in Beirut, Lebanon, in an attempt to provide support to U.S.-backed Lebanese forces and an element of calming stability to the city. In order to fulfill its pacifying political mission, the Marine contingent exhibited a "low military profile" in order to appear as unthreatening as possible. However, before the Marines could have much of a political effect, the building used as their barracks was blown up and many Marines were killed. Assessing the causes of the disaster is difficult because no blame was ever really established.

References

Breckinridge, Scott D. *The CIA and the U.S. Intelligence System.* Boulder, CO: Westview Press, 1986.

Brinkley, David A., and Hull, Andrew W. *Estimative Intelligence: A Textbook on the History, Products, Uses and Writing of Intelligence Estimates.* Columbus, OH: Battelle, 1979.

Clancy, Tom. *The Cardinal of the Kremlin.* New York: Putnam, 1988.

Cline, Ray S. *The CIA Under Reagan, Bush, and Casey.* Washington, DC: Acropolis Books, 1981.

Crawford, David J. *Volunteers: The Betrayal of National Defense Secrets by Air Force Traitors.* Washington, DC: GPO, 1988.

Laqueur, Walter. *The Age of Terrorism.* Boston: Little, Brown, 1987.

Lowenthal, Mark M. *U.S. Intelligence: Evolution and Anatomy.* New York: Praeger, 1984.

Quirk, John; Phillips, David; Cline, Ray; and Pforzheimer, Walter. *The Central Intelligence Agency: A Photographic History.* Guilford, CT: Foreign Intelligence Press, 1986.

Turner, Stansfield. *Secrecy and Democracy: The CIA in Transition.* Boston: Houghton Mifflin, 1985.

U.S. Congress. Senate. *Alleged Assassination Plots Involving Foreign Leaders: An Interim Report of the Select Committee to Study Governmental Operations with Respect to Intelligence Activities.* 94th Congress, 1st sess., Nov. 20, 1975. S. Rept. 94-465.

U.S. Congress. Senate. *Final Report of the Senate Select Committee to Study Government Operations with Respect to Intelligence Activities. Report 94-755. Book I, Foreign and Military Intelligence.* Washington, DC: GPO, 1976.

Von Hoene, John P. A. *Intelligence User's Guide.* Washington, DC: DIA, 1983.

—**LEDBETTER, GARY L.,** attached to the U.S. Navy, was convicted in 1967 of espionage offenses concerning attempting to pass classified information to a foreign intelligence service. His motives were apparently monetary. He was sentenced to six months in prison.

References

Crawford, David J. *Volunteers: The Betrayal of National Defense Secrets by Air Force Traitors.* Washington, DC: GPO, 1988.

—**LEE, ANDREW D.,** while working for a company under contract to the Central Intelligence Agency, was arrested in 1977 for selling secrets to the Soviet Union. His partner, Christopher Boyce, was also arrested. Lee was convicted and sentenced to life in prison.

References

Allen, Thomas B., and Polmar, Norman. *Merchants of Treason: America's Secrets for Sale.* New York: Delacorte Press, 1988.

Becket, Henry S. A. *The Dictionary of Espionage: Spookspeak into English.* New York: Stein and Day, 1986.

Corson, William R. *The Armies of Ignorance: The Rise of the American Intelligence Empire.* New York: Dial Press, 1977.

Deacon, Richard. *Spyclopedia: An Encyclopedia of Spies, Secret Services, Operations, Jargon, and All Subjects Related to the World of Espionage.* London: Macdonald, 1987.

Godson, Roy, ed. *Intelligence Problems for the 1980s, Number 3: Counterintelligence.* Washington, DC: National Strategy Information Center, 1980.

Turner, Stansfield. *Secrecy and Democracy: The CIA in Transition.* Boston: Houghton Mifflin, 1985.

—**LEGAL** is clandestine and covert intelligence operations jargon for an intelligence officer who works abroad with no attempt to hide his identity. He is generally attached to his embassy or to another open activity of his government. However, this association is merely a means to cover his true mission. *See also:* Agent, Case Officer, Illegal Residency, Legal, Legal Residency.

References

Allen, Thomas B., and Polmar, Norman. *Merchants of Treason: America's Secrets for Sale.* New York: Delacorte Press, 1988.

Becket, Henry S. A. *The Dictionary of Espionage: Spookspeak into English.* New York: Stein and Day, 1986.

—LEGAL OPERATIONS are operations conducted by intelligence agents, officers, co-opted workers, or employees who are under the control of a legal residency. *See also:* Legal.

References

Becket, Henry S. A. *The Dictionary of Espionage: Spookspeak into English.* New York: Stein and Day, 1986.

Deacon, Richard. *Spyclopedia: An Encyclopedia of Spies, Secret Services, Operations, Jargon, and All Subjects Related to the World of Espionage.* London: Macdonald, 1987.

Kessler, Ronald. *Spy vs. Spy: Stalking Soviet Spies in America.* New York: Charles Scribner's Sons, 1988.

—LEGAL RESIDENCY is a clandestine and covert intelligence operations term for an intelligence location in a foreign country. A legal residency is staffed with intelligence officers assigned as overt representatives of their nation who may or may not be identified as intelligence officers. *See also:* Legal.

References

Department of Defense, Defense Intelligence College. *Glossary of Intelligence Terms and Definitions.* Washington, DC: DIC, 1987.

Kessler, Ronald. *Spy vs. Spy: Stalking Soviet Spies in America.* New York: Charles Scribner's Sons, 1988.

Treverton, Gregory F. *Covert Action: The Limits of Intervention in the Postwar World.* New York: Basic Books, 1987.

—LEGEND is a term used in clandestine and covert intelligence operations. It is an invented name and biography to hide the identity of a spy. In *Mortal Games,* Pierre Salinger and Leonard Gross provide a detailed and fascinating description of the efforts that go into a legend. *See also:* Agent Authentication, Alias, Cover, Cover Name, Cover Organizations, Cover Story, Naked, Pocket Litter, Pseudonym, Sanctification, Singleton.

References

Becket, Henry S. A. *The Dictionary of Espionage: Spookspeak into English.* New York: Stein and Day, 1986.

Deacon, Richard. *Spyclopedia: An Encyclopedia of Spies, Secret Services, Operations, Jargon, and All Subjects Related to the World of Espionage.* London: Macdonald, 1987.

Kessler, Ronald. *Spy vs. Spy: Stalking Soviet Spies in America.* New York: Charles Scribner's Sons, 1988.

Quirk, John; Phillips, David; Cline, Ray; and Pforzheimer, Walter. *The Central Intelligence Agency: A Photographic History.* Guilford, CT: Foreign Intelligence Press, 1986.

Salinger, Pierre, and Gross, Leonard. *Mortal Games.* New York: Doubleday, 1988.

—LEGITIMATE is CIA jargon for an outsider who is exactly what he claims to be.

References

Becket, Henry S. A. *The Dictionary of Espionage: Spookspeak into English.* New York: Stein and Day, 1986.

Deacon, Richard. *Spyclopedia: An Encyclopedia of Spies, Secret Services, Operations, Jargon, and All Subjects Related to the World of Espionage.* London: Macdonald, 1987.

Kessler, Ronald. *Spy vs. Spy: Stalking Soviet Spies in America.* New York: Charles Scribner's Sons, 1988.

Ranelagh, John. *The Agency: The Rise and Decline of the CIA.* New York: Simon and Schuster, 1986.

Treverton, Gregory F. *Covert Action: The Limits of Intervention in the Postwar World.* New York: Basic Books, 1987.

—LETTER DROP is a place where an agent can leave secret correspondence to be retrieved by his controller or another agent. *See also:* Accommodation Address, Illegal Communication, Live Letter Boxes, Live Letter Drops, Mail Cover.

References

Becket, Henry S. A. *The Dictionary of Espionage: Spookspeak into English.* New York: Stein and Day, 1986.

Ranelagh, John. *The Agency: The Rise and Decline of the CIA.* New York: Simon and Schuster, 1986.

—LEVELS OF PRECISION, in imagery interpretation, from low to high, are as follows: detection, general identification, precise identification, description, and specific characteristics. *See also:* Image; Image Motion Compensation; Imagery; Imagery Exploitation; Imagery Intelligence;

Imagery Interpreter; Photographic Coverage; Photographic Intelligence; Photographic Interpretation; Photographic Reading.

References

Reeves, Robert; Anson, Abraham; and Landen, David. *Manual of Remote Sensing*. Falls Church, VA: American Society of Photogrammetry, 1975.

—**LIAISON** is a general intelligence term. It is contact or communication maintained between elements of military forces to insure mutual understanding, cooperation, and coordination.

References

Department of Defense, Joint Chiefs of Staff. *Department of Defense Dictionary of Military and Related Terms*. Washington, DC: GPO, 1986.

—**LIBRARY ACCESSIONS LIST (LAL)** is a monthly listing of all the items that have been cataloged and added to the Defense Intelligence Agency library collection during the previous month. *See also:* Defense Intelligence Agency.

References

Von Hoene, John P. A. *Intelligence User's Guide*. Washington, DC: DIA, 1983.

—**LIBYA** played a continuing role in the Reagan administration years, and in each episode, intelligence performed successfully. The first incident involved provocative Libyan Air Force moves against U.S. naval operations in and near the Gulf of Sirte. In this instance, U.S. intelligence detected indications that Libya might operate aggressively against the forces. As the U.S. exercises were continued, U.S. warning aircraft detected and tracked an approaching hostile Libyan fighter that was about to fire its missiles. The aircraft was warned, and when it failed to heed the warning by breaking off the attack, it was shot down. That this incident was an intelligence success was obvious. But another aspect of the episode is interesting because it revealed the type of role that the President intended to play in intelligence and in military operations. Specifically, when the attack was about to occur, the President was not awakened with news of the incident. Rather, he was allowed to sleep through the night. This was in such stark contrast to previous presidential micromanagement of the *Mayaguez* incident and the Iran hostage rescue attempt that some members of the press began to question President Reagan's actions. The Presi-

dent responded by stating his belief that the decision for the U.S. action had been made on the proper operational level, implying that he should not become involved in tactical decisions of that nature. He went on to add that it was his feeling that the higher such decisions were pushed up the management ladder the greater the chances were that the wrong decision would be made.

The second Libyan incident, Operation "Eldorado Canyon," involved punitive air attacks on Libya in response to Libyan support for Arab international terrorism. The operation was a joint operation, involving the U.S. Navy, which launched aircraft from its carrier off the Libyan coast, and the U.S. Air Force, which staged long-range sorties from bases in the United Kingdom. The operation was an impressive military success, primarily because, although it was a joint operation, it in fact was run as independent naval and air force operations that were timed to occur concurrently over Libya.

Equally important, politically, the operation was, with one exception, a resounding success. Intelligence reporting was accurate and complete, providing the operating forces with complete targeting information for the operation. As a result, the targets were hit and had the desired political effect. Specifically, the sporadic reports that were received from Libya indicated that Muammar Qaddafi was completely unable to function after the raids, and that the colonels who were acting in his absence were pursuing a policy in which nothing would be allowed that might prompt a recurrence of the American raids. In this context, although Qaddafi had not been killed, the raids had so inhibited his actions that they were tantamount to an ideal use of military power for political affect.

References

Breckinridge, Scott D. *The CIA and the U.S. Intelligence System*. Boulder, CO: Westview Press, 1986.

Brinkley, David A. and Hull, Andrew W. *Estimative Intelligence: A Textbook on the History, Products, Uses and Writing of Intelligence Estimates*. Columbus, OH: Battelle, 1979.

Cline, Ray S. *The CIA Under Reagan, Bush, and Casey*. Washington, DC: Acropolis Books, 1981.

Crawford, David J. *Volunteers: The Betrayal of National Defense Secrets by Air Force Traitors*. Washington, DC: GPO, 1988.

Godson, Roy, ed. *Intelligence Problems for the 1980s, Number 2: Analysis and Estimates*. Washington, DC: National Strategy Information Center, 1980.

Laqueur, Walter. *The Age of Terrorism.* Boston: Little, Brown, 1987.

Lowenthal, Mark M. *U.S. Intelligence: Evolution and Anatomy.* New York: Praeger, 1984.

Quirk, John; Phillips, David; Cline, Ray; and Pforzheimer, Walter. *The Central Intelligence Agency: A Photographic History.* Guilford, CT: Foreign Intelligence Press, 1986.

Treverton, Gregory F. *Covert Action: The Limits of Intervention in the Postwar World.* New York: Basic Books, 1987.

Turner, Stansfield. *Secrecy and Democracy: The CIA in Transition.* Boston: Houghton Mifflin, 1985.

U.S. Congress. Senate. *Alleged Assassination Plots Involving Foreign Leaders: An Interim Report of the Select Committee to Study Governmental Operations with Respect to Intelligence Activities.* 94th Congress, 1st sess., Nov. 20, 1975. S. Rept. 94-465.

Von Hoene, John P. A. *Intelligence User's Guide.* Washington, DC: DIA, 1983.

—**LIGHT COVER** is the use of diplomatic credentials by a CIA officer who is stationed abroad.

References

Clancy, Tom. *The Cardinal of the Kremlin.* New York: Putnam, 1988.

—**LIMITED ACCESS AREA,** in communications security (COMSEC), means an area that contains classified information and in which uncleared people, if they were not monitored or accompanied by an individual who is cleared for access to the area, would have access to the information. Access to the information is therefore restricted by entry to the area and by accompanying uncleared individuals while they are in the area. *See also:* Access, Authorized, Classification, Classified Information, Code Word, Compromise, Declassification, Disclosure, Downgrade, Freedom of Information Act, Need-to-Know, Need-to-Know Principle, No-Lone Zone, Nondisclosure Agreement, Nondiscussion Area, Sanitization, Sanitize, Sanitized Area, Security Certification, Security Classification, Sensitive Compartmented Information, Sensitive Compartmented Information Facility, Two-Person Control.

References

Department of Defense, Defense Intelligence College. *Glossary of Intelligence Terms and Definitions.* Washington, DC: DIC, 1987.

—**LIMITED DISTRIBUTION (LIMDIS)** concerns data that has been formally restricted by the Intelligence Community Staff and that requires the originator's approval before it can be released. *See also:* Access, Authorized, Classification, Classified Information, Code Word, Compromise, Declassification, Disclosure, Downgrade, Freedom of Information Act, Need-to-Know, Need-to-Know Principle, No-Lone Zone, Nondisclosure Agreement, Nondiscussion Area, Sanitization, Sanitize, Sanitized Area, Security Certification, Security Classification, Sensitive Compartmented Information, Sensitive Compartmented Information Facility, Two-Person Control.

References

Department of Defense, Defense Intelligence College. *Glossary of Intelligence Terms and Definitions.* Washington, DC: DIC, 1987.

Godson, Roy, ed. *Intelligence Problems for the 1980s, Number 1: Elements of Intelligence.* Rev. ed. Washington, DC: National Strategy Information Center, 1983.

—**LIMITED MAINTENANCE,** in communications security (COMSEC), means maintenance that is performed by maintenance activities that are responsible for providing direct support to using organizations. Limited maintenance includes disassembly, isolating problems to a specific, removable subassembly, and replacing the subassembly without soldering. Limited maintenance facilities will also provide technical assistance to using facilities. *See also:* Communications Security.

References

Department of Defense, U.S. Army. *AIA: Threat Analysis.* Falls Church, VA: U.S. Army Intelligence Agency, 1987.

―――. *Counter-Signals Intelligence (C-SIGINT) Operations.* Field Manual FM 34-62. Washington, DC: Headquarters, Department of the Army, 1986.

—**LIMITED PROTECTION,** in communications security (COMSEC), means a form of short-term COMSEC protection that is applied to the electromagnetic or acoustic transmission of national security–related information. *See also:* Communications Security.

References

Department of Defense, U.S. Army. *AIA: Threat Analysis.* Falls Church, VA: U.S. Army Intelligence Agency, 1987.

————. *Counter-Signals Intelligence (C-SIGINT) Operations.* Field Manual FM 34-62. Washington, DC: Headquarters, Department of the Army, 1986.

—**LIMITED PROTECTION EQUIPMENT,** in communications security (COMSEC), means equipment that provides a limited degree of protection. This should advise the user that, while the equipment has a certain degree of shielding or protection, it is not invulnerable and therefore its transmissions or emanations can be intercepted by the enemy. *See also:* Communications Security.

References

Department of Defense, U.S. Army. *AIA: Threat Analysis.* Falls Church, VA: U.S. Army Intelligence Agency, 1987.

————. *Counter-Signals Intelligence (C-SIGINT) Operations.* Field Manual FM 34-62. Washington, DC: Headquarters, Department of the Army, 1986.

—**LINECROSSERS.** *See:* Border Crossers.

—**LINES OF COMMUNICATIONS (LOCS) STUDIES** are produced by the Defense Intelligence Agency. They are comprehensive studies of all types of communications within and between countries. They include data on ports, railways, highways, inland waterways, air transportation, beaches, and telecommunications. *See also:* Defense Intelligence Agency.

References

Von Hoene, John P. A. *Intelligence User's Guide.* Washington, DC: DIA, 1983.

—**LINK ENCRYPTION,** in communications security (COMSEC), means applying on-line cryptography to the individual links of an encryption system so that all the information that passes over each link is entirely encrypted. *See also:* Communications Security.

References

Department of Defense, Joint Chiefs of Staff. *Department of Defense Dictionary of Military and Related Terms.* Washington, DC: GPO, 1986.

U.S. Congress. Senate. *Final Report of the Senate Select Committee to Study Government Operations with Respect to Intelligence Activities. Report 94-755. Book I, Foreign and Military Intelligence.* Washington, DC: GPO, 1976.

—**LINKS OF COMMUNICATION,** as defined by the Church Committee, is a general term used to indicate the existence of a communications line between two points.

References

Department of Defense, Joint Chiefs of Staff. *Department of Defense Dictionary of Military and Related Terms.* Washington, DC: GPO, 1986.

U.S. Congress. Senate. *Final Report of the Senate Select Committee to Study Government Operations with Respect to Intelligence Activities. Report 94-755. Book I, Foreign and Military Intelligence.* Washington, DC: GPO, 1976.

—**LION-TAMER** is a term used in clandestine and covert intelligence operations. A lion-tamer is used when an agent who has been fired threatens to embarrass the intelligence agency. He is a muscle-man who is ordered to "soften up" the agent. Lion-tamers are also called upon to deal with errant "ladies" and "sisters." *See also:* Knuckle Draggers, Ladies, Sisters.

References

Becket, Henry S. A. *The Dictionary of Espionage: Spookspeak into English.* New York: Stein and Day, 1986.

Deacon, Richard. *Spyclopedia: An Encyclopedia of Spies, Secret Services, Operations, Jargon, and All Subjects Related to the World of Espionage.* London: Macdonald, 1987.

Ranelagh, John. *The Agency: The Rise and Decline of the CIA.* New York: Simon and Schuster, 1986.

—**LITERAL CRYPTOSYSTEM,** in communications security (COMSEC), means a cryptosystem that has been designed for literal communications, in which the plain-text elements are letters and sometimes include the numbers 1 through 9 and other symbols that are normally used in the written language. *See also:* Communications Security.

References

Department of Defense, U.S. Army. *AIA: Threat Analysis.* Falls Church, VA: U.S. Army Intelligence Agency, 1987.

————. *Counter-Signals Intelligence (C-SIGINT) Operations.* Field Manual FM 34-62. Washington, DC: Headquarters, Department of the Army, 1986.

—**LITMUS TEST** is a counterintelligence ploy in which false information is put before a suspected agent or informer and then the subject is watched to see if he passes the information to a hostile intelligence service. *See also:* Agent Provocateur,

Blow, Blown Agent, Co-opted Worker, Co-optees, Defector, Double Agent, Doubled, Establishing Bonafides, Flutter, Fluttered, Informant, Inside Man, Mole, Provocation Agent, Recruitment, Recruitment in Place, Walk-in.

References

Becket, Henry S. A. *The Dictionary of Espionage: Spookspeak into English.* New York: Stein and Day, 1986.

Deacon, Richard. *Spyclopedia: An Encyclopedia of Spies, Secret Services, Operations, Jargon, and All Subjects Related to the World of Espionage.* London: Macdonald, 1987.

Ranelagh, John. *The Agency: The Rise and Decline of the CIA.* New York: Simon and Schuster, 1986.

—**LIVE LETTER BOXES,** in clandestine and covert intelligence operations, are subagents who wittingly or unwittingly pass messages to other persons. *See also:* Accommodation Address, Dead Drop, Illegal Communication, Letter Drop, Live Letter Drops, Mail Cover.

References

Becket, Henry S. A. *The Dictionary of Espionage: Spookspeak into English.* New York: Stein and Day, 1986.

Deacon, Richard. *Spyclopedia: An Encyclopedia of Spies, Secret Services, Operations, Jargon, and All Subjects Related to the World of Espionage.* London: Macdonald, 1987.

Ranelagh, John. *The Agency: The Rise and Decline of the CIA.* New York: Simon and Schuster, 1986.

—**LIVE LETTER DROPS,** in clandestine and covert intelligence operations, are low-level agents who are recruited to receive letters and forward them to a case officer. *See also:* Live Letter Boxes.

References

Becket, Henry S. A. *The Dictionary of Espionage: Spookspeak into English.* New York: Stein and Day, 1986.

Deacon, Richard. *Spyclopedia: An Encyclopedia of Spies, Secret Services, Operations, Jargon, and All Subjects Related to the World of Espionage.* London: Macdonald, 1987.

Ranelagh, John. *The Agency: The Rise and Decline of the CIA.* New York: Simon and Schuster, 1986.

—**LIVE TAP,** in counterintelligence and covert and clandestine intelligence operations, is a telephone tap that is monitored by a listener, rather than being recorded for later study. *See also:* Electronic Surveillance.

References

Becket, Henry S. A. *The Dictionary of Espionage: Spookspeak into English.* New York: Stein and Day, 1986.

Deacon, Richard. *Spyclopedia: An Encyclopedia of Spies, Secret Services, Operations, Jargon, and All Subjects Related to the World of Espionage.* London: Macdonald, 1987.

Ranelagh, John. *The Agency: The Rise and Decline of the CIA.* New York: Simon and Schuster, 1986.

—**LOCK ON** is an electronics term that signifies that a tracking or target seeking system is continuously and automatically tracking a target in one or more coordinates (range, azimuth, elevation, or altitude). *See also:* Electronic Warfare.

References

Department of Defense, Joint Chiefs of Staff. *Department of Defense Dictionary of Military and Related Terms.* Washington, DC: GPO, 1986.

—**LOCK STUDIES** is a special FBI course in which agents are taught how to pick locks and open safes.

References

Becket, Henry S. A. *The Dictionary of Espionage: Spookspeak into English.* New York: Stein and Day, 1986.

—**LOG SUMMARIES** is a counterintelligence term. Log summaries are the notes that a wiretap team compiles during a shift of listening to telephone conversations. *See also:* Bug, Bugging, Electronic Surveillance.

References

Becket, Henry S. A. *The Dictionary of Espionage: Spookspeak into English.* New York: Stein and Day, 1986.

—**LOGIC BOMB** is a counterintelligence term used in the context of automatic data processing (ADP) system security. A logic bomb is a computer program that is executed at appropriate or periodic times in a computer system and determines the conditions or status of the computer that would facilitate the commission of an unauthorized act. An agent who has penetrated the system could plant a logic bomb in order to cause a complete system breakdown in a wartime emergency.

References

Blackburn, N. Glenn. "Computers: A Counterintelligence Concern." Unpublished paper provided to the editors. Washington, DC, 1987.

—**LONETREE, SERGEANT CLAYTON J.,** U.S. Marine Corps, served as a guard at the U.S. embassies in Vienna and Moscow. He was arrested on suspicion of espionage in 1987, was subsequently accused of giving Top Secret information to Soviet agents, and was tried, convicted, and sentenced to 30 years in prison. *See also:* Mozhno Girls, Swallow, Swallow's Nest.

References

Allen, Thomas B., and Polmar, Norman. *Merchants of Treason: America's Secrets for Sale.* New York: Delacorte Press, 1988.

—**LOOT** is a term used in clandestine and covert intelligence operations to describe the information that is obtained through an intelligence operation. *See also:* Debriefing, Processing the Take.

References

Becket, Henry S. A. *The Dictionary of Espionage: Spookspeak into English.* New York: Stein and Day, 1986.

—**LOW INTENSITY CONFLICT (LIC)** is a generic term that has no precise definition. However, of those available, the one provided by John Oseth is the most accurate. He defines low intensity conflict as "a wide variety of unconventional military or semi-military activities on both sides of the traditional distinction between peace and war. It includes coercive diplomacy, security assistance missions in relatively benign and varying degrees of hostile environments, insurgency and counterinsurgency operations, terrorism and counterterrorism, surgical direct action military operations, psychological warfare, and even operations by conventional or general-purpose forces in which ends and means are circumscribed by national policy." *See also:* Guerrilla Warfare.

References

Godson, Roy, ed. *Intelligence Problems for the 1980s, Number 1: Elements of Intelligence.* Rev. ed. Washington, DC: National Strategy Information Center, 1983.

Oseth, John M. "Intelligence and Low Intensity Conflict." *Naval War College Review* (Nov.–Dec. 1984): 19–36.

—**LOW PROBABILITY OF INTERCEPT,** in communications security (COMSEC), describes signals that are difficult to detect because their characteristics are hidden or disguised in some manner. *See also:* Communications Security.

References

Department of Defense, U.S. Army. *AIA: Threat Analysis.* Falls Church, VA: U.S. Army Intelligence Agency, 1987.

———. *Counter-Signals Intelligence (C-SIGINT) Operations.* Field Manual FM 34-62. Washington, DC: Headquarters, Department of the Army, 1986.

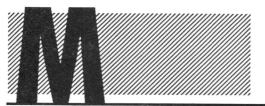

—**MI-5** is the United Kingdom's counterintelligence service and operates primarily in the British Isles. Its predecessor was established in 1909. It is under the supervision of a director-general who is responsible to the home secretary.

References

Allen, Thomas B., and Polmar, Norman. *Merchants of Treason: America's Secrets for Sale.* New York: Delacorte Press, 1988.

Corson, William R. *The Armies of Ignorance: The Rise of the American Intelligence Empire.* New York: Dial Press, 1977.

Deacon, Richard. *Spyclopedia: An Encyclopedia of Spies, Secret Services, Operations, Jargon, and All Subjects Related to the World of Espionage.* London: Macdonald, 1987.

Godson, Roy, ed. *Intelligence Problems for the 1980s, Number 1: Elements of Intelligence.* Rev. ed. Washington, DC: National Strategy Information Center, 1983.

Laqueur, Walter. *A World of Secrets.* New York: Basic Books, 1985.

Turner, Stansfield. *Secrecy and Democracy: The CIA in Transition.* Boston: Houghton Mifflin, 1985.

—**MI-6** is the United Kingdom's secret service. Established in 1909, it operates primarily overseas but is headquartered in London at Century House. Until 1953, its director-general was a naval or military officer.

References

Allen, Thomas B., and Polmar, Norman. *Merchants of Treason: America's Secrets for Sale.* New York: Delacorte Press, 1988.

American Bar Association. *Oversight and Accountability of the U.S. Intelligence Agencies: An Evaluation.* Washington, DC: ABA, 1985.

Corson, William R. *The Armies of Ignorance: The Rise of the American Intelligence Empire.* New York: Dial Press, 1977.

Deacon, Richard. *Spyclopedia: An Encyclopedia of Spies, Secret Services, Operations, Jargon, and All Subjects Related to the World of Espionage.* London: Macdonald, 1987.

Godson, Roy, ed. *Intelligence Problems for the 1980s, Number 1: Elements of Intelligence.* Rev.

ed. Washington, DC: National Strategy Information Center, 1983.

Laqueur, Walter. *A World of Secrets.* New York: Basic Books, 1985.

Maurer, Alfred C.; Turnstall, Marion D.; and Keagle, James M. *Intelligence Policy and Process.* Boulder, CO: Westview Press, 1985.

Turner, Stansfield. *Secrecy and Democracy: The CIA in Transition.* Boston: Houghton Mifflin, 1985.

—**MI-8** was an American organization set up by Herbert O. Yardley, an American cryptographer, after World War I. It was the cryptographic bureau of American intelligence and was a precursor to the National Security Agency. *See also:* National Security Agency.

References

Becket, Henry S. A. *The Dictionary of Espionage: Spookspeak into English.* New York: Stein and Day, 1986.

Corson, William R. *The Armies of Ignorance: The Rise of the American Intelligence Empire.* New York: Dial Press, 1977.

Deacon, Richard. *Spyclopedia: An Encyclopedia of Spies, Secret Services, Operations, Jargon, and All Subjects Related to the World of Espionage.* London: Macdonald, 1987.

Godson, Roy, ed. *Intelligence Problems for the 1980s, Number 1: Elements of Intelligence.* Rev. ed. Washington, DC: National Strategy Information Center, 1983.

Ranelagh, John. *The Agency: The Rise and Decline of the CIA.* New York: Simon and Schuster, 1986.

Treverton, Gregory F. *Covert Action: The Limits of Intervention in the Postwar World.* New York: Basic Books, 1987.

Turner, Stansfield. *Secrecy and Democracy: The CIA in Transition.* Boston: Houghton Mifflin, 1985.

—**MACHINE CRYPTOSYSTEM,** in communications security (COMSEC), means a cryptosystem in which the cryptographic processes are performed by crypto-equipment. *See also:* Communications Security.

References

Department of Defense, U.S. Army. *Counter-Signals Intelligence (C-SIGINT) Operations.* Field Manual FM 34-62. Washington, DC: Headquarters, Department of the Army, 1986.

————. *Military Intelligence Battalion Combat Electronic Warfare and Intelligence (Aerial Exploitation) (Corps).* Field Manual FM 34-22. Washington, DC: Headquarters, Department of the Army, 1984.

————. *Military Intelligence Company (Combat Electronic Warfare and Intelligence) (Armored Cavalry Regiment/Separate Brigade).* Field Manual FM 34-30. Washington, DC: Headquarters, Department of the Army, 1983.

—**MADSEN, LEE EUGENE,** attached to the U.S. Navy, was arrested in 1979 and charged with espionage offenses. He was apparently motivated by his ego and expected monetary gain. Madsen was convicted and sentenced to eight years in prison.

References

Allen, Thomas B., and Polmar, Norman. *Merchants of Treason: America's Secrets for Sale.* New York: Delacorte Press, 1988.

Crawford, David J. *Volunteers: The Betrayal of National Defense Secrets by Air Force Traitors.* Washington, DC: GPO, 1988.

Turner, Stansfield. *Secrecy and Democracy: The CIA in Transition.* Boston: Houghton Mifflin, 1985.

—**MAGIC** was translations of the intercepted Japanese code during World War II.

References

Lowenthal, Mark M. *U.S. Intelligence: Evolution and Anatomy.* New York: Praeger, 1984.

—**MAGPIE BOARD** is a term used in clandestine and covert intelligence operations to describe a small board or package that contains keys, wire, knives, and other materials that might aid in an escape.

References

Becket, Henry S. A. *The Dictionary of Espionage: Spookspeak into English.* New York: Stein and Day, 1986.

Deacon, Richard. *Spyclopedia: An Encyclopedia of Spies, Secret Services, Operations, Jargon, and All Subjects Related to the World of Espionage.* London: Macdonald, 1987.

Ranelagh, John. *The Agency: The Rise and Decline of the CIA.* New York: Simon and Schuster, 1986.

—**MAIL COVER** occurs when an intelligence or law enforcement agency requests permission from the U.S. Postal Service to examine the envelopes of mail addressed to an individual or organization. The person or organization is not told of the inspection, and the mail is not opened. *See also:* Flaps and Seals.

References

Becket, Henry S. A. *The Dictionary of Espionage: Spookspeak into English.* New York: Stein and Day, 1986.

Deacon, Richard. *Spyclopedia: An Encyclopedia of Spies, Secret Services, Operations, Jargon, and All Subjects Related to the World of Espionage.* London: Macdonald, 1987.

Ranelagh, John. *The Agency: The Rise and Decline of the CIA.* New York: Simon and Schuster, 1986.

Treverton, Gregory F. *Covert Action: The Limits of Intervention in the Postwar World.* New York: Basic Books, 1987.

Turner, Stansfield. *Secrecy and Democracy: The CIA in Transition.* Boston: Houghton Mifflin, 1985.

—**MAIN BATTLE AREA (MBA),** an Army tactical intelligence (TACINT) term, means that portion of the battlefield extending rearward from the forward edge of the battle area and in which the decisive battle is fought to defeat the enemy attack. Designation of the MBA may include the use of lateral and rear boundaries.

References

Department of Defense, U.S. Army. *Military Intelligence Group (Combat Electronic Warfare and Intelligence) (Corps).* Field Manual FM 34-20. Washington, DC: Headquarters, Department of the Army, 1983.

————. *U.S. Army Air Defense Artillery Employment.* Field Manual FM 44-1. Washington, DC: Headquarters, Department of the Army, 1983.

—**MAINTENANCE KEY,** in communications security (COMSEC), means cryptovariables that are intended only for off-the-air, in-shop use. *See also:* Communications Security.

References

Department of Defense, U.S. Army. *Counter-Signals Intelligence (C-SIGINT) Operations.* Field Manual FM 34-62. Washington, DC: Headquarters, Department of the Army, 1986.

————. *Military Intelligence Battalion (CEWI) (Tactical Exploitation) (Corps): Counterintelligence, Interrogation, Electronic Warfare.* Field Manual FM 34-23. Washington, DC: Headquarters, Department of the Army, 1985.

—**MAKE** is a term used in clandestine and covert intelligence operations. It occurs when a person who is under intelligence surveillance identifies his cover. The identified follower is said to have been made. *See also:* Agent, Cover, Go-Away, Meet Area, Movements Analysis, Pavement Artists, Shadow, Shaking Off the Dogs, Stroller, Surround, Surveillance, Thirty Threes, Walk-Past, What's Your Twenty?

References

Becket, Henry S. A. *The Dictionary of Espionage: Spookspeak into English.* New York: Stein and Day, 1986.

Deacon, Richard. *Spyclopedia: An Encyclopedia of Spies, Secret Services, Operations, Jargon, and All Subjects Related to the World of Espionage.* London: Macdonald, 1987.

Ranelagh, John. *The Agency: The Rise and Decline of the CIA.* New York: Simon and Schuster, 1986.

—**MAKING A PASS** is a term used in clandestine and covert intelligence operations to describe a situation when a message is physically handed or passed to a courier or agent. *See also:* Accommodation Address, Illegal Communication, Letter Drop, Live Letter Boxes, Live Letter Drops.

References

Becket, Henry S. A. *The Dictionary of Espionage: Spookspeak into English.* New York: Stein and Day, 1986.

Clancy, Tom. *The Cardinal of the Kremlin.* New York: Putnam, 1988.

—**MANAGEMENT BY OBJECTIVE** was a technique that William Colby introduced into the Central Intelligence Agency's Directorate for Operations. Its purpose was to link projects to specific program objectives and to key intelligence questions and to identify intelligence requirements more exactly and then establish the necessary collection and production requirements. *See also:* Central Intelligence Agency.

References

Corson, William R. *The Armies of Ignorance: The Rise of the American Intelligence Empire.* New York: Dial Press, 1977.

Fain, Tyrus G.; Plant, Katharine C.; and Milloy, Ross. *The Intelligence Community: History, Organization, and Issues.* Public Documents Series. New York: R.R. Bowker, 1977.

Godson, Roy, ed. *Intelligence Problems for the 1980s, Number 1: Elements of Intelligence.* Rev. ed. Washington, DC: National Strategy Information Center, 1983.

Lowenthal, Mark M. *U.S. Intelligence: Evolution and Anatomy.* New York: Praeger, 1984.

—**MANIPULATIVE COMMUNICATIONS COVER** is a term used in signals intelligence, communications security, communications intelligence, operations security, and signals analysis to describe measures that are taken to alter or conceal the characteristics of communications in order to prevent the enemy from identifying them. Manipulative communications cover is also known as communications cover. *See also:* Communications Security.

References

Department of Defense, Defense Intelligence College. *Glossary of Intelligence Terms and Definitions.* Washington, DC: DIC, 1987.

—**MANIPULATIVE COMMUNICATIONS DECEPTION.** *See:* Communications Deception, Manipulative Deception.

—**MANIPULATIVE DECEPTION,** in communications security (COMSEC), means altering or simulating friendly signals in order to deceive the enemy. *See also:* Communications Security.

References

Department of Defense, Defense Intelligence College. *Glossary of Intelligence Terms and Definitions.* Washington, DC: DIC, 1987.

Godson, Roy, ed. *Intelligence Problems for the 1980s, Number 1: Elements of Intelligence.* Rev. ed. Washington, DC: National Strategy Information Center, 1983.

———. *Intelligence Problems for the 1980s, Number 3: Counterintelligence.* Washington, DC: National Strategy Information Center, 1980.

—**MANUAL CRYPTOSYSTEM,** in communications security (COMSEC), means a cryptosystem in which the cryptographic processes are performed manually without the use of cryptoequipment, limited protection equipment, or auto-manual devices. *See also:* Communications Security.

References

Department of Defense, U.S. Army. *Counter-Signals Intelligence (C-SIGINT) Operations.* Field Manual FM 34-62. Washington, DC: Headquarters, Department of the Army, 1986.

———. *Military Intelligence Battalion Combat Electronic Warfare and Intelligence (Aerial Exploitation) (Corps).* Field Manual FM 34-22. Washington, DC: Headquarters, Department of the Army, 1984.

————. *Military Intelligence Battalion (CEWI) (Tactical Exploitation) (Corps): Counterintelligence, Interrogation, Electronic Warfare.* Field Manual FM 34-23. Washington, DC: Headquarters, Department of the Army, 1985.

————. *Military Intelligence Company (Combat Electronic Warfare and Intelligence) (Armored Cavalry Regiment/Separate Brigade).* Field Manual FM 34-30. Washington, DC: Headquarters, Department of the Army, 1983.

—**MAP** is a representation of the earth's surface at an established scale. It will have natural or artificial physical features and a means of orientation.

References
Reeves, Robert; Anson, Abraham; and Landen, David. *Manual of Remote Sensing.* Falls Church, VA: American Society of Photogrammetry, 1975.

—**MAPPING, CHARTING, AND GEODESY** is an official term that has been defined by the Defense Intelligence Agency for one of its functional areas. It means "activities involving the utilization of geographic, geodetic, gravimetric, cartographic, topographic, hydro-related oceanography, geomagnetic, and navigational data in the management of land, sea, and air surveys; and in the production of topographic maps, aeronautical charts, nautical charts and related items." *See also:* Defense Intelligence Agency.

References
Department of Defense, Defense Intelligence Agency. *Defense Intelligence Agency Manual 22-2.* Washington, DC: DIA, 1979.

—**MARCHETTI CASE** involved two court cases concerning Victor Marchetti, an employee of the Central Intelligence Agency who began writing fiction and then factual articles and books about the agency in 1972. The core issue in the Marchetti case concerned the power of an intelligence agency to prevent an employee from writing about the agency's affairs and operations. The first case was initiated by the CIA, which sought an injunction that would prevent Marchetti from publishing a magazine article that the agency claimed violated the secrecy agreement that he had signed as an agency employee. The court issued an injunction in this case, and, in spite of appeals, the injunction was not repealed.

The second case was initiated by Alfred A. Knopf, a publisher, and Marchetti and John Marks, coauthors of a book entitled *The CIA and the Cult of Intelligence.* This case cited the injunction that had been issued in the first case, and questioned the appropriateness of the deletions that had been made to the manuscript by the government. In this case, the court decided in favor of Marchetti, but this decision was overturned upon appeal by the government.

The implications of the case were significant. For the first time in history, the CIA had taken the initiative in the courts to prevent the unauthorized disclosure of intelligence sources and methods. In essence, the court "had affirmed the sanctity of a contract."

References
Godson, Roy, ed. *Intelligence Problems for the 1980s, Number 1: Elements of Intelligence.* Rev. ed. Washington, DC: National Strategy Information Center, 1983.

Kornblum, Allan. *Intelligence and the Law: Cases and Materials.* Vol. IV. Washington, DC: DIC, 1987.

Oseth, John M. *Regulating U.S. Intelligence Operations: A Study in the Definition of the National Interest.* Frankfurt: University of Kentucky Press, 1985.

Warner, John S. "The Marchetti Case: New Case Law." Unpublished manuscript, 1983.

—**MARK BIAS,** a baud-based system term used in communications intelligence, communications security, operations security, and signals analysis, is the consistent lengthening of the mark elements with a corresponding shortening of the space elements. *See also:* Communications Security.

References
Department of Defense, U.S. Army. *Counter-Signals Intelligence (C-SIGINT) Operations.* Field Manual FM 34-62. Washington, DC: Headquarters, Department of the Army, 1986.

————. *Military Intelligence Battalion Combat Electronic Warfare and Intelligence (Aerial Exploitation) (Corps).* Field Manual FM 34-22. Washington, DC: Headquarters, Department of the Army, 1984.

————. *Military Intelligence Battalion (CEWI) (Tactical Exploitation) (Corps): Counterintelligence, Interrogation, Electronic Warfare.* Field Manual FM 34-23. Washington, DC: Headquarters, Department of the Army, 1985.

————. *Military Intelligence Company (Combat Electronic Warfare and Intelligence) (Armored*

Cavalry Regiment/Separate Brigade). Field Manual FM 34-30. Washington, DC: Headquarters, Department of the Army, 1983.

—**MARKINGS CENTER BRIEFS (MCBS)** are prepared by the Defense Intelligence Agency. They are a compendium of special studies that provide production estimates on selected Communist-manufactured war matériel. *See also:* Defense Intelligence Agency.

References

Von Hoene, John P. A. *Intelligence User's Guide.* Washington, DC: DIA, 1983.

—**MARTIN, WILLIAM H.,** an employee at the National Security Agency, defected to the Soviet Union in 1960.

References

Allen, Thomas B., and Polmar, Norman. *Merchants of Treason: America's Secrets for Sale.* New York: Delacorte Press, 1988.

—**MASKING** is a term used in signals intelligence and electronic warfare. It is any active or passive jamming that is intended specifically to prevent the recognition of true information by a receiving system by masking true data with a high density of false data. *See also:* Jamming, Signals Intelligence.

References

Department of Defense, U.S. Army. *Counter-Signals Intelligence (C-SIGINT) Operations.* Field Manual FM 34-62. Washington, DC: Headquarters, Department of the Army, 1986.

———. *Military Intelligence Battalion Combat Electronic Warfare and Intelligence (Aerial Exploitation) (Corps).* Field Manual FM 34-22. Washington, DC: Headquarters, Department of the Army, 1984.

———. *Military Intelligence Battalion (CEWI) (Tactical Exploitation) (Corps): Counterintelligence, Interrogation, Electronic Warfare.* Field Manual FM 34-23. Washington, DC: Headquarters, Department of the Army, 1985.

———. *Military Intelligence Company (Combat Electronic Warfare and Intelligence) (Armored Cavalry Regiment/Separate Brigade).* Field Manual FM 34-30. Washington, DC: Headquarters, Department of the Army, 1983.

—**MATERIAL SYMBOL (MATSYM),** in communications security (COMSEC), means an unclassified identifier for certain key cards for resupply purposes. *See also:* Communications Security.

References

Department of Defense, U.S. Army. *Counter-Signals Intelligence (C-SIGINT) Operations.* Field Manual FM 34-62. Washington, DC: Headquarters, Department of the Army, 1986.

———. *Military Intelligence Battalion Combat Electronic Warfare and Intelligence (Aerial Exploitation) (Corps).* Field Manual FM 34-22. Washington, DC: Headquarters, Department of the Army, 1984.

———. *Military Intelligence Battalion (CEWI) (Tactical Exploitation) (Corps): Counterintelligence, Interrogation, Electronic Warfare.* Field Manual FM 34-23. Washington, DC: Headquarters, Department of the Army, 1985.

———. *Military Intelligence Company (Combat Electronic Warfare and Intelligence) (Armored Cavalry Regiment/Separate Brigade).* Field Manual FM 34-30. Washington, DC: Headquarters, Department of the Army, 1983.

—**MAYDAY BOOK** is a term used in clandestine and covert intelligence operations. It is a detailed book with the exact procedures to be followed if an agent believes that he is about to be arrested. *See also:* Surrounded.

References

Becket, Henry S. A. *The Dictionary of Espionage: Spookspeak into English.* New York: Stein and Day, 1986.

—**MC CONE, JOHN,** was born on January 4, 1902, in San Francisco, California. He attended the University of California and spent his early years in private business. In 1947 and 1948, he served as a member of the President's Air Policy Commission and then served as deputy to the secretary of defense from March to November 1948. In 1950, he became under secretary of the Air Force, serving in this capacity until 1951. From 1958 until 1960, he was chairman of the Atomic Energy Commission, and he was appointed by President Kennedy as director of Central Intelligence on September 27, 1961, was sworn in as a recess appointee on November 29, 1961, and was confirmed by the Senate on January 31, 1962. He resigned on April 25, 1965, and returned to private business. In 1983, he served on the President's Commission on Strategic Forces.

The appointment of McCone augured a significant change in the agency's orientation. McCone, who had pursued a successful career in business and government, was more interested in intelligence production than in operations, and this had a decidedly positive effect on the quality of the agency's intelligence output. In 1963, he established the National Intelligence Programs Evaluation (NIPE), to evaluate and review Intelligence Community programs, their cost-effectiveness, and the effectiveness of the United States Intelligence Board. Additionally, McCone took an active interest in the production of the National Intelligence Estimates, leading to a much more accurate intelligence picture of Cuba during the missile crisis in 1962 than had existed in 1961 during the Bay of Pigs invasion.

McCone's influence declined significantly after President Kennedy's assassination. President Johnson had less interest in intelligence than did Kennedy, and he preferred to work through the Departments of State and Defense. When McCone and Johnson disagreed over U.S. participation in Vietnam, with McCone arguing for a direct approach to the problem and Johnson preferring an incremental approach concerning U.S. involvement, McCone resigned.

In summary, McCone should be viewed as one of the best directors of Central Intelligence. He was the right man at the right time, in that he took an agency that was depressed from its role in the Bay of Pigs and he turned it around. His efforts for improving the analytical and estimative production of the agency met with substantial success, and the agency profited from his leadership. *See also:* Central Intelligence Agency.

References

Breckinridge, Scott D. *The CIA and the U.S. Intelligence System.* Boulder, CO: Westview Press, 1986.

Brinkley, David A., and Hull, Andrew W. *Estimative Intelligence: A Textbook on the History, Products, Uses and Writing of Intelligence Estimates.* Columbus, OH: Battelle, 1979.

Godson, Roy, ed. *Intelligence Problems for the 1980s, Number 1: Elements of Intelligence.* Rev. ed. Washington, DC: National Strategy Information Center, 1983.

Laqueur, Walter. *A World of Secrets.* New York: Basic Books, 1985.

Lowenthal, Mark M. *U.S. Intelligence: Evolution and Anatomy.* New York: Praeger, 1984.

Maurer, Alfred C.; Turnstall, Marion D.; and Keagle, James M. *Intelligence Policy and Process.* Boulder, CO: Westview Press, 1985.

Turner, Stansfield. *Secrecy and Democracy: The CIA in Transition.* Boston: Houghton Mifflin, 1985.

U.S. Congress. Senate. *Alleged Assassination Plots Involving Foreign Leaders: An Interim Report of the Select Committee to Study Governmental Operations with Respect to Intelligence Activities.* 94th Congress, 1st sess., Nov. 20, 1975. S. Rept. 94-465.

Von Hoene, John P. A. *Intelligence User's Guide.* Washington, DC: DIA, 1983.

—**MCMAHON, JOHN,** served as deputy director of Central Intelligence from June 10, 1982, until March 28, 1986. *See also:* Central Intelligence Agency.

References

Treverton, Gregory F. *Covert Action: The Limits of Intervention in the Postwar World.* New York: Basic Books, 1987.

Turner, Stansfield. *Secrecy and Democracy: The CIA in Transition.* Boston: Houghton Mifflin, 1985.

—**MEACONING** is an electronic warfare term. It is a system of receiving beacon signals and then rebroadcasting them on the same frequency to confuse navigation. Meaconing stations cause inaccurate bearings to be obtained by aircraft and ground stations. *See also:* Jamming.

References

Department of Defense, Joint Chiefs of Staff. *Department of Defense Dictionary of Military and Related Terms.* Washington, DC: GPO, 1986.

—**MEACONING, INTRUSION, JAMMING, AND INTERFERENCE (MIJI)** is a form of electronic warfare that is used to disrupt hostile navigational or communications equipment.

References

Department of Defense, Joint Chiefs of Staff. *Department of Defense Dictionary of Military and Related Terms.* Washington, DC: GPO, 1986.

—**MEASLES** is a term used in clandestine and covert intelligence operations. It refers to a killing that is done so expertly that it appears that the death was due to natural causes. *See also:* Active Measures, Assassination, Demote Maximally, Executive Action, Heavy Mob, Special Activities, Terminate With Extreme Prejudice.

References

Becket, Henry S. A. *The Dictionary of Espionage: Spookspeak into English.* New York: Stein and Day, 1986.

Deacon, Richard. *Spyclopedia: An Encyclopedia of Spies, Secret Services, Operations, Jargon, and All Subjects Related to the World of Espionage.* London: Macdonald, 1987.

—**MEASUREMENT AND SIGNATURE INTELLI-GENCE (MASINT)** is scientific and technical intelligence information that is obtained by the quantitative and qualitative analysis of metric, angle, spatial, wavelength, modulation, plasma, hydromagnetic, and other data derived from specific technical sensors in order to identify any distinctive features associated with the source, emitter, or sender and to enable the subsequent identification and measurement of the same. MASINT includes but is not limited to the following disciplines: radar intelligence (RADINT); nuclear intelligence (NUCINT); radiation intelligence (RINT); acoustical intelligence (ACOUSTINT or ACINT); electro-optical intelligence (ELECTRO-OPINT); event-related dynamic measurements photography (OPTINT); and debris collection. *See also:* Scientific and Technical Intelligence.

References

Department of Defense, Defense Intelligence College. *Glossary of Intelligence Terms and Definitions.* Washington, DC: DIC, 1987.

Department of Defense, Joint Chiefs of Staff. *Department of Defense Dictionary of Military and Related Terms.* Washington, DC: GPO, 1986.

Department of Defense, U.S. Army. *Military Intelligence Battalion (CEWI) (Tactical Exploitation) (Corps): Counterintelligence, Interrogation, Electronic Warfare.* Field Manual FM 34-23. Washington, DC: Headquarters, Department of the Army, 1985.

Laqueur, Walter. *A World of Secrets.* New York: Basic Books, 1985.

—**MEDICAL INTELLIGENCE (MEDINT).** (1) Medical intelligence is foreign intelligence concerning all aspects of foreign natural and man-made environments that could affect the health of military forces. Medical intelligence includes general medical intelligence, which is concerned with foreign biological and medical capabilities and health situations, and medical scientific and technical intelligence, which assesses and pre-

dicts technological advances that have medical significance, including defense against chemical, biological, and radiological warfare. Medical intelligence has applicability to both tactical and strategic planning and operations, including military and humanitarian efforts. (2) Medical intelligence has also been defined by the Defense Intelligence Agency for one of its functional areas. It means "professional activities dealing with the collection, evaluation, analysis, classification, interpretation, and production of intelligence of foreign medical, bio-scientific materiel and environmental information, epidemiological information, flora, fauna, sanitary conditions, foreign field medical delivery systems, and capabilities for strategic and tactical military medical planning and operations."

References

Department of Defense, Defense Intelligence Agency. *Defense Intelligence Agency Manual 22-2.* Washington, DC: DIA, 1979.

Department of Defense, Defense Intelligence College. *Glossary of Intelligence Terms and Definitions.* Washington, DC: DIC, 1987.

Department of Defense, Joint Chiefs of Staff. *Department of Defense Dictionary of Military and Related Terms.* Washington, DC: GPO, 1986.

Godson, Roy, ed. *Intelligence Problems for the 1980s, Number 1: Elements of Intelligence.* Rev. ed. Washington, DC: National Strategy Information Center, 1983.

Laqueur, Walter. *A World of Secrets.* New York: Basic Books, 1985.

Treverton, Gregory F. *Covert Action: The Limits of Intervention in the Postwar World.* New York: Basic Books, 1987.

—**MEDICAL INTELLIGENCE INFORMATION AGENCY (MIIA).** *See:* Armed Forces Medical Intelligence Center (AFMIC).

—**MEDIUM-RANGE BALLISTIC MISSILE (MRBM)** is a ballistic missile with a range from 600 to 1,500 nautical miles.

References

Department of Defense, Joint Chiefs of Staff. *Department of Defense Dictionary of Military and Related Terms.* Washington, DC: GPO, 1986.

—**MEET AREA,** in FBI terminology, is the area surrounding a meeting site. *See also:* Alternate Meet, Blind Dating, Movements Analysis, Pavement Artists, Riding Shotgun, Shadow, Shaking Off the Dogs, Shaking the Tree, Stroller, Walk-Past, Wash, What's Your Twenty?

References

Kessler, Ronald. *Spy vs. Spy: Stalking Soviet Spies in America.* New York: Charles Scribner's Sons, 1988.

—**MEMORANDUM OF AGREEMENT (MOA)** is a written agreement between different military units that explains how they will support each other. Tenant commands, i.e., those that are located on the property or in the facilities of a parent command, will have an MOA regarding the use of the parent command's facilities.

References

Department of Defense, Defense Intelligence Agency. *Defense Intelligence Agency Manual.* Washington, DC: DIA, 1987.

—**MERCHANT INTELLIGENCE (MERINT)** is intelligence handling and communications instructions for merchant ship crews so that they can report vital intelligence sightings.

References

Department of Defense, Joint Chiefs of Staff. *Department of Defense Dictionary of Military and Related Terms.* Washington, DC: GPO, 1986.

—**MESSAGE** is any thought or idea that is expressed briefly in plain, coded, or secret language and is prepared in any form that is suitable for transmission by any means of communication. *See also:* Communications Security.

References

Department of Defense, Joint Chiefs of Staff. *Department of Defense Dictionary of Military and Related Terms.* Washington, DC: GPO, 1986.

Godson, Roy, ed. *Intelligence Problems for the 1980s, Number 1: Elements of Intelligence.* Rev. ed. Washington, DC: National Strategy Information Center, 1983.

Laqueur, Walter. *A World of Secrets.* New York: Basic Books, 1985.

—**MESSAGE INDICATOR** is a communications term that means a group of symbols that are usually placed at the beginning of the text of an encrypted text or transmission and that establish the starting point of the key cycle. *See also:* Communications Security.

References

Department of Defense, Defense Intelligence Agency. *Defense Intelligence Agency Manual.* Washington, DC: DIA, 1987.

Department of Defense, Defense Intelligence College. *Glossary of Intelligence Terms and Definitions.* Washington, DC: DIC, 1987.

Department of Defense, Joint Chiefs of Staff. *Department of Defense Dictionary of Military and Related Terms.* Washington, DC: GPO, 1986.

—**METEOROLOGICAL INTELLIGENCE.** *See:* Geographical Intelligence.

—**MICE** is a CIA acronym that addresses the four most common reasons for KGB defections: money, ideology, compromise, and ego.

References

Becket, Henry S. A. *The Dictionary of Espionage: Spookspeak into English.* New York: Stein and Day, 1986.

Deacon, Richard. *Spyclopedia: An Encyclopedia of Spies, Secret Services, Operations, Jargon, and All Subjects Related to the World of Espionage.* London: Macdonald, 1987.

Ranelagh, John. *The Agency: The Rise and Decline of the CIA.* New York: Simon and Schuster, 1986.

—**MICROFICHE** is a sheet of microfilm that contains rows of microimages of pages of printed matter.

References

Department of Defense, Defense Intelligence Agency. *Defense Intelligence Agency Manual.* Washington, DC: DIA, 1987.

Department of Defense, Joint Chiefs of Staff. *Department of Defense Dictionary of Military and Related Terms.* Washington, DC: GPO, 1986.

Laqueur, Walter. *A World of Secrets.* New York: Basic Books, 1985.

—**MICROFILM** is a film that bears a photographic record of printed or other graphic matter on a reduced scale.

References

Department of Defense, Joint Chiefs of Staff. *Department of Defense Dictionary of Military and Related Terms.* Washington, DC: GPO, 1986.

Laqueur, Walter. *A World of Secrets.* New York: Basic Books, 1985.

—**MICROWAVE.** *See:* Radar Intelligence, Side-looking Airborne Radar (SLAR).

—**MICROWAVE RELAY,** as defined by the Church Committee, is a process for propagating tele-communications over long distances by using radio signals that are relayed by several stations that are located within "line of sight" of each other.

References

U.S. Congress. Senate. *Final Report of the Senate Select Committee to Study Government Operations with Respect to Intelligence Activities. Report 94-755. Book I, Foreign and Military Intelligence.* Washington, DC: GPO, 1976.

—**MILITARY CAPABILITIES** is an official term that has been defined by the Defense Intelligence Agency for one of its functional areas. It means "the study and analysis of intelligence on military ground, naval, air, and paramilitary forces to include their organization and equipment, order of battle, doctrine, tactics and training; the evaluation of capabilities, vulnerabilities, and ability by the governments, and military forces of an assigned geographic area to execute a specified or probable course of action."

References

Department of Defense, Defense Intelligence Agency. *Defense Intelligence Agency Manual 22-2.* Washington, DC: DIA, 1979.

Department of Defense, Joint Chiefs of Staff. *Department of Defense Dictionary of Military and Related Terms.* Washington, DC: GPO, 1986.

—**MILITARY CAPABILITIES STUDY** of NATO countries is produced by the Defense Intelligence Agency. It describes the NATO organization, analyzes both the military and the political postures of NATO countries, and provides a comprehensive description of each country's armed forces. *See also:* Defense Intelligence Agency.

References

Treverton, Gregory F. *Covert Action: The Limits of Intervention in the Postwar World.* New York: Basic Books, 1987.

Von Hoene, John P. A. *Intelligence User's Guide.* Washington, DC: DIA, 1983.

—**MILITARY DECEPTION,** an Army tactical intelligence (TACINT) term, means the actions that are executed to mislead foreign decisionmakers, causing them to derive and accept certain estimates of their opponent's military capabilities, intentions, operations, or other activities that will prompt actions or responses from these decisionmakers that will contribute to the achievement of their opponent's objectives.

References

Department of Defense, U.S. Army. *Counter-Signals Intelligence (C-SIGINT) Operations.* Field Manual FM 34-62. Washington, DC: Headquarters, Department of the Army, 1986.

Military Intelligence Battalion Combat Electronic Warfare and Intelligence (Aerial Exploitation) (Corps). Field Manual FM 34-22. Washington, DC: Headquarters, Department of the Army, 1984.

————. *Military Intelligence Battalion (CEWI) (Tactical Exploitation) (Corps): Counterintelligence, Interrogation, Electronic Warfare.* Field Manual FM 34-23. Washington, DC: Headquarters, Department of the Army, 1985.

————. *Military Intelligence Company (Combat Electronic Warfare and Intelligence) (Armored Cavalry Regiment/Separate Brigade).* Field Manual FM 34-30. Washington, DC: Headquarters, Department of the Army, 1983.

—**MILITARY DEPARTMENT INTELLIGENCE CHIEFS (MDICS)** are the deputy chief of staff for intelligence, Department of the Army, the assistant chief of naval operations (intelligence), and the assistant chief of staff, intelligence, Department of the Air Force.

References

Corson, William R. *The Armies of Ignorance: The Rise of the American Intelligence Empire.* New York: Dial Press, 1977.

—**MILITARY GEOGRAPHICAL INTELLIGENCE.** *See:* Geographical Intelligence.

—**MILITARY INTELLIGENCE (MI)** is basic, current, or estimative intelligence on any foreign military or military-related situation or activity that is significant to military policymaking or to the planning and conduct of military operations and activities. In the indications and warning (I&W) context, military intelligence means analyzed, evaluated, and interpreted information on foreign nations that: (a) describes and defines the military forces of the country and their capabilities for both offense and defense, and assesses the military strategy, tactics and doctrine of a nation, as well as estimating its probable use of military force; and (b) provides decisionmakers, planners, and commanders with the data that is needed to chose courses of action required to counter foreign military threats, and to conduct operations with U.S. forces, if necessary.

References

Corson, William R. *The Armies of Ignorance: The Rise of the American Intelligence Empire.* New York: Dial Press, 1977.

Department of Defense, Defense Intelligence College. *Glossary of Intelligence Terms and Definitions.* Washington, DC: DIC 1987.

Department of Defense, Joint Chiefs of Staff. *Department of Defense Dictionary of Military and Related Terms.* Washington, DC: GPO, 1986.

Department of Defense, U.S. Army. *Counter-Signals Intelligence (C-SIGINT) Operations.* Field Manual FM 34-62. Washington, DC: Headquarters, Department of the Army, 1986.

Godson, Roy, ed. *Intelligence Problems for the 1980s, Number 4: Covert Action.* Washington, DC: National Strategy Information Center, 1981.

Kent, Sherman. *Strategic Intelligence for American World Policy.* Princeton, NJ: Princeton University Press, 1966.

Laqueur, Walter. *A World of Secrets.* New York: Basic Books, 1985.

Quirk, John; Phillips, David; Cline, Ray; and Pforzheimer, Walter. *The Central Intelligence Agency: A Photographic History.* Guilford, CT: Foreign Intelligence Press, 1986.

Turner, Stansfield. *Secrecy and Democracy: The CIA in Transition.* Boston: Houghton Mifflin, 1985.

—**MILITARY INTELLIGENCE BATTALION COMBAT ELECTRONIC WARFARE AND INTELLIGENCE (AERIAL EXPLOITATION) (CORPS) (AEB)** provides aerial reconnaissance, surveillance, and electronic warfare target acquisition support to the corps. It is organized in three companies:

Headquarters, Headquarters and Service Company provides command and control and support for all elements assigned or attached to the battalion. It is composed of a company headquarters, a food service section, a telecommunications center section, and a service platoon.

Aerial Surveillance Company provides surveillance and reconnaissance support to the corps. The company plans and conducts aerial

reconnaissance and surveillance of routes, zones, areas, coastlines, and borders using side-looking airborne radar (SLAR), infrared, photographic, and visual means. Combat information and imagery intelligence (IMINT) are reported to the supported unit and to the Corps Tactical Operations Center (CTOC) support element. The aerial surveillance company is composed of the following: (1) Company headquarters. (2) Two flight platoons, which assure that aircraft and crews are available to meet mission requirements (each flight platoon has two flight sections that provide near all-weather day and night surveillance using day and night sensors and visual means). (3) An imagery interpretation section, which processes infrared and photographic imagery that is obtained by the company. (4) A service platoon, which maintains the aircraft and systems, and is composed of a platoon headquarters, an aviation unit maintenance section, and a surveillance systems repair section. (5) A data terminal section, which provides combat information to the corps.

Aerial Electronic Warfare Company provides signals collection and processing support to the corps. It plans and conducts aerial signals collection missions, processes the intercepted signals, and reports on them. This company is organized in the following manner: (1) Company headquarters. (2) A flight platoon, which provides aerial communications intelligence (COMINT) and electronic intelligence (ELINT) collection support to the corps. It is subdivided into a platoon headquarters; a communications intelligence aircraft section, which provides the GUARDRAIL aircraft and crews that are needed to accomplish the aerial COMINT collection mission; and a noncommunications electronic intelligence aircraft section, which provides the QUICKLOOK aircraft and pilots to accomplish the noncommunications ELINT collection mission. (3) An operations platoon, which performs ground-based processing and reporting of collected SIGINT data. It is subdivided into a platoon headquarters; a collection and direction finding section that remotely operates the collection and direction finding (DF) subsystems onboard GUARDRAIL aircraft from ground-based processing facilities; an analysis and reporting section, which analyzes the data that is received from the GUARDRAIL aircraft, and for reporting combat information, electronic warfare data, and special intelligence (SI) technical information to designated recipients; and a noncommunications electronic intelligence processing section, which provides the ground processing, reporting, and tasking effort for the QUICK-LOOK system. (4) A service platoon, which maintains the aircraft and the collection systems.

References

Department of Defense, U.S. Army. *Counter-Signals Intelligence (C-SIGINT) Operations.* Field Manual FM 34-62. Washington, DC: Headquarters, Department of the Army, 1986.

———. *Military Intelligence Battalion Combat Electronic Warfare and Intelligence (Aerial Exploitation) (Corps).* Field Manual FM 34-22. Washington, DC: Headquarters, Department of the Army, 1984.

———. *Military Intelligence Battalion (CEWI) (Tactical Exploitation) (Corps): Counterintelligence, Interrogation, Electronic Warfare.* Field Manual FM 34-23. Washington, DC: Headquarters, Department of the Army, 1985.

———. *Military Intelligence Company (Combat Electronic Warfare and Intelligence) (Armored Cavalry Regiment/Separate Brigade).* Field Manual FM 34-30. Washington, DC: Headquarters, Department of the Army, 1983.

—MILITARY INTELLIGENCE BATTALION (COMBAT ELECTRONIC WARFARE AND IN-TELLIGENCE) (CEWI) (OPERATIONS) (CORPS),

commonly referred to as the operations battalion, is the nerve center of corps intelligence operations. The operations battalion is organic to the Military Intelligence Brigade at corps level. It is composed of operating elements that perform a variety of functions in support of corps intelligence and electronic warfare (IEW) operations. The key functions of the battalion are to provide a corps tactical operations center (CTOC) support element, a technical control and analysis element (TCAE), and communications to support MI group operations.

References

Department of Defense, U.S. Army. *Counter-Signals Intelligence (C-SIGINT) Operations.* Field Manual FM 34-62. Washington, DC: Headquarters, Department of the Army, 1986.

———. *Military Intelligence Battalion Combat Electronic Warfare and Intelligence (Aerial Exploitation) (Corps).* Field Manual FM 34-22. Washington, DC: Headquarters, Department of the Army, 1984.

———. *Military Intelligence Battalion (CEWI) (Tactical Exploitation) (Corps): Counterintelligence, Interrogation, Electronic Warfare.* Field Manual FM 34-23. Washington, DC: Headquarters, Department of the Army, 1985.

———. *Military Intelligence Company (Combat Electronic Warfare and Intelligence) (Armored Cavalry Regiment/Separate Brigade).* Field Manual FM 34-30. Washington, DC: Headquarters, Department of the Army, 1983.

—MILITARY INTELLIGENCE BATTALION (CEWI) (TACTICAL EXPLOITATION) (CORPS)

provides electronic warfare, enemy prisoner of war (EPW) interrogation and document review, counterintelligence (CI), and operations security (OPSEC) support to the Army corps. Its specific mission is defined as providing: EPW, linecrosser, and refugee interrogation and document exploitation; CI and OPSEC support; ground-based signals intelligence (SIGINT) collection, processing, and reporting; and ground-based electronic countermeasures (ECM) and electronic support measures (ESM).

In order to accomplish this mission, the battalion is organized in the following manner: (1) A battalion headquarters, headquarters and service company. (2) An interrogation company, consisting of (a) a company headquarters; (b) an operations platoon, which provides support to interrogation operations, consisting of an operations and processing section; a document exploitation section, which reads and exploits captured enemy documents; and a signals intelligence/electronic warfare (SIGINT/EW) exploitation section; (c) an interrogation platoon, which will interrogate prisoners of war, line crossers, and detainees. (3) A counterintelligence company, consisting of (a) a company headquarters; (b) an operations section, which plans, coordinates, and schedules counterintelligence operations; (c) a counterintelligence (CI) platoon, which conducts CI operations; and (d) a signals security platoon, which provides radio and telephone monitoring in support of the corps OPSEC program. (4) An electronic warfare company, consisting of (a) a company headquarters; (b) an operations platoon, which is designed to exploit enemy electronic command and control, weapons, radar, and communication systems, composed of a platoon headquarters; a report and analysis team, which is part of the company's command and control system; a transcription and analysis team, which supports the platoon's voice collection teams; voice collection teams, which intercept and record enemy voice and Morse communications; electronic intelligence intercept teams, which intercept and report on enemy noncommunications electronic emissions; VHF electronic countermeasures teams, which conduct jamming and deception operations; and a multichannel intercept section, which intercepts, processes, and reports on enemy multichannel communications; (c) an HF intercept platoon, which can intercept and can jam enemy HF communications, composed of a platoon headquarters; an HF analysis team, which processes collected information; an HF intercept section, which intercepts enemy HF communications; and HF electronic countermeasures teams, which can disrupt enemy voice and other HF communications by jamming and intrusion.

References

Department of Defense, U.S. Army. *Counter-Signals Intelligence (C-SIGINT) Operations.* Field Manual FM 34-62. Washington, DC: Headquarters, Department of the Army, 1986.

————. *Military Intelligence Battalion Combat Electronic Warfare and Intelligence (Aerial Exploitation) (Corps).* Field Manual FM 34-22. Washington, DC: Headquarters, Department of the Army, 1984.

————. *Military Intelligence Company (Combat Electronic Warfare and Intelligence) (Armored Cavalry Regiment/Separate Brigade).* Field Manual FM 34-30. Washington, DC: Headquarters, Department of the Army, 1983.

—MILITARY INTELLIGENCE BRIGADE (COMBAT ELECTRONIC WARFARE AND INTELLIGENCE) (CEWI) (CORPS)

is structured to support a corps having combat divisions, and an Armored Cavalry Regiment (ACR). Brigade assets are task organized to support corps combat operations as well as similar operations by the corps' subordinate commands. The MI Brigade is composed of the following:

Headquarters and Headquarters Detachment (HHD) provides command and control of assigned or attached units or elements, including specialized intelligence, electronic warfare (EW) and operations security (OPSEC) support attachments.

Tactical Exploitation Battalion (TEB) provides interrogation, counterintelligence (CI), ground-based SIGINT and EW, and OPSEC support for the corps.

Aerial Exploitation Battalion (AEB) provides SIGINT collection, analysis, processing, and reporting; aerial surveillance (AS) support; and exploitation of collected imagery. Aerial reconnaissance is provided by the AS company using side-looking airborne radar (SLAR), infrared (IR), photographic, and visual means.

Operations Battalion, which is organized as follows: (1) Headquarters, Headquarters and Service Company (HH&S) provides command and control of assigned and attached elements. The H&HS, in turn, is composed of headquarters and service companies, service platoons and sections. (2) Operations Company, which is composed of (a) company headquarters, which provides command and control of assigned and attached elements; and (b) a Corps Tactical Operations Center (CTOC) support element, which provides the Corps G2 with intelligence and counterintelligence planning and intelligence collection, management, production and dissemination. The element is composed of:

- the collection management and dissemination (CM&D) section, which provides collection management and intelligence dissemination;
- the intelligence production section (IPS), which provides all-source intelligence production, maintains the intelligence data base, and identifies gaps in the intelligence effort (it, with the assistance of the terrain team (corps) and the USAF weather team, performs intelligence preparation of the battlefield);
- the OPSEC management and analysis (M&A) section, which provides counterintelligence, OPSEC, and deception planning and assistance;
- the electronic warfare (EW) section, which plans EW operations and recommends task organization and allocation of EW resources;
- the tactical command post (TACCP) section, which provides limited intelligence and electronic warfare (IEW) support to the corps TACCP while maintaining continuous communications with the CM&D section;
- the imagery interpretation (II) section, which exploits imagery for the corps;
- the USAF weather team, which provides the staff weather officer, weather observation, and forecast support to the corps;
- the terrain team, which provides terrain intelligence assistance and performs other functions as well;
- the mission control section, which provides technical control of SIGINT and EW assets;
- the process and analysis section, which establishes and maintains the technical data base in support of EW and SIGINT tasking;

- the traffic analysis team, which performs second-level analysis of intercepted enemy communications;
- the cryptanalysis team, which provides an enemy code and cipher exploitation capability;
- the electronic intelligence (ELINT) analysis team, which correlates and analyzes all enemy noncommunications intercepts;
- the language support team, which transcribes, translates, and processes selected plain-text communications; and
- the SIGINT integration and reporting section, which produces SIGINT-derived intelligence.

(3) Communications Company provides communications support to the group, including: radiotypewriter (RATT) communications; telecommunications centers (TCC); wire and switchboard services; secure FM voice retransmission; and organic maintenance of equipment and maintenance of the USAF weather team communications equipment. It is composed of the following:

- the company headquarters, which provides command and control of assigned and attached elements;
- the CTOC TCC platoon, which operates a message center and terminals for the corps CTOC support element and the special security officer (SSO);
- the CTOC RATT platoon, which operates RATT equipment at the CTOC in support of the CM&D section and the SSO; it also supports divisions, brigades and platoons by sending teams;
- the TCAE RATT platoon, which provides RATT support to the TCAE and deployed RATT teams and other entities;
- the staff/administrative RATT section, which provides additional RATT links for the CTOC and other elements;
- the support/maintenance platoon, which is organized with a platoon headquarters, a C-E maintenance section, a tactical wire section, and a radio transmission section; it provides C-E and COMSEC maintenance support for the battalion and the group HHD, tactical wire communications support for the group CP and the CTOC support element, and radio transmission stations for critical group FM nets; and
- the USAF weather team, which provides communications equipment that is used by the USAF team.

References
Department of Defense, U.S. Army. *Military Intelligence Battalion (CEWI) (Operations) (Corps)*. Field Manual 34-21. Washington, DC: Headquarters, Department of the Army, 1982.

———. *Military Intelligence Group (Combat Electronic Warfare and Intelligence) (Corps)*. Field Manual FM 34-20. Washington, DC: Headquarters, Department of the Army, 1983.

—MILITARY INTELLIGENCE COMPANY (COMBAT ELECTRONIC WARFARE AND INTELLIGENCE) (ARMORED CAVALRY REGIMENT/SEPARATE BRIGADE) has been developed specifically to support the Armored Cavalry Regiment (ACR) and separate brigade on the battlefield. It provides intelligence collection, integration, multisource analysis, electronic warfare and operations security (OPSEC) support on a task organized basis. The company is organized to provide centralized control and decentralized execution. It operates under the command and control of the regimental/brigade commander and the staff supervision of the regimental/brigade S2/S3. In order to accomplish its missions, the MI company is organized in the following manner: (1) Company headquarters, which provides command and control for assigned and attached elements. It is composed of a commander, a first sergeant and administrative personnel. (2) A service platoon, which provides essential services. (3) A communications platoon, which provides the company's telecommunications and radio teletypewriter (RATT) support. This platoon is composed of (a) a platoon headquarters; (b) a telecommunications center section, which provides telecommunications; (c) a radio teletypewriter (RATT) section, which mans the RATTs; and (d) the equipment for the USAF weather section. (4) A tactical operations center support platoon, which assists in analyzing and directing the electronic warfare, OPSEC and intelligence missions. This platoon is composed of (a) a platoon headquarters; (b) a collection management and dissemination section, which drafts collection plans and provides inputs to intelligence reports, plans, annexes, and other intelligence documents; (c) an intelligence production section, which performs all-source analysis and production, and maintains the electronic warfare data base; and (d) a technical control and analysis section, which provides detailed mission tasking to the electronic warfare and flight platoons. (5) Electronic warfare platoons, which are organized in the following manner: (a) a transcription/analysis team; (b) a voice collection team, which intercepts enemy HF and VHF communications; (c) a noncommunications collection team, which provides information on noncommunications emitters; (d) an HF/VHF electronic countermeasures team, which can jam enemy HF and VHF communications; (e) a VHF electronic countermeasures team, which can jam enemy VHF communications; and (f) a remote sensor team, which provides warning, combat surveillance and target acquisition support. (6) A surveillance platoon, consisting of (a) a platoon headquarters; (b) surveillance squads, which provide radar surveillance; (c) ground surveillance radar teams, which provide additional radar surveillance support; and (d) an operations support section, which is composed of a section headquarters; an interrogation team, which will question prisoners of war, refugees and detainees, and review captured documents; and an OPSEC support team, which provides counterintelligence and operations security support. (7) A flight platoon, which provides airborne intercept, direction finding, and jamming support.

References

Department of Defense, U.S. Army. *Military Intelligence Company (Combat Electronic Warfare and Intelligence) (Armored Cavalry Regiment/ Separate Brigade).* Field Manual FM 34-30. Washington, DC: Headquarters, Department of the Army, 1983.

————. *Military Intelligence Battalion (CEWI) (Tactical Exploitation) (Corps): Counterintelligence, Interrogation, Electronic Warfare.* Field Manual FM 34-23. Washington, DC: Headquarters, Department of the Army, 1985.

—**MILITARY INTELLIGENCE DIVISION (MID)** was an early intelligence branch of the U.S. Army. It carried on military intelligence operations in the United States during World War I. It continued into World War II and rapidly became the Army's largest staff element. However, in a significant reorganization in 1942, the MID became the Military Intelligence Service, which remained subordinate to the General Staff.

References

Corson, William R. *The Armies of Ignorance: The Rise of the American Intelligence Empire.* New York: Dial Press, 1977.

Finnegan, John P. *Military History: A Picture History.* Arlington, VA: U.S. Army Intelligence and Security Command, 1984.

Lowenthal, Mark M. *U.S. Intelligence: Evolution and Anatomy.* New York: Praeger, 1984.

—**MILITARY INTELLIGENCE INTEGRATED DATA SYSTEM (MIIDS)** is an intelligence management system. The Project Management Office for the MIIDS is the Defense Intelligence Agency's Directorate for Foreign Intelligence (VP). *See also:* Defense Intelligence Agency.

References

Department of Defense, Defense Intelligence Agency. *Organization, Mission, and Key Personnel.* Washington, DC: DIA, 1986.

—**MILITARY INTELLIGENCE SERVICE (MIS)** was created in 1942 as a result of a massive Army reorganization. It was set up to fulfill the mission of the Military Intelligence Division, which was abolished by the reorganization. The MIS collected and produced intelligence that it received from its overseas teams and headquarters production elements. It also administered a semiautonomous multidisciplined intelligence element, the American Intelligence Service, and disseminated sensitive cryptological intelligence through its Special Branch.

References

Corson, William R. *The Armies of Ignorance: The Rise of the American Intelligence Empire.* New York: Dial Press, 1977.

Finnegan, John P. *Military Intelligence: A Picture History.* Arlington, VA: U.S. Army Intelligence and Security Command, 1984.

Laqueur, Walter. *A World of Secrets.* New York: Basic Books, 1985.

Treverton, Gregory F. *Covert Action: The Limits of Intervention in the Postwar World.* New York: Basic Books, 1987.

—**MILITARY INTELLIGENCE SUMMARIES (MIS)** are produced by the Defense Intelligence Agency on individual countries. They are an eight-volume compilation (by broad geographic area) of intelligence data on ground, naval, air, missile, and paramilitary forces of foreign nations. They include assessments of military capabilities, political and economic stability, and the extent of insurgency and Communist influence. *See also:* Defense Intelligence Agency.

References

Laqueur, Walter. *A World of Secrets.* New York: Basic Books, 1985.

Treverton, Gregory F. *Covert Action: The Limits of Intervention in the Postwar World.* New York: Basic Books, 1987.

Von Hoene, John P. A. *Intelligence User's Guide.* Washington, DC: DIA, 1983.

—**MILITARY MISSION OPTIONS.** The Department of Defense has organized the U.S. warfighting capability so that the Unified and Specified Commanders (commanders-in-Chief [CINCs]) are the agents of the National Command Authority (NCA) who are responsible for implementing military action. The military options that are available to the CINC and the NCA as a possible solution to a problem cover a range of force options. The specific option that is chosen for a given situation represents a finite description (a snapshot) of what is on the continuum of force possibilities. When faced with a problem, the CINC would look at his overall military capability as well as what would be the most appropriate action for the circumstances. The CINC's regional view of the problem could be balanced by the global view of the NCA and Joint Chiefs of Staff (JCS). The NCA perspective is most sensitive to the political, diplomatic, and economic factors that would influence the solution finally chosen to satisfy national objectives. The military factor may not determine the solution to a particular problem, but it may be a part of many solutions. If the use of military force were contemplated, the NCA could provide the CINC with guidance as to the level of military force that is envisioned. Whether the CINC is involved with regional or global planning, within his area of responsibility he would most likely want to prepare for the "worst case" conditions that are envisioned in a scenario, even if a lesser application of force may be applied. As the CINC develops his mission statement, from the spectrum of force possibilities he might consider the following types of force options:

Presence. Presence is best visualized in connection with the current unified command structure. With its established unified commands, the U.S. government shows resolve on a global basis. The size or permanence of the force can vary according to the situation. Presence could be a large number of forward-deployed forces as are currently deployed in Europe, or it could be just one ship making a port call to a certain port at a critical time. The timeliness of the force may have more to do with the success of this option than the size of the force. The presence of the Military Assistance Advisory Groups (MAAGs), missions, and security assistance operations around the world relates to our level of interest and our assessment of the threat. Forward-deployed forces provide an added dimension to the U.S. global influence and represent a U.S. initiative in maintaining that influence. Presence has much to do with "showing the flag." U.S. military presence, when properly executed, is a significant source of international goodwill as well.

Show of force. A show of force is an extension of presence that stops short of bringing opposing forces together in conflict. It has been referred to as "muscle flexing" or "saber-rattling." Properly applied and timed correctly, a show of force may provide just the deterrent that is required to prevent any further escalation of hostilities. To be properly applied, the show of force must be credible in the eyes of the party that the United States is trying to influence.

Demonstration. A show of force and a demonstration are similar, but they differ in the degree of the implied threat. The purpose of a demonstration is not to seek a decision. However, the demonstration actually employs force, but it does so in a manner that is designed to warn or threaten the opposition rather than to engage in combat. A demonstration can warn the potential aggressor that the United States has the capability and the will to get as tough as necessary for the situation. A demonstration can also be staged to deceive the enemy as to our true actions. Feints of "cover and deception" movements are a form of demonstration. Normally, deception operations are used in conjunction with another action, such as an invasion.

Quarantine. This term was used during the 1962 Cuban Missile Crisis to mean, "A collective, peaceful process involving limited coercive measures interdicting the unreasonable movement of certain types of offensive military weapons and associated material by one state into the territory of another." The word, in the classic sense, means a period during which a ship is detained in isolation until it is free of a contagious disease. When both definitions are combined, the meaning becomes an act short of war that is designed to exclude specific items from movement into or from a state.

Blockade. Of the different degrees of blockade, one type is absolute, and its objective is to cut off enemy communications and commerce.

It attempts to isolate a place or region, and it could apply to all means of transportation regardless of whether the nation of registry is participating in the conflict. The target nation may consider such a total blockade as an "act of war." A lesser degree of blockade has been called a "pacific blockade." This type may or may not be perceived as an act of war. It is often limited to carriers flying the flag of the state against which retaliatory measures are taken. A blockade is a method of bringing pressure to bear on the opposition.

Force entry. This option can involve the actual use of military forces in an objective area. It is the most extreme of the mission options that are available to the CINC. In this option, U.S. forces are moved forward with the intention of engaging in combat if necessary, in order to accomplish their mission. Whether armed conflict occurs will depend on the resistance that is met. Combat operations could range from an administrative landing in order to conduct police-type operations to an outright invasion under a state of war. With an invasion, a combat assault is made against armed forces in order to gain entry into a hostile area. The point of armed conflict takes place at the point of entry. However, many U.S. plans result in administrative landings that are intended to support a friendly government. If armed conflict were to result in this case, the point of armed conflict would not be coincident with the point of entry. This option could employ some or all of the less drastic force options previously discussed.

Psychological operations (PSYOPS)/unconventional warfare (UW)/civil affairs. The joint force commander may plan for these options along with and as a part of his major operations plans. In some situations, he may use these options independently. PSYOPS try to create attitudes and behavior favorable to achieving plan objectives. UW can be military or paramilitary operations. Psychological operations and unconventional warfare operations may range from clandestine to overt actions. Civil affairs operations are those activities that embrace the relationship between our military forces and the civilian authorities and people in the objective area. Civil affairs activities normally are in support of other operations.

References

Department of Defense, Defense Intelligence Agency. *Defense Intelligence Agency Manual.* Washington, DC: DIA, 1987.

Department of Defense, Joint Chiefs of Staff. *Department of Defense Dictionary of Military and Related Terms.* Washington, DC: GPO, 1986.

Kent, Sherman. *Strategic Intelligence for American World Policy.* Princeton, NJ: Princeton University Press, 1966.

Laqueur, Walter. *A World of Secrets.* New York: Basic Books, 1985.

—**MILITARY ORDER SIGNED JUNE 13, 1942,** by President Roosevelt, entitled "Office of Strategic Services." This order disbanded the Office of Coordinator of Information and established the Office of Strategic Services (OSS). The OSS was placed under the Joint Chiefs of Staff; its duties were to collect strategic intelligence for the Joint Chiefs of Staff and to plan and conduct those special operations that were directed by the Joint Chiefs of Staff. The order also established the position of director and assigned William J. Donovan to that position.

The significance of the order was that it reflected President Roosevelt's continued dissatisfaction with the state of U.S. intelligence. The President had established the Office of Coordinator of Information in the summer of 1941 due to such apprehensions, and the Japanese success at Pearl Harbor confirmed his misgivings. In creating the OSS, Roosevelt hoped to provide the centralized intelligence entity that he felt the country needed. However, the OSS was placed under the Joint Chiefs of Staff, where it competed with the JCS's own intelligence body. This, and patent military dissatisfaction with the new entity, did much to inhibit the success of the OSS in World War II. Nonetheless, the order is significant in that it created the nation's first wartime centralized intelligence service. *See also:* Office of Strategic Services.

References

Office of the President of the United States. *Military Order, Office of Strategic Services.* Washington, DC, June 13, 1942.

—**MILITARY STRATEGY** is the component of national strategy that is concerned with using the armed forces to secure national policy objectives through the use or threatened use of force. *See also:* Strategy.

References

Department of Defense, Joint Chiefs of Staff. *Department of Defense Dictionary of Military and Related Terms.* Washington, DC: GPO, 1986.

Kent, Sherman. *Strategic Intelligence for American World Policy.* Princeton, NJ: Princeton University Press, 1966.

Laqueur, Walter. *A World of Secrets.* New York: Basic Books, 1985.

Treverton, Gregory F. *Covert Action: The Limits of Intervention in the Postwar World.* New York: Basic Books, 1987.

—**MILLER, RICHARD W.,** an FBI agent, was arrested in Baltimore, Maryland, on October 2, 1984. He was convicted on espionage charges on June 19, 1986, and was sentenced to life in prison.

References

Allen, Thomas B., and Polmar, Norman. *Merchants of Treason: America's Secrets for Sale.* New York: Delacorte Press, 1988.

Crawford, David J. *Volunteers: The Betrayal of National Defense Secrets by Air Force Traitors.* Washington, DC: GPO, 1988.

—**MILLISECOND,** a baud-based system term used in communications intelligence, communications security, operations security, and signals analysis, is a measure of time that is equal to one thousandth of a second. *See also:* Communications Security.

References

Department of Defense, U.S. Army. *Counter-Signals Intelligence (C-SIGINT) Operations.* Field Manual FM 34-62. Washington, DC: Headquarters, Department of the Army, 1986.

—**MINIMAL ACCESS** is exposure to sensitive compartmented information (SCI) that results in the gaining of little, if any, knowledge of value. *See also:* Sensitive Compartmented Information.

References

Laqueur, Walter. *A World of Secrets.* New York: Basic Books, 1985.

—**MINTKENBAUGH, JAMES ALLEN,** attached to the U.S. Army, was convicted of espionage offenses relating to passing classified information to the Soviet KGB in 1965. He was motivated by revenge. He was sentenced to 25 years in prison.

References

Allen, Thomas B., and Polmar, Norman. *Merchants of Treason: America's Secrets for Sale.* New York: Delacorte Press, 1988.

Crawford, David J. *Volunteers: The Betrayal of National Defense Secrets by Air Force Traitors.* Washington, DC: GPO, 1988.

—**MIRA, FRANCISCO DE ASIS,** an Air Force computer technician, was convicted of providing photographs of classified code books, maintenance schedules, and status boards to East German intelligence. Mira was apparently motivated by financial gain and a desire to be accepted. A court-martial convicted him in 1983, awarding him a dishonorable discharge and a seven-year prison sentence.

References

Crawford, David J. *Volunteers: The Betrayal of National Defense Secrets by Air Force Traitors.* Washington, DC: GPO, 1988.

—**MIRV ICBM** is a ballistic missile with a multiple independently targetable reentry vehicle capability. The MX became an intelligence issue in 1969, when Richard Helms, then director of Central Intelligence, conflicted with Henry Kissinger and Secretary of Defense Melvin Laird as to whether the Soviet SS-9 ICBM had a MIRV capability or merely an MRV (multiple but not independently guided vehicle) capability. Kissinger and his staff believed that the SS-9 had a MIRV capability, Helms did not, and Laird maintained that it probably did have such a capability. The immediate relevance of the controversy was that it had an impact on the question of whether the United States should MIRV its missiles and deploy ABMs. However, on another level, the issue reemphasized the chronic dissatisfaction with the National Intelligence Estimates (NIEs). *See also:* Helms, Richard.

References

Lowenthal, Mark M. *U.S. Intelligence: Evolution and Anatomy.* New York: Praeger, 1984.

—**MISSILE AND SPACE INTELLIGENCE CENTER, HUNTSVILLE, ALABAMA,** is a component of the Army Intelligence Agency. The center provides detailed, all-source analysis on foreign strategic air defense, tactical air defense, short-range ballistic and anti-tank guided missiles, and related technologies. The center also manages the Army development and acquisition of threat simulators.

References

Department of Defense, U.S. Army. *AIA: Threat Analysis*. Falls Church, VA: U.S. Army Intelligence Agency, 1987.

—**MISSILE GAP** was an intelligence controversy in the late 1950s. Because of the dramatic Soviet advances in nuclear weaponry, missiles, and satellites, the public and Congress expressed increasing concern about Soviet military developments and questioned the validity of public U.S. estimates concerning the Soviet missile capability. Although President Eisenhower adamantly denied the charges that U.S. estimates were too low, President Kennedy and Senator Stuart Symington made them a major issue in the 1960 election. Although subsequent analysis by the Kennedy administration revealed that the missile gap in fact did not exist, the entire controversy reflected the great concern over the accuracy of the National Intelligence Estimates. This problem of accuracy has been a chronic one and led to the Team A/Team B controversy of the mid-1970s and the argument for competitive analysis. *See also:* Competitive Analysis, Team A/Team B.

References

Brinkley, David A., and Hull, Andrew W. *Estimative Intelligence: A Textbook on the History, Products, Uses and Writing of Intelligence Estimates*. Columbus, OH: Battelle, 1979.

Laqueur, Walter. *A World of Secrets*. New York: Basic Books, 1985.

Lowenthal, Mark M. *U.S. Intelligence: Evolution and Anatomy*. New York: Praeger, 1984.

Treverton, Gregory F. *Covert Action: The Limits of Intervention in the Postwar World*. New York: Basic Books, 1987.

—**MISSION** is an Army term that has two meanings. (1) A mission is the task, together with the purpose, that clearly indicates the action to be taken and the reason why the action is to be taken. (2) In common usage, especially when it is applied to lower military units, a mission is a duty or task that is assigned to an individual or a unit.

References

Department of Defense, Joint Chiefs of Staff. *Department of Defense Dictionary of Military and Related Terms*. Washington, DC: GPO, 1986.

Department of Defense, U.S. Army. *Counter-Signals Intelligence (C-SIGINT) Operations*. Field Manual FM 34-62. Washington, DC: Headquarters, Department of the Army, 1986.

———. *Military Intelligence Battalion Combat Electronic Warfare and Intelligence (Aerial Exploitation) (Corps)*. Field Manual FM 34-22. Washington, DC: Headquarters, Department of the Army, 1984.

———. *Military Intelligence Battalion (CEWI) (Tactical Exploitation) (Corps): Counterintelligence, Interrogation, Electronic Warfare*. Field Manual FM 34-23. Washington, DC: Headquarters, Department of the Army, 1985.

Godson, Roy, ed. *Intelligence Problems for the 1980s, Number 1: Elements of Intelligence*. Rev. ed. Washington, DC: National Strategy Information Center, 1983.

—**MISSION MANAGEMENT,** in Army tactical intelligence (TACINT), has two meanings. (1) Mission management can mean the specific planning, direction, and control of operations that are needed to satisfy the commander's needs for intelligence, electronic warfare, counterintelligence, and operations security support. (2) Mission management can also mean the translation of general requirements into specific needs and the identification and tasking of the organization or organizations that can best satisfy those needs.

References

Department of Defense, U.S. Army. *Counter-Signals Intelligence (C-SIGINT) Operations*. Field Manual FM 34-62. Washington, DC: Headquarters, Department of the Army, 1986.

———. *Military Intelligence Battalion Combat Electronic Warfare and Intelligence (Aerial Exploitation) (Corps)*. Field Manual FM 34-22. Washington, DC: Headquarters, Department of the Army, 1984.

———. *Military Intelligence Battalion (CEWI) (Tactical Exploitation) (Corps): Counterintelligence, Interrogation, Electronic Warfare*. Field Manual FM 34-23. Washington, DC: Headquarters, Department of the Army, 1985.

———. *Military Intelligence Company (Combat Electronic Warfare and Intelligence) (Armored Cavalry Regiment/Separate Brigade)*. Field Manual FM 34-30. Washington, DC: Headquarters, Department of the Army, 1983.

—**MISSION STATEMENT** is a general intelligence term. It is a concise, thorough description of an organization's functions.

References

Department of Defense, Defense Intelligence Agency. *Defense Intelligence Agency Manual.* Washington, DC: DIA, 1987.

Godson, Roy, ed. *Intelligence Problems for the 1980s, Number 1: Elements of Intelligence.* Rev. ed. Washington, DC: National Strategy Information Center, 1983.

—**MISSION STATEMENT MATRIX** is a form that a command uses in order to identify its nonrecurring signals intelligence requirements.

References

Department of Defense, Defense Intelligence Agency. *Defense Intelligence Agency Manual.* Washington, DC: DIA, 1987.

Department of Defense, U.S. Army. *Counter-Signals Intelligence (C-SIGINT) Operations.* Field Manual FM 34-62. Washington, DC: Headquarters, Department of the Army, 1986.

———. *Military Intelligence Battalion Combat Electronic Warfare and Intelligence (Aerial Exploitation) (Corps).* Field Manual FM 34-22. Washington, DC: Headquarters, Department of the Army, 1984.

———. *Military Intelligence Battalion (CEWI) (Tactical Exploitation) (Corps): Counterintelligence, Interrogation, Electronic Warfare.* Field Manual FM 34-23. Washington, DC: Headquarters, Department of the Army, 1985.

———. *Military Intelligence Company (Combat Electronic Warfare and Intelligence) (Armored Cavalry Regiment/Separate Brigade).* Field Manual FM 34-30. Washington, DC: Headquarters, Department of the Army, 1983.

—**MISSION TASKING** is an Army tactical intelligence term that means the assignment of a mission to an organization.

References

Department of Defense, U.S. Army. *Counter-Signals Intelligence (C-SIGINT) Operations.* Field Manual FM 34-62. Washington, DC: Headquarters, Department of the Army, 1986.

———. *Intelligence and Electronic Warfare Operations.* Field Manual FM 34-1. Washington, DC: Headquarters, Department of the Army, 1984.

———. *Military Intelligence Battalion (CEWI) (Operations) (Corps).* Field Manual FM 34-21. Washington, DC: Headquarters, Department of the Army, 1982.

—**MITCHELL, BERNON F.,** an employee at the National Security Agency, defected to the Soviet Union in 1960.

References

Allen, Thomas B., and Polmar, Norman. *Merchants of Treason: America's Secrets for Sale.* New York: Delacorte Press, 1988.

Bamford, James. *The Puzzle Palace: A Report on America's Most Secret Agency.* New York: Penguin Books, 1983.

Turner, Stansfield. *Secrecy and Democracy: The CIA in Transition.* Boston: Houghton Mifflin, 1985.

—**MKNAOMI** was the first Central Intelligence Agency operation that was associated with the use of chemical weapons.

References

Fain, Tyrus G.; Plant, Katharine C.; and Milloy, Ross. *The Intelligence Community: History, Organization, and Issues.* Public Documents Series. New York: R.R. Bowker, 1977.

—**MOBILE COMSEC FACILITY,** in communications security (COMSEC), means a facility that contains classified COMSEC material and can operate while it is in motion. *See also:* Communications Security.

References

Department of Defense, U.S. Army. *Counter-Signals Intelligence (C-SIGINT) Operations.* Field Manual FM 34-62. Washington, DC: Headquarters, Department of the Army, 1986.

———. *Military Intelligence Battalion Combat Electronic Warfare and Intelligence (Aerial Exploitation) (Corps).* Field Manual FM 34-22. Washington, DC: Headquarters, Department of the Army, 1984.

———. *Military Intelligence Battalion (CEWI) (Tactical Exploitation) (Corps): Counterintelligence, Interrogation, Electronic Warfare.* Field Manual FM 34-23. Washington, DC: Headquarters, Department of the Army, 1985.

———. *Military Intelligence Company (Combat Electronic Warfare and Intelligence) (Armored Cavalry Regiment/Separate Brigade).* Field Manual FM 34-30. Washington, DC: Headquarters, Department of the Army, 1983.

—**MODIFICATION,** in communications security (COMSEC), means a National Security Agency (NSA)–approved mechanical, electrical, or software change that affects the characteristics of a

COMSEC end item. The classes of modifications are: (1) Mandatory modification, which is a change that the NSA requires to be accomplished. It must be done and reported by a specified Time Compliance Date. (This should not be confused with those changes that the NSA considers optional but that have been declared to be mandatory by another department, agency, or service.) (2) Optional/special mission modification, which is a change that is tailored to specific operational or environmental requirements that the NSA has determined does not require universal application. (3) Repair action, which is an optional change that can be made by holders. It will enhance the operation, maintainability, or reliability of a COMSEC end item. *See also:* Communications Security.

References

Department of Defense, U.S. Army. *Counter-Signals Intelligence (C-SIGINT) Operations.* Field Manual FM 34-62. Washington, DC: Headquarters, Department of the Army, 1986.

————. *Military Intelligence Battalion Combat Electronic Warfare and Intelligence (Aerial Exploitation) (Corps).* Field Manual FM 34-22. Washington, DC: Headquarters, Department of the Army, 1984.

————. *Military Intelligence Battalion (CEWI) (Tactical Exploitation) (Corps): Counterintelligence, Interrogation, Electronic Warfare.* Field Manual FM 34-23. Washington, DC: Headquarters, Department of the Army, 1985.

————. *Military Intelligence Company (Combat Electronic Warfare and Intelligence) (Armored Cavalry Regiment/Separate Brigade).* Field Manual FM 34-30. Washington, DC: Headquarters, Department of the Army, 1983.

—**MODULATE** is to vary in amplitude, frequency, or phase of a wave in accordance with some type of information that is being transmitted.

References

Department of Defense, U.S. Army. *Counter-Signals Intelligence (C-SIGINT) Operations.* Field Manual FM 34-62. Washington, DC: Headquarters, Department of the Army, 1986.

————. *Military Intelligence Battalion Combat Electronic Warfare and Intelligence (Aerial Exploitation) (Corps).* Field Manual FM 34-22. Washington, DC: Headquarters, Department of the Army, 1984.

————. *Military Intelligence Battalion (CEWI) (Tactical Exploitation) (Corps): Counterintelligence, Interrogation, Electronic Warfare.* Field Manual FM 34-23. Washington, DC: Headquarters, Department of the Army, 1985.

————. *Military Intelligence Company (Combat Electronic Warfare and Intelligence) (Armored Cavalry Regiment/Separate Brigade).* Field Manual FM 34-30. Washington, DC: Headquarters, Department of the Army, 1983.

—**MOLE** is a term used in clandestine and covert intelligence operations to describe a hostile spy who works his way into an intelligence organization in order to report to an enemy one. *See also:* Agent in Place, Case, Co-Opted Worker, Co-Optees, Double Agent, Penetration, Recruitment, Recruitment in Place, Sleeper.

References

Clancy, Tom. *The Cardinal of the Kremlin.* New York: Putnam, 1988.

Deacon, Richard. *Spyclopedia: An Encyclopedia of Spies, Secret Services, Operations, Jargon, and All Subjects Related to the World of Espionage.* London: Macdonald, 1987.

Godson, Roy, ed. *Intelligence Problems for the 1980s, Number 1: Elements of Intelligence.* Rev. ed. Washington, DC: National Strategy Information Center, 1983.

Quirk, John; Phillips, David; Cline, Ray; and Pforzheimer, Walter. *The Central Intelligence Agency: A Photographic History.* Guilford, CT: Foreign Intelligence Press, 1986.

Turner, Stansfield. *Secrecy and Democracy: The CIA in Transition.* Boston: Houghton Mifflin, 1985.

—**MONGOOSE.** Operation Mongoose was an operation that President Kennedy directed the CIA to undertake in November 1961. Its goal was to overthrow the communist regime of Fidel Castro, and its actions included a wide range of operations, from simple intelligence and propaganda activities to sabotage of factories and installations, bombing power lines, spreading nonlethal chemicals on sugar fields to sicken the cane cutters, and several plots to murder Fidel Castro. *See also:* Assassination; Central Intelligence Agency; Kennedy, John F.

References

American Bar Association. *Oversight and Accountability of the U.S. Intelligence Agencies: An Evaluation.* Washington, DC: ABA, 1985.

Becket, Henry S. A. *The Dictionary of Espionage: Spookspeak into English.* New York: Stein and Day, 1986.

Breckinridge, Scott D. *The CIA and the U.S. Intelligence System.* Boulder, CO: Westview Press, 1986.

Corson, William R. *The Armies of Ignorance: The Rise of the American Intelligence Empire*. New York: Dial Press, 1977.

Fain, Tyrus G.; Plant, Katharine C.; and Milloy, Ross. *The Intelligence Community: History, Organization, and Issues*. Public Documents Series. New York: R.R. Bowker, 1977.

Godson, Roy, ed. *Intelligence Problems for the 1980s, Number 1: Elements of Intelligence*. Rev. ed. Washington, DC: National Strategy Information Center, 1983.

————. *Intelligence Problems for the 1980s, Number 4: Covert Action*. Washington, DC: National Strategy Information Center, 1981.

Laqueur, Walter. *A World of Secrets*. New York: Basic Books, 1985.

Lefever, Ernest W., and Godson, Roy. *The CIA and the American Ethic: An Unfinished Debate*. Washington, DC: Ethics and Public Policy Center, Georgetown University, 1979.

Maurer, Alfred C.; Turnstall, Marion D.; and Keagle, James M. *Intelligence Policy and Process*. Boulder, CO: Westview Press, 1985.

Turner, Stansfield. *Secrecy and Democracy: The CIA in Transition*. Boston: Houghton Mifflin, 1985.

U.S. Congress. Senate. *Alleged Assassination Plots Involving Foreign Leaders: An Interim Report of the Select Committee to Study Governmental Operations with Respect to Intelligence Activities*. 94th Congress, 1st sess., Nov. 20, 1975. S. Rept. 94-465.

—**MONITOR** is a term used in signals intelligence, communications security, communications intelligence, operations security, and signals analysis. It is to observe, listen to, intercept, record, or transcribe any form of communication or media for collecting intelligence information or communications security purposes. Monitoring can be either overt or covert. *See also:* Communications Security, Signals Intelligence.

References
Department of Defense, Defense Intelligence College. *Glossary of Intelligence Terms and Definitions*. Washington, DC: DIC, 1987.

Godson, Roy, ed. *Intelligence Problems for the 1980s, Number 1: Elements of Intelligence*. Rev. ed. Washington, DC: National Strategy Information Center, 1983.

Kent, Sherman. *Strategic Intelligence for American World Policy*. Princeton, NJ: Princeton University Press, 1966.

Treverton, Gregory F. *Covert Action: The Limits of Intervention in the Postwar World*. New York: Basic Books, 1987.

Turner, Stansfield. *Secrecy and Democracy: The CIA in Transition*. Boston: Houghton Mifflin, 1985.

—**MONITORING** is a term used in electronic warfare and in counterintelligence. It is the act of listening to and reviewing the enemy's, one's own, or allied communications for the purpose of maintaining standards, improving communications, or for reference, as applicable. As defined by the Church Committee, monitoring is the "observing, listening to, or recording of foreign or domestic communications for intelligence collection or intelligence security (COMSEC) purposes." *See also:* Counterintelligence.

References
Department of Defense, Joint Chiefs of Staff. *Department of Defense Dictionary of Military and Related Terms*. Washington, DC: GPO, 1986.

Godson, Roy, ed. *Intelligence Problems for the 1980s, Number 1: Elements of Intelligence*. Rev. ed. Washington, DC: National Strategy Information Center, 1983.

Kent, Sherman. *Strategic Intelligence for American World Policy*. Princeton, NJ: Princeton University Press, 1966.

Lowenthal, Mark M. *U.S. Intelligence: Evolution and Anatomy*. New York: Praeger, 1984.

Quirk, John; Phillips, David; Cline, Ray; and Pforzheimer, Walter. *The Central Intelligence Agency: A Photographic History*. Guilford, CT: Foreign Intelligence Press, 1986.

Turner, Stansfield. *Secrecy and Democracy: The CIA in Transition*. Boston: Houghton Mifflin, 1985.

U.S. Congress. Senate. *Final Report of the Senate Select Committee to Study Government Operations with Respect to Intelligence Activities. Report 94-755. Book I, Foreign and Military Intelligence*. Washington, DC: GPO, 1976.

—**MOONLIGHT EXTRADITION** is a term used in clandestine and covert intelligence operations to describe the deporting of a person sought by intelligence or law enforcement agencies without the benefit of extradition procedures.

References
Becket, Henry S. A. *The Dictionary of Espionage: Spookspeak into English*. New York: Stein and Day, 1986.

Deacon, Richard. *Spyclopedia: An Encyclopedia of Spies, Secret Services, Operations, Jargon, and All Subjects Related to the World of Espionage.* London: Macdonald, 1987.

Ranelagh, John. *The Agency: The Rise and Decline of the CIA.* New York: Simon and Schuster, 1986.

—**MOORE, EDWIN G., II,** a disgruntled Central Intelligence Agency employee, was arrested in 1976, convicted, and sentenced to fifteen years in prison for attempting to sell information to the Soviets.

References

Allen, Thomas B., and Polmar, Norman. *Merchants of Treason: America's Secrets for Sale.* New York: Delacorte Press, 1988.

—**MOORE, MICHAEL R.,** Lance Corporal, U.S. Marine Corps, was arrested with photographs and other materials and was alleged to be preparing to contact the Soviets while absent without leave in the Philippines. He was given a convenience-of-the-government discharge.

References

Allen, Thomas B., and Polmar, Norman. *Merchants of Treason: America's Secrets for Sale.* New York: Delacorte Press, 1988.

—**MORISON, SAMUEL LORING,** a naval analyst at the Naval Information Support Center in Suitland, Maryland, was arrested on October 10, 1984, in Baltimore. He had passed classified photography to *Jane's Defence Weekly,* which was subsequently published. Morison was convicted of espionage charges on October 17, 1985, and was sentenced to two years in prison.

References

Allen, Thomas B., and Polmar, Norman. *Merchants of Treason: America's Secrets for Sale.* New York: Delacorte Press, 1988.

Crawford, David J. *Volunteers: The Betrayal of National Defense Secrets by Air Force Traitors.* Washington, DC: GPO, 1988.

Lardner, George. "Morison Espionage Conviction Affirmed." *The Washington Post,* April 5, 1988, p. A-6.

—**MORNING SUMMARY (MS)** is a summary of current intelligence reports of interest to national-level policymakers. One of the contributors to the MS is the Defense Intelligence Agency's Directorate for Current Intelligence (JSI). *See also:* Defense Intelligence Agency.

References

Department of Defense, Defense Intelligence Agency. *Organization, Mission, and Key Personnel.* Washington, DC: DIA, 1986.

—**MOSAIC** is an intelligence imagery and photoreconnaissance term for an assembly of overlapping photographs that have been matched to form a continuous photographic representation. *See also:* Aerial Photograph.

References

Department of Defense, Joint Chiefs of Staff. *Department of Defense Dictionary of Military and Related Terms.* Washington, DC: GPO, 1986.

Department of Defense. U.S. Army. *Intelligence Imagery.* Army Field Manual FM 34-55. Washington, DC: Headquarters, Department of the Army, 1985.

—**MOSSADDEQ, MUHAMMED.** *See:* Iran.

—**MOVEMENTS ANALYSIS** is a term used in counterintelligence and refers to the constant surveillance of the movements of officials from the Soviet embassy, other bloc embassies, Aeroflot airline, and TASS news agency. Through such shadowing, counterintelligence agents can tell which officials are legitimate diplomats and which are spies. *See also:* Alternate Meet, Between the Lines Entry, Exfiltration, Go-Away, Pavement Artists, Shadow, Shaking Off the Dogs, Stroller, Surround, Surveillance, Walk-Past, What's Your Twenty?

References

Becket, Henry S. A. *The Dictionary of Espionage: Spookspeak into English.* New York: Stein and Day, 1986.

Deacon, Richard. *Spyclopedia: An Encyclopedia of Spies, Secret Services, Operations, Jargon, and All Subjects Related to the World of Espionage.* London: Macdonald, 1987.

Godson, Roy, ed. *Intelligence Problems for the 1980s, Number 1: Elements of Intelligence.* Rev. ed. Washington, DC: National Strategy Information Center, 1983.

Ranelagh, John. *The Agency: The Rise and Decline of the CIA.* New York: Simon and Schuster, 1986.

—**MOZHNO GIRLS** or "permitted girls" are KGB women who attempt to seduce Western officials and agents in order to collect information of intelligence value. *See also:* Agent, Fur-Lined Seat Cover, Honey Trap, Ladies, Raven, Sisters, Stable, Swallow, Swallow's Nest, Taxi.

References

Becket, Henry S. A. *The Dictionary of Espionage: Spookspeak into English.* New York: Stein and Day, 1986.

Deacon, Richard. *Spyclopedia: An Encyclopedia of Spies, Secret Services, Operations, Jargon, and All Subjects Related to the World of Espionage.* London: Macdonald, 1987.

Ranelagh, John. *The Agency: The Rise and Decline of the CIA.* New York: Simon and Schuster, 1986.

—**MUELLER, GUSTAV ADOLPH,** an Air Force enlisted student at the European Command Intelligence School at Oberammergau, Germany, was arrested on October 26, 1949, by counterintelligence agents posing as Soviet intelligence officers. He was apparently motivated ideologically, although immaturity and a desire for adventure may have also been motives. He was apprehended before he could pass any information. On April 15, 1950, he was convicted of attempting to pass classified information to Soviet officials and was sentenced to prison for five years and was dishonorably discharged. David Crawford notes that Mueller was probably the first individual to attempt to betray the United States in the post–World War II period.

References

Crawford, David J. *Volunteers: The Betrayal of National Defense Secrets by Air Force Traitors.* Washington, DC: GPO, 1988.

—**MUGBOOKS** are photo albums that are kept in CIA stations. They contain photographs and biographical sketches of hostile agents who are operating in the area.

References

Becket, Henry S. A. *The Dictionary of Espionage: Spookspeak into English.* New York: Stein and Day, 1986.

Deacon, Richard. *Spyclopedia: An Encyclopedia of Spies, Secret Services, Operations, Jargon, and All Subjects Related to the World of Espionage.* London: Macdonald, 1987.

Ranelagh, John. *The Agency: The Rise and Decline of the CIA.* New York: Simon and Schuster, 1986.

—**MULTILEVEL SECURITY** is a term used in counterintelligence, counterespionage, and counterinsurgency. Such security applies to automatic data processing systems and involves the provisions for safeguarding information in a multilevel information handling system. Such a system concurrently stores and processes several levels, categories, and compartments of material in a remotely accessed resource sharing ADP system. It allows the stored material to be selectively accessed and manipulated from variously controlled terminals by people having different security levels and access approvals. The security measures are intended to ensure that there are proper matches between information security and personnel security. *See also:* Communications Security.

References

Department of Defense, Defense Intelligence College. *Glossary of Intelligence Terms and Definitions.* Washington, DC: DIC, 1987.

Godson, Roy, ed. *Intelligence Problems for the 1980s, Number 1: Elements of Intelligence.* Rev. ed. Washington, DC: National Strategy Information Center, 1983.

—**MULTIPLEX (MUX),** a baud based system term used in communications intelligence, communications security, operations security, and signals analysis, is the transmission of two or more channels of information in time division or frequency division on a single transmitter. Frequency division multiplex (FDM) is a device or process for transmitting two or more signals over the same path by sending each one over a different frequency band. Time division multiplex (TDM) is a process of transmitting two or more channels of information over a common path by allocating a different time interval for the transmission of each channel. (The time available is divided among two or more channels.) *See also:* Communications Security.

References

Department of Defense, Joint Chiefs of Staff. *Department of Defense Dictionary of Military and Related Terms.* Washington, DC: GPO, 1986.

Department of Defense, U.S. Army. *Counter-Signals Intelligence (C-SIGINT) Operations.* Field Manual FM 34-62. Washington, DC: Headquarters, Department of the Army, 1986.

————. *Military Intelligence Battalion Combat Electronic Warfare and Intelligence (Aerial Exploitation) (Corps).* Field Manual FM 34-22. Washington, DC: Headquarters, Department of the Army, 1984.

————. *Military Intelligence Battalion (CEWI) (Tactical Exploitation) (Corps): Counterintelligence, Interrogation, Electronic Warfare.* Field Manual FM 34-23. Washington, DC: Headquarters, Department of the Army, 1985.

—**MULTIPLEXING,** as defined by the Church Committee, is a technique that allows one signal to carry several communications (e.g., conversations, messages) simultaneously. *See also:* Communications Security.

References

U.S. Congress. Senate. *Final Report of the Senate Select Committee to Study Government Operations with Respect to Intelligence Activities. Report 94-755. Book I, Foreign and Military Intelligence.* Washington, DC: GPO, 1976.

—**MULTITARGET JAMMING** is an electronic warfare term for any jamming that is meant to simultaneously, or on some type of time sharing basis, present interference to two or more receiving systems or families of receiving systems. *See also:* Barrage Jamming, Jamming.

References

Department of Defense, Joint Chiefs of Staff. *Department of Defense Dictionary of Military and Related Terms.* Washington, DC: GPO, 1986.

Department of Defense, U.S. Army. *Counter-Signals Intelligence (C-SIGINT) Operations.* Field Manual FM 34-62. Washington, DC: Headquarters, Department of the Army, 1986.

————. *Military Intelligence Battalion Combat Electronic Warfare and Intelligence (Aerial Exploitation) (Corps).* Field Manual FM 34-22. Washington, DC: Headquarters, Department of the Army, 1984.

————. *Military Intelligence Battalion (CEWI) (Tactical Exploitation) (Corps): Counterintelligence, Interrogation, Electronic Warfare.* Field Manual FM 34-23. Washington, DC: Headquarters, Department of the Army, 1985.

—**MURPHY COMMISSION** involved a series of hearings held by the Subcommittee on Legislation of the House Committee on Intelligence in 1979. Its purpose was to examine the difficulties that had been caused by the restrictive rules and procedures that had been placed on the intelligence agencies. It provided an opportunity for the intelligence agencies to explain and criticize the effects that the congressional intelligence reform movement was having on intelligence production. Later in the same year, the commission held hearings on the impact of the Freedom of Information Act and the Privacy Act on intelligence operations, and on a third occasion it held hearings on the "graymail" issue, in which a defendant in an espionage trial argues that he must use classified information in his case, with the aim of forcing the government to give up its case rather than release the information. In these hearings, as well, the intelligence agencies were given a chance to present their views on these issues. The Murphy Commission was proof that Congress was moving back toward its support of the Intelligence Community and away from the stances of the Church and Pike committees. *See also:* Congressional Oversight.

References

Godson, Roy, ed. *Intelligence Problems for the 1980s, Number 1: Elements of Intelligence.* Rev. ed. Washington, DC: National Strategy Information Center, 1983.

Kornblum, Allan. *Intelligence and the Law: Cases and Materials.* Vol. IV. Washington, DC: DIC, 1987.

Oseth, John M. *Regulating U.S. Intelligence Operations: A Study in the Definition of the National Interest.* Frankfurt: University of Kentucky Press, 1985.

Turner, Stansfield. *Secrecy and Democracy: The CIA in Transition.* Boston: Houghton Mifflin, 1985.

Warner, John S. *National Security and the First Amendment.* McLean, VA: Association of Former Intelligence Officers, 1985.

—**MURPHY, MICHAEL R.,** a crewman on board the USS *Polk,* a ballistic missile–equipped submarine, approached the Soviets in 1981, making an offer. Murphy, who had a secret clearance, was honorably discharged from the Navy.

References

Allen, Thomas B., and Polmar, Norman. *Merchants of Treason: America's Secrets for Sale.* New York: Delacorte Press, 1988.

Crawford, David J. *Volunteers: The Betrayal of National Defense Secrets by Air Force Traitors.* Washington, DC: GPO, 1988.

—**MUSIC BOX** is a clandestine and covert intelligence operations term for a radio transmitter.

References

Deacon, Richard. *Spyclopedia: An Encyclopedia of Spies, Secret Services, Operations, Jargon, and All Subjects Related to the World of Espionage.* London: Macdonald, 1987.

Quirk, John; Phillips, David; Cline, Ray; and Pforzheimer, Walter. *The Central Intelligence Agency: A Photographic History.* Guilford, CT: Foreign Intelligence Press, 1986.

—**MUSICIAN** is a clandestine intelligence operations term for a radio operator.

References

Becket, Henry S. A. *The Dictionary of Espionage: Spookspeak into English.* New York: Stein and Day, 1986.

Deacon, Richard. *Spyclopedia: An Encyclopedia of Spies, Secret Services, Operations, Jargon, and All Subjects Related to the World of Espionage.* London: Macdonald, 1987.

—**MYTHOLOGICAL DESIGNATOR,** in communications security (COMSEC), means a name from mythology that is assigned to a specific cryptoprinciple and its associated crypto-equipment for reference purposes. (Mythological designators are no longer assigned to new systems.) *See also:* Communications Security.

References

Department of Defense, U.S. Army. *Counter-Signals Intelligence (C-SIGINT) Operations.* Field Manual FM 34-62. Washington, DC: Headquarters, Department of the Army, 1986.

———. *Military Intelligence Battalion Combat Electronic Warfare and Intelligence (Aerial Exploitation) (Corps).* Field Manual FM 34-22. Washington, DC: Headquarters, Department of the Army, 1984.

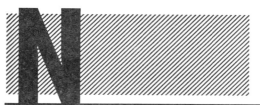

—**NADIR** is a term used in imagery and photoreconnaissance. The nadir is that point on the earth that is vertically below or beneath the observer. *See also:* Aerial Photograph.

References

Department of Defense, Joint Chiefs of Staff. *Department of Defense Dictionary of Military and Related Terms.* Washington, DC: GPO, 1986.

Reeves, Robert; Anson, Abraham; and Landen, David. *Manual of Remote Sensing.* Falls Church, VA: American Society of Photogrammetry, 1975.

—**NADIR, GROUND,** is a term used in imagery and photoreconnaissance. It is the point on the ground that is vertically beneath the center of the camera lens. *See also:* Nadir.

References

Reeves, Robert; Anson, Abraham; and Landen, David. *Manual of Remote Sensing.* Falls Church, VA: American Society of Photogrammetry, 1975.

—**NADIR, MAP,** is a term used in imagery and photoreconnaissance. It is the map position for the ground nadir. *See also:* Nadir.

References

Reeves, Robert; Anson, Abraham; and Landen, David. *Manual of Remote Sensing.* Falls Church, VA: American Society of Photogrammetry, 1975.

—**NADIR, PHOTOGRAPH** is a term used in imagery and photoreconnaissance. It is that point at which a vertical line through the perspective center of the camera lens pierces the plane of the photograph. This is also referred to as the nadir point. *See also:* Nadir.

References

Reeves, Robert; Anson, Abraham; and Landen, David. *Manual of Remote Sensing.* Falls Church, VA: American Society of Photogrammetry, 1975.

—**NAKED** is a term used in clandestine and covert intelligence operations. Naked indicates that an agent is working entirely alone, without any assistance from his or her intelligence organization. *See also:* Agent, Agent in Place, Double Agent, Illegal Agent, Illegal Operations, Mole, Sign of Life Signal, Silent School, Singleton.

References

Becket, Henry S. A. *The Dictionary of Espionage: Spookspeak into English.* New York: Stein and Day, 1986.

Deacon, Richard. *Spyclopedia: An Encyclopedia of Spies, Secret Services, Operations, Jargon, and All Subjects Related to the World of Espionage.* London: Macdonald, 1987.

Ranelagh, John. *The Agency: The Rise and Decline of the CIA.* New York: Simon and Schuster, 1986.

—**NASH** is a term used in clandestine and covert intelligence operations to describe a person belonging to one's own side. It is a corruption of a Russian word meaning "our."

References

Becket, Henry S. A. *The Dictionary of Espionage: Spookspeak into English.* New York: Stein and Day, 1986.

Deacon, Richard. *Spyclopedia: An Encyclopedia of Spies, Secret Services, Operations, Jargon, and All Subjects Related to the World of Espionage.* London: Macdonald, 1987.

Ranelagh, John. *The Agency: The Rise and Decline of the CIA.* New York: Simon and Schuster, 1986.

—**NATIONAL AGENCY CHECK** (NAC) is that part of a background investigation that involves a review of the files of all government agencies for derogatory information about an individual. *See also:* Access, Authorized, Background Investigation, Billet, Billet Realignment, Clearance, Compartmentation, Compromise, Debriefing, Defense Investigative Service, Need-to-Know, Need-to-Know Principle, Nondisclosure Agreement, Personnel Insecurity, Security, Security Classification, Sensitive Compartmented Information (SCI), Security Officer, Special Security Office System.

References

Allen, Thomas B., and Polmar, Norman. *Merchants of Treason: America's Secrets for Sale.* New York: Delacorte Press, 1988.

—**NATIONAL COMMITMENTS** is a term often used in formulating national security policy. National commitments are the specific undertakings that are waged to support a particular national strategy or policy.

References

Laqueur, Walter. *A World of Secrets.* New York: Basic Books, 1985.

Treverton, Gregory F. *Covert Action: The Limits of Intervention in the Postwar World.* New York: Basic Books, 1987.

—**NATIONAL COMPUTER SECURITY CENTER (NCSC),** established at the National Security Agency, is tasked with developing new security standards for computer systems and to evaluate computer systems for use within the Department of Defense. *See also:* Communications Security.

References

Laqueur, Walter. *A World of Secrets.* New York: Basic Books, 1985.

—**NATIONAL COMSEC ADVISORY MEMORANDUM (NACAM),** in communications security (COMSEC), is a document that provides advice and assistance to all government departments and agencies. Such a memorandum concerns broad communications security matters and is consistent with the policy guidance of the secretary of defense and the Special Subcommittee on Telecommunications protection. Such guidelines, which are approved by the committee, are signed by the chairman and are issued by the committee. *See also:* Communications Security.

References

Laqueur, Walter. *A World of Secrets.* New York: Basic Books, 1985.

—**NATIONAL COMSEC INFORMATION MEMORANDUM (NACSIM)** is a communications security (COMSEC) term. It is a document that provides instruction and establishes technical criteria that is to be implemented by departments and agencies on specific communications security matters. NACSIMs are issued by the director of the National Security Agency, after they have been coordinated with committee members and other affected departments and agencies. NACSIMs include legal guidelines, restrictions, and procedures that have been promulgated by the Department of Defense and approved by the attorney general. They are generally applicable to the conduct of communications security activities. *See also:* Communications Security.

References

Laqueur, Walter. *A World of Secrets.* New York: Basic Books, 1985.

—**NATIONAL CRYPTOLOGIC SCHOOL** is one of the ten branches of the National Security Agency. *See:* National Security Agency.

References

Bamford, James. *The Puzzle Palace: A Report on America's Most Secret Agency.* New York: Penguin Books, 1983.

—**NATIONAL DEFENSE EXPENDITURES,** a term used in intelligence program budgeting, is the Office of Management and Budget's classification. Within it, the item "Major National Security" includes military functions of the Department of Defense, atomic energy, foreign military aid, and stockpiling. *See also:* Budget.

References

Laqueur, Walter. *A World of Secrets.* New York: Basic Books, 1985.

Pickett, George. "Congress, the Budget, and Intelligence." In *Intelligence Policy and Process,* edited by Alfred C. Maurer, Marion D. Turnstall, and James M. Keagle. Boulder, CO: Westview Press, 1985.

—**NATIONAL DEFENSE UNIVERSITY (NDU),** located on Fort Leslie J. McNair, Washington, DC, consists of the Industrial College of the Armed Forces and the National War College. See these listings for institutional descriptions and curricula summaries.

References

Defense Intelligence Agency. *Training Compendium for General Defense Career Development Program (IDCP) Personnel DOD 1430.10M3-TNG.* Washington, DC: DIA, 1986.

—**NATIONAL EMERGENCY** is a condition that is declared by the President or Congress by virtue of powers vested in them. Such a declaration authorizes certain emergency actions to be taken in the national interest. These may include partial, full, or total mobilization of the national resources.

References

Department of Defense, Joint Chiefs of Staff. *Department of Defense Dictionary of Military and Related Terms.* Washington, DC: GPO, 1986.

Laqueur, Walter. *A World of Secrets*. New York: Basic Books, 1985.

Treverton, Gregory F. *Covert Action: The Limits of Intervention in the Postwar World*. New York: Basic Books, 1987.

—**NATIONAL ESTIMATE.** *See:* National Intelligence Estimate.

—**NATIONAL FOREIGN ASSESSMENT CENTER (NFAC)** was established by and is under the control and supervision of the director of Central Intelligence. The NFAC produces national intelligence. *See also:* Central Intelligence Agency.

References

Department of Defense, Defense Intelligence College. *Glossary of Intelligence Terms and Definitions*. Washington, DC: DIC, 1987.

Lefever, Ernest W., and Godson, Roy. *The CIA and the American Ethic: An Unfinished Debate*. Washington, DC: Ethics and Public Policy Center, Georgetown University, 1979.

Lowenthal, Mark M. *U.S. Intelligence: Evolution and Anatomy*. New York: Praeger, 1984.

Treverton, Gregory F. *Covert Action: The Limits of Intervention in the Postwar World*. New York: Basic Books, 1987.

—**NATIONAL FOREIGN INTELLIGENCE BOARD (NFIB).** The NFIB was established by Executive Order 12036, "United States Intelligence Activities," which was signed by President Carter on January 24, 1978. It replaced the United States Intelligence Board (USIB). According to the order, the NFIB was to be chaired by the director of Central Intelligence (DCI) and was to be staffed by members of the Intelligence Community. Its specific duties were to produce, review, and coordinate national foreign intelligence; advise the DCI on interagency exchanges of foreign intelligence information; advise the DCI concerning arrangements with foreign governments concerning intelligence matters; advise the DCI on the protection of intelligence sources and methods; advise the DCI on matters of common concern; and act on other matters that were referred to it by the DCI.

There was a further evolution in the NFIB's duties during the Reagan administration. Today, the board is a body that provides the DCI with advice concerning producing, reviewing, and coordinating national foreign intelligence; interagency exchanges of foreign intelligence information; arrangements with foreign governments on intelligence matters; protecting intelligence sources and methods; activities of common concern; and such others matters that the DCI refers to it. These duties are similar, if somewhat more substantive, than those defined in 1978. Its chairman is still the DCI, but its membership has received greater definition and is now composed of the appropriate officers from the Central Intelligence Agency, Office of the DCI, Department of State, Department of Defense, Department of Justice, Department of the Treasury, Department of Energy, the offices within the Department of Defense for reconnaissance programs, the Defense Intelligence Agency (represented by its Directorate for External Relations [DI]), the National Security Agency, and the Federal Bureau of Investigation. Senior intelligence officers of the Army, Navy, and Air Force participate as observers, and a representative of the assistant to the President for national security affairs may also attend the meetings as an observer.

The NFIB is also an official term that has been defined by the Defense Intelligence Agency for one of its functional areas. It means "activities involving full or part-time work on NFIB (formerly USIB) Committees or Committee staffs attempting to resolve community-wide intelligence problems."

References

Brinkley, David A., and Hull, Andrew W. *Estimative Intelligence: A Textbook on the History, Products, Uses and Writing of Intelligence Estimates*. Columbus, OH: Battelle, 1979.

Department of Defense, Defense Intelligence Agency. *Defense Intelligence Agency Manual 22-2*. Washington, DC: DIA, 1979.

Department of Defense, Defense Intelligence Agency. *Organization, Mission and Key Personnel*. Washington, DC: DIA, 1986.

Department of Defense, Defense Intelligence College. *Glossary of Intelligence Terms and Definitions*. Washington, DC: DIC, 1987.

Lowenthal, Mark M. *U.S. Intelligence: Evolution and Anatomy*. New York: Praeger, 1984.

Office of the President of the United States. *Executive Order 12036, United States Intelligence Activities*. Washington, DC, Jan. 24, 1978.

Oseth, John M. *Regulating U.S. Intelligence Operations: A Study in the Definition of the National Interest*. Frankfurt: University of Kentucky Press, 1985.

Quirk, John; Phillips, David; Cline, Ray; and Pforzheimer, Walter. *The Central Intelligence Agency: A Photographic History.* Guilford, CT: Foreign Intelligence Press, 1986.

Treverton, Gregory F. *Covert Action: The Limits of Intervention in the Postwar World.* New York: Basic Books, 1987.

Turner, Stansfield. *Secrecy and Democracy: The CIA in Transition.* Boston: Houghton Mifflin, 1985.

—NATIONAL FOREIGN INTELLIGENCE COMMUNITY. *See:* Intelligence Community.

—NATIONAL FOREIGN INTELLIGENCE COUNCIL (NFIC). The NFIC is an outgrowth of the National Foreign Intelligence Board (NFIB), which was created during the Reagan administration. Its purpose is to advise the director of Central Intelligence on budget issues. With the same membership as the NFIB, the NFIC meets quarterly to discuss budgetary priorities and budgetary matters.

References
Department of Defense, Defense Intelligence Agency. *Organization, Mission and Key Personnel.* Washington, DC: DIA, 1986.

Laqueur, Walter. *A World of Secrets.* New York: Basic Books, 1985.

Lowenthal, Mark M. *U.S. Intelligence: Evolution and Anatomy.* New York: Praeger, 1984.

Pickett, George. "Congress, the Budget, and Intelligence." In *Intelligence Policy and Process,* edited by Alfred C. Maurer, Marion D. Turnstall, and James M. Keagle. Boulder, CO: Westview Press, 1985.

Turner, Stansfield. *Secrecy and Democracy: The CIA in Transition.* Boston: Houghton Mifflin, 1985.

—NATIONAL FOREIGN INTELLIGENCE PROGRAM (NFIP) includes the following programs, but its composition is subject to review by the National Security Council and can be modified by the President: Central Intelligence Agency programs; the Consolidated Cryptologic Program, the General Defense Intelligence Program, and the Department of Defense reconnaissance programs except those elements that the director of Central Intelligence (DCI) and the secretary of defense agree should be excluded; other programs of Intelligence Community agencies that have been designated jointly by the DCI and the head of the department or by the President as national foreign intelligence or counterintelligence activities; and activities of the staff elements of the Office of the DCI.

Activities to acquire the intelligence required for planning and conducting tactical operations by the United States military forces are not included in the National Foreign Intelligence Program. However, the Defense Intelligence Agency's Directorate for Plans and Policies has a role in that it develops plans for acquiring the required intelligence to support the NFIP.

References
American Bar Association. *Oversight and Accountability of the U.S. Intelligence Agencies: An Evaluation.* Washington, DC: ABA, 1985.

Department of Defense, Defense Intelligence Agency. *Organization, Mission and Key Personnel.* Washington, DC: DIA, 1986.

Department of Defense, Defense Intelligence College. *Glossary of Intelligence Terms and Definitions.* Washington, DC: DIC, 1987.

Lowenthal, Mark M. *U.S. Intelligence: Evolution and Anatomy.* New York: Praeger, 1984.

Pickett, George. "Congress, the Budget, and Intelligence." In *Intelligence Policy and Process,* edited by Alfred C. Maurer, Marion D. Turnstall, and James M. Keagle. Boulder, CO: Westview Press, 1985.

Treverton, Gregory F. *Covert Action: The Limits of Intervention in the Postwar World.* New York: Basic Books, 1987.

—NATIONAL GOALS is a term often used in formulating national security policy. National goals are the broad ends to which a nation subscribes.

References
Laqueur, Walter. *A World of Secrets.* New York: Basic Books, 1985.

Pickett, George. "Congress, the Budget, and Intelligence." In *Intelligence Policy and Process,* edited by Alfred C. Maurer, Marion D. Turnstall, and James M. Keagle. Boulder, CO: Westview Press, 1985.

Treverton, Gregory F. *Covert Action: The Limits of Intervention in the Postwar World.* New York: Basic Books, 1987.

—NATIONAL IMAGERY INTERPRETABILITY RATING SCALE (NIIRS) is an intelligence imagery and photoreconnaissance term for a system that is used to rate the quality and interpretability of imagery. Ratings are expressed as

NIIRS 0 through NIIRS 9, with the ratings meaning the following: (0) imagery is useless for interpretation because of cloud cover, poor resolution, or other factors; (1) ground resolved distance is greater than 9 meters; (2) ground resolved distance of 4.5 to 9 meters; (3) ground resolved distance 2.5 to 4.5 meters; (4) ground resolved distance 1.2 to 2.5 meters; (5) ground resolved distance 0.75 to 1.2 meters; (6) ground resolved distance 40 to 75 centimeters; (7) ground resolved distance 20 to 40 centimeters; (8) ground resolved distance 10 to 20 centimeters; and (9) ground resolved distance of less than 10 centimeters. *See also:* Nadir.

References

Department of Defense, U.S. Army. *Intelligence Imagery.* Field Manual FM 34-55. Washington, DC: Headquarters, Department of the Army, 1985.

—**NATIONAL INDICATIONS CENTER** was created in 1954 and continued until 1974. Located in the Pentagon, its purpose was to support the Watch Committee, a Director of Central Intelligence Committee that was also begun in 1954. *See also:* Central Intelligence Agency.

References

Pickett, George. "Congress, the Budget, and Intelligence." In *Intelligence Policy and Process,* edited by Alfred C. Maurer, Marion D. Turnstall, and James M. Keagle. Boulder, CO: Westview Press, 1985.

Treverton, Gregory F. *Covert Action: The Limits of Intervention in the Postwar World.* New York: Basic Books, 1987.

—**NATIONAL INTELLIGENCE** is foreign intelligence that is produced under the aegis of the director of Central Intelligence and is intended to respond to the needs of the President, the National Security Council, and other federal officials who are involved in formulating and executing national security and foreign political or economic policy. It is intelligence that covers broad aspects of national policy and national security and transcends the competence of a single department or agency. *See also:* Central Intelligence Agency.

References

Department of Defense, Defense Intelligence College. *Glossary of Intelligence Terms and Definitions.* Washington, DC: DIC, 1987.

Department of Defense, Joint Chiefs of Staff. *Department of Defense Dictionary of Military and Related Terms.* Washington, DC: GPO, 1986.

Laqueur, Walter. *A World of Secrets.* New York: Basic Books, 1985.

Quirk, John; Phillips, David; Cline, Ray; and Pforzheimer, Walter. *The Central Intelligence Agency: A Photographic History.* Guilford, CT: Foreign Intelligence Press, 1986.

Treverton, Gregory F. *Covert Action: The Limits of Intervention in the Postwar World.* New York: Basic Books, 1987.

U.S. Congress. Senate. *Final Report of the Senate Select Committee to Study Government Operations with Respect to Intelligence Activities. Report 94-755. Book I, Foreign and Military Intelligence.* Washington, DC: GPO, 1976.

—**NATIONAL INTELLIGENCE ANALYTICAL MEMORANDUM (NIAM)** is a detailed analytical study of a complex subject that results in very tentative conclusions. Because it is a national document, it theoretically requires interagency coordination.

References

Brinkley, David A., and Hull, Andrew W. *Estimative Intelligence: A Textbook on the History, Products, Uses and Writing of Intelligence Estimates.* Columbus, OH: Battelle, 1979.

—**NATIONAL INTELLIGENCE ASSET** is one that is funded in the National Foreign Intelligence Program. Its primary purpose is to collect or process intelligence information or to produce national intelligence.

References

Department of Defense, Defense Intelligence College. *Glossary of Intelligence Terms and Definitions.* Washington, DC: DIC, 1987.

Laqueur, Walter. *A World of Secrets.* New York: Basic Books, 1985.

Treverton, Gregory F. *Covert Action: The Limits of Intervention in the Postwar World.* New York: Basic Books, 1987.

—**NATIONAL INTELLIGENCE AUTHORITY (NIA).** Presidential Directive of January 22, 1946, "Coordination of Federal Foreign Intelligence Activities," was issued by President Truman. Sent to the secretaries of War, State, and the Navy, it designated them, together with one other individual of the President's choosing, to be the National Intelligence Authority. The directive also formed the Central Intelligence Group and created the position of director of

Central Intelligence (DCI). The DCI would be appointed by the President, would sit as a non-voting member of the NIA, and would ensure that the group would fulfill its mission of supporting the NIA.

The creation of the NIA is best viewed in the context of a nation that was groping along the road to accepting its role as a world leader, a role that it was not sure it wished to accept. There are aspects of the bill that reflect Truman's and the nation's reservations concerning forming a clandestine intelligence agency, for fear that this would be a threat to democracy. Nonetheless, it also reflects a realization that the worldwide demands for U.S. leadership required a more centralized, professional Intelligence Community than that which had existed before the war.

In retrospect, the concept was flawed and failed to accomplish what Truman had envisioned. Nonetheless, the directive is a landmark because it redirected the federal government toward the centralization of intelligence, a trend that continues today. *See also:* Presidential Oversight.

References

Fain, Tyrus G.; Plant, Katharine C.; and Milloy, Ross. *The Intelligence Community: History, Organization, and Issues.* Public Documents Series. New York: R.R. Bowker, 1977.

Kent, Sherman. *Strategic Intelligence for American World Policy.* Princeton, NJ: Princeton University Press, 1966.

Lowenthal, Mark M. *U.S. Intelligence: Evolution and Anatomy.* New York: Praeger, 1984.

Office of the President of the United States. *Presidential Directive, Coordination of Federal Foreign Intelligence Activities.* Washington, DC, Jan. 22, 1946.

Quirk, John; Phillips, David; Cline, Ray; and Pforzheimer, Walter. *The Central Intelligence Agency: A Photographic History.* Guilford, CT: Foreign Intelligence Press, 1986.

Treverton, Gregory F. *Covert Action: The Limits of Intervention in the Postwar World.* New York: Basic Books, 1987.

U.S. Congress. Senate. *Final Report of the Senate Select Committee to Study Government Operations with Respect to Intelligence Activities. Report 94-755. Book I, Foreign and Military Intelligence.* Washington, DC: GPO, 1976.

—NATIONAL INTELLIGENCE COUNCIL (NIC).
See: Central Intelligence Agency.

—NATIONAL INTELLIGENCE DAILY (NID) is published by the Central Intelligence Agency. According to Henry Becket, only 60 copies of the daily are published. It is the most authoritative of any intelligence publication in the world, and, at the direction of William Colby, it presents its information in a newspaper style, with quick headline summaries and then in-depth analysis.

A major Department of Defense contributor to the NID is the Defense Intelligence Agency's Directorate for Current Intelligence (JSI). *See also:* Central Intelligence Agency, Defense Intelligence Agency.

References

Becket, Henry S. A. *The Dictionary of Espionage: Spookspeak into English.* New York: Stein and Day, 1986.

Department of Defense, Defense Intelligence Agency. *Organization, Mission and Key Personnel.* Washington, DC: DIA, 1986.

Fain, Tyrus G.; Plant, Katharine C.; and Milloy, Ross. *The Intelligence Community: History, Organization, and Issues.* Public Documents Series. New York: R.R. Bowker, 1977.

Turner, Stansfield. *Secrecy and Democracy: The CIA in Transition.* Boston: Houghton Mifflin, 1985.

—NATIONAL INTELLIGENCE ESTIMATE (NIE). NIE production is the responsibility of the National Intelligence Council, which is composed of the national intelligence officers (NIOs). They are then issued by the director of Central Intelligence with the advice of the National Foreign Intelligence Board. An NIE is a thorough assessment of a situation in a foreign nation that is relevant to the formulation of U.S. foreign, economic, or national security policy. Moreover, it projects probable future courses of action and developments. The NIE is structured in a way that differences within the Intelligence Community are highlighted. The Defense Intelligence Agency's action office for NIEs is the Directorate of Estimates (DE). National Intelligence Estimate was defined by the Church Committee in a slightly different way. To the committee, an NIE was an "estimate authorized by the Director of Central intelligence of the capabilities, vulnerabilities, and probable courses of action of foreign nations. It represents the composite views of the Intelligence Community." *See also:* Central Intelligence Agency.

References

American Bar Association. *Oversight and Accountability of the U.S. Intelligence Agencies: An Evaluation.* Washington, DC: ABA, 1985.

Brinkley, David A., and Hull, Andrew W. *Estimative Intelligence: A Textbook on the History, Products, Uses and Writing of Intelligence Estimates.* Columbus, OH: Battelle, 1979.

Department of Defense, Defense Intelligence Agency. *Organization, Mission and Key Personnel.* Washington, DC: DIA, 1986.

Department of Defense, Defense Intelligence College. *Glossary of Intelligence Terms and Definitions.* Washington, DC: DIC, 1987.

Department of Defense, Joint Chiefs of Staff. *Department of Defense Dictionary of Military and Related Terms.* Washington, DC: GPO, 1986.

Fain, Tyrus G.; Plant, Katharine C.; and Milloy, Ross. *The Intelligence Community: History, Organization, and Issues.* Public Documents Series. New York: R.R. Bowker, 1977.

Godson, Roy, ed. *Intelligence Problems for the 1980s, Number 2: Analysis and Estimates.* Washington, DC: National Strategy Information Center, 1980.

Laqueur, Walter. *A World of Secrets.* New York: Basic Books, 1985.

Lefever, Ernest W., and Godson, Roy. *The CIA and the American Ethic: An Unfinished Debate.* Washington, DC: Ethics and Public Policy Center, Georgetown University, 1979.

Quirk, John; Phillips, David; Cline, Ray; and Pforzheimer, Walter. *The Central Intelligence Agency: A Photographic History.* Guilford, CT: Foreign Intelligence Press, 1986.

Treverton, Gregory F. *Covert Action: The Limits of Intervention in the Postwar World.* New York: Basic Books, 1987.

Turner, Stansfield. *Secrecy and Democracy: The CIA in Transition.* Boston: Houghton Mifflin, 1985.

U.S. Congress. Senate. *Final Report of the Senate Select Committee to Study Government Operations with Respect to Intelligence Activities. Report 94-755. Book I, Foreign and Military Intelligence.* Washington, DC: GPO, 1976.

—**NATIONAL INTELLIGENCE OFFICER (NIO)** is the senior staff officer of the director of Central Intelligence (DCI) and the director's deputy for national intelligence for an assigned area for substantive responsibility. He manages estimative and interagency intelligence production on behalf of the DCI and is the principal point of contact between the DCI and the intelligence consumer below the cabinet level for matters pertaining to his subject.

Collectively, the NIOs form the National Intelligence Council (NIC). The NIC is subordinate to the deputy director for requirements and evaluation, intelligence staff, and produces the National Intelligence Estimates (NIEs) and Special National Intelligence Estimates (SNIEs), which are still considered to be products of the DCI. The NIOs are sources of national-level substantive guidance to Intelligence Community planners, collectors, and resource managers. They also interface with the defense intelligence officers to ensure that there is a defense input in national intelligence questions. The NIO system was organized in 1973 to replace the Office of National Estimates (ONE). *See also:* Central Intelligence Agency.

References

Brinkley, David A., and Hull, Andrew W. *Estimative Intelligence: A Textbook on the History, Products, Uses and Writing of Intelligence Estimates.* Columbus, OH: Battelle, 1979.

Department of Defense, Defense Intelligence Agency. *Organization, Mission and Key Personnel.* Washington, DC: DIA, 1986.

Department of Defense, Defense Intelligence College. *Glossary of Intelligence Terms and Definitions.* Washington, DC: DIC, 1987.

Fain, Tyrus G.; Plant, Katharine C.; and Milloy, Ross. *The Intelligence Community: History, Organization, and Issues.* Public Documents Series. New York: R.R. Bowker, 1977.

Laqueur, Walter. *A World of Secrets.* New York: Basic Books, 1985.

Lowenthal, Mark M. *U.S. Intelligence: Evolution and Anatomy.* New York: Praeger, 1984.

Treverton, Gregory F. *Covert Action: The Limits of Intervention in the Postwar World.* New York: Basic Books, 1987.

—**NATIONAL INTELLIGENCE PROGRAMS EVALUATION (NIPE)** was an office established by Director of Central Intelligence John McCone in 1963. Its purpose was to review and evaluate the programs of the Intelligence Community, their cost-effectiveness, and the effectiveness of the United States Intelligence Board in implementing the priority national intelligence objectives. The NIPE was limited in its ability to fulfill these tasks, but it went a long way toward providing the director of Central Intelligence with a greater role. *See also:* Central Intelligence Agency.

References

Brinkley, David A., and Hull, Andrew W. *Estimative Intelligence: A Textbook on the History, Products, Uses and Writing of Intelligence Estimates.* Columbus, OH: Battelle, 1979.

Laqueur, Walter. *A World of Secrets.* New York: Basic Books, 1985.

Lowenthal, Mark M. *U.S. Intelligence: Evolution and Anatomy.* New York: Praeger, 1984.

Treverton, Gregory F. *Covert Action: The Limits of Intervention in the Postwar World.* New York: Basic Books, 1987.

—**NATIONAL INTELLIGENCE PROGRAMS EVALUATION STAFF (NIPE STAFF)** was established in 1963 under the director of Central Intelligence to serve as a coordinating body for managing interdepartmental intelligence activities. It was replaced by the Intelligence Community Staff (IC Staff) in 1971. *See also:* Central Intelligence Agency.

References

Fain, Tyrus G.; Plant, Katharine C.; and Milloy, Ross. *The Intelligence Community: History, Organization, and Issues.* Public Documents Series. New York: R.R. Bowker, 1977.

Laqueur, Walter. *A World of Secrets.* New York: Basic Books, 1985.

—**NATIONAL INTELLIGENCE PROJECTIONS FOR PLANNING (NIPP)** is produced by the Joint Analysis Group (JAG). NIPPs are interagency assessments of future Soviet and Chinese military strengths.

References

Fain, Tyrus G.; Plant, Katharine C.; and Milloy, Ross. *The Intelligence Community: History, Organization, and Issues.* Public Documents Series. New York: R.R. Bowker, 1977.

—**NATIONAL INTELLIGENCE REFORM AND REORGANIZATION ACT OF 1978.** *See:* Senate Resolution 2525.

—**NATIONAL INTELLIGENCE RESOURCES BOARD (NIRB)** existed from 1968 to 1971. It was a senior-level Intelligence Community advisory group. It was replaced by the Intelligence Resources Advisory Committee (IRAC). *See also:* Central Intelligence Agency.

References

Laqueur, Walter. *A World of Secrets.* New York: Basic Books, 1985.

Lowenthal, Mark M. *U.S. Intelligence: Evolution and Anatomy.* New York: Praeger, 1984.

—**NATIONAL INTELLIGENCE SURVEY (NIS)** was a basic intelligence study produced on a coordinated interdepartmental basis and was concerned with the characteristics, basic resources, and relatively unchanging features of a foreign country or other area. The topics included: government, a general historical background summary, geography, economy, communications, transportation, science and technology, the military, and intelligence. The National Intelligence Survey program was discontinued in 1974.

References

Breckinridge, Scott D. *The CIA and the U.S. Intelligence System.* Boulder, CO: Westview Press, 1986.

Department of Defense, Joint Chiefs of Staff. *Department of Defense Dictionary of Military and Related Terms.* Washington, DC: GPO, 1986.

Treverton, Gregory F. *Covert Action: The Limits of Intervention in the Postwar World.* New York: Basic Books, 1987.

—**NATIONAL INTELLIGENCE TASKING CENTER (NITC)** was established by Executive order 12036, "United States Intelligence Activities," which was signed by President Carter on January 24, 1978.

According to the order, the NITC was directed by the director of Central Intelligence and was staffed by civilian and military personnel from the intelligence agencies. Its purpose was to assist the director of Central Intelligence in translating intelligence requirements and priorities into collection objectives; assigning targets and objectives to collection organizations; ensuing the timely dissemination of intelligence; providing advisory tasking to other agencies having intelligence information; and resolving conflicts among members of the Intelligence Community. *See also:* Presidential Oversight.

References

Department of Defense, Defense Intelligence College. *Glossary of Intelligence Terms and Definitions.* Washington, DC: DIC, 1987.

Godson, Roy, ed. *Intelligence Problems for the 1980s, Number 2: Analysis and Estimates.*

Washington, DC: National Strategy Information Center, 1980.

Office of the President of the United States. *Executive Order 12036, United States Intelligence Activities.* Washington, DC, Jan. 24, 1978.

Treverton, Gregory F. *Covert Action: The Limits of Intervention in the Postwar World.* New York: Basic Books, 1987.

Turner, Stansfield. *Secrecy and Democracy: The CIA in Transition.* Boston: Houghton Mifflin, 1985.

—**NATIONAL INTEREST** is a term often used in formulating national security policy and strategy. It involves actions that are considered to be vital to the survival of the state.

References

American Bar Association. *Oversight and Accountability of the U.S. Intelligence Agencies: An Evaluation.* Washington, DC: ABA, 1985.

Laqueur, Walter. *A World of Secrets.* New York: Basic Books, 1985.

Maurer, Alfred C.; Turnstall, Marion D.; and Keagle, James M. *Intelligence Policy and Process.* Boulder, CO: Westview Press, 1985.

Treverton, Gregory F. *Covert Action: The Limits of Intervention in the Postwar World.* New York: Basic Books, 1987.

—**NATIONAL MANAGER FOR TELECOMMUNICATIONS SECURITY AND AUTOMATED INFORMATION SYSTEMS SECURITY** was a position created by a proposed Presidential Directive signed on September 17, 1984, and entitled "National Policy on Telecommunications and Automated Information Systems Security." Under the prospective directive, the director of the National Security Agency (NSA) was designated as the national manager. He was to be responsible to the secretary of defense, who was designated as executive agent of the government for telecommunications and information systems security, in the same directive. The duties of the director of the NSA pertained to carrying out the responsibilities assigned to the secretary of defense in his capacity of executive agent of the government for telecommunications and information systems security. These duties were to be:

a. Ensure the development, in conjunction with NTISSC member departments and agencies, of plans and programs to fulfill the objectives of this Directive, including the development of necessary security architectures.

b. Procure for and provide to departments and agencies of the government and, where appropriate, to private institutions (including government contractors) and foreign governments, technical security material, other technical assistance, and other related services of common concern, as required to accomplish the objectives of this Directive.

c. Approve and provide minimum security standards and doctrine, consistent with provisions of the Directive.

d. Conduct, approve, or endorse the research and development of techniques and equipment for telecommunications and automated information systems security for national security information.

e. Operate, or coordinate the efforts of, government technical centers related to telecommunications and automated information systems security.

f. Review and assess for the Steering Group the proposed telecommunications security programs and budgets for the departments and agencies of the government for each fiscal year and recommend alternatives, where appropriate. The views of all affected departments and agencies shall be fully expressed to the Steering Group.

g. Review for the Steering Group the aggregated automated information systems security program and budget recommendations of the departments and agencies of the U.S. Government for each fiscal year.

In fulfilling these responsibilities, the director of the NSA was to be given the authority under the directive to:

a. Examine government telecommunications systems and automated information systems and evaluate their vulnerability to hostile interception and exploitation. Any such activities, including those involving monitoring of official telecommunications, shall be conducted in strict compliance with the law, Executive Orders and applicable Presidential Directives. No monitoring shall be performed without advising the heads of the agencies, departments or services concerned.

b. Act as government focal point for cryptography, telecommunications systems security, and automated information systems security.

c. Conduct, approve, or endorse research and development of techniques and equipment for telecommunications and automated information systems security for national security information.

d. Review and approve all standards, techniques, systems and equipments for telecommunications and automated information systems security.

e. Conduct foreign communications security liaison, including agreements with foreign governments and with international and private organizations for telecommunications and automated information systems security, except for those foreign intelligence relationships conducted for intelligence purposes by the Director of Central Intelligence. Agreements shall be coordinated with affected departments and agencies.

f. Operate such printing and fabrication facilities as may be required to perform critical functions related to the provision of cryptographic and other technical security material or services.

g. Assess the overall security posture and disseminate information on hostile threats to telecommunications and automated information systems security.

h. Operate a central technical center to evaluate and certify the security of telecommunications systems and automated information systems.

i. Prescribe the minimum standards, methods and procedures for protecting cryptographic and other sensitive technical security material, techniques, and information.

j. Review and assess annually the telecommunications systems security programs and budgets of the departments and agencies of the government, and recommend alternatives, where appropriate, for the Executive Agent and the Steering Group.

k. Review annually the aggregated automated information systems security program and budget recommendations of the departments and agencies of the U.S. Government for the Executive Agent and the Steering Group.

l. Request from the heads of departments and agencies such information and technical support as may be needed to discharge the responsibilities assigned herein.

m. Enter into agreements for the procurement of technical security material and other equipment, and their provision to government agencies and, where appropriate, to private organizations, including government contractors, and foreign governments.

("National Policy on Telecommunications and Automated Information Systems Security." Proposed Presidential Directive released Sept. 17, 1984, but never enacted.)

—**NATIONAL MILITARY COMMAND CENTER (NMCC).** Located in the Pentagon, the NMCC is the Joint Chiefs of Staff's watch center. Staffed around the clock, its watch teams provide the capability to react immediately to unforeseen events. Intelligence support for the NMCC is provided by the Defense Intelligence Agency's Directorate for NMIC Operations (JSO). The DIA staffs the National Military Intelligence Center,

which is located next to the NMCC so that it can provide the maximum degree of intelligence support to the NMCC team.

The NMCC is the result of a years-long search to find the appropriate system to provide adequate intelligence and operational response to both the President and other national-level personages and to the operational commanders. Today it is linked to the watch centers of the services, of the National Security Agency and of other Intelligence Community members through the National Operations and Intelligence Watch Officers' Net, and this allows all watch officers to converse immediately on events as they occur. In addition, the NMCC has the collection assets of the entire Intelligence Community at its disposal, and communications systems that allow it to converse with and support fully the operational commanders. In essence, the NMCC is the result of years of experience and research and is a system that is perceived to be the best one that can be provided to both field and national-level entities. *See also:* Defense Intelligence Agency.

References

Department of Defense, Defense Intelligence Agency. *Organization, Mission and Key Personnel.* Washington, DC: DIA, 1986.

—**NATIONAL MILITARY INTELLIGENCE ASSOCIATION (NMIA)** is a voluntary professional organization of military and civilian military intelligence experts. The organization's purpose is to promote the general understanding of the intelligence profession. The NMIA has several chapters, including ones in Washington, DC, Honolulu, and Europe, and it publishes the *American Intelligence Journal,* which contains articles on relevant contemporary and intelligence issues.

—**NATIONAL MILITARY INTELLIGENCE CENTER (NMIC).** *See:* Defense Intelligence Agency.

—**NATIONAL MILITARY INTELLIGENCE CENTER SUPPORT SYSTEM (NMICSS)** is managed by the Directorate for NMIC Operations (JSO), Defense Intelligence Agency, and provides technical support to the National Military Intelligence Center (NMIC). *See also:* Defense Intelligence Agency.

References

Department of Defense, Defense Intelligence Agency. *Organization, Mission and Key Personnel.* Washington, DC: DIA, 1986.

—**NATIONAL OBJECTIVES** are those fundamental aims, goals, or purposes of a nation—as opposed to the means for seeking these ends—toward which a policy is directed and efforts and resources of a country are applied. National objectives are usually articulated by the national leadership.

References

Department of Defense, Joint Chiefs of Staff. *Department of Defense Dictionary of Military and Related Terms.* Washington, DC: GPO, 1986.

Laqueur, Walter. *A World of Secrets.* New York: Basic Books, 1985.

Treverton, Gregory F. *Covert Action: The Limits of Intervention in the Postwar World.* New York: Basic Books, 1987.

—**NATIONAL OPERATIONS AND INTELLIGENCE ANALYSTS NET (NOIAN)** is a secure teleconferencing system that links the warning centers at the Central Intelligence Agency, Defense Intelligence Agency, National Security Agency, State Department, State Department's Bureau of Intelligence and Research, and Department of Defense Command Post (called the National Military Command Center [NMIC]) that can be activated to pass intelligence information on a particular issue or incident and to express points of view. The NOIAN and the National Operations and Intelligence Watch Officers Net (NOIWON) have the same subscribers, except for the White House, which is on the NOIWON, but not on the NOIAN.

References

Belden, Thomas. "Indications, Warning, and Crisis Options." *International Studies Quarterly* 21, no. 1 (Mar. 1977): 181–98.

—**NATIONAL OPERATIONS AND INTELLIGENCE WATCH OFFICERS NET (NOIWON)** is a secure teleconferencing system that links the warning centers at the Central Intelligence Agency, Defense Intelligence Agency, National Security Agency, State Department, State Department's Bureau of Intelligence and Research, White House, and Department of Defense Command Post (called the National Military Command Center [NMCC]) that is activated during crises or other situations that dictate a dialogue between these centers. It was designed by Dr. Thomas Belden and is intended to insure that all operations personnel concerned have the critical intelligence information they need to function properly. It is an operations-intelligence interface that is of inestimable value. When a secure voice conference is called among the watch officers, one of three possible results will occur. In most cases, the watch officers merely share the information that they have on a given situation. The second alternative concerns a situation in which one of the watch officers feels that it is necessary to take a particular action, such as notifying his agency director or putting his agency on alert. In this case, he will notify the other members of the NOIWON of his intention. The third alternative occurs when two or more watch officers decide that the situation is sufficiently important to issue an "Advisory," a short, formatted message that describes what is known and what is not known about the incident. The Advisory is distributed downward, upward, and laterally through each organization. It not only gives information but also seeks feedback from the recipients. Other NOIWON members may register their dissent, but they are required to distribute the Advisory through their own organization.

References

Belden, Thomas. "Indications, Warning, and Crisis Options." *International Studies Quarterly* 21, no. 1 (Mar. 1977): 181–98.

—**NATIONAL PHOTOGRAPHIC INTERPRETATION CENTER (NPIC)** was established in 1961 under the direction of the director of Central Intelligence to analyze photography from overhead reconnaissance. *See also:* Central Intelligence Agency.

References

Corson, William R. *The Armies of Ignorance: The Rise of the American Intelligence Empire.* New York: Dial Press, 1977.

Fain, Tyrus G.; Plant, Katharine C.; and Milloy, Ross. *The Intelligence Community: History, Organization, and Issues.* Public Documents Series. New York: R.R. Bowker, 1977.

Laqueur, Walter. *A World of Secrets.* New York: Basic Books, 1985.

Treverton, Gregory F. *Covert Action: The Limits of Intervention in the Postwar World.* New York: Basic Books, 1987.

—**NATIONAL POLICY** is a broad course of action or statements of guidance adopted by the government at the national level in pursuit of national objectives.

References

Department of Defense, Joint Chiefs of Staff. *Department of Defense Dictionary of Military and Related Terms.* Washington, DC: GPO, 1986.

Laqueur, Walter. *A World of Secrets.* New York: Basic Books, 1985.

Treverton, Gregory F. *Covert Action: The Limits of Intervention in the Postwar World.* New York: Basic Books, 1987.

—**NATIONAL PRINCIPLES** is a term often used in formulating national security policy. National principles are enduring modes of behavior or the relatively established guides to action that characterize nations.

References

Laqueur, Walter. *A World of Secrets.* New York: Basic Books, 1985.

Treverton, Gregory F. *Covert Action: The Limits of Intervention in the Postwar World.* New York: Basic Books, 1987.

—**NATIONAL PROGRAMS** is a term often used in formulating national security policy. National programs are what nations actually do to meet their commitments. Such programs are sometimes reflected in a nation's budget.

References

Laqueur, Walter. *A World of Secrets.* New York: Basic Books, 1985.

Treverton, Gregory F. *Covert Action: The Limits of Intervention in the Postwar World.* New York: Basic Books, 1987.

—**NATIONAL RECONNAISSANCE PROGRAMS** is a generic title that refers to overhead reconnaissance missions conducted by satellites and aircraft. The Department of Defense administers these programs, but the operation of specific programs is often delegated to the military services.

References

Corson, William R. *The Armies of Ignorance: The Rise of the American Intelligence Empire.* New York: Dial Press, 1977.

Dixon, James A. *National Security Policy Formulation: Institutions, Processes, and Issues.* Washington, DC: National Defense University, 1984.

Laqueur, Walter. *A World of Secrets.* New York: Basic Books, 1985.

—**NATIONAL SECURITY** is the territorial integrity, sovereignty, and international freedom of action of the United States. Intelligence activities relating to national security encompass all the military, economic, political, scientific and technological, and other aspects of foreign governments that pose actual or potential threats to U.S. interests. The Joint Chiefs of Staff define national security somewhat differently. They state that it is a collective term that encompasses both national defense and the foreign relations of the United States. Specifically, it is a condition provided by: (a) a military or defense advantage over any foreign nation or group of nations; or (b) a favorable foreign relations position; or (c) a defense posture capable of successfully resisting hostile or destructive action from within or without, overt or covert.

References

American Bar Association. *Oversight and Accountability of the U.S. Intelligence Agencies: An Evaluation.* Washington, DC: ABA, 1985.

Corson, William R. *The Armies of Ignorance: The Rise of the American Intelligence Empire.* New York: Dial Press, 1977.

Department of Defense, Defense Intelligence College. *Glossary of Intelligence Terms and Definitions.* Washington, DC: DIC: 1987.

Department of Defense, Joint Chiefs of Staff. *Department of Defense Dictionary of Military and Related Terms.* Washington, DC: GPO, 1986.

Kent, Sherman. *Strategic Intelligence for American World Policy.* Princeton, NJ: Princeton University Press, 1966.

Maurer, Alfred C.; Turnstall, Marion D.; and Keagle, James M. *Intelligence Policy and Process.* Boulder, CO: Westview Press, 1985.

—**NATIONAL SECURITY ACT OF 1947** established the Central Intelligence Agency and a director of Central Intelligence, which were under a new National Security Council that was presided over by the President. The CIA was given various duties concerning coordinating national intelligence. The act did not provide the director of Central Intelligence with a great deal of authority. Nonetheless an extremely comprehensive bill, it established the intelligence structure as we know it today. The act has been amended several times and appears in this encyclopedia as Appendix E.

In respect to its position on the Central Intelligence Agency, the act was an attempt to provide a central structure for the Intelligence Community and to centralize some of its functions. The act did not specifically authorize the CIA to participate in clandestine collection or operations. Indeed, it did not even address whether the agency should be involved in such activities. *See also:* Central Intelligence Agency, National Security Council.

References

Cline, Ray S. *The CIA Under Reagan, Bush, and Casey.* Washington, DC: Acropolis Books, 1981.

Corson, William R. *The Armies of Ignorance: The Rise of the American Intelligence Empire.* New York: Dial Press, 1977.

Godson, Roy, ed. *Intelligence Problems for the 1980s, Number 5: Clandestine Collection.* Washington, DC: National Strategy Information Center, 1982.

Kent, Sherman. *Strategic Intelligence for American World Policy.* Princeton, NJ: Princeton University Press, 1966.

Laqueur, Walter. *A World of Secrets.* New York: Basic Books, 1985.

Lefever, Ernest W., and Godson, Roy. *The CIA and the American Ethic: An Unfinished Debate.* Washington, DC: Ethics and Public Policy Center, Georgetown University, 1979.

Lowenthal, Mark M. *U.S. Intelligence: Evolution and Anatomy.* New York: Praeger, 1984.

Treverton, Gregory F. *Covert Action: The Limits of Intervention in the Postwar World.* New York: Basic Books, 1987.

Turner, Stansfield. *Secrecy and Democracy: The CIA in Transition.* Boston: Houghton Mifflin, 1985.

Warner, John S. "National Security and the First Amendment." Intelligence Profession Series, no. 2. McLean, VA: Association of Former Intelligence Officers, 1985.

—**NATIONAL SECURITY ADVISOR.** *See:* National Security Council.

—**NATIONAL SECURITY AGENCY (NSA).** (Editors' note: Unlike the other intelligence agencies, the NSA has maintained its shroud of secrecy. It does not publish brochures or narratives about its mission, organization, or staff, and it has traditionally offered very little about itself when its representatives have testified before Congress. The following discussion has been written without the benefit of government materials and has relied very heavily on James Bamford's *The Puzzle Palace,* which has been accepted at face value and is, by far, the most complete discussion of the agency available today.)

Of all the intelligence agencies, the least is known about the NSA, although it is one of the most powerful. It has complete responsibility for all U.S. communications security (COMSEC) activities and for producing signals intelligence (SIGINT) information. Among the agency's major functions are developing codes and cryptographic systems and producing SIGINT. It also processes counterintelligence information, provides SIGINT support to the military services, and conducts "foreign cryptological liaison relationships for intelligence purposes." The NSA was created on October 24, 1952, by President Truman to replace the Armed Forces Security Agency.

History

The state of the U.S. SIGINT on December 7, 1941, was a major factor in the disaster at Pearl Harbor. What compounded the tragedy, as Bamford observes, was that the community had foreknowledge of the attack but simply did not have the organization to process and disseminate the information quickly enough to warn U.S. forces of the impending catastrophe.

As a result of the attack, Secretary of War Henry Stimson appointed Alfred McCormack as his special assistant. McCormack's mission was to examine the entire U.S. collection and use of SIGINT material and to determine how the system could be improved. McCormack discovered almost immediately that the system was generally unsatisfactory. There were too few U.S. SIGINT intercept sites and the U.S. was not collecting as much information as it could. And even when information was collected, there were no standardized procedures for transmitting it to analysis centers. Rather, the existing procedures were haphazard at best. Assuming that the information did reach a production center, there were too few translators to translate all the material, and once the material was translated, there were too few analysts to process the information into intelligence. Finally, the dissemination of SIGINT was in an equally sorry state, with no established procedures for expeditiously delivering the material to the Washington leadership, and there were an inadequate number of secure means of transmitting the information to the field commanders who needed it in order to conduct operations.

McCormack's recommendation was to form a Special Branch in the War Department's Military Intelligence Service that would be independent. It would be charged with receiving raw SIGINT material, evaluating it, synthesizing it with intelligence information from other sources, analyzing it, and producing finished intelligence. Such a branch was created under the leadership of colonel Carter W. Clark. McCormack was commissioned as a colonel and became Clark's assistant.

While Clark and McCormack made great strides in the analysis of the intelligence that their Special Branch received, they worked under a significant handicap in that they had no operational control over the Signal Security Agency that collected the information. This meant that they had no control over which circuits were monitored, the prioritization of the sending of the traffic back to the analysis center, or where the intercept sites would be located. Nonetheless, SIGINT proved to be invaluable during the war and gave the U.S. the edge in such decisive conflicts as Coral Sea and the Battle of the Atlantic.

At war's end, the services again began competing for SIGINT missions. However, when the Army and Navy managed to resolve their differences, they began a consolidation that eventually resulted in the establishment in June 1946 of the United States Communications Intelligence Board (USCIB), composed of representatives from the Army, Navy, Air Force, Federal Bureau of Investigation, State Department, and Central Intelligence Group. In 1948, National Security Council Intelligence Directive (NSCID) No. 9 established the first charter for the U.S. SIGINT community. It designated the USCIB as the coordinator of communications intelligence, but it required a unanimous vote for all decisions, and it failed to give the board authority over the member agencies. As a result, the board was doomed to ineffectiveness. However, of equal significance was that the NSCID accorded communications intelligence a unique status and made it immune from normal Executive Orders that pertained to the Intelligence Community.

Thus, in 1948, while the nascent SIGINT community had great potential, it still was a fragmented composition of contending members. Secretary of Defense James Forrestal attempted unsuccessfully to change the situation. However, on May 20, 1949, his successor, Louis A. Johnson, established the Armed Forces Security Agency (AFSA) and placed it under the Joint Chiefs of Staff. Additionally, he created the Armed Forces Security Agency Council (AFSAC) to act as a governing council. Bamford notes that this arrangement was a cause of the failure to forewarn of the invasion of South Korea. As a result, AFSAC agreed to create the Intelligence Requirements Committee (IRC), which would convey Intelligence Community needs and priorities to the AFSA. Although this improved things to some extent, it still failed to create an acceptable situation. As a result of his dissatisfaction, President Truman created the Brownell Committee to investigate the SIGINT situation and make recommendations. The committee's report held the military services and the Joint Chiefs of Staff responsible for the problem. After considering several proposals, the committee recommended that the secretary of defense be made the executive agent for communications intelligence, that the AFSAC be abolished, and that the director of the AFSA be given far greater authority. The military services retained their service SIGINT organizations within the greater organizational framework. President Truman accepted the committee's recommendations with only one major exception: the name of the organization was changed to the National Security Agency.

The Tenure of Ralph J. Canine. Lieutenant General Ralph J. Canine, U.S. Army, a graduate of Northwestern, served as the director of the NSA from November 1952 until November 1956. Although he lacked a scientific background, Canine was considered an excellent director in that he was able to assuage the agency's two major personalities, the military and the civilian scientist. In his tenure, the agency settled into its new quarters and established its routines.

The Tenure of John A. Samford. With Canine's retirement, Lieutenant General John Alexander Samford, U.S. Air Force, became director and served in this capacity from November 1956 until November 1960. A graduate of West Point, Samford had spent almost his entire career in aviation. Under him, the worldwide field network of the agency was expanded considerably. However, his tour was marred when two NSA employees defected to the Soviet Union.

The Tenure of Laurence H. Frost. Vice Admiral Laurence H. Frost, U.S. Navy, served as director from November 1960 to June 1962. A graduate of Annapolis, Frost had an extensive communications background. Awarded a Bronze and two Silver Stars for his duty in the Pacific in World War II, Frost had also served in several intelligence billets and as chief of staff at the NSA from 1953 to 1955. He then served as director of naval intelligence and, in 1960, accepted assignment as director, NSA. Frost became director in the midst of the controversy of the defection of two NSA employees to the Soviet Union, and he spent most of his twenty-month tenure responding to inquests concerning the defections. However, it was during his tour that the NSA civilians were shifted from regular to excepted status, which meant that they now could be fired in the interests of national security. Following a dispute with the Pentagon in 1962, Frost was reassigned to the Potomac River Naval Command, from which he retired.

The Tenure of Gordon A. Blake. Lieutenant General Gordon A. Blake, U.S. Air Force, became director when Frost, in a controversy with the Pentagon, was forced to accept another command. Blake had extensive communications experience, having served as commander of the Army Airways Communications System in World War II and as director of Air Force Communications from 1953 to 1957. In 1957, he was appointed as commander, U.S. Air Force Security Service, the NSA's air arm.

He served as director from June 30, 1962, until June 1, 1965. He concentrated on, and succeeded in establishing, a closer relationship between the agency and the Service Cryptologic Organizations.

The Tenure of Marshall S. Carter. Lieutenant General Marshall S. Carter, U.S. Army, served as director of the NSA from June 1, 1965, until August 1, 1969. A graduate of West Point with a master's degree in engineering from MIT, Carter had served as deputy director of Central Intelligence under John McCone. When President Johnson replaced McCone with Vice Admiral William Rayborn, Carter was without a job, because the offices of director and deputy director of Central Intelligence could not be held by military officers. When the NSA directorship was offered, he quickly accepted it.

Carter was extremely popular with his employees. Gifted with a fine sense of humor, he worked arduously to improve the agency's image. He has been criticized by some because he expanded the civilian population at the agency. This was part of his effort to nationalize the NSA, but it did emphasize strategic over tactical SIGINT production, and it weakened the military's lines of control over the agency. These measures, of course, brought him into conflict with the military leadership, and his departure, and the assignment of Vice Admiral Noel Gayler, was the military's attempt to regain control.

The Tenure of Noel Gayler. Vice Admiral Noel Gayler, U.S. Navy, a naval aviator, was the sixth director of the NSA, serving from August 1, 1969, until August 24, 1972. A graduate of the Naval Academy, he had spent most of his career as a fighter pilot and had been awarded three Silver Stars for his service in World War II. His postwar tours included duty with the secretary of the navy, and then as naval attaché to London and as deputy director of the Joint Strategic Planning Staff. Gayler was unlike his predecessors at the NSA, who had been assigned to the agency as their last major job before retirement. He was young enough to anticipate an additional major tour before retirement, and when he left the NSA, it was to become commander in chief, Pacific (CINCPAC). Thus, beginning with Gayler, the directorship was no longer a dead-end job. Rather, it became a springboard to four-star rank.

The Tenure of Samuel C. Phillips. Lieutenant General Samuel C. Phillips, U.S. Air Force, served as director of the NSA from August 24, 1972, until August 15, 1973. Prior to assuming the directorship, he had had extensive experience in the Air Force missile program and possibly in the National Reconnaissance Program, which handles the U.S. spy satellites. He remained as director for barely a year and had little effect on the organization.

The Tenure of Lew Allen, Jr. Lieutenant General Lew Allen, Jr., U.S. Air Force, served as director of the NSA from August 15, 1973, until July 5, 1977. A graduate of West Point, he also held master's and doctoral degrees in physics from the University of Illinois. His experience included considerable work in the field of nuclear weapons, and he had also served in the Space Technology Office of the director of Defense Research and Engineering, Office of the Secretary of Defense, and in the National Reconnaissance Office. Allen spent a good deal of his time as director defending the agency in the White House and congressional investigations of the Intelligence Community. Upon being relieved as director, he served briefly as director, Air Force Systems Command, and then became chief of staff, U.S. Air Force.

The Tenure of Bobby Inman. Vice Admiral Bobby Ray Inman, U.S. Navy, served as director of the NSA from July 5, 1977, until March 10, 1981. Born in Rhonesboro, Texas, Inman was a career naval intelligence officer. In 1974, he was appointed as director of Naval Intelligence, and after a subsequent tour at the Defense Intelligence Agency, he became the director of the NSA. The youngest officer to ever hold the position, Inman was a skilled diplomat who was popular with Congress. In 1981, he left the agency to become the deputy director of Central Intelligence.

The Tenure of Lincoln D. Faurer. Lieutenant General Lincoln D. Faurer, U.S. Air Force, served as director of the NSA from March 1981 until 1985. A graduate of West Point, he held a master's degree in engineering management from Rensselaer Polytechnic Institute and a second master's in international affairs from George Washington University. With extensive experience in intelligence and strategic reconnaissance assignments, he was assigned to the Defense Intelligence Agency in 1964. In 1974, he returned to the agency to become its deputy director for intelligence, and then became its vice director for production. In 1977, he was transferred to Europe, where he was chief of intelligence for the U.S. European Command, and then became deputy chairman of NATO's Military Committee in Brussels. In 1981, he was selected as director of the NSA. Faurer's tenure had a positive affect on the agency, which continued to prosper under his leadership. A disagreement concerning reducing the funds to the agency led to Faurer's departure in 1985.

The Tenure of William Odom. Lieutenant General William Odom served as director of the NSA from 1985 to 1988. Numerous reports of his acerbic nature and of disgruntled agency employees indicated that he was one of the less popular directors.

The Tenure of William Studeman. Admiral William Studeman became director of the NSA in 1988. A career naval intelligence officer, Stude-

man was well prepared for the duties of the directorship. The major problems facing him as he assumed his responsibilities were the continued development of the agency, the low morale that had resulted from General Odom's tenure, and the possible changes that might occur as George Bush became President in 1989.

Organization

The NSA is composed of eleven major components: the headquarters, four operational branches, five support branches, and one training branch.

Headquarters. The headquarters is composed of the director, the vice director, and the support staff.

The duty of the director is to manage the NSA. After assuming the second responsibility of director of the Central Security Service, the director also became responsible for the interaction of the Service Cryptologic Agencies. The responsibilities of the position are awesome. He is responsible for the entire NSA complex, its security, its employees, and its production, and for all the field sites around the world. Additionally, given the nature of his work, he is often on a legal tightrope, as eavesdropping has been a continual concern of Congress, the White House, and the courts.

The following have served as deputy directors of the NSA:

Rear Admiral Joseph N. Wenger, U.S. Navy (vice director), November 1952–Autumn 1953.

Brigadier General John B. Ackerman, U.S. Air Force (vice director), Autumn 1953–June 1966.

Lieutenant General John S. Samford, U.S. Air Force (vice director), June 1956–October 1957.

Joseph H. Ream, November 1956–October 1957.

Dr. Howard T. Engstrom, October 1957–August 1958.

Dr. Louis W. Tordilla, August 1958–April 1974.

Benson K. Buffham, April 1974–May 1978.

Robert E. Drake, May 1978–April 1980.

Ann Z. Caracristi, April 1980–July 1982.

Robert E. Rich, July 1982–.

Of the deputies, Dr. Louis Tordilla, who served as deputy director for sixteen years, under seven different directors, was by far the most effective. He was responsible for the massive research and development program that produced the agency's advanced computer capabilities, and he offered a calming continuity to both U.S. and Allied leaders as the directors came and went. Primarily because of the imprint that Tordilla left on the position, the deputy director is intimately involved in the daily functioning of the agency. This allows the director to honor his responsibilities vis-à-vis Washington and to focus on the organization's major issues and problems.

Office of Signals Intelligence Operations (DDO). The DDO is managed by the deputy director for operations, and is the premiere office within the agency. Formerly known as the Office of Production (PROD), it has the largest staff, consisting of more "eavesdroppers, codebreakers, linguists, traffic and signals analysts" than any other office in the agency. Bamford states that "DDO encompasses the entire spectrum of signals intelligence, from intercept to cryptanalysis, traffic analysis to analysis of clear text, high-level diplomatic systems to low-level radio telephone. Its brief covers the analysis of systems belonging to friend as well as foe, to democracies as well as dictatorships, microcountries as well as superpowers. It is the Black Chamber's Black Chamber."

Over the years, the DDO has undergone its share of reorganizations. Today, it is believed to be composed of the following: A Group, which is the largest of the groups and is responsible for the analysis of all material concerning the Soviet Union and Warsaw Pact; B Group, which is responsible for China, Korea, Vietnam, and the rest of Communist Asia; G Group, which is responsible for the Third World and for international telecommunications to and from the United States; C Group, which provides computer support; W Group, which assures the coordination and management of all intercept operations; and a number of staff components, which provide support services such as computer liaison and plans and policy functions.

Office of Communications Security (COMSEC). COMSEC, better known as the S Organization, provides "the methods, principles, and equipment to protect the entire panoply of classified U.S. communications, including command and control, voice, data, teletype, and telemetry; it also prescribes the way in which the systems are to be used. This encompasses everything from the scrambler phone in the President's limousine to the banks of chattering crypto machines in the State Department's sixth-floor code room—and a great deal in between."

Office of Research and Engineering (R&E). R&E produces new systems to be used in fulfilling the agency's operational mission. It is composed of the following: REMP (Research, Engineering, Mathematics and Physics), which conducts general analysis of cryptanalytic problems; RADE (Research and Development), which constructs intercept and signals analysis hardware; STED (Standard Technical Equipment Development), which assists in producing advanced cryptologic equipment and was renamed the Cryptologic Equipment Division; and Computer Techniques Division, which accomplishes all computer research.

Office of Telecommunications and Computer Services. This office is responsible for the agency's computer research and development effort. It is also responsible for the Critical Intelligence Communications System (CRITICOMM). CRITICOMM is a worldwide circuit that is designed to flash to the President and a selected number of other high-level consumers news of an event within ten minutes of its occurrence. In 1973, the CRITICOMM/SPINTCOMM network became the Digital Network—Defense Special Security Communications System (DINDSSCS).

Office of Administration. This office is responsible for recruiting, clearing, training, and assigning personnel, runs the agency's security force, and enforces the agency's regulations.

Office of Installations and Logistics. This office is responsible for agency procurement, including all of its computer contracts, for growth planning in the NSA complex, for overseas installations development, and for various housekeeping chores.

Office of Plans and Policy (DDPP). The DDPP is a staff organization that is responsible for planning and policy development.

Office of Programs and Resources (DDPR). The DDPR prepares the community budget and the Consolidated Cryptologic Program (CCP), and it conducts liaison between the agency and the service cryptologic organizations.

Office of the General Counsel. This office is responsible for all of the agency's legal matters.

National Cryptologic School. This school is responsible for all of the agency's training.

The Plant. The National Security Agency complex lies on a thousand acres of Fort Meade, halfway between Washington and Baltimore and just off the Baltimore-Washington Parkway. The initial complex was a building with 1.4 million square feet of space and was completed in 1957. A second building, completed in 1966, provided an additional 512,000 square feet of space. Bamford provides some concept of the immensity of the complex. He says that it is "almost the size of the CIA building with the United States Capitol sitting on top . . . . Inside are 7,560,000 linear feet of telephone wire, 70,000 square feet of permanently sealed windows, 16,000 light fixtures, . . . and the nation's longest unobstructed corridor—980 feet—casting the 750-foot corridor of the Capitol in a distant second place." In 1968, a third building added an additional 261,516 square feet, and additional buildings, added in the 1970s and 1980s, have included dormitories, mess halls, and recreation facilities.

The NSA Seal. The NSA Seal has a proud, protective eagle, representative of the United States, with an ancient key in its talons. The key is representative of unlocking the secrets of others while guarding the secrets of the United States. Surrounding the eagle on the border of the seal are the words National Security Agency and United States of America. *See also:* communications security.

References

Allen, Thomas B., and Polmar, Norman. *Merchants of Treason: America's Secrets for Sale.* New York: Delacorte Press, 1988.

American Bar Association. Oversight and Accountability of the *U.S. Intelligence Agencies: An Evaluation.* Washington, DC: ABA, 1985.

Deacon, Richard. *Spyclopedia: An Encyclopedia of Spies, Secret Services, Operations, Jargon, and All Subjects Related to the World of Espionage.* London: Macdonald, 1987.

Godson, Roy, ed. *Intelligence Problems for the 1980s, Number 2: Analysis and Estimates.* Washington, DC: National Strategy Information Center, 1980.

———. *Intelligence Problems for the 1980s, Number 3: Counterintelligence.* Washington, DC: National Strategy Information Center, 1980.

———. *Intelligence Problems for the 1980s, Number 4: Covert Action.* Washington, DC: National Strategy Information Center, 1981.

———. *Intelligence Problems for the 1980s, Number 5: Clandestine Collection.* Washington, DC: National Strategy Information Center, 1982.

Lefever, Ernest W., and Godson, Roy. *The CIA and the American Ethic: An Unfinished Debate.* Washington, DC: Ethics and Public Policy Center, Georgetown University, 1979.

Maurer, Alfred C.; Turnstall, Marion D.; and Keagle, James M. *Intelligence Policy and Process.* Boulder, CO: Westview Press, 1985.

Quirk, John; Phillips, David; Cline, Ray; and Pforzheimer, Walter. *The Central Intelligence Agency: A Photographic History.* Guilford, CT: Foreign Intelligence Press, 1986.

U.S. Congress. Senate. *Final Report of the Senate Select Committee to Study Government Operations with Respect to Intelligence Activities. Report 94-755. Book I, Foreign and Military Intelligence.* Washington, DC: GPO, 1976.

—NATIONAL SECURITY AGENCY ACT OF 1959, 50 U.S.C.A. 402.

The National Security Agency had been granted considerable immunity when it was created by a Top Secret directive that was issued by President Truman on October 24, 1952, rather than by statute. However, Congress acted in 1959 to grant the NSA additional protection under the National Security Agency Act of 1959. In it, the NSA was exempt from having to provide any information concerning its mission and activities or the names, numbers, or ranks of its employees.

References

Warner, John S. "National Security and the First Amendment." Intelligence Profession Series. no. 2. McLean, VA: Association of Former Intelligence Officers, 1985.

—NATIONAL SECURITY COUNCIL (NSC)

was established by the National Security Act of 1947 and was placed in the Executive Office of the President in 1949, when the 1947 act was amended by the National Security Act Amendments of 1949.

Function

The NSC is the principal forum for consideration of national security policy issues that require presidential decision. The council advises the president with respect to the integration of domestic, foreign, and military policies relating to the national security, in order to enable the Executive departments and agencies to cooperate more effectively. For the purpose of making recommendations to the president, the NSC also assesses the objectives, commitments, and risks of the United States in relation to its actual and potential military power, and considers policies on matters of common interest to the Executive departments and agencies concerning national security.

Membership

The statutory members of the NSC are the president, the vice president, the secretary of state, and the secretary of defense.

The secretary of state is the president's principal foreign policy advisor. He formulates foreign policy in conjunction with the NSC process and the president's guidance, and he executes approved policy. The secretary of state has the authority and responsibility for the overall direction, coordination, and supervision of the interdepartmental duties that are incident to foreign policy formulation, and the activities of the Executive departments and agencies overseas.

The secretary of defense is the president's principal defense policy advisor. He is responsible for formulating general defense policy in conjunction with the NSC process and the president's guidance and for policy related to all matters of direct primary concern to the Department of Defense.

The director of Central Intelligence and the chairman of the Joint Chiefs of Staff are statutory advisors to the NSC. The director of Central Intelligence advises the council with respect to coordinating intelligence activities of the Executive departments and agencies in the interest of national security and otherwise as provided by law. The chairman of the Joint Chiefs of Staff is the principal military advisor to the president, the secretary of defense, and the NSC.

The directors of the United States Arms Control and Disarmament Agency and the United States Information Agency are special statutory advisors to the NSC. The director of the Arms Control and Disarmament Agency is the principal advisor to the president, the secretary of state, and the NSC on arms control and disarmament. The director of the United States Information Agency is the principal advisor to the president, the secretary of state, and the NSC on public diplomacy. In addition, the attorney general, the secretary of the treasury, and the chief of staff to the president attend council meetings at the president's invitation. As the meeting agenda dictates, heads of other Executive departments and agencies and senior officials of the Executive Office of the President participate in NSC meetings.

The Assistant to the President for National Security Affairs (national security advisor). The national security advisor has primary responsibility for the daily management of the NSC and the interagency coordination process. He serves as the principal White House staff advisor to the president with respect to all national security affairs. In this capacity, the national security advisor presents his own views and advice as well as the views of the other NSC members.

The National Security Council staff. The NSC staff is composed of people who have broad experience in national security affairs. Staff officers are balanced among the Executive departments and agencies and the private sector. The NSC staff organization sets clear, vertical lines of control and accountability to the national security advisor and his deputy, through the senior director of each directorate. The NSC legal advisor, a new position, ensures that the NSC actions conform to all legal requirements.

In their report to the president in February 1987, Senators John Tower and Edmund Muskie and Lieutenant General Brent Scowcroft noted that the NSC staff is a unique body in that it is highly personal to the president and has to respond to his working style. They said:

> At the time it established the National Security Council, Congress authorized a staff headed by an Executive Secretary appointed by the President. Initially quite small, the NSC staff expanded substantially under President Eisenhower.
>
> What emerges from this history is an NSC staff used by each President in a way that reflected his individual preferences and working style. Over time, it has developed an important role within the Executive Branch of coordinating policy review, preparing issues for Presidential decision, and monitoring implementation. But it has remained the President's creature, molded as he sees fit, to serve as his personal staff for national security affairs. For this reason, it has generally operated out of the public view and has not been subject to direct oversight by the Congress.

The NSC staff, through the executive secretary, assists the national security advisor in his roles both as manager of the NSC process and as the president's principal White House staff advisor on national security affairs.

The staff is composed of the following entities:

Assistant to the president for national security affairs is the president's chief advisor on national security affairs. He also has responsibility for the daily management of the NSC staff.

Deputy assistant to the president for national security affairs assists the assistant in fulfilling his duties and performs other duties as assigned.

Executive staff , which is composed of the executive secretary and his staff, the legal advisor, the legislative affairs advisor, a military assistant, and a counselor.

Ten staff directorates, five of which are geographic, and five of which are functional. The geographic directorates are:

- **European and Soviet Affairs,** which is concerned with U.S. national security policy as it applies to NATO, Western Europe, and the Soviet Union. This section plays a significant role in determining European disarmament and in detailing the president's schedule for summit talks.
- **Asian Affairs,** which probably played a significant role in Dr. Henry Kissinger's work concerning the U.S. recognition of the People's Republic of China. It also plays a significant role in any presidential trips to China.
- **African Affairs,** which advises the president on U.S. policy options concerning Africa.
- **Latin American Affairs,** which advises the president on U.S. policy options concerning Central and South America. Recently, this directorate has supported U.S. policymaking vis-à-vis the Nicaraguan government of Daniel Ortega, the Panama situation, and U.S. policy toward Honduras, El Salvador, and the Sandinistas.
- **Near East and South African Affairs,** which contributes to current policies toward Israel, Egypt, Jordan, and the other Middle Eastern nations, and toward South Africa. This directorate probably played a significant role in the U.S. strike against Libya and in the continuing U.S. policy concerning South Africa.

The functional directorates are:

- **Intelligence Programs,** which coordinates with the Central intelligence Agency, the Federal Bureau of Investigation, and the Defense Department in order to advise the president on these matters. This directorate would play a significant role in the formulation of special activities.
- **International Economic Affairs,** which would advise the president concerning U.S. international economic policy. This directorate probably played a significant

part in the U.S. program to devalue the U.S. dollar overseas in 1987 and 1988 in order to decrease the U.S. trade deficit.

- **International Programs/Technology Affairs,** which is concerned with many issues, including the transfer of U.S. technology overseas. This directorate probably played a significant role in the U.S. policy toward Japan, after a Japanese firm sold U.S. military technology to the Soviet Union.
- **Arms Control,** which works closely with the U.S. Arms Control and Disarmament Agency in developing arms control strategies.
- **Defense Policy.**

History

As James Dixon notes, the National Security Act of 1947 was considered a victory by those who felt that President Roosevelt had exceeded his powers as president of the United States. These individuals saw the NSC as a body that, by providing national security advice, would influence presidential decisionmaking. However, the council was not a decisionmaking body, and the president could accept or reject their positions as he saw fit. Additionally, there was no clearcut guidance as to how the NSC would be used, so each president was free to use the council as he wished. That each president has used the NSC in a different way has created a colorful history for the council.

President Harry S. Truman. President Truman faced some of the most difficult foreign policy problems that have ever confronted a president. Use of the atomic bomb, Soviet policy toward Eastern Europe, the creation of NATO, the Cold War, the Berlin airlift, the Marshall Plan, the creation of new nations out of old colonies, Soviet pressure on Greece, Turkey, Iran, and Austria, the Chinese revolution, and the Korean War were among the most pressing issues. Nonetheless, possibly because of his view that the president should not delegate his decisionmaking responsibilities, Truman did not attend NSC meetings until very late in his administration. His official reason for his absence was that he did not wish to influence the deliberations.

After the outbreak of the Korean War, Truman began attending the sessions and actively took part in the proceedings. However, in his memoirs, he stated, "I used the Council only as a place for recommendations to be worked out. The policy has to come down from the President, as all final decisions have to be made by him." Truman's assignation of the NSC to an advisory role has been continued by all subsequent presidents.

President Dwight D. Eisenhower. Unlike Truman, President Eisenhower preferred large, well-organized deliberative bodies, which, he felt, were the best means to the most accurate solutions. Under Robert Cutler, Truman's skeletal NSC was formalized, developed, and expanded. Procedures were established, and clear lines of authority and responsibility were defined. As a result, the NSC assumed a significant role in formulating and implementing national security policy decisions. Under this organization, the Planning Board and the Operations Coordinating Board were established and became very significant. The Planning Board assessed departmental recommendations, resolved differences between agencies, and prepared policy papers that outlined national security objectives. For its part, after a decision was made, the Operations Coordinating Board developed the operational guidelines and monitored policy implementation.

Eisenhower took a very active interest in national security affairs. He attended virtually every meeting, and his special assistant for national security affairs, General Andrew Goodpaster, presided over the NSC staff, which provided presidential liaison with this group as well.

Eisenhower's system has been criticized because it promoted "excessive compromise, logrolling, and minority domination." However, under Eisenhower, the system did work, and the nation pursued a coherent foreign policy. Thus, in the final analysis, although the system may have been too bureaucratic and formalized to support other presidents properly, the system functioned for Eisenhower by providing him the counsel that he needed to formulate U.S. policy.

President John F. Kennedy. With President Kennedy's accession to the presidency, the NSC organizational pendulum swung backward. In contrast to Eisenhower's penchant for large councils, Kennedy preferred a more informal system, in which national security issues would be handled by a group of trusted advisors. As a result, Kennedy dismantled the NSC system and abolished the Eisenhower boards. All that was left were the statutory members, who were the president, the vice president, the secretary of state, the secretary of defense, the director of the Office of Emergency Planning, and the president's special assistant for national security affairs. The

director of Central Intelligence and the chairman of the Joint Chiefs of Staff continued on in an advisory capacity. Many of the Kennedy apologists have praised his system and have labeled it a collegial system. However, while his approach resolved many of the problems that were inherent in the Eisenhower system, it nonetheless was not perfect. Among the justifiable criticisms that have been made are that Kennedy's system allowed the formal NSC structure to deteriorate and that his administration was sporadic. As Dixon notes, the Kennedy approach was basically one of "muddling through."

President Lyndon B. Johnson. Kennedy's assassination brought President Johnson, a man with little foreign policy experience, unexpectedly to the White House. Although Johnson attended the NSC meetings, he preferred to conduct the most important national security policy discussions at his "Tuesday Lunch" sessions, with only a few trusted advisors. This had two negative effects. First, it continued the erosive Kennedy trend in respect to the NSC, which was cut off from national security policy decisionmaking on many of the most important issues. Second, it meant that Johnson relied primarily on Secretary of State Dean Rusk and Secretary of Defense Robert McNamara, who were also fairly isolated from the NSC. As a result, Johnson deprived himself and his chief assistants from the support that the NSC could have provided, and the atrophying NSC was reduced to a role of keeping the minutes.

President Richard M. Nixon. President Nixon made the deterioration of the NSC under Kennedy and Johnson a campaign issue in the 1968 presidential election. Upon assuming office, he appointed Henry Kissinger as his assistant to the president for national security affairs and gave him the task of reestablishing the National Security Council. Although Kissinger did this, it is interesting to note that both he and Nixon distrusted bureaucracies and made most major policy decisions themselves. Not only was the NSC not permitted a significant role in U.S. foreign policy, but also the State Department was ignored as Nixon and Kissinger made many of the most important decisions themselves in the White House. Thus, although Nixon restored the NSC, he did not permit it to play a major role in policymaking.

President Gerald Ford. Like Johnson, President Ford had little foreign policy experience. As a result, he relied heavily on Kissinger, who virtually became the maker of U.S. foreign policy. The role of the NSC that was established in the Nixon administration was continued, until Ford was criticized for allowing Kissinger so much power. As result, Kissinger was forced to resign, and Ford appointed Lieutenant General Brent Scowcroft in his place.

In spite of the disuse of the NSC, the Nixon-Ford period has been labeled by some as a high point in U.S. foreign policy. America extricated itself from Vietnam, recognized China, and became very involved in the Middle East peace process.

President Jimmy Carter. President Carter had to change the role of the NSC when he took office, because the Nixon-Ford approach had so emphasized the role of Henry Kissinger that Kissinger's absence created a significant void. Carter's approach has been compared to Kennedy's because of his preference for small groups or teams to handle crisis issues. However, an additional element, Zbigniew Brzezinski, Carter's national security advisor, made Carter's administration unique. Brzezinski, like Kissinger, was a man of considerable reputation as a national strategist; he, like Kissinger, represented one of America's best universities; and he, like Kissinger, had a considerable ego. It would have been difficult not to compare the two during Brzezinski's tenure, and the comparisons were soon in coming and frequent in their appearance. As a result, there was a tendency for Brzezinski to attempt to maximize his role in U.S. foreign policymaking and an imperative to achieve significant accomplishments. Additionally, a humanistic presidential worldview and a presidential insistence on strengthening the role of the Cabinet officers were superimposed upon this structure. The system did not work because of Brzezinski's undue influence and the fact that he and Carter decided which issues the Cabinet would consider.

President Ronald Reagan. President Reagan's approach to national policy was to be presented with a list of alternative solutions from which he could choose. This harkened back, in a way, to President Truman's approach of taking clear responsibility for policy decisions.

Nonetheless, Reagan did make allowances for strong personalities in his administration. His choice of Alexander Haig as secretary of state and Jeane Kirkpatrick as U.S. ambassador to the United Nations are two examples of this. Additionally, Reagan deliberately deemphasized the profile of the assistant to the president for national security affairs so that he would not be-come a rival to the secretary of state or the president. Thus, the first three advisors—Richard Allen, William P. Clark, and Robert C. McFarlane—all were "low profile" administration figures.

The system seemed to function quite well for several years, but Reagan's final years in office were marred by the Iran-Contra scandal. Thus, while Reagan had taken several positive steps in reestablishing the role of the NSC during his administration, the scandal left the council in an unsettled state when he left office in 1989. It appeared that the dual problem of fully integrating the council into the decisionmaking structure so that it could interact effectively with the Department of State and the Intelligence Community still remained, to be tackled by George Bush when he took office in January 1989.

References

American Bar Association. *Oversight and Accountability of the U.S. Intelligence Agencies: An Evaluation.* Washington, DC: ABA, 1985.

Breckinridge, Scott D. *The CIA and the U.S. Intelligence System.* Boulder, CO: Westview Press, 1986.

Cline, Ray S. *The CIA Under Reagan, Bush, and Casey.* Washington, DC: Acropolis Books, 1981.

Corson, William R. *The Armies of Ignorance: The Rise of the American Intelligence Empire.* New York: Dial Press, 1977.

Fain, Tyrus G.; Plant, Katharine C.; and Milloy, Ross. *The Intelligence Community: History, Organization, and Issues.* Public Documents Series. New York: R.R. Bowker, 1977.

Laqueur, Walter. *A World of Secrets.* New York: Basic Books, 1985.

Lefever, Ernest W., and Godson, Roy. *The CIA and the American Ethic: An Unfinished Debate.* Washington, DC: Ethics and Public Policy Center, Georgetown University, 1979.

Lowenthal, Mark M. *U.S. Intelligence: Evolution and Anatomy.* New York: Praeger, 1984.

Maurer, Alfred C.; Turnstall, Marion D.; and Keagle, James M. *Intelligence Policy and Process.* Boulder, CO: Westview Press, 1985.

Office of the President of the United States. *Report of the President's Special Review Board.* Washington, DC: GPO, February 26, 1987.

Turner, Stansfield. *Secrecy and Democracy: The CIA in Transition.* Boston: Houghton Mifflin, 1985.

—NATIONAL SECURITY COUNCIL INTELLIGENCE DIRECTIVES (NSCIDS) are intelligence guidelines that are issued by the National Security Council to the intelligence agencies. They are often supplemented by more specific directives from the director of Central Intelligence and by internal or departmental guidance within the intelligence agencies. *See also:* National Security Council.

References

Corson, William R. *The Armies of Ignorance: The Rise of the American Intelligence Empire.* New York: Dial Press, 1977.

Fain, Tyrus G.; Plant, Katharine C.; and Milloy, Ross. *The Intelligence Community: History, Organization, and Issues.* Public Documents Series. New York: R.R. Bowker, 1977.

Laqueur, Walter. *A World of Secrets.* New York: Basic Books, 1985.

Quirk, John; Phillips, David; Cline, Ray; and Pforzheimer, Walter. *The Central Intelligence Agency: A Photographic History.* Guilford, CT: Foreign Intelligence Press, 1986.

Treverton, Gregory F. *Covert Action: The Limits of Intervention in the Postwar World.* New York: Basic Books, 1987.

Turner, Stansfield. *Secrecy and Democracy: The CIA in Transition.* Boston: Houghton Mifflin, 1985.

U.S. Congress. Senate. *Final Report of the Senate Select Committee to Study Government Operations with Respect to Intelligence Activities. Report 94-755. Book I, Foreign and Military Intelligence.* Washington, DC: GPO, 1976.

—**NATIONAL SECURITY COUNCIL INTELLIGENCE DIRECTIVE (NSCID) NO. 9**, issued in 1948, established the first charter for the U.S. SIGINT community. It designated the United States Communications Intelligence Board (USCIB) as the coordinator of Communications Intelligence, but it required a unanimous vote for all decisions, and it failed to give the board authority over the member agencies. As a result, the board was doomed to ineffectiveness. However, of equal significance was that the NSCID accorded communications intelligence a unique status and made it immune to normal Executive Orders that pertained to the Intelligence Community. *See also:* National Security Council.

References

Bamford, James. *The Puzzle Palace: A Report on America's Most Secret Agency.* New York: Penguin Books, 1983.

Corson, William R. *The Armies of Ignorance: The Rise of the American Intelligence Empire.* New York: Dial Press, 1977.

Laqueur, Walter. *A World of Secrets.* New York: Basic Books, 1985.

Turner, Stansfield. *Secrecy and Democracy: The CIA in Transition.* Boston: Houghton Mifflin, 1985.

—**NATIONAL SECURITY COUNCIL POLICY REVIEW COMMITTEE** was established by Executive Order 12036, "United States Intelligence Activities," which was signed by President Carter on January 24, 1978. The order established two committees, the NSC Policy Review Committee and the Special Coordinating Committee. The Policy Review Committee was to be chaired by the director of Central Intelligence and was composed of the vice president, the secretary of defense, the secretary of the treasury, the assistant to the president for national security affairs, the chairman of the Joint Chiefs of Staff, and other members, as appropriate. Its duties were to establish requirements and priorities for national foreign intelligence, review the budget proposals of the National Foreign Intelligence Program, conduct periodic reviews of intelligence products in order to assess their quality and responsiveness to intelligence requirements, and report annually on the activities of the National Security Council. *See also:* National Security Council.

References

Laqueur, Walter. *A World of Secrets.* New York: Basic Books, 1985.

Office of the President of the United States. *Executive Order 12036, United States Intelligence Activities.* Washington, DC, Jan. 24, 1978.

Treverton, Gregory F. *Covert Action: The Limits of Intervention in the Postwar World.* New York: Basic Books, 1987.

Turner, Stansfield. *Secrecy and Democracy: The CIA in Transition.* Boston: Houghton Mifflin, 1985.

—**NATIONAL SECURITY COUNCIL SPECIAL COORDINATING COMMITTEE (SCC)** was established by Executive Order 12036, "United States Intelligence Activities," which was signed by President Carter on January 24, 1978. The SCC was chaired by the assistant to the president for national security affairs, and was composed of the statutory members of the National Security Council and other senior officials, as appropriate. The duties of the SCC were to (1) Review each and every special activity that the Intelligence Community or National Security Council proposed and to make recommendations to the president. When meeting for this purpose, the SCC was to be composed of the secretary of state, secretary of defense, attorney general, director of Management and Budget, assistant to the president for national security affairs, chairman of the Joint Chiefs of Staff, and director of Central Intelligence. (2) Review sensitive foreign intelligence collection operations. When meeting for this purpose, only the secretary of state, secretary of defense, attorney general, assistant to the president for national security affairs, director of Central Intelligence, and such other members as designated by the chairman were to meet. (3) Develop policy for conducting counterintelligence. When meeting in this capacity, the members were to include the secretary of state, secretary of defense, attorney general, director of the Office of Management and Budget, assistant to the president for national security affairs, chairman of the Joint Chiefs of Staff, director of Central Intelligence, and director of the Federal Bureau of Investigation. Its responsibilities in this respect were to develop standards and doctrine for counterintelligence activity, resolve interagency differences, develop an annual threat assessment that would include an assessment of U.S. counterintelligence efforts, and approve specific counterintelligence activities. The SCC was also to conduct annual reviews of special activities and sensitive intelligence collection operations and report on these to the NSC, and it was to conduct such other actions as the president requested. *See also:* National Security Council.

References

Godson, Roy, ed. *Intelligence Problems for the 1980s, Number 2: Analysis and Estimates.* Washington, DC: National Strategy Information Center, 1980.

————. *Intelligence Problems for the 1980s, Number 3: Counterintelligence.* Washington, DC: National Strategy Information Center, 1980.

————. *Intelligence Problems for the 1980s, Number 4: Covert Action.* Washington, DC: National Strategy Information Center, 1981.

Kornblum, Allan. *Intelligence and the Law: Cases and Materials.* Vol. IV. Washington, DC: DIC, 1987.

Laqueur, Walter. *A World of Secrets.* New York: Basic Books, 1985.

Office of the President of the United States. *Executive Order 12036, United States Intelligence Activities.* Washington, DC, Jan. 24, 1978.

Oseth, John M. *Regulating U.S. Intelligence Operations: A Study in the Definition of the National Interest.* Frankfurt: University of Kentucky Press, 1985.

Treverton, Gregory F. *Covert Action: The Limits of Intervention in the Postwar World.* New York: Basic Books, 1987.

Turner, Stansfield. *Secrecy and Democracy: The CIA in Transition.* Boston: Houghton Mifflin, 1985.

—**NATIONAL SECURITY DECISION DIRECTIVE (NSDD).** *See:* National Security Decision Structure.

—**NATIONAL SECURITY DECISION STRUCTURE** involves the following National Security Council process. After a council member determines that a subject is sufficiently important to warrant further study, he will suggest this to the president. If the president agrees, he will sign a National Security Study Directive. All departments and agencies having an interest in the issue will then contribute to the answer, which is submitted to the president. After consideration, the president and the National Security Council will arrive at a decision, which is promulgated as a National Security Decision Directive and is signed by the president. This directive then becomes the basis for action by the appropriate departments and agencies. *See also:* National Security Council.

References

Breckinridge, Scott D. *The CIA and the U.S. Intelligence System.* Boulder, CO: Westview Press, 1986.

Corson, William R. *The Armies of Ignorance: The Rise of the American Intelligence Empire.* New York: Dial Press, 1977.

Laqueur, Walter. *A World of Secrets.* New York: Basic Books, 1985.

Treverton, Gregory F. *Covert Action: The Limits of Intervention in the Postwar World.* New York: Basic Books, 1987.

Turner, Stansfield. *Secrecy and Democracy: The CIA in Transition.* Boston: Houghton Mifflin, 1985.

—**NATIONAL SECURITY INFORMATION,** in communications security (COMSEC), means information that is related to the national defense or foreign policy of the United States and that was determined to be classified in accordance with the guidance of Executive Order 12356 or any preceding order. *See also:* Communications Security.

References

Laqueur, Walter. *A World of Secrets.* New York: Basic Books, 1985.

Turner, Stansfield. *Secrecy and Democracy: The CIA in Transition.* Boston: Houghton Mifflin, 1985.

—**NATIONAL SECURITY PLANNING GROUP.** The most cogent analysis of the National Security Planning Group was made by Senators John Tower and Edmund Muskie and Lieutenant General Brent Scowcroft, when they served on the President's Special Review Board to examine the National Security Council, the National Security Council staff, and the assistant to the president for national security affairs in 1987 in the wake of the Iran-Contra affair. They stated:

> The National Security Council has frequently been supported by committees made up of representatives of the relevant national security departments and agencies. These committees analyze issues prior to consideration by the Council. There are generally several levels of committees. At the top level, officials from each agency (at the Deputy Secretary or Under Secretary level) meet to provide a senior level policy review. These senior-level committees are in turn supported by more junior interagency groups (usually at the Assistant Secretary level). These in turn may overSee: staff level working groups that prepare detailed analysis of important issues.
>
> Administrations have differed in the extent to which they have used these interagency committees. President Kennedy placed little stock in them. The Nixon and Carter administrations, by contrast, made much use of them.
>
> President Reagan initially declared that the National Security Council would be the principal forum for consideration of national security issues. To support the work of the council, Reagan established an interagency committee system headed by three Senior Interagency Groups (SIGs), one each for foreign policy, defense policy, and intelligence. They were chaired by the secretary of state, the secretary of defense, and the director of Central Intelligence, respectively.
>
> President Reagan appointed several additional members to his National Security Council and allowed staff attendance at meetings. The resultant size of the meetings led the President to turn increasingly to a smaller group (called the National Security Planning Group [or NSPG]). Attendance at its meetings was more restricted but included the statutory principals of the NSC.

The NSPG was supported by the SIGs, and new SIGs were occasionally created to deal with particular issues. These were frequently chaired by the national security advisor. But generally the SIGs and many of their subsidiary groups (Interagency Groups ["IGs"]) fell into disuse. *See also:* National Security Council.

References

Laqueur, Walter. *A World of Secrets.* New York: Basic Books, 1985.

Office of the President of the United States. *Report of the President's Special Review Board.* Washington, DC: GPO, Feb. 26, 1987.

Turner, Stansfield. *Secrecy and Democracy: The CIA in Transition.* Boston: Houghton Mifflin, 1985.

—**NATIONAL SECURITY-RELATED INFORMATION,** in communications security (COMSEC), means unclassified information that is related to the national defense or foreign policy of the United States. *See also:* Communications Security.

References

Laqueur, Walter. *A World of Secrets.* New York: Basic Books, 1985.

Turner, Stansfield. *Secrecy and Democracy: The CIA in Transition.* Boston: Houghton Mifflin, 1985.

—**NATIONAL SECURITY STUDY DIRECTIVE.** *See:* National Security Decision Structure.

—**NATIONAL SIGINT OPERATIONS CENTER (NSOC),** located at the National Security Agency (NSA) complex at Fort Meade, Maryland, is the NSA's watch center. It is staffed constantly and the watch teams are constantly on the alert for incoming information of national intelligence value. The NSOC is a member of the National Warning System and is linked to the other warning centers via the National Operations and Intelligence Watch Officer Net (NOIWON). *See also:* National Security Agency.

References

Bamford, James. *The Puzzle Palace: A Report on America's Most Secret Agency.* New York: Penguin Books, 1983.

—**NATIONAL STRATEGY** is the art and science of developing and using the political, economic, and psychological powers of a nation, together with its armed forces, during peace and war, to secure national objectives.

References

Department of Defense, Joint Chiefs of Staff. *Department of Defense Dictionary of Military and Related Terms*. Washington, DC: GPO, 1986.

Kent, Sherman. *Strategic Intelligence for American World Policy*. Princeton, NJ: Princeton University Press, 1966.

Treverton, Gregory F. *Covert Action: The Limits of Intervention in the Postwar World*. New York: Basic Books, 1987.

—**NATIONAL/TACTICAL INTERFACE** is the relationship between national and tactical intelligence activities encompassing the full range of fiscal, technical, operational, and programmatic matters.

References

Department of Defense, Defense Intelligence College. *Glossary of Intelligence Terms and Definitions*. Washington, DC: DIC, 1987.

Kent, Sherman. *Strategic Intelligence for American World Policy*. Princeton, NJ: Princeton University Press, 1966.

—**NATIONAL TECHNICAL INFORMATION SERVICE (NTIS)** of the Department of Commerce is the focal point for public distribution of technical material that is produced by or obtained by the U.S. government agencies. Through agreements with more than 300 organizations, the NTIS adds about 70,000 new reports each year to its collection of over one million titles.

References

Department of Defense, U.S. Army. *RDTE Managers Intelligence and Threat Support Guide*. Alexandria, VA: Headquarters, Army Materiel Development and Readiness Command, 1983.

—**NATIONAL TECHNICAL MEANS (NTM)** was the term used in the SALT I agreement to refer to U.S. and Soviet reconnaissance and other satellites that could be used to monitor compliance with the agreement. The term has continued in use and means reconnaissance and other surveillance satellites.

References

American Bar Association. *Oversight and Accountability of the U.S. Intelligence Agencies: An Evaluation*. Washington, DC: ABA, 1985.

Godson, Roy, ed. *Intelligence Problems for the 1980s, Number 3: Counterintelligence*. Washington, DC: National Strategy Information Center, 1980.

Laqueur, Walter. *A World of Secrets*. New York: Basic Books, 1985.

Lowenthal, Mark M. *U.S. Intelligence: Evolution and Anatomy*. New York: Praeger, 1984.

Maurer, Alfred C.; Turnstall, Marion D.; and Keagle, James M. *Intelligence Policy and Process*. Boulder, CO: Westview Press, 1985.

Treverton, Gregory F. *Covert Action: The Limits of Intervention in the Postwar World*. New York: Basic Books, 1987.

—**NATIONAL TELECOMMUNICATIONS AND INFORMATION SYSTEMS SECURITY COMMITTEE (NTISSC)** was proposed under a proposed Presidential Directive, "National Policy on Telecommunications and Automated Information Systems Security," that was issued by the National Security Agency on September 17, 1984. According to the directive, the committee would operate under the direction of the System Security Steering Group, which was also established by the directive. Its purpose was to consider technical matters and develop operating policies as necessary to implement the provisions of the directive. The NTISSC would have been chaired by the assistant secretary of defense (command, control, communications, and intelligence) and would have been composed of a voting representative of each member of the Steering Group and of each of the following: the secretary of commerce; the secretary of transportation; the secretary of energy; the chairman, Joint Chiefs of Staff; administrator, General Services Administration; director, Federal Bureau of Investigation; director, Federal Emergency Management Agency; the chief of staff, U.S. Army; the chief of naval operations; the chief of staff, U.S. Air Force; commandant, U.S. Marine Corps; director, Defense Intelligence Agency; director, National Security Agency; and manager, National Communications System.

Under the directive, the duties of the NTISSC would have been to:

"(1) Develop such specific operating policies, objectives, and priorities as may be required to implement this Directive.

(2) Provide telecommunication and automated information systems security

guidance to the departments and agencies of the government.

(3) Submit annually to the Steering Group an evaluation of the status of national telecommunications and automated information systems security with respect to established objectives and priorities.

(4) Identify systems which handle sensitive, non-government information, the loss and exploitation of which could adversely affect the national security interest, for the purpose of encouraging, advising, and where appropriate, assisting the private sector in applying security measures.

(5) Approve the release of sensitive systems technical security material, information, and techniques to foreign governments or international organizations with the concurrence of the Director of Central Intelligence for those activities which he manages.

(6) Establish and maintain a national system for promulgating the operating policies, directives and guidance which may be issued pursuant to this Directive.

(7) Establish permanent and temporary subcommittees as necessary to discharge its responsibilities.

(8) Make recommendations to the Steering Group on Committee membership and establish criteria and procedures for permanent observers from other departments or agencies affected by specific matters under deliberation, who may attend meetings on invitation of the Chairman.

(9) Interact with the National Communications System Committee of Principals established by Executive Order 12472 to ensure the coordinated execution of assigned responsibilities."

("National Policy on Telecommunications and Automated Information Systems Security." Proposed Presidential Directive released September 17, 1984, but never enacted).

—**NATIONAL WAR COLLEGE (NWC),** located on Fort Leslie J. McNair, Washington, DC, is a part of the National Defense University. The college offers a ten-month curriculum to O5-O6 military officers and civilians in equivalent grades. It is the only U.S. government course that is dedicated to the study of national security policy formulation and the planning and implementation of national strategy. It is a senior service college course of study that is jointly sponsored by the Department of State and the Department of Defense. It is designed to promote excellence in the formulation of national security policy and strategy and to enhance the preparation of selected personnel in the Armed Forces, the Department of State, and other U.S. departments and agencies to perform high-level command and staff policy functions associated with national strategy formulation and implementation. The curriculum includes study and research in national security policy formulation, strategic planning and decisionmaking, trends in the international environment, security implications of major state and regional foreign and defense policies, and the role of joint and combined use of military power.

References

Defense Intelligence Agency. *Training Compendium for General Defense Career Development Program (IDCP) Personnel DOD 1430.10M3-TNG.* Washington, DC: DIA, 1986.

Turner, Stansfield. *Secrecy and Democracy: The CIA in Transition.* Boston: Houghton Mifflin, 1985.

—**NATO INTELLIGENCE SUBJECT CODE** is a numerical framework that has been developed for indexing the subject matter of intelligence documents. In addition to the subject outline, it includes a system of alphabetical or numerical symbols for geographic areas that are used with the subject classification.

References

Department of Defense, Joint Chiefs of Staff. *Department of Defense Dictionary of Military and Related Terms.* Washington, DC: GPO, 1986.

—**NAUTICAL MILE (NM)** is principally used in navigation. It is usually considered to be the length of one minute on any great circle of the earth. Because of confusion, in 1929, the International Hydrographic Bureau proposed a standard length of 1,852 meters, called the international nautical mile. However, varying lengths still exist. The U.S. nautical mile is 2,000 yards.

References

Reeves, Robert; Anson, Abraham; and Landen, David. *Manual of Remote Sensing.* Falls Church, VA: American Society of Photogrammetry, 1975.

—**NAVAL FIELD OPERATIONAL INTELLIGENCE OFFICE (NFOIO).** *See:* Naval Intelligence.

—**NAVAL FORCES INTELLIGENCE STUDY (NAFIS),** the production of which is managed by the Defense Intelligence Agency, provides detailed information on the organization, capabilities, and force levels of naval forces throughout the world. There are several volumes of the study, and each addresses a country. They provide good composition, identification, and strength summaries when they have been recently updated. *See also:* Defense Intelligence Agency.

References

Department of Defense, Defense Intelligence Agency. *Defense Intelligence Agency Manual.* Washington, DC: DIA, 1987.

—**NAVAL INTELLIGENCE.** Naval Intelligence has a long and prestigious history in the intelligence field. Today, it handles all aspects of collecting, analyzing, processing, and disseminating intelligence on foreign naval developments, and it interacts with other elements of the Intelligence Community to support the national leadership with the necessary intelligence.

Mission and Functions

The stated mission of the director of Naval Intelligence (DNI) is to implement the responsibilities of the chief of naval operations (CNO) with regard to intelligence, cryptology (less signal security), security, counterintelligence (including counterterrorism), law enforcement, and investigative matters; to serve as the principal staff advisor to the secretary of the Navy and the CNO in related planning, programming, and policy matters; and to represent the Department of the Navy on the National Foreign Intelligence Board and assist officials of the Department of the Navy in matters of protocol and liaison with foreign officials.

In support of this mission, the DNI has twenty functions. These range from advising and assisting the CNO in exercising command responsibilities over the Naval Intelligence Command, the Naval Security Group, and the Naval Investigative Service, to providing intelligence staff support to the secretary of the Navy and the CNO. His other major functions include: exercising cognizance over law enforcement, counterintelligence, physical security, and investigative matters; formulating policy concerning multidiscipline security, including the protection of classified material; participating in providing na-

tional, joint, and naval intelligence estimates; formulating policy concerning special intelligence and special activities materials within the Navy; exercising overall responsibility in matters pertaining to intelligence, requirements, collection, production, and dissemination; coordinating and directing undersea warfare intelligence and collaborating in the conduct of related special programs; ensuring that the intelligence and cryptologic requirements of the operational commanders are met; validating requirements for research and development, test and evaluation systems, equipment and techniques relating to intelligence, and other DNI functions; assuming OPNAV program sponsorship of validated intelligence and cryptologic requirements; coordinating program development for various programs of mutual interest with other appropriate offices within the Navy and Department of Defense; exercising cognizance over Navy portions of the General Defense Intelligence Program (GDIP), the tactical cryptologic program, and the program VIII cryptologic training resources; providing liaison for foreign officials accredited to the Navy; representing the Navy on the National Foreign Intelligence Board (NFIB) and other interdepartmental, DoD, and joint service committees; determining the responsiveness and effectiveness of intelligence and related functions to meet current, contingency, and mobilization requirements; collaborating with the Chief of Naval Personnel in establishing training, career development, and readiness programs relating to intelligence; acting as principal point of contact with the Defense Intelligence Agency (DIA), Central Intelligence Agency (CIA), National Security Agency (NSA), Federal Bureau of Investigation (FBI), State Department, other service intelligence agencies, and foreign and domestic agencies as appropriate; exercising program sponsorship for Naval Intelligence processing systems; and acting as senior intelligence officer of the Navy Department.

History

U.S. Naval Intelligence dates back to 1882, when the Office of Naval Intelligence (ONI) was established under the Bureau of Navigation. During its initial years, the office was not adequately funded, and personnel were borrowed from other offices in order to provide a civilian staff. However, with the commencement of the Spanish-American War, the situation was improved. In 1899, Congress appropriated $9,000 for a staff of eight people—five clerks, a translator, a draftsman, and two laborers.

The organization continued to function at about this size until the outbreak of World War I, when its responsibilities and size were both increased considerably. The organization grew from sixteen officers and civilians to 324 people by war's end.

The isolation of the interwar period took its toll on the entire military establishment, and the ONI was no exception. These were the decades when the organization, under severe funding restraints, was seeking an identity. There was no highly defined mission, the reliance was primarily on human intelligence (HUMINT) collection, but there were great opportunities for those with initiative. Naval Intelligence reflected the larger view of America an unfocused one as the United States sought to find its identity and to define its allies and potential adversaries in a changing international arena.

As the world approached World War II, the ONI began to emerge from a period of decline and, by June 1939, the DNI, Rear Admiral Walter S. Anderson, took steps to prepare the ONI for wartime intelligence operations. He sent naval attachés to several new posts, thereby improving the existing intelligence collection capability, and brought 225 Naval Reserve officers in to act as censors. A section was formed that would monitor the world's shipping routes, which reflected the admiral's faith in Alfred Mahan, who had stressed that protection of one's own sea lines of communication (SLOCs) and interdiction of the enemy's SLOCs were critically important aspects of naval warfare. Additionally, a Strategic Information Section provided information to the fleet, thereby assuring that the intelligence that was produced reached the fleet commanders as quickly as possible. Finally, a Secret Intelligence Section was formed to handle ONI's confidential agents.

In spite of these measures, Anderson still had his reservations. While he felt that the organizational initiatives that he had instituted would provide a good basis for operations should war occur, he believed that the ONI was critically understaffed.

Anderson's reservations were not ignored. In the following year, the ONI's capabilities were expanded considerably. Naval observers, liaison officers shipping advisors, and intelligence officers were assigned to ports and focal points around the world. The entire organization mushroomed during the war, to become a recognized

leader in intelligence collection and processing. These were exciting years, requiring great initiative from the office's intelligence officers. In his book, *Caviar and Commissars*, Admiral Kemp Tolley gives us a view of what the life was like. Officers were sent to collect intelligence and to do what they could do for the war effort. Beyond this broad assignment, there was little direction from headquarters. Rather, the officer was left to his own devices. Often he had no contact with his superiors for weeks at a time and was left to fend for himself. Intelligence was passed to headquarters when this was possible, but the most important imperative was to act and to inform those who needed the intelligence in time to enable them to use it to their benefit. The freewheeling life of Admiral Tolley contrasted greatly with the managed, directed careers of today's Naval Intelligence officers.

In the years immediately following World War II, there was a drastic reduction in the size of the U.S. Armed Forces as the country assumed a peacetime posture. However, the need for intelligence continued, and a selected number of career naval reservists were offered an opportunity to contribute when the restricted line (special duty intelligence) designator was created.

The ONI, like the other intelligence organizations, was affected dramatically by the postwar intelligence reorganizations. The most significant change was the passage of the National Security Act of 1947. This and the subsequent reorganizations were resisted adamantly by the Navy. As a result, when the Navy finally lost the battles, it found that the scope of its responsibilities was altered dramatically. In signals activity, a field in which Naval Intelligence had excelled, the ONI found that the primary responsibility was passed to the National Security Agency and naval participation in this effort was limited to its Naval Security Group, which participated as one of the three Service Cryptological Organizations. Likewise in covert operations, the Navy's role was curtailed drastically, with the primary responsibility passing to the Central Intelligence Agency.

Concurrently, the ONI was compelled to contribute to the production of national-level intelligence products. The creation of the Defense Intelligence Agency in 1962 was a continuation of the existing trend. The DIA further defined the ONI's role and responsibilities, while assuming responsibility for the overall supervision of departmental military intelligence.

The Korean and Vietnamese wars prompted a further expansion of the ONI's mission, and the accompanying technological revolution made worldwide intelligence collection the norm rather than the exception. The needs of both the fleet commanders and the national leadership were such that they compelled the expansion of Naval Intelligence to meet these needs.

In retrospect, the Navy's opposition to the trend of consolidation was myopic and detrimental. By refusing to cooperate, it lost its influence in the decisonmaking process, while its opposition to joint organizations, such as the Defense Intelligence Agency, meant that the other services, particularly the Air Force, by supporting the DIA, had much greater influence in the organization's decisions.

Today, the Naval Intelligence community is a highly professional organization. Equipped with the latest electronic and computer technology, its ocean surveillance system provides an extremely responsive, timely, and accurate intelligence collection capability. Naval Intelligence is composed of naval officers, specially trained enlisted personnel, and professional and nonprofessional civilians. The officers are regularly rotated through jobs in several major areas, including operational intelligence, scientific and technical intelligence, counterintelligence, attaché duty, joint staff duty, school and training assignments, and various support assignments.

The current emphasis is on the production of operational and scientific and technical (S&T) intelligence. Operational intelligence has the highest priority, and the best officers are normally assigned to these facilities. A close second is held by naval scientific and technical intelligence. Here the Navy, with its empirical orientation, has an impressive record, sporting the best naval S&T intelligence capability in the world.

Organization

Since World War II, Naval Intelligence has been expanded and its structure has been defined. Today, it is composed of 20,000 people and is under the direction of the director of Naval Intelligence. The DNI has six principal assistants, thirteen department heads, and three supporting commands: the Naval Intelligence Command, the Naval Security Group, and the Naval Investigative Service. Traditionally, the heads of these commands have also served as deputy directors on the chief of Naval Operations staff as OP-009B (Intelligence), OP-009C (Plans), and OP-009D (Security).

Naval Intelligence Command (NAVINTCOM or NIC). NAVINTCOM was organized in 1967 to implement the responsibilities of the DNI in fulfilling the intelligence requirements and responsibilities of the Navy department. NAVINTCOM employs 2,000 officers, enlisted personnel, and civilians. It has four component commands that produce a wide variety of intelligence:

1. *Navy Operations Intelligence Center (NOIC).* The result of a reorganization of the old Naval Ocean Surveillance Information Center (NOSIC) and Naval Field Operations Intelligence Office (NFOIO), the NOIC is located in Suitland, Maryland. Its mission is to produce finished operational intelligence, including indications and warning intelligence, ocean surveillance information, and detailed analyses of Soviet strategy, doctrine, tactics, and readiness in support of the Joint Chiefs of Staff, the Department of the Navy, the Defense Intelligence Agency, and the joint commands. Furthermore, it is to insure that this intelligence is distributed or disseminated in a timely manner so that adequate support to military and naval operational planning is assured. Finally, it performs other functions and tasks when directed to do so by higher authority. In fulfilling this mission, the NOIC accomplishes the following functions: it (a) provides current operational intelligence and ocean surveillance information on a continuous watch basis, reporting all-source information on foreign naval and naval air movements and operations (the NOIC fulfills this and other functions by maintaining the SEAWATCH automated data base that is tied to the Fleet Ocean Surveillance Intelligence Centers [FOSICs] in Rota, Spain, and Honolulu, Hawaii, the Fleet Ocean Surveillance Intelligence Facilities [FOSIFs] in London and in Kamisaya, Japan, and a multitude of reporting stations in what amounts to a very comprehensive and efficient ocean surveillance information system [OSIS]); (b) provides maritime-related indications and warning to the Department of the Navy and the Department of Defense; (c) provides current locating information on and operational histories of selected foreign merchant and fishing fleets; (d) maintains a current data base and an intelligence interface for the Navy Ocean Surveillance Information System; (e) conducts in-depth analyses and publishes all-source intelligence articles and studies on the organization, tactics, doctrine, and operational patterns of selected foreign naval and naval air forces and merchant and fishing fleets; (f) pro-

vides timely analytical support, data base maintenance, and feedback to special collection resources; (g) provides tactical and doctrinal intelligence support for the operating forces through production of naval warfare publications and related documents; (h) contributes to and reviews the drafts to the National Intelligence Estimates and various other studies that pertain to the Warsaw Pact, Soviet, and People's Republic of China navies and other topics of naval intelligence interest; (i) represents the intelligence interests of the Navy, conducts liaison, and acts as a single point of interface with the National Security Agency on all noncryptological matters; (j) provides operational intelligence support to the Center for War Gaming and the Center for Naval War Studies at the Naval War College, Newport, Rhode Island, and such other gaming efforts as appropriate; (k) provides direct support to the commander of NAVINTCOM in all matters relating to foreign antisubmarine warfare threats to the U.S. Navy strategic deterrent force; (l) provides specialized operational intelligence support for the U.S. Navy underseas warfare operations; and (m) provides graphic arts to support production of naval warfare publications and other assigned functions.

2. *Naval Technical Intelligence Center (NTIC).* The NTIC is the result of the combining of the Naval Scientific and Technical Intelligence Center (STIC), which had been located at the Naval Observatory in Washington, DC, and the Naval Reconnaissance and Technical Support Center (NRTSC) in Suitland, Maryland, shortly after the STIC moved to the NRTSC complex in 1970. The NTIC mission is to process, analyze, produce, and disseminate scientific and technical intelligence and develop threat assessments on foreign naval systems in order to support national and navy strategic plans, research and development, objectives, and programs, and perform such other functions and tasks as directed by higher authority.

In fulfilling this mission, the NTIC accomplishes the following functions: (a) provides scientific and technical intelligence support to the chief of naval operations; chief of naval material; director, Defense Intelligence Agency; director of Naval Intelligence; commander, Naval Intelligence Command; the naval establishment; the operating forces; and other authorized U.S. agencies; (b) develops and produces scientific and technical intelligence on the current and future technical characteristics and warfare capabilities of foreign naval surface, subsurface,

air, space, and merchant systems, including weapon, command, control, communications, and ocean surveillance systems, electromagnetics, and research and development; (c) provides Naval Intelligence threat support to the U.S. naval weapons system planning, development, and acquisition process by producing long-range threat assessments and projections; producing threat capabilities publications; developing threat assessments and threat support plans in support of specific programs and projects; and maintaining liaison with program sponsors, project managers, and other participants in the naval weapons systems planning, development, and acquisition process; (d) It conducts imagery analysis in support of navy technical and current intelligence programs. It exploits imagery obtained by special navy and national collection systems; (e) develops and maintains the Navy Intelligence data base, to include data from acoustic, nonacoustic, electronics, imagery, and national collection systems; (f) acts as the DNI's executive agent for acquiring foreign material and its exploitation within the Navy Foreign Material Exploitation Program (NFMP). (g) It provides representation on director of Central Intelligence committees, subcommittees, working groups, and other forums as directed by higher authority. Additionally, it provides technical support and liaison to national intelligence collection systems, and develops Naval Intelligence collection and exploitation requirements in support of national intelligence plans and programs. (h) It administers the NEC 0416 (ACINT specialist) Program and provides fully qualified personnel for temporary additional duty on board selected collection platforms. (i) It provides translation and other foreign language services, and disseminates the Naval Intelligence Processing System (NIPS) and Shipboard Microfilm (SMP) miniaturized data base. (j) It provides supply, fiscal, and reprographic support, as needed, to the Naval Intelligence Command and its subordinate activities. (k) It advises and assists the commander of NAVINTCOM and his subordinate commands in the formulation and execution of security policies and procedures.

3. *Naval Intelligence Operations Group CTF 168.* The mission of CTF 168 is to manage the levy and satisfaction of Naval Intelligence collection requirements, to conduct and support collection functions, and to conduct such other functions and tasks as may be directed by higher authority. In fulfilling this mission, CTF 168 accomplishes the following functions: it (a) pro-

vides qualified personnel, equipment, expendables, and initial processing to assist the operational forces in intelligence collection and reporting; (b) conducts intelligence collection operations and prepares the resulting intelligence information reports; (c) operates the Collection Advisory Center (CAC), facilitating time sensitive collection matters through direct communications with fleet commands, the Defense Intelligence Agency, and National Intelligence Systems; (d) advises the Navy in a timely manner of favorable collection opportunities, of related outstanding collection requirements, and of the availability of additional resources to assist them; (e) provides guidance to Navy collectors on the requirements, collection and reporting of intelligence information; (f) manages NAVINTCOM support of fleet intelligence collection, planning, implementation, and evaluation; (g) supervises the development, coordination, and appraisal of intelligence collection programs to satisfy Department of the Navy and Department of Defense intelligence information requirements; (h) provides intelligence collection support to U.S. naval and defense attachés; (i) plans and coordinates Navy human intelligence (HUMINT) operations and exploitation programs and coordinates them with other agencies; (j) in close coordination with research and development elements, provides acquisition and installation services, training and maintenance of intelligence collection equipment for a wide range of navy collectors; (k) develops program objectives and resource requirements for intelligence collection operations; and (l) administratively commands all Task Force 168 forward area support teams and scientific and technical collection task groups worldwide, and operationally commands the scientific and technical task groups.

4. *Naval Intelligence Processing System Support Activity (NIPSSA).* The NIPSSA's mission is to plan, sponsor, develop, and manage automated Naval Intelligence information processing and communications systems and to perform such other functions and tasks as directed by higher authority. In fulfilling this mission, the NIPSSA accomplishes the following functions and tasks:

(a) It advises the chief of naval operations (CNO) (OP-009) and the commander of NAVINTCOM, and, on their behalf, sponsors the Naval Intelligence Processing System (NIPS), Ocean Surveillance Information System (OSIS), all intelligence information systems (IIS), intelligence communications systems, and fleet tactical intelligence processing systems.

(b) It coordinates with appropriate OPNAV offices, other commands, and organizations on behalf of the CNO and the commander of NAVINTCOM regarding such systems, including establishing policy, planning, developing, programming, budgeting, managing, and evaluating their effectiveness, and suggesting actions to correct deficiencies.

(c) Additional specific functions by program include: the Ocean Surveillance Information System (OSIS), which coordinates and validates requirements, monitors the development and management of operational systems, manages NAVINTCOM participation in the operational aspects of the naval OSIS, and provides support on matters relating to the interface of the OSIS with the fleet command centers and the satisfaction of defense and national requirements for OSIS capabilities; the Naval Intelligence Processing System (NIPS), which supervises NAVINTCOM participation in the NIPS; the Fleet Tactical Intelligence Processing Systems, which coordinates, monitors and evaluates plans, programs, and procedures for the development, production, expansion, support, and operations of such systems to meet fleet tactical warfare requirements and which develops, coordinates, and promulgates guidance concerning standards, doctrine, and techniques for such systems and related equipment under development; the Intelligence Communications Systems, which manages Department of the Navy participation in such systems, monitors, reviews, and evaluates the plans, facilities, techniques, and procedures for such systems to insure optimum performance, economy of automation resources, and compatibility of effort, and studies and promotes the interface of intelligence communications systems with tactical intelligence command and control ADP systems and the development of mutually supporting intelligence and command management information systems.

(d) Manages the Department of the Navy participation in Department of Defense Intelligence Data Handling System (IDHS). It also monitors, reviews, and evaluates the plans, facilities, techniques, and procedures of Navy and Navy-supported IDHS to insure optimum performance, economy of automation resources, and compatibility of effort.

(e) Serves as a single manager, focal point, and coordinator for all NAVINTCOM present, proposed, and future automation and telecommunications activities.

(f) In support of the commander of NAV-INTCOM headquarters elements and commands, it operates and maintains the consolidated communications center and automated data processing centers located at Suitland, Maryland, and the Pentagon.

Commander, Naval Security Group (NSG). Headquartered in Washington, DC, the NSG provides security, cryptology, and electromagnetic support to fleet and national operations both ashore and at sea, around the world. The group has 14,750 people to fulfill this mission. The Naval Security Group is the Navy's Service Cryptologic Element, and therefore interacts closely with the National Security Agency. The officers in this group are designated 1610, restricted line (special duty cryptography), and serve their careers in cryptographic and security operations.

Naval Security and Investigative Command (NSIC). The NSIC is, for the most part, staffed by civilians. Its headquarters are located in the Washington, D.C. metropolitan area. Under the leadership of the director of the Naval Investigative Service, it is responsible for providing investigative support in matters involving serious crimes committed by or against Navy people. The director also serves as a staff advisor to the director of Naval Intelligence for counterintelligence matters, and the NSIC also has a criminal investigation function. The service has more than 140 offices (NISOs) worldwide, and it continually investigates fraud and other criminal activities. In 1987, the NSIC received some notoriety in the investigation of breaches in security at the U.S. Embassy in Moscow. The incident, involving alleged penetration of sensitive areas within the embassy by Soviet personnel who were admitted after Soviet women had allegedly compromised some of the U.S. Marine guards, received widespread attention. The role of the NSIC remains unclear, but some accounts indicate that their investigation was mismanaged and that, as a result, some of the evidence that they retrieved was inadmissible in court. The investigation did lead to the trial of one marine, Corporal Clayton Lonetree.

In addition to such investigations, the NSIC has responsibility for counterintelligence, counterterrorism, and information security. The organization employs 1,350 people, and the director is usually a naval captain, who serves both as the director and as the CNO deputy director of security (OP-009D).

References

American Bar Association. *Oversight and Accountability of the U.S. Intelligence Agencies: An Evaluation.* Washington, DC: ABA, 1985.

Corson, William R. *The Armies of Ignorance: The Rise of the American Intelligence Empire.* New York: Dial Press, 1977.

Godson, Roy, ed. *Intelligence Problems for the 1980s, Number 1: Elements of Intelligence.* Rev. ed. Washington, DC: National Strategy Information Center, 1983.

Kent, Sherman. *Strategic Intelligence for American World Policy.* Princeton, NJ: Princeton University Press, 1966.

Laqueur, Walter. *A World of Secrets.* New York: Basic Books, 1985.

Maurer, Alfred C.; Turnstall, Marion D.; and Keagle, James M. *Intelligence Policy and Process.* Boulder, CO: Westview Press, 1985.

Quirk, John; Phillips, David; Cline, Ray; and Pforzheimer, Walter. *The Central Intelligence Agency: A Photographic History.* Guilford, CT: Foreign Intelligence Press, 1986.

Turner, Stansfield. *Secrecy and Democracy: The CIA in Transition.* Boston: Houghton Mifflin, 1985.

—NAVAL INTELLIGENCE COMMAND (NAVINTCOM OR NIC). *See:* Naval Intelligence.

—NAVAL INTELLIGENCE OPERATIONS GROUP CTF 168. *See:* Naval Intelligence.

—NAVAL INTELLIGENCE PROCESSING SYSTEM (NIPS). *See:* Naval Intelligence.

—NAVAL INTELLIGENCE PROCESSING SYSTEMS SUPPORT ACTIVITY (NIPSSA). *See:* Naval Intelligence.

—NAVAL INTELLIGENCE PROCESSING SYSTEMS TRAINING FACILITY (NIPSTRAFAC), located on the Naval Air Station, Key West, Florida, offers a spate of course that run in length from two to eight weeks. The curricula is devoted almost entirely to training in the use of sea- and land-based naval intelligence computer systems, with a heavy emphasis on tactical intelligence systems. *See also:* Naval Intelligence.

References

Defense Intelligence Agency. *Training Compendium for General Defense Career Development Program (IDCP) Personnel DOD 1430.10M3-TNG.* Washington, DC: DIA, 1986.

—**NAVAL OCEANS SYSTEMS CENTER (NOSC).** *See:* Naval Intelligence.

—**NAVAL OPERATIONS INTELLIGENCE CENTER (NOIC).** *See:* Naval Intelligence.

—**NAVAL ORDER OF BATTLE (NOB)** is a Defense Intelligence Agency publication that presents information on the numerical strengths of navies, the types of ships that navies have, and the disposition of these forces. It contains detailed data on naval ships and craft by unit assignment, including name, type, identifying pendant number, condition and home port. *See also:* Defense Intelligence Agency.

References

Laqueur, Walter. *A World of Secrets.* New York: Basic Books, 1985.

Von Hoene, John P. A. *Intelligence User's Guide.* Washington, DC: DIA, 1983.

—**NAVAL ORDER OF BATTLE TEXTUAL SUMMARY (NOBTS),** is, in many ways, a companion to the Naval Order of Battle (NOB). It is less statistical and more analytical than the NOB, and attempts to place a nation's naval strengths, weaknesses, and accomplishments in perspective. *See also:* Defense Intelligence Agency.

References

Department of Defense, Defense Intelligence Agency. *Defense Intelligence Agency Manual.* Washington, DC: DIA, 1987.

—**NAVAL POST GRADUATE SCHOOL, MONTEREY, CALIFORNIA,** offers a twelve- to eighteen-month curriculum for U.S. military officers and civilian employees of the U.S. government. The school offers specialty programs that lead to a master's degree, including one in National Security Affairs.

References

Defense Intelligence Agency. *Training Compendium for General Defense Career Development Program (IDCP) Personnel DOD 1430.10M3-TNG.* Washington, DC: DIA, 1986.

—**NAVAL RECONNAISSANCE AND TECHNICAL SUPPORT CENTER (NRTSC).** *See:* Naval Intelligence.

—**NAVAL SECURITY AND INVESTIGATIVE COMMAND (NSIC).** *See:* Naval Intelligence.

—**NAVAL SECURITY GROUP.** *See:* Naval Intelligence.

—**NAVY SPACE COMMAND** was created in 1985. Located in Dahlgren, Virginia, the command was the focal point for establishing Navy space requirements and orbital operations plans before the establishment of the Space Command.

References

Boutacoff, David A. "Steering a Course Toward Space." *Defense Electronics* (Mar. 1986): 58-60, 62-63.

—**NAVAL TECHNICAL INTELLIGENCE CENTER (NTIC).** *See:* Naval Intelligence.

—**NAVAL WAR COLLEGE (NWC),** located on the U.S. Navy Base, Newport, Rhode Island, offers two ten-and-a-half-month courses. The College of Naval Command and Staff is for selected mid-career military officers and GS-11/13 civilians, and is meant to develop the students' command and management abilities and to enable them to conduct research leading to the development of advanced strategic and tactical concepts for the future employment of naval forces. The College of Naval Warfare is for O5-O6 military officers and GS-13/15 civilians and is similar in scope to the College of Naval Command and Staff, but is presented in the upper level management context. Both colleges are composed of three major areas of professional knowledge: strategy and policy, defense economics and decisionmaking, and naval operations.

In addition to its curriculum, the college also produces an excellent journal. Under the leadership of its editor-in-chief, Mr. Frank Uhlig, the *Naval War College Review* is one of the three best U.S. journals that deal with naval matters.

References

Defense Intelligence Agency. *Training Compendium for General Defense Career Development Program (IDCP) Personnel DOD 1430.10M3-TNG.* Washington, DC: DIA, 1986.

Turner, Stansfield. *Secrecy and Democracy: The CIA in Transition.* Boston: Houghton Mifflin, 1985.

—**NEAR-REAL TIME** is a general intelligence term. It is the brief interval of time between the collection of information concerning an event and the reception of this data at some other location. It is caused by the time required to process, communicate, and display the information.

References

Department of Defense, Defense Intelligence College. *Glossary of Intelligence Terms and Definitions.* Washington, DC: DIC, 1987.

—**NEED-TO-KNOW** is a general intelligence term. It means that an individual is not authorized access to classified material solely by virtue of his rank, office, position, or level of security clearance. Rather, access to such material is granted only when a valid need for the information exists. Verification of this "need to know" rests with the custodian of classified information, who must also verify that the recipient has the appropriate clearance. *See also:* Access, Authorized, Classification, Classified Information, Code Word, Compromise, Declassification, Disclosure, Downgrade, Freedom of Information Act, Limited Access Area, No-Lone Zone, Nondisclosure Agreement, Nondiscussion Area, Sanitization, Sanitize, Sanitized Area, Security Certification, Security Classification, Sensitive Compartmented Information, Sensitive Compartmented Information Facility, Two-Person Control.

References

Clancy, Tom. *The Cardinal of the Kremlin.* New York: Putnam, 1988.

Department of Defense, Defense Intelligence Agency. *Defense Intelligence Agency Manual.* Washington, DC: DIA, 1987.

Department of Defense, Joint Chiefs of Staff. *Department of Defense Dictionary of Military and Related Terms.* Washington, DC: GPO, 1986.

Godson, Roy, ed. *Intelligence Problems for the 1980s, Number 1: Elements of Intelligence.* Rev. ed. Washington, DC: National Strategy Information Center, 1983.

Treverton, Gregory F. *Covert Action: The Limits of Intervention in the Postwar World.* New York: Basic Books, 1987.

—**NEED-TO-KNOW PRINCIPLE** is a general intelligence term. It is a determination by an authorized holder of classified information that access to specific classified material in his or her possession is required by one or more persons so that they can perform a specific and authorized function that is essential to accomplish a national security task or as required by Federal Statute, Executive Order, or another directly applicable regulation. In addition to an established "need to know," a person must have an appropriate security clearance and access approval prior to being given the classified material. *See also:* Need-to-Know.

—**NEGATIVE INDICATION** is an indications and warning (I&W) term. It is evidence that an enemy is not doing something he normally would be expected to do if he were planning hostilities or other threatening actions; or it is evidence that positive actions are being taken that would reduce his capability to threaten U.S. security interests. *See also:* Indications and Warning.

References

Godson, Roy, ed. *Intelligence Problems for the 1980s, Number 1: Elements of Intelligence.* Rev. ed. Washington, DC: National Strategy Information Center, 1983.

Treverton, Gregory F. *Covert Action: The Limits of Intervention in the Postwar World.* New York: Basic Books, 1987.

—**NET ASSESSMENT** is a general intelligence term for an attempt to compare and evaluate the relative capabilities of two or more nations. It usually only involves foreign countries and is a comparative review and analysis of opposing national strengths, capabilities, vulnerabilities, and weaknesses. When a net assessment involves a comparison between the United States and the Soviet Union, it is often called a Red-Blue study.

References

Brinkley, David A., and Hull, Andrew W. *Estimative Intelligence: A Textbook on the History, Products, Uses, and Writing of Intelligence Estimates.* Columbus, OH: Battelle, 1979.

Department of Defense, Defense Intelligence College. *Glossary of Intelligence Terms and Definitions.* Washington, DC: DIC, 1987.

Godson, Roy, ed. *Intelligence Problems for the 1980s, Number 1: Elements of Intelligence.* Rev. ed. Washington, DC: National Strategy Information Center, 1983.

Treverton, Gregory F. *Covert Action: The Limits of Intervention in the Postwar World.* New York: Basic Books, 1987.

Turner, Stansfield. *Secrecy and Democracy: The CIA in Transition.* Boston: Houghton Mifflin, 1985.

—NET ASSESSMENT GROUP, as defined by the Church Committee, was the group within the National Security Council staff that was responsible for reviewing and evaluating all intelligence products and producing net assessments. It was abolished in June 1973. *See also:* Net Assessment.

References

Turner, Stansfield. *Secrecy and Democracy: The CIA in Transition.* Boston: Houghton Mifflin, 1985.

U.S. Congress. Senate. *Final Report of the Senate Select Committee to Study Government Operations with Respect to Intelligence Activities. Report 94-755. Book I, Foreign and Military Intelligence.* Washington, DC: GPO, 1976.

—NICARAGUA. The U.S. Intelligence Community performed excellently with respect to developments in communist Nicaragua. Reporting on the fall of the Somoza government, the rise of the Ortega regime and its human rights abuses, the delivery of Soviet arms to Cuba and their transference and subsequent delivery to Nicaragua, and Nicaraguan aggression against its neighbors was, for the most part, complete and accurate. In 1982, the U.S. Department of State chose to release much of this information, which enabled it to present a strong case against the Ortega government. Subsequent U.S. assistance to the Contras forced the communists to take the defensive; however, support for this cause was reduced greatly after the Iran-Contra scandal. By the end of 1989, the Nicaraguan communists remained on the defensive, indicating that the United States had, at least temporarily, managed to stop the communist offensive.

—NIXON, RICHARD. President Nixon may have come to the White House with a distrust of the Intelligence Community. The Community's role in the "missile gap" issue may have cost him the 1960 presidential election, and this may have been one of the reasons for his distrust. Unlike President Johnson, who preferred a minimal organization, Nixon preferred a large, formal arrangement similar to the one that existed during the Eisenhower administration. As a result, he restored much of the structure that had atrophied during the Johnson administration.

In intelligence issues, Nixon relied heavily on his National Security Advisor, Henry Kissinger, while minimizing his dependence on the Intelligence Community. Nixon retained Richard Helms as director of Central Intelligence (DCI) until 1973, when Helms accepted an appointment as U.S. ambassador to Iran.

With Helms's departure, Nixon appointed James Schlesinger as DCI. Schlesinger appears to have been a good choice, in that he made some astute organizational modifications and improved significantly the agency's production of National Intelligence Estimates (NIEs). Had he remained as DCI, he might have had an even more positive and significant impact on the agency, but in the continuous reassignments that accompanied the Watergate crisis, Schlesinger was named secretary of defense in the spring of 1973 and was shifted to that office less than six months after he had been appointed as DCI.

Nixon then named William Colby, a career intelligence professional, to replace Schlesinger. Colby, an astute appointment, continued many of Schlesinger's innovations. However, much of Colby's attention was directed to defending the agency in the congressional Watergate hearings, to the detriment of the general performance of the Intelligence Community. *See also:* Executive Oversight.

References

Breckinridge, Scott D. *The CIA and the U.S. Intelligence System.* Boulder, CO: Westview Press, 1986.

Brinkley, David A., and Hull, Andrew W. *Estimative Intelligence: A Textbook on the History, Products, Uses, and Writing of Intelligence Estimates.* Columbus, OH: Battelle, 1979.

Corson, William R. *The Armies of Ignorance: The Rise of the American Intelligence Empire.* New York: Dial Press, 1977.

Laqueur, Walter. *A World of Secrets.* New York: Basic Books, Inc., 1985.

Lowenthal, Mark M. *U.S. Intelligence: Evolution and Anatomy.* New York: Praeger, 1984.

Maurer, Alfred C.; Turnstall, Marion D.; and Keagle, James M. *Intelligence Policy and Process.* Boulder, CO: Westview Press, 1985.

Turner, Stansfield. *Secrecy and Democracy: The CIA in Transition.* Boston: Houghton Mifflin, 1985.

U.S. Congress. Senate. *Final Report of the Senate Select Committee to Study Government Operations with Respect to Intelligence Activities. Report 94-755. Book I, Foreign and Military Intelligence.* Washington, DC: GPO, 1976.

—**NOISE,** in electronic warfare, is any unwanted receiver response, other than another signal, that is interference. *See also:* Electronic Warfare.

References

Department of Defense, U.S. Army. *Counter-Signals Intelligence (C-SIGINT) Operations.* Field Manual FM 34-62. Washington, DC: Headquarters, Department of the Army, 1986.

————. *Military Intelligence Battalion Combat Electronic Warfare and Intelligence (Aerial Exploitation) (Corps).* Field Manual FM 34-22. Washington, DC: Headquarters, Department of the Army, 1984.

————. *Military Intelligence Battalion (CEWI) (Tactical Exploitation) (Corps): Counterintelligence, Interrogation, Electronic Warfare.* Field Manual FM 34-23. Washington, DC: Headquarters, Department of the Army, 1985.

—**NOISE JAMMING,** in electronic warfare (EW), are jamming signals that are random and are essentially unsynchronized with the target radar. *See also:* Electronic Warfare.

References

Department of Defense, U.S. Army. *Counter-Signals Intelligence (C-SIGINT) Operations.* Field Manual FM 34-62. Washington, DC: Headquarters, Department of the Army, 1986.

————. *Military Intelligence Battalion Combat Electronic Warfare and Intelligence (Aerial Exploitation) (Corps).* Field Manual FM 34-22. Washington, DC: Headquarters, Department of the Army, 1984.

————. *Military Intelligence Battalion (CEWI) (Tactical Exploitation) (Corps): Counterintelligence, Interrogation, Electronic Warfare.* Field Manual FM 34-23. Washington, DC: Headquarters, Department of the Army, 1985.

—**NOISE-MODULATED JAMMING,** in electronic warfare (EW), is random electronic noise that appears as background noise and tends to mask the desired signal. *See also:* Electronic Warfare.

References

Department of Defense, U.S. Army. *Counter-Signals Intelligence (C-SIGINT) Operations.* Field Manual FM 34-62. Washington, DC: Headquarters, Department of the Army, 1986.

————. *Military Intelligence Battalion Combat Electronic Warfare and Intelligence (Aerial Exploitation) (Corps).* Field Manual FM 34-22. Washington, DC: Headquarters, Department of the Army, 1984.

————. *Military Intelligence Battalion (CEWI) (Tactical Exploitation) (Corps): Counterintelligence, Interrogation, Electronic Warfare.* Field Manual FM 34-23. Washington, DC: Headquarters, Department of the Army, 1985.

—**NOLLE PROSEQUI,** in the intelligence context, means a notation on the record denoting that the individual whose access to sensitive compartmented information is being denied will proceed no further in his challenge of the denial.

References

Department of Defense, Defense Intelligence Agency. *Defense Intelligence Agency Manual.* Washington, DC: DIA, 1987.

—**NO-LONE ZONE,** in communications security (COMSEC), means an area, room, or space in which no person may have unaccompanied access and that, when staffed, must be occupied by two or more appropriately cleared individuals. *See also:* Access, Authorized, Classification, Classified Information, Code Word, Compromise, Declassification, Disclosure, Downgrade, Freedom of Information Act, Limited Access Area, Need-to-Know, Need-to-Know Principle, Nondisclosure Agreement, Nondiscussion Area, Sanitization, Sanitize, Sanitized Area, Security Certification, Security Classification, Sensitive Compartmented Information, Sensitive Compartmented Information Facility, Two-Person Control.

References

Department of Defense, Defense Intelligence Agency. *Defense Intelligence Agency Manual.* Washington, DC: DIA, 1987.

Godson, Roy, ed. *Intelligence Problems for the 1980s, Number 1: Elements of Intelligence*. Rev. ed. Washington, DC: National Strategy Information Center, 1983.

Godson, Roy, ed. *Intelligence Problems for the 1980s, Number 1: Elements of Intelligence*. Rev. ed. Washington, DC: National Strategy Information Center, 1983.

—**NOMENCLATORS,** a signals analysis term, is the substitution of letters, syllables, words, and names and may therefore be regarded as something between a cipher and a code. Nomenclators were used extensively in the fifteenth through the mid-nineteenth centuries.

References

Department of Defense, U.S. Army. *Counter-Signals Intelligence (C-SIGINT) Operations*. Field Manual FM 34-62. Washington, DC: Headquarters, Department of the Army, 1986.

———. *Military Intelligence Battalion Combat Electronic Warfare and Intelligence (Aerial Exploitation) (Corps)*. Field Manual FM 34-22. Washington, DC: Headquarters, Department of the Army, 1984.

———. *Military Intelligence Battalion (CEWI) (Tactical Exploitation) (Corps): Counterintelligence, Interrogation, Electronic Warfare*. Field Manual FM 34-23. Washington, DC: Headquarters, Department of the Army, 1985.

—**NONDISCLOSURE AGREEMENT,** sometimes referred to as a secrecy agreement, is a document that an individual signs before he is granted a clearance or is granted access to a compartmented program. In the agreement, the individual agrees not to disclose the information to which he will have access. Additionally, the individual agrees to submit any writings (books, articles, etc.) for security review before they are published. The legality of such agreements have been questioned by Victor Marchetti and others, and the courts have ruled that the agreements are indeed valid contracts. *See also:* Access, Authorized, Classification, Classified Information, Code Word, Compromise, Declassification, Disclosure, Downgrade, Freedom of Information Act, Limited Access Area, Need-to-Know, Need-to-Know Principle, No-Lone Zone, Nondiscussion Area, Sanitization, Sanitize, Sanitized Area, Security Certification, Security Classification, Sensitive Compartmented Information, Sensitive Compartmented Information Facility, Two-Person Control.

References

Department of Defense, Defense Intelligence Agency. *Defense Intelligence Agency Manual*. Washington, DC: DIA, 1987.

—**NONDISCUSSION AREA** is a clearly defined area that is within a sensitive compartmented information facility (SCIF) where classified discussions are not authorized. All such areas are clearly marked. *See also:* Access, Authorized, Classification, Classified Information, Code Word, Compromise, Declassification, Disclosure, Downgrade, Freedom of Information Act, Limited Access Area, Need-to-Know, Need-to-Know Principle, Nondisclosure Agreement, Sanitization, Sanitize, Sanitized Area, Security Certification, Security Classification, Sensitive Compartmented Information, Sensitive Compartmented Information Facility, Two-Person Control.

References

Department of Defense, Defense Intelligence Agency. *Defense Intelligence Agency Manual*. Washington, DC: DIA, 1987.

—**NON-LITERAL CRYPTOSYSTEM,** in communications security (COMSEC), means a cryptosystem that is intended for transmitting data in which the plain-text elements are signals or symbols other than the symbols (letters) that are normally used in the written language. *See also:* Communications Security.

References

Department of Defense, U.S. Army. *Counter-Signals Intelligence (C-SIGINT) Operations*. Field Manual FM 34-62. Washington, DC: Headquarters, Department of the Army, 1986.

———. *Military Intelligence Battalion Combat Electronic Warfare and Intelligence (Aerial Exploitation) (Corps)*. Field Manual FM 34-22. Washington, DC: Headquarters, Department of the Army, 1984.

———. *Military Intelligence Battalion (CEWI) (Tactical Exploitation) (Corps): Counterintelligence, Interrogation, Electronic Warfare*. Field Manual FM 34-23. Washington, DC: Headquarters, Department of the Army, 1985.

—**NONRECURRING DOCUMENT** is any finished or unfinished product that is produced by the Intelligence Community on a nonrecurring basis.

References

Department of Defense, Defense Intelligence
Agency. *Defense Intelligence Agency Manual.*
Washington, DC: DIA, 1987.

Godson, Roy, ed. *Intelligence Problems for the
1980s, Number 1: Elements of Intelligence.* Rev.
ed. Washington, DC: National Strategy Information
Center, 1983.

—**NONRECURRING FINISHED INTELLIGENCE**
(NRFI) is evaluated intelligence covering specific subjects or areas of research that has been
published on an unscheduled or one-time basis.
The production is considered completed and no
plans are made for revising or updating that
intelligence.

References

Department of Defense, Defense Intelligence
Agency. *Defense Intelligence Agency Manual.*
Washington, DC: DIA, 1987.

Godson, Roy, ed. *Intelligence Problems for the
1980s, Number 1: Elements of Intelligence.* Rev.
ed. Washington, DC: National Strategy Information
Center, 1983.

—**NORMAL INTELLIGENCE REPORTS** are a category of reports used to disseminate intelligence.
See also: Intelligence Reporting.

References

Department of Defense, Defense Intelligence
Agency. *Defense Intelligence Agency Manual.*
Washington, DC: DIA, 1987.

Department of Defense, Joint Chiefs of Staff.
*Department of Defense Dictionary of Military and
Related Terms.* Washington, DC: GPO, 1986.

Godson, Roy, ed. *Intelligence Problems for the
1980s, Number 1: Elements of Intelligence.* Rev.
ed. Washington, DC: National Strategy Information
Center, 1983.

Treverton, Gregory F. *Covert Action: The Limits of
Intervention in the Postwar World.* New York:
Basic Books, 1987.

—**NORTH, OLIVER.** *See:* Iran, Nicaragua.

—**NOTIONALS** are fictitious, private commercial
entities that exist on paper only. They serve as the
ostensible employers of intelligence personnel,
or as the ostensible sponsors of certain activities
in support of clandestine operations.

References

U.S. Congress. Senate. *Final Report of the Senate
Select Committee to Study Government Operations
with Respect to Intelligence Activities. Report 94-
755. Book I, Foreign and Military Intelligence.*
Washington, DC: GPO, 1976.

—**NOT RELEASABLE TO CONTRACTORS/**
CONSULTANTS (NOCONTRACT) is a caveat
placed on a document in addition to its classification that further restricts its distribution and
dissemination. In this case, the information cannot
be released to contractors or consultants—people
working on U.S. government contracts. The
caveat most often appears on materials relating
to government contracts, specifications, and other
data that would provide one contractor or consultant an unfair advantage over others when
contracting with the government. However, it
can also appear on sensitive intelligence data
and documents with the aim of limiting dissemination to U.S. military and government civilians.
See also: Access, Authorized, Classification,
Classified Information, Code Word, Compromise, Declassification, Disclosure, Downgrade,
Freedom of Information Act, Limited Access
area, Need-To-Know, Need-To-Know Principle,
Nondisclosure Agreement, Nondiscussion Area,
Sanitization, Sanitize, Sanitized Area, Security
Certification, Security Classification, Sensitive
Compartmented Information, Sensitive Com-
partmented Information Facility, Two-Person
Control.

References

Department of Defense, Defense Intelligence
Agency. *Defense Intelligence Agency Manual.*
Washington, DC: DIA, 1987.

Godson, Roy, ed. *Intelligence Problems for the
1980s, Number 1: Elements of Intelligence.* Rev.
ed. Washington, DC: National Strategy Information
Center, 1983.

—**NOT RELEASABLE TO FOREIGN NATIONALS**
(NOFORN) is a caveat that is placed on a document. It is in addition to the assigned classification and further restricts the document's distribution and dissemination. In this case, the information can be released only to U.S. citizens who
have been properly cleared to see the information and have a need to know the information.
See also: Access, Authorized, Classification,
Classified Information, Code Word, Compromise, Declassification, Disclosure, Downgrade,

Freedom of Information Act, Limited Access Area, Need-to-Know, Need-to-Know Principle, Nondisclosure Agreement, Nondiscussion Area, Sanitization, Sanitize, Sanitized Area, Security Certification, Security Classification, Sensitive Compartmented Information, Sensitive Compartmented Information Facility, Two-Person Control.

References

Department of Defense, Defense Intelligence Agency. *Defense Intelligence Agency Manual.* Washington, DC: DIA, 1987.

Godson, Roy, ed. *Intelligence Problems for the 1980s, Number 1: Elements of Intelligence.* Rev. ed. Washington, DC: National Strategy Information Center, 1983.

—**NOT WITTING** is a person who is not aware of a classified project, even though he may be working on a part of it. This person might be doing unclassified research or might be an errand boy who retrieves maps and other materials needed on a project.

References

Becket, Henry S. A. *The Dictionary of Espionage: Spookspeak into English.* New York: Stein and Day, 1986.

Deacon, Richard. *Spyclopedia: An Encyclopedia of Spies, Secret Services, Operations, Jargon, and All Subjects Related to the World of Espionage.* London: Macdonald, 1987.

Ranelagh, John. *The Agency: The Rise and Decline of the CIA.* New York: Simon and Schuster, 1986.

—**NUCLEAR INTELLIGENCE (NUCINT)** is intelligence information that is derived from collecting and analyzing radiation and the other effects that result from radioactive sources.

References

Department of Defense, Defense Intelligence College. *Glossary of Intelligence Terms and Definitions.* Washington, DC: DIC, 1987.

Godson, Roy, ed. *Intelligence Problems for the 1980s, Number 1: Elements of Intelligence.* Rev. ed. Washington, DC: National Strategy Information Center, 1983.

Laqueur, Walter. *A World of Secrets.* New York: Basic Books, 1985.

Treverton, Gregory F. *Covert Action: The Limits of Intervention in the Postwar World.* New York: Basic Books, 1987.

—**NUCLEAR PROLIFERATION INTELLIGENCE** is foreign intelligence relating to: (1) the scientific, technical, and economic capabilities and programs and the political plans and intentions of nations or foreign organizations that do not have nuclear weapons to acquire nuclear weapons or the research, development, and manufacturing of nuclear weapons; or (2) the attitudes, policies, and actions of foreign nations or organizations that have nuclear weapons to supply the technology, facilities, or special nuclear materials that could assist a nation or foreign organization that does not have nuclear weapons to acquire them.

References

Department of Defense, Defense Intelligence College. *Glossary of Intelligence Terms and Definitions.* Washington, DC: DIC, 1987.

Laqueur, Walter. *A World of Secrets.* New York: Basic Books, 1985.

Treverton, Gregory F. *Covert Action: The Limits of Intervention in the Postwar World.* New York: Basic Books, 1987.

—**NULL** is a cryptographic term that means a letter symbol or code group that is inserted in an encrypted message in order to delay or prevent its solution, or to complete encrypted groups for transmission, or for security purposes. It is a dummy letter. *See also:* Communications Security.

References

Department of Defense, U.S. Army. *Counter-Signals Intelligence (C-SIGINT) Operations.* Field Manual FM 34-62. Washington, DC: Headquarters, Department of the Army, 1986.

———. *Military Intelligence Battalion Combat Electronic Warfare and Intelligence (Aerial Exploitation) (Corps).* Field Manual FM 34-22. Washington, DC: Headquarters, Department of the Army, 1984.

———. *Military Intelligence Battalion (CEWI) (Tactical Exploitation) (Corps): Counterintelligence, Interrogation, Electronic Warfare.* Field Manual FM 34-23. Washington, DC: Headquarters, Department of the Army, 1985.

Ranelagh, John. *The Agency: The Rise and Decline of the CIA*. New York: Simon and Schuster, 1986.

Turner, Stansfield. *Secrecy and Democracy: The CIA in Transition*. Boston: Houghton Mifflin, 1985.

—**OBLIQUE AIR PHOTOGRAPH** is a term that is used in intelligence imagery and photoreconnaissance for a photograph that is taken with the camera axis directed between the horizontal and vertical planes. *See also:* Aerial Photograph.

References

Department of Defense, Joint Chiefs of Staff. *Department of Defense Dictionary of Military and Related Terms*. Washington, DC: GPO, 1986.

Reeves, Robert; Anson, Abraham; and Landen, David. *Manual of Remote Sensing*. Falls Church, VA: American Society of Photogrammetry, 1975.

—**OBLIQUE AIR PHOTOGRAPH STRIP** is a photographic strip that is composed of oblique air photographs.

References

Department of Defense, Joint Chiefs of Staff. *Department of Defense Dictionary of Military and Related Terms*. Washington, DC: GPO, 1986.

Reeves, Robert; Anson, Abraham; and Landen, David. *Manual of Remote Sensing*. Falls Church, VA: American Society of Photogrammetry, 1975.

—**OBSERVATION POSTS** is a term used in clandestine and covert intelligence operations to describe convenient locations, such as offices or apartments that overlook embassies and hangouts of citizens of potentially hostile nations. Henry Becket claims that the CIA pays the rent for non-agency people (grannies) to live in these places and, in turn, can use the places to photograph and surveil intelligence targets. *See also:* Doubled, Granny, Keeping Books, Movements Analysis, Pavement Artists, Shadow, Shaking Off The Dogs, Special Activities, Stroller, Surround, Surveillance, Thirty-Threes, Walk-Past.

References

Becket, Henry S. A. *The Dictionary of Espionage: Spookspeak into English*. New York: Stein and Day, 1986.

Deacon, Richard. *Spyclopedia: An Encyclopedia of Spies, Secret Services, Operations, Jargon, and All Subjects Related to the World of Espionage*. London: Macdonald, 1987.

—**OCEAN SURVEILLANCE INFORMATION SYSTEM (OSIS)** is a worldwide monitoring system that the U.S. Navy maintains to monitor naval and merchant maritime activity on the world's oceans. A system of aerial, surface, and subsurface systems continuously provide locating data on maritime activity. The main nodes of the system are both national and fleet oriented. The Navy Operational Intelligence Center, Suitland, Maryland, which monitors maritime activity worldwide and provides finished intelligence to both national-level customers and to the fleet commanders, provides the interface between national and fleet customers. On the next level are the Fleet Ocean Surveillance Information Centers (FOSICs), in Norfolk, Virginia, and Honolulu, Hawaii, which provide direct support to CINCLANT (commander-in-chief, Atlantic) and CINCPAC (commander-in-chief, Pacific), respectively. These centers monitor all maritime activity in the Atlantic and Pacific oceans, respectively, and together they perform a similar surveillance function in the Indian Ocean. There are also the Fleet Ocean Surveillance Intelligence Facilities in Rota, Spain, and Kamisea, Japan, which monitor maritime activity in the high-interest areas of the Mediterranean and Japanese seas. Finally, there are the afloat nodes. These are the fleet intelligence staffs and other intelligence elements on board U.S. ships that provide a mobile capability. Equipped with excellent communications, these units can detect and report events of interest on very short notice.

Together, these nodes compose an extremely effective intelligence system that is one of the strongest aspects of naval intelligence and one of the most capable and efficient systems in the U.S. Intelligence Community. *See also:* Fleet Ocean Surveillance Information Center, Fleet Ocean Surveillance Information Facility.

References

Watson, Bruce W. *Red Navy at Sea: Soviet Naval Operations on the High Seas, 1956–1980*. Boulder, CO: Westview Press, 1986.

Watson, Bruce W., and Watson, Susan M., eds. *The Soviet Navy: Strengths and Liabilities*. Boulder, CO: Westview Press, 1986.

—**OFFICE OF ADMINISTRATION.** *See:* National Security Agency.

—**OFFICE OF AFRICAN AND LATIN AMERICAN ANALYSIS.** *See:* Central Intelligence Agency.

—**OFFICE OF COLLECTION AND DISSEMINATION (OCD),** a component of the Directorate for Intelligence, Central Intelligence Agency, was charged with disseminating intelligence and with storing and retrieving unevaluated intelligence. It was renamed the office of Central Reference in 1955, and became the Central Reference Service in 1967. *See also:* Central Intelligence Agency.

References
Corson, William R. *The Armies of Ignorance: The Rise of the American Intelligence Empire.* New York: Dial Press, 1977.

Fain, Tyrus G.; Plant, Katharine C.; and Milloy, Ross. *The Intelligence Community: History, Organization, and Issues.* Public Documents Series. New York: R.R. Bowker, 1977.

Godson, Roy, ed. *Intelligence Problems for the 1980s, Number 1: Elements of Intelligence.* Rev. ed. Washington, DC: National Strategy Information Center, 1983.

—**OFFICE OF COMMUNICATIONS.** *See:* Central Intelligence Agency.

—**OFFICE OF COMMUNICATIONS SECURITY (COMSEC).** *See:* National Security Agency.

—**OFFICE OF THE COORDINATOR OF INFORMATION** was created by President Roosevelt in July 1941. It was an attempt to centralize intelligence and create a better intelligence organization. It was conceived by William J. Donovan, who was the first coordinator of information. A major problem that confronted the office was that, although the office had been created, the same order directed it not to interfere with the affairs of the Army or Navy.

The order of July 1941 reflected Roosevelt's concern about the state of U.S. intelligence and his belief that a centralized intelligence entity was needed. Signed less than five months before Pearl Harbor, the greatest intelligence failure in U.S. history, it reflects President Roosevelt's accurate perceptions of the state of U.S. intelligence. *See also:* Donovan, William J.; Office of Strategic Services.

References
Corson, William R. *The Armies of Ignorance: The Rise of the American Intelligence Empire.* New York: Dial Press, 1977.

Laqueur, Walter. *A World of Secrets.* New York: Basic Books, 1985.

Lowenthal, Mark M. *U.S. Intelligence: Evolution and Anatomy.* New York: Praeger, 1984.

Office of the President of the United States. *Order Signed by President Franklin D. Roosevelt, Coordinator of Information.* Washington, DC, July 11, 1941.

—**OFFICE OF CURRENT INTELLIGENCE (OCI)** was one of the results of General Walter Bedell Smith's 1950 reorganization of the Central Intelligence Agency. The OCI was tasked with producing current intelligence summaries, and the production of political intelligence was to be left to the Department of State. In spite of this arrangement, the OCI eventually began doing independent political research. *See also:* Central Intelligence Agency.

References
Fain, Tyrus G.; Plant, Katharine C.; and Milloy, Ross. *The Intelligence Community: History, Organization, and Issues.* Public Documents Series. New York: R.R. Bowker, 1977.

Laqueur, Walter. *A World of Secrets.* New York: Basic Books, 1985.

Lowenthal, Mark M. *U.S. Intelligence: Evolution and Anatomy.* New York: Praeger, 1984.

—**OFFICE OF CURRENT PRODUCTION AND ANALYTIC SUPPORT.** *See:* Central Intelligence Agency.

—**OFFICE OF DEVELOPMENT AND ENGINEERING.** *See:* Central Intelligence Agency.

—**OFFICE OF EAST ASIAN ANALYSIS.** *See:* Central Intelligence Agency.

—**OFFICE OF ECONOMIC RESEARCH (OER),** a component of the Directorate for Intelligence, Central Intelligence Agency, was established in 1967. It was tasked with producing economic intelligence. *See also:* Central Intelligence Agency.

References
Fain, Tyrus G.; Plant, Katharine C.; and Milloy, Ross. *The Intelligence Community: History, Organization, and Issues.* Public Documents Series. New York: R.R. Bowker, 1977.

—**OFFICE OF EUROPEAN ANALYSIS.** *See:* Central Intelligence Agency.

—**OFFICE OF FINANCE.** *See:* Central Intelligence Agency.

—**OFFICE OF THE GENERAL COUNSEL.** *See:* National Security Agency.

—**OFFICE OF GLOBAL ISSUES.** *See:* Central Intelligence Agency.

—**OFFICE OF IMAGERY ANALYSIS.** *See:* Central Intelligence Agency.

—**OFFICE OF INFORMATION RESOURCES.** *See:* Central Intelligence Agency.

—**OFFICE OF INFORMATION TECHNOLOGY.** *See:* Central Intelligence Agency.

—**OFFICE OF INSTALLATIONS AND LOGISTICS.** *See:* National Security Agency.

—**OFFICE OF LEADERSHIP ANALYSIS.** *See:* Central Intelligence Agency.

—**OFFICE OF LOGISTICS.** *See:* Central Intelligence Agency.

—**OFFICE OF MANAGEMENT AND BUDGET (OMB).** The Intelligence Branch of the National Security Division of the Office of Management and Budget has a staff that is charged with processing the National Foreign Intelligence Program (NFIP) budget, which is submitted annually by the director of Central Intelligence. The OMB reviews and evaluates the budget and makes a final recommendation to the president for inclusion before the NFIP budget is included in the budget that he presents to Congress. The recommendation of the OMB can be appealed by the agency concerned, and the president makes the final decision. *See also:* Defense Guidance (DG), Five-Year Defense Program (FYDP), National Defense Expenditures, National Intelligence Projections for Planning (NIPP), Office of Management and Budget (OMB), Program Budget Decision (PBD).

References

American Bar Association. *Oversight and Accountability of the U.S. Intelligence Agencies: An Evaluation.* Washington, DC: ABA, 1985.

Corson, William R. *The Armies of Ignorance: The Rise of the American Intelligence Empire.* New York: Dial Press, 1977.

Godson, Roy, ed. *Intelligence Problems for the 1980s, Number 1: Elements of Intelligence.* Rev. ed. Washington, DC: National Strategy Information Center, 1983.

Lowenthal, Mark M. *U.S. Intelligence: Evolution and Anatomy.* New York: Praeger, 1984.

Maurer, Alfred C.; Turnstall, Marion D.; and Keagle, James M. *Intelligence Policy and Process.* Boulder, CO: Westview Press, 1985.

Treverton, Gregory F. *Covert Action: The Limits of Intervention in the Postwar World.* New York: Basic Books, 1987.

—**OFFICE OF MEDICAL SERVICES.** *See:* Central Intelligence Agency.

—**OFFICE OF NATIONAL ESTIMATES (ONE)** was created during the tenure of General Walter Bedell Smith as director of Central Intelligence and was part of the reforms often referred to as the reorganization of 1950. The ONE was created to produce coordinated national intelligence estimates. The CIA's research was to be limited to economic intelligence, while political intelligence would be provided by the Department of State. However, under subsequent DCIs, the ONE acquired considerably more power. It was replaced by the National Intelligence Council in 1973. *See also:* Central Intelligence Agency.

References

American Bar Association. *Oversight and Accountability of the U.S. Intelligence Agencies: An Evaluation.* Washington, DC: ABA, 1985.

Corson, William R. *The Armies of Ignorance: The Rise of the American Intelligence Empire.* New York: Dial Press, 1977.

Fain, Tyrus G.; Plant, Katharine C.; and Milloy, Ross. *The Intelligence Community: History, Organization, and Issues.* Public Documents Series. New York: R.R. Bowker, 1977.

Laqueur, Walter. *A World of Secrets.* New York: Basic Books, Inc., 1985.

Lowenthal, Mark M. *U.S. Intelligence: Evolution and Anatomy.* New York: Praeger, 1984.

Maurer, Alfred C.; Turnstall, Marion D.; and Keagle, James M. *Intelligence Policy and Process.* Boulder, CO: Westview Press, 1985.

—**OFFICE OF NAVAL INTELLIGENCE (ONI)** has five major divisions: military information; intelligence research and development; intelligence policy and estimates; special projects; and plans, programs, and systems architecture. Each is assigned to the organization's secretariat, a body that also has staff assistants for Soviet strategy and doctrine, foreign liaison, interagency coordination, and other duties. The ONI is directed by the deputy director for plans, who also serves as the commander of the Naval Security Group Command, the navy's service cryptologic agency. *See also:* Naval Intelligence.

References

Corson, William R. *The Armies of Ignorance: The Rise of the American Intelligence Empire.* New York: Dial Press, 1977.

Godson, Roy, ed. *Intelligence Problems for the 1980s, Number 1: Elements of Intelligence.* Rev. ed. Washington, DC: National Strategy Information Center, 1983.

—**OFFICE OF NEAR EASTERN AND SOUTH ASIAN ANALYSIS.** *See:* Central Intelligence Agency.

—**OFFICE OF OPERATIONS (OO)** was an office that was placed in the Central Intelligence Agency's Directorate of Intelligence and under the deputy director for intelligence in 1952. Among its components were the Foreign Broadcast Information Service, which reported on open foreign broadcasts, overt collection entities that interviewed American tourists and businessmen who traveled abroad, and the Foreign Documents Division (FDD), which handled and translated foreign materials. It was dissolved in 1965. *See also:* Central Intelligence Agency.

References

Breckinridge, Scott D. *The CIA and the U.S. Intelligence System.* Boulder, CO: Westview Press, 1986.

Fain, Tyrus G.; Plant, Katharine C.; and Milloy, Ross. *The Intelligence Community: History, Organization, and Issues.* Public Documents Series. New York: R.R. Bowker, 1977.

—**OFFICE OF PERSONNEL/OEEO.** *See:* Central Intelligence Agency.

—**OFFICE OF PLANS AND POLICY.** *See:* National Security Agency.

—**OFFICE OF POLICY COORDINATION (OPC)** was created in 1948 and conducted covert action operations. In 1952, it was combined with the Office of Special Operations as the Clandestine Services under the deputy director for plans, which was later renamed the deputy director of operations. Although the OPC was located in the CIA, it reported to the Departments of State and Defense. Its purpose was to carry out those covert action missions that were assigned to the Central Intelligence Agency by the National Security Council. It was merged with the Office of Special Operations, Central Intelligence Agency, to form the Directorate for Plans. *See also:* Central Intelligence Agency.

References

Corson, William R. *The Armies of Ignorance: The Rise of the American Intelligence Empire.* New York: Dial Press, 1977.

Fain, Tyrus G.; Plant, Katharine C.; and Milloy, Ross. *The Intelligence Community: History, Organization, and Issues.* Public Documents Series. New York: R.R. Bowker, 1977.

Godson, Roy, ed. *Intelligence Problems for the 1980s, Number 3: Counterintelligence.* Washington, DC: National Strategy Information Center, 1980.

Laqueur, Walter. *A World of Secrets.* New York: Basic Books, Inc., 1985.

Treverton, Gregory F. *Covert Action: The Limits of Intervention in the Postwar World.* New York: Basic Books, 1987.

U.S. Congress. Senate. *Final Report of the Senate Select Committee to Study Government Operations with Respect to Intelligence Activities. Report 94-755. Book I, Foreign and Military Intelligence.* Washington, DC: GPO, 1976.

—**OFFICE OF PRIMARY RESPONSIBILITY** is the designated office of the military service or a National Foreign Intelligence Board (NFIB) member that produces a particular document.

References

Department of Defense, Defense Intelligence Agency. *Defense Intelligence Agency Manual.* Washington, DC: DIA, 1987.

Godson, Roy, ed. *Intelligence Problems for the 1980s, Number 1: Elements of Intelligence.* Rev. ed. Washington, DC: National Strategy Information Center, 1983.

—**OFFICE OF PRODUCTION.** *See:* National Security Agency.

—**OFFICE OF PROGRAMS AND RESOURCES (DDPR).** *See:* National Security Agency.

—**OFFICE OF REPORTS AND ESTIMATES (ORE)** was created in August 1946 by Lieutenant General Hoyt Vandenberg, U.S. Air Force, director of the Central Intelligence Group. The office was tasked with producing a current intelligence daily summary of foreign events and incidents and to conduct economic and scientific research. *See also:* Central Intelligence Agency.

References
Cline, Ray S. *The CIA Under Reagan, Bush, and Casey.* Washington, DC: Acropolis Books, 1981.

—**OFFICE OF RESEARCH AND DEVELOPMENT.** *See:* Central Intelligence Agency.

—**OFFICE OF RESEARCH AND ENGINEERING (R&E).** *See:* National Security Agency.

—**OFFICE OF RESEARCH AND EVALUATION (ORE)** was a component of the Central Intelligence Group (CIG) that was created by Lieutenant General Hoyt S. Vandenberg, U.S. Air Force, when he was director of Central Intelligence. The ORE was tasked with producing intelligence and national estimates. While the ORE's missions and operations seem modest when compared with those of later CIA departments, offices, and directorates, it was a significant expansion of the CIG's role and influence in U.S. intelligence production. *See also:* Central Intelligence Agency.

References
Lowenthal, Mark M. *U.S. Intelligence: Evolution and Anatomy.* New York: Praeger, 1984.

—**OFFICE OF RESEARCH AND REPORTS (ORR),** Central Intelligence Agency, was established in 1950 and became a component of the Directorate for Intelligence in 1952. It was responsible for scientific and strategic research and was dissolved in 1967. *See also:* Central Intelligence Agency.

References
Corson, William R. *The Armies of Ignorance: The Rise of the American Intelligence Empire.* New York: Dial Press, 1977.
Fain, Tyrus G.; Plant, Katharine C.; and Milloy, Ross. *The Intelligence Community: History, Organization, and Issues.* Public Documents Series. New York: R.R. Bowker, 1977.

Laqueur, Walter. *A World of Secrets.* New York: Basic Books, 1985.

—**OFFICE OF SCIENTIFIC INTELLIGENCE,** Central Intelligence Agency, was established in 1949. It was responsible for basic science and technical research. It became a component of the Directorate for Intelligence in 1952 and was transferred to the Directorate for Science and Technology in 1963. *See also:* Central Intelligence Agency.

References
Fain, Tyrus G.; Plant, Katharine C.; and Milloy, Ross. *The Intelligence Community: History, Organization, and Issues.* Public Documents Series. New York: R.R. Bowker, 1977.
Laqueur, Walter. *A World of Secrets.* New York: Basic Books, 1985.

—**OFFICE OF SCIENTIFIC AND WEAPONS RESEARCH.** *See:* Central Intelligence Agency.

—**OFFICE OF SECURITY.** *See:* Central Intelligence Agency.

—**OFFICE OF SECURITY (OS).** *See:* Defense Intelligence Agency.

—**OFFICE OF SIGINT OPERATIONS.** *See:* Central Intelligence Agency.

—**OFFICE OF SIGNALS OPERATIONS.** *See:* National Security Agency.

—**OFFICE OF SOVIET OPERATIONS.** *See:* Central Intelligence Agency.

—**OFFICE OF SPECIAL INVESTIGATIONS (OSI).** *See:* Air Force Intelligence.

—**OFFICE OF SPECIAL OPERATIONS** was established in 1946. It was the component of the Central Intelligence Agency that was responsible for espionage and counterespionage. In 1952, it was merged with the CIA's Office of Policy Coordination (OPC) to form the Directorate of Plans (DDP). *See also:* Central Intelligence Agency.

References
Corson, William R. *The Armies of Ignorance: The Rise of the American Intelligence Empire.* New York: Dial Press, 1977.

Fain, Tyrus G.; Plant, Katharine C.; and Milloy, Ross. *The Intelligence Community: History, Organization, and Issues.* Public Documents Series. New York: R.R. Bowker, 1977.

Godson, Roy, ed. *Intelligence Problems for the 1980s, Number 3: Counterintelligence.* Washington, DC: National Strategy Information Center, 1980.

Treverton, Gregory F. *Covert Action: The Limits of Intervention in the Postwar World.* New York: Basic Books, 1987.

U.S. Congress. Senate. *Final Report of the Senate Select Committee to Study Government Operations with Respect to Intelligence Activities. Report 94-755. Book I, Foreign and Military Intelligence.* Washington, DC: GPO, 1976.

—**OFFICE OF STRATEGIC RESEARCH (OSR),** Central Intelligence Agency, was established in 1967 as a component of the Directorate of Intelligence (DDI), thereby combining the military units in the Office of Current Intelligence and the Office of Research and Reports (ORR). *See also:* Central Intelligence Agency.

References
Fain, Tyrus G.; Plant, Katharine C.; and Milloy, Ross. *The Intelligence Community: History, Organization, and Issues.* Public Documents Series. New York: R.R. Bowker, 1977.

Godson, Roy, ed. *Intelligence Problems for the 1980s, Number 3: Counterintelligence.* Washington, DC: National Strategy Information Center, 1980.

Laqueur, Walter. *A World of Secrets.* New York: Basic Books, Inc., 1985.

—**OFFICE OF STRATEGIC SERVICES (OSS)** was a U.S. intelligence service that was active during World War II. It was established by President Roosevelt in June 1942, and was disbanded by President Truman on October 1, 1945.

President Roosevelt had recognized the need for a central intelligence unit even before the war began, and, in July 1941, he established the Office of the Coordinator of Information (COI) and appointed William Donovan, a World War I hero who had been awarded the Congressional Medal of Honor, to the position of coordinator. The COI had been Donovan's concept. With Pearl Harbor came the greater realization that a centralized intelligence organization was a necessity, and, in June 1942, the COI was reor-

ganized, renamed the Office of Strategic Services (OSS), and placed under the Joint Chiefs of Staff (JCS).

The OSS was to collect strategic intelligence for the JCS and plan and conduct those special operations as directed by the JCS. The order also established the position of director and assigned William J. Donovan to that position.

Initially, the OSS operated under several hardships. It had to compete with other intelligence organizations, particularly the Federal Bureau of Investigation and the Army's G-2. Additionally, by being under the JCS, it had to compete with the Joint Intelligence Committee (JIC) that had been created to fulfill the intelligence needs of the JCS. And, the United States was still a provincial nation, unaccustomed to a position of world leadership. An organization that specialized in subversion, covert operations, propaganda, and support of resistance groups somehow seemed un-American, and many questioned the need for such an organization or the methods it espoused.

The OSS was composed of eight branches: Research and Analysis (R&A) was responsible for producing estimates and studies; a second branch controlled training and assignments; and another five branches conducted clandestine collection, propaganda, subversion, sabotage, and paramilitary operations.

The TORCH operation, involving the Allied landings on North Africa in 1942, did much to further the OSS reputation, in that it acted as the principal intermediary between American and French forces. Nonetheless, OSS's contribution to the war effort must be assessed as modest. It competed with several other intelligence organizations in an atmosphere where there were poorly defined reporting lines. Nonetheless, it proved to be an operational training ground for the postwar analytical intelligence leaders and demonstrated the need for a single centralized intelligence entity. *See also:* Central Intelligence Agency.

References
American Bar Association. *Oversight and Accountability of the U.S. Intelligence Agencies: An Evaluation.* Washington, DC: ABA, 1985.

Becket, Henry S. A. *The Dictionary of Espionage: Spookspeak into English.* New York: Stein and Day, 1986.

Cline, Ray S. *The CIA Under Reagan, Bush, and Casey.* Washington: Acropolis Books, 1981.

Deacon, Richard. *Spyclopedia: An Encyclopedia of Spies, Secret Services, Operations, Jargon, and All Subjects Related to the World of Espionage.* London: Macdonald, 1987.

Godson, Roy, ed. *Intelligence Problems for the 1980s, Number 1: Elements of Intelligence.* Rev. ed. Washington, DC: National Strategy Information Center, 1983.

Laqueur, Walter. *A World of Secrets.* New York: Basic Books, 1985.

Lowenthal, Mark M. *U.S. Intelligence: Evolution and Anatomy.* New York: Praeger, 1984.

Maurer, Alfred C.; Turnstall, Marion D.; and Keagle, James M. *Intelligence Policy and Process.* Boulder, CO: Westview Press, 1985.

Office of the President of the United States. *Military Order, Office of Strategic Services.* Washington, DC, June 13, 1942.

Quirk, John; Phillips, David; Cline, Ray; and Pforzheimer, Walter. *The Central Intelligence Agency: A Photographic History.* Guilford, CT: Foreign Intelligence Press, 1986.

—**OFFICE OF TECHNICAL SERVICE.** *See:* Central Intelligence Agency.

—**OFFICE OF TELECOMMUNICATIONS AND COMPUTER SERVICES.** *See:* National Security Agency.

—**OFFICE OF TRAINING AND EDUCATION.** *See:* Central Intelligence Agency.

—**OFFICIAL.** *See:* Foreign Official.

—**OFFICIAL ESTABLISHMENTS** is a term used in counterintelligence, counterespionage, and counterinsurgency for any offices in a country that are controlled by a foreign government. *See also:* Accommodation Address, Case, Case Officer, Center, Chief of Base, Chief of Outpost, Chief of Station, Clean, Company, Cover, Cover Organizations, Firm, Illegal Residency, Legal Residency, Live Letter Boxes, Live Letter Drops, Suitable Cover.

References
Kessler, Ronald. *Spy vs. Spy: Stalking Soviet Spies in America.* New York: Charles Scribner's Sons, 1988.

—**OFFICIAL INFORMATION** is information that is subject to control by the U.S. government. *See also:* Classified Information.

References
Department of Defense, Defense Intelligence College. *Glossary of Intelligence Terms and Definitions.* Washington, DC: DIC, 1987.

Godson, Roy, ed. *Intelligence Problems for the 1980s, Number 1: Elements of Intelligence.* Rev. ed. Washington, DC: National Strategy Information Center, 1983.

Treverton, Gregory F. *Covert Action: The Limits of Intervention in the Postwar World.* New York: Basic Books, 1987.

—**OFFICIALS** is a term used in counterintelligence, counterespionage, and counterinsurgency to describe aliens assigned in the United States to official establishments or to the United Nations and its organizations. *See also:* Agent, Agent Net, Case Officer, Chief of Base, Chief of Outpost, Chief of Station, Illegal Agent, Illegal Support Officer, Legal, Legal Residency, Legitimate, Proprietaries, Proprietary Company, Singleton, Third Country Operation.

References
Kessler, Ronald. *Spy vs. Spy: Stalking Soviet Spies in America.* New York: Charles Scribner's Sons, 1988.

—**OFF-LINE CRYPTO-OPERATION,** in communications security (COMSEC), means the encryption or decryption that is performed separately and at a different time than the time of transmission or decryption. It is done by manual or machine crypto-equipments that are not electrically connected to the signal line. *See also:* Communications Security.

References
Department of Defense, U.S. Army. *Counter-Signals Intelligence (C-SIGINT) Operations.* Field Manual FM 34-62. Washington, DC: Headquarters, Department of the Army, 1986.

———. *Military Intelligence Battalion Combat Electronic Warfare and Intelligence (Aerial Exploitation) (Corps).* Field Manual FM 34-22. Washington, DC: Headquarters, Department of the Army, 1984.

———. *Military Intelligence Battalion (CEWI) (Tactical Exploitation) (Corps): Counterintelligence, Interrogation, Electronic Warfare.* Field Manual FM 34-23. Washington, DC: Headquarters, Department of the Army, 1985.

———. *Military Intelligence Company (Combat Electronic Warfare and Intelligence) (Armored Cavalry Regiment/Separate Brigade).* Field Manual FM 34-30. Washington, DC: Headquarters, Department of the Army, 1983.

—**OFFSET ARRANGEMENTS** is a CIA system that prevents deep cover agents from profiting from their cover jobs. Whatever these agents make from their cover jobs is deducted from their pay. If there is still a profit, then it goes to the U.S. Treasury.

References

Becket, Henry S. A. *The Dictionary of Espionage: Spookspeak into English.* New York: Stein and Day, 1986.

Deacon, Richard. *Spyclopedia: An Encyclopedia of Spies, Secret Services, Operations, Jargon, and All Subjects Related to the World of Espionage.* London: Macdonald, 1987.

Ranelagh, John. *The Agency: The Rise and Decline of the CIA.* New York: Simon and Schuster, 1986.

Quirk, John; Phillips, David; Cline, Ray; and Pforzheimer, Walter. *The Central Intelligence Agency: A Photographic History.* Guilford, CT: Foreign Intelligence Press, 1986.

—**OLMSTEAD VS. THE UNITED STATES** had established that government wiretapping was not a "search and seizure" subject to the Fourth Amendment's limitations. This meant that wiretapping did not involve a trespass into the subject's home or office. However, two 1967 court decisions, *Katz vs. United States* and *Berger vs. New York* indicated that the Supreme Court might overturn *Olmstead vs. United States* if it was asked to decide. *See: Katz vs. United States.*

References

Kornblum, Allan. *Intelligence and the Law: Cases and Materials.* Vol. IV. Washington, DC: DIC, 1987.

Oseth, John M. *Regulating U.S. Intelligence Operations: A Study in the Definition of the National Interest.* Frankfurt: University of Kentucky Press, 1985.

—**ONE-MAN BAY OF PIGS** is clandestine and covert intelligence operations jargon for an incompetent agent. It refers to the catastrophic Bay of Pigs operation and those who planned it.

References

Deacon, Richard. *Spyclopedia: An Encyclopedia of Spies, Secret Services, Operations, Jargon, and All Subjects Related to the World of Espionage.* London: Macdonald, 1987.

—**ONE-PART CODE** is a cryptographic term that means a code in which the plain-text elements are arranged in alphabetical, numerical, or an-other systematic order. It is accompanied by the code groups that are also arranged in alphabetical, numerical, or some other systematic order, so that one listing serves for both encoding and decoding. *See also:* Communications Security.

References

Department of Defense, U.S. Army. *Counter-Signals Intelligence (C-SIGINT) Operations.* Field Manual FM 34-62. Washington, DC: Headquarters, Department of the Army, 1986.

————. *Military Intelligence Battalion Combat Electronic Warfare and Intelligence (Aerial Exploitation) (Corps).* Field Manual FM 34-22. Washington, DC: Headquarters, Department of the Army, 1984.

————. *Military Intelligence Battalion (CEWI) (Tactical Exploitation) (Corps): Counterintelligence, Interrogation, Electronic Warfare.* Field Manual FM 34-23. Washington, DC: Headquarters, Department of the Army, 1985.

————. *Military Intelligence Company (Combat Electronic Warfare and Intelligence) (Armored Cavalry Regiment/Separate Brigade).* Field Manual FM 34-30. Washington, DC: Headquarters, Department of the Army, 1983.

—**ONE-SHOT** is a term used in clandestine and covert intelligence operations for an informant who thinks that he can make a one-time deal with an intelligence agency—that he can exchange a valuable piece of intelligence for a large sum of money. *See also:* Agent, Biographic Leverage, Blackmail, Co-Opted Worker, Co-Optees, Dirty Tricks, Disaffected Person, Doubled, Informant, Inside Man, Recruitment, Recruitment in Place, Turned.

References

Becket, Henry S. A. *The Dictionary of Espionage: Spookspeak into English.* New York: Stein and Day, 1986.

Clancy, Tom. *The Cardinal of the Kremlin.* New York: Putnam, 1988.

—**ONE-TIME CRYPTOSYSTEM,** a cryptographic term, is a cryptosystem that uses key variables that are used only once. *See also:* Communications Security.

References

Department of Defense, U.S. Army. *Counter-Signals Intelligence (C-SIGINT) Operations.* Field Manual FM 34-62. Washington, DC: Headquarters, Department of the Army, 1986.

———. *Military Intelligence Battalion Combat Electronic Warfare and Intelligence (Aerial Exploitation) (Corps)*. Field Manual FM 34-22. Washington, DC: Headquarters, Department of the Army, 1984.

———. *Military Intelligence Battalion (CEWI) (Tactical Exploitation) (Corps): Counterintelligence, Interrogation, Electronic Warfare*. Field Manual FM 34-23. Washington, DC: Headquarters, Department of the Army, 1985.

———. *Military Intelligence Company (Combat Electronic Warfare and Intelligence) (Armored Cavalry Regiment/Separate Brigade)*. Field Manual FM 34-30. Washington, DC: Headquarters, Department of the Army, 1983.

—**ONE-TIME PAD** is a cryptographic term that means a manual, one-time cryptosystem that is produced in pad form. *See also:* Communications Security.

References

Clancy, Tom. *The Cardinal of the Kremlin*. New York: Putnam, 1988.

—**ONE-TIME TAPE,** in communications security (COMSEC), means a punched paper tape that is used only once. It provides cryptovariables in certain machine cryptosystems. *See also:* Communications Security.

References

Department of Defense, U.S. Army. *Counter-Signals Intelligence (C-SIGINT) Operations*. Field Manual FM 34-62. Washington, DC: Headquarters, Department of the Army, 1986.

———. *Military Intelligence Battalion Combat Electronic Warfare and Intelligence (Aerial Exploitation) (Corps)*. Field Manual FM 34-22. Washington, DC: Headquarters, Department of the Army, 1984.

———. *Military Intelligence Battalion (CEWI) (Tactical Exploitation) (Corps): Counterintelligence, Interrogation, Electronic Warfare*. Field Manual FM 34-23. Washington, DC: Headquarters, Department of the Army, 1985.

———. *Military Intelligence Company (Combat Electronic Warfare and Intelligence) (Armored Cavalry Regiment/Separate Brigade)*. Field Manual FM 34-30. Washington, DC: Headquarters, Department of the Army, 1983.

—**ONE-WAY RADIO LINK (OWRL),** in FBI terminology, is the transmission of voice, key, or impulses by radio to intelligence personnel who,

by arrangement, can receive and decipher the message.

References

Kessler, Ronald. *Spy vs. Spy: Stalking Soviet Spies in America*. New York: Charles Scribner's Sons, 1988.

—**ON-LINE CRYPTO-OPERATION,** in communications security (COMSEC), means the use of crypto-equipment that is directly connected to a signal line, so that encryption and transmission are accomplished simultaneously. *See also:* Communications Security.

References

Department of Defense, U.S. Army. *Counter-Signals Intelligence (C-SIGINT) Operations*. Field Manual FM 34-62. Washington, DC: Headquarters, Department of the Army, 1986.

———. *Military Intelligence Battalion Combat Electronic Warfare and Intelligence (Aerial Exploitation) (Corps)*. Field Manual FM 34-22. Washington, DC: Headquarters, Department of the Army, 1984.

———. *Military Intelligence Battalion (CEWI) (Tactical Exploitation) (Corps): Counterintelligence, Interrogation, Electronic Warfare*. Field Manual FM 34-23. Washington, DC: Headquarters, Department of the Army, 1985.

———. *Military Intelligence Company (Combat Electronic Warfare and Intelligence) (Armored Cavalry Regiment/Separate Brigade)*. Field Manual FM 34-30. Washington, DC: Headquarters, Department of the Army, 1983.

—**OPEN CODE,** in FBI terminology, are seemingly innocuous messages that, by prearrangement, convey a different meaning.

References

Kessler, Ronald. *Spy vs. Spy: Stalking Soviet Spies in America*. New York: Charles Scribner's Sons, 1988.

—**OPEN SOURCE INFORMATION** is a generic term describing information that is of potential intelligence value and that is available to the public. *See also:* Classified Information.

References

Department of Defense, Defense Intelligence College. *Glossary of Intelligence Terms and Definitions*. Washington, DC: DIC, 1987.

Godson, Roy, ed. *Intelligence Problems for the 1980s, Number 1: Elements of Intelligence*. Rev. ed. Washington, DC: National Strategy Information Center, 1983.

Treverton, Gregory F. *Covert Action: The Limits of Intervention in the Postwar World*. New York: Basic Books, 1987.

Turner, Stansfield. *Secrecy and Democracy: The CIA in Transition*. Boston: Houghton Mifflin, 1985.

—**OPEN SOURCES** is a general intelligence term for primary and secondary source materials that are unclassified and may or may not be produced by the government. They are often the product of overt intelligence collection and often provide a valuable input to all source intelligence production. It is a common and valid observation that the availability of open source material is much greater in open democratic societies than in closed, autocratic societies such as that in the Soviet Union, and that this gives the latter an intelligence advantage. *See also:* Classified Information.

References

Godson, Roy, ed. *Intelligence Problems for the 1980s, Number 1: Elements of Intelligence*. Rev. ed. Washington, DC: National Strategy Information Center, 1983.

Oseth, John M. *Regulating U.S. Intelligence Operations: A Study in the Definition of the National Interest*. Frankfurt: University of Kentucky Press, 1985.

—**OPEN STORAGE** is an intelligence security term for the storage of classified information on desks, shelves, in metal containers, and elsewhere within an accredited facility. When an area is approved for open storage, it means that the security surrounding the area is sufficient to allow material to remain out of security containers while it is unattended. *See also:* Classified Information.

References

Department of Defense, Defense Intelligence Agency. *Defense Intelligence Agency Manual*. Washington, DC: DIA, 1987.

Department of Defense, Defense Intelligence College. *Glossary of Intelligence Terms and Definitions*. Washington, DC: DIC, 1987.

Godson, Roy, ed. *Intelligence Problems for the 1980s, Number 1: Elements of Intelligence*. Rev. ed. Washington, DC: National Strategy Information Center, 1983.

—**OPERATION CHAOS** was a domestic operation that was waged by the Central Intelligence Agency. The most complete discussion of the operation is by Dr. Ray Cline, who claims that both President Johnson and President Nixon were certain that U.S. dissident antiwar activity was being financed and directed from abroad. The activity was counterespionage in nature and was authorized expressly by a National Security Council directive. Cline claims that less than 30 people were involved in the operation. Americans were hired to join dissident groups so that they could establish their cover and would be attractive targets when they went abroad. Over a period of six years, the special task group compiled 13,000 files about these contacts, including files on 7,200 U.S. citizens. While the initial purpose of the operation was within the CIA's purview, the operation itself, it was later concluded, had entered the realm of domestic security and the agency had therefore exceeded its legal authority. All the major commentators on the operation stress the fact that both Johnson and Nixon adamantly and continuously demanded additional information so that they could cope with the dissident problem. *See also:* COINTELPRO.

References

American Bar Association. *Oversight and Accountability of the U.S. Intelligence Agencies: An Evaluation*. Washington, DC: ABA, 1985.

Corson, William R. *The Armies of Ignorance: The Rise of the American Intelligence Empire*. New York: Dial Press, 1977.

Godson, Roy, ed. *Intelligence Problems for the 1980s, Number 1: Elements of Intelligence*. Rev. ed. Washington, DC: National Strategy Information Center, 1983.

Maurer, Alfred C.; Turnstall, Marion D.; and Keagle, James M. *Intelligence Policy and Process*. Boulder, CO: Westview Press, 1985.

Oseth, John M. *Regulating U.S. Intelligence Operations: A Study in the Definition of the National Interest*. Frankfurt: University of Kentucky Press, 1985.

Treverton, Gregory F. *Covert Action: The Limits of Intervention in the Postwar World*. New York: Basic Books, 1987.

—**OPERATION ORDER (OPORD)** is a directive (usually formal) that is issued by a commander to his subordinate commanders with the goal of effecting the coordinated execution of an operation.

References

Department of Defense, Joint Chiefs of Staff. *Department of Defense Dictionary of Military and Related Terms*. Washington, DC: GPO, 1986.

Department of Defense, U.S. Army. *Military Intelligence Battalion Combat Electronic Warfare and Intelligence (Aerial Exploitation) (Corps)*. Field Manual FM 34-22. Washington, DC: Headquarters, Department of the Army, 1984.

————. *Military Intelligence Battalion (CEWI) (Tactical Exploitation) (Corps): Counterintelligence, Interrogation, Electronic Warfare*. Field Manual FM 34-23. Washington, DC: Headquarters, Department of the Army, 1985.

————. *Military Intelligence Company (Combat Electronic Warfare and Intelligence) (Armored Cavalry Regiment/Separate Brigade)*. Field Manual FM 34-30. Washington, DC: Headquarters, Department of the Army, 1983.

—**OPERATION PLANS** are plans for a single or a series of connected operations that are to be carried out simultaneously or in succession.

References

Department of Defense, Joint Chiefs of Staff. *Department of Defense Dictionary of Military and Related Terms*. Washington, DC: GPO, 1986.

Godson, Roy, ed. *Intelligence Problems for the 1980s, Number 1: Elements of Intelligence*. Rev. ed. Washington, DC: National Strategy Information Center, 1983.

Laqueur, Walter. *A World of Secrets*. New York: Basic Books, 1985.

Treverton, Gregory F. *Covert Action: The Limits of Intervention in the Postwar World*. New York: Basic Books, 1987.

—**OPERATIONAL CONTROL (OPCON)** is the authority delegated to a commander to direct the forces that have been assigned to him so that he can accomplish specific missions and tasks that are usually limited by time, function, or location, to deploy these forces, and to retain or assign tactical control of these forces.

References

Department of Defense, Defense Intelligence College. *Glossary of Intelligence Terms and Definitions*. Washington, DC: DIC, 1987.

Department of Defense, Joint Chiefs of Staff. *Department of Defense Dictionary of Military and Related Terms*. Washington, DC: GPO, 1986.

Laqueur, Walter. *A World of Secrets*. New York: Basic Books, 1985.

Treverton, Gregory F. *Covert Action: The Limits of Intervention in the Postwar World*. New York: Basic Books, 1987.

—**OPERATIONAL ELINT** is a category of electronic intelligence (ELINT) that is concerned with the introduction, disposition, movement, use,

tactics, and activity levels of known foreign noncommunications emitters and, where applicable, associated military systems. Operational ELINT may be used for satisfying current intelligence requirements and for indications and warning (I&W) purposes. *See also:* Electronic Intelligence.

References

Department of Defense, U.S. Army. *Counter-Signals Intelligence (C-SIGINT) Operations*. Field Manual FM 34-62. Washington, DC: Headquarters, Department of the Army, 1986.

————. *Military Intelligence Battalion Combat Electronic Warfare and Intelligence (Aerial Exploitation) (Corps)*. Field Manual FM 34-22. Washington, DC: Headquarters, Department of the Army, 1984.

————. *Military Intelligence Battalion (CEWI) (Tactical Exploitation) (Corps): Counterintelligence, Interrogation, Electronic Warfare*. Field Manual FM 34-23. Washington, DC: Headquarters, Department of the Army, 1985.

————. *Military Intelligence Company (Combat Electronic Warfare and Intelligence) (Armored Cavalry Regiment/Separate Brigade)*. Field Manual FM 34-30. Washington, DC: Headquarters, Department of the Army, 1983.

Godson, Roy, ed. *Intelligence Problems for the 1980s, Number 1: Elements of Intelligence*. Rev. ed. Washington, DC: National Strategy Information Center, 1983.

—**OPERATIONAL INTELLIGENCE (OPINTEL)** is the intelligence information that is needed to plan and execute operations. It may also be intelligence that is required to support the activities of intelligence agencies under the National Security Council. *See also:* Strategic Intelligence.

References

Department of Defense, Defense Intelligence College. *Glossary of Intelligence Terms and Definitions*. Washington, DC: DIC, 1987.

Department of Defense, Joint Chiefs of Staff. *Department of Defense Dictionary of Military and Related Terms*. Washington, DC: GPO, 1986.

Godson, Roy, ed. *Intelligence Problems for the 1980s, Number 1: Elements of Intelligence*. Rev. ed. Washington, DC: National Strategy Information Center, 1983.

Kent, Sherman. *Strategic Intelligence for American World Policy*. Princeton, NJ: Princeton University Press, 1966.

Treverton, Gregory F. *Covert Action: The Limits of Intervention in the Postwar World*. New York: Basic Books 1987.

U.S. Congress. Senate. *Final Report of the Senate Select Committee to Study Government Operations with Respect to Intelligence Activities. Report 94-755. Book I, Foreign and Military Intelligence.* Washington, DC: GPO, 1976.

—**OPERATIONAL KEY,** in communications security (COMSEC), refers to the cryptovariables that are intended for use on-the-air for the protection of mission-related, operational traffic. *See also:* Communications Security.

References

Department of Defense, U.S. Army. *Military Intelligence Battalion Combat Electronic Warfare and Intelligence (Aerial Exploitation) (Corps).* Field Manual FM 34-22. Washington, DC: Headquarters, Department of the Army, 1984.

————. *Military Intelligence Battalion (CEWI) (Tactical Exploitation) (Corps): Counterintelligence, Interrogation, Electronic Warfare.* Field Manual FM 34-23. Washington, DC: Headquarters, Department of the Army, 1985.

————. *Military Intelligence Company (Combat Electronic Warfare and Intelligence) (Armored Cavalry Regiment/Separate Brigade).* Field Manual FM 34-30. Washington, DC: Headquarters, Department of the Army, 1983.

—**OPERATIONAL SECURITY (OPSEC)** are the measures that are designed to protect information concerning planned, ongoing, or completed operations against unauthorized disclosure. *See also:* Communications Security.

References

Department of Defense, Defense Intelligence College. *Glossary of Intelligence Terms and Definitions.* Washington, DC: DIC, 1987.

Godson, Roy, ed. *Intelligence Problems for the 1980s, Number 1: Elements of Intelligence.* Rev. ed. Washington, DC: National Strategy Information Center, 1983.

Laqueur, Walter. *A World of Secrets.* New York: Basic Books, 1985.

Treverton, Gregory F. *Covert Action: The Limits of Intervention in the Postwar World.* New York: Basic Books, 1987.

—**OPERATIONAL USE** is a term used in clandestine intelligence operations to describe using a person, group, organization, or privileged information in an intelligence operation. *See also:* Concealment, Cover, Cover Name, Cover Or-

ganizations, Cover Story, Proprietaries, Proprietary Company, Putting in the Plumbing, Special Activities, Third Country Operation.

References

Becket, Henry S. A. *The Dictionary of Espionage: Spookspeak into English.* New York: Stein and Day, 1986.

Godson, Roy, ed. *Intelligence Problems for the 1980s, Number 1: Elements of Intelligence.* Rev. ed. Washington, DC: National Strategy Information Center, 1983.

U.S. Congress. Senate. *Final Report of the Senate Select Committee to Study Government Operations with Respect to Intelligence Activities. Report 94-755. Book I, Foreign and Military Intelligence.* Washington, DC: GPO, 1976.

—**OPERATIONS ADVISORY GROUP (OAG)** was established by President Ford in his Executive Order 11905, "United States Foreign Intelligence Activities," February 18, 1976. Composed of the assistant to the president for national security affairs, the secretary of state, the secretary of defense, the chairman of the Joint Chiefs of Staff, and the director of Central Intelligence, the OAG chairman was to be designated by the president. This group was to develop policy recommendations for the president prior to his decision on special activities, approve specific sensitive intelligence collection operations, and review ongoing special activities and sensitive collection operations periodically to ensure that they should be continued.

References

Office of the President of the United States. *Executive Order 11905, United States Foreign Intelligence Activities.* Washington, DC, Feb. 18, 1976.

Treverton, Gregory F. *Covert Action: The Limits of Intervention in the Postwar World.* New York: Basic Books, 1987.

—**OPERATIONS ANALYSIS (OPERATIONS RESEARCH)** is the analytical study of military problems that is undertaken to provide responsible commanders and staff agencies with a scientific basis for decision on action to improve military operations. This is also known as operational analysis.

References

Department of Defense, Joint Chiefs of Staff. *Department of Defense Dictionary of Military and Related Terms.* Washington, DC: GPO, 1986.

Godson, Roy, ed. *Intelligence Problems for the 1980s, Number 1: Elements of Intelligence.* Rev. ed. Washington, DC: National Strategy Information Center, 1983.

Treverton, Gregory F. *Covert Action: The Limits of Intervention in the Postwar World.* New York: Basic Books, 1987.

—**OPERATIONS CODE (OPCODE),** in communications security (COMSEC), means a code that is composed largely of words and phrases and that can be used for general communications. *See also:* Communications Security.

References

Department of Defense, U.S. Army. *Military Intelligence Battalion Combat Electronic Warfare and Intelligence (Aerial Exploitation) (Corps).* Field Manual FM 34-22. Washington, DC: Headquarters, Department of the Army, 1984.

————. *Military Intelligence Battalion (CEWI) (Tactical Exploitation) (Corps): Counterintelligence, Interrogation, Electronic Warfare.* Field Manual FM 34-23. Washington, DC: Headquarters, Department of the Army, 1985.

————. *Military Intelligence Company (Combat Electronic Warfare and Intelligence) (Armored Cavalry Regiment/Separate Brigade).* Field Manual FM 34-30. Washington, DC: Headquarters, Department of the Army, 1983.

—**OPERATIONS COORDINATING BOARD (OCB)** replaced the Psychological Strategy Board of the National Security Council on September 2, 1953. Its purpose was to act as a senior review body for covert operations. Its members included deputy-level officials from the Departments of State and Defense, from the Office of the President, and from the foreign aid program. It has been replaced by other oversight mechanisms. *See also:* Executive Oversight.

References

Fain, Tyrus G.; Plant, Katharine C.; and Milloy, Ross. *The Intelligence Community: History, Organization, and Issues.* Public Documents Series. New York: R.R. Bowker, 1977.

U.S. Congress. Senate. *Final Report of the Senate Select Committee to Study Government Operations with Respect to Intelligence Activities. Report 94-755. Book I, Foreign and Military Intelligence.* Washington, DC: GPO, 1976.

—**OPERATIONS SECURITY (OPSEC)** has two meanings. (1) In operations, operations security are those measures that are designed to protect information concerning planned, ongoing, or completed operations against unauthorized disclosure. (2) In communications security (COMSEC), it is a term that means the process of denying adversaries information about friendly capabilities and intentions by identifying, controlling, and protecting the indicators that are associated with the planning and conducting of military operations and other activities. *See also:* Communications Security.

References

Department of Defense, Joint Chiefs of Staff. *Department of Defense Dictionary of Military and Related Terms.* Washington, DC: GPO, 1986.

Laqueur, Walter. *A World of Secrets.* New York: Basic Books, 1985.

Treverton, Gregory F. *Covert Action: The Limits of Intervention in the Postwar World.* New York: Basic Books, 1987.

Turner, Stansfield. *Secrecy and Democracy: The CIA in Transition.* Boston: Houghton Mifflin, 1985.

—**OPERATIONS SECURITY (OPSEC) PROCESS** is an Army tactical intelligence (TACINT) term that refers to the procedures that an Army entity employs to ensure or to enhance its operations security (OPSEC). The process involves the continuous planning, data collection, analysis, reporting, and execution of orders and instructions. The process is cyclical in nature, taking into consideration the changing nature of both the threat and friendly vulnerabilities. It is normally composed of ten steps: identifying the hostile intelligence collection threat; identifying friendly force profiles and recommending essential elements of friendly information (EEFI); identifying friendly force vulnerabilities; performing risk analysis and select EEFI; recommending OPSEC procedures; selecting OPSEC measures; applying the OPSEC measures; directing the efforts to monitor the effectiveness of applied OPSEC measures; monitoring the effectiveness of OPSEC measures; and recommending adjustments to OPSEC measures. *See also:* Communications Security.

References

Department of Defense, U.S. Army. *Counter-Signals Intelligence (C-SIGINT) Operations.* Field Manual FM 34-62. Washington, DC: Headquarters, Department of the Army, 1986.

————. *Military Intelligence Battalion Combat Electronic Warfare and Intelligence (Aerial Exploitation) (Corps).* Field Manual FM 34-22. Washington, DC: Headquarters, Department of the Army, 1984.

———. *Military Intelligence Battalion (Combat Electronic Warfare Intelligence) (Division)*. Field Manual FM 34-10. Washington, DC: Headquarters, Department of the Army, 1981.

—**OPERATIVE.** *See:* Agent.

—**OPSCOMM** is a communications link that is established for the informal exchange of information on an informal basis. *See also:* Communications Security.

References

Department of Defense, U.S. Army. *Counter-Signals Intelligence (C-SIGINT) Operations*. Field Manual FM 34-62. Washington, DC: Headquarters, Department of the Army, 1986.

———. *Military Intelligence Battalion Combat Electronic Warfare and Intelligence (Aerial Exploitation) (Corps)*. Field Manual FM 34-22. Washington, DC: Headquarters, Department of the Army, 1984.

———. *Military Intelligence Battalion (Combat Electronic Warfare Intelligence) (Division)*. Field Manual FM 34-10. Washington, DC: Headquarters, Department of the Army, 1981.

—**OPSEC SUPPORT** is an Army tactical intelligence (TACINT) term that refers to those actions that support operations security (OPSEC) measures. *See also:* Communications Security.

References

Department of Defense, U.S. Army. *Counter-Signals Intelligence (C-SIGINT) Operations*. Field Manual FM 34-62. Washington, DC: Headquarters, Department of the Army, 1986.

———. *Military Intelligence Battalion Combat Electronic Warfare and Intelligence (Aerial Exploitation) (Corps)*. Field Manual FM 34-22. Washington, DC: Headquarters, Department of the Army, 1984.

———. *Military Intelligence Battalion (Combat Electronic Warfare Intelligence) (Division)*. Field Manual FM 34-10. Washington, DC: Headquarters, Department of the Army, 1981.

—**OPSEC SURVEY,** in communications security (COMSEC), refers to a technique of data acquisition and analysis that is used to construct the sequence of events that are associated with time-definable operations and functions. The objective is to identify activity that could be exploited by the enemy to gain a military, technical, diplomatic, or economic advantage and includes document reviews, interviews and observations, selected SIGSEC and COMSEC monitoring, and a review of all-source intelligence information that bears on the enemy threat. *See also:* Communications Security.

References

Department of Defense, U.S. Army. *Counter-Signals Intelligence (C-SIGINT) Operations*. Field Manual FM 34-62. Washington, DC: Headquarters, Department of the Army, 1986.

———. *Military Intelligence Battalion Combat Electronic Warfare and Intelligence (Aerial Exploitation) (Corps)*. Field Manual FM 34-22. Washington, DC: Headquarters, Department of the Army, 1984.

———. *Military Intelligence Battalion (CEWI) (Tactical Exploitation) (Corps): Counterintelligence, Interrogation, Electronic Warfare*. Field Manual FM 34-23. Washington, DC: Headquarters, Department of the Army, 1985.Department of

———. *Military Intelligence Company (Combat Electronic Warfare and Intelligence) (Armored Cavalry Regiment/Separate Brigade)*. Field Manual FM 34-30. Washington, DC: Headquarters, Department of the Army, 1983.

—**OPTICAL CHARACTER READER (OCR)** is a scanning device that reads and converts data from typed material to computer language, thereby eliminating the need to type all the information into an input that is acceptable for transmission. *See also:* Communications Security.

References

Department of Defense, U.S. Army. *Counter-Signals Intelligence (C-SIGINT) Operations*. Field Manual FM 34-62. Washington, DC: Headquarters, Department of the Army, 1986.

———. *Military Intelligence Battalion Combat Electronic Warfare and Intelligence (Aerial Exploitation) (Corps)*. Field Manual FM 34-22. Washington, DC: Headquarters, Department of the Army, 1984.

———. *Military Intelligence Battalion (CEWI) (Tactical Exploitation) (Corps): Counterintelligence, Interrogation, Electronic Warfare*. Field Manual FM 34-23. Washington, DC: Headquarters, Department of the Army, 1985.

———. *Military Intelligence Company (Combat Electronic Warfare and Intelligence) (Armored Cavalry Regiment/Separate Brigade)*. Field Manual FM 34-30. Washington, DC: Headquarters, Department of the Army, 1983.

—**OPTICAL INTELLIGENCE (OPTINT)** is the portion of electro-optical intelligence that deals with visible light. *See also:* Electro-Optical Intelligence.

References

Department of Defense, Defense Intelligence College. *Glossary of Intelligence Terms and Definitions.* Washington, DC: DIC, 1987.

—**ORCON** is a caveat placed on messages that contain information that clearly identifies or would reasonably permit ready identification of an intelligence source or method. Information bearing this caveat cannot be disseminated beyond the recipient headquarters without the permission of the originator.

References

Department of Defense, Defense Intelligence Agency. *Defense Intelligence Agency Manual.* Washington, DC: DIA, 1987.

—**ORDER OF BATTLE (OB)** is intelligence about the strength, identification, command structure, and disposition of the personnel, units, and equipment of any foreign force. In the Army tactical intelligence (TACINT) context, the counter-signals intelligence (C-SIGINT) section of the military intelligence unit develops OB data for enemy SIGINT units, and friendly OB as it pertains to the unit's electronic and communications systems. The data that can make up an OB list include composition, disposition, strength, training status, tactics, and communications-electronics emitters. *See also:* Defense Intelligence Agency.

References

Department of Defense, Defense Intelligence College. *Glossary of Intelligence Terms and Definitions.* Washington, DC: DIC, 1987.

Department of Defense, Joint Chiefs of Staff. *Department of Defense Dictionary of Military and Related Terms.* Washington, DC: GPO, 1986.

Department of Defense, U.S. Army. *Counter-Signals Intelligence (C-SIGINT) Operations.* Field Manual FM 34-62. Washington, DC: Headquarters, Department of the Army, 1986.

Quirk, John; Phillips, David; Cline, Ray; and Pforzheimer, Walter. *The Central Intelligence Agency: A Photographic History.* Guilford, CT: Foreign Intelligence Press, 1986.

U.S. Congress. Senate. *Final Report of the Senate Select Committee to Study Government Operations with Respect to Intelligence Activities. Report 94-755. Book I, Foreign and Military Intelligence.* Washington, DC: GPO, 1976.

—**ORDER OF BATTLE CARD** is a single, or master, standardized card that contains basic information on each enemy ground force unit or formation and provides all pertinent order of battle information. *See also:* Defense Intelligence Agency.

References

Department of Defense, Joint Chiefs of Staff. *Department of Defense Dictionary of Military and Related Terms.* Washington, DC: GPO, 1986.

—**ORGANIZATIONAL COVER** is a term used in clandestine and covert intelligence operations to describe the use of legitimate businesses as cover for covert agents. *See also*: Agent in Place, Case, Case Officer, Chief of Base, Chief of Outpost, Chief of Station, Clean, Cover Organizations, Cover Story, Illegal Residency, Legal, Legal Residency, Plumbing, Proprietaries, Proprietary Company, Putting in the Plumbing, Special Activities.

References

Becket, Henry S. A. *The Dictionary of Espionage: Spookspeak into English.* New York: Stein and Day, 1986.

Deacon, Richard. *Spyclopedia: An Encyclopedia of Spies, Secret Services, Operations, Jargon, and All Subjects Related to the World of Espionage.* London: Macdonald, 1987.

Ranelagh, John. *The Agency: The Rise and Decline of the CIA.* New York: Simon and Schuster, 1986.

Treverton, Gregory F. *Covert Action: The Limits of Intervention in the Postwar World.* New York: Basic Books, 1987.

—**OTT, BRUCE DAMIAN,** an Air Force sergeant, was arrested on July 16, 1982, by federal agents posing as Soviet intelligence officials, while passing classified information concerning the SR-71 reconnaissance aircraft. Ott was motivated by financial difficulties. On August 6, 1986, he was found guilty by court-martial for failing to report unauthorized contacts, for unauthorized removal of a classified document from his duty station, and for attempting to deliver a classified document to a foreign agent. He was sentenced to 25 years at hard labor.

References

Allen, Thomas B., and Polmar, Norman. *Merchants of Treason: America's Secrets for Sale*. New York: Delacorte Press, 1988.

Crawford, David J. *Volunteers: The Betrayal of National Defense Secrets by Air Force Traitors*. Washington, DC: GPO, 1988.

—**OUTLAY** is a budget term that has significance for the Intelligence Community. An outlay is the actual expenditure of money from the U.S. Treasury, which usually lags behind obligation. Congress, under the full funding concept, approves sufficient budget authority to complete a program even though completion and final payment may be several years away. This flow of funds naturally has an impact on the economy through the amount of money in circulation, inflation, interest rates, and employment. In recent years, Congress has attempted to adjust the budget authority in order to control outlays. *See also:* Office of Management and Budget.

References

Pickett, George. "Congress, the Budget, and Intelligence." In *Intelligence Policy and Process*, edited by Alfred C. Maurer, Marion D. Turnstall, and James M. Keagle. Boulder, CO: Westview Press, 1985.

—**OUT OF AREA** refers to Soviet naval deployments to the high seas, and is the method by which U.S. naval intelligence determines and judges the projection of Soviet naval power. Out of area encompasses all of the world's ocean areas except for Soviet inland waterways, coastal areas, and local exercise areas. Thus, whenever a Soviet ship travels westward from the North Cape and into the Norwegian Sea, exits from the Baltic Sea, passes southward through the Turkish Straits and into the Aegean, leaves the Sea of Japan, or proceeds eastward from the Sea of Okhotsk, it is considered to be out of area.

Soviet naval presence on the high seas is measured in terms of the out-of-area ship day. An out-of-area ship day is an entire day or a portion of a day that a ship spends outside of local Soviet waters. The out-of-area ship day is the basic measurement that U.S. naval intelligence uses to judge and measure Soviet naval operations and is invaluable for several reasons. Analyzing ship-day figures for several consecutive years can reveal trends in deployed naval strength. These statistics can be further refined in terms of ship type, geographic area, and nature of activity. Looking at ship days by ship type (surface combatant, amphibious warfare ship, submarine, auxiliary [supply] ship) yields a combatant-auxiliary ration that can provide an insight into the kind and quantity of auxiliary support the Soviet Navy needs in order to deploy a fleet of combatants. Comparing the surface combatant-submarine ratio is helpful in assessing the Soviet Union's motives in a given ocean area. For example, a traditionally high submarine presence in the Atlantic poses both a strategic missile threat and a significant antishipping threat to the West and is primarily defensive in nature. In contrast, one of several factors accounting for a high surface combatant presence in the Mediterranean is that these ships provide a highly visible manifestation of Soviet power in contrast to the low visibility of submerged submarines. This force comparison indicates that the Mediterranean Fleet is assigned a significant political mission in addition to its defense purpose.

The geographical distribution of ship days shows which areas of the world are most important to the Soviet Union at a particular time and, concurrently, the amount of power the Navy is either able to deploy or considers necessary in order to fulfill its assigned missions. Computing ship days in terms of ships' activities can help explain the purpose of a given contingent of ships. The major activities of naval ships include transit (movement from one location to another), exercises, patrols and other operations, time at anchor, and port visits.

References

Watson, Bruce W. *Red Navy at Sea: Soviet Naval Operations on the High Seas, 1956-1980*. Boulder, CO: Westview Press, 1986.

Watson, Bruce W., and Watson, Susan M., eds. *The Soviet Navy: Strengths and Liabilities*. Boulder, CO: Westview Press, 1986.

—**OUTSIDE MAN** is a CIA case officer who works overseas apparently as a private citizen with no overt ties with either the agency or the U.S. embassy. *See also:* Deep Cover, Singleton.

References

Becket, Henry S. A. *The Dictionary of Espionage: Spookspeak into English*. New York: Stein and Day, 1986.

Deacon, Richard. *Spyclopedia: An Encyclopedia of Spies, Secret Services, Operations, Jargon, and All Subjects Related to the World of Espionage.* London: Macdonald, 1987.

Ranelagh, John. *The Agency: The Rise and Decline of the CIA.* New York: Simon and Schuster, 1986.

Treverton, Gregory F. *Covert Action: The Limits of Intervention in the Postwar World.* New York: Basic Books, 1987.

—**OVERHEAD RECONNAISSANCE** is an intelligence imagery and photoreconnaissance term for collection missions involving aircraft or satellites to obtain photography and other intelligence data about target nations. *See also:* Aerial Photograph.

References
Breckinridge, Scott D. *The CIA and the U.S. Intelligence System.* Boulder, CO: Westview Press, 1986.

Godson, Roy, ed. *Intelligence Problems for the 1980s, Number 1: Elements of Intelligence.* Rev. ed. Washington, DC: National Strategy Information Center, 1983.

Turner, Stansfield. *Secrecy and Democracy: The CIA in Transition.* Boston: Houghton Mifflin, 1985.

—**OVEROBLIGATION** occurs when the total funds that a command has spent or reserved exceeds the amount of funds that the command has been authorized. *See also:* Office of Management and Budget.

References
Pickett, George. "Congress, the Budget, and Intelligence." In *Intelligence Policy and Process,* edited by Alfred C. Maurer, Marion D. Turnstall, and James M. Keagle. Boulder, CO: Westview Press, 1985.

—**OVERSIGHT.** *See:* Congressional Oversight, Executive Oversight.

—**OVERT** is a general intelligence term that means open or done without any attempt at concealment.

References
Department of Defense, Defense Intelligence College. *Glossary of Intelligence Terms and Definitions.* Washington, DC: DIC, 1987.

Kent, Sherman. *Strategic Intelligence for American World Policy.* Princeton, NJ: Princeton University Press, 1966.

Turner, Stansfield. *Secrecy and Democracy: The CIA in Transition.* Boston: Houghton Mifflin, 1985.

—**OVERT ACTIVITIES,** in FBI terminology, are actions that may be openly attributed to the government accountable for them.

References
Kent, Sherman. *Strategic Intelligence for American World Policy.* Princeton, NJ: Princeton University Press, 1966.

Kessler, Ronald. *Spy vs. Spy: Stalking Soviet Spies in America.* New York: Charles Scribner's Sons, 1988.

Laqueur, Walter. *A World of Secrets.* New York: Basic Books, 1985.

—**OVERT COLLECTION,** in intelligence collection, is acquiring information from the public media, observation, government-to-government dialogue, elicitation, and from sharing data that was acquired openly. The process of overt collection may be classified or unclassified. The target and the host government as well as the sources involved are usually aware of the general collection activity, although the specific acquisition, sites, and processes may be successfully concealed.

References
Department of Defense, Defense Intelligence College. *Glossary of Intelligence Terms and Definitions.* Washington, DC: DIC, 1987.

Godson, Roy, ed. *Intelligence Problems for the 1980s, Number 1: Elements of Intelligence.* Rev. ed. Washington, DC: National Strategy Information Center, 1983.

Kent, Sherman. *Strategic Intelligence for American World Policy.* Princeton, NJ: Princeton University Press, 1966.

Laqueur, Walter. *A World of Secrets.* New York: Basic Books, 1985.

Treverton, Gregory F. *Covert Action: The Limits of Intervention in the Postwar World.* New York: Basic Books, 1987.

—**OVERT INTELLIGENCE,** as defined by the Church Committee, is "information that is collected openly from public or open sources."

References

U.S. Congress. Senate. *Final Report of the Senate Select Committee to Study Government Operations with Respect to Intelligence Activities. Report 94-755. Book I, Foreign and Military Intelligence.* Washington, DC: GPO, 1976.

—**OVERT MEANS** is a definition that was established as a result of Presidential Order 12333, "United States Intelligence Activities," dated December 4, 1981. Overt means refers to methods of collection whereby the source of the information being collected is advised, or is otherwise aware, that he is providing such information to the Department of Defense or a component thereof.

References

Department of Defense. *Activities of DoD Intelligence Components that Affect U.S. Persons (Department of Defense Directive 5240.1).* Washington, DC: DoD, 1982.

—**OVERTAKEN BY EVENTS (OBE)** refers to information or decisions that were received or made prior to a significant occurrence that drastically altered the situation and made the information either irrelevant or inappropriate to the current situation. In the vernacular, it implies that the information or decision is dated.

References

Becket, Henry S. A. *The Dictionary of Espionage: Spookspeak into English.* New York: Stein and Day, 1986.

Deacon, Richard. *Spyclopedia: An Encyclopedia of Spies, Secret Services, Operations, Jargon, and All Subjects Related to the World of Espionage.* London: Macdonald, 1987.

Department of Defense, National Defense University. *Joint Staff Officer's Guide, 1986.* Washington, DC: GPO, 1986.

Department of Defense, U.S. Army. *Counter-Signals Intelligence (C-SIGINT) Operations.* Field Manual FM 34-62. Washington, DC: Headquarters, Department of the Army, 1986.

———. *Military Intelligence Battalion (CEWI) (Tactical Exploitation) (Corps): Counterintelligence, Interrogation, Electronic Warfare.* Field Manual FM 34-23. Washington, DC: Headquarters, Department of the Army, 1985.

———. *Military Intelligence Company (Combat Electronic Warfare and Intelligence) (Armored Cavalry Regiment/Separate Brigade).* Field Manual FM 34-30. Washington, DC: Headquarters, Department of the Army, 1983.

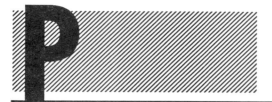

—**PACKED UP** is a term used in clandestine and covert intelligence operations to describe an intelligence operation that has been terminated, usually because it has failed or is about to be exposed. *See also:* Agent, Blow, Blown Agent, Burn, Burnt, Damage Assessment, Damage Control.

References

Becket, Henry S. A. *The Dictionary of Espionage: Spookspeak into English.* New York: Stein and Day, 1986.

Deacon, Richard. *Spyclopedia: An Encyclopedia of Spies, Secret Services, Operations, Jargon, and All Subjects Related to the World of Espionage.* London: Macdonald, 1987.

Kessler, Ronald. *Spy vs. Spy: Stalking Soviet Spies in America.* New York: Charles Scribner's Sons, 1988.

Ranelagh, John. *The Agency: The Rise and Decline of the CIA.* New York: Simon and Schuster, 1986.

—**PAGE PRINTER (PG PRTR)**, a baud-based system term used in communications intelligence, communications security, operations security, and signals analysis, is a teleprinter that types on a page (as opposed to a tape).

References

Department of Defense, U.S. Army. *Military Intelligence Battalion Combat Electronic Warfare and Intelligence (Aerial Exploitation) (Corps).* Field Manual FM 34-22. Washington, DC: Headquarters, Department of the Army, 1984.

———. *Military Intelligence Company (Combat Electronic Warfare and Intelligence) (Armored Cavalry Regiment/Separate Brigade).* Field Manual FM 34-30. Washington, DC: Headquarters, Department of the Army, 1983.

—**PANORAMIC AIR CAMERA** is an imagery and photoreconnaissance term. It is an air camera that, through a system of moving optics or mirrors, scans a wide area of the terrain, usually from horizon to horizon. The camera can be mounted vertically or obliquely within the aircraft to scan across or along the line of flight. *See also:* Aerial Photograph.

References

Department of Defense, Joint Chiefs of Staff. *Department of Defense Dictionary of Military and Related Terms.* Washington, DC: GPO, 1986.

—**PAPER MILL** is a term used in clandestine and covert intelligence operations to describe a fabricator who provides false information consistently and in volume. *See also:* Agent, Agent Authentication, Establishing Bonafides, Shopworn Goods.

References

Becket, Henry S. A. *The Dictionary of Espionage: Spookspeak into English.* New York: Stein and Day, 1986.

Deacon, Richard. *Spyclopedia: An Encyclopedia of Spies, Secret Services, Operations, Jargon, and All Subjects Related to the World of Espionage.* London: Macdonald, 1987.

Quirk, John; Phillips, David; Cline, Ray; and Pforzheimer, Walter. *The Central Intelligence Agency: A Photographic History.* Guilford, CT: Foreign Intelligence Press, 1986.

Ranelagh, John. *The Agency: The Rise and Decline of the CIA.* New York: Simon and Schuster, 1986.

—**PARAMETER** is a statistical or quantitative methodological term that is often used in intelligence analysis. It is a summary value that describes some characteristic of a population. Examples of parameters include means, standard deviations, proportions, and correlation coefficients. The correlation between height and weight for the population of adult women in the United States is a parameter.

References

Godson, Roy, ed. *Intelligence Problems for the 1980s, Number 1: Elements of Intelligence.* Rev. ed. Washington, DC: National Strategy Information Center, 1983.

—**PARAMILITARY FORCES**, as defined by the Church Committee, are "forces or groups which are distinct from the regular armed forces of a nation, although they may resemble regular forces in organization, equipment, training, or mission." *See also:* Guerrilla Operations, Guerrilla Warfare, Guerrillas.

References

Department of Defense, Joint Chiefs of Staff. *Department of Defense Dictionary of Military and Related Terms.* Washington, DC: GPO, 1986.

Godson, Roy, ed. *Intelligence Problems for the 1980s, Number 1: Elements of Intelligence.* Rev. ed. Washington, DC: National Strategy Information Center, 1983.

Laqueur, Walter. *The Age of Terrorism.* Boston: Little, Brown, 1987.

Treverton, Gregory F. *Covert Action: The Limits of Intervention in the Postwar World.* New York: Basic Books, 1987.

U.S. Congress. Senate. *Final Report of the Senate Select Committee to Study Government Operations with Respect to Intelligence Activities. Report 94-755. Book I, Foreign and Military Intelligence.* Washington, DC: GPO, 1976.

—**PARAMILITARY OPERATIONS** are those operations that provide covert military assistance and guidance to unconventional and conventional foreign forces and organizations. *See also:* Guerrilla Operations, Guerrilla Warfare, Guerrillas.

References

Department of Defense, Joint Chiefs of Staff. *Department of Defense Dictionary of Military and Related Terms.* Washington, DC: GPO, 1986.

Godson, Roy, ed. *Intelligence Problems for the 1980s, Number 1: Elements of Intelligence.* Rev. ed. Washington, DC: National Strategy Information Center, 1983.

———. *Intelligence Problems for the 1980s, Number 4: Covert Action.* Washington, DC: National Strategy Information Center, 1981.

Laqueur, Walter. *The Age of Terrorism.* Boston: Little, Brown, 1987.

Treverton, Gregory F. *Covert Action: The Limits of Intervention in the Postwar World.* New York: Basic Books, 1987.

Turner, Stansfield. *Secrecy and Democracy: The CIA in Transition.* Boston: Houghton Mifflin, 1985.

U.S. Congress. Senate. *Final Report of the Senate Select Committee to Study Government Operations with Respect to Intelligence Activities. Report 94-755. Book I, Foreign and Military Intelligence.* Washington, DC: GPO, 1976.

—**PAROLES** is a term used in clandestine and covert intelligence operations to describe the keywords for mutual identification among agents. *See also:* Agent Authentication, Alternate Meet, Establishing Bonafides, Making a Pass, Meet Area.

References

Kessler, Ronald. *Spy vs. Spy: Stalking Soviet Spies in America.* New York: Charles Scribner's Sons, 1988.

Quirk, John; Phillips, David; Cline, Ray; and Pforzheimer, Walter. *The Central Intelligence Agency: A Photographic History.* Guilford, CT: Foreign Intelligence Press, 1986.

—**PASSIVE COUNTERINTELLIGENCE**, in counterintelligence, counterinsurgency, and counterespionage, attempts to counter potentially hostile covert operations. It involves personnel security briefings and other preventive measures.

References

Godson, Roy, ed. *Intelligence Problems for the 1980s, Number 1: Elements of Intelligence.* Rev. ed. Washington, DC: National Strategy Information Center, 1983.

—**PASSIVE ELECTRONIC COUNTERMEASURES,** in electronic warfare (EW), involve searching for and analyzing electromagnetic radiations to determine their origin and pertinent characteristics of the radiations that the enemy may be using. *See also:* Electronic Countermeasures, Electronic Warfare.

References

Department of Defense, Joint Chiefs of Staff. *Department of Defense Dictionary of Military and Related Terms.* Washington, DC: GPO, 1986.

Department of Defense, U.S. Army. *Military Intelligence Battalion Combat Electronic Warfare and Intelligence (Aerial Exploitation) (Corps).* Field Manual FM 34-22. Washington, DC: Headquarters, Department of the Army, 1984.

———. *Military Intelligence Company (Combat Electronic Warfare and Intelligence) (Armored Cavalry Regiment/Separate Brigade).* Field Manual FM 34-30. Washington, DC: Headquarters, Department of the Army, 1983.

Godson, Roy, ed. *Intelligence Problems for the 1980s, Number 1: Elements of Intelligence.* Rev. ed. Washington, DC: National Strategy Information Center, 1983.

—**PASSIVE JAMMING,** in electronic warfare (EW), is using confusion reflectors to return spurious or confusing signals to the transmitting radar set. *See also:* Active Electronic Countermeasures, Active Jamming, Brute Force Jamming, Chaff, Combat Electronic Warfare Intelligence, Communications Jamming, Complex Barrage Jamming, Countermeasures, Deception, Deception Jammer, Deception Material, Dispenser, Drone, Electronic Camouflage, Electronic Counter-Countermeasures, Electronic Countermeasures, Electronic Deception, Electronic Jamming, Electronic Warfare, Electronic Warfare Support Measures, Escort Jamming, Garble, Jammer, Jammer Band (width), Jamming, Jamming Effectiveness, Jamming Platform, Jamming Signal, Jamming Target, Meaconing, Multitarget Jamming, Noise Jamming, Noise Modulated Jamming, Passive Jamming, Repeater Jammer, Self-Protection Jamming, Spot Jamming, Sweep Jamming.

References

Department of Defense, Joint Chiefs of Staff. *Department of Defense Dictionary of Military and Related Terms.* Washington, DC: GPO, 1986.

Department of Defense, U.S. Army. *Military Intelligence Battalion Combat Electronic Warfare and Intelligence (Aerial Exploitation) (Corps).* Field Manual FM 34-22. Washington, DC: Headquarters, Department of the Army, 1984.

———. *Military Intelligence Company (Combat Electronic Warfare and Intelligence) (Armored Cavalry Regiment/Separate Brigade).* Field Manual FM 34-30. Washington, DC: Headquarters, Department of the Army, 1983.

Godson, Roy, ed. *Intelligence Problems for the 1980s, Number 1: Elements of Intelligence.* Rev. ed. Washington, DC: National Strategy Information Center, 1983.

—**PATROL,** in tactical intelligence, is a detachment of ground, sea, or air forces that is sent out to gather information or to carry out a destructive, harassing, mopping-up, or security mission.

References

Department of Defense, Joint Chiefs of Staff. *Department of Defense Dictionary of Military and Related Terms.* Washington, DC: GPO, 1986.

—**PATTERN ANALYSIS** is an Army tactical intelligence (TACINT) term that refers to a detailed study of stereotyped actions that often occur in a given set of circumstances. Elements of the counter-signals intelligence (C-SIGINT) data base that could give the enemy a clue to a unit's type, disposition, activity, or capability are reviewed, and if vulnerabilities are identified, then corrective actions are initiated.

References

Department of Defense, U.S. Army. *Counter-Signals Intelligence (C-SIGINT) Operations.* Field Manual FM 34-62. Washington, DC: Headquarters, Department of the Army, 1986.

———. *Military Intelligence Company (Combat Electronic Warfare and Intelligence) (Armored*

Cavalry Regiment/Separate Brigade). Field Manual FM 34-30. Washington, DC: Headquarters, Department of the Army, 1983.

Treverton, Gregory F. *Covert Action: The Limits of Intervention in the Postwar World.* New York: Basic Books, 1987.

—**PATTERNS,** an Army tactical intelligence (TACINT) term, refers to stereotyped actions that so habitually occur in a given set of circumstances that they cue an observer, well in advance, to the type of military unit or activity, its identity, capabilities or intent. Stereotyping occurs in a variety of ways, such as through communications deployment techniques or historical association. Such patterns must be unique and detectable to be of military significance.

References

Department of Defense, U.S. Army. *Counter-Signals Intelligence (C-SIGINT) Operations.* Field Manual FM 34-62. Washington, DC: Headquarters, Department of the Army, 1986.

———. *Military Intelligence Company (Combat Electronic Warfare and Intelligence) (Armored Cavalry Regiment/Separate Brigade).* Field Manual FM 34-30. Washington, DC: Headquarters, Department of the Army, 1983.

—**PAVEMENT ARTISTS** is clandestine intelligence jargon for a surveillance team or an agent who is watching a house or apartment. *See also:* Clean, Cobbler, Make, Movements Analysis, Surround, Surveillance.

References

Becket, Henry S. A. *The Dictionary of Espionage: Spookspeak into English.* New York: Stein and Day, 1986.

Deacon, Richard. *Spyclopedia: An Encyclopedia of Spies, Secret Services, Operations, Jargon, and All Subjects Related to the World of Espionage.* London: Macdonald, 1987.

Kessler, Ronald. *Spy vs. Spy: Stalking Soviet Spies in America.* New York: Charles Scribner's Sons, 1988.

Ranelagh, John. *The Agency: The Rise and Decline of the CIA.* New York: Simon and Schuster, 1986.

—**PAYNE, LESLIE J.,** attached to the U.S. Army, was convicted of espionage offenses concerning passing classified information to East German intelligence. Payne may have been motivated by reasons of monetary gain. He was sentenced to four years in prison.

References

Crawford, David J. *Volunteers: The Betrayal of National Defense Secrets by Air Force Traitors.* Washington, DC: GPO, 1988.

—**PEARL HARBOR** was the greatest intelligence failure in U.S. history, and it was an intelligence failure on a number of levels. First, various pieces of information that might have indicated that a Japanese attack was about to take place were not coordinated. Second, intelligence mirror-imaged the Japanese, in that it rationalized Japanese behavior in the period before Pearl Harbor by discussing these actions in terms of how the United States would react under similar circumstances. This totally ignored the difference in U.S. and Japanese cultures, views, needs, and values. Third, U.S. intelligence grossly underestimated Japanese military capabilities. Fourth, U.S. intelligence was unable to identify and analyze accurately intelligence signals and signs. Fifth, the intelligence that was produced was poorly disseminated. Finally, some of the field commanders, who received only partial and, in some cases, misleading information, made incorrect decisions.

References

American Bar Association. *Oversight and Accountability of the U.S. Intelligence Agencies: An Evaluation.* Washington, DC: ABA, 1985.

Corson, William R. *The Armies of Ignorance: The Rise of the American Intelligence Empire.* New York: Dial Press, 1977.

Godson, Roy, ed. *Intelligence Problems for the 1980s, Number 1: Elements of Intelligence.* Rev. ed. Washington, DC: National Strategy Information Center, 1983.

———. *Intelligence Problems for the 1980s, Number 2: Analysis and Estimates.* Washington, DC: National Strategy Information Center, 1980.

Laqueur, Walter. *A World of Secrets.* New York: Basic Books, 1985.

Lefever, Ernest W., and Godson, Roy. *The CIA and the American Ethic: An Unfinished Debate.* Washington, DC: Ethics and Public Policy Center, Georgetown University, 1979.

Lowenthal, Mark M. *U.S. Intelligence: Evolution and Anatomy.* New York: Praeger, 1984.

Maurer, Alfred C.; Turnstall, Marion D.; and Keagle, James M. *Intelligence Policy and Process.* Boulder, CO: Westview Press, 1985.

Turner, Stansfield. *Secrecy and Democracy: The CIA in Transition.* Boston: Houghton Mifflin, 1985.

—**PEEP** is a term used in clandestine and covert intelligence operations. A peep is a photographic specialist who is known for his ability to take good pictures in difficult circumstances or is someone who plants hidden cameras. *See also:* Concealment Devices, Sound Man, Sound School, "Surreptitious Entry," Surround, Surveillance.

References

Becket, Henry S. A. *The Dictionary of Espionage: Spookspeak into English.* New York: Stein and Day, 1986.

Deacon, Richard. *Spyclopedia: An Encyclopedia of Spies, Secret Services, Operations, Jargon, and All Subjects Related to the World of Espionage.* London: Macdonald, 1987.

Kessler, Ronald. *Spy vs. Spy: Stalking Soviet Spies in America.* New York: Charles Scribner's Sons, 1988.

Ranelagh, John. *The Agency: The Rise and Decline of the CIA.* New York: Simon and Schuster, 1986.

—**PELTON, RONALD WILLIAM,** a former National Security Agency communications specialist, was arrested in Washington, DC, on November 25, 1985. He was convicted of espionage on June 5, 1986, and sentenced to life in prison. Pelton had received $35,000 from the Soviets for his espionage activity, which began after he left the National Security Agency in 1979.

References

Allen, Thomas B., and Polmar, Norman. *Merchants of Treason: America's Secrets for Sale.* New York: Delacorte Press, 1988.

Crawford, David J. *Volunteers: The Betrayal of National Defense Secrets by Air Force Traitors.* Washington, DC: GPO, 1988.

Gertz, Bill. "Intelligence Operation Red Star of Pelton Trial." *The Washington Times,* June 2, 1986, p. 2A.

Schmidt, Susan. "Pelton Convicted of Selling Secrets." *The Washington Post,* June 6, 1986, p. A1.

Tyler, Patrick. "Supersecret Work Revealed." *The Washington Post,* May 28, 1986, p. A1.

—**PENETRATION** is a term that has two meanings in intelligence. (1) In clandestine operations and as defined by the Church Committee, it is the recruiting of agents within a group, organization, or facility or the infiltrating of agents into or placing technical monitoring devices in a group, organization, or facility in order to collect information or influence events or activities. (2) In automatic data processing, it is extracting and identifying recognizable information from a protected ADP system without authorization. *See also:* Agent, Agent Authentication, Agent in Place, Agent Net, Agent of Influence, Agent Provocateur, Case, Co-opted Worker, Disaffected Person, Infiltration, Informant, Inside Man, Mole, Putting in the Plumbing, Recruitment, Recruitment in Place.

References

Becket, Henry S. A. *The Dictionary of Espionage: Spookspeak into English.* New York: Stein and Day, 1986.

Deacon, Richard. *Spyclopedia: An Encyclopedia of Spies, Secret Services, Operations, Jargon, and All Subjects Related to the World of Espionage.* London: Macdonald, 1987.

Department of Defense, Defense Intelligence College. *Glossary of Intelligence Terms and Definitions.* Washington, DC: DIC, 1987.

Department of Defense, Joint Chiefs of Staff. *Department of Defense Dictionary of Military and Related Terms.* Washington, DC: GPO, 1986.

Godson, Roy, ed. *Intelligence Problems for the 1980s, Number 1: Elements of Intelligence.* Rev. ed. Washington, DC: National Strategy Information Center, 1983.

———. *Intelligence Problems for the 1980s, Number 3: Counterintelligence.* Washington, DC: National Strategy Information Center, 1980.

Treverton, Gregory F. *Covert Action: The Limits of Intervention in the Postwar World.* New York: Basic Books, 1987.

U.S. Congress. Senate. *Final Report of the Senate Select Committee to Study Government Operations with Respect to Intelligence Activities. Report 94-755. Book I, Foreign and Military Intelligence.* Washington, DC: GPO, 1976.

—**PENETRATION AIDS** are techniques and devices that are used by aerospace systems to increase the probability of weapon systems penetrating the enemy's defenses. Such aids include, but are not limited to, electronic systems that defeat or deceive the enemy's defenses.

References

Department of Defense, Joint Chiefs of Staff. *Department of Defense Dictionary of Military and Related Terms.* Washington, DC: GPO, 1986.

Godson, Roy, ed. *Intelligence Problems for the 1980s, Number 1: Elements of Intelligence.* Rev. ed. Washington, DC: National Strategy Information Center, 1983.

———. *Intelligence Problems for the 1980s, Number 3: Counterintelligence.* Washington, DC: National Strategy Information Center, 1980.

Treverton, Gregory F. *Covert Action: The Limits of Intervention in the Postwar World.* New York: Basic Books, 1987.

—**PENETRATION INTELLIGENCE** is a term used in clandestine and covert intelligence operations to describe intelligence information that results from a penetration operation. (A penetration operation is one in which an agent joins—penetrates—a target organization and works within it.) It would include biographic information on an organization's leadership, information on its organizational structure, strategy and tactics, and data on its financial state and backing. *See also:* Penetration.

References

Department of Defense, Joint Chiefs of Staff. *Department of Defense Dictionary of Military and Related Terms.* Washington, DC: GPO, 1986.

Godson, Roy, ed. *Intelligence Problems for the 1980s, Number 1: Elements of Intelligence.* Rev. ed. Washington, DC: National Strategy Information Center, 1983.

———. *Intelligence Problems for the 1980s, Number 3: Counterintelligence.* Washington, DC: National Strategy Information Center, 1980.

Treverton, Gregory F. *Covert Action: The Limits of Intervention in the Postwar World.* New York: Basic Books, 1987.

U.S. Congress. Senate. *Final Report of the Senate Select Committee to Study Government Operations with Respect to Intelligence Activities. Report 94-755. Book I, Foreign and Military Intelligence.* Washington, DC: GPO, 1976.

—**PENETRATION OF A MASTER PROGRAM** is a counterintelligence term used in the context of automatic data processing (ADP) system security and refers to the most serious threat to any ADP system. It involves the seizure of the computer's master program (also known as the executive program) by a penetrator. Once in possession of this program, he or she can control the entire system.

References

Blackburn, N. Glenn. "Computers: A Counterintelligence Concern." Unpublished paper provided to the editors. Washington, DC, 1987.

Godson, Roy, ed. *Intelligence Problems for the 1980s, Number 3: Counterintelligence.* Washington, DC: National Strategy Information Center, 1980.

Martin, Paul H. "Communications-Computer Security." *Journal of Electronic Defense* (June 1987).

Muzerall, Joseph V., and Carty, Thomas P. "COMSEC and Its Need for Key Management." *DP&CS* (Spring 1987).

Treverton, Gregory F. *Covert Action: The Limits of Intervention in the Postwar World.* New York: Basic Books, 1987.

Ware, Willis H. "Information Systems, Security, and Privacy." *EDUCOM Bulletin* (Summer 1984).

—PENKOVSKY, COLONEL OLEG, was perhaps the most valuable agent in the history of the Central Intelligence Agency. A dissident Soviet official, Penkovsky volunteered his services to Western intelligence. With access to secret military, scientific and technological documents, Penkovsky provided thousands of pages of intelligence material concerning Soviet military technology. At first, the Penkovsky material was placed in a highly restricted category codenamed "Ironbark," but the value of the material was such that it was sanitized and given much greater distribution. The information that the colonel provided was invaluable and had a governing effect on such events as the Cuban missile crisis, in which the United States had a very accurate idea of the state of Soviet missile defenses. Colonel Penkovsky was arrested on October 22, 1962; he was tried and executed.

Many fictional writers have used Penkovsky in their works. Tom Clancy, for example, uses him in *The Cardinal of the Kremlin.* He pictures Penkovsky as a hero, who, realizing that he has been discovered, has the Cardinal betray or "burn" him so that the Cardinal can reinforce his credibility with the Soviet authorities.

References
Clancy, Tom. *The Cardinal of the Kremlin.* New York: Putnam, 1988.

Godson, Roy, ed. *Intelligence Problems for the 1980s, Number 3: Counterintelligence.* Washington, DC: National Strategy Information Center, 1980.

Laqueur, Walter. *A World of Secrets.* New York: Basic Books, 1985.

—PERIGREE is a term used in intelligence imagery and photoreconnaissance. It is the point in an orbit when the orbiting body is nearest to the body it is orbiting around.

References
Reeves, Robert; Anson, Abraham; and Landen, David. *Manual of Remote Sensing.* Falls Church, VA: American Society of Photogrammetry, 1975.

—PERIODIC INTELLIGENCE SUMMARY (PER-INTSUM) is a report on the intelligence situation in a tactical operation. It is normally produced at the corps level or higher and usually at 24-hour intervals.

References
Department of Defense, Joint Chiefs of Staff. *Department of Defense Dictionary of Military and Related Terms.* Washington, DC: GPO, 1986.

—PERIODIC REINVESTIGATION (PR), or special background investigation-periodic reinvestigation (SBI-PR), meets the periodic personnel reinvestigation requirements for access to sensitive compartmented information (SCI). SBI-PRs are initiated at the four-and-a-half year point after the completion of the subject's last SBI or SBI-PR. The SBI-PR updates the information contained in the individual's file and recertifies him or her for access to SCI. *See also:* Special Background Investigation.

References
Department of Defense, Defense Intelligence Agency. *Defense Intelligence Agency Manual.* Washington, DC: DIA, 1987.

—PERIODICAL is a recurring publication with a continuing policy as to content and purpose that is issued more than once within a twelve-month period, but less frequently than daily. Its purpose is to disseminate professional, technical, or substantive information.

References
Department of Defense, Defense Intelligence Agency. *Defense Intelligence Agency Manual.* Washington, DC: DIA, 1987.

—PERKINS, WALTER, an Air Force master sergeant, was arrested in Panama City, Florida, on October 18, 1971, by Air Force agents. He was charged with passing classified defense information to Soviet intelligence officers. Court-martialed and found guilty, he was sentenced to three years in prison and given a dishonorable discharge. He appears to have been motivated by financial gain.

References

Allen, Thomas B., and Polmar, Norman. *Merchants of Treason: America's Secrets for Sale.* New York: Delacorte Press, 1988.

Crawford, David J. *Volunteers: The Betrayal of National Defense Secrets by Air Force Traitors.* Washington, DC: GPO, 1988.

—**PERM-CERT** is the permanent certification of an individual for access to sensitive compartmented information (SCI). Although the situation has gotten better with the consolidation of clearance procedures and lists, most organizations still maintain their own lists and clearance procedures for access to SCI. When one wishes to visit another agency, it is necessary to have one's security clearances passed to the agency to be visited. This is an involved procedure, often involving several offices, and the system can be sidetracked. The result can be that an embarrassed visitor is left standing until the clearance is passed correctly. To minimize these situations and to ease the burden on security offices, those who visit other agencies frequently will ask their commands to PERM-CERT them at the commands that are often visited. These must be updated yearly, but in the interim, the visitor's name is placed on the agency's PERM-CERT list and is there at the security desk whenever the visitor arrives. The visitor's home agency makes a notation that such a PERM-CERT has been passed, so that if the employee is transferred or leaves the command before the year is up, the commands to which the PERM-CERT has been passed can be notified that the individual's name should be stricken from the list. *See also:* Clearance.

References

Department of Defense, Defense Intelligence Agency. *Defense Intelligence Agency Manual.* Washington, DC: DIA, 1987.

—**PERMUTER,** in communications security (COMSEC), refers to a device that is used in a crypto-equipment in order to change the order in which the contents of the shift register are used in various nonlinear combining circuits.

References

Department of Defense, U.S. Army. *Counter-Signals Intelligence (C-SIGINT) Operations.* Field Manual FM 34-62. Washington, DC: Headquarters, Department of the Army, 1986.

———. *Military Intelligence Company (Combat Electronic Warfare and Intelligence) (Armored Cavalry Regiment/Separate Brigade).* Field Manual FM 34-30. Washington, DC: Headquarters, Department of the Army, 1983.

—**PERSONA NON GRATA (PNG)** is a diplomatic term meaning that an individual has been told to leave the host nation because of unacceptable actions. Intelligence agents are often declared PNG when they are caught in intelligence operations, because they have immunity from arrest. In *The Charm School,* Nelson Demille gives an extensive discussion of the procedure and its effects. *See also:* Air Attaché, American Legation U.S. Naval Attaché (ALUSNA), American Legation U.S. Naval Liaison Officer (ALUSNLO), Attaché Activities, Army Attaché (ARMA), Defense Attaché (DATT), Defense Attaché Office (DAO), Defense Attaché System (DAS), Defense Intelligence Agency (DIA), United States Country Team.

References

Clancy, Tom. *The Cardinal of the Kremlin.* New York: Putnam, 1988.

Demille, Nelson. *The Charm School.* New York: Warner Books, 1988.

Kessler, Ronald. *Spy vs. Spy: Stalking Soviet Spies in America.* New York: Charles Scribner's Sons, 1988.

—**PERSONNEL INSECURITY,** in communications security (COMSEC), means the capture, unauthorized absence, defection, or control by a hostile intelligence entity of an individual having knowledge of, or access to, classified COMSEC information or material. *See also:* Communications Security.

References

Department of Defense, Defense Intelligence Agency. *Defense Intelligence Agency Manual.* Washington, DC: DIA, 1987.

—**PERSONNEL SECURITY** is a general intelligence term that has two slightly different meanings. (1) Personnel security is the means or procedures, such as selective investigations, record checks, personal interviews, and supervisory controls, that are designed to provide reasonable assurance that people being considered for access to classified information are loyal and trustworthy. (2) A second definition for personnel security resulted from the Department of Defense response to Presidential Executive Order 12333, "United States Intelligence Activities," dated December 4, 1981, which defined the types of activities that U.S. intelligence agencies could conduct in respect to U.S. citizens. It stated that "personnel security involved measures designed to insure that persons employed, or being considered for employment, in sensitive positions of trust are suitable for such employment with respect to loyalty, character, emotional stability, and reliability and that such employment is clearly consistent with the interests of national security. It includes measures designed to ensure that persons granted access to classified information remain suitable for such access and that access is consistent with the interests of national security." *See also:* Access; Authorized; Background Investigation; Billet; Billet Realignment; Compartmentation; Compromise; Debriefing; Defense Industrial Security Clearance Office; Defense Security Briefings; Defense Investigative Service; Need-to-Know; Need-to-Know Principle; No-Lone Zone; Nondisclosure Agreement; Personnel Insecurity; Security; Security Classification; Sensitive Compartmented Information (SCI); Security Officer; Special Security Office System.

References

Department of Defense. *Activities of DoD Intelligence Components that Affect U.S. Persons (Department of Defense Directive 5240.1).* Washington, DC: DoD, 1982.

Department of Defense, Defense Intelligence College. *Glossary of Intelligence Terms and Definitions.* Washington, DC: DIC, 1987.

Godson, Roy, ed. *Intelligence Problems for the 1980s, Number 1: Elements of Intelligence.* Rev. ed. Washington, DC: National Strategy Information Center, 1983.

Kent, Sherman. *Strategic Intelligence for American World Policy.* Princeton, NJ: Princeton University Press, 1966.

Turner, Stansfield. *Secrecy and Democracy: The CIA in Transition.* Boston: Houghton Mifflin, 1985.

—**PERSONNEL SECURITY INVESTIGATION** is an inquiry into the past of an individual that is intended to collect information pertaining to his or her trustworthiness and suitability for a position of trust as related to loyalty, character, emotional stability, and reliability. The Department of Defense implementation of Presidential Executive Order 12333, "United States Intelligence Activities," dated December 4, 1981, states that a personnel security investigation is:

(a) An inquiry into the activities of a person granted access to intelligence or other classified information; or a person who is being considered for access to intelligence or other classified information; including persons who are granted or may be granted access to facilities of the Department of Defense components; or a person to be assigned or retained in a position with sensitive duties. The investigation is designed to develop information pertaining to the suitability, eligibility, and trustworthiness of the individual with respect to loyalty, character, emotional stability and reliability.

(b) Inquiries or other activities directed against Department of Defense employees or members of a Military Service to determine the facts of possible voluntary or involuntary compromise of classified information by them.

(c) The collection of information about or from military personnel in the course of tactical training exercises for security training purposes.

See also: Background Investigation; National Agency Check; Special Background Investigation.

References

Department of Defense. *Activities of DoD Intelligence Components that Affect U.S. Persons (Department of Defense Directive 5240.1).* Washington, DC: DoD, 1982.

Department of Defense, Defense Intelligence Agency. *Defense Intelligence Agency Manual.* Washington, DC: DIA, 1987.

Department of Defense, Defense Intelligence College. *Glossary of Intelligence Terms and Definitions.* Washington, DC: DIC, 1987.

Department of Defense, Joint Chiefs of Staff. *Department of Defense Dictionary of Military and Related Terms.* Washington, DC: GPO, 1986.

Godson, Roy, ed. *Intelligence Problems for the 1980s, Number 1: Elements of Intelligence.* Rev. ed. Washington, DC: National Strategy Information Center, 1983.

—**PHILLIPS, LIEUTENANT GENERAL SAMUEL C., U.S. AIR FORCE,** served as the director of the National Security Agency from August 24, 1972, until August 15, 1973. Phillips had extensive experience in the Air Force missile program and possibly in the National Reconnaissance Program, which handles the U.S. spy satellites. He remained as director of the NSA for barely a year and had little effect on the organization. *See also:* National Security Agency.

References

Bamford, James. *The Puzzle Palace: A Report on America's Most Secret Agency.* New York: Penguin Books, 1983.

—**PHOTOGRAMMETRY** is the science or art of obtaining reliable measurements from photographic images.

References

Department of Defense, Joint Chiefs of Staff. *Department of Defense Dictionary of Military and Related Terms.* Washington, DC: GPO, 1986.

—**PHOTOGRAPHIC COVERAGE** is the extent to which an area has been covered photographically by one mission or a series of missions or during a period of time.

References

Department of Defense, Joint Chiefs of Staff. *Department of Defense Dictionary of Military and Related Terms.* Washington, DC: GPO, 1986.

Godson, Roy, ed. *Intelligence Problems for the 1980s, Number 1: Elements of Intelligence.* Rev. ed. Washington, DC: National Strategy Information Center, 1983.

Laqueur, Walter. *A World of Secrets.* New York: Basic Books, 1985.

Treverton, Gregory F. *Covert Action: The Limits of Intervention in the Postwar World.* New York: Basic Books, 1987.

—**PHOTOGRAPHIC INTELLIGENCE (PHOTINT)** is a category of imagery intelligence that involves the collected products of photographic interpretation that have been classified and interpreted for intelligence use. *See also:* Aerial Photograph.

References

Department of Defense, Joint Chiefs of Staff. *Department of Defense Dictionary of Military and Related Terms.* Washington, DC: GPO, 1986.

Godson, Roy, ed. *Intelligence Problems for the 1980s, Number 1: Elements of Intelligence.* Rev. ed. Washington, DC: National Strategy Information Center, 1983.

Laqueur, Walter. *A World of Secrets.* New York: Basic Books, 1985.

U.S. Congress. Senate. *Final Report of the Senate Select Committee to Study Government Operations with Respect to Intelligence Activities. Report 94-755. Book I, Foreign and Military Intelligence.* Washington, DC: GPO, 1976.

—**PHOTOGRAPHIC INTERPRETATION (PI)** is a category of imagery interpretation and is the process of locating, recognizing, identifying, and describing objects, activities, and terrain from photography. A photographic interpreter (PI), or photointerpreter, is an individual who has been specially trained in photographic interpretation. Because of this, he is better able to identify objects from their photographic images and can more accurately and completely assess the significance of these objects than can the untrained observer. *See also:* Photographic Intelligence.

References

Department of Defense, Defense Intelligence College. *Glossary of Intelligence Terms and Definitions.* Washington, DC: DIC, 1987.

Department of Defense, Joint Chiefs of Staff. *Department of Defense Dictionary of Military and Related Terms.* Washington, DC: GPO, 1986.

Godson, Roy, ed. *Intelligence Problems for the 1980s, Number 1: Elements of Intelligence.* Rev. ed. Washington, DC: National Strategy Information Center, 1983.

Laqueur, Walter. *A World of Secrets.* New York: Basic Books, 1985.

Treverton, Gregory F. *Covert Action: The Limits of Intervention in the Postwar World.* New York: Basic Books, 1987.

Turner, Stansfield. *Secrecy and Democracy: The CIA in Transition.* Boston: Houghton Mifflin, 1985.

—**PHOTOGRAPHIC READING** is the simple recognition of natural and man-made features from photographs not involving imagery interpretation techniques. *See also:* Photographic Intelligence.

References

Department of Defense, Joint Chiefs of Staff. *Department of Defense Dictionary of Military and Related Terms.* Washington, DC: GPO, 1986.

Laqueur, Walter. *A World of Secrets.* New York: Basic Books, 1985.

—**PHOTOGRAPHIC SCALE** is the ratio of the distance measured on a photograph or mosaic to the corresponding distance on the ground, classified as follows: (a) *very large scale,* 1:4,999 and higher; (b) *large scale,* 1:5,000 to 1:9,999; (c) *medium scale,* 1:10,000 to 1:14,999; (d) *small scale,* 1:25,000 to 1:49,000; and (e) *small scale,* 1:50,000 and smaller. *See also:* Photographic Intelligence.

References

Department of Defense, Joint Chiefs of Staff. *Department of Defense Dictionary of Military and Related Terms.* Washington, DC: GPO, 1986.

Laqueur, Walter. *A World of Secrets*. New York: Basic Books, 1985.

—**PHOTOGRAPHIC STRIP** is a series of successive overlapping photographs that are taken along a selected course or direction. *See also:* Photographic Intelligence.

References

Department of Defense, Joint Chiefs of Staff. *Department of Defense Dictionary of Military and Related Terms*. Washington, DC: GPO, 1986.

—**PHOTOGRAPHY** is the process of using optics to reproduce on film a viewed scene or object. *See also:* Photographic Intelligence.

References

Godson, Roy, ed. *Intelligence Problems for the 1980s, Number 1: Elements of Intelligence*. Rev. ed. Washington, DC: National Strategy Information Center, 1983.

Laqueur, Walter. *A World of Secrets*. New York: Basic Books, 1985.

Treverton, Gregory F. *Covert Action: The Limits of Intervention in the Postwar World*. New York: Basic Books, 1987.

—**PHOTOMAP** is a reproduction of a photograph or photomosaic upon which the grid lines, marginal data, contours, place names, boundaries, and other data may be added.

References

Department of Defense, Joint Chiefs of Staff. *Department of Defense Dictionary of Military and Related Terms*. Washington, DC: GPO, 1986.

Godson, Roy, ed. *Intelligence Problems for the 1980s, Number 1: Elements of Intelligence*. Rev. ed. Washington, DC: National Strategy Information Center, 1983.

—**PHYSICAL CHARACTERISTICS** are those military characteristics of equipment that are primarily physical in nature, such as weight, shape, volume, waterproofing, and sturdiness.

References

Department of Defense, Joint Chiefs of Staff. *Department of Defense Dictionary of Military and Related Terms*. Washington, DC: GPO, 1986.

—**PHYSICAL INSECURITY,** in communications security (COMSEC), means an occurrence (loss, theft, loss of control, capture, recovery by salvage, tampering, unauthorized viewing, access, or photographing) that results in the jeopardizing of COMSEC material. *See also:* Communications Security.

References

Department of Defense, Defense Intelligence Agency. *Defense Intelligence Agency Manual*. Washington, DC: DIA, 1987.

—**PHYSICAL SECURITY,** a term used in counterintelligence, counterespionage, and counterinsurgency, has two meanings. (1) Physical security is a component of communications security. It involves the physical measures used to protect classified equipment, material, and documents from disclosure to unauthorized persons. (2) Physical security is physical measures, such as safes, vaults, perimeter barriers, guard systems, alarms, and access controls, that are designed to safeguard installations against damage, disruption, or unauthorized entry, information, or material against unauthorized access or theft, and specified personnel against harm. *See also:* Authorized; Closed Storage; Communications Security; Compartmentation; Compromise; Controlled Area; Limited Access Area; No-Lone Zone; Nondiscussion Area; Open Storage; Physical Security Investigation; Secure Area; Secure Vault Area; Secure Vault Area Custodian; Secure Working Area; Security; Security Certification; Vault Door.

References

Department of Defense. *Activities of DoD Intelligence Components that Affect U.S. Persons (Department of Defense Directive 5240.1)*. Washington, DC: DoD, 1982.

Department of Defense, Defense Intelligence College. *Glossary of Intelligence Terms and Definitions*. Washington, DC: DIC, 1987.

Department of Defense, Joint Chiefs of Staff. *Department of Defense Dictionary of Military and Related Terms*. Washington, DC: GPO, 1986.

Department of Defense, U.S. Army. *Counter-Signals Intelligence (C-SIGINT) Operations*. Field Manual FM 34-62. Washington, DC: Headquarters, Department of the Army, 1986.

———. *Military Intelligence Company (Combat Electronic Warfare and Intelligence) (Armored Cavalry Regiment/Separate Brigade)*. Field Manual FM 34-30. Washington, DC: Headquarters, Department of the Army, 1983.

Godson, Roy, ed. *Intelligence Problems for the 1980s, Number 1: Elements of Intelligence.* Rev. ed. Washington, DC: National Strategy Information Center, 1983.

Kent, Sherman. *Strategic Intelligence for American World Policy.* Princeton, NJ: Princeton University Press, 1966.

—**PHYSICAL SECURITY INVESTIGATION** is a term that was developed when the Department of Defense responded to Presidential Executive Order 12333, "United States Intelligence Activities," dated December 4, 1981, which defined the types of activities that U.S. intelligence agencies could conduct concerning U.S. citizens. The term is defined as all inquiries, inspections, or surveys of the effectiveness of controls and procedures designed to provide physical security; and all inquiries and other actions undertaken to obtain information pertaining to physical threats to Department of Defense personnel or property. *See also:* Physical Security.

References

Department of Defense. *Activities of DoD Intelligence Components that Affect U.S. Persons (Department of Defense Directive 5240.1).* Washington, DC: DoD, 1982.

Godson, Roy, ed. *Intelligence Problems for the 1980s, Number 1: Elements of Intelligence.* Rev. ed. Washington, DC: National Strategy Information Center, 1983.

—**PHYSICAL VULNERABILITY (PV) PRODUCTS** are produced by the Defense Intelligence Agency. These include detailed physical vulnerability analytical studies and technical memoranda, physical vulnerability data on selected installations that are reflected in the Target Data Inventory (TDI), physical vulnerability handbooks for the employment of both nuclear and non-nuclear weapons, Communist World weapon effectiveness handbooks, and handbooks relating to bomb damage assessments. *See also:* Defense Intelligence Agency.

References

Von Hoene, John P. A. *Intelligence User's Guide.* Washington, DC: DIA, 1983.

—**PHYSICAL VULNERABILITY STUDY** is an official term that has been defined by the Defense Intelligence Agency for one of its functional areas. It means "the study of the susceptibility of potential targets to damage or impairment by the damage agents of a weapon; bomb damage assessment; weapons requirements estimation; damage prediction; weapons effect analysis." *See also:* Physical Security.

References

Department of Defense, Defense Intelligence Agency. *Defense Intelligence Agency Manual 22-2.* Washington, DC: DIA, 1979.

—**PIANO CONCERTO** is a term used in clandestine and covert intelligence operations. It means a message. *See also:* Piano Study.

References

Becket, Henry S. A. *The Dictionary of Espionage: Spookspeak into English.* New York: Stein and Day, 1986.

Deacon, Richard. *Spyclopedia: An Encyclopedia of Spies, Secret Services, Operations, Jargon, and All Subjects Related to the World of Espionage.* London: Macdonald, 1987.

Kessler, Ronald. *Spy vs. Spy: Stalking Soviet Spies in America.* New York: Charles Scribner's Sons, 1988.

Ranelagh, John. *The Agency: The Rise and Decline of the CIA.* New York: Simon and Schuster, 1986.

—**PIANO STUDY** is a term used in clandestine and covert intelligence operations to describe radio operating. *See also:* Piano Concerto.

References

Becket, Henry S. A. *The Dictionary of Espionage: Spookspeak into English.* New York: Stein and Day, 1986.

Deacon, Richard. *Spyclopedia: An Encyclopedia of Spies, Secret Services, Operations, Jargon, and All Subjects Related to the World of Espionage.* London: Macdonald, 1987.

Ranelagh, John. *The Agency: The Rise and Decline of the CIA.* New York: Simon and Schuster, 1986.

—**PICKERING, JEFFREY L.,** when stationed at the Naval Regional Medical Clinic, Seattle, Washington, admitted sending a secret document to the Soviet Embassy in Washington, DC. He was arrested in 1983, convicted, sentenced to five years at hard labor, and given a bad-conduct discharge.

References

Allen, Thomas B., and Polmar, Norman. *Merchants of Treason: America's Secrets for Sale.* New York: Delacorte Press, 1988.

—**PICKET SURVEILLANCE,** in FBI terminology, is placing surveillants at locations that encircle the area being watched. This is also known as perimeter surveillance. *See also:* Surveillance.

References

Becket, Henry S. A. *The Dictionary of Espionage: Spookspeak into English.* New York: Stein and Day, 1986.

Deacon, Richard. *Spyclopedia: An Encyclopedia of Spies, Secret Services, Operations, Jargon, and All Subjects Related to the World of Espionage.* London: Macdonald, 1987.

Kessler, Ronald. *Spy vs. Spy: Stalking Soviet Spies in America.* New York: Charles Scribner's Sons, 1988.

Ranelagh, John. *The Agency: The Rise and Decline of the CIA.* New York: Simon and Schuster, 1986.

—**PICKLE FACTORY** is intelligence jargon for the Central Intelligence Agency.

References

Quirk, John; Phillips, David; Cline, Ray; and Pforzheimer, Walter. *The Central Intelligence Agency: A Photographic History.* Guilford, CT: Foreign Intelligence Press, 1986.

—**PIGEON** is a term used in clandestine intelligence operations to describe the target of a surveillance operation. *See also:* Picket Surveillance, Surveillance.

References

Becket, Henry S. A. *The Dictionary of Espionage: Spookspeak into English.* New York: Stein and Day, 1986.

Deacon, Richard. *Spyclopedia: An Encyclopedia of Spies, Secret Services, Operations, Jargon, and All Subjects Related to the World of Espionage.* London: Macdonald, 1987.

Ranelagh, John. *The Agency: The Rise and Decline of the CIA.* New York: Simon and Schuster, 1986.

—**PIGGYBACK ENTRY** is a counterintelligence term used in the context of automatic data processing system (ADP) security and refers to a situation in which a penetrator taps the computer terminal lines. He then intercepts data that is being sent from the computer to a legitimate user and substitutes false data that is transmitted to the user.

References

Blackburn, N. Glenn. "Computers: A Counterintelligence Concern." Unpublished paper provided to the editors. Washington, DC, 1987.

Martin, Paul H. "Communications-Computer Security." *Journal of Electronic Defense* (June 1987).

Ware, Willis H. "Information Systems, Security, and Privacy." *EDUCOM Bulletin* (Summer 1984).

—**PIGGYBACKING** is a term used in clandestine and covert intelligence operations. It means relying on a friendly intelligence agency to reveal the results of an intelligence or counterintelligence operation.

References

Becket, Henry S. A. *The Dictionary of Espionage: Spookspeak into English.* New York: Stein and Day, 1986.

Deacon, Richard. *Spyclopedia: An Encyclopedia of Spies, Secret Services, Operations, Jargon, and All Subjects Related to the World of Espionage.* London: Macdonald, 1987.

Ranelagh, John. *The Agency: The Rise and Decline of the CIA.* New York: Simon and Schuster, 1986.

—**PIKE COMMITTEE.** As Watergate unraveled, it became obvious that the Intelligence Community had exceeded its authority and its operations were highly questionable. Both the Senate and the House formed investigative committees, and these groups not only investigated Watergate but also scrutinized all domestic intelligence activities that had been waged by the Intelligence Community in the 1960s and 1970s. The result was a definite shift in the focus of presidential and congressional oversight from concern about the quality of the intelligence produced to concern over the types of activities the Intelligence Community performed.

The House created the Select Committee on Intelligence, which was briefly chaired by Representative Lucien Nedzi. However, when it was revealed that Nedzi may have known about some of the intelligence activities and had not revealed them, his objectivity came into question, and he was replaced by Representative Otis Pike. Concurrently, the Senate created the Select Committee to Study Government Operations with Respect to Intelligence Activities, chaired by Senator Frank Church.

The Pike group focused on intelligence management, organization, and the quality of intelligence products, while the Church committee concentrated on intelligence abuses and illegalities.

The Pike Committee issued its report on January 29, 1976, recommending that the Defense Intelligence Agency be abolished, that the director of Central Intelligence be separated from the CIA so that he could concentrate on his management responsibilities, and that congressional and presidential oversight be enhanced. The committee decided to delay releasing its report until it was determined that it was unclassified. However, either a committee or a staff member leaked a copy of the report to Daniel Schorr, then of CBS news, who passed it to the *Village Voice*, which began publishing excerpts. The failure of the committee to keep its report secure played into the hands of its opponents, who claimed that sensitive intelligence matters could not be deliberated on Capitol Hill, because the committees simply could not guarantee adequate security. At a minimum, the divulgence of the report was unfortunate because it was so sensational that it overshadowed the report's contents, which did have some constructive suggestions concerning Intelligence Community reform.

Mark Lowenthal's assessment of the two committees is the most insightful and profound yet to appear. He believes that the Church Committee was the better of the two, in that it produced a very detailed 2,685-page report that comprehensively considered the CIA in its entirety. Similarly, Lowenthal feels that the Pike Committee, while it failed to prevent the leaking of its report to the *Village Voice* and thereby lost considerable degree of credibility, did concentrate on the really crucial issue of the quality of intelligence. *See also:* Congressional Oversight.

References

American Bar Association. *Oversight and Accountability of the U.S. Intelligence Agencies: An Evaluation.* Washington, DC: ABA, 1985.

Breckinridge, Scott D. *The CIA and the U.S. Intelligence System.* Boulder, CO: Westview Press, 1986.

Brinkley, David A., and Hull, Andrew W. *Estimative Intelligence: A Textbook on the History, Products, Uses, and Writing of Intelligence Estimates.* Columbus, OH: Battelle, 1979.

Cline, Ray S. *The CIA Under Reagan, Bush, and Casey.* Washington, DC: Acropolis Books, 1981.

Corson, William R. *The Armies of Ignorance: The Rise of the American Intelligence Empire.* New York: Dial Press, 1977.

Godson, Roy, ed. *Intelligence Problems for the 1980s, Number 1: Elements of Intelligence.* Rev. ed. Washington, DC: National Strategy Information Center, 1983.

————. *Intelligence Problems for the 1980s, Number 2: Analysis Analysis and Estimates.* Washington, DC: National Strategy Information Center, 1980.

————. *Intelligence Problems for the 1980s, Number 4: Covert Action.* Washington, DC: National Strategy Information Center, 1981.

Laqueur, Walter. *A World of Secrets.* New York: Basic Books, 1985.

Lefever, Ernest W., and Godson, Roy. *The CIA and the American Ethic: An Unfinished Debate.* Washington, DC: Ethics and Public Policy Center, Georgetown University, 1979.

Lowenthal, Mark M. *U.S. Intelligence: Evolution and Anatomy.* New York: Praeger, 1984.

Maurer, Alfred C.; Turnstall, Marion D.; and Keagle, James M. *Intelligence Policy and Process.* Boulder, CO: Westview Press, 1985.

Treverton, Gregory F. *Covert Action: The Limits of Intervention in the Postwar World.* New York: Basic Books, 1987.

Turner, Stansfield. *Secrecy and Democracy: The CIA in Transition.* Boston: Houghton Mifflin, 1985.

U.S. Congress. Senate. *Alleged Assassination Plots Involving Foreign Leaders: An Interim Report of the Select Committee to Study Governmental Operations with Respect to Intelligence Activities.* 94th Congress, 1st sess., Nov. 20, 1975. S. Rept. 94-465.

Von Hoene, John P. A. *Intelligence User's Guide.* Washington, DC: DIA, 1983.

—**PITCH** is a term used in clandestine and covert intelligence operations. A pitch is the act of persuading a person to be an agent. A cold pitch is made without any prior cultivation of the agent. *See also:* Cold Approach, Co-Opted Worker, Co-Optees, Recruitment, Recruitment in Place, Sweetener.

References

Becket, Henry S. A. *The Dictionary of Espionage: Spookspeak into English.* New York: Stein and Day, 1986.

Deacon, Richard. *Spyclopedia: An Encyclopedia of Spies, Secret Services, Operations, Jargon, and All Subjects Related to the World of Espionage.* London: Macdonald, 1987.

Quirk, John; Phillips, David; Cline, Ray; and Pforzheimer, Walter. *The Central Intelligence Agency: A Photographic History.* Guilford, CT: Foreign Intelligence Press, 1986.

—**PIZZO, FRANCIS XAVIER,** on duty with the U.S. Navy, was arrested in San Francisco on August 22, 1984. He was convicted of espionage on August 6, 1985.

References

Crawford, David J. *Volunteers: The Betrayal of National Defense Secrets by Air Force Traitors.* Washington, DC: GPO, 1988.

—**PLAIN TEXT,** in communications, is normal text or language, or any sign or signal that conveys information without a hidden or secret meaning. According to the Church Committee, plain text is "unencrypted communications; specifically, the original message of a cryptogram, expressed in ordinary language."

References

Department of Defense, Defense Intelligence College. *Glossary of Intelligence Terms and Definitions.* Washington, DC: DIC, 1987.

Department of Defense, Joint Chiefs of Staff. *Department of Defense Dictionary of Military and Related Terms.* Washington, DC: GPO, 1986.

Godson, Roy, ed. *Intelligence Problems for the 1980s, Number 1: Elements of Intelligence.* Rev. ed. Washington, DC: National Strategy Information Center, 1983.

Quirk, John; Phillips, David; Cline, Ray; and Pforzheimer, Walter. *The Central Intelligence Agency: A Photographic History.* Guilford, CT: Foreign Intelligence Press, 1986.

U.S. Congress. Senate. *Final Report of the Senate Select Committee to Study Government Operations with Respect to Intelligence Activities. Report 94-755. Book I, Foreign and Military Intelligence.* Washington, DC: GPO, 1976.

—**PLANNING,** in intelligence program budgeting, means the selection of courses of action through a systematic consideration of alternatives in order to attain organizational objectives. *See also:* Planning, Programming, and Budgeting System.

References

Godson, Roy, ed. *Intelligence Problems for the 1980s, Number 1: Elements of Intelligence.* Rev. ed. Washington, DC: National Strategy Information Center, 1983.

Kent, Sherman. *Strategic Intelligence for American World Policy.* Princeton, NJ: Princeton University Press, 1966.

Pickett, George. "Congress, the Budget, and Intelligence." In *Intelligence Policy and Process,* edited by Alfred C. Maurer, Marion D. Turnstall, and James M. Keagle. Boulder, CO: Westview Press, 1985.

Treverton, Gregory F. *Covert Action: The Limits of Intervention in the Postwar World.* New York: Basic Books, 1987.

Turner, Stansfield. *Secrecy and Democracy: The CIA in Transition.* Boston: Houghton Mifflin, 1985.

—**PLANNING AND DIRECTION.** *See:* Intelligence Cycle.

—**PLANNING AND COORDINATION GROUP (PCG),** as described by the Church Committee, was "a committee of the Operations Coordinating Board of the National Security Council. It became the normal channel for policy approval of covert operations under National Security Council Directive 5412/1 in 1955."

References

Godson, Roy, ed. *Intelligence Problems for the 1980s, Number 1: Elements of Intelligence.* Rev. ed. Washington, DC: National Strategy Information Center, 1983.

U.S. Congress. Senate. *Final Report of the Senate Select Committee to Study Government Operations with Respect to Intelligence Activities. Report 94-755. Book I, Foreign and Military Intelligence.* Washington, DC: GPO, 1976.

—**PLANNING, PROGRAMING, AND BUDGETING SYSTEM (PPBS)** is the means by which the Department of Defense is funded, and it is therefore crucial to the continuance of intelligence operations.

The assistant secretary of defense (comptroller) is responsible for the design, installation, and maintenance of the PPBS (DoDD 7000.1), which includes responsibility for establishing, improving, and maintaining procedural guidance for PPBS (DoDI 7045.7).

The PPBS is a cyclical process containing five distinct but interrelated phases: planning, programing, budgeting, execution and accountability. In the first three phases, prior decisions are reexamined and analyzed from the viewpoint of force structure/national security objectives and current environment (threat, economic, technological, and resource availability), and the decisions are either reaffirmed or modified as necessary. The cycle for a given fiscal year begins in the month of November almost two years prior to the beginning of that fiscal year. While the execution phase of that fiscal year might appear to be completed 35 months later, in reality obligations and expenditures against that fiscal year's program may continue, for some appropriations, for several years.

The Planning Phase

In the planning phase, the role and posture of the United States in the Department of Defense (DoD) and in the world environment are examined, with particular emphasis on presidential policies. Some of the facets analyzed are: (1) potential and probable enemy capabilities and threat; (2) potential and probable capabilities of U.S. Allies; (3) alternative U.S. policies and objectives in consideration of (1) and (2); (4) military strategies in support of these policies and objectives; (5) planning force levels that would achieve defense policy and strategy; and (6) planning assumptions for guidance in the following phases of the PPBS.

The first step in the PPBS is the preparation by the Joint Chiefs of Staff (JCS) and submission to the secretary of defense of the Joint Strategic Planning Document (JSPD) containing independent JCS military strategy advice and recommendations to be considered in the development of the draft Defense Guidance (DG) and subsequent PPBS documents. It contains a concise, comprehensive military appraisal of the threat to U.S. interests and objectives worldwide; a statement of recommended military objectives derived from national objectives; and the recommended military strategy to attain national objectives. A summary of the JCS planning force levels that successfully execute, with reasonable assurance, the approved national military strategy is included. JCS views on the attainability of the planning force in consideration of fiscal responsibility, manpower resources, material availability, technology, and industrial capacity are also stated. The JSPD provides an appraisal of the capabilities and risks associated with program force levels, based on planning forces that are considered necessary to execute the strategy, and recommends changes to the force planning and programing guidance where appropriate.

After consideration of the military advice of the JCS as expressed in the JSPD, the next milestone is the secretary of defense's Defense Guidance (DG). A draft of the DG covering the budget and program years is issued in January to solicit the comments of the DoD components and to provide a vehicle for an exchange of views on defense policy between the secretary of defense, the president, and the National Security Council. The final version of the DG, issued in March, serves as an authoritative statement of the fundamental strategy, issues, and rationale underlying the defense program, as seen by the leadership of the DoD. The DG, culminating the planning phase, provides definitive guidance, including fiscal constraints, for the development of the Program Objective Memorandum by the military departments of the defense agencies and continues as the primary DoD guidance until revised or modified by subsequent secretary of defense decisions.

The Programing Phase

Annually, in May, each military department and defense agency prepares and submits to the secretary of defense a Program Objective Memorandum (POM). POMs are based on the strategic concepts and guidance stated in the DG and include an assessment of the risk associated with the current and proposed forces and support programs. POMs express total program requirements for the years covered in the DG and provide the rationale for the proposed changes from the approved FYDP base. Dollar totals must be within the fiscal guidance issued by the secretary of defense. Major issues that are required to be resolved during the year of submission must be identified. Supporting information for POMs is in accordance with the annual POM Preparation Instructions.

After the POMs are submitted, the JCS submits the Joint Program Assessment Memorandum (JPAM) for consideration in reviewing the military department POMs, developing issue papers, and drafting Program Decision Memorandums (PDMs). The JPAM provides a risk assessment based on the composite of the POM force recommendations and includes the views of the JCS on the balance and capabilities of the overall POM force and support levels to execute the approved national military strategy. Where appropriate, the JCS recommends actions to achieve improvements in overall defense capabilities within, to the extent feasible, alternative POM funding levels directed by the secretary of defense. In addition, the JPAM develops SALT-constrained forces and provides recommendations on the nuclear weapons stockpiles considered necessary to support these forces, and on the security assistance program. The programing phase continues in accordance with the following steps:

(1) The POMs are analyzed at the OSD level and issue papers are generated that analyze the service proposals in relation to: (a) the Defense Guidance; (b) the balance between force structure, modernization, and readiness; and (c) efficiency tradeoffs. Significant issues raised by the POMs that require secretary of defense resolution are highlighted, decision alternatives are listed, and these alternatives are evaluated as to cost and capacity to implement DoD missions. These issue papers are developed in coordination with the DoD components to ensure completeness and accuracy of the information contained therein. The views of the JCS on risks involved in the POMs are considered during the preparation of the issue papers.

(2) Based on the issue papers and the JCS risk assessment, the secretary issues Program Decision Memoranda (PDM), which are transmitted to the DoD components for analysis and comment as appropriate.

(3) Comments on the PDMs may be prepared in a manner prescribed by the submitting activity, but must present precise program impact that may be expected as a result of the decision. If comments on the PDMs express a dissenting view, any additional or clarifying information or justification must accompany the statement to allow a reevaluation of the issue.

(4) Comments submitted by the JCS address the impact on total DoD program balance. The JCS provides the secretary of defense with an assessment of the risks involved and inherent in the PDMs and evaluation of strategic implications.

(5) Following a staff review on comments on the PDMs, meetings are held by the secretary of defense to discuss unresolved issues. If appropriate, Amended Program Decision Memoranda are then issued to incorporate any new decision, or to reiterate the previous decision.

The Budgeting Phase

With the establishment of program levels in the POM/PDM process, the budgeting phase begins with the DoD components formulating and submitting, by September 15, detailed budget estimates for the budget year portion of the approved program. The budget estimates include the prior year, current year, and budget year (budget year plus one for authorized programs) in accordance with the Budget Guidance Manual and supplementary memoranda. Budget estimates are prepared and submitted based on the approved program as well as economic assumptions related to pay and pricing policies that are contained in either the PDMs or in separately described detailed budget guidance revised and issued each year. The budget estimates are reviewed jointly by the Office of the Secretary of Defense (OSD) and the Office of Management and Budget (OMB). The entire budget is reviewed to insure that the requests are properly priced; to insure production schedules are within production capacity; and to insure that the estimates are consistent with the secretary's readiness objectives. Approval of the estimates for inclusion in the president's budget is documented by the secretary of defense budget decision documents. These decisions will evaluate, adjust, and approve all resources in the budget request within the appropriation and budget activity structures. The decisions will include the current year, the budget year, the authorization year (budget year +1), and an estimate of the resource impact on the three succeeding program years consistent with the president's requirement for multiyear planning estimates.

During the course of the budget review, the DoD components have an opportunity to express an appeal position on each decision. Prior to final decisions, the service secretaries and military chiefs have the opportunity for a meeting with the secretary of defense to present and resolve any outstanding issues of major significance.

The secretary then presents his budget for consideration within the overall federal requirements. Changes from that meeting are subsequently incorporated into the DoD submission and decision documentation is finalized. Following the printing process, the budget is submitted to Congress in January. The FYDP is updated to reflect the president's budget and related resource impact in the "outyears," thereby establishing a consistent base for the ensuing decision cycle.

The Execution and Accountability Phases

The execution and accountability phases follow the submission of the budget and its enactment by Congress. These phases are concerned with execution of the programs approved by Congress; the accountability and reporting of actual results for use in monitoring program execution; preparing future plans, programs, and budgets; and supplying financial status information to DoD managers. *See also:* Budget.

References

American Bar Association. *Oversight and Accountability of the U.S. Intelligence Agencies: An Evaluation.* Washington, DC: ABA, 1985.

Godson, Roy, ed. *Intelligence Problems for the 1980s, Number 1: Elements of Intelligence.* Rev. ed. Washington, DC: National Strategy Information Center, 1983.

Maurer, Alfred C.; Turnstall, Marion D.; and Keagle, James M. *Intelligence Policy and Process.* Boulder, CO: Westview Press, 1985.

Pickett, George. "Congress, the Budget, and Intelligence." In *Intelligence Policy and Process,* edited by Alfred C. Maurer, Marion D. Turnstall, and James M. Keagle. Boulder, CO: Westview Press, 1985.

—**PLANS AND PROGRAMS** is an official term that has been defined by the Defense Intelligence Agency for one of its functional areas. It means "the development of plans, policies, and programs for the overall operation and management of intelligence functions to include the strengthening of capabilities and support; long-range conceptual studies as a basis for planning guidance; contingency and war planning; and the continuous review and assessment of plans and program goals." *See also:* Defense Intelligence Agency.

References

Department of Defense, Defense Intelligence Agency. *Defense Intelligence Agency Manual 22-2.* Washington, DC: DIA, 1979.

—**PLANT,** a term used in clandestine and covert intelligence operations, has two meanings. (1) A plant is a listening or observation post that is used to watch a surveillance target. (2) A plant can also be someone who is sent to meet or work with someone who has a known or perceived weakness. *See also:* Agent in Place, Infiltration, Informant, Inside Man.

References

Becket, Henry S. A. *The Dictionary of Espionage: Spookspeak into English.* New York: Stein and Day, 1986.

Deacon, Richard. *Spyclopedia: An Encyclopedia of Spies, Secret Services, Operations, Jargon, and All Subjects Related to the World of Espionage.* London: Macdonald, 1987.

Ranelagh, John. *The Agency: The Rise and Decline of the CIA.* New York: Simon and Schuster, 1986.

—**PLAUSIBLE COVER** is an intelligence security term. It is a type of cover used to disguise the source of intelligence information so that it can be decompartmented, or released into collateral security channels. Plausible cover is an integral part of sanitization. The requirements for plausible cover will vary with the specific collector and the type of sensitive information that is involved. *See also:* Declassification, Downgrading.

References

Godson, Roy, ed. *Intelligence Problems for the 1980s, Number 1: Elements of Intelligence.* Rev. ed. Washington, DC: National Strategy Information Center, 1983.

Treverton, Gregory F. *Covert Action: The Limits of Intervention in the Postwar World.* New York: Basic Books, 1987.

—**"PLAUSIBLE DENIAL."** Although most covert actions will have overt results, the secrecy has as its aim the absence of an acknowledged sponsor. In modern international affairs, this lack of acknowledgment is called "plausible denial." Such denial has several benefits, and perhaps the most important is that the covert operation is not allowed to interfere with existing diplomatic relations, because the act has been neither acknowledged or proven. As defined by the Church Committee, plausible denial "was originally arranging, coordinating, and conducting covert operations so as to 'plausibly' permit official denial of U.S. involvement, sponsorship or support. Later this concept evolved so that it was employed by high officials and their subordinates to communicate without using precise language which would reveal authorization and involvement in certain activities and would be embarrassing and politically damaging if publicly revealed." *See also:* Iran, National Security Council.

References

American Bar Association. *Oversight and Accountability of the U.S. Intelligence Agencies: An Evaluation.* Washington, DC: ABA, 1985.

Breckinridge, Scott D. *The CIA and the U.S. Intelligence System.* Boulder, CO: Westview Press, 1986.

Godson, Roy, ed. *Intelligence Problems for the 1980s, Number 1: Elements of Intelligence.* Rev. ed. Washington, DC: National Strategy Information Center, 1983.

Maurer, Alfred C.; Turnstall, Marion D.; and Keagle, James M. *Intelligence Policy and Process.* Boulder, CO: Westview Press, 1985.

Treverton, Gregory F. *Covert Action: The Limits of Intervention in the Postwar World.* New York: Basic Books, 1987.

Turner, Stansfield. *Secrecy and Democracy: The CIA in Transition.* Boston: Houghton Mifflin, 1985.

U.S. Congress. Senate. *Final Report of the Senate Select Committee to Study Government Operations with Respect to Intelligence Activities. Report 94-755. Book I, Foreign and Military Intelligence.* Washington, DC: GPO, 1976.

—**PLAYBACK,** a term used in clandestine and covert intelligence operations, has two meanings. (1) Playback can be the reappearance in another country of false information that an intelligence agency managed to have published in one country in order to give additional credibility to the material. (2) Playback can also be an agent who is captured and is forced to continue transmitting information, usually false information, back home. *See also:* Agent, Agent Authentication, Blow, Blown Agent, Burn, Burnt, Co-Opted Worker, Co-Optees, Damage Assessment, Damage Control, Discard, Dispatched Agent, Doubled, Make, Packed Up, Rolling Up the Net, Toss, Turned.

References

Becket, Henry S. A. *The Dictionary of Espionage: Spookspeak into English.* New York: Stein and Day, 1986.

Deacon, Richard. *Spyclopedia: An Encyclopedia of Spies, Secret Services, Operations, Jargon, and All Subjects Related to the World of Espionage.* London: Macdonald, 1987.

Ranelagh, John. *The Agency: The Rise and Decline of the CIA.* New York: Simon and Schuster, 1986.

—**PLAY MATERIAL** is a term used in clandestine and covert intelligence operations to describe accurate information that an agent from one agency gives to an enemy agency in order to gain credibility so that he can infiltrate the agency. *See also:* Agent, Agent Authentication, Agent in Place, Cover, Cover Name, Cover Organizations, Cover Story, Cultivation, Establishing Bonafides, Legend, Litmus Test, Pocket Litter.

References

Becket, Henry S. A. *The Dictionary of Espionage: Spookspeak into English.* New York: Stein and Day, 1986.

Deacon, Richard. *Spyclopedia: An Encyclopedia of Spies, Secret Services, Operations, Jargon, and All Subjects Related to the World of Espionage.* London: Macdonald, 1987.

Ranelagh, John. *The Agency: The Rise and Decline of the CIA.* New York: Simon and Schuster, 1986.

—**PLUMBING** is a term used in clandestine and covert intelligence operations to describe the assets and services that support clandestine operations of CIA field stations, such as safe houses, unaccountable funds, investigative personnel, and surveillance teams. *See also:* Accommodation Address, Active Measures, Agent Authentication, Agent in Place, Cobbler, Cover, Cover Name, Cover Organizations, Cover Story, Establishing Bonafides, Honey Trap, Putting in the Plumbing, Stable, Sterile Funds, Sterile Telephone, Sterility Coding, Sterilize, Suitable Cover, Swallow's Nest, Taxi.

References

Deacon, Richard. *Spyclopedia: An Encyclopedia of Spies, Secret Services, Operations, Jargon, and All Subjects Related to the World of Espionage.* London: Macdonald, 1987.

Godson, Roy, ed. *Intelligence Problems for the 1980s, Number 1: Elements of Intelligence.* Rev. ed. Washington, DC: National Strategy Information Center, 1983.

Quirk, John; Phillips, David; Cline, Ray; and Pforzheimer, Walter. *The Central Intelligence Agency: A Photographic History.* Guilford, CT: Foreign Intelligence Press, 1986.

Treverton, Gregory F. *Covert Action: The Limits of Intervention in the Postwar World.* New York: Basic Books, 1987.

U.S. Congress. Senate. *Final Report of the Senate Select Committee to Study Government Operations with Respect to Intelligence Activities. Report 94-755. Book I, Foreign and Military Intelligence.* Washington, DC: GPO, 1976.

—**POCKET LITTER** is a term used in clandestine and covert intelligence operations to describe the false documents and materials that an agent carries with him to protect his identity and background if he is apprehended. *See also:* Agent, Agent Authentication, Double Agent, Handling Agent, Illegal Agent, Informant, Inside Man, Legend, Provocation Agent, Pseudonym, Putting in the Plumbing, Special Activities.

References

Becket, Henry S. A. *The Dictionary of Espionage: Spookspeak into English.* New York: Stein and Day, 1986.

Deacon, Richard. *Spyclopedia: An Encyclopedia of Spies, Secret Services, Operations, Jargon, and All Subjects Related to the World of Espionage.* London: Macdonald, 1987.

Quirk, John; Phillips, David; Cline, Ray; and Pforzheimer, Walter. *The Central Intelligence Agency: A Photographic History.* Guilford, CT: Foreign Intelligence Press, 1986.

Ranelagh, John. *The Agency: The Rise and Decline of the CIA.* New York: Simon and Schuster, 1986.

—**POINT DEFENSE,** in ground warfare, is a posture that is designed for the protection of a limited area, normally the defense of the vital elements of a force or the vital installations of the rear area. A point defense is characterized by the priority of defense that is given to specific assets. These assets can be either mobile or static, and they can be organizations or installations.

References

Department of Defense, U.S. Army. *U.S. Army Air Defense Artillery Employment.* Field Manual FM 44-1. Washington, DC: Headquarters, Department of the Army, 1983.

—**POLARITY,** a baud-based system term used in communications intelligence, communications security, operations security, and signals analysis, is the condition of a signal as to being positive or negative in comparison to the reference level. *Single polarity* is the condition in which all energized elements in each channel are transmitted in the same polarity. *Double polarity* is the condition in which the polarity of the energized elements of one or more channels is opposite the polarity of the energized elements in the remaining channels of the system. *Mixed polarity* is a condition in which the polarity of certain energized elements within a channel is opposite that of the other energized elements within the same channel. *See also:* Communications Security.

References

Department of Defense, U.S. Army. *Counter-Signals Intelligence (C-SIGINT) Operations.* Field Manual FM 34-62. Washington,] DC: Headquarters, Department of the Army, 1986.

———. *Military Intelligence Company (Combat Electronic Warfare and Intelligence) (Armored Cavalry Regiment/Separate Brigade).* Field Manual FM 34-30. Washington, DC: Headquarters, Department of the Army, 1983.

—**POLICY REVIEW COMMITTEE (PRC(I)).** The PRC was a committee established under the National Security Council that, when meeting under the chairmanship of the director of Central Intelligence, was empowered to establish requirements and priorities for national foreign intelligence and to evaluate the quality of the intelligence product. It was sometimes referred to as the Policy Review Committee (Intelligence). Its specific duties were defined in Executive Order No. 12036. It is now known as the Senior Interagency Group for Intelligence (SIG-I).

References

Department of Defense, Defense Intelligence College. *Glossary of Intelligence Terms and Definitions.* Washington, DC: DIC, 1987.

Godson, Roy, ed. *Intelligence Problems for the 1980s, Number 1: Elements of Intelligence.* Rev. ed. Washington, DC: National Strategy Information Center, 1983.

Laqueur, Walter. *A World of Secrets.* New York: Basic Books, 1985.

—**POLITICAL INTELLIGENCE,** one of the components of strategic intelligence, is intelligence concerned with the dynamics of the internal and external political affairs of foreign countries, regional groups, multilateral treaty arrangements, and organizations and foreign political movements directed against or having an impact on established governments or authority. The primary producer of political intelligence is the Department of State.

Political intelligence is intelligence concerning the foreign and domestic policies of foreign governments and the activities of political movements in foreign countries. The international position of any nation depends on such factors as the quality of its leadership, its domestic stability and economic position, manpower supply and physical resources, its military power in relation to other countries, its position in international trade, its success in obtaining allies against possible future danger, and the influence in other countries of its culture and its political system.

In studying the political aspects of strategic intelligence, the intelligence officer first considers the distribution and locus of political power, the political forces (dynamics) in the country, and its political equilibrium or stability. He often looks for the sources and sanctions of political power, since such power may be based on authority provided in tradition, or it may derive from democratic choice, political magnetism (charisma), skill and superior competence in handling the affairs of government, monopoly of organized force, or some combination of these. An understanding of the nature and sources of authority is particularly important in studying non-Western societies, where institutions differ from those familiar to the Western-trained intelligence officer.

The intelligence analyst also gives attention to the way decisions are made, taking account of both formal and informal processes. A study of decisionmaking includes analyses of (1) assigned responsibilities, (2) personal and professional background and motivations of policymakers, (3) mechanisms that are used to arrive at decisions, and (4) information on which policymakers must act.

Adequate political intelligence provides valuable indications concerning the probable courses of action of foreign nations. Therefore, it is necessary that a constant study be made of the form and internal dynamics of governments, their domestic and foreign policies, their parties, institutions, administrative procedures, and political personalities.

Basic Principles of Government

The structures and processes of any government are based on certain principles. The intelligence analyst obtains a knowledge of these principles is only obtained by a careful analysis of a government's past behavior, since they will be found only in partial form at best in written constitutions or other documents. In light of these principles, the government's future can be forecasted to some degree.

Therefore, it is necessary to compare the letter of the basic national law or constitutional system with its expression in actual practice. This comparison is made under the headings of the origin, history, and interpretation of the basic law; the legal position of the legislative, judicial, and executive branches of the government; and the civil and religious rights and privileges of the people. It is important to know the depth and extent of national devotion to basic rights, privileges and principles.

Governmental Structure

Structurally, governments are usually divided into central, regional, and local governments. In addition, some nations require a governmental structure for their colonies, possessions, dominions, mandates, and protectorates.

The operations of governmental organizations are studied by the intelligence analyst with a view toward determining their efficiency, integrity, and stability. Marked inefficiency and corruption in the operation of a government, if they indicate a change from past practices, may provide an opportunity for the emergence of new political forces. If such practices have been accepted for some time, they are indicative of popular apathy. Should the government become increasingly restrictive in regard to electoral procedures, the administration of justice, or the exercise of the basic rights and privileges of the people, it may mean that the government is embarking on a new course of action, either internal or international. Such action will often be accompanied by a change in the governmental structure that will ease the direction and control of the new policy. Consequently, information regarding changes in the structure or operation of a government is of great value in estimating the probable course of action of a nation.

Intelligence concerning the structural form of a government also contributes materially to the planning of the occupational phase that may follow the successful prosecution of a war. *See also:* Strategic Intelligence.

References

American Bar Association. *Oversight and Accountability of the U.S. Intelligence Agencies: An Evaluation.* Washington, DC: ABA, 1985.

Clauser, Jerome K., and Weir, Sandra M. *Intelligence Research Methodology.* State College, PA: HRB-Singer, 1975.

Department of Defense, Defense Intelligence College. *Glossary of Intelligence Terms and Definitions.* Washington, DC: DIC, 1987.

Department of Defense, Joint Chiefs of Staff. *Department of Defense Dictionary of Military and Related Terms.* Washington, DC: GPO, 1986.

Godson, Roy, ed. *Intelligence Problems for the 1980s, Number 1: Elements of Intelligence.* Rev.

ed. Washington, DC: National Strategy Information Center, 1983.

———. *Intelligence Problems for the 1980s, Number 4: Covert Action*. Washington, DC: National Strategy Information Center, 1981.

Kent, Sherman. *Strategic Intelligence for American World Policy*. Princeton, NJ: Princeton University Press, 1966.

Laqueur, Walter. *A World of Secrets*. New York: Basic Books, 1985.

Maurer, Alfred C.; Turnstall, Marion D.; and Keagle, James M. *Intelligence Policy and Process*. Boulder, CO: Westview Press, 1985.

Treverton, Gregory F. *Covert Action: The Limits of Intervention in the Postwar World*. New York: Basic Books, 1987.

Turner, Stansfield. *Secrecy and Democracy: The CIA in Transition*. Boston: Houghton Mifflin, 1985.

—**POLITICAL WARFARE** is the aggressive use of political means to achieve national objectives.

References

Department of Defense, Joint Chiefs of Staff. *Department of Defense Dictionary of Military and Related Terms*. Washington, DC: GPO, 1986.

—**POLLARD, JONATHAN JAY,** a naval intelligence analyst who worked with the Naval Investigative Service, was arrested on November 21, 1985, and accused of passing classified information to Israeli intelligence. He was convicted of espionage on June 4, 1986, and sentenced to life in prison.

References

Blitzer, Wolf. "Pollard: Not a Bumbler, But Israel's Master Spy." *The Washington Post*, Feb. 15, 1987, p. C1.

Crawford, David J. *Volunteers: The Betrayal of National Defense Secrets by Air Force Traitors*. Washington, DC: GPO, 1988.

Friedman, Robert I. "Pollard's Prison Letters: A Portrait of a Fanatic." *The Washington Post*, June 19, 1988, p. C2.

"Prosecutors Emphasize Damage Caused by Pollard." *The Washington Times*, Feb. 19, 1987, p. 5.

—**POLLARD, ANNE LOUISE HENDERSON,** wife of Jonathan Pollard, was arrested in Washington, DC, on November 22, 1985, and accused of helping her husband pass classified information to Israeli intelligence. She was convicted of espionage on June 4, 1986, and was sentenced to five years in prison.

References

Blitzer, Wolf. "Pollard: Not a Bumbler, But Israel's Master Spy." *The Washington Post*, Feb. 15, 1987, p. C1.

Crawford, David J. *Volunteers: The Betrayal of National Defense Secrets by Air Force Traitors*. Washington, DC: GPO, 1988.

Friedman, Robert I. "Pollard's Prison Letters: A Portrait of a Fanatic." *The Washington Post*, June 19, 1988, p. C2.

"Prosecutors Emphasize Damage Caused by Pollard." *The Washington Times*, Feb. 19, 1987, p. 5.

—**POLYGRAPH TESTING.** *See:* Personnel Security.

—**POLYPHONE**, a signals analysis term, is a symbol that has more than one meaning.

References

Department of Defense, U.S. Army. *Counter-Signals Intelligence (C-SIGINT) Operations*. Field Manual FM 34-62. Washington,] DC: Headquarters, Department of the Army, 1986.

———. *Military Intelligence Company (Combat Electronic Warfare and Intelligence) (Armored Cavalry Regiment/Separate Brigade)*. Field Manual FM 34-30. Washington, DC: Headquarters, Department of the Army, 1983.

—**PORT STUDIES** are detailed studies produced by the Defense Intelligence Agency as part of its Facilities and Installations Studies series. These are detailed studies of port facilities with text, tabular data, plans, and photography covering the harbor, landings, storage, clearance, naval facilities, supplies, utilities, port capability, and development. *See also:* Defense Intelligence Agency.

References

Kent, Sherman. *Strategic Intelligence for American World Policy*. Princeton, NJ: Princeton University Press, 1966.

Von Hoene, John P. A. *Intelligence User's Guide*. Washington, DC: DIA, 1983.

—**POSITIVE INTELLIGENCE** is a general intelligence term that has two meanings. (1) Positive intelligence is a term sometimes given to foreign intelligence to distinguish it from foreign counterintelligence. (2) In FBI terminology, positive intelligence is interpreted intelligence.

References

Department of Defense, Defense Intelligence College. *Glossary of Intelligence Terms and Definitions.* Washington, DC: DIC, 1987.

Godson, Roy, ed. *Intelligence Problems for the 1980s, Number 1: Elements of Intelligence.* Rev. ed. Washington, DC: National Strategy Information Center, 1983.

Kent, Sherman. *Strategic Intelligence for American World Policy.* Princeton, NJ: Princeton University Press, 1966.

Kessler, Ronald. *Spy vs. Spy: Stalking Soviet Spies in America.* New York: Charles Scribner's Sons, 1988.

Treverton, Gregory F. *Covert Action: The Limits of Intervention in the Postwar World.* New York: Basic Books, 1987.

—**POSITIVE MANAGEMENT** is a method of air battle management that relies on real-time data from radar, Identification Friend or Foe (IFF), computer digital data link, and communications equipment to provide air defense command and control and airspace management.

References

Department of Defense, U.S. Army. *U.S. Army Air Defense Artillery Employment.* Field Manual FM 44-1. Washington, DC: Headquarters, Department of the Army, 1983.

—**POSSIBLE FALSIFICATION EQUIPMENT** is an electronic surveillance term that refers to a variety of tools available to a forger that can be used to falsify an original recording. *See also:* Electronic Surveillance.

References

Kessler, Michael. *Wiretapping and Electronic Surveillance Commission Studies: Supporting Materials for the Report of the National Commission for the Review of Federal and State Laws Relating to Wiretapping and Electronic Surveillance, Washington, DC, 1976.* Townsend, PA: Loompanics Unlimited, 1976.

—**POSSIBLE SCI COMPROMISE** is a security violation or incident in which sensitive compartmented information (SCI) may have been exposed or compromised. *See also:* Compromise, Physical Security, Physical Security Investigation, Security, Sensitive Compartmented Information, Sensitive Compartmented Information Facility.

References

Godson, Roy, ed. *Intelligence Problems for the 1980s, Number 1: Elements of Intelligence.* Rev. ed. Washington, DC: National Strategy Information Center, 1983.

—**POWERS, FRANCIS GARY,** was a U-2 pilot who was shot down while flying a reconnaissance mission over the Soviet Union in 1960. His subsequent capture created an international incident and ended the highly successful U-2 program over the Soviet Union that had provided invaluable intelligence from 1956 to 1960. *See also:* U-2 Overhead Reconnaissance Program and U-2 spy plane.

References

Breckinridge, Scott D. *The CIA and the U.S. Intelligence System.* Boulder, CO: Westview Press, 1986.

—**PREASSAULT OPERATIONS,** in amphibious warfare operations, are those endeavors that are conducted in the objective area prior to the assault. They include reconnaissance, minesweeping, shore bombardment, bombing, underwater demolitions, and destroying beach obstacles.

References

Department of Defense, Defense Intelligence College. *Glossary of Intelligence Terms and Definitions.* Washington, DC: DIC, 1987.

Department of Defense, Joint Chiefs of Staff. *Department of Defense Dictionary of Military and Related Terms.* Washington, DC: GPO, 1986.

Von Hoene, John P. A. *Intelligence User's Guide.* Washington, DC: DIA, 1983.

—**PRECEDENCE** is a designation assigned to a message by the originator to indicate to communications personnel the relative order of handling and to the addressee the order in which the message is to be routed. The types of precedence are emergency, flash, immediate, priority, and routine. The drafter is responsible for assigning the proper precedence to a message. The precedence should be no higher than that which is necessary to insure that the message will be delivered in time to accomplish the required action. Specifically, precedence indicates *to the drafter*, the required speed of delivery to the addressee; *to the telecommunications center* *personnel*, the relative order of processing, transmitting, and delivering the messages; and *to the addressee*, the relative order in which to note and take action on messages. *See also:* Precedence Categories.

References

Department of Defense, Defense Intelligence Agency. *Defense Intelligence Agency Manual.* Washington, DC: DIA, 1987.

Department of Defense, Defense Intelligence College. *Glossary of Intelligence Terms and Definitions.* Washington, DC: DIC, 1987.

Department of Defense, Joint Chiefs of Staff. *Department of Defense Dictionary of Military and Related Terms.* Washington, DC: GPO, 1986.

Godson, Roy, ed. *Intelligence Problems for the 1980s, Number 1: Elements of Intelligence.* Rev. ed. Washington, DC: National Strategy Information Center, 1983.

—**PRECEDENCE CATEGORIES** pertain to U.S. message transmission and are the means that govern how quickly a message will be transmitted. The content of the message determines the precedence that should be assigned, and the drafter of the message is the person who assigns the precedence to the message. There are five precedence categories:

Emergency. This precedence may be used only National Command Authorities (NCAs), the Joint Chiefs of Staff, and certain designated commanders of Unified and Specified Commands. It is used for specifically designated emergency action command and control messages.

Flash. This precedence is reserved for initial enemy contact messages or operational combat messages of extreme urgency. Examples are: (1) initial enemy contact reports; (2) messages recalling or diverting friendly aircraft that are about to bomb targets that have been unexpectedly occupied by friendly forces, or messages taking emergency action to prevent conflict between friendly forces; (3) warning of imminent large-scale attacks; and (4) extremely urgent or critical (CRITIC) intelligence messages.

Immediate. This precedence is reserved for those messages relating to situations that gravely affect the security of national or allied forces or populations and that require immediate delivery to the addressee. Some examples are: (1) amplifying reports of initial enemy contact; (2) reports of unusual major movements of military forces of friendly powers in time of peace or strained

relations; (3) messages that report enemy counterattack or that request or cancel additional support; (4) attack orders to commit a force in reserve without delay; (5) messages concerning logistical support of special weapons when essential to sustained operations; (6) reports of widespread civil disturbance; (7) reports of warning of grave natural disaster (earthquake, flood, storm, hurricane, etc.); (8) requests for, or directions concerning, distress assistance; (9) urgent intelligence or diplomatic messages; (10) aircraft movement reports—messages relating to requests for news of aircraft in flight, flight plans, and cancellation messages to prevent unnecessary search and rescue actions; and (11) civil defense actions concerning the population and its survival.

Priority. This precedence is reserved for messages that require expeditious action by the addressee or furnish essential information for the conduct of operations in progress when ROUTINE will not suffice. This is the highest precedence normally authorized for administrative messages. Some examples are: (1) situation reports on positions on the front where an attack is impending or where fire or air support will soon be placed; (2) orders to aircraft formations or units to coincide with ground or naval operations; (3) messages concerning the immediate movement of naval, air, or ground forces; and (4) administrative, logistic, and personnel matters of an urgent and time-sensitive nature.

Routine. This is the precedence assigned to all types of messages that justify electrical transmission, but which are not of sufficient urgency or importance to require a higher precedence. Some examples are: (1) messages concerning normal peacetime military operations, programs, or projects; (2) messages concerning stabilized tactical operations; (3) operational plans concerning projects; (4) periodic or consolidated intelligence reports; (5) troop or ship movement messages, except when time factors dictate the use of a higher precedence; (6) supply and equipment requisition and movement messages, except when time factors dictate the use of a higher precedence; and (7) administrative, logistic, and personnel matters.

Although the time necessary to process a message will vary from command to command, the following guidelines, which are measured from the time that the message is delivered at the transmitting center to the time that it is available for delivery at the receiving center, are currently in effect: *emergency* overrides flash traffic; *flash* is handled as fast as possible, with the objective of less than ten minutes; *immediate* is handled within 30 minutes; *priority* is handled within 3 hours; and *routine* is handled within 6 hours. *See also:* Precedence.

References

Department of Defense, Defense Intelligence Agency. *Defense Intelligence Agency Manual.* Washington, DC: DIA, 1987.

Department of Defense, Joint Chiefs of Staff. *Department of Defense Dictionary of Military and Related Terms.* Washington, DC: GPO, 1986.

Laqueur, Walter. *A World of Secrets.* New York: Basic Books, Inc., 1985.

Von Hoene, John P. A. *Intelligence User's Guide.* Washington, DC: DIA, 1983.

—**PREDICTION.** *See:* Estimate, Estimative Intelligence.

—**PRELIMINARY INVESTIGATION** is the first phase of an FBI investigation of a suspect. It is intended to determine his or her culpability and whether enough evidence exists to warrant a full investigation.

References

Becket, Henry S. A. *The Dictionary of Espionage: Spookspeak into English.* New York: Stein and Day, 1986.

—**PREPRODUCTION MODEL,** in communications security (COMSEC), means a model that is suitable for complete evaluation of mechanical and electrical form, design, and performance. It is in final mechanical and electrical form, uses standard parts, whenever possible, and is completely representative of the final equipment. *See also:* Communications Security.

References

Department of Defense, U.S. Army. *Counter-Signals Intelligence (C-SIGINT) Operations.* Field Manual FM 34-62. Washington, DC: Headquarters, Department of the Army, 1986.

Martin, Paul H. "Communications-Computer Security." *Journal of Electronic Defense* (June 1987).

Muzerall, Joseph V., and Carty, Thomas P. "COMSEC and Its Need for Key Management." *DP&CS* (Spring 1987). Ware, Willis H. "Information Systems, Security, and Privacy." *EDUCOM Bulletin* (Summer 1984).

—**PRESIDENTIAL ORDER DATED JULY 11, 1941,** signed by President Roosevelt, established the Office of Coordinator of Information (COI) and appointed William J. Donovan to the post. This order was the result of Roosevelt's misgivings concerning the state of American intelligence and was the first attempt to centralize the intelligence world. The COI was basically the same position as Donovan had recommended and was the forerunner of the Office of Strategic Services. *See also:* Donovan, William J.; Office of Strategic Services (OSS).

References

Office of the President of the United States. *Order Signed by President Franklin D. Roosevelt, Coordinator of Information.* Washington, DC, July 11, 1941.

—**PRESIDENTIAL ORDER DATED JANUARY 22, 1946,** signed by President Truman, established a National Intelligence Authority (NIA), comprised of the secretary of war, secretary of state, secretary of the Navy, and the President's personal representative, Admiral William D. Leahy. The NIA was to oversee the work of a new body, the Central Intelligence Group. Funding and staffs for the new group were to come from the services, which retained their own intelligence services. Rear Admiral Sidney Souers was appointed as the first head of the CIG. *See also:* Central Intelligence Group; National Intelligence Authority; Souers, Sidney W.; Truman, Harry S.

References

Office of the President of the United States. *Presidential Directive, Coordination of Federal Foreign Intelligence Activities.* Washington, DC, Jan. 22, 1946.

—**PRESIDENTIAL OVERSIGHT.** *See:* Executive Oversight.

—**PRESIDENT'S BOARD OF CONSULTANTS ON FOREIGN INTELLIGENCE AFFAIRS (PBCFIA)** was in existence from 1956 until 1961. It was a predecessor to the President's Foreign Intelligence Advisory Board (PFIAB). Composed of a group of experienced private citizens, its role was to review periodically intelligence activities. *See also:* President's Foreign Intelligence Advisory Board (PFIAB).

References

Corson, William R. *The Armies of Ignorance: The Rise of the American Intelligence Empire.* New York: Dial Press, 1977.

Fain, Tyrus G.; Plant, Katharine C.; and Milloy, Ross. *The Intelligence Community: History, Organization, and Issues.* Public Documents Series. New York: R.R. Bowker, 1977.

Godson, Roy, ed. *Intelligence Problems for the 1980s, Number 1: Elements of Intelligence.* Rev. ed. Washington, DC: National Strategy Information Center, 1983.

Lowenthal, Mark M. *U.S. Intelligence: Evolution and Anatomy.* New York: Praeger, 1984.

Treverton, Gregory F. *Covert Action: The Limits of Intervention in the Postwar World.* New York: Basic Books, 1987.

Turner, Stansfield. *Secrecy and Democracy: The CIA in Transition.* Boston: Houghton Mifflin, 1985.

—PRESIDENT'S FOREIGN INTELLIGENCE AD-VISORY BOARD (PFIAB)

PRESIDENT'S FOREIGN INTELLIGENCE AD-VISORY BOARD (PFIAB) was established in 1961, disbanded in 1977, and reestablished in 1981. It is composed of a group of experienced individuals from outside the government who review intelligence operations and analyses. The members of the PFIAB serve at the pleasure of the president, and the president chooses a chairman and a vice chairman from among them. The members of the board are not compensated. According to Executive Order 12331, of October 20, 1981, the purpose of the board is to assess the quality, quantity, and adequacy of intelligence collection, analysis, and estimates, of counterintelligence, and of other intelligence activities. The board was given the authority to continually review the performance of all intelligence agencies involved in the collection, evaluation, and production of intelligence or the execution of intelligence policy. It reports directly to the president periodically, but at least semiannually.

The PFIAB continually reviews the performance of all government agencies that are engaged in intelligence collection, evaluation, or production or are involved in the execution of intelligence policy. The board also assesses the adequacy of personnel levels, management, and organization of the intelligence agencies and advises the president concerning their overall operations, making recommendations for improvements. These recommendations may be passed to the director of Central Intelligence or the subject agency.

References

American Bar Association. *Oversight and Accountability of the U.S. Intelligence Agencies: An Evaluation.* Washington, DC: ABA, 1985.

Becket, Henry S. A. *The Dictionary of Espionage: Spookspeak into English.* New York: Stein and Day, 1986.

Deacon, Richard. *Spyclopedia: An Encyclopedia of Spies, Secret Services, Operations, Jargon, and All Subjects Related to the World of Espionage.* London: Macdonald, 1987.

Godson, Roy, ed. *Intelligence Problems for the 1980s, Number 1: Elements of Intelligence.* Rev. ed. Washington, DC: National Strategy Information Center, 1983.

———. *Intelligence Problems for the 1980s, Number 5: Clandestine Collection.* Washington, DC: National Strategy Information Center, 1982.

Laqueur, Walter. *A World of Secrets.* New York: Basic Books, 1985.

Lowenthal, Mark M. *U.S. Intelligence: Evolution and Anatomy.* New York: Praeger, 1984.

Maurer, Alfred C.; Turnstall, Marion D.; and Keagle, James M. *Intelligence Policy and Process.* Boulder, CO: Westview Press, 1985.

Office of the President of the United States. *Executive Order 12331, President's Foreign Intelligence Advisory Board.* Washington, DC, Oct. 20, 1981.

Treverton, Gregory F. *Covert Action: The Limits of Intervention in the Postwar World.* New York: Basic Books, 1987.

Turner, Stansfield. *Secrecy and Democracy: The CIA in Transition.* Boston: Houghton Mifflin, 1985.

—PRESIDENT'S INTELLIGENCE OVERSIGHT BOARD (PIOB)

PRESIDENT'S INTELLIGENCE OVERSIGHT BOARD (PIOB) was established by President Ford in 1976 as part of his reform of the Intelligence Community. Its purpose was to monitor intelligence activities and report on any operations that were possibly illegal or improper. Although it was originally attached to the President's Foreign Intelligence Advisory Board (PFIAB), the PIOB continued to function in the Carter administration after the president abolished the PFIAB. President Reagan continued the PIOB, which he made a part of the Office of the President. It is composed of three members who are chosen from outside the government, and it continues to assess intelligence activities in terms of their propriety and legality.

References

Godson, Roy, ed. *Intelligence Problems for the 1980s, Number 1: Elements of Intelligence.* Rev. ed. Washington, DC: National Strategy Information Center, 1983.

Lowenthal, Mark M. *U.S. Intelligence: Evolution and Anatomy.* New York: Praeger, 1984.

Treverton, Gregory F. *Covert Action: The Limits of Intervention in the Postwar World.* New York: Basic Books, 1987.

Turner, Stansfield. *Secrecy and Democracy: The CIA in Transition.* Boston: Houghton Mifflin, 1985.

—**PRESIDENT'S SPECIAL REVIEW BOARD** was created by President Reagan by Executive Order 12575, "President's Special Review Board," which he signed on December 1, 1986. Created in the wake of the Iran-Contra scandal in which several National Security Council (NSC) staff members and the national security advisor had been implicated, the three-man special board was to investigate the NSC.

The functions of the Board were to examine the future role of the National Security Council staff; conduct an extensive study of the NSC staff's role in the "development, coordination, oversight, and conduct of foreign and national security policy"; review and examine the role of the NSC staff in operational activities, particularly those that were "extremely sensitive diplomatic, military, and intelligence missions"; provide recommendations to the president; and report to the president in 30 days.

Reagan was under a great deal of pressure to react to the Iran-Contra scandal. By creating the Special Review Board, he probably hoped that he would demonstrate that he had, indeed, reacted. Additionally, by appointing three extremely respected individuals, Senator John Tower (who was made chairman), Senator Edmund Muskie, and Lieutenant General Brent Scowcroft, the president averted accusations that the board would whitewash the issue. Conversely, the fact that the president gave the board only 30 days to complete its investigation and to report indicated that he wished to hurry its proceedings and to report as quickly as possible, thereby hopefully defusing the issue.

Working under severe time restraints, it is remarkable that the board produced a report that is so profound. Throughout, it is obvious that all three members were pained with having to make some of the statements that had to be made. Thus, in sum, the report stands as a noteworthy document that is unique and of great value for its penetrating analysis of the National Security Council. Major excerpts from the report appear in Appendix W. *See also:* Iran.

References

Office of the President of the United States. *Executive Order 12575, President's Special Review Board.* Washington, DC, Dec. 1, 1986.

—**PRIMARY ELEMENT** is a target intelligence term that pertains to the target that is to be destroyed. A primary element performs the principal function of an installation, site, or entity. At a radar site, the radar installation is a primary element.

References

Department of Defense, Defense Intelligence College. *Glossary of Intelligence Terms and Definitions.* Washington, DC: DIC, 1987.

Department of Defense, Joint Chiefs of Staff. *Department of Defense Dictionary of Military and Related Terms.* Washington, DC: GPO, 1986.

Von Hoene, John P. A. *Intelligence User's Guide.* Washington, DC: DIA, 1983.

—**PRIMARY INTELLIGENCE REQUIREMENT** is an Army tactical intelligence (TACINT) term referring to the critical items of information regarding the enemy and the environment that are needed by a commander by a particular time, so that he can relate it to other available information and intelligence, which, in turn, will assist him in reaching a logical decision. *See also:* Essential Elements of Information.

References

Department of Defense, U.S. Army. *Counter-Signals Intelligence (C-SIGINT) Operations.* Field Manual FM 34-62. Washington, DC: Headquarters, Department of the Army, 1986.

Kent, Sherman. *Strategic Intelligence for American World Policy.* Princeton, NJ: Princeton University Press, 1966.

Turner, Stansfield. *Secrecy and Democracy: The CIA in Transition.* Boston: Houghton Mifflin, 1985.

—**PRINCIPAL** is an intelligence officer or co-opted worker who is directly responsible for a principal agent or agent. He is also known as a handler. *See also:* Agent, Agent Authentication, Agent in Place, Agent Net, Chief of Base, Chief of Outpost, Chief of Station, Handling Agent, Illegal Support Officer.

References

Clancy, Tom. *The Cardinal of the Kremlin.* New York: Putnam, 1988.

Kessler, Ronald. *Spy vs. Spy: Stalking Soviet Spies in America.* New York: Charles Scribner's Sons, 1988.

—**PRINCIPAL AGENT,** in clandestine intelligence operations, is an agent who recruits other agents and then manages the resulting agent network. *See also:* Principal.

References

Becket, Henry S. A. *The Dictionary of Espionage: Spookspeak into English.* New York: Stein and Day, 1986.

Deacon, Richard. *Spyclopedia: An Encyclopedia of Spies, Secret Services, Operations, Jargon, and All Subjects Related to the World of Espionage.* London: Macdonald, 1987.

Quirk, John; Phillips, David; Cline, Ray; and Pforzheimer, Walter. *The Central Intelligence Agency: A Photographic History.* Guilford, CT: Foreign Intelligence Press, 1986.

Ranelagh, John. *The Agency: The Rise and Decline of the CIA.* New York: Simon and Schuster, 1986.

—**PRINTER CODES,** a baud-based system term used in communications intelligence, communications security, operations security, and signals analysis, are codes that are designed for use with teleprinter systems, in which an equal number of elements, varying only in their conditions of mark or space, are used to represent letters, numbers, or functions. *See also:* Communications Security.

References

Department of Defense, U.S. Army. *Counter-Signals Intelligence (C-SIGINT) Operations.* Field Manual FM 34-62. Washington, DC: Headquarters, Department of the Army, 1986.

———. *Military Intelligence Company (Combat Electronic Warfare and Intelligence) (Armored Cavalry Regiment/Separate Brigade).* Field Manual FM 34-30. Washington, DC: Headquarters, Department of the Army, 1983.

Martin, Paul H. "Communications-Computer Security." *Journal of Electronic Defense* (June 1987).

Muzerall, Joseph V., and Carty, Thomas P. "COMSEC and Its Need for Key Management." *DP&CS* (Spring 1987). Ware, Willis H. "Information Systems, Security, and Privacy." *EDUCOM Bulletin* (Summer 1984).

—**PRIORITY** is a value denoting a preferential rating or precedence in position that is used to discriminate between competing entities. In intelligence requirements, it is used to illustrate the relative importance of the requirements and to guide the actions planned, being planned, or in use to respond to the requirements. *See also:* Precedence.

References

Department of Defense, Defense Intelligence Agency. *Defense Intelligence Agency Manual.* Washington, DC: DIA, 1987.

Department of Defense, Defense Intelligence College. *Glossary of Intelligence Terms and Definitions.* Washington, DC: DIC, 1987.

Department of Defense, Joint Chiefs of Staff. *Department of Defense Dictionary of Military and Related Terms.* Washington, DC: GPO, 1986.

Kent, Sherman. *Strategic Intelligence for American World Policy.* Princeton, NJ: Princeton University Press, 1966.

Von Hoene, John P. A. *Intelligence User's Guide.* Washington, DC: DIA, 1983.

—**PRIORITY INTELLIGENCE REQUIREMENTS** are those requirements that a commander has anticipated and has assigned a priority in his planning and decisionmaking. *See also:* Information Requirements, Intelligence Cycle.

References

Department of Defense, Joint Chiefs of Staff. *Department of Defense Dictionary of Military and Related Terms.* Washington, DC: GPO, 1986.

Kent, Sherman. *Strategic Intelligence for American World Policy.* Princeton, NJ: Princeton University Press, 1966.

Turner, Stansfield. *Secrecy and Democracy: The CIA in Transition.* Boston: Houghton Mifflin, 1985.

—**PRIORITY NATIONAL INTELLIGENCE OBJECTIVES (PNIOs)** are a guide for coordinating intelligence collection and production in response to requirements relating to the formulation and execution of national security policy. They are compiled annually by the Intelligence Community and flow directly from the intelligence mission as established by the National Security Council. They are specific enough to provide a basis for planning the allocation of collection and research resources, but are not so specific as to constitute in themselves research and collection requirements. *See also:* Information Requirements, Intelligence Cycle.

References

Department of Defense, Joint Chiefs of Staff. *Department of Defense Dictionary of Military and Related Terms.* Washington, DC: GPO, 1986.

Godson, Roy, ed. *Intelligence Problems for the 1980s, Number 1: Elements of Intelligence.* Rev. ed. Washington, DC: National Strategy Information Center, 1983.

Kent, Sherman. *Strategic Intelligence for American World Policy*. Princeton, NJ: Princeton University Press, 1966.

Laqueur, Walter. *A World of Secrets*. New York: Basic Books, 1985.

—**PRISONER OF WAR CAGE** is a temporary construction, building, or enclosed area where prisoners of war are confined for interrogation and temporary detention pending further evacuation.

References

Department of Defense, Defense Intelligence College. *Glossary of Intelligence Terms and Definitions*. Washington, DC: DIC, 1987.

Department of Defense, Joint Chiefs of Staff. *Department of Defense Dictionary of Military and Related Terms*. Washington, DC: GPO, 1986.

—**PRISONER OF WAR CAMP** is a camp of semipermanent nature that is established for the internment and complete administration of prisoners of war. It may be located on, or may be independent of, other military installations.

References

Department of Defense, Defense Intelligence College. *Glossary of Intelligence Terms and Definitions*. Washington, DC: DIC, 1987.

Department of Defense, Joint Chiefs of Staff. *Department of Defense Dictionary of Military and Related Terms*. Washington, DC: GPO, 1986.

—**PRISONER OF WAR COLLECTION POINT** is a designated locality in a forward battle area where prisoners are assembled pending local examination for information of immediate tactical value and for subsequent evacuation.

References

Department of Defense, Defense Intelligence College. *Glossary of Intelligence Terms and Definitions*. Washington, DC: DIC, 1987.

Department of Defense, Joint Chiefs of Staff. *Department of Defense Dictionary of Military and Related Terms*. Washington, DC: GPO, 1986.

—**PRISONER OF WAR COMPOUND** is a subdivision of a prisoner of war camp.

References

Department of Defense, Defense Intelligence College. *Glossary of Intelligence Terms and Definitions*. Washington, DC: DIC, 1987.

Department of Defense, Joint Chiefs of Staff. *Department of Defense Dictionary of Military and Related Terms*. Washington, DC: GPO, 1986.

—**PRISONER OF WAR PERSONNEL RECORD** is a form for recording a photograph and fingerprints and other pertinent personal data concerning the prisoner of war, including that information required by the Geneva Convention.

References

Department of Defense, Defense Intelligence College. *Glossary of Intelligence Terms and Definitions*. Washington, DC: DIC, 1987.

—**PRIVACY ACT,** Section 552a, United States Code, established firm rules concerning the types of information that could be maintained on U.S. citizens and aliens who had been admitted for permanent residence. The most significant aspects of the act were that no agency could disclose any record to any person or other agency without the prior written consent of the subject of the record, unless the disclosure met very stringent restrictions; that each agency would keep detailed records of all disclosures of records; that each agency would permit a subject access to all records that were maintained on him; that the individual could request the record to be changed if it was in error; that no record be kept on how an individual exercises his or her rights under the First Amendment to the Constitution; that the agencies establish sufficient safeguards concerning the security and confidentiality of the records; that the agency could be held liable in a court of law if it failed to honor the provisions of this act; and that the president report annually the number of individuals who were denied access to their records and the reasons why access was denied.

References

Godson, Roy, ed. *Intelligence Problems for the 1980s, Number 1: Elements of Intelligence*. Rev. ed. Washington, DC: National Strategy Information Center, 1983.

Treverton, Gregory F. *Covert Action: The Limits of Intervention in the Postwar World*. New York: Basic Books, 1987.

—**PROBE MICROPHONE** is used in clandestine intelligence operations. It is a microphone that is put into a wall to transmit conversations to the next room. *See also:* Electronic Surveillance.

References

Becket, Henry S. A. *The Dictionary of Espionage: Spookspeak into English.* New York: Stein and Day, 1986.

Deacon, Richard. *Spyclopedia: An Encyclopedia of Spies, Secret Services, Operations, Jargon, and All Subjects Related to the World of Espionage.* London: Macdonald, 1987.

Ranelagh, John. *The Agency: The Rise and Decline of the CIA.* New York: Simon and Schuster, 1986.

—**PROCEDURAL MANAGEMENT** is a method of air battle management that relies on the use of techniques such as segmenting airspace by volume and time and weapons control statuses.

References

Department of Defense, U.S. Army. *U.S. Army Air Defense Artillery Employment.* Field Manual FM 44-1. Washington, DC: Headquarters, Department of the Army, 1983.

—**PROCESSING.** (1) Processing is a step in the intelligence cycle where information becomes intelligence through evaluation, analysis, integration, and interpretation. (2) Processing is also an official term that has been defined by the Defense Intelligence Agency for one of its functional areas. It means "data reduction and readout—those actions necessary to reduce raw data (obtained through photographic or technical resource exploitation, translation, or other means) to readable text or other forms usable by a researcher or analyst; or for storage in an automated data bank." *See also:* Defense Intelligence Agency, Intelligence Cycle.

References

Department of Defense, Defense Intelligence Agency. *Defense Intelligence Agency Manual 22-2.* Washington, DC: DIA, 1979.

Department of Defense, Defense Intelligence College. *Glossary of Intelligence Terms and Definitions.* Washington, DC: DIC, 1987.

Department of Defense, Joint Chiefs of Staff. *Department of Defense Dictionary of Military and Related Terms.* Washington, DC: GPO, 1986.

Godson, Roy, ed. *Intelligence Problems for the 1980s, Number 1: Elements of Intelligence.* Rev. ed. Washington, DC: National Strategy Information Center, 1983.

Turner, Stansfield. *Secrecy and Democracy: The CIA in Transition.* Boston: Houghton Mifflin, 1985.

U.S. Congress. Senate. *Final Report of the Senate Select Committee to Study Government Operations with Respect to Intelligence Activities. Report 94-755. Book I, Foreign and Military Intelligence.* Washington, DC: GPO, 1976.

Von Hoene, John P. A. *Intelligence User's Guide.* Washington, DC: DIA, 1983.

—**PROCESSING THE TAKE** is a term used in clandestine intelligence operations. It means translating, transcribing, and analyzing the information collected from telephone taps and room bugs. *See also:* Bleep Box, Bug, Bugging, Case, Concealment Devices, Dead Drop, Debriefing, Live Letter Boxes, Live Letter Drops, Rolling Up the Net, Special Activities.

References

Becket, Henry S. A. *The Dictionary of Espionage: Spookspeak into English.* New York: Stein and Day, 1986.

Deacon, Richard. *Spyclopedia: An Encyclopedia of Spies, Secret Services, Operations, Jargon, and All Subjects Related to the World of Espionage.* London: Macdonald, 1987.

Ranelagh, John. *The Agency: The Rise and Decline of the CIA.* New York: Simon and Schuster, 1986.

—**PRODUCER** is a general intelligence term. A producer is an organization that is specifically tasked by its department or command to analyze, interpret, and evaluate raw intelligence and information, and to produce finished intelligence materials from that information, so that the information can be distributed to customers. *See also:* Intelligence Cycle, Intelligence Production.

References

Department of Defense, Defense Intelligence College. *Glossary of Intelligence Terms and Definitions.* Washington, DC: DIC, 1987.

Department of Defense, Joint Chiefs of Staff. *Department of Defense Dictionary of Military and Related Terms.* Washington, DC: GPO, 1986.

Godson, Roy, ed. *Intelligence Problems for the 1980s, Number 1: Elements of Intelligence.* Rev. ed. Washington, DC: National Strategy Information Center, 1983.

———. *Intelligence Problems for the 1980s, Number 2: Analysis and Estimates.* Washington, DC: National Strategy Information Center, 1980.

Kent, Sherman. *Strategic Intelligence for American World Policy.* Princeton, NJ: Princeton University Press, 1966.

Turner, Stansfield. *Secrecy and Democracy: The CIA in Transition.* Boston: Houghton Mifflin, 1985.

Von Hoene, John P. A. *Intelligence User's Guide.* Washington, DC: DIA, 1983.

—**PRODUCT** is a general intelligence term that has two meanings. (1) A product is an intelligence report that is disseminated to customers by an agency. (2) In signals intelligence (SIGINT), it is intelligence information that is derived by analyzing SIGINT materials. It is published as either a report or a translation for dissemination to customers. *See also:* Intelligence Cycle, Intelligence Production.

References
Department of Defense, Defense Intelligence College. *Glossary of Intelligence Terms and Definitions.* Washington, DC: DIC, 1987.

Department of Defense, Joint Chiefs of Staff. *Department of Defense Dictionary of Military and Related Terms.* Washington, DC: GPO, 1986.

Godson, Roy, ed. *Intelligence Problems for the 1980s, Number 1: Elements of Intelligence.* Rev. ed. Washington, DC: National Strategy Information Center, 1983.

———. *Intelligence Problems for the 1980s, Number 2: Analysis and Estimates.* Washington, DC: National Strategy Information Center, 1980.

Kent, Sherman. *Strategic Intelligence for American World Policy.* Princeton, NJ: Princeton University Press, 1966.

Turner, Stansfield. *Secrecy and Democracy: The CIA in Transition.* Boston: Houghton Mifflin, 1985.

U.S. Congress. Senate. *Final Report of the Senate Select Committee to Study Government Operations with Respect to Intelligence Activities. Report 94-755. Book I, Foreign and Military Intelligence.* Washington, DC: GPO, 1976.

Von Hoene, John P. A. *Intelligence User's Guide.* Washington, DC: DIA, 1983.

—**PRODUCTION.** (1) The U.S. Army's definition of production is "the conversion of information or intelligence information into finished intelligence through the integration, analysis, evaluation, and interpretation of all available data, and the preparation of intelligence reports in support of known or anticipated consumer requirements." (2) Production is part of the intelligence cycle. (3) As defined by the Church Committee, production is "the preparation of reports based on an analysis of information to meet the needs of intelligence users (consumers) within and outside of the Intelligence Community." *See also:* Intelligence Cycle, Intelligence Production.

References
Department of Defense, Defense Intelligence College. *Glossary of Intelligence Terms and Definitions.* Washington, DC: DIC, 1987.

Department of Defense, Joint Chiefs of Staff. *Department of Defense Dictionary of Military and Related Terms.* Washington, DC: GPO, 1986.

Department of Defense, U.S. Army. *RDTE Managers Intelligence and Threat Support Guide.* Alexandria, VA: Headquarters, Army Materiel Development and Readiness Command, 1983.

Godson, Roy, ed. *Intelligence Problems for the 1980s, Number 1: Elements of Intelligence.* Rev. ed. Washington, DC: National Strategy Information Center, 1983.

———. *Intelligence Problems for the 1980s, Number 2: Analysis and Estimates.* Washington, DC: National Strategy Information Center, 1980.

Kent, Sherman. *Strategic Intelligence for American World Policy.* Princeton, NJ: Princeton University Press, 1966.

Turner, Stansfield. *Secrecy and Democracy: The CIA in Transition.* Boston: Houghton Mifflin, 1985.

U.S. Congress. Senate. *Final Report of the Senate Select Committee to Study Government Operations with Respect to Intelligence Activities. Report 94-755. Book I, Foreign and Military Intelligence.* Washington, DC: GPO, 1976.

Von Hoene, John P. A. *Intelligence User's Guide.* Washington, DC: DIA, 1983.

—**PRODUCTION DISTRIBUTION SYSTEM (PDS),** in communications security (COMSEC), means a wire line or fiber-optics system that includes adequate acoustical, electrical, electromagnetic, and physical safeguards that permit its use for transmitting classified information. Note that a complete PDS includes the subscriber and terminal equipment as well as the interconnecting lines. *See also:* Communications Security.

References
Blackburn, N. Glenn. "Computers: A Counterintelligence Concern." Unpublished paper provided to the editors. Washington, DC, 1987.

Department of Defense, U.S. Army. *Counter-Signals Intelligence (C-SIGINT) Operations.* Field Manual FM 34-62. Washington, DC: Headquarters, Department of the Army, 1986.

———. *Military Intelligence Company (Combat Electronic Warfare and Intelligence) (Armored Cavalry Regiment/Separate Brigade).* Field Manual FM 34-30. Washington, DC: Headquarters, Department of the Army, 1983.

Martin, Paul H. "Communications-Computer Security." *Journal of Electronic Defense* (June 1987).

Muzerall, Joseph V., and Carty, Thomas P. "COMSEC and Its Need for Key Management." *DP&CS* (Spring 1987). Ware, Willis H. "Information Systems, Security, and Privacy." *EDUCOM Bulletin* (Summer 1984).

—**PRODUCTION LINE** is published by the Defense Intelligence Agency. It is a newsletter for disseminating ideas and information throughout the intelligence production community. First published in 1981, it is issued semiannually. *See also:* Defense Intelligence Agency.

References

Von Hoene, John P. A. *Intelligence User's Guide.* Washington, DC: DIA, 1983.

—**PRODUCTION MODEL,** in communications security (COMSEC), means a model that is in its final mechanical and electrical form. It is the final production design and has been made by production tools, jigs, fixtures, and methods using standard parts, whenever possible. *See also:* Communications Security.

References

Blackburn, N. Glenn. "Computers: A Counterintelligence Concern." Unpublished paper provided to the editors. Washington, DC, 1987.

Muzerall, Joseph V., and Carty, Thomas P. "COMSEC and Its Need for Key Management." *DP&CS* (Spring 1987). Ware, Willis H. "Information Systems, Security, and Privacy." *EDUCOM Bulletin* (Summer 1984).

—**PRODUCTION PLANNING AND MANAGE-MENT** is an official term that has been defined by the Defense Intelligence Agency for one of its functional areas. It means "the coordination of the processing and production of intelligence to insure the substantive quality of intelligence products; the coordination of acquisition, exploitation and production activities; the evaluation of resources utilization; and the development and implementation of processing and production systems, schedules, inputs and requirements." *See also:* Defense Intelligence Agency.

References

Department of Defense, Defense Intelligence Agency. *Defense Intelligence Agency Manual.* Washington, DC: DIA, 1987.

———. *Defense Intelligence Agency Manual 22-2.* Washington, DC: DIA, 1979.

—**PRODUCTION RESPONSIBILITIES DOCU-MENT (PRD)** is published by the Defense Intelligence Agency. It is a comprehensive reference with an associated automated file reflecting geotopical production responsibilities of some 60 Department of Defense entities that are engaged in processing and producing general intelligence. *See also:* Defense Intelligence Agency.

References

Von Hoene, John P. A. *Intelligence User's Guide.* Washington, DC: DIA, 1983.

—**PRODUCTION SUPPORT AND PHOTO-GRAPHIC SERVICES** is an official term that has been defined by the Defense Intelligence Agency for one of its functional areas. It means "activities involved in facilitating and supporting intelligence production to include document storage and retrieval; reference and research; library operations; maps, chart, and target chart materials storage; publication of digests, visual presentation, graphic arts, cartographic and reproduction services; and photographic and laboratory services for mapping, charting, and intelligence photography." *See also:* Defense Intelligence Agency.

References

Department of Defense, Defense Intelligence Agency. *Defense Intelligence Agency Manual.* Washington, DC: DIA, 1987.

———. *Defense Intelligence Agency Manual 22-2.* Washington, DC: DIA, 1979.

Von Hoene, John P. A. *Intelligence User's Guide.* Washington, DC: DIA, 1983.

—**PROFILE** is an Army tactical intelligence (TAC-INT) term referring to the picture that is formed through the identification and analysis of elements, actions, equipment, and details of military units or activity. Patterns plus signature equal profile. *See also:* Signature.

References

Blackburn, N. Glenn. "Computers: A Counterintelligence Concern." Unpublished paper provided to the editors. Washington, DC, 1987.

Department of Defense, U.S. Army. *Counter-Signals Intelligence (C-SIGINT) Operations*. Field Manual FM 34-62. Washington, DC: Headquarters, Department of the Army, 1986.

————. *Military Intelligence Company (Combat Electronic Warfare and Intelligence) (Armored Cavalry Regiment/Separate Brigade)*. Field Manual FM 34-30. Washington, DC: Headquarters, Department of the Army, 1983.

Ware, Willis H. "Information Systems, Security, and Privacy." *EDUCOM Bulletin* (Summer 1984).

—**PROFORMA (PREDETERMINED FORMAT),** a baud-based system used in communications intelligence, communications security, operations security, and signals analysis, refers to systems that transmit limited, rigidly controlled information for a special purpose. The information is generally limited to numerals that equate to a response or direct an action. *See also:* Communications Security.

References

Blackburn, N. Glenn. "Computers: A Counterintelligence Concern." Unpublished paper provided to the editors. Washington, DC, 1987.

Department of Defense, U.S. Army. *Counter-Signals Intelligence (C-SIGINT) Operations*. Field Manual FM 34-62. Washington, DC: Headquarters, Department of the Army, 1986.

————. *Military Intelligence Company (Combat Electronic Warfare and Intelligence) (Armored Cavalry Regiment/Separate Brigade)*. Field Manual FM 34-30. Washington, DC: Headquarters, Department of the Army, 1983.

Ware, Willis H. "Information Systems, Security, and Privacy." *EDUCOM Bulletin* (Summer 1984).

—**PROGNOSIS** is a product of the Directorate of Estimates, Defense Intelligence Agency. It is generally a short document and is an uncoordinated estimative statement, generally about a single nation. *See also:* Defense Intelligence Agency.

References

Brinkley, David A., and Hull, Andrew W. *Estimative Intelligence: A Textbook on the History, Products, Uses, and Writing of Intelligence Estimates.* Columbus, OH: Battelle, 1979.

Godson, Roy, ed. *Intelligence Problems for the 1980s, Number 1: Elements of Intelligence.* Rev. ed. Washington, DC: National Strategy Information Center, 1983.

Pickett, George. "Congress, the Budget, and Intelligence." In *Intelligence Policy and Process*, edited by Alfred C. Maurer, Marion D. Turnstall, and James M. Keagle. Boulder, CO: Westview Press, 1985.

—**PROGRAM,** in intelligence program budgeting, has three meanings. (1) A program is a plan or scheme of action that is designed to accomplish a definite objective that is specific as to the time phasing of the work to be done and the means proposed for its accomplishment, particularly in quantitative terms, with respect to manpower, material, and facilities requirements. Thus a program provides a basis for budgeting. (2) A program can be a segment or element of a complete plan. (3) A program is also a budget account classification. *See also:* Budget.

References

Department of Defense, Defense Intelligence College. *Glossary of Intelligence Terms and Definitions.* Washington, DC: DIC, 1987.

Department of Defense, Joint Chiefs of Staff. *Department of Defense Dictionary of Military and Related Terms.* Washington, DC: GPO, 1986.

Godson, Roy, ed., *Intelligence Problems for the 1980s, Number 1: Elements of Intelligence.* Rev. ed. Washington, DC: National Strategy Information Center, 1983.

Kent, Sherman. *Strategic Intelligence for American World Policy.* Princeton, NJ: Princeton University Press, 1966.

Pickett, George. "Congress, the Budget, and Intelligence." In *Intelligence Policy and Process*, edited by Alfred C. Maurer, Marion D. Turnstall, and James M. Keagle. Boulder, CO: Westview Press, 1985.

Treverton, Gregory F. *Covert Action: The Limits of Intervention in the Postwar World.* New York: Basic Books, 1987.

Von Hoene, John P. A. *Intelligence User's Guide.* Washington, DC: DIA, 1983.

—**PROGRAM BUDGET DECISION (PBD),** in budgeting, is a secretary of defense decision document arising from the joint program and budget review conducted by the Office of the Secretary of Defense and the Office of Management and Budget. Its subject is deemed to be sufficiently important that it is presented to the secretary in a form that presents possible decision alternatives. *See also:* Program.

References

Pickett, George. "Congress, the Budget, and Intelligence." In *Intelligence Policy and Process*, edited by Alfred C. Maurer, Marion D. Turnstall, and James M. Keagle. Boulder, CO: Westview Press, 1985.

Turner, Stansfield. *Secrecy and Democracy: The CIA in Transition*. Boston: Houghton Mifflin, 1985.

—**PROGRAM CHANGE DECISION (PCD)** is a budgeting and finance term that is of importance in budgeting. It is a secretary of defense decision, in prescribed format, that authorizes changes to the Five-Year Defense Program (FYDP). *See also:* Program.

References

Pickett, George. "Congress, the Budget, and Intelligence." In *Intelligence Policy and Process*, edited by Alfred C. Maurer, Marion D. Turnstall, and James M. Keagle. Boulder, CO: Westview Press, 1985.

Turner, Stansfield. *Secrecy and Democracy: The CIA in Transition*. Boston: Houghton Mifflin, 1985.

—**PROGRAM CHANGE REQUEST (PCR)** is a budgeting and finance term that is of importance in budgeting. It is a proposal, in prescribed format, for out-of-cycle changes to the approved data in the Five-Year Defense Program (FYDP). *See also:* Program.

References

Pickett, George. "Congress, the Budget, and Intelligence." In *Intelligence Policy and Process*, edited by Alfred C. Maurer, Marion D. Turnstall, and James M. Keagle. Boulder, CO: Westview Press, 1985.

Turner, Stansfield. *Secrecy and Democracy: The CIA in Transition*. Boston: Houghton Mifflin, 1985.

—**PROGRAM COORDINATOR,** in intelligence data handling, is the overall program manager of a community development who is responsible for managing and coordinating the implementation of required capabilities of all affected General Defense Intelligence Community (GDIC) components. Normally he works with and through the GDIC component program managers. *See also:* Program.

References

Department of Defense, Defense Intelligence Agency. *Defense Intelligence Agency Manual.* Washington, DC: DIA, 1987.

—**PROGRAM COST,** in program budgeting, is the estimate of the total obligational authority (TOA) required to fund a program. *See also:* Program.

References

Pickett, George. "Congress, the Budget, and Intelligence." In *Intelligence Policy and Process*, edited by Alfred C. Maurer, Marion D. Turnstall, and James M. Keagle. Boulder, CO: Westview Press, 1985.

Turner, Stansfield. *Secrecy and Democracy: The CIA in Transition*. Boston: Houghton Mifflin, 1985.

—**PROGRAM COST REPORTING,** in budgeting, concerns the reporting requirements that are prescribed in the Department of Defense instructions that provide for comparable program cost and related data on research and development activities and hardware items for use in program cost validation and progress and status analyses. *See also:* Program.

References

Pickett, George. "Congress, the Budget, and Intelligence." In *Intelligence Policy and Process*, edited by Alfred C. Maurer, Marion D. Turnstall, and James M. Keagle. Boulder, CO: Westview Press, 1985.

—**PROGRAM DECISION MEMORANDUM,** in budgeting, is a document that records the secretary of defense's or deputy secretary of defense's final decisions on Program Objective Memorandum (POM) proposals and approves Department of Defense component POMs as modified by these decisions. *See also:* Program.

References

Pickett, George. "Congress, the Budget, and Intelligence." In *Intelligence Policy and Process*, edited by Alfred C. Maurer, Marion D. Turnstall, and James M. Keagle. Boulder, CO: Westview Press, 1985.

Turner, Stansfield. *Secrecy and Democracy: The CIA in Transition*. Boston: Houghton Mifflin, 1985.

—**PROGRAM DECISION PACKAGE (PDP),** in budgeting, describes all of the resources in dollars and manpower that are required to support an independent portion of the Air Force program. These are sometimes called "baseline PDPs," and the sum of all of them equals the total Air Force program. *See also:* Program.

References

Pickett, George. "Congress, the Budget, and Intelligence." In *Intelligence Policy and Process*, edited by Alfred C. Maurer, Marion D. Turnstall, and James M. Keagle. Boulder, CO: Westview Press, 1985.

—**PROGRAM ELEMENT (PE),** in budgeting, is the manpower, equipment, and facilities that are related to a mission capability or an activity. The program element is the basic building block in the Five-Year Defense Plan (FYDP).

Department of Defense intelligence activities constitute the largest portion of the National Foreign Intelligence Program (NFIP) and make up all of the intelligence-related activities (IRA). Each of these activities is also accounted for in the ten major programs of the Department of Defense budgeting system. At least four of the programs contain NFIP or IRA projects (Program 1 [Strategic Forces], Program 2 [General Purpose Forces], Program 3 [Communications and Intelligence], and Program 6 [Research and Development]). Within each program, an intelligence activity has a PE. The Department of Defense often discusses its projects in terms of PEs. *See also:* Program.

References

Godson, Roy, ed. *Intelligence Problems for the 1980s, Number 1: Elements of Intelligence*. Rev. ed. Washington, DC: National Strategy Information Center, 1983.

Pickett, George. "Congress, the Budget, and Intelligence." In *Intelligence Policy and Process*, edited by Alfred C. Maurer, Marion D. Turnstall, and James M. Keagle. Boulder, CO: Westview Press, 1985.

Turner, Stansfield. *Secrecy and Democracy: The CIA in Transition*. Boston: Houghton Mifflin, 1985.

—**PROGRAM ELEMENT SUMMARY DATA SHEET,** in budgeting, is the basic medium for presenting the details of the Five-Year Defense Program (FYDP). It includes forces for the prior and current fiscal years and eight years beyond the current fiscal year. It also lists costs (TOA) and manpower for the prior and current fiscal years and five years beyond the current fiscal year. *See also:* Program.

References

Pickett, George. "Congress, the Budget, and Intelligence." In *Intelligence Policy and Process*, edited by Alfred C. Maurer, Marion D. Turnstall, and James M. Keagle. Boulder, CO: Westview Press, 1985.

Turner, Stansfield. *Secrecy and Democracy: The CIA in Transition*. Boston: Houghton Mifflin, 1985.

—**PROGRAM MANAGEMENT,** in intelligence data handling, is the responsibility, within the Department of Defense Intelligence Information System (DODIIS) acquisition management process, for insuring that functional requirements are clearly, comprehensively, and accurately defined; that the DODIIS acquisition management process results in satisfying the defined requirements; and that organizations are effectively trained to use the ADP-T capabilities that have been developed. *See also:* Program.

References

Department of Defense, Defense Intelligence Agency. *Defense Intelligence Agency Manual.* Washington, DC: DIA, 1987.

Department of Defense, Defense Intelligence College. *Glossary of Intelligence Terms and Definitions.* Washington, DC: DIC, 1987.

Godson, Roy, ed. *Intelligence Problems for the 1980s, Number 1: Elements of Intelligence.* Rev. ed. Washington, DC: National Strategy Information Center, 1983.

Pickett, George. "Congress, the Budget, and Intelligence." In *Intelligence Policy and Process*, edited by Alfred C. Maurer, Marion D. Turnstall, and James M. Keagle. Boulder, CO: Westview Press, 1985.

Turner, Stansfield. *Secrecy and Democracy: The CIA in Transition*. Boston: Houghton Mifflin, 1985.

Von Hoene, John P. A. *Intelligence User's Guide.* Washington, DC: DIA, 1983.

—**PROGRAM MANAGER,** in intelligence data handling, is the individual charged by a functional sponsor to develop a new or revised functional architecture and, where appropriate, to develop the supporting ADP-T system architecture. The program manager is formally appointed by the chartering authority. *See also:* Program.

References

Department of Defense, Defense Intelligence Agency. *Defense Intelligence Agency Manual.* Washington, DC: DIA, 1987.

Department of Defense, Joint Chiefs of Staff. *Department of Defense Dictionary of Military and Related Terms.* Washington, DC: GPO, 1986.

Godson, Roy, ed. *Intelligence Problems for the 1980s, Number 1: Elements of Intelligence.* Rev. ed. Washington, DC: National Strategy Information Center, 1983.

Von Hoene, John P. A. *Intelligence User's Guide.* Washington, DC: DIA, 1983.

—**PROGRAM OBJECTIVE MEMORANDUM (POM)** is an annual submission memorandum that is presented to the secretary of defense by each military department and defense agency. It proposes the total program requirements for the next five years and includes a rationale for any planned changes from the approved Five-Year Defense Program (FYDP) baseline within the fiscal guidance.

Each military department and defense agency annually prepares a POM and submits it to the secretary of defense. The POM is based on the strategic concepts and guidance that are presented in the Defense Guidance, and it includes an assessment of the risk associated with current and proposed forces and support programs. *See also:* Program.

References

Department of Defense, Defense Intelligence Agency. *Organization, Mission, and Key Personnel.* Washington, DC: DIA, 1986.

Pickett, George. "Congress, the Budget, and Intelligence." In *Intelligence Policy and Process,* edited by Alfred C. Maurer, Marion D. Turnstall, and James M. Keagle. Boulder, CO: Westview Press, 1985.

—**PROGRAM REVIEW COMMITTEE (PRC)** pertains to budgeting. It reviews the budget proposals and makes recommendations that are relevant to resource allocation and the impact of resource limitations on Air Force program and force projections. *See also:* Program.

References

Pickett, George. "Congress, the Budget, and Intelligence." In *Intelligence Policy and Process,* edited by Alfred C. Maurer, Marion D. Turnstall, and James M. Keagle. Boulder, CO: Westview Press, 1985.

Von Hoene, John P. A. *Intelligence User's Guide.* Washington, DC: DIA, 1983.

—**PROGRAM YEAR (PY)** is a term used in budgeting. It is a fiscal year in the Five-Year Defense Program (FYDP) that does not end earlier than the second year beyond the current calendar year. Thus, during calendar year 1989, the first program year is 1991. *See also:* Program.

References

Pickett, George. "Congress, the Budget, and Intelligence." In *Intelligence Policy and Process,* edited by Alfred C. Maurer, Marion D. Turnstall, and James M. Keagle. Boulder, CO: Westview Press, 1985.

—**PROGRAMMING,** in budgeting, is the process of translating planned military force requirements into specific time-phased, scheduled actions and of identifying in relatively precise terms the resources required. It is the bridge between planning and budgeting. *See also:* Program.

References

Pickett, George. "Congress, the Budget, and Intelligence." In *Intelligence Policy and Process,* edited by Alfred C. Maurer, Marion D. Turnstall, and James M. Keagle. Boulder, CO: Westview Press, 1985.

Von Hoene, John P. A. *Intelligence User's Guide.* Washington, DC: DIA, 1983.

—**PROGRAMMING COST** is a budgeting and finance term that is of importance in intelligence budgeting. It is the cost data that are needed for making program decisions. Programming costs are based on sets of factors that will provide consistent cost data under the same or similar circumstances, and that are directly related to the explicit elements of the program decision. *See also:* Program.

References

Pickett, George. "Congress, the Budget, and Intelligence." In *Intelligence Policy and Process,* edited by Alfred C. Maurer, Marion D. Turnstall, and James M. Keagle. Boulder, CO: Westview Press, 1985.

Von Hoene, John P. A. *Intelligence User's Guide.* Washington, DC: DIA, 1983.

—**PROPAGANDA** is any form of communication, including information, ideas, doctrines, or special appeals, that supports national objectives and is designed to influence the opinions, emotions, attitudes, or behavior of any group in order to benefit the sponsor. *See also:* Black Propaganda, Gray Propaganda, White Propaganda.

References

Department of Defense, Joint Chiefs of Staff. *Department of Defense Dictionary of Military and Related Terms.* Washington, DC: GPO, 1986.

Godson, Roy, ed. *Intelligence Problems for the 1980s, Number 1: Elements of Intelligence.* Rev. ed. Washington, DC: National Strategy Information Center, 1983.

Kent, Sherman. *Strategic Intelligence for American World Policy.* Princeton, NJ: Princeton University Press, 1966.

Laqueur, Walter. *A World of Secrets.* New York: Basic Books, 1985.

Treverton, Gregory F. *Covert Action: The Limits of Intervention in the Postwar World.* New York: Basic Books, 1987.

Turner, Stansfield. *Secrecy and Democracy: The CIA in Transition.* Boston: Houghton Mifflin, 1985.

U.S. Congress. Senate. *Final Report of the Senate Select Committee to Study Government Operations with Respect to Intelligence Activities. Report 94-755. Book I, Foreign and Military Intelligence.* Washington, DC: GPO, 1976.

—**PROPER AUTHORITY (PA)** is an intelligence security and counterintelligence term. A proper authority is a senior official of the Intelligence Community (SOIC) or his or her designee who authorizes the sanitization or decompartmentation of sensitive compartmented information. *See also:* Declassification, Declassification and Downgrading Instructions, Decompartmentation, Sensitive Compartmented Information.

References

Godson, Roy, ed. *Intelligence Problems for the 1980s, Number 1: Elements of Intelligence.* Rev. ed. Washington, DC: National Strategy Information Center, 1983.

—**PROPOSED PRESIDENTIAL DIRECTIVE DATED SEPTEMBER 17, 1984,** entitled "National Policy on Telecommunications and Automated Information Systems Security," was proposed by the National Security Agency because of its concern over the poor state of existing security in the areas of telecommunications and automated information systems. Although it was never enacted, the directive was noteworthy because it would have extended the realm of security to civilian departments of the U.S. government that normally had almost no contact with the military, intelligence, and national security agencies and departments of the government. Furthermore, if liberally interpreted, it would have empowered the government to intrude into the private sector if it felt that there was an area affecting national security that was not protected by sufficient security. The wording of the directive was such that it could have been interpreted in a way that could have provided the groups and officers it created with substantial influence in the civilian sector of government and the private sector of the United States.

The objectives of the bill were to provide for:

(a) A reliable and continuing capability to assess threats and vulnerabilities, and to implement appropriate, effective countermeasures.

(b) A superior technical base within the government to achieve this security, and support for a superior technical base within the private sector in areas which complement and enhance government capabilities.

(c) A more effective application of government resources and encouragement of private sector security initiatives.

(d) Support and enhancement of other policy objectives for national telecommunications and automated information systems.

In order to support these objectives, the following policies were to be established:

(a) Systems which generate, store, process, transfer or communicate classified information in electrical form shall be secured by such means as are necessary to prevent compromise or exploitation.

(b) Systems handling other sensitive, but unclassified, government or government-derived information, the loss of which could adversely affect the national security interest, shall be protected in proportion to the threat of exploitation and the associated potential damage to the national security.

(c) The government shall encourage, advise, and, where appropriate, assist the private sector to: identify systems which handle sensitive non-government information, the loss of which could adversely affect the national security; determine the threat to, and vulnerability of, these systems; and formulate strategies and measures for providing protection in proportion to the threat of exploitation and the associated potential damage. Information and advice from the perspective of the private sector will be sought with respect to the implementation of this policy. In cases where implementation of security measures to non-governmental systems would be in the national security interest, the private sector shall be encouraged, advised, and, where appropriate, assisted in undertaking the application of such measures.

(d) Efforts and programs begun under PD-24 which support these policies shall be continued.

In order to implement the measures, the directive would have created several groups and positions. These were:

(a) The Systems Security Steering Group, which was to be chaired by the assistant to the president for national security affairs, was to be composed of the heads of the government departments and agencies concerned, and was to be tasked with overseeing the implementation of the directive.

(b) The National Telecommunications and Information Systems Security Committee, chaired by the assistant secretary of defense (command, control, communications, and intelligence) and composed of representatives from every department or agency represented on the Steering Group, plus several other heads of departments and agencies and other concerned persons, which would have been tasked with implementing the directive.

(c) The executive agent of the government for telecommunications and information systems security, who would have implemented the policies of the National Committee. The secretary of defense was designated as the executive agent.

(d) The national manager for telecommunications security and automated information systems security, who actually would have carried out the responsibilities of the executive agent. The director of the National Security Agency would have been designated as the national manager.

In addition, the directive would have tasked the secretary of commerce to develop the Public Federal Information Processing Standards, in order to disseminate the standards that the Steering Group approved, and would have tasked the director of the Office of Management and Budget to monitor and provide budget data.

Finally, the directive would have issued general guidance to the heads of all federal departments and agencies. These individuals would have been informed that they would:

(a) Be responsible for achieving and maintaining a secure posture for telecommunications and automated information systems within their departments or agencies.

(b) Ensure that the policies, standards and doctrines issued pursuant to this Directive are implemented within their departments or agencies.

(c) Provide to the Systems Security Steering Group, the NTISSC, Executive Agent, and the National Manager, as appropriate, such information as may be required to discharge responsibilities assigned herein, consistent with relevant law, Executive Order, and Presidential Directives.

In summary, because the directive proposed powers for the Intelligence Community in general and the National Security Agency in particular that far exceeded those that the Community had previously enjoyed, it would surely have met severe opposition that probably would have involved several court cases if it had been enacted. Nonetheless, the proposed directive was important in that it reflected the Community's concern for the lack of control over sensitive information resulting from both government- and privately sponsored research.

("National Policy on Telecommunications and Automated Information Systems Security." Presidential Directive issued on September 17, 1984, but never enacted.)

—**PROPRIETARIES** is a term used in clandestine and covert intelligence operations. Proprietaries are private commercial businesses that are capable of conducting business but have been created and are controlled by intelligence services in order to conceal the intelligence affiliation of the people employed, or the government sponsorship of some of the firm's activities that support clandestine operations. *See also:* Cover, Cover Name, Cover Organizations, Cover Story, Establishing Bonafides, Putting in the Plumbing, Suitable Cover.

References

Quirk, John; Phillips, David; Cline, Ray; and Pforzheimer, Walter. *The Central Intelligence Agency: A Photographic History.* Guilford, CT: Foreign Intelligence Press, 1986.

Treverton, Gregory F. *Covert Action: The Limits of Intervention in the Postwar World.* New York: Basic Books, 1987.

U.S. Congress. Senate. *Final Report of the Senate Select Committee to Study Government Operations with Respect to Intelligence Activities. Report 94-755. Book I, Foreign and Military Intelligence.* Washington, DC: GPO, 1976.

—**PROPRIETARY COMPANY** is a term used in clandestine and covert intelligence operations to describe a business entity owned, in whole or in part, or controlled by an intelligence organization and operated to provide commercial cover for an activity of that organization. *See also:* Cover.

References

Department of Defense, Defense Intelligence College. *Glossary of Intelligence Terms and Definitions.* Washington, DC: DIC, 1987.

Treverton, Gregory F. *Covert Action: The Limits of Intervention in the Postwar World.* New York: Basic Books, 1987.

Turner, Stansfield. *Secrecy and Democracy: The CIA in Transition.* Boston: Houghton Mifflin, 1985.

—**PROTECTED INFORMATION** is a term used in clandestine and covert intelligence operations to describe information that comes from clandestine sources and must be protected in order to protect the source. It is used to identify intelligence information that is provided by a commercial firm or private source. The information cannot be released without the permission of the originator.

References

Becket, Henry S. A. *The Dictionary of Espionage: Spookspeak into English.* New York: Stein and Day, 1986.

Deacon, Richard. *Spyclopedia: An Encyclopedia of Spies, Secret Services, Operations, Jargon, and All Subjects Related to the World of Espionage.* London: Macdonald, 1987.

Department of Defense, Defense Intelligence Agency. *Defense Intelligence Agency Manual.* Washington, DC: DIA, 1984.

Ranelagh, John. *The Agency: The Rise and Decline of the CIA.* New York: Simon and Schuster, 1986.

—**PROTECTION ELEMENT** is a target intelligence term pertaining to the target that is to be destroyed. Protection elements are passive or active measures that are usually layered. Such elements have at least some measures that provide protection to all elements of a target. For example, an antiair missile site would be a protection element at a radar site. *See also:* Target Intelligence, Targeting.

References

Department of Defense, Defense Intelligence College. *Glossary of Intelligence Terms and Definitions.* Washington, DC: DIC, 1987.

—**PROTECTIVE PACKAGING,** in communications security (COMSEC), means packaging techniques for keying material that discourages penetration and will reveal that a penetration has occurred. It will also prevent the viewing or copying of the keying material before the time it is exposed for use. *See also:* Communications Security.

References

Department of Defense, U.S. Army. *Counter-Signals Intelligence (C-SIGINT) Operations.* Field Manual FM 34-62. Washington, DC: Headquarters, Department of the Army, 1986.

———. *Military Intelligence Company (Combat Electronic Warfare and Intelligence) (Armored Cavalry Regiment/Separate Brigade).* Field Manual FM 34-30. Washington, DC: Headquarters, Department of the Army, 1983.

Martin, Paul H. "Communications-Computer Security." *Journal of Electronic Defense* (June 1987).

Muzerall, Joseph V., and Carty, Thomas P. "COMSEC and Its Need for Key Management." *DP&CS* (Spring 1987).

—**PROTECTIVE SECURITY** is a term used in counterintelligence, counterespionage, and counterinsurgency to describe an organized system of defensive measures that are instituted and maintained at all levels of command with the aim of maintaining the safety of people or objects. *See also:* Physical Security, Security.

References

Department of Defense, Joint Chiefs of Staff. *Department of Defense Dictionary of Military and Related Terms.* Washington, DC: GPO, 1986.

Godson, Roy, ed. *Intelligence Problems for the 1980s, Number 1: Elements of Intelligence.* Rev. ed. Washington, DC: National Strategy Information Center, 1983.

Laqueur, Walter. *A World of Secrets.* New York: Basic Books, 1985.

—**PROTOCOL OFFICE.** *See:* Defense Intelligence Agency.

—**PROVING IT OUT** is a term used in clandestine intelligence operations. It means verifying an agent's story by checking easily proven portions of his reports. *See also:* Agent Authentication, Establishing Bonafides, Legend.

References

Becket, Henry S. A. *The Dictionary of Espionage: Spookspeak into English*. New York: Stein and Day, 1986.

Deacon, Richard. *Spyclopedia: An Encyclopedia of Spies, Secret Services, Operations, Jargon, and All Subjects Related to the World of Espionage*. London: Macdonald, 1987.

Ranelagh, John. *The Agency: The Rise and Decline of the CIA*. New York: Simon and Schuster, 1986.

—**PROVOCATION,** in FBI terminology, is activity that is intended to make an individual, organization, intelligence service, or government do something that is self-damaging. *See also:* Provocation Agent.

References

Becket, Henry S. A. *The Dictionary of Espionage: Spookspeak into English*. New York: Stein and Day, 1986.

Deacon, Richard. *Spyclopedia: An Encyclopedia of Spies, Secret Services, Operations, Jargon, and All Subjects Related to the World of Espionage*. London: Macdonald, 1987.

Department of Defense, Defense Intelligence College. *Glossary of Intelligence Terms and Definitions*. Washington, DC: DIC, 1987.

Kessler, Ronald. *Spy vs. Spy: Stalking Soviet Spies in America*. New York: Charles Scribner's Sons, 1988.

Ranelagh, John. *The Agency: The Rise and Decline of the CIA*. New York: Simon and Schuster, 1986.

Treverton, Gregory F. *Covert Action: The Limits of Intervention in the Postwar World*. New York: Basic Books, 1987.

—**PROVOCATION AGENT,** in clandestine and covert intelligence operations, is an agent who provides false information in order to cause suspicion and throw rival intelligence organizations off guard. *See also:* Agent, Agent Authentication, Agent in Place, Agent Net, Agent of Influence, Agent Provocateur, Blow, Blown Agent, Burn, Burnt, Confusion Agent, Dispatched Agent, Double Agent, Handling Agent, Illegal Agent, Informant, Inside Man, Putting in the Plumbing, Recruitment, Recruitment in Place, Special Activities.

References

Becket, Henry S. A. *The Dictionary of Espionage: Spookspeak into English*. New York: Stein and Day, 1986.

Ranelagh, John. *The Agency: The Rise and Decline of the CIA*. New York: Simon and Schuster, 1986.

Treverton, Gregory F. *Covert Action: The Limits of Intervention in the Postwar World*. New York: Basic Books, 1987.

—**PSEUDONYM,** in FBI terminology, is a false name that looks like a true name. *See also:* agent, Agent Authentication, Agent in Place, Agent Net, Agent of Influence, Agent Provocateur, Illegal agent, Informant, Inside Man, Pocket Litter, Provocation Agent, Putting in the Plumbing, Recruitment, Recruitment in Place, Special Activities, Walk-in.

References

Kessler, Ronald. *Spy vs. Spy: Stalking Soviet Spies in America*. New York: Charles Scribner's Sons, 1988.

Ranelagh, John. *The Agency: The Rise and Decline of the CIA*. New York: Simon and Schuster, 1986.

—**PSYCHOLOGICAL ACTION** means using psychological media and supporting activities in peace and war to reduce the enemy's actual or potential prestige in potentially hostile or neutral nations while increasing friendly influence and feelings in the same. *See also:* Psychological Operations, Psychological Warfare.

References

American Bar Association. *Oversight and Accountability of the U.S. Intelligence Agencies: An Evaluation*. Washington, DC: ABA, 1985.

Department of Defense, Joint Chiefs of Staff. *Department of Defense Dictionary of Military and Related Terms*. Washington, DC: GPO, 1986.

Godson, Roy, ed. *Intelligence Problems for the 1980s, Number 3: Counterintelligence*. Washington, DC: National Strategy Information Center, 1980.

Laqueur, Walter. *A World of Secrets*. New York: Basic Books, 1985.

Maurer, Alfred C.; Turnstall, Marion D.; and Keagle, James M. *Intelligence Policy and Process*. Boulder, CO: Westview Press, 1985.

Treverton, Gregory F. *Covert Action: The Limits of Intervention in the Postwar World*. New York: Basic Books, 1987.

Turner, Stansfield. *Secrecy and Democracy: The CIA in Transition*. Boston: Houghton Mifflin, 1985.

—**PSYCHOLOGICAL CONSOLIDATION** involves actions that are intended to establish and maintain order and security in a combat zone and rear areas of friendly forces and to gain the support of the local population in a territory occupied by friendly forces. *See also:* Psychological Operations, Psychological Warfare.

References

American Bar Association. *Oversight and Accountability of the U.S. Intelligence Agencies: An Evaluation.* Washington, DC: ABA, 1985.

Department of Defense, Joint Chiefs of Staff. *Department of Defense Dictionary of Military and Related Terms.* Washington, DC: GPO, 1986.

Godson, Roy, ed. *Intelligence Problems for the 1980s, Number 3: Counterintelligence.* Washington, DC: National Strategy Information Center, 1980.

Maurer, Alfred C.; Turnstall, Marion D.; and Keagle, James M. *Intelligence Policy and Process.* Boulder, CO: Westview Press, 1985.

—**PSYCHOLOGICAL MEDIA** are the technical and nontechnical media that establish any kind of communication with a target audience. *See also:* Psychological Operations, Psychological Warfare.

References

American Bar Association. *Oversight and Accountability of the U.S. Intelligence Agencies: An Evaluation.* Washington, DC: ABA, 1985.

Department of Defense, Joint Chiefs of Staff. *Department of Defense Dictionary of Military and Related Terms.* Washington, DC: GPO, 1986.

Godson, Roy, ed. *Intelligence Problems for the 1980s, Number 3: Counterintelligence.* Washington, DC: National Strategy Information Center, 1980.

Maurer, Alfred C.; Turnstall, Marion D.; and Keagle, James M. *Intelligence Policy and Process.* Boulder, CO: Westview Press, 1985.

—**PSYCHOLOGICAL OPERATIONS (PSYOP)** are planned peacetime or wartime psychological activities that are directed toward enemy, friendly, or neutral audiences, with the goal of creating attitudes and behavior that will facilitate achieving one's political or military objectives. They include psychological action, psychological warfare, and psychological consolidation. They encompass those political, military, economic, ideological, and information activities that are designed to achieve a certain psychological effect. *See also:* Psychological Warfare.

References

American Bar Association. *Oversight and Accountability of the U.S. Intelligence Agencies: An Evaluation.* Washington, DC: ABA, 1985.

Department of Defense, Joint Chiefs of Staff. *Department of Defense Dictionary of Military and Related Terms.* Washington, DC: GPO, 1986.

Godson, Roy, ed. *Intelligence Problems for the 1980s, Number 1: Elements of Intelligence.* Rev. ed. Washington, DC: National Strategy Information Center, 1983.

———. *Intelligence Problems for the 1980s, Number 3: Counterintelligence.* Washington, DC: National Strategy Information Center, 1980.

Laqueur, Walter. *A World of Secrets.* New York: Basic Books, 1985.

Maurer, Alfred C.; Turnstall, Marion D.; and Keagle, James M. *Intelligence Policy and Process.* Boulder, CO: Westview Press, 1985.

Treverton, Gregory F. *Covert Action: The Limits of Intervention in the Postwar World.* New York: Basic Books, 1987.

Turner, Stansfield. *Secrecy and Democracy: The CIA in Transition.* Boston: Houghton Mifflin, 1985.

—**PSYCHOLOGICAL SITUATION** is the current emotional state, mental disposition, or other behavioral motivation of a target audience. It is founded primarily on national, political, social, economic, and psychological peculiarities but is subject to the influence of circumstances or events. *See also:* Psychological Operations, Psychological Warfare.

References

American Bar Association. *Oversight and Accountability of the U.S. Intelligence Agencies: An Evaluation.* Washington, DC: ABA, 1985.

Department of Defense, Joint Chiefs of Staff. *Department of Defense Dictionary of Military and Related Terms.* Washington, DC: GPO, 1986.

Godson, Roy, ed. *Intelligence Problems for the 1980s, Number 3: Counterintelligence.* Washington, DC: National Strategy Information Center, 1980.

Maurer, Alfred C.; Turnstall, Marion D.; and Keagle, James M. *Intelligence Policy and Process.* Boulder, CO: Westview Press, 1985.

Treverton, Gregory F. *Covert Action: The Limits of Intervention in the Postwar World.* New York: Basic Books, 1987.

—**PSYCHOLOGICAL STRATEGY BOARD (PSB)**, as defined by the Church Committee, was a National Security Council subcommittee that was established in 1951 to determine the desirability of proposed covert action programs and major covert action projects. Its members included departmental representatives and board staff members. It was replaced by the Operations Coordinating Board in 1953. *See also:* Psychological Operations, Psychological Warfare.

References

American Bar Association. *Oversight and Accountability of the U.S. Intelligence Agencies: An Evaluation*. Washington, DC: ABA, 1985.

Fain, Tyrus G.; Plant, Katharine C.; and Milloy, Ross. *The Intelligence Community: History, Organization, and Issues*. Public Documents Series. New York: R.R. Bowker, 1977.

U.S. Congress. Senate. *Final Report of the Senate Select Committee to Study Government Operations with Respect to Intelligence Activities. Report 94-755. Book I, Foreign and Military Intelligence*. Washington, DC: GPO, 1976.

—**PSYCHOLOGICAL THEME** is an idea or topic on which a psychological operation is based. *See also:* Psychological Operations, Psychological Warfare.

References

American Bar Association. *Oversight and Accountability of the U.S. Intelligence Agencies: An Evaluation*. Washington, DC: ABA, 1985.

Department of Defense, Joint Chiefs of Staff. *Department of Defense Dictionary of Military and Related Terms*. Washington, DC: GPO, 1986.

Godson, Roy, ed. *Intelligence Problems for the 1980s, Number 3: Counterintelligence*. Washington, DC: National Strategy Information Center, 1980.

Maurer, Alfred C.; Turnstall, Marion D.; and Keagle, James M. *Intelligence Policy and Process*. Boulder, CO: Westview Press, 1985.

Treverton, Gregory F. *Covert Action: The Limits of Intervention in the Postwar World*. New York: Basic Books, 1987.

—**PSYCHOLOGICAL WARFARE.** The official definition of psychological warfare is the use of the communications media and other psychological means, in a declared emergency or war, with the purpose of bringing psychological pressure to bear on the enemy and to influence favorably the attitudes of hostile groups and other target audiences in areas that are under enemy control. The primary goals are to weaken the enemy's will to engage in or continue hostilities and to reduce his capacity for waging war. As defined by the Church Committee, psychological warfare has a slightly different meaning. It is the planned use of propaganda and other psychological actions to influence opinions, emotions, attitudes, and behavior of hostile foreign groups so as to support the achievement of national policy objectives. *See also:* Psychological Operations, Psychological Warfare Consolidation.

References

American Bar Association. *Oversight and Accountability of the U.S. Intelligence Agencies: An Evaluation*. Washington, DC: ABA, 1985.

Department of Defense, Joint Chiefs of Staff. *Department of Defense Dictionary of Military and Related Terms*. Washington, DC: GPO, 1986.

Godson, Roy, ed. *Intelligence Problems for the 1980s, Number 1: Elements of Intelligence*. Rev. ed. Washington, DC: National Strategy Information Center, 1983.

———. *Intelligence Problems for the 1980s, Number 3: Counterintelligence*. Washington, DC: National Strategy Information Center, 1980.

Laqueur, Walter. *A World of Secrets*. New York: Basic Books, 1985.

Maurer, Alfred C.; Turnstall, Marion D.; and Keagle, James M. *Intelligence Policy and Process*. Boulder, CO: Westview Press, 1985.

Treverton, Gregory F. *Covert Action: The Limits of Intervention in the Postwar World*. New York: Basic Books, 1987.

U.S. Congress. Senate. *Final Report of the Senate Select Committee to Study Government Operations with Respect to Intelligence Activities. Report 94-755. Book I, Foreign and Military Intelligence*. Washington, DC: GPO, 1976.

—**PSYCHOLOGICAL WARFARE CONSOLIDATION** is psychological warfare that is directed toward people in friendly rear areas or in territory occupied by friendly military forces with the goal of facilitating military operations and promoting maximum cooperation among the civilian population. *See also:* Psychological Operations, Psychological Warfare.

References

American Bar Association. *Oversight and Accountability of the U.S. Intelligence Agencies: An Evaluation*. Washington, DC: ABA, 1985.

Department of Defense, Joint Chiefs of Staff. *Department of Defense Dictionary of Military and Related Terms*. Washington, DC: GPO, 1986.

Maurer, Alfred C.; Turnstall, Marion D.; and Keagle, James M. *Intelligence Policy and Process*. Boulder, CO: Westview Press, 1985.

Treverton, Gregory F. *Covert Action: The Limits of Intervention in the Postwar World*. New York: Basic Books, 1987.

—**PUBLIC AFFAIRS.** *See:* Central Intelligence Agency.

—**PUBLIC CRYPTOGRAPHY,** in communications security (COMSEC), means the body of crypto-graphic-related knowledge, study, techniques, and applications that are, or are intended to be, in the public domain. *See also:* Communications Security, Cryptography.

References

Department of Defense, U.S. Army. *Counter-Signals Intelligence (C-SIGINT) Operations*. Field Manual FM 34-62. Washington, DC: Headquarters, Department of the Army, 1986.

————. *Military Intelligence Company (Combat Electronic Warfare and Intelligence) (Armored Cavalry Regiment/Separate Brigade)*. Field Manual FM 34-30. Washington, DC: Headquarters, Department of the Army, 1983.

—**PUBLIC KEY CRYPTOGRAPHY,** in communica-tions security (COMSEC), means a type of cryp-tography in which the encryption process is publicly available and unprotected, but in which part of the decryption process is protected so that only a party with knowledge of both parts of the decryption process can decrypt the enciphered text. *See also:* Communications Security.

References

Department of Defense, U.S. Army. *Counter-Signals Intelligence (C-SIGINT) Operations*. Field Manual FM 34-62. Washington, DC: Headquarters, Department of the Army, 1986.

————. *Military Intelligence Company (Combat Electronic Warfare and Intelligence) (Armored Cavalry Regiment/Separate Brigade)*. Field Manual FM 34-30. Washington, DC: Headquarters, Department of the Army, 1983.

—**PUBLIC LAW 95-111,** entitled "Electronic Sur-veillance Within the United States for Foreign Intelligence Purposes," was enacted by the 95th Congress on October 25, 1978. It placed strin-gent restrictions on the use of electronic surveil-lance. The most significant aspects of the law were that (1) the president, through the attorney general, could authorize electronic surveillance without a court order if the attorney general certified in writing that such surveillance was directed against a foreign power and that there was no likelihood the surveillance would over-hear the conversation of a U.S. person (in this instance, the attorney general was required to notify the congressional intelligence committees of the surveillance); (2) the chief justice of the Supreme Court would appoint seven judges to rule, and three additional judges to sit in review, on warrants requesting permission to conduct surveillance in situations in which information might be collected against U.S. persons; (3) the provisions concerning applying for such permis-sion be followed; (4) the dissemination of the results of such surveillance be highly restricted; (5) the attorney general forward an annual report to Congress identifying the number of requests that had been made, the number that had been approved, the number modified, and the number denied; and (6) the attorney general report to Congress twice a year on the status of all elec-tronic surveillance activity. The law also estab-lished fines that were to be paid to citizens who had been unjustly surveilled as well as fines and sentences that could be imposed on those who had accomplished the improper surveillance.

The significance of the law was that it reflected the current outrage in Congress concerning the intelligence activities that had been revealed in the recent congressional investigations. This law and other congressional actions, including cre-ating standing oversight committees and passing additional legislation, reflected congressional intention not to permit additional excesses by the Intelligence Community.

—**PUBLIC LAW 96-456,** the "Classified Informa-tion Procedures Act," was approved by Congress on October 15, 1980. The law attempted to deal with the problem of "graymail." Graymail in-volved situations in which defendants in spy cases threatened to reveal or request classified information during their trials. In this way they hoped to discourage the government from prose-cuting them, for fear that the classified informa-tion would be compromised. Conversely, if they were tried and were denied permission to admit the information into evidence, then there was a good chance that a mistrial would be declared.

Responding to this problem, Congress passed Public Law 96-456 (which appears as Appendix N to this book), thereby establishing lengthy but nonetheless workable procedures for trying such cases.

The significance of the act was twofold. First, it rather effectively prevented the further use of the graymail tactic in trials. Second, the act indicated a moderation of the outrage that Congress had felt earlier concerning the excesses of the Intelligence Community. *See also:* Graymail.

—**PUDDING (OR PUDDING CLUB)** is a derogatory or sarcastic term used by Western intelligence agents to refer to the United Nations.

References

Deacon, Richard. *Spyclopedia: An Encyclopedia of Spies, Secret Services, Operations, Jargon, and All Subjects Related to the World of Espionage.* London: Macdonald, 1987.

—**PUGH, ERNEST C.,** while a sailor stationed at the Defense Language Institute, Monterey, California, in 1982, went to the Soviet Consulate in San Francisco and attempted to defect. He was discharged from the Navy.

References

Allen, Thomas B., and Polmar, Norman. *Merchants of Treason: America's Secrets for Sale.* New York: Delacorte Press, 1988.

—**PUT HIM ON THE BOX** is intelligence jargon for administering a lie detector test to an individual. *See also:* Flutter, Fluttered.

References

Clancy, Tom. *The Cardinal of the Kremlin.* New York: Putnam, 1988.

—**PUTTING IN THE PLUMBING** is a term used in clandestine and covert intelligence operations. It means to organize the support necessary for an impending operation. The 1960s television show "Mission Impossible" had fascinating scenes of the detail and trouble that went into such preparations. *See also:* Agent Authentication, Agent in Place, Agent of Influence, Agent Provocateur, Pocket Litter, Pseudonym, Special Activities.

References

Becket, Henry S. A. *The Dictionary of Espionage: Spookspeak into English.* New York: Stein and Day, 1986.

Deacon, Richard. *Spyclopedia: An Encyclopedia of Spies, Secret Services, Operations, Jargon, and All Subjects Related to the World of Espionage.* London: Macdonald, 1987.

Ranelagh, John. *The Agency: The Rise and Decline of the CIA.* New York: Simon and Schuster, 1986.

—**PUZZLE PALACE** is a nickname for the National Security Agency. It also the title of an excellent book by James Bamford, which is the only available study of the agency. *See also:* National Security Agency.

References

Bamford, James. *The Puzzle Palace: A Report on America's Most Secret Agency.* New York: Penguin Books, 1983.

Deacon, Richard. *Spyclopedia: An Encyclopedia of Spies, Secret Services, Operations, Jargon, and All Subjects Related to the World of Espionage.* London: Macdonald, 1987.

Laqueur, Walter. *A World of Secrets.* New York: Basic Books, 1985.

—**Q** is a special clearance that governs access to nuclear information. It is assigned by the Department of Energy.

References

Allen, Thomas B., and Polmar, Norman. *Merchants of Treason: America's Secrets for Sale.* New York: Delacorte Press, 1988.

—**QUARTERLY INTELLIGENCE PRODUCTION LISTING (QUIP)** is a catalog of Defense Intelligence Agency documents published during a three-month period and is one of the most formal methods for analysts to identify documents that have been recently published. *See also:* Intelligence Product, Product, Production.

References

Von Hoene, John P. A. *Intelligence User's Guide.* Washington, DC: DIA, 1983.

—**QUICKLOOK AIRCRAFT** is an Army tactical intelligence (TACINT) airborne ELINT collection and emitter location system. Mounted in the RV-1D aircraft, QUICKLOOK provides classification and location of electronic emitters to a ground-based data collection and emitter location facility via digital downlink. Like GUARD-RAIL, QUICKLOOK missions are flown in a stand-off mode. *See also:* Reconnaissance.

References

Department of Defense, U.S. Army. *Military Intelligence Battalion Combat Electronic Warfare and Intelligence (Aerial Exploitation) (Corps).* Field Manual FM 34-22. Washington, DC: Headquarters, Department of the Army, 1984.

—**QUICK REACTION REQUIREMENT (QRR)** is an Army intelligence term for a requirement for immediate production in order to satisfy a consumer's urgent need for intelligence. *See also:* Battlefield Intelligence.

References

Department of Defense, U.S. Army. *RDTE Managers Intelligence and Threat Support Guide.* Alexandria, VA: Headquarters, Army Materiel Development and Readiness Command, 1983.

—**QUICK TRIP AROUND THE HORN** is a term used in clandestine and covert intelligence operations. It is a radio operator's check on communications activity. *See also:* Illegal Communication, Sign of Life Signal.

References

Deacon, Richard. *Spyclopedia: An Encyclopedia of Spies, Secret Services, Operations, Jargon, and All Subjects Related to the World of Espionage.* London: Macdonald, 1987.

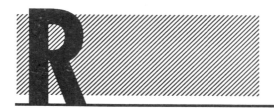

R-12 is a term used in clandestine intelligence operations. It is a small bug that can be inserted in a telephone and then called up from anywhere in the world to eavesdrop on conversations. *See also:* Bug, Bugging, Concealment, Concealment Devices, Harmonica Bug, Putting in the Plumbing, Sterile Telephone.

References

Deacon, Richard. *Spyclopedia: An Encyclopedia of Spies, Secret Services, Operations, Jargon, and All Subjects Related to the World of Espionage.* London: Macdonald, 1987.

RABBLE ROUSER INDEX, according to Henry Becket, was an FBI file used to target individuals for its COINTELPRO operations. It eventually included people in the Black Panthers, Southern Christian Leadership Conference, Ku Klux Clan, and Students for a Democratic Society. It has been abolished. *See also:* COINTELPRO.

References

Becket, Henry S. A. *The Dictionary of Espionage: Spookspeak into English.* New York: Stein and Day, 1986.

Treverton, Gregory F. *Covert Action: The Limits of Intervention in the Postwar World.* New York: Basic Books, 1987.

RADAR is an acronym for RAdio Detection And Ranging. It is a method, system, or a technique for using beamed, reflected, and timed electromagnetic radiation to detect, locate, or track objects or to measure altitude.

References

Godson, Roy, ed. *Intelligence Problems for the 1980s, Number 1: Elements of Intelligence.* Rev. ed. Washington, DC: National Strategy Information Center, 1983.

Laqueur, Walter. *A World of Secrets.* New York: Basic Books, 1985.

Maurer, Alfred C.; Turnstall, Marion D.; and Keagle, James M. *Intelligence Policy and Process.* Boulder, CO: Westview Press, 1985.

Reeves, Robert; Anson, Abraham; and Landen, David. *Manual of Remote Sensing.* Falls Church, VA: American Society of Photogrammetry, 1975.

Turner, Stansfield. *Secrecy and Democracy: The CIA in Transition.* Boston: Houghton Mifflin, 1985.

RADAR ABSORBENT MATERIAL is used as a radar camouflage device in order to reduce the radar cross section or echo area of an object. *See also:* Radar.

References

Department of Defense, U.S. Army. *Counter-Signals Intelligence (C-SIGINT) Operations.* Field Manual FM 34 62. Washington, DC: Headquarters, Department of the Army, 1986.

———. *Military Intelligence Battalion Combat Electronic Warfare and Intelligence (Aerial Exploitation) (Corps).* Field Manual FM 34-22. Washington, DC: Headquarters, Department of the Army, 1984.

———. *Military Intelligence Company (Combat Electronic Warfare and Intelligence) (Armored Cavalry Regiment/Separate Brigade).* Field Manual FM 34-30. Washington, DC: Headquarters, Department of the Army, 1983.

Turner, Stansfield. *Secrecy and Democracy: The CIA in Transition.* Boston: Houghton Mifflin, 1985.

RADAR BUTTON is a device that pinpoints the carrier's location back to a base so that his intelligence agency knows where he is at all times and can send help if it is needed. *See also:* Radar.

References

Deacon, Richard. *Spyclopedia: An Encyclopedia of Spies, Secret Services, Operations, Jargon, and All Subjects Related to the World of Espionage.* London: Macdonald, 1987.

RADAR EXPLOITATION REPORT (RADAREXREP) is a report used to disseminate the results that have been obtained from the rapid analysis of radar imagery and debriefing the air crew that flew the radar imagery mission. The report discusses those targets that were cited in the mission tasking, addressing each target separately. *See also:* Radar.

References

Department of Defense, U.S. Army. *Intelligence Imagery.* Field Manual FM 34-55. Washington, DC: Headquarters, Department of the Army.

————. *Military Intelligence Battalion Combat Electronic Warfare and Intelligence (Aerial Exploitation) (Corps)*. Field Manual FM 34-22. Washington, DC: Headquarters, Department of the Army, 1984.

————. *Military Intelligence Battalion (Combat Electronic Warfare Intelligence) (Division)*. Field Manual FM 34-10. Washington, DC: Headquarters, Department of the Army, 1981.

————. *Military Intelligence Company (Combat Electronic Warfare and Intelligence) (Armored Cavalry Regiment/Separate Brigade)*. Field Manual FM 34-30. Washington, DC: Headquarters, Department of the Army, 1983.

—**RADAR INTELLIGENCE (RADINT)** is an intelligence imagery and photoreconnaissance term for intelligence information that is derived from information collected by radar. The vulnerability of the platform's operating radars is generally offset by the penetrating capability, resolution, and geometric fidelity of radar over extreme distances. Because microwaves can penetrate virtually all atmospheric conditions, airborne radars are limited only by the ability of their platforms to operate in adverse weather conditions. *See also:* Radar.

References

Department of Defense, Defense Intelligence College. *Glossary of Intelligence Terms and Definitions*. Washington, DC: DIC, 1987.

Department of Defense, U.S. Army. *Intelligence Imagery*. Field Manual FM 34-55. Washington, DC: Headquarters, Department of the Army, 1985.

————. *Military Intelligence Battalion Combat Electronic Warfare and Intelligence (Aerial Exploitation) (Corps)*. Field Manual FM 34-22. Washington, DC: Headquarters, Department of the Army, 1984.

————. *Military Intelligence Battalion (Combat Electronic Warfare Intelligence) (Division)*. Field Manual FM 34-10. Washington, DC: Headquarters, Department of the Army, 1981.

————. *Military Intelligence Company (Combat Electronic Warfare and Intelligence) (Armored Cavalry Regiment/Separate Brigade)*. Field Manual FM 34-30. Washington, DC: Headquarters, Department of the Army, 1983.

Godson, Roy, ed. *Intelligence Problems for the 1980s, Number 5: Clandestine Collection*. Washington, DC: National Strategy Information Center, 1982.

Laqueur, Walter. *A World of Secrets*. New York: Basic Books, 1985.

Maurer, Alfred C.; Turnstall, Marion D.; and Keagle, James M. *Intelligence Policy and Process*. Boulder, CO: Westview Press, 1985.

—**RADAR RECONNAISSANCE** is reconnaissance by means of radar to collect information on enemy activity and to determine the nature of the terrain. *See also:* Radar, Triangulation.

References

Department of Defense, Joint Chiefs of Staff. *Department of Defense Dictionary of Military and Related Terms*. Washington, DC: GPO, 1986.

Department of Defense, U.S. Army. *Military Intelligence Battalion Combat Electronic Warfare and Intelligence (Aerial Exploitation) (Corps)*. Field Manual FM 34-22. Washington, DC: Headquarters, Department of the Army, 1984.

————. *Military Intelligence Battalion (Combat Electronic Warfare Intelligence) (Division)*. Field Manual FM 34-10. Washington, DC: Headquarters, Department of the Army, 1981.

————. *Military Intelligence Company (Combat Electronic Warfare and Intelligence) (Armored Cavalry Regiment/Separate Brigade)*. Field Manual FM 34-30. Washington, DC: Headquarters, Department of the Army, 1983.

Turner, Stansfield. *Secrecy and Democracy: The CIA in Transition*. Boston: Houghton Mifflin, 1985.

—**RADIATION INTELLIGENCE (RINT)** is a general intelligence term. Radiation intelligence concerns the functions and characteristics that are derived from information obtained from unintentional electromagnetic energy emanating from foreign sources. It does not include such energy emanating from nuclear detonations or radioactive sources. *See also:* Active Electronic Countermeasures, Active Jamming, Brute Force Jamming, Combat Electronic Warfare Intelligence, Communications Jamming, Complex Barrage Jamming, Countermeasures, Deception, Deception Jammer, Deception Material, Drone, Electronic Camouflage, Electronic Counter Countermeasures, Electronic Countermeasures, Electronic Deception, Electronic Jamming, Electronic Warfare, Electronic Warfare Support Measures, Escort Jamming, Garble, Jammer, Jammer Band (width), Jamming, Jamming Effectiveness, Jamming Platform, Jamming Signal, Jamming Target, Multitarget Jamming, Noise Jamming, Noise Modulated Jamming, Passive Jamming, Repeater Jammer, Self-Protection Jamming, Spot Jamming, Sweep Jamming.

References

Department of Defense, Defense Intelligence College. *Glossary of Intelligence Terms and Definitions.* Washington, DC: DIC, 1987.

Department of Defense, Joint Chiefs of Staff. *Department of Defense Dictionary of Military and Related Terms.* Washington, DC: GPO, 1986.

Godson, Roy, ed. *Intelligence Problems for the 1980s, Number 1: Elements of Intelligence.* Rev. ed. Washington, DC: National Strategy Information Center, 1983.

Maurer, Alfred C.; Turnstall, Marion D.; and Keagle, James M. *Intelligence Policy and Process.* Boulder, CO: Westview Press, 1985.

Turner, Stansfield. *Secrecy and Democracy: The CIA in Transition.* Boston: Houghton Mifflin, 1985.

—**RADIO DECEPTION** is a term used in signals intelligence, communications security, communications intelligence, operations security, and signals analysis. It means using a radio to deceive the enemy. It includes sending false messages and using deceptive headings and enemy call signs. *See also:* Communications Security, Electronic Warfare.

References

Department of Defense, Joint Chiefs of Staff. *Department of Defense Dictionary of Military and Related Terms.* Washington, DC: GPO, 1986.

Department of Defense, U.S. Army. *Military Intelligence Battalion Combat Electronic Warfare and Intelligence (Aerial Exploitation) (Corps).* Field Manual FM 34-22. Washington, DC: Headquarters, Department of the Army, 1984.

———. *Military Intelligence Company (Combat Electronic Warfare and Intelligence) (Armored Cavalry Regiment/Separate Brigade).* Field Manual FM 34-30. Washington, DC: Headquarters, Department of the Army, 1983.

Turner, Stansfield. *Secrecy and Democracy: The CIA in Transition.* Boston: Houghton Mifflin, 1985.

—**RADIO DIRECTION FINDING (RDF)** is a term used in signals intelligence, communications security, communications intelligence, operations security, and signals analysis. It is radio location in which only the direction of a station can be determined by means of its emissions if there is only one line of bearing, or its location, if more than one station can determine a line of bearing or direction to the transmitter. *See also:* Communications Security, Radio Fix.

References

Department of Defense, Joint Chiefs of Staff. *Department of Defense Dictionary of Military and Related Terms.* Washington, DC: GPO, 1986.

Department of Defense, U.S. Army. *Military Intelligence Company (Combat Electronic Warfare and Intelligence) (Armored Cavalry Regiment/ Separate Brigade).* Field Manual FM 34-30. Washington, DC: Headquarters, Department of the Army, 1983.

Godson, Roy, ed. *Intelligence Problems for the 1980s, Number 1: Elements of Intelligence.* Rev. ed. Washington, DC: National Strategy Information Center, 1983.

Laqueur, Walter. *A World of Secrets.* New York: Basic Books, 1985.

Maurer, Alfred C.; Turnstall, Marion D.; and Keagle, James M. *Intelligence Policy and Process.* Boulder, CO: Westview Press, 1985.

Turner, Stansfield. *Secrecy and Democracy: The CIA in Transition.* Boston: Houghton Mifflin, 1985.

—**RADIOELECTRONIC COMBAT (REC)** is an Army tactical intelligence (TACINT) term that means the total integration of electronic warfare with the physical destruction of resources in order to deny the enemy the use of his electronic control systems, while protecting one's own electronic control systems.

References

Department of Defense, U.S. Army. *Intelligence and Electronic Warfare Operations.* Field Manual FM 34-1. Washington, DC: Headquarters, Department of the Army, 1984.

———. *Military Intelligence Battalion (Combat Electronic Warfare Intelligence) (Division).* Field Manual FM 34-10. Washington, DC: Headquarters, Department of the Army, 1981.

———. *Military Intelligence Battalion (CEWI) (Operations) (Corps).* Field Manual FM 34-21. Washington, DC: Headquarters, Department of the Army, 1982.

———. *Military Intelligence Company (Combat Electronic Warfare and Intelligence) (Armored Cavalry Regiment/Separate Brigade).* Field Manual FM 34-30. Washington, DC: Headquarters, Department of the Army, 1983.

———. *Military Intelligence Group (Combat Electronic Warfare and Intelligence) (Corps).* Field Manual FM 34-20. Washington, DC: Headquarters, Department of the Army, 1983.

—**RADIO FIX** is a term used in signals intelligence, communications security, communications intelligence, operations security, and signals analysis. It is the location of a friendly or enemy radio transmitter and is determined by finding the direction of the transmitter from three or more listening stations. *See also:* Communications Security.

References

Department of Defense, Joint Chiefs of Staff. *Department of Defense Dictionary of Military and Related Terms.* Washington, DC: GPO, 1986.

————. *Military Intelligence Battalion (CEWI) (Operations) (Corps).* Field Manual FM 34-21. Washington, DC: Headquarters, Department of the Army, 1982.

————. *Military Intelligence Company (Combat Electronic Warfare and Intelligence) (Armored Cavalry Regiment/Separate Brigade).* Field Manual FM 34-30. Washington, DC: Headquarters, Department of the Army, 1983.

————. *Military Intelligence Group (Combat Electronic Warfare and Intelligence) (Corps).* Field Manual FM 34-20. Washington, DC: Headquarters, Department of the Army, 1983.

Laqueur, Walter. *A World of Secrets.* New York: Basic Books, 1985.

—**RADIO FREE EUROPE AND RADIO LIBERTY** have been targeted against Eastern Europe and the Soviet Union, respectively. For years they were funded covertly by the Central Intelligence Agency, but as result of the congressional debates of 1971, they were made independent in 1973 under a congressionally chartered Board for International Broadcasting and are now funded openly by the U.S. government. While both may be considered by some to be instruments of propaganda, their credibility rests on their objectivity and accuracy, and the fact that both have been successful for decades attests to the reputations they have developed.

References

Breckinridge, Scott D. *The CIA and the U.S. Intelligence System.* Boulder, CO: Westview Press, 1986.

Corson, William R. *The Armies of Ignorance: The Rise of the American Intelligence Empire.* New York: Dial Press, 1977.

Godson, Roy, ed. *Intelligence Problems for the 1980s, Number 1: Elements of Intelligence.* Rev. ed. Washington, DC: National Strategy Information Center, 1983.

————. *Intelligence Problems for the 1980s, Number 5: Clandestine Collection.* Washington, DC: National Strategy Information Center, 1982.

Maurer, Alfred C.; Turnstall, Marion D.; and Keagle, James M. *Intelligence Policy and Process.* Boulder, CO: Westview Press, 1985.

Treverton, Gregory F. *Covert Action: The Limits of Intervention in the Postwar World.* New York: Basic Books, 1987.

Turner, Stansfield. *Secrecy and Democracy: The CIA in Transition.* Boston: Houghton Mifflin, 1985.

—**RANDOMIZER,** in communications security (COMSEC), refers to a random bit generator that produces patterns used to modify the key variable of crypto-equipment in order to establish a unique point on the key cycle where encryption is to begin. *See also:* Communications Security.

References

Department of Defense, U.S. Army. *Military Intelligence Battalion Combat Electronic Warfare and Intelligence (Aerial Exploitation) (Corps).* Field Manual FM 34-22. Washington, DC: Headquarters, Department of the Army, 1984.

————. *Military Intelligence Battalion (Combat Electronic Warfare Intelligence) (Division).* Field Manual FM 34-10. Washington, DC: Headquarters, Department of the Army, 1981.

————. *Military Intelligence Company (Combat Electronic Warfare and Intelligence) (Armored Cavalry Regiment/Separate Brigade).* Field Manual FM 34-30. Washington, DC: Headquarters, Department of the Army, 1983.

—**RAVEN** is a term used in clandestine and covert intelligence operations to describe a male seducer who lures women into a honey trap. *See also:* Agent, Fur-Lined Seat Cover, Honey Trap, Ladies, Mozhno Girls, Recruitment, Recruitment in Place, Sisters, Taxi.

References

Deacon, Richard. *Spyclopedia: An Encyclopedia of Spies, Secret Services, Operations, Jargon, and All Subjects Related to the World of Espionage.* London: Macdonald, 1987.

Quirk, John; Phillips, David; Cline, Ray; and Pforzheimer, Walter. *The Central Intelligence Agency: A Photographic History.* Guilford, CT: Foreign Intelligence Press, 1986

—**RAW INTELLIGENCE** is a general intelligence term. It is collected intelligence information that has not yet been converted into intelligence. *See also:* Intelligence Cycle, Intelligence Information.

References

Department of Defense, Defense Intelligence College. *Glossary of Intelligence Terms and Definitions.* Washington, DC: DIC, 1987.

Godson, Roy, ed. *Intelligence Problems for the 1980s, Number 1: Elements of Intelligence*. Rev. ed. Washington, DC: National Strategy Information Center, 1983.

Kent, Sherman. *Strategic Intelligence for American World Policy*. Princeton, NJ: Princeton University Press, 1966.

Laqueur, Walter. *A World of Secrets*. New York: Basic Books, 1985.

Maurer, Alfred C.; Turnstall, Marion D.; and Keagle, James M. *Intelligence Policy and Process*. Boulder, CO: Westview Press, 1985.

Treverton, Gregory F. *Covert Action: The Limits of Intervention in the Postwar World*. New York: Basic Books, 1987.

Turner, Stansfield. *Secrecy and Democracy: The CIA in Transition*. Boston: Houghton Mifflin, 1985.

Treverton, Gregory F. *Covert Action: The Limits of Intervention in the Postwar World*. New York: Basic Books, 1987.

U.S. Congress. Senate. *Alleged Assassination Plots Involving Foreign Leaders: An Interim Report of the Select Committee to Study Governmental Operations with Respect to Intelligence Activities*. 94th Congress, 1st sess., Nov. 20, 1975. S. Rept. 94-465.

————. *Final Report of the Senate Select Committee to Study Government Operations with Respect to Intelligence Activities. Report 94-755. Book I, Foreign and Military Intelligence*. Washington, DC: GPO, 1976.

Von Hoene, John P. A. *Intelligence User's Guide*. Washington, DC: DIA, 1983.

—**RAYBORN, VICE ADMIRAL WILLIAM F., JR., U.S. NAVY,** was born on June 8, 1905, in Decatur, Texas. He graduated from the U.S. Naval Academy in 1928 and from the U.S. Naval War College in 1952. His naval career included a tour as director of the Special Projects Office, U.S. Navy, which developed the Polaris missile for the Fleet Ballistic Missile System, and as deputy chief of naval operations (development) from 1962 to 1963. He retired from the Navy on September 1, 1963, and worked in private industry until 1965. He was appointed director of Central Intelligence by President Johnson on April 11, 1965. His appointment was confirmed by the Senate on April 22, and he was sworn in on April 28, 1965. He resigned on June 30, 1966, to return to private industry. *See also:* Central Intelligence Agency.

References
Breckinridge, Scott D. *The CIA and the U.S. Intelligence System*. Boulder, CO: Westview Press, 1986.

Brinkley, David A., and Hull, Andrew W. *Estimative Intelligence: A Textbook on the History, Products, Uses, and Writing of Intelligence Estimates*. Columbus, OH: Battelle, 1979.

Cline, Ray S. *The CIA Under Reagan, Bush, and Casey*. Washington, DC: Acropolis Books, 1981.

Corson, William R. *The Armies of Ignorance: The Rise of the American Intelligence Empire*. New York: Dial Press, 1977.

Lowenthal, Mark M. *U.S. Intelligence: Evolution and Anatomy*. New York: Praeger, 1984.

Quirk, John; Phillips, David; Cline, Ray; and Pforzheimer, Walter. *The Central Intelligence Agency: A Photographic History*. Guilford, CT: Foreign Intelligence Press, 1986.

—**REACTIVE THREAT** is an Army term for devices, tactical techniques, and systems that could be adopted by a potential enemy in response to a U.S. system that is being developed.

References
Department of Defense, U.S. Army. *RDTE Managers Intelligence and Threat Support Guide*. Alexandria, VA: Headquarters, Army Materiel Development and Readiness Command, 1983.

—**READINESS CONDITION (REDCON).** *See:* Operational Readiness.

—**REAGAN, RONALD.** President Reagan inherited a difficult situation from the Carter administration. The Intelligence Community had been decimated by the congressional and presidential investigations and by its association with the intelligence failures in Iran and the Soviet brigade in Cuba. Reagan's administration was noteworthy for its many positive and for its few negative effects on the Intelligence Community.

In respect to positive accomplishments, Reagan shifted the focus of presidential oversight away from the types of intelligence operations that were being conducted to the quality of intelligence collection, analysis, and reporting. His appointment of William Casey as director of Central Intelligence (DCI), although controversial, initially had a positive affect on the CIA. The President also issued Executive Orders that protected the identities of intelligence agents and curtailed the information that had to be provided in response to Freedom of Information requests. Finally, he restored the President's Foreign Intelligence Advisory Board (PFIAB) and directed its focus toward contributing constructively to improving the quality of U.S. intelligence. However, as impressive as these accomplishments were, they were diminished somewhat by the Iran-Contra scandal.

In summary, President Reagan's performance vis-à-vis the Intelligence Community should be given high marks. He reversed the restrictions of the Carter administration, appointed a DCI who substantially improved the morale and performance of the agency, and reestablished the presidential oversight mechanisms. The Iran-Contra operation and its divulgence were unfortunate, but in 1989 it was still too early to judge the long-term effects, if any, that the operation would have on the Intelligence Community. *See also:* Executive Oversight, Iran.

References

American Bar Association. *Oversight and Accountability of the U.S. Intelligence Agencies: An Evaluation.* Washington, DC: ABA, 1985.

Breckinridge, Scott D. *The CIA and the U.S. Intelligence System.* Boulder, CO: Westview Press, 1986.

Brinkley, David A., and Hull, Andrew W. *Estimative Intelligence: A Textbook on the History, Products, Uses, and Writing of Intelligence Estimates.* Columbus, OH: Battelle, 1979.

Laqueur, Walter. *A World of Secrets.* New York: Basic Books, 1985.

Lowenthal, Mark M. *U.S. Intelligence: Evolution and Anatomy.* New York: Praeger, 1984.

Maurer, Alfred C.; Turnstall, Marion D.; and Keagle, James M. *Intelligence Policy and Process.* Boulder, CO: Westview Press, 1985.

Treverton, Gregory F. *Covert Action: The Limits of Intervention in the Postwar World.* New York: Basic Books, 1987.

Turner, Stansfield. *Secrecy and Democracy: The CIA in Transition.* Boston: Houghton Mifflin, 1985.

U.S. Congress. Senate. *Alleged Assassination Plots Involving Foreign Leaders: An Interim Report of the Select Committee to Study Governmental Operations with Respect to Intelligence Activities.* 94th Congress, 1st sess., Nov. 20, 1975. S. Rept. 94-465.

Von Hoene, John P. A. *Intelligence User's Guide.* Washington, DC: DIA, 1983.

—**REAL TIME** is the absence of delay, except for the time necessary to transmit the information, between the occurrence of an event and the receipt of the news at some other location. *See also:* Near Real Time, Reporting Interval.

References

Department of Defense, Joint Chiefs of Staff. *Department of Defense Dictionary of Military and Related Terms.* Washington, DC: GPO, 1986.

Godson, Roy, ed. *Intelligence Problems for the 1980s, Number 1: Elements of Intelligence.* Rev. ed. Washington, DC: National Strategy Information Center, 1983.

Maurer, Alfred C.; Turnstall, Marion D.; and Keagle, James M. *Intelligence Policy and Process.* Boulder, CO: Westview Press, 1985.

—**REAM, JOSEPH H.,** served as deputy director of the National Security Agency from November 1956 to October 1957. Although he served less than a year and left in order to work with CBS, the practice of appointing of a civilian to the deputy directorship was continued. *See also:* National Security Agency.

References

Bamford, James. *The Puzzle Palace: A Report on America's Most Secret Agency.* New York: Penguin Books, 1983.

—**REAR AREA** is an Army tactical term that means the area to the rear of the main battle area in which supply, maintenance, support, communication centers, and administrative echelons are located.

References

Department of Defense, U.S. Army. *Intelligence and Electronic Warfare Operations.* Field Manual FM 34-1. Washington, DC: Headquarters, Department of the Army, 1984.

————. *Military Intelligence Battalion (CEWI) (Operations) (Corps).* Field Manual FM 34-21. Washington, DC: Headquarters, Department of the Army, 1982.

————. *Military Intelligence Group (Combat Electronic Warfare and Intelligence) (Corps).* Field Manual FM 34-20. Washington, DC: Headquarters, Department of the Army, 1983.

—**REASONABLE BELIEF** is a term that resulted from the Department of Defense implementation of Presidential Executive Order 12333, "United States Intelligence Activities," dated December 4, 1981. It is defined as a belief that arises when the facts and circumstances are such that a reasonable person would hold the belief. Reasonable belief must rest on facts and circumstances that can be articulated; hunches or intuition are not sufficient. It can be based on experience, training, and knowledge of foreign intelligence or counterintelligence work applied to the facts and circumstances at hand, so that a trained and experienced "reasonable person" might hold a reasonable belief sufficient to satisfy this criterion when someone unfamiliar with foreign intelligence or counterintelligence might not.

References

Department of Defense. *Activities of DoD Intelligence Components that Affect U.S. Persons (Department of Defense Directive 5240.1).* Washington, DC: DoD, 1982.

Godson, Roy, ed. *Intelligence Problems for the 1980s, Number 1: Elements of Intelligence.* Rev. ed. Washington, DC: National Strategy Information Center, 1983.

Maurer, Alfred C.; Turnstall, Marion D.; and Keagle, James M. *Intelligence Policy and Process.* Boulder, CO: Westview Press, 1985.

Turner, Stansfield. *Secrecy and Democracy: The CIA in Transition.* Boston: Houghton Mifflin, 1985.

—**REASONABLE DOUBT** concerns the need to classify a given piece of information. When such a doubt exists, the information is treated as if it were classified until an authoritative determination is made. Once such a determination is made, the information is classified accordingly or, if it has been declared to be unclassified, then it is not given a classification. *See also:* Classification, Classification Authority, Classification Review, Classified Information, Declassification, Decompartmentation, Information Security, Open Source Information, Open Sources, Security, Sensitive Compartmented Information.

References

Department of Defense. Information Security Oversight Office. *Directive No. 1: National Security Information.* As reproduced in *Federal Register,* June 25, 1982, pp. 27836- 27841.

Godson, Roy, ed. *Intelligence Problems for the 1980s, Number 1: Elements of Intelligence.* Rev. ed. Washington, DC: National Strategy Information Center, 1983.

Maurer, Alfred C.; Turnstall, Marion D.; and Keagle, James M. *Intelligence Policy and Process.* Boulder, CO: Westview Press, 1985.

Turner, Stansfield. *Secrecy and Democracy: The CIA in Transition.* Boston: Houghton Mifflin, 1985.

—**RECIPIENT** is a intelligence security and counterintelligence term for a person who is authorized to receive or have knowledge of sensitive compartmented information (SCI) activities. *See also:* Authorized, Classification, Classified Information, Compartmentation, Controlled Area, Controlled Dissemination, Information Security, Need-to-Know, Need-to-Know Principle, Security Clearance, Sensitive Compartmented Information, Sensitive Compartmented Information Facility, Special Security Office, Special Security Officer System.

References

Godson, Roy, ed. *Intelligence Problems for the 1980s, Number 1: Elements of Intelligence.* Rev. ed. Washington, DC: National Strategy Information Center, 1983.

Maurer, Alfred C.; Turnstall, Marion D.; and Keagle, James M. *Intelligence Policy and Process.* Boulder, CO: Westview Press, 1985.

—**RECLAMA** pertains to budgeting. It is a formal restatement and presentation of budget requirements to the Office of the Secretary of Defense (OSD), Office of Management and Budget (OMB), or the Congress in further justification of that portion of a service's requirements that the reviewing authorities have not funded. *See also:* Budget.

References

Pickett, George. "Congress, the Budget, and Intelligence." In *Intelligence Policy and Process,* edited by Alfred C. Maurer, Marion D. Turnstall, and James M. Keagle. Boulder, CO: Westview Press, 1985.

—**RECOGNITION SIGNAL** is a term used in clandestine and covert intelligence operations to describe a discreet but visible sign that is made to an unknown agent that you are an agent that he should contact. *See also:* Alternate Meet, Establishing Bonafides, Go-Away, Make, Making a Pass, Meet Area, Movements Analysis, Shadow, Surveillance.

References

Becket, Henry S. A. *The Dictionary of Espionage: Spookspeak into English.* New York: Stein and Day, 1986.

Department of Defense, Joint Chiefs of Staff. *Department of Defense Dictionary of Military and Related Terms.* Washington, DC: GPO, 1986.

Kessler, Ronald. *Spy vs. Spy: Stalking Soviet Spies in America.* New York: Charles Scribner's Sons, 1988.

—**RECONNAISSANCE (RECCE or RECON).** (1) Reconnaissance is an operation intended to gather information either on the activities, resources, or forces of a foreign nation or on the meteorological, hydrographic, or geographic characteristics of an area. Reconnaissance can be through visual observation or another means. (2) Reconnaissance is also an Army tactical intelligence (TACINT) term that means a mission undertaken to obtain, by visual observation or other detection methods, information about the activities and resources of an enemy or a potential enemy; or to collect data concerning the meteorological, hydrographic, or geographic characteristics of a particular area. (3) As defined by the Church Committee, reconnaissance is a mission that is undertaken to obtain, by observation or other detection methods, information about the activities and resources of foreign states. *See also:* Aerial Reconnaissance.

References

Department of Defense, Defense Intelligence College. *Glossary of Intelligence Terms and Definitions.* Washington, DC: DIC, 1987.

Department of Defense, Joint Chiefs of Staff. *Department of Defense Dictionary of Military and Related Terms.* Washington, DC: GPO, 1986.

Department of Defense, U.S. Army. *Military Intelligence Battalion Combat Electronic Warfare and Intelligence (Aerial Exploitation) (Corps).* Field Manual FM 34-22. Washington, DC: Headquarters, Department of the Army, 1984.

————. *Military Intelligence Company (Combat Electronic Warfare and Intelligence) (Armored Cavalry Regiment/Separate Brigade).* Field Manual FM 34-30. Washington, DC: Headquarters, Department of the Army, 1983.

Maurer, Alfred C.; Turnstall, Marion D.; and Keagle, James M. *Intelligence Policy and Process.* Boulder, CO: Westview Press, 1985.

—**RECONNAISSANCE AND SURVEILLANCE** is an official term that has been defined by the Defense Intelligence Agency for one of its functional areas. It means "obtaining through observation or other detection methods, information about foreign activities and resources and data concerning the meteorological, hydrographic or geographic characteristics of a particular area and maintaining systemic watch of air, surface, or subsurface areas by visual, electronic, photographic or other means. *See also:* Reconnaissance.

References

Department of Defense, Defense Intelligence Agency. *Defense Intelligence Agency Manual 22-2.* Washington, DC: DIA, 1979.

Godson, Roy, ed. *Intelligence Problems for the 1980s, Number 1: Elements of Intelligence.* Rev. ed. Washington, DC: National Strategy Information Center, 1983.

Kent, Sherman. *Strategic Intelligence for American World Policy.* Princeton, NJ: Princeton University Press, 1966.

Laqueur, Walter. *A World of Secrets.* New York: Basic Books, 1985.

Maurer, Alfred C.; Turnstall, Marion D.; and Keagle, James M. *Intelligence Policy and Process.* Boulder, CO: Westview Press, 1985.

Treverton, Gregory F. *Covert Action: The Limits of Intervention in the Postwar World.* New York: Basic Books, 1987.

Turner, Stansfield. *Secrecy and Democracy: The CIA in Transition.* Boston: Houghton Mifflin, 1985.

—**RECONNAISSANCE EXPLOITATION REPORT (RECCEXREP)** is an intelligence imagery and photoreconnaissance term for the format used to report the results of a tactical air reconnaissance mission. Whenever possible, it should include the interpretation of sensor imagery resulting from the mission. It provides the first rapid analysis of imagery and debriefing of the air crew that flew the reconnaissance mission. The report addresses the targets that were requested in the mission tasking, addressing each of the targets separately. *See also:* Reconnaissance.

References

Department of Defense, Joint Chiefs of Staff. *Department of Defense Dictionary of Military and Related Terms.* Washington, DC: GPO, 1986.

—**RECONNAISSANCE IN FORCE** is an offensive operation that is intended to discover or test the enemy's strength or to obtain other information. *See also:* Reconnaissance.

References

Department of Defense, Joint Chiefs of Staff. *Department of Defense Dictionary of Military and Related Terms.* Washington, DC: GPO, 1986.

—**RECONNAISSANCE PATROL.** *See:* Patrol.

—**RECONNAISSANCE PHOTOGRAPHY** is an intelligence imagery and photoreconnaissance term for photography that has been taken to obtain information on the results of bombing, or on enemy movements, concentrations, activities or forces. *See also:* Aerial Photography.

References

Department of Defense, Joint Chiefs of Staff. *Department of Defense Dictionary of Military and Related Terms.* Washington, DC: GPO, 1986.

Turner, Stansfield. *Secrecy and Democracy: The CIA in Transition.* Boston: Houghton Mifflin, 1985.

—**RECORDING,** in the Army tactical intelligence (TACINT) context, is a step in the signals intelligence (SIGINT) process. *See:* SIGINT Process.

References

Department of Defense, Joint Chiefs of Staff. *Department of Defense Dictionary of Military and Related Terms.* Washington, DC: GPO, 1986.

Department of Defense, U.S. Army. *Counter-Signals Intelligence (C-SIGINT) Operations.* Field Manual FM 34-62. Washington, DC: Headquarters, Department of the Army, 1986.

Treverton, Gregory F. *Covert Action: The Limits of Intervention in the Postwar World.* New York: Basic Books, 1987.

—**RECOUPMENT** is a budgeting and finance term that is of importance in intelligence budgeting. It refers to funds that become excess to programs for the current or previous years and that are transferred in order to finance approved requirements of another program year. *See also:* Reclama.

References

Pickett, George. "Congress, the Budget, and Intelligence." In *Intelligence Policy and Process,* edited by Alfred C. Maurer, Marion D. Turnstall, and James M. Keagle. Boulder, CO: Westview Press, 1985.

—**RECRUITMENT,** in FBI terminology, is the enlisting of an individual to work for an intelligence or counterintelligence service. *See also:* Agent, Agent in Place, Agent of Influence, Agent Provocateur, Confusion Agent, Dispatched Agent, Double Agent, Handling Agent, Illegal Agent, Informant, Inside Man, Provocation Agent, Pseudonym, Recruitment in Place, Special Activities, Walk-In.

References

Godson, Roy, ed. *Intelligence Problems for the 1980s, Number 2: Analysis and Estimates.* Washington, DC: National Strategy Information Center, 1980.

———. *Intelligence Problems for the 1980s, Number 5: Clandestine Collection.* Washington, DC: National Strategy Information Center, 1982.

Turner, Stansfield. *Secrecy and Democracy: The CIA in Transition.* Boston: Houghton Mifflin, 1985.

—**RECRUITMENT IN PLACE** is a term used in clandestine and covert intelligence operations. It occurs when a person agrees to become an agent and stay in his position in his organization or government while reporting on it to an intelligence or security organization of a foreign nation. *See also:* Agent, Agent Authentication, Agent in Place, Agent of Influence, Agent Provocateur, Confusion Agent, Dispatched Agent, Double Agent, Handling Agent, Illegal Agent, Informant, Inside Man, Provocation Agent, Recruitment, Special Activities, Walk-In.

References

Godson, Roy, ed., *Intelligence Problems for the 1980s, Number 2: Analysis and Estimates.* Washington, DC: National Strategy Information Center, 1980.

———. *Intelligence Problems for the 1980s, Number 5: Clandestine Collection.* Washington, DC: National Strategy Information Center, 1982.

Kessler, Ronald. *Spy vs. Spy: Stalking Soviet Spies in America.* New York: Charles Scribner's Sons, 1988.

Turner, Stansfield. *Secrecy and Democracy: The CIA in Transition.* Boston: Houghton Mifflin, 1985.

—**RED/BLACK CONCEPT** is a communications security (COMSEC) term. The red/black concept involves separating electrical and electronic circuits, components, equipment, and systems that handle classified plain language information in electric signal form (red) from those that handle encrypted or unclassified information (black). Red and black terminology is used to clarify specific criteria relating to and differentiating between such circuits, components, equipment, and systems and the areas in which they are contained. *See also:* Jamming.

References

Department of Defense, Defense Intelligence College. *Glossary of Intelligence Terms and Definitions.* Washington, DC: DIC, 1987.

Department of Defense, Joint Chiefs of Staff. *Department of Defense Dictionary of Military and Related Terms.* Washington, DC: GPO, 1986.

Department of Defense, U.S. Army. *Intelligence and Electronic Warfare Operations.* Field Manual FM 34-1. Washington, DC: Headquarters, Department of the Army, 1984.

————. *Military Intelligence Battalion (CEWI) (Operations) (Corps).* Field Manual 34-21. Washington, DC: Headquarters, Department of the Army, 1982.

————. *Military Intelligence Battalion (CEWI) (Tactical Exploitation) (Corps): Counterintelligence, Interrogation, Electronic Warfare.* Field Manual FM 34-23. Washington, DC: Headquarters, Department of the Army, 1985.

————. *Military Intelligence Battalion (Combat Electronic Warfare Intelligence) (Division).* Field Manual FM 34-10. Washington, DC: Headquarters, Department of the Army, 1981.

————. *Military Intelligence Group (Combat Electronic Warfare and Intelligence) (Corps).* Field Manual FM 34-20. Washington, DC: Headquarters, Department of the Army, 1983.

—**RED DESIGNATION** is a communications security (COMSEC) term. It is a designation applied to telecommunications circuits, components, equipment, and systems that handle classified plain text or other information that requires protection during electrical transmission. The term is also applied to areas in which such information exists. *See also:* Red/Black Concept.

References

Department of Defense, U.S. Army. *Military Intelligence Battalion (CEWI) (Operations) (Corps).* Field Manual FM 34- 21. Washington, DC: Headquarters, Department of the Army, 1982.

————. *Military Intelligence Battalion (Combat Electronic Warfare Intelligence) (Division).* Field Manual FM 34-10. Washington, DC: Headquarters, Department of the Army, 1981.

————. *Military Intelligence Company (Combat Electronic Warfare and Intelligence) (Armored Cavalry Regiment/Separate Brigade).* Field Manual FM 34-30. Washington, DC: Headquarters, Department of the Army, 1983.

————. *Military Intelligence Group (Combat Electronic Warfare and Intelligence) (Corps).* Field Manual FM 34-20. Washington, DC: Headquarters, Department of the Army, 1983.

—**RED POWER** is a communications security (COMSEC) term. It is power that is filtered on the equipment side and is used to power red equipment. *See also:* Red/Black Concept.

References

Department of Defense, U.S. Army. *Intelligence and Electronic Warfare Operations.* Field Manual FM 34-1. Washington, DC: Headquarters, Department of the Army, 1984.

————. *Military Intelligence Battalion (Combat Electronic Warfare Intelligence) (Division).* Field Manual FM 34-10, 3 July 1981. Washington, DC: Headquarters, Department of the Army, 1981.

————. *Military Intelligence Group (Combat Electronic Warfare and Intelligence) (Corps).* Field Manual FM 34-20. Washington, DC: Headquarters, Department of the Army, 1983.

—**RED SIGNALS** is a intelligence security and counterintelligence term. Red signals are those that are encrypted and carry national security information. *See also:* Red/Black Concept.

References

Department of Defense, U.S. Army. *Military Intelligence Battalion (CEWI) (Tactical Exploitation) (Corps): Counterintelligence, Interrogation, Electronic Warfare.* Field Manual FM 34-23. Washington, DC: Headquarters, Department of the Army, 1985.

————. *Military Intelligence Battalion (Combat Electronic Warfare Intelligence) (Division).* Field Manual FM 34-10. Washington, DC: Headquarters, Department of the Army, 1981.

————. *Military Intelligence Company (Combat Electronic Warfare and Intelligence) (Armored Cavalry Regiment/Separate Brigade).* Field Manual FM 34-30. Washington, DC: Headquarters, Department of the Army, 1983.

—**REFERENCE SERVICE** pertains to a request for a subject search rather than a request to borrow a specific document.

References

Department of Defense, Defense Intelligence Agency. *Defense Intelligence Agency Manual.* Washington, DC: DIA, 1987.

—**REFUGEE** is a term used in clandestine and covert intelligence operations to describe a person who is outside the country or area of his former residence and who, because of fear of being prosecuted or because of hostilities in that area or country, is unwilling or unable to return to it.

References
Department of Defense, Defense Intelligence College. *Glossary of Intelligence Terms and Definitions.* Washington, DC: DIC, 1987.

—**REGIMENTAL LANDING TEAM (RLT),** in amphibious operations, is a task organization of an infantry regiment, battle group, or similar unit, reinforced by those elements that are required for initiating combat operations ashore. This will normally be composed of the assault battalion landing teams and a regimental landing team in reserve.

References
Department of Defense, Defense Intelligence College. *Glossary of Intelligence Terms and Definitions.* Washington, DC: DIC, 1987.

Department of Defense, Joint Chiefs of Staff. *Department of Defense Dictionary of Military and Related Terms.* Washington, DC: GPO, 1986.

—**REGIONALIZATION,** in communications security (COMSEC), means a cryptovariable distribution concept in which a group of subscribers in a secure telecommunications system assigned to a designated region or area are serviced by a specific key distribution center. *See also:* Communications Security.

References
Department of Defense, U.S. Army. *Military Intelligence Battalion (CEWI) (Operations) (Corps).* Field Manual FM 34- 21. Washington, DC: Headquarters, Department of the Army, 1982.

———. *Military Intelligence Battalion (Combat Electronic Warfare Intelligence) (Division).* Field Manual FM 34-10. Washington, DC: Headquarters, Department of the Army, 1981.

———. *Military Intelligence Company (Combat Electronic Warfare and Intelligence) (Armored Cavalry Regiment/Separate Brigade).* Field Manual FM 34-30. Washington, DC: Headquarters, Department of the Army, 1983.

———. *Military Intelligence Group (Combat Electronic Warfare and Intelligence) (Corps).* Field Manual FM 34-20. Washington, DC: Headquarters, Department of the Army, 1983.

—**REGISTER OF INTELLIGENCE PUBLICATIONS (RIP)** is a semiannual publication of the Defense Intelligence Agency that lists, with brief abstracts, significant studies received by the Defense Intelligence Agency Library. It includes products of the Intelligence Community, selected Central Intelligence Agency publications, and some foreign produced materials. *See also:* Defense Intelligence Agency.

References
Department of Defense, Defense Intelligence Agency. *Defense Intelligence Agency Manual.* Washington, DC: DIA, 1987.

Von Hoene, John P. A. *Intelligence User's Guide.* Washington, DC: DIA, 1983.

—**REGULARLY SUPERCEDED KEYING MATERIAL,** in communications security (COMSEC), refers to the keying material that is designated for use during a specific period of time and that is superceded regardless of whether the key is or is not used. *See also:* Communications Security.

References
Department of Defense, U.S. Army. *Military Intelligence Battalion (CEWI) (Operations) (Corps).* Field Manual FM 34-21. Washington, DC: Headquarters, Department of the Army, 1982.

———. *Military Intelligence Battalion (CEWI) (Tactical Exploitation) (Corps): Counterintelligence, Interrogation, Electronic Warfare.* Field Manual FM 34-23. Washington, DC: Headquarters, Department of the Army, 1985.

—**REINFORCING** is an Army tactical intelligence (TACINT) term that means the providing of support to one military intelligence (MI) unit by another. Such support is responsive to the needs of the reinforced unit. The reinforcing MI unit is under the operational control of the reinforced unit.

References
Department of Defense, U.S. Army. *Intelligence and Electronic Warfare Operations.* Field Manual FM 34-1. Washington, DC: Headquarters, Department of the Army, 1984.

———. *Military Intelligence Battalion (Combat Electronic Warfare Intelligence) (Division).* Field Manual FM 34-10. Washington, DC: Headquarters, Department of the Army, 1981.

———. *Military Intelligence Company (Combat Electronic Warfare and Intelligence) (Armored Cavalry Regiment/Separate Brigade).* Field Manual FM 34-30. Washington, DC: Headquarters, Department of the Army, 1983.

———. *Military Intelligence Group (Combat Electronic Warfare and Intelligence) (Corps).* Field Manual FM 34-20. Washington, DC: Headquarters, Department of the Army, 1983.

—**REKEYING VARIABLE,** in communications security (COMSEC), refers to a cryptovariable that
is used for encrypting other key variables when
they are electrically transmitted. *See also:* Communications Security.

References

Department of Defense, U.S. Army. *Military
Intelligence Battalion (CEWI) (Operations) (Corps).*
Field Manual FM 34-21. Washington, DC:
Headquarters, Department of the Army, 1982.

————. *Military Intelligence Battalion (Combat
Electronic Warfare Intelligence) (Division).* Field
Manual FM 34-10. Washington, DC: Headquarters,
Department of the Army, 1981.

—**RELEASE,** in communications security
(COMSEC), means the authorized divulgence of
U.S. cryptographic information or issuance of
U.S. COMSEC material to foreign nations, inter-
national organizations, or U.S. contractors. *See
also:* Communications Security.

References

Department of Defense, U.S. Army. *Military
Intelligence Battalion Combat Electronic Warfare
and Intelligence (Aerial Exploitation) (Corps).* Field
Manual FM 34-22, Washington, DC: Headquarters,
Department of the Army, 1984.

————. *Military Intelligence Battalion (Combat
Electronic Warfare Intelligence) (Division).* Field
Manual FM 34-10. Washington, DC: Headquarters,
Department of the Army, 1981.

————. *Military Intelligence Company (Combat
Electronic Warfare and Intelligence) (Armored
Cavalry Regiment/Separate Brigade).* Field Manual
FM 34-30. Washington, DC: Headquarters, U.S.
Army, 1983.

—**RELEASE PREFIX,** in communications security
(COMSEC), refers to a prefix that is used in the
short titles of U.S.-produced keying material that
has been marked "CRYPTO" to indicate its foreign release status. An "A" is used for material
that is releasable to specific Allied nations, while
"US" indicates that the information is intended
exclusively for U.S. use. *See also:* Communications Security.

References

Department of Defense, U.S. Army. *Intelligence and
Electronic Warfare Operations.* Field Manual FM
34-1. Washington, DC: Headquarters, Department
of the Army, 1984.

————. *Military Intelligence Battalion (Combat
Electronic Warfare Intelligence) (Division).* Field
Manual FM 34-10. Washington, DC: Headquarters,
Department of the Army, 1981.

—**RELEASING AGENCIES** is an intelligence term
used on the joint intelligence and national level
to describe Department of Defense agencies and
offices to which the director of the Defense
Intelligence Agency has delegated authority to
release classified material to their contractors, as
well as those military service offices and agencies to which authority to release has been
delegated by the assistant chiefs of staff for intelligence, Army and Air Force, and the director of
Naval Intelligence. *See also:* Defense Intelligence Agency.

References

Department of Defense, Defense Intelligence
Agency. *Defense Intelligence Agency Manual.*
Washington, DC: DIA, 1987.

Department of Defense, Defense Intelligence
College. *Glossary of Intelligence Terms and
Definitions.* Washington, DC: DIC, 1987.

—**RELEASING OFFICIAL** is a general intelligence
term. In message preparation, a releasing official is a person who has been authorized to
approve a message for electrical transmission.
He is the last person to read a message before it
is sent. As a result, he must assure himself that:
(1) the message is necessary and should be sent;
(2) it sufficiently important or time sensitive
that it should be sent by message; (3) the message has been given the appropriate security
classification.

References

Department of Defense, Defense Intelligence
Agency. *Defense Intelligence Agency Manual.*
Washington, DC: DIA, 1987.

Department of Defense, Defense Intelligence
College. *Glossary of Intelligence Terms and
Definitions.* Washington, DC: DIC, 1987.

—**REMOTE REKEYING,** in communications security (COMSEC), means the encrypted transmission of cryptographic key variables from a
remote source. *See also:* Communications
Security.

References

Department of Defense, U.S. Army. *Intelligence and
Electronic Warfare Operations.* Field Manual FM
34-1. Washington, DC: Headquarters, Department
of the Army, 1984.

————. *Military Intelligence Battalion (CEWI)
(Operations) (Corps).* Field Manual 34-21.
Washington, DC: Headquarters, Department of the
Army, 1982.

——. *Military Intelligence Battalion (Combat Electronic Warfare Intelligence) (Division)*. Field Manual FM 34-10. Washington, DC: Headquarters, Department of the Army, 1981.

—**REMOTE SENSING** is an intelligence imagery and photoreconnaissance term for the measuring or acquiring of information about some property or phenomenon by a recording device that is not in physical or intimate contact with the subject of the study.

References

Reeves, Robert; Anson, Abraham; and Landen, David. *Manual of Remote Sensing*. Falls Church, VA: American Society of Photogrammetry, 1975.

—**REPEATER JAMMER** is a term used in signals intelligence, communications security, operations security, and signals analysis. It is a jamming transmitter that is used to confuse or deceive the enemy by causing the enemy's equipment to present false information. This is done by a system that intercepts and reradiates a signal on the frequency of the enemy's equipment. The reradiated signal is modified, causing the enemy's equipment to present an erroneous range, azimuth or number of targets. *See also:* Jammer.

References

Department of Defense, Joint Chiefs of Staff. *Department of Defense Dictionary of Military and Related Terms*. Washington, DC: GPO, 1986.

—**REPETITIVE INTERCEPTS** is an electronic intelligence term. These are multiple intercepts of the same emitter over a period of time. *See also:* Electronic Intelligence.

References

Department of Defense, U.S. Army. *Military Intelligence Battalion (CEWI) (Operations) (Corps)*. Field Manual FM 34-21. Washington, DC: Headquarters, Department of the Army, 1982.

——. *Military Intelligence Group (Combat Electronic Warfare and Intelligence) (Corps)*. Field Manual FM 34-20. Washington, DC: Headquarters, Department of the Army, 1983.

—**REPORT.** *See:* Intelligence Information Report, Intelligence Report.

—**REPORTED UNIT** is a term used in intelligence operations. It is a unit designation that has been mentioned in an agent report, captured document, or interrogation report, but for which there is not sufficient information to include the unit in the accepted order of battle holdings.

References

Department of Defense, Joint Chiefs of Staff. *Department of Defense Dictionary of Military and Related Terms*. Washington, DC: GPO, 1986.

—**REPORTING TIME INTERVAL** is a general intelligence term. It is the time interval between the detection of an event and the receipt of a report by the intelligence customer.

References

Department of Defense, Joint Chiefs of Staff. *Department of Defense Dictionary of Military and Related Terms*. Washington, DC: GPO, 1986.

Kent, Sherman. *Strategic Intelligence for American World Policy*. Princeton, NJ: Princeton University Press, 1966.

—**REQUIREMENT** is a general intelligence term. It is a general or specific request for intelligence information that is made by a member of the Intelligence Community. *See also:* Collection Requirement, Intelligence Requirement, Task.

References

Department of Defense, Defense Intelligence College. *Glossary of Intelligence Terms and Definitions*. Washington, DC: DIC, 1987.

Department of Defense, Joint Chiefs of Staff. *Department of Defense Dictionary of Military and Related Terms*. Washington, DC: GPO, 1986.

Godson, Roy, ed. *Intelligence Problems for the 1980s, Number 1: Elements of Intelligence*. Rev. ed. Washington, DC: National Strategy Information Center, 1983.

Maurer, Alfred C.; Turnstall, Marion D.; and Keagle, James M. *Intelligence Policy and Process*. Boulder, CO: Westview Press, 1985.

Pickett, George. "Congress, the Budget, and Intelligence." In *Intelligence Policy and Process*, edited by Alfred C. Maurer, Marion D. Turnstall, and James M. Keagle. Boulder, CO: Westview Press, 1985.

Quirk, John; Phillips, David; Cline, Ray; and Pforzheimer, Walter. *The Central Intelligence Agency: A Photographic History*. Guilford, CT: Foreign Intelligence Press, 1986.

Treverton, Gregory F. *Covert Action: The Limits of Intervention in the Postwar World*. New York: Basic Books, 1987.

Turner, Stansfield. *Secrecy and Democracy: The CIA in Transition*. Boston: Houghton Mifflin, 1985.

U.S. Congress. Senate. *Final Report of the Senate Select Committee to Study Government Operations with Respect to Intelligence Activities. Report 94-755. Book I, Foreign and Military Intelligence*. Washington, DC: GPO, 1976.

—**REQUIREMENTS MANAGEMENT** is an Army tactical intelligence (TACINT) term that means the translation of the commander's guidance and the concept of the operation into basic intelligence, electronic warfare, counterintelligence, and operations security requirements; and the general planning, direction, and control necessary to satisfy those requirements.

References

Department of Defense, Defense Intelligence College. *Glossary of Intelligence Terms and Definitions*. Washington, DC: DIC, 1987.

Department of Defense, Joint Chiefs of Staff. *Department of Defense Dictionary of Military and Related Terms*. Washington, DC: GPO, 1986.

Department of Defense, U.S. Army. *Intelligence and Electronic Warfare Operations*. Field Manual FM 34-1. Washington, DC: Headquarters, Department of the Army, 1984.

Treverton, Gregory F. *Covert Action: The Limits of Intervention in the Postwar World*. New York: Basic Books, 1987.

Turner, Stansfield. *Secrecy and Democracy: The CIA in Transition*. Boston: Houghton Mifflin, 1985.

—**RESEARCH AND ANALYSIS (R&A)** was the analytical branch of the Office of Strategic Services. After the disestablishment of the OSS in 1945, R&A was given to the State Department, where it was united with other units to form the Interim Research and Intelligence Service. *See also:* Office of Strategic Services.

References

Corson, William R. *The Armies of Ignorance: The Rise of the American Intelligence Empire*. New York: Dial Press, 1977.

Kent, Sherman. *Strategic Intelligence for American World Policy*. Princeton, NJ: Princeton University Press, 1966.

Lowenthal, Mark M. *U.S. Intelligence: Evolution and Anatomy*. New York: Praeger, 1984.

Treverton, Gregory F. *Covert Action: The Limits of Intervention in the Postwar World*. New York: Basic Books, 1987.

—**RESEARCH AND DEVELOPMENT (R&D).** (1) Research and development involves basic and applied research in the sciences and engineering, and the design and development of prototypes and processes. It excludes routine product testing, market research, sales promotion, sales service, and other nontechnological activities or technical services. Basic research includes original investigations for the advancement of scientific knowledge that do not have specific practical objectives, while applied research is the practical application of knowledge, material, and techniques toward a solution to an existing or anticipated military or technological requirement. Finally, development includes technical activities of a nonroutine nature that are concerned with translating research findings or other scientific knowledge into products or processes. Development does not include routine technical services or other activities excluded from the above definition of research and development. (2) Research and development is an official term that has been defined by the Defense Intelligence Agency for one of its functional areas. It means "the examination of basic and applied research efforts and programs; the initiation of technical feasibility studies of new concepts; the evaluation, assessment, and review of requirements and projects pertaining to research, exploratory development, advanced development, engineering development and operational systems development. The above effort may also be applied to solution of intelligence problems."

References

Department of Defense, Defense Intelligence Agency. *Defense Intelligence Agency Manual 22-2*. Washington, DC: DIA, 1979.

Department of Defense, Defense Intelligence College. *Glossary of Intelligence Terms and Definitions*. Washington, DC: DIC, 1987.

Department of Defense, Joint Chiefs of Staff. *Department of Defense Dictionary of Military and Related Terms*. Washington, DC: GPO, 1986.

Godson, Roy, ed. *Intelligence Problems for the 1980s, Number 1: Elements of Intelligence*. Rev. ed. Washington, DC: National Strategy Information Center, 1983.

Kent, Sherman. *Strategic Intelligence for American World Policy*. Princeton, NJ: Princeton University Press, 1966.

Maurer, Alfred C.; Turnstall, Marion D.; and Keagle, James M. *Intelligence Policy and Process*. Boulder, CO: Westview Press, 1985.

—**RESEARCH AND DEVELOPMENT (RADE)** is a component of one of the ten branches that constitute the National Security Agency. *See:* National Security Agency.

References

Bamford, James. *The Puzzle Palace: A Report on America's Most Secret Agency*. New York: Penguin Books, 1983.

Kent, Sherman. *Strategic Intelligence for American World Policy*. Princeton, NJ: Princeton University Press, 1966.

RESEARCH, ENGINEERING, MATHEMATICS, AND PHYSICS (REMP) is a component of one of the ten branches that constitute the National Security Agency. *See:* National Security Agency.

References

Bamford, James. *The Puzzle Palace: A Report on America's Most Secret Agency*. New York: Penguin Books, 1983.

—**RESERVE KEYING MATERIAL,** in communications security (COMSEC), refers to uncommitted keying material that is held in reserve and will be used to satisfy unplanned keying material requirements. *See also:* Communications Security.

References

Department of Defense, Defense Intelligence College. *Glossary of Intelligence Terms and Definitions*. Washington, DC: DIC, 1987.

—**RESIDENCY, ILLEGAL.** *See:* Illegal Residency.

—**RESIDENCY, LEGAL.** *See:* Legal Residency.

—**RESIDENT,** in FBI terminology, is the head of a legal or illegal residency who supervises subordinate intelligence personnel. *See also:* Accommodation Address, Agent, Illegal Agent, Illegal Communication, Illegal Net, Illegal Operations, Illegal Residency, Illegal Support Officer, Legal, Legal Residency, Legend, Legitimate, Submerge.

References

Kessler, Ronald. *Spy vs. Spy: Stalking Soviet Spies in America*. New York: Charles Scribner's Sons, 1988.

—**RESOLUTION (PHOTOGRAPHIC)** is an intelligence imagery and photoreconnaissance term. It is the ability of the entire photographic system (including lens, exposure, processing, etc.) to render a sharply defined image.

References

Department of Defense, Joint Chiefs of Staff. *Department of Defense Dictionary of Military and Related Terms*. Washington, DC: GPO, 1986.

Turner, Stansfield. *Secrecy and Democracy: The CIA in Transition*. Boston: Houghton Mifflin, 1985.

—**RESOURCE ALLOCATION,** in intelligence data handling, is the planned acquisition of the needed resources through the program and budget process so that the Department of Defense Intelligence Information System (DODIIS) acquisition management process can be executed. *See also:* Reclama.

References

Department of Defense, Defense Intelligence Agency. *Defense Intelligence Agency Manual*. Washington, DC: DIA, 1987.

Godson, Roy, ed. *Intelligence Problems for the 1980s, Number 1: Elements of Intelligence*. Rev. ed. Washington, DC: National Strategy Information Center, 1983.

Maurer, Alfred C.; Turnstall, Marion D.; and Keagle, James M. *Intelligence Policy and Process*. Boulder, CO: Westview Press, 1985.

Pickett, George. "Congress, the Budget, and Intelligence." In *Intelligence Policy and Process*, edited by Alfred C. Maurer, Marion D. Turnstall, and James M. Keagle. Boulder, CO: Westview Press, 1985.

—**RESOURCE MANAGEMENT SYSTEMS,** in budgeting, includes all recurring quantitative data that is used at all management levels in the Department of Defense for planning and controlling the acquisition, use, and disposition of resources. Such systems include, but are not restricted to: (1) programming and budgeting systems, (2) systems for managing resources for operating activities, (3) systems for managing inventory and similar costs, and (4) systems for managing the acquisition, use, and disposition of capital assets. *See also:* Reclama.

References

Godson, Roy, ed. *Intelligence Problems for the 1980s, Number 1: Elements of Intelligence*. Rev. ed. Washington, DC: National Strategy Information Center, 1983.

Maurer, Alfred C.; Turnstall, Marion D.; and Keagle, James M. *Intelligence Policy and Process*. Boulder, CO: Westview Press, 1985.

Pickett, George. "Congress, the Budget, and Intelligence." In *Intelligence Policy and Process*, edited by Alfred C. Maurer, Marion D. Turnstall, and James M. Keagle. Boulder, CO: Westview Press, 1985.

—**RESPONSIBILITY** is the obligation to carry forward an assigned task to a successful conclusion. With responsibility goes the authority to direct and take the necessary action to insure success. *See also:* Indications and Warning.

References

Department of Defense, Joint Chiefs of Staff. *Department of Defense Dictionary of Military and Related Terms*. Washington, DC: GPO, 1986.

Turner, Stansfield. *Secrecy and Democracy: The CIA in Transition*. Boston: Houghton Mifflin, 1985.

—**RESTRICTED DATA (RD)** is a marking placed on documents in addition to the security classification. It is applied to all data concerning: (a) the design, manufacture and use of atomic weapons; (b) the production of special nuclear material; or (c) the use of special nuclear material to produce energy.

References

Allen, Thomas B., and Polmar, Norman. *Merchants of Treason: America's Secrets for Sale*. New York: Delacorte Press, 1988.

Department of Defense, Defense Intelligence Agency. *Defense Intelligence Agency Manual*. Washington, DC: DIA, 1987.

—**RETRACING THE ANALYSIS** is a process used to determine how an intelligence estimate was in error. *See also:* Estimative Intelligence, Intelligence Estimate.

References

Becket, Henry S. A. *The Dictionary of Espionage: Spookspeak into English*. New York: Stein and Day, 1986.

—**RHODES, ROY ADIR,** a sergeant in the U.S. Army, was convicted of espionage crimes associated with passing classified information to the Soviet KGB while he was stationed at the U.S.

Embassy in Moscow in the 1950s. Rhodes, who was blackmailed into committing the crime, was sentenced to five years in prison.

References

Allen, Thomas B., and Polmar, Norman. *Merchants of Treason: America's Secrets for Sale*. New York: Delacorte Press, 1988.

Crawford, David J. *Volunteers: The Betrayal of National Defense Secrets by Air Force Traitors*. Washington, DC: GPO, 1988.

—**RIDING SHOTGUN** is a term used in clandestine and covert intelligence operations. It means to send a second agent to surveil an intelligence officer who is meeting a dangerous contact or is meeting a contact under dangerous circumstances. Nelson Demille has an excellent example of riding shotgun in his novel *The Charm School*, in which the CIA station chief and enforcements follow the U.S. air attaché when he meets a KGB officer. *See also:* Blind Dating, Heavy Mob.

References

Demille, Nelson. *The Charm School*. New York: Warner Books, 1988.

—**RINGING THE GONG** is when a CIA station predicts that a revolution is about to occur in the host country.

References

Becket, Henry S. A. *The Dictionary of Espionage: Spookspeak into English*. New York: Stein and Day, 1986.

—**RISK,** in communications security (COMSEC), refers to the probability that an enemy will successfully exploit a specific telecommunications or COMSEC system for its intelligence content. The factors of risk are threat and vulnerability. *See also:* Communications Security.

References

Department of Defense, Defense Intelligence College. *Glossary of Intelligence Terms and Definitions*. Washington, DC: DIC, 1987.

Department of Defense, Joint Chiefs of Staff. *Department of Defense Dictionary of Military and Related Terms.* Washington, DC: GPO, 1986.

Department of Defense, U.S. Army. *Counter-Signals Intelligence (C-SIGINT) Operations.* Field Manual FM 34-62. Washington, DC: Headquarters, Department of the Army, 1986.

Kent, Sherman. *Strategic Intelligence for American World Policy.* Princeton, NJ: Princeton University Press, 1966.

Treverton, Gregory F. *Covert Action: The Limits of Intervention in the Postwar World.* New York: Basic Books, 1987.

Turner, Stansfield. *Secrecy and Democracy: The CIA in Transition.* Boston: Houghton Mifflin, 1985.

—**RISK ANALYSIS** is an Army tactical intelligence (TACINT) term that means the process of determining the risks to operations when no operations security (OPSEC) measures are applied to protect or control friendly vulnerabilities from hostile intelligence collection, and the comparison of these risks to the cost of implementing the OPSEC measures (in terms of time, equipment, funds, and manpower) and their probable effectiveness.

References

Department of Defense, Defense Intelligence College. *Glossary of Intelligence Terms and Definitions.* Washington, DC: DIC, 1987.

Department of Defense, Joint Chiefs of Staff. *Department of Defense Dictionary of Military and Related Terms.* Washington, DC: GPO, 1986.

Department of Defense, U.S. Army. *Military Intelligence Battalion Combat Electronic Warfare and Intelligence (Aerial Exploitation) (Corps).* Field Manual FM 34-22. Washington, DC: Headquarters, U.S. Army, 1984.

———. *Military Intelligence Battalion (Combat Electronic Warfare Intelligence) (Division).* Field Manual FM 34-10. Washington, DC: Headquarters, Department of the Army, 1981.

———. *Military Intelligence Battalion (CEWI) (Tactical Exploitation) (Corps): Counterintelligence, Interrogation, Electronic Warfare.* Field Manual FM 34-23. Washington, DC: Headquarters, Department of the Army, 1985.

———. *Military Intelligence Company (Combat Electronic Warfare and Intelligence) (Armored Cavalry Regiment/Separate Brigade).* Field Manual FM 34-30. Washington, DC: Headquarters, Department of the Army, 1983.

Treverton, Gregory F. *Covert Action: The Limits of Intervention in the Postwar World.* New York: Basic Books, 1987.

Turner, Stansfield. *Secrecy and Democracy: The CIA in Transition.* Boston: Houghton Mifflin, 1985.

—**ROCKEFELLER COMMISSION.** In 1974, President Ford, who had only been in office for about four months but who had inherited the intelligence crisis from his predecessor, President Nixon, requested a report from William Colby, who was then serving as the director of Central Intelligence. After reviewing the report, Ford established a presidential panel chaired by Vice President Nelson Rockefeller to investigate the CIA's domestic activities and operations.

Rockefeller's appointment was certainly politically motivated in that it was meant to signal Ford's displeasure with the Intelligence Community and his intention to create a committee of sufficient stature that it would not be cowed into producing a "whitewash." The appointment of Rockefeller, a distinguished Republican in his own right who had been brought on board the Ford administration because of his perceived integrity, was probably intended as a message to Congress that the president intended to lead the investigation and wanted Congress to defer to his leadership. If this was the case, the commission was partially successful, in that the objectivity and thoroughness of the Rockefeller Commission were never seriously questioned. However, the existence of the commission did not dissuade Congress, which proceeded to create two investigative bodies, the Church and Pike committees, to investigate the Intelligence Community.

Nonetheless, the Rockefeller Commission did complete its investigation and submitted its report in June 1975. It confirmed the accusations of illegal CIA activities, including domestic surveillance and spying. Among the commission's recommendations was one that called for a Joint Oversight Committee in Congress to oversee intelligence activities. *See also:* Executive Oversight.

References

Breckinridge, Scott D. *The CIA and the U.S. Intelligence System.* Boulder, CO: Westview Press, 1986.

Lowenthal, Mark M. *U.S. Intelligence: Evolution and Anatomy.* New York: Praeger, 1984.

Maurer, Alfred C.; Turnstall, Marion D.; and Keagle, James M. *Intelligence Policy and Process.* Boulder, CO: Westview Press, 1985.

Turner, Stansfield. *Secrecy and Democracy: The CIA in Transition.* Boston: Houghton Mifflin, 1985.

U.S. Congress. Senate. *Alleged Assassination Plots Involving Foreign Leaders: An Interim Report of the Select Committee to Study Governmental Operations with Respect to Intelligence Activities.* 94th Congress, 1st sess., Nov. 20, 1975. S. Rept. 94-465.

Von Hoene, John P. A. *Intelligence User's Guide.* Washington, DC: DIA, 1983.

—**ROGALSKY, IVAN,** was arrested for espionage crimes associated with attempting to pass classified information concerning the space shuttle program to a foreign intelligence service. He may have been motivated by expectations of monetary reward. Ruled psychologically incompetent, he was not tried.

References

Crawford, David J. *Volunteers: The Betrayal of National Defense Secrets by Air Force Traitors.* Washington, DC: GPO, 1988.

—**ROLLING UP THE NET** is a term used in clandestine and covert intelligence operations. It means arresting members of an intelligence organization after the organization has been discovered.

References

Becket, Henry S. A. *The Dictionary of Espionage: Spookspeak into English.* New York: Stein and Day, 1986.

—**ROSENBERG, JULIUS AND ETHEL,** leaders of the "Atomic Spy Ring," were accused of espionage. Members of a spy ring spanning the United States, the United Kingdom, and Canada that was controlled by the Soviet Union and operated during the 1940s and 1950s, they were convicted of espionage during wartime, sentenced to death, and executed on June 19, 1953. Ideological fervor was exploited as a motive to inspire

the ring. Thomas Allen and Norman Polmar correctly note that the Rosenberg ring was the last of the ideological spies and that from then on, with one exception, spying for money became the vogue.

References

Allen, Thomas B., and Polmar, Norman. *Merchants of Treason: America's Secrets for Sale.* New York: Delacorte Press, 1988.

—**ROUTINE MESSAGE** is a message of the lowest priority. It means that the information the message contains should be transmitted by rapid means but is not sufficiently urgent to require a higher precedence. *See also:* Precedence.

References

Department of Defense, Joint Chiefs of Staff. *Department of Defense Dictionary of Military and Related Terms.* Washington, DC: GPO, 1986.

—**RUMOR** is a term used in clandestine and covert intelligence operations. It is a false story that is started with the intention of damaging a rival intelligence organization. *See also:* Black Bag Job, Black Bag Operation, Blow, Blown Agent, Dirty Tricks, Snitch Jacket.

References

Becket, Henry S. A. *The Dictionary of Espionage: Spookspeak into English.* New York: Stein and Day, 1986.

—**RUN DOWN A CASE** is a term used in clandestine and covert intelligence operations. It is the decision to cancel a double agent operation, usually because it is suspected that the other side has become aware that it is being deceived. *See also:* Blow, Blown Agent, Co-Opted Worker, Co-Optees, Double Agent, Doubled, Recruitment, Recruitment in Place, Special Activities.

References

Becket, Henry S. A. *The Dictionary of Espionage: Spookspeak into English.* New York: Stein and Day, 1986.

—S&T HIGHLIGHTS-EURASIAN COMMUNIST COUNTRIES, produced by the Defense Intelligence Agency, provides a concise assessment of the more significant military-related scientific and technical developments of the Warsaw Pact countries, China, and North Korea. It includes intelligence on deployed weapons, new systems under development, and technologies with implications for future military capabilities. *See also:* Defense Intelligence Agency.

References

Department of Defense, Defense Intelligence Agency. *Defense Intelligence Agency Manual.* Washington, DC: DIA, 1987.

———. *Organization, Mission and Key Personnel.* Washington, DC: DIA, 1986.

Von Hoene, John P.A. *Intelligence User's Guide.* Washington, DC: Defense Intelligence Agency, 1983.

—SABOTAGE. (1) Sabotage is an action against material, premises or utilities or their production that injures, interferes with, or obstructs the national security or ability of a nation to prepare for or wage a war. (2) Sabotage is a counterintelligence term used in the context of automatic data system security and refers to a situation in which "sleeper" agents who have been blended into the mainstream of society are issued orders to sabotage critical Department of Defense computer facilities prior to or during the outbreak of hostilities. Such agents could physically attack power sources, air conditioning systems, and water supplies. Although access to such facilities is tightly controlled, few installations are hardened to withstand the effects of well-placed, high explosive demolitions.

References

Blackburn, N. Glenn. "Computers: A Counterintelligence Concern." Unpublished paper provided to the editors. Washington, DC, 1987.

Department of Defense, Defense Intelligence College. *Glossary of Intelligence Terms and Definitions.* Washington, DC: DIC, 1987.

Department of Defense, Joint Chiefs of Staff. *Department of Defense Dictionary of Military and Related Terms.* Washington, DC: GPO, 1986.

Godson, Roy, ed. *Intelligence Problems for the 1980s, Number 1: Elements of Intelligence.* Rev. ed. Washington, DC: National Strategy Information Center, 1983.

Turner, Stansfield. *Secrecy and Democracy: The CIA in Transition.* Boston: Houghton Mifflin, 1985.

—SAFE. *See:* Support for Analysts' File Environment.

—SAFE AREA INTELLIGENCE BRIEF (SAIB) is a briefing about a safe area within hostile territory that is presented to those who will be in the territory and may be in danger of being captured. The purpose of the briefing is to help them avoid apprehension. *See also:* Evasion and Escape, Evasion and Escape Intelligence.

References

Department of Defense, Defense Intelligence College. *Glossary of Intelligence Terms and Definitions.* Washington, DC: DIC, 1987.

Department of Defense, Joint Chiefs of Staff. *Department of Defense Dictionary of Military and Related Terms.* Washington, DC: GPO, 1986.

—SAFE AREA INTELLIGENCE DESCRIPTION (SAID) is the information that is available about an area that is assembled to help people avoid capture. *See also:* Safe Area Intelligence Brief (SAIB).

References

Department of Defense, Defense Intelligence College. *Glossary of Intelligence Terms and Definitions.* Washington, DC: DIC, 1987.

Department of Defense, Joint Chiefs of Staff. *Department of Defense Dictionary of Military and Related Terms.* Washington, DC: GPO, 1986.

—SAFE HOUSE is a term used in clandestine and covert intelligence operations to describe a house or premises that is controlled by an intelligence organization and that provides at least temporary security for individuals involved in or equipment used in clandestine operations. *See also:* Accommodation Address, Clean, Concealment, Cover, Go to Ground, Illegal Residency, Suitable Cover.

References

Clancy, Tom. *The Cardinal of the Kremlin.* New York: Putnam, 1988.

Department of Defense, Defense Intelligence College. *Glossary of Intelligence Terms and Definitions.* Washington, DC: DIC, 1987.

Department of Defense, Joint Chiefs of Staff. *Department of Defense Dictionary of Military and Related Terms.* Washington, DC: GPO, 1986.

U.S. Congress. Senate. *Final Report of the Senate Select Committee to Study Government Operations with Respect to Intelligence Activities. Report 94-755. Book I, Foreign and Military Intelligence.* Washington, DC: GPO, 1976.

—SAFEGUARDING NATIONAL SECURITY IN-FORMATION, National Security Decision Directive No. 4, issued by President Reagan on March 11, 1983, was promulgated in order to stop the leakage of security information. It was meant to supplement Executive Order 12356 and stipulated:

(1) Each Executive Branch agency that handled classified information was directed to establish procedures to safeguard against the unauthorized disclosure of classified information. At a minimum, these procedures would include the following: (a) that all individuals authorized access to classified information had to sign a nondisclosure agreement that stated that they would not divulge the classified information that they would be permitted to see; (b) that all individuals granted access to sensitive compartmented information also sign a nondisclosure statement and that this statement also include a specific passage concerning prepublication review (such review concerned any materials that the individual might write and wish to have published, and such materials had to be reviewed for classified material and the individual was obliged to accept the decision of the reviewing office); (c) that the nondisclosure statements be in a form that would be enforceable in a court of law; and (d) that the agency develop procedures to restrict media contact with intelligence agency employees.

(2) Each agency was to develop investigative procedures that were to be employed in the event of an unauthorized disclosure.

(3) Such unauthorized disclosures were to be reported to the Department of Justice, which would determine whether they were serious enough to warrant referral to the Federal Bureau of Investigation for further action.

(4) The Office of Management and Budget was to develop procedures that would require intelligence agency employees to submit to polygraph tests in the event of an unauthorized disclosure.

(5) The attorney general, in consultation with the Director of the Office of Personnel Management, was to establish an intergovernmental group to examine the federal personnel security program and recommend revisions to the same.

The significance of this directive was that it focused the attention of intelligence agency employees on unauthorized disclosures. Congress later limited the use of polygraph testing, and urinalysis testing, covered under another directive, was also curtailed. Nonetheless, the directive was successful, because it appeared that there were far fewer cases of unauthorized disclosure in the late 1980s.

References

Godson, Roy, ed. *Intelligence Problems for the 1980s, Number 1: Elements of Intelligence.* Rev. ed. Washington, DC: National Strategy Information Center, 1983.

Office of the President of the United States. *National Security Decision Directive No. 4, Safeguarding National Security Information.* Washington, DC, Mar. 11, 1983.

—SAFFORD, LEONARD J., attached to the U.S. Army, was convicted of espionage crimes associated with passing classified material to a Soviet intelligence service. Safford's motive was expected monetary gain. He was sentenced to 25 years in prison.

References

Crawford, David J. *Volunteers: The Betrayal of National Defense Secrets by Air Force Traitors.* Washington, DC: GPO, 1988.

—SALT I and SALT II. The fate of the SALT agreements was influenced significantly by the perceived state of U.S. intelligence. Certainly it would be simplistic to claim that intelligence was the only or even the overriding factor in the success of SALT I and the failure of SALT II. Other significant factors included the degree of Executive commitment to the agreements, the skill of the White House in convincing Congress of their value, and the disposition of Congress when it considered each agreement. Nonetheless, the intelligence factor was significant and should not be underrated.

SALT I was approved as much because of the efforts of Henry Kissinger, who had been crucial to the writing of the agreement, as it was because of the U.S. intelligence capability. However, SALT I was a task that the Intelligence Community could accomplish, in that the U.S. national technical means, as the U.S. satellite reconnaissance capability has been euphemized, was capable of verifying Soviet obedience.

SALT II, on the other hand, presented many factors that the Intelligence Community would have difficulty monitoring. First of all, since SALT II involved missile quality as well as quantity, the Intelligence Community would have to report on *types* as well as on *numbers*, a considerably more complex task, and one that the national technical means might not be able to monitor accurately. Second, the U.S. intelligence capability had been weakened by the loss of crucially important intelligence posts in Iran after the fall of the Shah. Third, as Mark Lowenthal notes, the KH-11 satellite system had been seriously compromised when the Soviets received detailed material on the systems first from Christopher Boyce and later from William Kampiles. Such information might aid the Soviets in defeating the U.S. overhead reconnaissance capability if they wished to violate the treaty. Fourth, U.S. intelligence estimates had continued to be inaccurate, bringing into question the Community's ability to produce accurate intelligence, and finally, as the intelligence reporting on the Irani hostage situation demonstrated, intelligence was not infallible. If these factors were not enough, the failure of intelligence to report on the Soviet brigade in Cuba was the last straw, because it highlighted not only the fallibility of U.S. intelligence but also called into question the seriousness of the Soviet desire for peace. These and other equally important factors resulted in the treaty's failure. *See also:* National Technical Means.

References

Breckinridge, Scott D. *The CIA and the U.S. Intelligence System.* Boulder, CO: Westview Press, 1986.

Brinkley, David A., and Hull, Andrew W. *Estimative Intelligence: A Textbook on the History, Products, Uses, and Writing of Intelligence Estimates.* Columbus, OH: Battelle, 1979.

Lowenthal, Mark M. *U.S. Intelligence: Evolution and Anatomy.* New York: Praeger, 1984.

Maurer, Alfred C.; Turnstall, Marion D.; and Keagle, James M. *Intelligence Policy and Process.* Boulder, CO: Westview Press, 1985.

U.S. Congress. Senate. *Final Report of the Senate Select Committee to Study Government Operations with Respect to Intelligence Activities. Report 94-755. Book I, Foreign and Military Intelligence.* Washington, DC: GPO, 1976.

—**SAMFORD, LIEUTENANT GENERAL JOHN A., U.S. AIR FORCE,** served as the director of the National Security Agency (NSA) from November 1956 until November 1960. A graduate of West Point, Samford had spent almost his entire career in aviation. In World War II, he served in various capacities, including chief of staff of the Eighth Air Force. In 1944, he was assigned to Washington as assistant chief of staff for Air Force Intelligence, and then had teaching assignments at the Air Command and Staff School and Air War College. During the Korean War, he served as director of Air Force Intelligence and then became vice director of the NSA, serving in that capacity from June until November 1956, when he relieved Lieutenant General Ralph J. Canine as director of the NSA. He retired from the NSA in 1960 in the midst of a scandal resulting from the defection of two NSA employees to Moscow. *See also:* National Security Agency.

References

Bamford, James. *The Puzzle Palace: A Report on America's Most Secret Agency.* New York: Penguin Books, 1983.

—**SANCTIFICATION** is a term used in covert operations. It is to blackmail someone with the aim of extracting political favors from him. *See also:* Blackmail, Biographic Leverage, Honey Trap, Ladies, Raven, Sisters, Swallow, Swallow's Nest.

References

Deacon, Richard. *Spyclopedia: An Encyclopedia of Spies, Secret Services, Operations, Jargon, and All Subjects Related to the World of Espionage.* London: Macdonald, 1987.

Treverton, Gregory F. *Covert Action: The Limits of Intervention in the Postwar World.* New York: Basic Books, 1987.

—**SANCTION** is a term used in covert operations. It is an intelligence agency's approval for a killing. *See also:* Active Measures, Assassination, Executive Action, Terminate with Extreme Prejudice.

References

Becket, Henry S. A. *The Dictionary of Espionage: Spookspeak into English.* New York: Stein and Day, 1986.

Deacon, Richard. *Spyclopedia: An Encyclopedia of Spies, Secret Services, Operations, Jargon, and All Subjects Related to the World of Espionage.* London: Macdonald, 1987.

Ranelagh, John. *The Agency: The Rise and Decline of the CIA.* New York: Simon and Schuster, 1986.

Treverton, Gregory F. *Covert Action: The Limits of Intervention in the Postwar World.* New York: Basic Books, 1987.

—SANITIZATION is a general intelligence term that has two meanings. (1) Sanitization is the process of editing or otherwise altering intelligence information or reports in order to protect sensitive intelligence sources, methods, capabilities, analytical procedures, or privileged information so that the document can be disseminated more widely. (2) In FBI terminology, to sanitize is to alter information to conceal how, where, and from whom the information was obtained. *See also:* Access, Authorized, Classification, Classified Information, Code Word, Compromise, Declassification, Disclosure, Downgrade, Freedom of Information Act, Limited Access Area, Need-to-Nnow, Need-to-Know Principle, No-Lone Zone, Nondisclosure Agreement, Nondiscussion Area, Sanitize, Sanitized Area, Security Certification, Security Classification, Sensitive Compartmented Information, Sensitive Compartmented Information Facility, Two-Person Control.

References

Department of Defense, Defense Intelligence College. *Glossary of Intelligence Terms and Definitions.* Washington, DC: DIC, 1987.

Department of Defense, Joint Chiefs of Staff. *Department of Defense Dictionary of Military and Related Terms.* Washington, DC: GPO, 1986.

Godson, Roy, ed. *Intelligence Problems for the 1980s, Number 1: Elements of Intelligence.* Rev. ed. Washington, DC: National Strategy Information Center, 1983.

Turner, Stansfield. *Secrecy and Democracy: The CIA in Transition.* Boston: Houghton Mifflin, 1985.

—SANITIZE, as defined by the Church Committee, means "deleting or revising a report or document in order to prevent the identification of intelligence sources and methods that contributed to or are dealt with in the report." *See also:* Sanitization.

References

Department of Defense, Defense Intelligence College. *Glossary of Intelligence Terms and Definitions.* Washington, DC: DIC, 1987.

Department of Defense, Joint Chiefs of Staff. *Department of Defense Dictionary of Military and Related Terms.* Washington, DC: GPO, 1986.

Godson, Roy, ed. *Intelligence Problems for the 1980s, Number 1: Elements of Intelligence.* Rev. ed. Washington, DC: National Strategy Information Center, 1983.

Turner, Stansfield. *Secrecy and Democracy: The CIA in Transition.* Boston: Houghton Mifflin, 1985.

U.S. Congress. Senate. *Final Report of the Senate Select Committee to Study Government Operations with Respect to Intelligence Activities. Report 94-755. Book I, Foreign and Military Intelligence.* Washington, DC: GPO, 1976.

—SANITIZED AREA is an intelligence security and counterintelligence term. It is an area from which all sensitive compartmented information (SCI) has been removed so that individuals who have not been indoctrinated for SCI can enter the area for legitimate reasons and on a temporary basis. These personnel, who may be accomplishing janitorial, maintenance, or other legitimate business, must be escorted by an SCI-indoctrinated individual at all times. *See also:* Sanitization, Sanitize.

References

Department of Defense, Defense Intelligence College. *Glossary of Intelligence Terms and Definitions.* Washington, DC: DIC, 1987.

Department of Defense, Joint Chiefs of Staff. *Department of Defense Dictionary of Military and Related Terms.* Washington, DC: GPO, 1986.

Godson, Roy, ed. *Intelligence Problems for the 1980s, Number 1: Elements of Intelligence.* Rev. ed. Washington, DC: National Strategy Information Center, 1983.

—SATELLITE is a body that revolves around another body or a man-made object that revolves around a spatial body.

References

Laqueur, Walter. *A World of Secrets.* New York: Basic Books, 1985.

Reeves, Robert; Anson, Abraham; and Landen, David. *Manual of Remote Sensing.* Falls Church, VA: American Society of Photogrammetry, 1975.

Treverton, Gregory F. *Covert Action: The Limits of Intervention in the Postwar World.* New York: Basic Books, 1987.

Turner, Stansfield. *Secrecy and Democracy: The CIA in Transition.* Boston: Houghton Mifflin, 1985.

—**SCALP HUNTERS** is a term used in intelligence operations to describe experts in defection who are trained in distinguishing true defectors from fakes. Their purpose is to keep a watch out for foreign diplomats and other foreigners who may be willing to defect. *See also:* Agent, Co-Opted Worker, Co-Optees, Defector, Disaffected Person, Double Agent, Informant, Inside Man, Mole, Sleeper.

References

Becket, Henry S. A. *The Dictionary of Espionage: Spookspeak into English.* New York: Stein and Day, 1986.

Deacon, Richard. *Spyclopedia: An Encyclopedia of Spies, Secret Services, Operations, Jargon, and All Subjects Related to the World of Espionage.* London: Macdonald, 1987.

Ranelagh, John. *The Agency: The Rise and Decline of the CIA.* New York: Simon and Schuster, 1986.

—**SCAN,** in electronic warfare and signals intelligence, is the movement of an electronic beam through space searching for a target. Scanning is done by moving the antenna or by lobe watching. As defined by the Church Committee, scan is also "one complete rotation of an antenna in the electromagnetic and acoustic contexts." *See also:* Electronic Warfare.

References

Department of Defense, Joint Chiefs of Staff. *Department of Defense Dictionary of Military and Related Terms.* Washington, DC: GPO, 1986.

U.S. Congress. Senate. *Final Report of the Senate Select Committee to Study Government Operations with Respect to Intelligence Activities. Report 94-755. Book I, Foreign and Military Intelligence.* Washington, DC: GPO, 1976.

—**SCHLESINGER, JAMES RODNEY,** was born on February 15, 1929, in New York City. He received his bachelor's degree from Harvard University in 1950, and he earned a master's in 1952 and a Ph.D. in 1956 from the same university. His early years were spent in academia and business. He was an assistant and then an associate professor of economics at the University of Virginia from 1955 to 1963. He then served as a staff member at the Rand Corporation from 1963 until 1967, and then as its director of strategic studies from 1967 until 1969. In 1969, he was made assistant director and acting deputy director of the Bureau of the Budget, and he served in this capacity until 1970. In 1970 and 1971, he served as assistant director of the Office of Management and Budget and then as chairman of the Atomic Energy Commission in 1972. He was appointed to serve as director of Central Intelligence (DCI) by President Nixon on December 21, 1972. His appointment was confirmed by the Senate on January 23, 1973, and he was sworn in on February 2, 1973. He resigned on July 2, 1973, to become secretary of defense, and he served in this position until 1975. In 1977, he became the secretary of energy and served until 1979. In 1979, he became a private consultant and became counselor to the President's Commission on Strategic Forces in 1983.

Although Schlesinger served as DCI for only six months, his tenure had a decided effect on the Intelligence Community. Schlesinger reduced drastically the size of the Directorate for Operations and the analytic staff, and he took an active role in the production of the National Intelligence Estimates. He probably would have had an even more dramatic effect on the agency had he been permitted to remain as DCI, but the president appointed him as secretary of defense in the spring of 1973. *See also:* Central Intelligence Agency.

References

Breckinridge, Scott D. *The CIA and the U.S. Intelligence System.* Boulder, CO: Westview Press, 1986.

Brinkley, David A., and Hull, Andrew W. *Estimative Intelligence: A Textbook on the History, Products, Uses, and Writing of Intelligence Estimates.* Columbus, OH: Battelle, 1979.

Cline, Ray S. *The CIA Under Reagan, Bush, and Casey.* Washington, DC: Acropolis Books, 1981.

Corson, William R. *The Armies of Ignorance: The Rise of the American Intelligence Empire.* New York: Dial Press, 1977.

Laqueur, Walter. *A World of Secrets.* New York: Basic Books, 1985.

Lowenthal, Mark M. *U.S. Intelligence: Evolution and Anatomy.* New York: Praeger, 1984.

Maurer, Alfred C.; Turnstall, Marion D.; and Keagle, James M. *Intelligence Policy and Process.* Boulder, CO: Westview Press, 1985.

Turner, Stansfield. *Secrecy and Democracy: The CIA in Transition.* Boston: Houghton Mifflin, 1985.

U.S. Congress. Senate. *Final Report of the Senate Select Committee to Study Government Operations with Respect to Intelligence Activities. Report 94-755. Book I, Foreign and Military Intelligence.* Washington, DC: GPO, 1976.

Von Hoene, John P. A. *Intelligence User's Guide.* Washington, DC: DIA, 1983.

—**SCIENCE AND TECHNOLOGY** is an official term that has been defined by the Defense Intelligence Agency for one of its functional areas. It means "activities using the basic knowledge of a professional discipline such as engineering, biological, physical, medical, and social sciences, and mathematics as they relate to foreign scientific research and development as it concerns the national economy and military potential; and foreign technological development, performance, and operational capabilities of foreign material which now, or may eventually have a practical application for military purposes." *See also:* Scientific and Technical Intelligence.

References

Department of Defense, Defense Intelligence Agency. *Defense Intelligence Agency Manual 22-2.* Washington, DC: DIA, 1979.

Godson, Roy, ed. *Intelligence Problems for the 1980s, Number 1: Elements of Intelligence.* Rev. ed. Washington, DC: National Strategy Information Center, 1983.

Turner, Stansfield. *Secrecy and Democracy: The CIA in Transition.* Boston: Houghton Mifflin, 1985.

—**SCIENTIFIC ADVISORY COMMITTEE (SAC).** *See:* Defense Intelligence Agency *under* Directorate for Scientific and Technical Intelligence.

—**SCIENTIFIC AND TECHNICAL INTELLIGENCE (S&T or S&TI),** one of the eight components of strategic intelligence, is intelligence concerns foreign developments in basic and applied scientific and technical research and development. These include engineering and production techniques, new technology, and weapon systems and their capabilities and characteristics. It also includes intelligence that requires scientific or technical expertise on the part of the analyst, such as medicine, physical health studies, and behavioral analyses. The Defense Intelligence Agency, the various service scientific and technological organizations, and the Central Intelligence Agency all have responsibilities in the production of scientific and technical intelligence.

General

Scientific and technical intelligence is the study of the scientific and technical capacities and activities of all nations. No significant changes are likely to occur in the techniques of modern war or in the production of new weapons without the aid of science. Hence, the intelligence officer learns about the activities of foreign scientists, the research and development programs and scientific organization of foreign nations, the funds available for scientific study and the discoveries and inventions that result from these activities. Scientific intelligence, moreover, is contributory to other components of strategic intelligence, especially economic, telecommunications, and armed forces intelligence.

Scientific activities may be divided into basic or pure research and applied science. The military research and development program is a particular phase of the latter that is of primary interest to the intelligence analyst. Applied science is of most importance to the military and is often identified as technical intelligence. Pure scientific research, however, is a key national potential.

Potential

The history and traditions of a nation's scientific endeavor will largely determine the government's attitude toward science. A knowledge of this attitude helps the intelligence officer estimate the role of the scientists in the country under consideration and the particular fields of research that are receiving major attention. An important factor in determining scientific potential is the rate at which a country is training its new scientists and the quality of their training.

New Weapons and Equipment

An important task of scientific and technical intelligence is forecasting new weapons and equipment of foreign armed forces. A study of the scientific research that is being accomplished in a country will reveal discoveries that may later be applied in the development of new weapons and techniques. These discoveries occur in the obvious fields of scientific endeavor such as electronics and atomic energy. However, the possibility that important events may occur in fields of scientific endeavor that are less obvious than electronics and atomic energy should not be ignored. Synthetic materials or substitutes that have been developed by science have allowed nations to wage war in spite of shortages in materials that were previously considered essential—for instance, synthetic fuels, lubricants, and synthetic rubber.

Scientific and technical intelligence is concerned with all scientific developments that may have military application until the time when such developments result in weapons that are adopted in a foreign nation as standard equipment. The weapons then become the concern of the armed forces intelligence analyst.

Collection

The task of collecting scientific and technical information is usually complicated by the fact that most countries take extreme measures to conceal scientific and technical activities. The problem is further aggravated by the lack of sufficient technically trained personnel for fieldwork. The scientific researcher must depend to a large extent on information that is furnished to him by observers who are not specialists in this field.

Scientific and technical intelligence should identify the main research and development organizations of a nation and their types; their interrelationships and how their efforts are coordinated; and where and how research projects originate. The researcher must ascertain the governmental structure that controls or supervises scientific research and development, both within and outside the armed forces.

National academies of science can provide valuable material for the intelligence analyst. Not only does the membership roster of an academy list the nation's leading scientists, but the academy frequently publishes scholarly papers that reveal trends in their research program. This applies also to organizations that sponsor or engage in research. Another source is technical publications, which frequently mirror the scientific developments in a country.

Colleges and universities, especially those whose scientific or technical schools are outstanding, also can be sources of valuable intelligence information. The types of science that are stressed in their curricula may yield valuable information on those items that the nation is emphasizing in its research and development programs.

In many countries, there are privately owned research organizations. Their relationship with the government, their significance and caliber, and the types of research in which they are engaged should be carefully studied. Also, it should be determined whether the research

organizations have any international affiliations. The research projects that are receiving major attention may be conspicuous by the allocation of both public and private funds. The information will be even more valuable if the intelligence analyst can ascertain what amounts are allocated to specific projects or to individual scientists. Citations accompanying prizes, scholarships, and other awards often recite the accomplishments for which the honor was conferred.

Other intelligence targets that can be exploited in the scientific and technical field include (1) exports and imports of materials or equipment that pertain to a particular or specific type of scientific research or development; (2) stockpiling certain raw materials; (3) erecting or expanding facilities that are appropriate to specific categories of research or manufacture; (4) imposing extreme security precautions around an installation; and (5) higher wages or other inducements for certain types of scientists or workers.

The whereabouts of scientists is especially important, for the location of specialists is often a key to the type of research activity being conducted by a particular installation.

Scientists in one country frequently correspond and exchange visits with scientists in other countries, including those of the Soviet bloc. This type of scientific contact can often be exploited to obtain useful or significant information on Soviet bloc scientific activities.

Of particular importance to the military aspects of scientific and technical intelligence is the development of new collection techniques, based upon scientific principles, that can be used to collect important technical information.

Conclusions

The key functions of scientific and technical intelligence are to project the future threat potential against the United States; to aid in U.S. research and development; to evaluate the vulnerability and survivability of U.S. weapons; and to aid in the development of U.S. countermeasures.

The key sources of scientific and technical information on a given nation are: (1) Human intelligence (HUMINT), which should be helpful in providing intelligence on the nation's policy, military strategy, military requirements, research, specifications and tests, production and facilities construction. In addition, it should provide even better information, which is of medium value (potentially useful) in the production of intelligence in the areas of the nation's design and development focus and its military operations. (2) Open literature (LITINT), which can provide low value (helpful) information on the nation's military requirements, resource allocation, threat assessment, and military operations, medium value (potentially useful) information in the areas of policy, military strategy, design and development, specifications and tests, and technology exploitation, and high value (virtually sufficient) data on the nation's research. (3) Photography, which can provide medium value (potentially useful) data on the nation's design and development operations, military operations, and its production, and high value (virtually sufficient) data on facilities construction. (4) Communications intelligence (COMINT), which can provide low value (helpful) data on military requirements, resource allocation, and specifications and tests, medium value (potentially useful) information on design and development, military operations, and facilities construction, and high value (virtually sufficient) information on production. (5) Material exploitation, which can provide medium value (potentially useful) information on design and development and on production.

References

Clauser, Jerome K., and Weir, Sandra M. *Intelligence Research Methodology*. State College, PA: HRB-Singer, 1975.

Department of Defense, Defense Intelligence College. *Glossary of Intelligence Terms and Definitions*. Washington, DC: DIC, 1987.

Department of Defense, Joint Chiefs of Staff. *Department of Defense Dictionary of Military and Related Terms*. Washington, DC: GPO, 1986.

Godson, Roy, ed. *Intelligence Problems for the 1980s, Number 1: Elements of Intelligence*. Rev. ed. Washington, DC: National Strategy Information Center, 1983.

———. *Intelligence Problems for the 1980s, Number 2: Analysis and Estimates*. Washington, DC: National Strategy Information Center, 1980.

———. *Intelligence Problems for the 1980s, Number 5: Clandestine Collection*. Washington, DC: National Strategy Information Center, 1982.

U.S. Congress. Senate. *Final Report of the Senate Select Committee to Study Government Operations with Respect to Intelligence Activities. Report 94-755. Book I, Foreign and Military Intelligence*. Washington, DC: GPO, 1976.

—SCIENTIFIC AND TECHNICAL INTELLIGENCE CENTER (STIC) (NAVY). *See:* Naval Intelligence.

—SCIENTIFIC AND TECHNICAL INTELLIGENCE COMMITTEE (STIC). *See:* Director of Central Intelligence Committee.

—SCIENTIFIC AND TECHNICAL INTELLIGENCE INFORMATION SERVICES PROGRAM (STIISP). This Department of Defense program is coordinated by the Directorate for Scientific and Technical Intelligence (DT) of the Defense Intelligence Agency. It includes the operation of the Central Information Reference and Control (CIRC) system, which supports the intelligence and research and development communities, other government agencies, and government contractors by maintaining a central source of references to scientific and technical intelligence information. The Air Force Systems Command's Foreign Technology Division is the executive agent for the CIRC.

References

Clauser, Jerome K., and Weir, Sandra M. *Intelligence Research Methodology*. State College, PA: HRB-Singer, 1975.

Department of Defense, Defense Intelligence Agency. *Defense Intelligence Agency Manual*. Washington, DC: DIA, 1987.

———. *Organization, Mission, and Key Personnel*. Washington, DC: DIA, 1986.

Von Hoene, John P. A. *Intelligence User's Guide*. Washington, DC: DIA, 1983.

—SCIENTIFIC AND TECHNICAL INTELLIGENCE PRODUCTION SCHEDULE (STIPS) is a quarterly schedule produced by the Defense Intelligence Agency, and it provides information on what scientific and technical intelligence topics have been approved for production (a necessary step before intelligence production can begin) and when production on these projects is scheduled to be completed.

References

Department of Defense, Defense Intelligence Agency. *Defense Intelligence Agency Manual*. Washington, DC: DIA, 1987.

———. *Organization, Mission, and Key Personnel*. Washington, DC: DIA, 1986.

Von Hoene, John P. A. *Intelligence User's Guide*. Washington, DC: DIA, 1983.

—SCIENTIFIC AND TECHNICAL INTELLIGENCE REGISTER (STIR) is produced semiannually by the Defense Intelligence Agency and identifies and catalogues the current scientific and technical intelligence products that have been published under DIA tasking for the Department of Defense. It also includes selected departmental scientific and technical products of interest to consumers who are outside of the producing military department. *See also:* Defense Intelligence Agency.

References
Department of Defense, Defense Intelligence Agency. *Defense Intelligence Agency Manual.* Washington, DC: DIA, 1987.

———. *Organization, Mission, and Key Personnel.* Washington, DC: DIA, 1986.

Von Hoene, John P. A. *Intelligence User's Guide.* Washington, DC: DIA, 1983.

—**SCIENTIFIC ESTIMATES COMMITTEE (SEC),** a subcommittee of the Intelligence Advisory Committee (IAC), was established in 1952. Its duties were to accomplish the interagency coordination of scientific intelligence as well as the production of intelligence. It was renamed the Scientific Intelligence Committee in 1959.

References
Fain, Tyrus G.; Plant, Katharine C.; and Milloy, Ross. *The Intelligence Community: History, Organization, and Issues.* Public Documents Series. New York: R.R. Bowker, 1977.

—**SCIENTIFIC INTELLIGENCE COMMITTEE (SIC)** was in existence from 1959, when it replaced the Scientific Estimates Committee, until 1976, when it was replaced by the Scientific and Technical Intelligence Committee. The SIC was a production committee of the director of Central Intelligence and had Community representation on the committee staff.

References
Laqueur, Walter. *A World of Secrets.* New York: Basic Books, 1985.

Maurer, Alfred C.; Turnstall, Marion D.; and Keagle, James M. *Intelligence Policy and Process.* Boulder, CO: Westview Press, 1985.

Von Hoene, John P. A. *Intelligence User's Guide.* Washington, DC: DIA, 1983.

—**SCRANGE, SHARON MARIE,** an employee in CIA Operations Support, was arrested on July 11, 1985, in Springfield, Virginia. She was convicted of espionage on September 27, 1985, and sentenced to five years in prison. She was paroled after serving eighteen months.

References
Allen, Thomas B., and Polmar, Norman. *Merchants of Treason: America's Secrets for Sale.* New York: Delacorte Press, 1988.

Crawford, David J. *Volunteers: The Betrayal of National Defense Secrets by Air Force Traitors.* Washington, DC: GPO, 1988.

—**SCREEN.** In surveillance, camouflage, and concealment, a screen is any natural or artificial material that is placed between the collection sensor and the object to be camouflaged or concealed.

References
Department of Defense, Joint Chiefs of Staff. *Department of Defense Dictionary of Military and Related Terms.* Washington, DC: GPO, 1986.

—**SEA ECHELON** is the portion of the assault shipping that withdraws from or remains out of the transport area during an amphibious landing, operates in designated areas that are farther out to sea from the beach, and is on-call to assist if necessary.

References
Department of Defense, Defense Intelligence College. *Glossary of Intelligence Terms and Definitions.* Washington, DC: DIC, 1987.

Department of Defense, Joint Chiefs of Staff. *Department of Defense Dictionary of Military and Related Terms.* Washington, DC: GPO, 1986.

—**SEARCH.** (1) Search is a step in the Army tactical signals intelligence (SIGINT) production process. *See also:* Artificial Intelligence, Signals Intelligence Process.

References
Department of Defense, Joint Chiefs of Staff. *Department of Defense Dictionary of Military and Related Terms.* Washington, DC: GPO, 1986.

Department of Defense, U.S. Army. *Military Intelligence Battalion Combat Electronic Warfare and Intelligence (Aerial Exploitation) (Corps).* Field Manual FM 34-22. Washington, DC: Headquarters, Department of the Army, 1984.

———. *Military Intelligence Battalion (Combat Electronic Warfare Intelligence) (Division).* Field Manual FM 34-10. Washington, DC: Headquarters, Department of the Army, 1981.

————. *Military Intelligence Battalion (CEWI) (Tactical Exploitation) (Corps): Counterintelligence, Interrogation, Electronic Warfare.* Field Manual FM 34-23. Washington, DC: Headquarters, Department of the Army, 1985.

————. *Military Intelligence Company (Combat Electronic Warfare and Intelligence) (Armored Cavalry Regiment/Separate Brigade).* Field Manual FM 34-30. Washington, DC: Headquarters, Department of the Army, 1983.

—**SECONDARY DISTRIBUTION** is a general intelligence term for issuing a copy of a publication from available stock in response to a specific request after the initial dissemination has been accomplished. It can also mean the loan of a copy of a publication from a library collection. *See also:* Dissemination, Intelligence Cycle.

References

Department of Defense, Defense Intelligence Agency. *Defense Intelligence Agency Manual.* Washington, DC: DIA, 1987.

—**SECONDARY ELEMENTS** is a target intelligence term that pertains to the target. Secondary elements are those parts of the target that are not directly relevant to the principal mission or functions of target. Thus, if the secondary elements are left undamaged they will affect neither positively nor negatively the continued functioning of the target in respect to its fulfilling its mission. If a radar site, for example, were a target, then the mess hall would be a secondary element, while the radar facility and its support facilities would be the critical primary elements, because they are critical to the site's mission. *See also:* Targeting.

References

Department of Defense, Joint Chiefs of Staff. *Department of Defense Dictionary of Military and Related Terms.* Washington, DC: GPO, 1986.

Department of Defense, Defense Intelligence College. *Glossary of Intelligence Terms and Definitions.* Washington, DC: DIC, 1987.

—**SECRET.** *See:* Security Classification.

—**SECRET INTELLIGENCE BRANCH OF THE OFFICE OF STRATEGIC SERVICES (OSS).** *See:* Office of Strategic Services, Strategic Services Unit.

—**SECRET WRITING** is a term used in clandestine and covert intelligence operations to describe messages that are written with an invisible substance, ranging from lemon juice to sophisticated chemicals, that will appear under certain conditions.

References

Quirk, John; Phillips, David; Cline, Ray; and Pforzheimer, Walter. *The Central Intelligence Agency: A Photographic History.* Guilford, CT: Foreign Intelligence Press, 1986.

—**SECRETARIAT.** *See:* Defense Intelligence Agency.

—**SECURE AREA** is an intelligence security and counterintelligence term for an accredited facility that is used for storing, handling, discussing, and processing sensitive compartmented information (SCI). *See also:* Access, Authorized, Classification, Classified Information, Code Word, Compromise, Declassification, Disclosure, Downgrade, Freedom of Information Act, Limited Access Area, Need-to-Know, Need-to-Know Principle, No-Lone Zone, Nondisclosure Agreement, Nondiscussion Area, Sanitization, Sanitize, Sanitized Area, Security Certification, Security Classification, Sensitive Compartmented Information, Sensitive Compartmented Information Facility, Two-Person Control.

References

Department of Defense, Defense Intelligence Agency. *Defense Intelligence Agency Manual.* Washington, DC: DIA, 1987.

Department of Defense, Defense Intelligence College. *Glossary of Intelligence Terms and Definitions.* Washington, DC: DIC, 1987.

Department of Defense, Joint Chiefs of Staff. *Department of Defense Dictionary of Military and Related Terms.* Washington, DC: GPO, 1986.

Godson, Roy, ed. *Intelligence Problems for the 1980s, Number 1: Elements of Intelligence.* Rev. ed. Washington, DC: National Strategy Information Center, 1983.

—**SECURE PHONE** is one that is equipped with scramblers or other devices so that conversations cannot be monitored. *See also:* Access, Authorized, Classification, Classified Information, Code Word, Compromise, Declassification, Disclosure, Downgrade, Freedom of Information Act, Limited Access Area, Need-to-Know, Need-to-

Know Principle, No-Lone Zone, Nondisclosure Agreement, Nondiscussion Area, Sanitization, Security Certification, Security Classification, Sensitive Compartmented Information, Sensitive Compartmented Information Facility, Two-Person Control.

References

Department of Defense, Defense Intelligence Agency. *Defense Intelligence Agency Manual.* Washington, DC: DIA, 1987.

Department of Defense, Defense Intelligence College. *Glossary of Intelligence Terms and Definitions.* Washington, DC: DIC, 1987.

Department of Defense, Joint Chiefs of Staff. *Department of Defense Dictionary of Military and Related Terms.* Washington, DC: GPO, 1986.

—**SECURE SUBSCRIBER FACILITY,** in communications security (COMSEC), refers to a secure telecommunications facility in which user-operated secure voice, data, facsimile, or video circuits terminate. *See also:* Communications Security.

References

Department of Defense, Defense Intelligence Agency. *Defense Intelligence Agency Manual.* Washington, DC: DIA, 1987.

Department of Defense, Defense Intelligence College. *Glossary of Intelligence Terms and Definitions.* Washington, DC: DIC, 1987.

Department of Defense, Joint Chiefs of Staff. *Department of Defense Dictionary of Military and Related Terms.* Washington, DC: GPO, 1986.

—**SECURE TELECOMMUNICATIONS FACILITY,** in communications security (COMSEC), refers to a telecommunications facility that uses cryptomaterial to protect the transmission of national security information. *See also:* Communications Security.

References

Department of Defense, Defense Intelligence Agency. *Defense Intelligence Agency Manual.* Washington, DC: DIA, 1987.

Department of Defense, Defense Intelligence College. *Glossary of Intelligence Terms and Definitions.* Washington, DC: DIC, 1987.

Department of Defense, Joint Chiefs of Staff. *Department of Defense Dictionary of Military and Related Terms.* Washington, DC: GPO, 1986.

—**SECURE VAULT AREA (SVA)** is an intelligence security and counterintelligence term for a sensitive compartmented information facility (SCIF)

that is under the security jurisdiction of the designated SVA custodian. It is identical in operation to a Special Security Office (SSO) except that it normally has no SCI communications capability. *See also:* Sensitive Compartmented Information Facility.

References

Department of Defense, Defense Intelligence Agency. *Defense Intelligence Agency Manual.* Washington, DC: DIA, 1987.

Department of Defense, Defense Intelligence College. *Glossary of Intelligence Terms and Definitions.* Washington, DC: DIC, 1987.

Department of Defense, Joint Chiefs of Staff. *Department of Defense Dictionary of Military and Related Terms.* Washington, DC: GPO, 1986.

—**SECURE VAULT AREA (SVA) CUSTODIAN** is the person who is responsible to the appointing senior intelligence officer (SIO) in matters concerning sensitive compartmented information (SCI) security of his or her SVA. *See also:* Secure Vault Area.

—**SECURE WORKING AREA (SWA)** is an intelligence security and counterintelligence term for a sensitive compartmented information facility (SCIF) that is used daily for handling, processing, or discussing SCI material but where no SCI material is stored. *See also:* Sensitive Compartmented Information Facility.

References

Department of Defense, Defense Intelligence Agency. *Defense Intelligence Agency Manual.* Washington, DC: DIA, 1987.

Department of Defense, Defense Intelligence College. *Glossary of Intelligence Terms and Definitions.* Washington, DC: DIC, 1987.

Department of Defense, Joint Chiefs of Staff. *Department of Defense Dictionary of Military and Related Terms.* Washington, DC: GPO, 1986.

—**SECURITY.** (1) In the general sense, security involves establishing and maintaining protective measures that are intended to ensure a state of inviolability from hostile acts and influences. The types of security include: automatic data processing system security; communications security; computer security; cryptographic security; electronic emission security; electronic security; emanation security; emission security; information security; multilevel security; national security; operations security; personnel security; physical security; signals security; transmission security; and uni-level security.(2) In Army tactical intelligence (TACINT), the term has three meanings: (a) security means the measures that are taken by a military unit, activity, or installation to protect itself against all acts that are designed to, or that may, impair its effectiveness; (b) security is a condition that results from establishing and maintaining protective measures that ensure a state of inviolability from hostile acts or influences; (c) with respect to classified matter, security is a condition that prevents unauthorized persons from having access to official information that is safeguarded in the interests of national security. *See also:* Access, Authorized, Classification, Classified Information, Code Word, Compromise, Declassification, Disclosure, Downgrade, Freedom of Information Act, Limited Access Area, Need-to-Know, Need-to-Know Principle, No-Lone Zone, Nondisclosure Agreement, Nondiscussion Area, Sanitization, Sanitize, Sanitized Area, Security Certification, Security Classification, Sensitive Compartmented Information, Sensitive Compartmented Information Facility, Two-Person Control.

References

Department of Defense, Defense Intelligence College. *Glossary of Intelligence Terms and Definitions.* Washington, DC: DIC, 1987.

Department of Defense, Joint Chiefs of Staff. *Department of Defense Dictionary of Military and Related Terms.* Washington, DC: GPO, 1986.

Department of Defense, U.S. Army. *Counter-Signals Intelligence (C-SIGINT) Operations.* Field Manual FM 34-62. Washington, DC: Headquarters, Department of the Army, 1986.

Godson, Roy, ed. *Intelligence Problems for the 1980s, Number 1: Elements of Intelligence.* Rev. ed. Washington, DC: National Strategy Information Center, 1983.

———. *Intelligence Problems for the 1980s, Number 3: Counterintelligence.* Washington, DC: National Strategy Information Center, 1980.

Kent, Sherman. *Strategic Intelligence for American World Policy.* Princeton, NJ: Princeton University Press, 1966.

Laqueur, Walter. *A World of Secrets.* New York: Basic Books, Inc., 1985.

Treverton, Gregory F. *Covert Action: The Limits of Intervention in the Postwar World.* New York: Basic Books, Inc., 1987.

—**SECURITY CERTIFICATION** is issued by a competent national authority and indicates that a person has been investigated and is eligible for access to classified material to the extent stated on the certification. *See also:* Security Classification.

References

American Bar Association. *Oversight and Accountability of the U.S. Intelligence Agencies: An Evaluation.* Washington, DC: ABA, 1985.

Department of Defense, Joint Chiefs of Staff. *Department of Defense Dictionary of Military and Related Terms.* Washington, DC: GPO, 1986.

Kent, Sherman. *Strategic Intelligence for American World Policy.* Princeton, NJ: Princeton University Press, 1966.

Maurer, Alfred C.; Turnstall, Marion D.; and Keagle, James M. *Intelligence Policy and Process.* Boulder, CO: Westview Press, 1985.

Turner, Stansfield. *Secrecy and Democracy: The CIA in Transition.* Boston: Houghton Mifflin, 1985.

—**SECURITY CLASSIFICATION** is a categorization by which national security information and material can be assigned a level of security that provides adequate safety for the information contained in the item. There are three security categories:

TOP SECRET is assigned to national security information or material that requires the highest degree of protection. Its unauthorized disclosure could reasonably be expected to cause exceptionally grave damage to the national security. Examples of "exceptionally grave damage" include armed hostilities against the United States or its allies; disruption of foreign relations vitally affecting the national security; the compromise of vital defense plans or complex cryptologic and communications intelligence systems; the revelation of sensitive intelligence operations; and the disclosure of scientific or technological developments vital to national security.

SECRET is assigned to national security information that requires a substantial degree of protection. Its unauthorized disclosure could reasonably be expected to cause serious damage to the national security. Examples of "serious damage" include disruption of foreign relations significantly affecting the national security; significantly impairing a program or policy directly related to the national security; revealing significant military plans or intelligence operations; and compromising significant scientific or technological developments relating to the national security.

CONFIDENTIAL is assigned to national security information that requires protection. Its unauthorized disclosure could reasonably be expected to cause damage to the national security. *See also:* Access, Authorized, Classification, Classified Information, Code Word, Compromise, Declassification, Disclosure, Downgrade, Freedom of Information Act, Limited Access Area, Need-to-Know, Need-to-Know Principle, No-Lone Zone, Nondisclosure Agreement, Nondiscussion Area, Sanitization, Sanitize, Sanitized Area, Security Certification, Security Classification, Sensitive Compartmented Information, Sensitive Compartmented Information Facility, Two-Person Control.

References

American Bar Association. *Oversight and Accountability of the U.S. Intelligence Agencies: An Evaluation.* Washington, DC: ABA, 1985.

Department of Defense, Joint Chiefs of Staff. *Department of Defense Dictionary of Military and Related Terms.* Washington, DC: GPO, 1986.

Godson, Roy, ed. *Intelligence Problems for the 1980s, Number 1: Elements of Intelligence.* Rev. ed. Washington, DC: National Strategy Information Center, 1983.

Kent, Sherman. *Strategic Intelligence for American World Policy.* Princeton, NJ: Princeton University Press, 1966.

Maurer, Alfred C.; Turnstall, Marion D.; and Keagle, James M. *Intelligence Policy and Process.* Boulder, CO: Westview Press, 1985.

Turner, Stansfield. *Secrecy and Democracy: The CIA in Transition.* Boston: Houghton Mifflin, 1985.

—SECURITY CLEARANCE is an administrative determination that an individual is eligible, from a security standpoint, for access to classified information. *See also:* Access, Authorized, Classification, Classified Information, Code Word, Compromise, Declassification, Disclosure, Downgrade, Freedom of Information Act, Limited Access Area, Need-to-know, Need-to-Know Principle, No-Lone Zone, Nondisclosure Agreement, Nondiscussion Area, Sanitization, Sanitize, Sanitized Area, Security Certification, Security Classification, Sensitive Compartmented Information, Sensitive Compartmented Information Facility, Two-Person Control.

References

American Bar Association. *Oversight and Accountability of the U.S. Intelligence Agencies: An Evaluation.* Washington, DC: ABA, 1985.

Department of Defense, Joint Chiefs of Staff. *Department of Defense Dictionary of Military and Related Terms.* Washington, DC: GPO, 1986.

Godson, Roy, ed. *Intelligence Problems for the 1980s, Number 1: Elements of Intelligence.* Rev. ed. Washington, DC: National Strategy Information Center, 1983.

Kent, Sherman. *Strategic Intelligence for American World Policy.* Princeton, NJ: Princeton University Press, 1966.

Maurer, Alfred C.; Turnstall, Marion D.; and Keagle, James M. *Intelligence Policy and Process.* Boulder, CO: Westview Press, 1985.

Turner, Stansfield. *Secrecy and Democracy: The CIA in Transition.* Boston: Houghton Mifflin, 1985.

—SECURITY COMMITTEE (CIA). *See:* Director of Central Intelligence Committee.

—SECURITY COUNTERMEASURES, in counterintelligence, counterespionage, and counterinsurgency, are measures that are designed to impair the effectiveness of an unfriendly or hostile attack upon security.

References

American Bar Association. *Oversight and Accountability of the U.S. Intelligence Agencies: An Evaluation.* Washington, DC: ABA, 1985.

Department of Defense, Joint Chiefs of Staff. *Department of Defense Dictionary of Military and Related Terms.* Washington, DC: GPO, 1986.

Kent, Sherman. *Strategic Intelligence for American World Policy.* Princeton, NJ: Princeton University Press, 1966.

Maurer, Alfred C.; Turnstall, Marion D.; and Keagle, James M. *Intelligence Policy and Process.* Boulder, CO: Westview Press, 1985.

—SECURITY EDUCATION AND SELF-INSPECTION PROGRAM. *See:* Defense Intelligence Agency.

—SECURITY INTELLIGENCE is intelligence on the identity, capabilities, and intentions of hostile organizations or individuals who are, or may be, engaged in espionage, sabotage, subversion, or terrorism. *See also:* Counterintelligence, Intelligence, Security.

References

Department of Defense, Joint Chiefs of Staff. *Department of Defense Dictionary of Military and Related Terms.* Washington, DC: GPO, 1986.

Godson, Roy, ed. *Intelligence Problems for the 1980s, Number 3: Counterintelligence.* Washington, DC: National Strategy Information Center, 1980.

Kent, Sherman. *Strategic Intelligence for American World Policy.* Princeton, NJ: Princeton University Press, 1966.

Treverton, Gregory F. *Covert Action: The Limits of Intervention in the Postwar World.* New York: Basic Books, 1987.

Turner, Stansfield. *Secrecy and Democracy: The CIA in Transition.* Boston: Houghton Mifflin, 1985.

—SECURITY MEASURES, as defined by the Church Committee, are "steps taken by the government and intelligence departments and agencies, among others, for protection from espionage, observation, sabotage, annoyance, or surprise. With respect to classified materials, it is the condition which prevents unauthorized persons from having access to official information which is safeguarded in the interests of national defense."

References
American Bar Association. *Oversight and Accountability of the U.S. Intelligence Agencies: An Evaluation.* Washington, DC: ABA, 1985.

Godson, Roy, ed. *Intelligence Problems for the 1980s, Number 1: Elements of Intelligence.* Rev. ed. Washington, DC: National Strategy Information Center, 1983.

———. *Intelligence Problems for the 1980s, Number 3: Counterintelligence.* Washington, DC: National Strategy Information Center, 1980.

Kent, Sherman. *Strategic Intelligence for American World Policy.* Princeton, NJ: Princeton University Press, 1966.

Maurer, Alfred C.; Turnstall, Marion D.; and Keagle, James M. *Intelligence Policy and Process.* Boulder, CO: Westview Press, 1985.

U.S. Congress. Senate. *Final Report of the Senate Select Committee to Study Government Operations with Respect to Intelligence Activities. Report 94-755. Book I, Foreign and Military Intelligence.* Washington, DC: GPO, 1976.

—SEED VARIABLE, in communications security (COMSEC), means a cryptovariable that is intentionally loaded into cryptoequipment and from which a sequence of updated variables is subsequently derived. *See also:* Communications Security.

References
Department of Defense, U.S. Army. *Counter-Signals Intelligence (C-SIGINT) Operations.* Field Manual FM 34-62. Washington, Headquarters, Department of the Army, 1986.

—SELF-AUTHENTICATION, in communications security (COMSEC), means the implicit authentication of transmission on a secure telecommunications system or cryptonet to a predetermined classification level, through the use of the appropriate key. *See also:* Communications Security.

References
Department of Defense, U.S. Army. *Counter-Signals Intelligence (C-SIGINT) Operations.* Field Manual FM 34-62. Washington, Headquarters, Department of the Army, 1986.

—SELF-PROTECTION JAMMING, in electronic warfare (EW), is jamming that is performed by an aircraft in order to protect itself. *See also:* Electronic Warfare.

References
Department of Defense, Defense Intelligence College. *Glossary of Intelligence Terms and Definitions.* Washington, DC: DIC, 1987.

Department of Defense, Joint Chiefs of Staff. *Department of Defense Dictionary of Military and Related Terms.* Washington, DC: GPO, 1986.

Department of Defense, U.S. Army. *Counter-Signals Intelligence (C-SIGINT) Operations.* Field Manual FM 34-62. Washington, Headquarters, Department of the Army, 1986.

—SENATE INTELLIGENCE COMMITTEE. *See:* Senate Select Committee on Intelligence (SSCI).

—SENATE RESOLUTION 21, passed by the 94th Congress, established the Select Committee on Government Operations with Respect to Intelligence Activities. *See:* Church Committee.

—SENATE RESOLUTION 400, passed by the 94th Congress, established the Senate Select Committee on Intelligence. The purpose of the committee was to continually monitor the activities and programs of the U.S. Intelligence Community and to report to the Senate on the same. The committee was to be composed of sixteen members; eight members, including the chairman, from the majority party; and eight members, including the vice chairman, from the minority party. No member was to serve on the committee for more than eight years. The following were the significant aspects of the resolution: (1) All proposed legislation concerning the community was to be referred to the Committee for consideration. (2) The Committee was to establish provisions to ensure adequate security for the classified materials that were passed to it. (3) The committee could release classified material to the public, but first had to notify the president. The president had five days to respond if he opposed releasing the information to the public. (4) The Resolution provided for the full funding of the committee, which was to receive all the files of the Senate Select Committee on Government Operations with Respect to Intelligence Activities (the Church Committee), when that committee expired. (5) Among the specific duties assigned to the committee were to study the quality of the analytical capabilities of the U.S. foreign intelligence agencies, to investigate the authority of the intelligence agencies to conduct different types of intelligence activities, to investigate the organization of the intelligence community, to investigate how Congress is informed of covert and clandestine activities, to investigate the desirability of a joint congressional committee on intelligence, and to investigate how Intelligence Community funds were allocated. (6) The Committee was to report regularly to the Senate on its findings.

References

Godson, Roy, ed. *Intelligence Problems for the 1980s, Number 1: Elements of Intelligence.* Rev. ed. Washington, DC: National Strategy Information Center, 1983.

U.S. Congress. Senate. *Senate Resolution 400, A Resolution Establishing a Select Committee on Intelligence.* 94th Congress.

—**SENATE RESOLUTION 2525,** the National Intelligence Reorganization and Reform Act of 1978, was a massive compendium about intelligence organization, control, accountability, and oversight that was introduced by Senator Walter Huddleston in February 1978. It was an attempt to develop a legislative charter for the Intelligence Community and was purportedly meant as a vehicle for discussion on the issue. It failed because Congress could not decide on the types of abuses and excesses to legislate against. Nonetheless, it was significant for several reasons. First, it culminated the attempt by Congress

to fulfill its oversight responsibilities concerning the Intelligence Community. The failure of the bill or another bill like it to pass signified that Congress would henceforth be much less assertive in its relations with the community. Second, the bill culminated a trend to develop charter legislation for the intelligence agencies. Failure of the bill also signified that such efforts would also meet with failure. *See also:* Congressional Oversight.

References

Godson, Roy, ed. *Intelligence Problems for the 1980s, Number 1: Elements of Intelligence.* Rev. ed. Washington, DC: National Strategy Information Center, 1983.

Lefever, Ernest W., and Godson, Roy. *The CIA and the American Ethic: An Unfinished Debate.* Washington, DC: Ethics and Public Policy Center, Georgetown University, 1979.

Oseth, John M. *Regulating U.S. Intelligence Operations: A Study in the Definition of the National Interest.* Frankfurt: University of Kentucky Press, 1985.

—**SENATE SELECT COMMITTEE ON INTELLIGENCE (SSCI)** was founded in 1976. As the Watergate scandal unraveled, it appeared that the Intelligence Community may have exceeded its authority and that its operations may have been illegal. Both Houses created investigative committees. The Senate created the Select Committee to Study Government Operations with Respect to Intelligence Activities, chaired by Senator Frank Church, which concentrated on intelligence abuses and illegalities. Although it completed its investigation and issued its report in April 1976, the Senate maintained its SSCI, and congressional oversight was therefore continued into the Carter administration. The Senate Select Committee reported in May 1977 that the intelligence agencies were now properly accountable to Congress and that presidential oversight was working—relatively high marks when one considers the recent past. *See also:* Congressional Oversight.

References

Breckinridge, Scott D. *The CIA and the U.S. Intelligence System.* Boulder, CO: Westview Press, 1986.

Corson, William R. *The Armies of Ignorance: The Rise of the American Intelligence Empire.* New York: Dial Press, 1977.

Godson, Roy, ed. *Intelligence Problems for the 1980s, Number 1: Elements of Intelligence.* Rev.

ed. Washington, DC: National Strategy Information Center, 1983.

————. *Intelligence Problems for the 1980s, Number 2: Analysis and Estimates.* Washington, DC: National Strategy Information Center, 1980.

Laqueur, Walter. *A World of Secrets.* New York: Basic Books, 1985.

Lowenthal, Mark M. *U.S. Intelligence: Evolution and Anatomy.* New York: Praeger, 1984.

Maurer, Alfred C.; Turnstall, Marion D.; and Keagle, James M. *Intelligence Policy and Process.* Boulder, CO: Westview Press, 1985.

U.S. Congress. Senate. *Final Report of the Senate Select Committee to Study Government Operations with Respect to Intelligence Activities. Report 94-755. Book I, Foreign and Military Intelligence.* Washington, DC: GPO, 1976.

—SENATE SELECT COMMITTEE TO STUDY GOVERNMENT OPERATIONS WITH RESPECT TO INTELLIGENCE ACTIVITIES. *See:* Church Committee.

—SENIOR INTELLIGENCE OFFICER (SIO) is the highest ranking individual within a given command, component, or element of the Intelligence Community organization. He is charged with direct foreign intelligence missions, functions, and responsibilities.

References

Department of Defense, Defense Intelligence Agency. *Defense Intelligence Agency Manual.* Washington, DC: DIA, 1987.

Department of Defense, Defense Intelligence College. *Glossary of Intelligence Terms and Definitions.* Washington, DC: DIC, 1987.

Department of Defense, Joint Chiefs of Staff. *Department of Defense Dictionary of Military and Related Terms.* Washington, DC: GPO, 1986.

—SENIOR INTERAGENCY GROUP FOR INTELLIGENCE (SIG I) is a committee of the National Security Council and is composed of the director of Central Intelligence, the assistant to the president for national security affairs, the deputy secretary of state, the deputy secretary of defense, the chairman of the Joint Chiefs of Staff, the deputy attorney general, the director of the Federal Bureau of Investigation, and the director of the National Security Agency. The chairman varies in accordance with the meeting's agenda, and is charged to advise and assist the National Security Council in fulfilling its responsibilities

for intelligence policy and intelligence matters. It ensures that there is communication between the agencies on problems requiring interagency involvement, and it monitors the execution of previously approved policies and decisions.

References

Laqueur, Walter. *A World of Secrets.* New York: Basic Books, 1985.

—SENIOR INTERAGENCY GROUPS (SIGS). The most complete and incisive discussion of the SIGs was provided by a Special Review Board, composed of Senator John Tower, Senator Edmund Muskie, and Lieutenant General Brent Scowcroft, that was created by President Reagan to examine the National Security Council, the National Security Council staff, and the assistant to the president for national security affairs, in the wake of the Iran Contra affair. The board made the following observation:

The National Security Council has frequently been supported by committees made up of representatives of the relevant national security departments and agencies. These committees analyze issues prior to consideration by the Council. There are generally several levels of committees. At the top level, officials from each agency (at the Deputy Secretary or Under Secretary level) meet to provide a senior level policy review. These senior level committees are in turn supported by more junior interagency groups (usually at the Assistant Secretary level). These in turn may oversee staff level working groups that prepare detailed analysis of important issues.

Administrations have differed in the extent to which they have used these interagency committees. President Kennedy placed little stock in them. The Nixon and Carter Administrations, by contrast, made much use of them.

President Reagan initially declared that the National Security Council would be the principal forum for consideration of national security issues. To support the work of the Council, President Reagan established an interagency committee system headed by three Senior Interagency Groups (or "SIGs"), one each for foreign policy, defense policy, and intelligence. They were chaired by the Secretary of State, the Secretary of Defense, and the Director of Central Intelligence, respectively.

President Reagan appointed several additional members to his National Security Council and allowed staff attendance at meetings. The resultant size of the meetings led the President to turn increasingly to a smaller group (called the National Security Planning Group or "NSPG"). Attendance at its meetings was more restricted but included the statutory principals of the NSC. The NSPG was supported by the SIGs, and new SIGs were occasionally created to deal with particular issues. These were frequently chaired by the National Security Advisor. But generally the SIGs and many of their subsidiary groups (called Interagency Groups or "IGs") fell into disuse.

References

Godson, Roy, ed. *Intelligence Problems for the 1980s, Number 1: Elements of Intelligence.* Rev. ed. Washington, DC: National Strategy Information Center, 1983.

Laqueur, Walter. *A World of Secrets.* New York: Basic Books, 1985.

Office of the President of the United States. *Report of the President's Special Review Board.* Washington, DC: GPO, Feb. 26, 1987.

—**SENSITIVE** indicates that the subject requires special protection from disclosure in order to avoid a compromise or a threat to the security of the sponsor. It may be applied to an agency, installation, person, position, document, material, or activity. *See also:* Sensitive Compartmented Information (SCI).

References

Department of Defense, Defense Intelligence College. *Glossary of Intelligence Terms and Definitions.* Washington, DC: DIC, 1987.

Department of Defense, Joint Chiefs of Staff. *Department of Defense Dictionary of Military and Related Terms.* Washington, DC: GPO, 1986.

Laqueur, Walter. *A World of Secrets.* New York: Basic Books, 1985.

Treverton, Gregory F. *Covert Action: The Limits of Intervention in the Postwar World.* New York: Basic Books, 1987.

U.S. Congress. Senate. *Final Report of the Senate Select Committee to Study Government Operations with Respect to Intelligence Activities. Report 94-755. Book I, Foreign and Military Intelligence.* Washington, DC: GPO, 1976.

—**SENSITIVE COMPARTMENTED INFORMATION (SCI)** is information requiring special controls, access requirements, and restricted handling within compartmented intelligence systems and for which compartmentation has been established. *See also:* Access, Authorized, Classification, Classified Information, Code Word, Compromise, Declassification, Disclosure, Downgrade, Freedom of Information Act, Limited Access Area, Need-to-Know, Need-to-Know Principle, No-Lone Zone, Nondisclosure Agreement, Nondiscussion Area, Sanitization,

Sanitize, Sanitized Area, Security Certification, Security Classification, Sensitive Compartmented Information (SCI), Sensitive Compartmented Information Facility, Two-Person Control.

References

Department of Defense, Defense Intelligence Agency. *Defense Intelligence Agency Manual.* Washington, DC: DIA, 1987.

Department of Defense, Defense Intelligence College. *Glossary of Intelligence Terms and Definitions.* Washington, DC: DIC, 1987.

Department of Defense, Joint Chiefs of Staff. *Department of Defense Dictionary of Military and Related Terms.* Washington, DC: GPO, 1986.

Maroni, Alice C. *Special Access Programs: Understanding the "Black Budget."* Washington, DC: Foreign Affairs and National Defense Division, Congressional Research Service, Library of Congress, 1987.

Turner, Stansfield. *Secrecy and Democracy: The CIA in Transition.* Boston: Houghton Mifflin, 1985.

—**SENSITIVE COMPARTMENTED INFORMATION BILLET STRUCTURE (SCIBS)** is a listing of billets or positions for which an SCI need to know has been established by a proper authority. It identifies those billets by billet number, descriptive title, organization, and similar data. *See also:* Sensitive Compartmented Information (SCI), Sensitive Compartmented Information Facility.

References

Department of Defense, Defense Intelligence Agency. *Defense Intelligence Agency Manual.* Washington, DC: DIA, 1987.

———. *Organization, Mission and Key Personnel.* Washington, DC: DIA, 1986.

Turner, Stansfield. *Secrecy and Democracy: The CIA in Transition.* Boston: Houghton Mifflin, 1985.

—**SENSITIVE COMPARTMENTED INFORMATION FACILITY (SCIF)** is an accredited area, room, group of rooms, or installation where SCI may be stored, used, discussed, and/or electronically processed. SCI procedural and physical measures prevent the free access of persons unless they have been formally indoctrinated for the particular SCI that is authorized for use and storage within the SCIF.

Qualification of the facility is a continuous process, with periodic reinspections concerning the facility's physical security, emissions security, and personnel security. The key individual in this process is the special security officer, who is the point of contact for the special access programs. *See also:* Sensitive Compartmented Information (SCI).

References

Department of Defense, Defense Intelligence Agency. *Defense Intelligence Agency Manual.* Washington, DC: DIA, 1987.

————. *Organization, Mission and Key Personnel.* Washington, DC: DIA, 1986.

—**SENSITIVE INTELLIGENCE SOURCES AND METHODS** refers to intelligence that has been developed from information available from a single, very vulnerable source or from a very vulnerable method. Revealing the intelligence will enable the enemy to easily identify the source or the method and to take measures to deny the passage of further information. Leaks of this type of information are probably the most devastating, because not only is the information compromised, but the source from which the information originated or the method by which it was obtained may be permanently destroyed. Such damage usually extends into the future if we cannot develop alternative sources to provide information.

References

Department of Defense, Defense Intelligence Agency. *Defense Intelligence Agency Manual.* Washington, DC: DIA, 1987.

Department of Defense, Defense Intelligence College. *Glossary of Intelligence Terms and Definitions.* Washington, DC: DIC, 1987.

—**SENSOR** is a technical device that is designed to detect and respond to one or more particular stimulae and that may record or transmit a resultant impulse for interpretation or measurement. It is often called a *technical sensor.* A *special sensor* is an unclassified term that is used as a matter of convenience to refer to a highly classified or controlled technical sensor.

References

Department of Defense, Defense Intelligence Agency. *Defense Intelligence Agency Manual.* Washington, DC: DIA, 1987.

Department of Defense, Defense Intelligence College. *Glossary of Intelligence Terms and Definitions.* Washington, DC: DIC, 1987.

—**SEQUENTIAL (ELEMENT ARRANGEMENT),** a baud-based system term used in communications intelligence, communications security,

operations security, and signals analysis, is the characterizing of a multiplex signal in which the elements of each channel are adjacent to each other. When all the elements of a channel have been sent, those of the succeeding channel are sent. *See also:* Communications Security.

References

Department of Defense, U.S. Army. *Counter-Signals Intelligence (C-SIGINT) Operations.* Field Manual FM 34-62. Washington, Headquarters, Department of the Army, 1986.

—**SERVICE CRYPTOLOGIC AGENCIES (SCAs),** as defined by the Church Committee, are the Army Security Agency, the Naval Security Group Command, and Air Force Security Service. Their signals intelligence collection functions were brought under the operational control of the director of the National Security Agency (NSA) when the SCAs were confederated into the Central Security Service (CSS) in 1971, and the director of the NSA was given the additional responsibility of chief of the CSS. *See also:* Service Cryptologic Elements.

References

Laqueur, Walter. *A World of Secrets.* New York: Basic Books, Inc., 1985.

U.S. Congress. Senate. *Final Report of the Senate Select Committee to Study Government Operations with Respect to Intelligence Activities. Report 94-755. Book I, Foreign and Military Intelligence.* Washington, DC: GPO, 1976.

—**SERVICE CRYPTOLOGIC ELEMENTS** are U.S. Army, Navy, and Air Force elements that perform cryptologic functions. They are also known as service cryptologic agencies or service cryptologic organizations.

References

Department of Defense, Defense Intelligence College. *Glossary of Intelligence Terms and Definitions.* Washington, DC: DIC, 1987.

Laqueur, Walter. *A World of Secrets.* New York: Basic Books, 1985.

—**SERVICE CRYPTOLOGIC ORGANIZATIONS (SCOs).** *See:* Service Cryptologic Elements.

—**SETTING UP** is a term used in clandestine and covert intelligence operations to describe when secret agents frame or trap a target. *See also:* Ladies, Raven, Sisters, Taxi.

References

Becket, Henry S. A. *The Dictionary of Espionage: Spookspeak into English.* New York: Stein and Day, 1986.

Deacon, Richard. *Spyclopedia: An Encyclopedia of Spies, Secret Services, Operations, Jargon, and All Subjects Related to the World of Espionage.* London: Macdonald, 1987.

Ranelagh, John. *The Agency: The Rise and Decline of the CIA.* New York: Simon and Schuster, 1986.

—**SHADOW** is to surveil or to follow. *See:* Surveillance.

References

Becket, Henry S. A. *The Dictionary of Espionage: Spookspeak into English.* New York: Stein and Day, 1986.

Deacon, Richard. *Spyclopedia: An Encyclopedia of Spies, Secret Services, Operations, Jargon, and All Subjects Related to the World of Espionage.* London: Macdonald, 1987.

Kessler, Ronald. *Spy vs. Spy: Stalking Soviet Spies in America.* New York: Charles Scribner's Sons, 1988.

Ranelagh, John. *The Agency: The Rise and Decline of the CIA.* New York: Simon and Schuster, 1986.

—**SHADRIN, NICHOLAS,** is one of the most puzzling individuals to ever confront the Intelligence Community. The captain of a Soviet destroyer, Shadrin and the Polish woman whom he loved fled across the Baltic Sea in 1959 in a daring escape.

Shadrin married and came to the United States. With a master's degree in engineering, a doctoral degree that he earned at George Washington University, an infectious personality, and a keen mind, Shadrin quickly became everyone's friend. By the accounts of almost everyone he met, Shadrin did not pry, did not seek information. Rather, his motive always seemed to be a desire to be accepted. Several people referred to him as like a lovable Russian bear.

Shadrin sought employment and was hired by the Defense Intelligence Agency (DIA). Because of his background, he was denied high-level security clearances and therefore was placed in the DIA spaces in the Old Post Office Building on Pennsylvania Avenue with all the other Soviet and East European defectors that had been hired by the agency. There they were to scan the open literature—newspapers, magazines, and journals—and identify items of intelligence interest.

According to Henry Hurt, Shadrin's desire for acceptance became focused on his gaining a security clearance, and, in 1975, he purportedly agreed to act as a double agent for U.S. intelligence in the hopes of being granted a clearance as a reward. At any rate, he and his wife traveled to Vienna for a meeting with Soviet intelligence. Hurt points out the many errors in the operation, including assigning inexperienced personnel and the lack of adequate protection for Shadrin. One thing is certain: Shadrin never returned to his wife from the meeting, and the assumption is that he was picked up by Soviet intelligence.

A damage assessment was then made concerning the kidnapping or defection of Shadrin. Initially, it appeared that the damage was slight, if any at all. The DIA had placed him in the Old Post Office Building and had made certain that he did not have access to classified information. But then the investigation was expanded and it was found that everyone knew him. He frequented the Georgetown cocktail circuit and had friends in the Intelligence Community. He was also on very friendly terms with many people at George Washington and Georgetown universities. And many of his government friends had talked. In sum, the conductors of the damage assessment concluded that the damage could not be calculated, but that it was severe.

To this day, no one knows whether Shadrin was a Soviet agent or whether he was kidnapped. It is assumed that the Soviets now have whatever information Shadrin had because, whether willingly or under interrogation, it is assumed that he would have told them everything that he knew. *See also:* Double Agent.

References

Hurt, Henry. *The Spy Who Never Came Back.* New York: Reader's Digest Press, 1981.

—**SHAKING OFF THE DOGS,** a clandestine and covert intelligence operations term, is the process of losing a surveillance team. *See also:* Alternate Meet, Fur-Lined Seat Cover, Go-Away, Go to Ground, Meet Area, Movements Analysis, Riding Shotgun, Stroller, Surround, Surveillance, What's Your Twenty?

References

Becket, Henry S. A. *The Dictionary of Espionage: Spookspeak into English.* New York: Stein and Day, 1986.

Deacon, Richard. *Spyclopedia: An Encyclopedia of Spies, Secret Services, Operations, Jargon, and All Subjects Related to the World of Espionage.* London: Macdonald, 1987.

Ranelagh, John. *The Agency: The Rise and Decline of the CIA.* New York: Simon and Schuster, 1986.

—**SHAKING THE TREE** is a counterintelligence technique that uses disinformation or some other means to throw the opponent off guard, with the hopes that these actions will provide additional information. *See also:* Black Bag Job, Black Bag Operation, Black List, Confusion Agent, Dirty Tricks, Infiltration, Informant, Inside Man, Penetration.

References

Becket, Henry S. A. *The Dictionary of Espionage: Spookspeak into English.* New York: Stein and Day, 1986.

Deacon, Richard. *Spyclopedia: An Encyclopedia of Spies, Secret Services, Operations, Jargon, and All Subjects Related to the World of Espionage.* London: Macdonald, 1987.

Ranelagh, John. *The Agency: The Rise and Decline of the CIA.* New York: Simon and Schuster, 1986.

Treverton, Gregory F. *Covert Action: The Limits of Intervention in the Postwar World.* New York: Basic Books, 1987.

—**SHEEP DIPPING.** (1) Sheep dipping is a term used in clandestine and covert intelligence operations. It means using a military instrument (such as an airplane) or an officer in a clandestine operation. He is usually in a civilian capacity or under civilian cover, although the instrument or officer will covertly retain his military identity or its ownership. (2) Sheep dipping also means placing individuals in organizations or groups where they become active, establish their credentials, and then collect information of intelligence interest. *See also:* Agent, Agent Authentication, Agent in Place, Agent Net, Agent of Influence, Agent Provocateur, Case, Case Officer, Clean, Cover, Cover Name, Cover Organizations, Cover Story, Dirty Tricks, Illegal Operations, Penetration, Penetration Aids, Pseudonym, Recruitment, Recruitment in Place, Special Activities, Submerge, Suitable Cover.

References

Becket, Henry S. A. *The Dictionary of Espionage: Spookspeak into English.* New York: Stein and Day, 1986.

Deacon, Richard. *Spyclopedia: An Encyclopedia of Spies, Secret Services, Operations, Jargon, and All Subjects Related to the World of Espionage.* London: Macdonald, 1987.

Ranelagh, John. *The Agency: The Rise and Decline of the CIA.* New York: Simon and Schuster, 1986.

Quirk, John; Phillips, David; Cline, Ray; and Pforzheimer, Walter. *The Central Intelligence Agency: A Photographic History.* Guilford, CT: Foreign Intelligence Press, 1986.

U.S. Congress. Senate. *Final Report of the Senate Select Committee to Study Government Operations with Respect to Intelligence Activities. Report 94-755. Book I, Foreign and Military Intelligence.* Washington, DC: GPO, 1976.

—**SHIELDED ENCLOSURE,** in communications security (COMSEC), means an area (a room or a container) that is specifically designed to attenuate electromagnetic radiation or acoustic emanations that originate from either inside or outside of the area. *See also:* Communications Security.

References

Department of Defense, Defense Intelligence College. *Glossary of Intelligence Terms and Definitions.* Washington, DC: DIC, 1987.

Department of Defense, Joint Chiefs of Staff. *Department of Defense Dictionary of Military and Related Terms.* Washington, DC: GPO, 1986.

Maurer, Alfred C.; Turnstall, Marion D.; and Keagle, James M. *Intelligence Policy and Process.* Boulder, CO: Westview Press, 1985.

—**SHOE,** a clandestine and covert intelligence operations term, means a false passport. *See also:* Establishing Bonafides, Legend, Pocket Litter.

References

Becket, Henry S. A. *The Dictionary of Espionage: Spookspeak into English.* New York: Stein and Day, 1986.

Deacon, Richard. *Spyclopedia: An Encyclopedia of Spies, Secret Services, Operations, Jargon, and All Subjects Related to the World of Espionage.* London: Macdonald, 1987.

Ranelagh, John. *The Agency: The Rise and Decline of the CIA.* New York: Simon and Schuster, 1986.

Quirk, John; Phillips, David; Cline, Ray; and Pforzheimer, Walter. *The Central Intelligence Agency: A Photographic History.* Guilford, CT: Foreign Intelligence Press, 1986.

—**SHOPPING LIST** is a term used in counterintelligence operations. It is the list of Western technical, electronic, and industrial equipment that the KGB wants to obtain, either through purchasing or by stealing. The list is updated at least annually. *See also:* Intelligence Requirements.

References

Becket, Henry S. A. *The Dictionary of Espionage: Spookspeak into English.* New York: Stein and Day, 1986.

Deacon, Richard. *Spyclopedia: An Encyclopedia of Spies, Secret Services, Operations, Jargon, and All Subjects Related to the World of Espionage.* London: Macdonald, 1987.

Ranelagh, John. *The Agency: The Rise and Decline of the CIA.* New York: Simon and Schuster, 1986.

Turner, Stansfield. *Secrecy and Democracy: The CIA in Transition.* Boston: Houghton Mifflin, 1985.

—**SHOPWORN GOODS** is a term used in counterintelligence operations to describe information that a defector gives the other side. The information is so dated that it is worthless.

References

Becket, Henry S. A. *The Dictionary of Espionage: Spookspeak into English.* New York: Stein and Day, 1986.

Deacon, Richard. *Spyclopedia: An Encyclopedia of Spies, Secret Services, Operations, Jargon, and All Subjects Related to the World of Espionage.* London: Macdonald, 1987.

Ranelagh, John. *The Agency: The Rise and Decline of the CIA.* New York: Simon and Schuster, 1986.

—**SHORAN** is an electronic measuring system that indicates the distance from an airborne station to each of two ground stations.

References

Department of Defense, Defense Intelligence College. *Glossary of Intelligence Terms and Definitions.* Washington, DC: DIC, 1987.

Department of Defense, Joint Chiefs of Staff. *Department of Defense Dictionary of Military and Related Terms.* Washington, DC: GPO, 1986.

—**SIBLINGS** is a Central Intelligence Agency euphemism for employees of the Defense Intelligence Agency.

References

Becket, Henry S. A. *The Dictionary of Espionage: Spookspeak into English.* New York: Stein and Day, 1986.

Deacon, Richard. *Spyclopedia: An Encyclopedia of Spies, Secret Services, Operations, Jargon, and All Subjects Related to the World of Espionage.* London: Macdonald, 1987.

Ranelagh, John. *The Agency: The Rise and Decline of the CIA.* New York: Simon and Schuster, 1986.

—**SIDE-LOOKING AIRBORNE RADAR (SLAR)** is an airborne radar, viewing at right angles to the axis of the vehicle, which produces a presentation of terrain or targets. SLAR can provide stand-off surveillance of large areas, has a near–all-weather capability, is equally effective day or night, and has a stand-off capability that places it out of range of enemy forward defense systems.

References

Department of Defense, Defense Intelligence College. *Glossary of Intelligence Terms and Definitions.* Washington, DC: DIC, 1987.

Department of Defense, Joint Chiefs of Staff. *Department of Defense Dictionary of Military and Related Terms.* Washington, DC: GPO, 1986.

—**SIGINT ACTIVITY** involves the necessary actions that are conducted in order to produce signals intelligence. *See also:* SIGINT-Related Activity.

References

Department of Defense, Defense Intelligence College. *Glossary of Intelligence Terms and Definitions.* Washington, DC: DIC, 1987.

Department of Defense, U.S. Army. *Counter-Signals Intelligence (C-SIGINT) Operations.* Field Manual FM 34-62, Washington, DC: Headquarters, Department of the Army, 1986.

Godson, Roy, ed. *Intelligence Problems for the 1980s, Number 1: Elements of Intelligence.* Rev. ed. Washington, DC: National Strategy Information Center, 1983.

Maurer, Alfred C.; Turnstall, Marion D.; and Keagle, James M. *Intelligence Policy and Process.* Boulder, CO: Westview Press, 1985.

Turner, Stansfield. *Secrecy and Democracy: The CIA in Transition.* Boston: Houghton Mifflin, 1985.

—**SIGINT PROCESS.** The process used to perform signals intelligence (SIGINT) in the Army tactical intelligence (TACINT) context involves search, identification, interception, direction finding, recording, analysis, and dissemination. Each of these steps are defined as follows:

Search is the beginning of the SIGINT process. In this step, intercept operators are assigned a portion of the frequency spectrum and are told to look for signals of interest. Once a signal is intercepted, the intelligence portion of the process begins.

Identification is the analysis of the content of the communications or signal characteristics of the emitter in order to identify the signal for further exploitation. Analysis can be as simple as identifying a language or as complicated as determining a special code that is being used by a unit.

Direction finding (DF) is the determining of an emitter's location. DF is used to determine the approximate direction or bearing of a transmitting antenna. When the DF station obtains a line of bearing (LOB), it provides an approximate direction to the emitter, but not the distance. (The exception is the single station locator system, which can provide a location with one bearing.) Two or three LOBs are needed to provide a more definite location.

Recording is the placing of all intercepted traffic with other associated data in the appropriate files or logging information in a way that it can be easily retrieved, collated, or cross-referenced. This information can then be used to assist in analysis.

Analysis is a systematic examination of intercepted data in order to identify significant facts and derive conclusions. All information on the intercepted signals, including messages and traffic from communications emitters, is passed to an analysis center. There it is combined with information gathered from numerous sources and analyzed to determine the enemy's locations, make-up, capabilities, and intentions.

Dissemination is rapidly passing **usable** information and intelligence to the decisionmaker, for use in developing plans or for immediate action.

References

Department of Defense, Defense Intelligence College. *Glossary of Intelligence Terms and Definitions.* Washington, DC: DIC, 1987.

Department of Defense, Joint Chiefs of Staff. *Department of Defense Dictionary of Military and Related Terms.* Washington, DC: GPO, 1986.

Department of Defense, U.S. Army. *Counter-Signals Intelligence (C-SIGINT) Operations.* Field Manual FM 34-62, Washington, DC: Headquarters, Department of the Army, 1986.

Godson, Roy, ed. *Intelligence Problems for the 1980s, Number 1: Elements of Intelligence.* Rev. ed. Washington, DC: National Strategy Information Center, 1983.

Maurer, Alfred C.; Turnstall, Marion D.; and Keagle, James M. *Intelligence Policy and Process.* Boulder, CO: Westview Press, 1985.

Turner, Stansfield. *Secrecy and Democracy: The CIA in Transition.* Boston: Houghton Mifflin, 1985.

—**SIGINT-RELATED ACTIVITY** is any operation that is intended primarily for a purpose other than producing signals intelligence (SIGINT), but which can be used to produce SIGINT or produces SIGINT as a by-product of its principal purpose. *See also:* SIGINT Activity.

References

Department of Defense, Defense Intelligence College. *Glossary of Intelligence Terms and Definitions.* Washington, DC: DIC, 1987.

Godson, Roy, ed. *Intelligence Problems for the 1980s, Number 1: Elements of Intelligence.* Rev. ed. Washington, DC: National Strategy Information Center, 1983.

Maurer, Alfred C.; Turnstall, Marion D.; and Keagle, James M. *Intelligence Policy and Process.* Boulder, CO: Westview Press, 1985.

Turner, Stansfield. *Secrecy and Democracy: The CIA in Transition.* Boston: Houghton Mifflin, 1985.

—**SIGINT TECHNICAL INFORMATION** is information concerning or derived from intercepted foreign transmissions or radiations. It is technical information as opposed to intelligence and requires further collection or analysis before it is signals intelligence.

References

Department of Defense, Defense Intelligence College. *Glossary of Intelligence Terms and Definitions.* Washington, DC: DIC, 1987.

Godson, Roy, ed. *Intelligence Problems for the 1980s, Number 1: Elements of Intelligence.* Rev. ed. Washington, DC: National Strategy Information Center, 1983.

Maurer, Alfred C.; Turnstall, Marion D.; and Keagle, James M. *Intelligence Policy and Process.* Boulder, CO: Westview Press, 1985.

Turner, Stansfield. *Secrecy and Democracy: The CIA in Transition.* Boston: Houghton Mifflin, 1985.

—**SIGNAL.** (1) A signal is anything intentionally transmitted by visual, electromagnetic, nuclear, or acoustic methods for either communications or noncommunications purposes. (2) In FBI terminology, a signal is a prearranged sign that a dead drop box has been filled and needs to be emptied, or that a meeting is needed. (3) A signal, as defined by the Church Committee and as applied to electronics, is any transmitted electrical impulse.

References

Department of Defense, Defense Intelligence College. *Glossary of Intelligence Terms and Definitions.* Washington, DC: DIC, 1987.

Department of Defense, Joint Chiefs of Staff. *Department of Defense Dictionary of Military and Related Terms.* Washington, DC: GPO, 1986.

Godson, Roy, ed. *Intelligence Problems for the 1980s, Number 1: Elements of Intelligence.* Rev. ed. Washington, DC: National Strategy Information Center, 1983.

Kessler, Ronald. *Spy vs. Spy: Stalking Soviet Spies in America.* New York: Charles Scribner's Sons, 1988.

Maurer, Alfred C.; Turnstall, Marion D.; and Keagle, James M. *Intelligence Policy and Process.* Boulder, CO: Westview Press, 1985.

Turner, Stansfield. *Secrecy and Democracy: The CIA in Transition.* Boston: Houghton Mifflin, 1985.

U.S. Congress. Senate. *Final Report of the Senate Select Committee to Study Government Operations with Respect to Intelligence Activities. Report 94-755. Book I, Foreign and Military Intelligence.* Washington, DC: GPO, 1976.

—**SIGNAL SECURITY (SIGSEC)** is an Army tactical intelligence term. It means the measures that are taken to protect friendly electromagnetic emissions from exploitation by the enemy. It is a generic term that includes both communications security (COMSEC) and electronic security (ELSEC). *See also:* Communications Security, Electronic Security.

References

Department of Defense, Joint Chiefs of Staff. *Department of Defense Dictionary of Military and Related Terms.* Washington, DC: GPO, 1986.

Godson, Roy, ed. *Intelligence Problems for the 1980s, Number 1: Elements of Intelligence.* Rev. ed. Washington, DC: National Strategy Information Center, 1983.

Maurer, Alfred C.; Turnstall, Marion D.; and Keagle, James M. *Intelligence Policy and Process.* Boulder, CO: Westview Press, 1985.

Treverton, Gregory F. *Covert Action: The Limits of Intervention in the Postwar World.* New York: Basic Books, 1987.

—**SIGNAL SECURITY AGENCY (SSA).** In 1942, the Signal Intelligence Service (SIS) was moved to Arlington Hall Station in Virginia, was expanded, and was eventually renamed the Signal Security Agency (SSA). During the war, the SSA broke and exploited the Imperial Japanese Army code systems. In the first years of the war, the SSA was controlled by the chief signal officer, and the intelligence it produced was analyzed and disseminated by the Special Branch of the Military Intelligence Service. However, in 1944, in a reorganization that made the SSA more responsive to Army intelligence needs, the SSA was placed under the operational control of the Military Intelligence Division.

References

Finnegan, John P. *Military Intelligence: A Picture History.* Arlington, VA: U.S. Army Intelligence and Security Command, 1984.

—**SIGNAL VICINITY,** in FBI terminology, is the area surrounding the place where a signal has been transmitted or is located.

References

Kessler, Ronald. *Spy vs. Spy: Stalking Soviet Spies in America.* New York: Charles Scribner's Sons, 1988.

—**SIGNALS ANALYSIS (SA)** is a step in the Army tactical intelligence (TACINT) signals intelligence (SIGINT) process. *See:* SIGINT Process.

References

Department of Defense, U.S. Army. *Counter-Signals Intelligence (C-SIGINT) Operations.* Field Manual FM 34-62. Washington, DC: Headquarters, Department of the Army, 1986.

—**SIGNALS INTELLIGENCE (SIGINT)** is intelligence information that is composed of any or all of the following: communications intelligence, electronics intelligence, and foreign instrumentation signals intelligence, regardless of how this information is transmitted. As defined by the Church Committee, signals intelligence is "the general term for the foreign intelligence mission of the National Security Agency/Central Security Service (NSA/CSS). SIGINT involves the interception, processing, analysis and dissemination of information that is derived from foreign electrical communications and other signals. It is composed of three elements: Communications Intelligence (COMINT), Electronics Intelligence (ELINT), and Telemetry Intelligence (TELINT). Most SIGINT is collected by personnel of the Service Cryptologic Agencies." *See also:* Communications Intelligence, Electronics Intelligence, SIGINT Activity, SIGINT Process, SIGINT-Related Activity, SIGINT Technical Information, Telemetry Intelligence (TELINT).

References

Breckinridge, Scott D. *The CIA and the U.S. Intelligence System*. Boulder, CO: Westview Press, 1986.

Department of Defense, Defense Intelligence College. *Glossary of Intelligence Terms and Definitions*. Washington, DC: DIC, 1987.

Department of Defense, Joint Chiefs of Staff. *Department of Defense Dictionary of Military and Related Terms*. Washington, DC: GPO, 1986.

Godson, Roy, ed. *Intelligence Problems for the 1980s, Number 1: Elements of Intelligence*. Rev. ed. Washington, DC: National Strategy Information Center, 1983.

————. *Intelligence Problems for the 1980s, Number 2: Analysis and Estimates*. Washington, DC: National Strategy Information Center, 1980.

Lowenthal, Mark M. *U.S. Intelligence: Evolution and Anatomy*. New York: Praeger, 1984.

Maurer, Alfred C.; Turnstall, Marion D.; and Keagle, James M. *Intelligence Policy and Process*. Boulder, CO: Westview Press, 1985.

U.S. Congress. Senate. *Final Report of the Senate Select Committee to Study Government Operations with Respect to Intelligence Activities. Report 94-755. Book I, Foreign and Military Intelligence*. Washington, DC: GPO, 1976.

—SIGNALS INTELLIGENCE COMMITTEE was a Director of Central Intelligence Committee that was established in 1946 and had community representation.

References

Corson, William R. *The Armies of Ignorance: The Rise of the American Intelligence Empire*. New York: Dial Press, 1977.

Laqueur, Walter. *A World of Secrets*. New York: Basic Books, 1985.

—SIGNALS INTELLIGENCE ON-LINE INTELLIGENCE (OR INFORMATION) SYSTEM (SOLIS) is an automated file that provides access to full text retrieval on appropriate intelligence subjects. The documents in the products file are automatically indexed and remain online for a minimum of ten months.

References

Department of Defense, Defense Intelligence Agency. *Defense Intelligence Agency Manual*. Washington, DC: DIA, 1987.

Von Hoene, John P. A. *Intelligence User's Guide*. Washington, DC: DIA, 1983.

—SIGNALS INTELLIGENCE SERVICE (SIS). When the U.S. Army's cryptologic unit, MI-8, was dissolved in 1929, the Signal Corps assumed responsibility for cryptanalysis and formed the SIS to both make and break cryptosystems. The first person to direct the SIS was William F. Friedman. He and his assistants, Frank B. Rowlett, Abraham Sinkov, Solomon Kullback, and John B. Hurt, would all become leaders in the field. In the 1930s, they developed an electro-mechanical cipher device, which would later be modified into SIGABA, the backbone of high-level communications in World War II. Equally significant was the fact that the SIS broke the Japanese PURPLE machine cipher in 1940. The intelligence derived from this cipher by the SIS, known as MAGIC, allowed U.S. policymakers to monitor Japanese diplomatic traffic up to the attack on Pearl Harbor.

References

Corson, William R. *The Armies of Ignorance: The Rise of the American Intelligence Empire*. New York: Dial Press, 1977.

Finnegan, John P. *Military Intelligence: A Picture History*. Arlington, VA: U.S. Army Intelligence and Security Command, 1984.

—SIGNALS SECURITY ACQUISITION AND ANALYSIS, in communications security (COMSEC), means collecting and then analyzing electronic emissions in order to determine the susceptibility of these emissions to interception and exploitation by hostile intelligence services. It includes cataloging the transmission spectrum and taking signal parameter measurements as required. It does not include acquiring information that is carried on the system, which is in the realm of signals security surveillance. *See also:* Communications Security, Signals Security Surveillance.

References

Department of Defense, Defense Intelligence College. *Glossary of Intelligence Terms and Definitions*. Washington, DC: DIC, 1987.

Laqueur, Walter. *A World of Secrets*. New York: Basic Books, 1985.

Von Hoene, John P. A. *Intelligence User's Guide*. Washington, DC: DIA, 1983.

—SIGNALS SECURITY SURVEILLANCE, in electronic warfare, signals intelligence, communications security, operations security, and signals analysis, involves systematically surveilling one's own electronic emissions in order to determine if the existing signals security measures are adequate, to provide data from which to predict the effectiveness of proposed signals security measures, and to confirm that these measures are adequate after they are implemented. *See also:* Communications Security, Operations Security, Signals Intelligence.

References

Department of Defense, Defense Intelligence College. *Glossary of Intelligence Terms and Definitions.* Washington, DC: DIC, 1987.

Godson, Roy, ed. *Intelligence Problems for the 1980s, Number 1: Elements of Intelligence.* Rev. ed. Washington, DC: National Strategy Information Center, 1983.

Laqueur, Walter. *A World of Secrets.* New York: Basic Books, 1985.

Maurer, Alfred C.; Turnstall, Marion D.; and Keagle, James M. *Intelligence Policy and Process.* Boulder, CO: Westview Press, 1985.

—**SIGNALS SECURITY (SIGSEC) SURVEY** is the primary means for accomplishing a SIGSEC vulnerability assessment. Such a vulnerability assessment is a SIGSEC support function and is performed to determine the extent to which U.S. military noncommunications and communications emitter systems and it electromagnetic radiations from those systems can be exploited and disrupted. It compares enemy communications intelligence (COMINT) and electronic intelligence (ELINT) collection capabilities with friendly force electromagnetic profiles, and it identifies friendly force vulnerabilities to the enemy collection threat. This function involves identifying the vulnerabilities and providing follow-on assistance in developing and implementing countermeasures. The procedure for estimating the electromagnetic vulnerability of a unit or activity is the electromagnetic vulnerability assessment. *See also:* Communications Security.

References

Department of Defense, U.S. Army. *Counter-Signals Intelligence (C-SIGINT) Operations.* Field Manual FM 34-62, Washington, DC: Headquarters, Department of the Army, 1986.

—**SIGNATURE.** (1) In communications and communications security (COMSEC), signature refers to the touch of a wireless radio operator that indicates his personal transmitting pattern. Each operator has a certain touch that is so idiosyncratic that an experienced receiver can tell immediately if the operator has been switched. (2) In Army tactical intelligence (TACINT) signature means the identification of a military unit or activity resulting from the unique and detectable, visual, imagery, electromagnetic, olfactory, or acoustical display of key equipment that is normally associated with that type of unit or activity. Signatures fall into four categories: imagery (visual, photographic, or infrared); electromagnetic (communications and noncommunications); acoustical; and olfactory. Signatures are detected because different units have different types of equipment, are of differing sizes, emit different electromagnetic signals, deploy differently, and have different noises and smells associated with them. Detection of individual signatures can be used by enemy analysts to locate entire units, key activities, groups, and so forth. *See also:* Communications Security.

References

Becket, Henry S. A. *The Dictionary of Espionage: Spookspeak into English.* New York: Stein and Day, 1986.

Department of Defense, Joint Chiefs of Staff. *Department of Defense Dictionary of Military and Related Terms.* Washington, DC: GPO, 1986.

Department of Defense, U.S. Army. *Counter-Signals Intelligence (C-SIGINT) Operations.* Field Manual FM 34-62, Washington, DC: Headquarters, Department of the Army, 1986.

—**SIGNIFICANT SOVIET ACTIVITIES** is an annual publication of the Defense Intelligence Agency that describes significant Soviet events and activities that have occurred during the previous year. *See also:* Defense Intelligence Agency.

References

Department of Defense, Defense Intelligence Agency. *Defense Intelligence Agency Manual.* Washington, DC: DIA, 1987.

Von Hoene, John P. A. *Intelligence User's Guide.* Washington, DC: DIA, 1983.

—**SIGN OF LIFE SIGNAL,** in FBI terminology, is a signal that is sent periodically to indicate that an agent is still safe. *See also:* Agent, Concealment, Cover, Damage Assessment, Damage Control, Quick Trip Around the Horn, Submerge.

References

Becket, Henry S. A. *The Dictionary of Espionage: Spookspeak into English.* New York: Stein and Day, 1986.

Deacon, Richard. *Spyclopedia: An Encyclopedia of Spies, Secret Services, Operations, Jargon, and All Subjects Related to the World of Espionage.* London: Macdonald, 1987.

Kessler, Ronald. *Spy vs. Spy: Stalking Soviet Spies in America.* New York: Charles Scribner's Sons, 1988.

Ranelagh, John. *The Agency: The Rise and Decline of the CIA.* New York: Simon and Schuster, 1986.

—**SILENT SCHOOL** is a clandestine and covert intelligence operations term for individual instruction of an intelligence agent who will assume deep cover. The purpose is to isolate him so that as few people as possible will know his identity. An excellent example of a silent school was presented by Pierre Salinger and Leonard Gross in *Mortal Games,* when the hero is secreted to the Cotswalds in the United Kingdom and trained in his new identity. *See also:* Agent, Informant, Inside Man, Mole, Singleton.

References

Salinger, Pierre, and Gross, Leonard. *Mortal Games.* New York: Doubleday, 1988.

—**SINGLE INTEGRATED OPERATIONS PLAN (SIOP)** pertains to the targeting of U.S. land- and sea-based ICBMs. It lists the targets that will be struck by U.S. ICBMs in a general war and is necessary in that it insures that there is no duplication of targeting between the Navy and Air Force, and that the targets are hit in a priority order. Initially, the Air Force controlled such targeting, but with the advent of U.S. ballistic missile-equipped submarines, targeting responsibilities have been shared by the Navy and Air Force.

References

Breckinridge, Scott D. *The CIA and the U.S. Intelligence System.* Boulder, CO: Westview Press, 1986.

Department of Defense, Defense Intelligence Agency. *Defense Intelligence Agency Manual.* Washington, DC: DIA, 1987.

Turner, Stansfield. *Secrecy and Democracy: The CIA in Transition.* Boston: Houghton Mifflin, 1985.

—**SINGLETON** is a term used in clandestine and covert intelligence operations to describe an individual agent working alone, rather than in a net. Perhaps the most famous singleton was the fictional James Bond. *See also:* Silent School.

References

Becket, Henry S. A. *The Dictionary of Espionage: Spookspeak into English.* New York: Stein and Day, 1986.

Kessler, Ronald. *Spy vs. Spy: Stalking Soviet Spies in America.* New York: Charles Scribner's Sons, 1988.

—**SINO-VIETNAMESE WAR OF 1979.** Intelligence support to the national decisionmakers concerning the Sino-Vietnamese War of 1979 was remarkable in its consistency, thoroughness, and accuracy. The war began with the Chinese stating that their war aim was to punish the Vietnamese for their ill treatment of Chinese citizens living in Vietnam, while the Vietnamese stated that they intended to expel the Chinese invaders. The Chinese experienced greater resistance than they had anticipated, and the war ended inconclusively. For its part, the Soviet Union proceeded more cautiously than it had in its other recent crisis responses. This probably reflected Soviet uncertainty concerning the intentions of the Chinese, whom they considered unpredictable. Thus, their response was to direct Soviet ships that were on the high seas to stations off the Chinese coast, and to deploy two groups of combatants. The first assumed a station due east of Shanghai, where it stayed throughout the war, while the second sailed into the South China Sea, where it operated. Additionally, some of these ships entered Vietnamese ports to provide port security, lest the Chinese opt to conduct air strikes. The Soviets also waged intense reconnaissance activity along the Chinese coast, and increased Soviet Ground Forces activity along the Sino-Soviet border.

Throughout the period leading up to the war and throughout the war, the U.S. intelligence reporting was complete, timely, and accurate. It reported of the increase in tension between China and Vietnam, predicted that hostilities might occur, reported on these hostilities in depth, noted the war's inconclusive end, and predicted that another, more violent war might occur in the future. One unfortunate aspect of the reporting was that it initially called the Soviet ships that were assuming stations off the Chinese coast an intelligence collection force. Once labeled by the American press, no subsequent reporting could change this label. Thus, the Soviet force, which eventually numbered 29 ships, including several surface combatants—a force that far exceeded one that would have been assembled for intelligence collection purposes—was never reported to the public as the significant projection of Soviet military power that it in fact was.

This show of Soviet military support was very successful: from it the Soviets gained naval and air access to Vietnamese facilities that permitted them to further isolate China and permitted them a vital base in Southeast Asia. From here they have been able to monitor and, in a foreign policy sense, neutralize to a certain extent the U.S. presence in the Philippines. Additionally, the presence was also significant in respect to the projection of Soviet power into the Indian Ocean. Prior to 1979, the Soviet Union had tried to respond to crises by deploying naval power to the Indian Ocean, specifically the Indo-Pakistani War of 1971 and the Arab-Israeli War of 1973, but in both cases they failed to the extent that their naval power was far less than what the United States deployed for the same crisis, and arrived long after U.S. naval forces arrived. This was due to the fact that reacting Soviet naval forces were isolated and had to travel all the way from their bases in Vladivostok, situated in Northeast Asia. This long distance affected very adversely both the reaction time and the amount of power that could be supported logistically. Now, however, the Soviets can stage naval forces from Danang, which is on roughly the same parallel as the U.S. facilities at Subic, and will therefore be able to react as quickly as U.S. naval forces, and with much greater power. *See also:* Carter, Jimmy; National Security Council.

References

Brinkley, David A., and Hull, Andrew W. *Estimative Intelligence: A Textbook on the History, Products, Uses, and Writing of Intelligence Estimates.* Columbus, OH: Battelle, 1979.

Godson, Roy, ed. *Intelligence Problems for the 1980s, Number 1: Elements of Intelligence.* Rev. ed. Washington, DC: National Strategy Information Center, 1983.

Laqueur, Walter. *A World of Secrets.* New York: Basic Books, 1985.

Lowenthal, Mark M. *U.S. Intelligence: Evolution and Anatomy.* New York: Praeger, 1984.

Maurer, Alfred C.; Turnstall, Marion D.; and Keagle, James M. *Intelligence Policy and Process.* Boulder, CO: Westview Press, 1985.

Treverton, Gregory F. *Covert Action: The Limits of Intervention in the Postwar World.* New York: Basic Books, 1987.

Turner, Stansfield. *Secrecy and Democracy: The CIA in Transition.* Boston: Houghton Mifflin, 1985.

U.S. Congress. Senate. *Final Report of the Senate Select Committee to Study Government Operations with Respect to Intelligence Activities. Report 94-755. Book I, Foreign and Military Intelligence.* Washington, DC: GPO, 1976.

Watson, Bruce W. *Red Navy at Sea: Soviet Naval Operations on the High Seas, 1956-1980.* Boulder, CO: Westview Press, 1986.

Watson, Bruce W., and Watson, Susan M., eds. *The Soviet Navy: Strengths and Liabilities.* Boulder, CO: Westview Press, 1986.

—**SISTERS** is a term used in clandestine and covert intelligence operations to describe the lower ranks of the "ladies." They usually receive the tougher assignments and are often called upon to seduce targets. *See also:* Ladies.

References

Becket, Henry S. A. *The Dictionary of Espionage: Spookspeak into English.* New York: Stein and Day, 1986.

Deacon, Richard. *Spyclopedia: An Encyclopedia of Spies, Secret Services, Operations, Jargon, and All Subjects Related to the World of Espionage.* London: Macdonald, 1987.

Ranelagh, John. *The Agency: The Rise and Decline of the CIA.* New York: Simon and Schuster, 1986.

—**SITUATION MAPS** is an Army tactical term that refers to maps that provide a temporary graphic display of the current, known dispositions, and major activities of friendly and enemy forces. The basic SITMAP provides a format for accurate notations of friendly and enemy forces that are relative to friendly boundaries. Electronic order of battle overlays are used to graphically depict communications and noncommunications emitters and associated units, facilities, and activities.

References

Department of Defense, U.S. Army. *Counter-Signals Intelligence (C-SIGINT) Operations.* Field Manual FM 34-62. Washington, DC: Headquarters, Department of the Army, 1986.

—**SITUATION REPORT** is a general intelligence term. It is a narrative report that is prepared by a subordinate commander to inform his superiors of his evaluation of the significant factors that substantially improve or impair his operational readiness.

References

Department of Defense, Defense Intelligence College. *Glossary of Intelligence Terms and Definitions*. Washington, DC: DIC, 1987.

Department of Defense, Joint Chiefs of Staff. *Department of Defense Dictionary of Military and Related Terms*. Washington, DC: GPO, 1986.

Godson, Roy, ed. *Intelligence Problems for the 1980s, Number 1: Elements of Intelligence*. Rev. ed. Washington, DC: National Strategy Information Center, 1983.

Kent, Sherman. *Strategic Intelligence for American World Policy*. Princeton, NJ: Princeton University Press, 1966.

Von Hoene, John P. A. *Intelligence User's Guide*. Washington, DC: DIA, 1983.

—**SKEWED.** A skewed frequency distribution is not symmetric in shape. If more than half the scores in a distribution fall below its mean, the distribution is called positively skewed; if more than half the scores in a distribution fall above the mean, the distribution is called negatively skewed.

References

Department of Defense, Defense Intelligence College. *Glossary of Intelligence Terms and Definitions*. Washington, DC: DIC, 1987.

—**SKEWNESS** is a statistical or quantitative methodological term that is often used in intelligence analysis. It means the extent to which a distribution of data points is concentrated at one end or the other; the lack of symmetry.

References

Department of Defense, Defense Intelligence College. *Glossary of Intelligence Terms and Definitions*. Washington, DC: DIC, 1987.

—**SKUNK WORKS** is a secret section of Lockheed Aircraft in Burbank, California, where the U-2 aircraft was built. *See also:* SR-71 Aircraft, U-2 Overhead Reconnaissance Program and U-2 Spy Plane.

References

Becket, Henry S. A. *The Dictionary of Espionage: Spookspeak into English*. New York: Stein and Day, 1986.

Turner, Stansfield. *Secrecy and Democracy: The CIA in Transition*. Boston: Houghton Mifflin, 1985.

—**SLAVENS, BRIAN E.,** Corporal, U.S. Marine Corps, while a guard at a naval installation in Alaska, deserted his post and went to the Soviet embassy, offering to sell classified information. He was given a dishonorable discharge and was sentenced to two years in prison. He was freed after serving eighteen months of his sentence.

References

Allen, Thomas B., and Polmar, Norman. *Merchants of Treason: America's Secrets for Sale*. New York: Delacorte Press, 1988.

—**SLEEPER** is a term used in clandestine and covert intelligence operations to describe a previously placed spy who is ready to be activated at a suitable moment. In *The Charm School*, Nelson Demille describes a rather far-fetched Soviet operation that trains and places thousands of Soviet sleepers in the United States. *See also:* Mole, Singleton.

References

Demille, Nelson. *The Charm School*. New York: Warner Books, 1988.

Kessler, Ronald. *Spy vs. Spy: Stalking Soviet Spies in America*. New York: Charles Scribner's Sons, 1988.

Quirk, John; Phillips, David; Cline, Ray; and Pforzheimer, Walter. *The Central Intelligence Agency: A Photographic History*. Guilford, CT: Foreign Intelligence Press, 1986.

—**SMITH, GENERAL WALTER BEDELL,** was born on October 5, 1895, in Indianapolis, Indiana. He briefly attended Butler University and then pursued a career in the Army. During World War II, he served as chief of staff of the Allied Forces in North Africa and the Mediterranean, and then as chief of staff to General Dwight D. Eisenhower, Supreme Headquarters, Allied Expeditionary Forces. He was promoted to lieutenant general on January 13, 1944, was U.S. ambassador to the Soviet Union from 1946 to 1949 and commanding general of the First Army from 1949 to 1950. He was appointed by President Truman to be director of Central Intelligence (DCI) on August 21, 1950. His appointment was confirmed by the Senate on August 28, and he was sworn in on October 7, 1950. He was promoted to general, U.S. Army, on August 1, 1951. He retired from the Army on February 9, 1953, and resigned as DCI on the same date to become secretary of state. He subsequently pursued a career in private business and died on August 9, 1961.

Smith, who had been Eisenhower's chief of staff when the general was supreme commander in Europe, was aggressive and an extremely competent administrator. With his deputy DCI, William Jackson, Smith instituted a number of reforms. He created the Office of National Estimates, whose only task was to produce coordinated national estimates. An Office of Research and Reports was created to report on economic changes in the Soviet bloc, and in 1952, the Directorate for Intelligence (DDI) was formed to produce finished intelligence.

In summary, Smith was one of the best people ever appointed to the office of DCI. He was ambitious and intelligent, and under his leadership the agency continued to grow and prosper. He appears to have had a sense of morality that was imposed upon the agency and kept it on an even keel, away from politics and illegal or questionable enterprises. *See also:* Central Intelligence Agency.

References

Breckinridge, Scott D. *The CIA and the U.S. Intelligence System.* Boulder, CO: Westview Press, 1986.

Brinkley, David A., and Hull, Andrew W. *Estimative Intelligence: A Textbook on the History, Products, Uses, and Writing of Intelligence Estimates.* Columbus, OH: Battelle, 1979.

Godson, Roy, ed. *Intelligence Problems for the 1980s, Number 1: Elements of Intelligence.* Rev. ed. Washington, DC: National Strategy Information Center, 1983.

Lowenthal, Mark M. *U.S. Intelligence: Evolution and Anatomy.* New York: Praeger, 1984.

Maurer, Alfred C.; Turnstall, Marion D.; and Keagle, James M. *Intelligence Policy and Process.* Boulder, CO: Westview Press, 1985.

U.S. Congress. Senate. *Final Report of the Senate Select Committee to Study Government Operations with Respect to Intelligence Activities. Report 94-755. Book I, Foreign and Military Intelligence.* Washington, DC: GPO, 1976.

—**SNITCH JACKET** is a term used in clandestine intelligence operations. It is a means of neutralizing an agent by labeling him an informant (snitch) so that he will no longer be trusted. *See also:* Co-opted Worker, Co-optees, Dirty Tricks.

References

Becket, Henry S. A. *The Dictionary of Espionage: Spookspeak into English.* New York: Stein and Day, 1986.

Deacon, Richard. *Spyclopedia: An Encyclopedia of Spies, Secret Services, Operations, Jargon, and All Subjects Related to the World of Espionage.* London: Macdonald, 1987.

Kessler, Ronald. *Spy vs. Spy: Stalking Soviet Spies in America.* New York: Charles Scribner's Sons, 1988.

Ranelagh, John. *The Agency: The Rise and Decline of the CIA.* New York: Simon and Schuster, 1986.

—**SNUGGLING** is a term used in clandestine and covert intelligence operations. Snuggling is a black propaganda technique in which a clandestine radio program is broadcast on a frequency very close to a legitimate station, with the hopes that listeners will confuse their bogus program for the real one.

References

Becket, Henry S. A. *The Dictionary of Espionage: Spookspeak into English.* New York: Stein and Day, 1986.

Deacon, Richard. *Spyclopedia: An Encyclopedia of Spies, Secret Services, Operations, Jargon, and All Subjects Related to the World of Espionage.* London: Macdonald, 1987.

Kessler, Ronald. *Spy vs. Spy: Stalking Soviet Spies in America.* New York: Charles Scribner's Sons, 1988.

Ranelagh, John. *The Agency: The Rise and Decline of the CIA.* New York: Simon and Schuster, 1986.

Treverton, Gregory F. *Covert Action: The Limits of Intervention in the Postwar World.* New York: Basic Books, 1987.

—**SOAP** is a term used in clandestine and covert intelligence operations. It is an acronym for a truth drug, a special type of sodium (so-) pentothal (pe), hence sope or soap.

References

Deacon, Richard. *Spyclopedia: An Encyclopedia of Spies, Secret Services, Operations, Jargon, and All Subjects Related to the World of Espionage.* London: Macdonald, 1987.

—**SOCIOLOGICAL INTELLIGENCE,** one of the eight components of strategic intelligence, is concerned with social stratification, value systems, beliefs, and other social characteristics of selected populations. The Department of State is the primary producer of sociological intelligence.

General

The Intelligence Community accepts the following definition of sociology: Sociology is the study of society, as well as of the groups within society, their composition, organization, purposes, and habits, and the role of the individual in relation to social institutions. Each foreign society should be viewed as a distinctive culture with its own combination of social and cultural features, including history, language, and values.

From this, the Community believes that the factors that influence the group behavior of human beings are best studied through examining a nation's social institutions and folkways. These include social groupings with special reference to stratification and mobility, the churches, national morality and taboos, national traditions and habits of thought, and slow or rapid trends toward change.

Factors that affect the cohesion and stability of societies may be seen in the means whereby societies transmit information, influence, and authority—which may be through a variety of social channels ranging from distinctive ways of inculcating values and habits in rearing children to elaborate systems of mass communication for developing viewpoints and attitudes.

For strategic intelligence purposes, the Intelligence Community says that the sociological factors that relate to groups of people may be studied under six headings: demography—the study of population, manpower and labor; social characteristics; public opinion; education; religion; and public welfare and health.

Demography

Demographic intelligence consists primarily of statistics that describe the size, distribution, and characteristics of a population, together with the changes in these aspects. Such statistics are normally derived from censuses and vital statistics covering the entire population being described, or from a survey of a sample of the population. Estimates derived in other ways have proved to be highly inaccurate and are of little value for intelligence purposes. Fortunately, the international apparatus for gathering and integrating these statistics has steadily improved, and in general it can be said that from the point of view of intelligence the problems involved are more those of interpretation than of collection.

On another level, demography should be understood to include the study of factors that affect rates of population growth. Social conditions such as the standard of living, may have marked effects. Medical conditions may diminish death rates with striking results. Governmental policies, furthermore, may strengthen or weaken these factors, or, as through propaganda and suggestion, exert influence upon trends in

the population. Information about these factors is less readily available and they require attention in the field.

Certainly the size and rate of growth of the total population, taken in conjunction with resources, trade and existing technology, determines the level of economic well-being in the country. The rate of population growth, taken in conjunction with the rate of economic growth, determines the rate of per capita economic growth. The level of economic well-being and the rate of per capita economic growth are, in turn, major factors in a country's military potential and political power.

Statistics on the characteristics and the distribution of the population can be compiled by using a wide variety of categories. Among the most useful are age-and-sex groups, geographical groups, geographical categories, proportions living in urban and rural areas, ethnic categories, educational categories, proportion participating in the labor force, and the distribution of the labor force among the various types of economic activity. Among the most important characteristics of a population are its birth and death rates, its rates of marriage and divorce, and its rates of internal and external migration. In addition to the significance of these rates for population growth, they can provide the demographic specialist with a wealth of information about the economic, social and cultural characteristics of the population to which they refer.

Characteristics of the People

Intelligence on this subject includes considering both the physical and cultural characteristics of a people and their national attitudes and social organization. Physical characteristics of most peoples can be readily studied in reference works, but intelligence should take note of variable factors such as physical vigor, and perhaps also stature and carriage. The cultural characteristics include command and distribution of languages and dialects; social stratification, including cleavages and divisions and their effect on the political and military solidarity of the national society; and trends in the composition and size of social groups and levels. Business and professional groups, secret societies including revolutionary movements, and military and aristocratic orders are considered under this heading.

Public Opinion

Public opinion is the expression of attitudes of significant segments of the population on questions of general interest to the state and society. It is not a monolithic entity, since it may be made up of many conflicting viewpoints. Nor should it necessarily be identified with a majority consensus on a distinctive set of opinions. Intelligence should therefore pay attention to the opinions of minority groups, especially of groups that are capable of exerting pressure on governments by virtue of their organized energy, politico-economic power, para-military resources, special influence, personal contacts, or articulateness.

Given understanding of the basic attitudes that are prevalent in a society, propagandists, particularly in totalitarian countries, can direct the flow of opinion into channels that lead to powerful mass movements, forceful national action, and even war. The role and formulation of public opinion (and its political consequences) vary considerably in different societies. Consequently, it is important to secure intelligence on both the basic social attitudes of a country and the ease with which these attitudes are directed toward certain pre-conceived aims or are susceptible to being so directed.

The mechanism that shapes opinion requires observation at three levels. Intelligence production is largely a matter of biographic intelligence about editors, writers, and information staffs, including specialized advisors such as psychologists. Dissemination is accomplished by the media, including the press, radio, magazines, movies, and educational institutions, but front organizations and other interest or pressure groups may also play an important role. Finally, the content of the information or propaganda naturally caps the structure. It is well to remember that sophisticated techniques have been developed for analyzing the substance of public opinion, and the intelligence collector must take account of those techniques in order to avoid many pitfalls.

Education

A study of the level of education provides one factor that is required for estimating the possible future progress of a nation in political development, economics, and science. Public policy is one major element, because public authorities at the local or often the national level exercise close supervision over the school system and some infuse paramilitary training at an early stage. Intelligence focuses on the general level and character of education in a country and the quality of its secondary schools, trade schools,

colleges, and graduate schools. It includes statistics on literacy, the philosophy of education and training, the quality of artistic and cultural interest, the number of students who go to foreign countries, the extent to which foreign languages are taught, and the values and attitudes that the schools seek to inculcate.

Religion

The distribution of adherents to various religions, the presence or absence of an official state church, the attitude of church groups toward the government, and the attitude of the government toward religious groups have an important bearing on national psychology, public opinion, and education. The type of religious organization and the extent to which religious values and codes are operative also must be considered.

Some religions glorify war, and others vilify it, while there are an infinite number of attitudes between these two extremes. The intelligence analyst tries to remain constantly aware of the enormous extent to which religion pervades every aspect of the way of life in certain countries. These countries' leaders and their policies cannot be understood outside of the context of their religion.

Public Welfare

Public welfare concerns itself with matters such as health, living conditions, organizations for social service, social insurance, and social problems that have a bearing on national strength and stability. These problems include the extent and significance of divorce, broken homes, slums, narcotics, crime, and the ways in which a society copes with these problems.

Intelligence in the field of public welfare has many uses outside the purely sociological interest. National health, for example, is a key to the vitality of a nation and its people. It bears on the industrial potential of a nation, the effects of a possible blockade and restrictive buying programs, and the degree to which a nation may withstand the rigors of war. Moreover, the status of public health and sanitization in a foreign country would be of paramount importance to our planning in the event our troops should be required to conduct operations there.

References

Clauser, Jerome K., and Weir, Sandra M. *Intelligence Research Methodology*. State College, PA: HRB-Singer, 1975.

Godson, Roy, ed. *Intelligence Problems for the 1980s, Number 1: Elements of Intelligence*. Rev. ed. Washington, DC: National Strategy Information Center, 1983.

Maurer, Alfred C.; Turnstall, Marion D.; and Keagle, James M. *Intelligence Policy and Process*. Boulder, CO: Westview Press, 1985.

—**SOFT TARGETS** are friendly or neutral nations in which the CIA has only a routine interest in terms of intelligence coverage. *See also:* Hard Targets.

References

Becket, Henry S. A. *The Dictionary of Espionage: Spookspeak into English*. New York: Stein and Day, 1986.

Deacon, Richard. *Spyclopedia: An Encyclopedia of Spies, Secret Services, Operations, Jargon, and All Subjects Related to the World of Espionage*. London: Macdonald, 1987.

Kent, Sherman. *Strategic Intelligence for American World Policy*. Princeton, NJ: Princeton University Press, 1966.

Ranelagh, John. *The Agency: The Rise and Decline of the CIA*. New York: Simon and Schuster, 1986.

Turner, Stansfield. *Secrecy and Democracy: The CIA in Transition*. Boston: Houghton Mifflin, 1985.

—**SOLD** is a term used in clandestine intelligence operations. It is an agent who has been deliberately betrayed by his own side. *See also:* Agent, Burn, Burnt, Demote Maximally, Executive Action, Surround, Surveillance, Turned.

References

Becket, Henry S. A. *The Dictionary of Espionage: Spookspeak into English*. New York: Stein and Day, 1986.

Deacon, Richard. *Spyclopedia: An Encyclopedia of Spies, Secret Services, Operations, Jargon, and All Subjects Related to the World of Espionage*. London: Macdonald, 1987.

Ranelagh, John. *The Agency: The Rise and Decline of the CIA*. New York: Simon and Schuster, 1986.

—**SORBEL, MORTON,** was a member of the "Atomic Spy Ring," led by Julius and Ethel Rosenberg. Sorbel was tried, convicted, and sentenced to 30 years in prison. Eligible for parole in 1962, he was released in 1969. *See also:* Rosenberg, Julius and Ethel.

References

Allen, Thomas B., and Polmar, Norman. *Merchants of Treason: America's Secrets for Sale*. New York: Delacorte Press, 1988.

—**SORENSON, THEODORE.** When President Carter took office in 1977, the Intelligence Community was emerging from the Watergate scandal. George Bush was then the director of Central Intelligence (DCI). Carter's first choice for DCI was Theodore Sorenson. However, Sorenson's support of Daniel Ellsberg during the *Pentagon Papers* case in 1972 and his draft status as a conscientious objector prompted considerable congressional opposition, and it was doubtful that Sorenson would receive congressional approval. As a result, Sorenson subsequently withdrew his name from nomination, and Carter then nominated Admiral Stansfield Turner, U.S. Navy, who became the next DCI.

References

Lowenthal, Mark M. *U.S. Intelligence: Evolution and Anatomy*. New York: Praeger, 1984.

Turner, Stansfield. *Secrecy and Democracy: The CIA in Transition*. Boston: Houghton Mifflin, 1985.

—**SORTIE NUMBER,** in photoreconnaissance and imagery intelligence collection, is a reference number that is used to identify all the imagery that was taken by all of the sensors during one air reconnaissance sortie. *See also:* Aerial Photograph.

References

Department of Defense, Defense Intelligence College. *Glossary of Intelligence Terms and Definitions*. Washington, DC: DIC, 1987.

Department of Defense, Joint Chiefs of Staff. *Department of Defense Dictionary of Military and Related Terms*. Washington, DC: GPO, 1986.

—**SOUERS, REAR ADMIRAL SIDNEY WILLIAM, U.S. NAVAL RESERVE,** was born on March 30, 1892, in Dayton, Ohio. He attended Purdue University and Miami University of Ohio, earning a bachelor's degree in 1914. His earlier career was spent in private business, and he was commissioned a lieutenant commander in the U.S. Naval Reserve in 1929. He volunteered for active duty in July 1940, was promoted to rear admiral, and was made deputy chief of Naval Intelligence in 1945. He was appointed director of Central Intelligence (DCI) by President Truman and was sworn in on January 23, 1946. His tenure lasted a little over three months, and he resigned on June 10, 1946, to return to civilian life. Because his tenure was so short, Souers had practically no lasting affect on the CIG. He returned to private business, but accepted the position of secretary of the National Security Council. He died on January 14, 1973. *See also:* Central Intelligence Agency.

References

Breckinridge, Scott D. *The CIA and the U.S. Intelligence System.* Boulder, CO: Westview Press, 1986.

Brinkley, David A., and Hull, Andrew W. *Estimative Intelligence: A Textbook on the History, Products, Uses, and Writing of Intelligence Estimates.* Columbus, OH: Battelle, 1979.

Cline, Ray S. *The CIA Under Reagan, Bush, and Casey.* Washington, DC: Acropolis Books, 1981.

Laqueur, Walter. *A World of Secrets.* New York: Basic Books, 1985.

Quirk, John; Phillips, David; Cline, Ray; and Pforzheimer, Walter. *The Central Intelligence Agency: A Photographic History.* Guilford, CT: Foreign Intelligence Press, 1986.

Treverton, Gregory F. *Covert Action: The Limits of Intervention in the Postwar World.* New York: Basic Books, 1987.

—**SOUND MAN** is a term used in clandestine and covert intelligence operations for a wiretapping or bugging expert. *See also:* Sound School.

References

Becket, Henry S. A. *The Dictionary of Espionage: Spookspeak into English.* New York: Stein and Day, 1986.

Deacon, Richard. *Spyclopedia: An Encyclopedia of Spies, Secret Services, Operations, Jargon, and All Subjects Related to the World of Espionage.* London: Macdonald, 1987.

Ranelagh, John. *The Agency: The Rise and Decline of the CIA.* New York: Simon and Schuster, 1986.

—**SOUND SCHOOL** is the FBI course that is taught on bugging and wiretapping.

References

Becket, Henry S. A. *The Dictionary of Espionage: Spookspeak into English.* New York: Stein and Day, 1986.

Deacon, Richard. *Spyclopedia: An Encyclopedia of Spies, Secret Services, Operations, Jargon, and All Subjects Related to the World of Espionage.* London: Macdonald, 1987.

Ranelagh, John. *The Agency: The Rise and Decline of the CIA.* New York: Simon and Schuster, 1986.

—**SOURCE** is a general intelligence term that has several meanings. (1) It is a person, device, system, or activity from which intelligence information is obtained. (2) In clandestine activity, a source is an agent, normally a foreign national, who works for an intelligence activity. (3) In interrogation activities, a source is any person who furnishes intelligence information, either with or without the knowledge that the information is being used for intelligence purposes. (4) An uncontrolled source is a voluntary contributor of information who may or may not know that the information will be used for intelligence purposes. (5) As defined by the Church Committee, source is "a person, thing, or activity which provides intelligence information. In clandestine activities, the term applies to an agent or asset, normally a foreign national, being used in an intelligence activity for intelligence purposes. In interrogations, it refers to a person who furnishes intelligence information with or without knowledge that the information is being used for intelligence purposes." *See also:* Agent, Collection Agency, Human Source, Sensitive Intelligence Sources and Methods.

References

Clancy, Tom. *The Cardinal of the Kremlin.* New York: Putnam, 1988.

Department of Defense, Defense Intelligence College. *Glossary of Intelligence Terms and Definitions.* Washington, DC: DIC, 1987.

Department of Defense, Joint Chiefs of Staff. *Department of Defense Dictionary of Military and Related Terms.* Washington, DC: GPO, 1986.

Godson, Roy, ed. *Intelligence Problems for the 1980s, Number 1: Elements of Intelligence.* Rev. ed. Washington, DC: National Strategy Information Center, 1983.

Kessler, Ronald. *Spy vs. Spy: Stalking Soviet Spies in America.* New York: Charles Scribner's Sons, 1988.

Maurer, Alfred C.; Turnstall, Marion D.; and Keagle, James M. *Intelligence Policy and Process.* Boulder, CO: Westview Press, 1985.

Quirk, John; Phillips, David; Cline, Ray; and Pforzheimer, Walter. *The Central Intelligence Agency: A Photographic History.* Guilford, CT: Foreign Intelligence Press, 1986.

Turner, Stansfield. *Secrecy and Democracy: The CIA in Transition.* Boston: Houghton Mifflin, 1985.

U.S. Congress. Senate. *Final Report of the Senate Select Committee to Study Government Operations*

with Respect to Intelligence Activities. Report 94-755. Book I, Foreign and Military Intelligence. Washington, DC: GPO, 1976.

—**SOURCE PROTECT,** a communications term, is a warning at the start of a message that its contents are to be very tightly restricted. *See also:* Access, Authorized, Classification, Code Word, Compromise, Declassification, Disclosure, Downgrade, Freedom of Information Act, Limited Access Area, Need-to-Know, Need-to-Know Principle, No-Lone Zone, Nondisclosure Agreement, Nondiscussion Area, Sanitization, Sanitize, Sanitized Area, Security Certification, Security Classification, Sensitive Compartmented Information, Sensitive Compartmented Information Facility, Two-Person Control.

References

Becket, Henry S. A. *The Dictionary of Espionage: Spookspeak into English.* New York: Stein and Day, 1986.

—**SOUTHER, GLENN,** a naval intelligence employee, disappeared in 1986 after being questioned by the FBI. In July 1988, he surfaced in the Soviet Union requesting asylum. In the same month, Souther was interviewed on Soviet radio. The interview was extremely propagandistic and was very much out of tune with the prevailing Gorbachev theme of cooperation with the West. In the interview, Souther discussed his involvement in Eldorado Canyon, the U.S. attack on Libya. He claimed that he had been told to recover photographs of the French embassy in Libya because the United States intended to attack the embassy as well as Libyan targets. In a general reference to the U.S. satellite photographic capability, Souther said that it was very good, and that if you exposed an object to the skies, you should assume that the Americans could photograph and identify it.

References

Allen, Thomas B., and Polmar, Norman. *Merchants of Treason: America's Secrets for Sale.* New York: Delacorte Press, 1988.

AP and UPI bulletins in July 1988 that discussed the Souther interview.

—**SOVIET BRIGADE IN CUBA.** In 1971, President Carter restricted the number of SR-71 flights over Cuba in 1971 as a part of his program of stringent control over intelligence operations. The result was that the amount of data on Cuban developments that the Intelligence Community was receiving was restricted, and this led to the failure of intelligence to report on the existence of the Soviet brigade in Cuba more promptly than it did.

Once news of the brigade was made public, the situation quickly escalated. However, in spite of Executive and congressional outrage at the presence of the brigade, the United States was unable to force the Soviets to withdraw their troops.

References

Breckinridge, Scott D. *The CIA and the U.S. Intelligence System.* Boulder, CO: Westview Press, 1986.

Cline, Ray S. *The CIA Under Reagan, Bush, and Casey.* Washington, DC: Acropolis Books, 1981.

Laqueur, Walter. *A World of Secrets.* New York: Basic Books, 1985.

Lowenthal, Mark M. *U.S. Intelligence: Evolution and Anatomy.* New York: Praeger, 1984.

Treverton, Gregory F. *Covert Action: The Limits of Intervention in the Postwar World.* New York: Basic Books, 1987.

—*SOVIET MILITARY POWER* is an unclassified publication that has been issued annually since 1981 by the secretary of defense. It is an impressively complete and detailed presentation of the Soviet military services, and annually discusses most of the latest military hardware. Given its great exposure and wide public appeal, the photographic layouts and graphics are of exceptionally high quality for a government publication. More important, however, is the statistical material that is presented. A concerted and noteworthy effort is made to present as much unclassified data on the Soviet military as is possible. Additionally, while the tenor of the prose at times becomes jingoistic, it is evident that the Department of Defense attempts to present the information objectively.

—*SOVIET NAVAL SHIPBUILDING* is a publication that is produced by the Defense Intelligence Agency as part of its Military Economic and Production Studies series. The publication summarizes general trends and presents current naval programs and production data on naval combatants and various auxiliary (logistical support) ships. *See also:* Defense Intelligence Agency.

References

Department of Defense, Defense Intelligence Agency. *Defense Intelligence Agency Manual.* Washington, DC: DIA, 1987.

———. *Organization, Mission and Key Personnel.* Washington, DC: DIA, 1986.

Von Hoene, John P. A. *Intelligence User's Guide.* Washington, DC: DIA, 1983.

—**SPACE AND NAVAL WARFARE SYSTEMS COMMAND (SPAWAR)** is a new Naval Command. While the Navy has been reticent concerning the details, it is believed to be an attempt to help the Navy compete with the Air Force in the Unified Space Command, since it may allow the Navy a larger voice in space warfare policy and management.

References

Boutacoff, David A. "Steering a Course Toward Space." Defense Electronics (Mar. 1986): 58-60, 62-63.

—**SPACE ORDER OF BATTLE (SOB)** is prepared by the Defense Intelligence Agency and provides a good summary of the few countries currently involved in space operations. *See also:* Defense Intelligence Agency.

References

Department of Defense, Defense Intelligence Agency. *Defense Intelligence Agency Manual.* Washington, DC: DIA, 1987.

———. *Organization, Mission and Key Personnel.* Washington, DC: DIA, 1986.

—**SPECIAL ACCESS PROGRAM** is a general intelligence term. It is any program imposing "need to know" or access controls beyond those normally required for access to Confidential, Secret, or Top Secret information. Such a program may include special clearance, adjudication, or investigative requirements, special designations of officials authorized to determine "need to know," or special lists of persons that have been determined to have a "need to know." *See also:* Sensitive Compartmented Information.

References

Maroni, Alice C. *Special Access Programs: Understanding the "Black Budget."* Washington, DC: Foreign Affairs and National Defense Division, Congressional Research Service, Library of Congress, 1987.

Turner, Stansfield. *Secrecy and Democracy: The CIA in Transition.* Boston: Houghton Mifflin, 1985.

—**SPECIAL ACTIVITIES** are defined in Executive Order No. 12036, which states that they are "activities conducted abroad in support of national foreign policy objectives which are designed to further official U.S. programs and policies abroad and which are planned and executed so that the role of the United States government is not apparent or acknowledged publicly, and functions in support of such activities, but not including diplomatic activity or the collection or production of intelligence or related support functions." They are also known as *covert action. See also:* Covert Action.

References

American Bar Association. *Oversight and Accountability of the U.S. Intelligence Agencies: An Evaluation.* Washington, DC: ABA, 1985.

Department of Defense, Defense Intelligence College. *Glossary of Intelligence Terms and Definitions.* Washington, DC: DIC, 1987.

Godson, Roy, ed. *Intelligence Problems for the 1980s, Number 1: Elements of Intelligence.* Rev. ed. Washington, DC: National Strategy Information Center, 1983.

Maurer, Alfred C.; Turnstall, Marion D.; and Keagle, James M. *Intelligence Policy and Process.* Boulder, CO: Westview Press, 1985.

Treverton, Gregory F. *Covert Action: The Limits of Intervention in the Postwar World.* New York: Basic Books, 1987.

Turner, Stansfield. *Secrecy and Democracy: The CIA in Transition.* Boston: Houghton Mifflin, 1985.

—**SPECIAL ACTIVITIES OFFICER (SAO)** is an obsolete term. When it was in use, it meant a type of sensitive compartmented information office or the officer who was responsible for the security of that information. He or she was also called the special intelligence/special activities officer (SI/SAO) if the facility or officer handled the appropriate types of information. The term special activities officer was abolished because it was confused with special activities, which are covert operations that are conducted by operational intelligence personnel. The special activities officer fulfilled administrative and security roles, and, at times, a limited intelligence production role. However, he or she was not involved in any type of covert or clandestine activity. *See also:* Access, Authorized, Classification, Code Word, Compromise, Declassification, Disclosure, Downgrade, Freedom of Information Act, Limited Access Area, Need-to-Know, Need-to-Know Principle, No-Lone Zone, Nondisclosure Agreement, Nondiscussion Area, Sanitization, Sanitize, Sanitized Area, Security Certification, Security Classification, Sensitive Compartmented Information, Sensitive Compartmented Information Facility, Two-Person Control.

References

Department of Defense, Defense Intelligence Agency. *Defense Intelligence Agency Manual.* Washington, DC: DIA, 1987.

————. *Organization, Mission and Key Personnel.* Washington, DC: DIA, 1986.

Department of Defense, Defense Intelligence College. *Glossary of Intelligence Terms and Definitions.* Washington, DC: DIC, 1987.

Laqueur, Walter. *A World of Secrets.* New York: Basic Books, 1985.

—**SPECIAL AGENT,** as defined by the Church Committee, is a U.S. military or civilian who is a specialist in military security or in the collection of intelligence or counterintelligence information.

References

Department of Defense, Joint Chiefs of Staff. *Department of Defense Dictionary of Military and Related Terms.* Washington, DC: GPO, 1986.

Treverton, Gregory F. *Covert Action: The Limits of Intervention in the Postwar World.* New York: Basic Books, 1987.

U.S. Congress. Senate. *Final Report of the Senate Select Committee to Study Government Operations with Respect to Intelligence Activities. Report 94-755. Book I, Foreign and Military Intelligence.* Washington, DC: GPO, 1976.

—**SPECIAL BACKGROUND INVESTIGATION (SBI)** is an inquiry into an individual's background history, in which, in addition to the information verified for a background investigation, the subject's employment and records are checked for fifteen years and his reputation is checked through visits to his neighborhood. When completed, it meets the investigative requirements for access to sensitive compartmented information (SCI). *See also:* Access, Authorized, Background Investigation, National Agency

Check, Need-to-Know, Need-to-Know Principle, No-Lone Zone, Nondisclosure Agreement, Nondiscussion Area.

References

Allen, Thomas B., and Polmar, Norman. *Merchants of Treason: America's Secrets for Sale.* New York: Delacorte Press, 1988.

Department of Defense, Defense Intelligence Agency. *Defense Intelligence Agency Manual.* Washington, DC: DIA, 1987.

Department of Defense, Defense Intelligence College. *Glossary of Intelligence Terms and Definitions.* Washington, DC: DIC, 1987.

Department of Defense, Joint Chiefs of Staff. *Department of Defense Dictionary of Military and Related Terms.* Washington, DC: GPO, 1986.

—**SPECIAL COORDINATION COMMITTEE (SCC) OF THE NATIONAL SECURITY COUNCIL (NSC)** was an NSC committee that dealt with oversight of sensitive intelligence activities, such as covert actions, which were undertaken on presidential authority, under President Carter. *See also:* National Security Council.

References

Department of Defense, Defense Intelligence College. *Glossary of Intelligence Terms and Definitions.* Washington, DC: DIC, 1987.

Godson, Roy, ed. *Intelligence Problems for the 1980s, Number 1: Elements of Intelligence.* Rev. ed. Washington, DC: National Strategy Information Center, 1983.

Laqueur, Walter. *A World of Secrets.* New York: Basic Books, 1985.

Treverton, Gregory F. *Covert Action: The Limits of Intervention in the Postwar World.* New York: Basic Books, 1987.

Turner, Stansfield. *Secrecy and Democracy: The CIA in Transition.* Boston: Houghton Mifflin, 1985.

—**SPECIAL COORDINATING COMMITTEE (INTELLIGENCE) (SCCI)** was established by President Carter and had the duties previously assigned to the Operations Advisory Group. Specifically, it had responsibility for reviewing and recommending to the president on covert action proposals and sensitive intelligence operations, and conducting periodic reviews of programs that were previously considered and approved. It was composed of the secretary of defense, the secretary of state, the director of Central Intelligence, and the chairman of the Joint Chiefs of Staff, with the attorney general and the chief of the Office of Management and Budget as observers.

The committee's powers were expanded further under Presidential Executive Order 12036. In it the committee was to develop a national counterintelligence policy. In addition, the attorney general was made a full member of the committee, thereby expanding his oversight role.

References

Laqueur, Walter. *A World of Secrets.* New York: Basic Books, 1985.

Oseth, John M. *Regulating U.S. Intelligence Operations: A Study in the Definition of the National Interest.* Frankfurt: University of Kentucky Press, 1985.

Treverton, Gregory F. *Covert Action: The Limits of Intervention in the Postwar World.* New York: Basic Books, 1987.

Turner, Stansfield. *Secrecy and Democracy: The CIA in Transition.* Boston: Houghton Mifflin, 1985.

—**SPECIAL DEFENSE INTELLIGENCE ESTIMATE (SDIE)** is similar to the Defense Intelligence Estimate in respect to length, target audience, and coordination, but is much narrower in scope. In addition, it is often produced to respond to a specific request from a high-level intelligence customer. Alternatively, an SDIE can be initiated by the Defense Intelligence Agency to report on a significant military intelligence development that has occurred on short notice. *See also:* Estimate, Estimative Intelligence.

References

Brinkley, David A., and Hull, Andrew W. *Estimative Intelligence: A Textbook on the History, Products, Uses and Writing of Intelligence Estimates.* Columbus, OH: Battelle, 1979.

Department of Defense, Defense Intelligence Agency. *Defense Intelligence Agency Manual.* Washington, DC: DIA, 1987.

Department of Defense, Defense Intelligence College. *Glossary of Intelligence Terms and Definitions.* Washington, DC: DIC, 1987.

—**SPECIAL DEFENSE INTELLIGENCE NOTICE (SDIN)** is a notice, the purpose of which is to give the Joint Chiefs of Staff, the Unified and Specified Commands, the military services, and selected government agencies timely intelligence about events that could have an immediate and significant effect on planning and operations.

References

Department of Defense, Defense Intelligence Agency. *Defense Intelligence Agency Manual.* Washington, DC: DIA, 1987.

Department of Defense, Defense Intelligence College. *Glossary of Intelligence Terms and Definitions.* Washington, DC: DIC, 1987.

Department of Defense, National Defense University. *Joint Staff Officer's Guide, 1986.* Washington, DC: GPO, 1986.

—**SPECIAL GROUP (AUGMENTED)**, as defined by the Church Committee, is "a National Security Council (NSC) subcommittee that was established in 1962 to oversee Operation Mongoose, a major Central Intelligence Agency covert action program to overthrow Fidel Castro." *See also:* Central Intelligence Agency, Mongoose.

References

Corson, William R. *The Armies of Ignorance: The Rise of the American Intelligence Empire.* New York: Dial Press, 1977.

Treverton, Gregory F. *Covert Action: The Limits of Intervention in the Postwar World.* New York: Basic Books, 1987.

U.S. Congress. Senate. *Final Report of the Senate Select Committee to Study Government Operations with Respect to Intelligence Activities. Report 94-755. Book I, Foreign and Military Intelligence.* Washington, DC: GPO, 1976.

—**SPECIAL GROUP (CI)**, as defined by the Church Committee, was the Special Group on Counterinsurgency that was established by National Security Action Memorandum 124 on January 1, 1983, to ensure the design of effective interagency programs to prevent and resist insurgency. Paramilitary programs were a major focus of the group.

References

Corson, William R. *The Armies of Ignorance: The Rise of the American Intelligence Empire.* New York: Dial Press, 1977.

Treverton, Gregory F. *Covert Action: The Limits of Intervention in the Postwar World.* New York: Basic Books, 1987.

U.S. Congress. Senate. *Final Report of the Senate Select Committee to Study Government Operations with Respect to Intelligence Activities. Report 94-755. Book I, Foreign and Military Intelligence.* Washington, DC: GPO, 1976.

—**SPECIAL INTELLIGENCE (SI)** is an unclassified term used to describe a category of sensitive compartmented information (SCI). *See also:* Access, Authorized, Classification, Code Word, Compromise, Declassification, Disclosure, Downgrade, Freedom of Information Act, Limited Access Area, Need-to-Know, Need-to-Know Principle, No-Lone Zone, Nondisclosure Agreement, Nondiscussion Area, Sanitization, Sanitize, Sanitized Area, Security Certification, Security Classification, Sensitive Compartmented Information, Sensitive Compartmented Information Facility, Two-Person Control.

References

Allen, Thomas B., and Polmar, Norman. *Merchants of Treason: America's Secrets for Sale.* New York: Delacorte Press, 1988.

Department of Defense, Defense Intelligence College. *Glossary of Intelligence Terms and Definitions.* Washington, DC: DIC, 1987.

Treverton, Gregory F. *Covert Action: The Limits of Intervention in the Postwar World.* New York: Basic Books, 1987.

—**SPECIAL INTELLIGENCE COMMUNICATIONS (SPINTCOMM)** is a communications network that was designed to handle all special intelligence and consists of those facilities under the operational and technical control of the chief of intelligence of each of the military departments, under the management of the Defense Intelligence Agency, and under the technical and security specification criteria established and monitored by the National Security Agency. In 1973, it became part of the DINDSSCS. *See also:* Communications Security.

References

Department of Defense, Defense Intelligence Agency. *Defense Intelligence Agency Manual.* Washington, DC: DIA, 1987.

———. *Organization, Mission and Key Personnel.* Washington, DC: DIA, 1986.

Department of Defense, Defense Intelligence College. *Glossary of Intelligence Terms and Definitions.* Washington, DC: DIC, 1987.

—**SPECIAL INTELLIGENCE/SPECIAL ACTIVITIES OFFICE (SI/SAO).** *See:* Special Activities Officer.

—**SPECIAL NATIONAL INTELLIGENCE ESTIMATE (SNIE)** is a National Intelligence Estimate (NIE) that is relevant to a specific policy problem that needs to be addressed in the immediate future. An SNIE is usually unscheduled, shorter, and prepared more quickly than an NIE and is coordinated within the Intelligence Community to the extent that time permits. The Defense Intelligence Agency's contributions to the SNIEs are prepared by the agency's Directorate for Estimates (DE). *See also:* National Intelligence Estimate (NIE).

References

American Bar Association. *Oversight and Accountability of the U.S. Intelligence Agencies: An Evaluation.* Washington, DC: ABA, 1985.

Department of Defense, Defense Intelligence Agency. *Organization, Mission and Key Personnel.* Washington, DC: DIA, 1986.

Department of Defense, Defense Intelligence College. *Glossary of Intelligence Terms and Definitions.* Washington, DC: DIC, 1987.

Fain, Tyrus G.; Plant, Katharine C.; and Milloy, Ross. *The Intelligence Community: History, Organization, and Issues.* Public Documents Series. New York: R.R. Bowker, 1977.

Lowenthal, Mark M. *U.S. Intelligence: Evolution and Anatomy.* New York: Praeger, 1984.

Maurer, Alfred C.; Turnstall, Marion D.; and Keagle, James M. *Intelligence Policy and Process.* Boulder, CO: Westview Press, 1985.

—**SPECIAL OPERATIONS** are operations conducted by specially trained, equipped, and organized Department of Defense forces against strategic and tactical targets in pursuit of national military, political, economic, or psychological objectives. These operations may be conducted during peace or wartime. They may support conventional operations or may be waged independently if the use of conventional forces is either inappropriate or unfeasible.

References

American Bar Association. *Oversight and Accountability of the U.S. Intelligence Agencies: An Evaluation.* Washington, DC: ABA, 1985.

Corson, William R. *The Armies of Ignorance: The Rise of the American Intelligence Empire.* New York: Dial Press, 1977.

Department of Defense, Joint Chiefs of Staff. *Department of Defense Dictionary of Military and Related Terms.* Washington, DC: GPO, 1986.

Laqueur, Walter. *A World of Secrets.* New York: Basic Books, 1985.

Maurer, Alfred C.; Turnstall, Marion D.; and Keagle, James M. *Intelligence Policy and Process.* Boulder, CO: Westview Press, 1985.

Treverton, Gregory F. *Covert Action: The Limits of Intervention in the Postwar World.* New York: Basic Books, 1987.

Turner, Stansfield. *Secrecy and Democracy: The CIA in Transition.* Boston: Houghton Mifflin, 1985.

—**SPECIAL OPERATIONS DIVISION (SOD),** as defined by the Church Committee, was "a facility at Fort Detrick, Maryland, that was the site for research and some testing and storage of biological and chemical agents and toxins."

References

U.S. Congress. Senate. *Final Report of the Senate Select Committee to Study Government Operations with Respect to Intelligence Activities. Report 94-755. Book I, Foreign and Military Intelligence.* Washington, DC: GPO, 1976.

—**SPECIAL PROCEDURES GROUP (SPG)** was established in 1947 and was responsible for conducting covert psychological operations.

References

Fain, Tyrus G.; Plant, Katharine C.; and Milloy, Ross. *The Intelligence Community: History, Organization, and Issues.* Public Documents Series. New York: R.R. Bowker, 1977.

Laqueur, Walter. *A World of Secrets.* New York: Basic Books, 1985.

—**SPECIAL SECURITY GROUP (SSG),** which controls the dissemination of sensitive compartmented information (SCI) to the U.S. Army worldwide, became part of the U.S. Army Intelligence and Security Command (INSCOM) in 1980. *See also:* Sensitive Compartmented Information.

References

Finnegan, John P. *Military Intelligence: A Picture History.* Arlington, VA: U.S. Army Intelligence and Security Command, 1984.

—**SPECIAL SECURITY OFFICER (SSO)** is the control point for security procedures within any activity that is authorized to have sensitive compartmented information. The most significant duties of the special security officer are to: (1) supervise the operation of the Special Security Office and administer the special compartmented information security program to include special compartmented information security oversight for other local special compartmented information facilities that are under his cognizance; (2) maintain all relevant directives, regulations, manuals, and guidelines that are needed to adequately fulfill the SSO responsibilities; (3) insure that special compartmented information is properly used, accounted for, controlled, safeguarded, packaged, transmitted, and destroyed; (4) provide advice and assistance concerning special compartmented information classification, control systems, sanitization, downgrading, decompartmentation, operational use, and emergency use; (5) insure that special compartmented information is disseminated only to persons who are authorized to have access to the material and only to those who have a need to know; (6) manage the special compartmented information, personnel, communications/TEMPEST, and physical security procedures and actions; (7) maintain the command's special compartmented information billet structure; (8) conduct security briefings, education programs, indoctrinations and debriefings, obtain signed nondisclosure agreements and perform other related personnel security actions pertaining to special compartmented information programs; (9) annually inspect all the subordinate special compartmented information facilities, document the inspection results, recommend corrective actions, and follow-up on the corrective measures; (10) insure that each subordinate special security officer and other security personnel perform an annual self-inspection of their facilities; (11) investigate security infractions, make recommendations, and prepare the required reports; (12) maintain listings of available products and assure the dissemination of products to authorized users; (13) provide privacy communications support to general/flag officers residing on or transiting through the installation; (14) maintain a telephone log of special security office personnel; and (15) develop a continuing security education training and awareness program.

References

Department of Defense, Defense Intelligence Agency. *Defense Intelligence Agency Manual.* Washington, DC: DIA, 1987.

———. *Organization, Mission and Key Personnel.* Washington, DC: DIA, 1986.

Department of Defense, Defense Intelligence College. *Glossary of Intelligence Terms and Definitions.* Washington, DC: DIC, 1987.

Department of Defense, Joint Chiefs of Staff. *Department of Defense Dictionary of Military and Related Terms.* Washington, DC: GPO, 1986.

—**SPECIAL SECURITY OFFICER SYSTEM** is one through which the director of the Defense Intelligence Agency, the service intelligence chiefs, and the Unified and Specified Commands perform their responsibilities concerning the security, use, and dissemination of sensitive compartmented information (SCI), to include both physical and electrical means. The acronym SSO is used to refer to both the office and the officer. *See also:* Defense Intelligence Agency, Sensitive Compartmented Information, Special Security Officer.

References
Department of Defense, Defense Intelligence Agency. *Defense Intelligence Agency Manual.* Washington, DC: DIA, 1987.

————. *Organization, Mission and Key Personnel.* Washington, DC: DIA, 1986.

Department of Defense, Defense Intelligence College. *Glossary of Intelligence Terms and Definitions.* Washington, DC: DIC, 1987.

—**SPECIAL SECURITY REPRESENTATIVE (SSR)** is a person who is responsible for the daily management and implementation of sensitive compartmented information (SCI) security and administrative instruction. *See also:* Special Security Officer.

References
Department of Defense, Defense Intelligence Agency. *Defense Intelligence Agency Manual.* Washington, DC: DIA, 1987.

Department of Defense, Defense Intelligence College. *Glossary of Intelligence Terms and Definitions.* Washington, DC: DIC, 1987.

—**SPECIAL SENSOR** is a term used in signals intelligence (SIGINT) and signals analysis for a piece of equipment on an instrumented platform and in installations that is designed to collect measurements of signature data that can be processed further into intelligence information that intelligence analysts can use. *See also:* Sensor.

References
Department of Defense, U.S. Army. *Counter-Signals Intelligence (C-SIGINT) Operations.* Field Manual FM 34-62. Washington, DC: Headquarters, Department of the Army, 1986.

————. *Military Intelligence Battalion (Combat Electronic Warfare Intelligence) (Division).* Field Manual FM 34-10. Washington, DC: Headquarters, Department of the Army, 1981.

————. *Military Intelligence Company (Combat Electronic Warfare and Intelligence) (Armored Cavalry Regiment/Separate Brigade).* Field Manual FM 34-30. Washington, DC: Headquarters, Department of the Army, 1983.

————. *RDTE Managers Intelligence and Threat Support Guide.* Alexandria, VA: Headquarters, Army Materiel Development and Readiness Command, 1983.

—**SPECIAL WEATHER INTELLIGENCE (SWI).** *See:* Geographical Intelligence.

—**SPECIALIST INTELLIGENCE REPORTS** is a category of specialized, technical reports that are used in disseminating intelligence.

References
Department of Defense, Joint Chiefs of Staff. *Department of Defense Dictionary of Military and Related Terms.* Washington, DC: GPO, 1986.

—**SPECIFIC INTELLIGENCE COLLECTION REQUIREMENT (SICR)** is an identified gap in intelligence that can be satisfied only by additional collection. It has been replaced by the Intelligence Collection Requirement (ICR). *See also:* Intelligence Requirement.

References
Department of Defense, Defense Intelligence Agency. *Defense Intelligence Agency Manual.* Washington, DC: DIA, 1987.

Department of Defense, Joint Chiefs of Staff. *Department of Defense Dictionary of Military and Related Terms.* Washington, DC: GPO, 1986.

—**SPECIFIED COMMAND** is one that has a broad continuing mission and is normally composed of one service. The specified commands are the Strategic Air Command (SAC), a command with responsibility for worldwide strategic nuclear operations, and the Force Command (FORSCOM), the strategic land force reserve of the free world. FORSCOM provides a reserve of combat-ready ground forces to reinforce the other unified and specified commands, and plans for the defense of the United States and Alaska.

The Unified and Specified Commands are force packages that are to be employed in military operations. The operational chain of command proceeds from the president to the secretary of defense through the chairman of the Joint Chiefs of Staff to the Unified and Specified Commands to their component commands. This concept is difficult for many to understand, because of the popular belief that the services control and command their own forces and commands. The services do in terms of administration and maintenance, but do not in terms of operational employment. Rather, the above-described chain-of-command prevails.

The Unified and Specified Command concept emerged in the years following World War II, as the United States military realized that the nature of warfare had progressed beyond theater warfare, where the several military forces could operate in isolation. Rather, the development of modern weapons meant that warfare in one theater could affect drastically the events in another theater. Now, it was realized, what was needed was the combined arms package that could provide adequate coordination among the several forces operating in a given region. The Unified and Specified Command approach was the response to this problem. *See also:* Unified Command.

References

Department of Defense, Joint Chiefs of Staff. *Department of Defense Dictionary of Military and Related Terms.* Washington, DC: GPO, 1986.

U.S. Congress. Senate. *Final Report of the Senate Select Committee to Study Government Operations with Respect to Intelligence Activities. Report 94-755. Book I, Foreign and Military Intelligence.* Washington, DC: GPO, 1976.

—**SPLIT CAMERAS** is an intelligence imagery and photoreconnaissance term for an assembly of two cameras disposed at a fixed overlapping angle relative to each other. *See also:* Fan Cameras, Sortie Number.

References

Department of Defense, Joint Chiefs of Staff. *Department of Defense Dictionary of Military and Related Terms.* Washington, DC: GPO, 1986.

Reeves, Robert; Anson, Abraham; and Landen, David. *Manual of Remote Sensing.* Falls Church, VA: American Society of Photogrammetry, 1975.

—**SPLIT KNOWLEDGE,** in communications security (COMSEC), refers to the separation of data into two or more parts. Each part of the data is constantly keep under the control of separate authorized individuals or teams, so that no one individual will be knowledgeable of the total data involved. *See also:* Communications Security.

References

Department of Defense, U.S. Army. *Counter-Signals Intelligence (C-SIGINT) Operations.* Field Manual FM 34-62. Washington, DC: Headquarters, Department of the Army, 1986.

————. *Military Intelligence Battalion (Combat Electronic Warfare Intelligence) (Division).* Field Manual FM 34-10. Washington, DC: Headquarters, Department of the Army, 1981.

————. *Military Intelligence Company (Combat Electronic Warfare and Intelligence) (Armored Cavalry Regiment/Separate Brigade).* Field Manual FM 34-30. Washington, DC: Headquarters, Department of the Army, 1983.

————. *RDTE Managers Intelligence and Threat Support Guide.* Alexandria, VA: Headquarters, Army Materiel Development and Readiness Command, 1983.

—**SPLIT VERTICAL PHOTOGRAPHY** is an intelligence imagery and photoreconnaissance term for photographs that are taken simultaneously by two cameras mounted at an angle from the vertical. One camera is tilted to the left, and one to the right, in order to obtain a small overlap. *See also:* Sortie Number.

References

Department of Defense, Joint Chiefs of Staff. *Department of Defense Dictionary of Military and Related Terms.* Washington, DC: GPO, 1986.

Reeves, Robert; Anson, Abraham; and Landen, David. *Manual of Remote Sensing.* Falls Church, VA: American Society of Photogrammetry, 1975.

—**SPONSORING AGENCY** is that element of a government agency that is responsible for a contractor's performance under a contract.

References

Department of Defense, Defense Intelligence Agency. *Defense Intelligence Agency Manual.* Washington, DC: DIA, 1987.

—**SPOOF** is a term used in signals intelligence, communications security, operations security, and signals analysis. It means to use equipment or procedures that intentionally mislead the enemy. An example would be to continue to use a frequency after it has been jammed, and, at the same time, introduce new frequencies. Another spoof is to establish decoy radio transmitters in order to prompt the enemy to engage in a considerable jamming effort because he believes that the decoys are part of a navigation system. *See also:* Communications Security.

References

Department of Defense, Joint Chiefs of Staff. *Department of Defense Dictionary of Military and Related Terms*. Washington, DC: GPO, 1986.

—**SPOOK** is American slang for a spy. *See also:* Agent, Agent in Place, Agent of Influence, Agent Provocateur, Cobbler, Confusion Agent, Co-Opted Worker, Co-Optees, Defector, Disaffected Person, Dispatched Agent, Double Agent, Flaps and Seals Man, Fur-Lined Seat Cover, Granny, Handling Agent, Heavy Mob, Honey Trap, Illegal Agent, Inside Man, Ladies, Lion Tamer, Mole, Mozhno Girls, Musician, Paroles, Pavement Artists, Pigeon, Provocation Agent, Raven, Scalp Hunters, Singleton, Sisters, Sleeper, Sound Man, Stable, Swallow, Taxi.

References

Clancy, Tom. *The Cardinal of the Kremlin*. New York: Putnam, 1988.

Deacon, Richard. *Spyclopedia: An Encyclopedia of Spies, Secret Services, Operations, Jargon, and All Subjects Related to the World of Espionage*. London: Macdonald, 1987.

Laqueur, Walter. *A World of Secrets*. New York: Basic Books, 1985.

Quirk, John; Phillips, David; Cline, Ray; and Pforzheimer, Walter. *The Central Intelligence Agency: A Photographic History*. Guilford, CT: Foreign Intelligence Press, 1986.

—**SPOT INTELLIGENCE REPORT (SPIREP)** is a narrative report submitted by the Unified and Specified Commands, the military services, and military organizations of the divisional (two-star) level whenever critical developments appear imminent or are of potentially high interest to U.S. national-level decisionmakers. Its purpose is to give the Joint Chiefs of Staff, the National Military Intelligence Center, the Unified and Specified Commands, and selected government agencies timely intelligence information on developments that could have an immediate and

significant affect on current planning and operations. The initial SPIREP will not be delayed for verifying the information or for getting more details. Rather, amplifying or clarifying information should be transmitted in a followup SPIREP. *See also:* Dissemination, Intelligence Cycle.

References

Department of Defense, Defense Intelligence Agency. *Defense Intelligence Agency Manual*. Washington, DC: DIA, 1987.

Department of Defense, National Defense University. *Joint Staff Officer's Guide, 1986*. Washington, DC: GPO, 1986.

Turner, Stansfield. *Secrecy and Democracy: The CIA in Transition*. Boston: Houghton Mifflin, 1985.

—**SPOT JAMMING,** in electronic warfare (EW), is jamming a specific frequency or channel. *See also:* Barrage Jamming, Electronic Jamming, Electronic Warfare, Jamming.

References

Department of Defense, Joint Chiefs of Staff. *Department of Defense Dictionary of Military and Related Terms*. Washington, DC: GPO, 1986.

—**SPOT REPORT** is a concise narrative report of essential information covering events or conditions that may have an immediate and significant effect on current planning and operations. A spot report is given the fastest means of transmission. *See also:* Dissemination, Intelligence Cycle.

References

Department of Defense, Defense Intelligence Agency. *Defense Intelligence Agency Manual*. Washington, DC: DIA, 1987.

Department of Defense, Joint Chiefs of Staff. *Department of Defense Dictionary of Military and Related Terms*. Washington, DC: GPO, 1986.

Turner, Stansfield. *Secrecy and Democracy: The CIA in Transition*. Boston: Houghton Mifflin, 1985.

—**SPOTTER** is an agent or an illegal agent who is assigned to locate and assess individuals who might be of service to an intelligence agency.

References

Becket, Henry S. A. *The Dictionary of Espionage: Spookspeak into English*. New York: Stein and Day, 1986.

Deacon, Richard. *Spyclopedia: An Encyclopedia of Spies, Secret Services, Operations, Jargon, and All Subjects Related to the World of Espionage*. London: Macdonald, 1987.

Kessler, Ronald. *Spy vs. Spy: Stalking Soviet Spies in America.* New York: Charles Scribner's Sons, 1988.

Ranelagh, John. *The Agency: The Rise and Decline of the CIA.* New York: Simon and Schuster, 1986.

—**SPY.** *See:* Agent, Intelligence Officer.

—**SQUIRT TRANSMITTER** is a term used in clandestine and covert intelligence operations. It is a device that an agent can use to transmit his material extremely rapidly. The message is punched onto tape and the tape is fed through a transmitter at approximately 300 words per minute. This allows the agent to be off the air before directional homing equipment can locate him.

References

Becket, Henry S. A. *The Dictionary of Espionage: Spookspeak into English.* New York: Stein and Day, 1986.

Deacon, Richard. *Spyclopedia: An Encyclopedia of Spies, Secret Services, Operations, Jargon, and All Subjects Related to the World of Espionage.* London: Macdonald, 1987.

Kessler, Ronald. *Spy vs. Spy: Stalking Soviet Spies in America.* New York: Charles Scribner's Sons, 1988.

Ranelagh, John. *The Agency: The Rise and Decline of the CIA.* New York: Simon and Schuster, 1986.

—**SR-71 AIRCRAFT (BLACKBIRD)** is a high altitude reconnaissance aircraft that replaced the U-2 aircraft. *See:* U-2 Overhead Reconnaissance Program and U-2 Spy Plane.

References

Breckinridge, Scott D. *The CIA and the U.S. Intelligence System.* Boulder, CO: Westview Press, 1986.

Clancy, Tom. *The Cardinal of the Kremlin.* New York: Putnam, 1988.

Godson, Roy, ed. *Intelligence Problems for the 1980s, Number 5: Clandestine Collection.* Washington, DC: National Strategy Information Center, 1982.

Laqueur, Walter. *A World of Secrets.* New York: Basic Books, 1985.

—**STABLE** is a term used in clandestine and covert intelligence operations to describe the inventory of "ladies" and "sisters" who are available for assignments. It may also include the "taxis" and

"fairies." *See also:* Ladies, Sisters, Taxis, Swallow, Swallow's Nest.

References

Becket, Henry S. A. *The Dictionary of Espionage: Spookspeak into English.* New York: Stein and Day, 1986.

Deacon, Richard. *Spyclopedia: An Encyclopedia of Spies, Secret Services, Operations, Jargon, and All Subjects Related to the World of Espionage.* London: Macdonald, 1987.

Kessler, Ronald. *Spy vs. Spy: Stalking Soviet Spies in America.* New York: Charles Scribner's Sons, 1988.

Ranelagh, John. *The Agency: The Rise and Decline of the CIA.* New York: Simon and Schuster, 1986.

—**STAGING** is sending an illegal agent to an area where he can be trained and can establish a legend before he enters the target country. *See also:* Legend, Silent School.

References

Becket, Henry S. A. *The Dictionary of Espionage: Spookspeak into English.* New York: Stein and Day, 1986.

Deacon, Richard. *Spyclopedia: An Encyclopedia of Spies, Secret Services, Operations, Jargon, and All Subjects Related to the World of Espionage.* London: Macdonald, 1987.

Kessler, Ronald. *Spy vs. Spy: Stalking Soviet Spies in America.* New York: Charles Scribner's Sons, 1988.

Ranelagh, John. *The Agency: The Rise and Decline of the CIA.* New York: Simon and Schuster, 1986.

Turner, Stansfield. *Secrecy and Democracy: The CIA in Transition.* Boston: Houghton Mifflin, 1985.

—**STANDARD TECHNICAL EQUIPMENT DEVELOPMENT (STED)** is a component of one of the ten branches that constitute the National Security Agency. *See:* National Security Agency.

References

Bamford, James. *The Puzzle Palace: A Report on America's Most Secret Agency.* New York: Penguin Books, 1983.

—**START (RELEASE) ELEMENT,** a baud-based system term used in communications intelligence, communications security, operations security, and signals analysis, is an element that serves to prepare the receiving mechanism for the reception and registration of a character. *See also:* Communications Security.

References

Department of Defense, U.S. Army. *Counter-Signals Intelligence (C-SIGINT) Operations.* Field Manual FM 34-62.Washington, DC: Headquarters, Department of the Army, 1986.

————. *Military Intelligence Battalion (Combat Electronic Warfare Intelligence) (Division).* Field Manual FM 34-10. Washington, DC: Headquarters, Department of the Army, 1981.

————. *Military Intelligence Company (Combat Electronic Warfare and Intelligence) (Armored Cavalry Regiment/Separate Brigade).* Field Manual FM 34-30. Washington, DC: Headquarters, Department of the Army, 1983.

————. *RDTE Managers Intelligence and Threat Support Guide.* Alexandria, VA: Headquarters, Army Materiel Development and Readiness Command, 1983.

—STATEMENT OF INTELLIGENCE INTEREST (SII) is a customer's entire requirement for intelligence information reports (IIRs), nonrecurring finished intelligence (NRFI), finished recurring intelligence (FRI), and signals intelligence (SIGINT) that makes up a detailed profile of a customer's mission, function, and areas of responsibility. This documentation is the basis for disseminating information reports, nonrecurring finished intelligence, and the initial issue of finished recurring intelligence publications. Previously, an SII referred only to IIRs and NRFI. *See also:* Defense Intelligence Thesaurus (DIT) Worksheet.

References

Department of Defense, Defense Intelligence Agency. *Defense Intelligence Agency Manual.* Washington, DC: DIA, 1987.

Department of Defense, U.S. Army. *RDTE Managers Intelligence and Threat Support Guide.* Alexandria, VA: Headquarters, Army Materiel Development and Readiness Command, 1983.

—STATE, WAR, AND NAVY COORDINATING COMMITTEE (SWNCC) was established in 1944. It was a predecessor to the National Security Council.

References

Fain, Tyrus G.; Plant, Katharine C.; and Milloy, Ross. *The Intelligence Community: History, Organization, and Issues.* Public Documents Series. New York: R.R. Bowker, 1977.

—STENOGRAPHY OR CONCEALMENT CIPHER, a signals analysis term, is a cipher method that conceals, hides, or disguises the very existence of the secret message. Devices that are used are microdots or invisible inks. In electrical communications, stenography is represented by spurt or burst transmissions, which compress the messages. *See also:* Cipher.

References

Department of Defense, U.S. Army. *Counter-Signals Intelligence (C-SIGINT) Operations.* Field Manual FM 34-62. Washington, DC: Headquarters, Department of the Army, 1986.

—STEREO is an abbreviated version of stereoscopic. *See also:* Sortie Number.

References

Reeves, Robert; Anson, Abraham; and Landen, David. *Manual of Remote Sensing.* Falls Church, VA: American Society of Photogrammetry, 1975.

—STEREOSCOPIC COVER is an intelligence imagery and photoreconnaissance term. Stereoscopic cover involves taking photography with sufficient overlap to permit a complete stereoscopic examination. *See also:* Sortie Number.

References

Reeves, Robert; Anson, Abraham; and Landen, David. *Manual of Remote Sensing.* Falls Church, VA: American Society of Photogrammetry, 1975.

Turner, Stansfield. *Secrecy and Democracy: The CIA in Transition.* Boston: Houghton Mifflin, 1985.

—STEREOSCOPIC PAIR is an intelligence imagery and photoreconnaissance term for two photographs with sufficient overlap of detail so that it is possible to make a stereoscopic examination of an object or an area that appears in both photographs. *See also:* Sortie Number.

References

Department of Defense, Joint Chiefs of Staff. *Department of Defense Dictionary of Military and Related Terms.* Washington, DC: GPO, 1986.

Reeves, Robert; Anson, Abraham; and Landen, David. *Manual of Remote Sensing.* Falls Church, VA: American Society of Photogrammetry, 1975.

—STEREOSCOPIC VISION is an intelligence imagery and photoreconnaissance term. It is the capability to perceive three dimensional images. *See also:* Sortie Number.

References

Reeves, Robert; Anson, Abraham; and Landen, David. *Manual of Remote Sensing*. Falls Church, VA: American Society of Photogrammetry, 1975.

—**STEREOSCOPY** is an intelligence imagery and photoreconnaissance term for the science that concerns three-dimensional effects and how these effects are produced. *See also:* Sortie Number.

References

Reeves, Robert; Anson, Abraham; and Landen, David. *Manual of Remote Sensing*. Falls Church, VA: American Society of Photogrammetry, 1975.

—**STERILE FUNDS,** in FBI terminology, are currency that is used by an intelligence agency that cannot be traced to the agency.

References

Kessler, Ronald. *Spy vs. Spy: Stalking Soviet Spies in America*. New York: Charles Scribner's Sons, 1988.

Turner, Stansfield. *Secrecy and Democracy: The CIA in Transition*. Boston: Houghton Mifflin, 1985.

—**STERILE TELEPHONE** is a telephone that cannot be traced, even by the telephone company. The CIA has such phones both in the United States and overseas.

References

Becket, Henry S. A. *The Dictionary of Espionage: Spookspeak into English*. New York: Stein and Day, 1986.

Deacon, Richard. *Spyclopedia: An Encyclopedia of Spies, Secret Services, Operations, Jargon, and All Subjects Related to the World of Espionage*. London: Macdonald, 1987.

Ranelagh, John. *The Agency: The Rise and Decline of the CIA*. New York: Simon and Schuster, 1986.

Turner, Stansfield. *Secrecy and Democracy: The CIA in Transition*. Boston: Houghton Mifflin, 1985.

—**STERILITY CODING** is a term that is used in clandestine and covert intelligence operations. It is the use of intermediatory companies or people to sign for purchases or payments that the agency does not want to be identified with.

References

Becket, Henry S. A. *The Dictionary of Espionage: Spookspeak into English*. New York: Stein and Day, 1986.

Deacon, Richard. *Spyclopedia: An Encyclopedia of Spies, Secret Services, Operations, Jargon, and All Subjects Related to the World of Espionage*. London: Macdonald, 1987.

Ranelagh, John. *The Agency: The Rise and Decline of the CIA*. New York: Simon and Schuster, 1986.

—**STERILIZE** is a term used in clandestine and covert intelligence operations. To sterilize is to remove all marks and devices that can identify a piece of material as coming from an intelligence organization. This is done so that when the item is used in covert or clandestine operations, its source will not be revealed.

References

Becket, Henry S. A. *The Dictionary of Espionage: Spookspeak into English*. New York: Stein and Day, 1986.

Deacon, Richard. *Spyclopedia: An Encyclopedia of Spies, Secret Services, Operations, Jargon, and All Subjects Related to the World of Espionage*. London: Macdonald, 1987.

Kessler, Ronald. *Spy vs. Spy: Stalking Soviet Spies in America*. New York: Charles Scribner's Sons, 1988.

Ranelagh, John. *The Agency: The Rise and Decline of the CIA*. New York: Simon and Schuster, 1986.

Quirk, John; Phillips, David; Cline, Ray; and Pforzheimer, Walter. *The Central Intelligence Agency: A Photographic History*. Guilford, CT: Foreign Intelligence Press, 1986.

U.S. Congress. Senate. *Final Report of the Senate Select Committee to Study Government Operations with Respect to Intelligence Activities. Report 94-755. Book I, Foreign and Military Intelligence*. Washington, DC: GPO, 1976.

—**STOCK FUND,** in intelligence budgeting, is a type of working capital fund that is established to finance inventories of consumable materials.

References

Pickett, George. "Congress, the Budget, and Intelligence." In *Intelligence Policy and Process*, edited by Alfred C. Maurer, Marion D. Turnstall, and James M. Keagle. Boulder, CO: Westview Press, 1985.

—**STOP (LATCH) ELEMENT,** a baud-based system term used in communications intelligence, communications security, operations security, and signals analysis, is an element that serves to bring the receiving mechanism to rest in preparation for the reception of the next character. An "elongated" latch is an element that is of longer duration than the normal elements in a system. *See also:* Communications Security.

References

Department of Defense, U.S. Army. *Counter-Signals Intelligence (C-SIGINT) Operations.* Field Manual FM 34-62. Washington, DC: Headquarters, Department of the Army, 1986.

————. *Military Intelligence Battalion (Combat Electronic Warfare Intelligence) (Division).* Field Manual FM 34-10. Washington, DC: Headquarters, Department of the Army, 1981.

————. *Military Intelligence Company (Combat Electronic Warfare and Intelligence) (Armored Cavalry Regiment/Separate Brigade).* Field Manual FM 34-30. Washington, DC: Headquarters, Department of the Army, 1983.

————. *RDTE Managers Intelligence and Threat Support Guide.* Alexandria, VA: Headquarters, Army Materiel Development and Readiness Command, 1983.

—**STRATEGIC AIR COMMAND (SAC)** is one of three Specified Commands and is a major U.S. Air Force command. For years, the SAC's fleet of long-range bombers were the main U.S. strategic deterrent force, and the SAC was also responsible for the U.S. land-based ICBM force. Because of these interests, the Air Force inflated its estimates of Soviet bomber and missile production. This issue, which became known as the "missile gap," became a major campaign issue in the Kennedy-Nixon presidential contest of 1960. President Eisenhower knew that no such gap existed but was unable to state this publicly, because his evidence consisted of U-2 photography.

References

Breckinridge, Scott D. *The CIA and the U.S. Intelligence System.* Boulder, CO: Westview Press, 1986.

—**STRATEGIC ARMS LIMITATIONS TALKS.** *See:* SALT I and SALT II.

—**STRATEGIC INTELLIGENCE** is the intelligence that is needed for formulating policy and military plans at the national and international levels. It differs primarily from tactical intelligence in the level of its use, but may also vary in scope and detail. The components of strategic intelli-gence are biographic intelligence, economic intelligence, sociological intelligence, transportation and telecommunications intelligence, military geographic intelligence, armed forces intelligence, political intelligence, and scientific and technical intelligence. See the entries under each of these titles.

References

Clauser, Jerome K., and Weir, Sandra M. *Intelligence Research Methodology.* State College, PA: HRB-Singer, 1975.

Department of Defense, Defense Intelligence College. *Glossary of Intelligence Terms and Definitions.* Washington, DC: DIC, 1987.

Department of Defense, Joint Chiefs of Staff. *Department of Defense Dictionary of Military and Related Terms.* Washington, DC: GPO, 1986.

Department of Defense, U.S. Army. *Intelligence and Electronic Warfare Operations.* Field Manual FM 34-1. Washington, DC: Headquarters, Department of the Army, 1984.

Kent, Sherman. *Strategic Intelligence for American World Policy.* Princeton, NJ: Princeton University Press, 1966.

Laqueur, Walter. *A World of Secrets.* New York: Basic Books, 1985.

Quirk, John; Phillips, David; Cline, Ray; and Pforzheimer, Walter. *The Central Intelligence Agency: A Photographic History.* Guilford, CT: Foreign Intelligence Press, 1986.

Turner, Stansfield. *Secrecy and Democracy: The CIA in Transition.* Boston: Houghton Mifflin, 1985.

U.S. Congress. Senate. *Final Report of the Senate Select Committee to Study Government Operations with Respect to Intelligence Activities. Report 94-755. Book I, Foreign and Military Intelligence.* Washington, DC: GPO, 1976.

Von Hoene, John P. A. *Intelligence User's Guide.* Washington, DC: DIA, 1983.

—**STRATEGIC PSYCHOLOGICAL WARFARE** involves actions that pursue long-term and primarily political objectives, in a declared emergency or war, and that are designed to undermine the enemy's will to fight and to reduce his capacity for waging war. It can be directed against the enemy (the dominating political group, the government, and the executive agencies) or toward the population as a whole or certain elements of it.

References

Department of Defense, Joint Chiefs of Staff. *Department of Defense Dictionary of Military and Related Terms.* Washington, DC: GPO, 1986.

Treverton, Gregory F. *Covert Action: The Limits of Intervention in the Postwar World.* New York: Basic Books, 1987.

—**STRATEGIC SERVICES UNIT (SSU)** was the result of the disestablishment of the Office of Strategic Services (OSS) in 1945. The Research and Analysis Section of OSS went to the State Department, while the Secret Intelligence (clandestine collection) and X-2 (counterespionage) branches went to the War Department, where they were combined into the Strategic Service Unit. It was subsequently transferred to the Central Intelligence Group in 1946. *See also:* Office of Strategic Services.

References

Corson, William R. *The Armies of Ignorance: The Rise of the American Intelligence Empire.* New York: Dial Press, 1977.

Fain, Tyrus G.; Plant, Katharine C.; and Milloy, Ross. *The Intelligence Community: History, Organization, and Issues.* Public Documents Series. New York: R.R. Bowker, 1977.

Lowenthal, Mark M. *U.S. Intelligence: Evolution and Anatomy.* New York: Praeger, 1984.

Treverton, Gregory F. *Covert Action: The Limits of Intervention in the Postwar World.* New York: Basic Books, 1987.

—**STRATEGIC WARNING** is intelligence information or intelligence concerning the threat of the initiation of hostilities against the United States or of hostilities in which U.S. forces may become involved. Such a warning may be received at any time prior to the initiation of hostilities.

References

Department of Defense, Defense Intelligence College. *Glossary of Intelligence Terms and Definitions.* Washington, DC: DIC, 1987.

Department of Defense, Joint Chiefs of Staff. *Department of Defense Dictionary of Military and Related Terms.* Washington, DC: GPO, 1986.

Godson, Roy, ed. *Intelligence Problems for the 1980s, Number 1: Elements of Intelligence.* Rev. ed. Washington, DC: National Strategy Information Center, 1983.

Kent, Sherman. *Strategic Intelligence for American World Policy.* Princeton, NJ: Princeton University Press, 1966.

Maurer, Alfred C.; Turnstall, Marion D.; and Keagle, James M. *Intelligence Policy and Process.* Boulder, CO: Westview Press, 1985.

Treverton, Gregory F. *Covert Action: The Limits of Intervention in the Postwar World.* New York: Basic Books, 1987.

—**STRATEGIC WARNING LEAD TIME** is an indications and warning (I&W) term. It is that time between the receipt of strategic warning and the beginning of hostilities. This time may include two action periods: strategic warning pre-decision time and strategic warning post-decision time. *See also:* Indications and Warning.

References

Department of Defense, Defense Intelligence College. *Glossary of Intelligence Terms and Definitions.* Washington, DC: DIC, 1987.

Department of Defense, Joint Chiefs of Staff. *Department of Defense Dictionary of Military and Related Terms.* Washington, DC: GPO, 1986.

Kent, Sherman. *Strategic Intelligence for American World Policy.* Princeton, NJ: Princeton University Press, 1966.

—**STRATEGY,** according to the Joint Chiefs of Staff, is the art and science of developing and using political, economic, psychological, and military forces as necessary during peace and war, to afford the maximum support to policies, in order to increase the probabilities and favorable consequences of victory and to lessen the chances of defeat. *See also:* Military Strategy, National Strategy.

References

Department of Defense, Joint Chiefs of Staff. *Department of Defense Dictionary of Military and Related Terms.* Washington, DC: GPO, 1986.

Godson, Roy, ed. *Intelligence Problems for the 1980s, Number 1: Elements of Intelligence.* Rev. ed. Washington, DC: National Strategy Information Center, 1983.

Kent, Sherman. *Strategic Intelligence for American World Policy.* Princeton, NJ: Princeton University Press, 1966.

Maurer, Alfred C.; Turnstall, Marion D.; and Keagle, James M. *Intelligence Policy and Process.* Boulder, CO: Westview Press, 1985.

Treverton, Gregory F. *Covert Action: The Limits of Intervention in the Postwar World.* New York: Basic Books, 1987.

—**STRIKE PHOTOGRAPHY** is photography that is taken during an air strike. It is valuable in assessing the success of the strike. *See also:* Sortie Number.

References

Department of Defense, Joint Chiefs of Staff. *Department of Defense Dictionary of Military and Related Terms.* Washington, DC: GPO, 1986.

—**STRINGER** is a term used in clandestine intelligence operations to describe a low-level agent who lives or works near an intelligence target and passes along whatever he observes. He might also be used for letter drops, renting safe houses, or in short-notice surveillance.

References

Becket, Henry S. A. *The Dictionary of Espionage: Spookspeak into English.* New York: Stein and Day, 1986.

Quirk, John; Phillips, David; Cline, Ray; and Pforzheimer, Walter. *The Central Intelligence Agency: A Photographic History.* Guilford, CT: Foreign Intelligence Press, 1986.

—**STRIP PLOT** is an intelligence imagery and photoreconnaissance term for a portion of a map or overlay on which a number of photographs taken along a flight line are delineated without defining the outlines of the prints. *See also:* Sortie Number.

References

Department of Defense, Joint Chiefs of Staff. *Department of Defense Dictionary of Military and Related Terms.* Washington, DC: GPO, 1986.

—**STROLLER** is a term used in counterintelligence operations to describe an agent who is operating with a walkie-talkie set.

References

Becket, Henry S. A. *The Dictionary of Espionage: Spookspeak into English.* New York: Stein and Day, 1986.

Deacon, Richard. *Spyclopedia: An Encyclopedia of Spies, Secret Services, Operations, Jargon, and All Subjects Related to the World of Espionage.* London: Macdonald, 1987.

Ranelagh, John. *The Agency: The Rise and Decline of the CIA.* New York: Simon and Schuster, 1986.

—**SUBASSEMBLY,** in communications security (COMSEC), refers to a major subdivision of an assembly that consists of a package of parts, elements, and circuits that perform a specific function. *See also:* Communications Security.

References

Department of Defense, U.S. Army. *Counterintelligence.* Field Manual FM 34-60. Washington, DC: Headquarters, Department of the Army, 1985.

———. *Intelligence and Electronic Warfare Operations.* Field Manual FM 34-1. Washington, DC: Headquarters, Department of the Army, 1984.

———. *Military Intelligence Battalion (Combat Electronic Warfare Intelligence) (Division).* Field Manual FM 34-10. Washington, DC: Headquarters, Department of the Army, 1981.

———. *Military Intelligence Battalion (CEWI) (Tactical Exploitation) (Corps): Counterintelligence, Interrogation, Electronic Warfare.* Field Manual FM 34-23. Washington, DC: Headquarters, Department of the Army, 1985.

———. *Military Intelligence Company (Combat Electronic Warfare and Intelligence) (Armored Cavalry Regiment/Separate Brigade).* Field Manual FM 34-30. Washington, DC: Headquarters, Department of the Army, 1983.

—**SUBCHANNELING,** a baud-based system term used in communications intelligence, communications security, operations security, and signals analysis, is the process by which two or more separate subscribers, transmitting at a reduced rate, share the time normally allotted to one channel. This is also called channel subdivision. *See also:* Communications Security.

References

Department of Defense, U.S. Army. *Counterintelligence.* Field Manual FM 34-60. Washington, DC: Headquarters, Department of the Army, 1985.

———. *Intelligence and Electronic Warfare Operations.* Field Manual FM 34-1. Washington, DC: Headquarters, Department of the Army, 1984.

———. *Military Intelligence Battalion (Combat Electronic Warfare Intelligence) (Division).* Field Manual FM 34-10. Washington, DC: Headquarters, Department of the Army, 1981.

———. *Military Intelligence Battalion (CEWI) (Tactical Exploitation) (Corps): Counterintelligence, Interrogation, Electronic Warfare.* Field Manual FM 34-23. Washington, DC: Headquarters, Department of the Army, 1985.

———. *Military Intelligence Company (Combat Electronic Warfare and Intelligence) (Armored Cavalry Regiment/Separate Brigade).* Field Manual FM 34-30. Washington, DC: Headquarters, Department of the Army, 1983.

—**SUBCOMMITTEE ON LEGISLATION, U.S. PERMANENT SELECT COMMITTEE ON INTELLIGENCE.** *See:* Murphy Committee.

—**SUBMARINE-LAUNCHED BALLISTIC MISSILE (SLBM)** is a ballistic missile that can be launched from a submarine. Today's Soviet and U.S.

SLBMs can be launched while the submarine is submerged and can reach distances in excess of 4,000 miles. These factors, coupled with the submarine's intrinsic ability to avoid detection, make the ballistic missile-equipped submarine a most potent strategic weapon in both the Soviet and U.S. strategic arsenals.

References

Department of Defense, Joint Chiefs of Staff. *Department of Defense Dictionary of Military and Related Terms.* Washington, DC: GPO, 1986.

—**SUBMARINE-LAUNCHED CRUISE MISSILE (SLCM)** is a non-ballistic missile that is launched from submarines. SLCMs are intended primarily to attack targets at sea, although the newer cruise missiles are sufficiently accurate and powerful and have such great ranges that they can be used against land targets as well. In light of these capabilities and the fact that both U.S. and Soviet cruise missile-equipped submarines can launch their missiles while they are submerged means that these submarines pose a very severe anti-shipping threat.

References

Department of Defense, Joint Chiefs of Staff. *Department of Defense Dictionary of Military and Related Terms.* Washington, DC: GPO, 1986.

Laqueur, Walter. *A World of Secrets.* New York: Basic Books, Inc., 1985.

—**SUBMERGE** is a term used in clandestine and covert intelligence operations. It means to disappear from sight once an agent is within a target country. He may reappear later, usually with new identification and a new appearance. *See also:* Agent, Blow, Blown Agent, Burn, Burnt, Concealment, Cover, Damage Assessment, Damage Control, Go to Ground, Sign of Life Signal, Suitable Cover, Surfacing.

References

Becket, Henry S. A. *The Dictionary of Espionage: Spookspeak into English.* New York: Stein and Day, 1986.

Deacon, Richard. *Spyclopedia: An Encyclopedia of Spies, Secret Services, Operations, Jargon, and All Subjects Related to the World of Espionage.* London: Macdonald, 1987.

Ranelagh, John. *The Agency: The Rise and Decline of the CIA.* New York: Simon and Schuster, 1986.

—**SUBSIDIARY LANDING,** in amphibious warfare operations, is an amphibious landing that is usually made from outside of the designated landing area for the purpose of supporting the main amphibious landing.

References

Department of Defense, Joint Chiefs of Staff. *Department of Defense Dictionary of Military and Related Terms.* Washington, DC: GPO, 1986.

—**SUBVERSION,** as defined by the Church Committee, involves "actions that are designed to undermine the military, economic, political, psychological, or moral strength of a nation or entity. It can also apply to an undermining of a person's loyalty to a government or entity."

References

Department of Defense, Joint Chiefs of Staff. *Department of Defense Dictionary of Military and Related Terms.* Washington, DC: GPO, 1986.

Laqueur, Walter. *A World of Secrets.* New York: Basic Books, 1985.

Treverton, Gregory F. *Covert Action: The Limits of Intervention in the Postwar World.* New York: Basic Books, 1987.

U.S. Congress. Senate. *Final Report of the Senate Select Committee to Study Government Operations with Respect to Intelligence Activities. Report 94-755. Book I, Foreign and Military Intelligence.* Washington, DC: GPO, 1976.

—**SUITABILITY FILES** are files of highly personal information (sexual activities, drinking habits, indebtedness, etc.) that might reflect on the vulnerability or unreliability of an employee. The National Security Agency maintains such files, but to counsel and assist its employees, not to threaten them.

References

Bamford, James. *The Puzzle Palace: A Report on America's Most Secret Agency.* New York: Penguin Books, 1983.

Becket, Henry S. A. *The Dictionary of Espionage: Spookspeak into English.* New York: Stein and Day, 1986.

—**SUITABLE COVER** is an intelligence security and counterintelligence term. It is the existence of a plausible non-sensitive compartmented information (SCI) source to which an action or information based on SCI can be attributed. Its net effect is to conceal the relationship between the action and the SCI on which it is based. This method was devised during the Vietnam War, when SCI of great value to the Operational Commander or field forces could not be passed to them because of unsecure communications or uncleared personnel. This approach allows us to get the information to the person who needs it most—the commander.

References

Treverton, Gregory F. *Covert Action: The Limits of Intervention in the Postwar World.* New York: Basic Books, 1987.

—**SUNK COST,** in budgeting, is a past cost arising out of a decision that cannot now be revised, and associated with equipment or facilities not readily adaptable to present or future purposes.

References

Pickett, George. "Congress, the Budget, and Intelligence." In *Intelligence Policy and Process,* edited by Alfred C. Maurer, Marion D. Turnstall, and James M. Keagle. Boulder, CO: Westview Press, 1985.

—**SUPERSESSION,** in communications security (COMSEC), means a scheduled or unscheduled replacement of a COMSEC aid with a different edition. *See also:* Communications Security.

References

Department of Defense, U.S. Army. *Counterintelligence.* Field Manual FM 34-60. Washington, DC: Headquarters, Department of the Army, 1985.

———. *Intelligence and Electronic Warfare Operations.* Field Manual FM 34-1. Washington, DC: Headquarters, Department of the Army, 1984.

———. *Military Intelligence Battalion (Combat Electronic Warfare Intelligence) (Division).* Field Manual FM 34-10. Washington, DC: Headquarters, Department of the Army, 1981.

———. *Military Intelligence Battalion (CEWI) (Tactical Exploitation) (Corps): Counterintelligence, Interrogation, Electronic Warfare.* Field Manual FM 34-23. Washington, DC: Headquarters, Department of the Army, 1985.

———. *Military Intelligence Company (Combat Electronic Warfare and Intelligence) (Armored Cavalry Regiment/Separate Brigade).* Field Manual FM 34-30. Washington, DC: Headquarters, Department of the Army, 1983.

—**SUPPLEMENTAL PROGRAMMED INTERPRETATION REPORT (SUPIR)** is an intelligence imagery and photoreconnaissance term. It is a standardized imagery interpretation report that provides information on significant targets covered by the mission that has not been previously included in other reports. It may also be submitted when supplementary information is required. The conditions for the SUPIR are the same as for the IPIR.

References

Department of Defense, Defense Intelligence College. *Glossary of Intelligence Terms and Definitions.* Washington, DC: DIC, 1987.

Department of Defense, Joint Chiefs of Staff. *Department of Defense Dictionary of Military and Related Terms.* Washington, DC: GPO, 1986.

Department of Defense, U.S. Army. *Intelligence Imagery.* Field Manual FM 34-55. Washington, DC: Headquarters, Department of the Army, 1985.

—**SUPPORT FOR ANALYSTS' FILE ENVIRONMENT (SAFE)** is a joint Central Intelligence Agency-Defense Intelligence Agency project that is intended to develop a new computer and microfilm system that supports production analysts in reading, filing, and routing cable traffic, building and searching private and central files, and writing, editing, and routing intelligence memoranda and reports.

References

Department of Defense, Defense Intelligence College. *Glossary of Intelligence Terms and Definitions.* Washington, DC: DIC, 1987.

—**SUPPORTING ARMS COORDINATION CENTER (SACC),** in amphibious warfare operations, is a single location on board an Amphibious Command Ship in which all the communications links that are being used in coordinating the force support of the artillery, air, and naval gunfire are centralized. This is the naval counterpart to the fire support coordination center (FSCC) that is used by the landing force.

References

Department of Defense, Defense Intelligence College. *Glossary of Intelligence Terms and Definitions.* Washington, DC: DIC, 1987.

Department of Defense, Joint Chiefs of Staff. *Department of Defense Dictionary of Military and Related Terms.* Washington, DC: GPO, 1986.

—**SURFACING.** (1) Surfacing is the publicizing of a defector. (2) In FBI terminology, it is the public disclosure of an intelligence operation or of personnel. *See also:* Concealment, Cover, Exfiltration, Go to Ground, Packed Up, Sign of Life Signal, Submerge, Suitable Cover.

References

Becket, Henry S. A. *The Dictionary of Espionage: Spookspeak into English.* New York: Stein and Day, 1986.

Deacon, Richard. *Spyclopedia: An Encyclopedia of Spies, Secret Services, Operations, Jargon, and All Subjects Related to the World of Espionage.* London: Macdonald, 1987.

Kessler, Ronald. *Spy vs. Spy: Stalking Soviet Spies in America.* New York: Charles Scribner's Sons, 1988.

Ranelagh, John. *The Agency: The Rise and Decline of the CIA.* New York: Simon and Schuster, 1986.

—**SURREPTITIOUS ENTRY** is a term used in clandestine and covert intelligence operations, as well as in counterintelligence, counterespionage, and counterinsurgency to describe a warrantless entry into a target's property, either to install microphones or collect information. *See also:* "Least Intrusive Means."

References

Becket, Henry S. A. *The Dictionary of Espionage: Spookspeak into English.* New York: Stein and Day, 1986.

Deacon, Richard. *Spyclopedia: An Encyclopedia of Spies, Secret Services, Operations, Jargon, and All Subjects Related to the World of Espionage.* London: Macdonald, 1987.

Laqueur, Walter. *A World of Secrets.* New York: Basic Books, 1985.

Ranelagh, John. *The Agency: The Rise and Decline of the CIA.* New York: Simon and Schuster, 1986.

Treverton, Gregory F. *Covert Action: The Limits of Intervention in the Postwar World.* New York: Basic Books, 1987.

—**SURROUND** is a term used in counterintelligence operations. It is obvious surveillance, with no attempt to conceal the effort. When an agent realizes that he is surrounded, he knows that he will soon be arrested and that his operation has been discovered. *See also:* Concealment, Go-Away, Go to Ground, Movements Analysis, Pavement Artists, Shaking Off the Dogs, Stroller, Submerge, Suitable Cover, Surfacing, Surveillance, Walk-Past, What's Your Twenty?

References

Becket, Henry S. A. *The Dictionary of Espionage: Spookspeak into English.* New York: Stein and Day, 1986.

Deacon, Richard. *Spyclopedia: An Encyclopedia of Spies, Secret Services, Operations, Jargon, and All Subjects Related to the World of Espionage.* London: Macdonald, 1987.

Ranelagh, John. *The Agency: The Rise and Decline of the CIA.* New York: Simon and Schuster, 1986.

—**SURVEILLANCE.** (1) In a general sense, surveillance is the systematic observation or monitoring of places, persons, or things by visual, aural, electronic, photographic, or other means. (2) Surveillance is also an Army tactical intelligence (TACINT) term that means the all-weather, day and night systematic observation of a battle area for intelligence purposes. (3) Surveillance, as defined by the Church Committee, is simply the systematic observation of a target. *See also:* Surround.

References

American Bar Association. *Oversight and Accountability of the U.S. Intelligence Agencies: An Evaluation.* Washington, DC: ABA, 1985.

Department of Defense, Defense Intelligence College. *Glossary of Intelligence Terms and Definitions.* Washington, DC: DIC, 1987.

Department of Defense, Joint Chiefs of Staff. *Department of Defense Dictionary of Military and Related Terms.* Washington, DC: GPO, 1986.

Kent, Sherman. *Strategic Intelligence for American World Policy.* Princeton, NJ: Princeton University Press, 1966.

Laqueur, Walter. *A World of Secrets.* New York: Basic Books, 1985.

Maurer, Alfred C.; Turnstall, Marion D.; and Keagle, James M. *Intelligence Policy and Process.* Boulder, CO: Westview Press, 1985.

Treverton, Gregory F. *Covert Action: The Limits of Intervention in the Postwar World.* New York: Basic Books, 1987.

Turner, Stansfield. *Secrecy and Democracy: The CIA in Transition.* Boston: Houghton Mifflin, 1985.

U.S. Congress. Senate. *Final Report of the Senate Select Committee to Study Government Operations with Respect to Intelligence Activities. Report 94-755. Book I, Foreign and Military Intelligence.* Washington, DC: GPO, 1976.

—**SURVEILLANCE AND TARGET ACQUISITION (STA) PLATOON** is part of the Headquarters and Service Company of a U.S. Marine Corps battalion. It is composed of a platoon headquarters, a radar section, a night observation section, and a scout section. The STA platoon provides an electronic surveillance capability through the use of ground surveillance radars and low-light intensity observation devices.

References

Department of Defense, Joint Chiefs of Staff. *Department of Defense Dictionary of Military and Related Terms.* Washington, DC: GPO, 1986.

—**SUSCEPTIBILITY** is an Army tactical intelligence (TACINT) term that means the degree to which a device, equipment, or weapons system is open to effective attack due to one or more inherent weaknesses.

References

Department of Defense, U.S. Army. *Counter-Signals Intelligence (C-SIGINT) Operations.* Field Manual FM 34-62. Washington, DC: Headquarters, Department of the Army, 1986.

————. *Military Intelligence Battalion (Combat Electronic Warfare Intelligence) (Division).* Field Manual FM 34-10. Washington, DC: Headquarters, Department of the Army, 1981.

————. *Military Intelligence Battalion (CEWI) (Tactical Exploitation) (Corps): Counterintelligence, Interrogation, Electronic Warfare.* Field Manual FM 34-23. Washington, DC: Headquarters, Department of the Army, 1985.

————. *Military Intelligence Company (Combat Electronic Warfare and Intelligence) (Armored Cavalry Regiment/Separate Brigade).* Field Manual FM 34-30. Washington, DC: Headquarters, Department of the Army, 1983.

—**SWALLOW** is a clandestine and covert intelligence operations term that has differing interpretations. (1) One is that it is a woman who attempts to compromise a target sexually. The encounters are usually photographed and recorded, and the target is then blackmailed into providing intelligence. (2) However, Henry Becket maintains that a swallow is a female KGB spy, who is, in essence, a prostitute

Swallows, or at least Soviet females, figured prominently in the compromise of information at the U.S. Embassy in Moscow by Clayton Lonetree and possibly other U.S. Marine guards. The full extent of the compromise has not been made public, but one account stated that the women were allowed access to sensitive areas in the embassy. *See also:* Lonetree, Clayton.

References

Becket, Henry S. A. *The Dictionary of Espionage: Spookspeak into English.* New York: Stein and Day, 1986.

Deacon, Richard. *Spyclopedia: An Encyclopedia of Spies, Secret Services, Operations, Jargon, and All Subjects Related to the World of Espionage.* London: Macdonald, 1987.

Ranelagh, John. *The Agency: The Rise and Decline of the CIA.* New York: Simon and Schuster, 1986.

—**SWALLOW'S NEST** is a term used in clandestine and covert intelligence operations to describe the apartment or quarters that are used by a swallow to entrap a target. The place is fully equipped with cameras and recorders to tape the sexual play, for later use as blackmail. *See also:* Pigeon, Swallow, Raven.

References

Becket, Henry S. A. *The Dictionary of Espionage: Spookspeak into English.* New York: Stein and Day, 1986.

Deacon, Richard. *Spyclopedia: An Encyclopedia of Spies, Secret Services, Operations, Jargon, and All Subjects Related to the World of Espionage.* London: Macdonald, 1987.

Ranelagh, John. *The Agency: The Rise and Decline of the CIA.* New York: Simon and Schuster, 1986.

—**SWEEP JAMMING,** is an electronic warfare (EW) term. It is the jamming of a radar scope that is done by sweeping the atmosphere with electronic impulses that are on the same frequency as those received by the radarscope. *See also:* Jamming.

References

Department of Defense, Defense Intelligence College. *Glossary of Intelligence Terms and Definitions.* Washington, DC: DIC, 1987.

Department of Defense, Joint Chiefs of Staff. *Department of Defense Dictionary of Military and Related Terms.* Washington, DC: GPO, 1986.

—**SWEETENER** is a term used in clandestine and covert intelligence operations for gifts, inducements, and other means that an agent uses to soften up a target.

References

Becket, Henry S. A. *The Dictionary of Espionage: Spookspeak into English.* New York: Stein and Day, 1986.

Deacon, Richard. *Spyclopedia: An Encyclopedia of Spies, Secret Services, Operations, Jargon, and All Subjects Related to the World of Espionage.* London: Macdonald, 1987.

Ranelagh, John. *The Agency: The Rise and Decline of the CIA.* New York: Simon and Schuster, 1986.

—**SYLLABARY,** in communications security (COMSEC), refers to a list of individual letters, combinations of letters, or syllables in a code book. The list is accompanied by their equivalent code groups and is for use in spelling out words or proper names that do not appear in the vocabulary of a code. A syllabary is also known as a spelling table. *See also:* Communications Security.

References

Department of Defense, U.S. Army. *Counterintelligence.* Field Manual FM 34-60. Washington, DC: Headquarters, Department of the Army, 1985.

———. *Intelligence and Electronic Warfare Operations.* Field Manual FM 34-1. Washington, DC: Headquarters, Department of the Army, 1984.

———. *Military Intelligence Battalion (Combat Electronic Warfare Intelligence) (Division).* Field Manual FM 34-10. Washington, DC: Headquarters, Department of the Army, 1981.

———. *Military Intelligence Battalion (CEWI) (Tactical Exploitation) (Corps): Counterintelligence, Interrogation, Electronic Warfare.* Field Manual FM 34-23. Washington, DC: Headquarters, Department of the Army, 1985.

———. *Military Intelligence Company (Combat Electronic Warfare and Intelligence) (Armored Cavalry Regiment/Separate Brigade).* Field Manual FM 34-30. Washington, DC: Headquarters, Department of the Army, 1983.

—**SYNC ELEMENT,** a baud-based system term used in communications intelligence, communications security, operations security, and signals analysis, is a constant condition element that is transmitted every cycle to maintain speed adjustment between the transmitting and receiving equipments of a teleprinter system. *See also:* Communications Security.

References

Department of Defense, U.S. Army. *Counterintelligence.* Field Manual FM 34-60. Washington, DC: Headquarters, Department of the Army, 1985.

———. *Intelligence and Electronic Warfare Operations.* Field Manual FM 34-1. Washington, DC: Headquarters, Department of the Army, 1984.

———. *Military Intelligence Battalion (Combat Electronic Warfare Intelligence) (Division).* Field Manual FM 34-10. Washington, DC: Headquarters, Department of the Army, 1981.

———. *Military Intelligence Battalion (CEWI) (Tactical Exploitation) (Corps): Counterintelligence, Interrogation, Electronic Warfare.* Field Manual FM 34-23. Washington, DC: Headquarters, Department of the Army, 1985.

———. *Military Intelligence Company (Combat Electronic Warfare and Intelligence) (Armored Cavalry Regiment/Separate Brigade).* Field Manual FM 34-30. Washington, DC: Headquarters, Department of the Army, 1983.

—**SYNCHRONIZED,** a baud-based system term used in communications intelligence, communications security, operations security, and signals analysis, which means of or pertaining to a continuous running system that requires an additional element or elements for speed adjustment. *See also:* Communications Security.

References

Department of Defense, U.S. Army. *Counterintelligence.* Field Manual FM 34-60. Washington, DC: Headquarters, Department of the Army, 1985.

———. *Intelligence and Electronic Warfare Operations.* Field Manual FM 34-1. Washington, DC: Headquarters, Department of the Army, 1984.

———. *Military Intelligence Battalion (Combat Electronic Warfare Intelligence) (Division).* Field Manual FM 34-10. Washington, DC: Headquarters, Department of the Army, 1981.

———. *Military Intelligence Battalion (CEWI) (Tactical Exploitation) (Corps): Counterintelligence, Interrogation, Electronic Warfare.* Field Manual FM 34-23. Washington, DC: Headquarters, Department of the Army, 1985.

———. *Military Intelligence Company (Combat Electronic Warfare and Intelligence) (Armored Cavalry Regiment/Separate Brigade).* Field Manual FM 34-30. Washington, DC: Headquarters, Department of the Army, 1983.

—**SYNCHRONOUS,** a baud-based system term used in communications intelligence, communications security, operations security, and signals analysis, which means of or pertaining to a system that does not require any additional element or elements for speed adjustment. *See also:* Communications Security.

References

Department of Defense, U.S. Army. *Counterintelligence*. Field Manual FM 34-60. Washington, DC: Headquarters, Department of the Army, 1985.

————. *Intelligence and Electronic Warfare Operations*. Field Manual FM 34-1. Washington, DC: Headquarters, Department of the Army, 1984.

————. *Military Intelligence Battalion (Combat Electronic Warfare Intelligence) (Division)*. Field Manual FM 34-10. Washington, DC: Headquarters, Department of the Army, 1981.

————. *Military Intelligence Battalion (CEWI) (Tactical Exploitation) (Corps): Counterintelligence, Interrogation, Electronic Warfare*. Field Manual FM 34-23. Washington, DC: Headquarters, Department of the Army, 1985.

————. *Military Intelligence Company (Combat Electronic Warfare and Intelligence) (Armored Cavalry Regiment/Separate Brigade)*. Field Manual FM 34-30. Washington, DC: Headquarters, Department of the Army, 1983.

—**SYNCHRONOUS CRYPTO-OPERATION,** in communications security (COMSEC), means a method of on-line crypto-operation in which the terminal crypto-equipments have timing systems that keep them in step. *See also:* Communications Security.

References

Department of Defense, U.S. Army. *Counterintelligence*. Field Manual FM 34-60. Washington, DC: Headquarters, Department of the Army, 1985.

————. *Intelligence and Electronic Warfare Operations*. Field Manual FM 34-1. Washington, DC: Headquarters, Department of the Army, 1984.

————. *Military Intelligence Battalion (Combat Electronic Warfare Intelligence) (Division)*. Field Manual FM 34-10. Washington, DC: Headquarters, Department of the Army, 1981.

————. *Military Intelligence Battalion (CEWI) (Tactical Exploitation) (Corps): Counterintelligence, Interrogation, Electronic Warfare*. Field Manual FM 34-23. Washington, DC: Headquarters, Department of the Army, 1985.

————. *Military Intelligence Company (Combat Electronic Warfare and Intelligence) (Armored Cavalry Regiment/Separate Brigade)*. Field Manual FM 34-30. Washington, DC: Headquarters, Department of the Army, 1983.

—**SYNCH SECTION,** a baud-based system term used in communications intelligence, communications security, operations security, and signals analysis, is the portion of a cycle of a communications signal that contains all the synch elements for the system. *See also:* Communications Security.

References

Department of Defense, U.S. Army. *Counterintelligence*. Field Manual FM 34-60. Washington, DC: Headquarters, Department of the Army, 1985.

————. *Intelligence and Electronic Warfare Operations*. Field Manual FM 34-1. Washington, DC: Headquarters, Department of the Army, 1984.

————. *Military Intelligence Battalion (Combat Electronic Warfare Intelligence) (Division)*. Field Manual FM 34-10. Washington, DC: Headquarters, Department of the Army, 1981.

————. *Military Intelligence Battalion (CEWI) (Tactical Exploitation) (Corps): Counterintelligence, Interrogation, Electronic Warfare*. Field Manual FM 34-23. Washington, DC: Headquarters, Department of the Army, 1985.

————. *Military Intelligence Company (Combat Electronic Warfare and Intelligence) (Armored Cavalry Regiment/Separate Brigade)*. Field Manual FM 34-30. Washington, DC: Headquarters, Department of the Army, 1983.

—**SYSTEM** is a term often used in intelligence budgeting. (1) A weapon system is composed of equipment, skills, and techniques, the composite of which forms an instrument of combat. The complete weapon system includes all related facilities, equipment, materials, services, and personnel required solely for its operation, so that the instrument of combat becomes a self-sufficient unit of striking power in its intended operational environment. (2) A support system is a composite of equipment, skills and techniques that, while not an instrument of combat, is capable of performing a clearly defined function in support of a mission. A complete support system includes all related facilities, equipment, materials, services, and personnel required for operation of the system, so that it can be considered a self-sufficient unit in its intended operational environment. *See also:* Appropriation or Fund Account.

References

Department of Defense, Joint Chiefs of Staff. *Department of Defense Dictionary of Military and Related Terms*. Washington, DC: GPO, 1986.

Godson, Roy, ed. *Intelligence Problems for the 1980s, Number 1: Elements of Intelligence.* Rev. ed. Washington, DC: National Strategy Information Center, 1983.

Maurer, Alfred C.; Turnstall, Marion D.; and Keagle, James M. *Intelligence Policy and Process.* Boulder, CO: Westview Press, 1985.

Pickett, George. "Congress, the Budget, and Intelligence." In *Intelligence Policy and Process,* edited by Alfred C. Maurer, Marion D. Turnstall, and James M. Keagle. Boulder, CO: Westview Press, 1985.

—**SYSTEM ANALYSIS (SA),** in intelligence budgeting, is a formal inquiry that is intended to advise a decisionmaker on the policy choices involved in major decisions. In the Department of Defense, a systems analysis may be concerned with such matters as weapon development, force posture design, or the determination of strategic objectives. To qualify as a system analysis, a study must consider the entire problem. Characteristically, it will involve a systematic investigation of the decisionmaker's objectives, and of the relevant criteria; a comparison—quantitative when possible—of the costs, effectiveness, and risks associated with the alternative policies or strategies for achieving each objective; and an attempt to formulate additional alternatives if those examined are deficient. *See also:* System.

References

Pickett, George. "Congress, the Budget, and Intelligence." In *Intelligence Policy and Process,* edited by Alfred C. Maurer, Marion D. Turnstall, and James M. Keagle. Boulder, CO: Westview Press, 1985.

—**SYSTEM DEVELOPMENT COORDINATOR,** in intelligence data handling, is the overall system development manager of a community development responsible for managing and coordinating the development of Department of Defense Intelligence Information System (DODIIS) subsystems at all the affected General Defense Intelligence Community (GDIC) components. *See also:* Community Development, Program Manager, System Development Manager.

References

Department of Defense, Defense Intelligence Agency. *Defense Intelligence Agency Manual.* Washington, DC: DIA, 1987.

—**SYSTEM DEVELOPMENT MANAGEMENT,** in intelligence data handling, is the responsibility for insuring that the ADP-T systems developed in response to the data handling requirements defined by the functional design, do so effectively and economically.

References

Department of Defense, Defense Intelligence Agency. *Defense Intelligence Agency Manual.* Washington, DC: DIA, 1987.

—**SYSTEM DEVELOPMENT MANAGER (SDM),** in intelligence data handling, is the individual who is in charge of a system development office or responsible for the technical aspects of a Department of Defense Intelligence Information System (DODIIS) subsystem or enhancement of an existing DODIIS subsystem. Where this is established with General Defense Intelligence Program (GDIP) resources, the SDM is formally appointed by the Chartering Authority. *See also:* Chartering Authority, System Development Office.

References

Department of Defense, Defense Intelligence Agency. *Defense Intelligence Agency Manual.* Washington, DC: DIA, 1987.

—**SYSTEM DEVELOPMENT OFFICE,** in intelligence handling, is the office that is responsible for the design, development, test, and deployment of an ADP-T system architecture (Department of Defense Intelligence Information [DODIIS] subsystem) or a portion of such a subsystem. *See also:* Defense Intelligence Agency.

References

Department of Defense, Defense Intelligence Agency. *Defense Intelligence Agency Manual.* Washington, DC: DIA, 1987.

—**SYSTEM INDICATOR,** in communications security (COMSEC), means a symbol or group of symbols that appear in an encrypted message, that identify the specific cryptosystems or keying material that is used in the encryption. *See also:* Communications Security.

References

Department of Defense, U.S. Army. *Military Intelligence Battalion (Combat Electronic Warfare Intelligence) (Division).* Field Manual FM 34-10. Washington, DC: Headquarters, Department of the Army, 1981.

———. *Military Intelligence Battalion (CEWI) (Tactical Exploitation) (Corps): Counterintelligence, Interrogation, Electronic Warfare.* Field Manual FM 34-23. Washington, DC: Headquarters, Department of the Army, 1985.

———. *Military Intelligence Company (Combat Electronic Warfare and Intelligence) (Armored Cavalry Regiment/Separate Brigade).* Field Manual FM 34-30. Washington, DC: Headquarters, Department of the Army, 1983.

—**SYSTEM OPERATING ACTIVITY (SOA),** in intelligence data handling, is the organization responsible for operating and maintaining one or more ADP-T systems supporting one or more functional architectures. All or a portion of an SOA may be designated to function as a system development office or provide support to a program management office. *See also:* Program Management Office, System Development Office.

References

Department of Defense, Defense Intelligence Agency. *Defense Intelligence Agency Manual.* Washington, DC: DIA, 1987.

—**SYSTEM SPEED,** a baud-based system term used in communications intelligence, communications security, operations security, and signals analysis, is a signal parameter that is given in operations per minute (i.e. the number of complete signal cycles sent in one minute). *See also:* Communications Security.

References

Department of Defense, U.S. Army. *Intelligence and Electronic Warfare Operations.* Field Manual FM 34-1. Washington, DC: Headquarters, Department of the Army, 1984.

———. *Military Intelligence Battalion (Combat Electronic Warfare Intelligence) (Division).* Field Manual FM 34-10. Washington, DC: Headquarters, Department of the Army, 1981.

———. *Military Intelligence Battalion (CEWI) (Tactical Exploitation) (Corps): Counterintelligence, Interrogation, Electronic Warfare.* Field Manual FM

34-23. Washington, DC: Headquarters, Department of the Army, 1985.

———. *Military Intelligence Company (Combat Electronic Warfare and Intelligence) (Armored Cavalry Regiment/Separate Brigade).* Field Manual FM 34-30. Washington, DC: Headquarters, Department of the Army, 1983.

—**SYSTEMS SCIENCE** is an official term that has been defined by the Defense Intelligence Agency for one of its functional areas. It means "professional activities that are directly related to information science, systems analysis, operations research, and computer sciences; work in this area support, to varying degrees, all other areas, to include the management and administrative operations of the intelligence community." *See also:* Defense Intelligence Agency.

References

Department of Defense, Defense Intelligence Agency. *Defense Intelligence Agency Manual.* Washington, DC: DIA, 1987.

—**SYSTEMS SECURITY STEERING GROUP** was proposed by "National Policy on Telecommunications and Automated Information Systems Security," a proposed directive that was issued on September 17, 1984, but was never enacted. The steering group was to consist of the secretary of state, the secretary of the treasury, the secretary of defense, the attorney general, the director of the Office of Management and Budget, and the director of Central Intelligence, and was to be chaired by the assistant to the president for national security affairs. The mission of the group was to be:

(1) to oversee and implement the directive which established the group and provided guidelines for security in the subject areas;

(2) to monitor the activities of the operating level National Telecommunications and Information Systems Security Committee and provide guidance for its activities;

(3) to review and evaluate the security status of those telecommunications and automated information systems that handle classified or sensitive government or government-derived information with respect to established objectives and priorities, and report findings and recommendations through

the National Security Council to the President.

(4) to review consolidated resources program and budget proposals for telecommunications systems security, including the COMSEC Resources Program, for the U.S. Government and provide recommendations to OMB for the normal budget review process.

(5) to review in aggregate the program and budget proposals for the security of automated information systems of the departments and agencies of the government.

(6) to review and approve matters referred to it by the Executive Agent in fulfilling its responsibilities.

(7) on matters pertaining to the protection of intelligence sources and methods, to be guided by the policies of the Director of Central Intelligence.

(8) to interact with the Steering Group on National Security Communications to ensure that the objectives and policies of this Directive and NSDD-97, National Security Communications Policy, are addressed in a coordinated manner.

(9) to recommend for Presidential approval additions or revisions to this Directive as national interests may require.

(10) to identify categories of sensitive non-government information, the loss of which could adversely affect the national security interest, and recommend steps to protect such information.

References

"National Policy on Telecommunications and Automated Information Systems Security." Proposed Presidential Directive released Sept. 17, 1984, but never enacted.

—**TACTICAL AIR CONTROL CENTER (TACC)**, in amphibious warfare operations, is the principal air operations installation (land or ship-based) from which all aircraft and all air warning functions of tactical air operations are controlled.

References

Department of Defense, Joint Chiefs of Staff. *Department of Defense Dictionary of Military and Related Terms.* Washington, DC: GPO, 1986.

—**TACTICAL AIR CONTROL PARTY (TACP)**, in amphibious warfare operations, is a subordinate Marine or Air Force operational component of the landing force tactical air control system that is designed to provide air liaison functions and for the control of aircraft from a forward observation post. The tactical air control party operates at division, regimental, and battalion levels. *See also:* Tactical Air Control Center.

References

Department of Defense, Joint Chiefs of Staff. *Department of Defense Dictionary of Military and Related Terms.* Washington, DC: GPO, 1986.

—**TACTICAL AIR DIRECTION CENTER (TADC)**, in amphibious warfare operations, is an air operations installation under the overall control of the tactical air control command center from which aircraft and aircraft warning service functions of tactical air operations in an area of responsibility are directed.

References

Department of Defense, Joint Chiefs of Staff. *Department of Defense Dictionary of Military and Related Terms.* Washington, DC: GPO, 1986.

—**TACTICAL AIR OPERATIONS CENTER (TAOC)**, in amphibious warfare operations, is a subordinate operational component of the Marine Air Control System that is designed for control and direction of air defense. It is under operational control of a tactical air command or direction center, as appropriate.

References

Department of Defense, Joint Chiefs of Staff. *Department of Defense Dictionary of Military and Related Terms.* Washington, DC: GPO, 1986.

—**TACTICAL EXPLOITATION OF NATIONAL CAPABILITIES (TENCAP)** allows the services to use the products from national reconnaissance programs for tactical purposes. The national programs have capabilities that far exceed those of the service tactical organizations and can provide the information at much less cost than can the services. The purpose of the TENCAP is to allow the services to exploit the current and future capabilities of the national systems and to permit the integration of this information into tactical decisionmaking as quickly as possible.

References

Department of Defense, U.S. Army. *Intelligence and Electronic Warfare Operations.* Field Manual FM 34-1. Washington, DC: Headquarters, Department of the Army, 1984.

———. *Military Intelligence Battalion (Combat Electronic Warfare Intelligence) (Division).* Field Manual FM 34-10. Washington, DC: Headquarters, Department of the Army, 1981.

—**TACTICAL INFORMATION PROCESSING AND INTERPRETATION SYSTEM (TIPI)** is a tactical, mobile, land-based, automated information handling system that is designed to store and retrieve intelligence information and to process and interpret imagery or non-imagery data.

References

Department of Defense, Joint Chiefs of Staff. *Department of Defense Dictionary of Military and Related Terms.* Washington, DC: GPO, 1986.

—**TACTICAL INTELLIGENCE (TACINT OR TAC-INTEL).** (1) Tactical intelligence is foreign intelligence that is produced under the aegis of the secretary of defense and is intended primarily to respond to the needs of military field commanders so that they can maintain the readiness of operating forces for combat operations and to support the planning and conduct of combat operations. (2) Tactical intelligence, as defined by the Church Committee, is "intelligence supporting military plans and operations at the military unit level. Tactical intelligence and strategic intelligence differ only in scope, point of view, and level of employment." (3) Tactical intelligence is also an indications and warning (I&W) term. In this context, it means intelligence that is required for the planning and conduct of tactical operations. Essentially tactical intelligence and strategic intelligence differ only in scope, point of view, and level of employment. *See also:* Combat Intelligence.

References

Department of Defense, Defense Intelligence College. *Glossary of Intelligence Terms and Definitions.* Washington, DC: DIC, 1987.

Department of Defense, Joint Chiefs of Staff. *Department of Defense Dictionary of Military and Related Terms.* Washington, DC: GPO, 1986.

Department of Defense, U.S. Army. *Military Intelligence Battalion (Combat Electronic Warfare Intelligence) (Division).* Field Manual FM 34-10. Washington, DC: Headquarters, Department of the Army, 1981.

———. *Military Intelligence Company (Combat Electronic Warfare and Intelligence) (Armored Cavalry Regiment/Separate Brigade).* Field Manual FM 34-30. Washington, DC: Headquarters, Department of the Army, 1983.

Godson, Roy, ed. *Intelligence Problems for the 1980s, Number 1: Elements of Intelligence.* Rev. ed. Washington, DC: National Strategy Information Center, 1983.

Maurer, Alfred C.; Turnstall, Marion D.; and Keagle, James M. *Intelligence Policy and Process.* Boulder, CO: Westview Press, 1985.

U.S. Congress. Senate. *Final Report of the Senate Select Committee to Study Government Operations with Respect to Intelligence Activities. Report 94-755. Book I, Foreign and Military Intelligence.* Washington, DC: GPO, 1976.

—**TACTICAL INTELLIGENCE AND RELATED ACTIVITIES (TIARA).** The Defense Intelligence Agency office that develops the agency's requisite intelligence and support capabilities for TIARA is the Directorate for Plans and Policies (VP), while its policies and plans are developed by the Directorate for Operations, Plans, and Training (VO).

References

Department of Defense, Defense Intelligence Agency. *Organization, Mission, and Key Personnel.* Washington, DC: DIA, 1986.

Maroni, Alice C. *Special Access Programs: Understanding the "Black Budget."* Washington, DC: Foreign Affairs and National Defense Division, Congressional Research Service, Library of Congress, 1987.

—**TACTICAL INTELLIGENCE ASSET** is an intelligence asset that is funded in Department of Defense programs. Its primary purpose is to collect or process intelligence information or to produce tactical intelligence. *See also:* Intelligence Asset, Tactical Intelligence.

References

Department of Defense, Defense Intelligence College. *Glossary of Intelligence Terms and Definitions.* Washington, DC: DIC, 1987.

—**TACTICAL PSYCHOLOGICAL WARFARE** involves actions that are designed to bring pressure to bear on enemy forces and civilians in support of tactical military ground, air, or sea operations in areas where these operations are planned or conducted. It must conform to the overall strategic psychological warfare policy, but will be conducted as an integral part of combat operations.

References

Department of Defense, Joint Chiefs of Staff. *Department of Defense Dictionary of Military and Related Terms.* Washington, DC: GPO, 1986.

—**TACTICAL WARNING** is an indications and warning (I&W) term that has two meanings. (1) Tactical warning is a notification that the enemy has initiated hostilities. Such warning may be received at any time from the launching of the attack until the attack reaches its target. (2) In satellite missile surveillance, tactical warning is a notification to operational command centers that a specific threat is occurring. The component elements that describe events are Country of Origin (the country or countries initiating the hostilities); Event Type and Size (identification of the type of event and the determination of its size or the number of weapons); and Event Time (the time that the hostile event occurred). *See also:* Indications and Warning.

References

Department of Defense, Joint Chiefs of Staff. *Department of Defense Dictionary of Military and Related Terms.* Washington, DC: GPO, 1986.

—**TACTICS** are the employment of units in combat and the ordered arrangement and maneuver of units in relation to each other and to the enemy in order to use their full potentialities. Tactics require the specific application of doctrinal principles.

References

Department of Defense, Joint Chiefs of Staff. *Department of Defense Dictionary of Military and Related Terms.* Washington, DC: GPO, 1986.

Department of Defense, U.S. Army. *U.S. Army Air Defense Artillery Employment.* Field Manual FM 44-1. Washington, DC: Headquarters, Department of the Army, 1983.

—**TAIL** is slang for following someone. *See:* Surveillance.

References

Clancy, Tom. *The Cardinal of the Kremlin.* New York: Putnam, 1988.

—**TALENT SPOTTER** is a term used in clandestine and covert intelligence operations. A talent spotter is a deep cover agent who identifies people who are suitable recruits for intelligence work. *See also:* Co-Opted Worker, Co-Optees, Cultivation, Defector, Disaffected Person, Double Agent, Handling Agent, Litmus Test, Nash, Notionals, Not Witting, Recruitment, Recruitment in Place.

References

Becket, Henry S. A. *The Dictionary of Espionage: Spookspeak into English.* New York: Stein and Day, 1986.

Deacon, Richard. *Spyclopedia: An Encyclopedia of Spies, Secret Services, Operations, Jargon, and All Subjects Related to the World of Espionage.* London: Macdonald, 1987.

Ranelagh, John. *The Agency: The Rise and Decline of the CIA.* New York: Simon and Schuster, 1986.

—**TALKING PAPER** is a paper that is intended for use by an informed principal as a memory aid for advocating a particular view or objective in an oral discussion.

References

Department of Defense, Defense Intelligence College. *Glossary of Intelligence Terms and Definitions.* Washington, DC: DIC, 1987.

—**TAMPERING,** in communications security (COMSEC), refers to an unauthorized modification that alters the proper functioning of a COMSEC equipment or system in a manner that degrades the security that it provides. *See also:* Communications Security.

References

Department of Defense, U.S. Army. *Military Intelligence Battalion (Combat Electronic Warfare Intelligence) (Division).* Field Manual FM 34-10. Washington, DC: Headquarters, Department of the Army, 1981.

———. *Military Intelligence Company (Combat Electronic Warfare and Intelligence) (Armored Cavalry Regiment/Separate Brigade).* Field Manual FM 34-30. Washington, DC: Headquarters, Department of the Army, 1983.

—**TANK.** (1) The tank is a sound-secure room in the larger CIA stations around the world, where conversations can occur without detection. (2) It is also a briefing room of the Joint Chiefs of Staff.

References

Becket, Henry S. A. *The Dictionary of Espionage: Spookspeak into English.* New York: Stein and Day, 1986.

—**TAPE MIXER,** in communications security (COMSEC), means teletypewriter security equipment that encrypts plain text and decrypts ciphered text by combining them with data from a one-time tape. *See also:* Communications Security.

References

Department of Defense, U.S. Army. *Intelligence and Electronic Warfare Operations.* Field Manual FM 34-1. Washington, DC: Headquarters, Department of the Army, 1984.

———. *Military Intelligence Battalion (CEWI) (Tactical Exploitation) (Corps): Counterintelligence, Interrogation, Electronic Warfare.* Field Manual FM 34-23. Washington, DC: Headquarters, U.S. Army, 1985.

—**TARGET.** (1) A target is a country, area, installation, organization, weapon system, military force, political, or economic situation, signal, person, or other entity against which intelligence operations are conducted. (2) A target is a target intelligence term that pertains to the entity that is to be destroyed. In this context, it is a geographic area, complex, or installation that is planned for capture or destruction by military forces, or an area that has been designated for future firing. (3) A target, as defined by the Church Committee, is a person, agency, facility, area, or country against which intelligence operations are directed.

References

Deacon, Richard. *Spyclopedia: An Encyclopedia of Spies, Secret Services, Operations, Jargon, and All Subjects Related to the World of Espionage.* London: Macdonald, 1987.

Department of Defense, Defense Intelligence College. *Glossary of Intelligence Terms and Definitions.* Washington, DC: DIC, 1987.

Department of Defense, Joint Chiefs of Staff. *Department of Defense Dictionary of Military and Related Terms.* Washington, DC: GPO, 1986.

Kent, Sherman. *Strategic Intelligence for American World Policy.* Princeton, NJ: Princeton University Press, 1966.

Kessler, Ronald. *Spy vs. Spy: Stalking Soviet Spies in America.* New York: Charles Scribner's Sons, 1988.

Laqueur, Walter. *A World of Secrets.* New York: Basic Books, 1985.

Treverton, Gregory F. *Covert Action: The Limits of Intervention in the Postwar World.* New York: Basic Books, 1987.

U.S. Congress. Senate. *Final Report of the Senate Select Committee to Study Government Operations with Respect to Intelligence Activities. Report 94-755. Book I, Foreign and Military Intelligence.* Washington, DC: GPO, 1976.

—**TARGET ACQUISITION** is a target intelligence term that pertains to the target that is to be destroyed. It means detecting, identifying, and locating a target in sufficient detail to permit the effective use of weapons. *See also:* Targeting.

References

Department of Defense, Joint Chiefs of Staff. *Department of Defense Dictionary of Military and Related Terms.* Washington, DC: GPO, 1986.

Kent, Sherman. *Strategic Intelligence for American World Policy.* Princeton, NJ: Princeton University Press, 1966.

—**TARGET ANALYSIS.** (1) Target analysis is a target intelligence term that pertains to the target that is to be destroyed. It is an examination of potential targets to determine their relative military importance so that they can be prioritized, and the weapons that will be required to incur the desired level of damage or casualties. (2) Target analysis is an official term that has been defined by the Defense Intelligence Agency for one of its functional areas. It means "the study and analysis of targets in support of weapons systems development, force determinations, contingency plans, and the evaluation of plans for the deployment of forces and weapons." *See also:* Targeting.

References

Department of Defense, Defense Intelligence Agency. *Defense Intelligence Agency Manual.* Washington, DC: DIA, 1987.

Department of Defense, Joint Chiefs of Staff. *Department of Defense Dictionary of Military and Related Terms.* Washington, DC: GPO, 1986.

Kent, Sherman. *Strategic Intelligence for American World Policy.* Princeton, NJ: Princeton University Press, 1966.

—**TARGET CHARACTERISTICS** is a target intelligence term that pertains to the target that is to be destroyed. Every target has many distinctive characteristics by which it can be detected, located, and identified for future action. Such characteristics generally are classified as being functional, physical, environmental, or psychosocial. Additional information will often be provided concerning the mobility of the target. *See also:* Targeting.

References

Department of Defense, Joint Chiefs of Staff. *Department of Defense Dictionary of Military and Related Terms.* Washington, DC: GPO, 1986.

Kent, Sherman. *Strategic Intelligence for American World Policy.* Princeton, NJ: Princeton University Press, 1966.

—**TARGET CORRELATION** is a target intelligence term that pertains to the target that is to be destroyed. It occurs when information from one or more than one source is used to determine targeting data. This normally requires only a short period of time to verify. Target correlation is an Army tactical intelligence (TACINT) term. *See also:* Targeting.

References

Department of Defense, U.S. Army. *Military Intelligence Battalion (Combat Electronic Warfare Intelligence) (Division).* Field Manual FM 34-10. Washington, DC: Headquarters, Department of the Army, 1981.

————. *Military Intelligence Company (Combat Electronic Warfare and Intelligence) (Armored Cavalry Regiment/Separate Brigade).* Field Manual FM 34-30. Washington, DC: Headquarters, Department of the Army, 1983.

Kent, Sherman. *Strategic Intelligence for American World Policy.* Princeton, NJ: Princeton University Press, 1966.

—**TARGET DEVELOPMENT** is an Army tactical intelligence (TACINT) term that refers to a process of intelligence analysis. It includes locating, identifying, and tracking targets to permit engaging them at the greatest possible range. Target development is essential to the delay, attrition, and destruction of second-echelon and other follow-on forces. *See also:* Targeting.

References

Department of Defense, U.S. Army. *Military Intelligence Battalion (Combat Electronic Warfare Intelligence) (Division)*. Field Manual FM 34-10. Washington, DC: Headquarters, Department of the Army, 1981.

———. *Military Intelligence Battalion (CEWI) (Tactical Exploitation) (Corps): Counterintelligence, Interrogation, Electronic Warfare*. Field Manual FM 34-23. Washington, DC: Headquarters, Department of the Army, 1985.

———. *Military Intelligence Company (Combat Electronic Warfare and Intelligence) (Armored Cavalry Regiment/Separate Brigade)*. Field Manual FM 34-30. Washington, DC: Headquarters, Department of the Army, 1983.

———. *Military Intelligence Group (Combat Electronic Warfare and Intelligence) (Corps)*. Field Manual FM 34-20. Washington, DC: Headquarters, Department of the Army, 1983.

Kent, Sherman. *Strategic Intelligence for American World Policy*. Princeton, NJ: Princeton University Press, 1966.

—**TARGET INTELLIGENCE (TI).** (1) Target intelligence is intelligence that portrays and locates the components of a target or target complex and indicates its identification, vulnerability, and relative importance. Target intelligence is special purpose military intelligence that is derived from all sources to support decisionmakers, operational forces, and supporting staff functions in planning for and executing strikes and attacks against selected enemy forces, facilities, and functions. Target intelligence also supports the development of U.S. policy and planning guidance and military planners who are engaged in weapons acquisition and force structure decisionmaking. Target intelligence is included in automated data bases, for example, the Automated Installation Intelligence File, and in imagery-based products, such as automated tactical target graphics. (2) Target intelligence is an official term that has been defined by the Defense Intelligence Agency for one of its functional areas. It means "the development and preparation of data serving to identify the loca-

tion, nature, function, relative importance, vulnerability of an installation, place, position or concentration to assist planners in making selection of targets in support of a given strategy. *See also:* Targeting.

References

Department of Defense, Defense Intelligence Agency. *Defense Intelligence Agency Manual*. Washington, DC: DIA, 1987.

Department of Defense, Joint Chiefs of Staff. *Department of Defense Dictionary of Military and Related Terms*. Washington, DC: GPO, 1986.

Kent, Sherman. *Strategic Intelligence for American World Policy*. Princeton, NJ: Princeton University Press, 1966.

Laqueur, Walter. *A World of Secrets*. New York: Basic Books, 1985.

—**TARGET OF OPPORTUNITY.** (1) A target of opportunity is a target that appears during combat that can be reached by ground fire, naval fire, or aircraft fire, and against which fire has not been scheduled. (2) In clandestine intelligence, it is an entity that becomes available to an intelligence service or agency by chance, and provides the opportunity to collect needed information. (3) A target of opportunity, as defined by the Church Committee, is "a term describing an entity (e.g., governmental entity, installation, political organization, or individual) that becomes available to an intelligence agency or service by chance, and provides the opportunity for the collection of needed information."

References

Department of Defense, Joint Chiefs of Staff. *Department of Defense Dictionary of Military and Related Terms*. Washington, DC: GPO, 1986.

Quirk, John; Phillips, David; Cline, Ray; and Pforzheimer, Walter. *The Central Intelligence Agency: A Photographic History*. Guilford, CT: Foreign Intelligence Press, 1986.

U.S. Congress. Senate. *Final Report of the Senate Select Committee to Study Government Operations with Respect to Intelligence Activities. Report 94-755. Book I, Foreign and Military Intelligence*. Washington, DC: GPO, 1976.

—**TARGET STUDY** is a term used in clandestine intelligence operations. It is a compilation of all the available information on an individual who is being considered for recruitment as an intelligence source. The study includes amassing all documents, extensive surveillance, and an assessment on why the person might be vulnerable to an offer.

References

Becket, Henry S. A. *The Dictionary of Espionage: Spookspeak into English.* New York: Stein and Day, 1986.

Deacon, Richard. *Spyclopedia: An Encyclopedia of Spies, Secret Services, Operations, Jargon, and All Subjects Related to the World of Espionage.* London: Macdonald, 1987.

Kent, Sherman. *Strategic Intelligence for American World Policy.* Princeton, NJ: Princeton University Press, 1966.

Ranelagh, John. *The Agency: The Rise and Decline of the CIA.* New York: Simon and Schuster, 1986.

—**TARGET SYSTEM** is a target intelligence term that pertains to the target that is to be destroyed. It is all the targets situated in a particular geographic area that are functionally related. *See also:* Targeting.

References

Department of Defense, Joint Chiefs of Staff. *Department of Defense Dictionary of Military and Related Terms.* Washington, DC: GPO, 1986.

—**TARGET SYSTEM COMPONENTS** is a target intelligence term that pertains to the target that is to be destroyed. These are a set of targets belonging to one or more groups of industries and basic utilities that are required to produce component parts of an end product or system. A ball bearing factory would be a component of a target system pertaining to enemy tank production. *See also:* Targeting.

References

Department of Defense, Joint Chiefs of Staff. *Department of Defense Dictionary of Military and Related Terms.* Washington, DC: GPO, 1986.

—**TARGETING.** Targeting is a key function during peace, exercises, crises, and war. Targeting includes policy, operations, logistics, cartography, demography, intelligence, and automated data processing personnel, products, processes, and procedures. Complementary aspects of targeting are performed at each level of air, ground, naval, and joint headquarters. The intelligence targeting function is the bridge that unifies and links these many disciplines, levels of command, and air, ground, and naval offensive forces and operations. During peacetime, it is the daily task of targeting personnel to plan for eventualities that the United States hopes will be deterred but that the nation nevertheless must be prepared for. For targeting to be done well during hostilities, preparation during peacetime and training during exercises are at least as important as target selection during a war. Without extensive, coordinated preparation, targeting will not be accomplished effectively when it is most critical, thus squandering valuable resources and potentially resulting in defeat.

Targeting is the process of selecting targets and matching these targets with the operational capabilities in order to support the commander's guidance as stated in his concept of operations. The targeting process is a logical sequence of interdependent planning functions that occur at all levels of command and that result in offensive plans and operations that have the highest probability of success. Target intelligence is a crucial factor at every stage of the targeting process, as it may continually provide data that either continues to justify consideration of the target or it may provide information that indicates that the target should be dropped from considera-tion. Moreover, other target intelligence may be of crucial value in planning the type of opera-tion that will be conducted against the target. Hence, target intelligence is an integral part of the targeting process. This process has the following major steps:

Concept of operations. This is a verbal or graphic statement, in broad outline, of a commander's assumptions or intentions concerning an operation or a series of operations, is reviewed and used as guidance for the remainder of the process.

Target development. This includes systematically identifying and analyzing target systems and the component installations, sites, and entities in order to determine which critical and vulnerable elements our military operations should be directed against in order to achieve the specified tactical or strategic objective.

Weaponeering. This is the process of estimating the quantity of specific types of munitions, fuzing, and delivery vehicles that are required to achieve a predetermined level of damage to a specific target or type of target, while minimizing the collateral damage to friendly forces and civilian objects, property, and people.

Force and weapon availability and application. Offensive delivery assets and weapons are optimally matched against the proposed targets, based on weaponeering recommendations, in order to apply the available offensive, destructive systems as effectively, economically and quickly as possible.

Execution. In this phase, U.S. forces attack the target.

Assessment. This final phase involves analyzing the mission results in order to determine if the mission was accomplished. Assessment goes beyond bomb damage assessment (BDA) and includes determining the capability of the target to continue functioning or to recover.

Finally, the purposes or objectives of targeting are deterrence, attrition of enemy forces and capabilities, reprisal or retaliation, sending a signal, denying the enemy the ability to achieve his aims, inhibiting enemy reconstruction, terminating hostilities on terms favorable to the United States and its Allies, or obtaining a better peace.

In the context of communications intelligence, targeting is the intentional selection or collection of telecommunications for intelligence purposes. *See also:* Target, Target Acquisition, Target Analysis, Target Characteristics, Target Correlation, Target Development, Target Intelligence, Target Study, Target System, Target System Components.

References

Department of Defense, Defense Intelligence College. *Glossary of Intelligence Terms and Definitions.* Washington, DC: DIC, 1987.

Department of Defense, Joint Chiefs of Staff. *Department of Defense Dictionary of Military and Related Terms.* Washington, DC: GPO, 1986.

Godson, Roy, ed. *Intelligence Problems for the 1980s, Number 1: Elements of Intelligence.* Rev. ed. Washington, DC: National Strategy Information Center, 1983.

Maurer, Alfred C.; Turnstall, Marion D.; and Keagle, James M. *Intelligence Policy and Process.* Boulder, CO: Westview Press, 1985.

U.S. Congress. Senate. *Final Report of the Senate Select Committee to Study Government Operations with Respect to Intelligence Activities. Report 94-755. Book I, Foreign and Military Intelligence.* Washington, DC: GPO, 1976.

—**TASK.** A task is a general intelligence term. (1) It is a particular undertaking or assignment for intelligence personnel. (2) Task, as defined by the Church Committee, is a term connoting the assignment or direction of an intelligence unit to perform a specified function." *See also:* Intelligence Requirement.

References

Department of Defense, Joint Chiefs of Staff. *Department of Defense Dictionary of Military and Related Terms.* Washington, DC: GPO, 1986.

Godson, Roy, ed. *Intelligence Problems for the 1980s, Number 1: Elements of Intelligence.* Rev. ed. Washington, DC: National Strategy Information Center, 1983.

Maurer, Alfred C.; Turnstall, Marion D.; and Keagle, James M. *Intelligence Policy and Process.* Boulder, CO: Westview Press, 1985.

Treverton, Gregory F. *Covert Action: The Limits of Intervention in the Postwar World.* New York: Basic Books, 1987.

Turner, Stansfield. *Secrecy and Democracy: The CIA in Transition.* Boston: Houghton Mifflin, 1985.

U.S. Congress. Senate. *Final Report of the Senate Select Committee to Study Government Operations with Respect to Intelligence Activities. Report 94-755. Book I, Foreign and Military Intelligence.* Washington, DC: GPO, 1976.

—**TASK ELEMENT (TE),** in amphibious warfare operations, is a component of a naval task unit that is organized by the commander of a task unit or a higher authority.

References

Department of Defense, Joint Chiefs of Staff. *Department of Defense Dictionary of Military and Related Terms.* Washington, DC: GPO, 1986.

—**TASK FORCE (TF).** (1) In intelligence, particularly in the Defense Intelligence Agency, task forces are formed to handle crises or other major requirements. Using the task force approach, the agency is able to garner all the personnel and material resources that are necessary to fully handle a major crisis or project. (2) In operations, a task force can be a temporary grouping of units under one commander that is formed for the purpose of carrying out a specific operation or mission. (3) A task force can also be a semipermanent organization of units that are under one commander and are assembled in order to carry out a continuing specific task. (4) Finally, a task force can also be a component of a fleet that is organized by the commander of a task fleet or a higher authority in order to accomplish a specific task.

References

Department of Defense, Joint Chiefs of Staff. *Department of Defense Dictionary of Military and Related Terms.* Washington, DC: GPO, 1986.

—**TASK GROUP (TG),** in naval operations, is a component of a naval task force that is organized by the commander of a task force or higher authority. *See also:* Task Force.

References

Department of Defense, Joint Chiefs of Staff. *Department of Defense Dictionary of Military and Related Terms.* Washington, DC: GPO, 1986.

—**TASK UNIT (TU),** in naval operations, is a component of a naval task group that is organized by the task group commander or by a higher authority. *See also:* Task Force.

References

Department of Defense, Joint Chiefs of Staff. *Department of Defense Dictionary of Military and Related Terms.* Washington, DC: GPO, 1986.

—**TASKING** is a general intelligence term. It is the assignment or direction of an individual or activity to perform in a specified way to achieve an objective or goal.

References

Department of Defense, Defense Intelligence College. *Glossary of Intelligence Terms and Definitions.* Washington, DC: DIC, 1987.

Turner, Stansfield. *Secrecy and Democracy: The CIA in Transition.* Boston: Houghton Mifflin, 1985.

—**TAXI** is a term used in clandestine and covert intelligence operations. A taxi is a homosexual member of a stable, who is called upon to entrap a target sexually. The term is passé, as taxis are now called "ladies," "sisters," or "swallows." *See also:* Ladies, Sisters, Swallows, Swallow's Nest, Stable.

References

Deacon, Richard. *Spyclopedia: An Encyclopedia of Spies, Secret Services, Operations, Jargon, and All Subjects Related to the World of Espionage.* London: Macdonald, 1987.

—**TAYLOR, VICE ADMIRAL RUFUS L., U.S. NAVY,** served as deputy director of Central Intelligence from October 13, 1966, until January 31, 1969. *See also:* Central Intelligence Agency.

References

Lowenthal, Mark M. *U.S. Intelligence: Evolution and Anatomy.* New York: Praeger, 1984.

—**TEAM A/TEAM B.** In 1975, after examining a National Intelligence Estimate (NIE) and questioning its accuracy, the President's Foreign Intelligence Advisory Board recommended a competitive analysis. When Director of Central Intelligence George Bush agreed, Team A and Team B were created. Team A was composed of Intelligence Community analysts, while Team B was composed of three outside groups, chaired by Professor Richard Pipes of Harvard University. Both were given the same data and were asked to see if it would support differing views on the USSR. Team B arrived at significantly different conclusions from Team A, attacked the validity of "mirror image" assumptions, and argued that the USSR sought military superiority. When news of the differences in views was made public, Team B members were accused of being hawks. *See also:* Estimate, Intelligence Estimate.

References

Lowenthal, Mark M. *U.S. Intelligence: Evolution and Anatomy.* New York: Praeger, 1984.

—**TECHNICAL COVERAGE** is an FBI euphemism for a wiretap or bug. *See also:* Bug, Concealment Devices, Dry Cleaning, Exterminators, Granny, Harmonica Bug, Penetration, Penetration Aids, Plumbing, Putting in the Plumbing, Sound Man, Sound School, Special Activities, Sterile Telephone, Surveillance.

References

Becket, Henry S. A. *The Dictionary of Espionage: Spookspeak into English.* New York: Stein and Day, 1986.

Laqueur, Walter. *A World of Secrets.* New York: Basic Books, 1985.

—**TECHNICAL ELINT** is electronic intelligence (ELINT) that provides a detailed knowledge of the technical characteristics of a given emitter that permits estimation of its primary function, capabilities, modes of operation (including malfunctions), and state-of-the-art as well as its specific role within a complex weapons system or defense network. *See also:* Electronic Intelligence.

References

Turner, Stansfield. *Secrecy and Democracy: The CIA in Transition.* Boston: Houghton Mifflin, 1985.

—**TECHNICAL INTELLIGENCE (TI)** is intelligence on the characteristics and performance of foreign weapons and equipment. It is a part of scientific and technical intelligence and is distinct from order of battle. *See also:* Scientific and Technical Intelligence.

References

Department of Defense, Defense Intelligence College. *Glossary of Intelligence Terms and Definitions.* Washington, DC: DIC, 1987.

Department of Defense, Joint Chiefs of Staff. *Department of Defense Dictionary of Military and Related Terms.* Washington, DC: GPO, 1986.

Godson, Roy, ed. *Intelligence Problems for the 1980s, Number 1: Elements of Intelligence.* Rev. ed. Washington, DC: National Strategy Information Center, 1983.

Kent, Sherman. *Strategic Intelligence for American World Policy.* Princeton, NJ: Princeton University Press, 1966.

Laqueur, Walter. *A World of Secrets.* New York: Basic Books, 1985.

Treverton, Gregory F. *Covert Action: The Limits of Intervention in the Postwar World.* New York: Basic Books, 1987.

Turner, Stansfield. *Secrecy and Democracy: The CIA in Transition.* Boston: Houghton Mifflin, 1985.

—**TECHNICAL SECURITY MATERIAL** was a term that was created and defined in "National Policy on Telecommunications and Automated Information Systems Security," a proposed Presidential Directive that appeared on September 17, 1984, but was never enacted. Under that proposed directive, technical security material "means equipment, components, devices, and associated documentation or other media which pertain to cryptography, or to the securing of telecommunications and automated information systems."

—**TECHNICAL SENSOR.** *See:* Sensor.

—**TECHNICAL SERVICES DIVISION,** a component of the Directorate for Plans, Central Intelligence Agency, was engaged in research and development to provide operational support for clandestine activities. It was transferred to the Directorate for Science and Technology in 1973. *See also:* Central Intelligence Agency.

References

Corson, William R. *The Armies of Ignorance: The Rise of the American Intelligence Empire.* New York: Dial Press, 1977.

Fain, Tyrus G.; Plant, Katharine C.; and Milloy, Ross. *The Intelligence Community: History, Organization, and Issues.* Public Documents Series. New York: R.R. Bowker, 1977.

—**TECHNICAL SIGINT** is intelligence information that provides a detailed knowledge of the technical characteristics of a given emitter and thus permits estimates to be made about its primary function, capabilities, modes of operation (including malfunctions), and state-of-the-art, as well as its specific role within a complex weapon system or defense network. Technical SIGINT is a contributor to technical intelligence. *See also:* Technical Intelligence.

References

Department of Defense, Defense Intelligence College. *Glossary of Intelligence Terms and Definitions.* Washington, DC: DIC, 1987.

Turner, Stansfield. *Secrecy and Democracy: The CIA in Transition.* Boston: Houghton Mifflin, 1985.

—**TECHNICAL SURVEILLANCE COUNTERMEASURES (TSCM) SURVEY** is a thorough physical, electronic, and visual examination by special agents in and about an area in order to detect technical surveillance devices, technical security hazards, and physical security weaknesses. TSCM surveys differ from TEMPEST surveys in that the latter are limited to investigation and studies of compromising emanations, whereas the TSCM surveys are basically designed to prevent the technical penetration efforts of hostile intelligence services.

References

Godson, Roy, ed. *Intelligence Problems for the 1980s, Number 3: Counterintelligence.* Washington, DC: National Strategy Information Center, 1980.

Turner, Stansfield. *Secrecy and Democracy: The CIA in Transition.* Boston: Houghton Mifflin, 1985.

—**TECHNOLOGICAL TRANSFER (T^2 OR TT)** is a counterintelligence term used in the context of automatic data system security. Recent Soviet acquisitions of Western computer technology have made U.S. military-related computer systems even more vulnerable. More than one-third of all known Soviet integrated circuits have been copied from U.S. designs. In copying them, they are also able to examine them in order to determine systems vulnerabilities, which allow for the development of exploitation techniques.

References

Blackburn, N. Glenn. "Computers: A Counterintelligence Concern." Unpublished paper provided to the editors. Washington, DC, 1987.

Laqueur, Walter. *A World of Secrets*. New York: Basic Books, 1985.

Turner, Stansfield. *Secrecy and Democracy: The CIA in Transition*. Boston: Houghton Mifflin, 1985.

—**TELECOMMUNICATIONS (TELECOM).** (1) In a general sense, telecommunications are any transmission, emission, or reception of signs, signals, writing, images, and sounds or information of any nature by wire, radio, visual, electromechanical, electro-optical, or other electromagnetic means. (2) Under a proposed Presidential Directive entitled "National Policy on Telecommunications and Automated Information Systems Security," released on September 17, 1984, telecommunications are "the preparation, transmission, communication or related processing of information by electrical, electromagnetic, electromechanical or electro-optical means." *See also:* Transportation and Telecommunications Intelligence.

References

Department of Defense, Defense Intelligence College. *Glossary of Intelligence Terms and Definitions*. Washington, DC: DIC, 1987.

Department of Defense, Joint Chiefs of Staff. *Department of Defense Dictionary of Military and Related Terms*. Washington, DC: GPO, 1986.

Godson, Roy, ed. *Intelligence Problems for the 1980s, Number 1: Elements of Intelligence*. Rev. ed. Washington, DC: National Strategy Information Center, 1983.

Maurer, Alfred C.; Turnstall, Marion D.; and Keagle, James M. *Intelligence Policy and Process*. Boulder, CO: Westview Press, 1985.

"National Policy on Telecommunications and Automated Information Systems Security." Proposed Presidential Directive released Sept. 17, 1984, but never enacted.

U.S. Congress. Senate. *Final Report of the Senate Select Committee to Study Government Operations with Respect to Intelligence Activities. Report 94-755. Book I, Foreign and Military Intelligence*. Washington, DC: GPO, 1976.

—**TELECOMMUNICATIONS AND AUTOMATED INFORMATION SYSTEMS SECURITY** was defined in "National Policy on Telecommunications and Automated Information Systems Security," a proposed Presidential Directive that was released on September 17, 1984, but was never put into effect, as the "protection afforded to telecommunications and automated information systems, in order to prevent exploitation through interception, unauthorized electronic access, or related technical intelligence threats, and to ensure authenticity. Such protection results from the application of security measures (including cryptosecurity, transmission security, emission security, and computer security) to systems which generate, store, process, transfer, or communicate information of use to an adversary, and also includes the physical protection of sensitive technical security material and sensitive technical security information."

—**TELEGRAPH** is a clandestine and covert intelligence operations term. It is a prearranged signal that tells an agent that he should pick up material from a dead drop. *See also:* Dead Drop.

References

Becket, Henry S. A. *The Dictionary of Espionage: Spookspeak into English*. New York: Stein and Day, 1986.

Deacon, Richard. *Spyclopedia: An Encyclopedia of Spies, Secret Services, Operations, Jargon, and All Subjects Related to the World of Espionage*. London: Macdonald, 1987.

Ranelagh, John. *The Agency: The Rise and Decline of the CIA*. New York: Simon and Schuster, 1986.

—**TELEMETRY** is the measurement of a quantity, transmitting the measurement data to a remote station, where the material is interpreted and recorded. *See also:* Telemetry Intelligence.

References

Reeves, Robert; Anson, Abraham; and Landen, David. *Manual of Remote Sensing*. Falls Church, VA: American Society of Photogrammetry, 1975.

Turner, Stansfield. *Secrecy and Democracy: The CIA in Transition*. Boston: Houghton Mifflin, 1985.

—**TELEMETRY INTELLIGENCE (TELINT)** is technical and intelligence information derived from intercepting, processing, and analyzing foreign telemetry. It is a subcategory of foreign instrumentation signals intelligence (FISINT). *See also:* Telemetry.

References

Department of Defense, Defense Intelligence College. *Glossary of Intelligence Terms and Definitions.* Washington, DC: DIC, 1987.

Department of Defense, Joint Chiefs of Staff. *Department of Defense Dictionary of Military and Related Terms.* Washington, DC: GPO, 1986.

Godson, Roy, ed. *Intelligence Problems for the 1980s, Number 5: Clandestine Collection.* Washington, DC: National Strategy Information Center, 1982.

Laqueur, Walter. *A World of Secrets.* New York: Basic Books, 1985.

Maurer, Alfred C.; Turnstall, Marion D.; and Keagle, James M. *Intelligence Policy and Process.* Boulder, CO: Westview Press, 1985.

Turner, Stansfield. *Secrecy and Democracy: The CIA in Transition.* Boston: Houghton Mifflin, 1985.

—**TELEPRINTER (PRTR),** a baud-based system term used in communications intelligence, communications security, operations security, and signals analysis, is an electrically operated instrument that is used in the transmission and reception-printing of messages by proper sensing and interpretation of electrical signals. Teleprinter is a general name applied to all types of baud-based printing equipments. *See also:* Communications Security.

References

Department of Defense, U.S. Army. *Military Intelligence Battalion (Combat Electronic Warfare Intelligence) (Division).* Field Manual FM 34-10. Washington, DC: Headquarters, Department of the Army, 1981.

————. *Military Intelligence Group (Combat Electronic Warfare and Intelligence) (Corps).* Field Manual FM 34-20. Washington, DC: Headquarters, Department of the Army, 1983.

—**TELEPROCESSING** is the overall function of an information transmission system that combines telecommunications, automatic data processing, and man-machine interface equipment and their interaction as an integrated whole.

References

Department of Defense, Defense Intelligence College. *Glossary of Intelligence Terms and Definitions.* Washington, DC: DIC, 1987.

Department of Defense, Joint Chiefs of Staff. *Department of Defense Dictionary of Military and Related Terms.* Washington, DC: GPO, 1986.

—**TELEPROCESSING SECURITY,** in communications security (COMSEC), refers to the protection that results from all the measures that are designed to prevent the deliberate or inadvertent unauthorized disclosure, acquisition, manipulation, or modification of information in a teleprocessing system. *See also:* Communications Security.

References

Department of Defense, Joint Chiefs of Staff. *Department of Defense Dictionary of Military and Related Terms.* Washington, DC: GPO, 1986.

—**TELEVISION IMAGERY** is imagery that is acquired by a television camera and is recorded or transmitted electronically.

References

Department of Defense, Joint Chiefs of Staff. *Department of Defense Dictionary of Military and Related Terms.* Washington, DC: GPO, 1986.

—**TELL-TALE** is used in clandestine and covert intelligence operations. It is a form of talcum powder that is invisible. If examined under ultraviolet light, it will show whether the documents on which it has been placed have been disturbed.

References

Becket, Henry S. A. *The Dictionary of Espionage: Spookspeak into English.* New York: Stein and Day, 1986.

Deacon, Richard. *Spyclopedia: An Encyclopedia of Spies, Secret Services, Operations, Jargon, and All Subjects Related to the World of Espionage.* London: Macdonald, 1987.

Ranelagh, John. *The Agency: The Rise and Decline of the CIA.* New York: Simon and Schuster, 1986.

—**TEMPEST** is a term referring to technical investigations for compromising emanations from electrically operated information processing equipment. The Defense Intelligence Agency TEMPEST program is managed by the agency's Directorate for Security and Counterintelligence (OS). Within the U.S. Army, the term TEMPEST is synonymous with emissions security (EMSEC) and control of compromising emanations. *See also:* Defense Intelligence Agency.

References

Department of Defense, Defense Intelligence Agency. *Organization, Mission, and Key Personnel.* Washington, DC: DIA, 1986.

Department of Defense, Defense Intelligence College. *Glossary of Intelligence Terms and Definitions.* Washington, DC: DIC, 1987.

Department of Defense, U.S. Army. *Counterintelligence.* Field Manual FM 34-60. Washington, DC: Headquarters, Department of the Army, 1985.

———. *Counter-Signals Intelligence (C-SIGINT) Operations.* Field Manual FM 34-62. Washington, DC: Headquarters, Department of the Army, 1986.

—**TEMPLATE** is an Army tactical intelligence (TACINT) term that means a graphic illustration of an enemy capability, drawn to scale. It is an analytical tool that integrates enemy doctrine, capabilities, and vulnerabilities and applies them to specific terrain, weather, and tactical scenarios. There are several types of templates. Among them are (1) a doctrinal template, which depicts how the enemy would like to fight if he were not restricted by terrain and weather; (2) a situation template, which depicts how the enemy might adjust his doctrine to fit terrain and weather constraints; (3) an event template, which depicts time-related, logically sequenced indications or events that are keyed to a series of situation templates (event templating determines the what, when and where of collection planning); (4) a decision support template, which is keyed to the event template and identifies critical events that are relative to time, location, and current situation and that require tactical decisions.

References

Department of Defense, U.S. Army. *Intelligence and Electronic Warfare Operations.* Field Manual FM 34-1. Washington, DC: Headquarters, Department of the Army, 1984.

———. *Military Intelligence Battalion (CEWI) (Operations) (Corps).* Field Manual FM 34-21. Washington, DC: Headquarters, Department of the Army, 1982.

—**TEMPORARY SECURE AREA (TSA)** is a temporarily accredited facility that is used for storing, handling, discussing, or processing sensitive compartmented information (SCI). TSAs are normally established for a nonrenewable period of six months or less. *See also:* Sensitive Compartmented Information, Sensitive Compartmented Information Facility.

References

Department of Defense, Defense Intelligence College. *Glossary of Intelligence Terms and Definitions.* Washington, DC: DIC, 1987.

—**TEMPORARY SECURE WORKING AREA (TSWA)** is an intelligence security and counterintelligence term. It is an area, room, or group of rooms that have been properly secured against physical and audio penetration for the temporary use of sensitive compartmented information (SCI). No storage of SCI is permitted in a TSWA, and the time of use is not to exceed 40 hours per month.

References

Department of Defense, Defense Intelligence College. *Glossary of Intelligence Terms and Definitions.* Washington, DC: DIC, 1987.

—**10/5 PANEL,** as defined by the Church Committee, is a predecessor to the 40 Committee of the National Security Council.

References

U.S. Congress. Senate. *Final Report of the Senate Select Committee to Study Government Operations with Respect to Intelligence Activities. Report 94-755. Book I, Foreign and Military Intelligence.* Washington, DC: GPO, 1976.

—**TERMINATE WITH EXTREME PREJUDICE** was a term, popular in the 1960s, which meant murdering someone. *See also:* Assassination, Demote Maximally, Executive Action.

References

Becket, Henry S. A. *The Dictionary of Espionage: Spookspeak into English.* New York: Stein and Day, 1986.

Deacon, Richard. *Spyclopedia: An Encyclopedia of Spies, Secret Services, Operations, Jargon, and All Subjects Related to the World of Espionage.* London: Macdonald, 1987.

Ranelagh, John. *The Agency: The Rise and Decline of the CIA.* New York: Simon and Schuster, 1986.

Treverton, Gregory F. *Covert Action: The Limits of Intervention in the Postwar World.* New York: Basic Books, 1987.

—**TERPIL, FRANK, AND EDWIN WILSON** were two Central Intelligence Agency employees who left the agency. Their subsequent business activities involved selling restricted material and arms to Libya and providing former Green Berets to train the Libyans in the use of the equipment. In the ensuing congressional investigation, it appeared that Terpil and Wilson had used their former contacts in the CIA to arrange the Libyan deal, and that some CIA employees may even have helped them. Wilson was arrested in 1982 and was subsequently convicted on a number of charges. Mark Lowenthal astutely notes that the Wilson-Terpil case highlighted the problem of controlling agents who leave the CIA, the issue of the relationship between CIA employees and former employees, and the inadequacy of the existing laws governing the transfer of U.S. technology.

References

Lowenthal, Mark M. *U.S. Intelligence: Evolution and Anatomy.* New York: Praeger, 1984.

—**TERRAIN INTELLIGENCE** is processed information on the military significance of natural and man-made characteristics of an area.

References

Department of Defense, Joint Chiefs of Staff. *Department of Defense Dictionary of Military and Related Terms.* Washington, DC: GPO, 1986.

Godson, Roy, ed. *Intelligence Problems for the 1980s, Number 1: Elements of Intelligence.* Rev. ed. Washington, DC: National Strategy Information Center, 1983.

Kent, Sherman. *Strategic Intelligence for American World Policy.* Princeton, NJ: Princeton University Press, 1966.

Maurer, Alfred C.; Turnstall, Marion D.; and Keagle, James M. *Intelligence Policy and Process.* Boulder, CO: Westview Press, 1985.

—**TERRAIN STUDY** is an analysis and interpretation of natural and man-made features of an area, their effects on military operations, and the effect of weather and climate on these features.

References

Department of Defense, Joint Chiefs of Staff. *Department of Defense Dictionary of Military and Related Terms.* Washington, DC: GPO, 1986.

—**TERRORISM** is "the unlawful use of force or violence against persons or property to intimidate or coerce a government, the civilian population or any segment thereof, in furtherance of political or social objectives."

References

American Bar Association. *Oversight and Accountability of the U.S. Intelligence Agencies: An Evaluation.* Washington, DC: ABA, 1985.

Department of Defense, Defense Intelligence College. *Glossary of Intelligence Terms and Definitions.* Washington, DC: DIC, 1987.

Godson, Roy, ed. *Intelligence Problems for the 1980s, Number 1: Elements of Intelligence.* Rev. ed. Washington, DC: National Strategy Information Center, 1983.

Laqueur, Walter. *The Age of Terrorism.* Boston: Little, Brown, 1987.

———. *A World of Secrets.* New York: Basic Books, 1985. 1985.

Treverton, Gregory F. *Covert Action: The Limits of Intervention in the Postwar World.* New York: Basic Books, 1987.

Turner, Stansfield. *Secrecy and Democracy: The CIA in Transition.* Boston: Houghton Mifflin, 1985.

—**TERRORIST ORGANIZATION** is a group that engages in terrorist activities. *See also:* International Terrorist Activity.

References

Department of Defense, Defense Intelligence College. *Glossary of Intelligence Terms and Definitions.* Washington, DC: DIC, 1987.

Godson, Roy, ed. *Intelligence Problems for the 1980s, Number 1: Elements of Intelligence.* Rev. ed. Washington, DC: National Strategy Information Center, 1983.

———. *Intelligence Problems for the 1980s, Number 3: Counterintelligence.* Washington, DC: National Strategy Information Center, 1980.

Laqueur, Walter. *The Age of Terrorism.* Boston: Little, Brown, 1987.

Treverton, Gregory F. *Covert Action: The Limits of Intervention in the Postwar World.* New York: Basic Books, 1987.

—**TERRORIST THREAT CONDITION** is a level of terrorist threat to U.S. military facilities and personnel. It is also called THREATCON. There are three levels of THREATCON:

THREATCON WHITE means that there is a nonspecific terrorist threat against U.S. military personnel or facilities in a general geographic area. This threat may be based on information that the terrorist elements in the area have general plans against military facilities.

THREATCON YELLOW means that there is a specific threat against U.S. military personnel or facilities in a particular geographic area. This threat may be based on information that terrorist elements are actively preparing for operations in a particular area.

THREATCON RED means that there is an imminent threat of terrorist acts against specific U.S. military personnel or facilities. This threat may be based on information regarding plans or preparations for terrorist attacks against specific persons or facilities.

References

Department of Defense, Defense Intelligence College. *Glossary of Intelligence Terms and Definitions.* Washington, DC: DIC, 1987.

Godson, Roy, ed. *Intelligence Problems for the 1980s, Number 1: Elements of Intelligence.* Rev. ed. Washington, DC: National Strategy Information Center, 1983.

———. *Intelligence Problems for the 1980s, Number 3: Counterintelligence.* Washington, DC: National Strategy Information Center, 1980.

Laqueur, Walter. *The Age of Terrorism.* Boston: Little, Brown, 1987.

Treverton, Gregory F. *Covert Action: The Limits of Intervention in the Postwar World.* New York: Basic Books, 1987.

—**THERMAL DETECTOR** is a device that determines where people have been sitting or lying.

References

Deacon, Richard. *Spyclopedia: An Encyclopedia of Spies, Secret Services, Operations, Jargon, and All Subjects Related to the World of Espionage.* London: Macdonald, 1987.

—**THERMAL IMAGERY (INFRARED)** is imagery produced by measuring and recording electronically the thermal radiation of objects.

References

Department of Defense, Joint Chiefs of Staff. *Department of Defense Dictionary of Military and Related Terms.* Washington, DC: GPO, 1986.

—**THIRD COUNTRY OPERATION,** in FBI terminology, is one that is conducted by an intelligence agency in one country, based in a second country, and aimed at a third country. *See also:* Agent, Agent in Place, Agent Net, Agent of Influence, Agent Provocateur, Between the Lines Entry, Confusion Agent, Double Agent, Handling Agent, Infiltration, Inside Man, Moonlight

Extradition, Penetration, Sign of Life Signal, Silent School, Singleton, Special Activities.

References

Kessler, Ronald. *Spy vs. Spy: Stalking Soviet Spies in America.* New York: Charles Scribner's Sons, 1988.

—**THIRTY THREES** is a term used in clandestine and covert intelligence operations to indicate an emergency. *See also:* Blow, Blown Agent, Burn, Burnt, Damage Assessment, Damage Control, Dangle, Demote Maximally, Discard, Doubled, Go to Ground, Packed Up, Rolling up the Net, Sign of Life Signal, Special Activities, Submerge, Surround.

References

Deacon, Richard. *Spyclopedia: An Encyclopedia of Spies, Secret Services, Operations, Jargon, and All Subjects Related to the World of Espionage.* London: Macdonald, 1987.

—**THOMPSON, ROBERT G.,** a former Air Force airman second class, may have been an illegal agent trained by the KGB when he was captured by the Soviet Army in 1945. He provided the Soviets with information concerning Air Force counterintelligence activities and intelligence information on a variety of U.S. military operations and programs. He was tried, found guilty, and received a 30-year sentence. In 1978, he was traded to East Germany in exchange for an Israeli pilot who was being held in Mozambique.

References

Allen, Thomas B., and Polmar, Norman. *Merchants of Treason: America's Secrets for Sale.* New York: Delacorte Press, 1988.

Crawford, David J. *Volunteers: The Betrayal of National Defense Secrets by Air Force Traitors.* Washington, DC: GPO, 1988.

—**THREAT.** (1) A threat is force or activity that is viewed as being inimical to the interests of a nation. With respect to a nation's armed forces, a threat is usually viewed as the armed forces of another nation. In many instances, however, the threat from forces in the nation is viewed as more serious than any external threat. This is particularly true in Third World countries. The threat is usually the object of a nation's major intelligence effort, because it is through intelligence that the threat is defined and measured. This, in turn, drives the majority of such things as the defense budget, strength of the armed forces, military deployments, and modernization. For these reasons, the threat is an important starting point in the intelligence process. (2) Threat is also a communications security (COMSEC) term that means the technical or operational capability of a hostile entity to detect, exploit, or subvert friendly telecommunications and the demonstrated, presumed, or inferred intent of that entity to conduct such activity. (3) Threat is also an Army tactical intelligence (TACINT) term that refers to the technical and operational capability of an enemy to detect, exploit, or subvert friendly telecommunications and the demonstrated, presumed or inferred intent of that enemy to conduct such activity. As applied to this concept, there are two aspects to the threat: the *threat from*, and the *threat to*. The threat from is represented by the general or "generic" threat posed by a hostile SIGINT capability. The threat to is the identification of a specific threat that is targeted against a specific unit or activity. The threat to is derived from analysis of the generic threat (templates) and available information concerning SIGINT capabilities and intentions that are facing a unit or activity. (4) Threat is also an indications and warning (I&W) term. In this context, it means the extant military, economic, and/or political capability of a foreign country coupled with the aggressive intentions to use this capability to undertake any action whose consequence will be detrimental to the interests of the United States.

References

American Bar Association. *Oversight and Accountability of the U.S. Intelligence Agencies: An Evaluation*. Washington, DC: ABA, 1985.

Department of Defense, Defense Intelligence College. *Glossary of Intelligence Terms and Definitions*. Washington, DC: DIC, 1987.

Department of Defense, U.S. Army. *Counter-Signals Intelligence (C-SIGINT) Operations*. Field Manual FM 34-62. Washington, DC: Headquarters, Department of the Army, 1986.

———. *RDTE Managers Intelligence and Threat Support Guide*. Alexandria, VA: Headquarters, Army Materiel Development and Readiness Command, 1983.

Godson, Roy, ed. *Intelligence Problems for the 1980s, Number 1: Elements of Intelligence*. Rev. ed. Washington, DC: National Strategy Information Center, 1983.

Laqueur, Walter. *A World of Secrets*. New York: Basic Books, 1985.

Maurer, Alfred C.; Turnstall, Marion D.; and Keagle, James M. *Intelligence Policy and Process*. Boulder, CO: Westview Press, 1985.

—**THREAT APPROVAL** is an Army intelligence term that means the same as validation (in the Army context), but is done at the Headquarters, Department of the Army, ITAC, or MACOM level. *See also:* Threat.

References

Department of Defense, U.S. Army. *RDTE Managers Intelligence and Threat Support Guide*. Alexandria, VA: Headquarters, Army Materiel Development and Readiness Command, 1983.

—**THREAT VALIDATION** is an Army intelligence term that refers to the Defense Intelligence Agency's evaluation of and concurrence with threat documentation. The DIA evaluations of service-produced threats stress the appropriateness and completeness of the intelligence, accuracy of the judgments, the consistency with existing intelligence positions, the logic of the extrapolations from existing intelligence, and the suitability of the methodologies that have been used. Validation indicates the general acceptability of the intelligence for use in support of a specific plan, program, study, materiel acquisition milestone, or combat development activity. *See also:* Threat.

References

Department of Defense, U.S. Army. *RDTE Managers Intelligence and Threat Support Guide*. Alexandria, VA: Headquarters, Army Materiel Development and Readiness Command, 1983.

—**THRESHOLDS,** in intelligence program budgeting and for purposes of the PPBS, are a set of criteria that, if met or exceeded, require the submission of a program change request to the Office of the Secretary of Defense. *See also:* Program Change Request.

References

Pickett, George. "Congress, the Budget, and Intelligence." In *Intelligence Policy and Process,* edited by Alfred C. Maurer, Marion D. Turnstall, and James M. Keagle. Boulder, CO: Westview Press, 1985.

—**TIARA.** *See:* Tactical Iintelligence and Related Activities.

—**TIME COMPLIANCE DATE,** in communications security (COMSEC),is the date by which a mandatory modification to a COMSEC end item must be incorporated, if the item is to remain approved for operational use. *See also:* Communications Security.

References

Department of Defense, U.S. Army. *Military Intelligence Battalion (Combat Electronic Warfare Intelligence) (Division).* Field Manual FM 34-10. Washington, DC: Headquarters, Department of the Army, 1981.

————. *Military Intelligence Company (Combat Electronic Warfare and Intelligence) (Armored Cavalry Regiment/Separate Brigade).* Field Manual FM 34-30. Washington, DC: Headquarters, Department of the Army, 1983.

—**TIME ON TARGET (TT)** is the time when an aircraft is scheduled to attack or photograph a target. *See also:* Targeting.

References

Department of Defense, Joint Chiefs of Staff. *Department of Defense Dictionary of Military and Related Terms.* Washington, DC: GPO, 1986.

—**TIME-PHASED COSTS,** in intelligence budgeting, are a presentation of the cost results that are broken down by the time period in which the costs occur rather than a single total cost figure. *See also:* Thresholds.

References

Pickett, George. "Congress, the Budget, and Intelligence." In *Intelligence Policy and Process,* edited by Alfred C. Maurer, Marion D. Turnstall, and James M. Keagle. Boulder, CO: Westview Press, 1985.

—**TIP-OFF** is an Army tactical intelligence (TAC-INT) term that means data that can be used for fire or maneuver decisions as received without further processing, interpretation, or integration with other data.

References

Department of Defense, U.S. Army. *Counter-Signals Intelligence (C-SIGINT) Operations.* Field Manual FM 34-62. Washington, DC: Headquarters, Department of the Army, 1986.

—**TITLING STRIP** is an intelligence imagery and photoreconnaissance term. It is the information that is added to photographic negatives or posi-

tives to identify them and provide reference information. *See also:* Aerial Photograph.

References

Department of Defense, Joint Chiefs of Staff. *Department of Defense Dictionary of Military and Related Terms.* Washington, DC: GPO, 1986.

—**TOBIAS, MICHAEL TIMOTHY,** Radioman Third Class, U.S. Navy, was arrested and charged with espionage in San Francisco on August 22, 1984. He was convicted on August 14, 1985, and sentenced to twenty years in prison.

References

Crawford, David J. *Volunteers: The Betrayal of National Defense Secrets by Air Force Traitors.* Washington, DC: GPO, 1988.

—**TONGUE-TANGLER** is a term used in clandestine and covert intelligence operations. It is a thin layer of flesh-colored plastic that a person wears to give him a slight lisp. It is not popular because it is uncomfortable.

References

Becket, Henry S. A. *The Dictionary of Espionage: Spookspeak into English.* New York: Stein and Day, 1986.

—**TOP SECRET (TS).** *See:* Security Classification.

—**TOP SECRET CODEWORD (TSCW)** appears on a piece of information to indicate that it is to be kept within special compartmented intelligence channels. *See also:* Access, Authorized, Classification, Code Word, Compromise, Declassification, Disclosure, Downgrade, Freedom of Information Act, Limited Access Area, Need-to-Know, Need-to-Know Principle, No-Lone Zone, Nondisclosure Agreement, Nondiscussion Area, Sanitization, Sanitize, Sanitized Area, Security Certification, Security Classification, Sensitive Compartmented Information, Sensitive Compartmented Information Facility, Two-Person Control.

References

Department of Defense, Defense Intelligence Agency. *Defense Intelligence Agency Manual.* Washington, DC: DIA, 1987.

Department of Defense, Defense Intelligence College. *Glossary of Intelligence Terms and Definitions.* Washington, DC: DIC, 1987.

—**TOP SECRET CONTROL (TSC)** is a system that controls the storage, accountability, and dissemination of Top Secret material. The system includes physical security, in that the material can only be retained in certain approved areas; dissemination, in that only those who have been cleared for access to Top Secret can be allowed to see it and must sign on a cover sheet that they have seen it; and accountability, in that periodic inventories must be held in order to account for all the Top Secret material. *See also:* Top Secret Codeword.

References

Department of Defense, Defense Intelligence Agency. *Defense Intelligence Agency Manual.* Washington, DC: DIA, 1987.

————. *Organization, Mission and Key Personnel.* Washington, DC: DIA, 1986.

Department of Defense, Defense Intelligence College. *Glossary of Intelligence Terms and Definitions.* Washington, DC: DIC, 1987.

Department of Defense, Joint Chiefs of Staff. *Department of Defense Dictionary of Military and Related Terms.* Washington, DC: GPO, 1986.

Maurer, Alfred C.; Turnstall, Marion D.; and Keagle, James M. *Intelligence Policy and Process.* Boulder, CO: Westview Press, 1985.

—**TOP SECRET CONTROL OFFICER (TSCO)** is an individual who has been designated to receive, transmit, and maintain current access and accountability records for Top Secret information. He is responsible for the physical security of the command's Top Secret information and, unless he is given an exemption, must conduct an inventory of all Top Secret materials at least annually. *See also:* Top Secret Codeword.

References

Department of Defense, Information Security Oversight Office. *Directive No. 1: National Security Information.* As reproduced in *Federal Register,* June 25, 1982, pp. 27836- 27841.

Department of Defense, Defense Intelligence Agency. *Organization, Mission, and Key Personnel.* Washington, DC: DIA, 1986.

————. *Defense Intelligence Agency Manual.* Washington, DC: DIA, 1987.

Department of Defense, Defense Intelligence College. *Glossary of Intelligence Terms and Definitions.* Washington, DC: DIC, 1987.

Department of Defense, Joint Chiefs of Staff. *Department of Defense Dictionary of Military and Related Terms.* Washington, DC: GPO, 1986.

—**TORCH** was the first significant Office of Strategic Services (OSS) overseas operation in World War II, and it involved the Allied landings on North Africa in 1942. Ray Cline notes that the OSS involvement very quickly took the form not only of intelligence collection, but also of clandestine operations, in that the OSS was the primary intermediary between U.S. and French forces. Although the OSS had only moderate success in its attempts to solicit the assistance of French General Henri Giraud and Admiral Jean Darlan, the role that the OSS played as primary interface between the Americans and French drastically improved its reputation, thereby allowing it to play a more significant role in the remainder of the war. *See also:* Office of Strategic Services.

References

Cline, Ray S. *The CIA Under Reagan, Bush, and Casey.* Washington: Acropolis Books, 1981.

—**TORDILLA, DR. LOUIS,** served as deputy director of the National Security Agency from August 1958 until April 21, 1974, under seven different DIRNSAs. Tordilla was responsible for the massive research and development program that produced the agency's advanced computer capabilities. Additionally, he offered a calming continuity to both U.S. and Allied leaders as the DIRNSAs came and went. He did much to further civilian influence in the agency and left an imprint on the deputy DIRNSA position that remains to this day. *See also:* National Security Agency.

References

Bamford, James. *The Puzzle Palace: A Report on America's Most Secret Agency.* New York: Penguin Books, 1983.

—**TOSS** is a term used in clandestine intelligence and in counterintelligence, counterespionage, and counterinsurgency operations. It means to enter surreptitiously the office or living quarters of someone suspected of espionage or criminal activity. *See also:* Agent Authentication, Damage Assessment, Establishing Bonafides, Shadow, Shaking Off the Dogs, Sound Man, Sound School, Special Activities, Surreptitious Entry, Surround, Surveillance.

References

Becket, Henry S. A. *The Dictionary of Espionage: Spookspeak into English.* New York: Stein and Day, 1986.

Deacon, Richard. *Spyclopedia: An Encyclopedia of Spies, Secret Services, Operations, Jargon, and All Subjects Related to the World of Espionage.* London: Macdonald, 1987.

Ranelagh, John. *The Agency: The Rise and Decline of the CIA.* New York: Simon and Schuster, 1986.

—TOTAL OBLIGATIONAL AUTHORITY (TOA) is a Department of Defense budgeting term that is of significance to the Intelligence Community. It is the total direct financial requirements of the Five-Year Defense Plan (FYDP), or any component of the FYDP, that is necessary to support the approved program in a given fiscal year. It is almost synonymous with the budget authority (BA) provided by Congress. It is the authority to enter into obligations for immediate or future payment (outlay) of government funds. Obligations may be incurred for several years, depending on the type of appropriation. *See also:* Thresholds.

References
Pickett, George. "Congress, the Budget, and Intelligence." In *Intelligence Policy and Process,* edited by Alfred C. Maurer, Marion D. Turnstall, and James M. Keagle. Boulder, CO: Westview Press, 1985.

—TOTAL SYSTEM COST, in program budgeting, is the total research and development, investment, and operating costs (for a specified number of years of operation) that are required to develop, procure, and operate a particular weapon system. *See also:* Thresholds.

References
Pickett, George. "Congress, the Budget, and Intelligence." In *Intelligence Policy and Process,* edited by Alfred C. Maurer, Marion D. Turnstall, and James M. Keagle. Boulder, CO: Westview Press, 1985.

—TOXINS, as defined by the Church Committee, "are chemicals which are not living organisms, but are produced by living organisms and are lethal."

References
U.S. Congress. Senate. *Final Report of the Senate Select Committee to Study Government Operations with Respect to Intelligence Activities. Report 94-755. Book I, Foreign and Military Intelligence.* Washington, DC: GPO, 1976.

—TRADECRAFT is a term used in clandestine and covert intelligence operations to describe the methods and operations that an intelligence agency uses to conduct its business. *See also:* Active Measures, Agent, Agent Authentication, Between the Lines Entry, Biographic Leverage, Black Bag Job, Black Bag Operation, Black List, Blackmail, Bleep Box, Blind Dating, Bug, Burn, Cacklebladder, Canister, Case, Chief of Base, Chief of Outpost, Chief of Station, Cobbler, Cold Approach, Concealment, Cover Organizations, Demote Maximally, Dirty Tricks, Discard, Dispatched Agent, Dispenser, Double Agent, Edible Paper, Flaps and Seals, Game, Inside Man, Keeping Books, Litmus Test, Mole, Moonlight Extradition, Movements Analysis, Musician, Paper Mill, Penetration, Plumbing, Pocket Litter, Putting in the Plumbing, Recruitment in Place, Riding Shotgun, Shopping List, Shopworn Goods, Sign of Life Signal, Silent School, Singleton, Soap, Sound Man, Sound School, Special Activities, Third Country Operation.

References
Becket, Henry S. A. *The Dictionary of Espionage: Spookspeak into English.* New York: Stein and Day, 1986.

Kessler, Ronald. *Spy vs. Spy: Stalking Soviet Spies in America.* New York: Charles Scribner's Sons, 1988.

Quirk, John; Phillips, David; Cline, Ray; and Pforzheimer, Walter. *The Central Intelligence Agency: A Photographic History.* Guilford, CT: Foreign Intelligence Press, 1986.

—TRAFFIC, as defined by the Church Committee, are "messages that are carried over a communications network."

References
U.S. Congress. Senate. *Final Report of the Senate Select Committee to Study Government Operations with Respect to Intelligence Activities. Report 94-755. Book I, Foreign and Military Intelligence.* Washington, DC: GPO, 1976.

—TRAFFICABILITY is the capability of terrain to bear traffic and refers to the extent that terrain will permit the continued movement of all types of traffic.

References
Department of Defense, Joint Chiefs of Staff. *Department of Defense Dictionary of Military and Related Terms.* Washington, DC: GPO, 1986.

—**TRAFFIC ANALYSIS (TA)** is a cryptologic discipline that develops information from communications about the composition and operation of communication systems and the organizations that they serve. The process involves studying the external characteristics of the radio traffic and related materials and reconstructing communication plans in order to produce signals intelligence.

References

Department of Defense, Defense Intelligence College. *Glossary of Intelligence Terms and Definitions.* Washington, DC: DIC, 1987.

—**TRAFFIC-FLOW SECURITY,** in communications security (COMSEC), means the capability of certain on-line, machine cryptosystems to conceal the presence of valid traffic. *See also:* Communications Security.

References

Department of Defense, Joint Chiefs of Staff. *Department of Defense Dictionary of Military and Related Terms.* Washington, DC: GPO, 1986.

—**TRAFFIC INTELLIGENCE** is the communications intelligence that is produced by all means except cryptanalysis or decryption of intercepted communications.

References

Department of Defense, Defense Intelligence College. *Glossary of Intelligence Terms and Definitions.* Washington, DC: DIC, 1987.

—**TRAINING SUPPORT BASE (TSB),** in intelligence data handling, is composed of defense or military service schools and training centers, agencies, or commands that provide both functional and ADP courses of instruction and the resources to accomplish the instruction. Vendor or contractor training on vendor or contractor ADP systems is considered a part of the TSB.

References

Department of Defense, Defense Intelligence Agency. *Defense Intelligence Agency Manual.* Washington, DC: DIA, 1987.

—**TRAITOR** is a person who reveals his country's secrets, regardless of his motive. *See also:* Co-Optee, Defector, Disaffected Worker.

References

Becket, Henry S. A. *The Dictionary of Espionage: Spookspeak into English.* New York: Stein and Day, 1986.

Deacon, Richard. *Spyclopedia: An Encyclopedia of Spies, Secret Services, Operations, Jargon, and All Subjects Related to the World of Espionage.* London: Macdonald, 1987.

Ranelagh, John. *The Agency: The Rise and Decline of the CIA.* New York: Simon and Schuster, 1986.

Turner, Stansfield. *Secrecy and Democracy: The CIA in Transition.* Boston: Houghton Mifflin, 1985.

—**TRAN, DAI KIEM,** was a research physicist at the Naval Research Laboratory in Washington, DC. In 1983, Tran was exposed as a Vietnamese intelligence officer. He left the laboratory but was not prosecuted.

References

Allen, Thomas B., and Polmar, Norman. *Merchants of Treason: America's Secrets for Sale.* New York: Delacorte Press, 1988.

—**TRANSEC VARIABLE,** in communications security, refers to a cryptovariable that is used to maintain transmission security. *See also:* Communications Security.

References

Department of Defense, U.S. Army. *Counterintelligence.* Field Manual FM 34-60. Washington, DC: Headquarters, Department of the Army, 1985.

———. *Intelligence and Electronic Warfare Operations.* Field Manual FM 34-1. Washington, DC: Headquarters, Department of the Army, 1984.

———. *Military Intelligence Battalion (Combat Electronic Warfare Intelligence) (Division).* Field Manual FM 34-10. Washington, DC: Headquarters, Department of the Army, 1981.

—**TRANSFER OF ACCOUNTABILITY,** in communications security, refers to the process of transferring the accountability of COMSEC material from the Central Office of Record of the shipping organization, to the Central Office of Record of the receiving organization, or between commands or between COMSEC custodians. *See also:* Communications Security.

References

Department of Defense, U.S. Army. *Counterintelligence.* Field Manual FM 34-60. Washington, DC: Headquarters, Department of the Army, 1985.

———. *Intelligence and Electronic Warfare Operations.* Field Manual FM 34-1. Washington, DC: Headquarters, Department of the Army, 1984.

————. *Military Intelligence Battalion (Combat Electronic Warfare Intelligence) (Division)*. Field Manual FM 34-10. Washington, DC: Headquarters, Department of the Army, 1981.

—**TRANSMISSION AUTHENTICATION,** in communications security, is a procedure whereby a station may establish the authenticity of its own communication. *See also:* Communications Security.

References

Department of Defense, U.S. Army. *Counterintelligence*. Field Manual FM 34-60. Washington, DC: Headquarters, Department of the Army, 1985.

————. *Intelligence and Electronic Warfare Operations*. Field Manual FM 34-1. Washington, DC: Headquarters, Department of the Army, 1984.

————. *Military Intelligence Battalion (Combat Electronic Warfare Intelligence) (Division)*. Field Manual FM 34-10. Washington, DC: Headquarters, Department of the Army, 1981.

—**TRANSMISSION SECURITY (TRANSEC),** in communications security (COMSEC), is a component of communications security. It results from all measures designed to protect transmissions from interception and exploitation by means other than cryptanalysis. In the Army tactical environment, this includes using only authorized operations procedures on radiotelephone nets; maintaining net discipline at all times; using authentication procedures; encrypting all classified and sensitive information before transmitting it; and using radio and telephone only for official business and keeping all conversations (transmissions) as brief as possible. *See also:* Communications Security.

References

Department of Defense, Defense Intelligence College. *Glossary of Intelligence Terms and Definitions*. Washington, DC: DIC, 1987.

Department of Defense, Joint Chiefs of Staff. *Department of Defense Dictionary of Military and Related Terms*. Washington, DC: GPO, 1986.

Department of Defense, U.S. Army. *Counterintelligence*. Field Manual FM 34-60. Washington, DC: Headquarters, Department of the Army, 1985.

—**TRANSMITTER-DISTRIBUTOR (TD),** a baud-based system term used in communications intelligence, communications security, operations security, and signals analysis, is a motor-driven device that translates teleprinter code combina-

tions from perforated tape into electrical impulses, which it relays to other equipment, such as a radio transmitter. *See also:* Communications Security.

References

Department of Defense, U.S. Army. *Counterintelligence*. Field Manual FM 34-60. Washington, DC: Headquarters, Department of the Army, 1985.

————. *Intelligence and Electronic Warfare Operations*. Field Manual FM 34-1. Washington, DC: Headquarters, Department of the Army, 1984.

————. *Military Intelligence Battalion (Combat Electronic Warfare Intelligence) (Division)*. Field Manual FM 34-10. Washington, DC: Headquarters, Department of the Army, 1981.

—**TRANSPONDER** is a combined receiver and transmitter whose function is to automatically send a signal when triggered by an interrogating signal.

References

Department of Defense, Joint Chiefs of Staff. *Department of Defense Dictionary of Military and Related Terms*. Washington, DC: GPO, 1986.

—**TRANSPORTABLE COMSEC FACILITY,** in communications security (COMSEC), means a facility that contains classified COMSEC material and can be readily moved from one location to another, but is not equipped to be operated while it is in motion. *See also:* Communications Security.

References

Department of Defense, U.S. Army. *Counterintelligence*. Field Manual FM 34-60. Washington, DC: Headquarters, Department of the Army, 1985.

————. *Intelligence and Electronic Warfare Operations*. Field Manual FM 34-1. Washington, DC: Headquarters, Department of the Army, 1984.

————. *Military Intelligence Battalion (Combat Electronic Warfare Intelligence) (Division)*. Field Manual FM 34-10. Washington, DC: Headquarters, Department of the Army, 1981.

—**TRANSPORTATION AND LOGISTICS** is an official term that has been defined by the Defense Intelligence Agency for one of its functional areas. It means "the study and analysis of the complete system of lines of communication (overland, water, and air travel) including their capacities and all means of transport available which connect and support an operating military force with one or more bases of operations along which supplies and reinforcements move; activities relating to the science of planning and carrying out the movement and maintenance of forces; the design and development, acquisition, storage, movement, distribution, maintenance, evacuation, and disposition of material; movement, evacuation, and hospitalization of personnel; acquisition or construction, maintenance, operation, and disposition of facilities; and acquisition of furnishing of services." *See also:* Defense Intelligence Agency, Transportation and Telecommunications Intelligence.

References

Department of Defense, Defense Intelligence Agency. *Defense Intelligence Agency Manual.* Washington, DC: DIA, 1987.

————. *Organization, Mission and Key Personnel.* Washington, DC: DIA, 1986.

—**TRANSPORTATION AND TELECOMMUNICATIONS INTELLIGENCE,** one of the eight components of strategic intelligence, examines transportation networks, including the highways, railroads, inland waterways, and civil air capability, as well as a nation's telephone, telegraph, and civil broadcast capabilities. The Defense Intelligence Agency has primary responsibility for the production of transportation and communications intelligence.

General

Transportation intelligence is concerned with the operation and facilities of transportation systems in foreign countries. This subject includes railways, highways, inland waterways, petroleum pipelines, ports, the merchant marine, and aviation.

Telecommunications intelligence is concerned with the operation and facilities of fixed military communications systems in foreign countries. This includes radio, television, telephone, telegraph, submarine cable, and related communications media. The ultimate purpose of this intelligence is to permit evaluation: (1) of the military potential and vulnerability of a country's total telecommunications systems, and (2) the compatibility between local communications equipment and U.S. equipment.

The nature of these systems is closely tied to the nation's social and economic life. The more interdependent these factors become, the more vulnerable they are to all forms of attack. Conversely, the more complex and diversified they become, the more flexible they are and consequently the more difficult to destroy. Similarly,

the more extensive and well-integrated transportation systems become, the less vulnerable they are to attack. By integration, we mean the effective interconnection of the various regional systems.

Thus, a transportation system may be extensive if it covers a large area, but will not be well integrated unless it is interconnected, and the rail gauges, weight-carrying capacities, and operating techniques are common throughout the system. The same is true in the case of a telecommunications system. A complex, dispersed, and diversified telecommunications system is less vulnerable to destruction and provides more flexibility in operation.

In measuring the effectiveness of a transportation or a telecommunications system from a military point of view, it must be recognized that the military uses of these systems in wartime will be superimposed upon the normal domestic requirements. For example, a comparison of the number of telephones and the number of miles of telephone wire in a country with those of another country is meaningless unless the degree to which each country depends on these systems to support its normal domestic economy is also compared. This necessity for comparison on the basis of need and capacity is equally important in evaluating all types of transportation and telecommunications facilities.

The possibility of substituting an alternate means must also be considered. The overall vulnerability of a transportation system is lessened if adequate alternative means exist, as in the case where railroads are supplemented by inland waterways. The same is true of telecommunications if telephone and telegraph can be rerouted through other systems or readily supplemented by radio in the event of bombing, sabotage or local disruption.

There is usually a close affinity between the telecommunications and transportation systems of a country. Major telecommunications routes almost invariably follow the basic pattern of transportation routes. This is true because: (1) telecommunications emerged in the nineteenth century, after the transportation routes had been established; (2) the location of the major economic centers determined the transportation routes and subsequently the telecommunications routes; and (3) telecommunications routes are easier to construct, maintain, supply, and repair if they are located along the readily accessible transportation routes.

In the Middle East, the overall pattern of some telecommunications does not differ appreciably from the transportation pattern that was established over 7,000 years ago. The major exception to this parallel pattern is found in radio relay systems, which are beginning to depart from the established transportation routes. Individual towers can be placed on high ground, reached by helicopter, and spaced many miles apart. These factors lessen the requirements for easy road access and mile-by-mile servicing, which are mandatory in the case of pole lines. Line-of-sight characteristics of the radio relay systems tend to follow the shortest straight distance between major terminals and avoid the frequently winding routes of the transportation system.

Operationally, telecommunications have enormously increased the tonnage capacities of transportation systems by providing speedier scheduling, and coordination and control of shipments. Reciprocally, the control lines along transportation routes may provide additional communications circuits in a military emergency. As an index to the volume of military requirements on telecommunications, over 100,000 telephone calls may be required in the production, assembly, and shipment of one modern prototype aircraft.

Transportation

Railroads. A well-integrated and efficiently operated railway system is a vital necessity to the economy of a modern highly industrialized nation. The size and efficiency of the railway network are important indices of the economic and military potential of a country. An expanding railway system is often indicative of an expanding economy. Railroad construction without apparent economic justification, or the apparently needless duplication of railway facilities, is often important evidence of strategic military planning.

Railway traffic flow studies are essential in estimating the economic position and potential of a nation in peace and war. Sensitive railway junctions, bridges, tunnels, yards, and control facilities must be studied carefully from the standpoint of the acute effect of their loss to the economy and military capabilities of a nation.

Knowledge of their susceptibility to interdiction by military action or sabotage provides an index to their vulnerability. In addition, data are required on routes, mileage, gauges, multiplicity of track, curves and grades, the condition and

composition of roadbeds, spurs, rolling stock, repair facilities, classification yards, lubricants, and supplies of all kinds.

Highways. A well-integrated and extensive highway net is essential to any country with a highly developed economy. Most of the general remarks concerning railways in the preceding paragraph are applicable to the study of highway systems. The highways of a country include its primary and secondary road nets, overland routes, and trails.

To assess the adequacy of a country's highways it is necessary to collect extensive data on capacities both as to weight and volume, surface conditions, the effect of water and climate on the surfaces, constructions, defiles, bridges, and bypasses. Operational data required include numbers and types of motor vehicles available, repair facilities and supplies. Traffic density studies provide valuable information concerning the normal level of use of highways, and provide a valuable means of measuring changes in the character of highway activity.

Inland waterways. Inland waterways may be of prime importance to a nation's economy. Although operating at slow speeds, inland waterway carriers provide great weight-carrying capacities and often supplement both the rail and highway transportation systems. To determine the importance of waterways to the peacetime economy of a nation and to estimate the degree to which traffic may be increased in time of war, it is necessary to collect the same type of data required for rail and highway transport. In addition, data peculiar to waterways, such as depths of channels, locations of dams, locks, bridges, inland ports, and the availability of ships and boats must be considered.

Air transport. Although air transport is still only a supplementary mode of transportation providing a high speed, long distance medium with definite weight-carrying limitations, it is becoming increasingly important in relation to older forms of transportation. Some countries lacking adequate railways, highways, and waterways are depending to a great extent on air transport to support an expanding economy. This is particularly true of countries that have undergone extensive economic development since the advent of the airplane.

In addition, commercial aviation provides a ready means of reinforcing military aviation in time of war. Necessary data on air transport include that of organization, personnel, airline companies, air and ground equipment, repair facilities, fuel, routes, navigational aids, and airports.

Pipelines. Pipelines are practical only for the transportation of extremely limited types of materials in great bulk over comparatively long distances. The materials transported are primarily liquid and gaseous, such as petroleum products, chemicals, and illuminating gas. However, pipelines provide a speedy means of transporting their specialized loads over difficult terrain in mountainous and desert areas. Because pipelines are generally laid in straight lines, the distances traversed by them are often shorter than for other means of transportation.

Pipelines are extremely vulnerable to sabotage, but usually they can be camouflaged since they can be buried or covered with vegetation. The length, diameter, capacity, type of construction, type of material transported, and the location and type of pumping stations, are important items of information concerning pipelines.

Merchant marine. Sea transport is a basic necessity for the participation of any nation in world trade. Where nations do not possess adequate shipping facilities, they must depend on the merchant marines of other countries. Nearly every nation of the world would be seriously hampered in both peace and war if it were denied the use of maritime shipping facilities. Moreover, the nation possessing a strong merchant fleet has an important auxiliary to its navy in wartime. The importance of any merchant marine depends on the size of its fleet, the quality of its seamanship, the newness of its ships, the adequacy and extent of repair and construction facilities, the distribution of its shipping, and its routes and ports of call.

Ports and harbors. Although the study of ports and harbors is a part of transportation and telecommunications intelligence, it is also an important aspect of economic intelligence. In wartime this factor becomes even more important since, in addition to their normal peacetime significance, there is their added importance to the attacker, who needs to capture port facilities to support his landings, and for the subsequent supply of the ground, naval and air offensives.

To estimate the value of a port it is necessary to know its location, the type of shelter afforded, the average length, channels, bottom and silting, hydrographic conditions, warehousing facilities, types of piers and wharves, tonnage capacities for both long and short periods, availability of marine supplies, and the extent of repair and construction facilities.

The development of modern engineering techniques, which permit the construction of emergency port facilities at beach locations for temporary wartime use, has not detracted from the basic necessity to control conventional harbors and ports.

Telecommunications

Telecommunications can be defined as any means or method for transmitting information by use of electrical energy or the electromagnetic spectrum. Any portion of this spectrum might be used in a telecommunications system; for example, radio frequencies, audible frequencies, visible light, infrared and ultraviolet. Theoretically, even alpha, beta, gamma, or cosmic rays could be used to transmit information. The most common types of telecommunications equipment appearing in modern civil systems are the telephone, telegraph, radio and television, and submarine cable. Many combinations, such as radiotelegraph, variants such as wired broadcasting and facsimile, or specialized developments such as microwave relay equipment are becoming more prevalent each year. Variations in telecommunications systems are almost infinite. As an example, a communication between two distant cities may begin with one individual speaking into a telephone, travel over a coaxial cable, be amplified at a repeater station, be relayed by microwave relay towers, be carried on overhead lines, thence underwater by submarine cable, before finally reaching a listener at another city. These variations, while increasing the technical problem, actually decrease the vulnerability of the system as a whole, because alternate routes and facilities are available for rerouting messages in the event of damage to a part of the system.

In wartime, if these means for rapid communication were destroyed or even interrupted, all types of surface and air transportation might be seriously impaired. Modern nations have become so dependent on telecommunications for government, industry, education, propaganda, coordination and control purposes that they would be paralyzed if the telecommunications system were destroyed.

Intelligence on telecommunications should provide an overall picture that shows its background and its significance to the nation, as well as information on its top administration and control. This picture should be supported by detailed data on all existing civil equipment, facilities, and systems both domestic and international. Connections with surrounding countries and electronic warfare (jamming and electronic countermeasures) aspects are especially important. Details should include accurate locations, routes, capacities, technical characteristics of equipment, vulnerability, repair and maintenance, facilities, administration, and usage patterns in peace and war. *See also:* strategic intelligence.

References

Clauser, Jerome K., and Weir, Sandra M. *Intelligence Research Methodology.* State College, PA: HRB-Singer, 1975.

Department of Defense, Defense Intelligence College. *Glossary of Intelligence Terms and Definitions.* Washington, DC: DIC, 1987.

Department of Defense, Joint Chiefs of Staff. *Department of Defense Dictionary of Military and Related Terms.* Washington, DC: GPO, 1986.

—**TRANSPOSITION,** a signals analysis term, is a system in which the letters of the plain-text message are taken out of their normal order and rearranged to a pattern or key that has been previously agreed upon by the correspondents. For example, the word transposition might become noitsnartisop.

References

Department of Defense, U.S. Army. *Counterintelligence.* Field Manual FM 34-60. Washington, DC: Headquarters, Department of the Army, 1985.

————. *Intelligence and Electronic Warfare Operations.* Field Manual FM 34-1. Washington, DC: Headquarters, Department of the Army, 1984.

————. *Military Intelligence Battalion (Combat Electronic Warfare Intelligence) (Division).* Field Manual FM 34-10. Washington, DC: Headquarters, Department of the Army, 1981.

—**TREE-SHAKER.** *See:* Agent Provocateur, Shaking the Tree.

—**TRENDS AND DEVELOPMENTS IN FOREIGN TECHNOLOGY, WEAPONS, AND SYSTEMS** is an all-source weekly periodical that is published by the Defense Intelligence Agency in order to provide senior Department of Defense officials and military commanders with the results of indepth analyses of foreign scientific and technical developments. *See also:* Defense Intelligence Agency.

References

Von Hoene, John P. A. *Intelligence User's Guide.* Washington, DC: DIA, 1983.

—**TRIANGULATION** is a term used both in signals intelligence and in clandestine intelligence operations. (1) It is a signals intelligence technique of locating a secret transmitter by using three directional receivers that each take a bearing on the transmitter. The three bearings are then plotted on a map and their intersection will indicate the transmitter's location. (2) In counterintelligence, it means providing different versions of the same intelligence to different people suspected of passing intelligence to the enemy and then monitoring the intelligence fed back from the enemy to determine who compromised the material. *See also:* Surveillance.

References

Becket, Henry S. A. *The Dictionary of Espionage: Spookspeak into English.* New York: Stein and Day, 1986.

Deacon, Richard. *Spyclopedia: An Encyclopedia of Spies, Secret Services, Operations, Jargon, and All Subjects Related to the World of Espionage.* London: Macdonald, 1987.

Kent, Sherman. *Strategic Intelligence for American World Policy.* Princeton, NJ: Princeton University Press, 1966.

Kessler, Ronald. *Spy vs. Spy: Stalking Soviet Spies in America.* New York: Charles Scribner's Sons, 1988.

Laqueur, Walter. *A World of Secrets.* New York: Basic Books, 1985.

Ranelagh, John. *The Agency: The Rise and Decline of the CIA.* New York: Simon and Schuster, 1986.

—**TRI-CAMERA PHOTOGRAPHY,** in imagery and photoreconnaissance, is photography that is obtained by the simultaneous exposure of three cameras that have been systematically placed at fixed overlapping angles relative to each other. The purpose of such photography is to cover a wide field. *See also:* Titling Strip.

References

Department of Defense, Defense Intelligence College. *Glossary of Intelligence Terms and Definitions.* Washington, DC: DIC, 1987.

—**TROJAN HORSE** is a counterintelligence term used in the context of automatic data system security and refers to a situation in which an agent places a secret instruction in the software of a computer that is activated under special circumstances. Once a trojan horse is in place, it is likely to remain hidden from even the most skilled experts.

References

Blackburn, N. Glenn. "Computers: A Counterintelligence Concern." Unpublished paper provided to the editors. Washington, DC, 1987.

—**TRUJILLO, RAFAEL.** *See:* Dominican Republic.

—**TRUMAN, HARRY.** Presidential oversight has been a problem that has plagued all the postwar presidents. President Truman, possibly fearing the dangers of a centralized intelligence organization, disbanded the Office of Strategic Services in 1945 and placed its branches within the Departments of State and War. It was his hope that the Department of State would take the lead in centralized intelligence collection and production. When this did not occur, Truman favored the creation of the Central Intelligence Group, which later became the Central Intelligence Agency. He was instrumental in the passage of the National Security Act of 1947 and the CIA Act of 1949.

In terms of his choices for director of Central Intelligence (DCI), Truman's first two choices were individuals who were not assertive in Washington politics and may not really have wanted the job. However, his third DCI, Lieutenant General Hoyt Vandenberg, U.S. Air Force, was aggressive and dynamic. Under his leadership, the CIA expanded in size, mission, and power.

In the final analysis, Truman kept the embryonic central intelligence entity alive and permitted it to grow during his administration, thereby producing the basis on which Lieutenant General Walter Bedell Smith and others continued to build. *See also:* Presidential Oversight.

References

American Bar Association. *Oversight and Accountability of the U.S. Intelligence Agencies: An Evaluation.* Washington, DC: ABA, 1985.

Breckinridge, Scott D. *The CIA and the U.S. Intelligence System.* Boulder, CO: Westview Press, 1986.

Corson, William R. *The Armies of Ignorance: The Rise of the American Intelligence Empire.* New York: Dial Press, 1977.

Laqueur, Walter. *A World of Secrets.* New York: Basic Books, 1985.

Lefever, Ernest W., and Godson, Roy. *The CIA and the American Ethic: An Unfinished Debate.* Washington, DC: Ethics and Public Policy Center, Georgetown University, 1979.

Maurer, Alfred C.; Turnstall, Marion D.; and Keagle, James M. *Intelligence Policy and Process.* Boulder, CO: Westview Press, 1985.

Treverton, Gregory F. *Covert Action: The Limits of Intervention in the Postwar World.* New York: Basic Books, 1987.

—**TSEC NOMENCLATURE,** in communications security (COMSEC), refers to a system for identifying the type and purpose of COMSEC material over which the National Security Agency exercises configuration control. TSEC is an abbreviation for telecommunications security. *See also:* Communications Security.

References

Department of Defense, U.S. Army. *Counterintelligence.* Field Manual FM 34-60. Washington, DC: Headquarters, Department of the Army, 1985.

———. *Intelligence and Electronic Warfare Operations.* Field Manual FM 34-1. Washington, DC: Headquarters, Department of the Army, 1984.

———. *Military Intelligence Battalion (Combat Electronic Warfare Intelligence) (Division).* Field Manual FM 34-10. Washington, DC: Headquarters, Department of the Army, 1981.

—**TURNED** is an individual who is working for an intelligence organization and who has been persuaded to work for the other side. After he is persuaded, he is said to be "turned." *See also:* Blackmail, Cold Approach, Co-Opted Worker, Co-Optees, Cultivation, Defector, Disaffected Person, Double Agent, Honey Trap, Litmus Test, Special Activities, Swallow, Swallow's Nest.

References

American Bar Association. *Oversight and Accountability of the U.S. Intelligence Agencies: An Evaluation.* Washington, DC: ABA, 1985.

Becket, Henry S. A. *The Dictionary of Espionage: Spookspeak into English.* New York: Stein and Day, 1986.

Deacon, Richard. *Spyclopedia: An Encyclopedia of Spies, Secret Services, Operations, Jargon, and All Subjects Related to the World of Espionage.* London: Macdonald, 1987.

Maurer, Alfred C.; Turnstall, Marion D.; and Keagle, James M. *Intelligence Policy and Process.* Boulder, CO: Westview Press, 1985.

Quirk, John; Phillips, David; Cline, Ray; and Pforzheimer, Walter. *The Central Intelligence Agency: A Photographic History.* Guilford, CT: Foreign Intelligence Press, 1986.

—**TURNER, ADMIRAL STANSFIELD, U.S. NAVY,** was born on December 1, 1923, in Highland Park, Illinois. He attended Amherst College and later graduated from the U.S. Naval Academy in 1946. A Rhodes Scholar, he attended Oxford University. Highlights of his naval career include serving as director of the Systems Analysis Division, Office of the Chief of Naval Operations, in 1971 and 1972; president of the U.S. Naval War College from 1972 to 1974; commander of the U.S. Second Fleet from 1974 to 1975; and commander-in-chief of the Allied Forces Southern Europe from 1975 to 1977. He was promoted to vice admiral in 1972, and to admiral in 1975. He was appointed director of Central Intelligence by President Jimmy Carter on February 8, 1977. The appointment was confirmed by the Senate on February 24, and he was sworn in on March 9, 1977. He retired from active duty in the U.S. Navy on December 31, 1978, and from the directorship on January 20, 1981. As of 1990 he was employed as a private consultant and writer. *See also:* Central Intelligence Agency.

References

American Bar Association. *Oversight and Accountability of the U.S. Intelligence Agencies: An Evaluation.* Washington, DC: ABA, 1985.

Breckinridge, Scott D. *The CIA and the U.S. Intelligence System.* Boulder, CO: Westview Press, 1986.

Corson, William R. *The Armies of Ignorance: The Rise of the American Intelligence Empire.* New York: Dial Press, 1977.

Laqueur, Walter. *A World of Secrets.* New York: Basic Books, 1985.

Lowenthal, Mark M. *U.S. Intelligence: Evolution and Anatomy.* New York: Praeger, 1984.

Maurer, Alfred C.; Turnstall, Marion D.; and Keagle, James M. *Intelligence Policy and Process.* Boulder, CO: Westview Press, 1985.

Treverton, Gregory F. *Covert Action: The Limits of Intervention in the Postwar World.* New York: Basic Books, 1987.

Von Hoene, John P. A. *Intelligence User's Guide.* Washington, DC: DIA, 1983.

—**TWO-PART CODE,** in communications security (COMSEC), is a code consisting of two sections or parts: an encoding section in which the vo-cabulary items are arranged in alphabetical or other systematic order accompanied by their code equivalents; and a decoding section in which the code groups are arranged in alphabetical or numerical order and are accompanied by their plain-text meanings. *See also:* Communications Security.

References

Department of Defense, U.S. Army. *Counterintelligence.* Field Manual FM 34-60. Washington, DC: Headquarters, Department of the Army, 1985.

———. *Intelligence and Electronic Warfare Operations.* Field Manual FM 34-1. Washington, DC: Headquarters, Department of the Army, 1984.

———. *Military Intelligence Battalion (Combat Electronic Warfare Intelligence) (Division).* Field Manual FM 34-10. Washington, DC: Headquarters, Department of the Army, 1981.

—**TWO-PERSON CONTROL,** in communications security (COMSEC), means the continuous close surveillance and control of certain COMSEC materials by at least two appropriately cleared and authorized individuals, each (all) of whom have been trained to be able to detect incorrect and unauthorized procedures concerning the tasks to be performed and with the established security requirements. *See also:* Access, Authorized, Classification, Code Word, Compromise, Declassification, Disclosure, Downgrade, Freedom of Information Act, Limited Access Area, Need-to-Know, Need-to-Know Principle, No-Lone Zone, Nondisclosure Agreement, Nondiscussion Area, Sanitization, Sanitize, Sanitized Area, Security Certification, Security Classification, Sensitive Compartmented Information, Sensitive Compartmented Information Facility, Two-Person Control.

References

Department of Defense, U.S. Army. *Counterintelligence.* Field Manual FM 34-60. Washington, DC: Headquarters, Department of the Army, 1985.

—**TWO-WAY RADIO LINK,** in FBI terminology, is the transmission of radio messages between intelligence officers and their command centers.

References

Kessler, Ronald. *Spy vs. Spy: Stalking Soviet Spies in America.* New York: Charles Scribner's Sons, 1988.

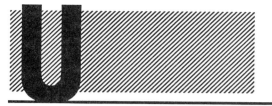

—U-2 OVERHEAD RECONNAISSANCE PROGRAM AND U-2 SPY PLANE.

In the post-World War II period, it became apparent that modern airborne reconnaissance systems would greatly enhance U.S. intelligence collection of Soviet military activities. In 1953, the Central Intelligence Agency began to develop new cameras and film of unprecedented quality. Concurrently, the "Skunk Works" designed and produced the U-2 aircraft. The U-2 first flew in 1955 and was first used for operational flights over the Soviet Union in 1956. Initially, President Eisenhower had doubts about the plane's invulnerability and would have preferred a single massive one-time penetration of Soviet airspace by several U-2 aircraft. However, he demurred and individual flights were made over the Soviet Union in a highly successful program that ran until 1960, when the plane piloted by Francis Gary Powers was shot down over Soviet airspace. Follow-on programs were begun in anticipation of the U-2's obsolescence. The two most important were the SR-71 aircraft and the satellite reconnaissance program. The capture of Powers did create a short hiatus in U.S. collection over the Soviet Union until the reconnaissance satellites became operational in 1961. The SR-71 "Blackbird" has been a highly successful reconnaissance vehicle.

References

American Bar Association. *Oversight and Accountability of the U.S. Intelligence Agencies: An Evaluation.* Washington, ABA, 1985.

Breckinridge, Scott D. *The CIA and the U.S. Intelligence System.* Boulder, CO: Westview Press, 1986.

Godson, Roy, ed. *Intelligence Problems for the 1980s, Number 1: Elements of Intelligence.* Rev. ed. Washington, DC: National Strategy Information Center, 1983.

———. *Intelligence Problems for the 1980s, Number 5: Clandestine Collection.* Washington, DC: National Strategy Information Center, 1982.

Laqueur, Walter. *A World of Secrets.* New York: Basic Books, 1985.

Maurer, Alfred C.; Turnstall, Marion D.; and Keagle, James M. *Intelligence Policy and Process.* Boulder, CO: Westview Press, 1985.

Treverton, Gregory F. *Covert Action: The Limits of Intervention in the Postwar World.* New York: Basic Books, 1987.

Turner, Stansfield. *Secrecy and Democracy: The CIA in Transition.* Boston: Houghton Mifflin, 1985.

—ULTRA

was the code word for the Allied program that involved transmission intercepts of German traffic during World War II. During the war the Germans used the Enigma machine, a battery-powered electromechanical cipher device that had three wheels and permitted 1,560,000 permutations for each character. A plug-board further scrambled each character, and the message keys were changed every 24 hours. Early in the war, Enigma was broken by British cryptanalysts, who built upon the work of Polish and French analysts. The Ultra traffic, intercepts of high-level German military communications, was of inestimable value during the war. *See also:* Donovan, William; Office of Strategic Services.

References

Finnegan, John P. *Military Intelligence: A Picture History.* Arlington, VA: U.S. Army Intelligence and Security Command, 1984.

Godson, Roy, ed. *Intelligence Problems for the 1980s, Number 5: Clandestine Collection.* Washington, DC: National Strategy Information Center, 1982.

Laqueur, Walter. *A World of Secrets.* New York: Basic Books, 1985.

Lowenthal, Mark M. *U.S. Intelligence: Evolution and Anatomy.* New York: Praeger, 1984.

Maurer, Alfred C.; Turnstall, Marion D.; and Keagle, James M. *Intelligence Policy and Process.* Boulder, CO: Westview Press, 1985.

—UNAUTHORIZED DISCLOSURE. *See:* Compromise.

—UNAUTHORIZED INDIVIDUAL

is an intelligence security and counterintelligence term. He or she is a person who is not authorized to have access to classified information. *See also:* Access, Authorized, Classification, Classified Information.

References

Department of Defense, Defense Intelligence College. *Glossary of Intelligence Terms and Definitions.* Washington, DC: DIC, 1987.

Department of Defense, Joint Chiefs of Staff. *Department of Defense Dictionary of Military and Related Terms.* Washington, DC: GPO, 1986.

—**UNCLASSIFIED MATTER** is official material that does not require security safeguards, but the disclosure of which may be controlled for other reasons. *See also:* Classification, Classified Information.

References

Department of Defense, Joint Chiefs of Staff. *Department of Defense Dictionary of Military and Related Terms.* Washington, DC: GPO, 1986.

Godson, Roy, ed. *Intelligence Problems for the 1980s, Number 1: Elements of Intelligence.* Rev. ed. Washington, DC: National Strategy Information Center, 1983.

Maurer, Alfred C.; Turnstall, Marion D.; and Keagle, James M. *Intelligence Policy and Process.* Boulder, CO: Westview Press, 1985.

—**UNCONVENTIONAL WARFARE** involves a broad spectrum of military and paramilitary operations that are conducted in enemy-held, enemy-controlled, or politically sensitive territory. Unconventional warfare includes, but is not limited to, the interrelated fields of guerrilla warfare, evasion and escape, subversion, sabotage, and other operations of a low visibility, covert, or clandestine nature. These interrelated aspects of unconventional warfare may be prosecuted singly or collectively by predominantly indigenous personnel, usually supported and directed in varying degrees by an external source during all conditions of war and peace. *See also:* Guerrilla Operations, Guerrilla Warfare, Guerrillas, Low Intensity Conflict.

References

Department of Defense, Joint Chiefs of Staff. *Department of Defense Dictionary of Military and Related Terms.* Washington, DC: GPO, 1986.

Laqueur, Walter. *A World of Secrets.* New York: Basic Books, 1985.

Treverton, Gregory F. *Covert Action: The Limits of Intervention in the Postwar World.* New York: Basic Books, 1987.

—**UNCONVENTIONAL WARFARE FORCES** are United States military forces that have an existing unconventional warfare capability and consist of Army Special Forces and such Navy, Air Force, and Marine units as are assigned to these operations. *See also:* Unconventional Warfare.

References

Department of Defense, Joint Chiefs of Staff. *Department of Defense Dictionary of Military and Related Terms.* Washington, DC: GPO, 1986.

Treverton, Gregory F. *Covert Action: The Limits of Intervention in the Postwar World.* New York: Basic Books, 1987.

—**UNDERWATER DEMOLITION TEAM (UDT),** in naval operations, is a group of officers and men who have been specially trained and equipped for making hydrographic reconnaissance of approaches to prospective amphibious landing beaches, for demolishing obstacles, and for clearing mines, marking channels, and performing other underwater and surface tasks.

References

Department of Defense, Joint Chiefs of Staff. *Department of Defense Dictionary of Military and Related Terms.* Washington, DC: GPO, 1986.

—**UNEVALUATED INFORMATION** is a generic team for raw data, information that has been collected but has not been processed into intelligence. Because it has not been processed, it still lacks an assessment as to its accuracy and reliability. *See also:* Intelligence Cycle.

References

Department of Defense, Defense Intelligence College. *Glossary of Intelligence Terms and Definitions.* Washington, DC: DIC, 1987.

Godson, Roy, ed. *Intelligence Problems for the 1980s, Number 1: Elements of Intelligence.* Rev. ed. Washington, DC: National Strategy Information Center, 1983.

Maurer, Alfred C.; Turnstall, Marion D.; and Keagle, James M. *Intelligence Policy and Process.* Boulder, CO: Westview Press, 1985.

Treverton, Gregory F. *Covert Action: The Limits of Intervention in the Postwar World.* New York: Basic Books, 1987.

—**UNIFIED COMMAND** is one with a broad continuing mission under a single commander and composed of significant assigned components of two or more services. The Unified and Specified Commands are force packages that are to be employed in military operations. The operational chain of command proceeds from the president to the secretary of defense to the chairman of the Joint Chiefs of Staff to the Unified and Specified Commands to their component commands. This concept is difficult for many to understand, because the popular belief is that the services control and command their own forces and commands. The services do in terms of administration and maintenance, but do not in terms of operational employment. Rather, the above-described chain of command prevails.

The Unified and Specified Command concept emerged in the years following World War II, as the United States realized that the nature of warfare had progressed beyond theater warfare, where the several military forces could operate in isolation. Rather, the development of modern weapons meant that warfare in one theater could affect drastically the events in another theater. Now, it was realized, what was needed was the combined arms package that could provide adequate coordination among the several forces operating in a given region. The Unified and Specified Command approach was the response to this problem. The Unified Commands are:

U.S. Atlantic Command (USLANTCOM) defends the eastern approaches to the United States and the sea lines of communication in the Atlantic area. CINCLANT is also SACLANT, a major NATO commander.

U.S. Southern Command (USSOUTHCOM) defends the Panama Canal and fulfills U.S. military responsibilities throughout the Latin American region.

U.S. European Command (USEUCOM) is responsible for the U.S. contribution to NATO and for commanding U.S. forces assigned to Europe. Its area of responsibility also includes the Middle East and the African states bordering on the Mediterranean. CINCEUR is also SACEUR, a major NATO commander, and as such is responsible for Allied Command Europe.

U.S. Pacific Command (USPACOM) is responsible for the defense of the United States from attack in the Pacific, and for U.S. defense interests in the Pacific and Indian Ocean area.

U.S. Central Command (USCENTCOM) is responsible primarily for the Southwest Asia area for the conduct of operational planning for contingencies.

U.S. Special Operations Command (USSOCOM) is responsible for providing combat-ready special operations forces for rapid deployment to the other unified commands.

U.S. Space Command (USSPACECOM) is responsible for space control, directing space support operations for assigned systems, and operating Joint Chiefs of Staff-designated space systems in support of the National Command Authorities, the Joint Chiefs of Staff, and other unified and specified commands.

U.S. Transportation Command (USTRANSCOM) is responsible for providing common-user airlift, sealift, terminal services, and U.S. commercial air and land transportation to deploy, employ, and sustain U.S. forces worldwide.

Where the United States has no significant forces assigned, unified operations, if required, would be conducted by deploying a joint task force headquarters to provide the necessary command and control. *See also:* Specified Command.

References

Department of Defense, Joint Chiefs of Staff. *Department of Defense Dictionary of Military and Related Terms.* Washington, DC: GPO, 1986.

"The Unified and Specified Commands." *Defense 87* (Nov.-Dec. 1987): 2-58.

—**UNILATERAL** is a term used in clandestine and covert intelligence operations. It is a CIA agent who operates in a foreign country without overt ties to the agency or the embassy. His cover is constructed so that he can be officially disavowed if his operation fails. *See also:* Agent, Illegal Agent, Singleton.

References

Becket, Henry S. A. *The Dictionary of Espionage: Spookspeak into English.* New York: Stein and Day, 1986.

Ranelagh, John. *The Agency: The Rise and Decline of the CIA.* New York: Simon and Schuster, 1986.

—**UNI-LEVEL SECURITY** concerns automatic data processing systems. It provides for safeguarding the information within a single information handling system by protecting the highest level of classification of the material in the system. It assigns the most restrictive dissemination caveats and instructions to all the material in the system, and is therefore different from a system that has multi-level security. *See also:* Multilevel Security.

References

Department of Defense, Defense Intelligence College. *Glossary of Intelligence Terms and Definitions.* Washington, DC: DIC, 1987.

—**UNIQUE VARIABLE (UV),** in communications security (COMSEC), means a rekeying variable that is held by only one crypto-equipment and its associated key distribution center.

References

Department of Defense, U.S. Army. *Counterintelligence*. Field Manual FM 34-60. Washington, DC: Headquarters, Department of the Army, 1985.

—**UNITED STATES.** A definition of United States was provided in the Department of Defense implementation of Presidential Executive Order 12333, "United States Intelligence Activities," dated December 4, 1981, which defined the types of intelligence activities that could be conducted by U.S. intelligence activities against U.S. citizens. It stated that the United States, when used to describe a place, shall include the territories under the sovereignty of the United States.

References

Corson, William R. *The Armies of Ignorance: The Rise of the American Intelligence Empire*. New York: Dial Press, 1977.

Department of Defense. *Activities of DoD Intelligence Components that Affect U.S. Persons (Department of Defense Directive 5240.1)*. Washington, DC: DoD, 1982.

—**U.S. ARMY COUNTERINTELLIGENCE CORPS** (CIC) replaced the Corps of Intelligence Police at the beginning of 1942. The CIC was larger and had a more centralized organization and its own chief and school. Its mission was to recruit and train Army counterintelligence personnel. The local G-2s still supervised local CIC operations, and the corps conducted investigations in the United States and furnished tactical detachments to the field forces. Criticism of some of CIC's activities led to its assimilation into the short-lived Security Intelligence Corps, but its overseas units continued to function. The CIC became independent once more at the end of World War II.

References

Finnegan, John P. *Military Intelligence: A Picture History*. Arlington, VA: U.S. Army Intelligence and Security Command, 1984.

Lefever, Ernest W., and Godson, Roy. *The CIA and the American Ethic: An Unfinished Debate*. Washington, DC: Ethics and Public Policy Center, Georgetown University, 1979.

—**U.S. ARMY DOMESTIC INTELLIGENCE OPERATIONS.** During the upheavals of the 1960s, the Army was directed to increase its surveillance of dissident groups. The Army responded by establishing files on several groups and by harassing some of them. The program was terminated in 1970. *See also:* Domestic Activities, Domestic Collection, Domestic Contacts Division, Domestic Contacts Service, Domestic Intelligence.

References

Breckinridge, Scott D. *The CIA and the U.S. Intelligence System*. Boulder, CO: Westview Press, 1986.

—**U.S. ARMY INTELLIGENCE** provides intelligence to the U.S. Army and to the Department of Defense. In this capacity, it "is responsible for collecting, producing and disseminating military and military-related foreign intelligence, including intelligence on indications and warning, capabilities, weapons, and equipment; conducts counterintelligence operations and produces and disseminates counterintelligence reports; and develops, buys and manages tactical intelligence systems and equipment."

The major components of Army Intelligence are the Army Intelligence and Security Command (INSCOM), which performs the necessary signals intelligence, human intelligence, and counterintelligence functions, and the Army Intelligence Agency (AIA). In addition to its headquarters staff, the AIA is composed of the Missile and Space Intelligence Center, located at Redstone Arsenal, Huntsville, Alabama, the Intelligence Threat and Analysis Center, located in the Washington Navy Yard, Washington, DC, and the Foreign Science and Technology Center, located in Charlottesville, Virginia. *See also:* Army Intelligence Agency, Army Intelligence and Security Command, Counterintelligence, Foreign Science and Technology Center, Human Intelligence, Intelligence Threat and Analysis Center.

References

Kent, Sherman. *Strategic Intelligence for American World Policy*. Princeton, NJ: Princeton University Press, 1966.

Laqueur, Walter. *A World of Secrets*. New York: Basic Books, 1985.

Lefever, Ernest W., and Godson, Roy. *The CIA and the American Ethic: An Unfinished Debate*. Washington, DC: Ethics and Public Policy Center, Georgetown University, 1979.

Treverton, Gregory F. *Covert Action: The Limits of Intervention in the Postwar World*. New York: Basic Books, 1987.

—U.S. ARMY INTELLIGENCE AGENCY (USAINTA) was responsible for the Army's counterintelligence program until 1975, when USAINTA was merged with other U.S. Army elements to form the U.S. Army Intelligence and Security Command (INSCOM). It was reactivated in 1985 as the Army Intelligence Agency (AIA). Presently composed of the Intelligence and Threat Analysis Center, the Foreign Science and Technology Center, and the Missile and Space Intelligence Center, it provides intelligence users with short- to long-range scientific and technological as well as general military intelligence assessments. Serving tactical and strategic planners, policy-makers, and weapons developers, the AIA's all-source analysis is significant in U.S. force modernization, operational planning, materiel acquisition, weapons modeling, strategic space systems, technology transfer, arms control, and operations security.

References

Breckinridge, Scott D. *The CIA and the U.S. Intelligence System.* Boulder, CO: Westview Press, 1986.

Department of Defense, U.S. Army. *AIA: Threat Analysis.* Falls Church, VA: AIA, 1987.

Finnegan, John P. *Military Intelligence: A Picture History.* Arlington, VA: U.S. Army Intelligence and Security Command, 1984.

—U.S. ARMY INTELLIGENCE AND SECURITY COMMAND (INSCOM) was created on January 1, 1977, as the result of a reorganization that was intended to improve the Army's intelligence activities. It combined certain elements of the Army Security Agency, the U.S. Army Intelligence Agency, the U.S. Army Forces Command, and the assistant chief of staff, Department of the Army.

INSCOM is a major Army command. Its mission is to accomplish intelligence, security, and electronic warfare operations for Army echelons above the corps level. It produces Army-level general intelligence and threat analysis, and it monitors intelligence and threat production by other Army elements. It is also tasked with responding to actions from the Department of the Army. INSCOM has more than 16,000 military and civilian employees.

INSCOM has three basic types of units. Its *field stations* are part of the worldwide U.S. communications network and provide rapid relay and secure communications; its *single disciplinary military intelligence units* provide intelligence and security support to the Army; and the *multidiscipline military intelligence units* provide security support to deployable and deployed Army forces and have resources such as counterintelligence, operations security support, and signals security support units.

In addition, INSCOM has several unique units. Its Army Russian Institute in Garmisch, Federal Republic of Germany, provides the Army with Russian area specialists. The institute's program includes Soviet area studies, travel in the Soviet Union, and two years of advanced Russian language training. INSCOM's Central Security Facility, located at Fort George Meade, Maryland, provides information to more than 400 requesters worldwide, including the Defense Investigative Service. The facility also processes requests that are submitted under the Freedom of Information Act. Finally, the command's Special Security Group, headquartered at Arlington Hall Station, Virginia, provides the secure means to disseminate sensitive compartmented information to Army organizations.

INSCOM is currently headquartered at Arlington Hall Station, Virginia, and at Fort George Meade, Maryland, with field stations in Germany, Japan, Korea, Panama, Turkey, and the United States, and military intelligence units in Panama, Korea, Germany, Japan, and the United States.

References

Department of Defense, U.S. Army. *INSCOM: United States Army Intelligence and Security Command.* Arlington Hall Station, VA: Public Affairs Office, U.S. Army Intelligence and Security Command, 1985.

———. *RDTE Managers Intelligence and Threat Support Guide.* Alexandria, VA: Headquarters, Army Materiel Development and Readiness Command, 1983.

—U.S. ARMY INTELLIGENCE AND THREAT CENTER (ITAC). ITAC was created in 1977 as the merger of six independent Army intelligence organizations. A further consolidation occurred in 1985, when ITAC was joined with the Foreign Science and Technology Center and the Missile and Space Intelligence Center to form the Army Intelligence Agency.

ITAC's mission is to provide the Department of the Army and the Department of Defense with comprehensive general intelligence and counterintelligence analysis and production reflecting the capabilities, vulnerabilities, and current and future threats to the Army from foreign military and security forces. In accomplishing its mission, ITAC produces studies that analyze the military capabilities of foreign forces against conventional and unconventional attack, project hostile capabilities in certain geographic areas, and assess the political and military environments that can influence Army force and operations planning.

ITAC is composed of a command element (with the Command Office, a Special Security detachment, a Special Research detachment, an administrative office, and management office), and six divisions. The names and purposes of these divisions are as follows:

The Automated Services Division provides automation and operations research analytical support. It establishes and administers all ITAC computer systems and oversees the design, development, and use of the Automated Threat Intelligence Production System (ATIPS).

The Counterintelligence and Terrorism Division collates, analyzes, and evaluates information of counterintelligence significance and prepares estimates and studies of foreign intelligence services and international terrorist activities. It supports the U.S. Army Subversion and Espionage Directed Against the U.S. Army (SAEDA) and Operational Security (OPSEC) programs through studies and analyses of the multidiscipline threats that are posed by foreign intelligence services. It supports contingency planning and major exercises through hostile intelligence threat assessments. The division provides assessments in support of the Army's technology transfer control program. It also monitors the internal security situation of key countries and gives spot security evaluations to high-level Army travelers prior to their departure overseas.

The Imagery Division produces detailed imagery exploitation reports and keys on foreign ground forces equipment and weaponry and responds to imagery-exploitation support requirements from the Department of the Army, Department of Defense, and other agencies. Exploitation and retasking of targets of Army interest is performed daily. Many capabilities of weapon systems can be deduced from the imagery analysis and mensuration provided by division analysts. Imagery reports are produced for users at all levels in addition to supporting projects for other ITAC divisions and Army Intelligence Agency centers. This information supplies imagery-de-

rived intelligence to contingency forces in times of crisis.

The Regional Division conducts research and analysis on assigned areas of the world where U.S. forces may be employed, and produces short-, mid-, and long-range forecasts and assessments of these areas. These studies cover military capabilities as well as the political, economic, demographic, sociological, cultural, and geographic aspects of certain countries. For example, long-range planning estimates are made to determine U.S. strategic requirements and to develop and prioritize force capabilities and structures. Additionally, this division participates in the Department of Defense-delegated production programs for ground order of battle and associated installations. In this capacity, it has a major input into the DIA ground order of battle estimates.

The Warsaw Pact Division conducts research and analysis of Soviet and Warsaw Pact forces, tactics, operations, and materiel. It produces short-, mid-, and long-range forecasts of Warsaw Pact organization tactics, operational art, and strategy. Projections are made as far as twenty years into the future to assess the threats the Army may encounter. When considering the cost of major Army materiel development systems, it is essential that they not become prematurely obsolete through corresponding enemy countermeasures that could have been forecast.

The Special Research Detachment is collocated with the National Security Agency at Fort Meade, Maryland. It is responsible for all-source, SIGINT-intensive research, analysis, and production on the Warsaw Pact, Latin American, and Middle Eastern countries. The detachment focuses on specific intelligence issues dealing with current and near-term national security questions. It also provides direct support to other ITAC divisions when required and provides analytical assistance for high interest study task forces.

The Production Support Division provides editorial, graphic, photographic, audiovisual, printing, and research support.

References

Department of Defense, U.S. Army. *United States Army Intelligence and Threat Analysis Center.* Washington, DC: USAITC, 1987.

—**U.S. ARMY INTELLIGENCE CENTER AND SCHOOL (USAICS)** is located at Fort Huachuca, Arizona. The school offers a plethora of courses in intelligence collection, counterintelligence, intelligence and imagery analysis, terrorism, interrogation, and all-source intelligence. The school is located in one of the most beautiful areas of the United States, and its facilities and staff are impressive.

References

Defense Intelligence Agency. *Training Compendium for General Defense Career Development Program (IDCP) Personnel DOD 1430.10M3-TNG.* Washington, DC: DIA, 1986.

—**U.S. ARMY INTELLIGENCE COMMAND (USAINTC)** was established in 1965 and took control of the seven counterintelligence groups in the continental United States. As a result of the significant disturbances in U.S. cities in the 1960s, USAINTC became deeply involved in domestic intelligence collection operations. When the command's role was revealed in the early 1970s, there was a significant public reaction. USAINTC's responsibilities concerning conducting background investigations of prospective government intelligence employees were given to the newly formed Defense Intelligence Service. Since these duties accounted for about 90 percent of the command's workload, it ceased to have a mission. It was finally discontinued in 1974 and was replaced by the U.S. Army Intelligence Agency (USAINTA).

References

Finnegan, John P. *Military Intelligence: A Picture History.* Arlington, VA: U.S. Army Intelligence and Security Command, 1984.

—**U.S. ARMY SECURITY AGENCY (ASA),** as one of the Service Cryptologic Agencies, collected information under the direction of the director of the National Security Agency in his dual role as chief of the Central Security Service (CSS). It was created on September 15, 1945, to "exercise command over all signals intelligence and communications security establishments, units, and personnel of the U.S. Army," and later became part of INSCOM. Operating under the command of the director of intelligence (a former title of the Army's deputy chief of staff for intelligence), the agency replaced the Signal Security Agency. In addition, it absorbed the theater and Army commanders' COMINT and COMSEC detachments. In 1948 and 1949, the ASA was partially dismantled, with some of its

responsibilities going to the newly established Air Force Security Service. Then, many of its most important functions were transferred to a new joint-service organization, the Armed Forces Security Agency, which later evolved into the National Security Agency. *See also:* Armed Forces Security Agency.

References

Lefever, Ernest W., and Godson, Roy. *The CIA and the American Ethic: An Unfinished Debate.* Washington, DC: Ethics and Public Policy Center, Georgetown University, 1979.

Finnegan, John P. *Military Intelligence: A Picture History.* Arlington, VA: U.S. Army Intelligence and Security Command, 1984.

Quirk, John; Phillips David; Cline, Ray; and Pforzheimer, Walter. *The Central Intelligence Agency: A Photographic History.* Guilford, CT: Foreign Intelligence Press, 1986.

—**U.S. ARMY WAR COLLEGE (AWC),** located at Carlisle Barracks, Pennsylvania, offers a 44-week course of instruction for military officers of the ranks of O5 and O6 and civilians of equivalent rank. The course is intended to prepare the student for senior command and staff positions in the Army and the Department of Defense, and to promote an understanding of the art and science of land warfare. It includes an examination of the national and international environment, national security policy formulation, and the decisionmaking process within the Department of Defense; a detailed study of land warfare to include the historical aspects of warfare, development of U.S. military strategy, force planning and structuring, command, management, and employment of Army forces, and future considerations for the conduct of land battle.

References

Defense Intelligence Agency. *Training Compendium for General Defense Career Development Program (IDCP) Personnel DOD 1430.10M3-TNG.* Washington, DC: DIA, 1986.

Lefever, Ernest W., and Godson, Roy. *The CIA and the American Ethic: An Unfinished Debate.* Washington, DC: Ethics and Public Policy Center, Georgetown University, 1979.

—**U.S. COMMUNICATIONS INTELLIGENCE BOARD (USCIB)** was created in 1946 and was continued until 1958, when it was merged with the U.S. Intelligence Board. It was a senior level

Intelligence Community advisory group, composed of representatives from the Army, Navy, Air Force, Federal Bureau of Investigation, State Department, and Central Intelligence Group, that made recommendations on communications intelligence operations to the secretary of defense. *See also:* U.S. Intelligence Board.

References

Bamford, James. *The Puzzle Palace: A Report on America's Most Secret Agency.* New York: Penguin Books, 1983.

Fain, Tyrus G.; Plant, Katharine C.; and Milloy, Ross. *The Intelligence Community: History, Organization, and Issues.* Public Documents Series. New York: R.R. Bowker, 1977.

—**UNITED STATES COUNTRY TEAM,** as described by the Church Committee, "is the senior, in-country, United States coordinating and supervising body. It is headed by the Chief of the United States diplomatic mission (usually an ambassador) and is composed of the senior member of each represented United States department or agency." *See also:* Defense Attaché System.

References

U.S. Congress. Senate. *Final Report of the Senate Select Committee to Study Government Operations with Respect to Intelligence Activities. Report 94-755. Book I, Foreign and Military Intelligence.* Washington, DC: GPO, 1976.

—**U.S. FOREIGN INTELLIGENCE ACTIVITIES.** *See:* Executive Order 11905.

—**U.S. INTELLIGENCE BOARD (USIB)** existed from 1958 until 1976 and was responsible for coordinating and managing intelligence among the various agencies. According to the Church Committee, until its abolition in Executive Order 11905 of February 18, 1976, the USIB was the National Security Council's central coordinating committee for the Intelligence Community.

References

American Bar Association. *Oversight and Accountability of the U.S. Intelligence Agencies: An Evaluation.* Washington, DC: ABA, 1985.

Corson, William R. *The Armies of Ignorance: The Rise of the American Intelligence Empire.* New York: Dial Press, 1977.

Fain, Tyrus G.; Plant, Katharine C.; and Milloy, Ross. *The Intelligence Community: History, Organization, and Issues.* Public Documents Series. New York: R.R. Bowker, 1977.

Laqueur, Walter. *A World of Secrets.* New York: Basic Books, 1985.

Lowenthal, Mark M. *U.S. Intelligence: Evolution and Anatomy.* New York: Praeger, 1984.

Maurer, Alfred C.; Turnstall, Marion D.; and Keagle, James M. *Intelligence Policy and Process.* Boulder, CO: Westview Press, 1985.

Treverton, Gregory F. *Covert Action: The Limits of Intervention in the Postwar World.* New York: Basic Books, 1987.

U.S. Congress. Senate. *Final Report of the Senate Select Committee to Study Government Operations with Respect to Intelligence Activities. Report 94-755. Book I, Foreign and Military Intelligence.* Washington, DC: GPO, 1976.

—**UNITED STATES PERSON** is a citizen of the United States, an alien known by the intelligence agency concerned to be a permanent resident alien, an unincorporated association organized in the United States or substantially composed of U.S. citizens or permanent resident aliens, or a corporation incorporated in the United States, except for a corporation directed or controlled by a foreign government or governments. *See also:* Bug, Bugging, Movements Analysis, Pavement Artists, Shadow, Shaking Off the Dogs, Surround, Surveillance.

References

American Bar Association. *Oversight and Accountability of the U.S. Intelligence Agencies: An Evaluation.* Washington, DC: ABA, 1985.

Kornblum, Allan. *Intelligence and the Law: Cases and Materials.* Vol. IV. Washington, DC: DIC, 1987.

Maurer, Alfred C.; Turnstall, Marion D.; and Keagle, James M. *Intelligence Policy and Process.* Boulder, CO: Westview Press, 1985.

Oseth, John M. *Regulating U.S. Intelligence Operations: A Study in the Definition of the National Interest.* Frankfurt: University of Kentucky Press, 1985.

Turner, Stansfield. *Secrecy and Democracy: The CIA in Transition.* Boston: Houghton Mifflin, 1985.

U.S. Government, Department of Defense. *Activities of DoD Intelligence Components that Affect U.S. Persons (Department of Defense Directive 5240.1).* Washington, DC: DoD, 1982.

—**UNITED STATES PERSON-INFORMATION THAT MAY BE COLLECTED ABOUT.** In the Department of Defense enactment of the guidance provided by Presidential Executive Order

12333, "United States Intelligence Activities," dated December 4, 1981, the deputy director of defense stated that information that identifies a United States person may be collected by a Department of Defense intelligence component only if it is necessary to the conduct of a function assigned the collecting component, and only if it falls within one of the following categories:

Information obtained with consent. Information may be collected about a U.S. person who consents to such collection.

Publicly available information. Information may be collected about a United States person if it is publicly available.

Foreign intelligence. Subject to the special limitation contained in (5) below, information may be collected about a United States person if the information constitutes foreign intelligence, provided the intentional collection of foreign intelligence about the United States persons shall be limited to persons who are: (1) individuals reasonably believed to be foreign officers or employees, or otherwise acting on behalf, of a foreign power; (2) an organization reasonably believed to be owned or controlled, directly or indirectly, by a foreign power; (3) persons or organizations reasonably believed to be engaged or about to engage, in international terrorist or international narcotics activities; (4) persons who are reasonably believed to be prisoners of war; missing in action; or are the targets, the hostages, or victims of international terrorist organizations; or (5) corporations or other commercial organizations believed to have some relationship with foreign powers, organizations, or persons.

Counterintelligence. Information may be collected about a United States person if the information constitutes counterintelligence, provided that the intentional collection of counterintelligence about the United States persons must be limited to: (1) persons who are reasonably believed to be engaged in, or about to engage in, intelligence activities on behalf of a foreign power, or international terrorist activities; or (2) persons in contact with persons described above, for the purpose of identifying such person and assessing their relationship with persons described above.

Potential sources of assistance to intelligence activities. Information may be collected about United States persons reasonably believed to be potential sources of intelligence, or potential sources of assistance to intelligence activities, for the purpose of assessing their suitability or credi-

bility. This category does not include investigations undertaken for personnel security purposes.

Protection of intelligence sources and methods. Information may be collected about a United States person who has access to, had access to, or is otherwise in possession of, information that reveals foreign intelligence and counterintelligence sources and methods, when collection is reasonably believed to protect against the unauthorized disclosure of such information; provided that within the United States, intentional collection of such information shall be limited to persons who are: (1) present and former DoD employees; (2) present or former employees of a present or former DoD contractor; and (3) applicants for employment at DoD or at a contractor of DoD.

Physical security. Information may be collected about a United States person who is reasonably believed to threaten the physical security of DoD employees, installations, operations, or official visitors. Information may also be collected in the course of a lawful physical security investigation.

Personnel security. Information may be collected about a United States person that arises out of a lawful personnel security investigation.

Communications security. Information may be collected about a United States person that arises out of a lawful communications security investigation.

Narcotics. Information may be collected about a United States person who is reasonably believed to be engaged in international narcotics activities.

Threats to security. Information may be collected about a United States person when the information is needed to protect the safety of any person or organization, including those who are targets, victims, or hostages of international terrorist organizations.

Overhead reconnaissance. Information may be collected from overhead reconnaissance not directed at specific United States persons.

Administrative purposes. Information may be collected about a United States person that is necessary for administrative purposes. *See also:* United States Person.

References

American Bar Association. *Oversight and Accountability of the U.S. Intelligence Agencies: An Evaluation.* Washington, DC: ABA, 1985.

Department of Defense. *Activities of DoD Intelligence Components that Affect U.S. Persons*

(Department of Defense Directive 5240.1). Washington, DC: DoD, 1982.

Godson, Roy, ed. *Intelligence Problems for the 1980s, Number 1: Elements of Intelligence.* Rev. ed. Washington, DC: National Strategy Information Center, 1983.

Kornblum, Allan. *Intelligence and the Law: Cases and Materials.* Vol. IV. Washington, DC: DIC, 1987.

Maurer, Alfred C.; Turnstall, Marion D.; and Keagle, James M. *Intelligence Policy and Process.* Boulder, CO: Westview Press, 1985.

Oseth, John M. *Regulating U.S. Intelligence Operations: A Study in the Definition of the National Interest.* Frankfurt: University of Kentucky Press, 1985.

Turner, Stansfield. *Secrecy and Democracy: The CIA in Transition.* Boston: Houghton Mifflin, 1985.

—USS *LIBERTY,* a naval ship that was designed for intelligence collection operations, was attacked deliberately by Israeli naval ships and aircraft as she operated in international waters off the coast of the Middle East in 1967. The *Liberty* was attacked continuously until Israeli forces were certain that they had destroyed the ship's ability to communicate. Israeli forces then offered assistance to the ship. By this time, several members of the crew had been killed and several more were wounded. Israel subsequently apologized and the United States, for political reasons, did not make an issue of the incident. Rather it accepted Israel's position that it had attacked the ship by mistake.

The question of why the Israelis attacked the ship remains unanswered. One reason that has been given is that Israel did not want the United States to know that it was succeeding as well as it was on the Sinai during the June 1967 war, lest the United States attempt to compel Israel to cease operations before it had captured Jerusalem and its objectives on the Golan Heights.

The attack on the *Liberty* and the seizure of another ship, the *Pueblo,* by North Korea in 1968 prompted the United States to conduct subsequent intelligence gathering activities from armed ships, so that incidents like the *Liberty* and *Pueblo* would not recur. *See also:* USS *Pueblo.*

References

Watson, Bruce W. *Red Navy at Sea: Soviet Naval Operations on the High Seas, 1956-1980.* Boulder, CO: Westview Press, 1986.

Watson, Bruce W., and Watson, Susan M., eds. *The Soviet Navy: Strengths and Liabilities.* Boulder, CO: Westview Press, 1986.

—USS *PUEBLO,* under the command of Commander Lloyd Bucher, U.S. Navy, was seized by North Korean ships while conducting intelligence collection operations in international waters in 1968. The ship was escorted to a North Korean port, where all equipment and intelligence materials were examined by both North Korean and Soviet intelligence. This, in itself, was a major catastrophe for the Intelligence Community in that it provided the Koreans and Soviets with valuable knowledge concerning the state of U.S. intelligence collection. Additionally, the publications and instructions that were seized provided detailed information on U.S. intelligence collection programs and procedures.

The crew of the *Pueblo* was held for a prolonged period by the North Koreans in what became a political exercise of the first order. After extended negotiations, the crew was returned. The seizure of the *Pueblo* and the premeditated Israeli attack on the *Liberty* a year before convinced the United States that such intelligence collection operations from unarmed ships was simply too risky. Thenceforth, such operations were conducted from armed ships, which could defend themselves should they be attacked. *See also:* USS *Liberty.*

References

Watson, Bruce W. *Red Navy at Sea: Soviet Naval Operations on the High Seas, 1956-1980.* Boulder, CO: Westview Press, 1986.

Watson, Bruce W., and Watson, Susan M., eds. *The Soviet Navy: Strengths and Liabilities.* Boulder, CO: Westview Press, 1986.

—U.S. SIGNALS INTELLIGENCE DIRECTIVE (USSID) is a document produced by the National Security Agency that prescribes policy and procedures concerning signals intelligence matters. *See also:* National Security Agency.

References

Laqueur, Walter. *A World of Secrets.* New York: Basic Books, 1985.

—U.S. SIGNALS INTELLIGENCE SYSTEM (USSS) is composed of the National Security Agency and elements of the military departments and of the Central Intelligence Agency that perform signals intelligence activities. It also includes elements from other departments or agencies that may be authorized occasionally to perform signals intelligence activities. When these elements are authorized, they are under the direction of the U.S. Signals Intelligence Direction System.

References

Department of Defense, Defense Intelligence College. *Glossary of Intelligence Terms and Definitions.* Washington, DC: DIC, 1987.

Laqueur, Walter. *A World of Secrets.* New York: Basic Books, 1985.

—UNITED STATES VS. BUTENKO was a court case that considered the question of whether judicial review was required in a case involving the electronic surveillance of an American who was passing intelligence information to foreign agents. The defense held that the surveillance had been conducted to obtain intelligence information, not to obtain information to be used to prosecute Butenko, and that such activities required a warrant. A Court of Appeals held that such warrantless surveillance was not illegal and the Supreme Court declined to consider the case. This and a second case, *United States vs. U.S. District Court*, did much to delineate the boundaries between domestic and foreign intelligence operations.

References

Kornblum, Allan. *Intelligence and the Law: Cases and Materials.* Vol. IV. Washington, DC: DIC, 1987.

Oseth, John M. *Regulating U.S. Intelligence Operations: A Study in the Definition of the National Interest.* Frankfurt: University of Kentucky Press, 1985.

—UNITED STATES VS. U.S. DISTRICT COURT was a Supreme Court decision concerning the electronic surveillance of dissident American groups. The Court refused to accept the argument that national security was sufficient justification to waive the requirement for a warrant. The significance of the decision was that the Court more clearly delineated the boundaries between domestic and foreign intelligence operations.

References

Kornblum, Allan. *Intelligence and the Law: Cases and Materials.* Vol. IV. Washington, DC: DIC, 1987.

Oseth, John M. *Regulating U.S. Intelligence Operations: A Study in the Definition of the National Interest.* Frankfurt: University of Kentucky Press, 1985.

—UPGRADE is a general intelligence term. After it has been determined that a piece of classified information requires, in the interest of national security, a higher degree of protection against unauthorized disclosure than that which is currently provided, it is upgraded. This involves changing the security classification to a higher one, and changing the classification designation on the document to the higher classification. *See also:* Security Classification.

References

Department of Defense, Defense Intelligence College. *Glossary of Intelligence Terms and Definitions.* Washington, DC: DIC, 1987.

—USER. (1) In respect to intelligence consumption, user is now a passé term; it has been replaced by "customer." User is also a communications security (COMSEC) term that means an individual who is required to use COMSEC material in the performance of his official duties and who is responsible for safeguarding this material while it is in his custody.

References

Godson, Roy, ed. *Intelligence Problems for the 1980s, Number 1: Elements of Intelligence.* Rev. ed. Washington, DC: National Strategy Information Center, 1983.

Kent, Sherman. *Strategic Intelligence for American World Policy.* Princeton, NJ: Princeton University Press, 1966.

Maurer, Alfred C.; Turnstall, Marion D.; and Keagle, James M. *Intelligence Policy and Process.* Boulder, CO: Westview Press, 1985.

Treverton, Gregory F. *Covert Action: The Limits of Intervention in the Postwar World.* New York: Basic Books, 1987.

—**VACUUM CLEANER** is a term used in clandestine intelligence operations to describe an informant who divulges information about every aspect of his target organization, regardless of its relevance to his assignment.

References

Becket, Henry S. A. *The Dictionary of Espionage: Spookspeak into English.* New York: Stein and Day, 1986.

Deacon, Richard. *Spyclopedia: An Encyclopedia of Spies, Secret Services, Operations, Jargon, and All Subjects Related to the World of Espionage.* London: Macdonald, 1987.

Ranelagh, John. *The Agency: The Rise and Decline of the CIA.* New York: Simon and Schuster, 1986.

—**VALIDATE,** in intelligence data handling, is the act of concurring in pursuit of subsequent actions for approval.

References

Department of Defense, Defense Intelligence Agency. *Defense Intelligence Agency Manual.* Washington, DC: DIA, 1987.

Department of Defense, Defense Intelligence College. *Glossary of Intelligence Terms and Definitions.* Washington, DC: DIC, 1987.

Department of Defense, Joint Chiefs of Staff. *Department of Defense Dictionary of Military and Related Terms.* Washington, DC: GPO, 1986.

—**VALIDATION** is a process normally associated with collecting intelligence information. It is the affirming or acknowledging of a statement of need, or production requirement, for finished intelligence, and includes the essentiality and feasibility of tasking the requirement for production action. Thus, it provides official status to an identified intelligence requirement, confirms that the requirement is appropriate for a given collector, and confirms that the requirement has not been previously satisfied. *See also:* Intelligence Collection, Intelligence Cycle.

References

Department of Defense, Defense Intelligence College. *Glossary of Intelligence Terms and Definitions.* Washington, DC: DIC, 1987.

Department of Defense, U.S. Army. *RDTE Managers Intelligence and Threat Support Guide.* Alexandria, VA: Headquarters, Army Materiel Development and Readiness Command, 1983.

Godson, Roy, ed. *Intelligence Problems for the 1980s, Number 1: Elements of Intelligence.* Rev. ed. Washington, DC: National Strategy Information Center, 1983.

—**VANDENBERG, LIEUTENANT GENERAL HOYT S., U.S. ARMY,** was born on January 24, 1899, in Milwaukee, Wisconsin. He graduated from the U.S. Military Academy in 1923, and from the Army War College in 1936. Highlights of his army career included duty as commander, Ninth Air Force in Europe during World War II and as assistant chief of staff, G-2, War Department General Staff from January to June 1946. He was appointed as director of Central Intelligence (DCI) by President Truman on June 7 and was sworn in on June 10, 1946. He served until May 1, 1947, when he was assigned as deputy commander, U.S. Army Air Forces. On October 1, 1947, he became vice chief of staff of the U.S. Air Force with the rank of general. He served as chief of staff of the Air Force from 1948 until 1953. He retired from the Air Force on June 30, 1953, and died on April 2, 1954.

Vandenberg, the third DCI, was much more forceful than either of his predecessors. His efforts did much to increase the influence of the agency, and he seemed to view the directorship as a stepping stone to his goal of becoming chief of staff of the U.S. Air Force. Vandenberg did manage to gain greater budget independence for the CIG and expanded the group's clandestine collection, research, and analysis roles. Thus, under his auspices, the CIG's function was changed from that of an organization that merely coordinated national estimates to one that produced intelligence. Additionally, the Office of Research and Evaluation was formed, and the CIG continued to expand in size and scope. Finally, under him, the group produced its first national estimate, which dealt with Soviet intentions and capabilities.

Vandenberg also played a pivotal role in delineating the proposed Central Intelligence Agency's role in intelligence. Through his influence, the National Security Act of 1947 stated that the agency would have several missions. It would advise the National Security Council and the president on intelligence activities. Second, it would make recommendations to the National Security Council on intelligence activities. Additionally, it would correlate, evaluate, and disseminate intelligence. Finally, it would perform intelligence functions that the National Security Council felt could best be handled by a central intelligence organization; and would perform such other duties as the National Security Council directed.

In summary, Vandenburg's tenure as DCI benefited the CIA significantly. More assertive than either of his two predecessors, he expanded significantly the organization's size, missions, and managerial power. In spite of the fact that his efforts have been overshadowed by those of his successor, General Walter Bedell Smith, they were both significant in and beneficial to the evolution of central intelligence.

References

Breckinridge, Scott D. *The CIA and the U.S. Intelligence System.* Boulder, CO: Westview Press, 1986.

Brinkley, David A., and Hull, Andrew W. *Estimative Intelligence: A Textbook on the History, Products, Uses, and Writing of Intelligence Estimates.* Columbus, OH: Battelle, 1979.

Cline, Ray S. *The CIA Under Reagan, Bush, and Casey.* Washington, DC: Acropolis Books, 1981.

Corson, William R. *The Armies of Ignorance: The Rise of the American Intelligence Empire.* New York: Dial Press, 1977.

Crawford, David J. *Volunteers: The Betrayal of National Defense Secrets by Air Force Traitors.* Washington, DC: GPO, 1988.

Kent, Sherman. *Strategic Intelligence for American World Policy.* Princeton, NJ: Princeton University Press, 1966.

Laqueur, Walter. *A World of Secrets.* New York: Basic Books, 1985.

Lowenthal, Mark M. *U.S. Intelligence: Evolution and Anatomy.* New York: Praeger, 1984.

U.S. Congress. Senate. *Alleged Assassination Plots Involving Foreign Leaders: An Interim Report of the Select Committee to Study Governmental Operations with Respect to Intelligence Activities.* 94th Congress, 1st sess., Nov. 20, 1975. S. Rept. 94-465.

Von Hoene, John P. A. *Intelligence User's Guide.* Washington, DC: DIA, 1983.

—**VARIANT,** in communications security (COMSEC), means one of two or more code symbols that have the same plain-text equivalent.

References

Department of Defense, Defense Intelligence College. *Glossary of Intelligence Terms and Definitions.* Washington, DC: DIC, 1987.

Department of Defense, Joint Chiefs of Staff. *Department of Defense Dictionary of Military and Related Terms.* Washington, DC: GPO, 1986.

Department of Defense, U.S. Army. *Counter-Signals Intelligence (C-SIGINT) Operations.* Field Manual FM 34-62. Washington, DC: Headquarters, Department of the Army, 1986.

—**VAULT DOOR** is an intelligence security and counterintelligence term. It is a General Services Administration maximum security vault door (Class 5, Type 1 or Class 6, Type 1) that is equipped with a Group 1 lock and drill resistant 1/8 inch hard plate that is installed between the door and the locking device. *See also:* Classified Information, Closed Storage, Controlled Area, Controlled Dissemination, Information Security, Open Storage, Physical Security, Secure Area, Secure Vault Area, Secure Vault Area Custodian, Secure Working Area, Security, Special Security Officer System.

References

Department of Defense, Defense Intelligence Agency. *Defense Intelligence Agency Manual.* Washington, DC: DIA, 1987.

Department of Defense, Defense Intelligence College. *Glossary of Intelligence Terms and Definitions.* Washington, DC: DIC, 1987.

—**VERTICAL AIR PHOTOGRAPH,** in imagery intelligence and photoreconnaissance, is a photograph that is taken with the optical axis of the camera perpendicular to the surface of the earth. *See also:* Aerial Photograph.

References

Department of Defense, Defense Intelligence College. *Glossary of Intelligence Terms and Definitions.* Washington, DC: DIC, 1987.

Department of Defense, Joint Chiefs of Staff. *Department of Defense Dictionary of Military and Related Terms.* Washington, DC: GPO, 1986.

—**VITAL GROUND** is a tactical intelligence term. It is territory, that if possessed by the enemy, will seriously interfere with the successful defense of a position.

References

Department of Defense, Defense Intelligence College. *Glossary of Intelligence Terms and Definitions.* Washington, DC: DIC, 1987.

Department of Defense, Joint Chiefs of Staff. *Department of Defense Dictionary of Military and Related Terms.* Washington, DC: GPO, 1986.

—**VULNERABILITY.** (1) In the communications security (COMSEC) context, vulnerability is a term that refers to the characteristics of a friendly telecommunications system that are potentially exploitable by the enemy. (2) When vulnerability is used in an Army tactical intelligence (TACINT) sense, vulnerability is a susceptibility in the presence of a threat. Susceptibility in the absence of a threat does not constitute a vulnerability. Vulnerabilities are those profiles that disclose indicators of a unit's planning or operational procedures which, unless adequate operations security (OPSEC) procedures are implemented, will be detected by hostile collection resources. If collected, these vulnerabilities could comprise the unit's essential elements of friendly information (EEFI), thus jeopardizing the success of the plan or operation. Vulnerabilities may include any activity that is undertaken by a military unit, and they are determined by comparing the friendly force profile (all indicators key to the current operation) to the hostile collection threat. Time, date, location, and type of collector are the first important considerations when considering vulnerability. (3) Vulnerability can also be specified in the following manner. An *enemy vulnerability* is any condition or circumstance of the enemy situation or the area of operations that makes the enemy especially liable to damage, deception, or defeat. *National vulnerabilities* are those susceptibilities of a nation to any action, by any means, in peace or war through which its war potential may be reduced or its will to fight diminished.

References

Department of Defense, U.S. Army. *Counter-Signals Intelligence (C-SIGINT) Operations.* Field Manual FM 34-62. Washington, DC: Headquarters, Department of the Army, 1986.

Treverton, Gregory F. *Covert Action: The Limits of Intervention in the Postwar World.* New York: Basic Books, 1987.

—**VULNERABILITY ASSESSMENT,** in communications security (COMSEC), refers to the systematic examination of telecommunications in order to determine the adequacy of existing COMSEC measures, to identify existing COMSEC deficiencies, to provide data that can be used to predict the effectiveness of proposed COMSEC measures, and to confirm that such proposed measures are adequate after they have been implemented.

References

Department of Defense, U.S. Army. *Counter-Signals Intelligence (C-SIGINT) Operations.* Field Manual FM 34-62. Washington, DC: Headquarters, Department of the Army, 1986.

Godson, Roy, ed. *Intelligence Problems for the 1980s, Number 3: Counterintelligence.* Washington, DC: National Strategy Information Center, 1980.

—**VULNERABLE-CRITICAL ELEMENTS** is a target intelligence term that pertains to the target that is to be destroyed. These elements are targeted for attack because their destruction means the most economic, effective, and safe way to negate the principal functions of an installation, site, or entity.

References

Department of Defense, Defense Intelligence College. *Glossary of Intelligence Terms and Definitions.* Washington, DC: DIC, 1987.

Department of Defense, Joint Chiefs of Staff. *Department of Defense Dictionary of Military and Related Terms.* Washington, DC: GPO, 1986.

—**VULNERABLE ELEMENTS** is a target intelligence term that pertains to the target that is to be destroyed. Such elements are susceptible to detection, identification, collection, or neutralization.

References

Department of Defense, Defense Intelligence College. *Glossary of Intelligence Terms and Definitions.* Washington, DC: DIC, 1987.

Department of Defense, Joint Chiefs of Staff. *Department of Defense Dictionary of Military and Related Terms.* Washington, DC: GPO, 1986.

Godson, Roy, ed. *Intelligence Problems for the 1980s, Number 3: Counterintelligence.* Washington, DC: National Strategy Information Center, 1980.

—**W GROUP** is a component of one of the ten branches that constitute the National Security Agency. *See:* National Security Agency.

References

Bamford, James. *The Puzzle Palace: A Report on America's Most Secret Agency.* New York: Penguin Books, 1983.

—**WAIVER** is an intelligence security and counter-intelligence term that means the withdrawal or modification of certain requirements for a position, facility, or action so that it can meet existing requirements.

References

Department of Defense, Defense Intelligence Agency. *Defense Intelligence Agency Manual.* Washington, DC: DIA, 1987.

Department of Defense, Defense Intelligence College. *Glossary of Intelligence Terms and Definitions.* Washington, DC: DIC, 1987.

—**WALKER, ARTHUR,** brother of John Walker and a former naval officer, was arrested on May 29, 1985, in Norfolk, Virginia. He was convicted on August 9, 1985, of passing secrets to John Walker, who sold them to the Soviets. He was sentenced to life imprisonment. *See also:* Walker, John; Walker, Michael; Whitworth, Jerry.

References

Allen, Thomas B., and Polmar, Norman. *Merchants of Treason: America's Secrets for Sale.* New York: Delacorte Press, 1988.

Crawford, David J. *Volunteers: The Betrayal of National Defense Secrets by Air Force Traitors.* Washington, DC: GPO, 1988.

Kornblum, Allan. *Intelligence and the Law: Cases and Materials.* Vol. IV. Washington, DC: DIC, 1987.

—**WALKER, JOHN,** a retired naval warrant officer and communications specialist, spied for the Soviets for at least seventeen years and was leader of the Walker spy ring. Arrested on May 20, 1985, in Baltimore, Maryland, and charged with espionage, he was convicted on October 28, 1985, and sentenced to life in prison. *See also:* Walker, John; Walker, Michael; Whitworth, Jerry.

References

Allen, Thomas B., and Polmar, Norman. *Merchants of Treason: America's Secrets for Sale.* New York: Delacorte Press, 1988.

Crawford, David J. *Volunteers: The Betrayal of National Defense Secrets by Air Force Traitors.* Washington, DC: GPO, 1988.

Kornblum, Allan. *Intelligence and the Law: Cases and Materials.* Vol. IV. Washington, DC: DIC, 1987.

—**WALKER, MICHAEL,** son of John Walker and on active duty with the U.S. Navy, was arrested while on board the USS *Nimitz,* then in port in Haifa, Israel, on May 22, 1985. He was convicted of stealing and then giving classified documents to his father for sale to the Soviets. Convicted on October 28, 1985, he was sentenced to 25 years in prison. *See also:* Walker, Arthur; Walker, John; Whitworth, Jerry.

References

Allen, Thomas B., and Polmar, Norman. *Merchants of Treason: America's Secrets for Sale.* New York: Delacorte Press, 1988.

Crawford, David J. *Volunteers: The Betrayal of National Defense Secrets by Air Force Traitors.* Washington, DC: GPO, 1988.

Kornblum, Allan. *Intelligence and the Law: Cases and Materials.* Vol. IV. Washington, DC: DIC, 1987.

—**WALK-IN** is a term used in clandestine intelligence operations to describe a person who, on his own initiative, contacts a representative of a foreign country and who volunteers intelligence information or requests political asylum. *See also:* Agent, Agent Authentication, Agent in Place, Agent Net, Agent of Influence, Agent Provocateur, Confusion Agent, Dispatched \Agent, Double Agent, Handling Agent, Illegal Agent, Informant, Inside Man, Provocation Agent, Recruitment, Recruitment in Place, Special Activities.

References

Allen, Thomas B., and Polmar, Norman. *Merchants of Treason: America's Secrets for Sale.* New York: Delacorte Press, 1988.

Deacon, Richard. *Spyclopedia: An Encyclopedia of Spies, Secret Services, Operations, Jargon, and All Subjects Related to the World of Espionage.* London: Macdonald, 1987.

Department of Defense, Defense Intelligence College. *Glossary of Intelligence Terms and Definitions.* Washington, DC: DIC, 1987.

Kessler, Ronald. *Spy vs. Spy: Stalking Soviet Spies in America.* New York: Charles Scribner's Sons, 1988.

Quirk, John; Phillips, David; Cline, Ray; and Pforzheimer, Walter. *The Central Intelligence Agency: A Photographic History.* Guilford, CT: Foreign Intelligence Press, 1986.

—**WALK-PAST** is a term used in clandestine intelligence operations to describe when an agent who has recently arrived in a target country walks past another at a set time and place. No contact is made. Rather, his appearance means that he has successfully entered the target country and provides an opportunity for the second agent to see if the arrival is under surveillance.

References

Becket, Henry S. A. *The Dictionary of Espionage: Spookspeak into English.* New York: Stein and Day, 1986.

Deacon, Richard. *Spyclopedia: An Encyclopedia of Spies, Secret Services, Operations, Jargon, and All Subjects Related to the World of Espionage.* London: Macdonald, 1987.

Ranelagh, John. *The Agency: The Rise and Decline of the CIA.* New York: Simon and Schuster, 1986.

—**WALTERS, LIEUTENANT GENERAL VERNON A., U.S. ARMY,** served as deputy director of Central Intelligence from May 2, 1972, until July 7, 1976.

References

Breckinridge, Scott D. *The CIA and the U.S. Intelligence System.* Boulder, CO: Westview Press, 1986.

—**WARNING** is an indications and warning (I&W) term. It is a notification of impending activities on the part of a foreign power or powers, including hostilities, that may affect U.S. military forces or security interests. *See also:* Indications and Warning.

References

Department of Defense, Defense Intelligence College. *Glossary of Intelligence Terms and Definitions.* Washington, DC: DIC, 1987.

Department of Defense, Joint Chiefs of Staff. *Department of Defense Dictionary of Military and Related Terms.* Washington, DC: GPO, 1986.

Godson, Roy, ed. *Intelligence Problems for the 1980s, Number 1: Elements of Intelligence.* Rev. ed. Washington, DC: National Strategy Information Center, 1983.

Laqueur, Walter. *A World of Secrets.* New York: Basic Books, 1985.

Maurer, Alfred C.; Turnstall, Marion D.; and Keagle, James M. *Intelligence Policy and Process.* Boulder, CO: Westview Press, 1985.

Treverton, Gregory F. *Covert Action: The Limits of Intervention in the Postwar World.* New York: Basic Books, 1987.

—**WARNING INTELLIGENCE** is an indications and warning (I&W) term. It is an intelligence product upon which one can base or justify a notification of impending activities by foreign powers, including hostilities, that may adversely affect U.S. military forces or security interests. *See also:* Indications and Warning.

References

Department of Defense, Defense Intelligence College. *Glossary of Intelligence Terms and Definitions.* Washington, DC: DIC, 1987.

Department of Defense, Joint Chiefs of Staff. *Department of Defense Dictionary of Military and Related Terms.* Washington, DC: GPO, 1986.

Godson, Roy, ed. *Intelligence Problems for the 1980s, Number 1: Elements of Intelligence.* Rev. ed. Washington, DC: National Strategy Information Center, 1983.

Laqueur, Walter. *A World of Secrets.* New York: Basic Books, 1985.

Maurer, Alfred C.; Turnstall, Marion D.; and Keagle, James M. *Intelligence Policy and Process.* Boulder, CO: Westview Press, 1985.

Treverton, Gregory F. *Covert Action: The Limits of Intervention in the Postwar World.* New York: Basic Books, 1987.

—**WARNING INTELLIGENCE APPRAISAL** is produced by the Defense Intelligence Agency. It is an alerting document on a developing intelligence and warning (I&W) situation, providing a more in-depth analysis and assessment than the Defense Intelligence Notice (DIN). The warning appraisal is prepared, printed, and disseminated on an urgent basis whenever a short assessment of an imminent development is of considerable interest to high-level U.S. officials. *See also:* Indications and Warning.

References

Godson, Roy, ed. *Intelligence Problems for the 1980s, Number 1: Elements of Intelligence*. Rev. ed. Washington, DC: National Strategy Information Center, 1983.

Maurer, Alfred C.; Turnstall, Marion D.; and Keagle, James M. *Intelligence Policy and Process*. Boulder, CO: Westview Press, 1985.

Von Hoene, John P. A. *Intelligence User's Guide*. Washington, DC: DIA, 1983.

—**WARNING NET** is an indications and warning (I&W) term. It is a communications system that is established for the purpose of disseminating warning information of enemy movements or action to all interested commands. *See also:* Indications and Warning.

References

Department of Defense, Joint Chiefs of Staff. *Department of Defense Dictionary of Military and Related Terms*. Washington, DC: GPO, 1986.

—**WARNING ORDER** is a preliminary notice of an order or an action that is to follow. It is designed to give subordinates time to make the necessary plans and preparations. In Navy jargon, a warning order is often called a "heads up."

References

Department of Defense, Joint Chiefs of Staff. *Department of Defense Dictionary of Military and Related Terms*. Washington, DC: GPO, 1986.

—**WASH** is a term used in clandestine intelligence operations. It means to recycle a valid passport by removing the writing and photograph and reissuing it with a new name and photograph. *See also:* Shoe.

References

Becket, Henry S. A. *The Dictionary of Espionage: Spookspeak into English*. New York: Stein and Day, 1986.

Deacon, Richard. *Spyclopedia: An Encyclopedia of Spies, Secret Services, Operations, Jargon, and All Subjects Related to the World of Espionage*. London: Macdonald, 1987.

Ranelagh, John. *The Agency: The Rise and Decline of the CIA*. New York: Simon and Schuster, 1986.

—**WASHINGTON NATIONAL RECORDS CENTER (WNRC)** is the National Archive where public records and historical documents are preserved.

References

Von Hoene, John P. A. *Intelligence User's Guide*. Washington, DC: DIA, 1983.

—**WATCH CENTER** is an indications and warning (I&W) term. It is a center for the review of all incoming intelligence information, and it possesses or has access to extensive communications for alerting local intelligence personnel and contacting appropriate external reporting sources and other nodes in the Department of Defense I&W system. *See also:* Indications and Warning.

References

Department of Defense, National Defense University. *Joint Staff Officer's Guide, 1986*. Washington, DC: GPO, 1986.

Godson, Roy, ed. *Intelligence Problems for the 1980s, Number 1: Elements of Intelligence*. Rev. ed. Washington, DC: National Strategy Information Center, 1983.

Maurer, Alfred C.; Turnstall, Marion D.; and Keagle, James M. *Intelligence Policy and Process*. Boulder, CO: Westview Press, 1985.

Von Hoene, John P. A. *Intelligence User's Guide*. Washington, DC: DIA, 1983.

—**WATCH COMMITTEE** was created in 1954 and abolished in 1974. It was a production committee of the director of Central Intelligence and was supported by the National Indications Center, which was located in the Pentagon. *See also:* Indications and Warning.

References

Corson, William R. *The Armies of Ignorance: The Rise of the American Intelligence Empire*. New York: Dial Press, 1987.

—**WATCH LIST** is a term used in intelligence and counterintelligence operations for a compilation of names of people who are of interest to the Intelligence Community. As defined by the Church Committee, a watch list is a list of words—such as names, entities, or phrases—that can be employed by a computer to select out the required information from a mass of data.

References

Becket, Henry S. A. *The Dictionary of Espionage: Spookspeak into English*. New York: Stein and Day, 1986.

Corson, William R. *The Armies of Ignorance: The Rise of the American Intelligence Empire*. New York: Dial Press, 1987.

Quirk, John; Phillips David; Cline, Ray; and Pforzheimer, Walter. *The Central Intelligence Agency: A Photographic History.* Guilford, CT: Foreign Intelligence Press, 1986.

U.S. Congress. Senate. *Final Report, Senate Select Committee on Intelligence, 26 February 1976.* Washington, DC: GPO, 1976.

—**WATCHERS** is a term used in clandestine and covert intelligence operations to describe intelligence personnel who are keeping someone under surveillance. *See also:* Pavement Artists, Shadow, Shaking Off the Dogs, Surround, Surveillance.

References

Quirk, John; Phillips David; Cline, Ray; and Pforzheimer, Walter. *The Central Intelligence Agency: A Photographic History.* Guilford, CT: Foreign Intelligence Press, 1986.

—**WEAPON AND SPACE SYSTEMS INTELLI-GENCE COMMITTEE (WSSIC).** *See:* Director of Central Intelligence Committee.

—**WEATHER INTELLIGENCE.** *See:* Geographic Intelligence.

—**WEEKLY INTELLIGENCE PRODUCTION (WIP)** is a listing of intelligence products that have been published by the Defense Intelligence Agency during the week and that are deemed to be of sufficient importance that they should be brought to the attention of high-level officials. Distribution of the WIP is limited to the Washington, DC, area.

References

Von Hoene, John P. A. *Intelligence User's Guide.* Washington, DC: DIA, 1983.

—**WEEKLY INTELLIGENCE SUMMARY (WIS)** is produced by the Defense Intelligence Agency and is designed to provide military commanders, planners, and operational personnel worldwide with a summary of recent developments that have occurred throughout the world. It also serves as a vehicle for disseminating maps, photographs, and other graphics, as well as scientific and technical information.

References

Von Hoene, John P. A. *Intelligence User's Guide.* Washington, DC: DIA, 1983.

—**WHALEN, WILLIAM H., U.S. ARMY,** a military intelligence officer, was convicted, in 1966, of espionage crimes concerning his association with a Soviet intelligence service while he was stationed at the Pentagon. His motive was apparently anticipated monetary gain. He was sentenced to fifteen years in prison.

References

Crawford, David J. *Volunteers: The Betrayal of National Defense Secrets by Air Force Traitors.* Washington, DC: GPO, 1988.

—**WHAT'S YOUR TWENTY?** is a term used in clandestine and covert intelligence operations. It means what is your location?

References

Becket, Henry S. A. *The Dictionary of Espionage: Spookspeak into English.* New York: Stein and Day, 1986.

Deacon, Richard. *Spyclopedia: An Encyclopedia of Spies, Secret Services, Operations, Jargon, and All Subjects Related to the World of Espionage.* London: Macdonald, 1987.

Ranelagh, John. *The Agency: The Rise and Decline of the CIA.* New York: Simon and Schuster, 1986.

—**WHITE HOUSE SITUATION ROOM (WHSR)** serves as the White House watch center. It has the necessary communications with the Intelligence Community watch centers and receives their periodic intelligence reports. In times of crisis, the WHSR can communicate immediately with the relevant watch centers, thereby providing the president with the most current and accurate information on any given situation.

References

Department of Defense, National Defense University. *Joint Staff Officer's Guide, 1986.* Washington, DC: GPO, 1986.

—**WHITE INTELLIGENCE** is information collected from foreign newspapers, digests, broadcasts, and other open source material.

References

Becket, Henry S. A. *The Dictionary of Espionage: Spookspeak into English.* New York: Stein and Day, 1986.

Deacon, Richard. *Spyclopedia: An Encyclopedia of Spies, Secret Services, Operations, Jargon, and All Subjects Related to the World of Espionage.* London: Macdonald, 1987.

Ranelagh, John. *The Agency: The Rise and Decline of the CIA.* New York: Simon and Schuster, 1986.

Ranelagh, John. *The Agency: The Rise and Decline of the CIA.* New York: Simon and Schuster, 1986.

—**WHITE PROPAGANDA** is propaganda that is disseminated and acknowledged by the sponsor or by an accredited agency of the sponsor. *See also:* Gray Propaganda, Propaganda, White Propaganda.

References

Department of Defense, Joint Chiefs of Staff. *Department of Defense Dictionary of Military and Related Terms.* Washington, DC: GPO, 1986.

Treverton, Gregory F. *Covert Action: The Limits of Intervention in the Postwar World.* New York: Basic Books, 1987.

—**WHITWORTH, JERRY,** a former Navy man, was arrested and charged with passing cryptographic materials to John Walker for sale to the Soviets. Convicted in 1986, he was sentenced to 365 years in prison. *See also:* Walker, Arthur; Walker, John; Walker, Michael.

References

Allen, Thomas B., and Polmar, Norman. *Merchants of Treason: America's Secrets for Sale.* New York: Delacorte Press, 1988.

Crawford, David J. *Volunteers: The Betrayal of National Defense Secrets by Air Force Traitors.* Washington, DC: GPO, 1988.

—**WILSON, EDWIN P.** *See:* Terpil, Frank.

—**WIRETAPPING.** *See:* Electronic Surveillance.

—**WITTING** is a term used in intelligence operations to describe a person who knowingly cooperates with an intelligence agency. *See also:* Agent in Place, Agent Net, Agent of Influence, Agent Provocateur, Co-Opted Worker, Co-Optees, Defector, Infiltration, Informant, Inside Man, Recruitment, Recruitment in Place.

References

Becket, Henry S. A. *The Dictionary of Espionage: Spookspeak into English.* New York: Stein and Day, 1986.

Deacon, Richard. *Spyclopedia: An Encyclopedia of Spies, Secret Services, Operations, Jargon, and All Subjects Related to the World of Espionage.* London: Macdonald, 1987.

—**WOLD, HANS P.,** was arrested in 1983 while being absent without leave (AWOL) from the USS *Ranger.* He had photographed Top Secret information and was accused of intending to pass the information to the Soviets. Prompted by expected monetary reward, Wold was tried, given a dishonorable discharge, and sentenced to four years at hard labor.

References

Allen, Thomas B., and Polmar, Norman. *Merchants of Treason: America's Secrets for Sale.* New York: Delacorte Press, 1988.

—**WOLFF, JAY CLYDE,** a former Navy member, was arrested on December 15, 1984, in Albuquerque, New Mexico. He was convicted of espionage on May 17, 1985.

References

Crawford, David J. *Volunteers: The Betrayal of National Defense Secrets by Air Force Traitors.* Washington, DC: GPO, 1988.

—**WOOD, JAMES D.,** an Air Force technical sergeant, was arrested by FBI agents in Queens, New York, on July 21, 1973, as he met a Soviet intelligence officer. An inspection of his rented automobile revealed that he had over 100 classified Air Force, Department of Defense, and FBI documents. He admitted that financial problems and gambling debts had prompted him to contact the Soviets. He was apprehended before he could pass considerable amounts of information and he therefore caused only minor damage. Wood was convicted in a court-martial and received a dishonorable discharge and a seven-year prison sentence.

References

Allen, Thomas B., and Polmar, Norman. *Merchants of Treason: America's Secrets for Sale.* New York: Delacorte Press, 1988.

Crawford, David J. *Volunteers: The Betrayal of National Defense Secrets by Air Force Traitors.* Washington, DC: GPO, 1988.

—**WORK-CAPITAL FUND,** in budgeting, is a revolving fund that has been established to finance inventories of supplies or other stores, or to provide working capital for industrial-type activities.

References

Pickett, George. "Congress, the Budget, and Intelligence." In *Intelligence Policy and Process*, edited by Alfred C. Maurer, Marion D. Turnstall, and James M. Keagle. Boulder, CO: Westview Press, 1985.

—**WORKING VARIABLE,** in communications security (COMSEC), means a cryptovariable that is distributed by a key generation facility for use on a specific interstation call.

References

Muzerall, Joseph V., and Carty, Thomas P. "COMSEC and Its Need for Key Management." *DP&CS* (Spring 1987). Ware, Willis H. "Information Systems, Security, and Privacy." *EDUCOM Bulletin* (Summer 1984).

—**WORLDWIDE MILITARY COMMAND AND CONTROL SYSTEM (WWMCCS),** according to the Joint Chiefs of Staff, is "the system that provides the means for operational direction and technical administrative support involved in the function of command and control of U.S. military forces." Components of the system are the National Military Command System (NMCS); the WWMCCS-related management/information systems of the headquarters of the military departments; the command and control systems of the headquarters of the service component commands; and the command and control support systems of Department of Defense agencies.

The requirement for the system was identified in the Defense Reorganization Act of 1958 and was subsequently formalized as a system that established a set of command and control capabilities that were to support the National Command Authorities (NCA), the Joint Chiefs of Staff, and the major field commanders. The goal of the system was to insure effective connectivity among the NCA, Joint Chiefs of Staff, and other compo-

nents of the National Military Command System down to the service component commanders.

The system provides a multipath channel of secure communications to transmit information from primary sources to those who must make decisions (including the president) and to transmit their decisions, in the form of military orders, to their subordinates.

The WWMCCS is not a single system, nor are there plans for it to become one. It is a system of systems that range from the national to the theater level. Some of the systems are unique to the WWMCCS, but most are ones that were designed, developed, bought, and used to satisfy the command and control requirements of the services or the commands that normally use them. Their primary function is to support the national-level command and control function.

There are five elements of the WWMCCS: warning systems; communications; data collection and processing; executive aids; and facilities. Each of these permeates various levels of command and control, and together their operation forms a worldwide information system.

Finally, the system supports four basic functional areas: resource and unit monitoring (RUM); conventional planning and execution (CPE); nuclear planning and execution (NPE); and tactical warning and attack assessment (TW/AA). *See also:* Indications and Warning.

References

Department of Defense, Defense Intelligence Agency. *Defense Intelligence Agency Manual.* Washington, DC: DIA, 1987.

Department of Defense, Defense Intelligence College. *Glossary of Intelligence Terms and Definitions.* Washington, DC: DIC, 1987.

Department of Defense, National Defense University. *Joint Staff Officer's Guide, 1986.* Washington, DC: GPO, 1986.

—**WRIGHT, BRIGADIER GENERAL EDWIN K., U.S. ARMY,** served as the deputy director of Central Intelligence from January 20, 1947, to March 9, 1949.

References

Quirk, John; Phillips, David; Cline, Ray; and Pforzheimer, Walter. *The Central Intelligence Agency: A Photographic History.* Guilford, CT: Foreign Intelligence Press, 1986.

—**X-2** was the counterintelligence unit of the Office of Strategic Services (OSS). When President Truman ordered the end of OSS operations as of October 1, 1945, the War Department took control of Secret Intelligence (clandestine collection) and X-2 (counterintelligence) and combined them into the Strategic Service Unit (SSU). *See also:* Office of Strategic Services.

References

Corson, William R. *The Armies of Ignorance: The Rise of the American Intelligence Empire.* New York: Dial Press, 1977.

Lowenthal, Mark M. *U.S. Intelligence: Evolution and Anatomy.* New York: Praeger, 1984.

—**YAGER, CORPORAL JOEL, U.S. MARINE CORPS,** was arrested in 1977 for attempting to sell classified material to a foreign national, who actually was a Naval Investigative Service agent. His motive appears to have been profit. Yager was not court-martialed.

References

Allen, Thomas B., and Polmar, Norman. *Merchants of Treason: America's Secrets for Sale.* New York: Delacorte Press, 1988.

Crawford, David J. *Volunteers: The Betrayal of National Defense Secrets by Air Force Traitors.* Washington, DC: GPO, 1988.

—**YARDLEY, HERBERT O.** After World War I, the U.S. Army's cryptologic service, MI-8, continued to operate out of a brownstone apartment building in New York City. Under its director, Herbert O. Yardley, its small staff made a number of breakthroughs, including breaking the Japanese diplomatic code. In 1929, the new secretary of state, Henry Stimson, made his famous "gentlemen do not read each other's mail" statement, and MI-8 was discontinued shortly thereafter. Yardley, disillusioned with the government's reversal in position, wrote *The American Black Chamber,* in which he detailed American operations, thereby inflicting grave damage on U.S. intelligence operations.

References

Corson, William R. *The Armies of Ignorance: The Rise of the American Intelligence Empire.* New York: Dial Press, 1977.

Finnegan, John P. *Military Intelligence: A Picture History.* U.S. Army Intelligence and Security Command, 1984.

—**Z VARIABLE,** in communications security (COMSEC), means a cryptovariable that is used in certain cryptosystems in order to protect the other variables that are contained in a key distribution data base.

References

Martin, Paul H. "Communications-Computer Security." *Journal of Electronic Defense* (June 1987).

Muzerall, Joseph V., and Carty, Thomas P. "COMSEC and Its Need for Key Management." *DP&CS* (Spring 1987). Ware, Willis H. "Information Systems, Security, and Privacy." *EDUCOM Bulletin* (Summer 1984).

—**ZENITH** is a term used in intelligence imagery and photoreconnaissance. It is the point in the celestial sphere that is exactly overhead; as opposed to nadir. *See also:* Aerial Photograph, Nadir, Photographic Intelligence.

References

Reeves, Robert; Anson, Abraham; and Landen, David. *Manual of Remote Sensing.* Falls Church, VA: American Society of Photogrammetry, 1975.

—**ZEROIZE,** in communications security (COMSEC), means to remove or eliminate the cryptovariable from crypto-equipment or a fill device.

References

Martin, Paul H. "Communications-Computer Security." *Journal of Electronic Defense* (June 1987).

Muzerall, Joseph V., and Carty, Thomas P. "COMSEC and Its Need for Key Management."

DP&CS (Spring 1987). Ware, Willis H. "Information Systems, Security, and Privacy." *EDUCOM Bulletin* (Summer 1984).

—**ZOO** is the police station. *See also:* Doctor.

References

Becket, Henry S. A. *The Dictionary of Espionage: Spookspeak into English.* New York: Stein and Day, 1986.

Deacon, Richard. *Spyclopedia: An Encyclopedia of Spies, Secret Services, Operations, Jargon, and All Subjects Related to the World of Espionage.* London: Macdonald, 1987.

Ranelagh, John. *The Agency: The Rise and Decline of the CIA.* New York: Simon and Schuster, 1986.

The Appendixes

Contents

Appendix A

Presidential Order, July 11, 1941
Coordinator of Information

By virtue of the authority vested in me as President of the United States and as Commander in Chief of the Army and Navy of the United States, it is ordered as follows:

1. There is hereby established the position of Coordinator of Information, with authority to collect and analyze all information and data, which may bear upon national security; to correlate such information and data, and to make such information and data available to the President and to such departments and officials of the Government as the President may determine; and to carry out, when requested by the President, such supplementary activities as may facilitate the securing of information important for national security not now available to the Government.

2. The several departments and agencies of the Government shall make available to the Coordinator of Information all and any such information and data relating to national security as the Coordinator, with the approval of the President, may from time to time request.

3. The Coordinator of Information may appoint such committees, consisting of appropriate representatives of the various departments and agencies of the Government, as he may deem necessary to assist him in the performance of his functions.

4. Nothing in the duties and responsibilities of the Coordinator of Information shall in any way interfere with or impair the duties and responsibilities of the regular military and naval advisers of the President as Commander in Chief of the Army and Navy.

5. Within the limits of such funds as may be allocated to the Coordinator of Information by the President, the Coordinator may employ necessary personnel and make provision for the necessary supplies, facilities, and services.

6. William J. Donovan is hereby designated as Coordinator of Information.

Franklin D. Roosevelt

THE WHITE HOUSE

July 11, 1941

Appendix B

Military Order, June 13, 1942
Office of Strategic Services

By virtue of the authority vested in me as President of the United States and as Commander in Chief of the Army and Navy of the United States, it is ordered as follows:

1. The Office of Coordinator of Information established by Order of July 11, 1941, exclusive of the foreign information activities transferred to the Office of War Information by Executive Order of June 13, 1942, shall hereafter be known as the Office of Strategic Services, and is hereby transferred to the jurisdiction of the United States Joint Chiefs of Staff.

2. The Office of Strategic Services shall perform the following duties:

   a. Collect and analyze such strategic information as may be required by the United States Joint Chiefs of Staff.

   b. Plan and operate such special services as may be directed by the United States Joint Chiefs of Staff.

3. At the head of the Office of Strategic Services shall be a Director of Strategic Services who shall be appointed by the President and who shall perform his duties under the direction and supervision of the United States Joint Chiefs of Staff.

4. William J. Donovan is hereby appointed as Director of Strategic Services.

5. The Order of July 11, 1941, is hereby revoked.

FRANKLIN D. ROOSEVELT

Commander in Chief

Appendix C

Executive Order 9621, September 30, 1945
Termination of the Office of Strategic Services
and Disposition of Its Functions

By virtue of the authority vested in me by the Constitution and Statutes, including Title I of the First War Powers Act, 1941, and as President of the United States and Commander in Chief of the Army and the Navy, it is hereby ordered as follows:

1. There are transferred to and consolidated in an Interim Research and Intelligence Service, which is hereby established in the Department of State, (a) the functions of the Research and Analysis Branch and of the Presentation Branch of the Office of Strategic Services (provided for by the Military Order of June 13, 1942) excluding such functions performed within the countries of Germany and Austria, and (b) those other functions of the Office of Strategic Services (hereinafter referred to as the Office) which relate to the functions of the said Branches transferred by this paragraph. The functions of the Director of Strategic Services and of the United States Joint Chiefs of Staff, relating to the functions transferred to the Service by this paragraph, are transferred to the Secretary of State. The personnel, property, and records of the said Branches, except such thereof as is located in Germany and Austria, and so much of the other personnel, property and records of the Office and of the funds of the Office as the Director of Bureau of the Budget shall determine to relate primarily to the functions transferred by this paragraph, are transferred to the said Service. Military personnel now on duty in connection with the activities transferred by this paragraph may, subject to applicable law and to the extent mutually agreeable to the Secretary of State and to the Secretary of War or the Secretary of the Navy, as the case may be, continue on such duty in the Department of State.

2. The Interim Research and Intelligence Service shall be abolished as of the close of business December 31, 1945, and the Secretary of State shall provide for winding up its affairs. Pending such abolition, (a) the Secretary of State may transfer from the said Service to such agencies of the Department of State as he shall designate any function of the Service, (b) the Secretary may curtail the activities carried on by the Service, (c) the head of the Service, who shall be designated by the Secretary, shall be responsible to the Secretary or to such other officer of the Department of State as the Secretary shall direct, and (d) the Service shall, except as otherwise provided in this order, be administered as an organizational entity in the Department of State.

3. All functions of the Office not transferred by paragraph 1 of this order, together with all personnel, records, property, and funds of the Office not

so transferred, are transferred to the Department of War; and the Office, including the Office of the Director of Strategic Services, is terminated. The functions of the Director of Strategic Services, and of the United States Joint Chiefs of Staff, relating to the functions transferred by this paragraph, are transferred to the Secretary of War. Naval personnel on duty with the Office in connection with the activities transferred by this paragraph may, subject to applicable law and to the extent mutually agreeable to the Secretary of War and the Secretary of the Navy, continue on such duty in the Department of War. The Secretary of War shall, whenever he deems it compatible with the national interest, discontinue any activity transferred by this paragraph and wind up all affairs relating thereto.

4. Such further measures and dispositions as may be determined by the Director of the Bureau of the Budget to be necessary to effectuate the transfer or redistribution of functions provided for in this order shall be carried out in such manner as the Director may direct and by such agencies as he may designate.

5. All provisions of prior orders of the President which are in conflict with this order are amended accordingly.

6. This order shall, except as otherwise specifically provided, be effective as of the opening of business October 1, 1945.

Harry S. Truman

THE WHITE HOUSE

September 20, 1945

Appendix D

Presidential Order, January 22, 1946
Coordination of Federal Foreign Intelligence Activities

THE WHITE HOUSE
Washington, January 22, 1946

To the Secretary of State, the Secretary of War,
and the Secretary of the Navy.

1. It is my desire, and I hereby direct, that all Federal foreign intelligence activities be planned, developed and coordinated so as to assure the most effective accomplishment of the intelligence mission related to the national security. I hereby designate you, together with another person to be named by me as my personal representative, as the National Intelligence Authority to accomplish this purpose.

2. Within the limits of available appropriations, you shall each from time to time assign persons and facilities from your respective Departments, which persons shall collectively form a Central Intelligence Group and shall, under the direction of a Director of Central Intelligence, assist the National Intelligence Authority. The Director of Central Intelligence shall be designated by me, shall be responsible to the National Intelligence Authority, and shall sit as a non-voting member thereof.

3. Subject to the existing law, and to the direction and control of the National Intelligence Authority, the Director of Central Intelligence shall:

    a. Accomplish the correlation and evaluation of intelligence relating to the national security, and the appropriate dissemination within the Government of the resulting strategic and national policy intelligence. In so doing, full use shall be made of the staff and facilities of the intelligence agencies of your Departments.

    b. Plan for the coordination of such of the activities of the intelligence agencies of your Departments as relate to the national security and recommend to the National Intelligence Authority the establishment of such over-all policies and objectives as will assure the most effective accomplishment of the national intelligence mission.

    c. Perform, for the benefit for said intelligence agencies, such services of common concern as the National Intelligence Authority determines can be more efficiently accomplished centrally.

    d. Perform such other functions and duties related to intelligence affecting the national security as the President and the National Intelligence Authority may from time to time direct.

4. No police, law enforcement or internal security functions shall be exercised under this directive.

5. Such intelligence received by the intelligence agencies of your Departments as may be designated by the National Intelligence Authority shall be freely available to the Director of Central Intelligence for correlation, evaluation or dissemination. To the extent approved by the National Intelligence Authority, the operations of said intelligence agencies shall be open to inspection by the Director of Central Intelligence in connection with planning functions.

6. The existing intelligence agencies of your Departments shall continue to collect, evaluate, correlate and disseminate departmental intelligence.

7. The Director of Central Intelligence shall be advised by an Intelligence Advisory Board consisting of the heads (or their representatives) of the principal military and civilian intelligence agencies of the Government having functions related to national security, as determined by the National Intelligence Authority.

8. Within the scope of existing law and Presidential directives, other departments and agencies of the executive branch of the Federal Government shall furnish such intelligence information relating to the national security as is in their possession, and as the Director of Central Intelligence may from time to time request pursuant to regulations of the National Intelligence Authority.

9. Nothing herein shall be construed to authorize the making of investigations inside the continental limits of the United States and its possessions, except as provided by law and Presidential directives.

10. In the conduct of their activities the National Intelligence Authority and the Director of Central Intelligence shall be responsible for fully protecting intelligence sources and methods.

Sincerely yours,

HARRY S. TRUMAN

Appendix E

National Security Act of 1947, July 26, 1947

An act to promote the national security by providing for a Secretary of Defense; for a National Military Establishment; for a Department of the Army, a Department of the Navy, and a Department of the Air Force; and for the coordination of the activities of the National Military Establishment with other departments and agencies of the Government concerned with the national security.

Be it enacted by the Senate and House of Representatives of the United States of America in Congress assembled,

SHORT TITLE

That [50 U.S.C. 401 note] this Act may be cited as the "National Security Act of 1947."

DECLARATION OF POLICY

Section 2. [50 U.S.C. 401] In enacting this legislation, it is the intent of Congress to provide a comprehensive program for the future security of the United States; to provide for the establishment of integrated policies and procedures for the departments, agencies, and functions of the Government relating to the national security; to provide a Department of Defense, including the three military Departments of the Army, the Navy (including naval aviation and the United States Marine Corps), and the Air Force under the direction, authority, and control of the Secretary of Defense; to provide that each military department shall be separately organized under its own Secretary and shall function under the direction, authority, and control of the Secretary of Defense; to provide for their unified direction under civilian control of the Secretary of Defense but not to merge these departments or services; to provide for the establishment of unified or specified combatant commands, and a clear and direct line of command to such commands; to eliminate unnecessary duplication in the Department of Defense, and particularly in the field of research and engineering by vesting its overall direction and control in the Secretary of Defense; to provide more effective, efficient, and economical administration in the Department of Defense; to provide for the unified strategic direction of the combatant forces, for their operation under unified command, and for their integration into an efficient team of land, naval, and air forces but not to establish a single Chief of Staff over the armed forces nor an overall armed forces general staff.

TITLE I—COORDINATION FOR NATIONAL SECURITY

NATIONAL SECURITY COUNCIL

Section 101. [50 U.S.C. 402]

    (a)   There is hereby established a council to be known as the National Security Council (thereinafter in this section referred to as the "Council").

The President of the United States shall preside over meetings of the Council: *Provided*, That in his absence he may designate a member of the Council to preside in his place.

The function of the Council shall be to advise the President with respect to the integration of domestic, foreign, and military policies relating to the national security so as to enable the military services and the other departments and agencies of the Government to cooperate more effectively in matters involving the national security.

The Council shall be composed of[1]—

(1) the President;

(2) the Vice President;

(3) the Secretary of State;

(4) the Secretary of Defense;

(5) the Director for Mutual Security;

(6) the Chairman of the National Security Resources Board; and

(7) the Secretaries and Under Secretaries of other executive departments and the military departments, the Chairman of the Munitions Board, and the Chairman of the Research and Development Board, when appointed by the President by and with the advice and consent of the Senate, to serve at his pleasure.

(b) In addition to performing such other functions as the President may direct, for the purpose of more effectively coordinating the policies and functions of the departments and agencies of the Government relating to the national security, it shall, subject to the direction of the President, be the duty of the Council—

(1) to assess and appraise the objectives, commitments, and risks of the United States in relation to our actual and potential military power, in the interest of national security, for the purpose of making recommendations to the President in connection therewith; and

(2) to consider policies on matters of common interest to the departments and agencies of the Government concerned with the national security, and to make recommendations to the President in connection therewith.

(c) The Council shall have a staff to be headed by a civilian executive secretary who shall be appointed by the President, and who shall receive compensation at the rate of $10,000 a year.[2] The executive secretary, subject to the direction of the Council, is hereby authorized, subject to the civil-service laws and the Classification Act of 1923, as amended,[3] to appoint and fix the compensation of such personnel as may be necessary to perform such duties as may be prescribed by the Council in connection with the performance of its functions.

(d) The Council shall, from time to time, make such recommendations, and such other reports to the President as it deems appropriate or as the President may require.

CENTRAL INTELLIGENCE AGENCY

Section 102. [50 U.S.C. 403]

(a) There is hereby established under the National Security Council a Central Intelligence Agency with a Director of Central Intelligence who shall be the head thereof, and with a Deputy Director of Central Intelligence who shall act for, and exercise the powers of, the Director during his absence or disability. The Director and the Deputy Director shall be appointed by the President, by and with the advice and consent of the Senate, from among the commissioned officers of the armed services, whether in an active or retired status, or from among individuals in civilian life: *Provided, however,* That at no time shall the two positions of the Director and Deputy Director be occupied simultaneously by commissioned officers of the armed forces, whether in an active or retired status.

(b)

(1) If a commissioned officer of the armed forces is appointed as Director, or Deputy Director, then—

(A) in the performance of his duties as Director, or Deputy Director, he shall be subject to no supervision, control, restriction, or prohibition (military or otherwise) other than would be operative with respect to him if he were a civilian in no way connected with the Department of the Army, the Department of the Navy, the Department of the Air Force, or the armed services or any component thereof; and

(B) he shall not possess or exercise any supervision, control, powers, or functions (other than such as he possesses, or is authorized or directed to exercise, as Director, or Deputy Director) with respect to the armed forces or any other component thereof, the Department of the Army, the Department of the Navy, or the Department of the Air Force, or any branch, bureau, unit, or division thereof, or with respect to any of the personnel (military or civilian) of any of the foregoing.

(2) Except as provided in paragraph (1), the appointment to the office of Director, or Deputy Director, of a commissioned officer of the armed services, and his acceptance of and service in such office, shall in no way affect any status, office, rank or grade he may occupy or hold in the armed services, or any emolument, perquisite, right, privilege, or benefit incident to or arising out of any such status, office, rank or grade. Any such commissioned officer shall, while in the office of Director, or Deputy Director, continue to hold rank and grade not lower than that in which serving at the time of his appointment and to receive the military pay and allowance (active or retired, as the case may be, including personal money allowance) payable to a commissioned officer of his grade and length of service for which the appropriate department shall be reimbursed from any funds available to defray the expenses of the Central Intelligence Agency. He also shall be paid by the Central Intelligence Agency from such funds as annual compensation at a rate equal to the amount by which the compensation established for such position exceeds the amount of his annual military pay and allowances.

(3) The rank or grade of any such commissioned officer shall, during the period in which such commissioned officer occupies the office of the Director of Central Intelligence, or Deputy Director of Central Intelligence,

be in addition to the numbers and percentages otherwise authorized and appropriated for the armed service of which he is a member.

(c) Notwithstanding the provisions of section 6 of the Act of August 24, 1912 (37 Stat. 555),[4] or the provisions of any other law, the Director of Central Intelligence may, in his discretion, terminate the employment of any officer or employee of the Agency whenever he shall deem such termination necessary or advisable in the interests of the United States, but such termination shall not affect the right of such officer or employee to seek or accept employment in any other department or agency of the Government if declared eligible for such employment by the United States Civil Service Commission.[5]

(d) For the purpose of coordinating the intelligence activities of the several government departments and agencies in the interest of national security, it shall be the duty of the Agency, under the direction of the National Security Council—

(1) to advise the National Security Council in matters concerning such intelligence activities of the Government departments and agencies as relate to the national security;

(2) to make recommendations to the National Security Council for the coordination of such intelligence activities of the departments and agencies of the Government as relate to the national security;

(3) to correlate and evaluate intelligence relating to the national security, and provide for the appropriate dissemination of such intelligence within the Government using where appropriate existing agencies and facilities: *Provided*, That the agency shall have no police, subpoena, law-enforcement powers, or internal security functions: *Provided further*, That the departments and other agencies of the Government shall continue to collect, evaluate, correlate and disseminate departmental intelligence: *And provided further*, That the Director of Central Intelligence shall be responsible for protecting intelligence sources and methods from unauthorized disclosure;

(4) to perform, for the benefit of existing intelligence agencies, such additional services of common concern as the National Security Council determines can be more efficiently accomplished centrally;

(5) to perform such other functions and duties related to intelligence affecting the national security as the National Security Council may from time to time direct.

(e) To the extent recommended by the National Security Council and approved by the President, such intelligence of the departments and agencies of the Government, except as hereinafter provided, relating to the national security shall be open to the inspection of the Director of Central Intelligence, and such intelligence as relates to the national security and is possessed by such departments and other agencies of the Government, except as hereinafter provided, shall be made available to the director of Central Intelligence for correlation, evaluation, and dissemination: *Provided however*, That upon written request of the Director of Central Intelligence, the Director of the Federal Bureau of Investigation shall make available to the Director of Central Intelligence such information for correlation, evaluation, and dissemination as may be essential to the national security.

(f) Effective when the Director first appointed under subsection (a) has taken office—

(1) the National Intelligence Authority (11 Fed. Reg. 1337, 1339, February 5, 1946) shall cease to exist; and

(2) the personnel, property, and records of the Central Intelligence Group are transferred to the Central Intelligence Agency, and such Group shall cease to exist. Any unexpended balances of appropriations, allocations, or other funds available or authorized to be made available for such Group shall be available and shall be authorized to be made available in like manner for expenditure by the Agency.

APPOINTMENT OF DIRECTOR OF INTELLIGENCE COMMUNITY STAFF

Section 102a.

(1) If a commissioned officer of the Armed Forces is appointed as Director of the Intelligence Community Staff, such commissioned officer, while serving in such a position—

(A) shall not be subject to supervision, control, restriction, or prohibition by the Department of Defense or any component thereof; and

(B) shall not exercise, by reason of his status as a commissioned officer, any supervision, control, powers, or functions (other than as authorized as Director of the Intelligence Community Staff) with respect to any of the military or civilian personnel thereof.

(2) Except as provided in subsection (1), the appointment of a commissioned officer of the Armed Forces to the position of Director of the Intelligence Community Staff, his acceptance of such appointment and his service in such position shall in no way affect his status, promotion, rank, or grade in the Armed Forces, or any emolument, perquisite, right, privilege, or benefit incident to or arising out of any such status, position, rank, or grade. Any such commissioned officer, while serving in the position of Director of the Intelligence Community Staff, shall continue to hold a rank and grade not lower than that in which he was serving at the time of his appointment to such position and to receive the military pay and allowances (including retired or retainer pay) payable to a commissioned officer of his grade and length of service for which the appropriate military department shall be reimbursed from any funds available to defray the expenses of the Intelligence Community Staff. In addition to any pay or allowance payable under the preceding sentence, such commissioned officer shall be paid by the Intelligence Community Staff, from funds available to defray the expenses of such staff, an annual compensation at a rate equal to the excess of the rate of compensation payable for such position over the annual rate of his military pay (including retired and retainer pay) and allowances.

(3) Any commissioned officer to which subsection (1) applies, during the period of his service as Director of the Intelligence Community Staff, shall not be counted against the numbers and percentages of commissioned officers of the rank and grade of such officer authorized for the Armed

Force of which he is a member, except that only one commissioned officer of the Armed Forces occupying the position of Director of Central Intelligence or Deputy Director of Central Intelligence as provided for in section 102, or the position of Director of the Intelligence Community Staff, under this section, shall be exempt from such numbers and percentage at any one time.

NATIONAL SECURITY RESOURCES BOARD[6]

Section 103. [50 U.S.C.404]

(a) The Director of the Office of Defense Mobilization,[7] subject to the direction of the President, is authorized, subject to the civil-service laws and the Classification Act of 1949,[8] to appoint and fix the compensation of such personnel as may be necessary to assist the Director in carrying out his functions.

(b) It shall be the function of the Director of the Office of Defense Mobilization to advise the President concerning the coordination of military, industrial, and civilian mobilization, including—

(1) policies concerning industrial and civilian mobilization in order to assure the most effective mobilization and maximum utilization of the Nation's manpower in the event of war.

(2) programs for the effective use in time of war of the Nation's natural and industrial resources for military and civilian needs, for the maintenance and stabilization of the civilian economy in time of war, and for the adjustment of such economy to war needs and conditions;

(3) policies for unifying, in time of war, the activities of Federal agencies and departments engaged in or concerned with production, procurement, distribution, or transportation of military or civilian supplies, materials, and products;

(4) the relationship between potential supplies of, and potential requirements for, manpower, resources, and productive facilities in time of war;

(5) policies for establishing adequate reserves of critical and strategic material, and for conservation of these resources;

(6) the strategic relocation of industries, services, government, and economic activities, the continuous operation of which is essential to the Nation's security.

(c) In performing his functions, the Director of the Office of Defense Mobilization shall utilize to the maximum extent the facilities and resources of the Departments and Agencies of the Government.

TITLE II—THE DEPARTMENT OF DEFENSE

Section 201. [Subsections (a) and (b) were repealed by section 307 of Public Law 87-651 (Act of September 7, 1962, 76 Stat. 526). Subsection (c) consisted of an amendment to another Act.]

(d) [50 U.S.C. 408] Except to the extent inconsistent with the provisions of this Act, the provisions of title IV of the Revised Statutes[9] as now of hereafter amended shall be applicable to the Department of Defense.

[Sections 202-204 were repealed by section 307 of Public Law 87-651 (Act of September 7, 1962, 76 Stat. 526).]

DEPARTMENT OF THE ARMY

Section 205. [Subsections (a), (d), and (e) were repealed by the law enacting titles 10 and 32, United States Code (Act of August 10, 1956, 70A Stat. 676).]

(b)   All laws, orders, regulations, and other actions relating to the Department of War or to any officer or activity whose title is changed under this section shall, insofar as they are not inconsistent with the provisions of this Act, be deemed to relate to the Department of the Army within the Department of Defense or to such officer or activity designated by his or its new title.

(c)   [50 U.S.C. 409(a)] The term "Department of the Army" as used in this Act shall be construed to mean the Department of the Army at the seat of government and all field headquarters, forces, reserve components, installations, activities, and functions under the control or supervision of the Department of the Army.

DEPARTMENT OF THE NAVY

Section 206.

(a)   [50 U.S.C. 409(b)] The term "Department of the Navy" as used in this Act shall be construed to mean the Department of the Navy at the seat of government; the headquarters, United States Marine Corps; the entire operating forces of the United States Navy, including naval aviation, and of the United States Marine Corps, including the reserve components of such forces; all field activities, headquarters, forces, bases, installations, activities and functions under the control or supervision of the Department of the Navy; and the United States Coast Guard when operating as a part of the Navy pursuant to law.

[Subsections (b) and (c) were repealed by the law enacting titles 10 and 32, United States Code (Act of August 10, 1956, 70A Stat. 676).]

DEPARTMENT OF THE AIR FORCE

Section 207. [Subsections (a), (b), (d), (e), and (f) were repealed by the law enacting titles 10 and 32, United States Code (Act of August 10, 1956, 70A stat. 676).]

(c)   [50 U.S.C. 409(c)] The term "Department of the Air Force" as used in this Act shall be construed to mean the Department of the Air Force at the seat of government and all field headquarters, forces, reserve components, installations, activities, and functions under the control or supervision of the Department of the Air Force.

[Section 208 (less subsection (c)) was repealed by the law enacting titles 10 and 32, United States Code (Act of August 10, 1956, 70A Stat. 676). Section 208(c) was repealed by the law enacting title 5, United States Code (Public Law 89-544, September 6, 1966, 80 Stat. 654).]

[Sections 209-214 were repealed by the law enacting titles 10 and 32, United States Code (Act of August 10, 1956, 70A Stat. 676).]

TITLE III—MISCELLANEOUS

[Section 301 was repealed by the law enacting title 5, United States Code (Public Law 89-544, September 6, 1966, 80 Stat. 654).]

[Section 302 was repealed by the law enacting titles 10 and 32, United States Code (Act of August 10, 1956, 70A Stat. 676).]

ADVISORY COMMITTEES AND PERSONNEL

Section 303. [50 U.S.C.405]

(a) The Director of the Office of Defense Mobilization, the Director of Central Intelligence, and the National Security Council, acting through its Executive Secretary, are authorized to appoint such advisory committees and to employ, consistent with other provisions of this Act, such part-time advisory personnel as they may deem necessary in carrying out their respective functions and the functions of agencies under their control. Persons holding other offices or positions under the United States for which they receive compensation, while serving as members of such committees, shall receive no additional compensation for such service. Other members of such committees and other part-time advisory personnel so employed may serve without compensation or may receive compensation at a daily rate not to exceed the daily equivalent of the rate of pay in effect for grade GS-18 of the General Schedule established by section 5332 of title 5, United States Code, as determined by appointing authority.

(b) Service of an individual as a member of any such advisory committee, or in any other part-time capacity for a department or agency hereunder, shall not be considered as service bringing such individual within the provisions of section 203, 205, or 207, of title 18, United States Code, unless the act of such individual, which by such section is made unlawful when performed by an individual referred to in such section, is with respect to any particular matter which directly involves a department or agency which such person is advising or in which such department or agency is directly interested.

[Sections 304-306 were repealed by the law enacting title 5, United States Code (Public Law 89-544, September 6, 1966, 80 Stat. 654).]

AUTHORIZATION FOR APPROPRIATIONS

Section 307. [50 U.S.C. 411] There are hereby authorized to be appropriated such sums as may be necessary and appropriate to carry out the provisions and purposes of this Act.

DEFINITIONS

Section 308. [50 U.S.C. 410]

(a)[10] As used in this Act, the term "function" includes functions, powers, and duties.

(b)   As used in this Act, the term "Department of Defense" shall be deemed to include the military departments of the Army, the Navy, and the Air Force, and all agencies created under title II of this Act.

SEPARABILITY

Section 309. [50 U.S.C. 401 note] If any provision of this Act or the application thereof to any person or circumstances is held invalid, the validity of the remainder of the Act and of the application of such provision to other persons and circumstances shall not be affected thereby.

EFFECTIVE DATE

Section 310. [50 U.S.C. 401 note]

(a) The first sentence of section 202(a) and sections 1, 2, 307, 308, 309, and 310 shall take effect immediately upon the enactment of this Act.

(b)   Except as provided in subsection (a), the provisions of this Act shall take effect on whichever the following days is the earlier: the day after the day upon which the Secretary of Defense first appointed takes office, or the sixtieth day after the date of the enactment of this Act.

SUCCESSION TO THE PRESIDENCY

Section 311. [Section 311 consisted of an amendment to the Act entitled "An Act to provide for the performance of the duties of the office of President in case of removal, resignation, death, or inability of both the President and Vice President."]

[Title IV *less* section 411 was repealed by section 307 of Public Law 87-651 (Act of September 7, 1962, 76 Stat. 526).]

REPEALING AND SAVING PROVISIONS

Section 411. [50 U.S.C. 412] All laws, orders, regulations inconsistent with the provisions of this title are repealed insofar as they are inconsistent with the powers, duties, and responsibilities enacted hereby: *Provided,* That the powers, duties, and responsibilities of the Secretary of Defense under this title shall be administered in conformance with the policy and requirements for administration of budgetary and fiscal matters in the Government generally, including accounting and financial reporting, and that nothing in this title shall be construed as eliminating or modifying the powers, duties, and responsibilities of any other department, agency, or officer of the Government in connection with such matters, but no such department, agency, or officer shall exercise any such powers, duties, or responsibilities in a manner that will render ineffective the provisions of this title.

TITLE IV ACCOUNTABILITY FOR INTELLIGENCE ACTIVITIES[11]

CONGRESSIONAL OVERSIGHT

Section 501. [50 U.S.C. 413]

(a) To the extent consistent with all applicable authorities and duties, including those conferred by the Constitution upon the executive and legislative branches of the Government, and to the extent consistent with due regard for the protection from unauthorized disclosure of classified information and information relating to intelligence sources and methods, the Director of Central Intelligence and the heads of all departments, agencies, and other entities of the United States involved in intelligence activities shall—

(1) keep the Select Committee on Intelligence of the Senate and the Permanent Select Committee on Intelligence of the House of Representatives (hereinafter in this section referred to as "intelligence committees") fully and currently informed of all intelligence activities which are the responsibility of, are engaged in by, or are carried out for or on behalf of, any department, agency, or entity of the United States, including any significant anticipated intelligence activity, except that (A) the foregoing provision shall not require approval of the intelligence committees as a condition precedent to the initiation of any such anticipated intelligence activity, and (B) if the President determines it is essential to limit prior notice to meet extraordinary circumstances affecting vital interests of the United States, such notice shall be limited to the chairman and ranking minority members of the intelligence committees, the Speaker and minority leader of the House of Representatives, and the majority and minority leaders of the Senate;

(2) furnish any information or material concerning intelligence activities which is in the possession, custody, or control of any department, agency, or entity of the United States and which is requested by either of the intelligence committees in order to carry out its authorized responsibilities; and

(3) report in a timely fashion to the intelligence committees any illegal intelligence activity or significant intelligence failure and any corrective action that has been taken or is planned to be taken in connection with such illegal activity or failure.

(b) The President shall inform the intelligence committees in a timely fashion of intelligence operations in foreign countries, other than activities intended solely for obtaining necessary intelligence, for which prior notice was not given under subsection (a) and shall provide a statement for the reasons for not giving prior notice.

(c) The President and the intelligence committees shall each establish such procedures as may be necessary to carry out the provisions of subsections (a) and (b).

(d) The House of Representatives and the Senate, in consultation with the Director of Central Intelligence, shall each establish, by rule or resolution of such House, procedures to protect from unauthorized disclosure all classified information and all information relating to intelligence sources and methods furnished to intelligence committees or to Members of the Congress under this section. In accordance with such procedures, each of the intelligence committees shall promptly call to the attention of its respective House, or to any appropriate committee or committees of its respective House, any matter relating to intelligence activities requiring the attention of such House or such committee or committees.

(e) Nothing in this Act shall be construed as authority to withhold information from the intelligence committees on the grounds that providing the information to the intelligence committees would constitute the unauthorized disclosure of classified information or information relating to intelligence sources and methods.

TITLE VI—PROTECTION OF CERTAIN NATIONAL SECURITY INFORMATION[12]

Section 601.

(a) Whoever, having or having had authorized access to classified information that identifies a covert agent, intentionally discloses any information identifying such covert agent to any individual not authorized to receive classified information, knowing that the information disclosed so identifies such covert agent and that the United States is taking affirmative measures to conceal such covert agent's intelligence relationship to the United States, shall be fined not more than $50,000 or imprisoned not more than ten years, or both.

(b) Whoever, as a result of having authorized access to classified information, learns the identity of a covert agent and intentionally discloses any information identifying such covert agent to any individual not authorized to receive classified information, knowing that the information disclosed so identifies such covert agent and that the United States is taking affirmative measures to conceal such covert agent's intelligence relationship to the United States, shall be fined not more than $25,000 or imprisoned not more than five years, or both.

(c) Whoever, in the course of a pattern of activities intended to identify and expose covert agents and with reason to believe that such activities would impair or impede the foreign intelligence activities of the United States, discloses any information that identifies an individual as a covert agent to any individual not authorized to receive classified information, knowing that the information disclosed so identifies such individual and that the United States is taking affirmative measures to conceal such individual's classified intelligence relationship to the United States, shall be fined not more than $15,000 or imprisoned not more than three years, or both.

DEFENSES AND EXCEPTIONS

Section 602.

(a) It is a defense to a prosecution under section 601 that before the commission of the offense with which the defendant is charged, the United States had publicly acknowledged or revealed the intelligence relationship to the United States of the individual the disclosure of whose intelligence relationship to the United States is the basis for the prosecution.

(b)

(1) Subject to paragraph (2), no person other than a person committing an

offense under section 601 shall be subject to prosecution under such section by virtue of section 2 or 4 of title 18, United States Code, or shall be subject to prosecution for conspiracy to commit an offense under such section.

(2) Paragraph (1) shall not apply

    (A)   in the case of a person who acted in the course of a pattern of activities intended to identify and expose covert agents and with reason to believe that such activities would impair or impede the foreign intelligence activities of the United States, or

    (B)   in the case of a person who has authorized access to classified information.

(c)   It shall not be an offense under section 601 to transmit information described in such section directly to the Select Committee on Intelligence of the Senate or to the Permanent Select Committee on Intelligence of the House of Representatives.

(d)   It shall not be an offense under section 601 for an individual to disclose information that solely identifies himself as a covert agent.

REPORT

Section 603.

    (a)   The President, after receiving information from the Director of Central Intelligence, shall submit to the Select Committee on Intelligence of the Senate and the Permanent Select Committee on Intelligence of the House of Representatives an annual report on measures to protect the identities of covert agents, and on any other matter relevant to the protection of the identities of covert agents.

    (b)   The report described in subsection (a) shall be exempt from any requirement for publication or disclosure. The first such report shall be submitted no later than February 1, 1983.

EXTRATERRITORIAL JURISDICTION

Section 604. There is jurisdiction over an offense under section 601 committed outside the United States if the individual committing the offense is a citizen of the United States or an alien lawfully admitted to the United States for permanent residence (as defined in section 101(a)(20) of the Immigration and Nationality Act).

PROVIDING INFORMATION TO CONGRESS

Section 605. Nothing in this title may be construed as authority to withhold information from the Congress or from a committee of either House of Congress.

DEFINITIONS

Section 606. For purposes of this title:

    (1)   The term "classified information" means information or material designated and clearly marked or clearly represented, pursuant to the provi-

sions of a statute or Executive order (or a regulation or order issued pursuant to a statute or Executive order), as requiring a specific degree of protection against unauthorized disclosure for reasons of national security.

(2) The term "authorized," when used with respect to access to classified information, means having authority, right, or permission pursuant to the provisions of a statute, Executive order, directive of the head of any department or agency engaged in foreign intelligence or counterintelligence activities, order of any United States court, or provisions of any Rule of the House of Representatives or resolution of the Senate which assigns responsibility within the respective House of Congress for the oversight of intelligence activities.

(3) The term "disclose" means to communicate, provide, impart, transmit, transfer, convey, publish, or otherwise make available.

(4) The term "covert agent" means—

(A) an officer or employee of an intelligence agency or a member of the Armed Forces assigned to duty with an intelligence agency—

(i) whose identity as such an officer, employee, or member is classified information, and

(ii) who is serving outside the United States or has within the last five years served outside the United States; or

(B) a United States citizen whose intelligence relationship to the United States is classified information, and—

(i) who resides and acts outside the United States as an agent of, or informant or source of operational assistance to, an intelligence agency, or

(ii) who is at the time of the disclosure acting as an agent of, or informant to, the foreign counterintelligence or foreign counterterrorism components of the Federal Bureau of Investigation; or

(C) an individual, other than a United States citizen, whose past or present intelligence relationship to the United States is classified information and who is a present or former agent of, or a present or former informant or source of operational assistance to, an intelligence agency.

(5) The term "intelligence agency" means the Central Intelligence Agency, a foreign intelligence component of the Department of Defense, or the foreign counterintelligence or foreign counterterrorism components of the Federal Bureau of Investigation.

(6) The term "informant" means any individual who furnishes information to an intelligence agency in the course of a confidential relationship protecting the identity of such individual from public disclosure.

(7) The terms "officer" and "employee" have the meanings given such terms by section 2104 and 2105, respectively, of title 5, United States Code.

(8) The term "Armed Forces" means the Army, Navy, Air Force, Marine Corps, and Coast Guard.

(9) The term "United States," when used in a geographic sense, means all areas under the territorial sovereignty of the United States and the Trust Territory of the Pacific Islands.

(10) The term "pattern of activities" requires a series of acts with a common purpose or objective.

TITLE VII—PROTECTION OF OPERATIONAL FILES OF THE CENTRAL INTELLIGENCE AGENCY

EXEMPTION OF CERTAIN OPERATIONAL FILES FROM SEARCH, REVIEW, PUBLICATION, OR DISCLOSURE

Section 701.

(a) Operational files of the Central Intelligence Agency may be exempted by the Director of Central Intelligence from the provisions of section 552 of title 5, United States Code (Freedom of Information Act), which require publication or disclosure, or search or review in connection therewith.

(b) For the purposes of this title the term "operational files" means—

(1) files of the Directorate of Operations which document the conduct of foreign intelligence or counterintelligence operations or intelligence or security liaison arrangements or information exchanges with foreign governments or their intelligence or security services;

(2) files of the Directorate for Science and Technology which document the means by which foreign intelligence or counterintelligence is collected through scientific and technical systems; and

(3) files of the Office of Security which document investigations conducted to determine the suitability of potential foreign intelligence or counterintelligence sources; except that files which are the sole repository of disseminated intelligence are not operational files.

(c) Notwithstanding subsection (a) of this section, exempted operational files shall continue to be subject to search and review for information concerning—

(1) United States citizens or aliens lawfully admitted for permanent residence who have requested information on themselves pursuant to the provisions of section 552 of title 5, United States Code (Freedom of Information Act), or section 552a of title 5, United States Code (Privacy Act of 1974);

(2) any special activity the existence of which is not exempt from disclosure under the provisions of section 552 of title 5, United States Code (Freedom of Information Act); or

(3) the specific subject matter of an investigation by the intelligence committees of the Congress, the Intelligence Oversight Board, the Department of Justice, the Office of General Counsel of the Central Intelligence Agency, the Office of Inspector General of the Central Intelligence Agency, or the Office of the Director of Central Intelligence for an impropriety, or violation of law, Executive order, or Presidential directive, in the conduct of an intelligence activity.

(d)

(1) Files that are not exempted under subsection (a) of this section which contain information derived or disseminated from exempted operational files shall be subject to search and review.

(2) The inclusion of information from exempted operational files in files that are not exempted under subsection (a) of this section shall not affect the exemption under subsection (a) of this section of the originating operational files from search, review, publication, or disclosure.

(3) Records from exempted operational files which have been disseminated to and referenced in files that are not exempted under subsection (a) of this section and which have been returned to exempted operational files for sole retention shall be subject to search and review.

(e) The provisions of subsection (a) of this section shall not be superceded except by a provision of law which is enacted after the date of enactment of subsection (a), and which specifically cites and repeals or modifies its provisions.

(f) Whenever any person who has requested agency records under section 552 of title 5, United States Code (Freedom of Information Act), alleges that the Central Intelligence Agency has improperly withheld records because of failure to comply with any provision of this section, judicial review shall be available under the terms set forth in section 552(a)(4)(B) of title 5, United States Code, except that—

(1) in any case in which information specifically authorized under criteria established by an Executive order to be kept secret in the interest of national defense or foreign relations is filed with, or produced for, the court by the Central Intelligence Agency, such information shall be examined ex parte, in camera by the court;

(2) the court shall, to the fullest extent practicable, determine issues of fact based on sworn written submissions of the parties;

(3) when a complainant alleges that requested records are improperly withheld because of improper placement solely in exempted operational files, the complainant shall support such allegation with a sworn written submission, based upon personal knowledge or otherwise admissible evidence;

(4)

(A) when a complainant alleges that requested records were improperly withheld because of improper exemption of operational files, the Central Intelligence Agency shall meet its burden under section 552(a)(4)(B) of title 5, United States Code, by demonstrating to the court by sworn written submission that exempted operational files likely to contain responsive records currently perform the functions set forth in subsection (b) of this section; and

(B) the court may not order the Central Intelligence Agency to review the content of any exempted operational file or files in order to make the demonstration required under subparagraph (A) of this paragraph, unless the complainant disputed the Central Intelligence Agency's showing with a sworn written submission based on personal knowledge or otherwise admissible evidence;

(5) in proceedings under paragraphs (3) and (4) of this subsection, the parties shall not obtain discovery pursuant to rules 26 through 36 of the Federal Rules of Civil Procedure, except that requests for admission may be made pursuant to rules 26 and 36;

(6) if the court finds under this subsection that the Central Intelligence Agency

has improperly withheld requested records because of failure to comply with any provision of this section, the court shall order the Central Intelligence Agency to search and review the appropriate exempted operational file or files for the requested records and make such records, or portions thereof, available in accordance with the provisions of section 552 of title 5, United States Code (Freedom of Information Act), and such order shall be the exclusive remedy for failure to comply with this section; and

(7) if at any time following the filing of a complaint pursuant to this subsection the Central Intelligence Agency agrees to search the appropriate exempted operational file or files for the requested records, the court shall dismiss the claim based upon such complaint.

DECENNIAL REVIEW OF EXEMPTED OPERATIONAL FILES

Section 702.

(a) Not less than once every ten years, the Director of Central Intelligence shall review the exemptions in force under subsection (a) of section 701 of this Act to determine whether such exemptions may be removed from any category of exempted files or any portion thereof.

(b) The review required by subsection (a) of this section shall include consideration of the historical value or other public interest in the subject matter of the particular category of files or portions thereof and the potential for declassifying a significant part of the information contained therein.

(c) A complainant who alleges that the Central Intelligence Agency has improperly withheld records because of failure to comply with this section may seek judicial review in the district court of the United States of the district in which any of the parties reside, or in the District of Columbia. In such a proceeding, the court's review shall be limited to determining (1) whether the Central intelligence Agency has conducted the review required by subsection (a) of this section within ten years of the enactment of this title or within ten years after the last review, and (2) whether the Central Intelligence Agency, in fact, considered the criteria set forth in subsection (b) of this section in conducting the required review.

Notes

1. The positions of Director for Mutual Security, Chairman of the National Security Resources Board, and Chairman of the Research and Development Board have been abolished by various Reorganization Plans. The statutory members of the National Security Council are the President, Vice President, Secretary of State, and Secretary of Defense.
2. The specification of the salary of the head of the National Security Council staff is obsolete and has been superseded.
3. The Classification Act of 1923 was repealed by the Classification Act of 1949. The Classification Act of 1949 was repealed by the law enacting title 5, United States Code (Public Law 89–544, Sept. 6, 1966, 80 Stat. 378), and its provisions were codified as chapter 51 and subchapter 53 of title 5. Section 7(b) of that Act (80 Stat. 631) provided: "A reference to a law replaced by sections 1–6 of this Act, including a reference in a regulation, order, or other law, is deemed to refer to the corresponding provision enacted by this Act."

4. The cited Act of August 24, 1912, was repealed by the law enacting title 5, United States Code (Public Law 89–544, Sept. 6, 1966, 80 Stat. 378). The provisions of section 6 of that Act were codified as section 7501 of title 5.

5. The functions of the Civil Service Commission were transferred to the Director of the Office of Personnel Management by section 102 of Reorganization Plan No. 2 of 1978 (92 Stat. 3783; 5 U.S.C. 1101 note).

6. Section 103 deals with emergency preparedness. Section 50 of the Act of September 3, 1954 (68 Stat. 1244), eliminated former subsection (a), relating to the establishment of the National Security Resources Board, and redesignated former subsections (b)–(d) as subsections (a)–(c). The section heading was not amended accordingly.

7. The functions of the Director of the Office of Defense Mobilization under this section which previously were transferred to the President, were delegated to the Director of the Federal Emergency Management Agency by section 4–102 of Executive Order No. 12148 (July 20, 1979, 44 F.R. 43239, 50 U.S.C. App. 2251 note).

8. The Classification Act of 1949 was repealed by the law enacting title 5, United States Code (Public Law 89–544, September 6, 1966, 80 Stat. 378), and its provisions were codified as chapter 51 and subchapter 53 of that title.

9. Title IV of the Revised Statutes consisted of sections 158-198 of the Revised Statutes. Sections 176 and 193 are codified as sections 492–1 and 492–2 of title 31, United States Code. The remainder of those sections have been repealed or replaced by provisions of title 5, United States Code, as enacted. See the "Tables" volume of the United States Code for the distribution of specific sections.

10. Section 307 of Public Law 87–651 (Act of Sept. 7, 1962, 76 Stat. 526)repealed section 308(a) *less* its applicability to sections 2, 101–103, and 103.

11. This title is also set out *post* at page 211 along with other materials relating to congressional oversight of intelligence activities.

12. Title VI was added by the Intelligence Identities Protection Act of 1982 (Public Law 97–200).

Appendix F

Section 552, Title 5, United States Code
Freedom of Information Act, 1967

552. Public information: agency rules, opinions, orders, records, and proceedings.

(a)   Each agency shall make available to the public information as follows:

(1) Each agency shall separately state and currently publish in the Federal register for the guidance of the public—

(A)   descriptions of its central and field organization and the established places at which, the employees (and in the case of the uniformed service, the members) from whom, and the methods whereby, the public may obtain information, make submittals or requests, or obtain decisions;

(B)   statements of the general course and method by which its functions are channeled and determined, including the nature and requirements of all formal and informal procedures available;

(C)   rules of procedure, descriptions of forms available or the places at which forms may be obtained, and instructions as to the scope and contents of all papers, reports, and examinations;

(D)   substantive rules of general applicability adopted as authorized by law, and statements of general policy or interpretations of general applicability formulated and adopted by the agency; and

(E)   each amendment, revision, or repeal of the foregoing.

Except to the extent that a person has actual and timely notice of the terms thereof, a person may not in any manner be required to resort to, or be adversely affected by, a matter required to be published in the Federal Register and not so published. For the purpose of this paragraph, matter reasonably available to the class of persons affected thereby is deemed published in the Federal Register when incorporated by reference therein with the approval of the Director of the Federal Register.

(2) Each agency, in accordance with published rules, shall make available for public inspection and copying—

(A)   final opinions, including concurring and dissenting opinions, as well as orders, made in the adjudication of cases;

(B)   those statements of policy and interpretations which have been adopted by the agency and are not published in the Federal Register; and

(C) administrative staff manuals and instructions to staff that affect a member of the public; unless the materials are promptly published and copies offered for sale. To the extent required to prevent a clearly unwarranted invasion of personal privacy, an agency may delete identifying details when it makes available or publishes an opinion, statement of policy, interpretation, or staff manual or instruction. However, in each case the justification for the deletion shall be explained fully in writing. Each agency shall also maintain and make available for public inspection and copying current indexes providing identifying information for the public as to any matter issued, adopted, or promulgated after July 4, 1967, and required by this paragraph to be made available and published. Each agency shall promptly pub-lish, quarterly or more frequently, and distribute (by sale or otherwise) copies of each index or supplements thereto unless it determines by order published in the Federal Register that the publication would be unnecessary and impracticable, in which case the agency shall nonetheless provide copies of such index on request at a cost not to exceed the direct cost of duplication. A final order, opinion, statement of policy, interpretation, or staff manual or instruction that affects a member of the public may be relied on, used, or cited as precedent by an agency against a party other than an agency if—

(i) it has been indexed and either made available or published as provided by this paragraph; or

(ii) the party has actual and timely notice of the terms thereof.

(3) Except with respect to the records made available under paragraphs (1) and (2) of this subsection, each agency, upon any request for records which (A) reasonably describes such records and (B) is made in accordance with published rules stating the time, place, fees (if any) and procedures to be followed, shall make the records promptly available to any person.

(4)

(A) In order to carry out the provisions of this section, each agency shall promulgate regulations, pursuant to notice and receipt of public com-ments, specifying a uniform schedule of fees applicable to all constitu-ent units of such agency. Such fees shall be limited to reasonable standard charges for document search and duplication and provide for recovery of only the direct costs of such search and duplication. Documents shall be furnished without charge or at a reduced charge where the agency determines that waiver or reduction of the fee is in the public interest because furnishing the information can be consid-ered as primarily benefiting the general public.

(B) On complaint, the district court of the United States in the district in which the complainant resides, or has his principal place of business, or in which the agency records are situated, or in the District of Columbia, has jurisdiction to enjoin the agency from withholding agency records and to order the production of any agency records improperly withheld from the complainant. In such a case the court shall determine the matter de novo, and may examine the contents of such agency records in camera to determine whether such records or any part thereof shall be withheld under any of the exemptions set forth in subsection (b) of this section, and the burden is on the agency to sustain its action.

(C) Notwithstanding any other provision of law, the defendant shall serve an answer or otherwise plead to complaint made under this subsection within thirty days after service upon the defendant of the pleading in which such complaint is made, unless the court otherwise directs for good cause shown.

(D) The court may assess against the United States reasonable attorney fees and other litigation costs reasonably incurred in any case under this section in which the complainant has substantially prevailed.

(E) Whenever the court orders the production of any agency records improperly withheld from the complainant and assesses against the United States reasonable attorney fees and other litigation costs, and the court additionally issues a written finding that the circumstances surrounding the withholding raise questions whether agency personnel acting arbitrarily or capriciously with respect to the withholding, the Special Counsel shall promptly initiate a proceeding to determine whether disciplinary action is warranted against the officer or employee who was primarily responsible for the withholding. The Special Counsel, after investigation and consideration of the evidence submitted, shall submit his findings and recommendations to the administrative authority of the agency concerned and shall send copies of the findings and recommendations to the officer or employee or his representative. The administrative authority shall take the corrective action that the Special Counsel recommends.

(F) In the event of noncompliance with the order of the court, the district court may punish for contempt the responsible employee, and in the case of a uniformed service, the responsible member.

(5) Each agency having more than one member shall maintain and make available for public inspection a record of the final votes of each member in every agency proceeding.

(6)

(A) Each agency, upon any request for records made under paragraph (1), (2), or (3) of this subsection, shall—

(i) determine within ten days (excepting Saturdays, Sundays, and legal holidays) after the receipt of any such request whether to comply with such request and shall immediately notify the person making such request of such determination and the reasons therefor, and of the right of such person to appeal to the head of the agency any adverse determination; and

(ii) make a determination with respect to any appeal within twenty days (excepting Saturdays, Sundays, and legal public holidays) after the receipt of such appeal. If on appeal the denial of the request for records is in whole or in part upheld, the agency shall notify the person making such request of the provisions for judicial review of that determination under paragraph (4) of this subsection.

(B) In unusual circumstances as specified in this subparagraph, the time limits prescribed in either clause (i) or clause (ii) of subparagraph (A) may be extended by written notice to the person making such request setting forth the reasons for such extension and the date on which a determination is expected to be dispatched. No such notice shall specify a date that would result in an extension for more than ten working days. As used in this subparagraph, "unusual circumstances" means, but only to the extent reasonably necessary to the proper processing of the particular request—

(i) the need to search for and collect the requested records from field facilities or other establishments that are separate from the office processing the request;

(ii) the need to search for, collect, and appropriately examine a voluminous amount of separate and distinct records which are demanded in a single request; or

(iii) the need for consultation, which shall be conducted with all practicable speed, with another agency having a substantial interest in the determination of the request or among two or more components of the agency having substantial subject-matter interest therein.

(C) Any person making a request to any agency for records under paragraph (1), (2), or (3) of this subsection shall be deemed to have exhausted his administrative remedies with respect to such request if the agency fails to comply with the applicable time limit provisions of this paragraph. If the Government can show exceptional circumstances exist and that the agency is exercising due diligence in responding to the request, the court may retain jurisdiction and allow the agency additional time to complete its review of the records. Upon any determination by an agency to comply for a request for records, the records shall be made promptly available to such person making such request. Any notification of denial of any request for records under this subsection shall set forth the names and titles or positions of each person responsible for the denial of such request.

(b) This section does not apply to matters that are:

(1) (A) specifically authorized under criteria established by an Executive order to be kept secret in the interest of national defense or foreign policy and (B) are in fact properly classified pursuant to such Executive order;

(2) related solely to the internal personnel rules and practices of an agency;

(3) specifically exempted from disclosure by statute (other than section 552b of this title), provided that such statute (A) requires that the matters be withheld from the public in such a manner as to leave no discretion on the issue, or (B) establishes particular criteria for withholding or refers to particular types of matters to be withheld;

(4) trade secrets and commercial or financial information obtained from a person and privileged or confidential;

(5) inter-agency or intra-agency memorandums or letters which would not be available by law to a party other than an agency in litigation with the agency;

(6) personnel and medical files and similar files the disclosure of which would constitute a clearly unwarranted invasion of personal privacy;

(7) investigatory records compiled for law enforcement purposes, but only to the extent that the production of such records would (A) interfere with enforcement proceedings, (B) deprive a person of a right to a fair or impartial adjudication, (C) constitute an unwarranted invasion of personal privacy, (D) disclose the identity of a confidential source and, in the case of a record compiled by a criminal law enforcement authority in the course of a criminal investigation, or by an agency conducting a lawful national security intelligence investigation, confidential information furnished only by the confidential source, (E) disclose investigative techniques and procedures, or (F) endanger the life or physical safety of law enforcement personnel;

(8) contained in or related to examination, operating, or condition reports prepared by, on behalf of, or for the use of an agency responsible for the regulation or supervision of financial institutions; or

(9) geological or geophysical information and data, including maps, concerning wells.

Any reasonably segregable portion of a record shall be provided to any person requesting such record after deletion of the portions which are exempt under this subsection.

(c) This section does not authorize withholding of information or limit the availability of records to the public, except as specifically stated in this section. This section is not authority to withhold information from Congress.

(d) On or before March 1 of each calendar year, each agency shall submit a report covering the preceding calendar year to the Speaker of the House of Representatives and President of the Senate for referral to the appropriate committees of the Congress. The report shall include—

(1) the number of determinations made by such agency not to comply with requests for records made to such agency under subsection (a) and the reasons for each such determination;

(2) the number of appeals made by persons under subsection (a)(6), the result of such appeals, and the reason for the action upon each appeal that results in a denial of information;

(3) the names and titles or positions of each person responsible for the denial of records requested under this section, and the number of instances of participation for each;

(4) the results of each proceeding conducted pursuant to subsection (a)(4)(F), including a report of the disciplinary action taken against the officer or employee who was primarily responsible for improperly withholding records or an explanation of why disciplinary action was not taken;

(5) a copy of every rule made by such agency regarding this section;

(6) a copy of the fee schedule and the total amount of fees collected by the agency for making records available under this section; and

(7) such other information as indicates efforts to administer fully this section.

The Attorney General shall submit an annual report on or before March 1 of each calendar year which shall include for the prior calendar year a listing of the number of cases arising under this section, the exemption involved in each case, the disposition of such case, and the cost, fees, and penalties assessed under subsections (a)(4)(E), (F), and (G). Such reports shall also include a description of the efforts undertaken by the Department of Justice to encourage agency compliance with this section.

(e) For purposes of this section, the term "agency" as defined in section 551(1) of this title includes any executive department, military department, Government corporation, Government controlled corporation, or other establishment in the executive branch of the Government (including the Executive Office of the President), or any independent regulatory agency.

Appendix G

Public Law 93-148 [H.J. Res. 542], 87 Stat. 555, 50 U.S.C. 1541-1548
War Powers Resolution, 1973

JOINT RESOLUTION

Concerning the war powers of Congress and the President.

Resolved by the Senate and the House of Representatives of the United States of America in Congress assembled,

SHORT TITLE

SECTION 1. This joint resolution may be cited as the "War Powers Resolution."

PURPOSE AND POLICY

SEC. 2.

(a) It is the purpose of this joint resolution to fulfill the intent of the framers of the Constitution of the United States and insure that the collective judgment of both the Congress and the President will apply to the introduction of the United States Armed Forces into hostilities, or into situations where imminent involvement in hostilities is clearly indicated by the circumstances, and to the continued use of such forces in hostilities or in such situations.

(b) Under article I, section 8, of the Constitution, it is specifically provided that the Congress shall have the power to make all laws necessary and proper for carrying into execution, not only its own powers but also all other powers vested by the Constitution in the Government of the United states, or in any department or officer thereof.

(c) The constitutional powers of the President as Commander-in-Chief to introduce United States Armed Forces into hostilities, or into situations where imminent involvement in hostilities is clearly indicated by the circumstances, are exercised only pursuant to (1) a declaration of war, (2) specific statutory authorization, or (3) a national emergency created by attack upon the United States, its territories or possessions, or its armed forces.

CONSULTATION

SEC. 3. The President in every possible instance shall consult with Congress before introducing United States Armed Forces into hostilities or into situations where imminent involvement in hostilities is clearly indicated by the circumstances, and after every such introduction shall consult regularly with the Congress until United States Armed Forces are no longer engaged in hostilities or have been removed from such situations.

REPORTING

SEC. 4.

(a) In the absence of a declaration of war, in any case in which United States Armed Forces are introduced—

(1) into hostilities or into situations where imminent involvement in hostilities is clearly indicated by the circumstances;

(2) into the territory, airspace or waters of a foreign nation, while equipped for combat, except for deployments which relate solely to supply, replacement, repair, or training of such forces; or

(3) in numbers which substantially enlarge United States Armed Forces equipped for combat already located in a foreign nation; the President shall submit within 48 hours to the Speaker of the House of Representatives and to the President pro tempore of the Senate a report, in writing, setting forth—

(A) the circumstances necessitating the introduction of United States Armed Forces;

(B) the constitutional and legislative authority under which such introduction took place; and

(C) the estimated scope and duration of the hostilities or involvement.

(b) The President shall provide such other information as the Congress may request in the fulfillment of its constitutional responsibilities with respect to committing the Nation to war and to the use of United States Armed Forces abroad.

(c) Whenever United States Armed forces are introduced into hostilities or into any situation described in subsection (a) of this section, the President shall, so long as such armed forces continue to be engaged in such hostilities or situation, report to the Congress periodically on the status of such hostilities or situation as well as on the scope and duration of such hostilities or situation, but in no event shall he report to Congress less often than once every six months.

CONGRESSIONAL ACTION

SEC. 5.

(a) Each report submitted pursuant to section (4)(a)(1) shall be transmitted to the Speaker of the House of Representatives and to the President pro tempore of the Senate on the same calendar day. Each report so transmitted shall be referred to the Committee on Foreign Affairs of the House of Representatives and to the Committee on Foreign Relations of the Senate for appropriate action. If, when the report is transmitted, the Congress has adjourned sine die or has adjourned for any period in excess of three calendar days, the Speaker of the House of Representatives and the President pro tempore of the Senate, if they deem it advisable (or if petitioned by at least 30 percent of the membership of their respective Houses) shall jointly request the President to convene the Congress in order that it may consider the report and take appropriate action pursuant to this section.

(b) Within sixty calendar days after a report is submitted or is required to be submitted pursuant to section (4)(a)(1), whichever is earlier, the President shall terminate any use of United States Armed Forces with respect to which such report was submitted (or required to be submitted), unless the Congress (1) has declared war or has enacted a specific authorization for such use of United States Armed Forces, (2) has extended by law such sixty-day period, or (3) is physically unable to meet as a result of an armed attack upon the United States. Such sixty-day period shall be extended for not more than an additional thirty days if the President determines and certifies to the Congress in writing that unavoidable military necessity respecting the safety of United States Armed Forces requires the continued use of such armed forces in the course of bringing about a prompt removal of such forces.

(c) Notwithstanding subsection (b), at any time that United States Armed Forces are engaged in hostilities outside the territory of the United States, its possessions and territories without a declaration of war or a specific statutory authorization, such forces shall be removed by the President if the Congress so directs by concurrent resolution.

CONGRESSIONAL PRIORITY PROCEDURES FOR JOINT RESOLUTION OR BILL

SEC. 6.

(a) Any joint resolution or bill introduced pursuant to section 5(b) at least thirty calendar days before the expiration of the sixty-day period specified in such section shall be referred to the Committee on Foreign Affairs of the House of Representatives or the Committee on Foreign Relations of the Senate, as the case may be, and such committee shall report one such joint resolution or bill, together with its recommendations, not later than twenty-four calendar days before the expiration of the sixty-day period specified in such section, unless such House shall otherwise determine by the yeas and nays.

(b) Any joint resolution or bill so reported shall become the pending business of the House in question (in the case of the Senate the time for debate shall be equally divided between the proponents and the opponents), and shall be voted on within three calendar days thereafter, unless such House shall otherwise determine by yeas and nays.

(c) Such a joint resolution or bill passed by one House shall be referred to the committee of the other House named in subsection (a) and shall be reported out not later than fourteen calendar days before the expiration of the sixty-day period specified in section 5(b). The joint resolution or bill so reported shall become the pending business of the House in question and shall be voted on within three calendar days after it has been reported, unless such House shall otherwise determine by yeas and nays.

(d) In the case of any disagreement between the two Houses of Congress with respect to a joint resolution or bill passed by both Houses, conferees shall be promptly appointed and the committee of conference shall make and file a report with respect to such resolution or bill not later than four calendar days before the expiration of the sixty-day period specified in section 5(b). In the event the conferees are unable to agree within 48 hours, they shall report back to their respective Houses in disagreement. Notwithstanding any rule in either House concerning the printing of conference reports in the Record or concerning any delay in the consideration of such reports, such report shall be acted on by both Houses not later than the expiration of such sixty-day period.

CONGRESSIONAL PRIORITY PROCEDURES FOR CONCURRENT RESOLUTION

SEC. 7.

(a) Any concurrent resolution introduced pursuant to section 5(c) shall be referred to the Committee on Foreign Affairs of the House of Representatives or the Committee on Foreign Relations of the Senate, as the case may be, and one such concurrent resolution shall be reported out by such committee together with its recommendations within fifteen calendar days, unless such House shall otherwise determine by yeas and nays.

(b) Any concurrent resolution so reported shall become the pending business of the House in question (in the case of the Senate the time for debate shall be equally divided between the proponents and the opponents) and shall be voted on within three calendar days thereafter, unless such House shall otherwise determine by yeas and nays.

(c) Such a concurrent resolution passed by one House shall be referred to the committee of the other House named in subsection (a) and shall be reported out by such committee together with its recommendations within fifteen calendar days and shall thereupon become the pending business of such House and shall be voted upon within three calendar days, unless such House shall otherwise determine by yeas and nays.

(d) In the case of any disagreement between the two Houses of Congress with respect to a concurrent resolution passed by both Houses, conferees shall be promptly appointed and the committee of conference shall make and file a report with respect to such concurrent resolution within six calendar days after the legislation is referred to the committee of conference. Notwithstanding any rule in either House concerning the printing of conference reports in the Record or concerning any delay in the consideration of such reports, such report shall be acted on by both Houses not later than six calendar days after the conference report is filed. In the event the conferees are unable to agree within 48 hours, they shall report back to their respective Houses in disagreement.

INTERPRETATION OF JOINT RESOLUTION

SEC. 8.

(a) Authority to introduce United States Armed Forces into hostilities or into situations wherein involvement in hostilities is clearly indicated by the circumstances shall not be inferred—

(1) from any provision or law (whether or not in effect before the date of the enactment of this joint resolution), including any provision contained in any appropriation Act, unless such provision specifically authorizes the introduction of United States Armed Forces into hostilities or into such

situations and states that it is intended to constitute specific statutory authorization within the meaning of this joint resolution; or

(2) from any treaty heretofore or hereafter ratified unless such treaty is implemented by legislation specifically authorizing the introduction of United States Armed Forces into hostilities or into such situations and stating that it is intended to constitute specific statutory authorization within the meaning of this joint resolution.

(b) Nothing in this joint resolution shall be construed to require any further specific statutory authorization to permit members of United States Armed Forces to participate jointly with members of the armed forces of one or more foreign countries in the headquarters operations of high-level military commands which were established prior to the date of enactment of this joint resolution and pursuant to the United Nations Charter or any treaty ratified by the United States prior to such date.

(c) For purposes of this joint resolution, the term "introduction of United States Armed Forces" includes the assignment of members of such armed forces to command, coordinate, participate in the movement of, or accompany the regular or irregular military forces of any foreign country or government when such military forces are engaged, or there exists an imminent threat that such forces will become engaged, in hostilities.

(d) Nothing in this joint resolution—

(1) is intended to alter the constitutional authority of the Congress or the President, or the provisions of existing treaties; or

(2) shall be construed as granting any authority to the President with respect to the introduction of United States Armed Forces into hostilities or into situations wherein involvement in hostilities is clearly indicated by the circumstances which authority he would not have had in the absence of this joint resolution.

SEPARABILITY CLAUSE

SEC. 9. If any provision of this joint resolution or the application thereof to any person or circumstances is held invalid, the remainder of the joint resolution and the application of such provision to any other person or circumstance shall not be affected thereby.

EFFECTIVE DATE

SEC. 10. This joint resolution shall take effect on the date of its enactment.

Appendix H

Executive Order 11905, February 18, 1976
United States Foreign Intelligence Activities

By virtue of the authority invested in me by the Constitution and statutes of the United States, including the National Security Act of 1947, as amended, and as President of the United States of America, it is hereby ordered as follows:

Section 1. *Purpose.* The purpose of this Order is to establish policies to improve the quality of intelligence needed for national security, to clarify the authority and responsibilities of the intelligence departments and agencies, and to establish effective oversight to assure compliance with law in the management and direction of intelligence agencies and departments of the national government.

Sec. 2. *Definitions.* For the purpose of this Order, unless otherwise indicated, the following terms shall have these meanings:

(a) *Intelligence* means:

(1) *Foreign intelligence* which means information, other than foreign counter-intelligence, on the capabilities, intentions and activities of foreign powers, organizations or their agents; and

(2) *Foreign counterintelligence* which means activities conducted to protect the United States and United States citizens from foreign espionage, sabotage, subversion, assassination or terrorism.

(b) *Intelligence Community* refers to the following organizations:

(1) Central Intelligence Agency;

(2) National Security Agency;

(3) Defense Intelligence Agency;

(4) Special offices within the Department of Defense for the collection of specialized intelligence through reconnaissance programs;

(5) Intelligence elements of the military services;

(6) Intelligence element of the Federal Bureau of Investigation;

(7) Intelligence element of the Department of State;

(8) Intelligence element of the Department of the Treasury; and

(9) Intelligence element of the Energy Research and Development Administration.

(c) *Special activities in support of national foreign policy objectives* means activities, other than the collection and production of intelligence and related support functions, designed to further official United States programs and policies abroad which are planned and executed so that the role of the United States Government is not apparent or publicly acknowledged.

(d) *National Foreign Intelligence Program* means the programs of the Central Intelligence Agency and the special offices within the Department of Defense for the collection of specialized intelligence through reconnaissance programs, the Consolidated Cryptologic Program, and those elements of the General Defense Intelligence Program and other programs of the departments and agencies, not including tactical intelligence, designated by the Committee on Foreign Intelligence as part of the Program.

Sec. 3. *Control and Direction of National Intelligence Organizations.*

(a) *National Security Council.*

(1) The National Security Council was established by the National Security Act of 1947 to advise the President with respect to the integration of domestic, foreign, and military policies relating to the national security. Statutory members of the National Security Council are the President, the Vice President, the Secretary of State, and the Secretary of Defense.

(2) Among its responsibilities, the National Security Council shall provide guidance and direction to the development and formulation of national intelligence activities.

(3) The National Security Council shall conduct a semi-annual review on intelligence policies and of ongoing special activities in support of national foreign policy objectives. These reviews shall consider the needs of users of intelligence and the timeliness and quality of intelligence products and the continued appropriateness of special activities in support of national foreign policy objectives. The National Security Council shall consult with the Secretary of the Treasury and such other users of intelligence as designated by the President as part of these reviews.

(b) *Committee on Foreign Intelligence.*

(1) There is established the Committee on Foreign Intelligence (hereinafter referred to as the CFI), which shall be composed of the Director of Central Intelligence, hereinafter referred to as the DCI, who shall be the Chairman; the Deputy Secretary of Defense for Intelligence; and the Deputy Assistant to the President for National Security Affairs. The CFI shall report directly to the National Security Council.

(2) The CFI shall (i) control budget preparation and resource allocation for the National Foreign Intelligence Program.

(A) The CFI shall, prior to submission to the Office of Management and Budget, review, and amend as it deems appropriate, the budget for the National Foreign Intelligence Program.

(B) The CFI shall also adopt rules governing the reprogramming of funds within this budget. Such rules may require that reprogrammings of certain types or amounts be given prior approval by the CFI.

(ii) Establish policy priorities for the collection and production of national intelligence.

(iii) Establish policy for the management of the National Foreign Intelligence Program.

    (iv)   Provide guidance on the relationship between tactical and national intelligence; however, neither the DCI nor the CFI shall have responsibility for tactical intelligence.

    (v)   Provide continuing guidance to the Intelligence Community in order to ensure compliance with policy directions of the NSC.

(3) The CFI shall be supported by the Intelligence Community staff headed by the Deputy to the Director of Central Intelligence for the Intelligence Community.

(4) The CFI shall establish such subcommittees as it deems appropriate to ensure consultation with members of the Intelligence Community on policies and guidance issued by the CFI.

(5) Decisions of the CFI may be reviewed by the National Security Council upon appeal by the Director of Central Intelligence or any member of the National Security Council.

(c)   *The Operations Advisory Group.*

(1) There is established the Operations Advisory Group (hereinafter referred to as the Operations Group), which shall be composed of the Assistant to the President for National Security Affairs; the Secretaries of State and Defense; the Chairman of the Joint Chiefs of Staff; and the Director of Central Intelligence. The Chairman shall be designated by the President. The Attorney General and the Director of the Office of Management and Budget or their representatives, and others who may be designated by the President, shall attend all meetings as observers.

(2) The Operations Group shall (i) consider and develop a policy recommendation, including any dissents, for the President prior to his decision on each special activity in support of national foreign policy objectives.

    (ii)   Conduct periodic reviews of programs previously considered by the Operations Group.

    (iii) Give approval for specific sensitive intelligence collection operations as designated by the Operations Group.

    (iv)   Conduct periodic reviews of ongoing sensitive intelligence collection operations.

(3) The Operations Group shall discharge the responsibilities assigned by subparagraphs (c)(2)(i) and (c)(2)(iii) of this section only after consideration in a formal meeting attended by all members and observers; or, in unusual circumstances when any member or observer is unavailable, when a designated representative of the member or observer attends.

(4) The staff of the National Security Council shall provide support to the Operations Group.

(d)   *Director of Central Intelligence.*

(1) The Director of Central Intelligence, pursuant to the National Security Act of 1947, shall be responsible directly to the National Security Council and the President. He shall:

    (i)   Chair the CFI.

(ii) Act as executive head of the CIA and Intelligence Community staff.

(iii) Ensure the development and submission of a budget for the National Foreign Intelligence Program to the CFI.

(iv) Act as the President's primary adviser on foreign intelligence and provide him and other officials in the Executive branch with foreign intelligence, including National Intelligence Estimates; develop national intelligence requirements and priorities; and supervise production and dissemination of national intelligence.

(v) Ensure appropriate implementation of special activities in support of national foreign policy objectives.

(vi) Establish procedures to ensure the propriety of requests, and responses thereto, from the White House Staff or other Executive departments and agencies to the Intelligence Community.

(vii) Ensure that appropriate programs are developed which properly protect intelligence sources, methods and analytical procedures. His responsibility within the United States shall be limited to:

(A) Protection by lawful means against disclosure by present or former employees of the Central Intelligence Agency or persons, or employees of persons or organizations, presently or formerly under contract with the Agency;

(B) providing leadership, guidance and technical assistance to other government departments and agencies performing foreign intelligence activities; and

(C) in cases involving serious or continuing security violations, recommending to the Attorney General that the case be referred to the Federal Bureau of Investigation for further investigation.

(viii) Establish a vigorous program to downgrade and declassify foreign intelligence information as appropriate and consistent with Executive Order No. 11652.

(ix) Ensure the existence of strong Inspector General capabilities in all elements of the Intelligence Community and that each Inspector General submits quarterly to the Intelligence Oversight Board a report which sets forth any questionable activities in which that intelligence organization has engaged or is engaged.

(x) Ensure the establishment, by the Intelligence Community, of common security standards for managing and handling foreign intelligence systems, information and products, and for granting access thereto.

(xi) Act as a principal spokesman to the Congress for the Intelligence Community and facilitate the use of foreign intelligence products by Congress.

(xii) Promote the development and maintenance by the Central Intelligence Agency of services of common concern to the Intelligence Community organizations, including multi-discipline analysis, national level intelligence products, and a national level current intelligence publication.

(xiii) Establish uniform criteria for the identification, selection, and designation of relative priorities for the transmission of critical intelligence, and provide the Secretary of Defense with continuing guidance as to the communications requirements of the Intelligence Community for the transmission of such intelligence.

(xiv) Establish such committees of collectors, producers and users of intelligence to assist in his conduct of his responsibilities as he deems appropriate.

(xv) Consult with users and producers of intelligence, including the Departments of State, Treasury, and Defense, the military services, the Federal Bureau of Investigation, the Energy Research and Development Administration, and the Council of Economic Advisors, to ensure the timeliness, relevancy and quality of the intelligence product.

(2) To assist the Director of Central Intelligence in the supervision and direction of the Intelligence Community, the position of Deputy Director of Central Intelligence for the Intelligence Community is hereby established (Committee on Foreign Intelligence).

(3) To assist the Director of Central Intelligence in the supervision and direction of the Central Intelligence Agency, the Director of Central Intelligence shall, to the extent consistent with his statutory responsibilities, delegate the day-to-day operation of the Central Intelligence Agency to the Deputy Director of Central Intelligence (50 U.S.C. 403(a)).

(4) To assist the Director of Central Intelligence in the fulfillment of his responsibilities, the heads of all departments and agencies shall give him access to all information relevant to the foreign intelligence needs of the United States. Relevant information requested by the DCI shall be provided, and the DCI shall take appropriate steps the maintain its confidentiality.

Sec. 4. *Responsibilities and Duties of the Intelligence Community.*

Purpose. The rules of operation prescribed by this section of the Order relate to the activities of our foreign intelligence agencies. In some instances, detailed implementation of this Executive order will be contained in classified documents because of the sensitivity of the information and its relation to national security. All such classified instructions will be consistent with this Order. Unless otherwise specified within this section, its provisions apply to activities both inside and outside the United States, and all references to law are to applicable laws of the United States. Nothing in this section of this Order shall be construed to interfere with any law-enforcement responsibility of any department or agency.

(a) *Senior Officials of the Intelligence Community.* The senior officials of the CIA, Departments of State, Treasury and Defense, ERDA and the FBI shall ensure that, in discharging the duties and responsibilities enumerated for their organizations which relate to foreign intelligence, they are responsive to the needs of the President, the National Security Council and other elements of the Government. In carrying out their duties and responsibilities, senior officials shall ensure that all policies and directives relating to intelligence activities are carried out in accordance with law and this Order, including Section 5, and shall:

(1) Make appropriate use of the capabilities of the other elements of the Intelligence Community in order to achieve maximum efficiency.

(2) Contribute in areas of his responsibility to the national intelligence products produced under auspices of the Director of Central Intelligence.

(3) Establish internal policies and guidelines governing employee conduct and ensuring that such are made known to, and acknowledged by, each employee.

(4) Provide for a strong and independent organization for identification and inspection of, and reporting on, unauthorized activity.

(5) Report to the Attorney General that information which relates to detection or prevention of possible violations of law by any person, including an employee of the senior official's department or agency.

(6) Furnish to the Director of Central Intelligence, the CFI, the Operations Group, the President's Foreign Intelligence Advisory Board, and the Intelligence Oversight Board all of the information required for the performance of their respective duties.

(7) Participate, as appropriate, in the provision of services of common concern as directed by the Director of Central Intelligence and provide other departments and agencies with such mutual assistance as may be within his capabilities and as may be required in the interests of the Intelligence Community for reasons of economy, effectiveness, or operational necessity.

(8) Protect intelligence and intelligence sources and methods within his department or agency, consistent with policies and guidance of the Director of Central Intelligence.

(9) Conduct a continuing review of all classified material originating within his organization and promptly declassifying such material consistent with Executive Order No. 11652, as amended.

(10) Provide administrative and support functions required by his department or agency.

(b) *The Central Intelligence Agency.* All duties and responsibilities of the Central Intelligence Agency shall be related to the foreign intelligence functions outlined below. As authorized by the National Security Act of 1947, as amended, the CIA Act of 1949, as amended, and other laws, regulations, and directives, the Central Intelligence Agency shall:

(1) Produce and disseminate foreign intelligence relating to the national security, including foreign political, economic, scientific, technical, military, sociological, and geographic intelligence, to meet the needs of the President, the National Security Council, and other elements of the United States Government.

(2) Develop and conduct programs to collect political, economic, scientific, technical, military, geographic, and sociological information, not otherwise obtainable, relating to foreign intelligence, in accordance with directives of the National Security Council.

(3) Collect and produce intelligence on foreign aspects of international terrorist activities and traffic in narcotics.

(4) Conduct foreign counterintelligence activities outside the United States and when inside the United States in coordination with the FBI subject to the approval of the Attorney General.

(5) Carry out such other special activities in support of national foreign policy objectives as may be directed by the President or the National Security Council and which are within the limits of applicable law.

(6) Conduct, for the Intelligence Community, services of common concern as directed by the National Security Council, such as monitoring of foreign public radio and television broadcasts and foreign press services, collection of foreign intelligence information from cooperating sources in the United States, acquisition and translation of foreign publications and photographic interpretation.

(7) Carry out or contract for research, development and procurement of technical systems and devices relating to the functions authorized in this subsection.

(8) Protect the security of its installations, activities, information and personnel. In order to maintain this security, the CIA shall conduct such investigations of applicants, employees, and other persons with similar associations with the CIA as are necessary.

(9) Conduct administrative, technical and support activities in the United States or abroad as may be necessary to perform the functions described in paragraphs (1) through (8) above, including procurement, maintenance and transport; communications and data processing; recruitment and training; the provision of personnel, financial and medical services; development of essential cover and proprietary arrangements; entering into contracts and arrangements with appropriate private companies and institutions to provide classified and unclassified research, analytical and developmental services and specialized expertise; and entering into similar arrangements with academic institutions, *provided* CIA sponsorship is known to the appropriate senior officials of the academic institutions and to senior project officials.

(c) *The Department of State.* The Secretary of State shall:

(1) Collect, overtly, foreign political, political-military, sociological, economic, scientific, technical and associated biographic information.

(2) Produce and disseminate foreign intelligence relating to United States foreign policy as required for the execution of his responsibilities and in support of policy-makers involved in foreign relations within the United States Government.

(3) Disseminate within the United States Government, as appropriate, reports received from United States diplomatic missions abroad.

(4) Coordinate with the Director of Central Intelligence to ensure that United States intelligence activities and programs are useful for and consistent with United States foreign policy.

(5) Transmit reporting requirements of the Intelligence Community to our Chiefs of Missions abroad and provide guidance for their collection effort.

(6) Contribute to the Intelligence Community guidance for its collection of intelligence based on the needs of those responsible for foreign policy decisions.

(7) Support Chiefs of Missions in discharging their responsibilities to direct and coordinate the activities of all elements of their missions.

(d) *The Department of the Treasury.* The Secretary of the Treasury shall:

(1) Collect, overtly, foreign financial and monetary information.

(2) Participate with the Department of State in the overt collection of general foreign economic information.

(3) Produce that intelligence required for the Secretary's interdepartmental responsibilities and the mission of the Department of the Treasury.

(4) Contribute intelligence and guidance required for the development of national intelligence.

(5) Disseminate within the United States Government, as appropriate, foreign intelligence information acquired.

(e) *Department of Defense.*

(1) The Secretary of Defense shall:

(i) Collect foreign military intelligence information as well as military-related foreign intelligence information, including scientific, technical, political and economic information as required for the execution of his responsibilities.

(ii) Produce and disseminate, as appropriate, intelligence emphasizing foreign military capabilities and intentions and scientific, technical and economic developments pertinent to his responsibilities.

(iii) Conduct such programs and missions necessary to fulfill national intelligence requirements as determined by the CFI.

(iv) Direct, fund and operate the National Security Agency, and national, defense and military intelligence and reconnaissance entities as required.

(v) Conduct, as the executive agent of the United States Government, signals intelligence activities and communications security, except as otherwise approved by the CFI.

(vi) Provide for the timely transmission of critical intelligence, as defined by the Director of Central Intelligence, within the United States Government.

(2) In carrying out these assigned responsibilities, the Secretary of Defense is authorized to utilize the following:

(i) The Defense Intelligence Agency (whose functions, authorities and responsibilities are currently publicly assigned by Department of Defense Directive No. 5105.21) to:

(A) Produce or provide military intelligence for the Secretary of Defense, the Joint Chiefs of Staff, other Defense components, and, as appropriate, non-Defense agencies.

(B) Coordinate all Department of Defense intelligence collection requirements and manage the Defense Attaché System.

(C) Establish substantive intelligence priority goals and objectives for the Department of Defense and provide guidance on substantive intelligence matters to all major defense intelligence activities.

(D) Review and maintain cognizance of all plans, policies and procedures for noncryptographic intelligence functions of the Department of Defense.

(E) Provide intelligence staff support as directed by the Joint Chiefs of Staff.

(ii) The National Security Agency, whose functions, authorities and responsibilities shall include:

(A) Establishment and operation of an effective unified organization for the signals intelligence activities of the United States Government, except for certain operations which are normally exercised through appropriate elements of the military command structure, or by the CIA.

(B) Exercise control over signals intelligence collection and processing activities of the Government, delegating to an appropriate agent specified resources for such periods and tasks as required for the direct support of military commanders.

(C) Collection, processing and dissemination of signals intelligence in accordance with objectives, requirements, and priorities established by the Director of Central Intelligence.

(D) Dissemination of signals intelligence to all authorized elements of the Government, including the Armed Services, as requested.

(E) Serving under the Secretary of Defense as the central communications security authority of the United States Government.

(F) Conduct of research and development to meet the needs of the United States for signals intelligence and communications security.

(iii) Special offices for the collection of specialized intelligence through reconnaissance programs, whose functions, authorities, and responsibilities shall include:

(A) Carrying out consolidated programs for reconnaissance.

(B) Assigning responsibility to the various departments and agencies of the Government, according to their capabilities, for the research, development, procurement, operations and control of designated means of collection.

(iv) Such other offices within the Department of Defense as shall be deemed appropriate for conduct of the intelligence missions and responsibilities assigned to the Secretary of Defense.

(f) *Energy Research and Development Administration.* The Administrator of the Energy Research and Development Administration shall:

(1) Produce intelligence required for the execution of his responsibilities and the mission of the Energy Research and Development Administration, hereinafter referred to as ERDA, including the area of nuclear and atomic energy.

(2) Disseminate such intelligence and provide technical and analytical expertise to other Intelligence Community organizations and be responsive to the guidance of the Director of Central Intelligence and the Committee on Foreign Intelligence.

(3) Participate with other Intelligence Community agencies and departments in formulating collection requirements where its special technical expertise can contribute to such collection requirements.

(g)   *The Federal Bureau of Investigation.* Under the supervision of the Attorney General and pursuant to such regulations as the Attorney General may establish, the Director of the FBI shall:

(1)   Detect and prevent espionage, sabotage, subversion, and other unlawful activities by or on behalf of foreign powers through such lawful counterintelligence operations within the United States, including electronic surveillance, as are necessary or useful for such purposes.

(2)   Conduct within the United States and its territories, when requested by officials of the Intelligence Community designated by the President, those lawful activities, including electronic surveillance, authorized by the President and specifically approved by the Attorney General, to be undertaken in support of foreign intelligence collection requirements of other intelligence agencies.

(3)   Collect foreign intelligence by lawful means within the United States and its territories when requested by officials of the Intelligence Community designated by the President to make such requests.

(4)   Disseminate, as appropriate, foreign intelligence and counterintelligence information which it acquires to appropriate Federal agencies, State and local law enforcement agencies and cooperating foreign governments.

(5)   Carry out or contract for research, development and procurement of technical systems and devices relating to the functions authorized above.

Sec. 5. Restrictions on Intelligence Activities. Information about the capabilities, intentions and activities of other governments is essential to informed decision-making in the field of national defense and foreign relations. The measures employed to acquire such information should be responsive to the legitimate needs of our Government and must be conducted in a manner which preserves and respects our established concepts of privacy and our civil liberties.

Recent events have clearly indicated the desirability of government-wide direction which will ensure a proper balancing of these interests. This section of this Order does not authorize any activity not previously authorized and does not provide exemption from any restrictions otherwise applicable. Unless otherwise specified, the provisions of this section apply to activities both inside and outside the United States. References to law are to applicable laws of the United States.

(a)   *Definitions.* As used in this section of this Order, the following terms shall have the meanings ascribed to them below:

(1)   "Collection" means any one or more of the gathering, analysis, dissemination or storage of non-publicly available information without the informed express consent of the subject of the information.

(2)   "Counterintelligence" means information concerning the protection of foreign intelligence or national security information and its collection from detection to disclosure.

(3)   "Electronic surveillance" means acquisition of a non-public communication by electronic means, without the consent of a person who is a party to, or, in the case of a non-electronic communication, visibly present at, the communication.

(4)   "Employee" means a person employed by, assigned or detailed to, or acting for a United States foreign intelligence agency.

(5) "Foreign intelligence" means information concerning the capabilities, intentions and activities of any foreign power, or of any non-United States person, whether within or outside the United States, or concerning areas outside the United States.

(6) "Foreign intelligence agency" means the Central Intelligence Agency, National Security Agency, and Defense Intelligence Agency; and further includes any other department or agency of the United States Government or component thereof while it is engaged in the collection of foreign intelligence or counterintelligence, but shall not include any such department, agency or component thereof to the extent that it is engaged in its authorized civil or criminal law enforcement functions; nor shall it include in any case the Federal Bureau of Investigation.

(7) "National security information" has the meaning ascribed to it in Executive Order No. 11652, as amended.

(8) "Physical surveillance" means continuing visual observation by any means; or acquisition of a non-public communication by a person not a party thereto or visibly present thereat through any means which does not involve electronic surveillance.

(9) "United States person" means United States citizens, aliens admitted to the United States for permanent residence and corporations or other organizations incorporated or organized in the United States.

(b) *Restrictions on Collection.* Foreign intelligence agencies shall not engage in any of the following activities:

(1) Physical surveillance directed against a United States person, unless it is a lawful surveillance conducted pursuant to procedures approved by the head of the foreign intelligence agency and directed against any of the following:

(i) A present or former employee of such agency, its present or former contractors or their present or former employees, for the purpose of protecting foreign intelligence or counterintelligence sources or methods or national security information from unauthorized disclosure; or

(ii) a United States person, who is in contact with either such a present or former contractor or employee or with a non-United States person who is the subject of a foreign intelligence or counterintelligence inquiry, but only to the extent necessary to identify such United States person; or

(iii) a United States person outside the United States who is reasonably believed to be acting on behalf of a foreign power or engaging in international terrorist or narcotics activities or activities threatening the national security.

(2) Electronic surveillance to intercept a communication which is made from, or is intended by the sender to be received in, the United States, or directed against United States persons abroad, except lawful electronic surveillance under procedures approved by the Attorney General; *provided*, that the Central Intelligence Agency shall not perform electronic surveillance within the United States, except for the purpose of testing

equipment under procedures approved by the Attorney General consistent with law.

(3) Unconsented physical searches within the United States; or unconsented physical searches directed against United States persons abroad, except lawful searches under procedures approved by the Attorney General.

(4) Opening the mail or examination of envelopes of mail in United States postal channels except in accordance with applicable statutes and regulations.

(5) Examination of Federal tax returns or tax information except in accordance with applicable statutes and regulations.

(6) Infiltration or undisclosed participation within the United States in any organization for the purpose of reporting on or influencing its activities or members; except such infiltration or participation with respect to an organization composed primarily of non-United States persons which is reasonably believed to be acting on behalf of a foreign power.

(7) Collection of information, however acquired, concerning the domestic activities of United States persons except:

   (i)   Information concerning corporations or other commercial organizations which constitutes foreign intelligence or counterintelligence.

   (ii) Information concerning present or former employees, present or former contractors or their present or former employees, or applicants for any such employment or contracting, necessary to protect foreign intelligence or counterintelligence sources or methods or national security information from unauthorized disclosure; and the identity of persons in contact with the foregoing or with a non-United States person who is the subject of a foreign intelligence or counterintelligence inquiry.

   (iii) Information concerning persons who are reasonably believed to be potential sources or contacts, but only for the purpose of determining the suitability or credibility of such persons.

   (iv) Foreign intelligence or counterintelligence gathered abroad or from electronic surveillance conducted in compliance with Section 5(b)(2); or foreign intelligence acquired from cooperating sources in the United States.

   (v)   Information about a United States person who is reasonably believed to be acting on behalf of a foreign power or engaging in international terrorist or narcotics activities.

   (vi) Information concerning persons or activities that pose a clear threat to foreign intelligence agency facilities or personnel, *provided*, that such information is retained only by the foreign intelligence agency threatened and that proper coordination with the Federal Bureau of Investigation is accomplished.

(c) *Dissemination and Storage.* Nothing in this section of this Order shall prohibit:

(1) Lawful dissemination to the appropriate law enforcement agencies of incidentally gathered information indicating involvement in activities which may be a violation of law.

(2) Storage of information required by law to be retained.

(3) Dissemination to foreign intelligence agencies of information of the subject matter types listed in Section 5(b)(7).

(d) *Restrictions on Experimentation.* Foreign intelligence agencies shall not engage in experimentation with drugs on human subjects, except with the informed consent, in writing and witnessed by a disinterested third party, of each such human subject and in accordance with the guidelines issued by the National Commission for the Protection of Human Subjects for Biomedical and Behavioral Research.

(e) *Assistance to Law Enforcement Authorities.*

(1) No foreign intelligence agency shall, except as expressly authorized by law (i) provide services, equipment, personnel or facilities to the Law Enforcement Assistance Administration or to State or local police organizations of the United States or (ii) participate in or fund any law enforcement activity within the United States.

(2) These prohibitions shall not, however, preclude: (i) cooperation between a foreign intelligence agency and appropriate law enforcement agencies for the purpose of protecting the personnel and facilities of the foreign intelligence agency or preventing espionage or other criminal activity related to foreign intelligence or counterintelligence or (ii) provision of specialized equipment or technical knowledge for use by any other Federal department or agency.

(f) *Assignment of Personnel.* An employee of a foreign intelligence agency detailed elsewhere within the Federal Government shall be responsible to the host agency and shall not report to such employee's parent agency on the affairs of the host agency, except as may be directed by the latter. The head of the host agency, and any successor, shall be informed of the detailee's association with the parent agency.

(g) *Prohibition of Assassination.* No employee of the United States Government shall engage in, or conspire to engage in, political assassination.

(h) *Implementation.*

(1) This section of this Order shall be effective on March 1, 1976. Each department and agency affected by this section of this Order shall promptly issue internal directives to implement this section with respect to its foreign intelligence and counterintelligence operations.

(2) The Attorney General shall, within ninety days of the effective date of this section of this Order, issue guidelines relating to activities of the Federal Bureau of Investigation in the areas of foreign intelligence and counterintelligence.

Sec. 6. *Oversight of Intelligence Organizations.*

(a) There is hereby established an Intelligence Oversight Board, hereinafter referred to as the Oversight Board.

(1) The Oversight Board shall have three members who shall be appointed by the President and who shall be from outside the Government and be qualified on the basis of ability, knowledge, diversity of background and experience. The members of the Oversight Board may also serve on the

President's Foreign Intelligence Advisory Board (Executive Order No. 11460 of March 20, 1969). No member of the Oversight Board shall have any personal contractual relationship with any agency or department of the Intelligence Community.

(2) One member of the Oversight Board shall be designated by the President as its Chairman.

(3) The Oversight Board shall:

    (i) Receive and consider reports by Inspectors General and General Counsels of the Intelligence Community concerning activities that raise questions of legality and propriety.

    (ii) Review periodically the practices and procedures of the Inspectors General and General Counsels of the Intelligence Community designed to discover and report to the Oversight Board activities that raise questions of legality or propriety.

    (iii) Review periodically with each member of the Intelligence Community their internal guidelines to ensure their adequacy.

    (iv) Report periodically, at least quarterly, to the Attorney General and the President on its findings.

    (v) Report in a timely manner to the Attorney General and to the President any activities that raise serious questions about legality.

    (vi) Report in a timely manner to the President any activities that raise serious questions about propriety.

(b) Inspectors General and General Counsels within the Intelligence Community shall:

    (1) Transmit to the Oversight Board reports of any activities that come to their attention that raise questions of legality or propriety.

    (2) Report periodically, at least quarterly, to the Oversight Board on its findings concerning questionable activities, if any.

    (3) Provide to the Oversight Board all information requested about activities within their respective departments or agencies.

    (4) Report to the Oversight Board any occasion on which they were directed not to report any activity to the Oversight Board by their agency or department heads.

    (5) Formulate practices and procedures designed to discover and report to the Oversight Board activities that raise questions of legality or propriety.

(c) Heads of intelligence agencies or departments shall:

    (1) Report periodically to the Oversight Board on any activities of their organizations that raise questions of legality or propriety.

    (2) Instruct their employees to cooperate fully with the Oversight Board.

    (3) Ensure that Inspectors General and General Counsels of their agencies have access to any information necessary to perform their duties assigned by paragraph (4) of this section.

(d) The Attorney General shall:

(1) Receive and consider reports from the Oversight Board.

(2) Report periodically, at least quarterly, to the President with respect to activities of the Intelligence Community, if any, which raise questions of legality.

(e) The Oversight Board shall receive staff support. No person who serves on the staff of the Oversight Board shall have any contractual or employment relationship with any department or agency in the Intelligence Community.

(f) The President's Foreign Intelligence Advisory Board established by Executive Order No. 11460 of March 20, 1969, remains in effect.

Sec. 7. *Secrecy Protection.*

(a) In order to improve the protection of sources and methods of intelligence, all members of the Executive branch and its contractors given access to information containing sources or methods of intelligence shall, as a condition of obtaining access, sign an agreement that they will not disclose that information to persons not authorized to receive it.

(b) In the event of any unauthorized disclosure of information concerning sources or methods of intelligence, the names of any persons found to have made unauthorized disclosure shall be forwarded (1) to the heads of applicable departments or agencies for appropriate disciplinary action; and (2) to the Attorney General for appropriate legal action.

(c) In the event of any threatened unauthorized disclosure of information concerning sources or methods of intelligence by a person who has agreed not to make such disclosure, the details of the threatened disclosure shall be transmitted to the Attorney General for appropriate legal action, including the seeking of a judicial order to prevent such disclosure.

(d) In further pursuit of the need to provide protection for other significant areas of intelligence, the Director of Central Intelligence is authorized to promulgate rules and regulations to expand the scope of agreements secured from those persons who, as an aspect of their relationship with the United States Government, have access to classified intelligence material.

Sec. 8. *Enabling Data*

(a) The Committee on Foreign Intelligence and the Director of Central Intelligence shall provide for detailed implementation of this Order by issuing appropriate directives.

(b) All existing National Security Council and Director of Central Intelligence directives shall be amended to be consistent with this Order within ninety days of its effective date.

(c) This Order shall supersede the Presidential Memorandum of November 5, 1971, on the "Organization and Management of the U.S. Foreign Intelligence Community."

(d) Heads of departments and agencies within the Intelligence Community shall issue supplementary directives to their organizations consistent with this Order within ninety days of its effective date.

(e) This Order will be implemented within current manning authorizations of the Intelligence Community. To this end, the Director of the Office of

Management and Budget will facilitate the required realignment of personnel positions. The Director of the Office of Management and Budget will also assist in the allocation of appropriate facilities.

Gerald R. Ford

THE WHITE HOUSE

February 18, 1976

Appendix I

Senate Resolution 400, 94th Congress
A Resolution Establishing a Select Committee on Intelligence, May 1976

Resolved, That it is the purpose of this resolution to establish a new select committee of the Senate, to be known as the Select Committee on Intelligence, to oversee and make continuing studies of the intelligence activities and programs of the United States Government, and to submit to the Senate appropriate proposals for legislation and report to the Senate concerning such intelligence activities and programs. In carrying out this purpose, the Select Committee on Intelligence shall make every effort to assure that the appropriate departments and agencies of the United States provide informed and timely intelligence necessary for the executive and legislative branches to make sound decisions affecting the security and vital interests of the Nation. It is further the purpose of this resolution to provide vigilant legislative oversight over the intelligence activities of the United States to assure that such activities are in conformity with the Constitution and laws of the United States.

SEC. 2.

    (a)   (1) There is hereby established a select committee to be known as the Select Committee on Intelligence (hereinafter in this resolution referred to as the "select committee"). The select committee shall be composed of fifteen members appointed as follows:

        (A) two members from the Committee on Appropriations;

        (B) two members from the Committee on Armed Services;

        (C) two members from the Committee on Foreign Relations;

        (D) two members from the Committee on the Judiciary; and

        (E) seven members to be appointed from the Senate at large.

      (2) Members appointed from each committee named in clauses (A) through (D) of paragraph (1) shall be evenly divided between the two major political parties and shall be appointed by the President pro tempore of the Senate upon the recommendations of the majority and minority leaders of the Senate. Four of the members appointed under clause (E) of paragraph (1) shall be appointed by the President pro tempore of the Senate upon the recommendation of the majority leader of the Senate and three shall be appointed by the President pro tempore of the Senate upon the recommendation of the minority leader of the Senate.

      (3) The majority leader of the Senate and the minority leader of the Senate shall be ex officio members of the select committee but shall have no vote in the committee and shall not be counted for purposes of determining a quorum.

(b) No Senator may serve on the select committee for more than eight years of continuous service, exclusive of service by any Senator on such committee during the Ninety-fourth Congress. To the greatest extent practicable, one-third of the Members of the Senate appointed to the select committee at the beginning of the Ninety-seventh Congress and each Congress thereafter shall be Members of the Senate who did not serve on such committee during the preceding Congress.

(c) At the beginning of each Congress, the Members of the Senate who are members of the majority party of the Senate shall elect a chairman for the select committee, and the Members of the Senate who are the minority party of the Senate shall elect a vice chairman for such a committee. The vice chairman shall act in the place and stead of the chairman in the absence of the chairman. Neither the chairman nor the vice chairman of the select committee shall at the same time serve as chairman or ranking minority member of any other committee referred to in paragraph 6(f) of rule XXV of the Standing Rules of the Senate.

(d) For the purposes of paragraph 6(a) of rule XXV of the Standing Rules of the Senate, service of a Senator as a member of the select committee shall not be taken into account.

SEC. 3.

(a) There shall be referred to the select committee all proposed legislation, messages, petitions, memorials, and other matters relating to the following:

(1) The Central Intelligence Agency and the Director of Central Intelligence.

(2) Intelligence activities of all other departments and agencies of the Government, including, but not limited to, the intelligence activities of the Defense Intelligence Agency, the National Security Agency, and other agencies of the Department of Defense; the Department of State; the Department of Justice; and the Department of the Treasury.

(3) The organization or reorganization of any department or agency of the Government to the extent that the organization or reorganization relates to a function or activity involving intelligence activities.

(4) Authorization for appropriations, both direct and indirect, for the following:

(A) The Central Intelligence Agency and Director of Central Intelligence.

(B) The Defense Intelligence Agency.

(C) The National Security Agency.

(D) The intelligence activities of other agencies and subdivisions of the Department of Defense.

(E) The intelligence activities of the Department of State.

(F) The intelligence activities of the Federal Bureau of Investigation, including all activities of the Intelligence Division.

(G) Any department, agency, or subdivision which is the successor to any agency named in clause (A), (B), or (C); and the activities of any department, agency, or subdivision which is the successor to any department, agency, bureau,or subdivision named in clause (D), (E), or (F) to the extent that the activities of such successor department, agency, or subdivision are activities described in clause (D), (E), or (F).

(b) Any proposed legislation reported by the select committee, except any legislation involving matters specified in clause (1) or (4)(A) of subsection (a), containing any matter otherwise within the jurisdiction of any standing committee shall, at the request of the chairman of such standing committee, be referred to such standing committee for its consideration of such matter and be reported to the Senate by such standing committee within thirty days after the day on which such proposed legislation is referred to such standing committee; and any proposed legislation reported by any committee, other than the select committee, which contains any matter within the jurisdiction of the select committee shall, at the request of the chairman of the select committee, be referred to the select committee for its consideration of such matter and be reported to the Senate by the select committee within thirty days after the day on which such proposed legislation is referred to such committee. In any case in which a committee fails to report any proposed legislation referred to it within the time limit prescribed herein, such committee shall be automatically discharged from further consideration of such proposed legislation on the thirtieth day following the day on which such proposed legislation is referred to such committee unless the Senate provides otherwise. In computing any thirty-day period under this paragraph there shall be excluded from such computation any days on which the Senate is not in session.

(c) Nothing in this resolution shall be construed as prohibiting or otherwise restricting the authority of any other committee to study and review any intelligence activity to the extent that such activity directly affects a matter otherwise within the jurisdiction of such committee.

(d) Nothing in this resolution shall be construed as amending, limiting, or otherwise changing the authority of any standing committee of the Senate to obtain full and prompt access to the product of the intelligence activities of any department or agency of the Government relevant to a matter otherwise within the jurisdiction of such committee.

SEC. 4.

(a) The select committee, for the purposes of accountability to the Senate, shall make regular and periodic reports to the Senate on the nature and extent of the intelligence activities of the various departments and agencies of the United States. Such committee shall promptly call to the attention of the Senate or to any other appropriate committee or committees of the Senate any matters requiring the attention of the Senate or such other committee or committees. In making such reports, the select committee shall proceed in a manner consistent with section 8(c)(2) to protect national security.

(b) The select committee shall obtain an annual report from the Director of the Central Intelligence Agency, the Secretary of Defense, the Secretary of State, and the Director of the Federal Bureau of Investigation. Such reports shall review the intelligence activities of the agency or department concerned and the intelligence activities of foreign countries directed at the United States or its interests. An unclassified version of each report may be made available to the public at the discretion of the select committee. Nothing herein shall be construed as requiring the public disclosure in such reports of the names of individuals engaged in intelligence activities for the United States or the divulging of intelligence methods employed or the sources of information on which such reports are based or the amount of funds authorized to be appropriated for intelligence activities.

(c) On or before March 15 of each year, the select committee shall submit to the Committee on the Budget of the Senate the views and estimates described in section 301(c) of the Congressional Budget Act of 1974 regarding matters within the jurisdiction of the select committee.

SEC. 5.

(a) For the purposes of this resolution, the select committee is authorized in its discretion (1) to make investigations into any matter within its jurisdiction, (2) to make expenditures from the contingent funds of the Senate, (3) to employ personnel, (4) to hold hearings, (5) to sit and act at any time or place during the sessions, recesses, and adjourned periods of the Senate, (6) to require, by subpoena or otherwise, the attendance of witnesses and the production of correspondence, books, papers, and documents, (7) to take depositions and other testimony, (8) to procure the service of consultants or organizations thereof, in accordance with the provisions of section 202(i) of the Legislative Reorganization Act of 1946, and (9) with the prior consent of the Government department or agency concerned and the Committee on Rules and Administration, to use on a reimbursable basis the services of personnel of any such department or agency.

(b) The chairman of the select committee or any member thereof may administer oaths to witnesses.

(c) Subpoenas authorized by the select committee may be issued over the signature of the chairman, the vice chairman, or any member of the select committee designated by the chairman, and may be served by any person designated by the chairman or any member signing the subpoena.

SEC. 6. No employee of the select committee or any person engaged by contract or otherwise to perform service for or at the request of such committee shall be given access to any classified information by such committee unless such employee or person has (1) agreed in writing and under oath to be bound by the rules of the Senate (including the jurisdiction of the Select Committee on Standards and Conduct) and of such committee as to the security of such information during and after the period of his employment or contractual agreement with such committee; and (2) received an appropriate security clearance as determined by such committee in consultation with the Director of Central Intelligence. The type of security clearance to be required in the case of any such employee or person shall, within the determination of such committee in consultation with the Director of Central Intelligence, be commensurate with the sensitivity of the classified information to which such employee or person will be given access by such committee.

SEC. 7. The select committee shall formulate and carry out such rules and procedures as it deems necessary to prevent the disclosure, without the consent of the person or persons concerned, of information in the possession of such committee which unduly infringes upon the privacy or which violates the constitutional rights of such person or persons. Nothing herein shall be construed to prevent such committee from publicly disclosing any such information in any case in which such committee determines the national interest in the disclosure of such information clearly outweighs any infringement on the privacy of any person or persons.

SEC. 8.

(a) The select committee may, subject to the provisions of this section, disclose publicly any information in the possession of such committee after a determination by such committee that the public interest would be served by such disclosure. Whenever committee action is required to disclose any information under this section, the committee shall meet to vote on the matter within five days after any member of the committee requests such a vote. No member of the select committee shall disclose any information, the disclosure of which requires a committee vote, prior to a vote by the committee on the question of the disclosure of such information or after such vote except in accordance with this section.

(b)

(1) In any case in which the select committee votes to disclose publicly any information which has been classified under established security procedures, which has been submitted to it by the executive branch, and which the executive branch requests be kept secret, such committee shall notify the President of such vote.

(2) The select committee may disclose publicly such information after the expiration of a five-day period following the day on which notice of such vote is transmitted to the President, unless, prior to the expiration of such five-day period, the President, personally in writing, notifies the committee that he objects to the disclosure of such information, provides his reasons therefor, and certifies that the threat to the national interest of the United States posed by such disclosure is of such gravity that it outweighs any public interest in the disclosure.

(3) If the President, personally in writing, notifies the select committee of his objections to the disclosure of such information as provided in paragraph (2), such committee may, by majority vote, refer the question of the disclosure of such information to the Senate for consideration. The committee shall not publicly disclose such information without leave of the Senate.

(4) Whenever the select committee votes to refer the question of disclosure of any information to the Senate under paragraph (3), the chairman shall, not later than the first day on which the Senate is in session following the day on which the vote occurs, report the matter to the Senate for its consideration.

(5) One hour after the Senate convenes on the fourth day on which the Senate is in session following the day on which any such matter is reported to the Senate, or at such earlier time as the majority leader and the minority leader of the Senate jointly agree upon in accordance with section 133(f) of the Legislative Reorganization Act of 1946, the Senate shall go into closed session and the matter shall be the pending business. In considering the matter in closed session the Senate may—

(A) approve the public disclosure of all or any portion of the information in question, in which case the committee shall publicly disclose the information ordered to be disclosed,

(B) disapprove the public disclosure of all or any portion of the information in question, in which case the committee shall not publicly disclose the information ordered not to be disclosed, or

(C) refer all or any portion of the matter back to the committee, in which case the committee shall make the final determination with respect to the public disclosure of the information in question.

Upon conclusion of the consideration of such matter in closed session, which may not extend beyond the close of the ninth day on which the Senate is in session following the day on which such matter was reported to the Senate, or the close of the fifth day following the day agreed upon jointly by the majority and minority leaders in accordance with section 133(f) of the Legislative Reorganization Act of 1946 (whichever the case may be), the Senate shall immediately vote on the disposition of such matter in open session, without debate, and without divulging the information with respect to which the vote is being taken. The Senate shall vote to dispose of such matter by one or more of the means specified in clauses (A), (B), and (C) of the second sentence of this paragraph. Any vote of the Senate to disclose any information pursuant to this paragraph shall be subject to the right of a Member of the Senate to move for reconsideration of the vote within the time and pursuant to the procedures specified in rule XIII of the Standing Rules of the Senate, and the disclosure of such information shall be made consistent with that right.

(c) (1) No information in the possession of the select committee relating to the lawful intelligence activities of any department or agency of the United States which has been classified under established security procedures and which the select committee, pursuant to subsection (a) or (b) of this section, has determined should not be disclosed shall be made available to any person by a Member, officer, or employee of the Senate except in a closed session of the Senate or as provided in paragraph (2).

(2) The select committee may, under such regulations as the committee shall prescribe to protect the confidentiality of such information, make any information described in paragraph (1) available to any other committee or any other Member of the Senate. Whenever the select committee makes such information available, the committee shall keep a written record showing, in the case of any particular information, which committee or which Members of the Senate received such information. No Member of the Senate who, and no committee which, receives any information under this subsection, shall disclose such information except in a closed session of the Senate.

(d) It shall be the duty of the Select Committee on Standards and Conduct to investigate any unauthorized disclosure of intelligence information by a Member, officer or employee of the Senate in violation of subsection (c) and to report to the Senate concerning any allegation which it finds to be substantiated.

(e) Upon the request of any person who is subject to any such investigation, the Select Committee on Standards and Conduct shall release to such individual at the conclusion of its investigation a summary of its investigation together with its findings. If, at the conclusion of its investigation, the Select Committee on Standards and Conduct determines that there has been a significant breach of confidentiality or unauthorized disclosure by a Member, officer, or employee of the Senate, it shall report its findings to the Senate and recommend appropriate action such as censure, removal from committee membership, or expulsion from the Senate, in the case of Member, or removal from office or employment or punishment for contempt, in the case of an officer or employee.

SEC. 9. The select committee is authorized to permit any personal representative of the President, designated by the President to serve as a liaison to such committee, to attend any closed meeting of such committee.

SEC. 10. Upon expiration of the Select Committee on Governmental Operations With Respect to Intelligence Activities, established by Senate Resolution 21, Ninety-fourth Congress, all records, files, documents, and other materials in the possession, custody, or control of such committee, under appropriate conditions established by it, shall be transferred to the select committee.

SEC. 11.

(a) It is the sense of the Senate that the head of each department and agency of the United States should keep the select committee fully and currently informed with respect to intelligence activities, including any significant anticipated activities, which are the responsibility of or engaged in by such department or agency: *Provided,* That this does not constitute a condition precedent to the implementation of any such anticipated intelligence activity.

(b) It is the sense of the Senate that the head of any department or agency of the United States involved in any intelligence activities should furnish any information or documentation in the possession, custody, or control of the department or agency, or person paid by such department or agency, whenever requested by the select committee with respect to any matter within such committee's jurisdiction.

(c) It is the sense of the Senate that each department and agency of the United States should report immediately upon discovery to the select committee any and all intelligence activities which constitute violations of the constitutional rights of any person, violations of law, or violations of Executive orders, Presidential directives, or departmental or agency rules or regulations; each department and agency should further report to such committee what actions have been taken or are expected to be taken by the departments or agencies with respect to such violations.

SEC. 12. Subject to the Standing Rules of the Senate, no funds shall be appropriated for any fiscal year beginning after September 30, 1976, with the exception of a continuing bill or resolution, or amendment thereto, or conference report thereon, to, or for use of, any department or agency of the United States to carry out any of the following activities, unless such funds shall have been previously authorized by a bill or a joint resolution passed by the Senate during the same or preceding fiscal year to carry out such activity for such fiscal year:

(1) The activities of the Central Intelligence Agency and the Director of Central Intelligence.

(2) The activities of the Defense Intelligence Agency.

(3) The activities of the National Security Agency.

(4) The intelligence activities of other agencies and subdivisions of the Department of Defense.

(5) The intelligence activities of the Department of State.

(6) The intelligence activities of the Federal Bureau of Investigation, including all activities of the Intelligence Division.

SEC. 13.

(a) The select committee shall make a study with respect to the following matters, taking into consideration with respect to each such matter, all relevant aspects of the effectiveness of planning, gathering, use, security, and dissemination of intelligence:

(1) the quality of the analytical capabilities of United States foreign intelligence agencies and means for integrating more closely analytical intelligence and policy formulation;

(2) the extent and nature of the authority of the departments and agencies of the executive branch to engage in intelligence activities and the desirability of developing charters for each intelligence agency or department;

(3) the organization of intelligence activities in the executive branch to maximize the effectiveness of the conduct, oversight, and accountability of intelligence activities; to reduce duplication or overlap; and to improve the morale of the personnel of the foreign intelligence agencies;

(4) the conduct of covert and clandestine activities and the procedures by which Congress is informed of such activities;

(5) the desirability of changing any law, Senate rule or procedure, or any Executive order, rule, or regulation to improve the protection of intelligence secrets and provide for disclosure of information for which there is no compelling reason for secrecy;

(6) the desirability of establishing a standing committee of the Senate on intelligence activities;

(7) the desirability of establishing a joint committee of the Senate and the House of Representatives on intelligence activities in lieu of having separate committees in each House of Congress, or of establishing procedures under which separate committees on intelligence activities of the two Houses of Congress would receive joint briefings from the intelligence agencies and coordinate their policies with respect to the safeguarding of sensitive intelligence information;

(8) the authorization of funds for the intelligence activities of the Government and whether disclosure of any of the amounts of such funds is in the public interest; and

(9) the development of a uniform set of definitions for terms to be used in policies or guidelines which may be adopted by the executive or legislative branches to govern, clarify, and strengthen the operation of intelligence activities.

(b) The select committee may, in its discretion, omit from the special study required by this section any matter it determines has been adequately studied by the Select Committee to Study Governmental Operations With

Respect to Intelligence Activities, established by Senate Resolution 21, Ninety-fourth Congress.

(c) The select committee shall report the results of the study provided for by this section to the Senate, together with any recommendations for legislative or other actions it deems appropriate, no later than July 1, 1977, and from time to time thereafter as it deems appropriate.

SEC. 14.

(a) As used in this resolution, the term "intelligence activities" includes (1) the collection, analysis, production, dissemination, or use of information which relates to any foreign country, or any government, political group, party, military force, movement, or other association in such foreign country, and which relates to the defense, foreign policy, national security, or related policies of the United States, and other activity which is in support of such activities; (2) activities taken to counter similar activities directed against the United States; (3) covert or clandestine activities affecting the relations of the United States with any foreign government, political group, party, military force, movement or other association; (4) the collection, analysis, production, dissemination, or use of information about activities of persons within the United States, its territories and possessions, or nationals of the United States abroad whose political and related activities pose, or may be considered by any department, agency, bureau, office, division, instrumentality, or employee of the United States to pose, a threat to the internal security of the United States, and covert or clandestine activities directed against such persons. Such term does not include tactical foreign military intelligence serving no national policymaking function.

(b) As used in this resolution, the term "department or agency" includes any organization, committee, council, establishment, or office within the Federal Government.

(c) For purposes of this resolution, reference to any department, agency, bureau, or subdivision shall include a reference to any successor department, agency, bureau, or subdivision to the extent that such successor engages in intelligence activities now conducted by the department, agency, bureau, or subdivision referred to in this resolution.

SEC. 15. For the period from the date this resolution is agreed to through February 28, 1977, the expenses of the select committee under this resolution shall not exceed $275,000, of which amount not to exceed $30,000 shall be available for the procurement of the services of individual consultants, or organizations thereof, as authorized by section 202(i) of the Legislative Reorganization Act of 1946. Expenses of the select committee under this resolution shall be paid from the contingent fund of the Senate upon vouchers approved by the chairman of the select committee, except that vouchers shall not be required for the disbursement of salaries of employees paid at an annual rate.

SEC. 16. Nothing in this resolution shall be construed as constituting acquiescence by the Senate in any practice, or in the conduct of any activity, not otherwise authorized by law.

Appendix J

Rule XLVIII of the Rules of the House of Representatives
Permanent Select Committee on Intelligence

1. (a) There is hereby established a permanent select committee to be known as the Permanent Select Committee on Intelligence (hereinafter in this rule referred to as the "select committee"). The select committee shall be composed of not more than sixteen Members with representation to include at least one Member from

    (1) the Committee on Appropriations;

    (2) the Committee on Armed forces;

    (3) the Committee on Foreign Affairs; and

    (4) the Committee on the Judiciary.

    (b) The majority leader of the House and the minority leader of the House shall be ex officio members of the select committee but shall have no vote in the committee and shall not be counted for purposes of determining a quorum.

    (c) No Member of the House may serve on the select committee for more than six years of continuous service, exclusive of service by any Member of the House on such committee during the Ninety-fifth Congress. To the greatest extent practicable, at least four of the Members of the House appointed to the select committee at the beginning of the Ninety-seventh Congress and each Congress thereafter shall be Members of the House who did not serve on such committee during the preceding Congress.

2. (a) There shall be referred to the select committee all proposed legislation, messages, petitions, memorials, and other matters relating to the following:

    (1) The Central Intelligence Agency and the Director of Central Intelligence.

    (2) Intelligence and intelligence-related activities of all other departments and agencies of the Government, including, but not limited to, the intelligence and intelligence-related activities of the Defense Intelligence Agency, the National Security Agency, and other agencies of the Department of Defense; the Department of State; the Department of Justice; and the Department of the Treasury.

    (3) The organization or reorganization of any department or agency of the Government to the extent that the organization or reorganization relates to a function or activity involving intelligence or intelligence-related activities.

    (4) Authorizations or appropriations, both direct and indirect, for the following:

(A) The Central Intelligence Agency and Director of Central Intelligence.

(B) The Defense Intelligence Agency.

(C) The National Security Agency.

(D) The intelligence and intelligence-related activities of other agencies and subdivisions of the Department of Defense.

(E) The intelligence and intelligence-related activities of the Department of State.

(F) The intelligence and intelligence-related activities of the Federal Bureau of Investigation, including all activities of the Intelligence Division.

(G) Any department, agency, or subdivision which is the successor to any agency named in subdivision (A), (B), or (C), and the activities of any department, agency, or subdivision which is the successor to any department, agency, bureau, or subdivision named in subdivision (D), (E), or (F), to the extent that such activities of such successor department, agency, or subdivision are activities described in subdivision (D), (E), or (F).

(b) Any proposed legislation initially reported by the select committee, except any legislation involving matters specified in subparagraph (1) or (4)(A) of paragraph (a), containing any matter otherwise within the jurisdiction of any standing committee shall, at the request of the chairman of such standing committee, be referred to such standing committee by the Speaker for its consideration of such matter and be reported to the House by such standing committee within the time prescribed by the Speaker in the referral; and any proposed legislation initially reported by any committee, other than the select committee, which contains any matter within the jurisdiction of the select committee shall, at the request of the chairman of the select committee, be referred by the Speaker to the select committee for its consideration of such matter and be reported to the House within the time prescribed by the Speaker in the referral.

(c) Nothing in this rule shall be construed as prohibiting or otherwise restricting the authority of any other committee to study and review any intelligence or intelligence-related activity to the extent that such activity directly affects a matter otherwise within the jurisdiction of such committee.

(d) Nothing in this rule shall be construed as amending, limiting, or otherwise changing the authority of any standing committee of the House to obtain full and prompt access to the product of the intelligence or intelligence-related activities of any department or agency of the Government relevant to a matter otherwise within the jurisdiction of such committee.

3. (a) The select committee, for purposes of accountability to the House, shall make regular and periodic reports to the House on the nature and extent of the intelligence and intelligence-related activities of the various departments and agencies of the United States. Such committee shall promptly call to the attention of the House or to any other appropriate committee or committees of the House any matters requiring the attention of the House or such other committee or committees. In making such reports, the select

committee shall proceed in a manner consistent with clause 7 to protect national security.

(b) The select committee shall obtain an annual report from the Director of the Central Intelligence Agency, the Secretary of Defense, the Secretary of State, and the Director of the Federal Bureau of Investigation. Such reports shall review the intelligence and intelligence-related activities of the agency or department concerned and the intelligence and intelligence-related activities of foreign countries directed at the United States or its interest. An unclassified version of each report may be made available to the public at the discretion of the select committee. Nothing herein shall be construed as requiring the public disclosure in such reports of the names of individuals engaged in intelligence or intelligence-related activities for the United States or the divulging of intelligence methods employed or the sources of information on which such reports are based or the amount of funds authorized to be appropriated for intelligence and intelligence-related activities.

(c) On or before March 15 of each year, the select committee shall submit to the Committee on the Budget of the House the views and estimates described in section 301(a)(c) of the Congressional Budget Act of 1974 regarding matters within the jurisdiction of the select committee.

4. To the extent not inconsistent with the provisions of this rule, the provisions of 1, 2, 3, and 5(a), (b), (c), and 6(a), (b), and (c) of rule XI shall apply to the select committees, except that, notwithstanding the requirements of the first sentence of clause 2(g)(2) of rule XI, a majority of those present, there being in attendance the requisite number required under the rules of the select committee to be present for the purpose of taking testimony or receiving evidence, may vote to close a hearing whenever the majority determines that such testimony or evidence would endanger the national security.

5. No employee of the select committee or any person engaged by contract or otherwise to perform services for or at the request of such committee shall be given access to any classified information by such committee unless such employee or person has (1) agreed in writing and under oath to be bound by the rules of the House (including the jurisdiction of the Committee on Standards of Official Conduct and of the select committee as to the security of such information during and after the period of his employment of contractual agreement with such committee); and (2) received an appropriate security clearance as determined by such committee in consultation with the Director of Central Intelligence. The type of security clearance to be required in the case of any such employee or person shall, within the determination of such committee in consultation with the Director of Central Intelligence, be commensurate with the sensitivity of the classified information to which such employee or person will be given access by such committee.

6. The select committee shall formulate and carry out such rules and procedures as it deems necessary to prevent the disclosure, without the consent of the person or persons concerned, of information in the possession of such committee which unduly infringes upon the privacy or which violates the constitutional rights of such person or persons. Nothing herein shall be construed to prevent such committee from publicly disclosing

such information in any case in which such committee determines that national interest in the disclosure of such information clearly outweighs any infringement on the privacy of any person or persons.

7. (a) The select committee may, subject to the provisions of this clause, disclose publicly any information in the possession of such committee after a determination by such committee that the public interest would be served by such disclosure. Whenever committee action is required to disclose any information under this clause, the committee shall meet to vote on the matter within five days after any member of the committee requests such a vote. No member of the select committee shall disclosed any information, the disclosure of which requires a committee vote, prior to a vote by the committee on the question of the disclosure of such information or after such vote except in accordance with this clause.

(b) (1) In any case in which the select committee votes to disclose publicly any information which has been classified under established security procedures, which has been submitted to it by the executive branch, and which the executive branch requests be kept secret, such committee shall notify the President of such vote.

(2) The select committee may disclose publicly such information after the expiration of a five-day period following the day on which notice of such vote is transmitted to the President, unless prior to the expiration of such five-day period, the President, personally in writing, notifies the committee that he objects to the disclosure of such information, provides his reasons therefor, and certifies that the threat to the national interest of the United States posed by such disclosure is of such gravity that it outweighs any public interest in the disclosure.

(3) If the President, personally in writing, notifies the select committee of his objections to the disclosure of such information as provided in subparagraph (2), such committee may, by majority vote, refer the question of the disclosure of such information with a recommendation thereon to the House for consideration. The committee shall not publicly disclose such information without leave of the House.

(4) Whenever the select committee votes to refer the question of disclosure of any information to the House under subparagraph (3), the chair shall, not later than the first day on which the House is in session following the date on which the vote occurs, report the matter to the House for consideration.

(5) If within four calendar days on which the House is in session, after such recommendation is reported, no motion has been made by the chairman of the select committee to consider, in closed session, the matter reported under subparagraph (4), then such a motion will be deemed privileged and may be made by any Member. The motion under this subparagraph shall not be subject to debate or amendment. When made, it shall be decided without intervening motion, except one motion to adjourn.

(6) If the House adopts a motion to resolve into closed session, the Speaker shall then be authorized to declare a recess subject to the call of the Chair. At the expiration of such recess, the pending question, in closed session, shall be, "Shall the House approve the recommendations of the select committee?"

(7) After not more than two hours of debate on the motion, such debate to be equally divided and controlled by the chairman and ranking minority member of the select committee, or their designees, the previous question shall be considered as ordered and the House, without intervening motion except one motion to adjourn, shall immediately vote on the question, in open session but without divulging the information with respect to which vote is being taken. If the recommendation of the select committee is not agreed to, the question shall be deemed recommitted to the select committee for further recommendation.

(c) (1) No information in the possession of the select committee relating to the lawful intelligence or intelligence-related activities of any department or agency of the United States which has been classified under established security procedures and which the select committee, pursuant to paragraph (a) or (b) of this clause, has determined shall not be disclosed shall be made available to any person by a Member, officer, or employee of the House except as provided in subparagraph (2).

(2) The select committee shall, under such regulations as the committee shall prescribe, make any information described in subparagraph (1) available to any other committee or any other Member of the House and permit any other Member of the House to attend any hearing of the committee which is closed to the public. Whenever the select committee makes such information available, the committee shall keep a written record showing, in the case of any particular information, which committee or which members of the House received such information. No Member of the House who, and no committee which, receives any information under this subparagraph, shall disclose such information except in a closed session of the House.

(d) The Committee on Standards of Official Conduct shall investigate any unauthorized disclosure of intelligence or intelligence-related information by a Member, officer, or employee of the House in violation of paragraph (c) and report to the House concerning any allegation which it finds to be substantiated.

(e) Upon the request of any person who is subject to any such investigation, the Committee on Standards of Official Conduct shall release to such individual at the conclusion of its investigation a summary of its investigation, together with its findings. If, at the conclusion of its investigation, the Committee on Standards of Official Conduct determines that there has been a significant breach of confidentiality or unauthorized disclosure by a Member, officer, or employee of the House, it shall report its findings to the House and recommend appropriate action such as censure, removal from committee membership, or expulsion from the House, in the case of a Member, or removal from office or employment or punishment for contempt, in the case of an officer or employee.

8. The select committee is authorized to permit any personal representative of the President, designated by the President to serve as liaison to such committee, to attend any closed meeting of such committee.

9. Subject to the rules of the House, no funds shall be appropriated for any fiscal year beginning after September 30, 1978, with the exception of a continuing bill or resolution continuing appropriations, or amendment

thereto, or conference report thereon, to, or for use of, any department or agency of the United States to carry out any of the following activities, unless such funds shall have been previously authorized by a bill or joint resolution passed by the House during the same or preceding fiscal year to carry out such activity for such fiscal year.

(a) The activities of the Central Intelligence Agency and the Director of Central Intelligence.

(b) The activities of the Defense Intelligence Agency.

(c) The activities of the National Security Agency.

(d) The intelligence and intelligence-related activities of other agencies and subdivisions of the Department of Defense.

(e) The intelligence and intelligence-related activities of the Department of State.

(f) The intelligence and intelligence-related activities of the Federal Bureau of Investigation, including all activities of the Intelligence Division.

10. (a) As used in this rule, the term "intelligence and intelligence-related activities" includes (1) the collection, analysis, production, dissemination or use of information which relates to any foreign country, or any government, political group, party, military force, movement, or other association in such foreign country, and which relates to the defense, foreign policy, national security, or related policies of the United States, and other activity which is in support of such activities; (2) activities taken to counter similar activities directed against the United States; (3) covert or clandestine activities affecting the relations of the United States with any foreign government, political group, party, military force, movement, or other association; (4) the collection, analysis, production, dissemination, or use of information about activities of persons within the United States, its territories and possessions, or nationals of the United States abroad whose political and related activities pose, or may be considered by any department, agency, bureau, office, division, instrumentality, or employee of the United States to pose, a threat to the internal security of the United States, and covert or clandestine activities directed against such persons.

(b) As used in this rule, the term "department or agency" includes an organization, committee, council, establishment, or office within the Federal Government.

(c) For purposes of this rule, reference to any department, agency, bureau, or subdivision shall include reference to any successor department, agency, bureau, or subdivision to the extent that such successor engages in intelligence or intelligence-related activities now conducted by the department, agency, bureau, or subdivision referred to in this rule.

11. Clause 6(a) of rule XXVIII does not apply to conference committee meetings respecting legislation (or any part thereof) reported from the Permanent Select Committee on Intelligence.

Appendix K

Executive Order 12036, January 24, 1978
United States Intelligence Activities

By virtue of the authority vested in me by the Constitution and statutes of the United States of America including the National Security Act of 1947, as amended, and as President of the United States of America, in order to provide for the organization and control of United States foreign intelligence activities, it is hereby ordered as follows:

SECTION 1

DIRECTION, DUTIES AND RESPONSIBILITIES WITH RESPECT TO THE NATIONAL INTELLIGENCE EFFORT

1-1. *National Security Council.*

1-101. *Purpose.* The National Security Council (NSC) was established by the National Security Act of 1947 to advise the President with respect to the integration of domestic, foreign, and military policies relating to the national security. The NSC shall act as the highest Executive Branch that provides review of, guidance for, and direction to the conduct of all national foreign intelligence and counterintelligence activities.

1-102. *Committees.* The NSC Policy Review Committee and Special Coordinating Committee; in accordance with procedures established by the Assistant to the President for National Security Affairs, shall assist in carrying out the NSC's responsibilities in the foreign intelligence field.

1-2. *NSC Policy Review Committee.*

1-201. *Membership.* The NSC Policy Review Committee (PRC), when carrying out responsibilities assigned in this order, shall be chaired by the Director of Central Intelligence and composed of the Vice President, the Secretary of State, the Secretary of the Treasury, the Secretary of Defense, the Assistant to the President for National Security Affairs, and the Chairman of the Joint Chiefs of Staff, or their designees, and other senior officials, as appropriate.

1-202. *Duties.* The PRC shall:

    (a) Establish requirements and priorities for national foreign intelligence;

    (b) Review the National Foreign Intelligence Program and budget proposals and report to the President as to whether the resource allocations for intelligence capabilities are responsive to the intelligence requirements of the members of the NSC.

(c) Conduct periodic reviews of national foreign intelligence products, evaluate the quality of the intelligence product, develop policy guidance to ensure quality intelligence and to meet changing intelligence requirements; and

(d) Submit an annual report on its activities to the NSC.

1-203. *Appeals.* Recommendations of the PRC on intelligence matters may be appealed to the President or the NSC by any member of the PRC.

1-3. *NSC Special Coordination Committee.*

1-301. *Membership.* The NSC Special Coordination Committee (SCC) is chaired by the Assistant to the President for National Security Affairs and its membership includes the statutory members of the NSC and other senior officials, as appropriate.

1-302. *Special Activities.* The SCC shall consider and submit to the President a policy recommendation, including all dissents, on each special activity. When meeting for this purpose, the members of the SCC shall include the Secretary of State, the Secretary of Defense, the Attorney General, the Director of the Office of Management and Budget, the Assistant to the President for National Security Affairs, the Chairman of the Joint Chiefs of Staff, and the Director of Central Intelligence.

1-303. *Sensitive Foreign Intelligence Collection Operations.* Under standards established by the President, proposals for sensitive foreign intelligence collection operations shall be reported to the Chairman by the Director of Central Intelligence for appropriate review and approval. When meeting for the purpose of reviewing proposals for sensitive foreign intelligence collection operations, then members of the SCC shall include the Secretary of State, the Secretary of Defense, the Attorney General, the Assistant to the President for National Security Affairs, the Director of Central Intelligence, and such other members designated by the Chairman to ensure proper consideration of these operations.

1-304. *Counterintelligence.* The SCC shall develop policy with respect to the conduct of counterintelligence activities. When meeting for this purpose, the members of the SCC shall include the Secretary of State, the Secretary of Defense, the Attorney General, the Director of the Office of Management and Budget, the Assistant to the President for National Security Affairs, the Chairman of the Joint Chiefs of Staff, the Director of Central Intelligence, and the Director of the FBI. The SCC's counterintelligence functions shall include:

(a) Developing standards and doctrine for the counterintelligence activities of the United States;

(b) Resolving interagency differences concerning implementation of counterintelligence policy;

(c) Developing and monitoring guidelines consistent with this order for the maintenance of central records of counterintelligence information;

(d) Submitting to the President an overall annual assessment of the relative threat to United States interests from intelligence and security services of foreign powers and from international terrorist activities, including an assessment of the effectiveness of the United States counterintelligence activities; and (e)　approving counterintelligence activities which, under such standards as may be established by the President, require SCC approval.

1-305. *Required Membership*. The SCC shall discharge the responsibilities assigned by sections 1-302 through 1-304 only after consideration in a meeting at which all designated members are present or, in unusual circumstances when any such member is unavailable, when a designated representative of the member attends.

1-306. *Additional Duties*. The SCC shall also:

(a)　Conduct an annual review of ongoing special activities and sensitive national foreign intelligence collection operations and report thereon to the NSC; and

(b)　Carry out such other coordination and review activities as the President may direct.

1-307. *Appeals*. Any member of the SCC may appeal any decision to the President of the NSC.

1-4. *National Foreign Intelligence Board*.

1-401. *Establishment and Duties*. There is established a National Foreign Intelligence Board (NFIB) to advise the Director of Central Intelligence concerning:

(a)　Production, review, and coordination of national foreign intelligence;

(b)　The National Foreign Intelligence Program budget;

(c)　Interagency exchanges of foreign intelligence information;

(d)　Arrangements with foreign governments on intelligence matters;

(e)　The protection of intelligence sources and methods;

(f)　Activities of common concern; and

(g)　Other matters referred to it by the Director of Central Intelligence.

1-402. *Membership*. The NFIB shall be chaired by the Director of Central Intelligence and shall include other appropriate officers of the CIA, the Office of the Director of Central Intelligence, the Department of State, the Department of Defense, the Department of Justice, the Department of the Treasury, the Department of Energy, the Defense Intelligence Agency, the offices within the Department of Defense for reconnaissance programs, the National Security Agency and the FBI. A representative to the Assistant to the President for National Security Affairs may attend meetings of the NFIB as an observer.

1-403. *Restricted Membership and Observers*. When the NFIB meets for the purpose of section 1-40(a), it shall be composed solely of the senior intelligence officers of the designated agencies. The senior intelligence officers of the Army, Navy and Air Force may attend all meetings of the NFIB as observers.

1-5. *National Intelligence Tasking Center*.

1-501. *Establishment*. There is established a National Intelligence Tasking Center (NITC) under the direction, control and management of the Director of Central Intelligence for coordinating and tasking national foreign intelligence collection activities. The NITC shall be staffed jointly by civilian and military personnel including designated representatives of the chiefs of each of the Department of Defense intelligence organizations engaged in national foreign intelligence activities. Other agencies within the Intelligence Community may also designate representatives.

1-502. *Responsibilities.* The NITC shall be the central mechanism by which the Director of Central Intelligence:

(a) Translates national foreign intelligence requirements and priorities developed by the PRC into specific collection objectives and targets for the Intelligence Community;

(b) Assigns targets and objectives to national foreign intelligence collection organizations and systems;

(c) Ensures the timely dissemination and exploitation of data for national foreign intelligence purposes gathered by national foreign intelligence collection means, and ensures the resulting intelligence flow is routed immediately to relevant components and commands;

(d) Provides advisory tasking concerning collection of national foreign intelligence to departments and agencies having information collection capabilities or intelligence assets that are not a part of the National Foreign Intelligence Program. Particular emphasis shall be placed on increasing the contribution of departments or agencies to the collection of information through overt means.

1-503. *Resolution of Conflicts.* The NITC shall have the authority to resolve conflicts of priority. Any PRC member may appeal such a resolution to the PRC; pending the PRC's decision, the tasking remains in effect.

1-504. *Transfer of Authority.* All responsibilities and authorities of the Director of Central Intelligence concerning the NITC shall be transferred to the Secretary of Defense upon the express direction of the President. To maintain readiness for such transfer, the Secretary of Defense shall, with advance agreement of the Director of Central Intelligence, assume temporarily during regular practice exercises all responsibilities and authorities of the Director of Central Intelligence concerning the NITC.

1-6. *The Director of Central Intelligence.*

1-601. *Duties.* The Director of Central Intelligence shall be responsible directly to the NSC and, in addition to the duties specified elsewhere in this Order, shall:

(a) Act as the primary adviser to the President and the NSC on national foreign intelligence and provide the President and other officials in the Executive Branch with national foreign intelligence;

(b) Be the head of the CIA and of other such staff elements as may be required for discharge of the Director's Intelligence Community responsibilities;

(c) Act, in appropriate consultation with the departments and agencies, as the Intelligence Community's principal spokesperson to the Congress, the news media and the public, and facilitate the use of national foreign intelligence products by the Congress in a secure manner;

(d) Develop, consistent with the requirements and priorities established by the PRC, such objectives and guidance for the Intelligence Community as will enhance capabilities for responding to expected future needs for national foreign intelligence;

(e) Promote the development and maintenance of services of common concern by designated foreign intelligence organizations on behalf of the Intelligence Community;

(f) Ensure implementation of special activities;

(g) Formulate policies concerning intelligence arrangements with foreign governments, and coordinate intelligence relationships between agencies of the Intelligence Community and the intelligence or internal security services of foreign governments;

(h) Conduct a program to protect against overclassification of foreign intelligence information;

(i) Ensure the establishment by the Intelligence Community of common security and access standards for managing and handling foreign intelligence systems, information and products;

(j) Participate in the development of procedures required to be approved by the Attorney General governing the conduct of intelligence activities;

(k) Establish uniform criteria for the determination of relative priorities for the transmission of critical national foreign intelligence, and advise the Secretary of Defense concerning the communications requirements of the Intelligence Community for the transmission of such intelligence;

(l) Provide appropriate intelligence to departments and agencies not within the Intelligence Community; and

(m) Establish appropriate committees or other advisory groups to assist in the execution of the foregoing responsibilities.

1-602. *National Foreign Intelligence Program Budget.* The Director of Central Intelligence shall, to the extent consistent with applicable law, have full and exclusive authority for approval of the National Foreign Intelligence Program budget submitted to the President. Pursuant to this authority:

(a) The Director of Central Intelligence shall provide guidance for program and budget development to program managers and heads of component activities and to department and agency heads;

(b) The heads of the departments and agencies involved in the National Foreign Intelligence Program shall insure timely development and submission to the Director of Central Intelligence of proposed national programs and budgets in the format designated by the Director of Central Intelligence, by the program managers and heads of component activities, and shall also insure that the Director of Central Intelligence is provided, in a timely and responsive manner, all information necessary to perform the Director's program and budget responsibilities;

(c) The Director of Central Intelligence shall review and evaluate the national program and budget submissions and, with the advice of the NFIB and the departments and agencies concerned, develop the consolidated National Foreign Intelligence Program budget and present it to the President through the Office of Management and Budget;

(d) The Director of Central Intelligence shall present and justify the National Foreign Intelligence Program budget to the Congress;

(e)   The heads of the departments and agencies shall, in consultation with the Director of Central Intelligence, establish rates of obligation for appropriated funds;

(f)   The Director of Central Intelligence shall have full and exclusive authority for reprogramming National Foreign Intelligence Program funds, in accord with guidelines established by the Office of Management and Budget, but shall do so only after consultation with the head of the department affected and appropriate consultation with the Congress;

(g)   The departments and agencies may appeal to the President decisions by the Director of Central Intelligence on budget or reprogramming matters of the National Foreign Intelligence Program.

(h)   The Director of Central Intelligence shall monitor National Foreign Intelligence Program implementation and may conduct program and performance audits and evaluations.

1-603. *Responsibility for National Foreign Intelligence.* The Director of Central Intelligence shall have full responsibility for production and dissemination of national foreign intelligence and have the authority to levy analytic tasks on departmental intelligence production organizations, in consultation with those organizations. In doing so, the Director of Central Intelligence shall ensure that diverse points of view are considered fully and that differences of judgment within the Intelligence Community are brought to the attention of national policymakers.

1-604. *Protection of Sources, Methods and Procedures.* The Director of Central Intelligence shall ensure that programs are developed which protect intelligence sources, methods and analytical procedures, provided that this responsibility shall be limited within the United States to:

(a)   Using lawful means to protect against disclosure by present or former employees of the CIA or the Office of the Director of Central Intelligence, or by persons or organizations presently or formerly under contract with such entities; and

(b)   Providing policy, guidance and technical assistance to departments and agencies regarding protection of intelligence information, including information that may reveal intelligence sources and methods.

1-605. *Responsibility of Executive Branch Agencies.* The heads of all Executive Branch departments and agencies shall, in accordance with law and relevant Attorney General procedures, give the Director of Central Intelligence access to all information relevant to the national intelligence needs of the United States and shall give due consideration to the requests from the Director of Central Intelligence for appropriate support for CIA activities.

1-606. *Access to CIA Intelligence.* The Director of Central Intelligence shall, in accordance with law and relevant Attorney General procedures, give the heads of the departments and agencies access to all intelligence, developed by the CIA or the staff elements of the Office of the Director of Central Intelligence, relevant to the national intelligence needs of the departments and agencies.

1-7. *Senior Officials of the Intelligence Community.* The senior officials of each of the agencies within the Intelligence Community shall;

1-701. Ensure that all activities of their agencies are carried out in accordance with applicable law;

1-702. Make use of the capabilities of other agencies within the Intelligence Community in order to achieve efficiency and mutual assistance;

1-703. Contribute in their areas of responsibility to the national foreign intelligence products;

1-704. Establish internal policies and guidelines governing employee conduct and ensure that such are made known to each employee;

1-705. Provide for a strong, independent, internal means to identify, inspect, and report on unlawful or improper activity;

1-706. Report to the Attorney General evidence of possible violations of federal criminal law by an employee of their department or agency, and report to the Attorney General evidence of possible violations by any other person of those federal criminal laws specified in guidelines adopted by the Attorney General;

1-707. In any case involving serious or continuing breaches of security, re-commend to the Attorney General that the case be referred to the FBI for further investigation;

1-708. Furnish the Director of Central Intelligence, the PRC and the SCC, in accordance with applicable law and Attorney General procedures, the information required for the performance of their respective duties;

1-709. Report to the Intelligence Oversight Board, and keep the Director of Central Intelligence appropriately informed, concerning any intelligence activities of their organizations which raise questions of legality or propriety;

1-710. Protect intelligence and intelligence sources and methods consistent with guidance from the Director of Central Intelligence and the NSC;

1-711. Disseminate intelligence to cooperating foreign governments under arrange-ments established or agreed to by the Director of Central Intelligence;

1-712. Execute programs to protect against overclassification of foreign intelligence;

1-713. Instruct their employees to cooperate fully with the Intelligence Oversight Board; and

1-714. Ensure that the Inspectors General and General Counsel of their agencies have access to any information necessary to perform their duties assigned by this Order.

1-8. *The Central Intelligence Agency.* All duties and responsibilities of the CIA shall be related to the intelligence functions set out below. As authorized by the Na-tional Security Act of 1947, as amended, the CIA Act of 1949, as amended, and other laws, regulations and directives, the CIA, under the direction of the NSC, shall:

1-801. Collect foreign intelligence, including information not otherwise obtainable, and develop, conduct, or provide support for technical and other programs which collect national foreign intelligence. The collection of information within the United States shall be coordinated with the FBI as required by procedures agreed upon by the Director of Central Intelligence and the Attorney General;

1-802. Produce and disseminate foreign intelligence relating to the national security, including foreign political, economic, scientific, technical, military, geographic and sociological intelligence to meet the needs of the President, the NSC, and other elements of the United States Government;

1-803. Collect, produce and disseminate intelligence on foreign aspects of narcotics production and trafficking;

1-804. Conduct counterintelligence activities outside the United States and coordinate counterintelligence activities conducted outside the United States by other agencies within the Intelligence Community;

1-805. Without assuming or performing any internal security functions, conduct counterintelligence functions within the United States, but only in coordination with the FBI and subject to the approval of the Attorney General;

1-806. Produce and disseminate counterintelligence studies and reports;

1-807. Coordinate the collection outside the United States of intelligence information not otherwise obtainable;

1-808. Conduct special activities approved by the President and carry out such activities consistent with applicable law;

1-809. Conduct services of common concern for the Intelligence Community as directed by the NSC;

1-810. Carry out or contract for research, development and procurement of technical systems and devices relating to authorized functions;

1-811. Protect the security of its installations, activities, information and personnel by appropriate means, including such investigations of applicants, employees, contractors, and other persons with similar associations with the CIA as are necessary;

1-812. Conduct such administrative and technical support activities within and outside the United States as are necessary to perform the functions described in sections 1-801 through 1-811 above, including procurement and essential cover and proprietary arrangements.

1-813. Provide legal and legislative services and other administrative support to the Office of the Director of Central Intelligence.

1-9. *The Department of State.* The Secretary of State shall:

1-901. Overtly collect foreign political, sociological, economic, scientific, technical, political-military and associated biographic information;

1-902. Produce and disseminate foreign intelligence relating to United States foreign policy as required for the execution of the Secretary's responsibilities;

1-903. Disseminate, as appropriate, reports received from United States diplomatic and consular posts abroad;

1-904. Coordinate with the Director of Central Intelligence to ensure that national foreign intelligence activities are useful to and consistent with United States foreign policy;

1-905. Transmit reporting requirements of the Intelligence Community to the Chiefs of United States Missions abroad; and

1-906. Support Chiefs of Mission in discharging their statutory responsibilities for direction and coordination of mission activities.

1-10. *The Department of the Treasury.* The Secretary of the Treasury shall;

1-1001. Overtly collect foreign financial and monetary information;

1-1002. Participate with the Department of State in the overt collection of general foreign economic information;

1-1003. Produce and disseminate foreign intelligence relating to United States economic policy as required for the execution of the Secretary's responsibilities; and

1-1004. Conduct, through the United States Secret Service, activities to determine the existence and capability of surveillance equipment being used against the President of the United States, the Executive Office of the President, and, as authorized by the Secretary of the Treasury or the President, other Secret Service protectees and United States officials. No information shall be acquired intentionally through such activities except to protect against such surveillance, and those activities shall be conducted pursuant to procedures agreed upon by the Secretary of the Treasury and the Attorney General.

1-11. *The Department of Defense.* The Secretary of Defense shall:

1-1101. Collect foreign intelligence and be responsive to collection tasking by the NTIC;

1-1102. Collect, produce and disseminate foreign military and military-related intelligence information, including scientific, technical, political, geographic and economic information as required for execution of the Secretary's responsibilities;

1-1103. Conduct programs and missions necessary to fulfill national and tactical foreign intelligence requirements;

1-1104. Conduct counterintelligence activities in support of Department of Defense components outside the United States in coordination with the CIA, and within the United States in coordination with the FBI pursuant to procedures agreed upon by the Secretary of Defense and the Attorney General, and produce and disseminate counterintelligence studies and reports;

1-1105. Direct, operate, control and provide fiscal management for the National Security Agency and for defense and military intelligence and national reconnaissance entities;

1-1106. Conduct, as the executive agent of the United States Government, signals intelligence and communications security activities, except as otherwise directed by the NSC;

1-1107. Provide for the timely transmission of critical intelligence, as defined by the Director of Central Intelligence, within the United States Government;

1-1108. Review budget data and information on Department of Defense programs within the National Foreign Intelligence Program and review budgets submitted by program managers to the Director of Central Intelligence to ensure the appropriate relationship of the National Foreign Intelligence Program elements to the other elements of the Defense program;

1-1109. Monitor, evaluate and conduct performance audits of Department of Defense intelligence programs;

1-1110. Carry out or contract for research, development and procurement of technical systems and devices relating to authorized intelligence functions;

1-1111. Together with the Director of Central Intelligence, ensure that there is no unnecessary overlap between national foreign intelligence programs and Department of Defense intelligence programs and provide the Director of Central Intelligence all information necessary for this purpose;

1-1112. Protect the security of Department of Defense installations, activities, information and personnel by appropriate means including such investigations of applicants, employees, contractors and other persons with similar associations with the Department of Defense as are necessary; and

1-1113. Conduct such administrative and technical support activities within and outside the United States as are necessary to perform the functions described in sections 1-1101 through 1-1112 above.

1-12. *Intelligence Components Utilized by the Secretary of Defense.* In carrying out the responsibilities assigned in sections 1-1101 through 1-1113, the Secretary of Defense is authorized to utilize the following:

1-1201. *Defense Intelligence Agency,* whose responsibilities shall include:

(a) Production or, through tasking and coordination, provision of military and non-military-related intelligence for the Secretary of Defense, the Joint Chiefs of Staff, other Defense components, and, as appropriate, non-Defense agencies;

(b) Provision of military intelligence for national foreign intelligence products;

(c) Coordination of all Department of Defense intelligence collection requirements for departmental needs;

(d) Management of the Defense Attaché System; and

(e) Provision of foreign intelligence and counterintelligence staff support as directed by the Joint Chiefs of Staff.

1-1202. *National Security Agency (NSA),* whose responsibilities shall include:

(a) Establishment and operation of an effective unified organization for signals intelligence activities, except for the delegation of operational control over certain operations that are conducted through other elements of the Intelligence Community. No other department or agency may engage in signals intelligence activities except pursuant to a delegation by the Secretary of Defense;

(b) Control of signals intelligence and processing activities, including assignment of resources to an appropriate agent for such periods and tasks as required for the direct support of military commanders;

(c) Collection of signals intelligence information for national foreign intelligence purposes in accordance with tasking by the NTIC;

(d) Processing of signals intelligence data for national foreign intelligence purposes consistent with standards for timeliness established by the Director of Central Intelligence;

(e) Dissemination of signals intelligence information for national foreign intelligence purposes to authorized elements of the Government, including the military services, in accordance with guidance from the NTIC;

(f) Collection, processing, and dissemination of signals intelligence information for counterintelligence purposes;

(g) Provision of signals intelligence support for the conduct of military operations in accordance with tasking, priorities and standards of timeliness assigned by the Secretary of Defense. If provision of such support requires use of national collection systems, these systems will be tasked within existing guidance from the Director of Central Intelligence;

(h) Executing the responsibilities of the Secretary of Defense as executive agent for the communications security of the United States Government;

(i) Conduct of research and development to meet needs of the United States for signals intelligence and communications security;

(j) Protection of the security of its installations, activities, information and personnel by appropriate means including such investigations of applicants, employers, contractors and other persons with similar associations with the NSA as are necessary; and

(k) Prescribing, within its field of authorized operations, security regulations covering operating practices, including the transmission, handling and distribution of signals intelligence and communications security material within and among the elements under the control of the Director of the NSA, and exercising the necessary supervisory control to ensure compliance with the regulations.

1-1203. *Offices for the collection of specialized intelligence through reconnaissance programs*, whose responsibilities shall include:

(a) Carrying out consolidated reconnaissance programs for specialized intelligence;

(b) Responding to tasking through the NTIC; and

(c) Delegating authority to the various departments and agencies for research, development, procurement, and operation of designed means of collection.

1-1204. *The foreign intelligence and counterintelligence elements of the military services*, whose responsibilities shall include:

(a) Collection, production and dissemination of military and military related foreign intelligence, including information on indications and warnings, foreign capabilities, plans and weapons systems, scientific and technical developments and narcotics production and trafficking. When collection is conducted in response to national foreign intelligence requirements, it will be tasked by the NTIC. Collection of national foreign intelligence, not otherwise obtainable, outside the United States shall be coordinated with the CIA, and such collection within the United States shall be coordinated with the FBI;

(b) Conduct of counterintelligence activities outside of the United States in coordination with the CIA, and within the United States in coordination with the FBI, and production and dissemination of counterintelligence studies or reports; and

(c) Monitoring of the development, procurement and management of tactical intelligence systems and equipment and conducting related research, development, and test and evaluation activities.

1-1205. *Other offices within the Department of Defense* appropriate for conduct of the intelligence missions and responsibilities assigned to the Secretary of Defense. If such other offices are used for intelligence purposes, the provisions of Sections 2-101 through 2-309 of this Order shall apply to those offices when used for those purposes.

1-13. *The Department of Energy.* The Secretary of Energy shall:

1-1301. Participate with the Department of State in overtly collecting political, economic and technical information with respect to foreign energy matters;

1-1302. Produce and disseminate foreign intelligence necessary for the Secretary's responsibilities;

1-1303. Participate in formulating intelligence collection and analysis requirements where the special expert capability of the Department can contribute; and

1-1304. Provide expert technical, analytical and research capability to other agencies within the Intelligence Community.

1-14. *The Federal Bureau of Investigation.* Under the supervision of the Attorney General and pursuant to such regulations as the Attorney General may establish, the Director of the FBI shall:

1-1401. Within the United States conduct counterintelligence and coordinate counterintelligence activities of other agencies within the Intelligence Community. When a counterintelligence activity of the FBI involves military or civilian personnel of the Department of Defense, the FBI shall coordinate with the Department of Defense;

1-1402. Conduct counterintelligence activities outside the United States in coordination with the CIA, subject to the approval of the Director of Central Intelligence;

1-1403. Conduct within the United States, when requested by officials of the Intelligence Community designated by the President, lawful activities undertaken to collect foreign intelligence or to support foreign intelligence collection requirements of other agencies within the Intelligence Community;

1-1404. Produce and disseminate foreign intelligence, counterintelligence and counterintelligence studies and reports; and

1-1405. Carry out or contract for research, development and procurement of technical systems and devices relating to the functions authorized above.

1-15. *The Drug Enforcement Administration.* Under the supervision of the Attorney General and pursuant to such regulations as the Attorney General may establish, the Administrator of DEA shall:

1-1501. Collect, produce and disseminate intelligence on foreign and domestic aspects of narcotics production and trafficking in coordination with other agencies with responsibilities in these areas;

1-1502. Participate with the Department of State in the overt collection of general foreign political, economic and agricultural information relating to narcotics production and trafficking; and

1-1503. Coordinate with the Director of Central Intelligence to ensure that the foreign narcotics intelligence activities of the DEA are consistent with other foreign intelligence programs.

SECTION 2

RESTRICTIONS ON INTELLIGENCE ACTIVITIES

2-1. *Adherence to Law.*

2-101. *Purpose.* Information about the capabilities, intentions and activities of foreign powers, organizations or persons and their agents is essential to informed decision-making in the areas of national defense and foreign relations. The measures employed to acquire such information should be responsive to legitimate governmental needs and must be conducted in a manner that preserves and respects established concepts of privacy and civil liberties.

2-102. *Principles of Interpretation.* Sections 2-201 through 2-309 set forth limitations which, in addition to other applicable laws, are intended to achieve the proper balance between protection of individual rights and acquisition of essential information. Those actions do not authorize any activity not authorized by sections 1-101 through 1-1503 and do not provide any exemption from any other law.

2-2. *Restrictions on Certain Collection Techniques.*

2-201. *General Provisions.*

(a) The activities described in Sections 2-202 through 2-206 shall be undertaken only as permitted by this Order and by procedures established by the head of the agency concerned and approved by the Attorney General. Those procedures shall protect constitutional rights and privacy, ensure that information is gathered by the least intrusive means possible, and limit use of such information to lawful governmental purposes.

(b) Activities described in sections 2-202 through 2-205 for which a warrant would be required if undertaken for law enforcement rather than intelligence purposes shall not be undertaken against a United States person without a judicial warrant, unless the President has authorized the type of activity involved and the Attorney General has both approved the particular activity and determined that there is probably cause to believe that the United States person is an agent of a foreign power.

2-202. *Electronic Surveillance.* The CIA may not engage in any electronic surveillance within the United States. No agency within the Intelligence Community shall engage in any electronic surveillance directed against a United States person abroad or designed to intercept a communication sent from, or intended for receipt within, the United States except as permitted by the procedures established pursuant to section 2-201. Training of personnel by agencies in the Intelligence Community in the use of electronic communications equipment, testing by such agencies of such equipment, and the use of measures to determine the existence and capability of electronic surveillance equipment being used unlawfully shall not be prohibited and shall also be governed by such procedures. Such activities shall be limited in scope and duration to those necessary to carry out the training, testing or countermeasures purpose. No information derived from communications intercepted in the course of such training, testing or use of countermeasures may be retained or used for any other purpose.

2-203. *Television Cameras and Other Monitoring.* No agency within the Intelligence Community shall use any electronic or mechanical device surreptitiously and continuously to monitor any person within the United States, or any United States person abroad, except as permitted by the procedures established pursuant to Section 2-201.

2-204. *Physical Searches.* No agency within the Intelligence Community except the FBI may conduct any unconsented physical searches within the United States. All such searches conducted by the FBI, as well as all such searches conducted by any agency within the Intelligence Community outside the United States and directed against United States persons, shall be undertaken only as permitted by procedures established pursuant to section 2-201.

2-205. *Mail Surveillance.* No agency within the Intelligence Community shall open mail or examine envelopes within United States postal channels, except in accordance with applicable statutes and regulations. No agency within the Intelligence Community shall open mail of a United States person abroad except as permitted by procedures established pursuant to Section 2-201.

2-206. *Physical Surveillance.* The FBI may conduct physical surveillance directed against United States persons or others only in the course of a lawful investigation. Other agencies within the Intelligence Community may not undertake any physical surveillance directed against a United States person unless:

(a) The surveillance is conducted outside the United States and the person being surveilled is reasonably believed to be acting on behalf of a foreign power, engaging in international terrorist activities, or engaged in narcotics production or trafficking;

(b) The surveillance is conducted solely for the purpose of identifying a person who is in contact with someone who is the subject of a foreign intelligence or counterintelligence investigation; or

(c) That person is being surveilled for the purpose of protecting foreign intelligence and counterintelligence sources and methods from unauthorized disclosure or is the subject of a lawful counterintelligence, personnel, physical or communications security investigation.

(d) No surveillance under paragraph (c) of this section may be conducted within the United States unless the person being surveilled is a present employee, intelligence agency contractor or employee of such a contractor, or is a military person employed by a non-intelligence element of a military service. Outside the United States such surveillance may also be conducted against a former employee, intelligence agency contractor or employee of a contractor or a civilian person employed by a non-intelligence element of an agency within the Intelligence Community. A person who is in contact with such a present or former employee or contractor may also be surveilled, but only to the extent necessary to identify that person.

2-207. *Undisclosed Participation in Domestic Organizations.* No employees may join, or otherwise participate in, any organization within the United States on behalf of any agency within the Intelligence Community without disclosing their intelligence affiliation to appropriate officials of the organization, except as permitted by procedures established pursuant to Section 2-201. Such procedures shall provide for disclosure of such affiliation in all cases unless the agency head or a designee approved by the Attorney General finds that non-disclosure is essential to achieving lawful purposes, and that finding is subject to review by the Attorney General. Those procedures shall further limit undisclosed participation to cases where:

(a) The participation is undertaken on behalf of the FBI in the course of a lawful investigation;

(b) The organization concerned is composed primarily of individuals who are not United States persons and is reasonably believed to be acting on behalf of a foreign power; or

(c) The participation is strictly limited in its nature, scope and duration to that necessary for other lawful purposes relating to foreign intelligence and is a type of participation approved by the Attorney General and set forth in a public document. No such participation may be undertaken for the purpose of influencing the activity of the organization or its members.

2-208. *Collection of Nonpublicly Available Information.* No agency within the Intelligence Community may collect, disseminate or store information concerning the activities of United States persons that is not available publicly, unless it does so with their consent or as permitted by procedures established pursuant to Section 2-201. Those procedures shall limit collection, storage or dissemination to the following types of information:

(a) Information concerning corporations or other commercial organizations or activities that constitutes foreign intelligence or counterintelligence;

(b) Information arising out of a lawful counterintelligence or personnel, physical or communications security investigation;

(c) Information concerning present or former employees. present or former intelligence agency contractors or their present or former employees, or applicants for any such employment or contracting, which is needed to protect foreign intelligence or counterintelligence sources or methods from unauthorized disclosure;

(d) Information needed solely to identify individuals in contact with those persons described in paragraph (c) of this section or with someone who is the subject of a lawful foreign intelligence or counterintelligence investigation;

(e) Information concerning persons who are reasonably believed to be potential sources or contacts, but only for the purpose of determining the suitability or credibility of such persons;

(f) Information constituting foreign intelligence or counterintelligence gathered abroad from electronic surveillance conducted in compliance with Section 2-202 or from cooperating sources in the United States;

(g) Information about a person who is reasonably believed to be acting on behalf of a foreign power, engaging in international terrorist activities or narcotics production or trafficking, or endangering the safety of a person protected by the United States Secret Service or the Department of State;

(h) Information acquired by overhead reconnaissance not directed at specific United States persons;

(i) Information concerning United States persons abroad that is obtained in response to requests from the Department of State for support of its consular responsibilities relating to the welfare of those persons;

(j) Information collected, received, disseminated or stored by the FBI and necessary to fulfill its lawful investigative responsibilities; or

(k) information concerning persons or activities that pose a clear threat to any facility or personnel of an agency within the Intelligence Community. Such information may be retained only by the agency threatened and, if appropriate, by the United States Secret Service and FBI.

2-3. *Additional Restrictions.*

2-301. *Tax Information.* No agency within the Intelligence Community shall examine tax returns or tax information except as permitted by applicable law.

2-302. *Restrictions on Experimentation.* No agency within the Intelligence Community shall sponsor, contract for, or conduct research on human subjects except in accordance with guidelines issued by the Department of Health, Education and Welfare. The subject's informed consent shall be documented as required by those guidelines.

2-303. *Restrictions on Contracting.* No agency within the Intelligence Community shall enter into a contract or arrangement for the provision of goods or services with private companies or institutions in the United States unless the agency sponsorship is known to the appropriate officials of the company or institution. In the case of a company or institution other than an academic institution, intelligence agency sponsorship may be concealed where it is determined, pursuant to procedures approved by the Attorney General, that such concealment is necessary to maintain essential cover or proprietary arrangements for authorized intelligence purposes.

2-304. *Restrictions on Personnel Assigned to Other Agencies.* An employee detailed to another agency within the federal government shall be responsible to the host agency and shall not report to the parent agency on the affairs of the host agency unless so directed by the host agency. The head of the host agency, and any successor, shall be informed of the employee's relationship with the parent agency.

2-305. *Prohibition on Assassination.* No person employed by or acting on behalf of the United States Government shall engage in, or conspire to engage in, assassination.

2-306. *Restrictions on Special Activities.* No component of the United States Government except an agency within the Intelligence Community may conduct any special activity. No such agency except the CIA (or the military services in wartime) may conduct any special activity unless the President determines, with the SCC's advice, that another agency is more likely to achieve a particular objective.

2-307. *Restrictions on Indirect Participation in Prohibited Activities.* No agency of the Intelligence Community shall request or otherwise encourage, directly or indirectly, any person, organization, or government agency to undertake activities forbidden by this Order or applicable law.

2-308. *Restrictions on assistance to Law Enforcement Authorities.* Agencies within the Intelligence Community other than the FBI shall not, except as expressly authorized by law:

(a) Provide services, equipment, personnel or facilities to the Law Enforcement Assistance Administration (or its successor agencies) or to state or local police organizations of the United States; or

(b) Participate in or fund any law enforcement activity within the United States.

2-309. *Permissible Assistance to Law Enforcement Authorities.* The restrictions in Section 2-308 shall not include:

(a) Cooperation with appropriate law enforcement agencies for the purpose of protecting the personnel or facilities of any agency within the Intelligence Community;

(b) Participation in law enforcement activities, in accordance with law and this Order, to investigate or prevent clandestine intelligence activities by foreign powers, international narcotics production and trafficking, or international terrorist activities; or

(c) Provision of specialized equipment, technical knowledge, or assistance of expert personnel for use by any department or agency or, when lives are endangered, to support local law enforcement agencies. Provision of assistance by expert personnel shall be governed by procedures approved by the Attorney General.

2-310. *Permissible Dissemination and Storage of Information.* Nothing in Sections 2-201 through 2-309 of this Order shall prohibit:

(a) Dissemination of appropriate law enforcement agencies of information which indicates involvement in activities that may violate federal, state, local or foreign laws;

(b) Storage of information required by law to be retained;

(c) Dissemination of information covered by Section 2-208 (a)-(j) to agencies within the Intelligence Community or entities of cooperating foreign governments; or

(d) Lawful storage or dissemination of information solely for administrative purposes not related to intelligence or security.

SECTION 3

OVERSIGHT OF INTELLIGENCE ORGANIZATIONS

3-1. *Intelligence Oversight Board.*

3-101. *Membership.* The President's intelligence Oversight Board (IOB) shall function within the White house. The IOB shall have three members who shall be appointed by the President and who shall be from outside the government and be qualified on the basis of ability, knowledge, diversity of background and experience. No member shall have any personal interest in any contractual relationship with any agency within the Intelligence Community. One member shall be designated by the President as chairman.

3-102. *Duties.* The IOB shall:

    (a) Review periodically the practices and procedures of the Inspectors General and General Counsel with responsibilities for agencies within the Intelligence Community for discovering and reporting to the IOB intelligence activities that raise questions of legality or propriety, and consider written and oral reports referred under Section 3-201.

    (b) Review periodically for accuracy the internal guidelines of each agency within the Intelligence Community concerning the legality or propriety of intelligence activities;

    (c) Report periodically, at least quarterly, to the President on its findings; and report in a timely manner to the President any intelligence activities that raise serious questions of legality or propriety;

    (d) Forward to the Attorney General, in a timely manner, reports received concerning intelligence activities in which a question of legality has been raised or which the IOB believes to involve questions of legality;

    (e) Conduct such investigations of the intelligence activities of agencies within the Intelligence Community as the Board deems necessary to carry out its functions under this Order.

3-103. *Restriction on Staff.* No person who serves on the staff of the IOB shall have any contractual or employment relationship with any agency within the Intelligence Community.

3-2. *Inspectors General and General Counsel.* Inspectors General and General Counsel with responsibility for agencies within the Intelligence Community shall:

3-201. Transmit timely reports to the IOB concerning any intelligence activities that come to their attention and that raise questions of legality or propriety;

3-202. Promptly report to the IOB actions taken concerning the Board's findings on intelligence activities that raise questions of legality or propriety;

3-203. Provide the IOB information requested concerning the legality or propriety of intelligence activities within their respective agencies;

3-204. Formulate practices and procedures for discovering and reporting to the IOB intelligence activities that raise questions of legality or propriety; and

3-205. Report to the IOB any occasion on which the Inspectors General or General Counsel were directed not to report any intelligence activity to the IOB which they believed raised questions of legality or propriety.

3-3. *Attorney General.* The Attorney General shall:

3-301. Receive and consider reports from agencies within the Intelligence Community forwarded by the IOB;

3-302. Report to the President in a timely fashion any intelligence activities which raise questions of legality;

3-303. Report to the IOB and to the President in a timely fashion decisions made or actions taken in response to reports from agencies within the Intelligence Community forwarded to the Attorney General by the IOB;

3-304. Inform the IOB of legal opinions affecting the operations of the Intelligence Community; and

3-305. Establish or approve procedures, as required by this Order, for the conduct of intelligence activities. Such procedures shall ensure compliance with law, protect constitutional rights and privacy, and ensure that any intelligence activity within the United States or directed against any United States person is conducted by the least intrusive means possible. The procedures shall also ensure that any use, dissemination and storage of information about United States persons acquired through intelligence activities is limited to that necessary to achieve lawful governmental purposes.

3-4. *Congressional Intelligence Committees*. Under such procedures as the President may establish and consistent with applicable authorities and duties, including those conferred by the Constitution upon the Executive and Legislative Branches and by law to protect sources and methods, the Director of Central Intelligence and heads of departments and agencies of the United States involved in intelligence activities shall:

3-401. Keep the Permanent Select Committee on Intelligence of the House of Representatives and the Select Committee on Intelligence of the Senate fully and currently informed concerning intelligence activities, including any significant anticipated activities which are the responsibility of, or engaged in, by such department or agency. This requirement does not constitute a condition precedent to the implementation of such intelligence activities;

3-402. Provide any information or document in the possession, custody or control of the department or agency or person paid by such department or agency, within the jurisdiction of the Permanent Select Committee on Intelligence of the House of Representatives or the Select Committee on Intelligence of the Senate, upon request of such committee; and

3-403. Report in a timely fashion to the Permanent Select Committee on Intelligence of the House of Representatives and the Select Committee on Intelligence of the Senate information relating to intelligence activities that are illegal or improper and corrective actions that are taken or planned.

SECTION 4

GENERAL PROVISIONS

4-1. *Implementation.*

4-101. Except as provided in section 4-105 of this section, this Order shall supersede Executive Order 11905, "United States Foreign Intelligence Activities," dated February 18, 1976; Executive Order 11965, same subject, dated May 13, 1977; and Executive Order 11994, same subject, dated June 1, 1977.

4-102. The NSC, the Secretary of Defense, the Attorney General and the Director of Central intelligence shall issue such appropriate directives and procedures as are necessary to implement this Order.

4-103. Heads of agencies within the Intelligence Community shall issue appropriate supplementary directives and procedures consistent with this Order.

4-104. The Attorney General shall have sole authority to issue and revise procedures required by section 2-201 for the activities of the FBI relating to foreign intelligence and counterintelligence.

4-105. Where intelligence activities under this Order are to be conducted pursuant to procedures approved or agreed to by the Attorney General, those activities may be conducted under terms and conditions of Executive Order 11905 and any procedures promulgated thereunder until such Attorney General procedures are established. Such Attorney General procedures shall be established as expeditiously as possible after issuance of this Order.

4-106. In some instances, the documents that implement this Order will be classified because of the sensitivity of the information and its relation to national security. All instructions contained in classified documents will be consistent with this Order. All procedures promulgated pursuant to this Order will be made available to the Congressional intelligence committees in accordance with Section 3-402.

4-107. Unless otherwise specified, the provisions of this Order shall apply to activities both within and outside of the United States, and all references to law are to applicable laws of the United States, including the Constitution and this Order. Nothing in this Order shall be construed to apply to or interfere with any authorized civil or criminal law enforcement responsibility of any department or agency.

4-2. *Definitions.* For purposes of this Order, the following terms shall have these meanings:

4-201. *Communications security* means protective measures taken to deny unauthorized persons information derived from telecommunications of the United States Government related to national security and to ensure the authenticity of such telecommunications.

4-202. *Counterintelligence* means information gathered and activities conducted to protect against espionage and other clandestine intelligence activities, sabotage, international terrorist activities or assassinations conducted for or on behalf of foreign powers, organizations or persons, but not including personnel, physical, document, or communications security programs.

4-203. *Electronic surveillance* means acquisition of a nonpublic communication by electronic means without the consent of a person who is a party to an electronic communication or, in the case of a nonelectronic communication, without the consent of a person who is visibly present at the place of communication, but not including the use of radio direction finding equipment solely to determine the location of a transmitter.

4-204. *Employee* means a person employed by, assigned to, or acting for an agency within the Intelligence Community.

4-205. *Foreign Intelligence* means information relating to the capabilities, intentions and activities of foreign powers, organizations or persons, but not including counterintelligence except for information on international terrorist activities.

4-206. *Intelligence* means foreign intelligence and counterintelligence.

4-207. *Intelligence Community* and *agency or agencies within the Intelligence Community* refer to the following organizations:

    (a)   The Central Intelligence Agency (CIA);

(b)   The National Security Agency (NSA);

(c)   The Defense Intelligence Agency;

(d)   The Offices within the Department of Defense for the collection of specialized national foreign intelligence through reconnaissance programs;

(e)   The Bureau of Intelligence and Research of the Department of State;

(f)   The intelligence elements of the military services, the Federal Bureau of Investigation (FBI), the Department of the Treasury, the Department of Energy, and the Drug Enforcement Administration (DEA); and

(g)   The staff elements of the Office of the Director of Central Intelligence.

4-208. *Intelligence product* means the estimates, memoranda, and other reports produced from the analysis of available information.

4-209. *International terrorist activities* means any activity or activities which:

(a)   involves killing, causing serious bodily harm, kidnapping or violent destruction of property, or an attempt or credible threat to commit such acts; *and*

(b)   appears intended to endanger a protectee of the Secret Service or the Department of State or to further political, social or economic goals by intimidating or coercing a civilian population or an segment thereof, influencing the policy of a government or international organization by intimidation or coercion, or obtaining widespread publicity for a group or its cause; *and*

(c)   transcends national boundaries in terms of the means by which it is accomplished, the civilian population, government, or international organization it appears intended to coerce or intimidate, or the locale in which its perpetrators operate or seek asylum.

4-210. *The National Foreign Intelligence Program* includes the programs listed below, but its composition shall be subject to review by the National Security Council and modification by the President.

(a)   The programs of the CIA;

(b)   The Consolidated Cryptologic Program, the General Defense Intelligence Program, and the programs of the offices within the Department of Defense for the collection of specialized national foreign intelligence through reconnaissance except such elements as the Director of Central Intelligence and the Secretary of Defense agree should be excluded;

(c)   Other programs of agencies within the Intelligence Community designated jointly by the Director of Central Intelligence and the head of the department or by the President as national foreign intelligence or counterintelligence activities;

(d)   Activities of the staff elements of the Office of the Director of Central Intelligence;

(e)   Activities to acquire the intelligence required for the planning and conduct of tactical operations by the United States military forces are not included in the National Foreign Intelligence Program.

4-211. *Physical surveillance* means and unconsented, systematic and deliberate observation of a person by any means on a continuing basis, or unconsented acquisition of a nonpublic communication by a person not a party thereto or visibly present thereat through any means not involving electronic surveillance. This definition does not include overhead reconnaissance not directed at specific United States persons.

4-212. *Special activities* means activities conducted abroad in support of national foreign policy objectives which are designed to further official United States programs and policies abroad and which are planned and executed so that the role of the United States Government is not apparent or acknowledged publicly, and functions in support of such activities, but not including diplomatic activity or the collection and production of intelligence or related support functions.

4-213. *United States*, when used to describe a place, includes the territories of the United States.

4-214. *United States person* means a citizen of the United States, an alien lawfully admitted for permanent residence, an unincorporated association organized in the United States or substantially composed of United States citizens or aliens admitted for permanent residence, or a corporation incorporated in the United States.

Jimmy Carter

THE WHITE HOUSE

January 24, 1978

Appendix L

Foreign Intelligence Surveillance Act of 1978
Public Law 95-511, 95th Congress

Title I—Electronic Surveillance within the United States for Foreign Intelligence Purposes

DEFINITIONS

SEC. 101. As used in this title:

(a) "Foreign power" means—

    (1) a foreign government or any component thereof, whether or not recognized by the United States;

    (2) a faction of a foreign nation or nations, not substantially composed of United States persons;

    (3) an entity that is openly acknowledged by a foreign government or governments to be directed and controlled by such foreign government or governments;

    (4) a group engaged in international terrorism or activities in preparation therefor;

    (5) a foreign-based political organization, not substantially composed of United States persons; or

    (6) an entity that is directed and controlled by a foreign government or governments.

(b) "Agent of a foreign power" means—

    (1) any person other than a United States person, who—

        (A) acts in the United States as an officer or employee of a foreign power, or as a member of a foreign power as defined in subsection (a)(4);

        (B) acts for or on behalf of a foreign power which engages in clandestine intelligence activities in the United States contrary to the interests of the United States, when the circumstances of such person's presence in the United States indicate that such person may engage in such activities in the United States, or when such person knowingly aids or abets any person in the conduct of such activities or knowingly conspires with any person to engage in such activities; or

    (2) any person who—

        (A) knowingly engages in clandestine intelligence gathering activities for or on behalf of a foreign power, which activities involve or may involve a violation of the criminal statutes of the United States;

        (B) pursuant to the direction of an intelligence service or network of a foreign power, knowingly engages in any other clandestine intelligence activities for or on behalf of such foreign power, which activities involve or are about to involve a violation of the criminal statutes of the United States;

(C) knowingly engages in sabotage or international terrorism, or activities that are in preparation therefor, for or on behalf of a foreign power; or

(D) knowingly aids or abets any person in the conduct of activities described in subparagraph (A), (B), or (C), or knowingly conspires with any person to engage in activities described in subparagraph (A), (B), or (C).

(c) "International terrorism" means activities that—

(1) involve violent acts or acts dangerous to human life that are a violation of the criminal laws of the United States or of any State, or that would be a criminal violation if committed within the jurisdiction of the United States or any State;

(2) appear to be intended—

(A) to intimidate or coerce a civilian population;

(B) to influence the policy of a government by intimidation or coercion; or

(C) to affect the conduct of a government by assassination or kidnapping; and

(3) occur totally outside the United States, or transcend national boundaries in terms of the means by which they are accomplished, the persons they appear intended to coerce or intimidate, or the locale in which the perpetrators operate or seek asylum.

(d) "Sabotage" means activities that involve a violation of chapter 105 of title 18, United States Code, or that would involve such a violation if committed against the United States.

(e) "Foreign intelligence information" means—

(1) information that relates to, and if concerning a United States person is necessary to, the ability of the United States to protect against—

(A) actual or potential attack or other grave hostile acts of a foreign power or an agent of a foreign power;

(B) sabotage or international terrorism by a foreign power or an agent of a foreign power; or

(C) clandestine intelligence activities by an intelligence service or network of a foreign power or by an agent of a foreign power; or

(2) information with respect to a foreign power or foreign territory that relates to, and if concerning a United States person is necessary to—

(A) the national defense or the security of the United States; or

(B) the conduct of the foreign affairs of the United States.

(f) "Electronic surveillance" means—

(1) the acquisition by an electronic, mechanical, or other surveillance device of the contents of any wire or radio communication sent by or intended to

be received by a particular, known United States person who is in the United States, if the contents are acquired by intentionally targeting that United States person, under circumstances in which a person has a reasonable expectation of privacy and a warrant would be required for law enforcement purposes;

(2) the acquisition by an electronic, mechanical, or other surveillance device of the contents of any wire communication to or from a person in the United States, without the consent of any party thereto, if such acquisition occurs in the United States;

(3) the intentional acquisition by an electronic, mechanical, or other surveillance device of the contents of any radio communication, under circumstances in which a person has a reasonable expectation of privacy and a warrant would be required for law enforcement purposes, and if both the sender and all intended recipients are located within the United States; or;

(4) the installation or use of an electronic, mechanical, or other surveillance device in the United States for in the United States for monitoring to acquire information, other than from a wire or radio communication, under circumstances in which a person has a reasonable expectation of privacy and a warrant would be required for law enforcement purposes.

(g) "Attorney General" means the Attorney General of the United States (or Acting Attorney General) or the Deputy Attorney General.

(h) "Minimization procedures", with respect to electronic surveillance, means—

(1) specific procedures, which shall be adopted by the Attorney General, that are reasonably designed in light of the purpose and technique of the particular surveillance, to minimize the acquisition and retention, and prohibit the dissemination, of nonpublicly available information concerning unconsenting United States persons consistent with the need of the United States to obtain, produce, and disseminate foreign intelligence information;

(2) procedures that require that nonpublicly available information, which is not foreign intelligence information, as defined in subsection (e)(1), shall not be disseminated in a manner that identifies any United States person, without that person's consent, unless such person's identity is necessary to understand foreign intelligence information or assess its importance;

(3) notwithstanding paragraphs (1) and (2), procedures that allow for the retention and dissemination of information that is evidence of a crime which has been, is being, or is about to be committed and that is to be retained or disseminated for law enforcement purposes; and

(4) notwithstanding paragraphs (1), (2), and (3), with respect to any electronic surveillance approved pursuant to paragraph 102(a), procedures that require that no contents of any communication to which a United States person is a party shall be disclosed, disseminated, or used for any purpose or retained for longer than twenty-four hours unless a court order under section 105 is obtained or unless the Attorney General determines that the information indicates a threat of death or serious bodily harm to any person.

(i) "United States person" means a citizen of the United States, an alien lawfully admitted for permanent residence (as defined in section 101(a)(20) of the Immigration and Nationality Act), an unincorporated association a substantial number of members of which are citizens of the United States or aliens lawfully admitted for permanent residence, or a corporation which is incorporated in the United States, but does not include a corporation or an association which is a foreign power, as defined in subsection (a)(1), (2), or (3).

(j) "United States", when used in a geographic sense, means all areas under the territorial sovereignty of the United States and the Trust Territory of the Pacific Islands.

(k) "Aggrieved person" means a person who is the target of an electronic surveillance or any other person whose communications or activities were subject to electronic surveillance.

(l) "Wire communication" means any communication while it is being carried by a wire, cable, or other like connection furnished or operated by any person engaged as a common carrier in providing or operating such facilities for the transmission of interstate or foreign communications.

(m) "Person" means any individual, including any officer or employee of the Federal Government, or any group, entity, association, corporation, or foreign power.

(n) "Contents," when used with respect to communication, includes any information concerning the identity of the parties to such communication or the existence, substance, purport, or meaning of that communication.

(o) "State" means any State of the United States, the District of Columbia, the Commonwealth of Puerto Rico, the Trust Territory of the Pacific Islands, and any territory or possession of the United States.

AUTHORIZATION FOR ELECTRONIC SURVEILLANCE FOR FOREIGN INTELLIGENCE PURPOSES

SEC. 102.

(a)

(1) Notwithstanding any other law, the President, through the Attorney General, may authorize electronic surveillance without a court order under this title to acquire foreign intelligence information for periods up to one year if the Attorney General certifies in writing under oath that—

(A) the electronic surveillance is solely directed at—

(i) the acquisition of the contents of communications transmitted by means of communication used exclusively between or among foreign powers, as defined in section 101(a)(1), (2), or (3); or

(ii) the acquisition of technical intelligence, other than the spoken communications of individuals, from property or premises under the open and exclusive control of a foreign power, as defined in section 101(a)(1), (2), or (3);

(B) there is no substantial likelihood that the surveillance will acquire the contents of any communication to which a United States person is a party; and

(C) the proposed minimization procedures with respect to such surveillance meet the definition of minimization procedures under section 101(h); and if the Attorney General reports such minimization procedures and any changes thereto to the House Permanent Select Committee on Intelligence and the Senate Select Committee on Intelligence at least thirty days prior to their effective date, unless the Attorney General determines immediate action is required and notifies the committees immediately of such minimization procedures and the reason for their becoming effective immediately.

(2) An electronic surveillance authorized by this subsection may be conducted only in accordance with the Attorney General's certification and the minimization procedures adopted by him. The Attorney General shall assess compliance with such procedures and shall report such assessments to the House Permanent Select Committee on Intelligence and the Senate Select Committee on Intelligence under the provisions of section 108(a).

(3) The Attorney General shall immediately transmit under seal to the court established under section 103(a) a copy of his certification. Such certification shall be maintained under security measures established by the Chief Justice with the concurrence of the Attorney General, in consultation with the Director of Central Intelligence, and shall remain sealed unless—

(A) an application for a court order with respect to the surveillance is made under sections 101(h)(4) and 104; or

(B) the certification is necessary to determine the legality of the surveillance under section 106(f).

(4) With respect to electronic surveillance authorized by this subsection, the Attorney General may direct a specified communication common carrier to—

(A) furnish all information, facilities, or technical assistance necessary to accomplish the electronic surveillance in such a manner as will protect the secrecy and produce a minimum of interference with the services that such carrier is providing its customers; and

(B) maintain under security procedures approved by the Attorney General and the Director of Central Intelligence any records concerning the surveillance or the aid furnished which such carrier wishes to retain.

The Government shall compensate, at the prevailing rate, such carrier for furnishing such aid.

(b) Applications for a court order under this title are authorized if the President has, by written authorization, empowered the Attorney General to approve applications to the court having jurisdiction under section 103, and a judge to whom an application is made may, notwithstanding any other law, grant an order, in conformity with section 105, approving electronic surveillance of a foreign power or an agent of a foreign power for the purpose of obtaining foreign intelligence information, except that the court shall not have jurisdiction to grant any order approving electronic surveillance directed solely as described in paragraph (1)(A) of subsection (a) unless such surveillance may involve the acquisition of communications of any United States person.

DESIGNATION OF JUDGES

SEC. 103.

    (a)   The Chief Justice of the United States shall publicly designate seven district court judges from seven of the United States judicial circuits who shall constitute a court which shall have jurisdiction to hear applications for and grant orders approving electronic surveillance anywhere within the United States under the procedures set forth in this Act, except that no judge designated under this subsection shall hear the same application for electronic surveillance under this Act which has been denied previously by another judge designated under this subsection. If any judge so designated denies an application for an order authorizing electronic surveillance under this Act, such judge shall provide immediately for the record a written statement of each reason for his decision and, on motion of the United States, the record shall be transmitted, under seal, to the court of review established in subsection (b).

    (b)   The Chief Justice shall publicly designate three judges, one of whom shall be publicly designated as the presiding judge, from the United States district courts or court of appeals who together shall comprise a court of review which shall have jurisdiction to review the denial of any application made under this Act. If such court determines that the application was properly denied, the court shall immediately provide for the record a written statement of each reason for its decision and, on petition of the United States for a writ of certiorari, the record shall be transmitted under seal to the Supreme Court, which shall have jurisdiction to review such decision.

    (c)   Proceedings under this Act shall be conducted as expeditiously as possible. The record of proceedings under this Act, including applications made and orders granted, shall be maintained under security measures established by the Chief Justice in consultation with the Attorney General and the Director of Central Intelligence.

    (d)   Each judge designated under this section shall so serve for a maximum of seven years and shall not be eligible for redesignation, except that the judges first designated under subsection (a) shall be designated for terms of from one to seven years so that one term expires each year, and that judges first designated under subsection (b) shall be designated for terms of three, five, or seven years.

APPLICATION FOR AN ORDER

SEC. 104.

    (a)   Each application for an order approving electronic surveillance under this title shall be made by a Federal officer in writing upon oath or affirmation to a judge having jurisdiction under section 103. Each application shall require the approval of the Attorney General based upon his finding that it satisfies the criteria and requirements of such application as set forth in this title. It shall include—

       (1) the identity of the Federal officer making the application;

       (2) the authority conferred on the Attorney General by the President of the

United States and the approval of the Attorney General to make the application;

(3) the identity, if known, or a description of the target of the electronic surveillance;

(4) a statement of the facts and circumstances relied upon by the applicant to justify his belief that—

    (A) the target of the electronic surveillance is a foreign power or an agent of a foreign power; and

    (B) each of the facilities or places at which the electronic surveillance is being used, or is about to be used, by a foreign power or an agent of a foreign power.

(5) a statement of the proposed minimization procedures;

(6) a detailed description of the nature of the information sought and the type of communications or activities to be subjected to the surveillance;

(7) a certification or certifications by the Assistant to the President for National Security Affairs or an executive branch official or officials designated by the President from among those executive officers employed in the area of national security or defense and appointed by the President with the advice and the consent of the Senate—

    (A) that the certifying official deems the information sought to be foreign intelligence information;

    (B) that the purpose of the surveillance is to obtain foreign intelligence information;

    (C) that such information cannot be reasonably obtained by normal investigative techniques;

    (D) that designates the type of foreign intelligence information being sought according to the categories described in section 101(e); and

    (E) including a statement of the basis for the certification that—

        (i) the information sought is the type of foreign intelligence information designated; and

        (ii) such information cannot be reasonably obtained by normal investigative techniques;

(8) a statement of the means by which the surveillance will be effected and a statement whether physical entry is required to effect the surveillance;

(9) a statement of the facts concerning all previous applications that have been made to any judge under this title involving any of the persons, facilities, or places specified in the application, and the action taken on each previous occasion;

(10) a statement of the period of time for which the electronic surveillance is required to be maintained, and if the nature of the intelligence gathering is such that the approval of the use of electronic surveillance under this title should not automatically terminate when the described type of information has first been obtained, a description of facts supporting the belief that additional information of the same type will be obtained thereafter; and

(11) whenever more than one electronic, mechanical or other surveillance device is to be used with respect to a particular proposed electronic surveillance, the coverage of the devices involved and what minimization procedures apply to information acquired by each device.

(b) Whenever the target of the electronic surveillance is a foreign power, as defined in section 101(a) (1), (2), or (3), and each of the facilities or places at which the surveillance is directed or owned, leased, or exclusively used by that foreign power, the application need not contain the information required by paragraphs (6), (7)(E), (8), and (11) of subsection (a), but shall state whether physical entry is required to effect the surveillance and shall contain such information about the surveillance techniques and communications or other information concerning United States persons likely to be obtained as may be necessary to assess the proposed minimization procedures.

(c) The Attorney General may require any other affidavit or certification from any other officer in connection with the application.

(d) The judge may require the applicant to furnish such other information as may be necessary to make the determinations required by section 105.

ISSUANCE OF AN ORDER

SEC. 105.

(a) Upon an application made pursuant to section 104, the judge shall enter an ex parte order as requested or as modified approving the electronic surveillance if he finds that—

(1) the President has authorized the Attorney General to approve applications for electronic surveillance for foreign intelligence information;

(2) the application has been made by a Federal officer and approved by the Attorney General;

(3) on the basis of the facts submitted by the applicant there is probable cause to believe that—

(A) the target of the electronic surveillance is a foreign power or an agent of a foreign power: *Provided*, That no United States person may be considered a foreign power or an agent of a foreign power solely upon the basis of activities protected by the first amendment to the Constitution of the United States; and

(B) each of the facilitates or places at which the electronic surveillance is directed is being used, or is about to be used, by a foreign power or an agent of a foreign power;

(4) the proposed minimization procedures meet the definition of minimization procedures under section 101(h); and

(5) the application which has been filed contains all statements and certifications required by section 104 and, if the target is a United States person, the certification or certifications are not clearly erroneous on the basis of the statement made under section 104(a)(7) (E) and any other information furnished under section 104(d).

(b) An order approving an electronic surveillance under this section shall—

(1) specify—

(A) the identity, if known, or a description of the target of the electronic surveillance;

(B) the nature and location of each of the facilities or places at which the electronic surveillance will be directed;

(C) the type of information sought to be acquired and the type of communications or activities to be subjected to the surveillance;

(D) the means by which the electronic surveillance will be effected and whether physical entry will be used to effect the surveillance;

(E) the period of time during which the electronic surveillance is approved; and

(F) whenever more than one electronic, mechanical, or other surveillance device is to be used under the order, the authorized coverage of the devices involved and what minimization procedures shall apply to information subject to acquisition by each device; and

(2) direct—

(A) that the minimization procedures be followed;

(B) that, upon the request of the applicant, a specified communication or other common carrier, landlord custodian, or other specified person furnish the applicant forthwith all information, facilities, or technical assistance necessary to accomplish the electronic surveillance in such a manner as will protect its secrecy and produce a minimum of interference with the services that such carrier, landlord, custodian, or other person is providing that target of electronic surveillance;

(C) that such carrier, landlord, custodian, or other person maintain under security procedures approved by the Attorney General and the Director of Central Intelligence any records concerning the surveillance or the aid furnished that such person wishes to retain; and

(D) that the applicant compensate, at the prevailing rate, such carrier, landlord, custodian, or other person for furnishing such aid.

(c) Whenever the target of the electronic surveillance is a foreign power, as defined in section 101(a) (1), (2), or (3), and each of the facilities or places at which the surveillance is directed is owned, leased, or exclusively used by that foreign power, the order need not contain the information required by subparagraphs (C), (D), and (F) or subsection (b)(1), but shall generally describe the information sought, the communications or activities to be subjected to the surveillance, and the type of electronic surveillance involved, including whether physical entry is required.

(d)

(1) An order issued under this section may approve an electronic surveillance for the period necessary to achieve its purpose, or for ninety days, whichever is less, except that an order under this section shall approve an electronic surveillance targeted against a foreign power, as defined in section 101(a) (1), (2), or (3), for the period specified in the application or for one year, whichever is less.

(2) Extensions of an order issued under this title may be granted on the same basis as an original order upon an application for an extension and new findings made in the same manner as required for an original order, except that an extension of an order under this Act for a surveillance targeted against a foreign power, as defined in section 101(a) (5) or (6), or against a foreign power as defined in section 101(a) (4) that is not a United States person, may be for a period not to exceed one year if the judge finds probable cause to believe that no communication of any individual United States person will be acquired during the period.

(3) At or before the end of the period of time for which electronic surveillance is approved by an order or an extension, the judge may assess compliance with the minimization procedures by reviewing the circumstances under which information concerning United States persons was acquired, retained, or disseminated.

(e) Notwithstanding any other provision of this title, when the Attorney General reasonably determines that—

(1) an emergency situation exists with respect to the employment of electronic surveillance to obtain foreign intelligence information before an order authorizing such surveillance can with due diligence be obtained; and

(2) the factual basis for issuance of an order under this title to approve such surveillance exists; he may utilize the emergency employment of electronic surveillance if a judge having jurisdiction under section 103 is informed by the Attorney General or his designee at the time of such authorization that the decision has been made to employ emergency electronic surveillance and if an application in accordance with this title is made to that judge as soon as practicable, but not more than twenty-four hours after the Attorney General authorizes such surveillance. If the Attorney General authorizes such emergency employment of electronic surveillance, he shall require that the minimization procedures required by this title for the issuance of a judicial order be followed. In the absence of a judicial order approving such electronic surveillance, the surveillance shall terminate when the information sought is obtained, when the application for the order is denied, or after the expiration of twenty-four hours from the time of authorization by the Attorney General, whichever is earliest. In the event that such application for approval is denied, or in any other case where the electronic surveillance is terminated and no order is issued approving the surveillance, no information obtained or evidence derived from such surveillance shall be received in evidence or otherwise disclosed in any trial, hearing, or other proceeding in or before any court, grand jury, department, office, agency, regulatory body, legislative committee, or other authority of the United States, a State, or political subdivision thereof, and no information concerning any United States person acquired from such surveillance shall subsequently be used or disclosed in any other manner by Federal officers or employees without the consent of such person, except with the approval of the Attorney General if the information indicates a threat of death or serious bodily harm to any person. A denial of the application made under this subsection may be reviewed as provided in section 103.

(f) Notwithstanding any other provision of this title, officers, employees or agents of the United States are authorized in the normal course of their official duties to conduct electronic surveillance not targeted against the communications of any particular person or persons, under procedures approved by the Attorney General, solely to—

(1) test the capability of electronic equipment, if—

    (A) it is not reasonable to obtain the consent of the persons incidentally subjected to the surveillance;

    (B) the test is limited in extent and duration to that necessary to determine the capability of the equipment;

    (C) the contents of any communication acquired are retained and used only for the purpose of determining the capability of the equipment, are disclosed only to test personnel, and are destroyed before or immediately upon completion of the test; and:

    (D) *Provided,* That the test may exceed ninety days only with the prior approval of the Attorney General;

(2) determine the existence and capability of electronic surveillance equipment being used by persons not authorized to conduct electronic surveillance if—

    (A) it is not reasonable to obtain the consent of persons incidentally subjected to the surveillance;

    (B) such electronic surveillance is limited in extent and duration to that necessary to determine the existence and capability of such equipment; and

    (C) any information acquired by such surveillance is used only to enforce chapter 119 of title 18, United States Code, or section 705 of the Communications Act of 1934, or to protect information from unauthorized surveillance; or

(3) train intelligence personnel in the use of electronic surveillance equipment, if—

    (A) it is not reasonable to—

        (i) obtain the consent of the persons incidentally subjected to the surveillance;

        (ii) train persons in the course of surveillances otherwise authorized by this title; or

        (iii) train persons in the use of such equipment without engaging in electronic surveillance;

    (B) such electronic surveillance is limited in extent and duration to that necessary to train the personnel in the use of the equipment; and

    (C) no contents of any communication acquired are retained or disseminated for any purpose, but are destroyed as soon as reasonably possible.

(g) Certifications made by the Attorney General pursuant to section 102(a) and applications made and orders granted under this title shall be retained for a period of at least ten years from the date of the certification or application.

USE OF INFORMATION

SEC. 106.

(a) Information acquired from an electronic surveillance conducted pursuant to this title concerning any United States person may be used and disclosed by Federal officers and employees without the consent of the United States person only in accordance with the minimization procedures required by this title. No otherwise privileged communication obtained in accordance with, or in violation of, the provisions of this title shall lose its privileged character. No information acquired from an electronic surveillance pursuant to this title may be used or disclosed by Federal officers or employees except for lawful purposes.

(b) No information acquired pursuant to this title shall be disclosed for law enforcement purposes unless such disclosure is accompanied by a statement that such information, or any information derived therefrom, may only be used in a criminal proceeding with the advance authorization of the Attorney General.

(c) Whenever the Government intends to enter into evidence or otherwise use or disclose in any trial, hearing, or other proceeding in or before any court, department, officer, agency, regulatory body, or other authority of the United States, against an aggrieved person, any information obtained or derived from an electronic surveillance of that aggrieved person pursuant to the authority of this title, the Government shall, prior to the trial, hearing, or other proceeding or at a reasonable time prior to an effort to so disclose or so use that information or submit it in evidence, notify the aggrieved person and the court or other authority in which the information is to be disclosed or used that the Government intends to so disclose or so use such information.

(d) Whenever any State or political subdivision thereof intends to enter into evidence or otherwise use or disclose in any trial, hearing, or other proceeding in or before any court, department, officer, agency, regulatory body, or other authority of a State or a political subdivision thereof, against an aggrieved person any information obtained or derived from an electronic surveillance of that aggrieved person pursuant to the authority of this title, the State or political subdivision thereof shall notify the aggrieved person, the court or other authority in which the information is to be disclosed or used, and the Attorney General that the State or political subdivision thereof intends to so disclose or so use such information.

(e) Any person against whom evidence obtained or derived from an electronic surveillance to which he is an aggrieved person is to be, or has been, introduced or otherwise used or disclosed in any trial, hearing, or other proceeding in or before any court, department, officer, agency, regulatory body, or other authority of the United States, a State, or a political subdivision thereof, may move to suppress the evidence obtained or derived from such electronic surveillance on the grounds that—

(1) the information was unlawfully acquired; or

(2) the surveillance was not made in conformity with an order of authorization or approval. Such a motion shall be made before the trial, hearing, or other proceeding unless there was no opportunity to make such a motion or the person was not aware of the grounds of the motion.

(f)   Whenever a court or other authority is notified pursuant to subsection (c) or (d), or whenever a motion is made pursuant to subsection (e), or whenever any motion or request is made by an aggrieved person pursuant to any other statute or rule of the United States or any State before any court or any other authority of the United States or any State to discover or obtain applications or orders or other materials relating to electronic surveillance or to discover, obtain, or suppress evidence or information obtained or derived from electronic surveillance under this Act, the United States district court or, where the motion is made before another authority, the United States district court in the same district as the authority, shall, not withstanding any other law, if the Attorney General files an affidavit under oath that disclosure or an adversary hearing would harm the national security of the United States, review in camera and ex parte the application, order, and such other materials relating to the surveillance as may be necessary to determine whether the surveillance of the aggrieved person was lawfully authorized and conducted. In making this determination, the court may disclose to the aggrieved person, under appropriate security procedures and protective orders, portions of the application, order, or other materials relating to the surveillance only where such disclosure is necessary to make an accurate determination of the legality of the surveillance.

(g)   If the United States district court pursuant to subsection (f) determines that the surveillance was not lawfully authorized or conducted, it shall, in accordance with the requirements of law, suppress the evidence which was unlawfully obtained or derived from electronic surveillance of the aggrieved person or otherwise grant the motion of the aggrieved person. If the court determines that the surveillance was lawfully authorized and conducted, it shall deny the motion of the aggrieved person except to the extent that due process requires discovery or disclosure.

(h)   Orders granting motions or requests under subsection (g), decisions under this section that electronic surveillance was not lawfully authorized or conducted, and orders of the United States district court requiring review or granting disclosure of applications, orders, or other materials relating to a surveillance shall be final orders and binding upon all courts of the United States and the several States except a United States court of appeals and the Supreme Court.

(i)   In circumstances involving the unintentional acquisition by an electronic, mechanical, or other surveillance device of the contents of any radio communication, under circumstances in which a person has a reasonable expectation of privacy and a warrant would be required for law enforcement purposes, and if both the sender and all intended recipients are located within the United States, such contents shall be destroyed upon recognition, unless the Attorney General determines that the contents indicate a threat of death or serious bodily harm to any person.

(j)   If an emergency employment of an electronic surveillance is authorized under section 105(e) and a subsequent order approving the surveillance is not obtained, the judge shall cause to be served on any United States person named in the application and on such other United States persons subject to electronic surveillance as the judge may determine in his discretion it is in the interest of justice to serve, notice of—

(1) the fact of the application;

(2) the period of the surveillance; and

(3) the fact that during the period information was or was not obtained.

On an ex parte showing of good cause to the judge the serving of the notice required by this subsection may be postponed or suspended for a period not to exceed ninety days. Thereafter, on a further ex parte showing of good cause, the court shall forego ordering the serving of the notice required under this subsection.

REPORT OF ELECTRONIC SURVEILLANCE

SEC. 107. In April of each year, the Attorney General shall transmit to the Administrative Office of the United States Court and to Congress a report setting forth with respect to the preceding calendar year—

(a) the total number of applications made for orders and extensions of orders approving electronic surveillance under this title; and

(b) the total number of such orders and extensions either granted, modified, or denied.

CONGRESSIONAL OVERSIGHT

SEC. 108.

(a) On a semiannual basis the Attorney General shall fully inform the House Permanent Select Committee on Intelligence and the Senate Select Committee on Intelligence concerning all electronic surveillance under this title. Nothing in this title shall be deemed to limit the authority and responsibility of the appropriate committees of each House of Congress to obtain such information as they may need to carry out their respective functions and duties.

(b) On or before one year after the effective date of this Act and on the same day each year for four years thereafter, the Permanent Select Committee on Intelligence and the Senate Select Committee on Intelligence shall report respectively to the House of Representatives and the Senate, concerning the implementation of this Act. Said reports shall include but not be limited to an analysis and recommendations concerning whether this Act should be (1) amended, (2) repealed, or (3) permitted to continue in effect without amendment.

PENALTIES

SEC. 109.

(a) OFFENSE.—A person is guilty of an offense if he intentionally—

(1) engages in electronic surveillance under color of law except as authorized by statute; or

(2) discloses or uses information obtained under color of law by electronic surveillance, knowing or having reason to know that the information was obtained through electronic surveillance not authorized by statute.

(b) DEFENSE.—It is a defense to a prosecution under subsection (a) that the defendant was a law enforcement or investigative officer engaged in the course of his official duties and the electronic surveillance was authorized by and conducted pursuant to a search warrant or court order of a court of competent jurisdiction.

(c) PENALTY.—An offense described in this section is punishable by a fine of not more than $10,000 or imprisonment for not more than five years, or both.

(d) JURISDICTION.—There is Federal jurisdiction over an offense under this section if the person committing the offense was an officer or employee of the United States at the time the offense was committed.

CIVIL LIABILITY

SEC. 110. CIVIL ACTION.—An aggrieved person, other than a foreign power or an agent of a foreign power, as defined in section 101 (a) or (b)(1)(A), respectively, who has been subjected to an electronic surveillance or about whom information obtained by electronic surveillance of such person has been disclosed or used in violation of section 109 shall have a cause of action against any person who committed such violation and shall be entitled to recover—

(a) actual damages, but not less than liquidated damages of $1,000 or $100 per day for each day of violation, whichever is greater;

(b) punitive damages; and

(c) reasonable attorney's fees and other investigation and litigation costs reasonably incurred.

AUTHORIZATION DURING TIME OF WAR

SEC. 111. Notwithstanding any other law, the President, through the Attorney General, may authorize electronic surveillance without a court order under this title to acquire foreign intelligence information for a period not to exceed fifteen calendar days following a declaration of war by the Congress.

TITLE II—CONFORMING AMENDMENTS

AMENDMENTS TO CHAPTER 119 OF TITLE 18, UNITED STATES CODE

SEC. 201. Chapter 119 of title 18, United States Code, is amended as follows:

(a) Section 2511(2)(a)(ii) is amended to read as follows:

"(ii) Notwithstanding any other law, communication common carriers, their officers, employees, and agents, landlords, custodians, or other persons, are authorized to provide information, facilities, or technical assistance to persons authorized by law to intercept wire or oral communications or to conduct electronic surveillance, as defined in section 101 of the Foreign Intelligence Surveillance Act of 1978, if the common carrier, its officers, employees, or agents, landlord, custodian, or other specified person, has been provided with—

(A) a court order directing such assistance signed by the authorizing judge, or

(B) a certification in writing by a person specified in section 2518(7) of this title or the Attorney General of the United States that no warrant or court order is required by law, that all statutory requirements have been met, and that the specified assistance is required, setting forth the period of time during which the provision of the information, facilities, or technical assistance is authorized and specifying the information, facilities, or technical assistance required. No communication common carrier, officer, employee, or agent thereof, or landlord, custodian, or other specified person shall disclose the existence of any interception or surveillance or the device used to accomplish the interception or surveillance with respect to which the person has been furnished an order or certification under this subparagraph, except as may otherwise be required by legal process and then only after prior notification to the Attorney General or to the principal prosecuting attorney of a State or any political subdivision of a State, as may be appropriate. Any violation of this subparagraph by a communication common carrier or an officer, employee, or agent thereof, shall render the carrier liable for the civil damages provided in section 2520. No cause of action shall lie in any court against any communication common carrier, its officers, employees, or agents, landlord, custodian, or other specified person for providing information, facilities, or assistance in accordance with the terms of an order or certification under this paragraph."

(b) Section 2511(2) is amended by adding at the end thereof the following new provisions:

"(e) Notwithstanding any other provision of this title or section 605 or 606 of the Communications Act of 1934, it shall not be unlawful for an officer, employee, or agent of the United States in the normal course of his official duty to conduct electronic surveillance, as defined in section 101 of the Foreign Intelligence Surveillance Act of 1978, as authorized by that Act.

(f) Nothing contained in this chapter, or section 605 of the Communications Act of 1934, shall be deemed to affect the acquisition by the United States Government of foreign intelligence information from international or foreign communications by a means other than electronic surveillance as defined in section 101 of the Foreign Intelligence Surveillance Act of 1978, and procedures in this chapter and the Foreign Intelligence Surveillance Act of 1978 shall be the exclusive means by which electronic surveillance, as defined in section 101 of such Act, and the interception of domestic wire and oral communications may be conducted."

(c) Section 2511(3) is repealed.

(d) Section 2518(1) is amended by inserting "under this chapter" after "communication."

    (e) Section 2518(4) is amended by inserting "under this chapter" after both appearances of "wire or oral communication."

    (f) Section 2518(9) is amended by striking out "intercepted" and inserting "intercepted pursuant to this chapter" after "communication."

    (g) Section 2518(10) is amended by striking out "intercepted" and inserting "intercepted pursuant to this chapter" after the first appearance of "communication."

    (h) Section 2519(3) is amended by inserting "pursuant to this chapter" after "wire or oral communications" and after "granted or denied."

TITLE III—EFFECTIVE DATE

SEC 301. The provisions of this Act and the amendments made hereby shall become effective upon the date of enactment of this Act, except that any electronic surveillance approved by the Attorney General to gather foreign intelligence information shall not be deemed unlawful for failure to follow the procedures of this Act, if that surveillance is terminated or an order approving that surveillance is obtained under title I of this Act within ninety days following the designation of the first judge pursuant to section 103 of this Act.

Approved October 25, 1978.

Appendix M

Section 552a, Title 5, United States Code
Privacy Act, 1980

552a. Records maintained on individuals

(a) DEFINITIONS.—For purposes of this section—

    (1) the term "agency" means agency as defined in section 552(e) of this title;

    (2) the term "individual" means a citizen of the United States or an alien lawfully admitted for permanent residence;

    (3) the term "maintain" includes maintain, collect, use, or disseminate;

    (4) the term "record" means any item, collection, or grouping of information about an individual that is maintained by an agency, including, but not limited to, his education, financial transactions, medical history, and criminal or employment history and that contains his name, or the identifying number, symbol, or other identifying particular assigned to the individual, such as finger or voice print or photograph;

    (5) the term "system of records" means a group of any records under the control of any agency from which information is retrieved by the name of the individual or by some identifying number, symbol, or other identifying particular assigned to the individual;

    (6) the term "statistical record" means a record in a system of records maintained for statistical research or reporting purposes only and not used in whole or part in making any determination about an identifiable individual, except as provided by section 8 of title 13; and

    (7) the term "routine use" means, with respect to the disclosure of a record, the use of such record for a purpose which is compatible with the purpose for which it was collected.

(b) CONDITIONS OF DISCLOSURE.—No agency shall disclose any record which is contained in a series of records by an means of communication to any person, or to another agency, except pursuant to a written request by, or with the prior written consent of, the individual to which the record pertains, unless disclosure of the record would be—

    (1) to those officers and employees of the agency which maintains the record who have a need for the record in the performance of their duties;

    (2) required under section 552 of this title;

    (3) for a routine use as defined in subsection (a)(7) of this section and described under subsection (e)(4)(D) of this section;

    (4) to the Bureau of the Census for purposes of planning or carrying out a

census or survey or related activity pursuant to the provisions of title 13;

(5) to a recipient who has provided the agency with advance adequate written assurance that the record will be used solely as a statistical research or reporting record, and the record is to be transferred in a form that is not individually identifiable;

(6) to the National Archives of the United States as a record which has sufficient historical or other value to warrant its continued preservation by the United States Government, or for evaluation by the Archivist of the United States or the designee of the Archivist to determine whether the record has such value;

(7) to another agency or to an instrumentality of any governmental jurisdiction within or under the control of the United States for a civil or criminal law enforcement activity if the activity is authorized by law, and if the head of the agency or instrumentality has made a written request to the agency which maintains the record specifying the particular portion desired and the law enforcement activity for which the record is sought;

(8) to a person pursuant to a showing of compelling circumstances affecting the health or safety of an individual if upon such disclosure notification is transmitted to the last known address of such individual;

(9) to either House of Congress, or, to the extent of matter within its jurisdiction, any committee or subcommittee thereof, any joint committee of Congress or subcommittee of any such joint committee;

(10) to the Comptroller General, or any of his authorized representatives, in the course of the performance of the duties of the General Accounting Office;

(11) pursuant to the order of a court of competent jurisdiction; or

(12) to a consumer reporting agency in accordance with section 3(d) of the Federal Claims Collection Act of 1966 (31 U.S.C. 952(d)).

(c) ACCOUNTING OF CERTAIN DISCLOSURES.—Each agency, with respect to each system of records under its control, shall—

(1) except for disclosures made under subsections (b)(1) or (b)(2) of this section, keep an accurate accounting of—

(A) the date, nature, and purpose of each disclosure of a record to any person or to another agency made under subsection (b) of this section; and

(B) the name and address of the person or agency to whom the disclosure is made;

(2) retain the accounting made under paragraph (1) of this subsection for at least five years or the life of the record, whichever is longer, after the disclosure for which the accounting is made;

(3) except for disclosures made under subsection (b)(7) of this section, make the accounting made under paragraph (1) of this subsection available to the individual named in the record at his request; and

(4) inform any person or other agency about any correction or notification of dispute made by the agency in accordance with subsection (d) of this section of any record that has been disclosed to the person or agency if an

accounting of the disclosure was made.

(d) ACCESS TO RECORDS.—Each agency that maintains a system of records shall—

(1) upon request by any individual to gain access to his record or to any information pertaining to him which is contained in the system, permit him and upon his request, a person of his own choosing to accompany him, to review the record and have a copy made of all or any portion thereof in a form comprehensible to him, except that the agency may require the individual to furnish a written statement authorizing discussion of that individual's record in the accompanying person's presence;

(2) permit the individual to request amendment of a record pertaining to him and—

(A) not later than ten days (excluding Saturdays, Sundays, and legal public holidays) after the date of receipt of such request, acknowledge in writing such receipt; and

(B) promptly, either—

(i) make any correction of any portion thereof which the individual believes is not accurate, relevant, timely, or complete; or

(ii) inform the individual of its refusal to amend the record in accordance with his requests, the reason for the refusal, the procedures established by the agency for the individual to request a review of that refusal by the head of the agency or an officer designated by the head of the agency, and the name and business address of that official;

(3) permit the individual who disagrees with the refusal of the agency to amend his record to request a review of such refusal, and not later than 30 days (excluding Saturdays, Sundays, and legal public holidays) from the date on which the individual requests such review, complete such review and make a final determination unless, for good cause shown, the head of the agency extends such 30-day period; and, if after his review, the reviewing official also refuses to amend the record in accordance with the request, permit the individual to file with the agency a concise statement setting forth the reasons for his disagreement with the refusal of the agency, and notify the individual for the provisions for judicial review of the reviewing official's determination under subsection (g)(1)(A) of this section;

(4) in any disclosure, containing information about which the individual has filed a statement of disagreement, occurring after the filing of the statement under paragraph (3) of this subsection, clearly note any portion of the record which is disputed and provide copies of the statement and, if the agency deems it appropriate, copies of a concise statement of the reasons of the agency for not making the amendments requested, to persons or other agencies to whom the disputed record has been disclosed; and

(5) nothing in this section shall allow an individual access to any information compiled in reasonable anticipation of a civil action or proceeding.

(e) AGENCY REQUIREMENTS.—Each agency that maintains a system of records shall—

(1) maintain in its records only such information about an individual as is relevant and necessary to accomplish a purpose of the agency required to be accomplished by statute or by executive order of the President;

(2) collect information to the greatest extent practicable directly from the subject individual when the information may result in adverse determinations about the individual's rights, benefits, and privileges under Federal programs;

(3) inform each individual whom it asks to supply information on the form which it uses to collect the information or on a separate form that can be retained by the individual—

    (A) the authority (whether granted by statute, or by executive order of the President) which authorizes the solicitation of the information and whether disclosure of such information is mandatory or voluntary;

    (B) the principal purpose or purposes for which the information is intended to be used;

    (C) the routine uses which may be made of the information, as published pursuant to paragraph (4)(D) of this subsection; and

    (D) the effects on him, if any, of not providing all or any part of the requested information;

(4) subject to the provisions of paragraph (11) of this subsection, publish in the Federal Register at least annually a notice of the existence and character of the system of records, which notice shall include—

    (A) the name and location of the system;

    (B) the categories of individuals on whom records are maintained in the system;

    (C) the categories of records maintained in the system;

    (D) each routine use of the records maintained in the system, including the categories of users and the purpose of each use;

    (E) the policies and practices of the agency regarding storage, retrievability, access controls, retention, and disposal of records;

    (F) the title and business address of the agency official who is responsible for the system of records;

    (G) the agency procedures whereby an individual can be notified at his request if the system of records contains a record pertaining to him;

    (H) the agency procedures whereby an individual can be notified at his request how he can gain access to any record pertaining to him contained in the system of records, and how he can contest its content; and

    (I) the categories of sources of records in the system;

(5) maintain all records which are used by the agency in making any determination about an individual with such accuracy, relevance, timeliness, and completeness as is reasonably necessary to assure fairness to the individual in the determination;

(6) prior to disseminating any information about an individual to any person other than an agency, unless the dissemination is made pursuant to

subsection (b)(2) of this section, make responsible efforts to assure that such records are accurate, complete, timely, and relevant for agency purposes;

(7) maintain no record describing how any individual exercises rights guaranteed by the First Amendment unless expressly authorized by statute or by the individual about whom the record is maintained or unless pertinent to and within the scope of an authorized law enforcement activity;

(8) make reasonable efforts to serve notice on an individual when any record of such individual is made available to any person under compulsory legal process when such process becomes a matter of public record;

(9) establish rules of conduct for persons involved in the design, development, operation, or maintenance of any system of records, or in maintaining any record, and instruct each such person with respect to such rules and the requirements of this section, including any other rules and procedures adopted pursuant to this section and the penalties for noncompliance;

(10) establish appropriate administrative, technical, and physical safeguards to insure the security and confidentiality of records and to protect against any anticipated threats or hazards to their security or integrity which could result in their substantial harm, embarrassment, inconvenience, or unfairness to any individual on whom information is maintained; and

(11) at least 30 days prior to publication of information under paragraph (4)(D) of this subsection, publish in Federal Register notice of any new use or intended use of the information in the system, and provide an opportunity for interested persons to submit written data, views, or arguments, to the agency.

(f) AGENCY RULES.—In order to carry out the provisions of this section, each agency that maintains a system of records shall promulgate rules, in accordance with the requirements (including general notice) of section 553 of this title, which shall—

(1) establish procedures whereby an individual can be notified in response to his request if any system of records named by the individual contains a record pertaining to him;

(2) define reasonable times, places and requirements for identifying an individual who requests his record or information pertaining to him before the agency shall make the record or information available to the individual;

(3) establish procedures for the disclosure to an individual upon his request of his record or information pertaining to him, including special procedure, if deemed necessary, for the disclosure to an individual of medical records, including psychological records pertaining to him;

(4) establish procedures for reviewing a request from an individual concerning the amendment to any record or information pertaining to the individual, for making a determination on the request, for an appeal within the agency of an initial adverse agency determination, and for whatever additional means may be necessary for each individual to be able to exercise fully his rights under this section; and

(5) establish fees to be charged, if any, to any individual for making copies of his record, excluding the cost of any search for and review of the record.

The Office of the Federal Register shall annually compile and publish the rules promulgated under this subsection and agency notices published under subsection (e)(4) of this section in a form available to the public at low cost.

(g)

(1) CIVIL REMEDIES.—Whenever any agency—

(A) makes a determination under subsection (a)(3) of this section not to amend an individual's record in accordance with his request, or fails to make such review in conformity with that subsection;

(B) refuses to comply with an individual request under subsection (d)(1) of this section;

(C) fails to maintain any record concerning any individual with such accuracy, relevance, timeliness, and completeness as is necessary to assure fairness in any determination relating to the qualification, character, rights, or opportunities of, or benefits to the individual that may be made on the basis of such record, and consequently a determination is made which is adverse to the individual; or

(D) fails to comply with any other provision of this section, or any rule promulgated thereunder, in such a way as to have an adverse effect on an individual,

the individual may bring a civil action against the agency, and the district courts of the United States shall have jurisdiction in the matters under the provisions of this subsection.

(2)

(A) In any suit brought under the provisions of subsection (g)(1)(A) of this section, the court may order the agency to amend the individual's record in accordance with his request or in such other way as the court may direct. In such a case the court shall determine the matter de novo.

(B) The court may assess against the United States reasonable attorney fees and other litigation costs reasonably incurred in any case under this paragraph in which the complainant has substantially prevailed.

(3)

(A) In any suit brought under the provisions of subsection (g)(1)(B) of this section, the court may enjoin the agency from withholding the records and order the production to the complianant of any agency records improperly withheld from him. In such a case, the court shall determine the matter de novo, and may examine the contents of any agency records in camera to determine whether the records or any portion thereof may be withheld under any of the exemptions set forth in subsection (k) of this section, and the burden is on the agency to sustain its action.

(B) The court may assess against the United States reasonable attorney fees and other litigation costs reasonably incurred in any case under this paragraph in which the complainant has substantially prevailed.

(4) In any suit brought under the provisions of subsection (g)(1)(C) or (D) of this section in which the court determines that the agency acted in a manner

which was intentional or willful, the United States shall be liable to the individual in an amount equal to the sum of—

(A) actual damages sustained by the individual as the result of the refusal or failure, but in no case shall a person entitled to recovery receive less than the sum of $1,000; and

(B) the costs of the action together with reasonable attorney fees as determined by the court.

(5) an action to enforce any liability created under this section may be brought in the district court of the United states in the district in which the complainant resides, or has his principal place of business, or in which the agency records are situated, or in the District of Columbia, without regard to the amount in controversy, within two years from the date on which the cause of action arises, except that where an agency has materially and willfully misrepresented any information required under this section to be disclosed to an individual and the information so misrepresented is material to the establishment of the liability of the agency to the individual under this section, the action may be brought at any time within two years after the discovery by the individual of the misrepresentation. Nothing in this section shall be construed to authorize any civil action by reason of any injury sustained as the result of a disclosure of a record prior to September 27, 1975.

(h) RIGHTS OF LEGAL GUARDIANS.—For the purposes of this section, the parent of any minor, or the legal guardian of any individual who has been declared to be incompetent due to physical or mental incapacity or age by a court of competent jurisdiction, any act on behalf of the individual.

(i)

(1) CRIMINAL PENALTIES.—Any officer or employee of an agency, who by virtue of his employment or official position, has possession of, or access to, agency records which contain individually identifiable information the disclosure of which is prohibited by this section or by rules or regulations established thereunder, and who knowing that disclosure of the specific material is so prohibited, willfully discloses the material in any manner to any person or agency not entitled to receive it, shall be guilty of a misdemeanor and fined not more than $5,000.

(2) Any officer or employee of any agency who willfully maintains a system of records without meeting the notice requirements of subsection (e)(4) of this section shall be guilty of a misdemeanor and fined not more than $5,000.

(3) Any person who knowingly and willfully requests or obtains any record concerning an individual from an agency under false pretenses shall be guilty of a misdemeanor and fined not more than $5,000.

(j) GENERAL EXEMPTIONS.—The head of an agency may promulgate rules, in accordance with the requirements (including general notice) of sections 553 (b)(1), (2), and (3), (c) and (e) of this title, to exempt any system of records within the agency from any part of this section except subsections (b), (c)(1) and (2), (e)(4)(A) through (F), (e)(6), (7), (9), (10), and (11), and (i) if the system of records is—

(1) maintained by the Central Intelligence Agency; or (2) maintained by an agency or a component thereof which performs as its principal function

any activity pertaining to the enforcement of criminal laws, including police efforts to prevent, control, or reduce crime or to apprehend criminals, and the activities of prosecutors, courts, correctional, probation, pardon, or parole authorities, and which consists of (A) information compiled for the purpose of identifying individual criminal offenders and alleged offenders and consisting only of identifying data and notations of arrests, the nature and disposition of criminal charges, sentencing, confinement, release, and parole and probation status; (B) information compiled for the purpose of a criminal investigation, including reports of informants and investigators, and associated with an identifiable individual; or (C) reports identifiable to an individual compiled at any stage of the process of enforcement of the criminal laws from arrest or indictment through release from supervision.

At the time rules are adopted under this subsection, the agency shall include in the statement required under section 553(c) of this title, the reason why the system of records is to be exempted from a provision of this section.

(k) SPECIFIC EXEMPTIONS.—The head of any agency may promulgate rules, in accordance with the requirements (including general notice) of sections 553(b)(1), (2), and (3), (c), and (e) of this title, to exempt any systems of records within the agency from subsections (c)(3), (d), (e)(1), (e)(4) (G), (H), and (I) and (f) of this section if the system of records is—

(1) subject to the provisions of section 552(b)(1) of this title;

(2) investigatory material compiled for law enforcement purposes, other than material within the scope of subsection (j)(2) of this section: *Provided however,* That if any individual is denied any right, privilege, or benefit that he would otherwise be entitled by Federal law, or for which he would otherwise be eligible, as a result of the maintenance of such material, such material shall be provided to such individual, except to the extent that the disclosure of such material would reveal the identity of a source who furnished information to the Government under an express promise that the identity of the source would be held in confidence, or, prior to the effective date of this section [September 27, 1975], under an implied promise that the identity of the source would be held in confidence.

(3) maintained in connection with providing protective services to the President of the United States or other individuals pursuant to section 3056 of title 18;

(4) required by statue to be maintained and used solely as statistical records;

(5) investigatory material compiled solely for the purpose of determining suitability, eligibility, or qualifications for Federal civilian employment, military service, Federal contracts, or access to classified information, but only to the extent that the disclosure of such material would reveal the identity of a source who furnished information to the Government under an express promise that the identity of the source would be held in confidence, or, prior to the effective date of this section [September 27, 1975], under an implied promise that the identity of the source would be held in confidence.

(6) testing or examination material used solely to determine individual qualifications for appointment or promotion in the Federal service the disclosure

of which would compromise the objectivity or fairness of the testing or examination process; or

(7) evaluation material used to determine potential for promotion in the armed services, but only to the extent that the disclosure of such material would reveal the identity of a source who furnished information to the Government under an express promise that the identity of the source would be held in confidence, or, prior to the effective date of this section [September 27, 1975], under an implied promise that the identity of the source would be held in confidence.

At the time rules are adopted under this subsection, the agency shall include in the statement required under section 553(c) of this title the reasons why the system of records is to be exempted from a provision of this section.

(l)

(1) ARCHIVAL RECORDS.—Each agency record which is accepted by the Archivist of the United States for storage, processing, and servicing in accordance with section 3103 of title 44 shall, for the purposes of this section, be considered to be maintained by the agency which deposited the record and shall be subject to the provisions of this section. The Archivist of the United States shall not disclose the record except to the agency which maintains the record, or under rules established by that agency which are not inconsistent with the provisions of this section.

(2) Each agency record pertaining to an identifiable individual which was transferred to the National Archives of the United States as a record which has sufficient historical or other value to warrant its continued preservation by the United States Government, prior to the effective date of this section [September 27, 1975], shall, for the purposes of this section, be considered to be maintained by the National Archives and shall not be subject to the provisions of this section, except that a statement generally describing such records (modeled after the requirements relating to records subject to subsections (e)(4) (A) through (G) of this section) shall be published in the Federal Register.

(3) Each agency record pertaining to an identifiable individual which is transferred to the National Archives of the United States as a record that has sufficient historical or other value to warrant its continued preservation by the United States Government, on or after the effective date of this section [September 27, 1975], shall, for the purposes of this section, be considered to be maintained by the National Archives and shall be exempt from the requirements of this section except subsections (e)(4) (A) through (G) and (e)(9) of this section.

(m)

(1) GOVERNMENT CONTRACTORS.—When an agency provides by a contract for the operation by or on behalf of the agency of a system of records to accomplish an agency function, the agency shall, consistent with its authority, cause the requirements of this section to be applied to such system. For purposes of subsection (i) of this section any such contractor and any employee of such contractor, if such contract is agreed to on or after the effective date of this section, shall be considered to be an employee of an agency.

(2) A consumer reporting agency to which a record is disclosed under section 3(d) of the Federal Claims Collection Act of 1966 (31 U.S.C. 952(d)) shall not be considered a contractor for the purposes of this section.

(n) MAILING LISTS.—An individual's name and address may not be sold or rented by an agency unless such action is specifically authorized by law. This provision shall not be construed to require the withholding of names and addresses otherwise permitted to be made public.

(o) REPORT ON NEW SYSTEMS.—Each agency shall provide adequate advance notice to Congress and the Office of Management and Budget of any proposal to establish or alter any system of records in order to permit an evaluation of the probable or potential effect of such proposal on the privacy and other personal or property rights of individuals or the disclosure of information relating to such individuals, and its effect on the preservation of the constitutional principles of federalism and separation of powers.

(p) ANNUAL REPORT.—The President shall submit to the Speaker of the House and the President of the Senate, by June 30 of each calendar year, a consolidated report, separately listing for each Federal agency the number of records contained in any system of records which were exempted from the application of this section under the provisions of subsections (j) and (k) of this section during the preceding calendar year, and the reasons for the exemptions, and such other information as indicates efforts to administer fully this section.

(q)

(1) EFFECT OF OTHER LAWS.—No agency shall rely on any exemption contained in section 552 of this title to withhold from an individual any record which is otherwise accessible to such individual under the provisions of this section.

(2) No agency shall rely on any exemption in this section to withhold from an individual any record which is otherwise accessible to such individual under the provisions of section 552 of this title.

Appendix N

Public Law 96-456, 96th Congress, October 15, 1980
Classified Information Procedures Act

An Act

To provide certain pretrial, trial, and appellate procedures for criminal cases involving classified information.

Be it enacted by the Senate and the House of Representatives of the United States of America in Congress assembled.

DEFINITIONS

SECTION 1.

(a) "Classified information," as used in this Act, means any information or material that has been determined by the United States Government pursuant to an Executive order, statute, or regulation, to require protection against unauthorized disclosure for reasons of national security and any restricted data, as defined in paragraph r. of section 11 of the Atomic Energy Act of 1954 (42 U.S.C. 2014(y)).

(b) "National security," as used in this Act, means the national defense and foreign relations of the United States.

PRETRIAL CONFERENCE

SEC. 2. At any time after the filing of the indictment or information, any party may move for a pretrial conference to consider matters relating to classified information that may arise in connection with the prosecution. Following such motion, or on its own motion, the court shall promptly hold a pretrial conference to establish the timing of requests for discovery, the provision of notice required by section 5 of this Act, and the initiation of the procedure established by section 6 of this Act. In addition, at the pretrial conference the court may consider any matters which relate to classified information or which may promote a fair and expeditious trial. No admission made by the defendant or by any attorney for the defendant at such a conference may be used against the defendant unless the admission is in writing and is signed by the defendant and by the attorney for the defendant.

PROTECTIVE ORDERS

SEC. 3. Upon motion of the United States, the court shall issue an order to protect against the disclosure of any classified information disclosed by the United States to any defendant in any criminal case in a district court of the United States.

DISCOVERY OF CLASSIFIED INFORMATION BY DEFENDANTS

SEC. 4. The court, upon a sufficient showing, may authorize the United States to delete specified items of classified information from documents to be made available to the defendant through discovery under the Federal Rules of Criminal Procedure, to substitute a summary of the information for such classified documents, or to substitute a statement admitting relevant facts that the classified information would tend to prove. The court may permit the United States to make a request for such authorization in the form of a written statement to be inspected by the court alone. If the court enters an order granting relief following such an ex parte showing, the entire text of the statement of the United States shall be sealed and preserved in the records of the court to be made available to the appellate court in the event of an appeal.

NOTICE OF DEFENDANT'S INTENTION TO DISCLOSE CLASSIFIED INFORMATION

SEC. 5.

    (a)   NOTICE BY THE DEFENDANT.—If a defendant reasonably expects to disclose or to cause the disclosure of classified information in any manner in connection with any trial or pretrial proceeding involving the criminal prosecution of such defendant, the defendant shall, within the time specified by the court or, where no time is specified, within thirty days prior to trial, notify the attorney for the United States and the court in writing. Such notice shall include a brief description of the classified information. Whenever a defendant learns of additional classified information he reasonably expects to disclose at any such proceeding, he shall notify the attorney for the United States and the court in writing as soon as possible thereafter and shall include a brief description of the classified information. No defendant shall disclose any information known or believed to be classified in connection with a trial or pretrial proceeding until notice has been given under this subsection and until the United States has been afforded a reasonable opportunity to seek a determination pursuant to the procedure set forth in section 6 of this Act, and until the time for the United States to appeal such determination under section 7 has expired or any appeal under section 7 by the United States is decided.

    (b)   FAILURE TO COMPLY.—If the defendant fails to comply with the requirements of subsection (a) the court may preclude disclosure of any classified information not made the subject of notification and may prohibit the examination by the defendant of any witness with respect to any such information.

PROCEDURE FOR CASES INVOLVING CLASSIFIED INFORMATION

SEC. 6.

    (a)   MOTION FOR HEARING.—Within the time specified by the court for the filing of a motion under this section, the United States may request the court to conduct a hearing to make all determinations concerning the use, relevance, or admissibility of classified information that would otherwise be made during the trial or pretrial proceeding. Upon such a request, the court shall conduct such a hearing. Any hearing held pursuant to this subsection (or any portion of such hearing specified in the request of the Attorney General) shall be held in camera if the Attorney General certifies to the court in such petition that a public proceeding may result in the disclosure of classified information. As to each item of classified information, the court shall set forth in writing the basis for its determination. Where the United States motion under this subsection is filed prior to the trial or pretrial proceeding, the court shall rule prior to the commencement of the relevant proceeding.

(b) NOTICE.—

(1) Before any hearing is conducted pursuant to a request by the United States under subsection (a), the United States shall provide the defendant with notice of the classified information that is at issue. Such notice shall identify the specific classified information at issue whenever that information previously has been made available to the defendant by the United States. When the United States has not previously made the information available to the defendant in connection with the case, the information may be described by generic category, in such form as the court may approve, rather than by identification of the specific information of concern to the United States.

(2) Whenever the United States requests a hearing under subsection (a), the court, upon request of the defendant, may order the United States to provide the defendant, prior to trial, such details as to the portion of the indictment or information at issue in the hearing as are needed to give the defendant fair notice to prepare for the hearing.

(c) ALTERNATIVE PROCEDURE FOR DISCLOSURE OF CLASSIFIED INFORMATION.—

(1) Upon any determination by the court authorizing the disclosure of specific classified information under the procedures established by this section, the United States may move that, in lieu of the disclosure of such specific classified information, the court order—

(A) the substitution for such classified information of a statement admitting relevant facts that the specific classified information would tend to prove; or

(B) the substitution for such classified information of a summary of the specific classified information. The court shall grant such a motion of the United States if it finds that the statement or summary will provide the defendant with substantially the same ability to make his defense as would disclosure of the specific classified information. The court shall hold a hearing on any motion under this section. Any such hearing shall be held in camera at the request of the Attorney General.

(2) The United States may, in connection with a motion under paragraph (1), submit to the court an affidavit of the Attorney General certifying that the disclosure of classified information would cause identifiable damage to the national security of the United States and explaining the basis for the classification of such information. If so requested by the United States, the court shall examine such affidavit in camera and ex parte.

(d) SEALING OF RECORDS OF IN CAMERA HEARINGS.—If at the close of an in camera hearing under this Act (or any portion of a hearing under this Act that is held in camera) the court determines that the classified information at issue may not be disclosed or elicited at the trial or pretrial proceeding, the record of such in camera hearing shall be sealed and preserved by the court for use in the event of an appeal. The defendant may seek reconsideration of the court's determination prior to or during the trial.

(e) PROHIBITION ON DISCLOSURE OF CLASSIFIED INFORMATION BY DEFENDANT, RELIEF FOR DEFENDANT WHEN UNITED STATES OPPOSES DISCLOSURE.—

(1) Whenever the court denies a motion by the United States that it issue an order under subsection (c) and the United States files with the court and affidavit of the Attorney General objecting to disclosure of the classified information at issue, the court shall order that the defendant not disclose or cause the disclosure of such information.

(2) Whenever a defendant is prevented by an order under paragraph (1) from disclosing or causing the disclosure of classified information, the court shall dismiss the indictment or information; except that, when the court determines that the interests of justice would not be served by dismissal of the indictment or information, the court shall order such other action, in lieu of dismissing the indictment or information, as the court determines is appropriate. Such action may include, but need not be limited to—

(A) dismissing specified counts of the indictment or information

(B) finding against the United States on any issue as to which the excluded classified information relates; or

(C) striking or precluding all or part of the testimony of a witness.

An order under this paragraph shall not take effect until the court has afforded the United States an opportunity to appeal such order under section 7, and thereafter to withdraw its objection to the disclosure of the classified information at issue.

(f) RECIPROCITY.—Whenever the court determines pursuant to subsection (a) that classified information may be disclosed in connection with a trial or pretrial proceeding, the court shall, unless the interests of fairness do not so require, order the United States to provide the defendant with the information it expects to use to rebut the classified information. The court may place the United States under a continuing duty to disclose such rebuttal information. If the United States fails to comply with its obligation under this subsection, the court may exclude any evidence not made the subject of a required disclosure and may prohibit the examination by the United States of any witness with respect to such information.

INTERLOCUTORY APPEAL

SEC. 7.

(a) An interlocutory appeal by the United States taken before or after the defendant has been placed in jeopardy shall lie to a court of appeals from a decision or order of a district court in a criminal case authorizing the disclosure of classified information, imposing sanctions for nondisclosure of classified information, or refusing a protective order sought by the United States to prevent the disclosure of classified information.

(b) An appeal taken pursuant to this section either before or during trial shall be expedited by the court of appeals. Prior to trial, an appeal shall be taken within ten days after the decision or order appealed from and the trial shall not commence until the appeal is resolved. If an appeal is taken during trial, the trial court shall adjourn the trial until the appeal is resolved and the court of appeals (1) shall hear argument on such appeal within four days of the adjournment of the trial, (2) may dispense with written briefs other than the supporting materials previously submitted to the trial court, (3) shall render its decision within four days of argument on appeal, and (4) may dispense with the issuance of a written opinion in rendering its decision. Such appeal and decision shall not affect the right of the defendant, in a subsequent appeal from a judgment of conviction, to claim as error reversal by the trial court on remand of a ruling appealed from during trial.

INTRODUCTION OF CLASSIFIED INFORMATION

SEC. 8.

(a) CLASSIFICATION STATUS.—Writings, recordings, and photographs containing classified information may be admitted into evidence without change in their classification status.

(b) PRECAUTIONS BY THE COURT.—The court, in order to prevent unnecessary disclosure of classified information involved in any criminal proceeding, may order admission into evidence of only part of a writing, recording, or photograph, or may order admission into evidence of the whole writing, recording, or photograph with excision of some or all of the classified information contained therein, unless the whole ought in fairness be considered.

(c) TAKING OF TESTIMONY.—During the examination of a witness in any criminal proceeding, the United States may object to any question or line of inquiry that may require the witness to disclose classified information not previously found to be admissible. Following such an objection, the court shall take such suitable action to determine whether the response is admissible as will safeguard against the compromise of any classified information. Such action may include requiring the United States to provide the court with a proffer of the witness' response to the question or line of inquiry and requiring the defendant to provide the court with a proffer of the nature of the information he seeks to elicit.

SECURITY PROCEDURES

SEC. 9.

(a) Within one hundred and twenty days of the date of the enactment of this Act, the Chief Justice of the United States, in consultation with the Attorney General, the Director of Central Intelligence, and the Secretary of Defense, shall prescribe rules establishing procedures for the protection against unauthorized disclosure of any classified information in the custody of the United States district courts, courts of appeal, or Supreme Court. Such rules, and any changes in such rules, shall be submitted to the appropriate committees of Congress and shall become effective forty-five days after such submission.

(b) Until such time as rules under subsection (a) first become effective, the Federal courts shall in each case involving classified information adopt procedures to protect against the unauthorized disclosure of such information.

IDENTIFICATION OF INFORMATION RELATED TO THE NATIONAL DEFENSE

SEC. 10. In any prosecution in which the United States must establish that material relates to the national defense or constitutes classified information, the United States shall notify the defendant, within the time before trial specified by the court, of the portions of the material that it reasonably expects to rely upon to establish the national defense or classified information element of the offense.

AMENDMENT TO THE ACT

SEC. 11. Sections 1 through 10 of this Act may be amended as provided in section 2076, title 28, United States Code.

ATTORNEY GENERAL GUIDELINES

SEC. 12.

(a) Within one hundred and eighty days of enactment of this Act, the Attorney General shall issue guidelines specifying the factors to be used by the Department of Justice in rendering a decision whether to prosecute a violation of Federal law in which, in the judgment of the Attorney General, there is a possibility that classified information will be revealed. Such guidelines shall be transmitted to the appropriate committees of Congress.

(b) When the Department of Justice decides not to prosecute a violation of Federal law pursuant to subsection (a), an appropriate official of the Department of Justice shall prepare written findings detailing the reasons for the decision not to prosecute. The findings shall include—

(1) the intelligence information which the Department of Justice officials believe might be disclosed,

(2) the purpose for which the information might be disclosed,

(3) the probability that the information would be disclosed, and

(4) the possible consequences such disclosure would have on the national security.

REPORTS TO CONGRESS

SEC. 13.

(a) Consistent with applicable authorities and duties, including those conferred by the Constitution upon the executive and legislative branches, the Attorney General shall report orally or in writing semiannually to the Permanent Select Committee on Intelligence of the United States House of

Representatives, the Select Committee on Intelligence of the United States Senate, and the chairmen and ranking minority members of the Committees on the Judiciary of the Senate and House of Representatives on all cases where a decision not to prosecute a violation of Federal law pursuant to section 12(a) has been made.

(b)   The Attorney General shall deliver to the appropriate committees of Congress a report concerning the operation and effectiveness of this Act and including suggested amendments to this Act. For the first three years this Act is in effect, there shall be a report each year. After three years, such reports shall be delivered as necessary.

FUNCTIONS OF ATTORNEY GENERAL MAY BE EXERCISED BY DEPUTY ATTORNEY GENERAL OR A DESIGNATED ASSISTANT ATTORNEY GENERAL

SEC. 14. The functions and duties of the Attorney General under this Act may be exercised by the Deputy Attorney General or by an Assistant Attorney General designated by the Attorney General for such purpose and may not be delegated to any other official.

EFFECTIVE DATE

SEC. 15. The provisions of this Act shall become effective upon the date of the enactment of this Act, but shall not apply to any prosecution in which an indictment or information was filed before such date.

SHORT TITLE

SEC. 16. That this Act may be cited as the "Classified Information Procedures Act."

Approved October 15, 1980

Appendix O

Executive Order 12333, December 4, 1981
United States Intelligence Activities

Timely and accurate information about the activities, capabilities, plans, and intentions about foreign powers, organizations, and persons and their agents, is essential to the national security of the United States. All reasonable and lawful means must be used to ensure that the United States will receive the best intelligence available. For that purpose, by virtue of the authority invested in me by the Constitution and statutes of the United States of America, including the National Security Act of 1947, as amended, and as President of the United States of America, in order to provide for the effective conduct of United States intelligence activities and the protection of constitutional rights, it is hereby ordered as follows:

Part 1

Goals, Direction, Duties and Responsibilities With Respect to the National Intelligence Effort

1.1 *Goals.* The United States intelligence effort shall provide the President and the National Security Council with the necessary information on which to base decisions concerning the conduct and development of foreign, defense and economic policy, and the protection of United States national interests from foreign security threats. All departments and agencies shall cooperate fully to fulfill this goal.

(a) Maximum emphasis should be given to fostering analytical competition among the appropriate elements of the Intelligence Community.

(b) All means, consistent with applicable United States law and this Order, and with full consideration of the rights of United States persons, shall be used to develop intelligence information for the President and the National Security Council. A balanced approach between technical collection efforts and other means should be maintained and encouraged.

(c) Special emphasis should be given to detecting and countering espionage and other threats and activities directed by foreign intelligence services against the United States Government, or United States corporations, establishments, or persons.

(d) To the greatest extent possible consistent with applicable United States law and this Order, and with full consideration of the rights of United States persons, all agencies and departments should seek to ensure full and free exchange of information in order to derive maximum benefit from the United States intelligence effort.

1.2 *The National Security Council.*

(a) *Purpose.* The National Security council (NSC) was established by the National Security Act of 1947 to advise the President with respect to the integration of domestic, foreign, and military policies relating to the national security. The NSC shall act as the highest Executive Branch entity that provides review of, guidance for and direction to the conduct of all national foreign intelligence, counterintelligence, and special activities, and all attendant policies and programs.

(b) *Committees.* The NSC shall establish such committees as may be necessary to carry out its functions and responsibilities under this Order. The NSC, or committee established by it, shall consider and submit to the President a policy recommendation, including all dissents, on each special activity and shall review proposals for other sensitive intelligence operations.

1.3 *National Foreign Intelligence Advisory Groups.*

(a) *Establishment and Duties.* The Director of Central Intelligence shall establish such boards, councils, or groups as required for the purpose of obtaining advice from within the Intelligence Community concerning:

(1) Production, review and coordination of national foreign intelligence;

(2) Priorities for the National Foreign Intelligence Program budget;

(3) Interagency exchanges of foreign intelligence information;

(4) Arrangements with foreign governments on intelligence matters;

(5) Protection of intelligence sources and methods;

(6) Activities of common concern; and

(7) Such other matters as may be referred by the Director of Central Intelligence.

(b) *Membership.* Advisory groups established pursuant to this section shall be chaired by the Director of Central Intelligence or his designated representative and shall consist of senior representatives from organizations within the Intelligence community and from departments or agencies containing such organizations, as designated by the Director of Central Intelligence. Groups for consideration of substantive intelligence matters will include representatives of organizations involved in the collection, processing and analysis of intelligence. A senior representative of the Secretary of Commerce, the Attorney General, the Assistant to the President for National Security Affairs, and the Office of the Secretary of Defense shall be invited to participate in any group which deals with other than substantive intelligence matters.

1.4 *The Intelligence Community.* The Agencies within the Intelligence Community shall, in accordance with applicable United States law and with the other provisions of this Order, conduct intelligence activities necessary for the conduct of foreign relations and the protection of the national security of the United States, including:

(a) Collection of information needed by the President, the National Security Council, the Secretaries of State and Defense, and other Executive Branch officials for the performance of their duties and responsibilities;

(b)   Production and dissemination of intelligence;

(c)   Collection of information concerning, and the conduct of activities to protect against, intelligence activities directed against the United States, international terrorist and international narcotics activities, and other hostile activities directed against the United States by foreign powers, organizations, persons, and their agents;

(d)   Special activities;

(e)   Administrative and support activities within the United States and abroad necessary for the performance of authorized activities; and

(f)   Such other intelligence activities as the President may direct from time to time.

1.5   *Director of Central Intelligence.* In order to discharge the duties and responsibilities prescribed by law, the Director of Central Intelligence shall be responsible directly to the President and the NSC and shall:

(a)   Act as the primary adviser to the President and the NSC on national foreign intelligence and provide the President and other officials in the Executive Branch with national foreign intelligence;

(b)   Develop such objectives and guidance for the Intelligence Community as will enhance capabilities for responding to expected future needs for national foreign intelligence;

(c)   Promote the development and maintenance of services of common concern by designated intelligence organizations on behalf of the Intelligence Community;

(d)   Ensure implementation of special activities;

(e)   Formulate policies concerning foreign intelligence and counterintelligence arrangements with foreign governments, coordinate foreign intelligence and counterintelligence relationships between agencies of the Intelligence Community and the intelligence or internal security services of foreign governments, and establish procedures governing the conduct of liaison by any government or agency with such services on narcotics activities;

(f)   Participate in the development of procedures approved by the Attorney General governing criminal narcotics intelligence activities abroad to ensure that these activities are consistent with foreign intelligence programs;

(g)   Ensure the establishment by the Intelligence Community of common security and access standards for managing and handling foreign intelligence systems, information, and products;

(h)   Ensure that programs are developed which protect intelligence sources, methods, and analytical procedures;

(i)   Establish uniform criteria for the determination of relative priorities for the transmission of critical national foreign intelligence, and advise the Secretary of Defense concerning the communications requirements of the Intelligence Community for the transmission of such intelligence;

(j)   Establish appropriate staffs, committees, or other advisory groups to assist in the execution of the Director's responsibilities;

(k) Have full responsibility for production and dissemination of national foreign intelligence, and authority to levy analytic tasks on departmental intelligence production organizations, in consultation with those organizations, ensuring that appropriate mechanisms for competitive analysis are developed so that diverse points of view are considered fully and differences of judgment within the Intelligence Community are brought to the attention of national policymakers;

(l) Ensure the timely exploitation and dissemination of data gathered by national foreign intelligence collection means, and ensure that the resulting intelligence is disseminated immediately to appropriate government entities and military commands;

(m) Establish mechanisms which translate national foreign intelligence objectives and priorities approved by the NSC into specific guidance for the Intelligence Community, resolve conflicts in tasking priority, provide to departments and agencies having information collection capabilities that are not part of the National Foreign Intelligence Program advisory tasking concerning collection of national foreign intelligence, and provide for the development of plans and arrangements for transfer of required collection tasking authority to the Secretary of Defense when directed by the President;

(n) Develop, with the advice of the program managers and departments and agencies concerned, the consolidated National Foreign Intelligence Program budget, and present it to the President and to the Congress;

(o) Review and approve all requests for reprogramming National Foreign Intelligence Program funds, in accordance with the guidelines established by the Office of Management and Budget;

(p) Monitor National Foreign Intelligence Program implementation, and, as necessary, conduct program and performance audits and evaluations;

(q) Together with the Secretary of Defense, ensure that there is no unnecessary overlap between national foreign intelligence programs and Department of Defense intelligence programs consistent with the requirement to develop competitive analysis, and provide to and obtain from the Secretary of Defense all information necessary for this purpose;

(r) In accordance with law and relevant procedures approved by the Attorney General under this Order, give the heads of the departments and agencies access to all intelligence developed by the CIA or the staff elements of the Director of Central Intelligence, relevant to the national intelligence needs of the departments and agencies; and

(s) Facilitate the use of foreign intelligence products by Congress in a secure manner.

1.6 *Duties and Responsibilities of the Heads of Executive Branch Departments and Agencies.*

(a) The heads of all Executive Branch departments and agencies shall, in accordance with law and relevant procedures approved by the Attorney General under this Order, give the Director of Central Intelligence access to all information relevant to the national intelligence needs of the United States, and shall give due consideration to the requests from the Director of Central Intelligence for appropriate support for Intelligence Community activities.

(b) The heads of departments and agencies involved in the National Foreign Intelligence Program shall ensure timely development and submission to the Director of Central Intelligence by the program managers and heads of component activities of proposed national programs and budgets in the format designated by the Director of Central Intelligence, and shall also ensure that the Director of Central Intelligence is provided, in a timely and responsive manner, all information necessary to perform the Director's program and budget responsibilities.

(c) The heads of departments and agencies involved in the National Foreign Intelligence Program may appeal to the President decisions by the Director of Central Intelligence on budget or reprogramming matters of the National Foreign Intelligence Program.

1.7 *Senior Officials of the Intelligence Community.* The heads of departments and agencies with organizations in the Intelligence Community or the heads of such organizations, as appropriate, shall:

(a) Report to the Attorney General possible violations of federal criminal laws by employees and of specified criminal laws by any other person as provided in procedures agreed upon by the Attorney General and the head of the department or agency concerned, in a manner consistent with the protection of intelligence sources and methods, as specified in those procedures;

(b) In any case involving serious or continuing breaches of security, recommend to the Attorney General that the case be referred to the FBI for further investigation;

(c) Furnish the Director of Central Intelligence and the NSC, in accordance with applicable law and procedures approved by the Attorney General under this Order, the information required for the performance of their respective duties;

(d) Report to the Intelligence Oversight Board, and keep the Director of Central Intelligence appropriately informed, concerning any intelligence activities of their organizations that they have reason to believe may be unlawful or contrary to Executive order or Presidential directive;

(e) Protect intelligence and intelligence sources and methods from unauthorized disclosure consistent with guidance from the Director of Central Intelligence;

(f) Disseminate intelligence to cooperating foreign governments under arrangements established or agreed to by the Director of Central Intelligence;

(g) Participate in the development of procedures approved by the Attorney General governing production and dissemination of intelligence resulting from criminal narcotics intelligence activities abroad if their departments, agencies, or organizations have intelligence responsibilities for foreign or domestic narcotics production and trafficking;

(h) Instruct their employees to cooperate fully with the Intelligence Oversight Board; and

(i) Ensure that the Inspectors General and General Counsels for their organizations have access to any information necessary to perform their duties assigned by this Order.

1.8 *The Central Intelligence Agency.* All duties and responsibilities of the CIA shall be related to the intelligence functions set out below. As authorized by this Order, the National Security Act of 1947, as amended; the CIA Act of 1949, as amended; appropriate directives or other applicable law, the CIA shall:

(a) Collect, produce and disseminate foreign intelligence and counterintelligence, including information not otherwise obtainable. The collection of foreign intelligence or counterintelligence within the United States shall be coordinated with the FBI as required by procedures agreed upon by the Director of Central Intelligence and the Attorney General;

(b) Collect, produce and disseminate intelligence on foreign aspects of narcotics production and trafficking;

(c) Conduct counterintelligence activities outside the United States and, without assuming or performing any internal security functions, conduct counterintelligence activities within the United States in coordination with the FBI as required by procedures agreed upon by the Director of Central Intelligence and the Attorney General;

(d) Coordinate counterintelligence activities and the collection of information not otherwise obtainable when conducted outside the United States by other departments and agencies;

(e) Conduct special activities approved by the President. No agency except the CIA (or the Armed Forces of the United States in time of war declared by Congress or during any period covered by a report from the President to the Congress under the War Powers Resolution (87 Stat. 855)) may conduct any special activity unless the President determines that another agency is more likely to achieve a particular objective;

(f) Conduct services of common concern for the Intelligence Community as directed by the NSC;

(g) Carry out or contract for research, development and procurement of technical systems and devices relating to authorized functions;

(h) Protect the security of its installations, activities, information, property, and employees by appropriate means, including such investigations of applicants, employees, contractors, and other persons with similar associations with the CIA as are necessary; and

(i) Conduct such administrative and technical support activities within and outside the United States as are necessary to perform the functions described in sections (a) and through (h) above, including procurement and essential cover and proprietary arrangements.

1.9 *The Department of State.* The Secretary of State shall:

(a) Overtly collect information relevant to United States foreign policy concerns;

(b) Produce and disseminate foreign intelligence relating to United States foreign policy as required for the execution of the Secretary's responsibilities;

   (c)   Disseminate, as appropriate, reports received from United States diplomatic and consular posts;

   (d)   Transmit reporting requirements of the Intelligence Community to the Chiefs of United States Missions abroad; and

   (e)   Support Chiefs of Missions in discharging their statutory responsibilities for direction and coordination of mission activities.

1.10 *The Department of the Treasury.* The Secretary of the Treasury shall:

   (a)   Overtly collect foreign financial and monetary information;

   (b)   Participate with the Department of State in the overt collection of general foreign economic information;

   (c)   Produce and disseminate foreign intelligence relating to United States economic policy as required for the execution of the Secretary's responsibilities; and

   (d)   Conduct through the United States Secret Service, activities to determine the existence and capability of surveillance equipment being used against the President of the United States, the Executive Office of the President, and, as authorized by the Secretary of the Treasury or the President, other Secret Service protectees and United States officials. No information shall be acquired intentionally through such activities except to protect against such surveillance, and those activities shall be conducted pursuant to procedures agreed upon by the Secretary of the Treasury and the Attorney General.

1.11 *The Department of Defense.* The Secretary of Defense shall:

   (a)   Collect national foreign intelligence and be responsive to collection tasking by the Director of Central Intelligence;

   (b)   Collect, produce and disseminate military and military-related foreign intelligence and counterintelligence as required for execution of the Secretary's responsibilities;

   (c)   Conduct programs and missions necessary to fulfill national, departmental and tactical foreign intelligence requirements;

   (d)   Conduct counterintelligence activities in support of Department of Defense components outside the United States in coordination with the CIA, and within the United States in coordination with the FBI pursuant to procedures agreed upon by the Secretary of Defense and the Attorney General;

   (e)   Conduct, as the executive agent of the United States Government, signals intelligence and communications security activities, except as otherwise directed by the NSC;

   (f)   Provide for the timely transmission of critical intelligence, as defined by the Director of Central Intelligence, within the United States Government;

   (g)   Carry out or contract for research, development and procurement of technical systems and devices relating to authorized intelligence functions;

   (h)   Protect the security of Department of Defense installations, activities, property, information, and employees by appropriate means, including such investigations of applicants, employees, contractors, and other persons with similar associations with the Department of Defense as are necessary;

(i) Establish and maintain military intelligence relationships and military intelligence exchange programs with selected cooperative foreign defense establishments and international organizations, and ensure that such relationships and programs are in accordance with policies formulated by the Director of Central Intelligence;

(j) Direct, operate, control and provide fiscal management for the National Security Agency and for defense and military intelligence and national reconnaissance entities; and

(k) Conduct such administrative and technical support activities within and outside the United States as are necessary to perform the functions described in sections (a) through (j) above.

1.12 *Intelligence Components Utilized by the Secretary of Defense.* In carrying out the responsibilities assigned in section 1.11, the Secretary of Defense is authorized to utilize the following:

(a) *Defense Intelligence Agency*, whose responsibilities shall include:

(1) Collection, production, or, through tasking and coordination, provision of military and military-related intelligence for the Secretary of Defense, the Joint Chiefs of Staff, other Defense components, and, as appropriate, non-Defense agencies;

(2) Collection and provision of military intelligence for national foreign intelligence and counterintelligence products;

(3) Coordination of all Department of Defense intelligence collection requirements;

(4) Management of the Defense Attaché System; and

(5) Provision of foreign intelligence and counterintelligence staff support as directed by the Joint Chiefs of Staff.

(b) *National Security Agency*, whose responsibilities shall include:

(1) Establishment and operation of an effective unified organization for signals intelligence activities, except for the delegation of operational control over certain operations that are conducted through other elements of the Intelligence Community. No other department or agency may engage in signals intelligence activities except pursuant to a delegation by the Secretary of Defense;

(2) Control of signals intelligence collection and processing activities, including assignment of resources to an appropriate agent for such periods and tasks as required for the direct support of military commanders;

(3) Collection of signals intelligence information for national foreign intelligence purposes in accordance with guidance from the Director of Central Intelligence;

(4) Processing of signals intelligence data for national foreign intelligence purposes in accordance with guidance from the Director of Central Intelligence;

(5) Dissemination of signals intelligence information for national foreign intelligence purposes to authorized elements of the Government, including

the military services, in accordance with guidance from the Director of Central Intelligence;

(6) Collection, processing and dissemination of signals intelligence information for counterintelligence purposes;

(7) Provision of signals intelligence support for the conduct of military operations in accordance with tasking, priorities, and standards of timeliness assigned by the Secretary of Defense. If provision of such support requires use of national collection systems, these systems will be tasked within existing guidance from the Director of Central Intelligence;

(8) Executing the responsibilities of the Secretary of Defense as executive agent for the communications security of the United States Government;

(9) Conduct of research and development to meet the needs of the United States for signals intelligence and communications security;

(10) Protection of the security of its installations, activities, property, information, and employees by appropriate means, including such investigations of applicants, employees, contractors, and other persons with similar associations with the NSA as are necessary;

(11) Prescribing, within its field of authorized operations, security regulations covering operating practices, including the transmission, handling, and distribution of signals intelligence and communications security material within and among the elements under control of the Director of the NSA, and exercising the necessary supervisory control to ensure compliance with the regulations;

(12) Conduct of foreign cryptologic liaison relationships, with liaison for intelligence purposes conducted in accordance with policies formulated by the Director of Central Intelligence; and

(13) Conduct of such administrative and technical support activities within and outside the United States as are necessary to perform the functions described in sections (1) through (12) above, including procurement.

(c) *Offices for the collection of specialized intelligence through reconnaissance programs,* whose responsibilities shall include:

(1) Carrying out consolidated reconnaissance programs for specialized intelligence;

(2) Responding to tasking in accordance with procedures established by the Director of Central Intelligence; and

(3) Delegating authority to the various departments and agencies for research, development, procurement, and operation of designated means of collection.

(d) *The foreign intelligence and counterintelligence elements of the Army, Navy, Air Force, and Marine Corps,* whose responsibilities shall include:

(1) Collection, production and dissemination of military and military-related foreign intelligence and counterintelligence, and information on the foreign aspects of narcotics production and trafficking. When collection is conducted in response to national foreign intelligence requirements, it will be conducted in accordance with guidance from the Director of Central Intelligence. Collection of national foreign intelligence, not otherwise

obtainable, outside the United States shall coordinated with the CIA, and such collection within the United States shall be coordinated with the FBI;

(2) Conduct of counterintelligence activities outside the United States in coordination with the CIA, and within the United States in coordination with the FBI; and

(3) Monitoring of the development, procurement and management of tactical intelligence systems and equipment and conducting related research, development, and test and evaluation activities.

(e) *Other offices within the Department of Defense appropriate for conduct of the intelligence missions and responsibilities assigned to the Secretary of Defense.* If such other offices are used for intelligence purposes, the provisions of Part 2 of this Order shall apply to those offices when used for those purposes.

1.13 *The Department of Energy.* The Secretary of Energy shall:

(a) Participate with the Department of State in overtly collecting information with respect to foreign energy matters;

(b) Produce and disseminate foreign intelligence necessary for the Secretary's responsibilities;

(c) Participate in formulating intelligence collection and analysis requirements where the special expert capability of the Department can contribute; and

(d) Provide expert technical, analytical and research capability to other agencies within the Intelligence Community.

1.14 *The Federal Bureau of Investigation.* Under the supervision of the Attorney General and pursuant to such regulations as the Attorney General may establish, the Director of the FBI shall:

(a) Within the United States conduct counterintelligence and coordinate counterintelligence activities of other agencies within the Intelligence Community. When a counterintelligence activity of the FBI involves military or civilian personnel of the Department of Defense, the FBI shall coordinate with the Department of Defense;

(b) Conduct counterintelligence activities outside the United States in coordination with the CIA as required by procedures agreed upon by the Director of Central Intelligence and the Attorney General;

(c) Conduct, within the United States, when requested by officials of the Intelligence Community designated by the President, activities undertaken to collect foreign intelligence or support foreign intelligence collection requirements of other agencies within the Intelligence Community, or, when requested by the Director of National Security Agency to support the communications security activities of the United States Government;

(d) Produce and disseminate foreign intelligence and counterintelligence; and

(e) Carry out or contract for research, development and procurement of technical systems and devices relating to the functions authorized above.

Part 2

Conduct of Intelligence Activities

2.1 *Need.* Accurate and timely information about the capabilities, intentions and activities of foreign powers, organizations, or persons and their agents is essential to informed decisionmaking in the areas of national defense and foreign relations. Collection of such information is a priority objective and will be pursued in a vigorous, innovative and responsible manner that is consistent with the Constitution and applicable law and respectful of the principles upon which the United States was founded.

2.2 *Purpose.* This Order is intended to enhance human and technical collection techniques, especially those undertaken abroad, and the acquisition of significant foreign intelligence, as well as the detection and countering of international terrorist activities and espionage conducted by foreign powers. Set forth below are certain general principles that, in addition to and consistent with applicable laws, are intended to achieve the proper balance between the acquisition of essential information and protection of individual interests. Nothing in this Order shall be construed to apply to or interfere with any authorized civil or criminal law enforcement responsibility of any department or agency.

2.3 *Collection of Information.* Agencies within the Intelligence Community are authorized to collect, retain or disseminate information concerning United States persons only in accordance with procedures established by the head of the agency concerned and approved by the Attorney General, consistent with the authorities provided by Part 1 of this Order. Those procedures shall permit collection, retention and dissemination of the following types of information:

(a) Information that is publicly available or collected with the consent of the person concerned;

(b) Information constituting foreign intelligence or counterintelligence, including such information concerning corporations or other commercial organizations. Collection within the United States of foreign intelligence not otherwise obtainable shall be undertaken by the FBI or, when significant foreign intelligence is sought, by other authorized agencies of the Intelligence Community, provided that nor foreign intelligence collection by such agencies may be undertaken for the purpose of acquiring information concerning the domestic activities of United States persons;

(c) Information obtained in the course of a lawful foreign intelligence, counterintelligence, international narcotics or international terrorism investigation;

(d) Information needed to protect the safety of any persons or organizations, including those who are targets, victims or hostages of international terrorist organizations;

(e) Information needed to protect foreign intelligence or counterintelligence sources or methods from unauthorized disclosure. Collection within the United States shall be undertaken by the FBI except that other agencies of the Intelligence Community may also collect such information concerning present or former employees, present or former intelligence agency contractors or their present or former employees, or applicants for any such employment or contracting;

(f) Information concerning persons who are reasonably believed to be potential sources or contacts for the purpose of determining their suitability or credibility;

(g)   Information arising out of a lawful personnel, physical, or communications security investigation;

(h)   Information acquired by overhead reconnaissance not directed at specific United States persons;

(i)   Incidentally obtained information that may indicate involvement in activities that may violate federal, state, local or foreign laws; and

(j)   Information necessary for administrative purposes.

In addition, agencies within the Intelligence Community may disseminate information, other than information derived from signals intelligence, to each appropriate agency within the Intelligence Community for purposes of allowing the recipient agency to determine whether the information is relevant to its responsibilities and can be retained by it.

2.4 *Collection Techniques.* Agencies within the Intelligence Community shall use the least intrusive collection techniques feasible within the United States or directed against United States persons abroad. Agencies are not authorized to use such techniques as electronic surveillance, unconsented physical search, mail surveillance, physical surveillance, or monitoring devices unless they are in accordance with procedures established by the head of the agency concerned and approved by the Attorney General. Such procedures shall protect constitutional and other legal rights and limit use of such information to lawful government purposes. These procedures shall not authorize:

(a)   The CIA to engage in electronic surveillance within the United States except for the purpose of training, testing, or conducting countermeasures to hostile electronic surveillance;

(b)   Unconsented physical searches in the United States by agencies other than the FBI, except for:

   (1) Searches by counterintelligence elements of the military services directed against military personnel within the United States or abroad for intelligence purposes, when authorized by a military commander empowered to approve physical searches for law enforcement purposes, based upon a finding of probable cause to believe that such persons are acting as agents of foreign powers; and

   (2) Searches by CIA of personal property of non-United States persons lawfully in its possession.

(c)   Physical surveillance of a United States person in the United States by agencies other than the FBI, except for:

   (1) Physical surveillance of present or former employees, present or former intelligence agency contractors or their present or former employees, or applicants for any such employment or contracting; and

   (2) Physical surveillance of a military person employed by a nonintelligence element of a military service.

(d)   Physical surveillance of a United States person abroad to collect foreign intelligence, except to obtain significant information that cannot reasonably be acquired by other means.

2.5 *Attorney General Approval.* The Attorney General hereby is delegated the power to approve the use for intelligence purposes, within the United States or against a United States person abroad, of any technique for which a warrant would be required if undertaken for law enforcement purposes, provided that such techniques shall not be undertaken unless the Attorney General has determined in each case that there is probable cause to believe that the technique is directed against a foreign power or an agent of a foreign power. Electronic surveillance, as defined in the Foreign Intelligence Surveillance Act of 1978, shall be conducted in accordance with that Act, as well as this Order.

2.6 *Assistance to Law Enforcement Authorities.* Agencies within the Intelligence Community are authorized to:

    (a)   Cooperate with appropriate law enforcement agencies for the purpose of protecting the employees, information, property and facilities of any agency within the Intelligence Community;

    (b)   Unless otherwise precluded by law or this Order, participate in law enforcement activities to investigate or prevent clandestine intelligence activities by foreign powers, or international terrorist or narcotics activities;

    (c)   Provide specialized equipment, technical knowledge, or assistance of expert personnel for use by any department or agency, or, when lives are endangered, to support local law enforcement agencies. Provision of assistance by expert personnel shall be approved in each case by the General Counsel of the providing agency; and

    (d)   Render any other assistance and cooperation to law enforcement authorities not precluded by applicable law.

2.7 *Contracting.* Agencies within the Intelligence Community are authorized to enter into contracts or arrangements for the provision of goods or services with private companies or institutions in the United States and need not reveal the sponsorship of such contracts or arrangements for authorized intelligence purposes. Contracts or arrangements with academic institutions may be undertaken only with the consent of appropriate officials of the institution.

2.8 *Consistency With Other Laws.* Nothing in this Order shall be construed to authorize any activity in violation of the Constitution or statutes of the United States.

2.9 *Undisclosed Participation in Organizations Within the United States.* No one acting on behalf of agencies within the Intelligence Community may join or otherwise participate in any organization in the United States on behalf of any agency within the Intelligence Community without disclosing his intelligence affiliation to appropriate officials of the organization, except in accordance with procedures established by the head of the agency concerned and approved by the Attorney General. Such participation shall be authorized only if it is essential to achieving lawful purposes as determined by the agency head or designee. No such participation may be undertaken for the purpose of influencing the activity of the organization or its members except in cases where:

    (a)   The participation is undertaken on behalf of the FBI in the course of a lawful investigation; or

    (b)   The organization concerned is composed primarily of individuals who are not United States persons and is reasonably believed to be acting on behalf of a foreign power.

2.10 *Human Experimentation.* No agency within the Intelligence Community shall sponsor, contract for or conduct research on human subjects except in accordance with guidelines issued by the Department of Health and Human Services. The subject's informed consent shall be documented as required by those guidelines.

2.11 *Prohibition on Assassination.* No person employed by or acting on behalf of the United States Government shall engage in, or conspire to engage in, assassination.

2.12 *Indirect Participation.* No agency of the Intelligence Community shall participate in or request any person to undertake activities forbidden by this Order.

Part 3

General Provisions

3.1 *Congressional Oversight.* The duties and responsibilities of the Director of Central Intelligence and the heads of other departments, agencies, and entities engaged in intelligence activities to cooperate with the Congress in the conduct of its responsibilities for oversight of intelligence activities shall be as provided in title 50, United States Code, section 413. The requirements of section 662 of the Foreign Assistance Act of 1961, as amended (22 U.S.C. 2422), and section 501 of the National Security Act of 1947, as amended (50 U.S.C. 413), shall apply to all special activities as defined in this Order.

3.2 *Implementation.* The NSC, the Secretary of Defense, the Attorney General, and the Director of Central Intelligence shall issue such appropriate directives and procedures as are necessary to implement this Order. Heads of agencies within the Intelligence Community shall issue appropriate supplementary directives and procedures consistent with this Order. The Attorney General shall provide a statement of reasons for not approving any procedures established by the head of an agency in the Intelligence Community other than the FBI. The National Security Council may establish procedures in instances where the agency head and the Attorney General are unable to reach agreement on other than constitutional or other legal grounds.

3.3 *Procedures.* Until the procedures required by this Order have been established, the activities herein authorized which require procedures shall be conducted in accordance with existing procedures or requirements established under Executive Order No. 12036. Procedures required by this Order shall be established as expeditiously as possible. All procedures promulgated pursuant to this Order shall be made available to the congressional intelligence committees.

3.4 *Definitions.* For the purposes of this Order, the following terms shall have these meanings:

(a) *Counterintelligence* means information gathered and activities conducted to protect against espionage, other intelligence activities, sabotage, or assassinations conducted for or on behalf of foreign powers, organizations or persons, or international terrorist activities, but not including personnel, physical, document or communications security programs.

(b) *Electronic surveillance* means acquisition of a nonpublic communication by electronic means without the consent of a person who is a party to an electronic communication or, in the case of a nonelectronic communication, without the consent of a person who is visibly present at the place of communication, but not including the use of radio direction-finding equipment solely to determine the location of a transmitter.

(c) *Employee* means a person employed by, assigned to or acting for an agency within the Intelligence Community.

(d) *Foreign intelligence* means information relating to the capabilities, intentions and activities of foreign powers, organizations or persons, but not including counterintelligence except for information on international terrorist activities.

(e) *Intelligence activities* means all activities that agencies within the Intelligence Community are authorized to conduct pursuant to this Order.

(f) *Intelligence Community* and *agencies within the Intelligence Community* refer to the following agencies or organizations:

(1) The Central Intelligence Agency (CIA);

(2) The National Security Agency (NSA);

(3) The Defense Intelligence Agency (DIA);

(4) The offices within the Department of Defense for the collection of specialized national foreign intelligence through reconnaissance programs;

(5) The Bureau of Intelligence and Research of the Department of State;

(6) The intelligence elements of the Army, Navy, Air Force, and Marine Corps, the Federal Bureau of Investigation (FBI), the Department of the Treasury, and the Department of Energy; and

(7) The staff elements of the Director of Central Intelligence.

(g) *The National Foreign Intelligence Program* includes the programs listed below, but its composition shall be subject to review by the National Security Council and modification by the President:

(1) The programs of the CIA;

(2) The Consolidated Cryptologic Program, the General Defense Intelligence Program, and the programs of the offices within the Department of Defense for the collection of specialized national foreign intelligence through reconnaissance, except such elements as the Director of Central Intelligence and the Secretary of Defense agree should be excluded;

(3) Other programs of agencies within the Intelligence Community designated jointly by the Director of Central Intelligence and the head of the department or by the President as national foreign intelligence or counterintelligence activities;

(4) Activities of the staff elements of the Director of Central Intelligence;

(5) Activities to acquire the intelligence required for the planning and conduct of tactical operations by the United States military forces are not included in the National Foreign Intelligence Program.

(h) *Special activities* means activities conducted in support of national foreign policy objectives abroad which are planned and executed so that the role of the United States Government is not apparent or acknowledged publicly, and functions in support of such activities, but which are not intended to influence United States political processes, public opinion, policies, or media and do not include diplomatic activities or the collection and production of intelligence or related support functions.

(i)   *United States person* means a United States citizen, an alien known by the intelligence agency concerned to be a permanent resident alien, an unincorporated association substantially composed of United States citizens or permanent resident aliens, or a corporation incorporated in the United States, except for a corporation directed and controlled by a foreign government or governments.

3.5 *Purpose and Effect.* This Order is intended to control and provide direction and guidance to the Intelligence Community. Nothing contained herein or in any procedures promulgated hereunder is intended to confer any substantive or procedural right or privilege on any person or organization.

3.6 *Revocation.* Executive Order 12036 of January 24, 1978, as amended, entitled "United States Intelligence Activities," is revoked.

Ronald Reagan

THE WHITE HOUSE

December 4, 1981

Appendix P

Executive Order 12334, December 4, 1981
President's Intelligence Oversight Board

By the authority vested in me as President by the Constitution and statutes of the United States of America, and in order to enhance the security of the United States by assuring the legality of activities of the Intelligence Community, it is hereby ordered as follows:

Section 1. There is hereby established within the White House Office, Executive Office of the President, the President's Intelligence Oversight Board, which shall be composed of three members. One member, appointed from among the membership of the President's Foreign Intelligence Advisory Board, shall be designated by the President as Chairman. Members of the Board shall serve at the pleasure of the President and shall be appointed by the President from among trustworthy and distinguished citizens outside the Government who are qualified on the basis of achievement, experience and independence. The Board shall utilize such full-time staff and consultants as authorized by the President.

Sec. 2. The Board shall:

(a) Inform the President of Intelligence activities that any member of the Board believes are in violation of the Constitution or laws of the United States, Executive Orders, or Presidential directives;

(b) Forward to the Attorney General reports received concerning intelligence activities that the Board believes may be unlawful;

(c) Review the internal guidelines of each agency within the Intelligence Community concerning the lawfulness of intelligence activities;

(d) Review the practices and procedures of the Inspectors General and General Counsel of the Intelligence Community for discovering and reporting intelligence activities that may be unlawful or contrary to Executive order or Presidential directive; and

(e) Conduct such investigations as the Board deems necessary to carry out its functions under this Order.

Sec. 3. The Board shall, when required by this Order, report directly to the President. The Board shall consider and take appropriate action with respect to matters identified by the Director of Central Intelligence, the Central Intelligence Agency or other agencies of the Intelligence Community. With respect to matters deemed appropriate by the President, the Board shall advise and make appropriate recommendations to the Director of Central Intelligence, the Central Intelligence Agency, and other agencies of the Intelligence Community.

Sec. 4. The heads of departments and agencies of the Intelligence Community shall, to the extent permitted by the law, provide the Board with all the information necessary to carry out its responsibilities. Inspectors General and General Counsel of the Intelligence Community shall, to the extent permitted by the law, report to the Board concerning intelligence activities that they have reason to believe may be unlawful or contrary to Executive order or Presidential directive.

Sec. 5. Information made available to the Board shall be given all necessary security protection in accordance with applicable laws and regulations. Each member of the Board, each member of the Board's staff, and each of the Board's consultants shall execute an agreement never to reveal any classified information obtained by virtue of his or her service with the Board except to the President or to such persons as the President may designate.

Sec. 6. Members of the Board shall serve without compensation, but may receive transportation, expense, and per diem allowances as authorized by law. Staff and consultants to the Board shall receive pay and allowances as authorized by the President.

Ronald Reagan

THE WHITE HOUSE

December 4, 1981.

Appendix Q

Statement on the Issuance of a Presidential Directive, January 12, 1982
National Security Council Structure

I. National Security Council

The National Security Council (NSC) shall be the principal forum for consideration of national security policy issues requiring Presidential decision.

The functions and responsibilities of the NSC shall be as set forth in the National Security Act of 1947, as amended.

The NSC shall meet regularly. Those heads of departments and agencies who are not regular members shall participate as appropriate, when matters affecting their departments or agencies are considered.

The Assistant to the President for National Security Affairs, in consultation with the regular members of the NSC, shall be responsible for developing, coordinating, and implementing national security policy as approved by me. He shall determine and publish the agenda of NSC meetings. He shall ensure that the necessary papers are prepared and—except in unusual circumstances—distributed in advance to Council members. He shall staff and administer the National Security Council.

Decision documents shall be prepared by the Assistant to the President for National Security Affairs, and disseminated by him after the approval by the President.

II. NSC Responsibilities of the Secretary of State

The Secretary of State is my principal foreign policy adviser. As such, he is responsible for the formulation of foreign policy and for the execution of approved policy.

I have assigned to the Secretary of State authority and responsibility, to the extent permitted by law, for the overall direction, coordination, and supervision of the interdepartmental activities incident to foreign policy formulation, and the executive departments and agencies of the United States overseas. Such activities do not include those of the United States military forces operating in the field under the command of a United States area military commander, and such other military activities as I elect, as Commander in Chief, to conduct exclusively through military or other channels. Activities that are internal to the execution and administration of the approved programs of a single department or agency and which are not of such nature as to affect significantly the overall U.S. overseas program in a country or region are not considered to be activities covered within the meaning of this directive.

The Secretary of State is responsible for preparation of those papers addressing matters affecting the foreign policy and foreign relations of the United States for consideration by the NSC.

III. NSC Responsibilities of the Secretary of Defense

The Secretary of Defense is my principal defense policy adviser. As such, he is responsible for the formulation of general defense policy, policy related to all matters of direct and primary concern to the Department of Defense, and for the execution of approved policy. The Joint Chiefs of Staff are the principal military advisers to me, the Secretary of Defense and the NSC.

I have assigned to the Secretary of Defense authority and responsibility, to the extent permitted by law, for the overall direction, coordination, and supervision of the interdepartmental activities incident to defense policy formulation.

The Secretary of Defense is responsible for preparation of those papers addressing matters affecting the defense policy of the United States for consideration by the NSC.

IV. NSC Responsibilities of the Director of Central Intelligence

The Director of Central Intelligence is my principal adviser on intelligence matters. As such, he is responsible for the formulation of intelligence activities, policy, and proposals, as set forth in relevant Executive orders. I have assigned to the Director of Central Intelligence authority and responsibility, to the extent permitted by law and Executive order, for the overall direction, coordination, and supervision of the interdepartmental activities incident to intelligence matters.

The Director of Central Intelligence is responsible for the preparation of those papers addressing matters affecting the intelligence activities, policy, and proposals of the United States for consideration by the NSC.

V. Interagency Groups

To assist the NSC at large and its individual members in fulfilling their responsibilities, interagency groups are established as described herein. The focus of these interagency groups is to establish policy objectives, develop policy options, make appropriate recommendations, consider the implications of agency programs for foreign policy or overall national security policy, and undertake such other activities as may be assigned by the NSC.

A. The Senior Interagency Group—Foreign Policy (SIG-FP)

To advise and assist the NSC in exercising its authority and discharging its responsibilities for foreign policy and foreign affairs matters, the SIG-FP is established. The SIG-FP shall be composed of the Director of Central Intelligence; the Assistant to the President for National Security Affairs; the Deputy Secretary of State (Chairman); the Deputy Secretary of Defense or Under Secretary of Defense for Policy; and the Chairman, Joint Chiefs of Staff. Representatives of other departments and agencies with responsibility for specific matters to be considered will attend on invitation by the Chairman.

When meeting to consider arms control matters, the Group will be augmented by the Director, Arms Control and Disarmament Agency.

The SIG-FP will:

    1.   Ensure that important foreign policy issues requiring interagency attention

receive full, prompt, and systematic consideration;

2. Deal with interdepartmental matters raised by any member or referred to it by subordinate interagency groups, or, if such matters require higher level consideration, report them to the Secretary of State for decision or referral to the NSC;

3. Assure a proper selectivity of the foreign policy/foreign affairs areas and issues to which the United States applies its efforts;

4. Monitor the execution of approved policies and decisions; and

5. Evaluate the adequacy and effectiveness of interdepartmental overseas programs and activities.

A permanent secretariat, composed of personnel of the State Department augmented as necessary by personnel provided in response to the Chairman's request by the departments and agencies represented on the SIG-FP, shall be established.

B. The Senior Interagency Group—Defense Policy (SIG-FP)

To advise and assist the NSC in exercising its authority and discharging its responsibility for defense policy and defense matters, the SIG-DP is established. The SIG-DP shall consist of the Director of Central Intelligence; the Assistant to the President for National Security Affairs; the Deputy or an Under Secretary of State; the Deputy Secretary of Defense (Chairman); and the Chairman, Joint Chiefs of Staff. Representatives of other departments and agencies with responsibility for specific matters to be considered will attend on invitation by the Chairman.

The SIG-DP will:

1. Ensure that important defense policy issues requiring interagency attention receive full, prompt, and systematic consideration;

2. Deal with interdepartmental matters raised by any member or referred to it by subordinate interagency groups, or if such matters require higher level consideration, report them to the Secretary of Defense for decision or referral to the NSC; and

3. Monitor the execution of approved policies and decisions.

A permanent secretariat, composed of personnel of the Department of Defense augmented as necessary by personnel provided in response to the Chairman's request by the departments and agencies represented on the SIG-DP, shall be established.

C. The Senior Interagency Group—Intelligence (SIG-I)

To advise and assist the NSC in exercising its authority and discharging its responsibility for intelligence policy and intelligence matters, the SIG-I is established. The SIG-I shall consist of the Director of Central Intelligence (Chairman); the Assistant to the President for National Security Affairs; the Deputy Secretary of State; the Deputy Secretary of Defense; and the Chairman, Joint Chiefs of Staff. Representatives of other departments and agencies will attend on invitation by the Chairman when such departments and agencies have a direct interest in intelligence activities under consideration.

When meeting to consider sensitive intelligence collection activities referred by the

Director of Central Intelligence, the membership of the Group shall be augmented, as necessary, by the head of each organization within the intelligence community directly involved in the activity in question. When meeting to consider counterintelligence activities, the Group shall be augmented by the Director, Federal Bureau of Investigation, and the Director, National Security Agency.

The SIG-I will:

1. Establish requirements and priorities for national foreign intelligence;

2. Review such National Foreign Intelligence Program and budget proposals and other matters as are referred to it by the Director of Central Intelligence;

3. Review proposals for sensitive foreign intelligence collection operations referred by the Director of Central Intelligence;

4. Develop standards and doctrine for the counterintelligence activities of the United States; resolve interagency differences concerning the implementation of counterintelligence policy; and develop and monitor guidelines, consistent with applicable law and Executive orders, for the maintenance of central counterintelligence records;

5. Consider and approve any counterintelligence activity referred to the Group by the head of any organization in the intelligence community;

6. Submit to the NSC an overall, annual assessment of the relative threat to United States interests from intelligence and security services of foreign powers and from international terrorist activities, including an assessment of the effectiveness of the United States counterintelligence activities;

7. Conduct an annual review of ongoing, sensitive, national foreign intelligence collection operations and sensitive counterintelligence activities and report thereon to the NSC; and

8. Carry out such additional coordination review and approval of intelligence activities as the President may direct.

A permanent secretariat, composed of personnel of the Central Intelligence Agency augmented as necessary by personnel provided in response to the Chairman's request by the departments and agencies represented on the SIG-I, shall be established.

D. Regional and Functional Interagency Groups

To assist the SIG-FP, Interagency Groups (IG's) shall be established by the Secretary of State for each geographic region corresponding to the jurisdiction of the geographic bureaus in the Department of State, for Political-Military Affairs, and for International Economic Affairs. Each IG shall be comprised of the Director of Central Intelligence; the Assistant to the President for National Security Affairs; the Chairman, Joint Chiefs of Staff; the appropriate Assistant Secretary of State (Chairman); and a designated representative of the Secretary of Defense. Representatives of other departments and agencies with responsibility for specific matters to be considered will attend on invitation by the Chairman. The IG for International Economic Affairs will, in addition to the above membership, include representatives of the Secretary of the Treasury, the Secretary of Commerce, and the U.S. Trade Representative.

IG's for arms control matters will, in addition to the above membership, include a representative of the Director, Arms Control and Disarmament Agency. Arms control IG's will be chaired by the representative of the Secretary of State or the representative of the Director, Arms Control and Disarmament Agency, in accordance with guidelines to be provided by the SIG-FP.

To assist the SIG-DP, IG's shall be established by the Secretary of Defense corresponding to the functional areas within the Department of Defense. Each IG shall be comprised of the appropriate Under or Assistant Secretary of Defense (Chairman); a representative of the Secretary of State; the Director of Central Intelligence; the Assistant to the President for National Security Affairs; and the Chairman, Joint Chiefs of Staff. Representatives of other departments and agencies will attend on invitation by the Chairman.

Under and Assistant Secretaries, in their capacities as Chairmen of the IG's, will assure the adequacy of United States policy in the areas of their responsibility and of the plans, programs, resources, and performance for implementing that policy. They will be responsible for the conduct of interagency policy studies within the areas of their responsibility for consideration by the SIG.

The Regional IG's also shall prepare contingency plans pertaining to potential crises in their respective areas of responsibility. Contingency planning will be conducted in coordination with the Chairman of the Political-Military IG, with the exception of the military response option for employment of forces in potential crises, which will remain within the purview of the Department of Defense and will be developed by the Joint Chiefs of Staff.

To deal with specific contingencies, the IG's will establish full-time working groups, which will provide support to the crisis management operations of the NSC. These groups will reflect the institutional membership of the parent body, together with such additional members as may be required to respond to the contingency with the full weight of available expertise.

To assist the SIG-I, IG's shall be established by the Director of Central Intelligence. The IG for Counterintelligence shall consist of representatives of the Secretary of State; Secretary of Defense; the Director of Central Intelligence; the Director, Federal Bureau of Investigation; the Assistant to the President for National Security Affairs; Chairman, Joint Chiefs of Staff; the Director, National Security Agency; and a representative of the head of any other intelligence community organization directly involved in the activities under discussion. The IG for Counterintelligence will be under the chairmanship of the representative of the Director of Central Intelligence or the Director, Federal Bureau of Investigation, in accordance with guidelines to be provided by the SIG-I.

The operational responsibility or authority of a Secretary or other agency head over personnel from the department or agency concerned serving the IG's—including the authority to give necessary guidance to the representatives in the performance of IG duties—is not limited by this directive.

Appendix R

Executive Order 12356, April 1, 1982
National Security Information

This order prescribes a uniform system for classifying, declassifying, and safeguarding national security information. It recognizes that it is essential that the public be informed concerning the activities of its Government, but that the interests of the United States and its citizens require that certain information concerning the national defense and foreign relations be protected against unauthorized disclosure. Information may not be classified under this Order unless its disclosure reasonably could be expected to cause damage to the national security.

NOW, by the authority vested in me as President by the Constitution and laws of the United States of America, it is hereby ordered as follows:

PART 1 *Original Classification*

SECTION 1.1 *Classification Levels*

(a) National security information (hereinafter "classified information") shall be classified at one of the following three levels:

(1) "Top Secret" shall be applied to information, the unauthorized disclosure of which reasonably could be expected to cause exceptionally grave damage to the national security.

(2) "Secret" shall be applied to information, the unauthorized disclosure of which reasonably could be expected to cause serious damage to the national security.

(3) "Confidential" shall be applied to information, the unauthorized disclosure of which reasonably could be expected to cause damage to the national security.

(b) Except as otherwise provided by statute, no other terms shall be used to identify classified information.

(c) If there is reasonable doubt about the need to classify information, it shall be safeguarded as if it were classified pending a determination by an original classification authority, who shall make this determination within thirty (30) days. If there is reasonable doubt about the appropriate level of classification, it shall be safeguarded at the higher level of classification pending a determination by an original classification authority, who shall make this determination within thirty (30) days.

SEC. 1.2 *Classification Authority.*

(a) *Top Secret.* The authority to classify information originally as Top Secret may be exercised only by:

(1) the President;

(2) agency heads and officials designated by the President in the *Federal Register*; and

(3) officials delegated this authority pursuant to Section 1.2(d).

(b) *Secret.* The authority to classify information originally as Secret may be exercised only by:

(1) agency heads and officials designated by the President in the *Federal Register*;

(2) officials with original Top Secret classification authority; and

(3) officials delegated such authority pursuant to section 1.2(d).

(c) *Confidential.* The authority to classify information originally as Confidential may be exercised only by:

(1) agency heads and officials designated by the President in the *Federal Register*;

(2) officials with original Top Secret or Secret classification authority; and

(3) officials delegated such authority pursuant to Section 1.2(d).

(d) *Delegation of Original Classification Authority.*

(1) Delegations of original classification authority shall be limited to the minimum required to administer this Order. Agency heads are responsible for ensuring that designated subordinate officials have a demonstrable and continuing need to exercise this authority.

(2) Original Top Secret classification authority may be delegated only by the President; an agency head or official designated pursuant to Sections 1.2(a)(2); and the senior official designated under Section 5.3(a)(1) provided that official has been delegated original classification authority by the agency head.

(3) Original Secret classification authority may be delegated only by the President; and agency head or official designated pursuant to Sections 1.2(a)(2) and 1.2(b)(1); and official with original Top Secret classification authority; and the senior official designated under Section 5.3(a)(1), provided that official has been delegated original Secret classification authority by the agency head.

(4) Original Confidential classification authority may be delegated only by the President; an agency head or official designated pursuant to Sections 1.2(a)(2), 1.2(b)(1) and 1.2(c)(1); an official with original Top Secret classification authority; and the senior official designated under Section 5.3(a)(1), provided that official has been delegated original classification authority by the agency head.

(5) Each delegation of original classification authority shall be in writing and the authority shall not be redelegated except as provided in this Order. It shall identify the official delegated the authority by name or position title. Delegated classification authority includes the authority to classify information at the level granted and lower levels of classification.

(e) *Exceptional Cases.* When an employee, contractor, licensee, or grantee of an agency that does not have original classification authority originates information believed by that person to require classification, the information shall be protected in a manner consistent with this Order and its implementing directives. The information shall be transmitted promptly as provided under this Order or its implementing directives to the agency that has appropriate subject matter interest and classification authority with respect to this information. That agency shall decide within thirty (30) days whether to classify this information. If it is not clear which agency has classification responsibility for this information, it shall be sent to the Director of the Information Security Oversight Office. The Director shall determine the agency having primary subject matter interest and forward the information, with appropriate recommendations, to that agency for a classification determination.

SEC.1.3 *Classification Categories.*

(a) Information shall be considered for classification if it concerns:

(1) military plans, weapons, or operations;

(2) the vulnerabilities or capabilities of systems, installations, projects, or plans relating to the national security;

(3) foreign government information;

(4) intelligence activities (including special activities), or intelligence sources or methods;

(5) foreign relations or foreign activities of the United States;

(6) scientific, technological, or economic matters relating to the national security;

(7) United States Government programs for safeguarding nuclear materials or facilities;

(8) cryptology;

(9) a confidential source; or

(10) other categories of information that are related to the national security and require protection against unauthorized disclosure as determined by the President or by agency heads or other officials who have been delegated original classification authority by the President. Any determination made under this subsection shall be reported promptly to the Director of the Information Security Oversight Office.

(b) Information that is determined to concern one or more of the categories in Section 1.3(a) shall be classified when an original classification authority also determines that its unauthorized disclosure, either by itself or in the context of other information, reasonably could be expected to cause damage to the national security.

(c) Unauthorized disclosure of foreign government information, the identity of a confidential foreign source, or intelligence sources or methods is presumed to cause damage to the national security.

(d) Information classified in accordance with Section 1.3 shall not be declassified automatically as a result of any unofficial publication or inadvertent or unauthorized disclosure in the United States or abroad of identical or similar information.

SEC. 1.4 *Duration of Classifications.*

(a) Information shall be classified as long as required by national security considerations. When it can be determined, a specific date or event for declassification shall be set by the original classification authority at the time the information is originally classified.

(b) Automatic declassification determinations under predecessor orders shall remain valid unless the classification is extended by an authorized official of the originating agency. These extensions may be made by individual documents or categories of information. The agency shall be responsible for notifying holders of the information of such extensions.

(c) Information classified under predecessor orders and marked for declassification review shall remain classified until reviewed for declassification under the provisions of this Order.

SEC. 1.5 *Identification and Markings.*

(a) At the time of original classification, the following information shall be shown on the face of all classified documents, or clearly associated with other forms of classified information in a manner appropriate to the medium involved, unless this information itself would reveal a confidential source or relationship not otherwise evident in the document or information:

(1) one of the three classification levels defined in Section 1.1;

(2) the identity of the original classification authority if other than the person whose name appears as the approving or signing official;

(3) the agency and office of origin; and

(4) the date or event for declassification, or the notation "Originating Agency's Determination Required."

(b) Each classified document shall, by marking or other means, indicate which portions are classified, with the applicable classification level, and which portions are not classified. Agency heads may, for good cause, grant and revoke waivers of this requirement for specified classes of documents or information. The Director of the Information Security Oversight Office shall be notified of any waivers.

(c) Marking designations implementing the provisions of this Order, including abbreviations, shall conform to the standards prescribed in implementing directives issued by the Information Security Oversight Office.

(d) Foreign government information shall either retain its original classification or be assigned a United States classification that shall ensure a degree of protection at least equivalent to that required by the entity that furnished the information.

(e) Information assigned a level of classification under predecessor orders shall be considered as classified at that level of classification despite the omission of other required markings. Omitted markings may be inserted on a document by the officials specified in Section 3.1(b).

SEC 1.6 *Limitations on Classification.*

(a) In no case shall information be classified in order to conceal violations of law, inefficiency, or administrative error; to prevent embarrassment to a person, organization, or agency; to restrain competition; or to prevent or delay the release of information that does not require protection in the interest of national security.

(b) Basic scientific research information not clearly related to the national security may not be classified.

(c) The President or an agency head or official designated under Sections 1.2(a)(2), 1.2(b)(1), 1.2(c)(1) may reclassify information previously declassified and disclosed if it is determined in writing that (1) the information requires protection in the interest of national security; and (2) the information may reasonably be recovered. These reclassification actions shall be reported promptly to the Director of the Information Security Oversight Office.

(d) Information may be classified or reclassified after an agency has received a request for it under the Freedom of Information Act (5 U.S.C. 552) or the Privacy Act of 1974 (5 U.S.C. 552a), or the mandatory review provisions of this Order (Section 3.4) if such classification meets the requirements of this Order and is accomplished personally and on a document-by-document basis by the agency head, the deputy agency head, the senior agency official designated under Section 5.3(a)(1), or an official with original Top Secret classification authority.

PART 2 *Derivative Classification*

SEC. 2.1 *Use of Classified Information.*

(a) Derivative classification is (1) the determination that information is in substance the same as information currently classified, and (2) the application of the same classification markings. Persons who only reproduce, extract, or summarize classified information, or who only apply classification markings derived from source material or as directed by a classification guide, need not possess original classification authority.

(b) Persons who apply derivative classification markings shall:

(1) observe and respect original classification decisions; and

(2) carry forward to any newly created documents any assigned authorized markings. The declassification date or event that provides the longest period of classification shall be used for documents classified on the basis of multiple sources.

SEC. 2.2 *Classification Guides.*

(a) Agencies with original classification authority shall prepare classification guides to facilitate the proper and uniform derivative classification of information.

(b) Each guide shall be approved personally and in writing by an official who:

(1) has program or supervisory responsibility over the information or is the senior agency official designated under Section 5.3(a)(1); and

(2) is authorized to classify information originally at the highest level of classification prescribed in the guide.

(c) Agency heads may, for good cause, grant and revoke waivers of the requirement to prepare classification guides for specified classes of documents or information. The Director of the Information Security Oversight Office shall be notified of any waivers.

PART 3 *Declassification and Downgrading*

SEC. 3.1 *Declassification Authority.*

(a) Information shall be declassified or downgraded as soon as national security considerations permit. Agencies shall coordinate their review of classified information with other agencies that have a direct interest in the subject matter. Information that continues to meet the classification requirements prescribed by Section 1.3 despite the passage of time will continue to be protected in accordance with this Order.

(b) Information shall be declassified or downgraded by the official who authorized the original classification, if that official is still serving in the same position; the originator's successor; a supervisory official of either; or officials delegated such authority in writing by the agency head or the senior agency official designated pursuant to Section 5.3(a)(1).

(c) If the Director of the Information Security Oversight Office determines that information is classified in violation of this Order, the Director may require the information to be declassified by the agency that originated the classification. Any such decision by the Director may be appealed to the National Security Council. The information shall remain classified, pending a prompt decision on the appeal.

(d) The provisions of this Section shall also apply to agencies that, under the terms of this Order, do not have original classification authority, but that had such authority under predecessor orders.

SEC. 3.2 *Transferred Information.*

(a) In the case of classified information transferred in conjunction with a transfer of functions, and not merely for storage purposes, the receiving agency shall be deemed to be the originating agency for purposes of this Order.

(b) In the case of classified information that is not officially transferred as described in Section 3.2(a), but that originated in an agency that has ceased to exist and for which there is no successor agency, each agency in possession of such information shall be deemed to be the originating agency for purposes of this Order. Such information may be declassified or downgraded by the agency in possession after consultation with any other agency that has an interest in the subject matter of the information.

(c) Classified information accessioned into the National Archives of the United States shall be declassified or downgraded by the Archivist of the United States in accordance with this Order, the directives of the Information Security Oversight Office, and agency guidelines.

SEC. 3.3 *Systematic Review for Declassification.*

(a) The Archivist of the United States shall, in accordance with procedures and time frames prescribed in the Information Security Oversight Office's directives implementing this Order, systematically review for declassification or downgrading (1) classified records accessioned into the National

Archives of the United States, and (2) classified presidential papers or records under the Archivist's control. Such information shall be reviewed by the Archivist for declassification or downgrading in accordance with systematic review guidelines that shall be provided by the head of the agency that originated the information, or in the case of foreign government information, by the Director of the Information Security Oversight Office in consultation with interested agency heads.

(b) Agency heads may conduct internal systematic review programs for classified information originated by their agencies contained in records determined by the Archivist to be permanently valuable but that have not been accessioned into the National Archives of the United States.

(c) After consultation with affected agencies, the Secretary of Defense may establish special procedures for systematic review for declassification of classified cryptologic information, and the Director of Central Intelligence may establish special procedures for systematic review for declassification of classified information pertaining to intelligence activities (including special activities), or intelligence sources or methods.

SEC. 3.4 *Mandatory Review for Declassification.*

(a) Except as provided in Section 3.4 (b), all information classified under this Order or predecessor orders shall be subject to a review for declassification by the originating agency, if:

   (1) the request is made by a United States citizen or permanent resident alien, a federal agency, or a State or local government; and

   (2) the request describes the document or material containing the information with sufficient specificity to enable the agency to locate it with a reasonable amount of effort.

(b) Information originated by a President, the White House Staff, by committees, commissions, or boards appointed by the President, or others specifically providing advice and counsel to a President or acting on behalf of a President is exempted from the provisions of Section 3.4(a). The Archivist of the United States shall have the authority to review, downgrade and declassify information under the control of the Administrator of General Services of the Archivist pursuant to sections 2107, 2107 note, or 2203 of title 44, United States Code. Review procedures developed by the Archivist shall provide for consultation with agencies having primary subject matter interest and shall be consistent with the provisions of applicable laws or lawful agreements that pertain to the respective presidential papers or records. Any decision by the Archivist may be appealed to the Director of the Information Security Oversight Office. Agencies with primary subject matter interest shall be notified promptly of the Director's decision on such appeals and may further appeal to the National Security Council. The information shall remain classified pending a prompt decision on the appeal.

(c) Agencies conducting a mandatory review for declassification shall declassify information no longer requiring protection under this Order. They shall release this information unless withholding is otherwise authorized under applicable law.

(d) Agency heads shall develop procedures to process requests for the mandatory review of classified information. These procedures shall apply to information classified under this or predecessor orders. They shall also provide a means for administratively appealing a denial of a mandatory review request.

(e) The Secretary of Defense shall develop special procedures for the review of cryptographic information, and the Director of Central Intelligence shall develop special procedures for the review of information pertaining to intelligence activities (including special activities), or intelligence sources and methods, after consultation with affected agencies. The Archivist shall develop special procedures for the review of information accessioned into the National Archives of the United States.

(f) In response to a request for information under the Freedom of Information Act, the Privacy Act of 1974, or the mandatory review provisions of this Order:

(1) An agency shall refuse to confirm or deny the existence or non-existence of requested information whenever the fact of its existence or non-existence is itself classifiable under this Order.

(2) When an agency receives any request for documents in its custody that were classified by another agency, it shall refer copies of the request and the requested documents to the originating agency for processing, and may, after consultation with the originating agency, inform the requester of the referral. In cases in which the originating Agency determines in writing that a response under Section 3.4(f)(1) is required, the referring agency shall respond to the requester in accordance with that Section.

PART 4 *Safeguarding*

SEC. 4.1 *General Restrictions on Access.*

(a) A person is eligible for access to classified information provided that a determination of trustworthiness has been made by agency heads or designated officials and provided that such access is essential to the accomplishment of lawful and authorized Government purposes.

(b) Controls shall be established by each agency to ensure that classified information is used, processed, stored, reproduced, transmitted, and destroyed only under conditions that will provide adequate protection and prevent access by unauthorized persons.

(c) Classified information shall not be disseminated outside the executive branch except under conditions that ensure that the information will be given protection equivalent to that afforded within the executive branch.

(d) Except as provided by directives issued by the President through the National Security Council, classified information originating in one agency may not be disseminated outside any other agency to which it has been made available without the consent of the originating agency. For purposes of this Section, the Department of Defense shall be considered one agency.

SEC. 4.2 *Special Access Programs.*

(a) Agency heads designated pursuant to Section 1.2(a) may create special access programs to control access, distribution and protection of particularly sensitive information, classified pursuant to this Order or predecessor orders. Such programs may be created or continued only at the written direction of these agency heads. For special access programs pertaining to intelligence activities (including special activities but not including military operational, strategic and tactical programs), or intelligence sources and methods, this function will be exercised by the Director of Central Intelligence.

(b) Each agency head shall establish and maintain a system of accounting for special access programs. The Director of the Information Security Oversight Office, consistent with the provisions of Section 5.2(b)(4), shall have non-delegable access to such accountings.

SEC. 4.3 *Access by Historical Researchers and Former Presidential Appointees.*

(a) The requirement in Section 4.1(a) that access to classified information may be granted only as is essential to the accomplishment of authorized and lawful Government purposes may be waived as provided in Section 4.3(b) for persons who:

(1) are engaged in historical research projects, or

(2) previously have occupied policy-making positions to which they were appointed by the President.

(b) Waivers under Section 4.3(a) may be granted only if the originating agency:

(1) determines in writing that access is consistent with the interest of national security;

(2) takes appropriate steps to protect classified information from unauthorized disclosure or compromise, and ensures that the information is safeguarded in a manner consistent with this Order, and

(3) limits the access granted to former presidential appointees to items that the person originated, reviewed, signed, or received while serving as a presidential appointee.

PART 5 *Implementation and Review*

SEC. 5.1 *Policy Direction.*

(a) The National Security Council shall provide overall policy direction for the information security program.

(b) The Administrator of General Services shall be responsible for implementing and monitoring the program established pursuant to this Order. The Administrator shall delegate the implementation and monitorship functions of this program to the Director of the Information Security Oversight Office.

SEC. 5.2 *Information Security Oversight Office.*

(a) The Information Security Oversight Office shall have a full-time Director appointed by the Administrator of General Services subject to approval by the President. The Director shall have the authority to appoint a staff for the Office.

(b) The Director shall:

(1) develop, in consultation with the agencies, and promulgate, subject to the

approval of the National Security Council, directives for the implementation of this Order, which shall be binding on the agencies;

(2) oversee agency actions to ensure compliance with this Order and implementing directives;

(3) review all agency implementing regulations and agency guidelines for systematic declassification review. The Director shall require any regulation or guideline to be changed if it is not consistent with this Order or implementing directives. Any such decision by the Director may be appealed to the National Security Council. The agency regulations or guidelines shall remain in effect pending a prompt decision on the appeal;

(4) have the authority to conduct on-site reviews of the information security program of each agency that generates or handles classified information and to require of each agency those reports, information, and other cooperation that may be necessary to fulfill the Director's responsibilities. If these reports, inspections, or access to specific categories of classified information would pose an exceptional national security risk, the affected agency head or the senior official designated under Section 5.3(a)(1) may deny access. The Director may appeal denials to the National Security Council. The denial of access shall remain in effect pending a prompt decision on the appeal;

(5) review requests for original classification authority from agencies or officials not granted original classification authority and, if deemed appropriate, recommend presidential approval;

(6) consider and take action on complaints and suggestions from persons within or outside the Government with respect to the administration of the information security program;

(7) have the authority to prescribe, after consultation with affected agencies, standard forms that will promote the implementation of the information security program;

(8) report at least annually to the President through the National Security Council on the implementation of this Order; and

(9) have the authority to convene and chair interagency meetings to discuss matters pertaining to the information security program.

SEC. 5.3 *General Responsibilities.*

Agencies that originate or handle classified information shall:

(a) designate a senior agency official to direct and administer its information security program, which shall include an active oversight and security education program to ensure effective implementation of this Order;

(b) promulgate implementing regulations. Any unclassified regulations that establish agency information security policy shall be published in the *Federal Register* to the extent that these regulations affect members of the public;

(c) establish procedures to prevent unnecessary access to classified information, including procedures that (i) require that a demonstrable need for access to classified information is established before initiating administrative clearance procedures, and (ii) ensure that the number of persons granted access to classified information is limited to the minimum consistent with operational and security requirements and needs; and

(d) develop special contingency plans for the protection of classified information used in or near hostile or potentially hostile areas.

SEC. 5.4 *Sanctions.*

(a) If the Director of the Information Security Oversight Office finds that a violation of this Order or its implementing directives may have occurred, the Director shall make a report to the head of the agency or to the senior official designated under Section 5.3(a)(1) so that corrective steps, if appropriate, may be taken.

(b) Officers and employees of the United States Government, and its contractors, licensees, and grantees shall be subject to appropriate sanctions if they:

(1) knowingly, willfully, or negligently disclose to unauthorized persons information properly classified under this Order or predecessor orders;

(2) knowingly and willfully classify or continue the classification of information in violation of this Order or any implementing directive; or

(3) knowingly and willfully violate any other provision of this Order, or implementing directive.

(c) Sanctions may include reprimand, suspension without pay, removal, termination of classification authority, loss or denial of access to classified information, or other sanctions in accordance with applicable law and agency regulation.

(d) Each agency head or the senior official designated under Section 5.3(a)(1) shall ensure that appropriate and prompt corrective action is taken whenever a violation under Section 5.4(b) occurs. Either shall ensure that the Director of the Information Security Oversight Office is promptly notified whenever a violation under Section 5.4(b)(1) or (2) occurs.

PART 6 *General Provisions*

SEC. 6.1 *Definitions.*

(a) "Agency" has the meaning provided at 5 U.S.C. 522(e).

(b) "Information" means any information or material, regardless of its physical form or characteristics, that is owned by, produced by or for, or is under the control of the United States Government.

(c) "National security information" means information that has been determined pursuant to this Order or any predecessor order to require protection against unauthorized disclosure and that is so designated.

(d) "Foreign government information" means:

(1) information provided by a foreign government or governments, an international organization of governments, or any element thereof with the expectation, expressed or implied, that the information, the source of the information, or both, are to be held in confidence; or

(2) information produced by the United States pursuant to or as a result of a joint arrangement with a foreign government or governments or an interna-

tional organization of governments, or any element thereof, requiring that the information, the arrangement, or both, are to be held in confidence.

(e) "National security" means the national defense or foreign relations of the United States.

(f) "Confidential source" means any individual or organization that has provided, or that may reasonably be expected to provide, information to the United States on matters pertaining to the national security with the expectation, expressed or implied, that the information or relationship, or both, be held in confidence.

(g) "Original classification" means an initial determination that information requires, in the interest of national security, protection against unauthorized disclosure, together with a classification designation signifying the level of protection required.

SEC. 6.2 *General.*

(a) Nothing in this Order shall supersede any requirement made by or under the Atomic Energy Act of 1954, as amended. "Restricted Data" and "Formerly Restricted Data" shall be handled, protected, classified, downgraded, and declassified in conformity with the provisions of the Atomic Energy Act of 1954, as amended, and regulations issued under that Act.

(b) The Attorney General, upon request by the head of an agency or the Director of the Information Security Oversight Office, shall render an interpretation of this Order with respect to any question arising in the course of its administration.

(c) Nothing is this Order limits the protection afforded any information by other provisions of law.

(d) Executive Order No. 12065 of June 28,1978, as amended, is revoked as of the effective date of this Order.

(e) This Order shall become effective on August 1, 1982.

Ronald Reagan

THE WHITE HOUSE

April 2, 1982

Appendix S

National Security Decision Directive Number 84, March 11, 1983
Safeguarding National Security Information

As stated in Executive Order 12356, only that information whose disclosure would harm the national security interests of the United States may be classified. Every effort should be made to declassify information that no longer requires protection in the interest of national security.

At the same time, however, safeguarding against unlawful disclosures of properly classified information is a matter of grave concern and high priority for this Administration. In addition to the requirements set forth in Executive Order 12356, and based on the recommendations contained in the interdepartmental report forwarded by the Attorney General, I direct the following:

1. Each agency of the Executive Branch that originates or handles classified information shall adopt internal procedures to safeguard against unlawful disclosures of classified information. Such procedures shall at a minimum provide as follows:

   a. All persons with authorized access to classified information shall be required to sign a nondisclosure agreement as a condition of access. This requirement may be implemented prospectively by agencies for which the administrative burden of compliance would otherwise be excessive.

   b. All persons with authorized access to Sensitive Compartmented Information (SCI) shall be required to sign a nondisclosure agreement as a condition of access to SCI and other classified information. All such agreements must include a provision for prepublication review to assure deletion of SCI and other classified information.

   c. All agreements required in paragraphs 1.a. and 1.b. must be in a form determined by the Department of Justice to be enforceable in a civil action brought by the United States. The Director, Information Security Oversight Office (ISOO) shall develop standardized forms that satisfy these requirements.

   d. Appropriate policies shall be adopted to govern contacts between media representatives and agency personnel, so as to reduce the opportunity for negligent or deliberate disclosures of classified information. All persons with authorized access to classified information shall be clearly apprised of the agency's policies in this regard.

2. Each agency of the Executive Branch that originates or handles classified information shall adopt internal procedures to govern the reporting and investigation of unauthorized disclosures of such information. Such procedures shall at a minimum provide that:

a. All such disclosures that the agency considers to be seriously damaging to its mission and responsibilities shall be evaluated to ascertain the nature of the information disclosed and the extent to which it had been disseminated.

b. The agency shall conduct a preliminary internal investigation prior to or concurrently with seeking investigative assistance from other agencies.

c. The agency shall maintain records of disclosures so evaluated and investigated.

d. Agencies in possession of classified information originating with another agency shall cooperate with the originating agency by conducting internal investigations of the unauthorized disclosure of such information.

e. Persons determined by the agency to have knowingly made such disclosures or to have refused cooperation with investigations of such unauthorized disclosures will be denied further access to classified information and subjected to other administrative sanctions as appropriate.

3. Unauthorized disclosure of classified information shall be reported to the Department of Justice and the Information Security Oversight Office, as required by statute and Executive orders. The Department of Justice shall continue to review reported unauthorized disclosures of classified information to determine whether FBI investigation is warranted. Interested departments and agencies shall be consulted in developing criteria for evaluating such matters and in determining which cases should receive investigative priority. The FBI is authorized to investigate such matters as constitute potential violations of federal criminal law, even though administrative sanctions may be sought instead of criminal prosecution.

4. Nothing in this directive is meant to modify or preclude interagency agreements between FBI and other criminal investigative agencies regarding their responsibility for conducting investigations within their own agencies or departments.

5. The Office of Personnel Management and all departments and agencies with employees having access to classified information are directed to revise existing regulations and policies, as necessary, so that employees may be required to submit to polygraph examinations, when appropriate, in the course of investigations of unauthorized disclosures of classified information. As a minimum, such regulations shall permit an agency to decide that appropriate consequences will follow an employee's refusal to cooperate with a polygraph examination that is limited in scope to the circumstances of an unauthorized disclosure under investigation. Agency regulations may provide that only the head of the agency, or his delegate, is empowered to order an employee to submit to a polygraph examination. Results of polygraph examinations should not be relied upon to the exclusion of other information obtained during investigations.

6. The Attorney General, in consultation with the Director, Office of Personnel Management, is requested to establish an interdepartmental group to study the federal personnel security program and recommend appropriate revisions in existing Executive orders, regulations, and guidelines.

Ronald Reagan

Appendix T

Executive Order 12537, October 28, 1985
President's Foreign Intelligence Advisory Board

By the authority vested in me as President by the Constitution and statutes of the United States of America, and in order to enhance the security of the United States by improving the quality and effectiveness of intelligence available to the United States, it is ordered as follows:

Section 1. There is hereby established within the White House Office, Executive Office of the President, the President's Foreign Intelligence Advisory Board (the "Board"). The Board shall consist of not more than fourteen members, who shall serve at the pleasure of the President and shall be appointed by the President from among trustworthy and distinguished citizens outside the government who are qualified on the basis of achievement, experience, and independence. The President shall establish the terms of the members upon their appointment. To the extent practicable, one-third of the Board at any one time shall be comprised of members whose current term of service does not exceed two years. The President shall designate a Chairman and Vice Chairman from among the members. The Board shall utilize full-time staff and consultants as authorized by the President. Such staff shall be headed by an Executive Director, appointed by the President.

Sec. 2. The Board shall assess the quality, quantity, and adequacy of intelligence collection, of analysis and estimates, of counterintelligence, and other intelligence activities. The Board shall have the authority to continually review the performance of all agencies of the Federal government that are engaged in the collection, evaluation, or production of intelligence or the execution of intelligence policy. The Board shall further be authorized to assess the adequacy of management, personnel, and organization in the intelligence agencies.

Sec. 3. The Board shall report directly to the President and advise him concerning the objectives, conduct, management, and coordination of the various activities of the agencies of the intelligence community. The Board shall report periodically, but at least semiannually, concerning findings and appraisals and shall make appropriate recommendations for actions to improve and enhance the performance of the intelligence efforts of the United States.

Sec. 4. The Board shall receive, consider, and recommend appropriate action with respect to matters, identified to the Board by the Director of Central Intelligence, the Central Intelligence Agency, or other government agencies engaged in intelligence or related activities, in which the support of the Board will further the effectiveness of the national intelligence effort. With respect to matters deemed appropriate by the President, the Board shall advise and make recommendations to the Director of Central Intelligence, the Central Intelligence Agency, and other government agencies engaged in intelligence and related activities, concerning ways to achieve increased effectiveness in meeting national intelligence needs.

Sec. 5. The Board shall have access to the full extent permitted by applicable law to all information necessary to carry out its duties in the possession of any agency of the Federal government. Information made available to the Board shall be given all necessary security protection in accordance with applicable laws and regulations. Each member of the Board, each member of the Board's staff and each of the Board's consultants shall execute an agreement never to reveal any classified information obtained by virtue of his or her service with the Board except to the President or to such persons as the President may designate.

Sec. 6. Members of the Board shall serve without compensation, but may receive transportation, expenses, and per diem allowance as authorized by law. Staff and consultants to the Board shall receive pay and allowances as authorized by the President.

Sec. 7. Executive Order No. 12331 of October 20, 1981 is revoked.

Ronald Reagan

THE WHITE HOUSE,

October 28, 1985

Appendix U

Executive Order 12575, December 1, 1986
President's Special Review Board

By the authority vested in me as President by the Constitution and laws of the United States of America, and in order to establish, in accordance with the Federal Advisory Committee Act, as amended (5 U.S.C. App. I), a Special Review Board to review activities of the National Security Council, it is hereby ordered as follows:

Section 1. *Establishment.*

(a) There is established the President's Special Review Board on the future role of the National Security Council staff. The Board shall consist of three members appointed by the President from among persons with extensive experience in foreign policy and national security affairs.

(b) The President shall designate a Chairman from among the members of the Board.

Sec. 2. *Functions.*

(a) The Board shall conduct a comprehensive study of the future role and procedures of the National Security Council (NSC) staff in the development, coordination, oversight, and conduct of foreign and national security policy; review the NSC staff's proper role in operational activities, especially extremely sensitive diplomatic, military, and intelligence missions; and provide recommendations to the President based upon its analysis of the manner in which foreign and national security policies established by the President have been implemented by the NSC staff.

(b) The Board shall submit its findings and recommendations to the President within 60 days of the date of this Order.

Sec. 3. *Administration.*

(a) The heads of Executive departments, agencies, and independent instrumentalities, to the extent permitted by law, shall provide the Board, upon request, with such information as it may require for purposes of carrying out its functions.

(b) Members of the Board shall receive compensation for their work on the Board at the daily rate specified for GS-18 of the General Schedule. While engaged in the work of the Board, members appointed from among private citizens of the United States may be allowed travel expenses, including per diem in lieu of subsistence, as authorized by law for persons serving intermittently in the government service (5 U.S.C. 5701-5707).

(c) To the extent permitted by law and subject to the availability of appropriations, the Office of Administration, Executive Office of the President, shall provide the Board with such administrative services, funds, facilities, staff, and other support services as may be necessary for the performance of its functions.

Sec. 4. *General Provision.* The Board shall terminate 30 days after submitting its report to the President.

Ronald Reagan

THE WHITE HOUSE

December 1, 1986.

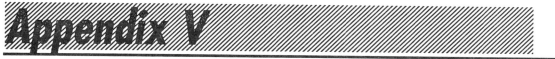

Appendix V

Letter from Senator John Tower, Senator Edmund Muskie, and Lieutenant General Brent Scowcroft forwarding the Report of the President's Special Review Board, February 26, 1987

Dear Mr. President:

We respectfully submit to you the Report of the Special Review Board. This Report is the product of our study of the National Security Council, its operation and its staff.

For the last three months, we have reviewed the evolution of the NSC system since its creation forty years ago. We had extensive discussions with almost every current and former senior official involved in national security affairs. Case studies from several Administrations were also conducted to inform our judgments.

At your direction, we also focused on the Iran/Contra matter and sought to follow your injunction that "all the facts come out." We attempted to do this as fairly as we knew how so that lessons for the future could be learned.

The Report is based in large part on information and documentation provided to us by U.S. departments and agencies and interviews of current and former officials. We relied upon others in the Executive Branch to conduct the search for materials or information we requested. In general, we received a positive response to our inquiries from every agency, including the White House, although the Independent Counsel and the Federal Bureau of Investigation responded negatively to our request for material. We found that the individuals from agencies that appeared before us generally did so in a forthcoming manner.

The portions of this Report that recite the facts were reviewed by appropriate agency representatives in order to identify classified material. This was done to enable you to make the Report public. These representatives performed this security review without regard for domestic political consequences. No material was deleted on the grounds that it might prove embarrassing to your Administration. There was, however, some information that we concluded had to remain in the classified domain. The appropriate Congressional committees may find this information of use.

While the publication of the material in this Report may be troublesome to some in the short term, we believe that, over time, the nation will clearly benefit from your decision to commission this review. We commend this Report to you and to future Presidents in the hope that it will enhance the effectiveness of the National Security Council.

We are honored to have had the opportunity to serve on this Board.

Sincerely,

Edmund S. Muskie
John Tower
Brent Scowcroft
[February 26, 1987]

Appendix W

Excerpts from the Report of the President's Special Review Board, February 26, 1987

[*Editors' note*: The following excerpts are presented in order to provide the reader with the *views of the Board concerning the problems of the National Security Council and, in a larger context, the Intelligence Community.* Conversely, Parts III and IV and the supporting appendixes, which focus on the Iran-Contra case, have been omitted because they pertain less to intelligence than to a particular incident, and, in respect to that incident, the Board was unable to interview three of its principal actors, Lieutenant Colonel Oliver North, Vice Admiral John Poindexter, and Ms. Fawn Hall, because they declined to be interviewed. Thus, we feel that the Board presented less information concerning the Iran-Contra operation than we have offered in this encyclopedia. As a result, the following consists of Parts I and II, which provide the Board's perceptions of the several participatory offices and departments, and Part V, their critical institutional analysis.]

PART I

INTRODUCTION

In November 1986, it was disclosed that the United States had, in August 1985, and subsequently, participated in secret dealings with Iran involving the sale of military equipment. There appeared to be a linkage between these dealings and efforts to obtain the release of U.S. citizens held hostage in Lebanon by terrorists believed to be closely associated with the Iranian regime. After the initial story broke, the Attorney General announced that proceeds from the arms transfers may have been diverted to assist U.S.-backed rebel forces in Nicaragua, known as the Contras. This possibility enlarged the controversy and added questions not only of policy and propriety but also violations of law.

These disclosures became the focus of substantial public attention. The secret arms transfers appeared to run directly counter to declared U.S. policies. The United States had announced a policy of neutrality in a six-year old Iran/Iraq war and had proclaimed an embargo on arms sales to Iran. It had worked actively to isolate Iran and other regimes known to give aid and comfort to terrorists. It had declared that it would not pay ransom to hostage-takers.

Public concern was not limited to the issues of policy, however. Questions arose as to the propriety of certain actions taken by the National Security Council staff and the manner in which the decision to transfer arms to Iran had been made. Congress was never informed. A variety of intermediaries, both private and governmental, some with motives open to question, had central roles. The NSC staff rather than the CIA seemed to be running the operation. The President appeared to be unaware of key elements of the operation. The controversy threatened a crisis of confidence in the manner in which national security decisions are made and the role played by the NSC staff.

It was this latter set of concerns that prompted the President to establish this Special Review Board on December 1, 1986. The President directed the Board to examine the proper role of the National Security Council staff in national security operations, including the arms transfers to Iran. The President made clear that he wanted "all the facts to come out."

The Board was not, however, called upon to assess individual culpability or be the final arbiter of the facts. These tasks have been properly been left to others. Indeed, the short deadline set by the President for completion of the Board's work and its limited resources precluded a separate and thorough field investigation. Instead, the Board has examined the events surrounding the transfer of arms to Iran as a principal case study in evaluating the operation of the National Security Council in general and the role of the NSC staff in particular.

The President gave the Board a broad charter. It was directed to conduct "a comprehensive study of the future role and procedures of the National Security Council (NSC) staff in the development, coordination, oversight, and conduct of foreign and national security policy."

It has been forty years since the enactment of the National Security Act of 1947 and the creation of the National Security Council. Since that time the NSC staff has grown in importance and the Assistant to the President for National Security Affairs has emerged as a key player in national security decision-making. This is the first Presidential Commission to have as its sole responsibility a comprehensive review of how these institutions have performed. We believe that, quite aside from the circumstances which brought about the Board's creation, such a review was overdue.

The Board divided its work into three major inquiries: the circumstances surrounding the Iran/Contra matter, other case studies that might reveal strengths and weaknesses in the operation of the National Security Council system under stress, and the manner in which the system has served eight different Presidents since its inception in 1947.

At Appendix B [editors' note: Appendix B has been omitted from this transcription] is a narrative of the information obtained from documents and interviews regarding the arms sales to Iran. The narrative is necessarily incomplete. As of the date of this report, some key witnesses had refused to testify before any forum. Important documents located in other countries had yet to be released, and important witnesses in other countries were not available. But the appended narrative tells much of the story. Although more information will undoubtedly come to light, the record thus far developed provides a sufficient basis for evaluating the process by which these events came about.

During the Board's work, it received evidence concerning the role of the NSC staff in support of the Contras during the period that such support was either barred or restricted by Congress. The Board had neither the time nor the resources to make a systematic inquiry into this area. Notwithstanding, substantial evidence came before the Board. A narrative of that evidence is contained in Appendix C [also omitted].

The Board found that the issues raised by the Iran/Contra matter are in most instances not new. Every Administration has faced similar issues, although arising in different factual contexts. The Board examined in some detail the performance of the National Security Council system in 12 different crises dating back to the Truman Administration. Former government officials participating in many of these crises were interviewed. This learning provided a broad historical perspective to the issues before the Board.

Those who expect from us a radical prescription for wholesale change may be disappointed. Not all major problems—and Iran/Contra has been a major one—can be solved simply by rearranging organizational blocks or passing new laws.

In addition, it is important to emphasize that the President is responsible for the national security policy of the United States. In the development and execution of that policy, the President is the decision-maker. He is not obliged to consult with or seek approval from anyone in the Executive Branch. The structure and the procedures of the National Security Council system should be designed to give the President every assistance in discharging these heavy responsibilities. It is not possible to make a system immune from error without paralyzing its capacity to act.

At its senior levels, the National Security Council is primarily the interaction of people. We have examined with care its operation in the Iran/Contra matter and have set out in considerable detail mistakes of omission, commission, judgment, and perspective. We believe that this record and analysis can warn future Presidents, members of the National Security Council, and National Security Advisors of the potential pitfalls they face even when they are operating with what they consider the best of motives. We would hope that this record would be carefully read and its lessons fully absorbed by all aspirants to senior positions in the National Security Council system.

This report will serve another purpose. In preparing it, we have contacted every living past President, three former Vice Presidents, and every living Secretary of State, Secretary of Defense, National Security Advisor, most Directors of Central Intelligence, and several Chairmen of the Joint Chiefs of Staff to solicit their views. We sought to learn how well, in their experience, the system had operated or, in the case of past Presidents, how well it served them. We asked all former participants how they would change the system to make it more useful to the President.

Our review validates the current National Security Council system. That system has been utilized by different Presidents in very different ways, in accordance with their individual work habits and philosophical predilections. On occasion over the years it has functioned with real brilliance; at other times serious mistakes have been made. The problems we examined in the case of Iran/Contra caused us deep concern. But their solution does not lie in revamping the National Security Council system.

That system is properly the President's creature. It must be left flexible to be molded by the President into the form most useful to him. Otherwise it will become either an obstacle to the President, and a source of frustration; or an institutional irrelevance, as the President fashions informal structures more to his liking.

Having said that, there are certain functions which need to be performed in some way for any President. What we have tried to do is to distill from the wisdom of those who have participated in the National Security Council system over the past forty years the essence of these functions and the manner in which that system can be operated so as to minimize the likelihood of major error without destroying the creative impulses of the President.

PART II

ORGANIZING FOR NATIONAL SECURITY

Ours is a government of checks and balances, of shared power and responsibility. The Constitution places the President and the Congress in dynamic tension. They both cooperate and compete in the making of national policy.

National security is no exception. The Constitution gives both the President and the Congress an important role. The Congress is critical in formulating national policies and in marshalling the resources to carry them out. But those resources—the nation's military personnel, its diplomats, its intelligence capability—are lodged in the Executive Branch. As Chief Executive and Commander-in-Chief, and with broad authority in the area of foreign affairs, it is the President who is empowered to act for the nation and protect its interests.

A. The National Security Council

The present organization of the Executive Branch for national security matters was established by the National Security Act of 1947. That Act created the National Security Council. As now constituted, its statutory members are the President, Vice President, Secretary of State and Secretary of Defense. The President is the head of the National Security Council.

Presidents have from time to time invited the heads of other departments or agencies to attend National Security Council meetings or to participate as de facto members. These have included the Director of Central intelligence (the "DCI") and the Chairman of the Joint Chiefs of Staff (the "CJCS"). The President (or, in his absence, his designee) presides.

The National Security Council deals with the most vital issues in the nation's national security policy. It is this body that discusses recent developments in arms control and the Strategic Defense Initiative; that discussed whether or not to bomb the Cambodia mainland after the *Mayaguez* was captured; that debated the timetable for the U.S. withdrawal from Vietnam; and that considered the risky and daring attempt to rescue U.S. hostages in Iran in 1980. The National Security Council deals with issues that are difficult, complex, and often secret. Decisions are often required in hours rather than weeks. Advice must be given under great stress and with imperfect information.

The National Security Council is not a decision-making body. Although its other members hold official positions in the Government, when meeting as the National Security Council they sit as advisors to the President. This is clear from the language of the 1947 Act:

> The function of the Council shall be to advise the President with respect to the integration of domestic, foreign, and military policies relating to the national security so as to enable the military services and the other departments and agencies of the Government to cooperate more effectively in matters involving the national security.

The National Security Council has from its inception been a highly personal instrument. Every President has turned for advice to those individuals and institutions whose judgment he has valued and trusted. For some Presidents, such as President Eisenhower, the National Security Council served as a primary forum for obtaining advice on national security matters. Other Presidents, such as President Kennedy, relied on more informal groupings of advisors, often including some but not all of the Council members.

One official summarized the way the system has been adjusted by different Presidents:

> The NSC is going to be pretty well what a President wants it to be and what he determines it should be. Kennedy—and these are some exaggerations and generalities of course—with an anti-organizational bias, disestablished all [the Eisenhower created] committees and put a tight group in the White House totally attuned to his philosophic approach. . . . Johnson didn't change that very much, except certain difficulties began to develop in the informality which was [otherwise] characterized by speed, unity of purpose, precision. . . . So it had great efficiency and responsiveness. The difficulties began to develop in . . . the informality of the thing.

The Nixon Administration saw a return to the use of the National Security Council as a principal forum for national security advice. This pattern was continued by President Ford and President Carter, and in large measure by President Reagan.

Regardless of the frequency of its use, the NSC has remained a strictly advisory body. Each President has kept the burden of decision for himself, in accordance with his Constitutional responsibilities.

B. The Assistant to the President for National Security Affairs

Although closely associated with the National Security Council in the public mind, the Assistant to the President for National Security Affairs is not one of its members. Indeed, no mention of this position is made in the National Security Act of 1947.

The position was created by President Eisenhower in 1953. Although its precise title has varied, the position has come to be known (somewhat misleadingly) as the National Security Advisor.

Under President Eisenhower, the holder of this position served as the principal executive officer of the council, setting the agenda, briefing the President on Council matters, and supervising the staff. He was not a policy advocate.

It was not until President Kennedy, with McGeorge Bundy in the role, that the position took on its current form. Bundy emerged as an important personal advisor to the President on national security affairs. This introduced an element of direct competition into Bundy's relationship with members of the National Security Council. Although President Johnson changed the title of the position to simply "Special Assistant," in the hands of Walt Rostow it continued to play an important role.

President Nixon relied heavily on his National Security Advisor, maintaining and even enhancing its prominence. In that position, Henry Kissinger became a key spokesman for the President's national security policies both to the U.S,. press and to foreign governments. President Nixon used him to negotiate on behalf of the United States with Vietnam, China, the Soviet Union, and other countries. The roles of spokesman and negotiator had traditionally been the province of the Secretary of State, not of the National Security Advisor. The emerging tension between the two positions was only resolved when Kissinger assumed them both.

Under President Ford, Lt. Gen. Brent Scowcroft became National Security Advisor, with Henry Kissinger remaining as Secretary of State. The National Security Advisor exercised major responsibility for coordinating for the President the advice of his NSC principals and overseeing the process of policy development and implementation within the Executive Branch.

President Carter returned in large part to the early Kissinger model, with a resulting increase in tensions with the Secretary of State. President Carter wanted to take the lead in matters of foreign policy, and used his National Security Advisor as a source of information, ideas, and new initiatives.

The role of the National Security Advisor, like the role of the NSC itself, has in large measure been a function of the operating style of the President. Notwithstanding, the National Security Advisor has come to perform, to a greater or lesser extent, certain functions which appear essential to the effective discharge of the President's responsibilities in national security affairs.

- He is an "honest broker" for the NSC process. He assures that issues are clearly presented to the President; that all reasonable options, together with an analysis of their disadvantages and risks, are brought to his attention; and that the views of the President's other principal advisors are accurately conveyed.

- He provides advice from the President's vantage point, unalloyed by institutional responsibilities and biases. Unlike the Secretaries of State and Defense, who have substantial organizations for which they are responsible, the President is the National Security Advisor's only constituency.

- He monitors the actions taken by the executive departments in implementing the President's national security policies. He asks the question whether these actions are consistent with Presidential decisions and whether, over time, the underlying policies continue to serve U.S. interests.

- He has a special role in crisis management. This has resulted from the need for prompt and coordinated action under Presidential control, often with secrecy being essential.

- He reaches out for new ideas and initiatives that will give substance to broad Presidential objectives for national security.

- He keeps the President informed about international developments and developments in Congress and the Executive Branch that affect the President's policies and priorities.

But the National Security Advisor remains the creature of the President. The position will be largely what he wants it to be. This presents any President with a series of dilemmas.

- The President must surround himself with people he trusts and to whom he can speak in confidence. To this end, the National Security Advisor, unlike the Secretaries of State and Defense, is not subject to confirmation by the Senate and does not testify before Congress. But the more the President relies on the National Security Advisor for advice, especially to the exclusion of his Cabinet officials, the greater will be the unease with this arrangement.

- As the "honest broker" of the NSC process, the National Security Advisor must ensure that the different and often conflicting views of the NSC principals are presented fairly to the President. But as an independent advisor to the President, he must provide his own judgment. To the extent that the National Security Advisor becomes a strong advocate for a particular point of view, his role as "honest broker" may be compromised and the President's access to the unedited views of the NSC principals may be impaired.

- The Secretaries of State and Defense, and the Director of Central Intelligence, head agencies of government that have specific statutory responsibilities and are subject to Congressional oversight for the implementation of U.S. national security policy. To the extent that the National Security Advisor assumes operational responsibilities, whether by negotiating with foreign governments or becoming heavily involved in military or intelligence operations, the legitimacy of that role and his authority to perform it may be challenged.

- The more the National Security Advisor becomes an "operator" in implementing policy, the less will he be able objectively to review that implementation—and whether the underlying policy continues to serve the interests of the President and the nation.

- The Secretary of State has traditionally been the President's spokesman on matters of national security and foreign affairs. To the extent that the National Security Advisor speaks publicly on these matters or meets with representatives of foreign governments, the result may be confusion as to what is the President's policy.

C. The NSC Staff

At the time it established the National Security Council, Congress authorized a staff headed by an Executive Secretary appointed by the President. Initially quite small, the NSC staff expanded substantially under President Eisenhower.

During the Eisenhower Administration, the NSC staff assumed two important functions: coordinating the executive departments in the development of national policy (through the NSC Planning Board) and overseeing the implementation of that policy (through the Operations Coordination Board). A systematic effort was made to coordinate policy development and its implementation by the various agencies through an elaborate set of committees. The system worked fairly well in bringing together for the President the views of the other NSC principals. But it had been criticized as biased toward reaching consensus among the principals rather than developing options for Presidential decision. By the end of his second term, President Eisenhower himself had reached the conclusion that a highly competent individual and a small staff could perform the needed functions in a better way. Such a change was made by President Kennedy.

Under President Kennedy, a number of the functions of the NSC staff were eliminated and its size was sharply reduced. The Planning and Operations Coordinating Boards were abolished. Policy development and policy implementation were assigned to individual Cabinet officers, responsible directly to the President. By late 1962 the staff was only 12 professionals, serving largely as an independent source of ideas and information to the President. The system was lean and responsive, but frequently suffered from a lack of coordination. The Johnson Administration followed much the same pattern.

The Nixon Administration returned to a model more like Eisenhower's but with something of the informality of the Kennedy/Johnson staffs. The Eisenhower system had emphasized coordination; the Kennedy-Johnson system tilted to innovation and the generation of new ideas. The Nixon system emphasized both. The objective was not inter-departmental consensus but the generation of policy options for Presidential decision, and then ensuring that those decisions were carried out. The staff grew to 50 professionals in 1970 and became a major factor in the national security decision-making process. This approach was largely continued under President Ford.

The NSC staff retained an important role under President Carter. While continuing to have responsibility for coordinating policy among the various executive agencies, President Carter particularly looked to the NSC staff as a personal source of independent advice. President Carter felt the need to have a group loyal only to him from which to launch his own initiatives and to move a vast and lethargic government. During his time in office, President Carter reduced the size of the professional staff to 35, feeling that a smaller group could do the job and would have a closer relationship to him.

What emerges from this history is an NSC staff used by each President in a way that reflected his individual preferences and working style. Over time, it has developed an important role within the Executive Branch of coordinating policy review, preparing issues for Presidential decision, and monitoring implementation. But it has remained the President's creature, molded as he sees fit, to serve as his personal staff for national security affairs. For this reason, it has generally operated out of the public view and has not been subject to direct oversight by the Congress.

D. The Interagency Committee System

The National Security Council has frequently been supported by committees made up of representatives of the relevant national security departments and agencies. These committees analyze issues prior to consideration by the Council. There are generally several levels of committees. At the top level, officials from each agency (at the Deputy Secretary or Under Secretary level) meet to provide a senior level policy review. These senior-level committees are in turn supported by more junior interagency groups (usually at the Assistant Secretary level). These in turn may oversee staff level working groups that prepare detailed analysis of important issues.

Administrations have differed in the extent to which they have used these interagency committees. President Kennedy placed little stock in them. The Nixon and Carter Administrations, by contrast, made much use of them.

E. The Reagan Model

President Reagan entered office with a strong commitment to cabinet government. His principal advisors on national security affairs were to be the Secretaries of State and Defense, and to a lesser extent the Director of Central Intelligence. The position of the National Security Advisor was initially downgraded in both status and access to the President. Over the next six years, five different people held that position.

The Administration's first National Security Advisor, Richard Allen, reported to the President through the senior White House staff. Consequently, the NSC staff assumed a reduced role. Mr. Allen believed that the Secretary of State had primacy in the field of foreign policy. He viewed the job of the National Security Advisor as that of a policy coordinator.

President Reagan initially declared that the National Security Council would be the principal forum for consideration of national security issues. To support the work of the Council, President Reagan established an interagency committee system headed by three Senior Interagency Groups (or "SIGs"), one each for foreign policy, defense policy, and intelligence. They were chaired by the Secretary of State, the Secretary of Defense, and the Director of Central Intelligence, respectively.

Over time, the Administration's original conception of the role of the National Security Advisor changed. William Clark, who succeeded Richard Allen in 1982, was a long-time associate of the President and dealt directly with him. Robert McFarlane, who replaced Judge Clark in 1983, although personally less close to the President, continued to have direct access to him. The same was true of VADM John Poindexter, who was appointed to the position in December 1985.

President Reagan appointed several additional members to his National Security Council and allowed staff attendance at meetings. The resultant size of the meetings led the President to turn increasingly to a smaller group (called the National Security Planning Group or

"NSPG"). Attendance at its meetings was more restricted but included the statutory principals of the NSC. The NSPG was supported by the SIGs, and new SIGs were occasionally created to deal with particular issues. These were frequently chaired by the National Security Advisor. But generally the SIGs and many of their subsidiary groups (called Interagency Groups or "IGs") fell into disuse.

As a supplement to the normal NSC process, the Reagan Administration adopted comprehensive procedures for covert actions. These are contained in a classified document, NSDD-159, establishing the process for deciding, implementing, monitoring, and reviewing covert activities.

F. The Problem of Covert Operations

Covert activities place a great strain on the process of decision in a free society. Disclosure of even the existence of the operation could threaten its effectiveness and risk embarrassment to the Government. As a result there is strong pressure to withhold information, to limit knowledge of the operation to a minimum number of people.

These pressures come into play with great force when covert activities are undertaken in an effort to obtain the release of U.S. citizens held hostage abroad. Because of the legitimate human concern all Presidents have felt over the fate of such hostages, our national pride as a powerful country with a tradition of protecting its citizens abroad, and the great attention paid by the news media to hostage situations, the pressures on any President to take action to free hostages are enormous. Frequently to be effective, this action must necessarily be covert. Disclosure would directly threaten the lives of the hostages as well as those willing to contemplate their release.

Since covert arms sales to Iran played such a central role in the creation of this Board, it has focused its attention in large measure on the role of the NSC staff where covert activity is involved. This is not to denigrate, however, the importance of other decisions taken by the government. In those areas as well the National Security Council and its staff play a critical role. But in many respects the best test of a system is its performance under stress. The conditions of greatest stress are often found in the crucible of covert activities.

PART V

RECOMMENDATIONS

"Not only . . . is the Federal power over external affairs in origin and essential character different from that over internal affairs, but participation in the exercise of the power is significantly limited. In this vast external realm, with its important, complicated, delicate and manifold problems, the President alone has power to speak or listen as a representative of the nation." *United States vs. Curtiss-Wright Export Corp.*, 299. U.S. 304, 319 (1936).

Whereas the ultimate power to formulate domestic policy resides in the Congress, the primary responsibility for the formulation and implementation of national security policy falls on the President.

It is the President who is the usual source of innovation and responsiveness in this field. The departments and agencies—the Defense Department, State Department, and CIA bureaucracies—tend to resist policy change. Each has its own perspective based on long experience. The challenge for the President is to bring his perspective to bear on these bureaucracies for they are his instruments for executing national security policy, and he must work through them. His task is to provide them leadership and direction.

The National Security Act of 1947 and the system that has grown up under it affords the President special tools for carrying out this important role. These tools are the National Security Council, the National Security Advisor, and the NSC Staff. These are the means through which the creative impulses of the President are brought to bear on the permanent government. The National Security Act, and custom and practice, rightly give the President wide latitude in fashioning exactly how these means are used.

There is no magic formula which can be applied to the NSC structure and process to produce an optimal system. Because the system is the vehicle through which the President formulates and implements his national security policy, it must adapt to each individual President's style and management philosophy. This means that NSC structures and processes must be flexible, not rigid. Overprescription would, as discussed in Part II, either destroy the system or render it ineffective.

Nevertheless, this does not mean there can be no guidelines or recommendations that might improve the operation of the system, whatever the particular style of the incumbent President. We have reviewed the operation of the system over the last 40 years, through good times and bad. We have listened carefully to the views of all the living former Presidents as well as those of most of the participants in their own national security systems. With the strong caveat that flexibility and adaptability must be at the core, it is our judgment that the national security system seems to have worked best when it has in general operated along the lines set forth below.

Organizing for National Security. Because of the wide latitude in the National Security Act, the President bears a special responsibility for the effective performance of the NSC system. A President must at the outset provide guidelines to the members of the National Security Council, his National Security Advisor, and the National Security Council staff. These guidelines, to be effective, must include how they will relate to one another, what procedures will be followed, what the President expects of them. If his advisors are not performing as he likes, only the President can intervene.

The National Security Council principals other than the President participate on the Council in a unique capacity. Although holding a seat by virtue of their official positions in the Administration, when they sit as members of the Council they sit not as cabinet secretaries or department heads but as advisors to the President. They are there not simply to advance or defend the particular positions of the departments or agencies they head but to give the best advice to the President. Their job—and their challenge—is to see the issue from this perspective, not from the narrower interests of their respective bureaucracies.

The National Security Council is only advisory. It is the President alone who decides. When the NSC principals receive those decisions, they do so as heads of the appropriate departments or agencies. They are then responsible to see that the President's decisions are carried out by those organizations accurately and effectively.

This is an important point. The policy innovation and creativity of the President encounters a natural resistance from the executing departments. While this resistance is a source of frustration to every President, it is inherent in the design of the government. It is up to the politically appointed agency heads to ensure that the President's goals, designs, and policies are brought to bear on this permanent structure. Circumventing the departments, perhaps by using the National Security Advisor or the NSC Staff to execute policy, robs the President of the experience and capacity resident in the departments. The President must act largely through them, but the agency heads must ensure that they execute the

President's policies in an expeditious and effective manner. It is not just the obligation of the National Security Advisor to see that the national security process is used. All of the NSC principals—and particularly the President—have that obligation.

This tension between the President and the Executive Departments is worked out through the national security process described in the opening sections of this report. It is through this process that the nation obtains both the best of the creativity of the President and the learning and expertise of the national security departments and agencies.

This process is extremely important to the President. His decisions will benefit from the advice and perspective of all the concerned departments and agencies. History offers numerous examples of this truth. President Kennedy, for example, did not have adequate consultation before entering upon the Bay of Pigs invasion, one of his greatest failures. He remedied this in time for the Cuban missile crisis, one of his greatest successes. Process will not always produce brilliant ideas, but history suggests it at least can help prevent bad ideas from becoming Presidential policy.

The National Security Advisor. It is the National Security Advisor who is primarily responsible for managing this process on a daily basis. The job requires skill, sensitivity, and integrity. It is his responsibility to ensure that matters submitted for consideration by the Council cover the full range of issues on which review is required; that those issues are fully analyzed; that a full range of options is considered; that the prospects and risks of each are examined; that all relevant intelligence and other information is available to the principals; that legal considerations are addressed; that difficulties in implementation are confronted. Usually, this can best be accomplished through interagency participation in the analysis of the issue and a preparatory policy review at the Deputy or Under Secretary level.

The National Security Advisor assumes these responsibilities not only with respect to the President but with respect to all the NSC principals. He must keep them informed of the President's thinking and decisions. They should have adequate notice and an agenda for all meetings. Decision papers should, if at all possible, be provided in advance.

The National Security Advisor must also ensure that adequate records are kept of NSC consultations and Presidential decisions. This is essential to avoid confusion among Presidential advisors and departmental staffs about what was actually decided and what is wanted. Those records are also essential for conducting a periodic review of a policy or initiative, and to learn from the past.

It is the responsibility of the National Security Advisor to monitor policy implementation and to ensure that policies are executed in conformity with the intent of the President's decision. Monitoring includes initiating periodic reassessments of a policy or operation, especially when changed circumstances suggest that the policy or operation no longer serves U.S. interests.

But the National Security Advisor does not simply manage the national security process. He is himself an important source of advice on national security matters to the President. He is not the President's only source of advice, but he is perhaps the one most able to see things from the President's perspective. He is unburdened by departmental responsibilities. The President is his only master. His advice is confidential. He is not subject to Senate confirmation and traditionally does not formally appear before Congressional committees.

To serve the President well, the National Security Advisor should present his own views, but he must at the same time represent the views of others fully and faithfully to the President. The system will not work well if the National Security Advisor does not have the trust of the NSC principals. He, therefore, must not use his proximity to the President to manipulate the process so as to produce his own position. He should not interpose himself between the President and the NSC principals. He should not seek to exclude the NSC principals from the decision process. Performing both these roles well is an essential, if not easy, task. In order for the National Security Advisor to serve the President adequately, he must have direct access to the President. Unless he knows firsthand the views of the President and is known to reflect them in his management of the NSC system, he will be ineffective. He should not report to the President through some other official. While the Chief of Staff or others can usefully interject domestic political considerations into national security deliberations, they should do so as additional advisors to the President.

Ideally, the National Security Advisor should not have a high public profile. He should not try to compete with the Secretary of State or the Secretary of Defense as the articulator of public policy. They, along with the President, should be the spokesmen for the policies of the Administration. While a "passion for anonymity" is perhaps too strong a term, the National Security Advisor should generally operate off-stage.

The NSC principals of course must have direct access to the President, with whatever frequency the President feels is appropriate. But these individual meetings should not be used by the principal to seek decisions or otherwise circumvent the system in the absence of the other principals. In the same way, the National Security Advisor should not use his scheduled intelligence or other daily briefings of the President as an opportunity to seek Presidential decision on significant issues.

If the system is to operate well, the National Security Advisor must promote cooperation rather than competition among himself and the other NSC principals. But the President is ultimately responsible for the operation of this system. If rancorous infighting develops among his principal national security functionaries, only he can deal with them. Public dispute over external policy by senior officials undermines the process of decision-making and narrows his options. It is the President's responsibility to ensure that it does not take place.

Finally, the National Security Advisor should focus on the advice and management, not implementation and execution. Implementation is the responsibility and the strength of the departments and agencies. The National Security Advisor and the NSC Staff generally do not have the depth of resources for the conduct of operations. In addition, when they take on implementation responsibilities, they risk compromising their objectivity. They can no longer act as impartial overseers of the implementation, ensuring that Presidential guidance is followed, that policies are kept under review, and that the results are serving the President's policy and the national interest.

The NSC Staff. The NSC staff should be small, highly competent, and experienced in the making of public policy. Staff members should be drawn both from within and from outside government. Those from within government should come from the several departments and agencies concerned with national security matters. No particular department or agency should have a predominate role. A proper balance must be maintained between people from within and outside the government. Staff members should generally rotate with a stay or more than four years viewed as the exception.

A large number of staff action officers organized along essentially horizontal lines enhances the possibilities for poorly supervised and monitored activities by individual staff members. Such a system is made to order for energetic self-starters to make unauthorized initiatives. Clear vertical lines of control and authority, responsibility and accountability, are essential to good management.

One problem affecting the NSC staff is lack of institutional memory. This results from the understandable desire of a President to replace the staff in order to be sure that it is responsible to him. Departments provide continuity that can help the Council, but the Council as an institution also needs some means to assure adequate records and memory. This was identified to the Board as a problem by many witnesses.

We recognize the problem and have identified a range of possibilities that a President might consider on the subject. One would be to create a small permanent executive secretariat. Another would be to have one person, the Executive Secretary, as a permanent position. Finally, a pattern of limited tenure and overlapping rotation could be used. Any of these would help reduce the problem of loss of institutional memory; none would be practical unless each succeeding President subscribed to it.

The guidelines for the role of the National Security Advisor also apply generally to the NSC staff. They should protect the process and thereby the President. Departments and agencies should not be excluded from participation in that process. The staff should not be implementors or operators and staff should keep a low profile with the press.

Principal Recommendation

The model we have outlined above for the National Security Council system constitutes our first and most important recommendation. It includes guidelines that address virtually all of the deficiencies in procedure and practice that the Board encountered in the Iran/Contra affair as well as in other case studies of this and previous administrations.

We believe this model can enhance the performance of a President and his administration in the area of national security. It responds directly to President Reagan's mandate to describe the NSC system as it ought to be.

The Board recommends that the proposed model be used by Presidents in their management of the National Security System.

Specific Recommendations

In addition to its principal recommendation regarding the organization and functioning of the NSC system and roles to be played by the participants, the Board has a number of specific recommendations.

1. *The National Security Act of 1947.* The flaws of procedure and failures of responsibility revealed by our study do not suggest any inadequacies in the provisions of the National Security Act of 1947 that deal with the structure and operation of the NSC system. Forty years of experience under that Act demonstrate to the Board that it remains a fundamentally sound framework for national security decision-making. It strikes a balance between formal structure and flexibility adequate to permit each President to tailor the system to fit his needs.

   As a general matter, the NSC Staff should not engage in the implementation of policy or the conduct of operations. This compromises their oversight role and usurps the responsibilities of the departments and agencies. But the inflexibility of a legislative restriction should be avoided. Terms such as "operation" and "implementation" are difficult to define, and a legislative proscription might preclude some future President from making a very constructive use of the NSC Staff.

Predisposition on sizing of the staff should be toward fewer rather than more. But a legislative restriction cannot foresee the requirements of future Presidents. Size is best left up to the discretion of the President, with the admonition that the role of the NSC staff is to review, not to duplicate or replace, the work of the departments and agencies.

We recommend that no substantive change be made in the provisions of the National Security Act dealing with the structure and operation of the NSC system.

2.   *Senate Confirmation of the National Security Advisor.* It has been suggested that the job of the National Security Advisor has become so important that its holder should be screened by the process of confirmation, and that once confirmed he should return frequently for questioning by the Congress. It is argued that this would improve the accountability of the National Security Advisor.

We hold a different view. The National Security Advisor does, and should continue, to serve only one master, and that is the President. Further, confirmation is inconsistent with the role the National Security Advisor should play. He should not decide, only advise. He should not engage in policy implementation or operations. He should serve the President, with no collateral and potentially diverting duties.

Confirmation would tend to institutionalize the natural tension that exists between the Secretary of State and the National Security Advisor. Questions would increasingly arise about who really speaks for the President in national security matters. Foreign governments could be confused or would be encouraged to engage in "forum shopping."

Only one of the former government officials interviewed favored Senate confirmation of the National Security Advisor. While consultation with Congress received wide support, confirmation and formal questioning were opposed. Several suggested that if the National Security Advisor were to become a position subject to confirmation, it could induce the President to turn to other internal staff or to people outside the government to play that role.

We urge the Congress not to require Senate confirmation of the National Security Advisor.

3.   *The Interagency Process.* It is the National Security Advisor who has the greatest interest in making the national security process work, for it is this process by which the President obtains the information, background, and analysis he requires to make decisions and build support for his programs. Most Presidents have set up interagency committees at both a staff and policy level to surface issues, develop options, and clarify choices. There has typically been a struggle for the chairmanships of these groups between the National Security Advisor and the NSC staff on the one hand, and the cabinet secretaries and department officials on the other.

> Our review of the operation of the present system and that of other administrations where committee chairmen came from the departments has led us to the conclusion that the system generally operates better when the committees are chaired by the individual with the greatest stake in making the NSC program work.

We recommend that the National Security Advisor chair the senior-level committees of the NSC system.

4. *Covert Actions.* Policy formulation and implementation are usually managed by a team of experts led by policymaking generalists. Covert action requirements are no different, but there is a need to limit, sometimes severely, the number of individuals involved. The lives of many people may be at stake, as was the case in the attempt to rescue the hostages in Teheran. Premature disclosure might kill the idea in embryo, as could have been the case in the opening of relations with China. In such cases, there is a tendency to limit those involved to a small number of top officials. This practice tends to limit severely the expertise brought to bear on the problem and should be used very sparingly indeed.

    The obsession with secrecy and preoccupation with leaks threaten to paralyze the government in its handling of covert operations. Unfortunately, the concern is not misplaced. The selective leak has become a principal means of waging bureaucratic warfare. Opponents of an operation kill it with a leak; supporters seek to build support through the same means.

    We have witnessed over the past years a significant deterioration in the integrity of process. Rather than a means to obtain results more satisfactory than the position of any of the individual departments, it has frequently become something to be manipulated to reach a specific outcome. The leak becomes a primary instrument in that process.

    This practice is destructive of orderly governance. It can only be reversed if the most senior officials take the lead. If senior decision-makers set a clear example and demand compliance, subordinates are more likely to conform.

    Most recent administrations have had carefully drawn procedures for the consideration of covert activities. The Reagan Administration established such procedures in January 1985, then promptly ignored them in their consideration of the Iran initiative.

We recommend that each administration formulate precise procedures for restricted consideration of covert action and that, once formulated, those procedures be strictly adhered to.

5. *The Role of the CIA.* Some aspects of the Iran arms sales raised broader questions in the minds of members of the Board regarding the role of CIA. The first deals with intelligence.

    The NSC staff was actively involved in the preparation of the May 20,

1985, update to the Special National Intelligence Estimate on Iran. It is a matter for concern if this involvement and the strong views of NSC staff members were allowed to influence the intelligence judgments contained in the update. It is also of concern that the update contained the hint that the United States should change its existing policy and encourage its allies to provide arms to Iran. It is critical that the line between intelligence and advocacy of a particular policy be preserved if intelligence is to retain its integrity and perform its proper function. In this instance, the CIA came close enough to the line to warrant concern.

We emphasize to both the intelligence community and policymakers the importance of maintaining the integrity and objectivity of the intelligence process.

6. *Legal Counsel.* From time to time issues with important legal ramifications will come before the National Security Council. The Attorney General is currently a member of the Council by invitation and should be in a position to provide legal advice to the Council and the President. It is important that the Attorney General and his department be available to interagency deliberations.

The Justice Department, however, should not replace the role of counsel in the other departments. As the principal counsel on foreign affairs, the Legal Advisor to the Secretary of State should also be available to all the NSC participants.

Of all the NSC participants, it is the Assistant for National Security Affairs who seems to have had the least access to expert counsel familiar with his activities.

The Board recommends that the position of Legal Advisor to the NSC be enhanced in stature and in its role within the NSC staff.

7. *Secrecy and Congress.* There is a natural tension between the desire for secrecy and the need to consult Congress on covert operations. Presidents seem to become increasingly concerned about leaks of classified information as their administrations progress. They blame Congress disproportionately. Various cabinet officials from prior administrations indicated to the Board that they believe Congress bears no more blame than the Executive Branch.

However, the number of Members and staff involved in reviewing covert activities is large; it provides cause for concern and a convenient excuse for Presidents to avoid Congressional consultation.

We recommend that Congress consider replacing the existing Intelligence Committees of the respective Houses with a new joint committee with a restricted staff to oversee the intelligence community, patterned after the Joint Committee on Atomic Energy that existed until the mid-1970s.

8. *Privatizing National Security Policy.* Careful and limited use of people outside the U.S. Government may be very helpful in some unique cases. But this practice raises substantial questions. It can create conflict of

interest problems. Private or foreign sources may have different policy interests or personal motives and may exploit their association with a U.S. government effort. Such involvement gives private and foreign sources potentially powerful leverage in the form of demands for return favors or even blackmail.

The U.S. has enormous resources invested in agencies and departments in order to conduct the government's business. In all but a very few cases, these can perform the functions needed. If not, then inquiry is required to find out why.

We recommend against having implementation and policy oversight dominated by intermediaries. We do not recommend barring limited use of private individuals to assist in United States diplomatic initiatives or in covert activities. We caution against use of such people except in very limited ways and under close observation and supervision.

Epilogue

If but one of the major policy mistakes we examined had been avoided, the nation's history would bear one less scar, one less embarrassment, one less opportunity for opponents to reverse the principles this nation seeks to preserve and advance in the world.

As a collection, these recommendations are offered to those who will find themselves in situations similar to the ones we reviewed; under stress, with high stakes, given little time, using incomplete information, and troubled by premature disclosure. In such a state, modest improvements may yield surprising gains. This is our hope.

Appendix X

Senate Resolution S.1721 (Proposed)
Intelligence Oversight Act of 1988

PURPOSE

The purpose of S.1721, as reported, is to clarify the legal requirements for congressional oversight of intelligence activities, including special activities, and to specify the procedures for authorization of special activities within the executive branch, so as to ensure that such activities are conducted in the national interest.

AMENDMENT

Strike all after the enacting clause and insert in lieu thereof the following:

That this Act may be cited as the "Intelligence Oversight Act of 1988".

SEC.1. Section 662 of the Foreign Assistance Act of 1961 (U.S.C. 2422) is hereby repealed.

SEC.2. Section 501 of title V of the National Security Act of 1947 (50 U.S.C. 413) is amended by striking the language contained there in, and substituting the following new sections:

GENERAL PROVISIONS

SEC. 501.

(a) The President shall ensure that the Select Committee on Intelligence of the Senate and the Permanent Select Committee of the House of Representatives (hereinafter in this title referred to as the "intelligence committees") are kept fully and currently informed of the intelligence activities of the United States, including any significant anticipated intelligence activities, as required by this title; provided, however, that nothing contained in this title shall be construed as requiring the approval of the intelligence committees as a condition precedent to the initiation of such activities; and provided further, however, That nothing contained herein shall be construed as a limitation on the power of the President to initiate such activities in a manner consistent with his powers conferred by the Constitution.

(b) The President shall ensure that any illegal intelligence activity is reported to the intelligence committees, as well as any corrective action that has been taken or is planned in connection with such illegal activity.

(c) The President and the intelligence committees shall each establish such procedures as may be necessary to carry out the provisions of this title.

(d) The House of Representatives and the Senate, in consultation with the Director of Central Intelligence, shall each establish, by rule or resolution of such House, procedures to protect from unauthorized disclosure all classified information and all information relating to intelligence sources and methods furnished to the intelligence committees or to Members of Congress under this title. In accordance with such procedures, each of the intelligence committees shall promptly call to the attention of its respective House, or to any appropriate committee or committees of its respective House, any matter relating to intelligence activities requiring the attention of such House or such committee or committees.

(e) Nothing in this Act shall be construed as authority to withhold information from the intelligence committees on the grounds that providing the information to the intelligence committees would constitute the unauthorized disclosure of classified information or information relating to intelligence sources and methods.

(f) As used in this section, the term "intelligence activities" includes, but is not limited to, "special activities" as defined in subsection 503(e), below.

REPORTING INTELLIGENCE ACTIVITIES OTHER THAN SPECIAL ACTIVITIES

SEC. 502. To the extent consistent with due regard for the protection from unauthorized disclosure of classified information relating to sensitive intelligence sources and methods or other exceptionally sensitive matters, the Director of Central Intelligence and the heads of all departments, agencies, and other entities of the United States Government involved in intelligence activities shall:

(a) keep the intelligence committees fully and currently informed of all intelligence activities, other than special activities, as defined in subsection 503(e), below, which are the responsibility of, are engaged in by, or are carried out for or on behalf of, any department, agency, or entity of the United States Government, including any significant anticipated intelligence activity and significant failures; and

(b) furnish the intelligence committees any information or material concerning intelligence activities other than special activities which is within their custody or control, and which is requested by the intelligence committees in order to carry out its authorized responsibilities.

PRESIDENTIAL APPROVAL AND REPORTING OF SPECIAL ACTIVITIES

SEC. 503.

(a) The President may authorize the conduct of "special activities," as defined herein below, by departments, agencies, or entities of the United States Government only when he determines such activities are necessary to support the foreign policy objectives of the United States and are important to the national security of the United States, which determination shall be set forth in a finding that shall meet each of the following conditions:

(1) Each finding shall be in writing unless immediate action by the United

States is required and time does not permit the preparation of a written finding, in which case a written record of the President's decision shall be contemporaneously made and shall be reduced to a written finding as soon as possible but in no event more than forty-eight hours after the decision is made;

(2) A finding may not authorize or sanction special activities, or any aspect of such activities, which have already occurred;

(3) Each finding shall specify each and every department, agency, or entity of the United States Government authorized to fund or otherwise participate in any significant way in such activities: Provided, That any employee, contractor, or contract agent of a department, agency, or entity of the United States Government other than the Central Intelligence Agency directed to participate in any way in a special activity shall be subject either to the policies and regulations of the Central Intelligence Agency, or to written policies or regulations adopted by such department, agency or entity, to govern such participation;

(4) Each finding shall specify whether it is contemplated that any third party which is not an element of, contractor or contract agent of, the United States Government, or is not otherwise subject to United States Government policies and regulations, will be used to fund or otherwise participate in any significant way in the special activity concerned, or be used to undertake the special activity concerned on behalf of the United States;

(5) A finding may not authorize any action intended to influence United States political processes, public opinion, policies or media; and

(6) A finding may not authorize any action that would violate any statute of the United States.

(b) To the extent consistent with due regard for the protection from unauthorized disclosure of classified information relating to sensitive intelligence sources and methods, or other exceptionally sensitive matters, the Director of Central Intelligence and the heads of all departments, agencies, and entities of the United States Government involved in a special activity shall:

(1) keep the intelligence committees fully and currently informed of all special activities which are the responsibility of, are engaged in by, or are carried out for or on behalf of, any department, agency or entity of the United States Government, including significant failures; and

(2) furnish to the intelligence committees any information or material concerning special activities which is in the possession, custody or control of any department, agency, or entity of the United States Government and which is requested by either of the intelligence committees in order to carry out its authorized responsibilities.

(c)

(1) Except as provided in subsection (2) through (4), below, the President shall ensure that any finding approved, or determination made, pursuant to subsection (a), above, shall be reported to the intelligence committees prior to the initiation of the activities authorized, and in no event later than 48 hours after such finding is signed or the determination is otherwise made by the President.

(2) On rare occasions when time is of the essence, the President may direct that special activities be initiated prior to reporting such activities to the intelligence committees; provided, however, That in such circumstances, notice shall be provided the intelligence committees as soon as possible thereafter but in no event later than 48 hours after the finding authorizing such activities is signed or such determination is made, pursuant to subsection (a), above.

(3) When the President determines it is essential to meet extraordinary circumstances affecting vital interests of the United States, the President may limit the reporting of findings or determinations pursuant to subsections (1) or (2) of this section, the chairmen and ranking minority members of the intelligence committees, the Speaker and Minority Leader of the House of Representatives, and the Majority and Minority Leaders of the Senate. In such case, the President shall provide a statement of the reasons for limiting access to such findings or determinations in accordance with this subsection.

(4) Notwithstanding the provisions of subsection (3) above, when the President determines it is essential to meet extraordinary circumstances affecting the most vital security interests of the United States and the risk of disclosure constitutes a grave risk to such vital interests, the President may limit the reporting of findings or determinations pursuant to subsections (1) or (2) of this section to the Speaker and Minority Leader of the House of Representatives, and the Majority and Minority Leaders of the Senate. In such cases, the President shall provide a statement of reasons explaining why notice to the intelligence committees is not being provided in accordance with subsection (c)(1), above. The President shall personally reconsider each week thereafter the reasons for continuing to limit such notice, and provide a statement to the members of Congress identified herein above on a weekly basis, confirming his decision, until such time as notice is, in fact, provided the intelligence committees.

(5) In all cases reported pursuant to subsections (c)(1), (c)(2), and (c)(3), above, a copy of the finding, signed by the President, shall be provided to the chairman of each intelligence committee. In all cases reported pursuant to subsection (c)(4), a copy of the finding, signed by the President, shall be shown to the members of Congress identified in such subsection at the time such finding is reported.

(d) The President shall ensure that the intelligence committees, or, if applicable, the members of Congress specified in subsection (c), above, are notified of any significant change in a previously-approved special activity, or any significant undertaking pursuant to a previously-approved finding, in the same manner as findings are reported pursuant to subsection (c), above.

(e) As used in this section, the term "special activity" means:

(1) any operation of the Central Intelligence Agency conducted in foreign countries, other than activities intended solely for obtaining necessary intelligence; and

(2) to the extent not consistent with subsection (1), above, any activity conducted by any department, agency, or entity of the United States Government in support of national foreign policy objectives abroad which is

planned and executed so that the role of the United States Government is not apparent or acknowledged publicly, and functions in support of such activity, but which does not include diplomatic and related support activities.

SEC. 3. Section 502 of title V of the National Security Act of 1947 (50 U.S.C. 414) is redesignated as section 504 of such Act, and is amended by deleting the number "501" in subsection (a)(2) of such section and substituting in lieu thereof "503"; and is further amended by adding the following new subsection (d):

"(d) No funds appropriated for, or otherwise available to, any department, agency, or entity of the United States Government, may be expended, or may be directed to be expended, for any special activity, as defined in subsection 503(e), above, unless and until a Presidential finding required by subsection (a), has been signed or otherwise issued in accordance with that subsection."

SEC. 4. Section 503 of title V of the National Security Act of 1947 (50 U.S.C. 415) is redesignated as section 505 of such Act.

Appendix Y

Other Congressional Legislation Affecting the Intelligence Community

SECTION 662 OF THE FOREIGN ASSISTANCE ACT OF 1961 (22 U.S.C. 2422) (THE "HUGHES-RYAN AMENDMENT")

SEC. 662. LIMITATION ON INTELLIGENCE ACTIVITIES.—No funds appropriated under the authority of this or any other Act may be expended by or on behalf of the Central Intelligence Agency for operations in foreign countries, other than activities intended solely for obtaining necessary intelligence, unless and until the President finds that each such operation is important to the national security of the United States. Each such operation shall be considered a significant anticipated intelligence activity for the purpose of section 501 of the National Security Act of 1947.

SECTION 118 OF THE INTERNATIONAL SECURITY AND DEVELOPMENT COOPERATION ACT OF 1980 (THE "CLARK AMENDMENT")
(22 U.S.C. 2293 note)

MILITARY OR PARAMILITARY OPERATIONS IN ANGOLA
SEC. 118.

(a) Notwithstanding any other provision of law, no assistance of any kind may be provided for the purpose, or which would have the effect, of promoting or augmenting, directly or indirectly, the capacity of any nation, group, organization, movement, or individual to conduct military or paramilitary operations in Angola unless and until—

(1) the President determines that such assistance should be furnished in the national security interests of the United States;

(2) the President submits to the Committee on Foreign Affairs of the House of Representatives and the Committee on Foreign Relations of the Senate a report containing—

(A) a description of the amounts and categories of assistance which he recommends be furnished and the identity of the proposed recipients of such assistance; and

(B) a certification that he has determined that the furnishing of such assistance is important to the national security interests of the United States and a detailed statement of the reasons supporting such a determination; and

(3) the Congress enacts a joint resolution approving the furnishing of such assistance.

(b)   If introduced within 30 days after the submission of the report required by paragraph (2) of subsection (a), a resolution under paragraph (3) of subsection (a) shall be considered in the Senate in accordance with the provisions of section 601(b) of the International Security Assistance and Arms Export Control Act of 1976 and in the House of Representatives in accordance with the procedures applicable to the consideration of resolutions of disapproval under section 36(b) of the Arms Export Control Act.

(c)   The prohibition contained in subsection (a) does not apply with respect to assistance which is furnished solely for humanitarian purposes.

(d)   The provisions of this section may not be waived under any other provision of law.

(e)   Section 404 of the International Security Assistance and Arms Export Control Act of 1976 is repealed.

SECTION 793 OF PUBLIC LAW 97-377 (THE "BOLAND AMENDMENT")

SEC. 793. None of the funds provided in this Act may be used by the Central Intelligence Agency or the Department of Defense to furnish military equipment, military training or advice, or other support for military activities, to any group or individual, not part of a country's armed forces, for the purpose of overthrowing the Government of Nicaragua or provoking a military exchange between Nicaragua and Honduras.

SECTION 775 OF PUBLIC LAW 98-212 (LIMIT ON 1984 FUNDING)

SEC. 775. During fiscal year 1984, not more than $24,000,000 of the funds available to the Central Intelligence Agency, the Department of Defense, or any other agency or entity of the United States involved in intelligence activities may be obligated or expended for the purpose or which would have the effect of supporting, directly or indirectly, military or paramilitary operations in Nicaragua by any nation, group, organization, movement, or individual.

SECTION 1540 OF PUBLIC LAW 98-525 (THE "DENTON AMENDMENT")
AUTHORIZATION FOR THE SECRETARY OF DEFENSE TO TRANSPORT HUMANITARIAN RELIEF SUPPLIES TO COUNTRIES IN CENTRAL AMERICA

SEC. 1540.

(a)   Notwithstanding any other provision of law, during fiscal year 1985, the Secretary of Defense may transport on a space available basis, at no charge, to any country in Central America goods and supplies which have been furnished by a nongovernmental source and which are intended for humanitarian assistance.

(b)

(1) The President shall institute procedures, including complete inspection prior to acceptance for transport, for determining that—

(A)   the transport of any goods and supplies transported under this section is consistent with foreign policy objectives;

(B) the goods and supplies to be transported are suitable for humanitarian purposes and are in usable condition;

(C) there is a legitimate humanitarian need for such goods and supplies;

(D) the goods and supplies will in fact be used for humanitarian purposes; and

(E) there are adequate arrangements for the distribution of such goods and supplies in the country of destination.

(2) Goods and supplies determined not to meet the criteria of paragraph (1) may not be transported under this section.

(3) It shall be the responsibility of the donor to insure that goods or supplies to be transported under this section are suitable for transport.

(c) Goods and supplies transported under this section may be distributed by an agency of the United States Government, a foreign government, or international organization, or private nonprofit relief organization. The Secretary of Defense may not accept any goods or supplies for transportation under this section unless verification of adequate arrangements has been received in advance for distribution of such goods and supplies.

(d) Goods or supplies transported under this section may not be distributed, directly or indirectly, to any individual, group, or organization engaged in military or paramilitary activity.

(e) No later than 90 days after the date of enactment of this section, and every 60 days thereafter, the Secretary of State shall report to the Congress concerning the origin, contents destination, and disposition of all goods and supplies transported under this section.